Historic Resource Study:
Chesapeake & Ohio Canal

By

Harlan D. Unrau

1,000,000 Books

are available to read at

Forgotten Books

www.ForgottenBooks.com

Read online
Download PDF
Purchase in print

ISBN 978-1-5285-2128-4
PIBN 10902832

This book is a reproduction of an important historical work. Forgotten Books uses state-of-the-art technology to digitally reconstruct the work, preserving the original format whilst repairing imperfections present in the aged copy. In rare cases, an imperfection in the original, such as a blemish or missing page, may be replicated in our edition. We do, however, repair the vast majority of imperfections successfully; any imperfections that remain are intentionally left to preserve the state of such historical works.

Forgotten Books is a registered trademark of FB &c Ltd.
Copyright © 2018 FB &c Ltd.
FB &c Ltd, Dalton House, 60 Windsor Avenue, London, SW19 2RR.
Company number 08720141. Registered in England and Wales.

For support please visit www.forgottenbooks.com

1 MONTH OF FREE READING

at

www.ForgottenBooks.com

By purchasing this book you are eligible for one month membership to ForgottenBooks.com, giving you unlimited access to our entire collection of over 1,000,000 titles via our web site and mobile apps.

To claim your free month visit:
www.forgottenbooks.com/free902832

* Offer is valid for 45 days from date of purchase. Terms and conditions apply.

English
Français
Deutsche
Italiano
Español
Português

www.forgottenbooks.com

Mythology Photography **Fiction**
Fishing Christianity **Art** Cooking
Essays Buddhism Freemasonry
Medicine **Biology** Music **Ancient Egypt** Evolution Carpentry Physics
Dance Geology **Mathematics** Fitness
Shakespeare **Folklore** Yoga Marketing
Confidence Immortality Biographies
Poetry **Psychology** Witchcraft
Electronics Chemistry History **Law**
Accounting **Philosophy** Anthropology
Alchemy Drama Quantum Mechanics
Atheism Sexual Health **Ancient History**
Entrepreneurship Languages Sport
Paleontology Needlework Islam
Metaphysics Investment Archaeology
Parenting Statistics Criminology
Motivational

Historic Resource Study: Chesapeake & Ohio Canal

By

Harlan D. Unrau

United States Department of Interior
National Park Service
Chesapeake & Ohio Canal National Historical Park
Hagerstown, Maryland
August 2007

Prepared by
Karen M. Gray
Headquarters Library Volunteer
Chesapeake &Ohio Canal National Historical Park

Historic Resource Study: Chesapeake & Ohio Canal

By

Harlan D. Unrau

United States Department of Interior
National Park Service
Chesapeake & Ohio Canal National Historical Park
Hagerstown, Maryland
August 2007

Prepared b
Karen M. Gra
Headquarters Library Volunte
Chesapeake &Ohio Canal National Historical Par

Chesapeake & Ohio Canal Historic Resource Study
By Harlan D. Unrau

CONTENTS

PREFACE 5

MONOGRAPHS:

1.	DESIGNERS OF THE C&O CANAL	7
2.	CONSTRUCTION ECONOMICS	45
3.	LABOR FORCE	107
4.	QUARRIES, MILLS AND KILNS	153
5.	CONSTUCTION CHRONOLOGY	175
6.	FLOODS	273
7.	BOATS AND NAVIGATION	327
8.	COMMERCE	427
9.	MAINTENANCE	535
10.	ECONOMIC IMPACT	633
11.	CANAL IN THE CIVIL WAR	703
12.	LOCKTENDERS AND BOATMEN	781

PREFACE

On January 8, 1971, President Richard M. Nixon signed into law the bill creating the Chesapeake & Ohio Canal National Historical Park. In the mid-1970s, National Park Service historian Harlan D. Unrau produced a major, handwritten, multi-volume study of the history, engineering, operation, maintenance, and other aspects of the Chesapeake & Ohio canal. A rough, unedited typed version was produced in the early 1980s for general use by park staff.

In 2006, C&O Canal NHP volunteers began the task of transcribing the Unrau work into MS Word. The present document lacks the benefit of information that has become available since the 1970s when Unrau created this work. Various imperfections will be apparent to the reader and some sources are not fully documented, but the work represents an early compilation of the canal's history and engineering that has never been surpassed and will be of incalculable value to researchers and those who simply desire to know more about this unique historic treasure.

It should be noted that the original work was developed as sixteen chapters organized in several volumes. The first four chapters are not included here and have not yet been transcribed. For the most part those early chapters contain information on the general state of canal building and engineering in the early 19th century, and background history—although there is also a section on certain C&O structures and engineering problems. Overall, however, the information is less specific to the C&O in chapters one through four than that in chapters five through sixteen treated as separate monographs in this volume.

Special appreciation for the preliminary transcription and minimal editing of the text goes to NPS volunteers William Bauman (who did the vast majority of the transcriptions), Rita Bauman, Karen Gray, Gary Petrichick, and Cecilia Thompson. Their work represents literally thousands of hours at their computers and in the C&O Canal NHP library. They, in turn, are indebted to C&O Canal NHP staff, especially William Justice and Sam Tamburro, who provided invaluable assistance in resolving many of the problems and uncertainties that the material presented; and Gary Scott from the regional office whose experience and advice in preparing the material for publication was also invaluable.

Karen M. Gray, Ph.D.
Volunteer and 2007 Draft Editor
C&O Canal National Historical Park
1850 Dual Highway, Suite 100
Hagerstown, MD 21740-6620
CHOH_information@nps.gov

HISTORIC RESOURCE STUDY
CHESAPEAKE & OHIO CANAL NHP

1.
DESIGNERS OF THE C & O CANAL

BY HARLAN D. UNRAU
HISTORIAN, C&O CANAL RESTORATION TEAM, SENECA
DENVER SERVICE CENTER
1976

CONTENTS

INTRODUCTION			11
I.	QUALIFICATIONS OF AN ENGINEER		12
II.	DESIGNERS WITH FULL LENGTH BIOGRAPHIES		13
	A.	JOHN JAMES ABERT (1788–1863)	13
	B.	CHARLES ELLET, JR. (1810–1862)	16
	C.	JAMES GEDDES (1763–1838)	20
	D.	WILLIAM RICH HUTTON (1826–1901)	22
	E.	CHARLES FENTON MERCER (1778–1858)	25
	F.	NATHAN S. ROBERTS (1776–1852)	30
	G.	BENJAMIN WRIGHT (1770–1842)	33
III.	DESIGNERS WITH PARTIAL BIOGRAPHIES		39
	A.	ALFRED CRUGER	39
	B.	CHARLES B. FISK	40
	C.	JOHN MARTINEAU	42
	D.	ELLWOOD MORRIS	43
	E.	THOMAS F. PURCELL	44

INTRODUCTION

The purpose of this document is to present the biographies of the engineers who played a prominent role in the design and construction of the Chesapeake & Ohio Canal. By studying the background of these men, one will gain a better understanding of the skills and experiences which they brought to the construction of the Chesapeake & Ohio. A look at the activities of these men after they left the canal will also enable one to place their services on the canal in the context of their professional engineering careers.

This chapter has been divided into two parts. The first section contains those individuals for whom biographical information is available to treat their entire lives. The second section includes those men for whom only limited biographical data is available. For the purpose of organization, the entries in both sections are alphabetized.

This chapter should not be considered as an exhaustive treatment of the aforementioned subjects. There are other lesser-known engineers who also played a role in the building of the canal. However, it can be argued that this chapter contains virtually all of the readily available biographical information on the lives of the most prominent engineers to be engaged in the construction of the Chesapeake & Ohio Canal.

I. QUALIFICATIONS OF AN ENGINEER

Before one studies the biographies of the principal engineers on the Chesapeake & Ohio Canal, it is imperative that he understand the qualifications for such a job as described by American canal promoters in the early nineteenth century. Civil engineering was just emerging from an infant state of development during this period. Furthermore, the canal era in the United States was just beginning to flourish when the Chesapeake & Ohio project was initially conceived and designed. Thus, one can more easily appreciate the training and expertise which the canal engineers brought to their task by understanding the qualification for such work as stated by contemporary writers active in the promotion of American canals.

Samuel Young, one of the New York canal commissioners, compiled his *A Treatise on Internal Navigation* at the request of the other commissioners in 1817 in order to familiarize New Yorkers with the standard engineering technique employed in Europe. Later, this book was widely read by canal enthusiasts throughout American. In the book, young listed seven qualifications for an engineer as follows:

1. A skillful engineer should undoubtedly possess a considerable degree of mathematical knowledge. Calculations, of which some are of the most obstruse [sic.] and laborious kind, will frequently occur; and he should therefore, be well acquainted with the principles on which all calculations are founded, and by which they are to be rightly applied in practice.
2. An engineer should also have studied the elements of most or all of the sciences, immediately connected with his profession; and he should particularly excel in an acquaintance with the various branches of mechanics, both theoretical and practical.
3. His knowledge should comprehend whatever has been written or done by other engineers, and he should have information in every department of his office from an accurate examination of the most considerable works that have been executed in all the various circumstances that are likely to occur.
4. It is necessary, that he should be a ready and correct, if not a finished, draughtsman.
5. He should also be conversant with the general principles of trade and commerce; with the various operations and improvements in agriculture; with the interests and connection of the different owners and occupiers of land, houses, mills, & c.; and with all the general laws and decisions of courts, pertaining to the objects connected with his profession.
6. By an extensive acquaintance with the disposition, inclination, and thickness of the various strata of matter, which compose the soil or land...he will be able to avoid many errors incident to those who are destitute of this knowledge, and to have the course and causes of springs, to which it leads.
7. "As the last, though not the least, of these qualifications of an engineer, which we shall enumerate, we shall add, that he should be a man of strict integrity."[1]

---

[1] Samuel Young, compl, *A Treatise on Internal Navigation* (Ballston Spa, 1817), 9–10

II DESIGNERS WITH FULL LENGTH BIOGRAPHIES

A. JOHN JAMES ABERT (1788–1863)

SIGNIFICANT CONTRIBUTIONS TO
THE CHESAPEAKE & OHIO CANAL

John J. Abert performed significant services for the Chesapeake & Ohio Canal both as a director of the company in 1833–1834 and 1836 and as a member of the U. S. Topographical Engineers. In 1824–25, he and his assistants conducted a detailed survey of the proposed route for the canal. A preliminary report submitted by Abert on February 14, 1825, supported the practicality of building an artificial waterway along the north bank of the Potomac from tidewater and of connecting the Potomac and Ohio River Valleys. Based on the results of this survey, Congress chartered the canal company in a measure signed by President James Monroe on March 3, 1825. Because his cost estimate for the canal's construction was considered extremely high, his survey was submitted to a reexamination in 1827 by James Geddes and Nathan S. Roberts, two civil engineers who confirmed the suitability of the route he had surveyed but at a lower estimated cost.

Shortly before the canal was opened to navigation between Georgetown and Seneca Falls in the summer of 1831, Abert and James Kearney, a fellow topographical engineer, were asked to inspect the canal's engineering works. In their report, they reported favorably on the quality of construction completed and described the existing conditions along the waterway.

During the late 1830s when talk was revived of an earlier project to connect Baltimore and the Chesapeake and Ohio via a crosscut canal, Abert was called to survey three possible routes for such a waterway. In his December 1838 report, he found that all three routes were impractical because of an insufficient water supply on the summit levels. Although he reported the discovery of a fourth, from Seneca to the Patapsco River via Brookeville, his projected high cost estimate for the waterway ended further speculation about the connection at that time.

BIOGRAPHICAL SKETCH

Early Years

Born probably in Shepherdstown, Virginia, (some sources place his birth at Frederick, Maryland), on September 17, 1788, John J. Abert was the son of John Abert, who is said to have emigrated to America as a soldier with Rochambeau in 1780, and Margarita Meng. On January 18, 1808, he was appointed from Virginia to the Military Academy at West Point where his scholarship soon won for him an assistantship to the professor of mathematics. In 1811 he left the Academy and for some three years he was an assistant to the chief clerk of the War Office in Washington, at the same time studying law. He was married to Ellen Matlack Stretch, granddaughter of Colonel Timothy Matlack, a Revolutionary War veteran, on January 25, 1812.[2]

He was admitted to the District of Columbia bar in 1813, practicing law there in 1813 and in Ohio in 1814. He served as a volunteer in the District of Columbia militia in 1814 and

---

[2] Asa M. Stackhouse, *Col. Timothy Matlack: Patriot and Soldier* (Haddonfield, 1910), 29–58. They had two daughters and four sons, three of which, James William, Silvanus Thayer, and William Stretch, served with distinction in the U.S. Army during the Civil War. *Appleton's Cyclopedia of American Biography*, I, 8–9.

fought as a private in the Battle of Bladensburg, August 24, 1814, and his services were acknowledged by a land grant of 160 acres in Wisconsin.[3]

Experience Prior to Service
On the Chesapeake & Ohio Canal

On November 22, 1814, Abert was appointed major in the Topographical Engineers and was attached to the northern division of the army from this date until January 15, 1829. He was engaged as an assistant under Ferdinand Rudolph Hassler and Isaac Roberdeau in geodetic surveys of the Atlantic Coast (1816–1818); in topographical surveys concerning harbor and river improvements, canals, and defenses, principally in the eastern United States; and in the preparation of extensive reports covering these activities. The wide scope of his work in making important surveys during the period of America's development after the War of 1812 is indicated by the following services, which form only part of those which he rendered during this time. He was an assistant in the reconnaissance of the East River in New York in 1818. That same year he served as superintending Topographical Engineer of Surveys in the Chesapeake Bay. The following year he held the same position in surveys of Dutch Island, Mount Hope Bay, Newport Neck, and the western entrance to Narragansett Bay, and the Narragansett roads in Rhode Island; the East River in New York; the Fall River in Massachusetts; and the Louisville Canal in Kentucky. After directing a survey of Cox's Head in 1821, he superintended a survey for the proposed Chesapeake & Ohio Canal in 1824–25, during the same period heading a reconnaissance of the Patuxent River in Maryland. Later in 1826–27, he made surveys in the State of Maine. In recognition of his abilities as well as his frankness in criticizing the organization and functions of the Topographical Bureau, he was brevetted lieutenant colonel on November 22, 1824.[4]

Service on the Chesapeake & Ohio Canal

During 1824–25, Abert and his assistants conducted a detailed survey of the proposed route of the Chesapeake & Ohio Canal. The survey was ordered by Congress which had appropriated $30,000 in response to the campaign growing out of the first Chesapeake & Ohio Canal Convention held in Washington in November 1823. The U.S. Board of Engineers made a preliminary report on February 14, 1825, supporting the practicability of building an artificial waterway along the north bank of the Potomac from tidewater and of connecting the Potomac and Ohio River Valleys.[5]

Based on the results of this survey, Congress chartered the canal company in a measure approved by President Monroe on March 3, 1825.[6] On October 13, 1826, however, the Board of Engineers made its full report, which the President transmitted to Congress on December 7, 1826.[7] The report reiterated the physical practicability of building the canal, but estimated the cost of the canal upon the dimensions required by the federal government at approximately

---

[3] *Dictionary of American Biography*, XI, 1
[4] George W. Cullum, *Biographical Register of the Officers and Graduates of the U.S. Military Academy at West Point, N.Y., from Its Establishment in 1802 to 1890* (3rd. ed., Boston, 1891) I, 101–102.
[5] U.S., Congress, House, Committee on Roads and Canals, Report of the Committee on Roads and Canals, H. Rept. 90, 19th ,Cong., 2d sess., 1827, Appendix 3, 37, 76.
[6] U.S., Congress, Senate, *Documents Relating to the Chesapeake & Ohio Canal*, S. Doc. 610, 26th Cong., 1st sess., 1840, 13. The charter called for the following minimum dimensions: 40 feet wide at the surface, 28 feet wide at the bottom, and 4 feet deep.
[7] The full report is printed in *Message of the President of the United States, Transmitting a Report from the Secretary of War with that of the Board of Engineers for Internal Improvement, on the Chesapeake & Ohio Canal*, H. Doc. 10, 19th Cong., 2d sess., 1826.

$22,000,000 for the eastern section.[8] The estimated cost had a devastating impact on the hopes of the canal supporters, who had been thinking in terms of a cost of $4,000,000 to $5,000,000. The result was the call for a second Chesapeake & Ohio Canal Convention in December 1826, which sought to discredit Abert's estimate and pressure President John Quincy Adams to submit the conflicting claims to two civil engineers, James Geddes and Nathan Roberts.[9]

Abert performed other services for the Chesapeake & Ohio Canal in subsequent years. Shortly before the line of the canal between Georgetown and Seneca Falls was opened to operation in the summer of 1831, an examination of the waterway was made by Abert and James Kearney at the request of the canal board. On June 13, the two engineers began their inspection, reporting favorably on the quality of construction completed and describing the existing condition along the waterway. The report, which is extant, is the earliest and generally most useful document that discusses in a comprehensive manner the problems encountered in the canal's construction and the engineering technology applied to their solution.[10]

Throughout the following decade, Abert was consulted frequently by the canal company engineers on matters of design and construction. During this period, he served as a company director in 1833-34 and 1836. When tales were revived in 1838 of an earlier project to connect Baltimore and the Chesapeake & Ohio via a cross-cut canal, he was called to examine three possible routes for such a waterway—the Westminster, the Monocacy–Lingamore, and the Seneca. In his report in December 1838, he confirmed the conclusions of earlier surveys that had found all three routes to be impractical because of an insufficient water supply of the summit levels. At the same time, he reported the discovery of a fourth, from Seneca to the Patapsco River via Brookeville. In response to a request for a further study of the Brookville route, he reported in February 1839 that for the 21 3/4 mile summit level, the probable cost of construction would be $11,570,000, a figure that ended all speculation about the connection at that time.[11]

Engineering Experience after Service
On the Chesapeake & Ohio Canal

Because of his engineering skills and executive acumen, Abert was made assistant to the chief engineer in charge of the Topographical Bureau on March 19, 1829. Some two years later on June 22, 1831, he was instrumental in having the bureau separated from the Engineer Department and made a distinct branch of the War Department.[12] During most of the period 1832 through 1834, he served as U.S. Commissioner for Indian Affairs in conducting the removal of Indian tribes to lands west of the Mississippi River. His principal efforts during 1833 and 1834 were directed toward attempts to locate reservations and to certify contracts for the Creeks and Wyandottes.[13]

---

[8] The detailed estimates were: $8,177,081.05 for the eastern section, $10,028,122.86 for the middle section, and $4,170,223.78 for the western section, making a total of $22,375,427.69.

[9] *Report of the Committee on Roads and Canals*, 1827, Appendix 13, 15, 82–87, and Forest G. Hill, *Roads, Rails and Waterways: The Army Engineers and Early Transportation* (Norman, 1957), 51–54.

[10] *Report of Col. John J. Abert and Col. James Kearney of the United States Topographical Engineers, Upon an Examination of the Chesapeake & Ohio Canal from Washington City to the "Point of Rocks;" Made by Order of the Secretary of War, at the Request of the Canal Company* (Washington, 1831)1–24.

[11] *Report from J. J. Abert ,In Reference to the Canal to Connect the Chesapeake & Ohio Canal with the City of Baltimore* (Washington, 1838), 1–42, the Proceedings of the President and Board of Directors, C, 400, D 119, #, 82.

[12] William H. Holcombe, "Col. John James Abert," in *Professional Memoirs, Corps of Engineers, U.S. Army and Engineer Department* (1915), VII, 204–205.

[13] See U.S., congress, Senate, *Correspondence on the Subject of the Emigration of Indians*, S. Doc. 512, 23d Cong., 1st sess., 1833.

From 1834 to 1861, as Chief of the Topographical Bureau, he was largely responsible for initiating and directing the topographic surveys of the United States, particularly in the West. To him fell the task of planning, organizing, and integrating the voluminous textual and cartographic products of these surveys, thereby placing him in the forefront of the American geographers of his time. His work was largely responsible for making the Topographical Bureau perhaps the most valuable repository of topographic description of the United States for this period. An act of Congress, approved July 7, 1838, elevated the Topographical Engineers to a staff corps of the army, and at that time he was appointed colonel, which rank he held until he was honorably retired from active duty on September 9, 1861.[14]

Abert had many professional affiliations aside from his duties with the Topographical Engineers. He was one of the founders and directors of the National Institute of Science in Washington, an organization that was a forerunner of the Smithsonian Institution.[15] An ardent supporter of scientific and historical associations, he was a member of the Geographical Society of Paris, the Washington National Monument Society, and the Board of Visitors to the United States Military Academy (1842). He befriended foreign scientists, such as Joseph Nicolas Nicollet and John James Audubon when they experienced difficulties in America, and occasionally enlisted their services in the Topographical Bureau. He died at his residence in Washington, D.C., on January 27, 1863, at the age of 74.[16]

B.   CHARLES ELLET, JR. (1810–1862)

SIGNIFICANT CONTRIBUTIONS TO
THE CHESAPEAKE & OHIO CANAL

During the summer of 1838, Charles Ellet, Jr., was hired as a volunteer assistant rodman by the Chesapeake & Ohio Canal Company. During the summer and fall, he aided in the surveys preparatory to the placement of the canal under contract, taking field notes, drawing maps, and making computations. Because of his initiative, Chief Engineer Benjamin Wright on November 22 appointed him Assistant Engineer of the Fifth Residency. He remained with the canal company until March 1830, when he resigned to continue his formal education in Paris.

BIOGRAPHICAL SKETCH

Early Years

Born at Penn's Manor in Bucks County, Pennsylvania, on January 1, 1810, Charles Ellet, Jr. was the sixth o the fourteen children of Charles Ellet, an eccentric Quaker farmer, and Mary Israel, the daughter of the one-time sheriff in Philadelphia. His maternal grandfather was a descendent of a family of Jewish diamond cutters originating in Holland, while his paternal ancestors were the

---

[4] Cullum, *Biographical Register of the Officers and Graduates of the U.S. Military Academy*, 101–102, and *Dictionary of American Biography*, xl, 3.

[15] *Reply of Col. Abert and Mr. Markoe to the Hon. Mr. Tappan, of the United States Senate* (Washington, 1843), 1–18.

[16] Washington *Daily National Intelligencer*, January 28, 1863; Francis H. Herrick, *Audubon the Naturalist* (2 vols., New York, 1917), II, 3–4, 64, 77, 155; and *Dictionary of American Biography*, XI, 3.

descendents of Samuel Carpenter, who had been secretary to William Penn and subsequently governor of Pennsylvania.[17]

After attending the country grammar schools along with the other children of his family, Ellet was able to attend a day school in Philadelphia for several months. As a youth, he gave early evidence of intellectual development and mathematical talent. About the age of 14, he began his own self-education, hiding his books in his pillow and feigning sickness to gain time to read, and carrying his books with him during his farm field work. His father being opposed to his becoming an engineer, he left home at age 17 to serve for several months as a rodman on the survey then being conducted by Canvass White along the North Branch of the Susquehanna River, where he acquired the rudiments of his profession.[18]

Service on the Chesapeake & Ohio Canal

During the summer of 1828, Ellet traveled to Maryland to begin work as a volunteer assistant on the Chesapeake & Ohio Canal, arriving in time to witness the groundbreaking ceremonies at Little Falls on July 4.[19]

While the board of directors relied heavily on experienced canal engineers from the North or those of foreign origin in making engineering appointments for the project, the rodmen were the principal exception to this policy. The directors accepted inexperienced applicants such as Ellet who were seeking a career in engineering. Some were appointed as apprentices and received their board and room, while others such as Ellet were only taken on as volunteer assistants without any fixed position or salary, thus making the canal a school in practical engineering.[20]

Throughout the summer and fall, Ellet did almost all the office work of his party, drawing the maps, making the computations, and walking from ten to twenty miles a day surveying the route. In recognition of his initiative and abilities, Chief Engineer Benjamin Wright on November 22 appointed him to the position of Assistant Engineer of the Fifth Residency at an annual salary of $800 on the supposition that he was "t least twenty two years of age" and had had considerable experience in engineering. During the period of his work on the canal, he devoted his leisure hours to the study of foreign languages, several of which he mastered. He remained with the canal company until March 1830 when he resigned to take up formal studies in Paris.[21]

After nearly two years on the canal, Ellet left for France in the spring of 1830 to complete his education in Paris at the Ecole Polytechnique. He witnessed the July revolution, made friends with Lafayette, and traveling by foot, inspected English, French, and German engineering works.[22]

---

[17] Herbert Pickens Gambrell, ed. *Memoirs of Mary Israel Ellet* (Doylestown, 1939), 15, 19, 28, and Charles Perrin Smith, *Lineage of the Lloyd and Carpenter Family* (Camden, 1870), 16–18, 64, 69–70, 78.)
[18] Charles B. Stuart, *Lives and Works of Civil and Military Engineers of America* (New York, 1871), 258.
[19] Ellet's diary, January 3, 1853, quoted in Gene D. Lewis, *Charles Ellet, Jr.: The Engineer As Individualist, 1810–1862* (Urbana, 1968), 14.
[20] Proceedings of the President and Board of Directors, A. 114–115, and Walter S. Sanderlin, *The Great National Project* (Baltimore, 1946), 62–63. Unless otherwise noted, all manuscript sources referred to in this chapter are located in the Chesapeake & Ohio Canal Records in the Department of the Interior files at the National Archives and are designated Record Group 79. [But such official support did not last. See Sanderlin, *The Great National Project*, 63, footnote 15: "In 1830, Judge Wright flatly vetoed President Mercer's plan to abolish the position of volunteer rodman by making the incumbents all inspectors of masonry, a job for which they were utterly unqualified." Wright to Mercer, February 24, 1830. –kg]
[21] Stuart, *Lives and Works of Civil and Military Engineers*, 258–259.
[22] *Dictionary of American Biography*, III, 87, and Stuart, *Lives and Works of Civil and Military Engineers*, 259

Upon his return from France in early 1832, the Chesapeake & Ohio Canal Company offered him his former position at a salary of $1,000 a year with the opportunity for promotion the next year to superintendent of a residency.[23]

In October 1832, he proposed to Congress a plan for the erection of a wire suspension bridge across the Potomac consisting of a 1,000-foot span, but the novel recommendation was rejected. The following summer, he was employed as an Assistant Engineer in the location of the western division of the Utica and Schenectady Railroad under William C. Young. In 1834 he conducted the first survey of the western division of the New York and Erie Railroad along with Benjamin Wright.[24]

Upon the recommendation of Wright, he was appointed assistant engineer of the James River and Kanawha Canal in June 1835. When Wright left full-time service with the canal the next year, Ellet became chief engineer, a job he held for nearly three years during which time the project was completed from Richmond to Lynchburg. While supervising the construction of the waterway, he made a survey for a ship canal from Richmond to Warwick and drew up a plan for the connection of the James River and Kanawha Improvement with tidewater.[25]

During his years with the James River and Kanawha Canal Company, he also wrote numerous pamphlets and reports on topics relative to the improvement and prosperity of the State of Virginia, especially advocating a continuous line of improvements from the Chesapeake Bay to the Ohio River.[26]

Ellet left the James River and Kanawha Canal in 1839 and returned to Philadelphia where he completed his *An Essay on the Laws of Trade*, a 283-page work devoted to the internal improvement in the United States. In the publication, he forecast sources and lines of trade, the tonnage and cost of transportation, the sources of capital, and the causes of the failure of transportation companies.[27]

During the next decade, Ellet was involved in a number of public improvement and private transportation projects. In 1840, he submitted to the St. Louis City Council a plan for a suspension bridge across the Mississippi River at that city.[28]

The following year he was employed to survey the city of Philadelphia and its surrounding environs. In 1842, he designed and constructed, at a cost of $35,000, the first important suspension bridge in the United States over the Schuylkill River at Fairmount.[29]

---

[23] Mercer to Ellet, February 7, 1832, Ltrs. Sent, C&O Co. Available evidence seems to indicate that Ellet rejected the offer because of the financial plight of the canal company and the competition of the Baltimore & Ohio Railroad. Lewis, *Charles Ellet, Jr.*, 26.
[24] *Appleton's Cyclopedia of American Biography*, II, 326.
[25] Charles Ellet, Jr., *Report on the Survey for a Ship Canal from Richmond to Warwick* (Richmond, 1836), 1–16, and Wayland Fuller Dunaway, *History of the James River and Kanawha Company* (New York, 1922), 240
[26] Among these works, the most notable were: *A Popular Exposition of the Incorrectness of the Tariffs of Toll in Use on the Public Improvements of the United States* (Philadelphia, 1839); *Report in Relation to the Water Power on the Line of the James River and Kanawha Canal* (Richmond, 1839); and *Report of the Chief Engineer on the Survey for the Extension of the James River and Kanawha Improvement from Lynchburg to the Ohio River* (Richmond, 1838).
[27] Charles Ellet, Jr., *An Essay on the Laws of Trade* (Richmond, 1839), 1–283.
[28] Charles Ellet, Jr., *Report and plan for a Wire Suspension Bridge: Proposed to be Constructed Across the Mississippi River at Saint Louis* (Philadelphia, 1840) 1–58.
[29] Charles Ellet, Jr., *A Popular Notice of Suspension Bridges, With a Brief Description of the Wire Bridge Across the Schuylkill at Fairmount* (Philadelphia, 1843), 1–18.

During 1846–47, he served as president of the Schuylkill Navigation Company, enlarging the channel of that important carrier of anthracite coal to a width of more than seventy feet and personally negotiating loans both at home and abroad for its reconstruction.[30]

In 1847, he left the presidency of the navigation company to design and build iron cable suspension bridges over the Niagara River, two miles below the falls; and over the Ohio at Wheeling. After he had erected a temporary bridge, the Niagara project was interrupted by court litigation and he withdrew his contract. His Wheeling Bridge, which was the completed in 1839, was 1,010 feet long—then the world's longest span. While a court suit brought a decree of abatement, he saved this bridge by convincing Congress to declare it a post-route, only to witness its destruction by a heavy storm in 1854.[31]

For more than twenty-five years, he urged the improvement of Western rivers. The Smithsonian Institution published his *Contributions to the Physical Geography of the United States* in 1850. His investigations into the causes of floods undertaken for the War Department in 1850–51 resulted in several reports and the publication in 1853 of his best known work, *The Mississippi and Ohio Rivers*. His plan for improving navigation and controlling floods or the principal western rivers by impounding surplus waters in upland reservoirs was considered to be the crowning conception of his professional career, but vigorous efforts to secure the necessary legislation to affect it failed.[32]

After brief service in laying out the western portion of the Baltimore & Ohio Railroad, Ellet became chief engineer for the Pennsylvania Railroad at Greensburg, in 1851. The following year he submitted to the Georgetown authorities a second plan and report for a suspension bridge across the Potomac River.[33]

In 1853 he was appointed chief engineer of the Virginia Central Railroad, for which in 1854 he built across the Blue Ridge a track of unprecedented curvature and grade.[34]

Later in 1858 he served as an engineer on the Kanawha River improvement in Virginia.[35]

Visiting Europe during the Crimean War, Ellet urged Russia to use "ram-boats" in the relief of Sebastopol (a bold innovation in naval warfare), and later offered similar plans to the allies. Returning home, he urged his ram-boat scheme to several secretaries of the navy and widely circulated his *Coast and Harbor Defences, or The Substitution of Steam Battering Rams for Ships of War* (1855).[36]

When the Merrimac demonstrated the effectiveness of a ram in 1862, he was commissioned a colonel by Secretary of War Edwin M. Stanton and assigned to protect the Mississippi

---

[30] Before becoming president of the Schuylkill Navigation Company, Ellet had written a pamphlet on the favorable possibilities for trade on the waterway. For more information on this topic, see hi *The Position and Prospects on the Schuylkill Navigation Company* (Philadelphia, 1834), 1–36.

[31] Charles Ellet, Jr., *The Wheeling Bridge* (Philadelphia, 1852), 1–6; and Charles Ellet, Jr., *Remarks Touching the Wheeling Bridge Suit, Addressed to the Hon. G. W. Thompson* (Philadelphia, 1852), 1–24.

[32] *The Cyclopedia of American biography*, II; Charles Ellet, Jr., *Contributions to the Physical Geography of the United States* (Washington, 1850), 1–65; Charles Ellet, Jr., *The Mississippi & Ohio and Rivers* (Philadelphia, 1853), 17–367; and Charles Ellet, Jr., *Report on the Overflows of the Delta of the Mississippi* (Washington, 1852), 1–96.

[33] Charles Ellet, Jr., *Report on a Suspension Bridge Across the Potomac, for Rail Road and Common Travel: Addressed to the Mayor and City Council of Georgetown, D.C.* (Philadelphia, 1852), 1–36.

[34] *Dictionary of American Biography*, III, 87; and Charles Ellet, Jr., *The Mountain Top Track* (Philadelphia, 1856), 1–23.

[35] *The Twentieth Century Biographical Dictionary of Notable Americans*, III; and Charles Ellet, Jr., *Report on the Improvement of the Kanawha and Incidentally of the Ohio River By Means of Artificial Lakes* (Philadelphia, 1858), 1–125.

[36] Charles Ellett, Jr., *Coast and Harbour Defences, or the Substitution of Steam Battering Rams for Ships of War* (Philadelphia, 1855), 1–17.

gunboat squadron against a fleet of Confederate rams. Hastily remodeling nine river boats on the Ohio River with heavy oak and railroad iron, he, with a volunteer crew, sank four Confederate boats near Memphis on June 5 and received the surrender of that city. Ellet, the only Union man injured in the battle, died as his boat touched shore at Cairo and his brother, Lieutenant-Colonel Alfred Washington Ellet, took command of the small fleet on June 21. Following services at Independence Hall in Philadelphia, he was buried in a nearby cemetery. His wife, Elvira, daughter of Judge William Daniel of Lynchburg, whom he had married in 1837, survived him by eight days.[37]

C. JAMES GEDDES. (1763–1838)

SIGNIFICANT CONTRIBUTIONS TO THE CHESAPEAKE & OHIO CANAL

James Geddes, an experienced engineer on the Erie, Champlain, and Ohio and Erie Canals, played a significant role in the design of the Chesapeake & Ohio Canal. In 1827, he, in association with Nathan S. Roberts, reviewed the estimates of the canal line for the secretary of War. The subsequent report, which estimated the cost of the canal to be considerably less than that proposed earlier by the U.S. Board of Engineers, enabled the project's supporters to extract from Congress a $1,000,000 stock subscription and thereby provided impetus to the commencement of actual construction of the waterway. Later, after the formal organization of the Chesapeake & Ohio Canal, the board of directors adopted for the line of the canal the route surveyed by the U.S. Board of Engineers and by Geddes and Roberts.

BIOGRAPHICAL SKETCH

Early Years

Born of Scottish ancestry near Carlisle, Pennsylvania, on July 22, 1763, James Geddes attended the public schools. As a young man he studied mathematics under a tutor and he studied languages on his own. In 1794 he moved to the vicinity of Syracuse, Onondaga County, New York, where he became one of the pioneers in the salt industry. The township of Geddes where he settled was named for him and remained his residence until his death on August 19, 1838, at the age of 75. In 1799 he was married to Lucy Jerome, daughter of Timothy Jerome of Fabius, New York. After studying law, he was admitted to the bar. In 1800 he was made a justice of the peace, and in 1809 he was appointed judge of the county court and of the court of common pleas. Becoming interested in public affairs, he was elected to the Assembly in 1804, the Thirteenth Congress, serving 1813–15, and again to the Assembly in 1822.[38]

Experience Prior to Service
On the Chesapeake & Ohio Canal

---

[37] Joel T. Headley, *Farragut and our Naval Commanders* (New York, 1867), 209–223; Warren D. Crandall and Isaac D. Newell, *History of the Ram Fleet and the Mississippi Marine Brigade...* (St. Louis, 1907), 1–28; and Washington *Evening Star*, June 23, 1862.

[38] *Biographical Dictionary of the American Congress, 1774–1971* (Washington, 1971), 993; *Dictionary of American Biography*, VII, 204–205; and Stuart, *Lives and Works of Civil and Military Engineers*, 45.

During his first term at Albany, Simon DeWitt, surveyor-general of New York, introduced Geddes to the possibility of constructing a canal from the Great Lakes to the Hudson River. Since the suggestion touched his imagination, he visited various sections of the state to secure information and launched a campaign, with the aid of DeWitt Clinton, to promote interest in the undertaking. When the state legislature appropriated $500 for a preliminary survey of the canal, the surveyor-general assigned the task to Geddes, although he was entirely without technical training, having used a level only on one previous occasion. The surveys he made in search of the most practicable route included: Oneida Lake to Lake Ontario where Salmon Creek enters it, down to Oswego River to Lake Ontario, the line from Lewiston to the navigable waters of the Niagara River above the falls, and from Buffalo east to the Seneca River. His report to the legislature, January 20, 1809, established the fact that a canal could be constructed without major difficulty along a route essentially the same as that later adopted for the Erie Canal.

When work on the Erie began in 1816, Geddes was engaged by the New York Canal commissioners as an engineer in charge of the section from the Seneca River to within eleven miles of the mouth of Tonawanda Creek. He remained on this section until 1818 when he was directed to superintend the location of the middle division between Rome and Utica. During this period, he made a remarkable test level between Rome and the eastern end of Oneida Lake, embracing nearly 100 miles of leveling. The difference at the junction in the levels was less than 1 ½ inches. In the summer of 1818, he was appointed by the Canal Commissioners as chief engineer of the Champlain Canal, commencing the final location of the work in September and continuing in charge of its construction until 1822.[39]

As a result of his work on the New York canals, Geddes was called by other states as well as by the federal government for assistance in promoting new waterways throughout the East. When the State of Ohio asked DeWitt Clinton in 1822 for the services of a good engineer, he recommended Geddes. Named chief engineer of the Ohio and Erie Canal that same year, he surveyed some 800 miles in less than eight months in the search for the most practicable route between the Ohio River and Lake Erie.[40]

The following year he went to Main to survey the route for the Cumberland and Oxford Canal, connecting tidewater with Sebago Pond.[41]

Service on the Chesapeake & Ohio Canal

At the request of the Secretary of War, Geddes, along with Nathan S. Roberts, made a survey of the proposed line of the Chesapeake & Ohio Canal from Georgetown to Cumberland in 1827. As the survey and cost estimate for the waterway by the U.S. Board of Engineers two years before had received widespread criticism from the canal's supporters, Geddes and Roberts were to review and revise the conflicting claims of the opposing sides. The two civil engineers completed their surveys in 1827 and reported in the same year that the canal could be constructed as far as Cumberland for approximately $4,500,000. This estimate was considerably less than the $8,200,000 proposed by the Board of Engineers for the same distance, and thus it enabled the ca-

---

[39] Merwin S. Hawley, "The Erie Canal: Its Origin Considered," Buffalo Historical Society Publications II (1880), 335–349; Henry Wayland Hill, "An Historical Review of Waterways and Canal Construction in New York State," Ibid, XII (1908), 95–103; and Joshua V.H. Clark, Onondaga (2 vols., Syracuse, 1849), II, 25ff.

[40] *Canal Report, Made by James Geddes, Esq., The Engineer Employed by the State of Ohio* (Columbus, 1823), 1–14.

[41] *The National Cyclopedia of American Biography*, X, 264.

nal project's supporters to extract from Congress a pledge to subscribe to $1,000,000 of stock in the company, thereby hastening the actual commencement of construction.[42]

After the canal company was formally organized, June 20–23, 1828, one of the first decisions of the board of directors was to adopt for the line of the canal the route surveyed by the United States Engineers and by Geddes and Roberts along the north branch of the Potomac River.[43]

Engineering Experience after Service
On the Chesapeake & Ohio Canal

Following the survey for the Chesapeake & Ohio Canal, Geddes was employed in 1828 by the State of Pennsylvania on its canal system. That same year he declined an appointment by the United States Government to investigate the feasibility of a route between the Tennessee and Alabama Rivers in the States of Tennessee, Alabama, and Georgia because of the distance from his home and ill health. In 1829 he terminated his professional career by reporting on the recently-completed Cumberland and Oxford Canal in Maine.

His death occurred on August 19, 1838, at the age of 75, and he was buried in Oakwood Cemetery in Syracuse, New York. Although urged to do so by his colleagues, he left no collection of papers, saying, "I attach no importance to what I have done, having simply performed my duty; therefore I ask no higher place in the public estimation than should be spontaneously given to me."[44]

D. WILLIAM RICH HUTTON. (1826–1901)

SIGNIFICANT CONTRIBUTIONS TO
THE CHESAPEAKE & OHIO CANAL

William R. Hutton played a significant role in the restoration and improvement of the Chesapeake & Ohio Canal as chief engineer in 1869–71 and consulting engineer in 1871–80. During the early 1870s when the canal enjoyed five years of unprecedented financial profits, he submitted two reports to the canal board that served as a basis for a program to recondition the waterway. As a result of his efforts, the canal regained its full prism by 1874 and the strength of its banks had been increased to withstand damage from periodic flooding. Among other improvements made on the canal at his urging were the dredging of Rock Creek Basin, an experiment in macadamizing the towpath, and the restoration of the masonry structures. One of his most noteworthy achievements was the promotion and the design of the Georgetown incline as a means of alleviating the congestion on the Georgetown level.

BIOGRAPHICAL SKETCH

---

[42] James Geddes and Nathan S. Roberts, *Chesapeake & Ohio Canal: Letter from the Secretary of War, Transmitting Estimates of the Cost of Making a Canal from Cumberland to Georgetown, March 10, 1828* (Washington, 1828), 1–100.
[43] Proceedings of the President and Board of Directors, A, 8.
[44] Quoted in Stuart, *Lives and Works of Civil and Military Engineers*, 45; *Biographical Dictionary of the American Congress*, 993; and Desmond Fitzgerald, "Early Engineering work in the United States," *Transactions of the American Society of Civil Engineers*, XLI (1899), 611.

Early Years

Born in Washington, D.C., on March 26, 1826, William Rich Hutton was the son of James[45] Hutton, a Navy department clerk, and Salome Rich. He was a descendent of John Hutton who had emigrated from Scotland to New York in the late seventeenth century. As a youth, he attended a private school in the District of Columbia taught by Mr. Abbott. Later, he studied mathematics, surveying, and drawing at the Benjamin Hollowell School in Alexandria, Virginia. In 1847, he was appointed as paymaster clerk in California and remained in that position until he returned to the Ease in 1853.[46]

Engineering Experience Prior to Service On the Chesapeake & Ohio Canal

Soon after his arrival in Washington, Hutton began his professional career in civil engineering by assisting General Montgomery C. Meigs in the construction of the Washington Aqueduct, carrying a large part of the water supply from the Great Falls of the Potomac to the city of Washington. This work involved not only the devising of methods to control the flow and distribution of the water, but also the design of the monumental bridge across Cabin John Branch which for some fifty years remained unsurpassed as the longest masonry arch in the world.[47]

In 1862–63, he served as chief engineer of the Annapolis Water works.[48]

Service on the Chesapeake & Ohio Canal

Hutton was associated with the Chesapeake & Ohio Canal during the most stable and prosperous periods of its history, serving as chief engineer in 1869–71 and consulting engineer in 1871–80. Familiar with the canal from his youth and from his work on the Washington Aqueduct, he played a significant role in the program of restoration and improvement of the waterway, particularly during the early 1870s when the canal enjoyed five years of unprecedented financial profits.[49]

Despite the repairs that had been made to the canal since the Civil War, there was still much to be done. Following an extensive survey of the canal, Hutton in 1871 recommended to the board of directors a thorough overhauling of the waterway, including repairs to locks, aqueducts, and the canal prism itself, at an estimated cost of $78,000.[50]

Following another Hutton report in August 1872 on the pressing need for renovation of the canal, a reconditioning program was begun that carried to completion the restoration of the

---

[45] Father's name is John according to biographical information on the Baltimore Architects Foundation web site: www.baltimorearchitecture.org/bios/hutton_wr.html. According to that site during the period 1873–1880 William Hutton apparently entered into a partnership with his brother, Major N. H. Hutton, (1834–1907), a leading Baltimore architect. —kg

[46] American Society of Civil Engineers, Committee on History and Heritage of American Civil Engineering, ed., *A Biographical Dictionary of American Civil Engineers* (New York, 1972), 64–65.

[47] *Dictionary of American Biography*, VI, 507.

[48] American Society of Civil Engineers, *Biographical Dictionary of American Civil Engineers*, 64–65.

[49] *The Twentieth Century Biographical Dictionary of Notable Americans*, V.

[50] Proceedings of the President and Board of Directors, L. 439, and *Report of the Year 1870* (Annapolis, 1871) 9.

canal to its original operating condition.[51] As a result of his efforts, the canal had regained its full prism by 1874, and the strength of its banks had so increased that a freshet which completely submerged the canal on the levels below Dams No. 4 and 5 in April of that year did not do appreciable damage.[52]

Among the other improvements made on the canal at Hutton's urging were the partial macadamization of the towpath on the Monocacy Division, the dredging of the Rock Creek Basin, the tightening of the lock chambers, the installation of new lock gates, and the rebuilding of the parapets and trunks of the Seneca and Tonoloway Aqueducts.[53]

In addition to the work of repair and improvement, provision was made to collect materials at periodic locations along the canal in anticipation of future trouble, thereby helping to expedite the actual work of repair and to reduce the interruptions to navigation.[54]

Perhaps the most noteworthy project with which he was associated was the promotion of the design of the Georgetown Incline as a means of alleviating the congestion on the Georgetown level by providing canal barges with direct access to the Potomac above the Alexandria Aqueduct.[55]

Engineering Experience after Service
On the Chesapeake & Ohio Canal

When he terminated his duties with the canal as chief engineer in 1871, Hutton took employment as chief engineer of the Western Maryland Railway, serving in this capacity from 1871–74. It was during this period that the Chesapeake & Ohio, in an effort to promote the expansion of its coal trade, sought to facilitate the construction of this railroad from Baltimore to Big Pool on the Potomac, expecting to carry most of the railroad's coal business between Big Pool terminus and Cumberland.[56]

From 1874 to 1878, he designed the first two locks and movable dams for the Kanawha River navigation in Virginia, receiving a *diplome d'Honneur* at the Paris Exposition in 1878 for his lock design.[57]

Hutton moved to New York City in 1880, and after a brief respite, he became a construction engineer on the New Croton Aqueduct in 1886. During 1886–87, he held a similar position with the Colorado Midland Railroad. From 1886–1889, he was chief engineer of the Washington Bridge over the Harlem River, and in 1889–91 he was chief engineer for the English syndicate that built the Hudson River Tunnel. In 1892, he was a member of a commission under the U.S. Board of Engineers concerned with obstructions in the Columbia River. His last major work was the drafting of plans for the Secretary of War for the proposed memorial bridge over the Potomac

---

[51] *Report of W.R. Hutton, Chief Engineer, As To Condition of Chesapeake & Ohio Canal, With Estimate of Cost of Extraordinary Repairs Required During the Current Year, August 14, 1872* (Annapolis, 1872), 4–30.
[52] *46th Annual Report* (1874), C&O Canal, 11–12, and *Proceedings of the President and Board of Directors*, M, 154–155.
[53] *Report of W.R. Hutton, 1872*, 4–30, and Forty-Second Annual Report (1870), C&O Co. 3–4.
[54] *Report of W.R. Hutton, 1879*, 4–30, and Hutton to Clarke, August 3, 1870, Ltrs. Recd., C&O Co.
[55] Virtually the entire section of the William R. Hutton collection concerned with the Chesapeake & Ohio Canal is composed of correspondence, plans, and drawings for the Georgetown Incline. The collection is located in the Division of Mechanical and Civil Engineering, the National Museum of American History [named the National Museum of History and Technology until 1980], the Smithsonian Institution, Washington, D.C.
[56] *45th Annual Report* (1873), C&O Co., 16–17.
[57] American Society of Civil Engineers, *Biographical Dictionary of American Civil Engineers*, 64–65

River between Washington and Arlington for which he received the second award of the four plans submitted.

After a six-week illness, he died on December 11, 1901 at Woodlands in Montgomery County, Maryland, and was buried in the cemetery of the nearby St. Rose Catholic Church. His wife, Mary Ann, the daughter of Francis Clopper of Montgomery County, four daughters, and one son, survived him.[58]

During his long career, he had many prestigious professional associations. In 1873, he became a member of the American Society of Civil Engineers; in 1880, of the Societe des Ingenieurs Civils de France; and in 1890, of the Institution of Civil Engineers of Great Britain. In 1891, he published his only book *The Washington Bridge over the Harlem River*, which traced the development of the design and construction of this famous structure.[59]

E. CHARLES FENTON MERCER. (1778–1858)

SIGNIFICANT CONTRIBUTIONS TO THE CHESAPEAKE & OHIO CANAL

Charles Fenton Mercer was active in the movement that resulted in the building of the Chesapeake & Ohio Canal and was for five years, 1828 to 1833, president of the company. An early advocate of internal improvements in his native Virginia, Mercer was elected to Congress in 1817 and later became chairman of the House Committee on Roads and Canals. As the chairman of the central committee of the Chesapeake & Ohio Canal Convention that met in Washington in November 1823, he played a prominent role in organizing public opinion behind the proposed connection between the Potomac and the Ohio Rivers and the creation of organizations to give effect to this rising interest.

When the Chesapeake & Ohio Canal company was formally organized at a meeting of the stockholders in Washington, June 20–23, 1828, Mercer was chosen the first president of the company. Though having no technical engineering training or experience, Mercer and the board of directors reserved to themselves the final decision on every question of design and construction no matter how specialized. Mercer frequently participated actively in the discussion of engineering technicalities, thus making himself of the most influential designers of the canal project in its early years. Throughout his tenure as president of the canal company, Mercer was a persistent advocate for "perfection" in construction, urging greater care and expenditure in construction in order to reduce subsequent repair and maintenance costs.

BIOGRAPHICAL SKETCH

Early Years

Born at Fredericksburg, Virginia, on June 16, 1778, Charles Fenton Mercer was the youngest son of Eleanor Dick, daughter of Mayor Charles Dick of Fredericksburg, and James Mercer, a prominent lawyer who had risen to the position of judge on the Virginia Court of Appeals. Charles Fenton was a grandson of John Mercer of Marlborough, a wealthy Virginia lawyer who had immi-

---

[58] Washington *Evening Star*, December 13, 1901.
[59] *Appleton's Annual Cyclopedia and Register of Important Events of the Year 1901*, VI, 438.

grated to Stafford County from Dublin, Ireland, in 1720 at the age of 17. Prominent in colonial affairs, John Mercer had written and published the first abridgement of the laws of Virginia.[60]

Left an orphan at the age of 15, Charles Fenton entered the College of New Jersey (later changed to Princeton University) in 1795 and graduated in 1797 at the head of his class. In college he began his lifelong friendship with John Henry Hobart, a prominent bishop in the Protestant Episcopal Church, and became a devout Episcopalian. From 1797 until 1802 he read law at Princeton and at Richmond. When war with France threatened in 1798, he sought commissions in the United States Army, appealing to family friend George Washington for assistance in obtaining them. However when the commissions were received—one as first lieutenant of the cavalry and the other as captain—he declined them since the threat had ceased.[61]

In 1802 he was licensed to practice law and soon afterward he went to England on business and also visited France. On his return to America, he settled on a large estate in the Bull Run Mountains at Aldie in Loudoun County, Virginia, and began the practice of his profession. He was never married.[62]

Mercer became a member of the Virginia House of Delegates in 1810 and served until he resigned in 1817 to enter Congress. While a member of the state legislature, he took a leading part in efforts to increase the banking capital of Virginia, to found a new bank, to promote the colonization in Africa of free Negroes from the United States, and to build roads and canals. He offered a bill to provide for a complete system of public education, from common-school to state university, which was defeated in the Senate in the spring of 1817 after having passed the House.[63]

He was also the author of the act by which a sword and pension were given to George Rogers Clark, the frontiersman and military leader who had won important victories against the British in the Old Northwest Territory during the American Revolution. During the War of 1812, Mercer was aide-de-camp to the governor and in command of the Second Virginia Brigade at Norfolk with the rank of brigadier-general.[64]

His interest in internal improvements began in 1812 when he acted with Chief Justice John Marshall and others as a commissioner appointed by the legislature to examine the Greenbrier and New Rivers, both sources of the Kanawha, and the headwaters of the James for the purpose of improving them for navigation and uniting them either by a railroad or by a continuous canal.

That same year he submitted a series of resolutions to the legislature for the establishment of a general fund for the internal improvement of the rivers and roads of the State. At the close of the war, he revised the resolutions he had earlier submitted to create a Fund for Internal

---

[60] James Mercer Garnett, *Biographical Sketch of Hon. Charles Fenton Mercer: 1778–1858* (Richmond, 1911), 3–5.
[61] This has largely been rewritten based on Robert Allen Carter, *Virginia Federalist in Dissent: A Life of Charles Fenton Mercer*, doctoral dissertation, University of Virginia, 1988, copy by UMI Dissertation Services, Ann Arbor, MI, 89–90. —kg
[62] *Dictionary of American Biography*, VI, 539. The Charles Fenton Mercer home at Aldie is still used as a private residence. It is located on U.S. 50, marked by a state sign noting Mercer's accomplishments.
[63] Throughout his political career, Mercer continued to press for a public education program. One of the most prominent speeches that he gave in behalf of his active interest in public education was *A Discourse on Popular Education; Delivered in the Church at Princeton, the Evening before the Annual Commencement of the College of New Jersey, September 26, 1826* (Princeton, 1826).
[64] *The Cyclopedia of American Biography*, IV. See also his Congressional bio at bio.congress.gov, which says: "During the War of 1812 [he] was appointed lieutenant colonel of a Virginia regiment and then major in command at Norfolk, Va.; inspector general in 1814; aide-de-camp to Governor Barbour and brigadier general in command of the Second Virginia Brigade."

Improvement to consist of all the stocks of the State derived from banking operations and all future acquisitions from the same source. To administer the fund he recommended the establishment of a Board of Public Works that would be empowered to hire a civil engineer and to propose to the legislature measures of improvement that were deemed expedient to the State. When the Board of Public Works was approved in 1816, Mercer became a member along with former president Thomas Jefferson and later James Madison.[65]

Mercer's enthusiasm for internal improvements, the suppression of the slave trade, and the colonization of free Negroes gave direction to his efforts when he became a member of the federal House of Representatives in 1817. He was chairman of the committees on roads and canal and on the District of Columbia.[66] Though a member of the Federalist Party until its dissolution, and then a Whig, he was never an ardent party man. He enjoyed the friendship of Presidents James Monroe and John Quincy Adams, but disliked the policies and personalities of Presidents Andrew Jackson and Martin Van Buren. One of his most famous addresses in Congress was delivered on January 26, 1819, in which he assailed Jackson's course in the Seminole War.[67]

He was a strong Unionist but was alarmed at the rapidly growing power of the executive branch of government under Jackson and was opposed to the President's control over federal patronage. He was a leader in the Virginia constitutional convention of 1829–30, in which he advocated manhood suffrage, equal representation, and the popular election of important officers. One of the originators of the plan for establishing the Free State of Liberia for American blacks, he became vice president of the Virginia Colonization Society in 1836.[68]

Service on the Chesapeake & Ohio Canal

As one of the leading advocates of internal improvements in Congress, Mercer became active in the movement that resulted in the construction of the Chesapeake & Ohio Canal. His second speech in the House favoring the constitutionality of the power of the federal government to appropriate funds for internal improvements received wide attention and was later published as a pamphlet. When interest in opening the Potomac Valley as a route for western trade began to increase in the early 1820s, he became a leading voice in calling for the first Chesapeake & Ohio Canal Convention to meet in Washington on November 5, 1823. Acting on behalf of a meeting he had convened earlier at Leesburg, Virginia, he invited delegates from Pennsylvania, Maryland, Virginia, and the three district cities to this convention to consider the expediency and practicality of improving the navigation of the Potomac and connecting it with the Ohio River at Pittsburgh. As chairman of the central committee, he exercised the guiding hand throughout the proceedings of the convention.[69]

---

[65] Garnett, *Biographical Sketch of C. F. Mercer*, 7, 13–14.
[66] He was initially a member of the Committee on the District of Columbia and later a member of and then, from 1831–39 (the 22nd through 25th Congresses), he was chair of the Committee on Roads and Canals.—kg
[67] *Annals of Congress*, 15 Cong., 2 Sess., 1818, Cols. 797–831. Also see, Charles Fenton Mercer, *Speech of the Hon. Mr. Mercer, in the House of Representatives, on the Seminole War* (Washington, 1829), 1–33.
[68] *Biographical Dictionary of the American Congress*, 1399; *Dictionary of American Biography*, VI, 539; and Matthew Carey, *Letters on the Colonization Society...addressed to the Hon. C. F. Mercer* (7th ed., Philadelphia, 1833) 5–32.
[69] U.S., Congress, House, Committee on Roads and Canals, *Chesapeake & Ohio Canal*, H. Rept. 414 to Accompany H.R. 94, 23d Cong., 1st sess., 1834, 4; U.S., Congress, House, Committee on Roads and Canals, *Report of the Committee on Roads and Canals*, H. Rept. 47, 20th Cong., 1st sess., 1828, 7–10, 16–23; *Proceedings of the Chesapeake & Ohio Canal Convention...1823...1826* (Washington, 1827), 1–4; and

The primary functions of the convention were the organization of public opinion behind the proposed connection between the Potomac and the Ohio and the creation of organizations to give effect to this arouse interest. The physical achievements of the convention were simply the adoption of Mercer's resolutions urging the connection with the West which read as follows:

> Whereas, a connection of the Atlantic and Western waters by a canal, leading from the seat of the National Government to the river Ohio, regarded as a local object, is one of the highest importance to the states immediately interested therein, and considered in a national view, is of unestimable [sic] consequences to the future union, security, and happiness of the United States.
>
> Resolved, that it is expedient to substitute for the present defective navigation of the Potomac River, above tide-water, a navigable canal from Cumberland to the Coal Banks at the eastern base of the Alleghany, and to extend such canal as soon thereafter as practicable to the highest constant steamboat navigation of the Monongahela or Ohio River.[70]

At a second meeting of the Chesapeake & Ohio Canal Convention on December 6, 1826, Mercer reported the progress which the central committee, of which he was virtually the only acting member, had made during the preceding three years. He had procured the cooperation of the three district cities and the Potomac Company in the enlarged venture. Moreover, sixteen acts of legislation had been passed by the three states most directly involved, in a measure approved by President Monroe on March 3, 1825.

Although the U.S. Board of Engineers had hurt the prospect for a congressional subscription to stock in the proposed canal by estimating the cost at $22,000,000, Mercer urged the delegates to support him in a two-fold course: to discredit the estimate of the Board of Engineers and to cause a new survey to be made to ascertain the true cost of the work. Through the efforts of Mercer and his supporters, the report of the government engineers was exhaustively examined and criticized by making comparisons with the actual cost of work don on the New York and Pennsylvania canals.

Later, Mercer played a leading role in the effort to have President John Quincy Adam submit the conflicting estimates made by the convention and the Board of Engineers to a review and revision by experienced civil engineers. Adams agreed and appointed James Geddes and Nathan S. Roberts, both former engineers on the Erie Canal. They completed their surveys in 1827 and reported that the canal could be constructed as far as Cumberland for approximately $4,500,000.[71]

Fortified with this estimate and reassured by the inaccuracy of the U.S. engineer's report, the canal supporters led by Mercer opened subscription books on October 1, 1827. In May 1828, after a brief struggle, Mercer and his fellow protagonists in Congress secured the passage of an act subscribing $1,000,000 of the public funds to the stock of the Chesapeake & Ohio Canal Company. The financial support of Congress triggered numerous celebrations throughout the Po-

---

Abner Lacock, *Great National Project: Proposed Connection of the Eastern and Western Waters, By a Communication through the Potomac Country* (Washington, 1822), 1–38.
[70] *Proceedings of the Chesapeake & Ohio Canal Convention, 1823 and 1826*, 4, and George Washington Ward, *The Early Development of the Chesapeake & Ohio Canal Project* (Baltimore, 1899), 50.
[71] *Report on the Committee on Roads and Canals*, 1827, Appendix 13, 15, 82–87, and *Documents Relating to the Chesapeake & Ohio Canal*, 1840, 13.

tomac Valley, one of the most noteworthy being a banquet given at Leesburg in honor of Mercer by the citizen of Loudoun County.[72]

The formal organization of the Chesapeake & Ohio Canal Company took place at a meeting of the stockholders in Washington, June 20–23, 1828. With the tacit approval of President Adams, Secretary of the Treasury Richard Rush, the proxy for the United States, placed Mercer's name in nomination for president of the company and Mercer was duly elected, although a small minority of stockholders favored former Secretary of the Treasury Albert Gallatin.[73]

During the early years of canal construction, Mercer and the canal board of directors reserved to themselves the final decision on every question of design and construction despite their selection of tested engineers and their own inexperience in canal technology. One of the best examples of this meddling in the affairs of the engineers occurred in November 1828 when a detailed set of "Rules and Regulations for the Engineering Department" was issued, virtually forcing the Engineers to sublimate their own expertise to the wishes of the board.[74]

In addition, President Mercer frequently participated actively in the discussion of engineering technicalities, notably in the proper dimensions of the canal prism through Georgetown and through the narrow passes near Point of Rocks and in the proper procedures to be followed in excavating the channel through rocky terrain.[75] Under such conditions, differences of opinion which arose between members of the engineering department were frequently carried over the head of Chief Engineer Benjamin Wright by appeals from ambitious underlings.

The five-year tenure of Mercer as president of the canal company was clouded by his political battles with the Jacksonian Democrats in Congress. Desperate for increased funding and denied extensions of large-scale aid by Maryland, Virginia, and the district cities, the canal company turned to congress as the last available source of aid. The prospects of assistance from the federal government, however, were slight after the victory of Andrew Jackson in 1828. The record of the administration clearly indicated its hostility toward national support for internal improvements in general and for the Chesapeake & Ohio in particular. By 1832, the administration was actively interfering in company affairs, and eventually Congress refused to accede to any of Mercer's petitions for further aid.

As president of the canal company, Mercer was a persistent advocate of "perfection" in construction. He urged greater care and expenditure in construction regardless of financial considerations in order to reduce subsequent repair and maintenance costs. This attitude was exemplified by his rejection of composite locks, slackwater navigation, and reduction of the cross-section of the canal prism in difficult terrain as temporary expedients that were not fitting for a work of national importance. Regardless of its economic and technical soundness, the policy of insisting on perfection regardless of the cost—which was generally supported by the directorate—proved to be a politically disastrous course for the company in the 1830s and 1840s, and left the future success of the canal clouded by a staggering capitalization.[76]

---

[72] Washington *National Intelligencer*, May 27, 1828; Charles Francis Adams, ed., *Memoirs of John Quincy Adams* (12 vols., Philadelphia, 1874–1877), VIII, 6; and Wilhelmus B. Bryan, *A History of the National Capital* (2 vols., New York, 1916), II, 111.
[73] *Proceedings of Stockholders*, A, 1–6; and Adams, *Memoirs of John Quincy Adams*, 8, 23–24, 26–27, 33–34, 36–37.
[74] *Proceedings of the President and Board of Directors*, A, 107, 109–110. Benjamin Wright, the well-known canal engineer who had been actively associated with the building of the Erie, had been hired as chief engineer upon the recommendation of Mercer.
[75] Mercer to Wright, February 2, 1830, and Wright to Mercer, February 2 and 3, 1830, Ltrs. Recd. C&O Co.
[76] Sanderlin, *The Great National Project*, 122–123.

In an effort to win the favor of the national administration, the canal company consented in 1833 to the replacement of Mercer by ex-Secretary of War John Eaton, a friend of Andrew Jackson, and a principal in the Peggy Eaton affair. At the annual stockholders' meeting in June of that year, the vote was 5,054 to 3,430 in favor of Eaton. However, 1,798 votes of Maryland and Georgetown were lost because of a division among the proxies. If cast for Mercer, as had been expected, they would have been sufficient to reelect him. As a final tribute to Mercer for his efforts on behalf of the canal, the stockholders later voted him a gift of $5,000.[77]

Discouraged by the obstacles to his efforts for the further development of internal improvements and for the gradual abolition of slavery and colonization of blacks, Mercer resigned from Congress on December 16, 1839.[78]

After spending several years working as a bank cashier in Tallahassee Florida, he became vice president of the National Society of Agriculture in 1842. He was an original grantee, partner, and agent of the Texas Association, a company which obtained a contract to settle colonists in Texas to receive pay from the Public in land. When the convention in 1845 declared colonization contracts unconstitutional, he and his associates brought suit to force payment, but the case was decided against them in the United States courts. In 1845 he published a vindictive pamphlet entitled "An Exposition of the Weakness and Inefficiency of the Government of the United States in North America.[79]

In 1847 Mercer built a house near Carrollton, Kentucky, which he made his home until 1853. Disposing of his property there in that year, he traveled for three years through Europe, working in the interest of the abolition of the slave trade. Ill with cancer of the lip, he returned to Fairfax County, Virginia, where he was nursed by relatives until his death on May 4, 1858. Initially buried in Leesburg's Episcopal Cemetery, his remains were later moved to Union Cemetery.[80]

F. NATHAN S. ROBERTS (1776–1852)

SIGNIFICANT CONTRIBUTIONS TO
THE CHESAPEAKE & OHIO CANAL

Nathan S. Roberts, an experienced engineer on the Erie, Chesapeake and Delaware, Pennsylvania Main Line, and Chenango Canals, played a significant role in the design and construction of the Chesapeake & Ohio Canal from 1827 to 1830. In 1827 he, in association with James Geddes, reviewed the estimates of the canal line for the Secretary of War. The subsequent report, which estimated the cost of the canal to be considerably less than that proposed by the U.S. Board of Engineers, enabled the project's supporters to elicit a $1,000,000 stock subscription from Congress and thereby provided impetus to the commencement of actual construction of the waterway. In December 1828 he became a member of the board of engineers, and, during the winter and spring, he, along with Benjamin Wright, completed the revision and location of the projected western section of the canal to Pittsburgh. In 1828 and 1829 he readied for construction the 12-

---

[77] "Proceedings of the Stockholders," A, 313; *Niles' Register*, XLIV (June 22, 1833), 270–271; and Garnett, *Biographical Sketch of C. F. Mercer*, 19–20.
[78] Charles Fenton Mercer, *The Farewell Address of the Hon. C. F. Mercer to his Constituents* (Washington, 1839), 1–16.
[79] In 1863 this booklet was reprinted in London under the title *The Weakness and Inefficiency of the Government of the United States of North America; By a Late American Statesman.*
[80] *Biographical Dictionary of the American Congress*, 1899, and *Dictionary of American Biography*, VI, 539.

mile stretch of the canal between Point of Rocks and Harpers Ferry. During the autumn and winter of 1830–31, he served in Washington as superintendent of the first division of the canal.

BIOGRAPHICAL SKETCH

Early Years

Born on July 28, 1776, Nathan S. Roberts was the son of Abraham Roberts, a native of New Hampshire whose Puritan forefathers had emigrated from England to Plymouth Colony in 1640 and settled in Auburn, Massachusetts. His grandfather, John Roberts, was slain in 1764 while serving as a soldier under Sir William Pepperell during the French and Indian War. As a young man, his father had gone to the West Indies and had acquired great wealth. Returning to America during the outbreak of the Revolution, he was captured by British cruisers, lost his fortune, and was forced to serve in the Royal Navy in several engagements against American vessels. Later he escaped and established his residence at Piles Grove, New Jersey, where Nathan was born.[81]

During his youth, Roberts aided in the support of his parents and younger brothers. After coming of age, he purchased 100 acres of new land in Vermont, where he began the cutting of timber, but he returned to Plainfield, New Jersey, and taught school in the winter. In 1803 he visited New York to examine some wild land that he had purchased in Oneida County. The following year he settled there and taught school at Oriskany until 1806, when he was appointed principal of the academy at Whitesboro. Here, on November 4, 1816, he married Lavinia, daughter of Ansel White and grand-daughter of Judge Hugh White, a pioneer settler of the region. That same year, he bought a farm in Lenox, Madison County, which was his home during the remainder of his life.[82]

Experience Prior to Service
On the Chesapeake & Ohio Canal

At the invitation of Benjamin Wright, Roberts began his career as a civil engineer on the Erie Canal in July 1816. His first job was to make a survey of the route of the middle section of the canal to Montezuma. He spent the winter of 1816–17 at Rome, preparing maps and profiles of the recently explored line. When the middle section was located and staked out the following spring, he was employed on it as an assistant engineer. In 1818 he was employed through the winter as a resident engineer in charge of the work from Rome to Syracuse, and in the spring was placed in charge of a party to locate the canal from Syracuse westward. Commencing on April 12, this location was completed to the Seneca River in July, and the work was contracted that summer.

In 1819 he located the canal from the Seneca River to the village of Clyde, and during the winter of 1819–20, he drafted plans for the locks between Clyde and Rochester. The following spring he located the canal down the Clyde River Valley and through the Cayuga marshes on the line he had explored the previous fall. He continued in charge of this work until near its completion in 1822, when he was directed by the Canal Commissioners to supervise the construction of the locks at Lockport and the building of the western section of the canal between Lockport and Lake Erie.

Roberts remained on the western section of the canal until its completion in 1825. He drafted the plan which was unanimously adopted for five pairs of locks at Lockport to overcome the barrier formed by a 60-foot rocky ridge—a more elaborate scheme of locks than had ever

---

[81] Stuart, *Lives and Works of Civil and Military Leaders*, 109–110.
[82] *Dictionary of American Biography*, XVI, 12.

been constructed in America. Construction of the locks began in July 1823, and they were opened to navigation in October 1825. Throughout his life, he took pleasure in alluding to the locks as the greatest accomplishment of his professional career.[83]

Upon completion of the Erie, Roberts became a consulting engineer for the Chesapeake and Delaware Canal in 1826. In January, 1826, he was employed by the State of New York to survey and to report on a route for a ship canal around Niagara Falls. Then followed service as chief engineer of the western section of the Pennsylvania Main Line Canal extending between Pittsburgh and Kiskiminetas. During a visit home he made an investigation and report for the New York State Canal Board on the practicality of supplying the summit level of the projected Chenango Canal with water.

Service on the Chesapeake & Ohio Canal

At the request of the Secretary of War, Roberts and James Geddes conducted a survey of the proposed line of the Chesapeake & Ohio Canal in 1827. As the survey and estimated cost of the canal made by the U.S. board of Engineers in 1825 had aroused fierce opposition by supporters of the project, these two civil engineers were to review and revise the conflicting claims of the two parties in the dispute. They completed their surveys in 1827 and reported in the same year that the canal could be constructed as far as Cumberland for approximately $4,500,000. This estimate was considerably less than that proposed by the Board of Engineers, and it enable the canal project's supporters to elicit a $1,000,000 stock subscription from Congress, thereby as enin the formal organization of the company and the actual commencement of construction.[84] t g

After the canal company was formally organized in June 1828, the board of directors adopted the route surveyed by the U.S. Board of Engineers and Roberts and Geddes along the north bank of the Potomac River for the line of the canal. Upon Wright's invitation in December 1828, Roberts became a member of the board of engineers to provide overall direction to the construction. During the winter and spring of 1828–29, he, along with Wright, completed the revision and location of the projected western section of the canal to Pittsburgh.[85]

In 1828–29, he surveyed the twelve-mile stretch through the narrow passes between Point of Rocks and Harpers Ferry, the area which was the focal point of the disputed right-of-way between the canal the Baltimore & Ohio Railroad.[86]

During the autumn and winter of 1830–31 as canal officials were readying the line between Little Falls and Seneca Falls for operation, he served in Washington as superintendent of the first division of the canal.[87]

---

[83] Stuart, *Lives and Works of Civil and Military Engineers*, 111–114; *Dictionary of American Biography*, XVI, 12; Fitzgerald, "Early Engineering Work," 610, John A. Krout, "New York's Early Engineers," *New York History*, XXVI (1945), 272; and Noble Earl Whitford *History of the Canal System of the State of New York Together with Brief Histories of the Canals of the United States and Canada* (2 vols., Albany, 1906), I, 797–798.

[84] Geddes and Roberts, *Chesapeake & Ohio Canal: Letter from the Secretary of War, Transmitting Estimates of the Cost of Making a Canal from Cumberland to Georgetown*, 1–100.

[85] Nathan S. Roberts and Benjamin Wright, "Report and Letters from the Engineers Employed in the Revised Location of the Western Section of the Chesapeake & Ohio Canal: With Estimates of the Cost of the Same," in *First Annual Report* (1829), C&O Co.

[86] *A complete Set of Maps, Drawings, and Tabular Statements; Relating to the Location of the Canal and Railroad, from the Point of Rocks to Harper's Ferry...Done Under and Order of the Chancellor of Maryland...Nathan S. Roberts, Commissioner, on the Part of the Chesapeake & Ohio Canal Company* (Georgetown, 1830), 1–56.

[87] *Proceedings of the President and Board of Directors*, B, 1771–174.

As the legal obstructions resulting form the dispute with the B&O Railroad were continuing to hamper construction, he requested a leave of absence from his employment with the canal company.[88]

Engineering Experience after Service
On the Chesapeake & Ohio Canal

After several more months rest at home, Roberts was appointed by the federal government to take charge of surveys for a ship canal around Muscle Shoals in the Tennessee River, Alabama. He held this position as chief engineer for two years. During this employment he was asked to take charge of the canal connecting the Mississippi River with Lake Pontchartrain in New Orleans, but he refused because of poor health and returned home to New York.[89]

In the spring of 1835, he was employed by the New York State Canal Board, along with John B. Jervis and Holmes Hutchinson, to make a series of examinations and surveys preparatory to enlarging the Erie. Four years later, he was named chief engineer of the western section and began the enlargement of the canal between Rochester and Buffalo, rebuilding one tier of the locks at Lockport and extending the dimensions of the canal prism. In 1841, while still engaged in the completion of his last great work, the Rochester Aqueduct, he was removed from office for political reasons by the new Whig administration which had risen to power in New York the previous year. He now retired to his farm in Madison County, where he died on November 24, 1852.[90]

G. BENJAMIN WRIGHT (1770–1842)

SIGNIFICANT CONTRIBUTIONS TO
THE CHESAPEAKE & OHIO CANAL

Benjamin Wright, sometimes called the "Father of American Civil Engineering," served as chief engineer on the Chesapeake & Ohio Canal from June 1828 to November 1830. In this position, he played a leading role in the design and construction of the waterway during its first years of existence. At Wright's urging, the board of directors relied heavily upon the available supply of men experienced on Northern or foreign canals to oversee the construction. During the 1828–29, he, along with Nathan S. Roberts, collaborated in an extensive survey of the projected western extension of the canal to the Ohio River.

BIOGRAPHICAL SKETCH

Early Years

Born in Wethersfield, Connecticut, on October 10, 1770, Benjamin Wright was the son of Ebenezer and Grace (Butler) Wright and a descendent of Thomas Wright, an early settler of Wethersfield. His father was a farmer of limited means and could only send his children to common

---

[88] Ibid, B, 295.
[89] Stuart, *Lives and Works of Civil and Military Engineers*, 116, and *Dictionary of American Biography*, XVI, 13.
[90] Alvin Fay Harlow, *Old Towpaths: The Story of the American Canal Era* (New York, 1926), 301–302; Krout, "New York's Early Engineers," 273–274; and Fitzgerald, "Early Engineering Work," 610.

schools during the winter months. Throughout his youth, he took a deep interest in mathematics and surveying. At the age of 16, he went to reside with an uncle at Plymouth in Litchfield County, where he had access to the best books and instruments which could then be obtained by country surveyors. With his growing knowledge of surveying, he absorbed the spirit of westward migration that was then sweeping New England as many settlers were moving toward the fertile Mohawk and Genesee Valleys of western New York. In those areas, flattering inducements were held out to young men who were capable of surveying land and preparing title deeds.

In 1789 Wright persuaded his father to move with his family to Fort Stanwix, now Rome, New York, which was then on the western border of settlement. For a short time, he assisted his father and brothers in clearing a field and erecting a long cabin. Soon he hired out as a surveyor, a job giving him access to the maps and drawing of very extensive tracts of land around Fort Stanwix. Originally, the surrounding area had been laid out in lots of 500 acres each. These he subdivided into such smaller lots as the settler purchased, which was rarely more than one-half or one-forth of the original lot. When not in the field, he devoted all his time to his studies, procuring from abroad the best books, maps, and instruments and patiently embodying his daily observations in topographical maps. His descriptions, estimates, and surveys became regarded as authoritative in boundary questions. Later, he would use his field notes and topographical information in locating the Erie Canal. Between 1792 and 1796, he laid out into farms more than 500,000 acres in Oneida and Oswego Counties.[91]

In 1798, Wright returned to Plymouth and on September 27 married Philomela Waterman, daughter of Simeon Waterman. They had nine children, eight of whom survived their parents. One son, Benjamin Hall Wright, was also a civil engineer and carried out some of the later projects on which his father had made reports.[92]

Experience Prior to Service
On the Chesapeake & Ohio Canal

As the Mohawk and Genesee Valleys developed into one of the most important agricultural sections in New York, Wright became interested in the problem of transporting surplus products to a market. Since roads were little better than trails and there seemed to be little hope of permanently improving them, he turned his attention to canals. In 1792 the Western Inland Lock Navigation Company had been formed and had completed some pioneer construction around Little Falls on the Mohawk River and thence from the river to Wood Creek at Fort Stanwix under an English engineer, William Weston. Several years after Weston's return to Britain, it was determined to improve the navigation of Wood Creek by dams and locks, there being a descent of 24 feet in some six miles of difficult navigation. Since it would be expensive to bring Weston back for the examination and the leveling, the directors of the company turned to Wright to make a map and profile of Wood Creek. This was his first work as an engineer, and it led to further work for the company.[93]

Philip Schuyler, a prominent general during the American Revolution and the president of the company, was especially pleased with Wright's work and in 1803 directed him to make a survey of Wood Creek from the point where the improvements ended down to Oneida Lake. Soon Schuyler had him survey some 100 miles of the Mohawk River from Fort Stanwix to

---

[91] Stuart, *Lives and Works of Civil and Military Engineers*, 48–50, and American Society of Civil Engineers, *Biographical Dictionary of American Civil Engineers*, 132–133.
[92] *Dictionary of American Biography*, XX, 544.
[93] Fitzgerald, "Early Engineering Work," 608–609, American Society of Civil Engineers, *Biographical Dictionary of American Civil Engineers*, 132–133.

Schenectady, "taking a regular traverse of the river, its windings, its breadth, the descent of each rapid, the descent between the rapids, the depth in each pool between rapids—at its lowest summer drought—the height of alluvial banks, and all other remarks and observations which he might think useful." In addition, he was to propose his own plan for improving the Mohawk in as economical a manner as possible. Wright finished this project in 1803, recommending a series of dams, locks, short canals, and slackwater navigation pools. The financial problems of the company never permitted the construction of any portion of the work.[94]

In 1811 Wright was employed by the state canal commissioners of New York to make an examination of the north side of the Mohawk River from Rome to Waterford on the Hudson. The following year he was directed to examine the country from Seneca Lake to Rome and from thence on the south side of the Mohawk to Albany. His report of this survey, accompanied by maps and profiles, was well-received and served as a preliminary examination for the future construction of the Erie Canal.[95]

During this period, Wright became the agent of the land proprietors in whose serve he had made the most extensive surveys. He thus became a leading member of the community, was repeatedly elected to the state legislature, and in 1813 was appointed county judge.[96]

In 1815, upon the more effective organization of the New York State Canal Board, the work of constructing the Erie project was launched. In the months just after its organization, the Canal Board was divided over the question of sending abroad for a chief engineer. But the views of Joseph Ellicott and others in western New York prevailed and the work was entrusted to Wright and James Geddes, another local surveyor-judge-engineer. Prior to the actual beginning of work, the Erie Canal project was divided into three divisions: Wright was appointed as chief engineer and was to have charge over the middle section between the Seneca River and Rome, Geddes of the western to Lake Erie, and Charles C. Broadhead of the eastern to the Hudson River. The first ground was broken July 4, 1817, at Rome. As the construction of the canal progressed, another engineer, David Thomas, took over the work on the western section, Geddes turned to the problems of the Champlain Canal, and Wright, having completed the middle section, because responsible for the difficult eastern division.[97]

With his abilities as a surveyor, his practical knowledge of construction, and his capacity for leadership, Wright had a significant impact on the design of the Erie and on succeeding generations of American engineers. He singly was responsible for surveying and locating the middle section of the canal, and he collaborated with Canvass White, his able young principal assistant, in determining the location of the line on the eastern division. Although he did not draw any plans of importance, he was, according to one of his assistants John B. Jervis, "a very sagacious critic of any presented."[98]

Wright and Geddes together solved the problem of securing an adequate flow of water for the western section of the canal by keeping the summit level from Buffalo to Lockport lower than the surface of Lake Erie. Among his chief structural engineering accomplishments was his supervision of the construction of the 801-foot aqueduct across the Genesee River at Rochester.

---

[94] Stuart, *Lives and Works of Civil and Military Engineers*, 52–53.
[95] Whitford, *History of the Canal System of New York*, I, 789.
[96] *Dictionary of American Biography*, XX, 543, and Stuart, *Lives and Works of Civil and Military Engineers*, 54.
[97] William A. Bird, "New York State Early Transportation," *Buffalo Historical Society Publications*, II (1880), 32; Merwin S. Hawley, "The Erie Canal: Its Origin, Its Resources, and Its Necessity," Ibid, 305–349; Fitzgerald, "Early Engineering Work," 608; and Stuart, *Lives and Works of Civil and Military Engineers*, 54–60, 68.
[98] John B. Jervis, "A Memoir of American Engineering," *Transactions of the American Society of Civil Engineers*, VI (1878), 42.

To conciliate the critics of the canal project and to prepare the public mind to meet the vast expense of the works near the Cohoes, the Little Falls, the Genesee River, and Lockport, he successfully urged the Canal Board to begin the work on the middle section, building both east and west simultaneously through the least difficult and costly parts.[99]

During his years on the Erie Canal, Wright gathered around him a remarkable group of young men, most of whom afterwards occupied important positions in the engineering field. Canvass White was assigned the duty of designing the locks and other mechanical structures and also contributed the important discovery that hydraulic cement could be produced from a deposit near the line of the canal. John B. Jervis, another assistant, later became one of the foremost American civil engineers of pre-civil war days. David Stanhope Bates had charge of the difficult crossing at the Irondequoit Valley and Nathan S. Roberts supervised the construction of the elaborate set of double locks at Lockport. The Erie Canal was thus the great American engineering school of the early nineteenth century, and Wright, as the presiding genius of the undertaking, has fairly been called the "Father of American Engineering."[100]

The success of the Erie Canal awakened a spirit of internal improvement throughout the developing nation. Wright acted as consulting engineer on a number of canal projects during the last years of the Erie work—the Northampton and New Haven Canal in 1821, the Blackstone Canal in 1822, and the Chesapeake and Delaware Canal in 1823. On the Chesapeake and Delaware project, he was associated with Colonel Joseph D. Totten and General Simon Bernard of the U.S. Board of Engineers, and Canvass White in determining the line of the canal. In 1825, he became consulting engineer for the Delaware and Hudson Canal, an undertaking completed by his associate Jervis.[101]

Service on the Chesapeake & Ohio Canal

Resigning as chief engineer of the Erie in 1827 and the Chesapeake and Delaware in 1828, Wright accepted the invitation of Charles F. Mercer to become chief engineer of the Chesapeake & Ohio Canal in the latter year. At Wright's urging, the board of directors relied almost exclusively upon the available supply of men experienced on Northern or foreign canals. Among his former associates on other canal projects that were employed to fill key engineering positions on

---

[99] Krout, "New York's Early Engineers," 273–275, and Stuart, *Lives and Works of Civil and Military Engineers*, 54–60.

[100] Richard Shelton Kirby and Philip Gustave Lawson, *The Early Years of Modern Civil Engineering* (New Haven, 1932), 46–47, and Harlow, *Old Towpaths*, 295–307. Some years later in 1870, Benjamin Hall Wright, the son of Benjamin Wright, wrote a 13–page booklet entitled *Origin of the Erie Canal Services of Benjamin Wright* in which he outlined the prominent role his father had played in the conception, design, and construction of the Erie and the significant impact of his father's work on subsequent American engineering.

[101] Henry D. Gilpin to Joshua Gilpin, May 28–29, 1823, Henry Dilworth Gilpin Papers, Historical Society of the Delaware, Wilmington; William Meredith to John C. Calhoun, May 19, 1823, quoted in Hill, *Roads, Rails, & Waterways*, 30; *The Act of Incorporation of the Farmington Canal Company, with the Reports of the Hon. Benjamin Wright and Andrew A. Bartow, esq., and of the Committee of the Legislature of Connecticut, on that Subject* (New Haven, 1822) 10–15; *Account of the Proposed canal from Worcester to Providence, Containing the Report of the Engineer, Together with Some Remarks Upon Inland Navigation* (Providence, 1825), 1–16; and *Report of Messrs. Benj. Wright and J.L. Sullivan, Engineers, Engaged in the Survey of the Route of the Proposed Canal from the Hudson, to the Headwaters of the Lackawaxen River* (Philadelphia, 1824), 1–70.

the Chesapeake & Ohio were John Martineau and Nathan S. Roberts, both of whom were appointed to the board of engineers to provide overall direction to the construction on the canal.[102]

During the first year of construction, Wright and Roberts collaborated in an extensive survey of the projected western section of the canal to Pittsburgh, revising the location and cost estimates that had been made by the U.S. Board of Engineers in 1825.[103]

After 2½ years as chief engineer, Wright resigned in November 1830 and refused several offers to return to the canal. While it is difficult to state the precise reasons for his separation from the company, his correspondence and other available documentation indicate several probably causes. His correspondence reveals that he often resented the frequent participation of President Mercer and other members of the board of directors in the discussion of engineering technicalities despite their inexperience in such matters. Under such conditions, differences of opinion which arose between members of the engineering department were frequently carried over the head of the chief engineer by appeals to the board from disgruntled underlings. Thus, the design and construction of the canal was often hampered by fractious infighting.[104]

The legal dispute between the Chesapeake & Ohio Canal Company and the Baltimore & Ohio Railroad over the right-of-way through the narrow passes above Point of Rocks may also have been a factor in Wright's decision to resign. Court injunctions prevented construction of the canal above Point of Rocks until 1832 by which time it was becoming apparent that the railroad would soon provide stiff competition to the financially hard-pressed canal company for the Potomac Valley trade.[105]

Engineering Experience after Service
On the Chesapeake & Ohio Canal

When Wright terminated his association with the Chesapeake & Ohio Canal, he desired to retire and be with his family which had already been removed to New York City. In 1832, he took an appointment as Street Commissioner in New York City, but he resigned at the end of the year because the work was confining and not suited to his interests. Soon he was appointed chief engineer of the Harlem Railroad Company, but he obtained leave of absence in the autumn of 1833 to become the consulting engineer on the St. Lawrence Ship Canal at Montreal. The following year he returned to Canada as the chief engineer on this canal and the consulting engineer on the Welland Canal between Lakes Erie and Ontario. During that year, he also was appointed by Governor Marcy of New York to survey the route for the New York and Erie Railroad under an appropriation from the State which duties occupied him intermittently for two years.[106]

During the years 1835 to 1839, Wright was engaged on several canal and railroad plans, but he remained principally in Virginia where he had been invited after the completion of the

---

[102] Proceedings of the President and Board of Directors, A, 2, 114–115; Proceedings of Stockholders, A, 16016; 1st Annual Report (1829), C&O Co., in ibid, A, 33, 48; and *Documents relating to the Chesapeake & Ohio Canal*, 1840, 126–127.

[103] Roberts and Wright, "Reports and Letters from the Engineers Employed in the Revised Location of the Section of the Chesapeake & Ohio Canal," in *First Annual Report*, (1829), C&O Co.

[104] Proceedings of the President and Board of Directors, A. 107, 109–110, and Wright to Mercer, February 9 and 24, 1830, and Van Slyke to Mercer, February 27, 1830, Ltrs. Recd., C&O Co. For example, in 1830 Wright vetoed Mercer's plan to abolish the position of volunteer rodman by making the incumbents all inspectors of masonry, a job for which they were unqualified.

[105] Sanderlin, *The Great National Project*, 122.

[106] Whitford, *History of the Canal System of New York*, II, 1171–1172; Hugh G. J. Aitken, *The Welland Canal Company: A Study in Canadian Enterprise* (Cambridge, 1954), 100; Fitzgerald, "Early Engineering Work,"611; and Stuart, *Lives and Works of Civil and Military Engineers*, 70–71.

New York and Erie Railroad survey. Earlier in 1824, he had briefly served as a special commissioner in Virginia to expand the James River Canal and make an examination for a connection between the James and the Ohio Rivers via the Kanawha. With the establishment of the James River and Kanawha Company in 1835, he became chief engineer of the project.[107]

Following a short period in this position, Wright had his duties reduced to that of a consultant so that he could participate in other ventures. In 1835, he was called by the Cuban authorities to visit Havana and advise on a railroad from that city to the interior of the island. The preliminary surveys of this work were examined and approved by him, and its subsequent execution was carried out under the superintendence of his son, Benjamin Hall Wright, and Alfred Cruger, an experienced engineer who had been an assistant of Wright on the Chesapeake & Ohio. In 36, he became chief engineer of the Tioga and Chemung Railroad, and in 1837 a consultant on the Illinois and Michigan Canal. He spent his last days in New York City, dying there on August 24, 1842, at the age of 72.[108]

---

[107] *First Annual Report of the President to the Stockholders of the James River and Kanawha Company* (Richmond, 1836), 11

[108] *Informe Sobre El Camino do Hierro de Puerto—Principe a Nuevitas, par D. Benjamin H. Wright* (Puerto Principe, 1827), 1-12; Fitzgerald, "Early Engineering Work," 611; Stuart, *Lives and Works of Civil and Military Engineers,* 71-72; and *New York Tribune,* August 25, 1842.

[II.] DESIGNERS WITH PARTIAL BIOGRAPHIES

A. ALFRED CRUGER

BIOGRAPHICAL SKETCH

Early Years and Experience Prior to Service
On the Chesapeake & Ohio Canal

There is little biographical information on the early life or experience of Alfred Cruger. All that is known is that his residence was in New York and that he surveyed and reported on the proposed route for the Saugatuck and New Milford Canal in Connecticut in 1827. It is likely that he gained some experience on civil engineering on the Erie Canal, although his role would have been minor as no sources on that canal mention his name.[109]

Service on the Chesapeake & Ohio Canal

Cruger was appointed a resident engineer on the fifth residency (Monocacy River to Point of Rocks) of the Chesapeake & Ohio Canal in November 1828.[110] Because of the dispute between the canal and the Baltimore & Ohio over the right-of-way above Point of Rocks, he was commissioned to assist Nathan S. Roberts in surveying the narrow passes from that point to Harpers Ferry.[111] After leaving the employment of the canal company for a short period in 1831 to make surveys for the Leesburg and Snicker's Gap Turnpike Company, he prepared plans and specifications for the Alexandria Aqueduct.[112] During the spring of 1834, he made an extensive survey for the location of the canal between Dams Nos. 5–6, but because of the mounting obstacles to the construction of the waterway he soon resigned to pursue engineering opportunities elsewhere.[113]

Engineering Experience after Service
On the Chesapeake & Ohio Canal

There is little available data on the later engineering career of Cruger except for his activities in Cuba which extended at least from 1835–1842. Shortly after he left the canal, he traveled to Cuba where he convinced the local authorities that their island would receive great financial benefit from building a railroad connecting Havana with the interior of the island.[114] In 1835 Benjamin Wright was called by the Cuban leaders to visit Havana and advise on the construction of such a railroad. After examining and approving the preliminary surveys for the work, he entrusted the superintendence of the project to his son, Benjamin Hall Wright, and Cruger, who remained on the project until at least 1842.[115]

---

[109] Alfred Cruger, *A Report of the Proposed Saugatuck and New Milford Canal* (New York, 1827), 1–11, and Proceedings of the President and Board of Directors, A, 114–115.
[110] Proceedings of the President and Board of Directors, A, 114–115.
[111] Sanderlin, *The Great National Project*, 88
[112] Proceedings of the President and Board of Directors, C. 176.
[113] *Chesapeake & Ohio Canal to Accompany H.R. No. 94,* 1834, 200–220, and Proceedings of the President and Board of Directors, D, 72.
[114] Stuart, *Lives and Works of Civil and Military Engineers*, 72.
[115] *Informe Presentado a la Comision Directiva del Camino de Hierro de Guines, por el Ingeniero Principal Director del Mismo D. Alfredo Cruger, Sobre el Projects de Construccion y Presupuesto del Ramal de*

B. CHARLES B. FISK

BIOGRAPHICAL SKETCH

Early Years and Experience Prior To Service
On the Chesapeake & Ohio Canal

Despite his substantial contribution to the engineering design of the Chesapeake & Ohio Canal, Charles B. Fisk is a relative unknown among nineteenth century American civil engineers. An extensive survey of biographical sources, including the files of the Biographical Archive of American Civil Engineers at the Smithsonian Institution, failed to turn up any information concerning Fisk. Thus the available biographical data on this man is limited to the records of the Chesapeake & Ohio and the James River & Kanawha, the two canal companies by which he is known to have been employed.

Service on the Chesapeake & Ohio Canal

In November 1828, Fisk was appointed as an assistant engineer on the fourth residency (Seneca Creek to Monocacy River) of the Chesapeake & Ohio Canal. The only data on his background found in the canal company records is that his residence was located in Connecticut. It is likely that he was young and relatively inexperienced in civil engineering since the canal directors generally selected for assistant engineers promising youths who were seeking careers in that field. The intention of the directors in adopting such a policy was to promote interest in internal improvements in the South and to follow the example of the Erie Canal in using the construction of the waterway as a "school of engineering."[116]

During the fall of 1833 when the financial plight of the company slowed construction operations on the canal, Fisk became the Superintendent of Repairs for the waterway between Dams Nos. 2 and 3. In April 1835, his duties as superintendent ceased, and he was advanced to equal rank with Thomas F. Purcell as resident engineer and given charge of the important third residency (the line between Dams Nos. 4 and 5) upon which all construction was then concentrated. He soon began to assume a prominent position among the canal company engineers, raising high the banner of perfection which former president Charles F. Mercer had carried so persistently, revising Alfred Cruger's earlier survey and cost estimate for building the 27-mile line between Dams Nos. 5 and 6, and participating on a survey team to locate the final fifty miles of the waterway between Dam No. 5 and Cumberland.[117]

Dicho Camino, desde Onivican al Batalano, Impreso por Acuerdo do la Real Juata de Formento, de Agricultura y Comercio de la Isla de Cuba (Habana, 1836), 1–36, and *Informe General del Ingeniero Director del Ferro-Carril de la Sabanilla, D. Alfredo Cruger, Presentado a la Junta Directors de la Empresa el 14 de Febraro do 1842.*

[116] Proceedings of the President and Board of Directors, A, 114–115, and First Annual Report (1829), C&O Co., in Proceedings of Stockholders, A, 33, 48. Further evidence of his lack of experience before entering service on the C&O Canal was his employment as a rodman on the early survey teams locating he canal in October 1828.

[117] See the first interrogatory and answer on1 of Maryland, General Assembly, Joint Committee on Expenditures for Internal Improvements, *Report of the Joint Committee Appointed to Inquire into the Expenditures of the State, in Works of Internal Improvement* (Annapolis, 1836); *Eighth Annual Report* (1836), C&O Co., 2–4; *Thirteenth Annual Report* (1841), C&O Co., 84–85; Proceedings of the President and Board of Directors, D, 311, 319; Fisk to Board of Directors, March 30, 1835, Ltrs. Recd., C&O Co.; and

When talk revived of connecting Baltimore with the Chesapeake & Ohio via a cross-cut canal, Fisk, with George W. Hughes, a state engineer, surveyed three possible routes for such an undertaking in March 1837. After examining the Westminster, the Monocacy–Linganore, and the Seneca routes, they reported that all three were impracticable because of an insufficient water supply on the summit levels.[118]

Because of his initiative and engineering abilities, Fisk was appointed on April 12, 1837, as chief engineer, a position he held until September 1852 with the exception of a six-month period in 1840–41. Thus, he performed a significant role in directing the design and construction of the canal from Dam No. 5 to Cumberland. Throughout his employment on the canal, his efforts were repeatedly complicated by the financial plight of the canal company and the meddling of the Maryland legislature in the affairs of the canal company.

His separation from the canal between October 1840 and April 1841 was partly the result of a disagreement with the canal directors over the policy of continuing construction on the basis of the unrestricted issuance of script and partly the result of the application of the spoils system in the operation of the canal. When the state authorities reorganized the canal board and launched a sweeping revival of the spoils system in June 1852, he resigned from his position three months later.[119]

Engineering Experience after Service
On the Chesapeake & Ohio Canal

There is little documentation concerning the later career of Fisk but a reference was found relating to his employment as an engineer for the James River and Kanawha Company in the fall of 1854. On October 21 of that year, he made a report to the directors of the company recommending sluice navigation as the best method in the improvement of the Kanawha River.[120]

At some point Fisk went to work for the Chesapeake & Ohio Railroad, as indicated in a important overview of his career on the C&O and his final years as an engineer. Written by James Worrall, a Pennsylvania engineer who worked briefly on the C&O as a young man, this account tell us that:

> Fisk came after Mr. Purcell on the C&O. He was a Connecticut man and a good engineer. He had a splendid corps—Elwood Morris, Gore, John A Byers, and others—but the canal was never finished and they had no great career. ...Fisk struggled along with the company, got poor with them, always respected but never adequately paid. The work was grand and his talents were worthy of it, but money was lacking. At length came up the Virginia railroad from Richmond to Ohio, afterwards called the Chesapeake & Ohio Railroad. Fisk was made Chief Engineer. He planned the mountain crossings via White Sulphur Springs—masterly work, great location, and all that; but in the midst came 1861, all was thrown into *pi*. It broke Fisk's heart; a fine intellect went down in disappointment.

Report of the Committee on the Location of the Canal from Dam No. 6 to Cumberland, October 9, 1835, Recd., C&O Co.

[118] Charles B. Fisk and George W. Hughes, *Report on the Examination of Canal Routes from the Potomac River to the City of Baltimore* (Annapolis, 1837), 1–56.

[119] *Thirteenth Annual Report* (1841), C&O Co., 67; *Twentieth Annual Report* (1848), C&O Co., 9; *Communication from the President of the Chesapeake & Ohio Canal Company to the Governor of Maryland* (Annapolis, 1842), 40–41; and Fisk to the Board of Directors, October 1, 1840, June 3, 1841, and September 27, 1852, Ltrs. Recd., C&O Co.

[120] *Twentieth Annual Report of the President of the Stockholders of the James River and Kanawha Company* (Richmond, 1854), 746–748.

Had he remained at home amongst the Yankees where he was born he would have been a distinguished man and to some purpose. But he starved down there in an abnormal environment. The great storm was brewing. It had to come, and Fisk sunk before it. The Chesapeake & Ohio Railroad was not finished until after the war.[121]

C. JOHN MARTINEAU

BIOGRAPHICAL SKETCH

Early Years and Experience Prior to Service
On the Chesapeake & Ohio Canal

An examination of available source material failed to turn up significant biographical material on the background of John Martineau. The only information that could be found indicated that he had been a pupil of Chief Engineer Benjamin Wright during the construction of the Erie Canal. The available evidence indicates that he played a minor role in the construction of the Erie, because no sources on that canal mention his name. However, he must have impressed Wright for in early September 1828, he was named to the Board of Engineers of the Chesapeake & Ohio at the recommendation of his former mentor.[122]

Service on the Chesapeake & Ohio Canal

It is apparent that Martineau was considered to be the junior member of the Board of Engineers because his salary was less than that of Benjamin Wright and Nathan S. Roberts. Throughout the summer and early fall, Martineau assisted his senior partners on the board in making the final location of the waterway from Little Falls to Seneca Falls preparatory to the initial letting of contracts. Later, he took a more direct role in the design of the canal, determining the final specification for Dams Nos. 1 and 2 and submitting the plan which was adopted for the construction of the early lockhouses. After survey the Monocacy River for the purpose of determining its utility as a feeder for the canal, he left the service of the company in June 1829 when the directors were forced to eliminate some engineering positions because of the continuing controversy with the Baltimore & Ohio.[123]

Engineering Experience after Service
On the Chesapeake & Ohio Canal

No readily-available information could be found relative to the subsequent engineering career of Martineau.

---

[121] *Memoirs of Colonel James Worrall, Civil Engineer.*, American Society of Civil Engineers, New York, 1887; 57–58.
[122] *The Alexandria Gazette*, September 13, 1828.
[123] Mercer to Bryant, August 27, 1828, Ltrs. Sent, C&O Co.; Martineau to Board of Directors, October 1, 1828, Ltrs. Recd., C&O Co.; and Proceedings of the President and Board of Directors, A, 48, 204–205, 294.

D. ELWOOD MORRIS

BIOGRAPHICAL SKETCH

Early Years and Experience Prior To Service On the Chesapeake & Ohio Canal

Little is known about the early life or engineering experience of Ellwood Morris prior to his employment on the Chesapeake & Ohio Canal. The only data that could be found for this period was that he was involved in making engineering surveys for the Winchester and Potomac Railroad in Virginia prior to obtaining a job on the canal.[124]

Service on the Chesapeake & Ohio Canal

In 1835 Morris was employed as an assistant engineer by the canal company upon the recommendation of Fisk. It is apparent that Morris rose rapidly through the ranks of the canal engineers because he was promoted to Principal Assistant Engineer in 1838. During the next two years, he supervised the construction above Dam No. 6 until October 1840 when he was named chief engineer to replace Fisk who left the company following a dispute with the new canal board. Following another reorganization of the canal company management in April 1841, Morris terminated his duties with the company and was replaced by Fisk.[125]

Engineering Experience after Service On the Chesapeake & Ohio Canal

There is little documentation for the later career of Morris except for the period 1851–61. In 1851–52 he, along with Benjamin Henry Latrobe, made preliminary surveys for the Cincinnati, Hillsborough, and Parkersburg Railroad, the Ohio River Valley line that would ultimately form a key section of the route between Baltimore and St. Louis.[126] Three years later in 1855, he surveyed the location for the Auburn, Pt. Clinton, and Allenton Railroad in northeastern Pennsylvania.[127] In 1857 he witnessed and published an article on the new method recently invented by Colonel Franklin Hewson for constructing temporary railroad bridges.[128] During the spring of 1857, he made surveys for the proposed improvement of the Ohio River.[129] In the spring of 1861 just prior to the firing of Fort Sumter, he made surveys for the U.S. Army for the fortification of the North Carolina coast.[130]

---

[124] *Proceedings of the Stockholders of the Chesapeake & Ohio Canal Company, In special General Meeting Commencing on the 8th of March, and Continuing, by Adjournment, to the 3d of April 1841* (Washington, 1841), 13

[125] *Ibid.*; Proceedings of the President and Board of Directors, F, 254, 257, 301–302, 308, 315; and Morris to Sprigg, April 7, 1841, and Fisk to President and Directors, April 29, 1841, Ltrs. Recd., C&O Co.

[126] Ellwood Morris, *Reconnaissance Made for the Cincinnati, Hillsborough, and Parkersburg Railway...December 1851*(Pittsburgh, 1852), 1–12, and Ellwood Morris, *Report on the Preliminary Surveys Made for the Cincinnati, Hillsborough, and Parkersburg Railway* (Cincinnati, 1852)1–48.

[127] Ellwood Morris, *Reconnaissance Made for the Auburn, Pt. Clinton, and Allentown Railroad...July 1855* (Pottsville, 1855), 1–22.

[128] *Railroad Bridge Drill, or Arrangements for the Speedy Erection of Temporary Bridges on Railroads by Col. Franklin Hawson, Reported from Personal Inspection by Ellwood Morris* (Philadelphia, 1857), 1–6

[129] Ellwood Morris, *Treatise on the Improvement of the Ohio River...June 1857* (Pottsville, 1857), 1–32.

[130] *The War of the Rebellion* (Washington, 1880–91), I, 51, 2.

E. THOMAS F. PURCELL

BIOGRAPHICAL SKETCH

Early Years and Experience Prior To Service
On the Chesapeake & Ohio Canal

An extensive survey of biographical sources and newspaper accounts of the early phases of the organization of the canal company failed to turn up any information concerning Thomas F. Purcell prior to his service on the Chesapeake & Ohio Canal. In the canal company records, it is noted that on November 22, 1828, he was formally appointed as a resident engineer on the first division and that his residence was in Virginia.[131] As is the case for many of the resident and assistant engineers on the canal, Purcell probably had some limited surveying experience in his background.

Service on the Chesapeake & Ohio Canal

After a short leave of absence from the canal company in the late fall of 1828 when he made surveys for the Rappahannock Company in Virginia, Purcell returned to direct the operations from Rock Creek Basin to Lock No. 8. When the legal dispute with the Baltimore & Ohio Railroad was resolved in early 1832, he was placed in charge of the construction from Point of Rocks to Dam No. 4, and in the fall of 1833 he was given responsibility for the work above the latter point. During the summer of 1835, he led a survey party in revising the location of the projected waterway between Dam No. 6 and Cumberland. A series of clashes with Fisk over the plans for the canal prism, locks, and dams on this stretch of the canal led to Purcell's bitter resignation in March 1836.[132]

Engineering Experience after Service
On the Chesapeake & Ohio Canal

Little information could be found on Purcell's career after he left the C&O Canal. The only reference that could be located concerned his activities for the Jeffersonville and New Albany Canal Company in 1837–38. During that period he surveyed and reported on the practicability and probable cost of the construction of a navigable canal for steamboats around the falls of the Ohio on the Indiana side of the river.[133]

---

[131] Proceedings of the President and Board of Directors, A, 114–115
[132] Proceedings of the President and Directors, C, 191, 246, 313, 400, E, 25, and Sanderlin, *The Great National Project*, 62, 95–96, 114, 118.
[133] See "Report...to the President and Directors of the Jeffersonville and New Albany Canal Company [Indiana]...January 8, 1838...by Thos. F. Purcell," in *An Act to Incorporate the Jeffersonville and New Albany Canal Company (Approved February 8, 1836)*.

**HISTORIC RESOURCE STUDY
CHESAPEAKE & OHIO CANAL NHP**

2.
THE ECONOMICS OF CONSTRUCTING THE C & O CANAL

BY HARLAN D. UNRAU
HISTORIAN, C&O CANAL RESTORATION TEAM, SENECA
DENVER SERVICE CENTER
1976

CONTENTS

I.	EMERGENCE OF THE C&O CANAL PROJECT: 1822–1828	49
II.	DISMAL COMMENCEMENT OF THE C&O CANAL PROJECT: 1828–1834	57
III.	MARYLAND ASSUMES CONTROL OF THE GREAT NATIONAL PROJECT: 1835–1842	80
IV.	THE BELATED COMPLETION OF THE C&O CANAL TO CUMBERLAND: 1842–1951	93
V.	SUMMARY	105

I. EMERGENCE OF THE C&O CANAL PROJECT: 1822–1828

The decline of the Potomac Company coincided with the dawn of the canal era in the United States. The age of simple river improvements had passed. In the nineteenth century attention turned to the feasibility of building permanent, artificial canals as an effective means of transportation. Canals combined the cheapness of water travel with the reliability of an independent waterway and the ease of a level, Stillwater route. Early efforts to enlist the support of the federal government of the various canal projects failed, and the states turned to their own resources. The commencement of the Erie Canal by the State of New York in 1817 marked the beginning of the active phase of the canal era. Pennsylvania followed with its main line of public works in 1826 as competition for the newly-completed Erie Canal. Ohio and other western states also began to participate in the canal-building race. In the 1820s Maryland and Virginia also began to lay plans for a canal to the west via the Potomac Valley.[1]

Promoters of the schemes to replace the Potomac Company were able to draw several valuable lessons from the financial experiences of that enterprise. Thus they might avoid the pitfalls of the earlier undertaking while striving to attain the fruits of success which eluded it. The most obvious lesson was the need of adequate financial support for a renewed undertaking. A vitally necessary corollary to the acquisition of adequate funding would be successful integration of the interests of Virginia, Maryland, and the federal government in the new endeavor.

In the years following the War of 1812, a number of proposals were made to construct independent canals along the Potomac River in the attempt to develop a viable route to the West. While none of these early projects materialized, they were significant in that they all embodied plans to abandon river improvements for artificial canals. They also led in part to a searching investigation of the whole Potomac Company undertaking, particularly after an inquiry by the newly-created Virginia Board of Public Works in 1816 led to the discovery that despite the expenditure of large sums, the company had failed to fulfill the requirements of its charter.[2]

Seeing the trend of public opinion and fearful of losing its vested rights, the Potomac Company formally requested a survey of its works in 1819. The State of Virginia authorized the Board of Public Works to conduct the inspection and to include a survey of the land between the Potomac and the southern branches of the Ohio for a possible connection of the two rivers. Thomas Moore, the engineer of the Board, made two examinations in 1820 and 1822. At the invitation of Virginia, the State of Maryland also sent and engineer, Isaac Briggs, to accompany Moore on his second trip. After the death of Moore during the second surveying expedition, Briggs completed the study under special authorization from the state of Virginia.[3]

The two reports issued by Moore and Briggs on their surveys added impetus to the call for an artificial waterway from tidewater on the Potomac to Cumberland and of a further connection with the Ohio River. Moore's report on the results of his first inspection confirmed the opinion that a connection between the two rivers was practicable, and estimated the cost of a canal along the Potomac from tidewater to Cumberland to be $1,114,300.[4]

---

[1] George Washington Ward, *The Early Development of the Chesapeake & Ohio Canal Project* (Baltimore, 1899), 36, and George Rogers Taylor, *The Transportation Revolution, 1815–1860* (New York, 1951), 32–48.

[2] Proceedings of the President and Directors of the Potomac Company, B, 340, and Peyton to President and Directors, November 8, 1816, and Mason to Peyton, December 8, 1817, ibid, 340–350.

[3] Ward, *Early Development of Chesapeake & Ohio Canal*, 40–45, and Proceedings of the President and Directors of the Potomac Company, B, 440–441.

[4] U.S., Congress, House, Committee on Roads and Canals, *Report of the Committee on Roads and Canals*, Rept. No. 90, 19th Cong., 2d sess., 1827, Appendix 3, 33–35.

In a more detailed report in December 1822, Briggs estimated the cost of an independent canal along the Potomac 30 feet wide at the surface, 20 feet wide at the bottom, and 3 feet deep, to be $1,578,954, or $8,676 per mile. If the average cost per mile were applied in exact proportion to a canal of the same dimensions as the Erie, Briggs noted that the cost would be $15,732 per mile, a sum that was approximately the same as that spent on those parts of the Erie where heavy excavation and extensive lockage were required.[5]

Simultaneously with the surveys by Briggs and Moore, a joint commission, appointed by the States of Virginia and Maryland, was conducting an investigation of the financial affairs of the Potomac Company. In their report to the governors of their respective states in December 1822, the commissioners found that the company had not only used all of its capital stock and collected tolls, but had incurred heavy debts which its resources would never enable it to discharge. From the commencement of operations in 1785 until August 1, 1822, the company had spent $729,387.29 on construction. The stock subscriptions to the company by the States of Virginia and Maryland and private investors amounted to $311,111.11, and beyond this sum the company had contracted loans totaling $175,886.59. Since August 1, 1799, the company had collected $221,927.67 in tolls, but these revenues had been exhausted in the construction expenditures. The commissioners concluded that the enterprise would never be able to meet the terms of its charter to provide an effective navigation between tidewater on the Potomac and Cumberland by means of river improvements and skirting canals around the rapids.[6]

After determining that the Potomac Company works were only providing an average annual navigation period of 45 days, the commissioners recommended the construction of the artificial waterway proposed by Briggs. The estimated cost of $1,578,954 should be divided by Virginia and Maryland, the money to be raised by 16 or 20 year loans. Once the loans were negotiated, the state legislature should open the books for individual subscriptions, the individuals to be entitled to the stock for which they subscribed provided they paid their annual interest on the amount to the state. All stock not sold in such manner should be held by the two states.[7]

After these reports were made, the question arose as to how this improvement should be put into effect. There were two alternative choices: an additional subscription to the Potomac Company, or the creation of a new company to take over the rights and privileges of the old one. Although the officials of the existing company argued for the adoption of the former alternative, it was decided to create a new enterprise, designated as the Potomac Canal Company to indicate its purpose and distinguish it from the older organization. The Virginia Assembly passed an act of incorporation, February 22, 1823.[8]

The act did not require the consent of Congress, but did stipulate that it must be confirmed by the State of Maryland to become operable. By its terms, Maryland was to subscribe $500,000, one third of its total capital. In Maryland, the act encountered the opposition of local interests, particularly the Baltimore merchants who saw the proposed canal as providing their competitors on the Potomac with the advantages of the western trade. At the public rally at the Baltimore Exchange on December 20, 1823, a major debate took place between Robert G. Harper, a former U.S. Senator, from Maryland representing the promoters of the canal, and George Winchester, a spokesman for the local business interests. Fearing that the projected canal

---

[5] *Message of the Governor of Maryland, Communicating the Report of the Commissioners Appointed to Survey the River Potomac* (Annapolis, 1822), Appendix, 77–84.

[6] *Letter from the Governor and Council of Maryland, Transmitting a Report of the Commissioners Appointed to Survey the River Potomac* (Washington, 1823), 5–9, 25–29.

[7] *Ibid*, 23–24.

[8] Annual Report (1823), Potomac Company, in Proceedings of the President and Directors of the Potomac Company, C, 14–15, and *The Potomac Canal: Papers Relating to the Practicability, Expediency, and Cost of the Potomac Canal* (Washington, 1823), Appendix, 30–39.

might establish the District of Columbia as a rival market to their city, those attending the meeting unanimously adopted resolutions opposing Maryland's subscription to the new company.[9] Largely as a result of the outcome of this meeting, the bill failed to pass the Maryland legislature, and lacking the consent required, the Virginia act became inoperative.[10] This ended the last attempt by Virginia and Maryland to effect a real improvement of the Potomac Valley route without federal support.

Nevertheless real progress had been made by 1823 in the effort to open the river as a route for western trade. The interest of the District cities and the States of Maryland and Virginia had been focused on the Potomac. A series of articles penned by Abner Lacock, a former U.S. Senator from Pennsylvania and internal improvements enthusiast, appeared in the Washington Intelligencer supporting the plans submitted by Moore and Briggs.[11] Even Briggs wrote a lengthy article in the newspaper defending his proposal with the following statement:

> In consequence of the long and narrow form of Maryland, this proposed improvement will bring almost to our very doors, the cheapest, safest, and most perfect of all possible modes of conveying our produce to market; and of bringing home its returns. It will...establish the predominance of, the agricultural interest. The western parts of Pennsylvania, the northern parts of Virginia, the rich state of Ohio, & c. by making their channel of commerce, will pour countless treasures into the lap of Maryland, and, at the same time, enrich themselves; for the benefits of commerce must be reciprocal, otherwise it cannot flourish, and will soon cease to exist.[12]

Numerous memorials from the inhabitants of Pennsylvania, Maryland, and Virginia, were referred to the House Committee on the District of Columbia requesting that the federal government aid the improvement of the Potomac route, and the chairman of the committee, Charles F. Mercer, proposed legislation to that effect.[13]

During the summer, James Shriver, a leading civil engineer and promoter of American canals, undertook a survey of the proposed route of the canal and later published his findings, concluding that a connection could be made from tidewater on the Potomac to Pittsburg on the Ohio for the sum of $5,566,564.[14]

In Congress, the friends of internal improvements were beginning to make headway in their campaign for federal support. The government appeared to be ready to undertake a general program of aid to public works. It was in this atmosphere that the first Chesapeake & Ohio Canal Convention met in Washington, November 6–8, 1823.

The convention assembled at the Capitol at the call of a meeting of the citizens of Loudoun County, Virginia. This earlier gathering had been held to discuss the proposals for the im-

---

[9] *Gen. Harpers' Speech to the Citizens of Baltimore, on the Expediency of Promoting a Connexion Between the Ohio, at Pittsburgh, and the Waters of the Chesapeake, at Baltimore, by a canal through the District of Columbia, with His Reply to Some of the Objections of Mr. Winchester* (Baltimore, 1824), 3, 62–63, 78.
[10] U.S., Congress, House, Committee on Roads and Canals, *Chesapeake & Ohio Canal, to Accompany Bill H.R. No 94*, H. Rept. 414, 23d Cong., 1st Sess., 1834, 4.
[11] All of the newspaper articles were collected into a single volume: Abner Lacock, *Great National Object: Proposed Connection of the Eastern and Western Waters by a Communication through the Potomac Country* (Washington, 1822)
[12] Washington *National Intelligencer; July 12, 1822* [date in source is 1828, which appears to be an error].
[13] All of the petitions and the proposed legislation appear in *Report of the Committee of the District of Columbia*, May 3, 1822 (Washington, 1822).
[4] James Shriver, *An Account of Surveys and Examinations, with Remarks and Documents, Relative to Chesapeake & Ohio, and Ohio and Lake Erie Canals* (Baltimore, 1824), 6-66.

provement of the Potomac route after the Potomac Canal Company project proved abortive, and to expand the scope of the project to include a canal all the way to the Ohio River. It requested similar meetings in other counties to support the citizens of Loudoun in their appeal for a general convention. In response to this plea many counties in Virginia, Maryland, and Pennsylvania chose delegates to the conference. In addition to these representatives there were members of the District Cities and several unofficial guests from Ohio. Among the most important men present were: Albert Gallatin of Pennsylvania; Bushrod C. Washington, Richard E. Byrd, and Charles F. Mercer of Virginia; Joseph Kent, Thomas Kennedy, and George C. Washington of Maryland; and Francis Scott Key, John Mason, and Thomas Corcoran of the District of Columbia. Governor Joseph Kent of Maryland, a long-time supporter of internal improvements, was the presiding officer of the convention, but Charles F. Mercer, United States Representative from Virginia who was serving on the Committee on the District of Columbia at that time,[15] exercised the guiding hand as chairman of the influential Central Committee.[16]

The primary functions of the convention were the mobilization of public opinion behind the proposed connection between the Potomac and the Ohio and the creation of organizations to give effect to this rising interest. Resolutions were adopted urging the connection with the West, and committees were named to formulate plans for the canal and to petition Congress and several states for consent and aid in the project. Relative to the financial arrangements for such an undertaking, the convention passed the following resolutions:

> That the most eligible mode of attaining this object will be by the incorporation of a joint stock company, empowered to cut the said Canal through the territory of the United States, in the District of Columbia, and of the States of Virginia, Maryland, and Pennsylvania...that...the completion of the Eastern section of the Canal...(tidewater to Cumberland)...be obtained through separate acts of the Governments and Corporations, of the states of Maryland and Virginia, of the United States, and of the three cities of the District of Columbia, a subscription to the amount, if necessary, of 2,750,000 dollars, in the following proportions, 2/11ths to be subscribed by the state of Maryland, 3/11ths by the state of Virginia, 4/11ths by the United States, and 2/11ths by the District cities, to be divided between them, according to an equitable ratio, to be fixed by themselves. In case a part of the sum aforesaid shall be subscribed by private individuals, in the mode provided by the act aforesaid, the several States and Corporations, within which such individual subscriptions are received, shall be requested to assume, as part of their aforesaid quotas, the amount of such subscription, under such security as they may deem expedient for the payment thereof, by the subscribers to them respectively:
>
> That the Government of the United States be earnestly solicited to obtain the whole of this sum on loan, receivable in four annual installments, upon the issue of certificates of stock, bearing an annual interest not exceeding five per cent and irredeemable for thirty years, and to guarantee the repayment thereof on a specific pledge of the public lots in the City of Washington, of the United States stock in the Canal and the public faith:
>
> That the first installment of the loan be made payable on the 1st of March, 1825, and the last on the 1st of March, 1829:

---

[15] Mercer was a member of the Committee on Roads and Canals in the 20th and 21st Congresses (March 4, 1827–March 3, 1831); and chairman in the 22nd through the 25th Congresses (March 4, 1831–March 3, 1839).

[16] House Report 414, 4 and Appendix A, 67–68, and *Proceedings of the Chesapeake & Ohio Canal Convention* (Washington, 1827), 1–6.

That the interest of each State and Corporation, upon its proportion of the said loan, be paid into the Treasury of the United States, according to the terms of the loan, and the principal sum at the expiration of thirty years, the period to be fixed for its redemption:

That, in the event of a refusal by the Government of the United States to negotiate the said loan, each State and Corporation shall provide the amount of its respective subscription, in such manner as may seem to it best.[17]

The success of the convention can best be measured by the course of events in the years immediately following. In his annual message in Congress in December 1823 President James Monroe referred to the convention's activities and urged Congress to give favorable consideration to the project, if its constitutional scruples would permit. Taking a relatively strong stand in favor of national aid to internal improvement companies, he indicated that his personal constitutional qualms were satisfied by the belief that the government could assist improvement projects if the operation of these works was turned over to the states or to private companies after completion. Although real participation by the general government in internal improvement projects had to await the presidency of John Quincy Adams, the President's message added momentum to the canal campaign.[18]

There was other evidence of success that emanated from the canal convention. Congress responded to President Monroe's message by providing $30,000 for a detailed survey of the proposed route by the United States Board of Engineers as part of a general program for studying possible routes for roads and canals "with a view to the transportation of the mail, the commercial intercourse, and military defense of the United States."[19] Upon receiving the memorial for an act of incorporation, the Virginia Assembly passed the necessary law on January 27, 1824.[20]

After the opposition of Baltimore interests and the indifference of the southern and eastern counties of the state had been overcome, the Maryland Assembly confirmed the Virginia act of incorporation on January 31, 1825.[21]

The petition to the Pennsylvania legislature failed both in 1824 and 1825, primarily because of the opposition of Philadelphia interests who were concerned that the canal would end the economic dependence of western Pennsylvania on their city.[22]

The U.S. Board of Engineers made a preliminary report on February 14, 1825. The Board concurred in the opinion if Thomas Moore and Isaac Briggs that the connection between tidewater on the Potomac and the Ohio at Pittsburgh via the Youghiogheny or Monongahela by an artificial canal was practicable. Although the U.S. engineers did not have sufficient data to estimate the expense of the work, they concluded that the cost would not bear any comparison with the

---

[17] *Proceedings of the Chesapeake & Ohio Canal Convention*, 13–17, and U.S., Congress, House of Representatives, Committee on Roads and Canals, *Chesapeake & Ohio Canal*, H. Rept. 47, 20th Cong., 1st sess., 1828, 10–14.

[18] James D. Richardson, ed., *A Compilation of the Messages and Papers of the Presidents* (10 vols., Washington, 1896), II, 216.

[19] *Proceedings of the Chesapeake & Ohio Canal Convention*, 42. [Note: The $30,000 was to fund the General Survey Act of 1824 as a whole. See Forest G. Hill, *Roads, Rails, & Waterways: The Army Engineers and Early Transportation*, 47, University of Oklahoma Press, 1957—kg]

[20] Act of State of Virginia, Acts of the States of Virginia, Maryland, and Pennsylvania, and of the Congress of the United States in relation to the Chesapeake & Ohio Canal company (Washington, 1828)2–15.

[21] *Laws Made and Passed by the General Assembly of the State of Maryland* (Annapolis, 1824), Ch. 79.

[22] Walter S. Sanderlin, *The Great National Project: A History of the Chesapeake & Ohio Canal* (Baltimore, 1946), 54.

political, commercial, and military advantages it would afford to the nation. Furthermore, the engineers concluded that

> The obstacle to a communication by the Potomac route with the Western states, lessens to a point, compared with the greatness of the object, whether in a commercial or political relation to the prosperity of the country. In Europe, their canals, even those of Governments, have all some definite limited object of utility. But here it is not alone the distance—the elevation—the vast natural navigation to be connected, which constitutes the grandeur of the design; but the immense interests it combines into an harmonious national whole.[23]

The report appeared to assure the ultimate success of the project by removing all remaining doubts as to its practicability. Congress confirmed the act of the Virginia Assembly, chartering the canal company in a measure approved by President Monroe on March 3, 1825, the last day of his administration.[24]

According to the terms of the charter, the Chesapeake & Ohio Canal Company was empowered to accept subscriptions for the purpose of financing the construction of an artificial waterway from tidewater on the Potomac in the District of Columbia to the highest point of permanent navigation on the Ohio River at Pittsburgh via the shortest possible route. The charter stipulated that the eastern section of the canal must be completed before the western section could be started. The act gave the canal company the power to condemn land and hold it in fee simple when used for canal purposes and granted it the right to use the water of the rivers for navigation purpose. The company was to be free forever from taxation. It must complete the entire project in twelve years. The dimensions of the waterway were to be at least 40 feet wide at the water surface, 28 feet wide at the bottom, and four feet deep. The use of injunctions was prohibited to allow the company officers to carry on their work with the least possible hindrance. The following year on February 26 Pennsylvania confirmed the charter with two principal reservations requiring the canal company to commence the construction of the western section within three years and to use Congressional funds equally for both eastern and western sections.[25]

Now that the company had hurdled the legal obstacles to its final organizations, friends of the project promptly began the campaign to obtain public support with renewed confidence.

On October 23, 1826, however, three U.S. Topographical Engineers, and John L. Sullivan, made their full report, which President John Quincy Adams formally transmitted to Congress on December 7, 1826. The report supported the earlier declarations that the proposed connection of the Potomac and Ohio Rivers was physically practicable, but estimated the cost of the canal with the enlarged dimensions of 48 feet in width at the surface, 33 feet in width at the bottom, and 5 feet in depth at $22,375,427.69. According to the report, the canal was to be divided into three sections: the eastern extending from Georgetown to Cumberland; the middle stretching from Cumberland to the mouth of the Casselman River on the Youghiogheny; and the western reaching

---

[23] Totten, Bernard, and Sullivan, to Macomb, February 3, 1825, *Reports on Internal Improvements, 1823–39*, Records of the Chief of Engineers; Record Group 77, National Arch9ives, and *Report of the Board of Engineers for Internal Improvements, As Communicated, by Message, from the President of the United States to Congress, February 14, 1825; and an Illustration of the Report by John L. Sullivan, A Member of the Board* (Washington, 1825), 3–22.

[24] Act of Congress, in U.S., Congress, Senate, *Documents Relating to the Chesapeake & Ohio Canal*, S. Doc. 610, 26th Cong., 1st sess., 1840, 13.

[25] Act of Pennsylvania, Senate Document 610, 31–34.

from there to Pittsburgh. The respective distances, elevation, and descent, lockage, and estimated cost of these sections was as follows[26]:

SECTION	DISTANCE		ASCENT & DESCENT— Ft.	NUMBER OF LOCKS	COST ESTIMATE
	MILES	YARDS			
Eastern	185	1078	578	74	$8,177,081.05
Middle	70	1010	1961	246	10,028,122.86
Western	85	348	619	78	4,170,223.78
	341	676	3158	398	$22,375,427.69

The estimated cost of the canal dashed the hopes of canal supporters. They had been thinking in terms of a canal with the general dimensions that had been recommended earlier by Engineers Moore and Briggs at a cost of between $4,000,000 and $5,000,000. They now sent out a call for a second Chesapeake & Ohio Canal Convention to be held in Washington on December 5, 1826.[27]

The principal task of the second assembling of the convention was to dispel the gloom which paralyzed the canal project's supporters. To accomplish this purpose the delegates, among whom were Andrew Stewart of Pennsylvania, George Washington Parke Custis of Alexandria County, D.C., and Henry Clay of the District of Columbia in addition to the majority of those who had attended the earlier meeting, sought to discredit the estimate of the U.S. Board of Engineers and to cause a new survey to be made to determine the true cost of the work on the enlarged dimensions. The report of the government engineers was exhaustively examined and compared with the actual cost of constructing the Erie, the Pennsylvania Main Line, the Ohio and Erie, and the Delaware and Hudson Canals. A committee appointed at the opening session of the convention and chaired by Andrew Steward of Pennsylvania reported that the allowances for labor costs were much too high and that the estimates for masonry, walling, and excavation were generally double or triple the prices paid on other canals. The convention delegates concluded that the Georgetown–Cumberland section of the canal could be built for $5,273,283, and the entire canal from Georgetown to Pittsburgh for $13,768,152, without changing the dimensions or durability of the waterway.[28]

At the same time, supporters of the canal in Congress urged President Adams to submit the conflicting estimates to a review by practical and experienced civil engineers. At the request of thirty-two members of Congress, the President appointed James Geddes and Nathan Roberts, both of whom had first gained renown as engineers on the Erie Canal and thereafter on the Ohio and Erie and Pennsylvania Main Line, to revise the estimates for the eastern section on the basis of actual wages and current prices for materials. They completed the surveys in 1827 and their report was submitted to Congress on March 10, 1828. In the document which was used as the primary source on which the initial stock subscriptions and early stages of construction were based, the two engineers applied their estimates to a canal of three different dimensions. The first plan was for a canal of 40 feet in width at the surface, 28 feet in width at the bottom, and 4 feet in depth. The second plan called for a canal based on the dimensions used by the U.S. Board of Engineers, while the third estimate was for an enlarged waterway of 60 feet in width at the surface, 42 feet in width at the bottom, and 5 feet in depth. The estimates for these plans, including a ten

---

[26] U.S. Congress, House, Message of the President of the United States, Transmitting a Report from the Secretary of War with that of the Board of Engineers for Internal Improvement, on the Chesapeake & Ohio Canal, H. Doc. 10, 19th Cong., 2nd sess., 1826.
[27] Sanderlin, Great National Project, 55.
[28] Proceedings of the Chesapeake & Ohio Canal Convention, 65-85.

percent allowance for contingencies but excluding any allowance for the purchase or condemnation of land or water rights, were $4,008,005.28 or $21,461.87 per mile; $4,330,991.68 or $23.191.38 per mile; and $4,479,346.93 or $23,985.79 per mile respectively.[29]

Fortified with this estimate, the canal supporters renewed their campaign to obtain federal and state funding for the project. The commissioners who had been appointed by the President of the United States and the Governors of Maryland and Virginia formally opened the books for the subscriptions of stock on October 1, 1827. In less than six weeks there had been subscribed more the $1,500,000.[30]

This sum was sufficient, under the provisions of the charter, to permit the organization of the canal company, but this action was delayed until Congress should act. After a lengthy debate, the friends of the canal project in Congress secured the passage of an act on May 24 directing the Secretary of the Treasury to subscribe for 10,000 shares of stock of the Chesapeake & Ohio Canal Company valued at $1,000,000. The act authorized the subscription to be paid out of the dividends accruing to the United States on account of the stock of the United States Bank.[31] The subscription on the part of the United States fulfilled the condition of an earlier Maryland subscription of $500,000 to the stock of the canal company, and that act now became effective.[32]

On the same day that it passed the subscription act, congress also approved an act providing its sanction to any subscriptions which had been or might be made to the stock of the canal company by the corporations of Washington, Georgetown, and Alexandria.[33] Washington had already subscribed 10,000 shares and soon Georgetown and Alexandria each subscribed 2,500 shares, thereby making a total investment of $1,500,000 in the new enterprise by these three debt-ridden cities. Shortly thereafter, Shepherdstown, Virginia, subscribed to $20,000 of the company stock.[34] These sums, together with private investments totaling $588,400, insured the successful launching of the long-awaited national project.[35]

The following month on June 20–23, the formal organization of the Chesapeake & Ohio Canal Company took place at a meeting of stockholders in the Washington City Hall, and the formal groundbreaking ceremonies were held near Little Falls on July 4.[36]

---

[29] Geddes and Roberts to Macomb, February 23, 1828, *Reports on Internal Improvements, 1823–39*, Records of the Chief of Engineers, Record Group 77, and U.S., Congress, House, *Letter from the Secretary of War Transmitting Estimates of the Cost of Making a Canal from Cumberland to Georgetown*, H. Doc. 192, 20th Cong., 1st sess., 1828, 5–6, 98.

[30] Richard W. Gill and John Johnson, *Reports of Cases Argued and Determined in the Court of Appeals of Maryland* (Baltimore, 1833), IV, 28–29, 57.

[31] Act of congress, *Chesapeake & Ohio Canal Company: Acts of the States of Virginia, Maryland, and Pennsylvania, and of the Congress of the United States, in Relation to the Chesapeake & Ohio Canal Company* (Washington, 1828), 44–45, and Washington *National Intelligencer*, May 31, 1828.

[32] *Laws Made and Passed by the General Assembly of the State of Maryland* (Annapolis, 1827), Ch. 61.

[33] Act of Congress, *Chesapeake & Ohio Canal Company: Acts*, 45–49.

[34] *Report to the Stockholders on the Completion of the Chesapeake & Ohio Canal to Cumberland, with a Sketch of the Potomac Company, and a General Outline of the History of the Chesapeake & Ohio Canal Company* (Frederick, 1851), 39–40, and *Ordinances of the Corporation of Georgetown* (Georgetown, 1829), 19

[35] U.S., Congress, House, Committee on Roads and Canals, Chesapeake & Ohio Canal, H. Rept. 141, 20th Cong., 1st sess., 1828, 50–59, and House Report 414,14.

[36] Proceedings of Stockholders, A, 1–3, and Washington National Intelligencer, July 7, 1828.

II. DISMAL COMMENCEMENT OF
THE C&O CANAL PROJECT: 1828–1834

During the early years of construction, the progress of the canal was repeatedly disrupted by problems growing out of the actual construction. These early trials of the canal project closely foreshadowed the future obstacles to its successful completion. The shortage of laborers was felt as soon as large-scale construction commenced a factor which caused the cost of wages to rise above earlier projections. Land disputes occupied much of the attention of the canal board as local landowners resisted the efforts of the company to keep costs at a minimum and sought instead to extract the maximum benefit from the loss of their lands. The late 1820s and early 1830s were also a period of rapid inflation, thereby contributing to the increase in costs of labor, land acquisition, and the supply and the transportation of construction materials.

As a result of these troubles, the canal company itself became involved in financial difficulties, a problem which it exacerbated by its own ill-advised enthusiasm. Among the actions of the board which illustrate the latter point were the decisions to build a canal with a much larger prism than had been proposed by most of the preliminary surveys and to purchase the strip of land between the canal and the river.

On top of these distractions, the company had to contend with a legal controversy growing out of a dispute with the Baltimore & Ohio Railroad Company over the right of way above Point of Rocks and the hostility of the Jackson administration toward national support for internal improvements in general and the Chesapeake & Ohio Canal in particular.

As early as the spring of 1829, many of the contractors were in financial difficulty despite the fact that the canal company had allowed higher estimates in the letting of its early contracts than had been made by Geddes and Roberts in 1827. For example, the two civil engineers had estimated the cost of common excavation at eight cents per cubic yard while the contracts let for Sections Nos. 1–34 from Little Falls to Seneca Falls, permitted an average of 9 1/6 cents.[37]

Before active construction operations resumed in the spring of 1830, Chief Engineer Benjamin Wright informed President Charles F. Mercer that "the truth is that we know the prices of these contractors are all very low, and that it yet remains doubtful whether they can sustain themselves."[38] He had made this statement after a general price increase of 25 percent had already been allowed, but the following month many of the lock contractors were again in financial distress. After Richard Holdsworth, the contractor for Aqueduct No. 1 and Locks Nos. 21, 23, and 24, complained on March 24 that his inability to obtain adequate funds had forced him to the brink of bankruptcy, Wright informed Mercer that "painful and unpleasant as this statement of Mr. Holdsworth is, I believe there is too much truth in it and…I do no believe the others (lock contractors) are in any better situated than Holdsworth."[39]

AMOUNT AND COST OF WORK DONE AS OF MAY 1, 1829

- 450,263 cubic yards of earth, gravel, and clay excavated, comprehending loose stone, of a weight each less than what it would require two men to lift on a cart or wheelbarrow, at an average price per cubic yard, of 8 53/100¢
- 45,452 cubic yards of hard pan, at an average price, per cubic yard, of 21¢

---

[37] Proceedings of the President and Board of Directors, A, 230–231, and Niles' Register, XXV (August 30, 1828), 6.
[38] Wright to Mercer, February 9, 1830, Ltrs. Recd., C&O Co.
[39] Proceedings of the President and Board of Directors, A, 202; B, 49; Wright to Mercer, March 25, 1830, Ltrs. Recd., C&O Co., and Leckie to Wright, July 1830, W. Robert Leckie Papers, Duke University.

- 14,437 cubic yards of rock quarried, at an average price, per cubic yard, of 28 35/100¢
- 43,930 cubic yards of rock blasted, at an average price per cubic yard, of 53¢
- 39,378 cubic yards of embankment, formed of earth from the canal excavations, at an average price, per cubic yard, of 10 76/100¢
- 52,352 cubic yards of embankment of earth not from the canal excavation, at an average price, per cubic yard, of 12 93/100¢
- 2,825 cubic yards of puddling, at an average price, per cubic yard, of 24 21/200¢
- 27,837 perches of 25 solid feet of external walling of rock excavated from the canal, at an average price per perch, of 54 82/100¢
- 2,066 perches of 25 solid feet of external walling of rock not excavated from the canal, at an average price, per perch, of 92 37/100¢

The extra work, so far, has not exceeded in cost $1,035, while the total expenditures on those items alone amount to $114,221.69 ½.

The common average of every species of excavation including every variety of earth, hard pan, and rock, is, as far as the work has gone, 13.58 cents per cubic yard.

Of embankment, whether of materials obtained from within or without the canal, 12 cents per cubic yard.

Of external, vertical, and slope wall, constructed of rock from within or without the canal, 57.42 cents per perch of twenty-five solid feet.

—Excerpted from *First Annual Report* (1829), C&O Co., 5–6

Even if the estimated cost of labor had been high enough for the prevailing level of wages and prices in 1828, some difficulty would have arisen from the general inflation which followed. In the first year the costs of construction were above the estimates of Geddes and Roberts and payments for lumber, stone, provisions, and labor all exceeded contract figures.[40]

The cost of water lime alone was nearly triple the original estimates. Contracts for some of the sections were not only relet but subdivided into as many as four parts in order to expedite their completion. Nearly all of the contracts for the locks had to be abandoned and relet several times, and one general increase of twenty-five per cent was granted.[41] By 1832 the rate of wages was almost double that prevailing in 1828, having risen from a monthly average of $8–$10 to $–$20.[42] By early 1834, the price of common earth excavation had risen from 9 1/6¢ to 11¢ per cubic yard; the cost of blasted rock had increased from 53¢ to 60¢ per cubic yard; and the cost of quarried rock had skyrocketed from 28 30/100¢ to 60¢ per cubic yard.[43]

The blasting which was necessary because of the rocky nature of the ground resulted in a series of annoying accidents, including the damage of several buildings from the concussion of the explosions and flying rocks.[44] To reduce the damage from this cause and to quiet the public outcry following such accidents, the canal board ordered the use of smaller charges and required that the blasting be covered with brush. The net result of this policy was more delay and increased expenses, in some cases nearly doubling the cost of certain sections.[45]

---

[40] *First Annual Report* (1829), C&O Co., 5–7.
[41] *Second Annual Report* (1830), C&O Co., 6; *First Annual Report* (1829), 7–8, and Proceedings of the President and Board of Directors, A, 178.
[42] Mercer to Maury, November 18, 1828, Ltrs. Sent, C&O Co., and *Fourth Annual Report* (1832), C&O Co., 15.
[43] House Report 414,194.
[44] Balch to President and Directors, August 28, 1830, Ltrs. Recd., C&O Co., and Proceedings of the President and Board.
[45] Proceedings of the President and Board of Directors, B, 87–88, 152, 191, 248, 257.

Company officials reported to Congress in 1834 that the difficult excavations above Georgetown were a leading cause of the increased cost of the canal:

> One cause of the higher price of the canal, below Seneca, should not be omitted. There was scarcely one-fourth of a mile of the entire line of 23 ½ miles, in which large detached stone, of the description called boulders, and ridges or strata of rock, more or less solid, did not occur. Whole sections, therefore, computed at 8 cents the cubic yard, prior to their construction, cost twelve times that sum for their mere excavation. In the bottom lands this occurred, as well as on the levels of the table land elevated more than sixty feet above the river. In some places the rock at the bottom of the canal, as on the low grounds below Seneca, for two feet of its depth, cost for excavation $1.25 the cubic yard, though the prior estimate of the engineer comprehended no rock whatever....[46]

The weather was responsible for other costly delays in digging the canal prism. The winter of 1838–29 was unusually severe, and the few contractors who had begun work during the fall were forced to suspend operations until spring.[47]

The freshets which occurred regularly in the spring and fall often filled the lock pits and portions of the canal trunk, further retarding the work and increasing the financial difficulties of the contractors as no provision had been made in the contracts for allowances to repair flood damage.[48]

The high banks on the river side of the canal were another source of increased costs. Extensive dry masonry walls were needed to protect the canal from the action of the Potomac as described by U.S. Engineer William Gibbs McNeill in 1833:

> Controlled as the engineer necessarily was, in his location of the canal, by the rocky and precipitous cliffs which, to a great extent, are washed by the Potomac, while an unusual quantity of rock excavation, on the one hand, was unavoidable, on the other he has judiciously disposed of his materials in the construction of permanent walls for the protection of the canal against the otherwise resistless action of the river....[49]

Contractors resorted to various expedients to avoid disastrous losses. The responsible ones sought redress in petitions for the payment of increased allowances from the money that had been retained by the company from their monthly estimates, usually a sum amounting to 10 percent.[50] Others sought to avoid losses by slipshod or fraudulent construction. On November 11, 1832, it was discovered that the contractors for Aqueduct No. 3 had instructed their stone cutters to scabble[51] their sheeting in the "roughest possible manner" instead of close cutting as they were being paid for and to reduce the beds of the stones nine inches under the requirements of their contract. As a result of these operations, Inspector of Masonry, A. B. McFarland predicted that "we are going to have a ridiculous piece of masonry."[52]

---

[46] House Report 414,194–195. of Directors, A, 149.
[47] *First Annual Report* (1829), 5, 21–22.
[48] Holdsworth and Isherwood to President and Directors, Sept. 24, 1829, Ltrs. Recd., C&O Co.
[49] Report of Captain Wm. G. McNeill on the Condition of the Chesapeake & Ohio Canal, December 1, 1833 in House Report 414,144–145.
[50] Proceedings of the President and Board of Directors, B, 388–389.
[51] To scabble is to work or dress stone roughly.
[52] McFarland to Ingle, November 11, 1832, Ltrs. Recd., C&O Co.

Earlier in May 1831 McFarland had reported on the fraudulent cost-saving building practices of Richard Holdsworth, the financially hard-pressed contractor for Aqueduct no. 1. During an inspection tour of the structure, he had detected:

> the sheeting of the arches laid nearly altogether without mortar, much of which is very deficient in beds, and as a substitute for mortar, the extrados of the sheeting are white washed with grout, with (the) pretension that the joints are perfectly filled. On a strict examination, however, this proves to be false. After removing this polish of grout, I discovered many vacuums below, which did not contain a particle of either grout or mortar, and in the spandrel and wing walls, depths of from 3 to 4 feet of the walls are laid up perfectly dry and grouted at the top, trusting for mere chance for it ever to reach the bottom.[53]

Still others absconded with the monthly payments on the estimates, leaving both laborers and creditors unpaid. This latter problem occurred as early as the winter of 1828–29, and it became a particularly acute problem over the next several years as financial conditions along the waterway continued to worsen.[54]

On the whole, many of the contractors were financially ruined by their experiences on the canal, and few if any prospered from their connection with it. In his speech at the formal dedicatory ceremonies opening the canal to navigation at Cumberland on October 10, 1850, William Price, one of the canal company directors, best summed up the plight of the contractors as follows:

> Many of us were young when this great work was commenced, and we have lived to see its completion, only because Providence has prolonged our lives until our heads are grey. During this interval of four and twenty years, we have looked with eager anxiety to the progress of the work up the valley of the Potomac. That progress has been slow—often interrupted and full of vicissitudes....Thousands have been ruined by their connection with the work, and but few in this region have had cause to bless it....
>
> Go view those magnificent aqueducts, locks, and culverts of hewn stone...look at all these things, and then think how soon the fortunes of individuals embarked in the prosecution of such an enterprise would be swallowed up, leaving upon it but little more impression than the bubbles which now float upon its waters. It will not be deemed out of place, if I here express the hope that those, whose losses have been gains of the company, should not in the hour of its prosperity be forgotten.[55]

Perhaps, the major problem with which the company had to contend during the actual construction of the canal was the supply of labor. The scarcity of workers and the consequently high rate of wages threatened to upset all the calculations of the contractors. There were few laborers available in the largely agricultural valley itself, and few could be attracted to it because of the reputation of the Potomac for periodic Asiatic cholera epidemics during the hot, humid summer construction season and because of the construction of other internal improvements in the East, notable the Baltimore & Ohio Railroad and the Pennsylvania Main Line Canal. As a result of these

---

[53] Ibid, May 25, 1831, Ltrs. Recd., C&O Co.
[54] Proceedings of the President and Board of Directors, A, 140, and W. Robert Leckie's notes, dated May 12, 1829, in his Diary and Account Book, 1828–1829, W. Robert Leckie Papers, Duke University.
[55] Cumberland Civilian, quoted in Report to the Stockholders on the Completion of the Chesapeake & Ohio Canal, 13–131.

recruitment problems, 2,113 men were working along the line of the canal in June 1829 while it was estimated that 6,000 were needed in order to complete the canal in the time specified in the contracts.[56]

As wages continued to rise from an average of $8–$10 per month for common labor in November 1828 to $12–$13 per month in July 1829, the canal directors undertook to encourage the migration of workers from all parts of the United States and from various European countries, especially Great Britain, the German states, and the Netherlands.[57] The experiment in using foreign laborers proved to be expensive and failed to solve the labor shortage in the long run.[58] Nevertheless, the use of imported laborers succeeded in temporarily stabilizing the rate of wages on the canal, as the total work force on the line rose from a low of about 1,800 in the summer months to over 3,100 by November 1829.[59]

Another major obstacle encountered in the construction of the canal was the high cost of land. Some of the landholders on the route over which the canal was to pass readily granted the company the title required, or at least rights to the use of the land. Many others obstructed the work and refused to surrender their property voluntarily in the hope of realizing great profits from forced sales. In his first annual report to the stockholders, on June 1, 1829, President Mercer stated:

> It was very soon apparent that the expectation of large indemnities had arisen among the proprietors of the ground and materials required for the canal, with the progress of the canal itself, and the certainty of its ultimate success. Efforts had been abortively made to profit by the uncertain hopes which preceded this state of absolute assurance. It was difficult to make them, with precision, as to the ground to be surrendered, because the final location of the canal, by the Engineer charged with it, remained uncertain until the moment o f contracting for its execution, and, even for some time after, so that promises, antecedently given, might be afterwards easily evaded. Some patriotic individuals, in the spirit of that provision of the charter of the company which now constitutes part of the standing law and usage of every State distinguished in the career of internal improvement, voluntarily surrendered their lands, without price, in the hope of aiding the company by the influence of their example. But the far greater number early indicated a disposition to exact prices for their property which left the President and Directors no alternative, but a resort to the process of condemnation, provided by the charter.[60]

The condemnation proceedings to which the canal directors resorted became more and more frequent as construction moved up the river and as speculation fever of the farmers rose.

Among those who resisted the condemnation efforts of the canal company were those who held out for the highest possible price, and those who would not sell at any price. The company records are filled with numerous instances where the land proprietors resisted the verdict of the juries, called for new trials, and attempted delaying tactics which raised their nuisance value. One such example was the lengthy negotiations and legal battle in the Montgomery County courts between the company and John P. C. Peter who owned some sixteen acres on the west side of

---

[56] *First Annual Report* (1829), 19–20, and *Second Annual Report* (1830), 5–6.
[57] *First Annual Report* (1829), 21–22, *and Proceedings of the President and Board of Directors*, A, 140, 153, 309.
[58] Washington Chronicle, October 24, 1829, and Sanderlin, *The Great National Project*, 77–78. A more complete discussion of the labor force and its effect on the construction of the canal appears in Chapter VI of this Historic Resource Study.
[59] Proceedings of the President and Board of Directors, A, 353–354.
[60] First Annual Report, 9–10. See also Hurd to Mercer, January 26, 1829, Ltrs. Recd., C&O Co.

Seneca Creek. Two condemnation proceedings were held, each followed by appeals and counter suits, over a 2½ year period before Peter accepted the second jury's assessment and agreed to the execution of the deed.[61]

Those who refused to sell at any price usually had motives in the background. For example, Charles Carroll of Carrollton, the sole surviving signer of the Declaration of Independence and one of the founders of the Baltimore & Ohio Railroad Company, bushed aside all offers for a relatively small parcel of his 10,000-acre estate in Frederick County. It was he who had laid the cornerstone of the railroad at the corner of Pratt and Amity Streets in Baltimore on the same day as the canal's groundbreaking ceremonies at Little Falls, saying: "I consider this among the most important acts of my life, second only to my signing of the Declaration of Independence, if second even to that."[62] He refused to accommodate the canal company, stressing the great inconveniences which his tenants would suffer during the construction operations; in return for this hardship to them, there was only the promise of increased land values for him if the canal were ever completed, a fact that he doubted.[63] His principal concern, however, was the struggle then taking place between the two rival transportation lines for the right of way above Point of Rocks.

The decision to extend the canal from Little Falls to Rock Creek brought on renewed difficulties with land proprietors. Georgetown merchants were reluctant to see the canal extended below its initial terminus, which was favorable to the commercial position of their town. But representatives of Washington interests maintained that the canal must terminate where shipping facilities were available and insisted that nothing less than a site in Washington, for example, the mouth of Tiber Creek, from which the city could construct a cross-town canal to the Eastern Branch, would be acceptable.[64]

Washington exerted great influence on the canal board by threatening to withhold payment on its $1,000,000 subscription to the company stock and by enlisting the support of Secretary of the Treasury Richard Rush. In the face of this overwhelming pressure, President Mercer and the stockholders agreed to Washington's demands at a general meeting on September 17, 1828.[65] While the canal company averted potential financial disaster by acceding to the demands of Washington, it also stirred the resentment of Georgetown business interests[66] because the new terminus paved the way for branch canals to Alexandria and Washington, their neighboring rivals for the commerce of the Potomac Valley.

The Merchants also dislike giving up what was and what promised to be valuable property in Georgetown. They were not satisfied that what they received then was a fair price in terms of the value the property might have if the town experienced the growth they anticipated. Thus, the awards for damages ran very high, and the company became embroiled in disputes with many of its early stockholders and supporters in Georgetown, including John Mason who had been an early advocate of the canal at the Chesapeake & Ohio Canal Conventions; Francis Scott Key, who

---

[61] Reference Book Concerning Land Titles, 1829–68, C&O Co.
[62] Edward Hungerford, *The Story of the Baltimore & Ohio Railroad* (2 vols, New York, 1928), I, 44.
[63] Carroll to Mercer, February 26, 1829, Ltrs. Recd., C&O Co.
[64] Washington National Intelligencer, September 10, 1828.
[65] Proceedings of the President and Directors of the Chesapeake & Ohio Canal Company, and of the Corporations of Washington, Georgetown, and Alexandria, in Relation to the Location of the Eastern Termination of the Chesapeake & Ohio Canal (Washington, 1828), 1–31. Following the meeting, Mercer sought the counsel of Attorney General William Wirt whether the company charter permitted the extension of the canal. On October 9, 1828, Wirt replied that the legislative acts of Virginia, Maryland, and the United States were vague on this point. However, since all the acts specified that the canal was to terminate at tidewater in the District of Columbia, it was his opinion that the company could locate the termination of the waterway anywhere in the District. *First Annual Report* (1829), Appendix, XXXVI–XL.
[66] Ordinances of the Corporation of Georgetown (Georgetown, 1830), 5

had attended the second convention and later rendered legal assistance to the company during the initial stages of its legal controversy with the railroad; and Walter Smith who served as one of the first directors of the company.[67]

The canal board made several significant decisions during the first year of construction that increased the expenditures of the canal company beyond the original estimates. Although the 1826 canal convention and the company's charter called for a canal of 40 feet wide at the surface, 28 feet wide at the bottom, and 4 feet deep, the U.S. Board of Engineers had recommended a waterway having the dimensions of 48, 33, and 5 feet respectively. However, when Geddes and Roberts reported that a canal 60 feet wide at the surface, 48 feet wide at the bottom, and 6 feet deep could be built for less than $5,000,000, the canal board decided to adopt the larger dimensions for the canal between Georgetown and Harpers Ferry because of the increased advantages attainable at what was projected as little additional cost. The greater size would give the canal a cross section of 306 square feet and a prism of 59,840 cubic yards as compared with 136 square feet and 25,595 5/9 cubic yards on the New York, Pennsylvania, and Ohio canals whose general dimensions were 40 feet wide at the surface, 28 feet wide at the bottom, and 4 feet deep.[68]

It was estimated that the increased prism would reduce water resistance to the equivalent of unimpeded sea navigation, and it was believed that much of the masonry would, the most expensive part of the construction, would be unaffected by the increase in size. On some sections, such as the Georgetown level, the larger dimensions would pay for themselves through the greater quantity of water which would be available for sale. The latter was dubious argument for the company did not have the right to sell water, and there was some doubt that the legislature would agree to it as a sizable block of Maryland citizens opposed the granting of such a privilege.[69]

To men who were fully convinced of the practicability and certain success of this national project, these supposed advantages far outweighed the increased cost of construction with Geddes and Roberts had estimated as $2,523.92 per mile and which ultimately more than doubled during the construction period.[70] It is interesting to note that by June 1830 when the rising cost of actual construction was beginning to surmount all of the original estimates, the board defended its initial enthusiasm for an enlarged canal by stating:

> If, in its plan, the Board have erred, it has arisen from their inability to forget, that a work destined to be the great central thoroughfare of so many States, and the firmest bond of their happy union, should be commensurate with its great end, and fulfill the wishes of the Government, Cities, and People, who have impressed upon it this high character.[71]

Another factor which increased the cost of building the canal was the directors' decision to purchase the strip of land between the canal and the river. The directors were obsessed with the idea of eliminating the construction of bridges over the canal, because the structures would obstruct the navigation of steamboats which the board hoped to introduce and their construction would

---

[67] Proceedings of the President and Board of Directors A, 59, 167, 182; and *Second Annual Report*, 11. For further information relative to the legal disputes between the canal company and these men, see Chesapeake & Ohio Canal Company vs. Key, U.S. Reports, 3 Cranch C.C. 599; Chesapeake & Ohio Canal Company vs. Mason, ibid, 4 Cranch C. C. 123; and Chesapeake & Ohio Canal Company vs. Union Bank, Ibid, 4 Cranch C. C. 75, 5 Cranch C.C. 509.
[68] First Annual Report, 9
[69] Ibid.
[70] Ibid, 8–15.
[71] *Second Annual Report*, 7.

cost more than the land was worth at any fair estimate of its value.[72] According to the company surveys, the entire quantity of land between the canal and the river from Georgetown to Point of Rocks did not exceed 1,300 acres of which more than 500 were reportedly inarable.[73] The acquisition of this land was not strictly within the terms of the charter which allowed the condemnation of private property for canal purposes only, and the attempts to purchase this land led to further costly and lengthy legal battle.

The cumulative effect of greater allowances to contractors, increased labor costs, and higher land payments led the canal company to the end of its financial resources. The company had begun its operations with a subscribed capital of $3,608,400, a total nearly $900,000 less than the estimated cost of $4,479,346.93 for the eastern section by Geddes and Roberts. The canal board and the stockholders felt secure nevertheless in commencing work with the available resources, confidently expecting further aid from Congress and from the interested states, especially Virginia which had as yet made no subscription. However, their optimistic expectations for more subscriptions were not forthcoming at this time from either public or private sources. Appeals to Congress and the legislatures of Maryland, Virginia and Pennsylvania proved futile, the most devastating blow to the company's finances occurring in Virginia where the Assembly failed to enact a measure subscribing $400,000 to the enterprise.[74] Thus, the canal company had to rely upon its existing resources for the prosecution of its work.

From the very beginning the directors encountered difficulties in securing the payment of the calls on the subscribed capital. Maryland insisted on paying part of its share in state bonds, a policy that the board was forced to accept because the railroad company had already agreed to it and because it was necessary to placate the canal's enemies in the state legislature. The company had so little success in selling the bonds that it resorted to hypothecations, or pledges of personal property as collateral security, in order to obtain loans from the local banks.[75]

The debt-ridden cities of the District of Columbia ran into trouble making payments on their subscriptions. Prior to their subscriptions to the canal company, the total indebtedness of the towns had been: Washington, $361,826; Georgetown, $155,149; and Alexandria, $277,776.[76] To this had been added $1,000,000, $250,000, and $250,000 respectively. To secure funds to meet the calls on the canal stock, the local authorities in April 1829 appointed ex-Secretary of the Treasury Richard Rush to act as the agent of the district cities to negotiate a loan in Europe.[77] After failing to secure a loan through the Barings and Rothschilds in London, Rush succeeded in obtaining the loan of $1,500,000 through the Dutch banking company of Daniel Crommelin & Sons in Amsterdam in November, 1829.[78] The terms of the loan were as follows:

---

[72] Mercer to Lee, January 17, 1829, Ltrs. Sent, C&O Co., and *Second Annual Report*, 11.

[73] *First Annual Report*, 15–16.

[74] U.S., Congress, House, Committee on Roads and Canals, Memorial of the Chesapeake & Ohio Canal Company, H.Doc. 12, 20th Cong., 2d sess., 1828, 108; ibid, Memorial of the Chesapeake & Ohio Canal Company, HY.Doc. 73, 20th Cong., 2d sess., 1829, 1–6; ibid, Committee on Internal Improvements, Memorial of the President and Directors of the Chesapeake & Ohio Canal Company, H.Doc. 53, 21st Congress, 2d sess., 1830, 1–10; Memorial from the Chesapeake & Ohio Canal Company to the Maryland Legislature (Annapolis, 1830); and *First Annual Report* (1829), 19.

[75] Kent to Mercer, October 4, 1828, and Smith to Ingle, January 4, 1831, Ltrs. Recd., C&O Co., and Proceedings of the President and Board of Directors, A, 373, 377–378.

[76] Wilhelmus B. Bryan, *A History of the National Capital* (1 vols., New York, 1916), II, 111.

[77] Gales, Cox, and Mason to Ingham, April 1829, in Washington, D.C., Georgetown, and Alexandria Collection, Holland Loan, Library of congress, and *Remarks on the Loan of a Million and a Half of Dollars, Proposed to be Raised by the City of Washington and the Towns of Georgetown and Alexandria, under an Act of the Congress of the United States* (London, 1829), 1–45.

[78] Niles' Register, XXXVII (October 3, 1829, January 23, 1830) 83, 360.

The said three thousand seven hundred and fifty bonds shall bear a fixed interest of five per cent per annum, upon their nominal capital of thousand guilders, Netherland currency each; the said interest will be payable in Amsterdam, at the counting house of the last underwritten, or of their successors, from six months to six months, say on the first January and the first July of each year; and when the said bonds therefore will be issued, there ill be added to them a set of half-yearly dividend warrants, each of twenty-five guilders, Netherland currency, payable in succession at the counting house of the last underwritten or of their cashiers, and the first of which dividend warrants will be payable first January, eighteen hundred thirty-one.[79]

During the early years of construction, the canal company also had the usual trouble with delinquent private stockholders and was forced to resort to threats and legal suits to obtain satisfaction.[80] By June 1832, the canal board had issued calls for the payment of nearly sixty per cent of its capital stock, a fact which clearly demonstrated the potential financial difficulties of the company since the only portion of the waterway that had been completed and opened for navigation was the 22-mile section from Georgetown to Seneca.[81]

As early as June 1829, the company officials realized that the higher costs would jeopardize the completion of the canal. This growing awareness was increasingly felt with the continuing difficulties in obtaining any new stock subscriptions. To offset this danger, the company hired Richard Rush, who was about to leave for London on behalf of the District cities, as its agent to open books in Europe to receive subscriptions up to $6,000,000 for the eastern section and $10,000,000 for the entire canal, but the attempt proved to be discouraging as no large subscriptions were forthcoming.[82]

As the railroad injunction continued in effect, the expense of a large engineering staff became a great burden on the company's financial condition. Accordingly the board released engineers as soon as they found positions elsewhere, reduced salaries, and eliminated some positions. The number of resident engineers was reduced from five to four in September 1829 and later to two in August 1830.[83] When Chief Engineer Wright resigned his position with the canal company in the fall of 1830, the canal directors abolished the position of Chief Engineer, noting that there was little need to employ a person in that position with construction prevented above Point of Rocks.[84] On April 1, 1831, after Nathan S. Roberts requested a leave of absence to return to his New York Home to regain his failing health, the board terminated his employment with the company and abolished his position for similar reasons.[85]

---

[79] *Letter and Accompanying Documents from the Hon. Richard Rush to Joseph Gales, Esq., Mayor of the City of Washington; Respecting the Loan of a Million and a Half Dollars, Negotiated by the Former, In Europe, for the said City and the Towns of Georgetown and Alexandria, under the Authority of an Act of Congress of the United States, Passed on the 24th of May, 1828* (Washington, 1830), 151.
[80] Proceedings of the President and Board of Directors, B, 291.
[81] Ringgold to Ingle, June 18, 1832, Ltrs. Recd., C&O Co., and *Washington National Intelligencer*, June 29, 1830.
[82] Sanderlin, *The Great National Project*, 82.
[83] Proceedings of the President and Board of Directors, A, 363, B, 173–174.
[84] Ibid, B, 172–173.
[85] Ibid, B. 295.

While not yet desperate, the financial condition of the company was rapidly deteriorating by 1832, a condition that was making some of its uneasy stockholders openly critical of company policies and forcing the canal directors to consider new initiatives to attract additional capital.[86]

The greatest deterrent to the westward progress of the canal after 1828 was the existence of a series of injunctions prohibiting the extension of the waterway above Point of Rocks. These injunctions were in turn the cause of a protracted and costly legal struggle between the canal company and the railroad company which ultimately increased the cost of constructing the waterway and further burdened the deteriorating financial condition of the Chesapeake & Ohio. The question involved in the cases was a dispute over the right of prior location of the respective transportation projects in the Potomac Valley, a matter that was not fully settled until early 1832 by the Maryland Court of Appeals.[87]

The legal controversy between the rival internal improvement companies was the culmination of a clash of commercial interests that had been developing since the early 1820s between the businessmen of Baltimore and those of Washington, Georgetown, and Alexandria. The Baltimore interests, originally active in support of the canal, lost their enthusiasm for the project as it became apparent that the canal, if built, would favor the development of the three District cities and as it became doubtful that the canal could be tapped far enough up the valley to allow Baltimore to share in its trade. Therefore, the Baltimore merchants adopted the proposal of building a railroad in February 1827 so that their city could compete with the commercial centers of New York and Philadelphia which were fed by the Erie and the Pennsylvania Main Line canals, respectively. On February 28, 1827, the charter of the railroad company was enacted into law, and after receiving stock subscriptions totaling $4,000,000, in just a few weeks, the company was organized on April 24.[88]

Both enterprises ultimately chose the Potomac Valley as the route of their respective works. While the canal company was still struggling to get organized in the late spring of 1828, the Baltimore & Ohio sent surveyors ahead to locate its line and secure land waivers, especially in the narrow passes of the valley at which a conflict with the canal might be expected.[89] To stop this usurpation of their rights, canal company stockholders applied to the Washington Country Court on June 10, 1828, and Judge Thomas Buchanan granted a preliminary injunction, prohibiting the railroad from acquiring land or rights of way along the projected route of the canal above Point of Rocks where it entered the valley.[90]

The railroad company countered with three injunctions against the canal which it obtained from Maryland Chancellor Theodoric Bland of the Court of Chancery at Annapolis on June 23, 24, and 25. The first enjoined interference with contract rights acquired by the railroad from local landowners; the second enjoined interference with condemnation proceedings; the third protected such additional rights as the railroad had acquired by being the first to physically locate its projected route on the ground.[91]

The canal company protested to the Chancellor in a lengthy brief filed on May 16, 1829, that the conduct of the Baltimore & Ohio was an infringement on the canal's chartered rights and

---

[86] *A Candid Appeal to the Stockholders of the Chesapeake & Ohio Canal Company* (Washington, 1832), 1–5.
[87] Sanderlin, *The Great National Project*, 83.
[88] John E. Semmes, *John H.B. Latrobe and his Times: 1803–1891* (Baltimore, 1917), 321–322; Hungerford, *Story of the Baltimore & Ohio Railroad*, I, 18–27; and Elihu S. Riley, *A History of the General Assembly of Maryland, 1635–1904* (Baltimore, 1905) 334
[89] Second Annual Report of the Baltimore & Ohio Railroad Company (1828), Appendix, 3–4.
[90] Gill and Johnson, Reports, IV, 36, *and Second Annual Report* (1830) 9.
[91] H.H. Walker Lewis, "The Great Case of the Canal vs. the Railroad", Maryland Law Review, XIX (winter, 1959), 11, and Gill and Johnson, Reports, IV, 13–16.

that the railroad officials had given the impression that their work would avoid the circuitous Potomac route for a more direct northwesterly course "straight across the mountains by means of inclined planes and stationary engines to Pittsburgh."[92]

The legal question involved was whether the Potomac Company's rights inherited by the Chesapeake & Ohio were still valid or whether the Baltimore & Ohio had acquired them by virtue of its charter from the State of Maryland the first exercise of the rights of location. The real issue, however, was the political-economic one between the City of Baltimore and the District of Columbia's three cities.[93]

The rivalry for the trade of the Potomac Valley was perhaps summed up best in a caustic speech by Representative George E. Mitchell, a railroad supporter from Cecil County, Maryland, on the House floor on February 26, 1829:

> I do not include in this estimate the cost of the Chesapeake & Ohio Canal. This, if it benefits any, will benefit more particularly the non-slaveholding states of the west. For us, it might as well be in china. The engineers of the United States have estimated the cost of this work at twenty-two million, five hundred thousand dollars. Whence is this sum to come? From the Chesapeake & Ohio Canal Company? Who does not know that Washington, Georgetown, and Alexandria are bankrupt? That the two last exhibit marks of decay? Who does not know that the company cannot sustain the expenditure, and that the burden must fall on the treasury of the United States? And that the states who can derive no early benefit from it will have to contribute most? Besides natural obstacles, almost insuperable, this canal, if ever completed, will have to contend against the competition of the Baltimore rail road—planned, and to be managed, by a company of individuals as distinguished for their activity, as for their capital—who have entered on their great work with the zeal which characterized the people of Baltimore—and who will have completed the road, and have it in full operation, pouring into their city the rich superabundance of the west, before this canal reaches the eastern base of the Alleghany. May success attend their undertaking.[94]

Throughout the legal struggle, the Baltimore & Ohio fought a delaying action in the courts, while its influence, and that of the city of Baltimore, had its effect in the Maryland General Assembly and in Congress. The Maryland legislature quickly became hostile to the canal company's claims, choosing to look upon the railroad as a purely Maryland project deserving of the state's protection.[95]

In Congress the influence of the canal company through its president, Charles F. Mercer, who doubled as the chairman of the House committee on Roads and Canals, was checked by numerous petitions by the railroad and by the hostility of the Jacksonian Democrats to federally

---

[92] Gill and Johnson, Reports, IV, 32-33, 47; and U.S., Congress, House, Memorial of the Chesapeake & Ohio Canal Company, H. Doc. 127, 20th Cong., 2d sess., 1829, 3

[93] The course of the controversy can be followed best in the series of letters apparently taken from the canal company's files for the purpose of publication in *Correspondence between the Chesapeake & Ohio Railroad Company, In Relation to the Disputes between those Companies Concerning the Right of Way for their Respective Works along the Potomac River* (Baltimore, 1830), 1–80.

[94] *Niles' Register*, XXXSVI (March 21, 1829), 53.

[95] Lee to Mercer, February 15, 1829, and Ingle to Mercer, February 2, 1831, Ltrs. Recd., C&O Co., and *Report from the President of the Chesapeake & Ohio Canal Company to the Legislature of Maryland* (Annapolis, 1831), 1-24.

sponsored internal improvements.[96] At the insistence of the railroad that both works be considered experiments until their relative merits had been tested, both companies became involved in periodically submitting lengthy reports concerning the historical advantages of railroads and canals in Europe and the United States.[97]

In the meantime, the Baltimore & Ohio was constructing its road from Baltimore to Frederick and then south to Point of Rocks. While its resources were limited, it had an obvious advantage in that its road began operating as soon as it was completed.[98] As the Court of Chancery showed little inclination of handing down an early verdict, the canal board soon became restless. The company had ample resources to undertake a large part of its intended work, and it was desirous of taking advantage of the relatively low prices for which the first contracts had been let.[99] In addition, the line of the canal above Seneca Falls feeder was useless until the next feeder was reached at Harper's Ferry.[100] Added to this difficulty was the charter requirement that one hundred miles of the canal must be completed in five years.[101]

Eventually the delay itself began to be costly, for after the canal was completed between tidewater at Georgetown and Seneca in the spring of 1831, the large staff of engineers represented a financial burden while construction came to a virtual halt. The aforementioned employment terminations of Chief Engineer Wright and Engineer Roberts and the subsequent elimination of their positions resulted in part from the construction delays caused by the legal battle with the railroad.[102] Moreover in a period of rising costs for labor, materials, and land acquisition, every delay in construction meant increased costs when work would resume.

The court battle followed a lackadaisical course as both companies turned to the Court of Chancery to adjudicate their rival claims. After receiving supplemental written arguments on behalf of the canal by former Attorney General William Wirt and on behalf of the railroad by John H.B. Latrobe, Roger Brook Taney, and Reverdy Johnson, a recognized leader of the Maryland Bar, during the summer of 1829, Chancellor Bland refused the canal company's motion to dissolve the injunctions against it on September 24.[103] Denying that there was any inconsistency between this proceeding and the prior suit in the Washington County Court, he observed that the earlier case involved the assertion by the canal company of a general right of priority whereas the railroad was merely seeking to preserve the status quo with respect to specific contract and other rights. Since both companies were authorized to acquire land for their corporate purposes, he felt

---

[96] Proceedings of the President and Board of Directors, B, 78 ff., and *Niles' Register*, XXXVIII (March 13, 1830) 62–63.
[97] *Report from the President of the Chesapeake & Ohio Canal Company to the Legislature of Maryland*, V–VIII, and House Report 414, 244–247.
[98] Sanderlin, *The Great National Project*, 85.
[99] Proceedings of Stockholders, A, 21.
[100] *Second Annual Report* (1830), 6.
[101] Act of Congress, Senate Document 610, 13.
[102] Proceedings of the President and Board of Directors, B, 171–174, 259.
[103] On November 22, 1828, the canal board had authorized President Mercer to employ William Wirt, the Attorney General of the United States, as an attorney for the canal company to assist Walter Jones in conducting the legal case with the railroad. See: Proceedings of the President and Board of Directors, A, 117. Although Wirt played a major role in the legal battle between the railroad and the canal, his personal papers, located at the Maryland Historical Society in Baltimore and in the Manuscript Collections of the Library of Congress, offer little substantive material relative to his participation. The great majority of his papers consist of correspondence with his wife, his children, and other relatives. While the letters give glimpses into the everyday workings of government and court life, the information generally tends to be peripheral to the major issues with which he was involved. Wirt resigned his position as Attorney General when Andrew Jackson became President in 1829, at which time he moved to Baltimore to open a private law practice. See: William Wirt, *Augments Delivered at Annapolis* (Washington, 1830), 3–206.

that the race should go to the diligent by stating: "Where two or more are allowed, by law, to purchase and acquire a title to lands...he who does the first requisite act for that purpose, shall not be hindered in his further progress...."[104]

Commissions to take evidence were issued to determine on the ground which company was entitled to priority and the extent to which it could proceed without interference with the other. The last of the commissions to take evidence was returned on May 27, 1831, at which point the canal company refused to spend further money and time in conducting the tedious evidentiary surveys and threatened to proceed with its own construction above Point of Rocks. The Chancellor eventually determined that enough ground had been covered (in fact only the 12-mile stretch between Point of Rocks and Harpers Ferry had been surveyed for the commissions),[105] AND ON November 9 the injunctions against the canal were made perpetual. Furthermore it was required to pay the costs of the suit, including the expenses of the additional surveys ordered by the Chancery Court. In making his decision, the Chancellor took the dubious position that this was not the proper time to consider the question of prior right.[106]

Arguing that the continued existence of the canal company was at stake, Walter Jones on December 7 applied to the Maryland Court of Appeals on behalf of the canal board to advance their appeal of the Chancellor's decision and hear it out of turn. The railroad opposed this move, stating that its senior counsel, Roger Brooke Taney, had recently been appointed U.S. Attorney General and would be unable to participate on such short notice. However, the canal company countered these objections by replying that its senior counsel, William Wirt, would also miss the trial because of a recent illness.[107]

On December 10, the Court of Appeals advanced the case and set it for argument on December 19, later changing it to December 26. The case was argued before the Court from December 26, 1831, through January 2, 1832. The canal company was represented by Walter Jones and Alexander C. Magruder, later a judge of the Court, while the railroad was represented by Reverdy Johnson and the venerable Massachusetts Senator Daniel Webster. Despite the absence of one of its members, the Court rendered its decision on January 4, reversing the decision of the Chancellor and confirming the canal company in its claim to the right of prior location by a vote of 3 to 2.[108]

In his opinion Chief Judge John Buchanan, who had presided over the original litigation in the Washington County Court when doing circuit duty, spoke for the majority that the canal company had the right of prior location because (1) the Potomac Company was entitled to priority and the Chesapeake & Ohio had succeeded to its rights and (2) the legislation chartering the canal company constituted a compact which would be impaired by the granting of any inconsistent rights to the railroad. Basing his reasoning on an 1819 Supreme Court decision by Chief Justice John Marshall declaring the sanctity of contract under the U.S. Constitution, he stated:

> And its charter, according to the decision of the Supreme Court in the case of the Trustees of Dartmouth College vs. Woodward, 4th Wheaton 518, being a contract between the states of Maryland, Virginia, and the Potomac Company, the obligation of which could not, without the assent of the corporation, be impaired, by any act of the legislature of ei-

---

[104] Gill and Johnson, Reports, IV, 54.
[105] *A Complete Set of Maps, Drawings, and Tabular Statements, Relating to the Locations of the Canal and Railroad, from the Point of Rocks to Harper's Ferry* (Georgetown, 1830), 1–56.
[106] Gill and Johnson, Reports, IV, 71.
[107] Jones to Mercer, December 2, 1831, and Wirt to Mercer, December 25, 1831, Ltrs. Recd., C&O Co.; and Magruder to Wirt, December 10, 1831, and Mercer to Ingle, January, 1833, Ltrs. Sent, C&O Co.
[108] Niles' Register, XLII (august 11, 1832), 219; Proceedings of the President and Board of Directors, C, 48; and Proceedings of Stockholders, A, 196.

ther of the States, nor the concurrent acts of both, consistently with the constitution of the United States, declaring that, no State shall pass any law impairing the obligation of contract, the chart4er of the Rail Road company, could not, without impairing the obligation of that contract, abolish, take away, or diminish the prior and paramount right of the Potomac Company, to select and appropriate by purchase or condemnation, and lands in the valley of the Potomac, for the route and site of a canal or canals, wherever it should think proper, along the borders of the river, either in terms, or by any construction of it, that would have authorized the Rail Road Company, to occupy any of the difficult passes, or other places along the river, for the route and site of the road, in such a manner, as either to exclude that company from a priority in the choice of a site or sites for the construction of the works authorized by its charter, or in any manner to restrict and circumscribe it, in the exercise of its prior right of election. But such an occupation of the Rail Road Company of the valley of the Potomac, would have been a violation of the vested corporate rights and privileges of the Potomac Company, and the charter of the Rail Road Company, in so far as it purports to be, or may be construed in derogation of those rights and privileges, is repugnant to the constitution of the United States, and void; there being no difference in principle, between a law, that in terms impairs the obligation of a contract, and one that produces the same effect, in the construction and practical execution of it....[109]

The successful termination of the controversy enabled the Chesapeake & Ohio Canal Company to resume construction of its waterway between Seneca and Point of Rocks and to place under contract the work above the latter village. The directors wasted little time in following up their advantage and placing the entire 100 miles under contract. It was now a two-fold race as the five years allowed by the charter for the construction of the first 100 miles would expire in 1833 and the exhaustion of the company's immediate financial resources was on the horizon. Within two months the 12-mile section of the canal between Point of Rocks and Harpers Ferry was let for contract, and during the spring and summer months canal officials let contracts to complete, with slackwater navigation at several points, approximately 117 miles of the canal all the way to Dam No. 5.[110]

To convince those who were skeptical of its assertion that it had sufficient funds to complete the contract, the canal board commissioned a comprehensive review of its financial condition. On December 15, 1832, President Mercer issued a published report indicating that the total amount of available company resources amounted to $60,419.16 in cash, $1,233,393.25 in uncollected stock, and $31,500.00 in estimated tolls for the approaching boating season, making a total of $1,325,812.41. According to the company estimates, it would cost $341,998.47 to complete the canal below Harpers Ferry, and $925,645.75 to finish it from Harpers Ferry to Dam No. 5. Added to these outlays, was the sum of $20,000 to operate the company during the coming year, thus making the total expenditures of the company to be $1, 287,644.22. By these projections, the company would have a surplus of $38,168.19 when the canal was finished to Dam No. 5. Admittedly, this was a thin margin of capital, but Mercer was optimistic that this amount would be augmented by additional grants from the interested states, higher toll collections once the canal

---

[109] Gill and Johnson, Reports, IV, 108-110. The full text of the opinions rendered in the case may be found in ibid, IV, 71-164, 164-226.
[110] Fourth Annual Report (1832), C&O Co., 5-8.

was opened to navigation for the 117 miles, and income from the sale of water power to manufacturers along the canal.[111]

At the same time, the indication of approaching financial duress was manifested in the revival of the proposal to substitute slackwater for canal navigation. Simultaneously with the aforementioned report, Mercer also submitted a study recommending the construction of a series of three dams and three canals, together with 20 miles of slackwater navigation, between Dam 5 and a point nine miles above Cumberland. According to the estimates of the company engineers, this plan would reduce the cost of the eastern section by over $500,000.[112]

The resumption of construction brought a renewal of the grievances of earlier years. Masonry work fell far behind schedule as the problem of stone and cement supplies reappeared, and there were more reports of absconding contractors.[113] Most serious of all, land costs continued high as the canal entered Washington County. The first land condemned was that of a bitter canal opponent, Gerard B. Wager, to whom very high damages were awarded thereby providing a discouraging precedent.[114]

The determination of the local land proprietors to extract maximum profits from the canal company was further intensified by the high award in the condemnation of Casper Wever's land. Wever, a civil engineer and an official of the Baltimore & Ohio Railroad, had purchased a 500-acre tract of land in the vicinity of present-day Weverton for the purpose of building a manufacturing town.[115] During the court proceedings, Wever traveled to Annapolis to obtain an injunction from Chancellor Bland to prevent construction of the canal on his land until he received full payment.[116]

After some of the landowners resorted to injunctions to enforce prompt payment of their awards, the board announced its intention to advertise the renewal of negotiations with Virginia landholders to shift the canal to the south side of the Potomac, but the notice failed to have any appreciable effect.[117]

The Baltimore & Ohio Railroad continued in active opposition to its arch rival, maintaining its agitation in the Maryland legislature and conducting a nuisance campaign in the Potomac Valley to hinder the progress of the canal. The purpose of this agitation was to stir up popular pressure to force joint construction of the two transportation systems.[118]

On top of the renewed construction difficulties, high land costs, and conflicts with the railroad, there was the disastrous epidemic of Asiatic cholera in the Potomac Valley during the summer of 1832.[119] The canal project had been plagued from its inception by the annual "sickly"

---

[111] Two Reports of the President to the Directors of the Chesapeake & Ohio Canal Company, *On the Present State of the Finances of the Company*, and *An Extension of the Navigation of the Potomac to a Point Nine Miles Above the Town of Cumberland, On a Plan Consistent with the Present Charter* (Washington, 1832), 3–8.

[112] Ibid, 8–12.

[113] McFarland to Mercer, November 5, 1832, and Purcell to President and Directors, August 24, 1833, Ltrs. Recd., C&O Co.

[114] Cruger to President and Director, August 3, 1832, and Mercer to Ingle, August 8, 1832, Ltrs. Recd., C&O Co.

[115] John Thomas Scharf, *History of Western Maryland* (2 vols., Philadelphia, 1882), II, 1285.

[116] Price to Ingle, August 25, 1832, and Price to Mercer, November 4, 1832, Ltrs. Recd., C&O Co.

[117] Price to Ingle, August 25, 1832, November 8, 1833, and June 10, 1834, Ltrs. Recd., C&O Co.

[118] Sanderlin, *The Great National Project*, 92–93, and *Proceedings of the President and Directors of the Chesapeake & Ohio Canal Company, on the Proposition of the Baltimore & Ohio Railroad Company, of the 19th day of January, 1832, for the Joint Construction of the Canal and Railroad....* (Washington, 1832), 1–34.

[119] *Niles' Register*, XLIII (September 22, 1832), 52.

season in the Potomac Valley causing the exodus of company officials, contractors, and laborers, but the 1832 epidemic proved to be the most devastating to occur during the construction period.[120] The epidemic spread along the entire line of construction from Point of Rocks to Williamsport causing immense suffering as described in the following account:

> As many as six persons are said to have been lying dead, at one time, in a single shantee, —while in others the dead and dying were mixed in awful confusion. Many had abandoned their employments and fled—and some of these were attacked on the roads, and died in the fence corners! The habits and exposures of these poor people fit them for the reception of the cholera, and their accommodations for the sick are wretched and scanty, indeed—for they are crowded in temporary sheds, and badly supplied even with the most common necessaries of life....[121]

Thus, the summer of 1832, the first one in which unrestricted construction was possible, witnessed a virtual suspension of work along the canal, and the opportunity to complete the first 100 miles of the waterway by 1833 was gone. In fact so little progress was made on the canal that not even the twelve miles between Point of Rocks and Harpers Ferry were finished in 1832.

With the coming of cooler weather in autumn, work slowly resumed on the canal, but the harm had been done. As a result of the many hindrances to construction the cost of the work had risen sharply, and the westward progress of the canal had virtually halted. By the latter part of 1832, the canal company was experiencing its first financial crisis. While it still possessed adequate resources on paper, it was having difficulty in securing the payment of its calls and consequently was becoming hard pressed for funds to push the construction. In June, President Mercer had sought unsuccessfully to obtain a $300,000 loan based on the pledge of company property.[122]

In October and November he made futile efforts to secure loans from private banks in Washington, New York, and Philadelphia on the pledge of Washington and Georgetown stock. Concurrently, the board asked the Pennsylvania, Virginia, and Maryland legislatures for additional subscriptions, but the requests were rejected.[123] Pennsylvania had shown initial interest only in the western section of the canal and was now completing its own extensive system of public works.[124] Virginia had failed to make any subscription to the Chesapeake & Ohio, principally because the canal was being built on the Maryland side of the Potomac and Virginia interests saw little advantage in supporting a transportation system that would render the commercial advantages of the Potomac trade on Washington and Georgetown. Furthermore, she was preparing to construct her own system of internal improvements connecting the Chesapeake Bay and the Ohio River via the James and Kanawha Rivers.[125]

To add to the financial woes of the company, simultaneous notices arrived in November 1832 from the Mayor of Washington indicating the city's inability to meet the twenty-ninth installment, and from the Secretary of the Treasury refusing to make further payments for the United States until the District cities caught up with their payments. The canal board prepared to suspend operations above Harpers Ferry when Washington defaulted.[126]

---

[120] House Report 414,237.
[121] Ibid, XLIII (September 15, 1832), 44
[122] Proceedings of the President and Board of Directors, C, 174.
[123] Proceedings of the President and Board of Directors, C, 174, 240, 243–244; and Mercer to Ingle, October 8, 25, 26, 31, 1833, Ltrs. Recd., C&O Co.
[124] *Niles' Register*, XL (April 9, 1831), 91.
[125] Wayland Fuller Dunaway, History of the James River and Kanawha Company (New York, 1922), 48–49, 123–162, 226–240.
[126] Proceedings of the President and Board of Directors, C, 236–237, 290

The canal company turned to the Maryland legislature for an extension of its charter and further large-scale aid. The general Assembly was decidedly hostile to the canal's petitions, and responded with a memorial to the canal company requesting joint construction of the two works to Harpers Ferry as a favor to the State, a policy that the railroad had recommended since its defeat in the Court of Appeals.[127] After a lengthy battle of proposals and counter-proposals over this issue, the Governor suggested that the state might force the canal to accommodate the railroad by withholding further financial aid.[128] A Senate committee responded with a report recommending the refusal of an extension of the charter and stating that they regarded the railroad "as decidedly and unqualifiedly a Maryland work" and that they did "not regard the canal in this light."[129]

The last source of aid still available for the canal Company was congress, but the prospects of assistance from the federal government were slight after the emergence of the Jacksonian Democrats in 2828. The early record of the administration clearly indicated its hostility toward federal support for internal improvements in general and for the Chesapeake & Ohio in particular. When he vetoed the Maysville Road Bill in May 1830, Jackson not only negated the proposed highway from Maysville to Lexington in Kentucky because it was an intrastate project, but he also challenged the principle that internal improvements were a federal responsibility. "If it be the wish of the people that the construction of roads and canals should be conducted by the Federal Government," he wrote, "it is not only highly expedient, but indispensably necessary, that a previous amendment to the Constitution, delegating the necessary power and defining and restricting its exercise with reference to the sovereignty of the States, should be made."[130]

An analysis of the position of the Chesapeake & Ohio Canal indicates that it failed to meet either of the criteria set down by Jackson for internal improvements deserving of federal support. While it originally had been projected as a great national project to connect tidewater on the Potomac with Pittsburgh on the Ohio, it was becoming more obvious with each passing day that the canal would do well to reach Cumberland, thus remaining an intrastate project tapping the largely agricultural Potomac Valley trade for the benefit of Washington and Georgetown. As there was little enthusiasm for the Constitutional amendment recommended by Jackson, there was little hope of overcoming his neo-Jeffersonian and laissez faire attitude toward the question of federal support for internal improvements.

Furthermore, the particular bitterness with which the Jacksonians viewed the Chesapeake & Ohio may have stemmed in part from the personal animosity that existed between President Jackson and Charles F. Mercer. As a young Congressman in 1819, Mercer had delivered an address on the House floor assailing Jackson's course in the Seminole War, a speech which Jackson—who was known to carry longstanding personal grudges—apparently never forgot.[131]

As chairman of the House Committee on Roads and Canals, Mercer had enjoyed the friendship of Presidents Monroe and John Quincy Adams, both of whom had supported the Chesapeake & Ohio Canal project. Jackson, on the other hand, had been a bitter antagonist of Adams since he lost the presidential election to him in 1824, and Jackson was little interested in

---

[127] Proceedings of Directors, C, 108, and *Report of the Committee Appointed on the 28th April, 1832, By the Stockholders of the Chesapeake & Ohio Canal Company, On the Resolution of the General Assembly of Maryland, Relative to the Joint construction of the Chesapeake & Ohio Canal and the Baltimore & Ohio Railroad, Between the "Point of Rocks" and Harper's Ferry* (Washington, 1832), 3–8.

[128] Maryland House Journal, 1832, 23–24.

[129] Maryland Senate Journal, 1832, Appendix I, 4.

[130] Richardson, Messages and Papers, II, 1341, and Journal of the House of Representatives of the United States, 21st Cong., 1st sess., 1829–30, 733–742. For more information on Jackson's general attitude toward internal improvements see Robert V. Remini, *Andrew Jackson* (New York, 1966), 126, and Harold C. Syrett, Andrew *Jackson: His Contribution to the American Tradition* (Indianapolis, 1953), 135–154.

[131] Annals of Congress, 15th Cong., 2d sess., cols. 797-831

bailing out a project that Adams had supported, particularly in the area of internal improvements.[132]

These political rivalries and personal animosities were exacerbated after 1828 when Mercer, still holding his chairmanship of the House committee, as well as doubling as the canal president, became a persistent critic of the increasing power of the presidency and the spoils system under Jackson at the very time that he was coming into frequent conflict with the Jacksonians by his advocacy of federal support for internal improvements.[133] Thus, Jackson and his supporters had particular disdain for the Chesapeake & Ohio and its president and consequently were not inclined to be receptive to its appeal for additional funding.

The actions of the Jacksonian Democrats in the early 1830s served to underline this policy of hostility toward federal support for internal improvements in general and for the Chesapeake & Ohio in particular. In December 1828 Jacksonians in Congress introduced a joint resolution against further aid to the Cumberland Road and opposing federal ownership of stock in private internal improvement companies.[134] In June 1829, the new administration failed to send a representative to the first annual meeting of the canal company stockholders.[135]

On March 1, 1830, the House Committee on Internal Improvements recommended that no further aid be granted to the project until the relative value of canals and railroads was proved by trial, thereby taking the position that had been advocated by the Baltimore & Ohio Railroad and causing canal officials to spend a great deal of time in collecting and publishing data on the subject.[136]

The administration reversed its former policy of ignoring canal company meetings and actively interfered in company affairs at the second annual meeting of the company stockholders in June 1830 when Secretary of the Treasury Samuel D. Ingham nominated Commodore George Washington Rodgers, a respected naval hero and Jacksonian loyalist, to replace Mercer.[137] Although Mercer was reelected by a margin of 5,831 to 3,531, the Jacksonians again tried to dislodge him at the 1832 annual meeting.[138]

Meanwhile Congress refused to accede to any of the canal company's petitions for further aid.[139] Finally, in a desperate effort to win the favor of the national administration, the canal company consented in June 1833, by a highly-contested vote of 5,054 to 3,430, to the replacement of Mercer by ex-Secretary of War John Eaton, a friend of Jackson from Tennessee and a

---

[132] Remini, *Andrew Jackson*, 125–126.
[133] James Mercer Garnett, *Biographical Sketch of Hon. Charles Fenton Mercer: 1778–1858* (Richmond, 1911), 3–15, and *Dictionary of American Biography*, VI, 539.
[134] U.S., Congress, Senate, Joint Resolution for the Care and Preservation of the Cumberland Road, and of Other Roads Made or To Be Made by the Federal Government within the Different States, S. Doc. 6, 20th Cong., 2d sess., 1828.
[135] Mercer to Ingle, September 1, 1829, Ltrs. Recd., C&O Co.
[136] U.S., Congress, House, Committee on Internal Improvement, Report of the Committee on Internal Improvement, to Which Were Referred Sundry Petitions, Praying for an Appropriation to the Chesapeake & Ohio Canal Company, to be expended on the Western Side of the Mountains, H. Rept. 280, 21st Cong., 1st sess., 1830, 1.
[137] Washington *National Intelligencer*, June 14, 1830.
[138] Boteler to Mercer, July 28, 1832, Ltrs. Recd., C&O Co.
[139] U.S. Congress, House, Committee on Roads and Canals, Memorial of the Chesapeake & Ohio Canal Company, H. Doc. 73, 20th Cong., 2d sess., 1829, 1-2; ibid, Memorial of Stockholders, & c. in the Chesapeake & Ohio Canal Company, H. Doc. 120, 20th Cong., 2d sess., 1829, 1-4; ibid, Memorial of the Chesapeake & Ohio Canal Company, H. Doc. 127, 20th Cong. 2d sess., 1829, 1-3; ibid, Committee of Internal Improvements, Memorial of the President and Directors of the Chesapeake & Ohio Canal Company, H. Doc. 53, 21st Cong., 2d sess., 1830, 1–10; and ibid, Committee for the District of Columbia, Chesapeake & Ohio Canal Co., H. Doc. 93, 22d Cong., 2d sess., 1833, 1-13.

principal in the well-publicized Peggy Eaton affair.[140] Fortified by this concession, the canal board memorialized Congress in the spring of 1834 for a further subscription by submitting a lengthy report describing the historical development, the progress of the construction, and numerous problems of the canal project.[141] Notwithstanding the influence of the new president and the support of Mercer, who still remained as the chairman of the House Committee on Roads and Canals, Congress refused further aid to the company.

Failing to secure relief from the federal government, the canal directors belatedly sought to make peace with Maryland. A subscription by Virginia for $250,000 in February 1833 was too small and too encumbered with stipulations concerning its use to provide any real assistance as the canal board agreed to apply some $80,000 of the amount subscribed to the construction of several river locks that would provide access to the canal for boats crossing the Potomac from the Virginia shore.[142]

Therefore in February 1833, even before the bill providing for the Virginia subscription passed, the directors indicated their willingness to compromise their differences with the state and railroad, a move undoubtedly prompted in part by the railroad company's petition to Congress in that month requesting that the financial relief sought by the District cities be denied.[143]

In March, the legislature passed an act proposing an arrangement in which the state, the canal, and the railroad could all participate.[144] According to the bill, which required the approval of both companies to become operable, the railroad company was to subscribe to $266,000 to the stock of the canal company in return for permission to construct its tracks from Point of Rocks to Harpers Ferry. This subscription covered the costs of extending the railway to Harpers Ferry on the right-of-way of between 20 and 30 feet in width. The canal company would undertake the actual location and construction of both lines through the 4.1 miles of difficult passes where both works came together. For its part, the railroad would agree not to use the Maryland side of the river above Harpers Ferry until the canal was completed to Cumberland or before 1840 if the canal had not been completed by that time. The legislature offered, as its part, to pass two acts, long the subject of dispute between it and the canal, when the railroad reached Harpers Ferry. These would permit the canal board to sell surplus water and to commence the western section before completing the canal to Cumberland.[145]

After the railroad signified its consent to some conditions designed by the canal company to protect its rights, the Chesapeake & Ohio formally accepted the Maryland act on May 9.[146] The acceptance of the compromise did not mark the end of the trouble between the railroad and the

---

[140] Washington *National Intelligencer*, June 7, 1833, and *Niles' Register*, XLIV (June 22, 1833), 270–271.

[141] Proceedings of Stockholders, A, 320–321; Eaton to Price, January 3, 1834, Ltrs. Sent, C&O Co.; Sixth Annual

[142] Richmond Compiler quoted in *Niles' Register*, XLIV (April 27, 1833), 132; Proceedings of the President and Board of Directors, C. 282–283; and *Report on a Survey and Estimate for the Improvement of the Navigation of Goose Creek, Little River, and Beaver Dam in Loudoun County, Va.* (Washington, 1832), 3–6.

[143] U.S., Congress, House, Memorial of the Baltimore & Ohio Railroad Company, H. Doc. 113, 22nd Cong., 2d sess., 1833, 1-0, and *Niles' Register*, XLII (August 18, 1832), 441–442.

[144] Laws Made and Passed by the General Assembly of the State of Maryland (Annapolis, 1833), Ch. 291, Fifth Annual Report (1833), C&O Co., 12–15; and Proceedings of the President and Board of Directors, C, 312.

[145] Proceedings of the President and Board of Directors, C, 312, 341–342; Hungerford, *Story of the Baltimore & Ohio Railroad*, I, 137–141; and Semomes, *Latrobe and His Times*, 341.

[146] Proceedings of the Stockholders, A, 268–269, and Washington *National Intelligencer*, May 10, 1833.

canal, but there did follow a brief period of cooperation that seemed to brighten the prospects for both companies.[147]

After the compromise of 1833, the canal company again turned to Virginia and Maryland for aid in the solution of its financial problems. In June 1833 it estimated that it would cost $1,106,000 to complete the navigation to Dam No. 5, while its resources to meet that sum amounted to $1,295,104.54, leaving only the small sum of $189,104.54 to be applied to the future extension of the canal.[148] The appeal to Virginia was unsuccessful, but the Maryland General Assembly voted an additional subscription of $125,000 in March 1834.[149] By the summer of 1834, the financial condition of the canal company was again desperate.[150]

COST OF EXCAVATION AND EMBANKMENT FOR CANAL PRISM - MAY 1, 1833			
	Cu.Yds.		Average per Yd.
Grubbing		$22,545.00	
Earth	5,006,642.00	610,475.76	12 19/100
Rock	907,698.00	599,003.65	65 99/100
Slate	8,150.00	1,841.00	22 59/100
Embankment from canal	1,017,809.00	124,382.23	12 22/100
Embankment not from canal	1,866,120.00	382,210.34	20 48/100
Puddling	134,709.00	30,273.75	
			Per Perch
Perches of stone pd.for as excavation	387,008.00	196,180.01	50 69/100
Perches of stone not pd.for as excavation	25,085.00	24,530.00	97 79/100
Extras		49,364.13	
TOTAL		$2,040,805.87	
Of the total sum, $1,619,625.65 had been done, and $421,180.22 still needed to be done.			
Excerpted from House Report 414,26			

The Financial statement presented to the annual meeting of the stockholders in June showed that the company had already spent $4,062,991.25. The available resources of the company totaled $439,912, but approximately $547,563 were needed to complete the work under contract to Dam No. 5, leaving a deficit of $107,651. Accordingly, President Eaton informed the stockholders:

> During the past twelve months, nothing has transpired to give any lively encouragement to the future progress and final completion of this important work. An embarrassed state of its finances has kept the officers, who have been engaged in superintending its affairs, under constant perplexity, and apprehension for its success; and with every practiced effort, they have been barely able to get on with its operation to the present time....The entire deficiency, over and above all the available means possessed by the company, it is

---

[147] Extracts from the Proceedings of the Baltimore & Ohio Railroad Company and the Chesapeake & Ohio Canal Company Respecting the Joint Construction of a Canal and Railroad Along 1–45; Fifth Annual Report (1833), 9, 15; and *Frederick Town Herald*, May 11, 1833.
[148] Fifth Annual Report (1833), 6.
[149] Laws Made and Passed by the General Assembly of the State of Maryland (Annapolis, 1834), ch. 241.
[150] *Williamsport Banner*, July 12, 1834.

believed, will not fall short of two hundred and forty or two hundred and fifty thousand dollars (when repairs and cost increases were counted).[151]

The deteriorating financial condition of the canal company was further aggravated by the monetary policies of the Jackson Administration. As a result of this continuing war against the Second Bank of the United States, the President in 1833 had forced the removal of the federal deposits from its vaults, distributing them among a select group of "pet banks." Excessive retrenchment by the bank's president, Nicholas Biddle, created a financial depression in 1834.[152]

COST OF CANAL CONSTRUCTION FROM ROCK CREEK BASIN TO DAM NO. 5 - MARCH 1, 1834	
Sections	$2,152,878.98
Locks	534,382.18
Lockhouses	21,725.22
Bridges and Aqueducts	291,014.75
Culverts	204,072.78
WasteWeirs	22,020.35
Dams and Feeders	209,891.00
TOTAL	$3,435,985.26
Excerpted from House Report 414,187	

Under the existing tight money market, the canal company could not convert $218,750 in Washington and Georgetown six percent bonds into money without taking a serious loss. The hard times also made it impossible for the company to collect $100,000 from the $250,000 due in March from the stockholders. Without any hope of obtaining substantial accretions to its resources, the canal directors determined:

> To issue promissory notes of five, ten, and twenty dollars, payable one year after date, with four per cent interest; and for the redemption of which, stocks of the State of Maryland, and of the corporations of Washington and Georgetown, will be placed in the hands of Phineas Janney, John P. Van Ness, and William Price, as trustees, to an amount ($150,000) greater than it is proposed to issue notes; with authority in the trust to sell the stocks, and apply the proceeds to the payment of the notes when at maturity.[153]

Once the decision had been made to issue canal script, the canal board renewed its efforts to secure bank loans. In mid-September, the Bank of the United States advanced $200,000 to the company and the boar immediately placed advertisements in the Potomac Valley newspapers to attract several hundred additional hands to complete the canal to Dam No. 5.[154]

---

[151] Sixth Annual Report (1834), C&O Co., 3–4, 6–7.
[152] John Spencer Bassett, *The Life of Andrew Jackson* (Rev. ed., New York, 1967), 631–655, and Glydon G. Van Deuser, *The Jacksonian Era, 1824–1848* (New York, 1959), 80–83.
[153] *Niles' Register*, XLVI (May 3, 1834), 149; *Williamsport Banner*, quoted in *Niles' Register*, XLIV (April 26, 1834), 133; and *Sixth Annual Report* (1834), 3–4.
[154] *Niles' Register*, XLVII (September 20, 1834, October 4, 1834); Proceedings of the President and Board of Directors, D 159; and Proceedings of Stockholders, A, 368.

Encouraged by this unexpected aid, the canal directors again directed appeals for additional funds to congress and the interested states in late 1834. They were supported in their petitions by the Internal Improvement Convention which met in Baltimore on December 8-10, 1834. The meeting assembled at the call of an earlier gathering at the Allegany Court House in Cumberland on October 18, at which supporters of the waterway in the western Maryland counties had urged further assistance for the project so that it could be completed to Cumberland.[155] About 200 representatives from Maryland, Virginia, Pennsylvania, Ohio, and the District cities attended the convention.[156]

Ostensibly called not only to consider measures "as should seem most likely to cause the Chesapeake & Ohio Canal to be soon finished," but also to undertake plans for other internal improvements "of a national character" to "advance the welfare to Maryland, and her sister states," the convention devoted its time almost exclusively to the problems of the waterway. The convention selected as its chairman, George Corbin Washington, a grandnephew of George Washington, Harvard-educated lawyer, and former Maryland Congressman who had been elected the third president of the canal company in June 1834.[157]

Among the important actions of the convention were the formal approval of memorials to the House of Representatives, the Mayor and City of Council of Baltimore, and the Virginia, Maryland, and Pennsylvania legislatures for more aid.[158] Two significant reports were submitted by committees appointed by the convention. One, by the principal committee headed by ex-president Mercer, examined the probably cost and time of completing the canal, and the other, chaired by Pennsylvania Congressman Andrew Stewart, reviewed the expected trade and revenue of the canal when it would reach Cumberland.[159]

The Mercer committee report noted the amount and quality of work already done on the canal and the work remaining to be done. Concerning the finances needed to complete the eastern section of the waterway, the report concluded:

> The completion of these works is expected to carry the total cost of the eastern section of the canal to the amount of very near $6,500,000. Of this sum, the first 107 miles with its appendages, will continue 4 ½ millions. This last sum allows $25,640 per mile, for each mile of the 78; and is believe to be sufficient; as well from the a reference to the actual cost of a large portion of the canal, above and below Williamsport, as from a survey and working estimate of the 25 ½ miles immediately below the Great Cacapon; at which point, it is contemplated to erect the next or sixth dam, across the Potomac. The total cost of these 26 ½ miles, it is confidently believed, will not exceed $600,000. So that, of the two millions, $1,400,000 will be applicable to the construction of 51 ½ miles above Cacapon; which allows about $17,184 per mile for the portion of the eastern section.

Altogether the report estimated that it would cost approximately $14,500,000 to complete the canal to Pittsburgh.[160]

The Stewart committee report studied the sources of trade of the canal when it would be completed to Cumberland. In glowing terms, it expressed the firm conviction that the Chesapeake

---

[155] *Journal of the Internal Improvement Convention Which Assembled in the City of Baltimore, On the 8th Day of December, 1834* (Baltimore, 1835), 3-7.
[156] Ibid, 7-10.
[157] *Niles' Register*, XLVI (July 5, 1834), 326.
[158] *Journal of the Internal Improvement Convention*, 27-44, 73-93, and *Niles' Register*, XLVII (December 13, 1834, January 1, 1835), 233, 308-310.
[159] *Journal of the Internal Improvement Convention*, 45-72.
[160] Ibid, 58-63.

& Ohio Canal will afford a more profitable investment of funds, than any similar work of internal improvement in the United States, possessing as it does, advantages in reference to climate, distance, structure, and sources of revenue, decidedly superior to any other, constructed or contemplated." The sources of revenue named by the report were coal, lumber, lime, iron, fish, agricultural produce, merchandise, and water power rentals, all of which would "force it (the canal) onward to its completion" to the Ohio River.[161]

Reassured by the convention reports and enthused over the prospects of a "geometrical increase of business" once the waterway reached Cumberland, the convention adjourned to press its quest for aid.

Once again the efforts were made to obtain the assistance of the United States. Despite the favorable recommendation of the House Committee on Roads and Canals, Congress again refused to grant the requested aid. After this rebuff to their petition, the canal supporters confirmed their efforts to obtain $500,000 from the dividend of the Second Bank of the United States, in return for which sum the company offered perpetual release from tolls for government business on the waterway. When this proposal failed to pass the Senate, it became clear to all concerned that the federal government had renounced all interest in the project.[162]

The failure of Congress to assume the support of the canal company placed the future of the work in the hands of the District cities and the interested states. The former were debt-ridden and incapable of rendering further aid, and the latter, except Maryland, were no longer interested. Supporters of the canal in the Virginia Assembly introduced a bill to guarantee a loan of $500,000 for the canal company in return for a mortgage of canal property to the state, but after passage in the lower house, the proposal was defeated by one vote in the Senate when it was called up during the absence of several known friends of the canal.[163] The canal was thus forced to rely solely upon the support of the state of Maryland.

---

[161] Ibid, 45–47, and *Niles' Register*, XLVII (January 17, 1835), 330, 341–344.

[162] Washington to Colston, January 31, 1835, Ltrs., Sent, C&O Co., and Proceedings of Stockholders, A, 365–370.

[163] *Niles' Register*, XLVII (February 21, 1835), 428; XLVIII (March 7, 1835), 2; and *Richmond Compiler* quoted in *Niles' Register*, XLVIII (March 14, 1835), 18.

III. MARYLAND ASSUMES CONTROL OF THE GREAT NATIONAL PROJECT: 1835-1842

The canal company vigorously pressed the Maryland General Assembly to pass a bill authorizing a loan of the entire $2,000,000 required to complete the canal to Cumberland. The campaign to acquire the loan was aided by the memorial of the politically impressive Internal Improvement Convention and the personal lobbying efforts of President Washington and certain influential members of the assembly.[164] After considerable debate, the Maryland legislature passed the act in March 1835 authorizing the loan, with members from Baltimore and the Eastern Shore supporting it as well as the canal supporters from the western counties.[165]

Apparently, two arguments had a great effect in winning support for the measure. It was widely believed that the future revenues of the canal, as outlined in the report of Andrew Stewart to the Internal Improvement Convention, would provide sizeable financial returns to the state in later years. To foster this hope, the pro-canal delegates, encouraged by President Washington, proposed to give the counties for educational purposes all receipts over the amount necessary to provide a sinking fund to redeem the debt.[166] The members were also afraid of the consequences of the concurrent deliberations in the Virginia legislature concerning the mortgage of the canal to that state for only $500,000, a sum clearly inadequate to complete it to Cumberland.[167]

The act provided for the payment of $600,000 on June 20, 1835, and $200,000 on October 1, 1835, $200,000 on January 1, 1836, and four quarterly installments of $250,000 each on the first of April, July, October, 1835, and January 1837. Upon the unanimous recommendation of the canal directors, the company stockholders formally accepted the load and authorized the mortgage at a special meeting on April 22.[168]

In reporting the $2,000,000 loan, the *Niles Register* editorialized that

> They cannot but congratulate the stockholders and the community upon the prospects which the act of Maryland affords of speedily realizing the sanguine anticipations in which they have long indulged for the completion of this great work of internal improvement.[169]

During the ensuing months, the canal company had little trouble in obtaining the money for the bonds issued to pay the loan as financial conditions both on the domestic and European scenes

---

[164] Proceedings of the President and Board of Directors, E, 83–84, 165; and *Memorial to the General Assembly of Maryland in Behalf of the Chesapeake & Ohio Canal* (Baltimore, 1835), 3–12.

[165] Ibid, 265; Washington to Ingle, March 1, 1835, Stewart to Ingle, March 6, 1835, and Nesbit to Washington, April 8, 1835, Ltrs. Recd., C&O Co.; *Laws Made and Passed by the General Assembly of the State of Maryland* (Annapolis, 1835), ch. 241; on Internal Improvement Maryland, General Assembly, House of Delegates, Committees *Report to the Committee on Internal Improvement to which Was Referred the Memorial of a Convention of Citizens of the States of Maryland, Virginia, Pennsylvania, & Ohio, and of the District of Columbia, Invoking Further Aid to the Chesapeake & Ohio Canal* (Annapolis, 1835), 1–7, and Ibid, Committee on Ways and Means, *To Whom Was Referred the Bill Reported by the Committee on the Internal Improvement, to Provide for the Completion of the Chesapeake & Ohio Canal to Cumberland* (Annapolis, 1835), 1–8.

[166] Washington to Ingle, March 1, 1835, Ltrs. Recd. C&O Co.

[167] Ingle to Barnard, March 6, 1835, Ltrs. Sent, C&O Co.

[168] Proceedings of the President and Board of Directors, 283; *Report of the President and Directors of the Chesapeake & Ohio Canal Company, to the Stockholders, Specially Concerned in General Meeting April 22, 1835* (Washington, 1835), 3–8; and Proceedings of Stockholders, A, 376–377.

[169] *Niles' Register*, XLVIII (April 25, 1835), 129.

were favorable to the disposal of the state bonds at a premium. Anxious to avoid speculation on future sales, the directors offered the bonds as a block and accepted the bid of a Baltimore house to take the bonds at a premium of $15.40 per $100.[170] A further indication of Maryland's interest in the completion of the eastern section was its decision as a one-sixth bondholder to forego dividends, thereby repaying her own loan to that extent.[171]

Upon receipt of the first installment of the $2,000,000 loan in June 1835, the company liquidated its entire debt of $559,771.05, retires its canal script, and resumed the construction of the waterway above Dam No. 5 with increased vigor.[172] However, the continued high cost of land and labor during the inflationary cycle of the 1830s, and increased construction difficulties in the upper Potomac Valley soon forced the actual cost of the canal far above the estimates which were the basis of the $2,000,000 loan. There were at least five factors that played a direct role in increasing the cost of construction, thus hindering the rapid completion of the work.

First, the work on the sections above Dam No. 5 proved more difficult and costly than had been anticipated in part because Charles B. Fisk, an assistant engineer who in May was placed in charge of the important new third residency on which all construction was then concentrated, again raised high the banner of perfection which former President Mercer had carried as persistently during the early years of the canal project. On March 30, 1835, he wrote to the canal board with apparently little knowledge of, or concern for, financial considerations, proposing a revision of building procedures in extending the canal and urging greater care and expenditure in construction in order to reduce subsequent repair and maintenance costs.[173]

Regardless of its economic or technical soundness, this plan proved to be politically disastrous course for the company in the 1830s and 1840s, leaving the future success of the canal clouded by a staggering capitalization, and in June 1837 it reiterated its insistence on perfection for the work above Dam No. 5 and rejected all proposals for expedients in construction:

> In the location and construction of the canal above Dam no. 5, as well as that designed from Cacapon to Cumberland, the Board has acted on the principal that temporary works and expedients, to hasten the opening of the navigation to the coal region, cannot accomplish the object for which this magnificent improvement was designed, and would prove a failure alike discreditable to its projectors and managers, as well as to the community concerned; neither would the interests of the stockholders have been consulted by a plan of operation looking only to saving in cost and time. False and imperfect construction and location would necessarily induce frequent costly repairs, amounting eventually to more than the first cost of a perfect work; and as to time, much more would be lost than gained, from the repeated and vexatious interruptions to trade, of breaches in the embankments, and failures in the masonry. Whilst, on the one hand, the Board has been actuated by the most scrupulous regard to the proper and judicious application of the funds of the company, on the other hand, they have endeavored to avoid false motions of economy in the construction of the work which is not designed to subserve the purposes of the present day or century, but is to endure for all time.[174]

---

[170] White to Washington, April 11, 1835, and Maclubin to Washington, June 5, 1835, Ltrs. Reed, C&O Co.
[171] Proceedings of Stockholder, A, 371.
[172] Maryland, General Assembly, Joint Committee on Expenditures for Internal Improvement, *Report of the Joint Committee Appointed to Inquire into the Expenditures of the State, In Works of Internal Improvement* (Annapolis, 1836), 4, and Proceedings of the President and Board of Directors, D, 342.
[173] Fish to President and Directors, March 30, 1835, Ltrs. Reed, C&O Co.; Proceedings of the President and Board of Directors, 311, 319.
[174] *Ninth Annual Report* (1837), C&O Co., 6–7.

The influence of such ideas by Fish would continue to affect the canal construction as he was promoted to chief engineer on April 12, 1837, and remained in that position, with the exception of a brief period in 1840–41, until 1852.

Second, construction costs increased because of the stone in the upper Potomac Valley. Contrary to earlier reports, new ground surveys by Resident Engineer Thomas F. Purcell and Superintendent of Masonry A. B. McFarland found a large part of the strata to be composed of normally friable red sandstone, much of it already rotten. Good supplies of limestone were discovered at scattered points on both sides of the river, notably near the mouth of the Great Cacapon on the Virginia side and at Town Hill on the Maryland side. But many of the deposits were at some distance from the projected line of the canal, thereby increasing transportation costs to move the materials to the construction site.[175]

Third, land damages added to the increasing expense of construction. Landholders in Washington and Allegany Counties continued to demand the highest possible prices, and juries in both jurisdictions continued to exact full satisfaction. Land costs averaged $2,290 per mile, more than double the estimates of 1834, ranging from 2 ½ to 25 times the company's original estimated costs. The general attitude of the Jacksonian-oriented western Maryland farmers appeared to be best summed up in the words of one of the proprietor's lawyers when he stated that "this great wealthy foreign Company should not be permitted to trespass upon the farmer without being made to pay ample for it."[176]

Fourth, the rise in construction costs was affected by the labor and provisions price increases of the 1830s. With resumption of large-scale operations the shortage of workers again became critical. To relieve this condition, A. B. McFarland went to New York and Philadelphia in early 1837 to recruit additional hands, as many other public works in the East had already been forced to suspend operations because of spiraling inflation.[177] Despite his efforts, the level of wages on the canal, which had averaged $5 to $10 per month on 1828, rose to nearly $35 per month.[178]

The contractors were experiencing severe financial problems by the summer of 1836. As a result, the canal board ratified a series of estimated increases among which were included an 8 per cent increase in the estimates for eighteen contractors between Dams No. 5 and 6 in August 1836, a further advance of $106,808 to the contractors on the same stretch of the canal in February 1837, and 30 per cent increase over January 1836 prices for the estimates on the "50-mile section" between the Cacapon River and Cumberland in August 1837.[179] Many contracts were abandoned and relet for increases of from 25 to 40 per cent.[180]

The steady rise in prices was also evidenced in a report in April 1838 which revealed that the following construction items had increased as follows within a five-month span:

Excavation from 11 and 14 cents to 20 cents a cubic yard
Puddling from 10 to 30 cents a cubic yard

---

[175] Purcell to Board of Directors, May 26, 1835, and McFarland to Bender, January 2, 1836, Ltrs. Recd., C&O Co.

[176] Price and Merrick to President and Directors, July 23, 1835; and Bender to President and Directors, August 10, 1835, and May 7, 1836, Ltrs. Recd., C&O Co.

[177] Tenth Annual Report (1838), C&O Co., Appendix 1, 22, and Proceedings of Stockholder, B, 81.

[178] G.M. and R.W. Watkins to President and Directors, February 15, 1837, and Fish to Bender, August 3, 1837, Ltrs., Recd., C&O Co.

[179] Proceedings of the President and Board of Directors, E, 126–127, 129; Fish to Bender, August 23, 1836, August 3, 1837, Ltrs. Sent, Chief Engineer; and Report of the Committee of Directors, February 4, 1837, Ltrs. Recd., C&O Co.

[180] Tenth Annual Report (1838), Appendix 3, 25 ff.

Walling from 45 cents to 75 cents a perch
Embankment from excavation from 18 cents to 30 cents a cubic yard[181]

Fifth, the adoption of the Paw Paw tunnel and deep cuts contributed to the increased costs of construction. One of the most expensive projects on the entire line, it was the proudest achievement of the company and its contractor, Lee Montgomery, a hard-working Methodist minister, was treated with greater deference by the canal directors than most other contractors. The importance of keeping the work moving on the heavy sections to prevent undue delay in the completion of the canal insured him of their continued financial assistance and by 1842 the company had paid over $616,478.65 for this partially-completed structure, a sum that was about 75 percent above earlier contract estimates.[182]

The escalation in land, labor, and construction costs soon forced the actual cost of the canal far above the estimates which were the basis of the $2,000,000 loan. In 1834, Engineer Alfred Cruger had allowed $663,676 for the construction of the 27 miles between Dam No. 5 and the Cacapon River.[183] Fisk revised this figure in June 1835 on the basis of work actually done, raising it to $1,022,534, and in June 1836 another revision raised the cost to $2,427,497.[184]

As a result of these developments, the resources of the company were inadequate for the job, and the canal board began curtaining its operations in January 1836 by suspending the letting of contracts and condemnation of land above the Cacapon.[185] As it had so many times in the past, the canal company again petitioned the District cities and the Virginia and Maryland legislature for further aid.[186]

The bankrupt District cities were in no position to offer assistance, their predicted declaration of foreclosure being prevented only by the assumption of their debts by the federal government in May 1836.[187] The petition to the Virginia Assembly produced a bill for an additional subscription to the company, but opposition from the James River and Kanawha Company prevented its passage.[188] When the company requested an additional $2,500,000 from the Maryland General Assembly, there was widespread support for the canal's appeal. The suspension of the work above the Cacapon in January 1836 was a serious blow to the Cumberland businessman as described in the *Niles' Register*:

> The stoppage of the work on the Chesapeake & Ohio Canal has caused a very considerable panic in Cumberland. Two hours after the arrival of the news, the price of produce came down at least 10 percent. Business still continues to be dull; our principal streets presenting an unusual barrenness; the merchant is idle; and the mechanic slow in the transaction of his business; the speculator is cut to the quick; and those who engaged to pay high rents on account of the prospects of the canal, have been suddenly and seriously

---

[181] Proceedings of the President and Board of Directors, E, 389–390.
[182] Bender to President and Directors, August 30, 1837, Ltrs. Recd., C&O Co.; Proceedings of the President and Board of Directors, E, 384; and Ledger Book A, C&O Co.
[183] The survey by Cruger is printed in its entirety in House Report 414, 200–220.
[184] *Eighth Annual Report* (1836), C&O Co., 3–4.
[185] Ingle to Bender, January 9, 16, 1836, Ltrs. Sent, C&O Co., and Bender to Ingle, January 19, 1836, Ltrs. Recd., C&O Co.
[186] *Memorial of the President and Directors of the Chesapeake & Ohio Canal company to the Honorable the General Assembly of Maryland, January 27, 1836* (Washington, 1836), 1–16.
[187] Proceedings of the President and Board of directors, E, 66. Also see, U.S., Congress, Senate, *Memorial of the Corporation of Georgetown, D.C., Praying to be Relieved from Pecuniary Embarrassments by Congress*, S. Doc. 48, 24th Cong., 1st sess., 136, 1–3.
[188] Sherrard to Hinderson, March 19, 1836, Ltrs. Recd, C&O Co.

disappointed. Indeed, the citizens of the town generally, and the farmers for many miles round, have great cause to regret this temporary suspension.

The proceeding has startled everybody. For after the great liberality of the legislature, in granting two millions, no one expected such a result. It was believed that the work would be very nearly completed at least....[189]

The popularity of the waterway had grown as it advanced westward and became an increasingly important factor in the projected regional economy. Town meetings, such as one held at Cumberland, passed resolutions urging the legislature to grant further aid.[190] The chances of the company's success in obtaining the increased aid were enhanced by the simultaneous need of the Baltimore & Ohio Railroad for further assistance and an internal improvements fever that was sweeping the state.

Despite these favorable circumstances, there was strong opposition in the Assembly to large appropriations for public works. Notwithstanding the recommendations of the Joint committee on Expenditures for Internal Improvement and the House Committee on Ways and Means, the bill providing $8,000,000 for various state canal and railroad projects failed to pass the House of Delegates by a vote of 35 to 34 on March 31, 1836.[191] Following the vote, the Assembly adjourned until May 4, when a special session would take up the proposal after the Maryland citizens had had an opportunity to discuss it.

The pro-internal improvements forces sponsored a series of rallies climaxed on May 2 by a mass meeting in Baltimore, attended by representatives from Maryland, Virginia, and Pennsylvania.[192] The rally adopted resolutions urging the state to:

1. complete the public works;
2. secure control of the Chesapeake & Ohio;
3. bring its trade to Baltimore by means of the long-discussed Maryland Cross-Cut Canal;
4. permit the extension of the Baltimore & Ohio to the west through Maryland;
5. encourage the development of local railroads, such as the Eastern Shore Railroad, in other parts of the state.[193]

The special session that met in Annapolis on May 20, 1836, referred the question of the condition of state finances and public works to the Joint Committee on Internal Improvements. Badly divided over this critical issue, the committee issued two separate reports. The majority noted that the exhausted condition of the state finances would not permit large expenditures for public works, and, at any rate, there was insufficient information on which to base major decisions on the proposed construction on the Baltimore & Ohio, the Maryland Cross-Cut Canal, and the Eastern Shore Railroad. The members could see no reason for extending the Chesapeake & Ohio if its

---

[189] *Niles' Register*, XLIX (February 20, 1836), 426.
[190] William H. Lowdermilk, *History of Cumberland* (Washington, 1878), 338–339.
[191] *Report of the Joint Committee Appointed to Inquire into the Expenditures of the State*, 3–4, "Report of the Committee on Ways and Means of the House of Delegates, on the Subject of the Finances and Internal Improvements," March 9, 1836, in *A Short History of the Public Debt of Maryland* (Baltimore, 1844), Appendix K, 52–62.
[192] *A Short History of the Public Debt of Maryland*, 23–25.
[193] "Address of the City of Baltimore to the People of Maryland," April 12, 1836, in Ibid, Appendix, 68-72, and *Journal of the Internal Improvement Convention*, May 2, 1836," in Ibid, 27–30.

terminus was to remain in Georgetown, and they found it difficult to see the need for extending both the canal and the railroad if one were more advantageous than the other.[194]

On the other hand, the minority report, written by Joseph Merrick, a long-time canal supporter who had helped engineer the 1834 and 1835 subscriptions through the Assembly, rejected the retrenchment policy of the majority. It urged the passage of the Eight Million Bill as a logical culmination of the state's efforts to acquire a share of the western trade and as a measure to provide for the future stability of the treasury.[195]

The Assembly paid little heed to the warnings of the majority report and adopted the views of the minority. The House of Delegates passed the internal improvements bill on June 3 by a vote of 48 to 39, and the Senate passed it the following day by a vote of 11 to 2. The act provided for the subscription of $8,000,000 to various internal improvement companies:

- $3,000,000 each to the Chesapeake & Ohio and the Baltimore & Ohio;
- $1,000,000 to the Baltimore and Susquehanna Railroad;
- $500,000 to the Maryland Canal Company for a branch canal from the Chesapeake & Ohio to Baltimore;
- And $250,000 each to the Annapolis and Elkridge Railroad and the Eastern Shore Railroad.

Before any payments would be made on the two major subscriptions, the Maryland Canal Company must be organized with sufficient funds to insure the construction of its work. The Baltimore & Ohio was released from the prohibition against extending its line in Maryland beyond Harpers Ferry before 1840. As had been the case in earlier subscriptions, the loans were in the form of state bonds.[196]

The citizens of Baltimore were delighted by the passage of the law. All the important provisions of the bill appeared to promote the commercial interests of their city over those of the District cities. Accordingly, a public meeting was held at the Exchange at which resolutions were unanimously adopted "for a public dinner—an exhibition of fires works—a salute of 100 guns—the ringing of bells of all the churches, engine houses, and other institutions—and the general display of the flags of the shipping and public buildings."[197] The celebrations were complemented by a report of the Baltimore Common Council urging both the railroad and canal companies to come to an agreement over any disputes which might arise between them and encouraging the efforts being taken to organize the Maryland Canal Company.[198]

The canal company and the District cities, particularly the Corporation of Washington, reacted with some displeasure to the Eight Million Dollar Bill. Their major objections centered on the provision of the act which required the Maryland Canal Company to construct a waterway by the "most northern practicable route," as the condition upon which the appropriation to the Chesapeake & Ohio depended and on the provision permitting the Baltimore & Ohio to extend its

---

[194] "Majority Report of the Joint Committee of Both Branches of the Legislature, Appointed to Investigate the Subject of Internal Improvement," in Ibid, 33–38.
[195] "Minority Report of the Joint Committee of Both Branches of the Legislature, Appointed to Investigate the Subject of Internal Improvement," in Ibid, 39
[196] *Eighth Annual Report* (1836), C&O Co., 6. For more information on the Maryland Crosscut Canal, see Walter S. Sanderlin, "The Maryland Canal Project—An Episode in the History of Maryland's Internal Improvements," *Maryland Historical Magazine*, XLI (March, 1946), 51–65.
[197] *Report to the Stockholders on the completion of the Chesapeake & Ohio Railroad to Cumberland*, 62–63.
[198] Baltimore, Common Council, Joint Committee on the Chesapeake & Ohio Canal, *Report, Presented by Mr. Maury* (Baltimore, 1836), 1–6.

line in Maryland above Harpers Ferry. Furthermore, by accepting the $3,000,000 subscription, the company would fall under the control of the State of Maryland, a long-standing ally of the railroad.[199]

Nevertheless, the provisions of the act were carried out in a relatively short time. The Chesapeake & Ohio and the Baltimore & Ohio reached an agreement on July 28 over the settlement of the disputes that might arise between the two companies. On the same day, the canal stockholders accepted the Maryland act by a vote of 4,101 to 2,333, the Corporation of Georgetown and Alexandria and the State of Maryland voting in the affirmative and the Corporation of Washington in the negative.[200]

Promoters of the cross-cut canal project obtained subscriptions from the Baltimore Citizenry and organized the company, despite the fact that earlier surveys by U.S. Engineer William Howard had shown the only practicable route for such a canal to lie through the District of Columbia.[201] The subscriptions to the Baltimore & Ohio and the Chesapeake & Ohio were then released from the legal restrictions of the act, and the State of Maryland, as a result of its 1834, 1835, and 1836 subscriptions, gained control of the company and a mortgage on its property. After this date, canal affairs were dominated by the state, and the future of the waterway was inseparably tied to the desires of the state.[202]

Although the $3,000,000 subscription appeared to assure the successful completion of the canal's construction, the company found itself in a precarious financial situation almost immediately. Three principal causes contributed to the desperate financial condition of the company: the monetary policies of the Jackson Administration that led to the severe economic Panic of 1837, the depression in England which brought a curtailment in the European money markets, and the political maneuvering by opponents of public works in Annapolis.

During his battle against the Second Bank of the United States, Jackson and his advisers gradually developed a theory of business cycles, in which paper money was the villain that caused alternated periods of inflation and depression. If the circulation of paper could be restricted and the proportion of gold and silver to paper increased, the cycle, and especially the ruinous inflation that was then occurring, could be brought under some measure of control. Wage earners and small farmers, the two groups that Jackson had championed as the epitome of the "common man," would then receive some protection from periodic disaster.[203]

When his efforts to persuade Congress to enact legislation limiting the circulation of bank votes failed, Jackson applied his hard-money tendencies to the sale of public lands. During the highly-inflationary mid-1830s, the purchase of public lands thereby fueling the uncontrolled inflation of the period increased by leaps and bounds. The banks, particularly in the West, had extended their loans beyond all reason, as much of the payment for government lands consisted of nothing more than paper of state banks, paper that was loaned out, returned to the banks, and again loaned out in a vicious cycle. Partly as a result of his concept of a sound currency and partly due to the public outcries against the land speculators, Jackson issued the Specie Circular on July

---

[199] *Report to the Stockholders on the Completion of the Chesapeake & Ohio Canal to Cumberland,* 63, Washington, D.C., Council, Joint Committee on the Chesapeake & Ohio Canal; *Report* (Washington, 1836), 1–6; and *Report of the General Committee of the Stockholders of the Chesapeake & Ohio Canal Company, Presented July 18, 1836* (Washington, 1836), 3–8.

[200] Proceedings of Stockholders, B, 40–49; and *Niles' Register,* L (August 6, 13, 1836), 377.

[201] U.S., Congress, House, *Letter of the Secretary of War, J. Barlow, Transmitting a Report of the Engineer on the Survey of a Route for the Proposed Canal to Connect the Chesapeake & Ohio Canal with Baltimore,* H. Doc. 58, 20th Cong., 1st sess., 1825, 6–8.

[202] Sanderlin, *Great National Project,* 111–112.

[203] Marquis James, *Andrew Jackson: Portrait of a President* (Indianapolis, 1937), 414, 426, 439–441.

11, 1836, prohibiting all federal government receivers of public money from accepting anything but specie in payment for the public lands.[204]

By the spring, the measure had created a demand for specie that many of the banks could not meet. Gold and silver were drained from the East to the West, making money very tight on the eastern seaboard. Western banks were forced to curtail their discounts, and bank failures in the West spread to the East, gripping the entire country in a sudden financial panic. Finding it virtually impossible to conduct its business in the specie shortage, the canal company resorted to the issue of change notes on June 20.[205]

The grave economic situation in America was worsened by a depression in England. To weather its crisis, the British government lowered the price of cotton from 17 ½ to 13 ½ cents, thereby undercutting the American cotton manufacturing industry. London investors also started a drain of specie from the United States as they began curtailing their commitments in North America.[206]

Against the background of national and international economic instability, the canal company had trouble from the start in obtaining the bonds issued by Maryland to cover the $3,000,000 subscription on the proceeds from the sale. First, there were delays in putting the law into effect as a result of a major political battle between the decreasing tobacco-raising and slaveholding counties of southern Maryland and the rapidly growing city and environs of Baltimore over the system of representation in Annapolis, a vicious conflict that led to constitutional amendments providing for the popular election of the governor and state senators, the abolition of the Governor's Council, and a slight increase in the representation of the city of Baltimore and the more populous counties.[207]

These political distractions caused the postponement of the appointment of state commissioners to negotiate the sale of the bonds until December 1836. One of the commissioners left immediately for London, but the other two remained in Maryland until the following spring.[208] By the end of March 1837, the directors, desperate for cash, decided to purchase the bonds on behalf of the company, and a provisional contract was drawn up accordingly.[209] When the commissioners failed to negotiate the sale of the bonds for the required 20 percent premium by December 1837, the board determined to undertake the task on the same terms.[210]

By this time more trouble was brewing for the canal company in Annapolis, as some members of the General Assembly had lost their enthusiasm for internal improvements as a result of the depression and the opponents of public works were demanding a reduction of governmental expenses and a limitation of the power of the General Assembly to contract debts.[211] After a considerable debate, during which time the legislature debated the repeal of the Eight Million

---

[204] Van Deusen, *Jacksonian Era*, 104–105, and *American State Papers, Public Land* (8 vols., Washington, 1832–61), VIII, 910.
[205] Van Deusen, *Jacksonian Era*, 116, and *Niles' Register*, LII (July 1, 1837), 273.
[206] Van Deusen, *Jacksonian Era*, 116–117.
[207] John Thomas Scharf, *History of Maryland from the Earliest Period to the Present Day* (3 vols., Baltimore, 1879), III, 192–196.
[208] Proceedings of Stockholders, B, 79, and *Report to the Stockholders on the Completion of the Chesapeake & Ohio Canal to Cumberland*, 75–76.
[209] Proceedings of the President and Board of Directors, E, 226; Proceedings of the Stockholders, B, 75; and Buchanan to Washington, March 7, 15, April 16, May 16, 1837, George Corbin Washington Papers, Maryland Historical Society, Baltimore.
[210] *Report to the Stockholders on the Completion of the Chesapeake & Ohio Canal to Cumberland*, 75–76.
[211] Richard Walsh and William Lloyd Fox, *Maryland: A History, 1632–1974* (Baltimore, 1974), 278–292.

Dollar Act and the withholding of bonds not already issued, the Assembly finally confirmed the bond issue in March 1838 and placed the certificates in the company's hands.[212]

The canal board divided the bonds into equal sums for sale in the United States and in Europe. There soon proved to be no market for the bonds either here or overseas because of the tightness of the financial communities after the economic depression. Accordingly, on the advice of their agents in London, both the railroad and canal companies prevailed upon the Maryland legislature to convert the bonds to 5 percent sterling, the canal company coupling with its request a petition for an additional $1,375,000 subscription.[213] After another debate on the advisability of refusing all further aid to the canal project, the Assembly in April 1839 consented to the company's requests.[214]

The company was released from the provisions of the 1836 act requiring state commissioners to negotiate the sale of the bonds at a 20 percent premium. Instead, the commissioners of loans was authorized to issue to the canal company five percent sterling bonds amounting to $3,200,000 in lieu of the $2,500,000 of six percent certificates which had been delivered to the company and $500,000 of six percent certifications which had been retained by the treasurer of Maryland as security for the payment of the premium. In return the company was required to redeem the six percents by a substitution of the five percents, where the former had been hypothecated, and return the entire amount to the state to be cancelled.[215] At the same time it subscribed an additional $1,375,000 to the canal stock, a loan that was the result of an admission as early as 1838 that because of the difficult construction and high building costs, $1,500,000 more would be needed above all available resources, to complete the waterway.[216]

During these lengthy negotiations, the canal company resorted to several temporary arrangements to keep the work going. Among these activities were the institution of suits against delinquent stockholders to force full payment, the shifting of their funds to specie-paying banks, and the procurement of loans from local banks on the pledge of Washington and Georgetown bonds. At first the efforts were successful only in Baltimore and Washington, but in November the Second Bank of the United States in Philadelphia granted a loan of $50,000 on the pledge of Washington stock. After that the company secured loans in the District of Columbia and in Baltimore amounting to over $300,000 by June 1838.[217]

---

[212] Proceedings of the President and Board of Directors, E, 380–381; *Tenth Annual Report* (1838), C&O Co., 3, 11; and *Laws Made and Passed by the General Assembly of the State of Maryland* (Annapolis, 1837), R68.

[213] Proceedings of the President and Board of Directors, E, 388; *Tenth Annual Report* (1838), 11; *Report to the Stockholders on the Completion of the Chesapeake & Ohio to Cumberland*, 78–80, and *Communication from George C. Washington, President of the Chesapeake & Ohio Canal Company in Answer to the Report Made to the House of Delegates, By the Chairman of the Committee on Internal Improvements, in Relation to Said Company* (Annapolis, 1839), 1–22. In his report, Washington reported that the current estimated cost to complete the canal from Dam No. 5 to Cumberland was $6,080,657, up 71 percent from the January 1836 estimate of $3,560,619.

[214] Baltimore *Sun*, March 14, 1839; and *Acts Relating to the Chesapeake & Ohio Canal Company, Passed by the General Assembly of Maryland, at December Session*, 1838, 1–6.

[215] "Report of the Committee on Ways and Means in Reference to the Chesapeake & Ohio Canal Company, March 14, 1839," *A Short History of the Public Debt of Maryland*, Appendix P, 76–78, and *Laws Made and Passed by the General Assembly of the State of Maryland* (Annapolis, 1838), ch. 386.

[216] *Laws Made and Passed by the General Assembly of the State of Maryland* (Annapolis, 1838), ch. 395; Baltimore *Sun*, April 6, 7, 1839; Proceedings of Stockholders, B, 188–189; and Washington to Ingle, February 5, 1838, Ltrs. Recd., C&O Co.

[217] Ingle to Schley, February 28, 1837, Ltrs. Sent, C&O Co.; and Proceedings of the President and Board of Directors, E, 223–334, 337, 346, 360, 370, 429–430; *Niles' Register*, LVII (October 5, 1839), 81.

Another temporary expedient was the renewed issuance of canal script. On June 29, 1837, the directors adopted this course of action but limited the issue to notes of less than $5.00 in value.[218] However, three months later, they began to issue larger notes of $5, $10, and $20 denominations and periodically expanded the script printing during the following year, until by May 1838, $376,513.50 in canal notes had been issued and $50,000 more had been authorized but not yet issued. Thus, what had started as a stop-gap measure became a regular practice with dangerous potentialities.[219]

The temporary measures were taken to enable the company to continue construction operations while it negotiated for the sale of the state bonds in England. Shortly after the Assembly confirmed the bond issue, the directors appointed George Peabody as their agent in England to effect the sale. Although Auguste Belmont, the New York agent for Rothschild and Son, of London, offered to purchase $1,500,000 of the 6 percent bonds, on May 1838, no bids were forthcoming which met the 20 percent premium required by the company's contract with the state.[220] Therefore the board decided to seek loans from banks on the pledge of the bonds while awaiting an improvement in the money markets. In a frenzy of hypothecation without effective safeguards, the board floated loans both in the United States and England on the pledge of Maryland bonds at 85. An example of such loan policies appeared in an advertisement in the Baltimore *Sun* on September 28, 1839:

> Public sale of six percent State of Maryland stock or bonds. By virtue of an agreement between the Chesapeake & Ohio Canal Company and the Commercial and Farmers Bank of Baltimore, and as authorized thereby, there will be offered at public auction at the Exchange, in the city of Baltimore, on Wednesday, the 9th of October, 1839, at 1 o'clock P.M. for cash, eight bonds of six percent loan of the state of Maryland Nos. 93 to 100 inclusive, for the sum of five thousand dollars each, amounting in the whole to forty thousand dollars with interest from the first of April 1838.[221]

By January 1, 1839, banks in the United States had loaned $490,000 and those in England, $1,258,925.08, including exchange differences.[222] After the substitution of 5 percent sterling for 6 percent dollar bonds had been effected and an additional subscription of $1,375,000 obtained, the company floated loans in America, bringing the total here to $1,110,000.[223] The wholesale hypothecation of Maryland bonds at 85 to secure loans totaling $2,368,925.08 put the canal company in an unpopular position. The directors' policy undermined the states' credit at home and abroad and threatened disaster to the company finances. The actions of the board were roundly criticized in the Assembly and the Committee on Ways and Means conducted a detailed investigation of the embarrassing conduct of canal affairs.[224]

The General condemnation of the directors' practices and the election of a Democrat, William Grason, in 1838 in the first popular election for Governor of the state enabled him to use influence in June 1839 to remove President Washington and the other members of the Whig-dominated canal board and appoint Democratic officials in their place.[225]

---

[218] *Niles Register*, LII (July 1, 1837), 237, and Proceedings of the President and Board of Directors, E. 268.
[219] Proceedings of the President and Board of Directors, E, 298–299, 317, 426.
[220] *Ibid*, E, 391–392, 410.
[221] Baltimore *Sun*, September 28, 1839.
[222] *Eleventh Annual Report* (1839), C&O Co., Appendix 1, 23.
[223] *Ibid*, 12
[224] "Report of the Committee on Ways and Means in Reference to the Chesapeake & Ohio Company, March 14, 1839," *A short History of the Public Debt of Maryland*, Appendix P, 76–78.
[225] Baltimore *Sun*, January 9, 1839, and Washington to Peabody, March 5, 1839, Ltrs. Sent, C&O Co.

The principal problem facing the new president, Francis Thomas, a five-term Jacksonian loyalist in Congress from Western Maryland, and the new directors in June 1839 was the liquidation of the staggering debt, while simultaneously finding some means of pushing the construction of the canal to a successful conclusion or suspending all operations. For several months Thomas personally negotiated for the liquidation of the debt, first making an agreement with the Baltimore & Ohio to cooperate in the sale of bonds to maintain the state's credit and prevent sacrifices.[226]

However as its creditors were pressing for payment and threatening to effect a forced sale of the bonds hypothecated to them, the canal company was forced to sell its bonds immediately in New York, Baltimore, Washington, and London.[227] The total loss for the company on the $4,065,444.42 of bonds sold was $1,048,022.09, or nearly 26 percent of the par value.[228] Despite a report by the Committee on Ways and Means finding these actions to be precipitous blunders, the *National Intelligencer* was able to report in January 1840:

> It is a gratification to us to be able to state...that information has been received by letters from long...of the sale of a sufficient amount of Maryland state five per cent bonds issued in behalf of the Chesapeake & Ohio Canal Company (added to the sales of said bonds made by the directors in this country) to pay all the old debts of the company to banks and bankers in the United States and in Europe, and leave a surplus for the redemption of the company's script (notes) now in circulation.[229]

Although the entire debt of the company arising from the hypothecation of the 5 percent bonds had been liquidated, the directors were still faced with the exhaustion of canal finances. To forestall this possibility, they authorized, on September 15, 1839, the issuance of $300,000 more in canal script and established a trust fund of 5 percent Maryland bonds to redeem the script as it was received for tolls and rents.[230] Insisting that they did not want to issue the notes except in dire necessity, the board suspended the issuance of the notes in April 1840 but resumed the practice in June with an issue of over $500,000 to pay the estimate of work done rather than abandon construction.[231]

The experiment with paper money again involved the company in legal and financial entanglement as disagreements with the trustees over the conduct of their affairs and the misappropriation of the trust fund led to a protracted legal controversy, a consequence of which was that over 80 percent of the latter issue was never redeemed.[232] Under the Thomas regime, the company continued to press the work on the unfinished portion of the canal above Dam No. 6. On the strength of its decision to issue script, the board relet abandoned contracts in December 1839.[233]

---

[226] McLane to Thomas, July 4, 1839; Proceedings of the President and Board of Directors, F, 95–96; and Baltimore *American*, September 15, 1841.
[227] Thomas to Peabody, July 18, 1839, Ltrs. Sent, C&O Co.
[228] *Thirteenth Annual Report* (1841), C&O Co., 27, and Baltimore *American*, September 11, 1841.
[229] Washington *National Intelligencer*, January 9, 1840.
[230] Proceedings of the President and Board of Directors, F, 108, 150–151.
[231] Proceedings of the President and Board of Directors, F, 233–234.
[232] Letter of John Gittings to the Stockholder of the Chesapeake & Ohio Canal Company (Baltimore, 1843), 1–19.
[233] Proceedings of the President and Board of Directors, F, 137–138.

| Chesapeake & Ohio Canal Company's Script ||||
| Issues: 1834-1841 ||||
When Issued	Amount	Redeemed	Outstanding Dec. 31, 1850
1834	$128,705.00	$128,155.00	$550.00
1837-38	418,000.00	410,706.25	7,293.75
1839	300,000.00	294,270.00	5,730.00
1840-41	555,400.00	110,970.00	444,430.00
	$1,402,105.00	$944,101.25	$458,003.75
Source	*Report to the Stockholders on the Completion of the Chesapeake & Ohio Canal to Cumberland*,86		

The board also made another application to the General Assembly on February 10, 1840, for further aid. According to the current engineers' estimates the canal from Dam No. 6 to Cumberland would cost $4,440,350 when it was completed. Of this sum $2,303,128 had been spent as of January 1, 1840. The company's available resources, consisting primarily of Maryland 5 percent bonds, totaled $1,489,571, but its liabilities amounted to $1,244,555, leaving a balance of $245,016.[234]

Despite the rejection of this request by the General Assembly in the spring of 1840,[235] the directors pushed the work rather than suspend operations, disperse the labor force of some 2,000, and sacrifice $150,000 worth of property, the sale of which it was thought would bring only 50 percent of its value. By continuing construction, the directors could also take advantage of the falling price of labor as the depressed economy had occasioned an average decrease in wages from $1.25 to $.87½ per day during the past year.[236]

The determination to continue construction of the waterway on the basis of the issuance of canal script was accompanied by the first large turnover of canal employees, a turn of events occasioned in part by a disagreement with the new policies and in part by the effect of the spoils system in the operation of the canal. Many old and reliable officials were dismissed or voluntarily retired, including Clerk John P. Ingle, Treasurer Thomas Filleboun, Chief Engineer Charles B. Fisk, and several divisional superintendents.[237] Beset by unfavorable publicity arising from the disgruntled comments of the ousted officials in the newspapers, inquiries by the new legislature concerning the directors' conduct of canal affairs, and the near exhaustion of the trust fund, the board reversed its former policy in March 1841, forbade the issuance of more script until means

---

[234] *Report from the Committee on Internal Improvement Transmitting a Communication from Francis Thomas President of the Chesapeake & Ohio Canal Company, to the Governor of Maryland* (Annapolis, 1840), 1–76.

[235] Maryland, General Assembly, House of Delegates, Committee on Internal Improvement, *A Report in Part from the Committee on Internal Improvement* (Annapolis, 1840), 1–18, and Ibid, *Report from the Committee on Internal Improvement, Transmitting a communication from Francis Thomas* (Annapolis, 1840) 1–76.

[236] *Twelfth Annual Report* (1840), C&O Co., 6; proceedings of the President and Board of Directors, F, 185–186, and *Proceedings of the President and Directors of the Chesapeake & Ohio Canal Company, in Relation to the Present Condition of the Work on the Line of the Canal; and the Report of the Chief Engineer on the Consequences of a Suspension of the Work* (Washington, 1840), 4–6.

[237] *Niles' Register*, LVIII (July 13, 1840), 308, and Proceedings of the President and Board of Directors, F, 246, 256–257, 259.

were provided to repay it, and prepared to suspend operations when the Assembly adjourned without providing effective aid.[238] Despite the criticism of the canal board's policies, the Assembly had passed a bill granting $2,000,000 in bonds to the company on the condition that the Cumberland coal mine owners would guarantee to pay the state $200,000 a year beginning six months after the completion of the waterway, but the latter had refused and the bill lapsed.[239]

In April 1841, the State of Maryland, as the controlling stockholders, ousted the Thomas directorate and installed a predominantly Whig board headed by Michael C. Sprigg as president. The new board proceeded to reform canal affairs by reinstating some of the old officials, forbidding company officers to interfere in state politics, continuing the edict against the issuance of script, and ordering that tolls be paid one-third in current money after August.[240]

[Anomalous citation appears on a page by itself in the Unrau text at this point: Committee on Internal Improvements, *Report of the Committee on Internal Improvements on the Condition of the Chesapeake & Ohio Canal* (Annapolis, 1841),1–27; and *ibid*; *Minority Report of the Committee on Internal Improvement on the subject of the Chesapeake & Ohio Canal*.]

With the canal company finances near total collapse, they authorized final suspensions in August, although they later agreed to accept drafts on the company by the contractors in order to encourage them to continue the work on their own until further aid was forthcoming. An order requiring the payment of tolls in cash after April 1, 1842, ended the period of disastrous financial experiments.[241]

Work on the canal continued haphazardly for several more months, and then it too came to an end, not to resume on a large scale until November 1847.[242]

---

[238] Proceedings of the President and Board of Directors, F, 279, 284, 297; Maryland, General Assembly, House of Delegates, 171A.
[239] Baltimore *American*, April 12, 1841, and January 14, 1842, and *Niles' Register*, LX (April 10, 1841), 89.
[240] Proceedings of the President and Board of Directors, F, 301–301, 308, 315, 359.
[241] *Ibid*, F, 377–378, 381.
[242] Fisk to Board of Directors, December 1, 1842, Ltrs. Recd., C&O Co.

IV. THE BELATED COMPLETION
OF THE C&O CANAL TO CUMBERLAND: 1842–1851

When construction came to a halt following the exhaustion of the company's immediate financial resources, the State of Maryland the canal company directorate reviewed the condition of the project. The waterway was open to navigation as far as Dam No. 6, a distance of approximately 135 miles above Georgetown. Of the 50 miles above the Cacapon River, all but 18 miles in scattered sections were finished, but these uncompleted miles included the costly tunnel and deep cuts as well as expensive masonry works in a region lacking good building stone. By May 1841, $10,275,034.98 had been applied to the construction of the canal, and $1,735,849.72 had gone into interest and losses.[243] The time limit of twelve years allowed by the charter for the completion of the eastern section had expired in 1840, but none of the parties to the charter had raised the question of forfeiture.[244]

The future success of the canal was clouded by the fact that the frontier had moved far to the West during the last decade and other established transportation lines were carrying the Ohio Valley trade, a development that would be more forcefully driven home by the completion of the Baltimore & Ohio Railroad to Cumberland in 1842.

The financial condition of the canal company by January 1842 was almost entirely helpless. In that month President Sprigg reported that the unfinished portion of the canal would cost nearly $1,545,000. The present debt of the company was $1,196,000 above all means, most of which were unavailable. Many of the company's resources were tied up in the few remaining 5 percent bonds it owned which had been deposited with the Barings in London, in January 1840. The tolls that had been collected on the navigable portion of the canal in 1841 amounted to only $52,500. Included in its debts was $521,339.25 in outstanding script. Present subscriptions to the capital stock of the company amounted to $8,359,400, of which $151,891.64 was unpaid and all but about $50,000 of this latter figure was lost. The State of Maryland still had a subscription of $163,724.44 to shares of stock in the former Potomac Company, and the Chesapeake & Ohio remained in debt to the state for the $2,000,000 loan in 1835. As a result, the state had mortgages upon the entire property of the company.[245]

The satisfactory sale and disposal of the 5 percent bonds in the hands of the Barings continued to be a primary goal of the canal company. There was no market for them because of the depression in England, but the situation was aggravated after Maryland failed to meet the semiannual interest payment on them beginning July 1, 1841.[246] Earlier in 1839 the Barings had agreed to accept the drafts of the company for amounts up to $200,000 providing not more than $30,000 were drawn a month, but after slightly over $30,000 had been advanced by December 1842, the Barings, hard pressed by the lingering tightness in the British money market, demanded some payment on the advances. If this was not forthcoming, they threatened to sell the bonds at market prices or purchase them in themselves at 50 percent, terms which the canal board flatly rejected.[247]

To counter the announcement of the Barings, the canal directors recommended that the coupons for 1841 and 1842, the receipt of which had been authorized in payment of state taxes by

---

[243] *Thirteenth Annual Report* (1841), C&O Co., 28.
[244] Coale to Price, December 8, 1843, Ltrs. Sent, C&O Co.
[245] *Communication from the President of the Chesapeake & Ohio Canal Company to the Governor of Maryland, December Session*, 1841 (Annapolis, 1842), 1–67, and *Niles' Register*, LXI (January 29, 1842), 352.
[246] Turner to Barings, January 10, 1843, and Turner to Ward, April 17, 1843, Ltrs. Sent, C&O Co.
[247] Barings to Peabody, November 27, December 6, 1839, quoted in Turner to Barings, January 10, 1843, Ltrs. Sent, C&O Co.

the Maryland General Assembly, be detached and sold to pay the interest due on the advanced made by the Barings. After the Barings consented to the sale of the coupons for July 1842, the canal board offered to settle the whole affair.[248] It proposed to sell the Barings at 65 all bonds necessary to repay the advances made and to allow the Barings to take at 85 all coupons necessary to pay the interest due on the drafts paid. The Barings promptly accepted this offer in November 1845.[249] The following March the transaction was formally completed when the Barings transferred the remaining bonds, comprising $15,500 5 percent Maryland bonds with coupons of July 1, 1844, from the other bonds to the canal company.[250]

Meanwhile, the State of Maryland had taken steps to compel the canal company to improve its financial condition. In the spring of 1842, the Assembly ordered the sale of all property owned by the company not strictly used for construction. The directors were to receive canal script and other evidences of company debts in payment of the land.[251] After Chief Engineer Fisk reported on a detailed survey of the entire line of the canal on July 20, the board ordered the required sales which were finally completed during the spring of 1844. The proceeds of the sales, considerably less than the cost of the lands to the canal company, amounted to $25,938, a pittance even when reckoned in depreciated canal script.[252]

Plans for the completion of the canal went on apace during the early 1840s as the canal company made repeated efforts to obtain adequate funding to finish the work. During the suspension of the work there were three principal plans advanced to accomplish this purpose.

- First, there was an attempt to secure the transfer of Chesapeake & Ohio stock held by the United States to the State of Maryland in return for a guarantee by the State to complete the eastern section of the canal.
- Second, there was a proposal to sell the state's interest in the canal to parties that would undertake the task of finishing the work.
- Third, an attempt was made to wave the state's prior liens on the canal revenues and permit the canal company to issue its own bonds to pay for the completion of the work.

The earliest form which the proposals to finish the canal took was the attempt to secure the transfer of Chesapeake & Ohio stock held by the United States to the State of Maryland. The federal government possessed $2,500,000 of the stock, including its own commitment for $1,000,000 and the subscriptions of the bankrupt District cities for $1,500,000. In return for the transfer of the stock, the State of Maryland offered a guarantee to complete the eastern section of the canal, a recommendation first made at the Assembly's Committee on Ways and Means, March 19, 1839, and later incorporated in the bill providing $1,375,000 for the canal.[253] Petitions to that effect were presented to Congress by Maryland Governor William Grason in 1840, Vermont Senator Samuel S. Phelps in 1840, the Maryland legislature in 1843–44, and Indiana Representative Robert D. Owen in 1844.[254]

---

[248] Turner to Ward, April 17, 1843, and Coale to Latrobe, September 30, 1843, Ltrs. Sent, C&O Co.
[249] Proceedings of the President and Board of Directors, G, 119–120.
[250] *Sixteenth Annual Report* (1844), C&O Co., 19–20.
[251] *Ibid*, 18.
[252] Fisk to President and Directors, July 20, 1842, and Ingle to Coale, June 11, 1844, Ltrs. Recd., C&O Co.
[253] "Report of the Committee on Ways and Means, March 19, 1839," *A Short History of the Public Debt of Maryland*, Appendix P, 76–78; *Laws Made and Passed by the General Assembly of the State of Maryland* (Annapolis, 1838), ch. 386; and Baltimore *Sun*, April 7, 1839.
[254] U.S. Congress, House, *Message on the Chesapeake & Ohio Canal from President Van Buren, Transmitting a Letter of the Maryland Governor, William Grason, on the Transfer of Stock in the Chesapeake & Ohio Canal Company*< H. Doc. 90, 26th Cong., 1st sess., 1840; *Ibid*, Senate, *Report of Senate S.S. Phelps on*

These petitions were supported by memorials from Maryland citizens, the most noteworthy of which was submitted by Allegany County in April 1843, and vigorously opposed by the District cities in two particularly strongly-worded statements in March and December 1840.[255]

After the senate passed a joint resolution providing for the transfer of the stock to the State of Maryland and the District cities on July 20, 1842, a committee of the city of Washington effectively denounced what it termed the selfish attitude of the State of Maryland towards the canal in a report that appeared to prevent passage of the resolution in the House.[256] The report stated in part:

> Coupled with the act (of 1839) authorizing this last subscription, was a direction to the Governor to ask of Congress a surrender to the State of the $2,500,000 of stock, originally subscribed by the United States, and the Corporation of Washington, Georgetown, and Alexandria; and if granted, the State pledged herself to buy out all individual stockholders at 50 per cent. But on the 23rd of February, 1841 (fifteen days after the Senate of the United States had passed a resolution giving her the said $2,500,000 of stock, and had sent it to the House of Representatives for concurrence and when it was expected that the House would also pass it), a bill was introduced into the Senate of Maryland, and instantly passed both branches of the legislature, quietly revoking this obligation to which she had pledged herself to Congress to pay the private stockholders 50 percent.[257]

Supporters of the transfer were unable to secure agreement in Congress on the resolutions providing for the transfer. Additional resolutions were introduced in either the House or the Senate annually from 1840 to 1844, but neither chamber could find grounds to approve the other's version.[258] The best chance for Congressional approval of the transfer came in 1842 when on July 20 the Senate passed a joint resolution providing for the transfer of the stock to the State of Maryland and the District cities, on the condition that Maryland would agree not to foreclose its mortgage.[259]

The District cities promptly consented to this solution, but at the same time condemned the passage of the aforementioned bill by the Maryland General Assembly revoking the state's

---

the Chesapeake & Ohio Canal Company Stock, S. Doc. 63, 26th Cong., 2d sess., 1841; Ibid, House Resolution of the Maryland Legislature for the Transfer of Chesapeake & Ohio Canal Company Stock by the United States to Maryland, H Doc. 71, 27th Cong., 3d sess., 1843; Ibid, House Report of Representative Owen on the Transfer of Chesapeake & Ohio Canal Company Stock, H Rept. 56, 28th Cong., 1st sess., 1844; Ibid, House Resolution of the Chesapeake & Ohio Canal Company Stock to Maryland, H. Doc. 227, 28th Cong., 1st sess., 1844.

[255] U.S., Congress, House, Memorial of the Citizens of Allegany County for the Surrender of the United States Stock in the Chesapeake & Ohio Canal Company to Maryland, H. Doc. 202, 27th Cong., 2d sess., 1843; Ibid, Senate, Memorial of the City of Washington Against the Transfer of Stock Held by the United States in the Chesapeake & Ohio Canal Company, S. Doc. 277, 26th Cong., 1st sess., 1840; and ibid, Senate, Memorial of the City of Washington Against the Transfer of Stock of the Chesapeake & Ohio Canal company, S. Doc. 30, 26th Cong., 2d sess., 1840.

[256] Niles' Register, LXII (July 23, 1842)

[257] The committee of the Corporation of Washington Appointed to Demonstrate Against the Surrender to the State of Maryland of the Stock Held by that Corporation in the Chesapeake & Ohio Canal (Washington, 1842), 1.

[258] Niles' Register, LVIII (July 18, 25, 1840); Ibid, LIX (January 16, February 13, 1841), 156, 233, 251, 283, 379; Ibid, LXII (May 7, June 11, June 18, July 2, August 13, 1842), 156, 233, 251, 283, 379; Ibid, LXV (December 23, 1843, Feb. 17, 1844), 271, 396; Ibid, LXVI (March 2, 9, April 20, 1844), 12-13, 17, 126; and Ibid, LXVII (December 21, 1844), 254.

[259] Ibid, LXII (July 23, 1842), 334.

pledge to pay the private stockholders 50 percent for their holdings.[260] Maryland insisted, however, that it must receive the stock before it would borrow further to complete the work, asserting that its position was based on the premise that the United States was responsible for the increased size and cost of the canal and therefore obligated to assist the state by assuming the expense of its completion, by direct relief, or by the transfer of the stock in its hands.[261] Because of the intransigence of Maryland, coupled with the apparent lack of unanimity in Congress and the seeming indifference of the canal company, efforts were dropped after 1844 to effect the stock transfer.[262]

A second scheme advanced to provide for the completion of the canal was the proposal to sell the state's interest in the canal to parties that would undertake the task of finishing the work.[263] Proposed even before the failure of the efforts to secure the stock transfer, this plan sought to connect the settlement of canal affairs with the solution of Maryland's financial problems. After the Whigs succeeded in breaking a Democratic filibuster, the General Assembly in March 1843 passed a bill setting the price for the state's interest in the canal at $5,000,000 in state bonds.[264]

However, the difficulties and uncertainties of completing the waterway were so great that no interest was shown in the sale. In the absence of any offers, the canal company undertook in 1844 to sell itself to prospective purchasers, arguing that $5,000,000 in Maryland bonds at the current depreciated value of 62½ would be a bargain.[265] The company, in a comic opera episode, even contemplated buying itself from the state by offering canal bonds to Maryland for $5,000,000, presumably to be exchanged by the state for its own bonds.[266]

A third proposal to complete the canal called for the state to waive its prior liens on canal revenues and permit the company to issue its own bonds to pay for the completion of the work. Like all the other projects designed to complete the eastern section of the canal, this plan was bitterly opposed by the Baltimore & Ohio and the City of Baltimore. This battle was graphically portrayed in an exchange of letters between "Delta" and "Maryland" in the Baltimore *Sun* and the Baltimore *American* ruing January–March 1841, for and against the completion of the canal respectively.[267] The proposal was also criticized because it did not provide relief for the financial condition of the state, a problem that made it appear to be a last-ditch effort to save the waterway.

The first attempt was made during the December session to the General Assembly in 1841. Disagreement between the House of Delegates and the Senate prevented the passage of the bill and provoked the following remonstrance in *Niles' Register*:

---

[260] Ibid, LXIII (January 21, 1843), 336; U.S., Congress, Senate, *Memorial of Georgetown Approving the Transfer of United States Stock in the Chesapeake & Ohio Canal Company to Maryland and the District of Columbia Cities*, S. Doc. 343, 27th Cong., 2d sess., 1842; and Ibid, Senate, *Resolution of Alexandria Approving the Transfer of the Stock of the United States in the Chesapeake & Ohio Canal Company to Maryland and the District of Columbia Cities*, S. Doc. 344, 27th Cong., 2d sess., 1842.
[261] *Niles' Register*, LXVI (March 2, 1844), 12, and *Speech of John M.S. Cousin, Esq., in the House of Delegates of Maryland, on the Preamble in the Resolution, Introduced by Him, on the Subject of Relief to the States, by the Issue of Two Hundred Millions of government Stock, Based Upon a Pledge of the Proceeds of Public Lands, Delivered Jan. 31st, & Feb. 1st, 1843* (Annapolis, 1843), 5–28.
[262] Coale to Young, December 13, 1843, Ltrs. Sent, C&O Co.
[263] Proceedings of the President and Board of Directors, G, 11.
[264] Baltimore *American*, March 9, 10, 13, 15, 1843; and *Laws Made and Passed by the General Assembly of the state of Maryland* (Annapolis, 1842), ch. 301.
[265] Coale to Ward, March 14, 1844, Ltrs. Sent, C&O Co.
[266] Proceedings of the President and Board of Directors, G, 40.
[267] Sanderlin, *The Great National Project*, 145, and *Delta: Or What Ought the State to Do with the Chesapeake & Ohio Canal* (Baltimore, 1841), 1–47.

> The unfortunate disagreement between the two houses of the legislature of Maryland, in relation to amendments to the bill for completing this stupendous work to the coal and iron regions of Allegany county, which alone can bring the work into profitable operation, will have the inevitable effect of suspending all operations for the year, and leave the unfinished work to certain dilapidation, the contracts subject to expensive litigation, and the state saddled with the interest occurring upon seven millions of dollars invested in the undertaking,—and this is the more to be regretted, because the bill contemplated no new demand upon the treasury, arrangements having been negotiated by which it is understood that capitalists, contractors, and engineers would undertake to finish the work to the mines, provided the state would agree to postpone its preference to the proceeds of the canal until the claims for advances now require to complete it, shall be satisfied.[268]

The legislature's inaction raised such an uproar in the Western counties that large meetings convened and sent appeals to Governor Francis Thomas to call a special session of the Assembly.[269]

The attempt was renewed in the December session 1842, with its proponents again advancing the often-used argument that "completion of the public works was forever to exonerate" the citizens of Maryland "from taxation on their or any other account." According to the supporters of the plan, the bill would allow the canal company to pay its "own way" and "never take one dollar out of the State Treasury."[270] Despite the pressure brought to bear for the bill, the enemies of the canal succeeded in defeating it a second time. Concerning this second defeat of the plan, *Niles' Register* remarked:

> This most splendid and amongst the most promising and important of all the canals in this country seems fated to have to encounter every species of the stock that can be conceived....Fated as we have been, to listen week after week to long labored speeches, and to watch, session after session, the under currents, of unnumerable little interests, each tugging as if for life, to accomplish its own design, without hardly for a moment regarding the public interest,—we grow almost sick at the contemplation of new difficulties and provoking obstacles to the progress of the work....
>
> The proposition to waive the lien of the state in favor of contractors who would undertake to finish the canal, was very earnestly debated in the legislature both last session and the session before, but did not prevail. The canal has been at a stand still, until the state either determines with its own resources or credit, to finish the work, or otherwise consent to forgo its liens in favor of whoever will, with their own resources, finish it. The actual opponents of the canal, of which there is a party (Democrats) in the state, sorry we are to say, throw their weight first in one and then in the other scale, and thereby prevent either expedient from being adopted.[271]

After a summer that saw increased agitation for a solution to the stalemate, the proposal to waive the state lien was re-introduced in the 1843 December session of the Assembly. The bill provided for the redemption of the existing script and certificates of indebtedness, principal, and interest by an issue of $100 six percent bonds of the company redeemable in twenty years. In return the state would surrender its liens against the canal, or it would permit the work to be paid for in company stock.

---

[268] *Niles' Register*, LXII (March 26, 1842), 52.
[269] *Ibid.*
[270] *A Short History of the Public Debt of Maryland*, 48.
[271] *Niles' Register*, LXIV (August 12, 1843), 372–373.

Opponents of the canal also inserted a provision authorizing a slackwater navigation to the mouth of the Savage River to be paid for by the issuance of 6 percent bonds redeemable in thirty years out of a sinking fund based on the revenue derived from that portion of the work. The latter provision stirred a serious controversy over the bill for the canal to Cumberland among those who were unalterably opposed to any further westward expansion.[272] Both the Whig and Democratic Party conventions in Frederick County came out in support of the measure. In his annual message to the legislature in December 1843, Governor Thomas observed that

> Whatever may be the opinions entertained, as to the policy of undertaking this great enterprize, with the means of Maryland almost alone, there ought to be now no diversity of sentiment, as to the justice and patriotism of essaying, to open a Canal communication from Cumberland to Tide Water.[273]

Opponents of the bill, principally the Baltimore & Ohio interests, used two persuasive arguments in the attempt to prevent the extension of the canal. First, the railroad already had been completed to Cumberland in 1842. Second, the canal and railroad companies had reached an agreement on September 21, 1843, whereby the latter would transport coal from Cumberland to the Canal at Dam No. 6, at 2 cents a ton per mile, providing that the amount of coal so carried would not interfere with its own business or require a material increase in facilities. Thus, the Baltimore & Ohio interests urged the Assembly to make this agreement permanent, that the railroad act as a feeder for the canal, thereby dispensing with the need for the completion of the waterway to Cumberland.[274]

The proponents of the bill, led by Delegate John Johnson of Anne Arundel County and canal company President James M. Coale, attempted to offset the effect of the railroad's arguments. In a major speech before the House of Delegates on February 27–28, Johnson urged that the canal's completion be funded from the future revenues of the waterway.[275]

President Coale made a thorough analysis of the whole question in a special report to the stockholders on November 16, 1843, which gained widespread publicity in the coming months. The decisive point of the report was his calculation of the amount of trade required to pay to the state annual occurring interest of $382,500 on the bonds it had issued for the canal:

> Taking it for granted—and we have no doubt of the fact—that the revenues from the other trade on the canal, intermediate and ascending, will hereafter be sufficient to pay expenses and keep the canal in repair and that the State of Maryland must look to the tolls from the coal trade as the means of enabling the Company to pay the interest on the State's investments, and the inquiry presents itself as to the amount of towage of that description that will be required for the purpose, from the point in question.
>
> From the depot at Dam No. 6 to Georgetown is 136 miles. The toll, at half a cent per ton per mile, with the usual boat duty, amounts to 73 7/10 cents per ton for said distance. To pay, therefore, $382,500 per annum, will require the transportation of 518,996 tons per annum, or 1,730 tons per day, allowing 300 days to a navigable year. The tonnage of the coal cars on the railroad is at present only five tons, but we understand that

---

[272] *Ibid*, LXV (February 3, 1844), 368.
[273] *Ibid*, LXV (September 9, December 30, 1843), 19, 276.
[274] Coale to Ward, March 14, 1844, Ltrs. Sent, C&O Co.; Proceedings of the President and Board of Directors, G, 97–100, 115; and Proceedings of Stockholders, C, 192–193.
[275] *Speech of John Johnson, Esq., on the Bill to Provide for Completing the Chesapeake & Ohio Canal from the Revenues of the Work* (Annapolis, 1844), 1–19.

the Company contemplates running cars which will carry six tons. To transport the requisite quantity, then, will require 289 cars to be running daily; and they can make but one trip per day. To keep up a constant trade, the same number must every day be at the mines or at Cumberland, receiving their loads, making in all 578 cars. Supposing 13 cars to be drawn by each locomotive and there would have to be 22 trains daily running on a single track between Cumberland and Dam No. 6—a distance of 45 miles! Clearly, the Railroad Company could not support the coal trade to this extent.[276]

The bill was defeated in the House of Delegates early in March 1844 by a vote of 42 to 35.[277]

A modified bill to accomplish the same purpose also lost out shortly therefore despite a mass meeting held by friends of the canal at the Allegany Court House in Cumberland to which "every man (who) is alive and well" was to attend to determine "the course necessary to be pursued by the people of Alleghany in the present crisis."[278] Ironically the canal company had enough influence in the Assembly to bring about the defeat in the same session of bills sponsored by the Baltimore & Ohio interests providing for the reduction of fares on the Washington branch of the railroad and for the extension of the main line west of Cumberland.[279]

During the protracted battle in Annapolis over the proposal to waive the state's prior lien, the directors prepared for the resumption of construction by soliciting contracts in the fall of 1841 and in each of the following two years in anticipation of aid from the Maryland legislature.[280] All the bids were conditioned on the waiver of Maryland's claims, except for the Letson-Rutter proposal in April 1843 which the directors rejected because of some undesirable conditions in its terms.[281] The board also sent inquiries to England concerning the availability of funds to complete its work if the state waiver became law.[282]

Despairing of aid from the Maryland legislature, the directors again appealed unsuccessfully to Congress, recommending an additional subscription of $2,500,000 or the setting aside of 2,000,000 acres of public land for the canal, as was proposed in pending legislation providing aid for the Illinois and Indiana canals.

As a result of the controversy over the Letson-Rutter contract proposal, the board on May 4, 1843, established the terms under which the contract for the completion of the canal would be negotiated. The contractors were to receive canal company bonds maturing in twenty years, bearing 6 percent interest payable every six months. Work was to begin in sixty days and the canal should be completed in two years. The maximum price at which the instrument would be negotiated was the $1,545,000 estimate made by Chief Engineer Fisk in 1842. The canal company would provide as security for the repayment of the bonds a pledge of all revenue, subject to existing mortgages, the latter phrase contingent on the state's willingness to waive its prior liens.[283]

At the urging of President Coale, the canal board devoted much of its attention to the task of securing legislature approval of the state waiver in the 1844 December session. There was considerable political excitement during 1844, which was both a national and state election year. Two major issues in the state campaign were the related questions of the state credit and the com-

---

[276] *Special Report of the President and Directors of the Chesapeake & Ohio Canal Company, to the Stockholders on the Subject of Completing the Canal to Cumberland* (Washington, 1843), 9–10.
[277] *Niles' Register*, LXVI (March 9, 1844), 17.
[278] *Niles' Register*, LXVI (March 16, 1844), 38; and *Cumberland Civilian*, March 14, 1844.
[279] *Niles' Register*, LXVI (March 16, 1844), 38
[280] Proceedings of the President and Board of Directors
[281] *Ibid*, G, 16, 37–39, 72–73, 75–87, and Proceedings of Stockholders, C, 153–161. For more information on the ill-fated Letson-Rutter proposal, see Sanderlin, *Great National Project*, 148–150.
[282] Coale to Peabody, August 23, 1843, Ltrs. Sent, C&O Co.
[283] Proceedings of the President and Board of Directors, G, 38–40.

pletion of the canal. On the whole, the election results were favorable to both issues, as the Whig governor-elect Thomas G. Pratt and many members of the new Assembly proved to be friendly to the waterway.[284]

Encouraged by the political changes at Annapolis, proponents of the canal introduced a bill in the new legislature to provide for the state lien. After a long and fractious fight, the canal bill and a stamp act to provide effective means of meeting the interest on the state debt, after being initially defeated, were reconsidered and passed in the crucial House of Delegates by the thin margin of 38 to 37.[285] The provisions of the important canal law were as follows:

1. The canal company was authorized to issue $1,700,000 of preferred construction bonds on the mortgage of its revenue.
2. The bonds were to be in $100 denominations, leaving 6 percent interest, and redeemable within 35 years.
3. The bonds could not be sold until the company received guarantees from the Alleghany coal companies for 195,000 tons of trade annually for five years commencing six moths after the completion of the canal to Cumberland.
4. The state's previous liens on the canal were waived in favor of the bonds.[286]

The passage of the two bills triggered the expected responses, with Western Maryland and the District cities celebrating the victory by staging gala parades, setting off large quantities of fireworks, and firing numerous canon while the furious city of Baltimore angrily demanded a redistribution of seats in the House of Delegates giving it greater representation and called for the repeal of both acts.[287]

President Coale and the canal board hastened to secure the required guarantees and to insure the full benefits of the act.[288] Coale went to Boston and New York to confer with officials of the Cumberland coal companies.[289] While in the east, an article reputedly inspired from Baltimore was published in the New York *Herald* casting great doubt on the value of the canal. It exaggerated the duration of enforced suspension of navigation during the winter months, and it emphasized the more frequent handling and transshipment of coal via the canal route and the greater damage to the coal. The canal president refuted these arguments, but the effect of their publication among financial interests in New York was undoubtedly harmful.[290] His attempts to submit the guarantees was further undermined by a resolution of the Baltimore City Council directing the

---

[284] *A Short History of the Public Debt of Maryland*, 49–50, and Mandeville to Price, October 5, 1844, Ltrs. Recd., C&O Co.
[285] *Niles' Register*, LXVII (February 22, 1845), 400; *Ibid,* LXVIII (March 8, 1845), 16; and *Communication from the President and Directors of the Chesapeake & Ohio Canal Company to the Governor of Maryland*, January 15, 1845 (Annapolis, 1845), 1–35.
[286] *Laws Made and Passed by the General Assembly of the State of Maryland* (Annapolis, 1844), ch. 281; and *Niles' Register*, LXVIII (March 15, 1845), 23–24. A mortgage according to the provisions of the sixth section of the act was executed on June 6, 1848.
[287] *Niles' Register*, LXVIII (March 15, 1845), 23; and *A Short History of the Public Debt of Maryland*, 49, 84.
[288] *Special Report of the President and directors of the Chesapeake & Ohio Canal Company, Submitting Certain Acts for the Acceptance of the Stockholders, 1845; Together with the Proceedings of the Stockholder Thereon* (Washington, 1845), 1–26, and *Niles Register*, LXVIII (May 3, 1845), 132.
[289] Proceedings of the President and Board of Directors, G, 228.
[290] Coale to Allen, May 13, 1845, Ltrs. Sent, C&O Co.

railroad to run its trains into the city with coal and iron ore and to lay tracks to a new depot on the south side of the Dam No. 6 basin where boats could dock free of port charges.[291]

At the same time, the board conducted an extensive correspondence throughout the spring of 1845 in its efforts to assure the guarantees. Many supporters of the canal participated in the campaign, holding public meetings and giving spirited addresses "to enlist confidence in the completion of the work." The Corporation of Alexandria passed an ordinance to indemnify any of their citizens that signed the guarantee bonds.[292]

As a result of these efforts, twenty-eight instruments, including both personal and corporate ones, were signed and delivered by mid-July for a total of 225,000 tons, an amount which included bonds guarantying 30,000 tons if it were necessary to fill out the total required. Governor Pratt formally accepted the guarantees and certified his approval in August 1845.[293]

After the guarantees were approved, the canal board made plans to let the contract. On September 23, 1845, the directors accepted the offer of Walter Gwynn, William Thompson, James Hunter, and Walter Cunningham. The state agents promptly gave their approval and the contract was drawn up and executed. The additional mortgage to the State of Maryland, required by the legislature as security for the payment of the loan made in 1834, was also drawn up and executed on January 5, 1846.[294] By the terms of the contract, Gwynn and Company agreed to:

1. Provide the materials of the required quality in workmanlike manner according to the modified December 1, 1842, plan and specifications drawn up by Chief Engineer Fisk.
2. Commence the work within thirty days and complete the canal by November 1, 1847.
3. Raise $100,000 to help the company pay its contingent expenses.
4. Cash the bonds of the canal company at par, paying the interest on them until January 1, 1848.

The price to be paid for the work was set at $1,625,000 in 6 percent canal bonds payable within 35 years.[295]

Work resumed on the canal within the specified 30-day time period. All the sections were sublet in mid-October, and the contractors placed a token force on the line by November 1, pending the successful negotiation for the necessary funds to finance large-scale construction.[296] The initial optimism engendered by the resumption of construction was echoed in a *Niles' Register* editorial that "Day is dawning again after a long gloomy night."[297] By May 1, 1846, however, the work done amount to only $55,384 and the work force had dwindled from some 300 to only 10 in June.[298]

The economic uncertainties caused by the outbreak of hostilities between the United States and Mexico on April 25, 1846, prevented any successful negotiations to acquire the necessary funding, and the negotiations totally collapsed in July when a $10,000,000 loan was floated

---

[291] *Niles' Register*, LXVIII (April 12, 1845), 85.
[292] *Ibid.*
[293] Proceedings of Stockholders, C, 497; Proceedings of the President and Board of Directors, G, 288, *Eighteenth Annual Report* (1846), C&O Co., 4–5; and *Niles' Register*, LXVIII (August 2, 1845), 341.
[294] Proceedings of the President and Board of Directors, G, 317–318, 320–323, 353–354.
[295] *Eighteenth Annual Report* (1846), 8–9.
[296] *Niles' Register*, LXIX (October 25, November 29, 1845), 128, 198; and *Eighteenth Annual report* (1846), 10–11.
[297] *Niles' Register*, LXIX (November 8, 1845), 147.
[298] *Eighteenth Annual report* (1846), 25; and Fisk to President and Directors, June 25, 1846, Ltrs. Recd. C&O Co.

by Congress to finance the war, thereby drawing off most of the available money.[299] Work on the canal ceased entirely that month and remained suspended through most of 1847.

The negotiations for the sale of the bonds had been under way since before the formal signing of the contract in September 1845. Efforts by the company itself and by Senator Daniel Webster, who as Secretary of State in the Harrison and Tyler administrations had made influential contacts in London, to effect a loan in England, failed in September 1845 when the Barings, undoubtedly influenced by the mounting tensions between the United States and Mexico over the American annexation of Texas, declined to take any part in it.[300]

Subsequent attempts to complete the necessary arrangements were progressing in the spring of 1846 when all efforts to interest London merchants failed with the outbreak of the Mexican War. The attitude of the Barings also was influenced by a report made at their request by William H. Swift and Nathan Hale in 1846, estimating the cost of completing the canal to Cumberland, the prospects of income to be derived from the coal trade once it was finished, and the comparison of transportation costs on the waterway and railroad.[301] The contractors then turned to American banking interests in New York, the District of Columbia, and Richmond for assistance, but these arrangements failed in July 1846 largely as the result of the federal monetary efforts to finance the war.[302]

As the tight money market eased somewhat in the spring of 1847, negotiations with the American capitalists resumed. By this time, several events had measurably improved the prospects affecting the sale of the bonds. On March 8, Maryland had shored up the credit of both the state and the canal company by making provision for the payment of the arrears of its debt and for prompt payment of the semi-annual interest in the future.[303] That same day the Virginia Assembly had authorized the state treasurer to guarantee $300,000 of the canal bonds.[304] The corporation of Georgetown and Washington had authorized the loan of $25,000 and $50,000, respectively to the contractors in exchange for the canal bonds, while the citizens of Alexandria took up a private subscription for $25,000 for the same purpose.[305]

Tentative arrangements made in Boston on May 11, provided for the distribution of the entire estimated sum of $1,100,000 cash needed to finish the canal among:

Virginia	$300,000
The District cities	$100,000
Boston interests	$200,000
The Barings	$300,000
The contractors	$200,000[306]

The negotiations were temporarily threatened by the withdrawal of the Barings because of a sudden growing tightness in the European money market, the rapid rise in the rate of interest charged by the Bank of England, and increasing apprehension of a large reduction of bullion and specie

---

[299] Justin Smith, *The War with Mexico* (2 vol., New York, 1919), II, 258–259; Cox to Coale, July 10, 1846, Ltrs. Recd., C&O Co.; and Proceedings of the President and Board of Directors, G, 443.
[300] *Ibid*, G, 311; and Karl Jack Bauer, *The Mexican War: 1846–1848* (New York, 1974), 3–11.
[301] William H. Swift and Nathan Hale, *Report on the Present State of the Chesapeake & Ohio Canal* (Boston, 1846), 1–99.
[302] *Eighteenth Annual Report* (1846), 11.
[303] *Nineteenth Annual Report* (1847), 4–5.
[304] *Report to the Stockholders on the Completion of the Chesapeake & Ohio Canal to Cumberland*, 106.
[305] *Ibid*.
[306] *Nineteenth Annual Report* (1847), C&O Co., 4–5, and *Niles' Register*, LXXII (May 22, 1847), 179. The actual estimated sum was $1,172,116.

by British banks. [A note appears at this point to "insert p. 213a," which is missing] However, it was fully expected that the rapid increase in the supply of money here would enable American bankers to make up the difference.[307]

The negotiations were finally carried to a successful conclusion by Nathan Hale and John Davis of Massachusetts and Horatio Allen of New York, acting as agents for the contractors. The Board drew up and executed the mortgage of the canal's revenues in the fall of 1847. It named Phineas Janney of Alexandria, W.W. Corcoran of Washington, David Henshaw, and George Morey of Boston, and Horatio Allen of New York, as representatives of the twenty-nine capitalists in New York, Boston, and Washington who had undertaken the sale of the bonds. Their withdrawal was influenced also by the opinion of their Boston agent that the canal could not be completed for the proposed $1,100,000 and that it is unlikely that the waterway could dispose of all of its authorized 1844 bonds without serious loss.[308]

By the terms of the final agreement, the capitalists agreed to take $500,000 of the bonds and the subcontractors $200,000, in addition to the $400,000 already pledged by the State of Virginia and the District Cities. The aggregate sum of these bonds and pledges sufficient, according to current estimates, for all the incidental expenses for engineering, salaries, damages for land, right of way, and interest on the bonds. In addition, the amount of $192,000 was left over and placed in the hands of the trustees to cover any deficit. The optimism created by this agreement was reflected by the *National Intelligencer* on October 5:

> We may therefore with entire confidence congratulate our fellow citizens of this District and of the states of Maryland and Virginia, not only them, but the country at large, that the managers of this important work have at length surmounted all the difficulties which have so long arrested it and that there is every prospect of its early completion to Cumberland.[309]

Active operations on the canal between Dam No. 6 and Cumberland resumed on November 18, 1847, under a modified contract. The old firm, Gwynn & Co., was reorganized as Gwyn and Cunningham retired. The remaining partners, Hunter and Thompson, continued with the addition of a third partner, Thomas G. Harris of Washington County, Maryland. The terms of the contract provided that the new firm, Hunter, Harris & Co., would receive no money until the canal was completed to Cumberland. The deadline for the completion of the work was set at October 1, 1849. Prices in the new contract were not to exceed the 1845 allowances by more than 12½ percent.[310]

To speed the work and reduce the cost of construction, the canal board incorporated in the contract some changes in the construction plans including the adoption of the composite plan for Locks Nos. 58–71 and the postponement of building lockhouses and of arching the Paw Paw Tunnel until after the canal was formally opened to Cumberland.[311]

With the resumption of construction, many of the old problems returned to hinder the progress of the work. Among the major obstacles to the work were the sickness and the scarcity of available laborers, the slow sale of the bonds, and the excess of costs over estimates. In spite of

---

[307] *Niles' Register*, LXXII (July 10, 1847), 293, and *Twentieth Annual Report* (1848), C&O Co., 3–5.

[308] *Report to the Stockholders on the Completion of the Chesapeake & Ohio Canal to Cumberland*, 106–107.

[309] Washington *National Intelligencer*, October 5, 1847; Proceedings of the President and Board of Directors, H, 92, 94–96; and *Twentieth Annual Report* (1848), 5–6.

[310] *Twentieth Annual Report*, 7–8, and Washington *National Intelligencer*, October 5, 1847.

[311] Proceedings of the President and Board of Directors, G, 285.

these distractions, however, the force employed on the line increased to 1,447 men and 594 work animals by May 1849.[312]

The difficulties experienced by the contractors in selling their bonds brought their financial trouble to a head on March 11, 1850. Work was suspended for several days, and the workers, who had been unpaid for some time, threatened violence unless they received their paychecks. The trustees, Davis, Hale, and Allen, took over the contract of assignment from Hunter, Harris & Co., and resumed work. The date for the completion of the canal was extended to July 1 and then August 1.[313]

These arrangements proved to be futile, for on July 15 the trustees' resources were exhausted and work again stopped. The canal board declared the contract abandoned two days later and negotiated a new one on July 18 with Michael Byrne, a Frederick County contractor who had done considerable work on the canal in the 1830s. Under this contract, Byrne was provided with $3,000 cash and $21,000 in bonds.[314]

By October 10, 1850, the work had progressed so that the "50-mile section" between the Cacapon River and Cumberland was formally opened to navigation. Gala ceremonies were held in Cumberland on that date celebrating the events with numerous speakers extolling the economic importance of the canal to the nation and more particularly to the State of Maryland. Two weeks later the Frederick *Examiner* commented that:

> We earnestly hope and feel persuaded that these expectations will not be long before Maryland can hold her head proudly up and say—I am out of debt, and prosperity is before me. I now take rank with the proudest of the Sister States of this glorious confederacy.[315]

After more than twenty-two years of alternating optimism and despair, the eastern portion of the waterway was completed nine years after the railroad had reached Cumberland and two years before it reached the Ohio River at Wheeling.

---

[312] *Ibid*, 14, 274–275; *Twenty-First Annual Report* (1849), C&O Co., 3–7, 24–25; and *Application of Hunter, Harris & Co. to the Chesapeake & Ohio Canal Company for Relief* (Baltimore, 1853), 1–45.

[313] Proceedings of the President and Board of Directors, H, 349, 365; and *Twenty-Second Annual Report* (1850), C&O Co., 5–7.

[314] Proceedings of the President and Board of Directors, H, 369–372.

[315] Frederick *Examiner*, October 23, 1850.

V. SUMMARY

Altogether the construction of the canal cost $11,071,075.21 or $59,618.61 per mile.[316] This large expenditure compares favorably with the original estimate for the canal by the U.S. Board of Engineers in 1826, but it compares rather poorly with the original estimate made by Geddes and Roberts. The estimate by the Board of Engineers for a canal 48 feet wide at the surface, 33 feet wide at the bottom, and 5 feet deep, extending from Georgetown to Cumberland was $8,177,081.05, or $43,963 per mile. However, this estimate made no allowance for land purchases, engineering expenses, or other contingencies, with the exception of a provision of $157,161 for fencing. Thus when the actual cost of land purchases ($424,723.91), engineering expenses ($429,845.94), incidental damages ($28,870.09), and company salaries (approximately $80,000) were added to the estimate, the total was $983,359.99 after subtracting the fencing provision. Comparing this figure with the actual cost of the canal, one finds that the cost over-run was $2,087,816.22, or 18.9 percent, a statistic that could easily be justified by the rising inflation of the period.[317]

On the other hand, a comparison of the actual cost of the canal with the 1827 estimate by Geddes and Roberts, on which the original stock subscription and construction operations were based, demonstrates the faulty financial presumptions under which the project was undertaken. The two civil engineers estimated that a canal 60 feet in width at the surface, 42 feet in width at the bottom, and 5 feet in depth extending from Georgetown to Cumberland would cost $4,479,346.93 or $23,985.79 per mile. Their estimate, like that of the Board of Engineers, did not contain any allowances for the purchase or condemnation of land, but, unlike the earlier estimate, it did include a ten percent allowance for contingencies. When the actual cost of land purchases, engineering expenses, incidental damages and company salaries is added to, the eastern section total is $5,412,786.87, a figure that includes the ten percent contingency allowance. Comparing this amount with the actual cost of the canal, one finds that the cost over-run was $5,658, 389.34, or 51.1 percent.[318]

This study of the financial origins, planning, and organization of the Chesapeake & Ohio Canal Company offers many clues as to the successes and failures of the waterway project. The various attempts to improve the Potomac River route as a channel for trade between the western hinterlands and the eastern seaboard originated in the rivalry between the merchants and capitalists of the eastern seaports. While the western merchants and farmers generally supported the canal proposals, the impetus and the capital, came from eastern sources, thereby reflecting the contemporary faith of eastern finances in the profit-making potential of this East–West transportation route in the period of American economic expansion after the War of 1812. Yet private support was insufficient for the realization of the projected improvement from Georgetown to Pittsburgh,

---

[316] *Report to the Stockholders on the Completion of the Chesapeake & Ohio Canal to Cumberland* 112–113. This sum was the figure given by President Coale to the stockholders on February 27, 1851, in his report on the completion of the canal. It does not include interest or repair costs. The interest on the capital stock and bonds borrowed by the company greatly enlarged this sum. As the company continually faced financial hardship, it generally was in arrears on its interest payments. For example, the unpaid interest on the Maryland stock and bonds amounted to $14,344,495 by May 1877, in Arthur Pue Gorman's scrapbooks, the Southern Historical Collection, University of North Carolina, Chapel Hill. See also, *Baltimore Gazette*, June 1872, in *Ibid.* [Note that "the aggregate length of the lines of the Baltimore & Ohio in 1850, including the Washington branch, and the extensions in Virginia, was 208 miles, which had cost $15,243,426." This represents a cost of $73,285.70. See ch. 20, *Development of Transportation Systems in the United States* by J.L. Ringwalt—Editor of Railway World—1888.—kg]

[317] *Ibid*, 112–113.

[318] House Document 192, 5–6, 98.

and from the very inception of the Chesapeake & Ohio, its promoters sought state and federal government subscriptions. Along with these subscriptions went active participation in, and control of the enterprise by the governments concerned, a seeming anomaly in the legendary age of *laissez faire*.

The experiences of the canal company during years of construction reflected the general pattern of the history of other American canals. Formally inaugurating its project with federal and state financial assistance, the company plunged into the race for the western waters in competition with rival works in the neighboring states and the Baltimore & Ohio Railroad in the same state. Its rapid progress was interrupted by a series of obstacles arising form the undertaking of such an extensive work in a thinly populated and rugged river valley with insufficient engineering expertise. Unexpected obstacles in excavation, the shortage of good building materials, the absence of an adequate labor force, widespread ill health during the summer construction season, disputes with local proprietors over land purchase, and trouble with contractors over rising costs, delayed the progress and increased the cost of the project.

These problems were exacerbated by the canal board's decision to build a 60-foot wide waterway, the general inflation and national economic cycles of the period, the difficulties in securing adequate funds on a continuing basis, the attitude of the Jackson Administration toward federal support of internal improvement projects, and the injection of Maryland state politics into canal affairs. The period of actual construction was thus characterized by alternating cycles of optimism and pessimism similar to those on other public works of the period.

**HISTORIC RESOURCE STUDY
CHESAPEAKE & OHIO CANAL NHP**

3.
LABOR FORCE OF THE C&O CANAL: 1828–1850

BY HARLAN D. UNRAU
HISTORIAN, C&O CANAL RESTORATION TEAM, SENECA
DENVER SERVICE CENTER
1976

CONTENTS

I.	A TIME OF EXPERIMENT: 1828–1831	111
II.	A TIME OF TROUBLE: 1832–1842	123
III.	A TIME OF RELATIVE CALM: 1847–1850	139

EPILOGUE

THE RELATIONSHIP OF THE IMPORTATION OF FOREIGN
IMMIGRANTS TO BUILD THE CHESAPEAKE & OHIO CANAL AND
THE RISE OF POLITICAL NATIVISM IN MARYLAND: 1829–1862 … 142

APPENDIXES

A	TREATY OF PEACE SIGNED AT WILLIAMSPORT JANUARY 27, 1834, BETWEEN THE CORKONIANS AND THE LONGFORDS	149
B:	REPORT OF CHARLES B. FISK, FEBRUARY 1838, REGARDING THE RELATIONSHIP BETWEEN LABOR DISORDERS AND THE COST OF THE CANAL	150

I.   A TIME OF EXPERIMENT: 1812–1831

When the actual digging of the canal commenced in the autumn of 1828, the main problem facing the company was the supply of labor. The scarcity of workers and the consequently high rate of wages threatened and upset all the financial calculations of the contractors. There were few laborers available in the largely agricultural valley itself, and few could be attracted to it because of the reputation of the Potomac for ill health during the long hot and humid summer and because of the construction of other railroads and the Pennsylvania Main Line Canal. Added to these considerations was the competition for workers between the railroad and the canal, with the farmers at harvest time, and among contractors themselves as a result of undertaking the construction of 48 miles of waterway to Point of Rocks within one year. The consequence of this scarcity was that labor costs were unexpectedly high and the average ability of the workers apparently rather low.[1]

The poor quality of the work performed by many of the laborers is graphically portrayed in the field notes of W. Robert Leckie, the newly-appointed inspector of masonry, during the spring of 1829. At one of the stone quar4ries being opened for use on the canal, he found the quarry and stonecutters so inexperienced that he "gave directions to have some clay joints cut off some of the stones, made a drawing of lewis and lewising tools, and gave also a drawing of a mallet and a description of the tools necessary to make them." The quality of the walls of the lockhouse at Lock No. 26 was "not good." Here he observed that both:

> Contractors and masons seem totally ignorant of what they should know, have neither skills nor tools to work with, everything done carelessly, and no attention paid to the mixing of the mortar.[2]

Following another inspection tour of the masonry works on the canal in August, he informed Chief Engineer Benjamin Wright that:

> The prospects of this important branch (masonry) are truly appalling. There are scarcely and masons on the line and the most of the small number are laborers totally ignorant of masonry, and who ought never be permitted to spoil such an important work.[3]

Despite the low assessment of the workers' capabilities by Leckie, not one of those laboring on the line of the canal were so ill-prepared. For example, contractor Mowry of Section No. 9, informed the company in July 1829 that he would bring an

> Experienced "canaller" to direct his work, who has been on the Eire and the Union, Susquehanna Division, and who is now collecting a set of his old hands, and will bring houses (horses), wagons, tools, and men to the C&OI Canal.[4]

---

[1] *First Annual Report* (1829), C&O Co., 19; *Second Annual Report* (1830), C&O Co., 5–6; *Baltimore & Ohio Railroad* (2 Vols., New York, 1928), I, 118–120.
[2] Diary and Account Book, 1828–1829 (April 11 and May 12, 1829), W. Robert Leckie Papers, Duke University Library.
[3] Leckie to Wright, August 21, 1829, Leckie Papers
[4] Mowry to Mercer, July 9, 1829, Ltrs. Recd. C&O Co., Records of the Chesapeake & Ohio Canal Company, Record Group 79, National Archives. (Unless otherwise noted, all document sources used in this chapter are located in this collection.)

Mounting wages proved inadequate to overcome the scarcity of workers in the Potomac Valley. Wages averaged $8 to $10 a month for common labor in November 1828, and continued to rise to $12 and $13 a month by mid-summer of the following year.[5]

A. W. Campbell, the contractor for Sections Nos. 30–31, complained in August 1829 that the rapid escalation in wages would bring on

> an average of 12 9/10 dollars per month, which is equal to 46 ½ cents per day. The board of the hands then at 1 50/100 dollars per week amounts to .25 cents for each working day. To this sum I add 5 cents for the board of men wet days and parts of days that their board is more than the proportion of work. The whiskey consumed is worth 4 cents per day. The use of barrows, picks, and shovels at the very low estimate is worth 6 cents. To this add a reasonable sum for superintendence and the expense of building, say 10 cents of the amount will stand thus:
>
> | | |
> |---|---|
> | For labor | 46½ cents per day |
> | For board | 30 cents per day |
> | For whiskey | 4 cents per day |
> | For use of tools | 6 cents per day |
> | For superintendence and buildings | <u>10</u> cents per day |
> | | 96½ cents per day[6] |

Yet despite this wage increase, inspector of masonry Leckie reluctantly reported in the spring of 1829 that there were only "about 50 stonecutters on the line." This deficiency was critical when one compared it with the number of stonecutters needed to complete the canal within the time limits set by company charter, for example, Leckie noted:

> There are in the Monocacy Aqueduct 160,000 feet of cutting which dissected into 180 parts the working days in 6 months would be 900 feet per day, and supposing every stonecutter to cut 8 feet per day it would require 112 stonecutters 6 months to do it.
>
> The Seneca Aqueduct if built of cut stone would require 16 stonecutters 6 months. There is 6,000 feet in a lock of [text missing] per day it will require 6 men 6 months to cut a lock.[7]

During the same period, Leckie also complained that the scarcity of masonry on the line was hindering construction. He informed Chief Engineer Benjamin Wright that there were fewer than fifty masons on the line, a fact that would make it difficult to complete the canal on schedule. Again using the locks and the Monocacy and Seneca Aqueducts as examples, he observed:

> Eight masons may set a lock in 40 days. There are in the Monocacy Aqueduct 11,000 perches and supposing each mason to lay three perches per day it would require 20 masons 6 months to lay it. Seneca Aqueduct would require 5 masons 6 months to lay it.[8]

---

[5] Mercer to Richards, July 8, 1829, Ltrs. Sent, C&O Co., and Proceedings of the President and Board of Directors, A, 140, 309.
[6] Campbell to Mercer, August 30, 1829, Ltrs. Recd., C&O Co.
[7] Diary and Account book, 1828–29 (May 26 and April 23, 1829), Leckie Papers.
[8] Diary and Account Book, 1828–29 (March 1829), and Leckie to Wright, August 21, 1829, Leckie Papers.

The board also took special note of the labor shortage and its effects on the construction of the canal in its first annual report to the stockholders in June 1829. According to the last weekly labor reports taken during the previous month the "number of hands, consisting of men and boys engaged on the works of the canal, was 2,113, of which 2,000 were men and the residue boys." However the directors estimated that the "number necessary to complete the canal under contract, in the time specified in the several contracts, cannot be short of 6,000."[9]

In desperation the canal company turned to various devices to relieve the labor shortage. As early as November 1828, the board had undertaken, through special agents and extensive correspondence, to encourage the migration of workers from all parts of the United States and from various European countries, especially Great Britain, Germany, and the Netherlands.[10] The company inserted advertisements in the newspaper of Dublin, Cork, Belfast, and Amsterdam, offering prospective workers meat three times a day, plenty of bread and vegetables, a reasonable allowance of liquor, and $8, $10, and $12 a month wages. Mercer estimated 2,000 or 3,000 were needed.[11] Supporters of the canal project in Congress even petitioned for the use of troops in the construction of the proposed tunnel on the mountain section through the Alleghenies, the most formidable undertaking of the projected connection between the Potomac and the Ohio.[12]

The efforts of the directors to secure an adequate number of workers at low wages led to a reversion to the colonial practice of using indentured servants. On January 31, 1829 the board authorized President Charles f. Mercer to make an agreement with Henry Richards, a Welshman formerly employed on the Erie and the Chesapeake and Delaware Canals.[13] Richards was to be the agent of the Chesapeake & Ohio Canal Company in Great Britain and was to recruit laborers to work on the line. The board also continued for a short period to negotiate for workers from the British Isles. In its general instructions to Maury and Richards in July, the company offered to pay all costs of transportation in return for the indentures of the immigrants for three months, each month computed at 26 working days. The directors requested that the workers be sent out in time to arrive between late September or early October. In this way they would avoid the "sickly" season and yet have three months of good working weather before winter. Quarrymen, stone cutters, and masons were most in demand for they were badly needed to stimulate the lagging masonry work, a fact demonstrated two months earlier when instructions were given by Mercer "to engage the services of 300 stone cutters and masons from Europe." The board discouraged the enlistment of farmers and if they came, required them to pay their own way and to find their own accommodations on the line.[14]

The detailed instructions to Richards included seven stipulations.

1. Upon his arrival in Britain he was to cooperate in every way with Maury.
2. He was to engage the services of English, Welsh, and Scottish laborers accustomed to digging.
3. Common laborers must sign obligations requiring three months' labor, while masons were to sign indentures for two months' service.

---

[9] *First Annual Report* (1829), 19–20.
[10] Mercer to Cope, November 18, 1828; and Mercer to Barbour, November 18, 1828, Ltrs. Sent C&O Co., and Proceedings of the President and Board of Directors, A, 105.
[11] Mercer to Maury, November 18, 1828, Ltrs. Sent C&O Co.; and Tear to Mercer, January 12, 1829, Ltrs. Recd. C&O Co.
[12] *Second Annual Report* (1830), 25–27.
[13] Proceedings of the President and Board of Directors, A, 153, 175.
[4] Mercer to Maury, July 8, 1829, and Mercer to Richards, July 8, 1829, Ltrs. Sent, C&O Co., and Proceedings of the President and Board of Directors, A, 226.

4. Any advances beyond the cost of transportation were to be repaid at the rate of $8 a month for common laborers and $15 a month for masons.
5. They were to receive the same subsistence as the other workers, but were to be boarded free of charge.
6. If necessary, Richards was authorized to offer wages as high as $10 a month for common laborers and $20 a month for masons and stone cutters.
7. Finally, the men so transported were to work on the canal for one year after the termination of their indentures at the prevailing rate of wages or at the stipulated rate, whichever the laborer in question desires. No contracts were to be made to extend beyond December 1, 1830.[15]

The mission of Richards on behalf of the canal company came at a most opportune time for the latter's purpose. Britain was in the midst of complex economic and social change, accompanied by unemployment, high prices, and unrest among the working classes. The effect of the Napoleonic Wars had stimulated British agriculture and given her a monopoly of the world carrying trade. The inevitable dislocation caused by rapid economic expansion produced sporadic riots and social discontent. The unrest was further fueled as farming and shipping slowly lost their wartime advantages. Demobilization as well as mechanization caused unemployment, and new jobs did not materialize in time to absorb surplus labor. Furthermore the antique borough system [somewhat analogous to U.S. legislative districts] left many fast-growing areas underrepresented in parliament. At the same time taxes were high for rich and poor alike because of the costs of the wars. In addition, the mounting cost of poor relief, borne by local property taxes, added to this tax load, while high prices and massive indirect taxation burdened the poor. Erratic fluctuation in production, wages, and prices, as well as import and exports, contributed to the social unrest. The instability in society was aggravated by a rapid population growth, the consequences of which included an enlarged labor force that outgrew the expanding economy and problems of urban life, housing, poverty, and crime. In London and the burgeoning industrial centers of northern Britain—Manchester, Birmingham, and Glasgow—organizations formed to angrily protest against the great variety of national ills, their memories of the French Revolution kept fresh and fired by agitators such as Henry Hunt. These working class and radical movements for political and economic reform to correct the inequities of British society were generally repressed with the aid of the military, the banning of public assemblies and the suspension of *habeus corpus*. Under these conditions, the Irish, Welsh, and English workers in the mines, mills, and factories were receptive to the terms offered by the Chesapeake and Ohio agent.[16]

While Richards was conducting his recruitment activities the board also took steps in July 1829 to attract additional workers to the Potomac Valley from other parts of the United States. The directors ordered that President Mercer be authorized

> To draw for and advance such sum of money as might be found necessary to pay the expense of transporting to the line of the canal, such number of laborers as the contractors will oblige themselves to employ, on the terms to be prescribed by the President.[17]

---

[15] Instructions to Richards, July 8, 1829, Ltrs. Sent, C&O Co.
[16] Walter Phelps Hall and William Steams Davis, *Course of Europe Since Waterloo* (New York, 1951), 47–56.
[17] Proceedings of the President and Board of Directors, A, 309.

The following month the board approved the expenditure of $975 for the transportation of laborers from New York under the direction of Joel Crittenden, on of the company agents in that state.[18]

Meanwhile Richards began sending the British laborers to America in August. The first group of about 320 workers crossed the Atlantic in the *Pioneer*, the *Julian*, and the *Boston*. Concerning the immigrants that he was sending, Richards wrote:

> I have been very careful to select men of good character, steady, and industrious...Some few Irishmen are among them but all these have worked some time in England & amongst Englishmen and are good workmen and peaceable.
>
> There are a great many miners and colliers chiefly in the *Boston*. The masons and quarry men have been selected from the quarries rail roads and canals in the different countries of England and Wales.
>
> ...Some few of the men are rather small and young—but most of these, if you think it is required, will serve for the longer time.
>
> According to your first instructions the men have agreed to work in lieu of their passage—the stone cutters, and masons and some blacksmiths & carpenters for three months, the laborers agree to work four months....The instructions received yesterday [missing text] shorter say 2 months for masons and 3 months for others, but as I shall be able to engage men on the same terms as before, I shall continue to do so leaving it to you to shorten their time after they arrive if you think proper. And this will perhaps be more satisfactory to the men themselves, who will think it a great favor.
>
> I have sent as few women and children as possible and those only the families of good workmen. I will send no more if I can possibly avoid it.
>
> ...I have sent with each vessel a careful and trusty man...(who will) see the workmen delivered to you.[19]

Another large contingent of laborers came over on the *Nimrod*.[20] Although Rice requested further instructions and authority to hire a thousand laborers, the group of 176 sent over on the *Shenandoah* which arrived late in October, was the last.[21]

The trip across the Atlantic was a harrowing affair for both the immigrants and their overseers. The latter were responsible for the safe delivery of the hands assigned to them and for the distribution of rations on board ship. On both counts they gained the hatred of the laborers. They differed widely in character, some being described as wretched, ignorant, and terrified men, and others as proud, arrogant, and disdainful of the workers.[22] The experience of the bosses was quite similar. The daily distribution of bread and meat often brought tempers to a boiling point as the immigrants complained of favoritism, (short) weight, and inedible provisions. At times they appealed to the ship captains, who invariably washed their hands of the quarrels and sometimes

---

[18] Ibid, A, 331, 337.
[19] Richards to President and Directors, August 21, 1829, Ltrs. Recd., C&O Co., quoted Walter S. Sanderlin, *The Great National Project: A History of the Chesapeake & Ohio Canal* (Baltimore, 1946), 73–74.
[20] Boteler and Reynolds to Ingle, November 1839, Ltrs. Recd., C&O Co.
[21] Proceedings of the President and Board of Directors, A, 380, and Ingle to Janney, October 26, 1829, Ltrs. Sent, C&O Co.
[22] Powell to President and Directors, November 18, 1829; and Gill to President and Directors, November 18, 1829, Ltrs. Recd., C&O Co.

urged the men to take matters into their own hands. Although the overseers were subjected to a constant stream of threats and abuse, all of them survived the journey.[23]

The company directed its agents to send the laborers to either Alexandria or Georgetown, fearing that if the men landed at another port, they might be diverted to some of the other internal improvement projects in the East. On their arrival they were assigned to directors Walter Smith at Georgetown and Phineas Janney at Alexandria.[24]

The latter paid the marine insurance on them, and completed arrangements for them to be housed in one large building in Alexandria.[25] They were then placed under supervision of a superintendent of imported laborers, one of the assistant engineers assigned to that duty, and those among them who were sick received medical attention from Dr. Joshua Riley prior to commencing work.[26] As the charges for the medical services were chargeable to the sick themselves, he was asked to reduce the charges in some degree to the ability of the workers to pay for such services. Subsequently they were turned over to the contractors and their indentures delinquent up to the latter upon receipt and upon the assumption of responsibility for the cost of transportation, a sum set at $32 per man by the board in September.[27] The contractors called the roll to have the indentures acknowledge by the laborer. If any of them refused they were [missing text].[28]

The experiences of the contractors with the immigrants varied widely, probably according to the character of the workers and the treatment given them. The 5 or 8 laborers and quarrymen assigned to Henry Boteler and George F. Reynolds, the proprietors of the Potomac Mill near Shepherdstown, were entirely satisfactory, although the mill owners attempted to reduce labor costs by paying wages below the $10 per month average for the canal and by failing to provide even a limited supply of clothing.[29] The men were described as lacking skills and initiative.[30]

Some of the laborers had real grievances in the treatment they received at the hands of the contractors. Those working for M. S. Wines left him and returned to Washington. They consented to resume work only on certain conditions that were agreed upon by their leaders and company officials. The demands they made were

> That they shall have as soon as it can be made so, a tight house with comfortable lodgings, as tight and comfortable as common board can make it; a sufficient supply of good bread, and meat, with such other things as are customary for laboring men, and these prepared in a cleanly manner; that their baggage shall be sent after them...and lastly that you (Wines) will open an account with each man and charge him with his passage over, and

---

[23] Powell to President and Directors, November 18, 1829, Gill to President and Directors, November 1829, and Jones to President and Directors, November 18, 1829, Ltrs. Recd., C&O Co.
[24] Mercer to Maury, July 8, 1829, and Mercer to Richards, July 8, 1829, Ltrs. Sent, C&O Co., and Proceedings of the President and Board of Directors, A, 380.
[25] Ingle to Riley, October 21, 1829, Ltrs. Sent, C&O Co., and Watts to President and Directors, November 4, 1829, Ltrs. Recd., C&O Co.
[26] Ingel to Riley, October 21, 1829, Ltrs. Sent, C&O Co., and watts to President and Directors, November 4, 1829, Ltrs. Recd., C&O Co.
[27] Proceedings of the President and Board of Directors, A, 364.
[28] Mercer to Ingle, September 30, 1829, Ltrs. Recd., C&O Co.
[29] Ingle to Boteler and Reynolds, October 22, and November 19, 1829, Ltrs. Sent, C&O Co., and Boteler and Reynolds to Ingle, November 5, 1829, Ltrs. Recd, C&O Co. Clerk Ingle also assigned a woman and child to Boteler and Reynolds to serve as a cook and clothes washer as the shanties along the line were too uncomfortable for women and children. The company continued to urge Boteller and Reynolds to accept more women and children as they had better housing facilities than were found elsewhere on the line.
[30] Diary and Account Book, 1829–1830, November 18, 1829, Leckie Papers.

with all other expenses incurred for him and credit him for his work at the customary price of labor until the account shall be given up to him.

In return the company promised that if Wines failed to live up to these conditions it would transfer them to another section. In notifying the contractor of these conditions, company John P. Ingle reminded Wines that:

> We should make some allowance for men in a strange country who have probably lived tolerably well at home and humanity requires that we should do all that is reasonable to make them contented. With kind treatment I really believe that everyone one of your men will faithfully serve you.[31]

These terms soon were ordered to apply to the entire line of the canal by the director, and Ingle was directed to go up the line and to investigate the complaints so generally made.[32]

One of the cases found by Ingle where friction between the contractors and the immigrants had led to a work stoppage was settled by a special meeting of the board with the disputing parties. It was agreed that the thirteen laborers who had left the line would return to work [missing text] paying the approved workmen and mechanics $1.12 ½ per day and the others according to merit down to $1 each besides their board. Thus the stage was set for still higher wages along the canal in the hope that this would avert further turmoil.[33]

Many of the dissatisfied workers were not so patient or conscientious. Some deserted the line of the canal and disappeared into the neighboring countryside. At first the board dealt leniently with the runaways that were captured and imprisoned, releasing them from jail on the promise that they would return to the canal.[34] The directors believed at this time that the grievances would be correct and the men retained. As they continued to abscond, the board began to lose faith in their good intentions and ordered effective steps taken to apprehend them.[35]

When it was reported that some of the men fled to the Baltimore & Ohio Railroad, the directors appealed directly to the President of the rival work not to hire the immigrants that had been brought to the Potomac Valley by the Canal Company.[36] Failing to receive full satisfaction from the railroad, the board ordered the preparation of a resume of the laws relative to indentured servants to be printed for distribution to the foreign laborers.[37]

Following a report in late October that 23 runaways had been caught and that many others had absconded, the board ordered that "immediate steps be taken to apprehend those now absent."[38] One of the principal consequences of the company's policy of taking a hard line against the apprehended runaways was a series of costly trials. On October 24, the *Washington Chronicle* reported that a number of such laborers had been brought before Judge Cranch in the District of Columbia court on a writ of habeas corpus. The workers had refused to comply with their contracts on the ground that they could not make themselves slaves and were under no obligation to serve the company. Hence they had left the line of the canal, only to be captured and imprisoned. The judge, at the urging of the company counsel, "wholly subverted" these "new-fangled notions

---

[31] Ingle to Wines, October 3, 1829, Ltrs. Sent, C&O Cao.
[32] Proceedings of the President and Board of Directors, A, 367.
[33] Proceedings of the President and Board of directors, A, 376.
[34] Ibid, A, 367–368
[35] Ibid, A. 379
[36] Jones to President and Directors, October 1829, Ltrs. Recd., C&O Co., and Proceedings of the President and Board of Directors, A, 369, 377.
[37] Proceedings of the President and Board of Directors, A, 378.
[38] Ibid, A, 379.

of American liberty" by sending the workers back to prison until they were willing to comply with the terms of their contracts.[39]

The series of trials in Baltimore where the company caught up with a large number of laborers and prosecuted them as runaways and debtors, proved to be a costly failure. Baltimore was hostile to the claims of the company, and the workers received the sympathetic assistance of lawyers, merchants, and tavern keepers who had been influenced by the emerging Jacksonian political philosophy. On one occasion in late October when agents of the canal company were about to take 20 captured runaways from Baltimore to Washington by steamboat, an innkeeper named Fox and an attorney named David Stewart informed the men that "they were of right perfectly free and therefore unlawfully arrested." After hearing this language, the workers "united in an effort and succeeded in an escape." Accordingly, the board ordered director Janney to consult with William Wirt, the former U.S. Attorney General who had set up a private practice in Baltimore shortly after leaving the government, concerning "the subject of prosecuting to the utmost rigor of the law this Mr. Stewart, Mr. Fox, and many others who may have aided in the escape of the men." The board was anxious that the escapees be captured, imprisoned as runaways, and prosecuted "in the hope that the question may be at once settled in Baltimore as it has been here (in Washington) on a writ of *habeas corpus*." If they did not act immediately, the board figured that Baltimore would become a haven for the runaways. The board settled on this procedure as it gave them a greater chance for success. Furthermore, a favorable decision in such a case would allow the canal company to hold the men to bail for their performance of their contract or to sue the men for their passage money.[40]

When Wirt reported that it would be difficult to prosecute Fox and Stewart, the canal board determined only to take the eleven runaways that had been captured to trial on a writ of *habeas corpus*. In early November the City Court of Baltimore ruled that the agreements between the company and the workers were not of a master-servant character, but were merely contracts for work. The men were freed, though subject to damages and costs. The company could still sue for debts, and for a short period the directors considered suing each of the men for the cost of their transportation or for the value of their services under the terms of the indentures which were computed at $50 for a common laborer and $75 for a mason.

It soon became evident that if such suits were filed, the immigrants could plead bankruptcy and either get off entirely or be sent to jail at the company's expense. In a jury trial there was always the possibility they might argue that the company had first broken the contract by providing inadequate or rotten food supplies on the voyage from Britain. With this argument, no court in Baltimore would convict them, especially when it might be composed of railroad men looking for workers themselves. In view of this unpromising prospect, the cases were dropped.[41]

An unhappy sequel to the Baltimore case occurred when the City Court attempted to charge the canal company for arresting and imprisoning the eleven runaways. Although canal agents assisted in locating and arresting the workers, the company was charged the full amount by law for taking the men into custody. Among the charges were items for the hire and the refreshment of the horses used by the court employees to arrest the men. Furthermore, the company was billed for the jail and tavern expenses of the men while they were awaiting trial.[42]

The immigrants who remained on the line, servants and freemen alike, suffered greatly from ill-health due to the rigors of the work and unhealthy atmosphere of the Potomac Valley. As early as August, 1829, sickness along the line of the canal forced many engineers as well as con-

---

[39] [citation missing]
[40] Ingle to Janney, October 26, 1829, Ltrs. Sent, C&O Co.
[41] Ingle to Wirt, October 29, November 6, 1829, and Ingle to Glenn, April, 1830, Ltrs. Sent, C&O Co.
[42] Ingle to Glen, November 17, 1829, Ltrs. Sent, C&O Co.

tractors and laborers to cease their work, thus causing the first of many health-related work slowdowns.[43]

During the following two months, the sick and destitute workers poured into Georgetown in ever-increasing numbers. By October they were being picked up off the streets of the town, sick and starving. [missing text] time, 126 had been cared for by the city authorities, and John Little, Trustee for the city of Georgetown, and John Brigum, Overseer of Poor, complained that these people were not Georgetown's poor and should be the responsibility of the canal company.[44] Accordingly, the canal board appropriated $150 for the care of the sick workers.[45]

In some cases the board agreed to pay for the care of entire families that had been imported. For example, the directors paid $9 per week for Evan, an "aged and infirm man" and his family only two of whom were capable of performing any work.[46]

The influx increased as winter approached, some finding their way to Washington where they were cared for by the city poor house and by private charity.[47] The miserable conditions of the laborers and the dismal tales of their treatment aroused city officials such as Washington Mayor Joseph Gales and humanitarian groups such as the Society of the sons of St. George, to well publicized attacks, thereby obliging the company to take official notice of the accusations and defend itself.[48] To counter some of the mounting criticism, the board in April 1830 appropriated an additional $117.45 to Georgetown and $267.45 to Washington for the medical care given the workers.[49]

The canal company was further put on the defensive by foreign visitors to Washington who observed the plight of the Irish immigrant workers and described their impressions in published journals of their travels. One of the most scathing indictments of the company's mistreatment of its imported workers was written by Frances Milton Trollope, and English lady who spent the summer of 1830 in the Potomac Valley. Her condemnation of the canal company's labor policy was published in her *Domestic Manners of the Americans* (1832):

> I have elsewhere stated my doubts if the laboring poor of our country mend their condition by emigrating to the United States, but it was not till the opportunity which a vicinity to the Chesapeake & Ohio Canal gave me, of knowing what their situation was after making the change, that I became fully aware how little it was to be desired for them. Of the white laborers on this canal, the great majority are Irishmen; their wages are from ten to fifteen dollars a month, with a miserable lodging, and the large allowance of whiskey. It

---

[43] Proceedings of the President and Board of Directors, A, 335.
[44] Little to President and Directors, October 13, 1829, enclosing the report of John Brigum, October 10, 1829, Ltrs. Recd., C&O Co.
[45] Proceedings of the President and Board of Directors, A, 380–381.
[46] Proceedings of the President and Board of Directors, A, 399. The directors, angered that such a man was permitted to emigrate to the Potomac Valley, order that Evan be discharged from his indenture and that expenses incurred in caring for him be charged to Richards.
[47] Whitwell to Mercer, March 9, 1830, enclosing the report of John McNerhany, Ltrs. Recd., C&O Co. Under the leadership of John McLeod, an Irish schoolmaster in the city, a group founded by the Washington Relief Society in 1830 to help the "indigent and disabled emigrants" and other distressed people who were unable to receive medical care or other treatment at city almshouse. In one winter, the organization boarded forty people in private homes or taverns, and in 1833 it opened an infirmary for destitute foreigners. Constance McLaughlin Green, *Washington: Village and Capital, 1800–1878*, (2 vols; Princeton, 1962), I, 133–134.
[48] Gales to Ingle, February 8, 1830, and Lenox and Herring to Ingle, February 17, 1830, Ltrs. Recd., C&O Co.
[49] Proceedings of the President and Board of Directors, B, 65.

is by means of this hateful poison that they are tempted, and indeed enabled for a time to stand the broiling heat of the sun in a most noxious climate: for through such, close to the romantic but unwholesome Potomac, the line of the canal has hitherto run. The situation of these poor strangers, when they sink at last in "the fever," which sooner or later is sure to overtake them, is dreadful. There is a strong feeling against the Irish in every part of the Union, but they will do twice as much work as a Negro, and therefore they are employed. When they fall sick, they may, and must look with envy on the slaves around them; for they are cared for; they are watched and physicked, as a valuable horse is watched and physicked: not so with the Irishman: he is literally thrown on one side, and a new comer takes his place. Details of their sufferings, and unheeded death, too painful to dwell upon, often reached us; on one occasion a farmer calling at the house, told the family that a poor man, apparently in a dying condition, was lying beside a little brook at the distance of a quarter of a mile. The spot was immediately visited by some of the family, and there in truth lay a poor creature, who was already past the power of speaking; he was conveyed to the house, and expired during the night. By inquiring at the canal, it was found that he was an Irish laborer, who having fallen sick, and spent his last cent, had left the stifling shantee where he lay, in the desperate attempt of finding his way to Washington, with what hope I know not. He did not appear above twenty, and as I looked on his pale young face, which even in death expressed suffering, I thought that perhaps he had left a mother and a home to seek wealth in America. I saw him buried under a group of locust trees, his very name unknown to those who laid him there, but the attendance of the whole family at the grave gave a sort of decency to his funeral, which rarely, in that country, honors the poor relics of British dust: but no clergyman attended, no prayer was said, no bell was tolled; these, indeed, are ceremonies unthought of, and in fact, unattainable without much expense, at such a distance from a town; had the poor youth been an American, he would have been laid in the earth in the same unceremonious manner. But had this poor Irish lad fallen sick in equal poverty and destitution among his own people, he would have found a blanket to wrap his shivering limbs and a kindred hand to close his eyes.

Trollope concluded her cryptic observations on American immigrant labor practices in general and those of the canal company in particular by stating:

> The poor of Great Britain, whom distress or a spirit of enterprise tempt to try another land, ought, for many reasons, to repair to Canada; there they would meet co-operation and sympathy, instead of malice, hatred, and all uncharitableness.[50]

The use of imported laborers succeeded in temporarily stabilizing and lowering the rate of wages on the canal.[51] The total working force on the line rose from a low of 1,600 or 2,000 in mid-summer to over 3,100 in November, 1829.[52] In the long run, however, the experiment was a failure and the difficulty of enforcing the terms of the contracts in the hostile atmosphere of the Jacksonian Era led to its suspension. The entanglements in law suits, in poor house claims, and in unfavorable notoriety, more than offset the immediate advantages. Even the statistics indicating a substantial rise in the labor force late in 1829 fails to prove the success of the experiment, for

---

[50] James E. Mooney, ed. *Domestic Manners of the Americans* by Francis Milton Trollope (Barre, 1969), 229–230.
[51] *Second Annual Report* (1830), 5–6.
[52] Proceedings of the President and Board of Directors, A, 352.

there was a suspension of work on the Pennsylvania Main Line and Chesapeake and Delaware Canals which might have caused migration to the Potomac Valley.[53]

Before the lessons of the episode had been learned, the directors at the urging of President Mercer, considered the purchase of 100 black slaves for the use of the company.[54] In taking this step, as in the case of the indentured servants, the board was following the example of the Potomac Company, despite the warning of the unfortunate results of the earlier experiments. As it would be necessary to instruct the slaves in the art of cutting stone and construction masonry, the directors took no action to carry out the recommendation. When a proposal to purchase 350 slaves came up before the annual meeting of the company stockholders in June 1830, it was decisively defeated.[55] By that time the company, believing the results were not commensurate with the effort, had given up on all schemes to provide cheap labor for the contractors.[56]

Aided in part by the completion of work on the Pennsylvania Main Line and the Chesapeake and Delaware Canals, the canal board had less difficulty in obtaining an adequate labor force in 1830. By May of that year some 6,000 workers and 700 horses were engaged on the line. However, as the legal controversy with the Baltimore & Ohio Railroad restricted construction above Point of Rocks and discouraged progress above Seneca Creek by preventing the building of the planned feeder at Harpers Ferry, far fewer laborers were needed in late 1830 and 1831. By mid-December 1830, there were 2,205 men and 379 horses engaged on the line.[57] By May 1831, the force working on the line of the canal had been reduced further to 1,326 men and 276 horses.[58]

As construction advanced, the canal directors were occupied with a series of problems related to the labor force. The presence of so large a body of laborers on such an extended line of the Potomac Valley created problems of morale and coordination. The annual sickly season continued to take its toll among the laborers and engineers alike, delaying construction and indirectly forcing wages up to unexpected levels.[59]

Compensation to laborers who had been injured in work-related accidents became an item of financial concern to the directors, thereby forcing them to encourage the contractors to take greater safety precautions when undertaking dangerous work such as blasting. One of the first of these cases was that of John Stubblefield, a free black, who was awarded a $2 monthly stipend for one year by the board after he lost his left arm while blasting rocks on the line in December 1828.[60]

Other petitions for aid from disabled workers soon were making their way to the board, including an appeal by Felix O'Neal, an Irish immigrant who had suffered a broken thigh bone and an injured hand while blasting on Section A in Georgetown.[61] The company also took steps to protect itself against liabilities when the worker on several different sections applied in February 1830 for the distribution of assessments made for work done in the month prior to the death of

---

[53] Ibid, A., 353–354
[54] Ibid, A, 310
[55] *Second Annual Report* (1830), 28
[56] All told, the company spent $37,300.54 on the recruitment, passage, and superintendence of the immigrants. Ledger A, C&O Co., 79. For his services in recruiting the laborers, Richards was paid $605.61. Ibid, 78.
[57] *Frederick Town Herald*, January 15, 1831.
[58] *Third Annual report* (1831), C&O Co. 4
[59] *Second Annual Report* (1830), 25.
[60] Proceedings of the President and Board of Directors, A, 149.
[61] O'Neal to President and Directors, April 13, 1831, Ltrs. Recd., C&O Co. The board later agreed to pay O'Neal $5 per month for five months.

one contractor and for the work done in the month prior to the abandonment of a contract by another.[62]

Some of the most important problems of morale among the labor force centered on such diverse considerations as communications, recreational diversion, and domestic home life. To solve the communication problem, a new postal route was established in the winter of 1828 with its own offices scattered along the canal. In September 1839, service was upgraded so that the mail was delivered twice daily along the line of the canal by horseback. By the following year, there were eight offices on the waterway at the following locations: Magazine, Section No. 8, Bear Island, Clementon, Seneca Mill, Edward's Ferry, Conrad's Ferry, Mouth of Monocacy, and Catoctin. In most cases, the contractor on the section was appointed the postmaster, on President Mercer's recommendation, but several were nearby landowners appointed on the recommendation of their Congressman.[63]

A critical problem facing the director was that of diversion or recreation. In the absence of other sources of amusement, drinking became almost the sole outlet for the workers.[64] Furthermore, many of the workers who were expected to put in long hours six days a week, ignored company regulations and insisted on taking an extended vacation over the Christmas holiday season to spend time with their families.[65] The board, after considerable prodding, also took steps in October 1829 to boost the morale of those workers who had brought their families with them from Europe. To meet the demands of rising inflation, the directors on October 12 increased the weekly allotment to $2.25 for board to each imported laborer. Furthermore, the workers having families were allowed an additional sum of 50 centers per week, thereby changing the company policies forbidding any aid for families coming with the recruits.[66]

Later, on December 2, the board determined to permit the foreign laborers who had brought families to receive and apply to their own board and wishing bills their earnings until April 1, 1830, after which time they were to use a portion of their earnings to repay the company for their passage and expenses. At the same time, any boys that Richards had recruited were discharged from their indentures and their expenses charged to his personal account.[67]

The company, anxious to rebut the charges of mistreating the immigrants, undertook the care of those imported families where a death made it difficult for the laborer to continue his work. One such case was that of John Wiley whose wife died several months after arriving on the line, leaving three children. Seeking to help the man care for his children, the board granted him a discharge from his indenture and authorized the contractors to pay him any wages he might have earned above the expenses of his passage. Within several weeks, Wiley abandoned the children and the directors determined to provide for the three children. As the directors had warned Richards not to send families, they charged the expenses to his personal account.[68]

---

[62] Proceedings of the President and Board of Directors, B, 28.
[63] Nelson to Mercer, September 28, 1829; Gardner to Mercer, September 29, 1829; and Hobbie to Mercer, February 19, 1830, Ltrs. Recd., C&O Co.
[64] Watts to President and Directors, December 9, 1829, Ltrs. Recd., C&O Co.
[65] Owens to Board of Directors, December 9, 1829, Ltrs. Recd., C&O Co.
[66] Proceedings of the President and Board of Directors, A, 374.
[67] Ibid, A, 410–411, and Ingle to Powell, December 8, 1829, Ltrs. Sent, C&O Co.
[68] Proceedings of the President and Board of Directors, A, 395, 424, and Ingle to Ford and Chapman, November 19, 1829, Ltrs. Sent, C&O Co.

II. A TIME OF TROUBLE: 1832–1842

The decade of construction from 1832 to 1842, which saw the completion of the canal to Dam No. 6 above Hancock, was a period marked by severe cholera epidemics among the workers and a series of labor disturbances often accompanied by violence. As a consequence, the construction of the waterway was hampered and the cost of the work rose sharply, thereby complicating the financial and legal problems of the canal company.

The canal project had been plagued from its inception by the annual 'sickly" season in the Potomac Valley, giving the region a reputation as an unhealthy area. In a report to the House Committee on Roads and canals in 1834, the canal board described the problem and the popular beliefs as to its causes:

> The autumnal diseases of the Potomac are by no means common to the whole river, which below tide water, as at Georgetown, is remarkable for the salubrity of its climate in autumn as well as at other seasons. Above tide water, which reaches three miles above Georgetown, and below Harpers Ferry, the banks of the Potomac are unhealthy from the last of July until the first hard frost of autumn, their inhabitants being subject for that period to intermittent, and agues and fevers, as on the Susquehanna and Juniata, and it is believed for the same reason, the great breadth of those rivers in proportion to the depth of their volume of water when reduced by autumnal droughts.
>
> One peculiarity is common to those rivers: it is the growth of several species of grass from their bottoms, the stems and blade of which attain, by the first hot weather of August, a considerable height and float on the surface of the water. Where this is shoal, and warmed by the action of the autumnal sun, this grass early undergoes a fermentation and decomposition, and emits an offensive odor, very perceptible by travelers who ford the river at night in the last of August, and throughout the month of September when the air is damp and still. May not this effluvia be the cause of the ill healthy of adjacent shored: In deep water, as opposite to Georgetown and Alexandria, and for the considerable distance above and below these towns, this grass does not appear on the surface of the Potomac, nor does it at Harper's Ferry, in consequence of the rapidity of the current, nor opposite to Shepherdstown, where a dam erected immediately below that town has deepened the water opposite to it.[69]

So firmly had these ideas become established in the minds of the valley inhabitants that there was usually a noticeable slacking of work on the canal during the summer months as company officials, contractors, and laborers left the region?

The inhabitants of the Potomac Valley were frightened perhaps more from the onslaught of cholera epidemics than any other disease because of its "fearful suddenness," its dreadful pain, and its "sudden termination." The afflicted patient

> would feel an uneasiness of the bowels with great heat and intense thirst; then would follow a feeling of heaviness and weakness, an almost total suspension of the pulse with a low, weak, and very plaintive voice; then the 'rice water' discharge would take place, violent vomiting, oppression of the stomach and an impeded respiration. The circulation of the blood became exceedingly sluggish, the forehead, tongue, and extremities became

---

[69] U.S., Congress, House, committee on Roads and Canals, Chesapeake & Ohio Canal, H. Rept. 414, 23d Cong., 1st sess., 1834, Appendix U, 237.

very cold. Cramps occurred in the legs, toes, and hands; the face of the patient became livid and cadaverous and the body presented a mottled appearance.

These symptoms were quickly succeeded by the final stage, which was a complete collapse of the whole system, greatly resembling the appearance of death, which quickly succeeded. The patient sometimes died in a tranquil stupor and sometimes in violent spasms and in great distress. The different stages of the disease followed each other occasionally with such rapidity that death occurred in a few hours after the appearance of the first symptom...The most popular treatment at first was hot applications, mustard plasters, calomel, and opium.[70]

The canal company resorted to unusual precautions to offset the threat of the 'sickly" season and to keep the work going when construction commenced above Point of Rocks following the successful resolution of the legal conflict with the Baltimore & Ohio Railroad in January 1832. The safeguards provided were the customary ones, but the attempt to prevent the effects of illness among the laborers was unprecedented on the canal. The board resolved to engage a physician to inspect the workers' shanties along the canal from July to October, to recommend measures for the health of the contractors and laborers, and to acquire and prescribe medicines for the sick.[71]
The office of Superintendent was created to let all the contracts above Point of Rocks and to provide "for the removal of the sick and then supply with such necessaries, hospital stores, and comfort, as their condition may need."[72]

In July, the directors relinquished the condition contained in the recently-let contracts prohibiting the contractors from providing spirituous liquors to the hands employed by them.[73]

When cholera first appeared among the workers near Harpers Ferry in August, the board authorized President Mercer to rent a suitable building near that town to be used as a hospital and appropriated the sum of $500 for the workers who would get the disease. As the cholera spread toward Point of Rocks, the board in early September authorized Mercer to provide for a second hospital near that village. Provision was to be made with both the contractors and the laborers to share the expenses of these hospitals with the company.[74]

In addition, steps were taken by the board to comply with a request from the Corporation of Georgetown that the water be drawn off that portion of the canal in the town at least once a week during the summer months as a sanitary measure.

By publicizing these measures for the care and prevention of sickness, the company sought to encourage workers and contractors alike to stay on the job, and perhaps to attract laborers from other public work.[75]

---

[70] Thomas J. C. Williams, *History of Washington County* (2 vols., Hagerstown, 1906), 221–222. According to Sanderlin, *Great National Project*, 93: "Officials of the Department of Health of the District of Columbia believe that the illnesses described were probably of various origins, coinciding in occurrence." Water-borne diseases such as typhoid and paratyphoid may have been the most prevalent. Insect-borne fevers undoubtedly accounted for many more. Dysentery from several causes and possibly milk-borne diseases seem best to fit the other symptoms described. On top of these were all the other human illnesses which when occurring in the sickly season, were attributed to the river. The occurrence of the water-borne and pest-borne diseases in late August and September coincided with the mosquito season in the Potomac Valley and the peak of the warm water period in the stream (at which time water-borne diseases are most potent."
[71] Proceedings of the President and Board of Directors, c, 174–174.
[72] Ibid, 175
[73] Ibid, C, 186
[74] Ibid, C, 212–214
[75] Ibid, C, 212

Despite all the precautions, the summer of 1832 proved to be the most disastrous to the health of the workers. Late in August, Asiatic cholera, which had gradually been spreading south from Montreal, made its appearance on the line near Harpers Ferry. The plague, soon popularly called the "the pestilence," spread rapidly down to Point of Rocks, causing a suspension of work on many sections as fear spread through the ranks of the labor force.[76]

Niles' Register described in ghastly terms the panic and confusion caused by the epidemic in the vicinity of Harpers Ferry:

> The cholera has raged dreadfully among the laborers on the Ohio & Chesapeake canal, in the neighborhood of Harper's Ferry. As many as six persons are said to have been lying dead, at one time, in a single shanty,—while in others the dead and the dying were mixed in awful confusion. Many had abandoned their employments and fled—and some of these were attached on the roads, and died in the fence corners! The habits and exposures of these poor people fit them for the reception of the cholera, and their accommodations for the sick and wretched and scanty, indeed-for they are crowded in temporary sheds, and badly supplied even with the most common necessaries of life. The laborers are chiefly Irishmen.[77]

After a hasty inspection of the Harpers Ferry—Point of Rocks area, President Mercer informed the directors that the panic had resulted in the dispersal of the terrified laborers. Accordingly, he observed:

> If the Board but imagine the panic produced by a mans turning black and dying in twenty four hours in the very room where his comrades are to sleep or to dine they will readily conceive the utility of separating the sick, dying and dead from the living.[78]

The cholera gradually spread up the river to the west of Harpers Ferry toward Sharpsburg and Shepherdstown. As it advanced, the same reports of the suspension of work and the panic of the laborers accompanied it. From Shepherdstown Henry Boteler, the proprietor of the Potomac Mill wrote:

> Before this letter reaches Washington, the whole line of canal from the point of rocks to WmsPort will be abandoned by the Contractors and Laborers—The Cholera has appeared amongst them, and had proved fatal in almost every case. There has been upwards of 30 deaths nearly opposite to us since Friday last, and the poor Exiles of Erin are flying in every direction...it is candidly my opinion, that by the last of this week you will not have a working man on the whole line.[79]

Similar scenes of suffering and panic were described by the company's counsel in Frederick:

---

[76] Williams, History of Washington County, I, 221, and Rush to President and Directors, August 5, 18) Ltrs. Recd., C&O Co. The cholera soon spread down the Potomac Valley to Washington where the Board of Health blamed the epidemic chiefly on the "large number of foreign emigrants...employed on the public works. Most of these were from Germany and Ireland, men who neither understood our language, nor were accustomed to our climate, habits and mode of living." Green, Washington: Village and Capital, I, 135.
[77] Niles' Register, XLIII (September 15, 1832), 44.
[78] Mercer to Ingle, September 3, 1832, quoted in Sanderlin, Great National Project, 95.
[79] Boteler to Ingle, September 4, 1832, Ltrs. Recd., C&O Co., quoted in Sanderlin, Great National Project, 95.

> They have since been suffering great mortality west of Harpers Ferry, [& c] fear that work is by this time suspended. The poor creatures, after seeing a few sudden & awful deaths amongst their friends, straggled off in all directions through the country; but for very many of them the panic came too late. They are dying in all parts of Washington County at the distance of 5 to 15 miles from the river. I myself saw numbers of them in carts & on foot making their way towards Pennsylvania.[80]

The scenes of suffering and death caused both anguish and alarm to the inhabitants of the valley, Engineer Thomas F. Purcell writing from Sharpsburg, described some of the occurrences of "inhuman outrage" as follows:

> Men deserted by their friends or comrades have been left to die in the fields, the highways, or in the neighboring barns & stables: in some instances, as I have been told; when the disease has attacked them, the invalid has been enticed from the shantee & left to die under the shade of some tree.
>
> Excited by the sufferings of the miserable victims of this disease; the citizens of this place have ministered to their wants, and sought to sooth their dying moments; but unfortunately for the cause of humanity, nearly every person who has been with the dead bodies or has assisted in burying them have paid the forfeit with their lives: and now it is scarcely possible to get the dead buried.[81]

During the first week of September the dead bodies of four canal workers were brought to Hagerstown to be buried in the only Roman Catholic cemetery in Washington County. Terrified by the spreading plague, the citizenry protests against bringing the dead within the town limits and the civic authorities passed ordinances forbidding the entry of any sick or dead canal workers for hospital care or internment. To aid the helpless workers, Father Timothy Ryan, the priest in charge of St. Mary's Church, in cooperation with Engineer Alfred Cruger of the canal company took steps to provide a burying aground near the canal.[82]

By late September the epidemic had reached its peak, but the laborers were still suffering and dying. Niles' Register reported that:

> The disease yet prevails severely on the line or in the neighborhood of the Chesapeake & Ohio Canal, about Harper's Ferry, & c. and at Sharpsburg, MD. The panic was awful, and the sufferings of the people, chiefly newly arrived foreigners, exceedingly stressing. The bodies of many laid on the roads unburied for days—being abandoned by their late relatives or associates.[83]

As the epidemic spread, the canal company adopted measures to care for the sick and to calm the panic. President Mercer made an effort to lease an abandoned mill owned by Caspar Wever near Lock No. 31 to be used as a hospital.[84]

---

[80] Price to Ingle, September 5, 1832, quoted in Sanderlin, Great National Project, 95.
[81] Purcell to President and Directors, September 11, 1832, quoted in Sanderlin, Great National Project, 95–96.
[82] Williams, History of Washington County, I, 222.
[83] Niles' Register, XLIII (September 22, 1832), 52.
[84] Mercer to Wever, September 11, 1832, Ltrs. Sent, C&O Co.

Wever, a longtime foe of the company, offered exorbitant terms of $350 per year, a rate double that when the long vacant mill had last been rented, plus all damages awarded by his agents upon examination after the mill would be relinquished[85]

The terms were so repulsive that they did not receive consideration.[86]

Two make-shift hospitals were finally established in some cabins rented near Harpers Ferry and in a large shanty at Section No. 112 just above Dam No. 3. Another was contemplated at Point of Rocks, while these temporary quarters left much to be desired, the permanent hospital at Harpers Ferry was not established until late in September.[87]

Even then the accommodations were not very elaborate, for as late as August 27, Mercer thought that it would only be necessary to purchase

> some hundred feet of plank for bunks and some blankets and sacks for straw and as few and as cheap articles for the Hospital as possible and place it in the charge of a physician of this place (Harpers Ferry) after engaging one or two nurses to attend the sick...[88]

The method by which the hospital was supported was a form of group insurance that the directorate had attempted unsuccessfully to introduce earlier in 1830.[89]

Each of the workers contributed 25 cents per month for the doctor's fees and the maintenance of the hospital.[90]

This system had worked successfully before on the James River Canal, but, as could be expected, it worked only as long as the fear of sickness was sufficiently great to cause the men to consent to the deduction from their wages. With the arrival of cooler weather and the disappearance of the cholera, the workers refused to approve further deductions and the program was discontinued. The following spring the hospital services were terminated and the equipment sold.[91]

Beginning in 1832, reports of unrest among the workers on the line appear in the company records. In that year the cause of the disturbance was an ill-advised attempt to enforce the prohibition of the use of spirituous liquors by the workers. In an effort to forestall the rioting and loss of time which resulted from excessive drinking, the directors ordered the enforcement of the condition contained in all contracts above Point of Rocks prohibiting the distribution of liquor to the workers. At the same time, President Mercer unsuccessfully sought to secure the passage of a law by the Maryland Assembly prohibiting the sale of liquor within two or three miles of the canal in Frederick, Washington, and Allegany Counties.[92]

The company had considerable difficulty enforcing its prohibition in the absence of supporting Maryland laws, as the contractors continually faced trouble with shopkeepers along the line who maintained grog shops or surreptitiously sold liquor to the men. Upon the report of Engineer Alfred Cruger that the enforcement of the prohibition was having the opposite effect from that intended, the directors repealed it.[93]

---

[85] Wever to Mercer, September 13, 1832, Ltrs. Recd., C&O Co.
[86] Mercer to Smith, September 24, 1832, Ltrs. Sent, C&O Co.
[87] Mercer to Smith, September 24, 1832, Ltrs. Sent, C&O Co., and Rush to President and Directors August 5, 1833, Ltrs. Recd., C&O Co.
[88] Mercer to Ingle, August 27, 1832, Ltrs. Recd., C&O Co.
[89] Proceedings of the President and Board of Directors, B, 49, 72.
[90] Mercer to Ingle, September 3, 1832; Mercer to Smith, September 24, 1832; and Rush to President and Directors, August 5, 1833, Ltrs. Recd., C&O Co.
[91] Mercer to Ingle, September 3, 1832, and Rush to President and Directors, August 5, 1833, Ltrs. Recd., C&O Co., and Proceedings of the President and Board of Directors, C, 263.
[92] Mercer to Ingle, January 23, 1832, Ltrs. Rec., C&O Co.
[93] Proceedings of the President and Board of Directors, C, 185-186.

Drunkenness had actually increased during the period of prohibition as the men, deprived of a steady supply of spirits during the day, drank excessive quantities of alcohol at neighboring grog shops in the evening. The intoxicated men rioted throughout most of the night, and morning found many of them lying on the ground where they had fallen exhausted, unfit for work that day.[94]

The laboring force was the cause of anxiety on the part of the directors for other reasons. For one thing there was the continued demand for more men, especially skilled masons and stonecutters. Mercer carried the search for hands as far north as Philadelphia on one of his trips to secure funds for the company. In the fall of that year, Mercer reported that he had hired eight men there. The terms which cost the company $130, included the advance of transportation money, the promise of bonus and the guarantee of work until December 10, 1832, at fair wages.[95]

Despite all the hindrance to the recruitment of laborers, the company had 4,700 men and 1,000 horses working on the line by May 1833.[96]

In the summer of 1833, there was another outbreak of the cholera sickness on a less serious scale. This time it broke out among the workers near Williamsport in July. After ten men died in one day, the symptoms of panic and threatened dispersal of the workers reappearance. The unrest spread to the neighboring village of Hagerstown because so many of the Irish workers were brought there for interment in the Catholic cemetery. Fear in the town increased as the death among the workers multiplied and at least one afflicted laborer came to the hamlet for treatment and died.[97]

A town meeting was held at which civic leaders expressed fear for the health and trade of the community. The town, the company, and the local Catholic parish took steps to provide other cemeteries closer to the line, thereby reducing the time lost from work during the solemnity and revelry of a funeral and removing the threat to the safety of the villagers.[98]

The directors rejected the recommendation of Engineer Thomas F. Purcell to purchase suitable lots for cemeteries, "considering it to be without the line of their duty." Instead they authorized the engineers "to use any waste ground owned by the Canal Company for the interment of persons dying upon the works of the Company."[99]

When the board refused to take further action to help the sick workers, Father Ryan, of St. Mary's Church in Hagerstown, established a burying ground and a hospital in a log house on the "Friend" farm along the Clear Spring road near Williamsport.[100]

The epidemic gradually retraced its previous course down the river to Harpers Ferry and then disappeared.

---

[94] Cruger to President and Directors, July 7, 1832, Ltrs. Recd., C&O Co.
[95] Mercer to Ingle, October 8, Ltrs. Recd., C&O Co., and Ledger A, C&O Co., 79.
[96] Mercer to Purcell, May 9, 1833, Ltrs. Sent, C&O Co. Of this force, 2,700 men and 655 horses were engaged between Harpers Ferry and Dam No. 5. Fifth Annual Report (1833), C&O Co., 3.
[97] Williams, History of Washington County, I, 223.
[98] "Resolutions of a Public Meeting in Hagerstown July 27, 1833," in Williams, Price, and Beatty to Purcell, July 31, 1833, Ltrs. Recd., C&O Co., and Purcell to President and Directors, August 1, 1833, Ltrs. Recd., C&O Co.
[99] Proceedings of the President and Board of Directors, C, 409. At least four such burying grounds were established pursuant to the Board's directive Williamsport Cemetery, just above the canal on a small hill in the town; Cacapon Cemetery, downstream from the mouth of the Cacapon River (between what are now the Western Maryland Railroad tracks and the canal; Paw Paw Cemetery, near the present intersection of Md. 51 and the canal next to the river; and Purslane Cemetery, at the upstream side of the mouth of Purslane Run. Edward McMillan Larrabee, "A Survey of histories and Prehistoric Archeological Sites Along the Chesapeake & Ohio Canal National Monument 1961–1962" (NPS Mss., 1962), 34, 41–42.
[100] Williams, History of Washington County, I, 480.

In 1834 and 1835 open warfare broke out between two long feuding rival factions of the Irish workers—the Corkonians and the Longfords, sometime called Fardowners—during the idle winter months.[101]

The first encounter in January 1834 was the result of a fight between on of the Corkonians and one of the Longfords named John Irons, the latter man being beaten badly that he soon died. The fight had been triggered by the long-threatened effort on the part of the rival factions to oust adherents of the other from the line of the canal, an event which would have led presumably to an increased rate of wages for those remaining. The skirmish between the Corkonians, who were working near Dam No. 5 above Williamsport, and the Fardowners from the vicinity of Dam No. 4, below the town, resulted in several deaths and many wounded in the clash before two companies of the Hagerstown Volunteers arrived on the scene to restore order. The following day the militia returned to Hagerstown with 34 prisoners who were sent to jail.[102]

After the battle there was general demoralization among the workmen, and the countryside took on the appearance of an armed camp. Within a week, a band of Corkonians "committed excesses" above Williamsport, and some of their number attempted to enter the town. However, they were met on the Conococheague Aqueduct by an opposing party of Irishmen in the town and driven back. In this affray one man was seriously beaten and wounded. The citizens of the town quickly took up arms and "soon put themselves in military order" for the protection of their homes and remained on patrol at the aqueduct "for the balance of the day, and the greater part of the night" to keep the warring factions apart.[103]

Notwithstanding these preventative measures a major battle erupted the following day January 24. A party of 300 Longfords, armed with guns, clubs and helves, were permitted to cross the aqueduct and march up to Dam No. 5, when they announced that their intentions were merely to make a show of force. Farther up the line they were joined by 300 to 400 more who had apparently crossed the Conococheague behind the town. In a field on a hill-top just above Middlekauff's Mill near Dam Mill near Dam No. 5, they met about 300 Corkonians armed with "military weapons." Accepting a challenge, the Longfords charged up the hill amid an exchange of volley that killed a number of men. Soon the Corkonians fell back and fled before the superior forces of the Longfords. A merciless pursuit took place until nightfall, and many of the fugitives that were over taken were savagely put to death. Later five men were found in one place with bullets through their heads. In addition, the bodies of other dead and wounded were strewn in every direction. All of the casualties were reported to have been of the Corkonian faction. About 10 o'clock that night the victorious Longfords marched back through Williamsport, disbanded, and returned to their shanties below the town.[104]

---

[101] The Corkonians had emigrated from Cork, Ireland's largest county which included much of the rugged southern coast. The seat of the county was the city of Cork, an emerging manufacturing and commercial center and the main seaport and the largest city on the southern coast. The Longfords emigrated from the county of Longford, a western county of the province of Leinster in north central Ireland. Located just east of the Shannon River, the county was largely agricultural hay and potatoes being its principal crops, with a few small industries in the towns of Longford, Granard, Ballymahon, and Edgeworthstown. Longford's land was poor, and much of the surface was under peat. Thus, it became one of the least populated regions of Ireland as a result of heavy emigration, especially after the partial failure of the potato crop in 1817, 1821, 1822, and 1829. Carl Wittke, the Irish in America (Baton Rouge, 1956), 3–12.

[102] Niles' Register, XLV (January 25, 1834), 366; Purcell to Ingle, January 23, 1834, Ltrs. Recd., C&O Co., and Williams, History of Washington County, I, 223.

[103] Williamsport Banner, January 18, 1834, quoted in Niles' Register, XLV (February 1, 1834) 382, and Williams, History of Washington County, I, 223–224.

[104] Williamsport Banner, January 18, 1834, in Niles' Register, XLV (February 1, 1834), 382.

The following day Colonel William H. Fitzhugh, the Washington County sheriff, arrived in Williamsport in command of two volunteer companies from Hagerstown, and one of the leading rioters was arrested. Shortly thereafter two companies of local militias, named the Williamsport Rifleman and the Clearspring Riflemen, were organized. But these forces were deemed insufficient for the emergency. An urgent request was sent to Washington to ask for federal troops. At the same time, deputations were sent out by the Williamsport civic leaders to the Corkonians and the Longfords to bring the leaders of the two factions together and effect reconciliation. About sunset on January 17, representatives of the two Irish factions met with the town leaders at Lyles' Tavern. A treaty of peace was prepared by the magistrates under the direction of General Otho Williams which the Irishmen signed.[105]

The town authorities warned the immigrants that if either side violated the agreement the citizens and the militia would unite with the other faction to drive the offender out of Washington County.

The Williamsport citizenry took other precautions to preserve the peace. One company of horse and two companies of infantry were organized. When word was received that a force of 100 armed Corkonians had passed Harpers Ferry and were on their way to reinforce their friends at Dam No., 5, the militia leaders were dispatched to meet the party near Dam No., 4. After hearing of the peace treaty, the Corkonians disbanded, surrendered their arms and returned to their work down the river. The forty prisoners in the Hagerstown jail were then released upon their own recognizance under the terms of the treaty.[106]

In the meantime on January 28, Dr. John O. Wharton, one of the representatives from Washington County in the Maryland House of Delegates, introduced a resolution asking the President of the United States to order out a sufficient number of troops to preserve the peace at Williamsport. The resolution passed the House, but the Senate substituted a resolution of its own authorizing the Governor to call out the state militia. Although the Senate's version was quickly accepted by the House, President Andrew Jackson had already issued orders to send two companies of the 1st regiment of the U.S., Cavalry stationed at Fort McHenry to proceed to the canal. Arriving via the Baltimore & Ohio Railroad, the federal force remained along the line of the waterway for several months.[107]

The presence of the feral troops triggered a lively debate among the officers of the canal company. John Eaton, the newly-elected company president, urged that the company to take advantage of the situation and discharge the trouble makers.[108]

This recommendation however was rejected by the directors because there was continual shortage of laborers and the likelihood that such an attempt would produce more violence.

Hostilities occurred briefly during February 1835 near Galloway's Mill. This time the workers on Sections Nos. 166 and 170–172 struck for higher wages and they made attempts to prevent all the laborers along the line from working. After a riot erupted, a "troop of horse, and company of riflemen" was dispatched from Hagerstown and "reduced the rioters to order and drove them away." The altercation, which had delayed the completion of the four sections by some fifteen days, so disgusted the editors of the Hagerstown Torchlight that they concluded their

---

[105] Niles' Register, XLV (February 8, 1834), 399. A copy of the treaty may be seen in Appendix A.
[106] Williams, History of Washington County, I, 224.
[107] Niles' Register, XLV (February 1, 1834), 382–383 Washington National Intelligences, January 30, 1834; and Williams, History of Washington County I, 224–225. According to Carl Wittke in his The Irish in America, 36, this was the first time that "President Jackson called out federal troops "in" a labor dispute."
[108] Eaton to Janney, Smith, and Gunton, January 31, 1834, Ltrs. Recd., C&O Co.

report by stating: "To refuse such persons employment is the surest way to check a riotous spirit."[1]

The company again attempted to eliminate drunkenness along the line in the summer of 1835 by placing provisions in the contracts for the work between Dams Nos. 5 and 6 prohibiting the contractors form giving liquor to the workers. As the "sickly" season approached, however, the board temporarily suspended the prohibition at the request of John Gorman, the contract for Sections Nos. 247–248 and Culvert No. 190. The prohibition was to be dispensed with for the duration of the "sickly" season in those cases where a contractor obtained a certificate from a reputable physician that the use of spirituous liquors was necessary to the health of his hands.[110]

The construction of the canal above Dam No. 5 was marred by recurring strike and clashes among the workers. In January 1836, violence flared between the Corkonians and the Longfords near Clear Spring. Two shanties were burned and several men were severely wounded in the encounter. It was said that the rival camps feared each other so much that they posed guards at night "with as much vigilance as would two threatening armies." In reporting the incident, the Hagerstown *Torchlight* urged the public authorities to "keep a close eye upon them (Irish), or much blood may yet be shed before spring, when their attention to their work will keep them from committing acts of violence on each other." The newspaper concluded its remarks by saying that "Thus are the ancient feuds of these foreign disturbing the peace of the country, and making life insecure."[111]

In 1836 violence occurred for the first time during the working months. The cause of these later disturbances appears to have been primarily economic. The faltering national economy as a result of the Jacksonian economic policies was beginning to produce widespread unemployment and consequently lower wages. Competition for the available jobs and for higher wages for found expression in the driving off of rivals and the creation of a scarcity of labor. Disturbances occurred all along the line, but the principal outbreak took place in April at Sections Nos. 229–230 about one mile below Lock No. 51. Here G.M. and R.W. Watkins had a large (under paid) force "principally of Dutch and country borns." These laborers were attacked by a party of Irish and beaten and dispersed with such ferocity that the contractors still had been unable to collect a work force ten months later.[112]

Lee Montgomery, the tunnel contractor, was better able to keep his men on the job and maintain order among them. The canal commissioner explained this as follows:

> Our Methodist parson-contractor upon being asked how he escaped, replied that his men were generally picked men, and had provided themselves, he believed, with some guns and few Little Sticks, and it was supposed they would use them rather than be intruded on, the rioters thought it best not to stop as they were passing by—The truth is that in a good cause few men would probably use a "Little Stick" more effectively than himself, although he would pay at the same time against being obliged to "hold them uneasy."[113]

The unrest continued throughout the summer and into the fall. Several of the contractors as well as some non-striking workmen were threatened. Beatings, vandalism, and other forms of physical violence were the common methods of punishment to those who defied the "desperadoes." Canal

---

[109] Hagerstown Torchlight quoted in Niles' Register, XLVII (February 21, 1835), 429, and Proceedings of the Proceedings of the President and Board of Directors, D, 234, 256–257.
[110] Proceedings of the President and Board of Directors, D, 403.
[111] Hagerstown Torchlight quoted in Niles' Register, XLIX (January 16, 1836), 337.
[112] [citation missing]
[113] Bender to Ingle, May 8, 1836, quoted in Sandelin, Great National Project, 119.

officials attributed the disturbances to the activities of a secret terrorist society from New York with branches in many states—probably an early labor union or Irish fraternal organization. As evidence of this charge was a placard that company men had taken from the door of a shanty near the tunnel. So great was the fear of those punished that none dared testify against their tormentors. While work on the canal gradually slowed because of the rising incidence of mob rule, the directors began to gather evidence for submission to the Governor of Maryland.[114]

When work resumed on the canal in March 1837, the directors determined to relive the labor shortage for recruiting workers from the depression-ridden cities of the Northeast. Accordingly, Superintendent of Masonry Alexander B. McFarland was authorized to journey to Philadelphia and New York to induce hands to come to the canal. However, remembering their past difficulties with contract labor and uncertain of how the national economic downturn would affect the finances of the canal company, the director instructed him "not to bind the Company to the payment of any money to men who may come on to the work, nor as security for the payment of wages." The following month when Chief Engineer Charles B. Fisk requested permission to employ an agent in New York City to send hands to the line of the canal, the board refused to act other than to make arrangements for such an agent "if it should hereafter be found necessary to appoint one."[115]

The economic plight of the nation forced the suspension of many internal improvement projects during 1837. The resulting layoffs of large numbers of workers made it easier for the Chesapeake & Ohio, which was continuing its sporadic construction operations with the aid of loans from the State of Maryland, to recruit additional laborers. Yet despite the influx of new workers, it was reported that the level of wages on the canal rose to $1.18 ¾ and $1.20 a day.[116]

Because of its own financial difficulties the company in late 1837 suspended construction above the Cacapon River (except for the heaviest sections and the masonry) and concentrated its operations on completing the waterway below that point. This curtailment in activities raised fears among company officials that they would lose some of the workers who had been employed above the Cacapon to the James River and the Kanawha Canal in Virginia. As these laborers, some of whom had come well-recommended from Philadelphia and New York, would be needed when additional funds were available to resume full-scale construction, Superintendent of Masonry McFarland urged Chief Engineer Fisk to consider some inducements to keep these reputable workers on the line. Since ten of them had the finances to engage in contracts, steps were taken to offer them contracts for the construction of the remaining culvers below the Cacapon.[117]

New outbreaks of rioting occurred in 1837 and 1838 among the Irish workers. In May and June 1837, the Paw Paw Tunnel was the site of disturbances, which were repeated in February and June of 1838. Here Parson Montgomery was working with his picked crew, augmented by laborers imported from England to increasing his force and to resist the strikers. Notwithstanding the efforts of the contracts the Irish succeeded in getting control of the work and bringing operations to a halt by commencing a "reign of terror." After surveying the situation in early June 1838, Engineer Ellwood Morris reported to Chief Engineer Fisk:

> Some scoundrels on Montgomery's Job (tunnel) whose names I cannot discover have taken up (recently) the plan of hammering all new comers. On the night of the 8th, 2 very

---

[114] Bender to Washington, November 17, 1836, Ltrs. Recd., C&O Co., and Proceedings of the President and Board of Directors, E, 172.
[115] Proceedings of the President and Board of Directors, E, 215, 244.
[116] Fisk to Bender, August 3, 1837, Ltrs. Sent, Chief Engineer, and Ninth Annual Report (1837), C&O Co., 9–10.
[117] McFarland to Fisk, December 7, 1837, Ltrs. Recd., Chief Engineer.

> steady & excellent miners who had been expressly written for by Montgomery & who had not been one week on the work, were assailed at midnight as they ascended from the lower workings (they being on the night shift) & on stepping from the bucket were knocked down & beaten with clubs.
>
> One of them the doctor told me yesterday had his thigh badly fractured. The other is very badly bruised.
>
> The attacking force, I learn form inquiring were 20 to 40 in number armed with shillelaghs.
>
> On the night of the 9th, some others of the shaft workmen were beaten & on Sunday last there was a mob fight in Athys Hollow.[118]

Four days later on June 14, Morris informed Fisk of the increasingly dangerous situation at Paw Paw Tunnel. On further examination he had found

> that the miner (Richardson) who was beaten at the shafts and had his thigh broken, is a boss, & what may appear singular on this work, he is started to have been a faithful one.
> There is every reason to believe from a variety of indirect information which I have become possessed of, that there is a regular conspiracy, embracing nearly all the men at the Tunnel; which has for its object to make time & get wages, without furnishing the usual equivalent in labor. Succeeding in this they seem to contemplate preserving so desirable a state of things to themselves, by either preventing the coming or instantly driving off, every man disposed to do a days work as well as every boss who seems inclined to exact it.
>
> To attain this end they will doubtless take life itself if their brutal beatings should fail.
>
> One of the best bosses now on the work (Williams) who is driving the bottoming, has received a solemn warning that he must decamp or take the usual consequences, this man has been disposed to do Montgomery justice; but he now stands in this position—he must either decamp, risk his life, or resort to the alternative which seems so well understood on this work....
>
> I find that of the 40 men who came over with Evans but 2 are left on the work, the rest have been driven away in part by their own interests in part by flogging & in part by threatening, but the two last are the chief causes....[119]

Again the company was partly to blame for its own misfortunes, for it had refused to press the cases against several of the trouble makers at the tunnel after they had been arrested for pulling down shanties in broad daylight. The other workers gained the impression that the company was unwilling to bear the expense of the trial and punishment of the terrorists.[120]

There were other disorders along the line of the canal in 1838, the most notable occurring at Oldtown on New Year's Day and at Prather's Neck in May. The fracas at Oldtown occurred when a large party of men working at the tunnel raided the village and nearly destroyed a tavern owned by Nicholas Ryan. Reacting quickly, Sheriff Thomas Dowden summoned the Cumberland Guards and other citizens to serve as a posse, but when they arrived at Oldtown the Irish had already left. Several ringleaders were arrested and jailed to see what effect that action would have on the others. Apparently it made little impression in the face of the continued uneasiness among

---

[118] Morris to Fisk, June 10, 1838, Ltrs. Recd., Chief Engineer.
[119] Ibid, June 14, 1838, Ltrs. Recd., Chief Engineer.
[120] Fisk to Bender, May 15, 1838, Ltrs. Recd., Commissioner.

the workers. They resorted to burning shanties in order to bring pressure to bear on contractors and to drive away German laborers and newcomers to the line whose presence threatened to reduce the jobs of the Irish and thus force down wages. As the troubles continued, a company of riflemen was organized in Cumberland, and the Governor of Maryland sent to the city 189 muskets and 120 rifles to arm the militia.[121]

In May 1838 violence occurred at Prather's Neck where the laborers "insisted" upon destroying the work they had done, since they were to receive no pay for it.[122]

The trouble was caused by the fact that David Lyles, the contractor for Sections Nos. 205-206, was engaged in a controversy with the company over the completion of his contract and, meanwhile, had refused to pay the wages of the laborers working on these sections. The company had made partial payment of the laborers' wages from $4,000 of money that had been withheld from Lyles' for the performance of his contract but refused to do more.[123]

Faced with the destruction of their works, the company asked the local militia to protect canal property, but the directors were embarrassed by the reluctance of the citizenry to turn out. The latter pointed out that both the state and the company had refused to pay their expenses last time. Besides many of them were convinced the company was partly to blame for withholding large sums from the contractors in such critical times.[124]

Some of the members of the local militia "positively refused to turn out while some went" so far as to declare, that if they did they would "fight for the Irish."[125]

Nevertheless, after the company promised to pay all the expenses, two companies of militia from Hagerstown and one from Smithsburg marched to the line, seized 140 kegs of gunpowder from the relatively quiet workers, and returned them to Hagerstown where they were stored on the courthouse lot in the center of town. Militia officers described the workers and their families as being "in suffering and deplorable condition" but determined to prevent work from being done until they were paid.[126]

They rejected an offer of 25 cents on the dollar and held fast to their positions. The local inhabitants assured them that they were in the right and supplied them with provisions on credit.[127]

Throughout the spring of 1838, there were repeated occurrences of work slowdown along the line of the canal, confirming in the minds [?] of the directors that there was a general conspiracy afloat. It was reported by Assistant Engineer Henry M. Dungan that

> It is of little use to blow the horn either in the mornings or after meals, as the men take their own time to come out on the work & I really do not think it would be safe for me to attempt to urge them to their duty....

---

[121] Fisk to Washington, February 5, 1838, Ltrs., Sent, Chief Engineer, and Will H. Lowdermil History of Cumberland (Washington, 1878), 342.
[122] Williams, History of Washington County, I, 233.
[123] Proceedings of the President and Board of Directors, E, 397-398, 400-404, 408-409, and Ingle to Fisk, May 9, 1838, Ltrs. Sent, C&O Co.
[124] Price to Washington, May 11, 1838, and Williams to Washington, May 16, 1838, Ltrs. Recd., C&O Co.
[125] Williams to Washington, May 16, 1838, Ltrs. Recd., C&O Co.
[126] Williams to Washington, May 17 and 18, 1833 Ltrs. Recd., C&O Co. On December 19, 1838, the directors authorized the payment of $231.99 to the militia of Washington County for their services in quieting the disorders of Prather's Neck in May. At the same time, they authorized the payment of $42.62 to the militia for their services in 1837. Proceedings of the President and Board of Directors, E, 52.
[127] Fisk to Ingle, May 19, 1838; Fillebrown to Ingle, May 19, 1838; and Williams to Washington May 24, 1838; Ltrs Recd., C&O Co.

A contractor wrote that his men had "flogged off one of his best bosses if not the very best." The only reason he could ascertain for the beating was that the boss had "endeavored to get there to work as men usually do."[128]

Prompted by a report submitted by Fisk in which he blamed much of the escalating cost of building the canal to the continuing labor disorders, the board finally took the long delayed steps to curb the violence and remove the troublemakers in the summer of 1838.[129]

A renewal of strife at the tunnel provided the opportunity for a series of decisive actions by the directors. Upon the recommendation of Montgomery and the concurrence of Fisk, the board on June 28 issued the following order:

> Whereas from representations made to the Board, that the laborers at the tunnel are in such a state of disorganization and insubordination that the work cannot be conducted without ruinous consequences to the Contractor; it is therefore ordered that the Contractor be and he is hereby authorized to discharge immediately all the hands now employed at the work on the tunnel, and to suspend said work until the further orders of the Board.[130]

In addition, the directors took steps toward the dismissal and black-listing of troublesome workers all along the line.[131]

On July 18, the directors formally resolved

> that the President of this company be and he is hereby authorized to direct the discharge of all disorderly men employed on the line of the Canal, and to forbid their employment hereafter, and to enable him to carry said order into effect, he is authorized to draw upon the Commissioner for the amount of wages due and necessary to be paid to the men so discharged which amount shall be charged to the contractors respectively, and that he be authorized to make the arrangements requisite to insure the application of the money for the object indicated.[132]

Accordingly on August 1, some 130 men were discharged and blacklisted, most from the Oldtown Deepcut and the Paw Paw Tunnel.[133]

Violence along the line of the canal subsided until October 30. On that day John Burbridge, who lived near the canal in the vicinity of Evitts Creek, was nearly beaten to death by a party of Irish workers. Two companies of militia under Captain King and Haller proceeded to the

---

[128] Morris to Fisk, June 16, 1838, Ltrs. Recd., Chief Engineer.
[129] The portion of Fisk's report that deals with the relationship of the escalating cost of building the canal and the labor disorders on the line may be seen in Appendix B. The report had been submitted to the Committee of Ways and Means of the Maryland House of Delegates in February 5, 1838, but it was also included as part of the company's annual report in June 1838. Tenth Annual report (1838), C&O Co., 27.
[130] Montgomery to Fisk, June 23, 1838, and Washington to Montgomery, June 28, 1838, Ltrs. Recd., Chief Engineer.
[131] Nisbet to Randolph, July 7, 1838, and Anonymous to Fisk, September 8, 1838, Ltrs. Recd., Chief Engineer.
[132] Proceedings of the President and Board of Directors, E, 466.
[133] Notice signed by C.B. Fisk, dated Chief Engineer's Office August 1, 1838, Ltrs. Recd., Chief Engineer. The blacklist, which came into general use in the United States after the Panic of 1837, was used as a weapon by employers to keep active labor organizers or those sympathetic to trade unionism from employment. Richard O. Boyer and Herbert M. Morris, *Labor's Untold Story* (3d. ed., New York, 1975)

canal where the men were working and arrested thirty suspects. The laborers were taken to the Cumberland jail for the hearing.[134]

There were no more incidents of violence among the 2,500 to 3,000 laborers on the canal until August and September 1839. At that time rioting broke out near Little Orleans, between Hancock and Cumberland. Determined to exterminate the Dutch whose general determination is to learn the line, "a large band of Irish attacked a group of Dutch workers on Section No. 281 on August 11:

> At an early hour on Sunday morning 11 inst. ninety one men from Watkins and the adjoining sections, while all the men on Section No. 281 were rapt in sleep attacked each shantee, and as the inmates attempted to escape were met by his armed band of outlawed desperadoes. Several succeeded in making their escape by swimming the river, & one while in the water was shot at twice, the last ball lodging in his arm.
> They also carried off whatever they could find of value by examining the men's trunks after forcing the locks. The property taken away was in cash one hundred and ten dollars, also three pistols, one gun and articles of clothing. Their intention was also to attack the Dutch on Sec. No. 280 but the day being too far advanced that was deferred.

Altogether there were 14 German casualties the most severe being a laborer almost beaten to death and one who was almost roasted alive. Most of the remaining Dutch workers on the line fled to Virginia fearing to return "not knowing at what hour they may be attacked."[135]

The unrest occasioned by the violence affected the surrounding countryside. The lives and property of citizens and contracts were "so utterly at the mercy of the ruffian that not one of the people within their ranks was willing to give information or even to be seen communicating with the troops." Furthermore, there were reports that a "regular organization among the laborers was forming." It was reported that the Irish possessed about "50 stand of arms" and that recently they had procured "50 large duck guns from Baltimore." There were also reports that numerous copies "of printed passwords and counters had been found," thereby fueling speculation that a large conspiracy was developing.[136]

Two days after the attack near Little Orleans the militia of Washington and Allegany Counties was called out to suppress the violence. A force of some 80 men moved from Cumberland under the command of Colonel Thruston and arrived at Little Orleans where they found "all laborers at work, without any suspicion of his approach." Thruston "captured all the men on the section, picked out such as could be identified as rioters, disarmed them all, destroyed the arms, and moved up the line. As they proceeded, the militiamen searched for concealed arms and pursued those that fled. Some ten men were shot and severely wounded. Those who attempted to escape across the Potomac were fired upon by the Cumberland Riflemen as they swam and as they clambered up the banks on the opposite shore, and there were reports of several casualties. Joined by several companies of cavalry, Thruston's increased force of 150 men proceeded to destroy some 50 shanties and shops, to burn 60 barrels of whiskey, to capture 120 guns and pistols, and to arrest 26 prominent leaders who were taken to the Cumberland jail. About $700 worth of firearms that were purchased for the rioter were intercepted by the troops. The militia was actively engaged for five days during which the soldiers marched 81 miles. The Baltimore Sun appeared to represent the vies of most valley residents when it observed that the "proceedings of the

---

[134] Lowdermilk, *History of Cumberland*, 344.
[135] Coote to Fisk, August 12, 1839 Ltrs. Recd., Chief Engineer; *Niles' Register*, LVII (September 1839), 37; and Eleventh Annual Report (1839), C&O Co., p ( )
[136] *Niles' Register*, LVII (September 14, 1839), 37.

troops seem harsh, but are not so viewed by those whose situation has made them acquainted with past acts of violence, and the immanency of future danger."[137]

Seeking to capitalize on the growing resentment of the local populace toward the lawlessness of the Irish, the company determined to prosecute those in the Cumberland jail to the full extent of the law. In well-publicized cases that extended from October 13 to 29, all but two of the Irish were convicted. One of the key prosecution witnesses was Thomas Conley, who had served temporarily since August as a Superintendent of Sections and may have played the dual role of labor spy. Those found guilty received fines and prison terms in the state penitentiary ranging from one to eighteen years.[138]

In the wake of violence, agent of the Chesapeake & Ohio and the Baltimore & Ohio agreed in October to take united action to regulate the rate of wages and preserve order among the workmen in the Potomac Valley. According to the terms of the agreement, the resident engineers on both lines would collect the names of men discharged by the contractors on a monthly basis. A general blacklist would be compiled from these lists and from 150 to 300 copies would be distributed to each contractor and resident engineer on the canal and railroad. In this way it was hoped that all troublesome workers would be driven out of the valley.[139]

Throughout the fall working season, both canal and railroad officials worked hard to implement the agreement, and the results were on the whole satisfactory.[140]

Nevertheless, the Irish workers were not ready to admit defeat. A large party formed between Hancock and Little Orleans, and it was reported that this band possessed 500 stands of arms. Sometime during October, a shipment of 500 additional duck guns arrived from Baltimore to reinforce the large cache of weapons that the Irish held. As news of the gun-running operations spread through Washington and Allegany Counties, there was general alarm and widespread fear. On October 14, a number of the contract petitioned the board to exert pressure on the Governor of Maryland to station a military force along the line of the canal to preserve peace among the workmen and to protect the waterway from destruction.[141]

A recurrence of the riot at Little Orleans on November 9 brought harsh retaliation similar to that of the preceding summer. This militia was summoned as quickly as possible, and three companies were soon on the scene—the Cumberland Riflemen under General Thruston, the Clear Spring Cavalry under Major Barnes, and the Smithsburg Company under Captain Hollings. Many of the rioters were arrested and their arms taken from them, thereby restoring order and ending the threat of armed rebellion.[142]

The drastic actions of the militia are the protests of some local residents who had not participated in the riots but whose property was destroyed. Apparently, the property of some innocent individuals was damaged when they refused, out of fear of reprisals by the Irish marauders, to cooperate with the militia in their search for the ringleaders and the hidden caches of weapons

---

[137] Ibid, and *Baltimore Sun*, September 4, 1833

[138] Lowdermilk, *History of Cumberland*, 344 and Byers to Fisk, November 12, 1839, Ltrs Recd., Chief Engineer. The canal company used an early form of labor spy in suppressing labor outbreaks among the workers in 1839. James Finney received $100 for his "services". Proceedings of the President and Board of Directors, F, 405. Labor spies did not come into general use until the 1870s and the 1880s when strikes in the burgeoning American industries made the hiring of such individuals big business. Soyer and Morais, Labor's Untold Story, 50

[139] Latrobe to Fisk, October 5, 1839, Ltrs. Recd., Chief Engineer.

[140] Byers to Fisk, November 8, 1839, and Patterson to Fisk, November 14, 1839, Ltrs. Recd., Chief Engineer.

[141] Williams, *History of Washington County*, I, 233, and Proceedings of the President and Board of Directors, F, 113.

[142] Williams, *History of Washington County*, 233.

of the rioters. Accordingly, a local man named McLaughlin, brought suit in the U.S. Circuit Court at Baltimore against Thruston, Hollingsworth, and Charles B. Fisk, chief engineer on the canal. After a lengthy trial, the defendants were found guilty of exceeding their authority and acting illegally. A judgment of $2,337—was rendered against them, and, after the state legislature refused to pay the sum, the canal company agreed to reimburse the men for the bill.[143]

There were no further outbreaks of violence on the canal after November 1839. The end of large-scale disorders was due in part to the harsh retaliatory tactics of the militia and the use of blacklists and labor spying by the canal company. Moreover, the worsening state of the nation economy weakened the workers' ability to resist.[144]

Construction on the canal continued sporadically from the fall of 1839 until the spring of 1842 when the faltering finances of the company finally brought all operations on the waterway to a halt. As the company faced the dismal prospect of curtailing its operations, canal officials increasingly blamed the escalating cost of labor as one of the leading causes of increasing the cost of construction above the original estimate. In August 1839, the General Committee of the Stockholders reported that:

> The actual cost of common labor to contractors during the last year had been $1.37½ per diem, including the usual allowances. Add a fair profit to the contractor, and we have the daily cost to the company $1.50. Until within the last 3 ½ years, it did not exceed $1.[145]

The following year in June the board made the same point in its annual report to the company stockholders:

> Whilst the first 107½ miles of the Chesapeake & Ohio Canal was being constructed, the average price of labor was less than ninety cents per day, and the total cost of that whole work, extending from the basin at Georgetown to dam No. 5 was $4,776,118. The Canal Company have already expended, since prices appreciated, on the 76½ miles west of dam No. 5 $4,162,000. And would have had to expend but for the depreciation of labor and produce to complete the same $2,152,663–$6,314,663. Making a difference of $1,538,545 in the cost of 76½ over and above the cost of 107½ of Canal.[146]

---

[143] Ibid, and Proceedings of the President and Board of Directors, F, 410–411.
[144] Walter S. Sanderlin, *A Study of the History of the Potomac River Valley* (Washington, 1952), 74.
[145] Report of the General Committee of the Stockholders of the Chesapeake & Ohio Canal Company (Washington, 1839), 30.
[146] Twelfth Annual Report (1840), C&O Co., 4. Although building operations were somewhat curtailed, there were still 1,902 workers on the line in May 1840. Ibid, 7.

III. A TIME OF RELATIVE CALM: 1847–1850

When work on the canal resumed November 1847 under a contract with Hunter Harris & Co., many of the old labor problems returned to hinder construction. Sickness and the scarcity of workers appear to have been the major problems facing the company in this period. President James M. Coale reported to the stockholders in June 1849 that:

> We are constrained to say, that during the year 1848, the force employed on the line was not as large as was desirable, although urgent appeals were made for its increase. It is true, that, for a part of the time, severe sickness prevailed among the laborers, and it was difficult to procure additional hands or even to retain those employed; but we think, that in the Spring months, and in the Fall after the frosts had produced a return of a healthy atmosphere, a larger force, than the one engaged, might reasonably have been expected.[147]

In spite of these distractions, however, the force employed on the line increased to 1,447 men and 594 horses, mules, and oxen in May 1849.[148]

Throughout the year 1849, the lack of sufficient labor force continued to hamper construction. This problem was the result of two ever-present difficulties—the financial troubles of the contractors and to attract workers to the Potomac Valley. By the end of the "sickly" season in late September, the number of workers had been reduced by more than one-half. It was estimated that 146 masons, 46 bricklayers, and 971 laborers were needed to complete the canal by December according to the term of the contract with Hunter, Harris & Co. However, there were only 60 masons, 18 bricklayers, and 458 laborers at work on the line. Furthermore, there were not enough quarrymen to keep the 60 masons working much longer. Of the 55 carpenters that it was estimated were needed, there were only a handful at work.[149]

While there were no reported outbreaks of violence on the canal during the last years of construction, the company took an increasingly hard line against those workers who were performing poorly. There were several instances in 1849 when the company discharged "poor quality" laborers. In October three such men were fired—Francis Crawford, a mason at Culvert No. 211, Patrick Connelly, a brick sorter at the tunnel, and Enos Belt, a boss at Locks Nos. 62, 63 1/3, 64 2/3, and 66.[150]

The following month, four workers, who had been part of a large group of men recruited in New York to make bricks at Paw Paw Tunnel, were removed from the payroll. The four workers—Patrick Lully, a packer [?], and George Brice, John Glassgow, and James Lynch all brick-

---

[147] Twenty-First Annual Report (1849), C&O Co., 5, and Fisk to Trustees, March 29, 1848, Ltrs. Recd. Chief Engineer.

[148] Twenty-First Annual Report (1849), 6–7. The number of men and work animals on the line was broken down into the following categories: 77 bosses, 39 blacksmiths, 54 carpenters, 75 drillers and blasters, 107 quarrymen, 59 stonecutters, 73 masons, 112 mason's tenders, 6 brick molders, 50 others engaged in making bricks, 16 bricklayers, 19 bricklayer's tenders, and 760 laborers. In addition, there were 233 drivers, 562 horses, 26 mules, and 6 oxen. The transportation vehicles and machinery in use was categorized as follows: 285 carts, 20 scoops, 13 ploughs, 11 two-horse wagons, 3 three-horse wagons, 28 four-horse wagons, 1 six-horse wagon, 5 one-horse railroad cars, 14 two-horse railroad cars, 10 three-horse railroad cars, 14 drags, 4 brick-molding machines, and numerous cranes. Fisk to President and Directors, June 2, 1849, in Twenty-First Annual Report (1849), Appendix A, 24.

[149] Fisk to Trustees, October 8, 1849, Ltrs. Recd., C&O Co.

[150] Dungan to Fisk, October 16, 1849, Ltrs. Recd., Chief Engineer.

layers—were said to be the work of a poor contingent of men at the tunnel. Hence they were singled out to serve as examples for the rest of the workers at Paw Paw.[151]

In March 1850, the financial difficulty of Hunter, Harris & Co. came to a head when they were unable to pay the workers on the line. There was suspension of work for several days, and the restless laborers threatened violence as they had been unpaid for some time. Nathan Hale, one of the agents and attorneys of the contractors, proceeded immediately to Cumberland and the other points along the line where the workers were gathering and succeeded in making arrangements with them for their wages. The laborers resumed operations, and Hunter, Harris & Co. assigned their contract to their trustees, the aforementioned Hale, John Davis and Horatio Allen, for the completion of the work.[152]

When work on the canal resumed under the new financial arrangement, the company faced a critical labor shortage. In early June, President Coale informed the company stockholders:

> The force at present employed on the line of the work, consists of 37 Bosses, 7 Blacksmiths, 70 Carpenters, 22 Quarrymen, 10 Stone-cutters, 20 Masons, 33 Mason Tenders, and 414 laborers, making the aggregate of all classes 613 men.
> There are also 104 Drivers and 215 Horses, together with the requisite carts, wagons, &c., for such numbers. The Chief Engineer is of opinion that it will be necessary for the contracts and assignees to increase the above mentioned force about fifty per cent, to enable them to complete the Canal for the admission of the water from Cumberland to Dam No. 6 by the first of July, and that with the present force it may be done by the middle of that month.[153]

During the summer of 1850, the final disruption of construction occurred. On July 18, the director negotiated a new contract with Michael Byrne, one of the major contractors in Frederick County who had constructed a number of works on the canal, and work was soon resumed. Construction proceeded without incident until the formal opening of the canal on October 10, 1850.[154]

At the inaugural ceremonies at Cumberland on that date, one of the two long speeches of welcome and eulogy was given by William Price, a citizen of Cumberland who had long been associated with the company. In his remarks, he reminded his listeners of the difficulties that had attended the construction of the waterway and of the sacrifices of those who had built it. His summary of the trials experienced by those who had constructed the canal is perhaps the most enduring epitaph ever uttered on their behalf:

> Many of us were young when this great work was commenced, and we have lived to see its completion, only because Providence has prolonged our lives until our heads are gray. During this interval of four and twenty years, we have looked with eager anxiety to the progress of the work up the valley of the Potomac. That progress has been slow—often interrupted and full of vicissitudes. At times the spectacle of thousands of busy workmen has animated the line of the work, when, to al human calculation, no cause was likely to intervene to prevent its early completion. But when we have turned to look at the scene again, it was all changed; contractors and laborers had departed and the stillness of deso-

---

[151] Dungan to Fisk, November 24 and 28, 1849, and McFarland to Fisk, November 27, 1849, Ltrs. Recd., Chief Engineer.
[152] Twenty-Second Annual Report (1850), C&O Co. 6–7
[153] Ibid, 4.
[154] Report to the Stockholders on the Completion of the Chesapeake & Ohio Canal to Cumberland (Frederick, 1851), 110–111.

lation reigned in their place. Thousands have been ruined by their connection with the work, and but few in this region have had cause to bless it.

Go view those magnificent aqueducts, locks and culverts, of hewn stone—those huge embankments, on which you may journey for days down the river; go view the great tunnel passing three fifths of a mile through rock, and arched with brick, its eastern portal opening upon a thorough-cut almost equal in magnitude to the tunnel itself. Look at the vessels lying in the basin, ready to commence the work of transportation, and large enough to navigate the Atlantic,—look at all these things, and then think how soon the fortunes of individuals embarked in the prosecution of such an enterprise would be swallowed up, leaving upon it but little more impression than the bubbles which now float upon its waters. It will not be deemed out of place, if I here express the hope that those whose losses have been gains of the company, should not in the hour of its prosperity be forgotten.[155]

---

[155] Cumberland Civilian, quoted in Report on the Completion of the Chesapeake & Ohio Canal, 130–131.

EPILOGUE

THE RELATIONSHIP OF THE IMPORTATION OF FOREIGN IMMIGRANTS TO BUILD THE CHESAPEAKE & OHIO CANAL AND THE RISE OF POLITICAL NATIVISM IN MARYLAND: 1829-1862.

The influx of foreign immigrants into the State of Maryland to provide a cheap pool of labor for the construction of its internal improvements projects had a profound impact on the social, religious, and political institutions of its people. This was particularly true of the largely Roman Catholic Irish workers who began to immigrate to the state in 1829-1830 to work on the Chesapeake & Ohio Canal and the Baltimore & Ohio Railroad. Despite an early colonial history of religious toleration and a continuing high proportion of Catholics in the population, Maryland proved to be no more immune to religious and national prejudice than any other state during the three decades of the ante-bellum period. Prompted by the accelerated immigration of the Irish and Germans after 1845, nativism—best defined as "intense opposition to an internal minority on grounds of its foreign connections"[156]—erupted into a political movement in the New England, mid-Atlantic, and Border States during the 1850s. Maryland, where the nativist tradition had been a latent force since the 1830s when the first waves of immigrants had arrived, emerged in the mid-1850s as one of the leading states in the political nativist movement[157]

As the earliest election successes of the nativist movement in Maryland occurred in the Potomac Valley towns of Hagerstown and Cumberland in 1854, it can be conjectured that the importation of foreigners by the canal company to build its works served as one of the earliest and most important episodes in the long chain of events that led to the formation of a political nativist movement in the state.[158]

The source of discontent which led to the formation of a political force, commonly known as the Know-Nothings but officially named the American Party, were related to the ultra-conservative sentiments of a nation caught up in the sweeping institutional changes of the ante-bellum period.[159]

The sources of discontent in Maryland were similar to those of the country as a whole. Native Marylanders despaired of the influx of foreigners particularly as the state was caught up in the accelerated rush of Irish and German immigrants who came to America in the late 1840s and early 1850s in response to famine and political unrest in their homelands. During these years, the foreign-born population of Maryland increased from 7 percent in 1840 to 12 percent in 1850, and the numbers kept climbing until 77,529 foreign-born persons lived in the state in 1860, comprising 15 percent of the total white population.[160]

The problem of the immigrants went beyond their numbers to the unwillingness of many of them to assimilate quickly, the political and economic radicalism of some of their leaders' the ease with which political machines often engineered them into voting in blocks, and the competition they presented to the American labor market. Distrust of the immigrants was closely linked to fear of Roman Catholicism the principal question in Maryland on this point being the loyalty or patriotism of the Catholics since they owed allegiance to the foreign hierarchy through their church. Distraught over the moral and social climate of the urban, industrial society that they saw

---

[156] John Higham, *Strangers in the Land* (New Brunswick, 1955), 4.
[157] Mary St. Patrick McConville, *Political Nativism in the State of Maryland* (Washington 1928), is the best reference to Maryland nativism prior to 1850.
[158] Lawrence Frederick Schmeckebier, *History of the Know-Nothing Party in Maryland* (Baltimore, 1899), 17.
[159] Richard Walsh and William Lloyd Fox, *Maryland A History, 1632-1974* (Baltimore, 1974), 304-305.
[160] William J. Evitts, *A Matter of Allegiances: Maryland from 1850 to 1861* (Baltimore, 1974), 68.

emerging around them, many old-line Americans blamed the sudden increase in crime pauperism, insanity, and drunkenness on the new immigrants. Perhaps, the greatest concern of the Know-Nothings was for the preservation of the Union as founded by the revolutionary generation. By returning to the "simpler politics" and the "purer precepts" of the Founding Fathers, the nation could overcome its social breakdown and political malaise.[161]

"Heed the warnings of Washington, Jefferson, Madison, Jackson," said the Hagerstown Herald and Torch, "and...inscribe the soul-stirring motto upon the Star-Spangled Banner— Americans shall Rule America."[162]

They hoped to cleanse politics of its demagoguery and corruption by extending the period of naturalization and electing qualified, statesmen like candidates to office.[163]

Traces of anti-Irish sentiments in Maryland and particularly in the Potomac Valley were manifested almost as soon as the first Irish workers arrived in mid-1829 [?] to work on the canal. The attitudes of some canal company officials undoubtedly represented the feelings of some of the valley residents. One of the overseers who was sent out with a boatload of immigrants to America referred to them as "clowns," "brutes," and "frauds."[164]

Clerk John P. Ingle described the newly-arrived immigrants as "plagues."[165]

Anti-Irish sentiment in Maryland and particularly in the Potomac Valley was very much on the mind of the English woman Francis Milton Trollope after she visited the line of the canal in the summer of 1830. Although she had had doubts that emigration to American would improve the living standards of e Irish, it was not until her examination of the squalid living conditions of the Irish on the line of the canal that she "became fully aware how little it was to be desired for them." During her stay in America she found "a strong feeling against the Irish in every part of the Union." Moreover, she "heard vehement complaints, and constantly met the same in the newspapers" of a practice "stated to be very generally adopted in Britain of sending out cargoes of parish paupers to the United States." These sentiments were particularly pronounced in Maryland newspapers. One such article told "of a cargo of aged paupers just arrived from England," with the remark "John Bull has squeezed the orange, and now insolent casts the skin in our faces." Such a feeling she declared, demonstrated "that these unfortunates are not likely to meet much kindness or sympathy in sickness, or in suffering of any kind." Stating that all—inquiries into the matter had failed to substantiate the newspaper charges, she observed:

> All I could ascertain was, that many English and Irish poor arrived yearly in the United States, with no other resources than what their labour furnished...It is generally acknowledge that the suffering among our labouring classes arises from the excess of our population; and it is impossible to see such a country as Canada, is extent, its fertility, its fine climate, and know that it is British ground, without feeling equal sorrow and astonishment that it is not made the means of relief.[166]

Mrs. Trollope was particularly incensed by the emerging anti-Irish customs already emerging in the Potomac Valley. An example of such a practice in Hagerstown and other communities was the "suspension," on the eve of St. Patrick's Day, in some conspicuous place, of a dummy figure, popularly denominated a 'Paddy' with the view of annoying the Irish residents of the town and

---

[161] Ibid, 67–80.
[162] Quoted in Walsh and Fox, *Maryland: A History*, 30.
[163] Bernard C. Steiner, Citizenship and Suffrage in Maryland (Baltimore, 1895), 29–47.
[164] Gill to President and Directors, November 18, 1839, Ltrs. Rec., C&O Co.
[165] Ingle to Janney, October 26, 1829, Ltrs. Sent, C&O Co.
[166] Mooney, ed., *Domestic Manners of the Americans*, 229–231.

vicinity. On numerous occasions, this practice provoked serious disturbances, but it continued to be condoned by the civil authorities.[167]

The arrival of large numbers of immigrants, particularly the Catholic Irish [....?] beliefs, disturbed the social tranquility of the Potomac Valley which up to this time had been characterized by its largely agricultural pursuits and its predominantly Protestant German and Scotch Irish community.[168]

The presence of large numbers of persons in crowded and filthy temporary quarters brought increasing health problems to the valley. During the major cholera epidemics of 1832 and 1833, fears that the sickness would spread from the workers to the local inhabitants led to town ordinances, such as those in Hagerstown, which prevented the stricken workers form entering the town limit for medical treatment and which permitted Catholic Irish workers who died to be buried only in cemeteries along the canal and away from inhabited areas.[169]

In addition, the existence of so many rough and tumble, unassimilated laborers in a limited area raised the question of the maintenance of law and order. Drunken brawls accompanying all night drinking bouts alarmed the valley.[170]

The clashes between the Irish factions in the winter months of 1834, 1835, and 1836 terrified citizens in the neighborhood form Williamsport to Clear Spring.[171]

The rising nativist sentiment in the valley could be seen in the Hagerstown Torch Light comments on the January 1836 riot near Clear Spring:

> The public authorities should keep a close eye upon them (the Irish), or much blood may yet be shed before spring, when their attention to their work will keep them from committing acts of violence on each other. Thus are the ancient feuds of these foreigners, disturbing the peace o the country, and making life insecure.[172]

The later disputes between the workers and the canal company in 1837, 1838, and 1839, at Paw Paw Tunnel, Old Town, and Little Orleans intensified the growing anti-foreign feeling in the valley by bringing the local inhabitants of the area into the difficult positions of militia, arbiters, and innocent victims.[173]

Nativist sentiment in Maryland erupted into a "Native American" party in Baltimore in 1844 and 1845.[174]

However, after receiving only 9 percent of the vote in Baltimore city elections in 1845, nativism left politics and went underground. Between 1845 and 1852 the nativism faith throughout the state was kept alive by fraternal orders carrying names like the United Sons of America, the Order of United Americans, and the Union of American Mechanics. Because their lodges were secret societies, no accurate estimate of their strength exists. By the early 1850s, however, these societies were certainly well attended.[175]

---

[167] John Thomas Scharf, *History of Western Maryland* (2 vols., Philadelphia, 1882), II, 1067.
[168] Sanderlin, *A Study of the History of the Potomac River Valley*, 89.
[169] Purcell to Eaton, June 24, 1833, and Stewart to Ingle, July 10, 1833, Ltrs. Recd., C&O Co.
[170] Cruger to President and Directors, July 7, 1832,—Ltrs. Recd., C&O Co., and Lowdermilk, *History of Cumberland*, 342.
[171] Williams, *History of Washington County*, I, 223–224; Niles' Register, XLV (January 25, 1834, and February 1, 1834), 336, 382–383; ibid, XLVII (January 16, 1836), 337.
[172] Hagerstown Torch Light, quoted in *Niles' Register* XLIX (January 16, 1836), 337.
[173] Price to Washington, May 11, 1838; Williams to Washington, May 16, 17, 18, 1838; Fisk to Ingle, May 19, 1838; and Fillebrown to Ingle, May 19, 1839; Ltrs. Recd., C&O Co.
[174] Benjamin Tuska, *Know-Nothingism in Baltimore*, 1854–1860 (New York, 1930), 2.
[175] Evitts, *Matter of Allegiances*, 64.

By 1853 the nativist societies had reversed their policy, as their numbers and influence warranted a more active pursuit of their principles. Their interest in politics was accentuated during this period by the statewide controversy over the Kerney School Bill, which would have provided public funds for parochial schools and the visit of the Papal legate Bedini to the United States and Baltimore.[176]

At first, the various Maryland nativist societies merged into one large body called the Order of the Star Spangled Banner or, more commonly, the Know-Nothing Order.[177]

Order retained secrecy, and members swore oaths to protect the American nation and the ideals it stood for from all subversion. In August 1853 the Order staged its first public demonstration in an effort to influence the House of Delegates election in Baltimore. Then in the spring of 1854, the Order scored its first political victories in the municipal elections of the western Maryland communities of Hagerstown and Cumberland. In both elections, all the candidates which the Order had secretly endorsed were swept into office.[178]

By fall 1854 the Know-Nothing movement had gained considerable momentum throughout Maryland. In Baltimore Samuel Hinks, the nativist candidate was elected by a margin of 2,744 votes, and the American Party also elected fourteen members to the upper chamber and eight to the lower chamber, thus gaining control over the city council.[179]

In the following year Americans added to their successes by expanding their political base to include victories in Annapolis and Williamsport.[180]

In the wake of the Whig Party's demise and with these nativist successes in Maryland and other victories in such states as Massachusetts and Delaware, the Americans threatened to become the second major national party. When the party's national council met in Philadelphia in 1855, it threw off the mantle of secrecy which had surrounded its activities and drew up a public platform of principles which stressed unionism, nationalism, and political reform. Among the planks in the platform were calls for: (1) a revision of state and national laws regulating immigration and the settlement of foreigners; (2) laws prohibiting the immigration of felons and paupers: (3) the repeal of laws allowing un-naturalized foreigners to vote or own land; (4) an end to corrupt political bossism, particularly as it related to the efforts to get the foreign minorities to vote as a block, and (5) resistance to the aggressive and corrupt policies of the Roman Catholic Church.[181]

By 1855 the emerging Know-Nothing movement had great appeal to the Protestant middle class in Maryland, and for its leadership it began to draw heavily on the upper-middle class business community. The organization was ready to make its assault on the state offices, and it did very well in the fall elections of 1855. Hinks won re-election as mayor in Baltimore by over 3,700 votes and the Americans retained control of the upper chamber of the city council. In November Know-Nothing William Purcell won the comptrollership; carrying twelve of Maryland's

---

[176] Schmeckebier, *History of the Know-Nothing Party in Maryland*, 15–17.

[177] Walsh and Fox, *Maryland: A History*, 311. Some nativists also temporarily cooperated with the Maine Law temperance movement, which was a political force advocating a state prohibition law similar to that passed by the State of Maine. The temperance movement also had nativist overtones, as it was basically a reaction by the old-line Marylanders of the corrupting influence of the temperance movement, which had built a program in Maryland by 1853, was the product of anti-saloon agitation which had begun in the 1830s shortly after the first waves of Irish began to immigrate to the state.

[178] Schmeckebier, *History of the Know-Nothing Party in Maryland*, 17.

[179] John Thomas Scharf, *History of Maryland from the Earliest Period to the Present Day* (3 Vols., Baltimore, 1879), III, 2.

[180] Walsh and Fox, *Maryland: A history*, 312.

[181] John Denig, *The Know-Nothing Manual* (Harrisburg, 1855), 1–64.

twenty-one counties plus Baltimore. The nativists elected one-half of the commissioners of Public works and filled all three available judgeships. Know-Nothing Daniel McPhail won the state lottery commissioner's job. Of the six Maryland Congressmen elected, four were Know-Nothings, one was an independent Whig, and one was an independent Democrat. Henry W. Hoffman, the American candidate from the Fifth Congressional District, won handily with a 749 majority, his most concentrated support coming particularly from Frederick and Washington Counties. Led by a sweep of Baltimore then House of Delegates seats, the Know-Nothings gained a 54 to 17 advantage over the Democrats in the lower chamber, while the makeup of the eleven State Senators elected consisted of 8 Know-Nothings, 2 Democrats, and 1 Whig. The know-Nothings had come a long way since their first cautious entry into politics two years earlier by capturing 51 percent of the state's vote.[182]

The Western Maryland counties played a significant role in the election of the American candidates to the state office in 1855. While Montgomery and Allegany Counties did not give the majority of their votes to Know-Nothing candidates, the total Know-Nothing vote in those two jurisdictions was nevertheless 49.6 and 49.1 percent respectively. On the other hand, Washington and Frederick Counties were in the Know-Nothing column giving 50.8 to 55.8 percent of their vote respectively to American candidates.[183]

With a series of brilliant successes in the 1855 elections, Maryland Know-Nothings looked optimistically towards the 1856 presidential election. However, schism over slavery and defections within the party's ranks over the issue fatally sapped the movement's strength on the national level. The only state that the American standard-bearer Millard Fillmore carried in that year was Maryland. Gaining more votes in the state than the Americans had in 1855, Fillmore won 55 percent of the electorate and carried fifteen of the twenty-one counties plus Baltimore. In Western Maryland, he carried Montgomery County (51.8%), Frederick County (53%) and Washington County (50.4%), losing only Allegany County (46.3%).[184]

Although the national American Party's demise quickly came the following year, it temporarily remained a viable political coalition in Maryland. After a spirited campaign, the American Thomas Hicks was elected governor in November 1857, getting 54.9 percent of the state vote. The Know-Nothings carried the other state offices, elected four Congressmen out of six, and continued their control of the state legislature. Yet the 1857 election marked the first obvious defect from the party, and the losses were nowhere more noticeable than in western Maryland. All four of the western counties gave a lesser percentage of the vote to Hicks than they had to Fillmore. Montgomery County's support dropped from 51.8 to 48 percent, Frederick from 53 to 51.3 percent, Washington from 50.4 to 50.2 percent, and Allegany from 46.3 to 43.6 percent. The American candidate, Henry W. Hoffman, who had won handily in 1855, now was defeated by the Democrat, Col. Jacob Kumkel, by 168 votes. These trends, coupled with a collapse national organization, were ominous signs for the American in Maryland.[185]

---

[182] Evitts, *Matter of Allegiances*, 80–88
[183] Thomas J.C. Williams, History of Frederick County, Maryland (Baltimore, 1910), 287–297; ibid, History of Washington County, 274–275; James Walter Thomas and Thomas J.C. Williams, History of Alleghany County, Maryland (Cumberland, 1923), 258; and Lowdermilk, *History of Cumberland* 383–385.
[184] Evitts, *Matter of Allegiances*, 100–101. In municipal elections in Baltimore in September, the American Thomas Swann was elected as mayor, and of the Know-Nothings won control of the lower chamber of the city council while splitting the upper chamber evenly with the Democrats.
[185] Walsh and Fox, *Maryland: A History*, 319–326, and Evitts, *Matter of Allegiances*, 106–107. The year 1859 also marked the election to Congress of Alexander Robinson Boteler, a member of an old-line Virginia family in Shepherdstown, Virginia. Active in the Whig Party during the late 1840s and early 1850s, he joined the American Party in the middle of the latter decade. He represented the Harpers Ferry District

While the Americans attempted to straddle the slavery issue, the Democrats, as the champions of Southern rights benefited from the growing sectional cleavage and especially from the widespread fear produced by John Brown's Raid on Harpers Ferry. In the 1859 elections, they nearly swept up all the state offices. In addition, they carried three of six congressional seats (including Western Maryland Fifth District), and won control of the House of Delegates, 45 to 29, and the Senate, 12 to 10. Only the comptrollership was kept in American hands, but that victory was achieved by a violence-studded campaign that produced a 12, 783—vote majority in Baltimore. By the following year as events were leading inexorably toward civil war, the Know-Nothings were in total eclipse in the state, particularly after a crushing defeat in the Baltimore mayoralty race.[186]

---

in Congress under the American Party label from 1857 until Virginia seceded from the Union in the spring of 1861, at which time he accepted appointment to the Confederate Provisional Congress in Montgomery, Alabama. Misc. Mss., Scrapbook I, Alexander Robinson Boteler Papers, Duke University Library and Ezra J. Warner And W. Buck Yearns, Biographical Register of the Confederate Congress (Baton Rouge, 1975), 25–26.

[186] Schmeckebier, *History of the Know-Nothing Party in Maryland*, 99–115.

APPENDIX A

The following is a copy of the treaty of peace made and concluded at Williamsport, on the 27th day of January, 1834, between the Corkonians and Longford men, the two contending parties of the Chesapeake & Ohio Canal laborers.

Whereas great commotions and divers riotous acts have resulted from certain misunderstandings and alleged grievances, mutually urged by two parties of laborers and mechanics, engaged on the line of the Chesapeake & Ohio Canal, and natives of Ireland; the one commonly known as the Longford men, the other as the Corkonians; and whereas it has been found that these riotous acts are calculated to disturb the public peace, without being in the least degree beneficial to the parties opposed to each other, but on the contrary are production of great injury and distress to the workmen and their families.

Therefore, we, the undersigned, representatives of each party, have agreed to, and do pledge ourselves to support and carry into effect the following terms of the agreement:

We agree, for ourselves, that we will not, either individually or collectively, interrupt or suffer to be interrupted in our presence, any person engaged on the line of the canal for or on account of a local difference or national prejudice, and that we will use our influence to destroy all these matters of difference growing out of this distinction of parties, known as Corkonians and Longfords; and we further agree and pledge ourselves in the most solemn manner, to inform on and bring to justice, any person or persons who may break the pledge contained in this agreement, either by interrupting any person passing along or near the line of the canal, or by secretly counseling or assisting any person or persons who may endeavor to excite riotous conduct among the above parties; and we further bind ourselves to the State of Maryland, each in the sum of twenty dollars, to keep the peace towards the citizens of the state. In witness thereof, we have hereunto signed our names, at Williamsport, this twenty-seventh day of January, eighteen hundred and thirty-four.

Timothy Kelly	Michael Tracy
William O'Brien	Thomas Mackey
Michael Collins	James Riley
John Bernes	Daniel Murrey
Thomas Bennett	Murty Dempsey
Michael Driscoll	James Carroll
Jeremiah Donovan	Thomas Cunningham
John Namack	Bathu S. McDade
Garret Donahue	James Clarke
Patrick McDonald	Michael Kain
James Slaman	Pat Purell
John O'Brien	William Moloney
Edward Farrell	Wm. Brown
Thomas Hill	Peter Conner

Signed before us, two justices of the peace, in and for Washington County and the State of Maryland this 27th day of January, 1834

Charles Heseltine
William Boullt[1]

---

[1] Excerpted from *Niles' Register*, XLV (February 8, 1834), 399.

APPENDIX B

REPORT OF CHARLES B. FISK, FEBRUARY 5, 1838, REGARDING THE RELATIONSHIP BETWEEN LABOR DISORDERS AND COST OF THE CANAL

In this connection, I will briefly allude to a very important cause of the great cost of work on our canal; one that has no reference to change of times, or the cost of provisions. I know not that a more appropriate occasion than this can be selected for the purpose, inasmuch as the influence of this cause, to which I am about to refer, has been more severely felt on the "7 ½ miles" than hitherto, and will continue to be felt, perhaps, in a still greater degree in our progress towards Cumberland, unless legislative action shall be efficiently exerted to prevent it.

Not one individual of the large body of Irish laborers along the line of the canal dares testify against another of their number in a court of justice. A murder may be committed—a hundred of them may witness it—and yet not one person can be found who knows anything about it. The remark upon all this, by the citizens of the State, is very apt to be, that these men do not interfere with the inhabitants; that their quarrels are among themselves, or between the two parties into which they are divided. Grant, for the moment, that their quarrels are among themselves. Who feel the consequences? The company, and, as a stockholder, the State. Let me mention a few facts. I have known a contractor on the "27 ½ miles" forced to give up his contract, his shanties burned, and death threatened, if he could be caught, simply because the engineer, as he had a right to do under the contract, had discharged from the line some notoriously worthless and disorderly men; and the contractor was suspected of having given information to the engineer.

Again: at the time of our greatest pressure for mechanics, several excellent masons, perfect strangers to all on the line, were induced to go up to the neighborhood of Hancock. They worked for one day, but were given to understand that they must not remain. They, in consequence, immediately returned to Washington.

Such are not solitary and rare occurrences. Many, and many, and many an instance have I known, in which quiet, peaceable, orderly, and well-disposed persons, from among the Irish laborers have been driven off from our canal, by their countrymen, simply from unwillingness to submit to the dictation of a tyrannical, secret, party organization, which, for the last two years, has been entirely beyond the read of all law, all authority.

True it is, these persons elsewhere have their quarrels and disputes among themselves; but they have rarely, as has been the case with us, been permitted to act with that organization as a body, that enables them to control the operations of a whole work.

The consequences of such a state of things will at once suggest themselves to everyone who reflects on the subject. Mechanics out of employ elsewhere often refuse to come upon our work for no other reason, than that the laws of the State afford them no protection when upon it. Other works, in other states, where the laws are respected, have a comparatively quiet and orderly body of laborers; the worthless leave them, and congregate, of course, where they will be least subject to the restraints of law.

But it is not the case, as admitted for the moment, that the quarrels of these persons are confined to themselves. I have known instances in which native citizens, laboring upon the "27 ½ miles" of canal, have been driven away from it, and repeatedly have German laborers been forced to quit the line.

This state of things, alone, I know has been very instrumental in keeping up the high prices of labor upon our canal. Its effects are felt in several ways. It keeps down the supply of labor below the demand. It gives us an inferior class of workmen. And afraid to give them directions contrary to their will, the contractor is sometimes, to all intents and purposes, under their control.

Notwithstanding all this, there are upon our canal many well-disposed and quiet laborers. Yet, although they may even be a majority in point of numbers, they are still under the control of that secret organization of which I have spoken. To these well-disposed persons I feel that I shall do a service, if by any means I can be instrumental, in the least, in inducing an action, by the competent authority that shall enforce quiet and good order upon our work. It is practicable; and recent movements on the part of the authorities of Washington and Allegany counties show that they have a willingness and disposition to give their aid. I will refer to a late occurrence.

Having been regardless of all civil authority on the "27 ½ miles" of the canal, along the narrow territory of the State of Maryland (at one point less than two miles in width), the idea at last became prevalent among the laborers, that in the mountains of Allegany County no force, in support of the laws of the State, could be brought to bear upon them. They conducted themselves accordingly. At length, upon the occurrence of an outrage, or rather of several—tearing down buildings and threatening lives, in one day, at Oldtown, in presence of many of the inhabitants, by upwards of four hundred men, who had come more than twelve miles for the purpose. The sheriff of the county, with a military force from Cumberland and other parts of the county, together with citizens from Virginia, assembled, arrested ten of the ringleaders, and have them now in jail awaiting their trial. The effect of this movement by the authorities of Allegany county, so far as we can judge in the short time that has since elapsed has been and will be of great service, and has satisfied me, in addition to previous observations, that provision be made by the Legislature that shall cause the laws of the State to be respected; and if so, one of the great difficulties we have to encounter for the last two years, in obtaining a sufficiency of laborers, will be done away. There will be a great improvement in the character of the line; and, as a necessary consequence, we shall do our work at less cost. So firmly convinced am I of good effect of the recent exercise of civil authority in Allegany county, that I have little doubt, should, unfortunately, our present embarrassments end in a total suspension of our work, we shall have much less to fear than we otherwise would have from the laborers who will be thrown out of employ. Indeed, had this authority not been exercised, I do not believe we should have escaped thus long from acts of violence on the part of the laborers, from want of confidence caused by the inability of the company, for the last two months, promptly to meet its engagements.

If the work should be entirely suspended, it can hardly be supposed that 3,000 laborers will quietly disperse—suddenly thrown out of employment, with money due to them, and many of them without the means of taking them elsewhere—especially little accustomed as they are to the restraints of law.[2]

---

[2] Excerpted from Tenth Annual Report (1838), C&O Co., 27-29

HISTORIC RESOURCE STUDY
CHESAPEAKE & OHIO CANAL NHP

4.
STONE QUARRIES AND MILLS ASSOCIATED WITH THE CONSTRUCTION OF THE C & O CANAL

BY HARLAN D. UNRAU
HISTORIAN, C&O CANAL RESTORATION TEAM, SENECA
DENVER SERVICE CENTER
1976

CONTENTS

I.	**STONE QUARRIES**		157
	A.	U.S. BOARD OF ENGINEERS SURVEY: 1824–1826	157
	B.	GEDDES AND ROBERTS SURVEY: 1827	157
	C.	STONE QUARRIES USED TO BUILD CANAL STRUCTURES	158
II.	**MILLS**		164
	A.	STONE CUTTING MILLS:	164
		SENECA RED SANDSTONE QUARRIES AND THE SENECA STONE MILL	164
	B.	CEMENT MILLS:	165
		1. POTOMAC MILL, SHEPHERDSTOWN	165
		2. TUSCARORA MILL	167
		3. HOOKS MILL	168
		4. SHAFER'S CEMENT MILL—ROUND TOP CEMENT COMPANY	169
		5. LEOPARD'S MILL	170
		6. LYNN MILL, CUMBERLAND	170
		7. IMPORTED CEMENT FROM NEW YORK AND ENGLAND	172
	C.	SAW MILLS:	173
		GREAT FALLS SAWMILL, MATILDAVILLE	173
	D.	BRICK KILNS:	174
		PAW PAW TUNNEL BRICK MAKING	174

I. STONE QUARRIES

A. U. S. BOARD OF ENGINEERS SURVEY: 1824–1826

When the U.S. Board of Engineers made their examination of the proposed route for the Chesapeake & Ohio Canal, they made a cursory survey of the surrounding lands to locate building materials. While their efforts to find building stone were negligible, they indicated that "along the whole line of the canal, good building stone will be easily procured." On the eastern section from Cumberland to Hancock, the banks of the Potomac were "formed of a variety of rocks, chiefly sandstone, schists, slates." On the Virginia side between these two towns, limestone was "found above the mouth of the South Branch." From Hancock down to Georgetown, the banks of the river presented "masses of limestone, sandstone and slate rocks." Although there was an abundant quantity of good building stone, the engineers reported that in some cases the stone would have to be transported to construction sites that were a distance away from the quarries, because there were some stretches along the route that contained almost no stone. The means of transportation would vary according to local circumstances. Among the modes of transportation they envisioned were boating, land carriage and inclined planes.

Concerning hydraulic lime, the engineers reported that lime abounded from Hancock to Great Falls, but it was "of a doubtful quality." In fact, it was their opinion that there was "very little hope" of finding "water lime of any kind" from Georgetown to Pittsburgh. Accordingly, they recommended the importation of the best hydraulic lime available. Considering the importance of the durability of the work, they urged, "that the distance of transportation and the expense attending it, ought not, in this case, to be taken too much into consideration."[1]

B. GEDDES AND ROBERTS SURVEY: 1827

During their survey of the canal route between Cumberland and tidewater in 1827, the two civil engineers, Geddes and Roberts, noted the location of the principal sources of available building materials along the line of the waterway. While they did not make an exhaustive survey of these sources, they did point out where the best stone quarries could be found and where there was lime for hydraulic mortar.

On the route between Cumberland and South Branch, Geddes and Roberts found that "stone for building locks, and for culverts and other necessary purposes, is very good, and found, generally, convenient to each place where it may be wanted." However, good cutting stone suitable for lock sills, hollow quoins, and face work was not so abundant. Lime and other materials for the locks could be obtained at reasonable prices in Cumberland. A cement mill some 4 ½ miles from the Potomac produced lime at a cost of 10 cents per barrel and delivered it for 2 ½ cents per bushel.

The engineers made very little comment on the availability of good building stone on the portion of the waterway between South Branch and Licking Creek. The only such references made were that there was an abundance of limestone about one-third mile above the mouth of the Cacapon River and about four miles west of Hancock. At the latter point, there were lime kilns producing water cement.

From Licking Creek to Conococheague Creek, the engineers observed that the "locks and other stone work can be built very reasonably" because "lime and stone, and other materials, are

---

[1] U.S., Congress, House, *Message from the President of the United States, Transmitting a Report from the Secretary of War with that of the Board of Engineers for Internal Improvement, Concerning the Proposed Chesapeake & Ohio Canal*, Exec. Doc. 10, 19th Cong., 2nd sess., 1826, 26–28.

in abundance, and convenient." Among the best locations of prospective limestone quarries were those about one mile west of North Mountain, near Charles Mill, and about three miles west of Williamsport.

Between Conococheague and Antietam Creeks, the engineers reported that there was a large quantity of good building limestone near Galoway's Mill and just below Shepherdstown. Over the distance from Antietam Creek to the Monocacy River, the engineers apparently found no prospective sources for building materials for none were reported.

Passing down the Monocacy River, Geddes and Roberts noted that there was a large quantity of limestone some four miles east of its mouth. Within another mile, there was a marble quarry where stone for the columns of the U. S. Capitol was obtained. Just above the mouth of Seneca Creek was the Seneca Red Sandstone Quarries, which had been in operation for more than 50 years. Some four miles below Great Falls was a stone quarry that would be of use to the canal. About one mile above the head of the old locks on the Little Falls Skirting Canal, there was a granite quarry.[2]

C. STONE QUARRIES USED TO BUILD CANAL STRUCTURES

During the period of construction, numerous stone quarries were opened throughout the Potomac Valley for the masonry works on the canal. In some cases, the quarries were already in existence prior to 1828. An effort has been made in this section to list the various quarries from which stone was obtained to build the individual masonry structures.

1. Tidelock and Locks Nos. 1–4: These five structures were built of Aquia Creek freestone. The backing of the walls of the tidelock, as well as that of Locks Nos. 1–4, was composed of granite, probably boated down the river from a quarry one-half mile from Lock No. 7.[3]
2. Georgetown Stone Bridges: The five stone bridges carrying streets across the canal in Georgetown were built of Aquia Creek freestone.[4]
3. Locks Nos. 5–6: The hammer dressed stone for the lower six feet of these two locks was obtained from a quarry less than one mile away. The cut stone, which comprised the rest of the locks, was from Aquia Creek.[5]
4. Lock No. 7: This lock was built of granite, except the coping, which was of Aquia Creek freestone. The granite was obtained from a quarry near Section No. 4 within one-eighth of a mile of the lock. This was the quarry referred to in the Geddes and Roberts report, indicating that it was in existence prior to the construction of the canal.[6]
5. Lock No. 8: This structure was built of Seneca Creek Red Sandstone, boated down the Potomac from the quarries just above the mouth of Seneca creek, some 14 ½ miles upstream.[7]
6. Lock No. 9: This lock was built of granite, except the coping, which was of Aquia Creek freestone and a few feet of ashlar, which were of Seneca Creek Red Sandstone. The granite,

---

[2] U.S., Congress, House, *Letter from the Secretary of War, Transmitting Estimates of the Cost of Making a Canal from Cumberland to Georgetown*, H. Doc. 192, 20th Cong., 1st sess., 1828, 15, 30, 46, 58, 64, 87, 94 and 99.
[3] *Report of Col. John J. Abert and Col. James Kearney, of the United States Topographical Engineers, Upon an Examination of the Chesapeake & Ohio Canal from Washington City to the "Point of Rocks"* (Washington, 1831), in U.S., Congress, House, Committee on Roads and Canal, *Chesapeake & Ohio Canal*, H. Rept. 414, 23rd Cong., 1st sess., 1834, 89–91; and Ibid, 158.
[4] *Abert and Kearney Report*, in *House Report 414*, 90–91.
[5] *House Report 414*, 158.
[6] Ibid, and Diary and Account Book, 1828–29, W. Robert Leckie Papers, Duke University Library.
[7] *House Report 414*, 158.

obtained from the quarry near Lock No. 7, was transported by wagon approximately 1¾ mile.[8]
7. Lock No. 10: This lock was built entirely of granite. Approximately one-half of the stone was obtained from the quarry near Lock No. 7, while the remaining portion was transported overland from a quarry four miles inland.[9]
8. Lock No. 11: The front ranges of this lock were Seneca Creek Red Sandstone, boated down the Potomac River some 14 miles. Its backing of rubble granite was probably obtained from the quarry near Lock No. 7.[10]
9. Lock No. 12: This lock was built entirely of granite obtained from the quarry near Lock No. 7. The stone was transported overland some 2 1/3 miles.[11]
10. Lock No. 13: This lock was built of granite from the country quarry referred to at Lock No. 10. The stone was transported overland some 4 1/3 miles. The coping and hollow quoins were of Seneca Creek Red Sandstone.[12]
11. Lock No. 14: This lock was built entirely of granite of which one-half was transported overland from the country quarry referred to at Lock No. 10 and the remainder was boated down the Potomac from a quarry near Great Falls some five miles upstream.[13]
12. Locks Nos. 15–20: These locks were all built of Seneca Creek Red Sandstone boated down the Potomac River some nine miles.[14]
13. Locks Nos. 21–24 and Guard Lock No. 2: These locks were all built of Seneca Creek Red Sandstone. The stone for Lock No. 21 was boated down the Potomac some 6 1/3 miles. The stone for Lock No. 22 was partially boated down the Potomac 3 ¼ miles. The stone for the other structures was hauled overland.[15]
14. Aqueduct No. 1: This aqueduct was built entirely of Seneca Creek Red Sandstone obtained from the nearby quarries some 200 yards away.[16]
15. Lock No. 25: This lock was built of Seneca Creek red sandstone and boated up the Potomac River some 8 ½ miles.[17]
16. Lock No. 26: This lock was built of Seneca Creek red sandstone boated up the Potomac some 16 2/3 miles and transported overland 1/3 mile.[18]
17. Lock No. 27: This lock was built primarily of red sandstone boated some five miles down the Potomac from a quarry near the river about 2 ½ miles below Point of Rocks. Stone for the coping was taken from Lee's quarry near Seneca. A few feet of ashlar were transported overland by railroad from the white granite quarry at Sugarloaf Mountain some 2½ miles away.[19]
18. Lock No. 28: One-seventh of the stone for this lock was brought 46 miles over the Baltimore & Ohio Railroad (at six cents per ton per mile) from the granite quarries on the Patapsco River near Ellicott City to Point of Rocks. From there, it was transported by wagon nearly

---

[8] *Ibid.*
[9] *Ibid.*
[10] *Abert and Kearney Report*, in *House Report 414*, 95; and *Ibid*, p.159.
[11] *House Report 414*, 159.
[12] *Ibid.*
[13] *Ibid.*
[14] *Ibid.*
[15] *Ibid.*
[16] *Abert and Kearney Report*, in *House Report 414*, 98–99.
[17] *House Report 414*, 159.
[18] *Ibid.*
[19] *Ibid.*

one mile to the lock. The remaining six-sevenths of the stone was transported in wagons from a quarry of hard white flint stone in Virginia, four miles distant.[20]

19. Aqueduct No. 2: This aqueduct was built of white granite obtained from the quarries on Sugarloaf Mountain less than three miles away. Having a dull white color, the stone split and hammered well, was fine grained, and considered to be very durable. A temporary railroad was constructed to the quarry.[21]

20. Lock No. 29: Two-thirds of the stone for this lock was obtained from the granite quarries on the Patapsco River near Ellicott City. The stone was transported over the Baltimore & Ohio Railroad to Point of Rocks from where it was taken by wagon some 2 2/3 miles to the lock. The remaining third of the face stone was obtained from the hard white flint stone quarry in Virginia referred to at Lock No. 28.[22]

21. Aqueduct No. 3: The face stone above the tops of the piers of this structure was obtained from the granite quarries on the Patapsco River near Ellicott City and transported 46 miles over the Baltimore & Ohio Railroad to Point of Rocks. From there, stone was taken by wagon to the aqueduct three miles distant. The masonry below the tops of the piers was of stone boated down the Potomac some seven miles from a quarry opposite Short Hill near Lock No. 31. This quarry was on the land of Casper Wever, a former employee of the federal government and the Baltimore & Ohio Railroad, who had purchased 500 acres on the site of what is now Weverton to establish a manufacturing town patterned after the plan of Lowell, Massachusetts.[23]

22. Lock No. 30: One-seventh of the stone for this lock was obtained from the granite quarries on the Patapsco River near Ellicott City and transported over the Baltimore & Ohio Railroad. One-seventh of the stone was found in various small quarries in the vicinity of the lock. The remaining five-sevenths of the stone was boated up the Potomac River some 32 ½ miles from the Seneca Creek red sandstone quarries.[24]

23. Lock No. 31: Stone for this lock was obtained from three sources. Some stone was obtained from the hard white flint stone quarry in Virginia referred to at Locks Nos. 28 and 29. Some stone was quarried within one-half mile of the lock on land owned by Casper Wever. The remaining stone was obtained from a granite quarry in Virginia. The latter was transported one mile overland and 1½ miles by water.[25]

24. Lock No. 32: One-fifth of the stone for this lock was obtained from the granite quarry in Virginia referred to at Lock No. 31. The transportation of this stone was by wagon for a distance of two miles, which included the crossing of the Shenandoah and Potomac Rivers. Four-fifths of the stone was obtained from different limestone quarries up the Potomac, varying in distance from two to 12 miles. The of the quarries that were most likely used were Knotts Quarry on the Virginia shore about 1/3 mile above Lock No. 37, a limestone quarry near the canal 1 ¾ mile below Lock No. 37, a quarry one-half mile from Lock No. 37 in Maryland, and a limestone quarry on the Virginia shore opposite Lock No. 38. The stone from these

---

[20] Ibid.
[21] Abert and Kearney Report, in House Report 414, 101–102.
[22] House Report 414I, 160.
[23] Report of Captain Wm. G. McNeill on the Condition of the Chesapeake & Ohio Canal, Dec. 1, 1833, in House Report 414, 149; John Thomas Scharf, A History of Western Maryland (3 Vols., Philadelphia, 1882), Vol. II, 1285;John R. Miele, The Chesapeake & Ohio Canal: A Physical History (NPS Mss., 1968), 133–135; Thomas F. Hahn, Towpath Guide to the Chesapeake & Ohio Canal, Section Two (York, 1972), 56–57; and Langley to Mercer, Oct. 28, 1828, Ltrs. Recd., C&O Co.
[24] House Report 414, 160.
[25] Ibid.

three quarries was boated down the river to Harpers Ferry and then taken by wagon the last mile to the lock.[26]
25. Lock No. 33: this lock was built mostly of granite from the Virginia quarry referred to at Locks Nos. 31 and 32. The stone was transported in wagons for a distance of 1½ miles, which included the crossing of the Shenandoah and Potomac Rivers. A small portion of the stone was from a quarry in Maryland one mile away.[27]
26. Lock No. 34: This lock was built of limestone from Knotts Quarry on the Virginia side of the Potomac River about 1/3 mile above Lock No. 37. The stone was boated down the river some five miles to Dam No. 3 and then wagoned about ¾ mile to the lock.[28]
27. Locks Nos. 35–36: These two locks were built of limestone from Knotts Quarry on the Virginia side of the Potomac about 1/3 mile above lock No. 37. The stone was boated down the river some five miles to the lock.[29]
28. Lock No. 37: This lock was built of limestone obtained from a quarry in Maryland about one-half mile away and transported by wagon to the site.[30]
29. Aqueduct No. 4: This aqueduct was built of limestone obtained from a quarry neat Antietam Village about ¾ of a mile distant. It is probable that the quarry was located on the Virginia side of the river.[31]
30. Lock No. 38: This lock was built of limestone obtained from a quarry directly opposite on the Virginia shore of the Potomac just below Shepherdstown.[32]
31. Lock No. 39: This lock was built of limestone obtained from a quarry in Virginia one mile distant. It could not be determined from the available records if this quarry was the same as that referred to at Lock No. 38.[33]
32. Lock No. 40: This lock was built of limestone obtained from a quarry about one-half mile distant.[34]
33. Dam No. 4, Guard Lock No. 4 and Locks Nos. 41–41: Available documentation does not indicate the precise location of the quarries from which stone was obtained for the rubble masonry of the Maryland abutment of the dam and guard lock or for the hammered masonry of the lock. Since these works are located in a heavy limestone area, it can be assumed that such stone was procured from nearby quarries or boated across the Potomac from quarries on Opequon Creek in Virginia.[35]
34. Lock No. 43: This lock was built of limestone from a quarry three miles distant on the Maryland side of the river. The stone was carried overland by wagon to the site.[36]
35. Lock No. 44 and Aqueduct No. 5: The lock and aqueduct were built of a "compact blue lime stone, of excellent quality, transported from almost exhaustless quarries within three miles" of the aqueduct. The quarry, then known as High Rock Quarry, was located 2 ½ miles west

---

[26] *Ibid,* and Thomas F. Hahn, *Towpath Guide to the Chesapeake & Ohio Canal, Section three* (York, 1972), 13, 16, and 28.
[27] *House Report 414*
[28] *Ibid.*
[29] *Ibid.*
[30] *Ibid.*
[31] *Report of McNeill,* in *House Report 414,* 149–150; and Purcell to president and Directors, Jun. 8, 1832, Ltrs. Recd., C&O Co.
[32] *House Report 414,* 161.
[33] *Ibid.*
[34] *Ibid.*
[35] *Ibid.*
[36] *Ibid.*

of the aqueduct on the berm side of the canal. Still in active operation, the quarry is now called Pinesburg Quarry.[37]
36. Dam No. 5, Guard Lock No. 5 and Locks Nos. 45–50: The dam abutments and the seven lock structures were built of Conococheague limestone obtained from a quarry within 200 feet of the pool behind the dam known as Prathers Neck quarry. The stone was taken by wagon to the individual construction sites, all of which were within two miles.[38]
37. Aqueduct No. 6: This aqueduct was built of Tonoloway gray limestone obtained from a quarry one-half mile north on the banks of Licking Creek. Stone for the sheeting was boated up the Potomac River some 7 ½ miles from the limestone quarry at Prathers Neck.[39]
38. Locks Nos. 51–52 and Aqueduct No. 7: These three structures were built of limestone obtained from Hart's Quarry on the Little Tonoloway "in the rear of Hancock" about two miles from the aqueduct. The stone was transported most of the distance over the Cumberland Road (National Road).[40]
39. Lock No. 53: This lock was built of sandstone taken from quarries about three miles distant and transported overland by wagon.[41]
40. Locks Nos. 54–55: These locks were constructed of limestone, portions of which were probably obtained from a Virginia quarry within one mile of Dam No. 6 and from Hart's Quarry on the Little Tonoloway near Hancock.[42]
41. Dam No. 6: The Virginia abutment of the dam was constructed of limestone from a Virginia quarry about one mile distant. The Maryland abutment was built of sandstone from several quarries in Maryland within the distance of one mile.[43]
42. Guard Lock No. 6: This lock was built of sandstone obtained from the Maryland quarries referred to at Dam No. 6.[44]
43. Lock No. 56: This lock was built of limestone, portions of which were obtained from the Virginia quarries about one mile from Dam No. 6 and from Hart's Quarry on the Little Tonoloway near Hancock.[45]
44. Aqueduct No. 8: The cut stone for the arch, the inside of the parapets, the coping, and the water table of the aqueduct were obtained from the limestone quarry in Virginia about one mile from Dam No. 6. The remainder of the stone was procured from several sandstone quarries a short distance across the Potomac on Sideling Hill Mountain.[46]
45. Lock No. 57: This lock was built of limestone obtained from a quarry in Virginia about one mile from Dam No. 6 and Hart's Quarry on the Little Tonoloway near Hancock.[47]
46. Aqueduct No. 9: This aqueduct was built chiefly of hard sandstone obtained from three quarries on Sideling Hill Mountain on the Virginia side of the Potomac, some 2 1/3 to 3 1/8 miles distant. The stone was hauled down to the river by wagon, boated across the Potomac to the "river road," and then carried overland for one mile by wagon.[48]

---

[37] *Ibid; Report of McNeill*, in *House Report 414*, 150–151; and Hahn, *Towpath Guide, Section Three*, 51, 54.
[38] Fisk to Board of Directors, June 16, 1835, Ltrs. Recd., C&O Co.
[39] *Ibid;* and Thomas F. Hahn, *Towpath Guide to the Chesapeake & Ohio Canal, Section Four* (York), 9
[40] *Report of the General Committee of the Stockholders of the Chesapeake & Ohio Canal Company* (Washington, 1839), 9; and Fisk to Board of Directors, June 16, 1835, Ltrs. Recd., C&O Co.
[41] *Report of the General Committee of the Stockholders*, 1839, 10.
[42] *Ibid*, 11–13.
[43] *Ibid*, 11.
[44] *Ibid*.
[45] *Ibid*, 12–13.
[46] *Ibid*, 13; and Harlan D. Unrau, *Single-Span Aqueducts, Historic Structures Report* (NPS Mss., 1974), 52, 54–55.
[47] *Ibid*.
[48] Byers to Fisk, Dec. 10, 1838, Ltrs Recd., Chief Engineer.

47. Locks Nos. 58–66: Stone for these composite locks was quarried in at least four different locations. The cut stone was quarried at Hart's Quarry on the Little Tonoloway near Hancock and boated up the Potomac over distances ranging between 19 ½ and 30 ½ miles. The remainder of the stone for the locks was quarried at (1) Twiggs Hollow just above Lock No. 61; (2) Purslane Mountain, about three miles from a point on the Virginia shore opposite Tunnel Hollow; and (3) Sideling Hill, some four miles from the mouth of Tunnel Hollow.[49]
48. Locks Nos. 67–68 and Aqueduct No. 10: These structures were built principally of limestone obtained from quarries on Town Hill on the Virginia side of the Potomac opposite the aqueduct, and from Hatch's Quarry at the mouth of South Branch.[50]
49. Locks Nos. 69–71: These three composite locks were built of limestone obtained from quarries on Warrior Mountain near the banks of the Potomac on the Virginia side of the river. Located just below and opposite to Oldtown, the quarries were about 1 ½ miles distant from Alum Hill.[51]
50. Locks Nos. 72–75 and Aqueduct No. 11: these five structures were built of limestone obtained principally from a quarry located some 1½ miles up Evitts Creek from the aqueduct. The stone was "a compact limestone, or rather marble, in some parts densely filled with marine shells." When polished, the limestone presented "a very interesting object" and was "admirably adapted for ornamental work." The limestone was brought from the quarry to the aqueduct by a temporary wooden railroad and was taken by wagon from the aqueduct to the four locks below, all of which were between five to six miles distant.[52]

---

[49] Lambie to Fisk, Feb. 28, 1839, Ltrs. Recd., Prin. Asst. Eng.; Fisk to President and Directors, May 27, 1839, Ltrs Sent, Chief Engineer; McFarland to Fisk, Sep. 11, 1839, Ltrs. Recd., Chief Engineer; and Fisk to Board of Directors, Sep. 25, 1839, Ltrs. Recd., C&O Co.

[50] McFarland to Bender, Jan. 2, 1836, Ltrs. Recd., Commissioner; and Morris to Fisk, Apr. 18, 1838, Ltrs. Recd., Chief Engineer.

[51] Purcell to Ingle, May 26, 1835, Ltrs. Recd., C&O Co.; Fisk to Sheriff of Hampshire County, Sep. 20, 1838, Ltrs. Sent, Chief Engineer; and McFarland to Fisk, Sep. 21, 1838, Ltrs. Recd., Chief Engineer.

[52] *Report of the General Committee of the Stockholders*, 1839, 19–20.

II. MILLS

A. STONE CUTTING MILLS

SENECA RED SANDSTONE QUARRIES AND THE SENECA STONE MILL

The Seneca Red Sandstone quarries, located on the high bluffs on the berm side of the canal turning basin just west of the mouth of Seneca Creek, were a widely used source of building stone from the late-eighteenth century until the mid-nineteenth century. This deposit, which underlies most of western Montgomery County, is Triassic Age and is part of a larger formation that runs erratically from Connecticut to the Carolinas. The stone, having a color that varied from a light reddish brown to a deep chocolate brown, was known in the building trade as "Seneca Red Stone."[53]

The texture of the Seneca Red Stone was exceptionally good. It was very fine grained and uniform and held up very well when exposed to the weather. One of its unique and valuable features was the ease with which it was carved and chiseled when it was first quarried. It was then quite soft and could be easily cut. Its fine and uniform texture made it very suitable for delicate carving. After exposure to the weather, the stone became hard, and as a result, remained well preserved over the years.[54]

The first use of Seneca Red Stone is not known, but it is known that it was used prior to the American Revolution.[55] The Seneca quarries supplied stone for the locks of the Potomac Company around Great Falls and for Aqueduct No. 1 and Locks Nos. 8, 9, 11, and 15–27 of the Chesapeake & Ohio Canal.[56] The stone was used in the construction of many houses and government buildings in Baltimore and Washington, among the most famous of which is the original Smithsonian Institution building on the Mall built in 1847.[57]

On the berm side of the canal turning basin just below the quarries was a stone mill that was built about 1837 to cut and dress the Seneca Red Stone for shipment by the Seneca Sandstone Company. Saws and polishers were powered by a water turbine fed by canal water diverted into a mill race. Gondolas pulled by mules and pushed by men carried the large stone blocks along narrow gauge rails to the mill. The large blocks were shaped by hammer and stone chisels before they were cut by tempered steel saws, six feet long, eight inches wide and 3/8 inch thick. An overhead pipe dripped water on the saws to keep the toothless blades cool. Progress was considered good if a saw cut one inch in a three-foot square block one foot thick per hour. For stone polishing, the cut stone was placed on a circular disk, which revolved from a belt attached to the water-driven shaft. Barriers around the disk kept the stone from being ejected by centrifugal force. By 1900,

---

[53] Department of Geology, Mines and Water Resources, State of Maryland, *Geography and Geology of Maryland* (Baltimore, 1957), 122; and Nancy Rosselli, Robert Rosselli, and Edwin F. Wesely, *Seneca Sandstone Biking Trail*, Sugarloaf Regional Trails, 1976.
[54] *Maryland Geological Survey* (Baltimore, 1906), Vol. VI, 186; and Miele, *Physical History*, 124–125.
[55] *Maryland Geological Survey*, 185.
[56] *Geology of Maryland*, 123; and *House Report 414*, 158–159.
[57] Miele, *Physical History*, 125.

the better quality Seneca Red Stone had been cut, the lower quality stone tending to flake and shatter.

As on of the major stone-cutting mills in the lower Potomac Valley, the mill cut red and gray sandstone boated from as far away as Goose Creek and Whites Ferry. In addition to the red sandstone used in the original Smithsonian building, stone cut at the Seneca mill was used in the construction of the old Congressional Library, the U. S. Capitol, and the Washington Monument.[58]

B. CEMENT MILLS

1. POTOMAC MILL, SHEPHERDSTOWN

As events were leading to the commencement of construction operations on the canal, Henry Boteler of Shepherdstown informed the waterway's chief supporter, Congressman Charles F. Mercer, in January 1828 that he had found large quantities of gray limestone that produced water lime near his flour mill on the banks of the Potomac some 240 yards upstream from Pack Horse Ford. The stone was visible on the surface of the ground as well as to a considerable depth below the surface. The hill where the stone had been found was some "200 feet high, and near half a mile around its base." The stone was easily accessible and could "be quarried with more facility than the common limestone."

Based on his experience, Boteler reported that he had prepared a mortar from the stone, which had hardened in water in a short time and had become "impervious." In preparing the stone for use, it required "only one-third of the time allotted to the burning of lime." Consequently, it needed "only a third of the wood necessary for calcining lime." He had found the stone to be harder than plaster of Paris, and, therefore, it could not be broken and ground to a powder as easily as gypsum. Accordingly, he was sending three specimens of the water lime, one in its natural state, one after burning, and one after calcining, together with "a small ball of the water lime, hardened to its present consistency in water, for a period of 48 hours."[59]

During the years 1828-29, Boteler and his associate, George F. Reynolds, were persuaded by canal company officials to convert a part of their prosperous flour mill to the manufacture of hydraulic cement.[60] By 1829, the flour mill was describe as "one of the finest manufacturing mills in America," producing 100 barrels of flour per day.

The mill was known as the Potomac Mill, later becoming the Potomac Cement Company.[61] The kiln, which Boteler and Reynolds built, was composed of 500 perches of stone and 26,000 bricks, and its total capacity was 1,625 bushels. Because the mill was able to grind about 2,000 bushels of lime per week, the canal company authorized the construction of a cement warehouse nearby to store the cement, until it was called for by the contractors.[62]

---

[58] Thomas F. Hahn, *Towpath Guide to the C&O Canal, Section Two* (York, 1971), 5-9.
[59] Boteler to Mercer, Jan 14 and 22, 1828, in U.S., Congress, House, Committee on Roads and Canals, *Chesapeake & Ohio Canal*, H. Rept. 141, 20th Cong. 1st sess., 1828, 38-39.
[60] *Proceedings of the President and Board of Directors*, A. 195-196; and Leckie to President and Directors, Mar. 9, 10, 29, 1829, Ltrs. Recd., C&O Co. Available documentation does not indicate the date of the construction of the flour mill. By 1829, the flour mill was described as "one of the finest manufacturing mills in America," producing 100 barrels of flour per day. Leckie to President and Directors, Mar. 10, 1829, Ltrs. Recd., C&O Co.
[61] Millard K. Bushong, *Historic Jefferson County* (Boyce, 1972), 4.
[62] *Proceedings of the President and Board of Directors*, A, 276; and Diary and Account Book, 1828-29, W. Robert Leckie Papers, Duke University Library.

Throughout the early period of construction, the company engineers experimented with the Shepherdstown lime and with limestone from other points in the Potomac Valley to find a high quality hydraulic mortar. More than 85 experiments were conducted with the Shepherdstown lime under the direction of Superintendent of Masonry Alexander B. McFarland for this purpose, using various hydrates, mixtures and burning times. Experiments were also made with limestone from Goose Creek, the Leesburg vicinity and Tuscarora Creek. It was finally determined during the spring of 1829 that the Shepherdstown cement was best because there would "be no danger whatever of its slaking or loosing its adhesion or bond."[63] In the course of their surveys, canal officials discovered a better grade blue lime some 500 feet from the kiln and adapted it for use on the waterway.[64] Accordingly, Boteler and Reynolds built two kilns near the blue stone deposit for its manufacture into lime.[65] By June 27, McFarland reported that one kiln was producing "extremely well" while the other was still being used for experimentation.[66]

By the summer of 1829, Boteler and Reynolds had their cement operations in full gear. On August 7th the canal company signed a contract purchasing 80,000 bushels of cement at 19 cents per bushel, the whole of which was to be delivered by May 15, 1830.[67]

Later in the fall, the company signed four separate contracts with Henry Strider, Joseph Hollman, Jacob Fouke and John Strider to transport the cement from Shepherdstown to the various construction sites below Seneca Creek at one-third cent per bushel per mile.[68] On January 28, 1830, a second contract was signed with Boteler and Reynolds to supply the line of the canal with 60,000 bushels of cement by September 1.[69] When work on the line above Point of Rocks began in 1832 following the resolution of the legal conflict with the Baltimore and Ohio Railroad, an agreement was made in May whereby Boteler and Reynolds would supply an unspecified quantity of cement to the contractors beyond the limits of the existing contracts at 20 cents per bushel.[70] The Potomac Mill was superseded by Shafer's Cement Mill at Round Top Hill as the principal supplier of cement to the canal company in the fall of 1838. By that time, it had provided more than 150,000 bushels of cement for use in the construction of the waterway at a cost of $32,909.42.[71]

The mill continued to play a significant role in the economic activity of the Shepherdstown vicinity. By 1861, it was owned by Alexander Boteler, a former Whig congressman who had recently been elected to serve in the Confederate Congress and who had recently entered the Confederate Army as an officer.[72] During the military activity that occurred in and around Shepherdstown in September 1861, Boteler's home as well as the mill and the bridge across the Poto-

---

[63] McFarland to Leckie, Mar. 31 and Apr. 18, 1829, Leckie Papers; and *Proceedings of the President and Board of Directors*, A, 184.

[64] Leckie to President and Directors, May 11, 1829, Ltrs. Recd., C&O Co.; and *Proceedings of the President and Board of Directors*, A, 195-196.

[65] Diary and Account Book, 1828-29, Leckie Papers. A diagram showing the location of the mill, the kilns and the lime supply was prepared on March 19, by Inspector of Masonry W. Robert Leckie.

[66] McFarland to President and Directors, Jun 27, 1829, Ltrs. Recd., C&O Co.

[67] *Contracts for Furnishing Hydraulic Cement*, Leckie Papers; and *Proceedings of the President and Board of Directors*, A, 320.

[68] *Contracts of Transporting Cement*, and *Contract [between] Chesapeake & Ohio Canal Company and Jacob Fouke, October 22, 1829*, Leckie Papers. Generally the canal company supplied the bags, boxes and boat covers for the cement, but the transporting contractors were allowed two cents per bushel if they supplied these items on their own.

[69] *Contracts for Furnishing Hydraulic Cement*, Leckie Papers.

[70] *Proceedings of the President and Board of Directors*, C, 140.

[71] Ledger A, C&O Co. 157-175. From November 1835 to June 1828, George F. Reynolds was the sole owner and operator of the Potomac Mill. *Ibid*, 157; and *Proceedings of the President and Board of Directors*, D, 407.

[72] Shepherdstown *Register*, July 16, 1914; and Aug. 21, 1924, in Scrapbook I, Alexander Robinson Boteler papers, Duke University.

mac, were destroyed by Federal troops. The mill was rebuilt after the Civil War and continued to operate until the end of the nineteenth century.[73]

Closely associated with the Potomac Mill was the dam, popularly called Boteler's Dam, across the Potomac that provided power for its operation. The impounded water formed a slackwater that occasioned the construction of a river lock to provide access to the canal from the river, thereby making it possible for the canal company to tap a lucrative Virginia trade. When the dam was destroyed, apparently by the 1889 flood, the slackwater was eliminated and the value of the river lock was negated. Its reason for existence gone, the lock was filled in and incorporated into the towpath bank of the canal prism.[74]

2.   TUSCARORA MILL

During the spring of 1829, Inspector of Masonry, W. Robert Leckie and his associate, James Alcott on New York, discovered a large quantity of stone "exactly like hydrate of lime about one-third of a mile" above the Tuscarora Mill on the creek of that name running through the estate of Charles Carroll of Carrollton in Frederick County.[75] Within a week, Leckie and Alcott were conducting experiments with the lime to test its binding qualities under water. Although the lime slaked in the early experiments, the two men continued making various mixtures until June when they made a cement that would set in water. Leckie was convinced that the Tuscarora Cement was equal to the blue hydrate of lime at Shepherdstown and was better than the general run of Parker Roman Cement.[76]

In June 1829, Leckie and Alcott agreed to take out a patent for the discovery and the manufacture of the hydraulic lime, the profits from its sale to be equally divided.[77] A draft of the letter that was sent to Secretary of State Martin Van Buren requesting the patent described the mineral content of the lime and the formula for preparing the cement. The letter read as follows:

> The mineral from which the cement is made is of several varieties and is an argillaceous ferruginous limestone found in the county of Frederick and state of Maryland; and in the county of Loudoun and state of Virginia. Our variety is a Camelottie meaguse limestone with alternate streaks of light blue and yellow gray: the other is a laminated light blue meaguse limestone with small chimney specks. Both effervesce slightly with acids, and the color where calcined is of a cream colored yellow, but not always the same, some parts being of a lighter and some of a darker color, it is found in ledges and in some places at the surface of the ground....
>
> It contains carbonic acid, lime, water, sibix, aluminum and oxide of iron.
>
> Preparation of the cement—the stone is first calcined 40 or 54 hours, then ground to a powder, and mixed with clean sand in the preparations of from one-third to one-half—adding as much water as will make it into a proper consistency for use.[78]

Apparently the patent was approved by August, for in that month Leckie informed Chief Engineer Benjamin Wright that his Tuscarora Cement was as good as the Shepherdstown blue lime. Accordingly, he requested that the canal company make arrangements to manufacture the Tus-

---

[73] John F. Luzader, *Historic Sites, Shepherdstown, W. Va.* (NPS Mss., 1962) 21.
[74] *Ibid.*
[75] Apr. 12, 1829, Diary and Account Book, 1828-29, Leckie Papers
[76] McFarland to Leckie, Apr. 18, 1829, and June 25, 1829, Diary and Account Book, 1828-29, Leckie Papers.
[77] *Agreement, James Alcott and Robert Leckie, June 26, 1829*, Leckie Papers
[78] Draft, Leckie and Alcott to Sec. Of St. [Van Buren], June 25, 1829, Leckie Papers

carora Cement on a large scale by constructing a draw kiln near the Tuscarora Mill that would contain 700 bushels.[79]

Although there is no documentary evidence as to the structures that were built near the Tuscarora Mill, the cement was soon being manufactured in large quantities. On February 3, 1830, the canal company signed a contract with Messrs. Brackett and Guy, the mill operators, to supply the line of the canal with 40,000 bushels of cement at 20 cents per 70 pound bushel. The cement was to be delivered by June 1, 1830.[80]

Despite the opposition of some canal officials to the use of the Tuscarora Cement on the canal, it began to be widely used as a supplement to the Shepherdstown lime, because there was frequently a shortage of the latter.

In June 1830, it was found that the quality of the Tuscarora Cement was too poor to be used on the canal. Accordingly, the board ordered the mill to be closed until the quality of the water lime could be improved by the use of coal in place of wood in the calcining process. No further use of the cement already manufactured was to be made on those parts of the masonry works that would be exposed to injury.[81]

At the recommendation of Engineer Alfred Cruger and Leckie, the board ordered the reactivatation of the mill in July. Henceforth, each kiln of lime that was burned would be tested before being shipped to the contractors.[82]

The canal company determined to contract for the unexpired seven-year lease of the mill by the Crommelin family in September 1832. At the same time. The board decided to procure by purchase or condemnation the land required for conducting a feeder from the dam and head race of the mill to the canal. While there is no record as to the final result of the negotiations leading to these two transactions, the mill continued to supply the canal with cement until the discovery of hydraulic lime at Round Top Hill.[83] During the more than six years that the Tuscarora Mill produced cement for the waterway, it supplied nearly 20,000 bushels of lime at a cost to the canal company of $4,088.17.[84]

3. HOOKS MILL

During the early 1830s, James Hook was associated with both Bracket and Guy at the Tuscarora Mill and Boteler and Reynolds at the Potomac Mill.[85] Sometime during the spring or summer of 1835, Hook established a mill on the Virginia side of the Potomac across from Hancock. Commencing in the fall of that year, he began supplying cement to the line of the canal. After two years of operating the mill, a period during which his business suffered because of the low level of the Potomac in the summer months, Hook died in August or September 1837. At that time, the canal company signed a contract with George Shafer, who had been operating a mill at Funkstown, paying him $300 to rent Hooks Mill and furnish cement to the contractors according to the provisions of Hooks uncompleted contract.[86] Hooks Mill continued to produce cement for the canal until the construction of Shafer's Cement Mill at Round Top Hill, some three miles west of

---

[79] Leckie to Wright, Aug. 21, 1829, Leckie Papers.
[80] *Contracts for Furnishing Hydraulic Cement*, Leckie Papers. In March 1830, the canal company awarded $100 to Alcott for his services in locating the Tuscarora water lime. *Proceedings of the President and Board of Directors*, B, 37–38.
[81] *Proceedings of the President and Board of Directors*, B, 125.
[82] *Ibid,* 146
[83] *Ibid,* C, 125; E, 62.
[84] Ledger A, C&O Co., 172–173.
[85] *Proceedings of the President and Board of Directors*, B, 143; D, 407.
[86] Fisk to Byrnes, Sep. 7, 1838, Ltrs. Sent, Chief Engineer.

Hancock. Altogether, Hooks Mill supplied nearly 31,000 bushels of cement for the construction of the canal.[87]

4.   SHAFER'S CEMENT MILL—ROUND TOP CEMENT COMPANY

In 1837, as the trunk of the canal was being excavated at Round Top Hill, it was discovered that the layers of "argillo-magnesian limestone" which cropped out in several places along the north bank of the Potomac had a "hydraulic character." The strata of rock were "exceedingly crooked and tortuous, bending up and down, and doubling upon each other in a very singular and complex manner," thus "forming a series of arches and counter-arches and concentrating a large quantity of the stone within easy and convenient reach." The aggregate thickness of the rock strata varied from eight to 12 feet. There were six distinct rock outcrops of the hydraulic stone exposed to view on the slope of the hill within a distance of about 200 yards along the canal.[88]

After the discovery of the rock, the canal company entered into a contract with George Shafer to rent Hooks Mill across the river from Hancock to grind the cement.[89] In May 1838, a contract was signed with Shafer to supply cement to the line of the canal from Dam No. 6 to the upper end of Paw Paw Tunnel.[90] At the same time, the board confirmed an agreement with Shafer authorizing him to build a mill on the berm side of the canal at Round Top Hill, some three miles west of Hancock. The canal company agreed to pay for the construction of the mills foundation and to rent the mill and the necessary water power for its operation to him for a period of 10 years. In addition, the company agreed to rent the land and stone quarries at Round Top Hill to him for the same period of time.[91]

By the spring of 1843, Shafer had supplied the canal company with some 80,000 bushels of hydraulic lime at a cost of $20,507.86.[92] Apparently, the mill was heavily damaged during the heavy spring freshet in 1843, because the board granted Shafer permission on June 6 of that year to transport toll-free upon the canal all the materials needed for its reconstruction.[93] When large-scale construction operations resumed on the canal in 1847, the contractors negotiated a contract with Shafer to deliver 120,000 bushels of cement to the line at a rate of 12,000 bushels per month if required, and the delivery began in early April 1848.[94]

Shafer continued to manufacture hydraulic lime under the brand name "Shafer Cement" until 1863. In that year, Robert Bridges and Charles W. Henderson purchased the mill and re-named the enterprise the Round Top Hydraulic Cement Company.[95] By 1882, the firm had grown

---

[87] *Proceedings of the President and Board of Directors*, D, 449; E, 62, 139; and Ledger A, C&O Co., 154.

[88] Thomas J. C. Williams, *A History of Washington County, Maryland, From the Earliest Settlements to the Present Time* (2 Vols., Hagerstown, 1906), Vol. I, 372.

[89] *Proceedings of the President and Board of Directors*, E, 488. Shafer had supplied hydraulic cement to the line of the canal from a small mill at Funktown since June 1835. No documentation could be found regarding the construction or operation of this mill. *Ibid,* D, 392; E, 1, 12; and McFarland to Bender, Feb. 10, 1836, Ltrs. Recd., Commissioner.

[90] *Proceedings of the President and Board of Directors*, E, 421.

[91] *Ibid,* E, 483–485.

[92] Ledger A, C&O Co., 152–153.

[93] *Proceedings of the President and Board of Directors*, G, 45–46.

[94] Davis, Hale and Allen to President and Directors, Apr. 11, 1848, in *Twentieth Annual Report* (1848), C&O Co., 16–21.

[95] Williams, *A History of Washington County*, Vol. I, 372. Bridges, the son of a Scotch immigrant and a long-time resident of Hancock, formed a business partnership with Henderson in 1850 that lasted some 48 years. His other business interests included the Berkeley Sand Company, located near Berkeley Springs, West Virginia, which manufactured glass sand, extensive farm holdings near Hagerstown, and timber and coal lands in West Virginia. In addition to his business interests, he served as a school commissioner in Washington County for many years; and in 1890, he was appointed as one of the receiver for the bankrupt canal company. *Ibid,* Vol. II, 1064–1065. Henderson, born in Bladensburg, Maryland, and raised in Berkeley County, Virginia, was a stockholder in many local banks and devoted

into one of the most important business enterprises of Washington County, employing 75 to 100 men. An adjacent cooper shop, where the barrels were produced in which the cement was shipped, employed 16 to 20 men.

The rock from which the cement was made was mined out of five tunnels in Round Top Hill, two of the tunnels running entirely through the hill. The stone was burned at the mill in eight kilns, each 21 feet deep and 10 feet in diameter at the base. The total daily capacity of the eight kilns was about 320 barrels of cement each weighting 300 pounds, or about 2,200 barrels per week. The mill that ground the cement was driven by "an overshot water-wheel, sixteen feet in diameter and sixteen feet width of breast, with buckets thirteen inched in depth." Water for turning the wheel was supplied by the canal. The grinding of the stone was accomplished by four pairs of French burrstones, each five feet in diameter. The total capacity of these grindstones was somewhat more than 400 bushels of cement in 24 hours. After the cement was packed in barrels, it was taken across the Potomac by cable and then shipped either east or west on the Baltimore and Ohio Railroad. The firm had about 300 acres on the West Virginia shore where there were located a warehouse for the deposit of the cement prior to shipment and switches that connected with the main tracks of the railroad. The canal was also used to ship the cement and to receive coal from the Allegany County mines for the mill's operation.[96]

As the Round Top Hydraulic Cement Company prospered, agency offices were established in the principal population centers of the Potomac Valley. One of the most important of these was operated by J. G. and J. M. Waters at 26 High Street fronting immediately on the canal in Georgetown. The business was located in one of the oldest commission houses in the city, having been established just prior to the Civil War by George Waters.[97]

5.   LEOPARD'S MILL

A mill operated by Jacob Leopard was located near Lock No. 53 some 2 ½ miles west of Round Top Hill.[98] The canal company purchased cement from Leopard on an irregular basis to supplement the company supply whenever Shafer's or Lynn's cement mills were unable to meet the needs of the canal contractors.[99] In November 1839, Leopard sued the canal company in the Washington County courts to obtain compensation for damage done to his mill and property by the construction of the canal. The case dragged through the courts for some five years before the two parties agreed to an out-of-court settlement in December 1844.[100]

6.   LYNN MILL, CUMBERLAND

In 1836, a cement mill was built on the banks of Wills Creek in Cumberland to produce the well known cement that carried the brand "Lynn Cement" and later "Cumberland Cement." The mill was probably built by John Galloway Lynn, the son of Captain David Lynn who had located at Cumberland before the outbreak of the American Revolution. John Galloway also built the Poto-

---

most of his attention to the mercantile side of business. His son, Raymond, purchased the holdings of Bridges in the Round Top Hydraulic Cement Company in 1903 after the plant burned. *Ibid,* Vol. II, 887–888.

[96] John Thomas Scharf, *A History of Western Maryland* (2 Vols., Philadelphia, 1882), Vol. II, 1256

[97] T. H. S. Boyd, *The History of Montgomery County, Maryland, From its earliest Settlement in 1650 to 1879* (Clarksburg, 1879), 153.

[98] Thomas F. Hahn, *Towpath Guide to the C&O Canal, Section Four* (York, 1973), 22.

[99] Fisk to Lynn, Sep. 18, 1838, Ltrs. Sent, C&O Co.

[100] *Proceedings of the President and Board of Directors,* F, 122; G, 214.

mac or Lynn Wharf on the Cumberland Basin above Dam No. 8 and operated it for many years for loading coal into canal boats to be transported down the waterway.[101]

As construction of the canal progressed above Dam No. 6, surveys were taken in the upper Potomac Valley to find new sources of hydraulic lime. On one of the surveys, it was discovered that "water lime" or "cement" rock cropped out in the northern part of Cumberland on the west bank of Wills Creek. Here the cement beds were folded and well exposed, allowing convenient access to the rock along the strike. The cement rock proper occurred in beds that varied in thickness from six to 17 feet. Quarrying operations were soon begun by the Lynn-owned Cumberland Hydraulic Cement and Manufacturing Company, and a mill was built on the banks of the creek near the quarries.[102]

The Lynn Mill had a peak capacity of producing 350 bushels of cement per week, a sum that was increased to 500 in 1848. After grinding 1,400 barrels of cement, the "midlings" were ground over to reduce the substance to powder form. The latter process generally required 36 hours to complete. The mill wheel was 16 feet high and was operated by water from Wills Creek.[103]

As early as September 1836, the Lynns offered to manufacture cement for the canal company.[104] Although the board took no action on this proposal, another offer by the Lynns in May 1838 to supply cement to the line between Paw Paw Tunnel and Cumberland led to an agreement the following month.[105] According to the contract, Lynn was to furnish 21,000 bushels of cement at 25 cents per bushel. Some of the cement was to be shipped to canal warehouses at Town Creek and Lock No. 67 for storage.[106] By May 1841, the Lynn Mill had supplied 50,394.14 bushels of cement to the company at a cost of $16,803.07.[107]

Charles Locker was operating the mill in the spring of 1848 when construction was resumed on the canal. A contract was signed whereby he agreed to supply the contractors with 60,000 bushels of cement at a rate of 6,000 bushels per month, if required. It was reported that the mill was full of cement and that delivery of articles to the line had begun in early April.[108]

The hydraulic cement manufactured at the mill received the commendation of noted engineers throughout the years, including Benjamin H. Latrobe, Charles P. Manning and Major Henry Brewerton. The cement was known "for the energy of its action" and for the fact that it would "bear a greater admixture of sand than any other natural cement." In the 1870s, a test comparing the relative strengths of the major cements in use in the United States revealed that "Cumberland Cement" was second only to English Portland Cement in the number of pounds it could sustain.[109] The cement mill continued to flourish into the 20th century.[110]

---

[101] James W. Thomas and Thomas J. C. Williams, *History of Allegany County, Maryland* (2 Vols., Cumberland, 1923), 784.

[102] *Maryland Geological Survey, Allegany County* (Baltimore, 1900), 185–186. Later in 1839, four additional cement quarries were discovered in the vicinity of Cumberland. Two quarries were located in the Little Bedford Valley about ¾ mile and 1¼ mile back from North Mountain—both being an extension of the vein Lynn was using. A third quarry was ¼ mile above Lynn's Backingstone Quarry and ¼ mile from the river on the hill side—also an extension southward of Lynn's vein. A fourth quarry was found about 2½ miles up from the mouth of North Branch. McFarland to Fisk, Aug. 8, 1839, Ltrs. Recd., Chief Engineer.

[103] Bryan to Fisk, Nov. 10, 1848, Ltrs. Recd., Chief Engineer.

[104] *Proceedings of the President and Board of Directors*, E, 135.

[105] *Ibid*, 421, 451.

[106] Fisk to President and Directors, June 25, 1838, and Fisk to Morris, Sep. 4, 1838, Ltrs. Sent, Chief Engineer.

[107] Ledger A, C&O Co., 154.

[108] Davis, Hale and Allen to president and Directors, Apr 11, 1848, in *Twentieth Annual Report* (1848), C&O Co., 16–21.

[109] C. J. Orick, comp., *The Mineral Resources and Manufacturing Facilities of the City of Cumberland, MD* (Cumberland, 1875), 23–24.

7. IMPORTED CEMENT FROM NEW YORK AND ENGLAND

Most of the cement used in the construction of the canal until the establishment of Shafer's Cement Mill at Round Top Hill in 1838 was produced at the Potomac Mill. However, the presence of large deposits of limestone did not insure that sufficient quantities of high-grade cement could be supplied to the contractors to fill their needs at all times. The Potomac Mill was creating a new industry in the region, necessitating an inevitable period of experimentation as a new science was being learned the hard way. This experimentation continued throughout the early construction period, and the lime, which the contractors received, was not always the high quality that was desired.[111] Furthermore, the capacity of the kilns was limited and often insufficient to supply heavy seasonal demands, thus frequently hindering progress on the masonry works.[112]

The problem of an adequate supply of high-grade lime continued to plague the directors throughout the early construction period. To fill the gaps in the local supply, the board imported large quantities of cement from New York and England. The earliest importation of cement occurred in November 1828 when the directors purchased 500 barrels of Parker's Roman Cement.[113] During the summer of 1829, the first season of full-scale operations, the canal board ordered that until good Shepherdstown cement was produced, the contractors were to use Roman Cement with Thomaston lime for backing.[114] Because the amount of Parker's Roman Cement on hand was insufficient to meet the needs of the contractors, the board purchased 332 barrels of Watts Roman Cement from a firm in Liverpool. The cement was to be shipped on the brig *Caledonia* bound for Baltimore, the insurance the company was forced to pay amounted to $1,770.67.[115] Since the company was in desperate need of cement, the board at the same time bought 50 casks of Rosendale water cement from Ulster County, New York, already on the Georgetown wharves and placed orders for 200 more.[116]

The canal company records are filled with references to further purchases of Rosendale or New York cement until September 1833. Altogether nearly 10,000 barrels, weighing 335 to

---

[110] *Maryland Geological Survey, Allegany County*, 185–186.
[111] McFarland to Ingle, May 29, 1829, and McFarland to Leckie, July 23, 1829, Ltrs. Recd., C&O Co.; and Ingle to Boteler and Reynolds, Apr. 22, 1830, Ltrs. Sent, C&O Co.
[112] Leckie to President and Directors, July 22, 1829, Wright to President and Directors, Mar 23, 1830; and Leckie to Cruger and President and Directors, July 1830, Ltrs. Recd., C&O Co.; and Ingle to McFarland, Jan 8, 1830; and Mercer to Boteler and Reynolds, May 5, 1830, Ltrs. Sent, C&O Co.
[113] *Proceedings of the President and Board of Directors*, A, 105. In 1796, Joseph Parker patented the so-called Roman Cement, the process consisting of a conversion by calcinations and pulverization of the nodules, or clay balls, found in the London clays. Henry Reid, *The Science and Art of the Manufacture of Portland Cement* (London, 1877), 29. For a description of the composition and the process of making Parker's Roman Cement see Appendix B.
[114] *Proceedings of the President and Board of Directors*, A, 278
[115] *Proceedings of the President and Board of Directors*, A, 287.
[116] *Ibid*, 283. Rock suitable for the manufacture of natural cement was first discovered in America in 1819 by Canvass White in Madison County, New York, during his service as an engineer on the Erie Canal. During the construction of the Delaware and Hudson Canal in 1825, natural cement rock was found near the Ulster County communities of High Falls and Rosendale, New York, and soon a large mill was erected at the latter town to produce Rosendale or New York water cement. Strictly speaking, natural, Roman, and Rosendale cements all belong to one class, their compositions and the process of their manufacture being similar. Natural or Rosendale cement was somewhat similar to hydraulic lime. Instead of slaking with water, however, after burning it was pulverized, exposed to the air to season, and marketed in powdered form. Instead of having a loss on ignition of 8 to 21 percent as in hydraulic limes, this loss was less than 5 percent and the resulting cement was considered to be much stronger. Richard K. Meade, *Manufacture of Cement* (Scranton, 1922), 3, 32; and Christopher Roberts, *The Middlesex Canal* (Cambridge, 1938), 99

350 pounds each, of the New York cement was purchased by the board for use on the canal at a cost of $24,307.03.[117]

C. SAW MILLS

GREAT FALLS SAWMILL, MATILDAVILLE

As construction on the canal commenced in the fall of 1828, the directors determined to build a sawmill near the waterway. In early September, a site was chosen at Matildaville on the Virginia side of the river near Great Falls; and Thomas Fairfax, on whose land the site was located, granted permission for the construction of the mill.[118] It was to be operated by water from the Potomac Company's skirting canal around the falls. In late September, the directors authorized the construction of the sawmill "for the purpose of supplying timber, scantling and plank, where deemed expedient, to the canal."[119] By early November, a contract had been let to William Apsey and work had begun under the direction of Superintendent of Wood Work Hezekiah Langley.[120] Because of the extended illness of the contractor, the mill was not completed until April 1830 at a cost of $2,445.92.[121]

The sawmill was built on a plan similar to that of Lewis Wernwag at Harpers Ferry with one saw and a machine for drawing the logs out of the water. At its peak capacity, the mill could cut 2,000 to 3,000 feet of "4 by 4" plank per day.[122]

During the construction of the sawmill, the canal company commissioned two surveys for the best supplies of timber in the Potomac Valley. Large quantities of good locust timber were in the Shenandoah and Opequon Valleys of Jefferson and Loudoun Counties in Virginia and the upper part of Frederick and the lower part of Washington Counties in Maryland. The Cacapon River Valley was also found to possess good stands of yellow pine, walnut, chestnut and white oak. The small locust, cedar, chestnut, white oak and black walnut trees that were in the path of the canal were considered to be sufficient for making fence posts and railing.[123]

In February 1831, the company leased the sawmill to George W. Smoot of Alexandria for five years at a yearly rental fee of $150.[124] When the Chesapeake & Ohio was opened between Georgetown and Seneca later in the year, the board solicited bids for the removal of the sawmill to an undetermined site on the new waterway. The expense of moving the mill would be repaid by allowing the mover to use the mill. Until a contract

---

[117] *Proceedings of the President and Board of Directors*, A, 408, 418; B, 28, 38, 51, 67, 143, 236; and Ledger A, C&O Co., 178–180.
[118] *Proceedings of the President and Board of Directors*, A, 57.
[119] *Ibid*, 84.
[120] *Ibid*, 394–395.
[121] *Ibid*, B, 31, 54, 64; and Ledger A, C&O Co., 180.
[122] Langley to Mercer, Oct. 28, 1828, Ltrs. Recd., C&O Co.
[123] Langley to Mercer, Oct. 28, 29, 1828; and Naylor to Mercer, Sep 30, 1828, Ltrs. Recd., C&O Co.
[124] *Proceedings of the President and Board of Directors*, B, 266.

was let for the move, all detachable parts of the mill were to be stored in the company warehouse in Georgetown for safekeeping.[125]

Although there is no available documentation concerning the relocation of the sawmill, there is evidence that Smoot took the canal company to court over this change in location. After a lengthy battle, the marshal of the District of Columbia in October 1835 ruled against Smoot by confirming the right of the canal company to break its rental agreement and to dispose of its property.[126]

There is no evidence that the canal company established other sawmills along the line of the canal during the construction period. Apparently, as the work progressed up the Potomac Valley, the timber products were supplied by mills in the area such as Lewis Wernwag's mill at Harpers ferry, Jacob Miller's mill about two-thirds of a mile below Pack Horse Ford, William Naylor's mill at the junction of the Cacapon and the Potomac and Young's sawmill at Cumberland. As the construction work progressed, the company increasingly began also to contract with individuals, such as Captain William Easby of Washington, for the manufacture, delivery and installation of lock gates and other timber-related products.[127]

D. BRICK KILNS

PAW PAW TUNNEL BRICK MAKING

Lee Montgomery, the contractor for Paw Paw Tunnel, began making bricks for the arching of the tunnel in 1837 or 1838. He used local building materials and a portable brick-making machine obtained in Baltimore. His kiln probably was located at the upstream end of the field adjacent to the canal section superintendent's house, because recent bulldozing at that location has revealed a large quantity of cinders and coal. In the spring of 1838, it was reported that Montgomery's bricks were of poor quality, and consequently, many of them were never used.[128]

When work resumed on the canal in November 1847 under the new contract with Hunter, Harris & Co., the work on the tunnel was subcontracted to McCullough & Day. Mr. Campbell, one of the workers of the latter firm, was assigned the task of making bricks for the tunnel arch. Upon examination, it was found that the excavation material from Section No. 311 at the upper end of the tunnel could be used for brick clay. Further examination of the ground indicated that there were sufficient quantities of clay within one-half mile of the upper portal of the tunnel to produce the 5,800,000 bricks required to arch the structure.[129]

To insure against future problems in producing good brick, Chief Engineer Fisk hired James McFarland to tour Hudson River Valley and to learn the mode of making bricks, the types of machinery used to mix and mould the clay, and the process of burning the bricks. This information was given to Campbell and presumably put to use.[130]

---

[125] *Ibid,* C, 21.
[126] *Ibid,* D, 415.
[127] Naylor to Mercer, Sep 30, 1828, Ltrs. Recd., C&O Co.; Miller to President and Board of Directors, May 1, 1863, Ltrs. Recd., C&O Co.; *Proceedings of the President and Board of Directors,* F, 215; Fisk to Easby, Aug 2, 15, 1838, Ltrs. Sent, C&O Co.; and Young to Fisk, Sep 28, 1848, Ltrs. Recd., Chief Engineer.
[128] Morris to Fisk, Mar 16, 1838, Ltrs. Recd., Chief Engineer, and Hahn, *Towpath Guide, Section Four,* 45.
[129] Morris to Fisk, Jun 5, 1839, and Dungan to Fisk, July 30, 1849, Ltrs. Recd., Chief Engineer.
[130] McFarland to Fisk, Feb 11, 1848, Ltrs. Recd., Chief Engineer.

HISTORIC RESOURCE STUDY
CHESAPEAKE & OHIO CANAL NHP

5.
A CHRONOLOGICAL DESCRIPTION OF THE CONSTRUCTION OF THE C & O CANAL: 1828–1850

BY HARLAN D. UNRAU
HISTORIAN, C&O CANAL RESTORATION TEAM, SENECA
DENVER SERVICE CENTER
1976

CONTENTS

I. GENERAL CHRONOLOGY OF THE CONSTUCTION
OF THE CHESAPEAKE & OHIO CANAL: 1828–1850 179

    1828 179
    1829 185
    1830 190
    1831 193
    1832 196
    1833 201
    1834 203
    1835 205
    1836 209
    1837 213
    1838 215
    1839 217
    1840 219
    1841 221
    1843: Alexandria Canal Opened 221
    1842–1847 221
    1847 222
    1848 222
    1849 224
    1850 224
    1851 226

II. CONSTRUCTION CHRONOLOGIES OF MAJOR STRUCTURES 227

    A. LIFT LOCKS 227
    B. TIDE LOCKS 237
    C. RIVER LOCKS 238
    D. GUARD LOCKS 238
    E. AQUEDUCTS 239
    F. DAMS 241
    G. LOCKHOUSES 242
    H. STOP LOCKS (STOP GATES) 249
    I. FEEDERS 250
    J. MISCELLANEOUS STRUCTURES 251

APPENDIXES 253

    A. PRESIDENT JOHN QUINCY ADAMS'S REMINISCENCES OF THE
       CANAL GROUND-BREAKING CEREMONIES ON JULY 4, 1828 253

    B. DESCRIPTION OF THE SEAL OF THE CHESAPEAKE & OHIO
       CANAL COMPANY, SEPTEMBER 3, 1828 254

    C. LIST OF CONTRACTORS FOR 34 SECTIONS BETWEEN
       LITTLE FALLS AND SENECA FALLS, AUGUST 20, 1828 255

D.	CONTRACTORS FOR SECTIONS BETWEEN SENECA FALLS AND POINT OF ROCKS, AND FOR MASONRY WORK BETWEEN LITTLE FALLS AND POINT OF ROCKS, OCTOBER 25, 1828	256
E.	LIST OF ENGINEERS APPOINTED ON THE FIRST DIVISION OF THE CHESAPEAKE & OHIO CANAL, NOVEMBER 22, 1828	257
F.	LIST OF CONTRACTORS FOR WORK ON THE CANAL BETWEEN ROCK CREEK AND LITTLE FALLS, DECEMBER 10, 1828	258
G.	LIST OF CONTRACTORS FOR LOCKHOUSES, DECEMBER 11, 1828	259
H.	LIST OF CONTRACTORS FOR RELET LOCKS, MARCH 14, 1829	260
I.	LIST OF LOCK TENDERS AND LOCATION OF LOCKHOUSES FROM LITTLE FALLS TO SENECA FALLS, AUGUST 7, 1830	261
J.	LIST OF CONTRACTORS FOR SECTIONS FROM POINT OF ROCKS TO HARPERS FERRY, MARCH 14, 1832	262
K.	LIST OF CONTRACTORS FOR SECTIONS NOS. 113–117 (DAMS NOS. 3–4), JUNE 2, 1832	263
L.	LIST OF MASONRY STRUCTURES AND DIFFICULT SECTIONS BETWEEN DAM NO. 5 AND THE CACAPON RIVER LET FOR CONTRACT, JULY 3, 1835	264
M.	LIST OF CONTRACTORS FOR SECTIONS BETWEEN DAM NO. 5 AND THE CACAPON RIVER, FEBRUARY 10, 1836	265
N.	LIST OF CONTRACTORS FOR 54 SECTIONS AND 4 LOCKS BETWEEN DAM NO. 6 AND CUMBERLAND, SEPTEMBER 27, 1837	266
O.	LIST OF CONTRACTORS FOR MASONRY WORK BETWEEN DAM NO. 6 AND CUMBERLAND, SEPTEMBER 29, 1837	267
P.	LIST OF CONTRACTORS FOR AQUEDUCT NO. 9 AND 17 SECTIONS LET UNDER APRIL 2 ORDER OF THE BOARD, MAY 23, 1838	268
Q.	LIST OF CONTRACTORS FOR LOCKS NOS. 57–67 AND CULVERTS NOS. 204, 210, 219–220, 225, AND 229 LET UNDER APRIL 2 ORDER OF THE BOARD, MAY 24, 1838	269
R.	LIST OF SUBCONTRACTORS FOR SECTIONS BETWEEN DAM NO. 6 AND CUMBERLAND, APRIL 11, 1848	270
S.	LIST OF CONTRACTORS FOR CULVERTS BETWEEN DAM NO. 6 AND CUMBERLAND, APRIL 11, 1848	271

I. GENERAL CHRONOLOGY OF THE CONSTUCTION OF THE CHESAPEAKE & OHIO CANAL: 1828-1850

1828

June 23: President Charles F. Mercer was authorized by the canal board to engage Benjamin Wright as chief engineer of the canal company. Additional surveyors and engineers were to be hired to aid Wright in preparing an unspecified section of the canal for immediate excavation.[1]

June 24: The company clerk was ordered to proceed immediately along both shores of the Potomac River between Seneca Creek and Cumberland for the purpose of obtaining land for the location of the canal. He was also authorized to purchase land on which was located materials for the construction of the waterway.[2]

June 24: Since the company stockholders and the citizens of the District of Columbia wanted the construction of the canal to commence on July 4, the canal board determined the work with the city authorities toward this goal. Following the passage of a resolution by the Washington Board of Aldermen and Common Council on July 1, the canal directors agreed to begin the excavation of the waterway with appropriate ceremonies on July 4, near the Powder Magazine at the head of Little Falls.[3]

June 26: President Mercer informed the canal board that notice had been served upon him on June 24 "of an injunction granted by Theodore Bland, Chancellor of the State of Maryland, at the suit of the Baltimore & Ohio Railroad Company." This injunction prevented the construction of the canal above Point of Rocks. The canal board, upon learning of this legal ploy by the railroad, resolved to engage Walter Jones, a local attorney, as counsel for the canal company and to hire additional legal counsel in Frederick, Maryland, to look after their interests. Later, on July 10, the board voted to retain Francis Scott Key, a lawyer in Georgetown, as an assistant counsel in the case.[4]

June 26: The canal board voted unanimously to adopt the route for the canal surveyed by the U. S. Board of Engineers and by James Geddes and Nathan S. Roberts along the north bank of the Potomac River below Cumberland.[5]

July 2: The canal board determined to take immediate steps to secure conveyances of land to the canal company in the states of Maryland and Pennsylvania for the commencement of the western section of the waterway between Cumberland and Pittsburgh as surveyed by the U. S. Board of Engineers in 1824-25. Andrew Stewart, a director of the company, was authorized to effect these land conveyances and, if necessary, to initiate condemnation proceedings under the state laws.[6]

July 4: On this date, groundbreaking ceremonies for the canal were held near the Powder Magazine at the head of Little Falls. To add to the significance of the occasion, the board invited Presi-

---

[1] *Proceedings of the President and Board of Directors*, A, 2.
[2] *Ibid*, 6.
[3] *Ibid*, 5, 9.
[4] *Ibid*, 8, 21.
[5] *Ibid*.
[6] *Ibid*, 10.

dent John Quincy Adams to attend the ceremonies and to turn the first spadeful of earth. Many representatives of official Washington and of the foreign delegations were among the dignitaries present at the ceremonies. After breakfasting in Georgetown, the directors and their guests proceeded up the river about five miles in boats especially provided for the occasion. They disembarked at the foot of Little Falls and went directly to the Powder Magazine at the head of the falls.

After a number of short speeches, President Adams gave his blessing to the undertaking by emphasizing the national character of the work. At the conclusion of his address, he took the spade and began to break the ground. Unfortunately, his spade struck a root and his effort was foiled. After a second failure, Adams took off his coat, again took up the shovel, and with the cheers of the audience finally succeeded in breaking the ground. The members of the official party returned to Georgetown where they partook of a lavish dinner. The affair was a huge success, focusing public attention on the Chesapeake & Ohio Canal as a national work and overshadowed the inaugural ceremonies of the Baltimore & Ohio Railroad in Baltimore on the same day.[7]

July 5: The directors authorized President Mercer to employ several principal engineers and a number of assistant engineers to survey and prepare for placing under contract the eastern section of the canal from Little Falls to Cumberland.

The board resolved that public notice should be given that proposals for the excavation, embankment and walling of the canal prism between Little Falls and Great Falls would be received at the C&O Canal Company office on August 14–16. Similar notice was also to be given that proposals for building from 18 to 20 locks and the masonry structures on this section of the canal were to be received October 1–20.

Immediate steps were authorized to locate the most convenient points along the Potomac River at which suitable stone could be obtained for the construction of the masonry works on the waterway. Similar inquires were to be made where suitable lime could be found near the river for making hydraulic cement. If necessary, a sum of $20 was to be offered as a reward to anyone who could discover large quantities of this material near the line of the canal.[8]

July 19: Chief Engineer Wright informed the board that the line of the canal from Great Falls to Seneca Creek was under survey and would be prepared for letting out contracts for the embankment, excavation and walling of the canal prism August 14–16. Proposals for the five locks and other masonry structures on this subdivision would be received October 1–20.[9]

July 30: After considerable pressure from the stockholders and citizens in Washington had been brought to bear on the directors to locate the eastern terminus of the canal in the District of Columbia, the board decided to hold a general meeting in the Washington City Hall on September 10 to resolve the question. Clerk John P. Ingle was instructed to place weekly notices of the meeting in the Philadelphia *American Daily Advertiser*, the Baltimore *American*, the *Virginia Free* and the Washington *National Intelligencer*. Two weeks later on August 9, the board appointed a

---

[7] Washington *National Intelligencer*, July 7, 1828, and Walter S. Sanderlin, *The Great National Project: A History of the Chesapeake & Ohio Canal* (Baltimore, 1946), 59–60. See Appendix A for President John Quincy Adams' reminiscences of the ground-breaking ceremonies which are excerpted from *Memoirs of John Quincy Adams*, Vol. 8, 49–50. The use of the Fourth of July for the formal inauguration of internal improvements projects was a common practice in those years. For example, the Erie Canal began construction on July 4, 1817.
[8] *Proceedings of the President and Board of Directors*, A, 11–13.
[9] *Ibid*, 24–25.

committee to consult with Attorney General William Wirt and members of Congress concerning the position the canal company should take at the general meeting.[10]

August 2: The board determined that President Mercer should direct the preparation, printing and distribution of proposals for the prospective contractors who were ready to bid for the excavation, embankment and walling of the canal prism. On August 9, Mercer submitted a printed form of the proposals; and on August 18, he submitted a second printed form of the contracts for work on the canal.[11]

July 10: Six newspapers were selected by the board to be used for advertising purposes by the canal. The newspapers were: the Washington *National Intelligencer*, Alexandria *Gazette*, *Virginia Free Press* (Charleston), Hagerstown *Herald*, Cumberland *Advocate*, and Pennsylvania *Democrat* (Uniontown).[12]

August 9: The board voted to give public notice that proposals would be received between October 15–20 for the entire section of the canal between Seneca Creek and Point of Rocks, a distance of about 27 miles. Bid would be accepted for the sections, socks, aqueduct and culverts on that stretch of the line. The forms for the proposals were to be ready for distribution by October 1. The letting of these contracts was to be published in all the newspapers of the counties bordering on the Potomac and in the Winchester papers, in addition to those that had been selected on July 10.[13]

August 20: After examining 462 proposals submitted by some 100 contractors, the board let contracts for the 34 sections between Little Falls and Seneca Creek. Most of the successful bidders had prior experience in the construction of canals in New York, Pennsylvania, Ohio, Connecticut and Canada, New York and Pennsylvania men secured 18 of the contracts, amounting to $160,000 of a total of $218,000 let.[14]

August 21: The canal company formally accepted the Potomac Company's surrender and conveyance "of all its rights and privileges."[15]

August 23: The board took action to organize its corps of engineers to direct the operations on the canal. The Board of Engineers was to consist of Chief Engineer Wright assisted by two directors, positions to be offered to Nathan S. Roberts and John Martineau. In addition, President Mercer was authorized to employ the number of resident and assistant engineers, rodmen and axemen that the Board of Engineers would require.

On this date, the Board of Engineers was also directed to survey and estimate the cost of building a feeder from the Monocacy River to the line of the canal.[16]

August 30: Upon the petition of several contractors, the board ordered that building materials and provisions for the contractors would be allowed to pass through the old Potomac Company locks

---

[10] *Ibid*, 31–32, 35–37.
[11] *Ibid*, 34, 35, 40.
[12] *Ibid*, 22.
[13] *Ibid*, 37–38.
[14] *Ibid*, 41–43, and Sanderlin, *The Great National project*, 67–68.
[15] *Proceedings of the President and Board of Directors*, A, 43–44.
[16] *Ibid*, 47–49, 54–55. Roberts and Martineau later accepted the positions offered to them.

at Little Falls and Great Falls without payment of toll charges. The move was made to hasten construction and lessen the impact of rising building costs.

The directors also instructed the Board of Engineers to construct a road or pathway along the line of the canal at the expense of the company.

Phineas Janney, a director of the company, was appointed to obtain Thomas Fairfax's consent for the construction of a saw mill at Great Falls for the use of the company. On September 3, Janney reported that Fairfax had given his consent.[17]

September 3: The canal company adopted an official seal commemorating the purposes of the waterway. Designed by Benjamin Chambers, the brass seal was to be impressed on all contracts of the company accompanied by the signature of the president or the director acting in his place.[18]

September 10: On this date, a general meeting of the stockholders of the canal company convened to determine the location of the eastern terminus of the waterway. President Mercer, on behalf of the directors, recommended to the stockholders that if Attorney General Wirt found that the company charter gave the authority for such action that the canal be extended from Little Falls to Rock Creek along the line surveyed by Wright and Martineau in August. When the Corporation of Washington built a basin at the mouth of Tiber Creek, the company would extend the canal to that point unless the corporation wished to construct the extension. A request would be made to Congress to aid the company in extending the canal to the Navy Yard and to Alexandria via an aqueduct across the Potomac, the northern abutment of which would be built by the company. The stockholders promptly agreed to the recommendation as it offered a compromise between those who desired the eastern terminus at Little Falls and those who wanted the company to extend its works to the Eastern Branch (Anacostia River).[19]

September 19: The board passed five resolutions relative to the construction of the canal: (1) each lock chamber was to be 15 feet wide in the clear so they would correspond with the locks on the canals in New York, Ohio and Western Pennsylvania; (2) the canal between its eastern terminus and the Shenandoah River at Harpers Ferry was to be six feet deep; (3) suitable places were to be selected for the immediate construction of as many lock-keepers' houses along the line of the canal as were needed by the Corps of Engineers in superintending its construction; (4) when the specifications for the October lettings were prepared, they were to be printed and distributed among the prospective contractors; and (5) the Board of Engineers was directed to locate and prepare for contract the portion of the canal between Little Falls and Rock Creek, including the basin at the latter location. As a part of this operation, the engineers were to report the plan and estimate of a road to replace the public highway which would be destroyed by the construction of this section of the canal.[20]

September 27: The board determined that proposals be received at the next letting for double and single locks and that the directors retain the alternative of adopting either plan. The board of en-

---

[17] *Ibid,* pp.53–54, 56–67. This saw mill was located at Matildaville on the Virginia side of the river and was contracted to William Apsey. See *Ibid,* B, 452; and Apsey to Mercer, June 17 and July 18, 1829, Ltrs. Recd., C&O Co.
[18] *Ibid,* 63–64. For a description of the seal, see Appendix B.
[19] *Ibid,* 76–78; *Proceedings of the Stockholders,* A, 23–32; *Proceedings of the President and Directors of the Chesapeake & Ohio Canal and of the Corporations of Washington, Georgetown and Alexandria, in Relation to the Location of the Eastern Termination of the Chesapeake & Ohio Canal* (Washington, 1828), 1–15.
[20] *Proceedings of the President and Board of Directors,* A, 80–82.

gineers was ordered to report on the relative cost and advantages of building single and double locks on the canal from its eastern terminus to the Shenandoah.

Walter Smith, one of the company directors, was authorized to speed the commencement of operations on the canal by making private contracts for the satisfaction of landowners through whose property the line of the canal would pass between Rock Creek and Seneca Creek. When he could not arrive at an agreement with the proprietor, he was to submit the case to outside arbitration. Where private contracts could be consummated by purchasing outright the right of the owner in the lot or part of the lot of the tract to be acquired, he was to do so for the benefit of the company.

The directors voted to appoint a superintendent of stone work and a superintendent of wood work to each division of the canal. These individuals would be treated as engineers and would work under the direction of the board of engineers.

President Mercer was instructed to have the superintendent of wood work construct a saw mill at Matildaville near the Great Falls on the Virginia side of the Potomac. The saw mill was to supply locust timber for the lock gates and scantling and plank to the contractors as needed during the construction of the waterway.[21]

October 16: Attorney General William Wirt submitted to President Mercer his legal opinion on the question of whether the canal company's charter permitted the extension of the waterway to Rock Creek. According to his understanding of the legislative acts of Virginia and Maryland and the company charter, the precise location of the canal's eastern termination was not defined. However, since the documents specified that the terminus of the canal was to be at tidewater in the District of Columbia, the company could legally locate its terminus anywhere in the District.[22]

October 18: The directors resolved that the portion of the canal between Rock Creek and Little Falls be placed under contract when Chief Engineer Wright reported that the company engineers had completed their surveys. The Seneca and Monocacy feeders and Dams Nos. 1 and 2 also were to be let for contract at his discretion. The time for this letting was subsequently fixed by Wright for December 4.[23]

October 21–25: After traveling up the canal from Georgetown and holding a three-day meeting at Leesburg, Virginia, President Mercer and the board of directors let 50 sections of the line from Seneca Creek to Point of Rocks and much of the masonry work between Little Falls and Point of Rocks. There were 1,308 proposals for these contracts. The work that was let included Sections Nos. 35–84, Locks Nos. 5–27, Aqueduct No. 1 and Culverts Nos. 10–12 and 17.[24]

October 31: The board accepted a proposal by Hovey and Hitchcock to construct Aqueduct No. 2 across the Monocacy.[25]

November 15: As there was an apparent labor shortage in the Potomac Valley, the board voted to begin advertising its need for workers in Europe.

---

[21] *Ibid*, 82–84.
[22] *Ibid*, 89.
[23] *Ibid*, 92.
[24] *Ibid*, 93–98; and Sanderlin, *The Great National project*, 68. See Appendix D for a list of the contractors.
[25] *Proceedings of the President and Board of Directors*, A, 100.

The directors determined to send a proposal to the authorities in Frederick that the company would convert the contemplated Monocacy feeder into a navigable canal provided the city and county would build an extension to the town.

The board decided that it was expedient to substitute ferries for bridges and fords across the canal. A petition was to be drawn up and presented to the Maryland legislature to authorize such substitution wherever the canal passed through the territory of that State. To achieve this goal with the least inconvenience to the landowners along the Potomac, the board wanted the State to grant it authority to acquire all the property between the canal and the river.[26]

November 22: The board organized the canal line and made assignments of the engineers to the administrative divisions of the canal. The directors divided the entire canal into three parts: eastern, middle and western. Inasmuch as the chapter required that construction begin to the east, that leg of the canal was subdivided into three parts of 120 sections each. The average section was half a mile in length, and twenty sections generally formed a residency.

A list of rules and regulations to govern the administration of the engineering corps was adopted and published. The engineer corps was divided into five grades: chief engineer, board of engineers, resident engineers, assistant engineers and rodmen. The board of engineers consisted of three members, each of whom also had charge of one division of the eastern section. The engineer in charge of the first division was automatically chief engineer.[27]

November 22: The board determined to stimulate the pride of the contractors in their work on the canal by announcing that rewards were to be given for quality construction. The rewards to be issued were as follows: (1) a silver cup valued at $50 for the best constructed lock on the first division completed within the specified time limit of the contracts; (2) a silver medal valued at $10 for the best constructed culvert of any letting; (3) a silver medal valued at $20 for the best portion of slope or vertical walling consisting of at least 500 perches of stone on a residency; (4) a silver medal valued at $30 for the best executed section of the first division; (5) a silver medal valued at $20 for the first section to be completed in any given letting; and (6) a silver medal valued at $10 for the greatest sum of common excavation done on any section in a given month.[28]

November 22: President Mercer informed the board that the Baltimore & Ohio Railroad had advertised to contract for the construction of their line across the right-of-way of the canal at Point of Rocks. Accordingly, the directors authorized him to apply for an injunction to prevent any further proceedings in the contemplated letting of such contracts. Mercer was also given permission to employ former Attorney General William Wirt as an attorney of the company to assist Walter Jones in conducting the legal suits between the two companies.[29]

November 29: Chief Engineer Wright submitted specifications for the pier at the Rock Creek Basin, the dams, the locks and the bridges. Accordingly, Clerk Ingle was ordered to print these documents for distribution.[30]

---

[26] *Ibid,* 104–105. Wilson M. C. Fairfax and Alfred Cruger were directed to survey all the land between the projected canal line and the river from Georgetown to Harpers Ferry preparatory to the land acquisition program.
[27] *First Annual Report* (1829), C&O Co., in *Proceedings of Stockholders,* A, 48; and *Proceedings of the President and Board of Directors,* A, 107–115. See Appendix E for a list of the engineers on the first division of the canal.
[28] *Proceedings of the President and Board of Directors,* A, 115–116.
[29] *Ibid,* 117.
[30] *Ibid,* 119.

November 29: When the board received word that the authorities at Frederick would not build a navigable canal to the contemplated feeder on the Monocacy River, they resolved to drop plans temporarily for the proposed feeder.[31]

December 3: The board agreed to advertise for the delivery to the company's saw mill at Great Falls of a large quantity of rough timber. The timber was to be used for sawed post and rail fences and for the posts and crossbars of the lock gates.[32]

December 10: After considering a number of proposals at the Engineer's Office in Georgetown, the board let contracts for the five miles between Rock Creek and Little Falls. This work included Sections A–H, Locks Nos. 1–4, Dams Nos. 1–2, bridges Nos. 1–2, seven culverts, and the pier, waste weir and tide lock at the Rock Creek Basin[33].

December 11: Chief Engineer Wright reported to the board on the number and location of the lockkeepers' houses necessary for the accommodation of the Resident Engineers. The board then accepted the bids for 12 lockhouses.[34]

1829

January 7: The board authorized President Mercer to commence advertisements in Virginia for the purpose of attracting laborers to the canal.[35]

January 21: The directors resolved to receive proposals for the supply of locust timber for the lock gates.[36]

January 31: To alleviate the continuing labor shortage along the line of the canal, the board authorized President Mercer to make an arrangement with Henry Richards, a Welshman formerly employed on the Erie and Chesapeake and Delaware Canals, to serve as the agent of the Chesapeake & Ohio Canal Company in Great Britain and to secure laborers to work on the project. The board also continued to negotiate for workers from the British Isles through James Maury, the American consul at Liverpool. On March 6, an agreement was made with Richards, and he was soon sent to England to recruit laborers in cooperation with Maury.[37]

March 6: Because of the continuing intransigence of many landowners along the line of the canal to surrender their properties to the company, the board ordered that condemnation proceedings be initiated to acquire the necessary land for the canal's right-of-way between Rock Creek and Point of Rocks. A jury was to be called for this purpose on March 24.[38]

---

[31] *Ibid*, 119.
[32] *Ibid*, 123.
[33] *Ibid*, 127. See Appendix F for a list of the contractors for this work.
[34] *Ibid*, 129. See Appendix G for a list of the contractors for the lockhouses.
[35] *Ibid*, 140.
[36] *Ibid*, 146.
[37] *Ibid*, 153, 175; Mercer to Maury, March 7 and July 8, 1829 and Mercer to Richards, July 8, 1829, Ltrs. Sent, C&O Co.
[38] *Proceedings of the President and Board of Directors*, A, 175.

March 14: Earlier on February 28, President Mercer had informed the directors that the contracts for Locks Nos. 5-8; 12; 15-18; 19-20; 23-24 and 26 had been abandoned. Accordingly, the board accepted new proposals to construct the locks, and on March 14, declared new contracts. The guard lock and feeder at Seneca Falls also were contracted to the firm of Holdsworth and Isherwood.[39]

March 17: The directors authorized Inspector of Masonry Alexander B. McFarland to make a contract with Boteler and Reynolds, who owned the Potomac Mills at Shepherdstown, for the delivery of 50,000 bushels of water lime to the canal works at 17 cents per bushel. Stone of a suitable quality for hydraulic lime had been discovered near Shepherdstown, on the Virginia side of the river, early in 1828, and a mill and kiln had been erected to grind and burn the lime.[40]

March 18: At a special meeting of the board, President Mercer announced that a suit brought by John Mason *et al.* of Georgetown to prevent the extension of the canal through Georgetown had been dismissed by the U.S. Supreme Court. Since the work on the canal between Little Falls and Rock Creek had been suspended pending the outcome of the suit, work on this portion of the waterway was to be rushed to completion.[41]

March 18: The directors decided that the plan of the canal should be changed so "as to form a berm bank...not exceeding forty feet in width" wherever the Chief Engineer recommended such a modification. Later on April 22, the board directed that the width of the canal prism be reduced in order to add six feet to the breadth of the berm bank between Georgetown and Little Falls. This berm was to serve as a new roadway between these two points, replacing the road which had been destroyed by the line of the canal.[42]

March 18: The board accepted the proposal submitted by James O'Brien for the construction of Lockhouse No. 6.[43]

April 4: As early as the spring of 1829, the company realized that the rising construction costs would jeopardize the completion of its work. To offset this danger and to increase the subscriptions to the level necessary to finish the canal, the board, on April 4, constituted Richard Rush as the agent of the company to open books in Europe to receive subscriptions up to $6,000,000 for the eastern section and $10,000,000 for the entire canal.[44]

April 8: Inspector of Masonry McFarland informed the board that he had discovered a blue hydrate of lime about 100 yards from the Potomac Mills in Shepherdstown. Because he considered this stone to be superior to that for which the company had contracted, the board ordered him to extend the existing contract with Boteler and Reynolds to 100,000 bushels of hydraulic cement using the blue stone.[45]

---

[39] *Ibid,* 178-179. See Appendix H for a list of the contractors for the relet locks. The locks were relet generally at prices 25 percent above those in the original contracts.
[40] *Ibid,* 181; and Boteler to Mercer, January 14 and 22, 1828, in U.S., Congress, House, Committee on Roads and Canals, *Report of the Committee on Roads and Canals,* H. Report 141, 20th Congress, 1st Session, 1828, Appendix 4, 38-39.
[41] *Proceedings of the President and Board of Directors,* A, 182.
[42] *Ibid,* 183-184, 204, 215. John W. Baker built the new road along Sections C. F.
[43] *Ibid,* 186-187.
[44] *Ibid,* 190-191, and *First Annual report* (1829), C&O Co., in *Proceedings of Stockholders,* A, 50.
[45] *Proceedings of the President and Board of Directors,* A, 195-196.

April 8: By the early spring of 1829, many contractors were facing financial hardship resulting from the rising cost of construction materials and labor. To prevent the bankruptcy of capable contractors who were willing to continue their operations, the board authorized President Mercer to provide additional compensation to them. This authority was given at first only for the lock contractors but was later extended to those on the aqueducts and sections.[46]

April 25: The board was informed that the local jury had completed the condemnation of land required for the construction of the canal through Georgetown to the Montgomery County line at a sum of $30,000. The board accepted the verdicts and appropriated the funds. The board also decided to sell the buildings and other improvements on the line of the canal in Georgetown at a public sale after five-days notice had been given in the Georgetown *Columbian*.[47]

April 25: Apparently the Potomac Mills were not supplying the canal works with sufficient quantities of water lime, because on this date, Chief Engineer Wright was ordered to purchase 4,000 bushels "of the best New York water lime."[48]

April 29: Despite delays caused by the legal dispute with the Baltimore & Ohio Railroad, the canal board began early preparations to extend their line up the Potomac Valley above Point of Rocks. On this date, Resident Engineer Alfred Cruger submitted to the board his plans, profiles and field notes from his recent survey of the line between Point of Rocks and Williamsport.[49]

May 20: The directors ordered the company engineers to build a berm bank or roadway 30 feet wide on each side of Rock Creek Basin.[50]

May 20: President Mercer was authorized to engage the services of 300 stonecutters and masons from Europe. He was also directed to make loans to the contractors to enable them to transport additional stonecutters and masons from other parts of the United States. Later, on June 10, he was instructed to provide for the importation of common laborers from Europe.[51]

June 1: The President and directors informed the canal company stockholders that the line of the canal between Rock Creek and Point of Rocks was under contract. This 48-mile distance included 92 sections, two aqueducts, about 60 culverts, two dams, 27 locks, 17 lockhouses and several basins. The contractors had commenced operations on 73 sections prior to May 1 and on the remaining sections after that date. Section No. 78, the first to be completed, had been constructed between January 15 and May 6. The previous winter had been so severe that the contractors who had begun construction after the August letting were no further ahead in their operations than those who had elected to begin after the arrival of spring. The contractors for the masonry works were generally further behind on their operations than were those for the excavation. The board had enlarged the general dimensions of the canal to 60 feet wide at the surface, 42 feet wide at the bottom, and six feet in depth to improve the course of the waterway at little additional cost. The enlarged dimensions, which were to apply to the canal between Georgetown and Harpers Ferry,

---

[46] *Ibid*, 196, 202, 205.
[47] *Ibid*, 209.
[48] *Ibid*, 209.
[49] *Ibid*, 213.
[50] *Ibid*, 228.
[51] *Ibid*, 226, 284.

had been prompted partially by the conditions attached to the Congressional subscription to canal company stock and partially by the intention of the board to provide water power to Georgetown manufacturers.[52]

June 6: At the urging of Alexander B. McFarland, the newly appointed Superintendent of Cement at Shepherdstown, the board ordered that a cement house be built near the Potomac Mills to protect the hydraulic lime until it was needed on the canal. The sum of $350 was appropriated for this purpose.[53]

June 8: The directors ordered Chief Engineer Wright to supply the contractors on the first and second residencies with adequate supplies of Roman cement. Thomaston lime was to be used as a cement for backing. These arrangements were to last until sufficient quantities of good water lime could be procured from Shepherdstown.[54]

June 10: The board authorized the purchase of locust and heart pine for the construction of lock gates. Nathaniel Billington's proposal for locust timber was accepted at 39 cents per cubic foot, and James Campbell's proposal to supply best heart pine in 2-inch plank was approved at $1.62½ per 100 feet, board measure.[55]

July 1: It was reported to the board that Messrs. R. and H. Fowler of New York, subcontractors under Hurd, Canfield & Co., had completed Section No. 78. As this was the first section to be completed on the canal, the Fowlers were entitled to a $20 silver medal. However, at their request, the board gave them $20 in cash in lieu of the medal.[56]

July 15: The problems caused by the continuing labor shortage in the Potomac Valley and by the stalemated legal dispute with the Baltimore & Ohio Railroad were much in evidence at the board's meeting on this date. President Mercer was directed to pay the expense of transporting workers from New York to the line of the canal. However, when Mercer recommended the purchase of 100 slaves who were to be instructed in the art of stonecutting and masonry, the board refused to support him. As a result of the work already executed and of the controversy with the railroad, the directors reduced the number of residencies from five to four and determined to terminate the services of an unspecified number of engineers.[57]

August 5: Upon the recommendation of Chief Engineer Wright, the board approved the use of cast iron paddle gates for the locks. Patented by John F. King of Washington, the lower lock gates were each to have two paddles, 2 feet by 18 inches and weighing about 160 to 180 pounds.[58]

The board was informed by Inspector of Masonry Robert Leckie that James O'Brien recently had completed Lockhouse No. 5. This was the first such structure on the canal to be fin-

---

[52] *First Annual Report* (1829), C&O Co., in *Proceedings of the President and Board of Directors*, A, 242–244; 256–257; 267–268.
[53] *Proceedings of the President and Board of Directors*, A, 276.
[54] *Ibid*, 278. Two days later, the directors purchased 50 casks of New York water cement already in Georgetown and ordered 200 more for immediate delivery.
[55] *Ibid*, 284.
[56] *Ibid*, 298.
[57] *Ibid*, 308–310; 363.
[58] *Ibid*, 318; Wright to President and Directors, July 30, 1829; and King to President and Directors, August 7, 1829, Ltrs. Recd., C&O Co. Earlier, the plan for the lower lock gates consisted of six wooden paddle gates opening from lateral culverts. *Proceedings of the Stockholders*, A, 19.

ished. According to Leckie, O'Brien was an excellent stone mason and had made one of the best stone jobs on the entire line.[59]

The board directed Inspector of Masonry Leckie to provide for the construction of suitable buildings along the line of the canal for storing cement.[60]

August 19: The directors appointed a committee to draw up a contract with O. H. Dibble for excavating and walling the Rock Creek Basin. After several weeks of negotiations, the signed contract was presented to the board and was promptly approved.[61]

August 26: It was reported to the board that work all along the line of construction was halted because of sickness. Because many of the engineers and contractors were away from the canal, the board was unable to push the work.[62]

September 11: Plagued by the late summer sickness and the rapidly rising cost of construction materials, many contractors had suspended their operations. In an effort to get the work resumed, the board voted to inform the contractors that it would consider as abandoned all works not under operation by October 5.[63]

September 24: The first flood to affect construction of the canal occurred in early August. The areas hardest hit by the freshet were Little Falls, Great Falls and Seneca. The contracts had not provided for additional compensation to cover damages from flooding during construction, the contractors began requesting supplemental aid to cover their losses.[64]

September 25: President Mercer informed the board that he had let the contracts for all the culverts, "except such as were before specially let," to two firms. The culverts below Seneca Creek were contracted to McCord & Mowry, while those above that point were let to Albert Hovey.[65]

September 29: C. K. Gardner of the U. S. Post Office Department notified President Mercer that seven post offices had been established along the canal during the winter of 1828-1829 for the convenience of canal officials and contractors. It is apparent that this had been accomplished after the canal company had put pressure on the postal service to do so. The canal company evidently felt that by providing mail service along the line of construction, faster and more effective communication could be had, which in turn would facilitate construction. The seven locations were as follows: Powder Magazine at Little Falls, Bear Island, Clementon, Seneca Mills, Conrad's Ferry, Mouth of Monocacy and Catoctin. Additional post offices would be established at other locations

---

[59] O'Brien to President and Directors, August 5, 1829; and Leckie to president and Directors, August 2, 1829, Ltrs. Recd., C&O Co.
[60] *Proceedings of the President Board of Directors*, A, 318-319.
[61] *Ibid*, 321, 331.
[62] *Ibid*, 335.
[63] *Ibid*, 346. An inspection tour by President Mercer in mid-September revealed that there were at work on the canal about 1,600 hands, the lowest number of laborers since the commencement of construction. The greatest number of workers was on the stretch between Little Falls and Georgetown, where the epidemic had not spread. The area most affected by the spread of the disease was the line between Seneca and Edward's Ferry. *Ibid*, 353.
[64] Holdsworth and Isherwood to president and Directors, September 24, 1829, and Wright to Mercer, October 3, 1829, Ltrs. Recd., C&O Co.; and *Proceedings of the President and Board of Directors*, A, 320-321.
[65] *Proceedings of the President and Board of Directors*, A, 357.

if they were at least four miles apart. Beginning immediately, the mail was to be delivered twice daily along the canal by horseback.[66]

October 6: Throughout the fall, the problems associated with importing foreign workers troubled the canal company. On October 6, the board directed Clerk Ingle to arrange for the release from prison of those imported laborers who had been incarcerated as "absconding servants" on the condition that they promised to return to the canal works. The following week on October 12, the directors learned that many of the imported laborers had run away and gained employment with the Baltimore & Ohio Railroad, while others had fled to Baltimore to seek the protection of the law. On October 21, Dr. John Little, a Trustee of the Poor in Georgetown, informed the board that 126 workmen from the canal had come destitute and sick to that town. Later, in early November, the company caught up with many of the deserters and prosecuted them as runaways and debtors.

November 7: Chief Engineer Wright submitted a plan for waste weirs along with a list of the number to be built below Seneca Creek. The board approved his report and ordered Clerk Ingle to advertise on the company's office door for the letting of the necessary contracts.[68]

1830

January 13

The directors notified the contractors on the line from Rock Creek to Seneca that their contracts had expired on December 31. However, as satisfactory progress had been made on most of the works, they agreed to set June 1 as the date when all work should be completed to Seneca Falls. The exceptions to this general extension were the heavy embankments requiring time to settle and the culverts. The former were to be completed by May 15 and the latter by April 15. Each contractor would be required to augment his work force to insure that his work would be finished within the specified time.[69]

January 29: The board ordered that a contract be negotiated with Boteler and Reynolds for the supply of 60,000 bushels of Shepherdstown cement in addition to the quantity previously authorized. All of the cement was to be delivered prior to September 1. While the terms of the contract would be the same as earlier ones, the company would pay an additional one cent per bushel for the lime that was delivered before June 1.[70]

January 29: President Mercer and Chief Engineer Wright were authorized to contract for the construction of waste weirs between Georgetown and Seneca Creek.[71]

---

[66] Gardner to Mercer, September 29, 1829, and Nelson to Mercer, September 28, 1829, Ltrs. Recd., C&O Co. Later on February 19, 1930, two more post offices were established at Section No. 8 and Edward's Ferry.
[67] *Proceedings of the President and Board of Directors*, A, 368, 374, 377–381, 389; Wirt to Ingle, October 28 and November 4, 1829; and Little to President and Directors, October 13, 1829, Ltrs. Recd., C&O Co.; and Sanderlin, *The Great National Project*, 74–78.
[68] *Proceedings of the President and Board of Directors*, A, 390.
[69] Ibid, B, 8–9.
[70] Ibid, 16–17.
[71] Ibid, 18.

February 3: The board directed President Mercer to contract with Brackett and Guy for the purchase of 40,000 bushels of water lime at 20 cents per bushel of 70 pounds. The cement was to be delivered by June 1 from their mill on the manor of Charles Carroll of Carrollton at Tuscarora near the Monocacy River.[72]

February 5: The directors ordered that public notice be given that bids for the construction of the culverts between Seneca and Point of Rocks and of Lock No. 25 would be accepted until February 24. The resident engineers were instructed to report those sections above Seneca that had been abandoned and to arrange for their reletting as soon as possible.[73]

February 12: Apparently, the canal company was still having difficulty in acquiring a sufficient supply of hydraulic lime, for on this date Clerk Ingle was instructed to advertise for the purchase of 20,000 bushels of New York water cement to be delivered at Georgetown in April.[74]

February 19: President Mercer was authorized to make a contract for raising the upper chamber and gates of the Old Potomac Company locks at Little Falls to adapt them for use with the increased depth on the new canal. The Little Falls Skirting Canal, which had been converted into a feeder for the Chesapeake & Ohio, had been four feet deep. To insure the new canal of an adequate supply of water, the old canal had been increased to a depth of six feet.[75]

March 3: Chief Engineer Wright was authorized to use Bradford Seymour's patent cast iron lattice gates for one of the locks as an experiment. Already in use on the Erie, Pennsylvania and Ohio Canals, the gates were later installed in the lower gates of Locks Nos. 26–27.[76]

May 31: The board ordered Chief Engineer Wright to prepare an estimate and specification for the northern abutment of the Alexandria Aqueduct prior to making a contract for its construction. Later on October 23, he submitted a design for the abutment to the directors. At that time, they instructed him to make a further study of its cost and to determine the expediency of immediate construction.[77]

June 7: The president and directors reported to the second annual meeting of the stockholders that they expected to bring into use "twenty of the new locks, and the entire canal, from Seneca to the old locks below Little Falls, by the next fourth of July." Although the original intention had been to complete the section by December 31, 1829, the company officials were encouraged that the works had been completed in "little more than eighteen months from the actual commencement" of the canal.

This good news was counterbalanced by the continuing controversy with the Baltimore & Ohio Railroad. After failing to quash the injunction in legal proceedings at Annapolis in August, 1829, the board had reduced the number of engineers and suspended the operations above Seneca, except for those on Aqueducts Nos. 1 and 2 and several difficult sections. They had made provision to relet the contracts for those masonry works above Seneca that had been abandoned but

---

[72] *Ibid*, 21. The contract was confirmed on February 19. Later on June 16, the directors discontinued this contract until the quality of the cement could be improved.
[73] *Ibid*, 23.
[74] *Ibid*, 25.
[75] *Ibid*, 27.
[76] *Ibid*, 34–35.
[77] *Ibid*, 87, 208.

with the stipulation that no cement would be supplied until the work below Seneca was finished.[78]

June 12: William Archer, who had been appointed by the stockholders to report on the progress of the construction in Georgetown, stated that work there was advancing. The Rock Creek Basin was progressing to rapid completion under the supervision of Chief Engineer Wright. The locks and bridges in Georgetown were nearly done as was the portion of the canal between the Foundry and the Market House. A short section of the canal above Georgetown had been filled with water, and the embankments had withstood the pressure of the water very well.[79]

June 25: After examining the canal from Little Falls to Seneca Creek, the directors determined not to water the canal on July 4 as had been discussed earlier except for certain sections that had been completed. Since the work was nearly finished on this section, the contractors were ordered to have their operations done by August 1. Two days earlier, the board extended the time for completion of the Georgetown level to September 25.[80]

July 24: The board authorized President Mercer to enlarge the lockkeepers' houses at Locks Nos. 20 and 23, provided the cost of the former did not exceed $1,300 and that of the latter $1,000. The company's shanties near Little Falls were to be taken down and the materials used to enclose the grounds around the two lockhouses.[81]

August 7: The directors ordered the engineers to advise the contractors that water would be admitted into the canal between Dams Nos. 1 and 2 on September 25. At the same time, lockkeepers were appointed for this portion of the canal.[82]

August 18: Clerk Ingle reported to the board that he had directed W. W. Fenlon to contract with Paterson, Wolcott & to paint some of the completed lock gates for the sum of $25 per lock.[83]

August 21: When the Alexandria Canal Company requested the services of an engineer to survey the route of its waterway, the board recommended that Chief Engineer Wright perform this job. Soon after submitting a design for the northern abutment of the Potomac Aqueduct on October 23, Wright left the Chesapeake & Ohio Canal and moved to New York City. On November 20, the directors selected Nathan S. Roberts to aid in the location of the Alexandria Canal whenever his services were needed.[84]

August 30: Benjamin Wright tendered his resignation from the office of chief engineer to become effective October 1. His stated reason for resigning was due to the fact that difficulties with the Baltimore & Ohio Railroad would hold up active construction operations above Seneca for the foreseeable future. The board accepted his resignation and agreed to abolish the position of chief

---

[78] *Second Annual Report* (1830), C&O Co., in *Proceedings of the President and Board of Directors*, B, 97–98.
[79] *Proceedings of the Stockholders*, A, 119–121.
[80] *Proceedings of the President and Board of Directors*, B, 128–130.
[81] *Ibid*, 148.
[82] *Ibid*, 156–159. See Appendix I for a list of the lockkeepers and the location of the lockhouses.
[83] Fenlon to Ingle, August 18, 1830, Ltrs. Recd., C&O Co. This price covered the cost of two common coats of paint.
[84] *Proceedings of the President and Board of Directors*, B, 167, 208, 224.

engineer when Section A, the Rock Creek Basin and Georgetown tidelock were completed.[85] Other engineering positions were to be eliminated also. After that time, there would be only two residencies covering the line between Georgetown and Point of Rocks: the first would extend from the tide lock to Section No. 40, and the second thence to Point of Rocks. The office of the first resident engineer, Thomas F. Purcell, would be near Seneca Creek, while the office of the second resident engineer, Daniel Van Slyke, who would double as superintendent of the canal, would be located near the mouth of the Monocacy River.[86]

September 25: The board determined that "suitable provision be made for passing horses and foot passengers across the locks from the towing path to the lockkeepers' houses in such manner as not to obstruct the navigation of the canal." The bridge across the canal at Little Falls was to be elevated so as not to hinder canal navigation.[87]

October 2: Before the canal was opened to regular navigation, experiments were made to test its capability of holding water and handling boats. Thus, the first recorded boat passed from Little Falls to Seneca on October 1. That night, a breach occurred in an embankment near the lower end of Section No. 15. Accordingly, the board ordered the construction of a wall, three feet high and eighteen inches thick, on the river side of the high embankment on Sections Nos. 12, 13, 15 and 18. The experiment also revealed the need for flumes around the locks, the directors instructed Superintendent Van Slyke to construct a flume around one lock to test its ability to handle the flow of water.[88]

November 26: In a supplementary report to the company stockholders, President Mercer observed that numerous boats had navigated the distance between Dams Nos. 1 and 2. Work on the Georgetown level was nearly done, with only a little masonry and embanking remaining to be done. Only several months' work would complete the canal to Point of Rocks with the exception of Aqueducts Nos. 1 and 2, Lock No. 24, and Dam No. 2. These structures would require from six to 12 months of labor. To permit navigation to Harpers Ferry, the board was considering a plan to feed the canal at Point of Rocks and from thence extend a slackwater navigation to the Shenandoah River.[89]

1831

January 4: Apparently, the canal was still only in partial use, for on this date, the board decided to suspend navigation on the canal until February 15 so that work on Sections Nos. 13 and 14 could be completed.[90]

March 19: Superintendent Van Slyke on April 2 informed Mercer that the canal between Little Falls and Seneca Falls had been opened to navigation on this date. During the first two weeks of navigation, the canal had been thronged with boats. Because it was difficult to preserve order among the boatmen, he recommended that navigation regulations be adopted and enforced. Later, on July 16, a list of regulations was drawn up and published.[91]

---

[85] *Ibid*, 170.
[86] *Ibid*, 171–174. Wright finally left the service of the company on November 13.
[87] *Ibid*, 189.
[88] *Ibid*, 191–192; and Van Slyke to President and Directors, October 2, 1830, Ltrs. Recd., C&O Co.
[89] *Proceedings of the President and Board of Directors*, B, 231–135.
[90] *Ibid*, 250
[91] Van Slyke to Mercer, April 2, 1831, Ltrs. Recd., C&O Co.

April 1: When Nathan S. Roberts asked for a temporary leave of absence, the board instructed President Mercer to inform him that the legal obstructions to the extension of the canal above Point of Rocks made it necessary for them to abolish his engineering position on the second division of the waterway.[92]

April 29: Prior to the introduction of water in the canal, the practice of the canal company had been to manure the banks and plant grass and trees on them. It was thought that these practices gave the banks greater strength and stability. On this date, the board ordered the suspension of these activities on the unfinished line above Seneca. Apparently, investigation of the operable waterway below that point had revealed the destructive tendencies of these earlier methods.[93]

May 6: President Mercer was authorized to request from the Secretary of War that several members of the U. S. Topographical Engineers examine the canal and report on its present condition, the adequacy of its plan, and the execution of its construction. Later on May 20, Colonel John J. Abert informed Mercer that he and Colonel James Kearney would undertake the examination in June.[94]

May 27: Following an inspection tour of the canal from Georgetown to Point of Rocks by the directors, they made several decisions affecting the lock bridges, the lock gates and the lock flumes. A pivot bridge for wagons and carriages was to be built over Lock No. 13, and broad planks were to be substituted for the plank and timber that had been thrown across the locks so as to enable the lockkeepers to discharge their duties more promptly. As an experiment in facilitating the filling of the locks, a small sluice gate operated by a lever was to be constructed around all the locks; the flumes were to be as far from the lock chamber as practicable, their bottoms were to be five feet above the bottom of the canal, and each was to have sills and gates.[95]

June 6: The president and directors reported to the third annual meeting of the company stockholders that early in the spring the navigation had been extended one mile below Little Falls and more recently one mile further to within sight of Georgetown. A packet boat carrying United States mail was already making daily trips to Seneca from where two public stage lines took the mail and passengers to Leesburg, Virginia via Edward's Ferry. The canal works in Georgetown were nearly completed, and it was anticipated that boats would pass through the tide lock by July 4.

The president and directors gave the stockholders a brief resume of the state of the unfinished line of the canal above Seneca. Locks Nos. 24 and 25 were nearly completed while the foundations of Locks Nos. 26 and 27 had been laid. Aqueduct No. 1 was nearing completion, but Aqueduct No. 2 which had been let to three different contractors was not expected to be finished until November. The culverts were in varying stages of construction, but all of them were expected to be finished by mid-September. Most of the sections were done, and the remainder could be completed within 90 days.

---

[92] *Proceedings of the President and Board of Directors*, B, 295.
[93] *Ibid*, 309.
[94] *Ibid*, 311, 319.
[95] *Ibid*, 324–325. Later on June 10, the board ordered that pivot bridges be constructed over Locks Nos. 26 and 27 and that ferries be provided in all other places where the company had been bound by agreement or by jury verdict to do so. It had been the original intention of the board to build as few bridges as possible and to provide access across the canal by ferries.

Because the controversy with the Baltimore & Ohio Railroad still prevented construction above Point of Rocks, three plans had been advanced for watering the 26 miles above Seneca. The plans, none of which had yet been adopted, included the use of the Monocacy River as a feeder, the construction of a dam below Point of Rocks, and the combined introduction of the Tuscarora, Little Monocacy and several lesser streams into the canal as feeders.[96]

June 10: The board took measures to protect the recently completed embankments from slippage. Where the embankments showed tendencies of washing, the directors ordered that back drains be constructed to catty off the water from the towpath and berm. In addition, the directors, reversing an earlier stand, voted to cover the bank slopes with manure or enriched soil and plant grass seed on the embankments.[97]

June 11: The directors authorized Clerk Ingle to arrange for the printing of 500 copies of the Albert and Kearney report on their recent examination of the canal. In their investigation of the canal, the two topographical engineers commented favorably upon the plan and the construction of the canal. The report is perhaps the earliest comprehensive examination of the engineering technology employed in the design and construction of the waterway. On this date, Abert was elected to a one-year term as a director of the canal company, thereby providing the company with the services of a well-known engineer.[98]

July 16: President Mercer submitted to the board the "Regulations for Navigating the Canal." After reviewing the rules, the directors approved them and ordered them to be printed and distributed. Six days later, the board formally announced that the canal "between the Seneca feeder and the wooden stock next above the foundry and the bridges and roadways within that distance, be declared open and free for trade and passing, subject to the Regulations of the Company."[99]

July 25: The canal company stockholders passed the following resolution relative to the extension of their works from the Rock Creek Basin to the mouth of Tiber Creek:

> Whereas the Corporation of Washington have purchased the Washington Canal and have advertised for proposals for excavating and completing the same, and whereas that part of said canal, from the mouth of the Tiber to 6th Street West is to form a basin for the reception of the waters of the Chesapeake & Ohio Canal; Therefore Resolved, That the President and Directors of the Chesapeake & Ohio Canal Company, be instructed to commence that part of the said Canal extending from the Basin at Rock Creek to the mouth of the Tiber to prosecute the same simultaneously with the work on said basin, provided the said President and Directors shall be satisfied upon a full consideration of all circumstances, be of opinion, that is properly chargeable to the said Corporation.[100]

August 12: Resident Engineer Purcell was directed to survey and locate the extension of the canal from the Rock Creek Basin to Tiber Creek. The extension was to be forty feet wide at the surface and six feet deep and its sides were to be dry-walled.[101]

---

[96] *Third Annual Report* (1831), C&O Co., 334–339.
[97] *Ibid*, 383–384.
[98] *Ibid*, B, 386–387, and U. S., Congress, House, Committee on Roads and Canal, *Chesapeake & Ohio Canal*, H. Report 414 to accompany H. R. 94, 23rd Congress, 1st Session, 1834, 88–105.
[99] *Ibid*, B, 410–419, 432.
[100] *Proceedings of the Stockholders*, A, 186–187.
[101] *Proceedings of the Stockholders*, B, 439

September 16: The board passed two measures relating to the canal in Georgetown. First, a 20-foot wide berm was to be built along the lower side of the canal between High and Frederick Streets. Second, in order to restore the 20-foot wide public highway on the upper side of the canal between High and Congress Street, condemnation proceedings were to be initiated to acquire title to the necessary properties. The proprietors were to be given the right to restore the buildings on the condemned property if they so desired.[102]

September 19: Resident Engineer Purcell informed the board that the canal through Georgetown had been watered. At the conclusion of their meeting, the directors embarked on their packet boat, the "C. F. Mercer," and passed through Locks Nos. 1–4 and landed on the pier at the Rock Creek Basin.[103]

October 28: The board ordered that proposals be received for removing the saw mill at Matildaville to a more suitable site on the Maryland side of the Potomac. All moveable parts of the saw mill were to be stored temporarily at the canal company store house in Georgetown for safekeeping.[104]

November 15: Resident Engineer Purcell reported to the board on his survey of extending the canal from the Rock Creek Basin to Tiber Creek. His report included "an experimental survey of the same thro' the 26th Street West." After considering the merits of his survey, the directors ordered Purcell to make another examination for the canal extension "through Virginia Avenue by tunneling where necessary—the tunnel to be protected by a brick arch." A letter from the Mayor of Washington was also read to the board giving notice that the City of Washington would not pay its $1,000,000 stock subscription to the C&O Canal Company until the Washington Canal was built. Accordingly, the directors ordered Clerk Ingle to inform the mayor that the extension would be placed under contract.[105]

December 17: After further surveys by Purcell and consultation with Abert, the board adopted a plan for the extension of the canal from the Rock Creek Basin to 17th Street. Purcell was ordered to locate the extension of the line and prepare specifications for the work. When this was done, Clerk Ingle was to advertise for job bids which would be received until December 12.[106]

1832

January 7: President Mercer informed the board that the Maryland Court of Appeals, by a vote of 3 to 2, had confirmed the canal company in its claim to the right of prior location *vis a vis* the Baltimore & Ohio Railroad in the disputed passes above Point of Rocks. In making this decision, the judges reversed the decision of the Chancellor, who in the September, 1831 term had released the railroad from the injunctions against it and made those against the canal permanent. The decision had a significant affect on the canal because it opened the way for construction above Point of Rocks.

---

[102] *Ibid,* C, 2–3.
[103] *Ibid,* 5.
[104] *Ibid,* p.21.
[105] *Ibid,* p.26.
[106] *Ibid,* 31, 38, 40, 42.

The directors immediately took steps to commence operations from Point of Rocks to Dam No. 4 above Williamsport. Public notice was to be given that the 12-mile stretch of the canal to Dam No. 3 at Harpers Ferry would be let in "convenient sections" at Harpers Ferry on February 23. At the same time, it was to be announced that the portion of the canal between Dams Nos. 3 and 4 would be let at Shepherdstown on April 4. This construction would allow the canal company to meet the terms of its charter which called for the building of 100 miles of waterway by 1833.

Engineers Purcell and Cruger were commissioned to locate the line all the way to Williamsport. They were to prepare for contract those sections which involved heavy embankments, steep side cutting, deep cutting and rock excavation by the aforementioned dates. In their preparations, they were to adhere to the plan of the canal already constructed as far as Harpers Ferry, but from that point, the canal was to be only 50 feet wide.[107]

January 14: Upon their receipt of the official copy of the decision by the Maryland Court of Appeals, the board determined that contracts would be let on February 23 for the 12 miles between Point of Rocks and Harpers Ferry. At the same time, the directors authorized President Mercer to make contracts for the two miles immediately above Point of Rocks without the usual public advertisement. The two miles included some of the narrowest of the disputed passes, and the directors were eager to occupy the most favorable location for their waterway.[108]

January 21: After considering the various proposals for extending the canal from the Rock Creek Basin to 17th Street, the board accepted the offer of John Carothers for Section I and the bid of J. W. Baker for Section K. The contractors were prohibited from sand blasting during the excavation operations, and they were liable for all damages done by their rock blasting.[109]

February 4: President Mercer informed the board that he had let contracts for Sections Nos. 85–89 pursuant to their order of January 14. Sections Nos. 85–86 were let to Hoffman and Lyles and Sections Nos. 87–89 to Williams and Dawes.[110]

February 4: The board unanimously voted to construct a lock at 17th Street in Washington to provide access for boats between the Washington branch canal and the Potomac River via Tiber Creek. That same day, a proposal by C. T. Le Baron and I. G. Camp was accepted for the construction of the lock. The contract called for a granite lock; but later, on April 30, the contract was changed to a lock of cut sandstone.[111]

---

[107] *Ibid*, 48–49; *Proceedings of the Stockholders*, A, 196; *Fourth Annual Report* (1832), C&O Co., in *Proceedings of the Stockholders*, A, 200; and Sanderlin, *The Great National Project*, 90–91. Apparently, contracts for masonry were not included in this letting, for in separate actions of the board it was determined to let contracts for Dam No. 3 and Aqueduct No. 3 on February 1 and to postpone the contracting for locks pending a study of the merits of filling the locks with water through lateral culverts and through the lock gate valves.
[108] *Proceedings of the President and Board of Directors*, C, 52–53; and Mercer to Cruger and Purcell, January 23, 1832, Ltrs. Sent, C&O Co.
[109] *Proceedings of the President and Board of Directors*, C, 56. The two sections were to be built according to the same dimensions of the canal through Georgetown, and both sides of the prism were to be protected by a vertical wall where it was practicable.
[110] *Ibid*, 63; and Ledger A, 1828–1841, 360, 362, 364, 366, 368.
[111] *Ibid*, 63–64; 130.

February 25: The board let contracts for the construction of Dam No. 3 and Aqueduct No. 3. The proposal of William Easby was accepted for the dam, while that of Tracy and Douglas was approved for the aqueduct.[112]

March 10: The board adopted the specifications for the locks and culverts between Point of Rocks and Harpers Ferry. The time set for receiving proposals for these structures was set at March 14.

The directors also ordered that the towpath in Georgetown between Congress Street and the west side of Frederick Street "be widened where practicable and where necessary." A wall was to be erected on the margin of the towpath to prevent slides.[113]

March 14: The directors took under consideration the proposals and declared contracts for Sections No. 90–112, covering the distance between Point of Rocks and Harpers Ferry. A contract was also let to Lewis Wernwag for the construction of Guard Lock No. 3. The contractors were to commence these works immediately and complete them by December 1.[114]

March 17: On this date, the board let the contracts for the locks and culverts between Point of Rocks and Harpers Ferry. The following contractors' proposals were accepted for the locks: Nos. 30–31 to Obediah Gordon, No. 32 to Lewis Wernwag, No. 33 to James O'Brien, and Nos. 34–35 to Henry Smith. The following contractors' proposals for the culverts were accepted: Nos. 75–79 to Dawes & Williams, Nos. 80–83 to James O'Brien, Nos. 84–87, 89 to Watson, Tainter & Co., and Nos. 88, 90–94 to the John Hay Co.[115]

March 31: The board entered into an agreement with H. B. Richards to quarry and lay stone coping on the front of the Rock Creek Pier and on the towpath wall in Georgetown.[116]

May 7: After receiving word from Resident Engineer Purcell that some 22 miles of the line above Harpers Ferry had been located, the directors resolved to receive job proposals for the construction of Sections Nos. 113–156 until May 30. The contracts for the 44 sections between Harpers Ferry and Dam No. 4 would be let on June 2 and those for the masonry works at a later time.[117]

May 15: Upon the recommendation of President Mercer, the board ordered the company engineers to locate and to prepare for contract the portion of the canal between Dam No. 4 and Licking Creek.[118]

May 31: The question of constructing the Alexandria Aqueduct continued in a stalemate in the face of opposition by Georgetown merchants and the indifference of the C&O Canal Company. As the site for its northern abutment still had not been chosen, the board ordered Purcell to determine its location in conjunction with the chief engineer of the Alexandria Canal Company. Later, on June 7, Alfred Cruger and Wilson M. C. Fairfax were appointed to assist Purcell. On June 23, the board directed Cruger to prepare a plan, specification and preliminary cost estimate for the

---

[112] *Ibid*, 78. Later, the contract with Easby was abrogated when the board decided to use the Government Dam for its water supply.
[113] *Ibid*, 99.
[114] *Ibid*, 104–105. A list of the contractors for these sections may be seen in Appendix J.
[115] *Ibid*, 109.
[116] *Ibid*, 117–118.
[117] *Ibid*, 136–137.
[118] *Ibid*, 139.

construction of the abutment. Two weeks later, on July 7, Purcell notified the directors that the site for the abutment had been selected.[119]

June 2: The board let contracts for Sections Nos. 113–157, covering the distance between Dams Nos. 3 and 4. The directors also accepted the following bids for some of the masonry work: Lock No. 36 to Fries and McDonnell, Lock No. 39 to Wilson and Bryan, and Culverts Nos. 95–99 to Tracy and Douglas.[120]

June 4: The president and directors reported to the fourth annual meeting of the company stockholders that great strides had been made to execute the construction of the canal since the favorable decision by the Maryland Court of Appeals. Furthermore, the line of the canal between Seneca and point of Rocks, on which operations generally had been suspended because of the lack of water from the proposed Dam No. 3, was nearly completed. The chief structure still to be finished was Aqueduct No. 2, but it was anticipated that the structure would be completed before the recently contracted works above Point of Rocks were ready for the admission of water.[121]

June 5: The board let contracts for the construction of Aqueduct No. 4 and the culverts between Harpers Ferry and Dam No. 4. The contract for Antietam Aqueduct was let to Gibson, Noonan, Medler & Fresh & Co. The contractors whose proposals for the culverts were accepted are as follows: Nos. 100–104, 106–107, 113–118 to Gibson, Noonan, Medler & Fresh & Co.; No. 105 to Moore and Temple; Nos. 108–110, 112 to George W. Hunter; and No. 111 to J. P. and J. Dougherty.[122]

June 7: The proposal of Joseph Hollman was accepted for the construction of Dam No. 4. After some modifications in their original bids, Gibson, Noonan, Medler & Fresh & Co. was given the contracts for Locks Nos. 37–38.[123]

June 23: The canal directors began to face two serious obstacles to the further progress of the canal: the five years allowed by the charter for the construction of the first 100 miles would expire in 1833, and the approaching exhaustion of the company's immediate financial resources. Accordingly, the board urged the engineers to consider the following temporary expedients in building the canal above Point of Rocks: deferring the construction of a dam at Harpers Ferry; substituting a suspension aqueduct with a wooden trunk for the proposed stone aqueduct across the Antietam; reducing the width of the canal to 20 feet and the depth to five feet on those sections requiring heavy excavation; dispensing with the coping of the culverts, aqueducts and locks except that required for hanging the lock gates; and slackwater navigation at various points.

The board also determined to hire two individuals who would expedite the construction. To prevent a serious work stoppage during the approaching "sickly season," a physician would be employed to inspect the line of the canal from July to October. His duties were to commence an investigation of the living conditions in and around the workers' shanties, to submit a list of recommendations to protect the health of the canal company personnel, contractors and laborers, and to insure an adequate supply of medicine for the workers.

---

[119] *Ibid,* 157, 165, 176, 184.
[120] *Ibid,* 159–161. A list of the contractors for Sections Nos. 113 157 may be seen in Appendix K.
[121] *Proceedings of the Stockholders,* A, 224.
[122] *Proceedings of the President and Board of Directors,* C, 163.
[123] *Ibid,* 165.

A superintendent of construction would be appointed to oversee the work above Point of Rocks. This man would henceforth make all contracts and inspect the works in progress subject to the general direction of the board. He was also to provide for the care of the sick in his jurisdiction.[124]

July 2: At the recommendation of the resident engineers, the board ordered that where it was expedient, hammer-dressed face work should be substituted for cut-stone face work on the masonry structures above Point of Rocks as a means of lowering construction expenses.[125]

July 17: The directors determined to let contracts for the portion of the canal from Sections Nos. 173–203 on August 23. The line of the canal immediately above Dam No. 4, comprising Sections Nos. 158–172, was to be designed for slackwater navigation and would not be let for construction until after the first 100 miles of the canal were completed. In this way, the canal company would meet the terms of its charter.[126]

August 18: At the recommendation of John J. Abert, the board determined to dispense with the construction of Dam No. 3. Instead, the company engineers were directed to make arrangements to use the water backed by the government dam at Harpers Ferry. Accordingly, a head gate or guard lock was designed for such a connection between the dam and the canal, and the contract for the work was let to Fries and McDonnell.[127]

August 25: The board approved the plan of a bridge and stop gate to be constructed on Section K at G Street in Washington. The proposal of Michael Corcoran was accepted for the masonry and that of Gideon Davis for the iron railing.[128]

August 25: The board let contracts for the sections, locks, culverts and aqueducts between Section No. 173 and Dam No. 5. William and Michael Byrne and Paul Provest were given contracts for Sections Nos. 173 and 187–200, Locks Nos. 43–44, Culverts Nos. 120 and 129–135, Aqueduct No. 5 and Dam No. 5. The other contractors whose proposals were accepted were as follows: No. 174, C. and M. Offutt and R. Anderson; No. 175, Philip Mays & Co.; No. 176, Patrick Kenney; No. 180, Chamberlain and Brown; No. 181, Monegan and Breslin; No. 182, Watkins and Magruder; No. 183, Polly and Draper; No. 184, James Gibbs; No. 185, Adam Young; and No. 186, P. Donovan. The contracts for all these structures specified that the work was to be completed within 12 months. At the same time, a private contract was entered into with Gibson, Noonan & Fresh for the construction of Lock No. 40, the letting of which had been suspended temporarily in June.[129]

August 31: The summer of 1832—the first in which unrestricted construction was possible—proved the most disastrous to the workers. Late in August, Asiatic cholera made its appearance on the line near Harpers Ferry, and it gradually spread westward to Williamsport. As a result of the plague, work was suspended on many of the sections, and fear spread rapidly among the workers. Despite the attempts by the company to aid the victims, many laborers died and many others fled

---

[124] *Ibid*, 174–175.
[125] *Ibid*, 179.
[126] *Ibid*, 181–182, 189.
[127] *Ibid*, 191–192, 207.
[128] *Ibid*, 209.
[129] *Ibid*, 209–211. Some time later, Sections Nos. 201 and 202 were let to the firm of William and Michael Byrne and Paul Provest.

the line of the canal in panic. By the early winter months when the epidemic began to subside, the westward progress of the waterway had all but halted.[130]

November 3: Despite the disruption to construction caused by the Asiatic cholera epidemic, the board continued to press for the completion of the waterway between Point of Rocks and Harpers Ferry. The directors voted to give discretion to President Mercer and the resident engineers to raise the prices for the unfinished masonry on that stretch of the canal as an incentive for the rapid completion of the works. In the future, no monthly estimates were to be made above Harpers Ferry that was under contract to a firm that had suspended work below that town.[131]

1833

February 23: President Mercer announced to the board that the General Assembly of Virginia had passed an act directing the State to purchase 2,500 shares of canal company stock. In return, the company on March 1 agreed to appropriate $80,000 for the construction of outlet locks to permit boats to pass to and from the river. The locks were to be located at the mouth of Goose Creek, the ferry at Shepherdstown, and the mouth of Opequon Creek. The locks were to be completed by November 1, 1835.[132]

April 20: The contract for the construction of Lock No. 45 was let to Byrne, Lathrop and Provest. The portion of the lock that would be underwater when Dam No. 5 was completed was to be constructed immediately. When the dam was finished, operations on the lock would resume so that it could be used as a means of passing boats from the slackwater pool behind the dam to the canal prism.[133]

May 4: The board authorized President Mercer to request the Secretary of the Treasury to order an inspection of the canal. During the current month, the directors anticipated that the canal below Harpers Ferry would be watered. In addition to the 64 miles of completed waterway, 38 miles were under contract.[134]

May 9: After a lengthy battle between the railroad and canal companies over the joint construction of their works between Point of Rocks and Harpers Ferry, an agreement was reached in which the state as well as the companies would participate. In return for permission to construct its tracks between the two towns, the railroad company subscribed to $266,000 of canal stock. The canal company undertook the grading of 4.1 miles of roadbed at the narrow pass where both works came together. As its part, the legislature offered to pass two acts, long the subject of dispute between it and the canal, when the railroad reached Harpers Ferry. These gave the canal

---

[130] *Ibid*, 212, 214–215; Charles N. Rush to president and Directors, August 5, 1832; Mercer to Ingle, September 3, 1832; Boteler to Ingle, September 4, 1832; B. price to Ingle, September 5, 1832; Purcell to President and Directors, September 11, 1832; and Rush to President and Directors, August 5, 1832, Ltrs. Recd., C&O Co.; and Sanderlin, *The Great National Project*, 93–97.

[131] *Proceedings of the President and Board of Directors*, C, 233. Later the board agreed to divide the sections in this area among several contractors in order to expedite the work.

[132] *Ibid*, 288, 293.

[133] *Ibid*, 313, 322.

[134] *Ibid*, 336. On June 5, Mercer was informed that Captain William Gibbs McNeill of the U.S. Topographical Engineers had been assigned to conduct the survey.

permission to sell surplus water and to begin the western section before completing the eastern part of the work.[135]

May 29-30: During an inspection tour of the canal from Georgetown to Williamsport, the directors made numerous decisions relative to the construction of the canal. At Shepherdstown on May 29, they let contracts for grading the 4.1 miles of railroad bed between Point of Rocks and Harpers Ferry. The first two miles below the Harpers Ferry Bridge were assigned to Thomas MacCubbin, the first 1-1/20 miles at the lower end of Point of Rocks were given to Hollman and Lyles, and the remaining portion at the upper end of Point of Rocks was let to Hugh Stewart. The contract for the Shepherdstown River Lock was given to John Cameron.

At Williamsport on the 30th, the directors determined that the canal under construction there be extended to the rock cliffs above the Galloway Mill. The outlet locks under construction above the mouth of the Opequon were to be transferred to the lower end of the extension. A towpath was to be constructed along the margin of the slackwater pool behind Dam No. 4 to facilitate navigation.[136]

June 3: The president and directors reported to the fifth annual meeting of the stockholders that the construction of the waterway had been impeded greatly by the cholera epidemic. However, the masonry between Point of Rocks and Harpers Ferry was expected to be completed within several days, and it was anticipated that the canal between the later town and Seneca would be watered by July1. Operations above Harpers Ferry had resumed on an active scale in April with an average force of 2,700 laborers and 655 work animals and a weekly use of 7,000 pounds of gunpowder.[137]

June 5: The board ordered that the wrought iron paddle gate made by William Easby for Guard Lock No. 3 should be used in a lift lock to test its practicality.[138]

June 28: A contract was let to J. and A Provest to build Sections Nos. 165–172. This work was to be completed by March 1, 1834.[139]

August 20: The board approved a specification drawn up by Engineer Purcell for the towpath along the slackwater above Dam No. 4. The towpath, comprising Section Nos. 157–165, would stretch from the Dam to Lock No. 41. Accordingly, the directors ordered that a contract be made immediately to execute the work.[140]

November 1: Charles B. Fisk, superintendent of the canal between Dams Nos. 2 and 3, reported to the board that water had been admitted into the canal at Harpers Ferry and that it had reached nearly to Seneca.[141]

---

[135] *Laws and Resolutions Relating to the Chesapeake & Ohio Canal* (Washington, 1855), 42–48; *Proceedings of the Stockholders*, A, 268–274; and *Proceedings of the President and Board of Directors*, C, 312, 340–346, 350–351.
[136] *Proceedings of the President and Board of Directors*, C, 357–360.
[137] *Proceedings of the Stockholders*, A, 276–277.
[138] *Proceedings of the President and Board of Directors*, C, 370.
[139] *Ibid,* 392.
[140] *Ibid,* 419; and Ledger A, 1828–1841, 505. A contract for the work was let shortly thereafter to Midler & Co., but the firm formally relinquished its contract on January 15, 1834.
[141] *Ibid,* D, 3.

November 15: Engineer Purcell reported to the board on the best means of providing for the Potomac River trade above Dam No. 5 prior to the completion of the canal below that point. After studying the possible alternatives, he concluded that a temporary lock around the south wing of the dam was most appropriate. The board accepted his recommendation and ordered him to draw up plans and specifications for a lock to be built of wood, or wood and stone combined. When he had determined which plan was best suited to the interests of the company, he was to let a contract for its construction to Stoughton & McGinley.[142]

November 22: Engineer Cruger was ordered to lead a group of company engineers in locating and estimating the cost of the canal from Dam No. 5 to Hancock on the Maryland shore of the Potomac River. At the same time, he was to examine the Virginia shore of the river between those two points and compare the costs of building the canal on the two side of the river.[143]

December 9: On this date, the report of Captain William Gibbs McNeill was read to the directors. At the request of the board, he had been assigned by the Secretary of War in June to survey the completed and unfinished portions of the canal from Georgetown to Dam No. 5. At the time of his survey, the line to Point of Rocks was ready for the admission of water except for several places where slight problems needed repairs. McNeill, as had Abert and Kearney several years before, commented favorably upon the quality of construction that he found.[144]

1834

January 6: The board ordered Clerk Ingle to arrange with the contractors employed on the line of the canal above Dam No. 4 for the temporary suspension of their work with the exception of the lock around Dam No. 5. If the contractors wished to continue their operations, they would have to accept payment with the stocks of the Corporations of Washington and Georgetown held by the canal company or with interest-bearing company bonds.[145]

January 18–24: Open warfare broke out between rival factions of the Irish laborers during the idle winter months. A preliminary skirmish took place between the Corkonians, who were working near Dam No. 5, above Williamsport, and the Longfords, or Fardowners, from the vicinity of Dam No. 4, below the town. Several were killed in the clash before the militia arrived on the scene to restore order. Despite the efforts of local citizen patrols, the Corkonians broke loose again in a few days, committing various acts of violence on the line. On January 24, some 700 Longfords met a force of 300 Corkonians on a hilltop near Dam No. 5. At least five Corkonians were killed in the short, pitched battle and many more in the woods during the flight that followed. After the victorious Longfords returned to their shanties at Williamsport, the local militia kept order until two companies of U. S. Troops arrived from Fort McHenry[146]

---

[142] *Ibid*, 13, 22. The lock was completed by May 2, 1834, and it was rebuilt by Wilcox and Stoughton in September 1834.
[143] *Ibid*, 18.
[144] *Ibid*, 29; and Report 414, pp.141–157.
[145] *Proceedings of the President and Board of Directors*, D, 39.
[146] *Niles' Register*, Vol. XLV (January 25, 1834), 336; *Ibid*, Vol. XLV (February 1, 1834), 382–383; and Purcell to Ingle, January 23, 1834; Raton to Janney, Smith and Gunton, January 31, 1834; and Purcell to President and Directors, January 29, 1834, Ltrs. Recd., C&O Co.

February 7: The canal directors agreed to construct and pay for the culverts that "were necessary on that part of the Baltimore & Ohio Railroad" which was to be graduated by the canal company.[147]

March 18: Superintendent Fisk informed the directors that it would be necessary to build several waste weirs on the line of the canal above Harpers Ferry now about to be opened to navigation. The board authorized the construction of those waste weirs that were indispensable to the security of the canal and that would be easily let for contract.[148]

April 11: Engineer Cruger submitted his report on the survey of the line of the canal between Dam No. 5 and the Cacapon River. Because the canal company finances were desperate, the report was filed away for future consideration.[149]

April 17: The canal company reported to the House Committee on Roads and Canals that 64 miles of the canal, stretching from Georgetown to Harpers Ferry, had been completed in October 1833. On the remaining portion of the canal under contract, only one lock and Aqueduct No. 4 remained to be finished, to complete the line to Dam No. 4. The distance between Dams Nos. 4 and 5 would be completed by the fall of 1834 as the majority of the work on this portion of the line was already done. As of March 1, the sum of $3,547,661.50 had been spent on building the canal.[150]

May 3: The contractors building the railroad for the canal company above Point of Rocks applied for ant extension of time in which to complete their contracts. Because the railroad consented to the time extension, the canal board directed that the contracts should be completed by July 1, 1834.[151]

June 2: The president and directors informed the sixth annual meeting of the company stockholders that operations on the canal during the preceding 12 months had been hampered by the desperate state of the company's finances. At that time, the canal had been completed to Dam No. 4, some 86 miles west of Washington. In addition, 20 miles of the canal above that point were nearly done, but work on this stretch had been suspended temporarily until more funds became available. The railroad above Point of Rocks, which the canal company had agreed to build, would be completed in July with funds supplied by the Baltimore & Ohio Railroad Company.[152]

September 18: The board appointed Directors John J. Abert and William Gunton to proceed to Williamsport for the purpose of putting under contract all work necessary to complete the canal to Dam No. 5. On October 1, the two men reported that the principal obstacle to the achievement of this objective had been the abandonment of Sections Nos. 165–172 by J. & A. Provest. Accordingly, the sections had been relet to the subcontractors of the Provests with the stipulation that the work be done by March 1, 1835. The contracts for Culverts Nos. 118 and 119 were also let, the former to William Broun and the latter to Slayman & Donley. After an inspection of the ground

---

[147] *Ibid*, 47.
[148] *Proceedings of the President and Board of Directors*, D, 56.
[149] *Ibid*, 72.
[150] Report 414, 16, 187.
[151] *Proceedings of the President and Board of Directors*, D, 85.
[152] *Sixth Annual Report* (1834), C&O Co., 3–5.

between Dams Nos. 4 and 5, the two directors urged the board to erect a stop gate at the upper end of the heavy work above Williamsport.[153]

October 18: The directors instructed Engineer Fisk to have the canal correctly measured from the tide lock at Georgetown to Shepherdstown. Stones or locust posts were to be placed on the berm side of the canal at intervals of one mile, designating the distance from the eastern terminus.[154]

December 3: Engineer Purcell notified the directors that water had been admitted into the canal at Dam No. 4. Thus it was necessary to provide for lockkeepers, the board authorized Fisk to take charge of the newly opened section of the canal, to appoint temporary lock operators, and to erect shanties for their accommodation.[155]

1835

January 21: Charles B. Fisk requested and received permission from the board to build three waste weirs on the recently completed section of the canal between Shepherdstown and Dam No. 4.[156]

February 25: The board moved to extend the date of completion of Sections Nos. 166, 170, 171 and 172 to March 15 because the Irish laborers on these sections had struck recently for higher wages. The strike had delayed operations on these sections, the last to be finished before the canal could be watered between Dams Nos. 4 and 5.[157]

March 20: The board was informed that the Maryland legislature had passed an act authorizing a loan of $2,000,000 to the canal company to complete the waterway to Cumberland. At a meeting of the company stockholders on April 22, the company formally accepted the loan.[158]

April 1: The board ordered Fisk to make immediate arrangements to revise the location of the line of the canal from Dam No. 5 to the Cacapon River that had been made in the spring of 1834 by Alfred Cruger. This stretch of the waterway was to be prepared for contract, although Fisk was instructed to designate which sections could be deferred temporarily.[159]

April 22: President George C. Washington informed the stockholders that since their June 1834 meeting, navigation had been opened 48 miles above Harpers Ferry. The canal was now open for a distance of 110 miles above Washington, in addition to an eight-to-ten-mile slackwater navigation above Dam No. 5.[160]

---

[153] *Proceedings of the President and Board of Directors*, D, 161, 166–168. The contract for the stop gate was let to E. & J. Stake on November 12, 1834.
[154] *Ibid*, 175.
[155] *Ibid*, 199.
[156] *Ibid*, 224. The contract for these three structures was let to John Cameron; they were completed in late April.
[157] *Ibid*, 234, 254–257; and Hagerstown *Torchlight* quoted in *Niles' Register*, Vol. XLVII (February 25, 1835), 429.
[158] *Proceedings of the Stockholders*, A, 363–378; and *Proceedings of the President and Board of Directors*, D, pp.261, 265, 281–183.
[159] *Proceedings of the President and Board of Directors*, D, 269–270.
[160] *Proceedings of the Stockholders*, A, 368.

April 29: Upon the acceptance of the $2,000,000 loan from the State of Maryland, the board appointed a committee to report on a plan to extend the canal from Dam No. 5 to Cumberland. In their first report on this date, the committee urged that this part of the canal be placed under the immediate superintendence of a commissioner to be appointed by the board. The work had moved so far westward that it was no longer possible for the directors, meeting in Washington, to maintain adequate control of operations. The commissioner, according to the committee, should have authority over lesser officials, land acquisition, company property utilization, and reletting abandoned contracts. After some discussion, the board accepted the committee's proposals and appointed one of its own members, George Bender, to fill the office of commissioner.[161]

April 29: In an effort to reduce construction expenses, the board resorted to building small, temporary lockhouses. On this date, Josephus Beall was paid for the building of three such structures. During the fall and winter of 1834–35, Isaac Williams also built four temporary lockhouses at Locks Nos. 28, 29 34 and 37.[162]

May 25: The board directed Engineer Purcell to examine and locate the line of the canal from the South Branch to Cumberland. The work was to be prepared for contract as soon as possible. Following this location, he was to locate the line from the Cacapon River to the South Branch.[163]

May 25: The board let a contract to Joseph Hollman to construct a flume around Lock No. 44 and a "suitable" brick or stone lockkeepers house near the lock. He also was given the privilege of constructing, at his own expense, a dry dock for the repair of boats. As part of the contract, Hollman was appointed lockkeeper at an annual salary of $150, and he agreed to pay an annual rent of $150 for the use of surplus water at the lock.[164]

May 27: Following negotiations with Alexandria Canal Company, the board appointed Captain William Turnbull to superintend the construction of the northern abutment of the Potomac Aqueduct. Preparatory to letting of a contract for the work, Turnbull was instructed to prepare a plan, specification and cost estimate for the structure.[165]

June 1: President George C. Washington informed the seventh annual meeting of the company stockholders that the $2,000,000 loan from the State of Maryland in March had afforded "the means for a spirited prosecution of the eastern section" and had strongly fortified "our belief in the ultimate connection with the Western waters." According to the president, a continuous canal was "now opened for navigation for the distance of one hundred and ten miles, from the basin in Washington to Dam No. 5, with the exception of about three miles of slack water above Dam No. 4, along Galloway's cliffs, where it is designed to construct a towpath, using the river (having a depth of from ten to fifteen feet) in place of a canal." During the past 12 months, the canal between Dams Nos. 4 and 5 had been finished and opened to navigation.

The board, anxious to begin construction above Dam No. 5, had sent out two surveying parties after the $2,000,000 loan. One group, led by Resident Engineer Fisk, was currently preparing the line between Dam No. 5 and the Cacapon River for contracting, while a small party, under Resident Engineer Purcell, was surveying the line from the South Branch to Cumberland.

---

[161] *Proceedings of the President and Board of Directors*, D, 270, 294–301.
[162] Ibid, 301; and *Articles of Agreement with Isaac Williams, October 2, 1834*, Ltrs. Recd., Chief Engineer.
[163] *Proceedings of the President and Board of Directors*, D, 311, 318–319.
[164] Ibid, 314.
[165] Ibid, 320. Turnbull submitted the requested documents on August 5.

As soon as the necessary arrangements could be made, the line between the Cacapon and South Branch would be made. During the summer, the board intended to let contracts for the masonry structures and the sections requiring heavy excavation. Since there was a lack of good building stone in the upper Potomac Valley, the board suggested the construction of temporary wooden locks where it was necessary.[166]

June 1: The board took several steps to expedite the future work on the canal above Dam No. 5. Contracts were ratified with James Hook of Hancock and George Reynolds of Cumberland to supply the line with hydraulic cement. A storehouse was to be built at McCoys Ferry to receive the cement, and Commissioner Bender was authorized to contract for the transportation of the cement to that point.[167]

June 17: A committee of the board was authorized to contract "for the construction of a Stop Gate at or near the site of the late temporary lock on Sect. D and also for the rubble stone wall proposed for the security of the embankment of Section B, both above and below the foundry.[168]

June 17: The board ordered Clerk Ingle to advertise for proposals for the construction of those sections, locks, aqueducts, culverts and dams between Dam No. 5 and the Cacapon that Resident Engineer Fisk certified as being ready for contract. The rime line for completion of the masonry was set at October 1, 1836, and that for the rest of the work at November 1, 1836.[169]

July 3: After examining the proposals for the masonry structures and difficult sections between Dam No. 5 and the Cacapon River, the board let a large number of contracts.[170]

July 8–22: During this period, the board examined the entire line of the canal from Georgetown to Cumberland. Among the most significant decisions that the directors made were the following:

> (1) A site was chosen for the Goose Creek River Lock as required by the 1833 act passed by the Virginia legislature. Resident Engineer Fisk was directed to prepare a plan and cost estimate preparatory to placing the lock under contract;
> (2) Upon finding that Sections Nos. 167–168 were located too close to the river, the directors ordered that new section be formed farther from the water provided that the additional land could be obtained at a reasonable cost;
> (3) The directors instructed Purcell to ascertain the best route for the canal and Dam No. 8 in the vicinity of Cumberland. Although somewhat undecided, they were inclined to pass the canal behind the town of Wills Creek, the shortest line to the west.[171]

August 5: The board directed that mile posts be erected on the towpath side of the recently opened portion of the canal.

---

[166] *Seventh Annual Report* (1835), C&O Co., 3–11.
[167] *Proceedings of the President and Board of Directors*, D, 324. On June 10, a contract was let to George Shafer, a Williamsport water lime manufacturer, to supply additional cement to the line.
[168] *Ibid,* 342. A contract for the stop gate was let to William Easby in August and the structure was completed in the spring of 1837.
[169] *Ibid,* 341.
[170] *Ibid,* 360–362. *Ibid,* 9.
[171] *Ibid,* 363–371.

The board approved a proposal by William Easby to construct the gates and other woodwork for the stop lock about to be constructed on Section C. Easby was also to build gates and other woodwork for the waste weir to be constructed at the Old Locks near Little Falls.[172]

September 2: The board accepted the bid of Michael Byrne to construct the river lock at Edward's Ferry and specified that the work was to be done by June 1, 1836. The proposal of John Cameron was approved for the building of Culverts Nos. 183–186.

The board ordered the division superintendents to determine the proper sites for lockhouses to be built along the canal. The locations of the houses were to be chosen having reference to the construction of flumes and the use of water power. Clerk Ingle was directed to advertise for proposals to build the lockhouses and to fence in the attached grounds.[173]

October 21: Periodically, the board let contracts for additional sections above Dam No. 5. On this date, the directors approved the bid of Enos Childs for Section No. 208, and later, on January 20, 1836, that of R. W. Watkins for Section No. 231.[174]

November 5: The discussion over the route of the waterway at Cumberland was long and heated. The directors were at first inclined to pass the canal behind the town of Wills Creek, the shortest line to the west. Upon receiving repeated protests from the local citizens and an offer of the city to waive all claims to property damages, the directors on this date reconsidered their plans and adopted a low-level route along the river into the center of the town.[175]

November 11: The board ordered that proposals would be received until December 21 for constructing the dams, the masonry, and the difficult sections of the line of the canal between the Cacapon River and Cumberland. Bids were also to be received for the northern abutment of the Potomac Aqueduct. The date for receiving the proposals was later extended to January 6.[176]

December 4: Resident Engineer Fisk was authorized to prepare for contract those sections (excluding sections of light excavation) between Dam No. 5 and the Cacapon that he considered it expedient to let.[177]

December 21: Purcell and Fisk recommended to the board that slackwater navigation be employed from Dam No. 5 to Lock No. 45. The directors accepted their report and ordered that this section of the canal be constructed according to the plans which they submitted.[178]

December 21: Upon the recommendation of Fisk, the board determined to build a tunnel about 3,000 feet long on the line below South Branch. The tunnel was to have a height above the water

---

[172] *Ibid*, 373, 377.
[173] *Ibid*, 394–395.
[174] *Ibid*, 416; E., 10.
[175] *Report of the Committee on the Location of the Canal from Dam No. 6 to Cumberland, October 9, 1835*, Ltrs, Recd., C&O Co.; *Proceedings of the Stockholders*, A, 417–421; *Proceedings of the President and Board of Directors*, D, 423–424; Sanderlin, *The Great National Project*, 114–115. Earlier, the board had decided to omit the construction of Dam No. 7 after considering several sites for its location near the mouth of the South Branch.
[176] *Proceedings of the President and Board of Directors*, D, 427, 434. Difficult sections were defined as those that would cost over $10,000 to construct.
[177] *Ibid*, 436.
[178] *Ibid*, 442–443.

line equal to the elevation of the permanent bridges on the canal. Fisk was directed to submit plans and estimates for the work.[179]

1836

January 16: On January 9, Fisk informed the directors that the current estimated cost of the line from Dam No. 5 to Cumberland was much greater than any former estimates. Accordingly, the board appointed a committee to consider what work below the Cacapon not then under contract should be let and what structures above that point should be placed under contract. Upon the recommendation of Fisk, the board determined to let contracts for all those sections not then under contracts below the Cacapon River. All work above that river was to be suspended with the exception of Sections Nos. 333–334 (deep cut at Oldtown), Locks Nos. 54–55, and Paw Paw Tunnel. After considering the proposals already received for the work above the Cacapon, the board accepted the bid of William Woodburn for Sections Nos. 333–334 and that of Henry Smith for Locks Nos. 54–55.[180]

January 20: On the recommendation of Resident Engineer Fisk, the board ordered that a lockkeeper's house be constructed near the site of Locks Nos. 62–66. When it was completed, the house was to be used by the engineer supervising the construction of Paw Paw Tunnel.[181]

February 10: Resident Engineer Fisk submitted to the board a plan and specification for the Paw Paw Tunnel and an improved specification of lockhouses. Both plans were adopted by the board. The latter plan was to be used for all the lockhouses that would be built except for one at Prathers Neck and one near the tunnel, both of which were to have dimensions of 30 by 22 feet and modified floor plans.[182]

February 10: The board considered the proposals for the sections between Dam No. 5 and the Cacapon River that were not under contract. On this date, the directors accepted bids for 34 sections.[183]

March 15: After considering the proposals received for the construction of Paw Paw Tunnel, the board accepted the bid of Lee Montgomery providing that the conditions of the contract, which still had to be drawn, were agreeable to the interests of the canal company.[184]

March 23: Two contracts were let on this date for masonry work between Dams Nos. 5 and 6. Henry Smith was given the contracts for the construction of a lockhouse at Lock No. 54 and of Culvert No. 198 on Section No. 258.[185]

March 30: The board received word that Thornton G. Bradley had offered to build the large lockhouse for Locks Nos. 62–66 at the site of Paw Paw Tunnel for $1,275. The directors voted to of-

---

[179] *Ibid*, 443.
[180] *Ibid*, E, 2–6.
[181] *Ibid*, 9.
[182] *Ibid*, 18.
[183] *Ibid*, 18–19. A list of the contractors for Sections Between Dam No. 5 and the Cacapon River may be seen in Appendix M.
[184] *Ibid*, 29. On April 6, the contract was written with the stipulation that the tunnel be completed by July 1, 1838.
[185] *Ibid*, 32.

fer contracts to Bradley for both the large lockhouses at Prathers Neck and at the tunnel for $1,200 each. They also determined to let contracts for the standard-sized lockhouses for $950 each.[186]

April 20: The board ordered the division superintendents to enclose the one-acre lots around the lockhouses with post and rail fences where the land for such purposes had been acquired by the canal company.[187]

April 27: The board formally accepted a new seal for the canal company. The seal incorporated scenes from industry, agriculture and shipping with a canal shown as the connecting link binding these sectors of the economy together. The motto inscribed around the edge of the seal was the fitting Latin phrase, "Esto Perpetua Perservando."[188]

May 4: Since many of the contractors were being forced to abandon their contracts because of the rising costs of construction and labor, the board became alarmed that construction on the canal might soon come to a standstill. Accordingly, the board agreed to adopt a new policy that when a contract was one-half completed, the contractor would be paid one-fourth of the retained money on his contract then in the hands of the canal company. When three-fourths of the contract was completed, all but ten percent of the retained money would be returned to the contractor.[189]

May 21: The board let contracts for 10 permanent lockhouses to three contractors. Contracts for lockhouses at Locks Nos. 28, 29 and 34 were let to Michael Foley, provided that one house be finished by the fall. John G. Grove was awarded contracts for six houses at $950 each, with the proviso that they were all to be enclosed and have their floors laid before 1837. The bid of Jonah Hood to build houses at Locks Nos. 35–36 was also accepted.[190]

May 27: The board let contracts for four culverts to two contractors: G. M. Watkins was given the contract for Culvert No. 162, while John Bain received the contracts for Culverts Nos. 160, 164 and 166, the latter two having been abandoned by James Lonergan.[191]

June 4: A major flood struck the canal in late May and early June, causing great damage to the canal below Dam No. 5 and hampering operations above that point. Navigation from Georgetown to Harpers Ferry was not restored until mid-June and from Harpers Ferry to Dam No. 5 until early July.[192]

June 8: President George C. Washington informed the directors that the Maryland legislature had passed an act four days earlier authorizing a state subscription of $3,000,000 to the stock of the canal company. The act was a comprehensive bill authorizing the expenditure of $8,000,000 to various internal improvements in the State.[193]

---

[186] *Ibid*, 36.
[187] *Ibid*, 47.
[188] *Ibid*, 49.
[189] *Ibid*, 53–54.
[190] *Ibid*, 63.
[191] *Ibid*, 66.
[192] *Ibid*, 70–71, 77, 89.
[193] *Ibid*, 72, 81, 88.

June 15: President Washington reported to the eighth annual meeting of the company stockholders that during the preceding year, the line of the canal between Dams Nos. 5 and 6 had been put under contract. Some sections were completed already, while others were nearly done. Paw Paw Tunnel and the deep cut at Oldtown, both requiring longer periods for their construction than any other works above the Cacapon, also had been placed under contract. While the work was progressing, the scarcity of laborers had prevented the work from progressing as rapidly as the board had wished.[194]

June 20: The board let contracts to John Moore to construct Culverts Nos. 147–148 and 151–152.[195]

June 20: The board authorized Resident Engineer Fisk to accept the Maryland governor's appointment to survey the country between the canal and Baltimore to determine the best location for a connecting cross-cut canal.
 The board confirmed contracts that the commissioner had made with Michael Byrne Co. for the construction of Locks Nos. 45–46 and 48–50.[196]

July 29: The directors let three contracts, the most important of which was for the construction of a towpath along the slackwater from Dam No. 4 to Lock No. 41. The board had adopted such a plan on April 14 and had accepted the specification for the work drawn up by Fisk on June 29. The contract was given to Joseph Hollman.
 The other contracts let by the board were as follows: Stop Gate in Maryland abutment to Dam No. 4 to G. W. Rogers; waste on Section No. 243 to Daniel K. Cahoon; and Culvert No. 188 to G. W. Higgins.[197]

August 10: The board let a contract to Thomas M. McCubbin for constructing a waste weir on Section No. 207.[198]

August 17: The board made three decisions concerning the construction of the canal: (1) mile posts were to be placed along the waterway above Harpers Ferry in the same manner as they were below; (2) The number of each lock and the elevation above tidewater were to be painted on the balance beams of the lower lock gates; and (3) the Williamsport Basin was to be walled as soon as the town council provided a conveyance for the wash of Potomac Street into Conococheague Creek.[199]

August 18: Upon the recommendation of Resident Engineer Fisk, the board adopted the use of "radiating shear paddle gates" in the locks between Dam No. 5 and the Cacapon River. A contract was let to Daniel Rodgers for finishing 10 sets of gates at $366 each. The gates were to be made at the Smith & Co. Foundry in Alexandria, Virginia.[200]

August 20: Mindful of the dire straits of the contractors caused by rapidly rising costs of labor and materials, the board authorized Resident Engineer Fisk to recommend measures to prevent

---

[194] *Eighth Annual Report* (1836), C&O Co., 8.
[195] *Proceedings of the President and Board of Directors*, E, 78.
[196] Ibid, 76.
[197] Ibid, 41, 84–85, 115, 123.
[198] Ibid, 118.
[199] Ibid, 122–123.
[200] Ibid, 124.

the continued abandonment of contracts. Fisk responded with a proposal to increase the estimates of 18 contractors by about eight percent, and the board quickly adopted the recommendation. Later, in February 1837, a directors' committee recommended a further advance of $106,808 to the contractors on the 27 miles. In August 1837, Fisk made out estimates for the 50 miles above Cacapon at a 30 percent increase over January 1836 prices.[201]

August 25: The board had intended originally to build a feeder canal from the Cacapon River to the waterway, but it finally determined upon the construction of Dam No. 6 near the mouth of the river. On this date, the board approved the plan and specification for the dam and its abutments and accompanying guard lock submitted by Fisk.

At the recommendation of Superintendent Elgin, the board let a contract to Jonah Hood for the construction of a lockhouse at Lock No. 32. So that the structure could be built at its approved location, Fisk was authorized to alter either the plan or size of the house.

Fisk was directed to employ temporary assistants to prepare the land on the line of the canal from the Cacapon River to the South Branch for jury condemnation or acquisition by the canal company.[202]

September 6: The board let contracts to Henry Wade for the construction of Culverts Nos. 144 and 145.[203]

September 14: After considering the proposals for the construction of the Dam No. 6 complex, the board accepted the proposal of Joseph Hollman and George Reynolds for the dam and that of George Weaver for the dam abutments and guard lock.[204]

September 21: The board let a contract to John Seales to construct a waste weir on Section No. 203 just above Dam No. 5.[205]

September 26: The board determined to purchase a house and Lot No. 3 in Berlin (now Brunswick) for use as a lockhouse at Lock No. 30. The directors agreed to pay Robert Kimble, the owner, the sum of $1,050 plus additional money to cover the cost of recent repairs to the house.[206]

October 14: The board let a contract to William Brown for the construction of Waste Weir No. 55.[207]

November 9: The board let a contract to Harvey Cogsil for constructing Waste Weir No. 59.[208]

November 16: The board let a contract to George W. Higgins for constructing Culvert No. 188.[209]

---

[201] *Ibid*, 126–127, 129; Fisk to Bender, August 22, 1836 and August 3, 1837, Ltrs. Sent, Chief Engineer; Ingle to Henderson, January 4, 1837, and Ingle to Bender, February 9, 1837, Ltrs. Recd., C&O Co.; and *Report of the Committee to the Directors*, February 4, 1837, Ltrs. Recd., C&O Co.
[202] *Proceedings of the President and Board of Directors*, E, 130–131.
[203] *Ibid*, 137.
[204] *Ibid*, 141–142.
[205] *Ibid*, 144. Available documentation indicates that this waste weir was identified as Waste No. 51.
[206] *Ibid*, 121–122, 146.
[207] *Ibid*, 156.
[208] *Ibid*, 167.
[209] *Ibid*, 168.

November 23: Commissioner Bender informed the board that labor disorders at Paw Paw Tunnel had hampered operations on that structure. The trouble had included beatings, destruction of property, and other forms of physical violence. He attributed the disturbances to the activities of a secret terrorist society from New York—probably an early labor union or Irish fraternal organization.[210]

December 7: The board authorized the construction of lockhouses at Tide Lock B (presently at the corner of 17th Street and Constitution Avenue) and at Lock No. 16.

December 28: The board approved a specification for the post and rail fence to be constructed on the towpath at various points between Point of Rocks and Harpers Ferry. Accordingly, the directors ordered that proposals be invited immediately for the construction of the fence.[211]

1837

January 4: To prevent future damage to the Nolands Ferry vicinity from high water, the board authorized Superintendent Elgin to construct a waste weir near the foot of Lock No. 28 and to place in charge of the lockkeeper of Lock No. 27 a double set of stop planks for use at Monocacy Aqueduct.[212]

February 15: Superintendent Elgin was authorized to let contracts to Elisha Howard and John Hoskinson to build a post and rail fence along the line of the canal at various points between Point of Rocks and Harpers Ferry. As part of the agreement between the canal company and the Baltimore & Ohio Railroad resulting from the Maryland Act of 1836 to promote internal improvements, the railroad paid $2,723 to the canal for the erection of the fence.[213]

March 1: When operations on the canal resumed, the construction was threatened by a critical labor shortage. Accordingly, the board sent Superintendent of Masonry McFarland to Philadelphia and New York to induce workers to come to the canal. However, he was instructed not to bind the canal company to any payment of funds to those who agreed to work on the waterway.[214]

April 1: To avoid the difficulties to construction, which had been experienced by the erection of Dam Nos. 4 and 5 and the consequent backing of water for miles, the board let a contract to John Cameron for the construction of Aqueduct No. 8. The contract was approved with the proviso that it could be terminated when the abutments had been built one foot above the apex of Dam No. 6.[215]

April 12: The canal board was anxious to begin operations on the 50 miles between Dam No. 6 and Cumberland, Chief Engineer Fisk was directed to report by May 10 on those sections, locks, aqueducts, culverts and dams which were ready for contract.[216]

---

[210] *Ibid*, 172; and Bender to Washington, November 17, 1836, Ltrs. Recd., C&O Co.
[211] *Proceedings of the President and Board of Directors*, E, 133, 179, 185.
[212] *Ibid*, 189.
[213] *Ibid*, 166, 173–175, 185, 209.
[214] *Ibid*, 215.
[215] *Ibid*, 230.
[216] *Ibid*, 233–234. On this date, Fisk had his position title changed from Resident Engineer to Chief Engineer.

May 3: The board let a contract to William W. Warrington for the construction of all culverts between Dam No. 6 and Aqueduct No. 8. The contract permitted the canal company to terminate the agreement once the work was built one foot above the comb of Dam No. 6.[217]

May 3: The board let a contract to James A. Foster to construct a lockhouse at Lock No. 33.[218]

May 10: The board authorized Commissioner Bender to accept proposals for the construction of lockhouses required on the line of the canal under contract between Dams Nos. 5 and 6. The price of the structures was not to exceed $950.[219]

May 17: The canal board authorized Commissioner Bender to accept proposals for the two large lockhouses at Prathers Neck and at Paw Paw Tunnel. The prices for the structures were not to exceed $1,250 each, and their dimensions were to be those adopted in February, 1836.[220]

May 26: The board let a contract to James Ellis to build Waste Weir No. 62 on Section No. 243.[221]

June 7: The board let a contract to William Broun for constructing a stop gate and bridge on Section No. 213.[222]

June 12: The board let a contract to John Seale for constructing a towpath along the slackwater from Dam No. 5 to Lock No. 45.[223]

June 12: President George C. Washington reported to the ninth annual meeting of the stockholders that the works on the canal had been "prosecuted with all possible vigor" during the past year. However, the construction had been hampered by the rising cost of construction and the competition for labor as a result of the numerous internal improvements under construction in the east. The 27-mile line between Dam No. 5 and 6 was still under construction, and the Paw Paw Tunnel and deep cut at Oldtown were underway. Under a provision of the law of the State of Virginia making a subscription of $250,000 to the stock of the canal company, two outlet locks had been built at Edwards Ferry and near the junction of the Shenandoah and the Potomac Rivers. Since the last annual meeting, the towpath for the slackwater pool behind Dam No. 4 had been put under contract; two miles of it were finished and in use, and the remaining 1-1/4 miles would be completed during the summer. Excellent progress had been made on Dam No. 6. To avoid the difficulties in construction which had been experienced by the erection of Dams Nos. 4 and 5 and the consequent backing of water for miles, the board had placed under contract the section above Dam No. 6, Aqueduct No. 8, and the culverts that opened into the pool. Many of the engineers were at work locating the line from the Cacapon to Cumberland so that by August 1 contracts for

---

[217] *Ibid*, 250. On June 19, the contract was reassigned to Robert Taylor prior to the commencement of construction.
[218] *Ibid*, 245–250.
[219] *Ibid*, 256.
[220] *Ibid*, 259.
[221] *Ibid*, 264–265.
[222] *Ibid*, 213.
[223] *Ibid*, 276.

the entire line between the latter and the Narrows could be let. Below the Narrows, the masonry works and the difficult sections would also be let.[224]

June 23: The board let a contract to Michael Byrne for the construction of a double square drain. The structure is identified as No. 138, indicating that it may have been numbered consecutively with the culverts.[225]

July 19: It was reported to the board that a lockhouse had been completed at Guard Lock No. 5 by George Fagen. This indicates that the contract, which did not appear in the written proceedings of the directors, probably had been let some time during the early spring.[226]

July 19: Clerk Ingle submitted to the board a revised form for contracts to be used in the approaching letting. This form was the printed 1837 specifications and contracts, many of which remain extant.[227]

July 24: The board let contracts for the construction of four lockhouses. The proposal of James A. Foster for a house 20-by-32 feet at Lock No. 38 was accepted, while the bids of Jesse Schofield for standard-size houses at Locks Nos. 46, 51 and 53 were approved.[228]

September 20: In order to construct the sections immediately above Dam No. 6 before the structure's backwater would affect them, the board let contracts for Sections Nos. 263–264 to John H. Mann and for Sections Nos. 265–266 to Barnard Groman.[229]

September 27: The board let contracts for the construction of 54 sections and four locks between Dam No. 6 and Cumberland. The sections were to be completed by December 15, 1839, and the locks by November 1, 1839.[230]

September 29: The board let contracts for the construction of Aqueducts Nos. 9–11, Locks Nos. 56–66 and 69–72, Dam No. 8, and Guard Lock No. 8. In addition, a contract was let to Timothy Cunningham to build a stop gate on Section No. 217.[231]

October 4: The board let a contract to E. M. Gatton for the construction of Culvert No. 213.[232]

November 15: Superintendent Elgin was authorized to construct a waste weir immediately below Lock No. 30.[233]

1838

---

[224] *Ninth Annual Report* (1837), C&O Co., 3–15.
[225] *Proceedings of the President and Board of Directors*, E, 282.
[226] *Ibid*, 293.
[227] *Ibid*.
[228] *Ibid*, 295.
[229] *Ibid*, 315–316.
[230] *Ibid*, 317–319. A list of the contractors may be seen in Appendix N.
[231] *Ibid*, 320–321. A list of the contractors for these works may be seen in Appendix O.
[232] *Ibid*, 324.
[233] *Ibid*, 336.

January 24: The board let three contracts for protection walls at various points along the canal. Enos Childs was to build rubble masonry walls at both ends of Aqueduct No. 6; Andrew Small was to build a rubble masonry wall from Aqueduct No. 7 to Lock No. 52; and John Bain was to build a dry wall to buttress the turnpike on Section No. 226.[234]

April 2: Clerk Ingle was ordered to advertise for proposals for the construction of those sections and masonry structures which were let in September 1837 but which had not been placed under formal contract. All the culverts from Dam No. 6 to Cumberland were also to be advertised for bids.[235]

May 18: The board reorganized the corps of engineers in order to expedite the work on the canal above Dam No. 6. Between the Cacapon River and Cumberland, there were to be four divisions, each under the supervision of a principal assistant. The first division extended from Dam No. 6 to Section No. 287 with John A. Byers in charge; the second division, covering Sections Nos. 288–323, was placed under Ellwood Morris; the third division, comprising Section Nos. 324–349, was assigned to Charles H. Randolph; and the fourth division, from Section No. 350 to Cumberland, was put in charge of Joshua Gore.[236]

May 23: The board confirmed a contract that had been negotiated with George Shafer to supply cement from his newly opened mill at Roundtop Hill to the line of the canal between Dam No. 6 and the upper end of Paw Paw Tunnel. At the same meeting, the board authorized Chief Engineer Fisk to negotiate a contract with James C. Lynn to supply cement from his mill at Cumberland to the works above the tunnel.[237]

The board considered the proposals that had been received under their order of April 2 and accepted bids for 17 sections and Aqueduct No. 9.[238]

May 24: The board considered additional proposals that had been received under their order of April 2 and accepted offers for Locks Nos. 57–67 and Culverts Nos. 204, 210, 219–220, 225 and 229.[239]

May 30: The board let a contract to Michael Byrne for the construction of five cement houses along the line of construction.[240]

June 4: President George C. Washington informed the tenth annual meeting of the company stockholders that the delay in putting into effect the June 1836 act by the Maryland legislature authorizing the subscription of $3,000,000 to the stock of the company had hampered operations on the canal during the preceding months. Other factors which had prevented the canal between Dams Nos. 5 and 6 from being opened to navigation on June 1 as had been anticipated were the extremely high water which suspended work on Dam No. 6 in the spring, the labor strife at

---

[234] *Ibid*, 359.
[235] *Ibid*, 382.
[236] *Ibid*, 412–415.
[237] *Ibid*, 421–422. The board confirmed a contract with Lynn on June 28.
[238] *Ibid*, 423. A list of the contractors for these works may be seen in Appendix P.
[239] *Ibid*, 424–425. Evidently, the canal company was having difficulty in getting bids for the culverts above Dam No. 6 because the board authorized Fisk to accept proposals for the remaining culverts at prices not exceeding ten percent above his cost estimates. A list of the contractors for these works may be seen in Appendix Q.
[240] *Ibid*, 428.

Prather's Neck which had led to a work stoppage, and the abandonment and reletting of numerous contracts for increases of from 25 to 40 percent. Despite these problems, the line between the two dams would be opened to navigation during the summer. Anxious to complete the canal to Cumberland, the heaviest sections and the aqueducts above the Cacapon had been placed under contract in September.[241]

September 25: The board let contracts to George G. Johnson for the construction of Culverts Nos. 234–241.[242]

July 4: Despite all the financial reverses of the canal company, the board still had not given up the idea of constructing the canal all the way to Pittsburg. Accordingly, Chief Engineer Fisk was directed to begin locating the line of the canal in Will's Creek Valley and on any other part of the "Summit Section" where it was likely that there would be competition for the right-of-way between the canal and the Baltimore & Ohio Railroad.[243]

July 18: The board authorized President Washington to initiate a policy of discharging disorderly men employed along the canal. Furthermore, he was to take steps to prevent their reemployment on the canal in the future. In this way, the directors attempted to expedite the work by eliminating the periodic labor strife which had hampered operations on the canal.[244]

July 18: Upon the recommendations of Chief Engineer Fisk, the board let the following contracts for the construction of culverts: James Brownlie, No. 206 on Section No. 283; No. 207 on Section No. 286; No. 208 on Section No. 291; John Riley, No. 209 on Section No. 296; John Waldron, No. 211 on Section No. 311; John Lobdell, No. 215 on Section No. 322; Robert McGregor, No. 216 on Section No. 330, No. 217 on Section No. 331; Robert McGregor, No. 216 on Section No. 330, No. 217 on Section No. 331; Patrick Crowley, Nos. 226–228 on Section No342; and William Lockwood, No. 232 on Section No. 347, No. 233 on Section Nor 348.[245]

September 28: The board let a contract to John Bain for constructing a stop gate on Section No. 228.[246]

October 17: Chief Engineer Fisk presented to the board a proposal from William Easby for completing the lock gates abandoned by Thornton C. Bradley and for several towpath bridges and gates for waste weirs and lock flumes. The proposal was accepted.[247]

1839

January 5: Chief Engineer Fisk informed the board that the line of the canal between Dams Nos. 5 and 6 was nearly ready to be watered. Accordingly, the board appointed John G. Stone to be superintendent of the new division.[248]

---

[241] *Tenth Annual Report* (1838), C&O Co., 3, 9, 12, 25.
[242] *Proceedings of the President and Board of Directors*, E, 446.
[243] *Ibid*, 456.
[244] *Ibid*, 466.
[245] *Ibid*, 467.
[246] *Ibid*, 498.
[247] *Ibid*, 507–508.
[248] *Ibid*, F, 3–4.

January 5: In an effort to economize and to hurry construction, the board began a policy of dispensing with certain culverts and other structures that were not deemed important to the construction of the canal. One of the first of the previously contracted culverts to be disposed of in such a manner was Culvert No. 146.[249]

March: The Alexandria Canal Company offered to contract for the construction of that part of the northern abutment of the Potomac Aqueduct which the C and O had agreed to fund. The board accepted this offer and authorized the letting of a contract.[250]

April 17: Superintendent Stone informed the board that water had been admitted into the canal between Dams Nos. 5 and 6. President Washington nominated, and the board approved, the following men to be lock tenders: Philip Trammel for Locks Nos. 45–46; Daniel Brewer for Locks Nos. 47–50; Henry Rowland for Locks Nos. 51–52; Hugh Connor for Lock No. 53; and James Neal for Guard Lock No. 6.[251]

May 15: Upon the recommendation of Chief Engineer Fisk, the board agreed to dispense with the construction of Culverts Nos. 202 ½, 203, 205, 209, 213, 214, 219, 220, 222, 225, 226, 227, 229 and 232. Because the canal finances were approaching exhaustion, this measure was taken as a step toward economy.[252]

June 3: President Washington informed the eleventh annual meeting of the company stockholders that construction was progressing as rapidly as possible. The entire line of the canal from Georgetown to Dam No. 6, embracing 135 miles, was open to navigation, the 27 ½-mile distance between Dams Nos. 5 and 6 having been watered early in April. This portion of the canal was completed with the exception of three lockhouses, the graveling of Dam No. 6, and some comparatively light work.

The line above the Cacapon River had been progressing with a force varying from 2,500 to 3,000 laborers. A number of sections were completed, and most of the heavy sections were nearly finished. It was intended by the board to let the abandoned sections and masonry as well as the previously uncontracted works in the near future to insure that the canal would be finished to Cumberland within two years. Good progress had been made on the tunnel, having two-thirds of its length already bored.[253]

August 5: The canal company stockholders considered and adopted a special report by its general committee relative to the condition of the canal from Georgetown to Cumberland. During the latter part of June, the general committee and several company officials had traveled the entire length of the canal, and the report included their observations on both the finished and unfinished portions of the waterway. On the 50 miles above Dam No. 6, there were under contract (including those already completed) 59 sections, 17 locks, 3 aqueducts, 13 culverts, 1 dam and guard lock, and 1 tunnel. In addition, the following had once been under contract but subsequently abandoned and not relet: 6 sections, 5 locks, 1 aqueduct, 9 culverts, and 1 lockhouse. Of the work that had never been under contract, there were: 34 sections, 7 culverts, 12 lockhouses, 16 wastes and waste weirs, 9 bridges and 4 stop gates. Nearly one-third of the work on the canal above the Ca-

---

[249] Ibid, 5.
[250] Ibid, 29.
[251] Ibid, 38.
[252] Ibid, 56.
[253] Eleventh Annual Report (1839), C&O Co., in Proceedings of the Stockholders, B, 210–214.

capon was completed, with the distance of about 15 miles at either end approximately one year ahead of the middle portion.[254]

September 25: The canal company was facing a complex two-fold problem in the summer and fall of 1839—that of liquidating its staggering debt and of finding some means to push the construction of the canal to a successful conclusion. The alternative was to suspend all operations until adequate funding could be obtained. On this date, the board initiated a new policy by authorizing the issuance of $200,000 in canal scrip and by establishing a trust fund of five percent Maryland bonds to redeem the scrip as it was received for tolls and rents, This policy was employed regularly until construction was suspended in 1841.[255]

October 14: Upon the recommendation of Chief Engineer Fisk, the board ordered President Francis Thomas to proceed to the canal and make arrangements with some of the contractors to suspend the construction of those works which could be delayed without serious injury to the ultimate completion of the waterway. Thomas was authorized to take further steps to reduce the expenditures of the company.

At the same time, the board received word from a number of contractors requesting that a military force be kept in the vicinity of the canal to preserve peace among the laborers. The board authorized the president to forward this request to the Governor of Maryland.[256]

December 21: After Chief Engineer Fisk reported that the following works were still unfinished and that their contracts had expired, the board declared the contracts to be abandoned: Sections Nos. 262, 264, 265, 269, 272, 293, 296, 297, 317, 318, 321, 329, 342, 347, 348, 350, 361, 367; Dam No. 8; Aqueducts Nos. 9 and 11; Locks Nos. 54, 56, 58, 72, 73, 74; and Culverts Nos. 206, 234–241. The board was willing to continue the construction of Sections Nos. 137–318, Aqueduct No 11 and Locks Nos. 72–74 providing satisfactory arrangements could be made with the contractors. Fisk was authorized to negotiate with the contractors for Sections Nos. 268, 279, 294, 320 and 324 for the suspension of their works.[257]

1840

February 27: The board approved modified contracts let to George Hoblitzell, William P. Sterritt and James Brounlie to recommence work on Section No. 367, Dam No. 8 and Culvert No. 206, respectively.[258]

May 27: The board let a contract to Lewis Wernwag for the construction of a pivot bridge at Nolands Ferry, which the directors had ordered to be built in February.[259]

---

[254] *Report of the General Committee of the Stockholders of the Chesapeake & Ohio Canal Company, August 5, 1839* (Washington, 1839), 22–23.
[255] *Proceedings of the President and Board of Directors*, F, 108, 120–121, 132; and Thomas to Pinckney, November 1, 1839, Ltrs. Sent, C&O Co.
[256] *Proceedings of the President and Board of Directors*, F, 112–113.
[257] *Ibid,* 137–138. Arrangements were made on January 22, 1840, to continue work on Sections Nos. 293 and 329 and Lock No. 72, the modified contracts calling for completion date by May or June, 1841. On January 23, 1840, the board agreed to a modified contract for the continuation of work on Sections Nos. 152–154; 156–157.
[258] *Ibid,* 177.
[259] *Ibid,* 215–216.

June 2: The president and directors reported to the twelfth annual meeting of the company stockholders that rising construction costs and deteriorating finances had caused a virtual suspension of operations on the "fifty-mile" section of the canal above Dam No. 6. Generally, the sections were far ahead of the masonry. Of the 99 sections on this line, 29 were completed, 18 were nearly finished, 17 were partially done but no longer under contract, and 35 had never been under contract. The masonry was largely suspended except for the 10 miles immediately above Dam No. 6 and the 10 immediately below Cumberland: of the 22 locks, five were nearly completed, materials had been prepared for five others, and 12 were not under contract; of the 30 culverts, five were finished, six others had been commenced, and nineteen were not under contract; of the four aqueducts, two were nearly done while two had hardly been started and were not presently under contract. Dam No. 8 and Guard Lock No. 8 at Cumberland were more than half done. However, none of the bridges, wastes, or waste weirs had been placed under contract. Within days, the heading of the Paw Paw Tunnel would be excavated from end to end while the lower half of the excavation was nearly one-third done.[260]

July 17: Chief Engineer Fisk notified Clement Cox, chairman of the committee of the stockholders, that work on the canal above Dam No. 6 was continuing at a spasmodic pace. Three thousand men were needed in constant employment to complete the waterway in two years, but only one-half that number was on the line. The masonry structures were about one year behind the sections, and the labor force was largely deficient in mechanics that were able to do masonry work. Of the masonry that was done, most was confined to the two ends of the line, leaving an intermediate distance of nearly 30 miles with its masonry scarcely begun.

From Dam No. 6 to the lower end of Seven-Mile Bottom, the sections were 80 percent done, and the five locks, two aqueducts, and five culverts about 50 percent completed. Between Seven-Mile Bottom and a point opposite the mouth of the South Branch, the sections were 40 percent completed, the Paw Paw Tunnel over 60 percent, and the nine locks, one aqueduct, and seven culverts less than 10 percent. On the next nine miles up to the lower entrance of The Narrows, the sections were over 60 percent completed, and the four locks and eleven culverts less than one percent. The sections on the remaining 10-½ miles to Cumberland were nearly 75 percent done, while the four locks, one aqueduct, seven culverts and Dam No. 8 complex were over 60 percent finished. The fifteen lockhouses and the numerous bridges and waste structures on the "fifty-mile" section were not presently under contract and were less than five percent done.[261]

July 19: Accompanying the board's determination to continue construction on the basis of the unrestricted issuance of scrip was the first large turnover of canal employees. This was partly the result of a disagreement with the new policies and partly the effect of the application of the spoils system in the operation of the canal. Many old and reliable officials were dismissed or voluntarily retired, including the clerk, the treasurer, Chief Engineer Fisk, and several division superintendents. Some of the ousted officials carried into the newspapers their opposition to the directorate, thereby further undermining public confidence in the canal project. The board met sporadically throughout the summer and fall, and construction continued at a spasmodic pace.[262]

---

[260] *Twelfth Annual report* (1840), C&O Co., 13–15.
[261] Fisk to Cox, July 17, 1840, in *Thirteenth Annual Report* (1841), C&O Co., 52–61.
[262] *Proceedings of the President and Board of Directors*, F, 246, 256–257, 259; and Ingle to President and Directors, June 10, 1840; Fisk to President and Directors, October 1, 1840; and Morris to Thomas, December 4, 1840, Ltrs. Recd., C&O Co.

September 26: President Thomas informed the board that the following works were the only ones in progress: 2 aqueducts, 1 culvert, 5 locks, 15 sections, 1 tunnel, 1 dam and the Deep Cut. Of these works, 8 sections, 1 culvert, 5 locks and 1 aqueduct were nearly completed. Accordingly, he recommended that several engineering positions be abolished as soon as Sections Nos. 268, 274–275, 279, 281, 312, 320 and 367, the culvert, Aqueduct No. 11, and Locks Nos. 55, 72 and 73 were completed.[263]

1841

March 16: When the Maryland Legislature adjourned in March without providing effective aid to the canal and with the trust fund near exhaustion, the board reversed its former policy by forbidding the issuance of more scrip until means were provided to repay it and by preparing to suspend operations.[264]

June 7: The board of directors informed the thirteenth annual meeting of the canal company stockholders that operations had nearly ceased on the waterway. Between 600 and 700 laborers were at work on seven sections, the tunnel, and Aqueduct No. 11. The contractors and workers were totally without money and were virtually destitute of credit. Unless the company bonds could be marketed in Europe or the Maryland Legislature provided effective aid, construction would be suspended. During the past year, approximately $467,000 worth of work had been done, but more then $1,600,000 still remained.[265]

August 7: When the board was informed that State of Maryland would not provide effective aid for the completion of the canal, it was determined to suspend operations indefinitely. The directors instructed the clerk to notify the contractors to stop their work and the chief engineer to commence making final estimates. At the same time, they agreed to accept drafts on the company by the contractors in order to encourage them to continue the work on their own until further aid was forthcoming. Work on the canal continued spasmodically a little longer and then it came to an end.[266]

1843: Alexandria Canal Opened

December 2: The Potomac Aqueduct was formally opened for use 10 years after work was begun on the Virginia side. The northern abutment which the canal company had paid for was completed in 1841. The entire structure had been built under the direction of Major William Turnbull of the U.S. Topographical Engineers.

1842–1847

Construction on the canal remained at a standstill until late 1845 while canal officials sought adequate funding to complete the canal. After attempting a number of schemes, friends of the canal induced the Maryland Legislature in March, 1845, to pass a canal bill authorizing the company to issue $1,700,000 of preferred construction bonds on the mortgage of its revenue when it received

---

[263] *Proceedings of the President and Board of Directors*, F, 256–257.
[264] *Ibid*, 297.
[265] *Thirteenth Annual Report* (1841), C&O Co., 9, 61–63.
[266] *Proceedings of the President and Board of Directors*, F, 377–378, 381; Fisk to President and Directors, December 1, 1842, Ltrs. Recd., C&O Co.; and *Fourteenth Annual Report* (1842), C&O Co., 3.

guaranties from interested coal companies for 195,000 tons of coal annually for five years. Following the approval of the guaranties by the Governor of Maryland in August 1845, the board on September 23 let a contract to Walter Gwynn, William Thompson, James Hunter and Walter Cunningham to complete the canal. By the terms of the contract, Messrs. Gwynn and Company agreed to provide the materials of the required quality according to the specifications of the chief engineer, to begin work in 30 days, and to complete the canal by November 1, 1847.

Gwynn and Company sublet all the sections in October 1845, and the contractors placed a token force on the line by November 1, pending successful negotiations for the necessary funding to finance large-scale construction. Conditions resulting from the Mexican War and the inability of canal officials to negotiate the sale of the bonds hampered the work. By May 1, 1846, the work done amounted to only $55,384, and by July, work on the canal had ceased entirely.

Following another year of negotiations, an agreement was reached whereby a group of 29 capitalists in New York, Boston and Washington took $500,000 of the bonds, the subcontractors $200,000, the Commonwealth of Virginia $300,000, and the District cities $100,000. Work was resumed on November 18, 1847, under a modified contract. The old company was reorganized and a new one succeeded to its contract with the canal board. Gwynn and Cunningham retired, but the remaining partners, Hunter and Thompson, continued, with the addition of a third partner, Thomas Harris.[267]

1847

December 8: The board approved a contract that President James M. Coale had negotiated with Owen Ardinger to construct a dry dock on the berm side of the canal near Williamsport. At the same time, the directors authorized Coale to grant permission to qualified persons who submitted requests for the right to build dry docks along the canal. All the dry docks were to be constructed under the direction of the chief engineer or the division superintendents.[268]

1848

April 11: John Davis, Nathan Hale and Horatio Allen, trustees of the parties that furnished the funds for the canal's completion and agents of Hunter, Harris & Co. informed the board that work was underway on the "fifty-mile" section. From Dam No. 6 to Cumberland, there were 84 sections, 16 locks, 1 dam, 3 aqueducts, 23 culverts, 10 waste weirs, 8 road bridges and ferries, 17 lockhouses and 2 stop gates. For administrative purposes, the 84 sections were divided into three classes: (1) 30 were finished before the work stoppage in 1841; (2) six were nearly finished and required final dressing work; and (3) 48 were hardly commenced. The first two classes comprised the heavy sections, and the contractors had placed their remaining work under the supervision of three work parties. The 48 sections in the third class were light sections and had been put under

---

[267] *Niles' Register*, Vol. LXVIII (March 8, 1845), 16; *Ibid*, Vol. LXVIII (March 15, 1845), 23–24; *Ibid*, Vol. LXXII (October 25, 1845), 128; *Proceedings of the President and Board of Directors*, G, 317–318, 320–323, 353–354, 443; *Eighteenth Annual Report* (1846), C&O Co., 8–11; *Twentieth Annual Report* (1848), C&O Co., 7–8; and Fisk to President and Directors, June 25, 1846; and C. Cox to Coale, July 10, 1846, Ltrs. Recd., C&O Co. During the interim of construction, the board had adopted various economy measures to facilitate the construction of the canal, including the substitution of Kyanized wood for stone in the locks, and the postponement of building lockhouses and arching the tunnel until after the canal was opened to Cumberland Sanderlin, *The Great National Project*, 157.

[268] *Proceedings of the President and Board of Directors*, H, 112. Earlier on October 2, the board had authorized John Moore, the lock tender at Georgetown, to construct a dry dock for the repair of boats near Lock No. 1.

subcontractors.[269] Work had been commenced on all of these sections except Nos. 295–296, 314 and 321, and preparations were nearly ready to begin on these. Within two months, it was anticipated that six-to-eight of these sections would be completed, at which time the laborers would be transferred to other sections still in progress.

Paw Paw Tunnel, located between Sections Nos. 299 and 311, had been contracted to McCullough & Day.

Arrangements had been made to complete the lift locks as follows: Locks Nos. 54 and 56 (masonry) to Moyle, Randal & Jones; Lock No. 58 (masonry) still not let; Locks Nos. 59–61 (composite) to Ritner & Co.; Locks Nos. 62–66 (composite) to Buell & Watt; Lock No. 67 (composite) to William P. Sterritt; and Locks Mos. 68–71 (masonry) to Fallan and Ambrose. The weigh lock at Cumberland was still not under contract.

The foundation of Dam No. 8 had been laid up to low water. Nearly one-fourth of the stone required for the dam was prepared and most of the timber was cut and delivered. The structure was under contract to William Lockwood.

Of the 23 culverts, 18 were let to contractors. The five remaining culverts were located between Section No. 352 and Cumberland and were about one-half completed. When the other masonry was more advanced, these culverts would be put under contract.

Three of the ten wastes and waste weirs had been put under contract to the following persons: one on Section No. 258 to Moyal, Randal and Jones; one on Section No. 320 to R. Sims and Co.; and one on Aqueduct No. 10 to Hunter, Harris and Co.

Three aqueducts were still not finished. Aqueduct No. 8 needed less than 300 perches of rubble masonry, a task apparently assigned to the Hunter, Harris and Co. construction team. The completion of Aqueduct No. 9 had been subcontracted to Thomas Bell who was expected to commence laying the arch within three weeks. Aqueduct No. 10, which had only one abutment laid, was assigned to the Hunter, Harris and Co. construction team.

Hunter, Harris and Co. made arrangements to furnish the cement required for the masonry works. They had contracted with George Shafer at the Round Top Cement Mill to burn, grind and deliver 12,000 bushels per month for 10 months, and with Charles Locker at Cumberland for 6,000 bushels per month for 10 months.[270]

June 5: President Coale reported to the twentieth annual meeting of the canal company stockholders that work on the waterway was progressing rapidly. It was anticipated that the canal would be completed to Cumberland before October 1, 1849, the date limited by the contract.[271]

October 10: To facilitate the construction of the waterway and to reduce the time and cost of completing the canal, the board determined to build Locks Nos. 68–71 on the composite plan and dispense with the erection of a bridge, forebay and Culvert No. 218 near Oldtown.[272]

December 8: The board authorized John G. Stone, Superintendent of the Third Division, to build a lockhouse on the company's land at Lock No. 44 at as low a rate as practicable.[273]

---

[269] *Twentieth Annual Report* (1847), C&O Co., Appendix D, 17–18.
[270] *Ibid*, 16–21.
[271] *Ibid*, 8–9.
[272] *Proceedings of the President and Board of Directors*, H, 214–216.
[273] *Ibid*, 228.

1849

June 4: Chief Engineer Fisk reported to the twenty-first annual Meeting of the canal company stockholders the construction was progressing at such a pace that it would probably be completed by December 10. To back his optimistic prediction, he submitted a list of work done and work to be done as follows:

	WORK DONE	WORK TO BE DONE	TOTAL
Sections	$297,385	$172,586	$469,971
Tunnel and its Deep Cuts	86,081	91,919	178,000
Composite & Masonry Locks	74,308	153,523	227,831
Aqueducts	30,337	41,370	71,707
Culverts	63,423	58,250	121,673
Wastes and Waste Weirs	2,283	39,703	41,986
Lockhouses, Bridges, Roads & Ferries	6,375	16,629	23,004
Dam No. 8 and Guard Lock No. 8	16,757	5,043	21,800
Miscellaneous	---	16,746	16,746
Cement Transportation	6,010	13,001	19,011
Weigh Lock and House	---	18,500	18,500
Totals	$583,209	$638,070	$1,221,279

As of May 25, the following numbers and classes of workers were employed on the line of the canal: 77 bosses, 39 blacksmiths, 54 carpenters, 75 drillers and blasters, 107 quarrymen, 59 stonecutters, 73 masons, 112 mason tenders, 6 brick molders, 50 brick makers, 16 bricklayers, 19 bricklayer tenders and 760 laborers. The total number of all classes of laborers and workmen was 1,447. There were also 233 drivers, 562 horses, 26 mules, and 6 oxen employed to drive and to work 285 carts, 20 scoops, 13 ploughs, 11 two-horse wagons, 3 three-horse wagons, 29 four-horse wagons, 1 six-horse wagon, 5 one-horse railroad cars, 14 two-horse railroad cars, 10 three-horse railroad cars, 14 drags, 4 brick-molding machines, and numerous cranes.

To facilitate the construction and reduce the cost of completing the canal, it had been determined to build Locks Nos. 68–71 on the composite plan and dispense with the erection of a bridge, forebay and Culvert No. 218 near Oldtown.[274]

September 27: The board extended the date for the completion of the canal after Hunter, Harris and Co. informed the directors that they were unable to finish construction in the specified time. Among the problems which had slowed their operations were the sickness and scarcity of workers and the ever-present financial troubles resulting from the slow sale of bonds and the excess of costs over estimates.[275]

1850

January 28: The Virginia and Maryland Bridge Company requested permission to build a bridge across the canal at Shepherdstown opposite the bridge they were then building across the Potomac River. Upon the recommendation of Chief Engineer Fisk, the board offered to contribute $1,000 toward the construction of the bridge over the canal provided that the bridge company

---

[274] *Twenty-First Annual Report* (1849), C&O Co., Appendix A, 23–27.
[275] *Proceedings of the President and Board of Directors*, H, 274–275; 300–301.

agreed to build it according to Fisk's specifications and to keep it in repair when it was completed.[276]

January 28: To speed the work and to reduce the cost of construction, Chief Engineer Fisk recommended that locust timber be substituted for stone in the coping of the towpath in the Paw Paw Tunnel. Anxious to economize and to see the work completed, the board adopted this measure.[277]

March 21: The board again took a step to save time and money in finishing the canal by ordering that the coping of the composite locks be changed from stone to wood.[278]

April 17: Troubles came to a head when the financial difficulties of Hunter, Harris and Co. brought about a suspension of the work for several days and the threat of violence. The workers, who had been unpaid for some time, were demanding satisfaction. The trustees, Davis, Hale and Allen, took over the contract on assignment from Hunter, Harris and Co. and resumed work. The date for the completion of the canal was extended to July 1 and then to August 1.[279]

June 3: President James M. Coale informed the twenty-second annual meeting of the canal company stockholders that water would be admitted into the first 10 miles of the canal between Cumberland and Lock No. 72 early the following week. With the present labor force at work on the canal, it was anticipated that the canal could be watered down to Dam No. 6 by mid-July. The current estimate of the chief engineer was that $49,227 worth of work needed to be done, and of this sum $9,000 could be executed after the admission of water. The labor force at work on the line at present consisted of 37 bosses, 7 blacksmiths, 70 carpenters, 22 quarrymen, 10 stonecutters, 20 masons, 33 mason tenders, and 414 laborers, making a total of 613 men. There were also 104 drivers, 215 horses, 147 carts, 14 two-horse railroad cars, 4 three-horse railroad cars and numerous wagons.

In order to hurry the work to completion, various steps had been taken to reduce the time and cost of construction. On one hand, there had been a substitution in the composite plan, for the masonry, in the construction of five lift locks, and of wooden, for stone coping, to a considerable extent upon the composite locks, the Paw Paw Tunnel towpath, and several wastes. On the other hand, numerous works had dispensed with, including two culverts, one bridge, one forebay, one stone and one wooden waste weir, and one lockhouse.[280]

June 25: The board determined to dispense with building the weigh lock at Cumberland until after the canal was completed.[281]

July 17–18: The resources of the trustees, Davis, Hale and Allen, were exhausted by mid-July and work again stopped. The board promptly declared the contract abandoned and negotiated a new one with Michael Byrne providing for the completion of the canal for $3,000 cash and $21,000 in bonds.[282]

---

[276] *Ibid*, 323.
[277] *Ibid*, 324–325.
[278] *Ibid*, 341–342.
[279] *Ibid*, 349, 365; and *Twenty-Second Annual Report* (1850), C&O Co., 6–7.
[280] *Twenty-Second Annual Report* (1850), C&O Co., 3–4, 13–15.
[281] *Proceedings of the President and Board of Directors*, H, 364.
[282] *Ibid*, 369–372.

October 10: The eastern section of the Chesapeake & Ohio Canal, the only part ever to be completed, was formally opened to trade at Cumberland. Following gala ceremonies at the basin, a procession of canal boats proceeded down the waterway toward Georgetown. After 22 years of intermittent enthusiasm and despair, the canal was navigable to Cumberland.[283]

November 27: The board ordered that a marble slab or block be placed "in a conspicuous position in the masonry of, or on the line of the canal" with the names of the president, directors, officers, state agents and the date of completion. The monument, a short obelisk, was built near the Wisconsin Avenue Bridge over the canal in Georgetown.[284]

1851

February 27: The president and directors reported to a special meeting of the canal company stockholders that Byrne had progressed with his operations to the point that, on October 10, the canal had been opened for navigation to Cumberland. Some light work still remained to be done which did not interfere with the passage of boats, and he had continued to press forward with the work through the winter. On February 17, the final payment was made to him pursuant to the provisions of his contract. This date marked, in a technical sense, the formal completion of the canal to Cumberland.

The canal, built at a total cost of $11,071,176.21, or $59,618.61 per mile was described as follows in the report:

The Chesapeake & Ohio Canal, between Georgetown and Cumberland, lies on the north, or Maryland side, of the river, with the advantages of a southern exposure, and pursues the immediate valley of the Potomac throughout its whole length, except at a point called Paw Paw Bend, about 27 miles below Cumberland, where it passes through the mountain by a tunnel 3,118 feet in length, and lined and arched with brick laid in cement, by which, about six miles, in distance, have been saved. From the Rock Creek Basin in Georgetown, where it first reaches tidewater, to the basin at Cumberland, is one hundred and eighty-four and four-tenths miles, and the total rise from the level of mid-tide, at Georgetown, to the Cumberland basin, is 609.7 feet. This ascent is overcome by 74 lift locks, and a tide lock that connects Rock Creek Basin with the Potomac River. At the terminus of the extension of the canal, at the mouth of the Tiber in the city of Washington, is another tide lock, which connects it with the Potomac River, and also with Washington city canal. The latter canal passes entirely through the city, and terminates on the eastern branch near the navy yard. From a point about a mile west of Rock Creek Basin, the Alexandria Canal, seven miles in length, diverges from the Chesapeake & Ohio Canal, crosses the Potomac River by an aqueduct 1600 feet long, and connects with tidewater at Alexandria. The Chesapeake & Ohio Canal is constructed for a depth of six feet throughout. From Georgetown to Harpers Ferry, 60 miles—it is 60 feet wide at the surface, and 42 feet at the bottom. From Harpers Ferry to Dam No. 5, 47 miles, the width of the surface is 50 feet, and at the bottom 32 feet, and from Dam No. 5 to Cumberland, 77½ miles, the surface width is 54 feet, and the bottom 30 feet. The average lift of the locks a little exceeds 8 feet. They are 100 feet long and 15 feet wide, in the clear, and are capable of passing boats carrying 120 tones (of 2,240 lbs.).

The present supply of water for the canal is drawn entirely from the Potomac. For this purpose, dams have been constructed across the river at seven different points.[285]

---

[283] *Ibid,* 379–380; Cumberland *Civilian,* October, 1850; and Georgetown *Advocate,* October 15, 1850.
[284] *Proceedings of the President and Board of Directors,* H, 384.
[285] *Report to the Stockholders on the Completion of the Chesapeake & Ohio Canal to Cumberland, with a Sketch of the Potomac Company, and a General Outline of the History of the Chesapeake & Ohio Canal Co., From Its Origin to February, 1851. . . . Made February 27th, 1851* (Frederick, 1851), 111–112.

II. INDIVIDUAL CHRONOLOGIES OF THE CONSTRUCTION OF MAJOR STRUCTURES ON THE CANAL: 1828–1850

A. LIFT LOCKS

Locks Nos. 1–4: Section A
December 10, 1828: Contract let to Dibble, Beaumont and McCord.
June–July, 1829: Work commenced on locks.
April, 1831: Work completed on locks.
Cost: $34,052.08

Locks Nos. 5–6: Section No. 1
October 25, 1828: Contract let to Bennett and Brackett.
March 14, 1829: Contract relet to Abram Knapp and Co.
May, 1829: Work commenced on locks.
September, 1830: Work completed on locks.
Cost: $18,985.67

Lock No. 7: Section No. 4
October 25, 1828: Contract let to Brackett and Hovey.
January, 1829: Work commenced on lock.
February, 1829: Contract abandoned.
March 14, 1829: Contract relet to Fenlon and Bosteder,
April, 1829: Work recommenced on lock.
September, 1829: Work completed on lock.
Cost: $9,493.43

Lock No. 8: Section No. 7
October 25, 1828: Contract let to Brackett and Hovey.
March 14, 1829: Contract relet to Abram Knapp and Co.
April, 1829: Work commenced on lock.
July, 1830: Work completed on lock.
Cost: $9,043.14

Lock No. 9: Section No. 8
October 25, 1828: Contract let to W. W. Fenlon and Co.
February, 1829: Work commenced on lock.
September, 1830: Work completed on lock.
Cost: $9,540.98

Lock No. 10: Section No. 8
October 25, 1828: Contract let to Kavenaugh, Knox, Hale and Nichols.
January, 1829: Work commenced on lock.
March 3, 1830: Contract abandoned.
March, 1830: Contract relet to Douglas and Small.
March, 1830: Work recommenced on lock.
August–September, 1830: Work completed on lock.
Cost: $9,729.22

Lock No. 11: Section No. 8
October 25, 1828: Contract let to Kavenaugh, Knox, Hale and Nichols.
January, 1829: Work commenced on lock.
July, 1830: Work completed on lock.
Cost: $10,089.18

Lock No. 12: Section No. 9
October 25, 1828: Contract let to J. and J. Maynard.
January, 1829: Work commenced on lock.
February, 1829: Contract abandoned.
March 14, 1829: Contract relet to Fenlon and Bosteder.
August, 1830: Work completed on lock.
Cost: $10,650.31

Lock No. 13: Section No. 9
October 25, 1828: Contract let to Patrick Donnelly.
December, 1829: Contract let to Charles Mowry.
December, 1829: Work commenced on lock.
September, 1830: Work completed on lock.
Cost: $9,300.81

Lock No. 14: Section No. 9
October 25, 1828: Contract let to Patrick Donnelly.
June, 1829: Contract relet to Wood and Kendall.
June, 1829: Work commenced on lock.
September, 1830: Work completed on lock.
Cost: $9,673.87

Lock No. 15: Section No. 17
October 25, 1828: Contract let to J. and J. Maynard.
January, 1829: Work commenced on lock.
February, 1829: Contract abandoned.
March 14, 1829: Contract relet to Abram Knapp and Co.
April, 1829: Work recommenced on lock.
July, 1829: Work completed on lock.
Cost: $10,349.83

Lock No. 16: Section No. 17
October 25, 1828: Contract let to J. and J. Maynard.
January, 1829: Work commenced on lock.
February, 1829: Contract abandoned.
March 14, 1829: Contract relet to Abram Knapp and Co.
April, 1829: Work recommenced on lock.
July, 1829: Work completed on lock.
Cost: $10,001.78

Lock No. 17: Section No. 18
October 25, 1828: Contract let to Henry and Roberts.
March 14, 1829: Contract relet to Abram Knapp and Co.

April, 1829: Work commenced on lock.
July, 1830: Work completed on lock.
Cost: $10,941.81

Lock No. 18: Section No. 18
October 25, 1828: Contract let to J. and J. Maynard.
January, 1829: Work commenced on lock.
February, 1829: Contract abandoned.
March 14, 1829: Contract relet to Abram Knapp and Co.
April, 1829: Work recommenced on lock.
July, 1830: Work completed on lock.]
Cost: $9,383.61

Lock No. 19: Section No. 18
October 25, 1828: Contract let to J. and J. Maynard.
January, 1829: Work commenced on lock.
February, 1829: Contract abandoned.
March 14, 1829: Contract relet to Fenlon and Bosteder.
November, 1829: Work recommenced on lock.
October–November, 1830: Work completed on lock.
Cost: $10,139.11

Lock No. 20: Section No. 18
October 25, 1828: Contract let to J. and J. Maynard.
January, 1829: Work commenced on lock.
February, 1829: Contract abandoned.
March 14, 1829: Contract relet to Abram Knapp and Co.
April, 1829: Work recommenced on lock.
July, 1830: Work completed on lock.
Cost: $9,355.52

Lock No. 21: Section No. 23
October 25, 1828: Contract let to Holdsworth and Isherwood.
July, 1829: Work commenced on lock.
October 12, 1829: Contract relinquished.
October 21, 1829: Contract relet to Richard Gorsline.
October, 1830: Work completed on lock.
Cost: $8,327.76

Lock No. 22: Section No. 29
October 25, 1828: Contract let to Kenney and Roberts.
March 14, 1829: Contract relet to F. C. Clopper.
April, 1829: Work commenced on lock.
May, 1831: Work completed on lock.
Cost: $7,969.28

Lock No. 23: Section No. 34
October 25, 1828: Contract let to Kenney and Roberts.
March 14, 1829: Contract relet to Holdsworth and Isherwood.

June, 1829: Work commenced on lock.
January, 1831: Work completed on lock.
Cost: $8,912.80

Lock No. 24: Section No. 35
October 25, 1828: Contract let to Holdsworth and Isherwood.
March, 1829: Work commenced on lock.
May 5, 1830: Contract assigned to Richard Holdsworth.
March, 1832: Work completed on lock.
Cost: $8,886.88

Lock No. 25: Section No. 51
October 25, 1828: Contract let to Lafferty and Boland.
July, 1829: Work commenced on lock.
January–February, 1830: Contract abandoned.
April 21, 1830: Contract relet to James Stewart.
June, 1830: Work recommenced on lock.
October, 1831: Work completed on lock.
Cost: $11,191.64

Lock No. 26: Section No. 68
October 25, 1828: Contract let to Amos Johnson.
March 14, 1829: Contract relet to Abram Knapp and Co.;
    firm subcontracted lock to Stewart and Douglas
January, 1831: Work commenced on lock.
July–August, 1832: Work completed on lock.
Cost: $10,376.30

Lock No. 27: Section No. 72
October 25, 1828: Contract let to Lafferty and Boland.
January, 1829: Work commenced on lock.
February, 1830: Contract abandoned.
February 12, 1830: Contract relet to D. Canfield.
November 26, 1830: Contract relet to Andrew Small.
March, 1831: Work recommenced on lock.
June, 1832: Work completed on lock.
Cost: $11,323.75

Lock No. 28: Section No. 87
March 24, 1832: Contract let to J. B. and D. K. Cahoon.
May, 1832: Work commenced on lock.
July, 1832: Work completed on lock.
Cost: $9,734.55

Lock No. 29: Section No. 90
March 17, 1832: Contract let to J. B. and D. K. Cahoon.
May, 1832: Work commenced on lock.
August 18, 1832: Contract abandoned.
August 25, 1832: Contract relet to Littlejohn and Thompson.

November, 1833: Contract abandoned and work recommenced by canal company.
April, 1834: Work completed on lock.
Cost: $9,457.05

Lock No. 30: Section No. 98
March 14, 1832: Contract let to Obadiah Gordon
June, 1832: Work commenced on lock.
July, 1832: Contract abandoned.
August – September, 1832: Contract relet to Andrew Small.
October, 1832: Work recommenced on lock.
October, 1833: Work completed on lock.
Cost: $11,694.51

Lock No. 31: Section No. 104
March 17, 1832: Contract let to Obadiah Gordon.
May, 1832: Work commenced on lock.
December 31, 1832: Contract abandoned.
January, 1833: Contract relet to John M. Moore.
January, 1833: Work recommenced on lock.
September, 1833: Work completed on lock.
Cost: $16,085.49

Lock No. 32: Section No. 108
March 17, 1832: Contract let to Lewis Wernwag.
September, 1832: Contract assigned to John Hay.
September, 1832: Work commenced on lock.
January 18, 1833: Contract abandoned and construction assigned to Charles B. Fisk, with John Hay as principal builder.
February, 1833: Contract relet to Gibson and Co.; firm subcontracted lock to Littlejohn and Co.
February, 1833: Work recommenced on lock.
July, 1833: Work completed on lock.
Cost: $11,298.85

Lock No. 33: Section No. 109
March 17, 1832: Contract let to James O'Brien.
April – May, 1832: Contract relet to Lewis Wernwag.
June, 1832: Work commenced on lock.
September, 1832: Contract abandoned.
September, 1832: Contract relet to Littlejohn and Co.
September, 1832: Work recommenced on lock.
September, 1833: Work completed on lock.
Cost: $20,728.05

Lock No. 34: Section No. 111
March 17, 1832: Contract let to Henry Smith.
April 21, 1832: Contract relet to Fries and McDonnell.
May, 1832: Work commenced on lock.
November, 1833: Work completed on lock.
Cost: $10,282.66

Lock No. 35: Section No. 112
March 17, 1832: Contract let to Henry Smith.
April 21, 1832: Contract relet to Fries and McDonnell.
June, 1832: Work commenced on lock.
October, 1834: Work completed on lock.
Cost: $10,809.19

Lock No. 36: Section No. 112
June 2, 1832: Contract let to Fries and McDonnell.
July, 1833: Work commenced on lock.
November, 1834: Work completed on lock.
Cost: $9,659.80

Lock No. 37: Section No. 122
June 7, 1832: Contract let to Gilson, Noonan, Midler and Fresh and Co.
September, 1832: Work commenced on lock.
August, 1833: Work completed on lock.
Cost: $11,453.13

Lock No. 38: Section No. 133
June 7, 1832: Contract let to Gilson, Noonan, Midler and Fresh and Co.
September, 1832: Work commenced on lock.
September, 1833: Work completed on lock.
Cost: $7,725.85

Lock No. 39: Section No. 135
June 2, 1832: Contract let to Wilson and Bryan.
July 17, 1832: Contract abandoned.
August 25, 1832: Contract relet to Gilson and Co.
January, 1833: Work commenced on lock.
April, 1833: Contract abandoned.
June 17, 1833: Contract relet to Jacob and Alexander Provest.
September, 1833: Work recommenced on lock.
September, 1834: Work completed on lock.
Cost: $9,265.00

Lock No. 40: Section No. 146
August 25, 1832: Contract let to Gibson, Noonan and Fresh.
January, 1833: Work commenced on lock.
June–July, 1834: Work completed on lock.
Cost: $10,202.00

Lock No. 41: Section No. 166
August 25, 1832: Contract let to Michael Byrne and Co.
January, 1833: Work commenced on lock.
November–December, 1834: Work completed on lock.
Cost: $10,930.66

Lock No. 42: Section No. 167
August 25, 1832: Contract let to Michael Byrne and Co,
February, 1833: Work commenced on lock.
November–December, 1834: Work completed on lock.
Cost: $8,349.96

Lock No. 43: Section No. 173
August 25, 1832: Contract let to Michael Byrne and Co.
February, 1833: Work commenced on lock.
January, 1835: Work completed on lock.
Cost: $9,634.40

Lock No. 44: Section No. 187
August 25, 1832: Contract let to Michael Byrne and Co.
September, 1832: Work commenced on lock.
November, 1834: Work completed on lock.
Cost: $10,485.82

Lock No. 45: Section No. 202
April 20, 1833: Contract let to Byrne, Lathrop and Provest to construct lock below water line.
June, 1833: Work commenced on lock.
November, 1834: Work completed under contract.
July 3, 1835: Contract let to W. Morrow to complete lock.
February 2, 1836: Contract abandoned.
June 20, 1836: Contract relet to Michael Byrne and Co.
August, 1836: Work recommenced on lock.
November, 1836: Work completed on lock.
Cost: $12,488.81

Lock No. 46: Section No. 203
July 3, 1835: Contract let to John C. Lissig.
February 2, 1836: Contract abandoned.
June 20, 1836: Contract relet to Michael Byrne and Co.
November, 1836: Work commenced on lock.
May, 1838: Work completed on lock.
Cost: $12,964.00

Lock No. 47: Section No. 206
July 3, 1835: Contract let to Daniel K. Cahoon.
January, 1836: Work commenced on lock.
November, 1837: Work completed on lock.
Cost: $10,546.05

Lock No. 48: Section No. 208
July 3, 1835: Contract let to Daniel K. Cahoon
December 9, 1835: Contract abandoned.
June 20, 1836: Contract relet to Michael Byrne.
January, 1837: Work commenced on lock.
May, 1838: Work completed on lock.
Cost: $13,232.82

Lock No. 49: Section No. 208
July 3, 1835: Contract let to Daniel K. Cahoon.
December 9, 1835: Contract abandoned.
June 20, 1836: Contract relet to Michael Byrne.
January, 1837: Work commenced on lock.
May, 1838: Work completed on lock.
Cost: $17,365.28

Lock No. 50: Section No. 208
July 3, 1835: Contract let to Daniel K. Cahoon.
December 9, 1835: Contract abandoned.
June 20, 1836: Contract relet to Michael Byrne.
April, 1837: Work commenced on lock.
May, 1838: Work completed on lock.
Cost: $13,783.30

Lock No. 51: Section No. 234
July 3, 1835: Contract let to Robert Brown.
January, 1836: Work commenced on lock.
August 9, 1837: Contract abandoned.
December 6, 1837: Contract relet to William Storey.
December, 1837: Work recommenced on lock.
April, 1838: Work completed on lock.
Cost: $16,257.24

Lock No. 52: Section No. 234
July 3, 1835: Contract let to Robert Brown.
January, 1836: Work commenced on lock.
August 9, 1837: Contract abandoned.
August 23, 1837: Modified contract relet to Robert Brown.
November, 1837: Work recommenced on lock.
April, 1839: Work completed on lock.
Cost: $15,191.61

Lock No. 53: Section No. 249
July 3, 1835: Contract let to Patrick McGinley.
September, 1835: Work commenced on lock.
January, 1836: Work stopped on lock.
March 15, 1836: Contract assigned to Thomas Fealey.
March, 1836: Work recommenced on lock.
January, 1837: Work completed on lock.
Cost: $11,387.62

Lock No. 54: Section No. 258
January 16, 1836: Contract let to Henry Smith.
May 1836: Work commenced on lock.
December 28, 1839: Contract abandoned.

No further work done on this lock until work resumed on the canal in November, 1847. At the time of its abandonment, the lock was 40 percent completed at a cost of $6,066.43. When work resumed in 1847, Hunter, Harris and Co. subcontracted this lock to Moyle, Randal and Jones for its completion.
1848–49: Work completed on lock.

Lock No. 55: Section No. 258
January 16, 1836: Contract let to Henry Smith.
November, 1836: Work commenced on lock.
October, 1840: Work completed on lock.
Cost: $13,621.54

Lock No. 56: Section No. 262
September 29, 1837: Contract let to John Cameron.
March, 1838: Work commenced on lock.
December 28, 1839: Contract abandoned.
No further work was done on this lock until work resumed on the canal in November, 1847. At the time of its abandonment, the lock was 50 percent completed; at a cost of $9,475.09. When work resumed in 1847, Hunter, Harris and Co. subcontracted this lock to Moyle, Randal and Jones for its completion.
1848–49: Work completed on lock.

Lock No. 57: Section No. 267
September 29, 1837: Contract let to W. C. Steedman.
May 24, 1838: Contract relet to James Wherry.
August, 1838: Work commenced on lock.
March, 1840: Work completed on lock.
Cost: $17,774.39

Lock No. 58: Section No. 276 (Composite Lock)
September 29, 1837: Contract let to W. C. Steedman.
May 24, 1838: Contract relet to James Wherry.
August, 1838: Work commenced on lock.
December 28, 1839: Contract abandoned.
No further work was done on this lock until work resumed on the canal in November, 1847. At the time of its abandonment, the lock was 40 percent completed; at a cost of $8,922.16. When work resumed in 1847, Hunter, Harris and Co. subcontracted this lock to an unnamed firm (according to available canal company records) for its completion.
1848–50: Work completed on lock.

Locks Nos. 59–66: Sections Nos. 282–299 (Composite Locks)
September 29, 1837: Contract for Lock No. 59 let to Edward H. Fielding.
September 29, 1837: Contract for Locks Nos. 60–66 let to Michael Byrne.
November, 1838: Work commenced on locks.
December 28, 1839: Work suspended on locks.
September, 1845: Contract let to Gwinn and Co.;
   subcontracted to Marcellus Ritner and Co.
April, 1846: Work recommenced on locks.
April–May, 1846: Contract abandoned.

November, 1847: Contract let to Hunter, Harris and Co.; Locks Nos. 59–61 were subcontracted to Ritner and Co.; and Locks Nos. 62–66 were subcontracted to Buell and Watt.
November, 1847: Work recommenced on locks.
June–July, 1850: Contract abandoned.
July, 1850: Contract relet to Michael Byrne.
July, 1850: Work recommenced on lock.
August, 1850: Work completed on Locks Nos. 61–66.
September, 1850: Work completed on Locks Nos. 59–60.

Lock No. 67: Section No. 322 (Composite Lock)
May 24, 1838: Contract let to Joshua Lobdell.
August, 1838: Work commenced on lock.
November 28, 1838: Contract abandoned.
No further work was done on this lock until work resumed on the canal in November, 1847. At the time of its abandonment, the lock was barely begun; only $740.56 worth of work had been done on it. When work resumed in 1847, Hunter, Harris and Co. subcontracted this lock to William P. Sterritt for its completion.
1848–50: Work completed on the lock.

Lock No. 68: Section No. 329 (Composite Lock)
September 27, 1837: Contract let to Robert McCoy.
May 16, 1838: Contract assigned to J. Noble Nisbet.
November 14, 1838: Contract abandoned.
No work had done on this lock at the time of its abandonment, and nothing was done on it until work resumed on the canal in November, 1847. At that time, Hunter, Harris and Co. subcontracted this lock to Fallan and Ambrose for its completion.
1849–50: Work completed on lock.

Lock No. 69: Section No. 331 (Composite Lock)
September 29, 1837: Contract let to William Pratt.
April, 1838: Work commenced on lock.
July 18, 1838: Contract abandoned.
No further work was done on this lock until work resumed on the canal in November, 1847. At the time of its abandonment, this lock was barely begun; only $759.12 worth of work had been done on it. When work resumed in 1847, Hunter, Harris and Co. subcontracted this lock to Fallan and Ambrose for its completion.
1849–50: Work completed on lock.

Lock No. 70: Section No. 332 (Composite Lock)
September 29, 1837: Contract let to William Pratt.
July 18, 1838: Contract abandoned.
No work had done on this lock at the time of its abandonment, and nothing was done on it until work resumed on the canal in November, 1847. At that time, Hunter, Harris and Co. subcontracted this lock to Fallan and Ambrose for its completion.
1849–50: Work completed on the lock.

Lock No. 71: Section No. 332 (Composite Lock)
September 29, 1837: Contract let to William Pratt.
July 18, 1838: Contract abandoned.

No work had done on this lock at the time of its abandonment, and nothing was done on it until work resumed on the canal in November, 1847. At that time, Hunter, Harris and Co. subcontracted this lock to Fallan and Ambrose for its completion.
1849–50: Work completed on lock.

Lock No. 72: Section No. 347
September 29, 1837: Contract let to G. W. Henry.
September 7, 1838: Contract relet to Thomas N. MacCubbin.
February, 1839: Work commenced on lock.
December 28, 1839: Contract abandoned.
January 22, 1840: Modified contract relet to Thomas N. MacCubbin.
November, 1841: Work completed on lock.
Cost: $20,853.85

Lock No. 73: Section No. 350
September 27, 1837: Contract let to George G. Johnson.
August, 1838: Work commenced on lock.
December 28, 1839: Contract abandoned.
January 23, 1840: Modified contract relet to George G. Johnson.
December, 1840: Work completed on lock.
Cost: $18,209.04

Lock No. 74: Section No. 350
September 27, 1837: Contract let to George G. Johnson.
April, 1838: Work commenced on lock.
December 28, 1839: Contract abandoned.
January 23, 1840: Modified contract relet to George G. Johnson.
March, 1841: Work completed on lock.
Cost: $20,547.35

Lock No. 75: Section No. 350
September 27, 1837: Contract let to George G. Johnson.
March, 1838: Work commenced on lock.
August, 1840: Work completed on lock.
Cost: $18,007.50

B. TIDE LOCKS

Tide Lock A: Section A
December 10, 1828: Contract let to Dibble, Beaumont and McCord.
April, 1830: Construction commenced on tide lock.
April, 1831: Construction completed on tide lock.
Cost: $16,620.42

Tide Lock B: Section I
February 4, 1832: Contract let to C. F. LeBaron and I. G. Camp.
April, 1832: Work commenced on tide lock.
December 1, 1832: Contract abandoned.

December, 1832: Work recommenced on tide lock with company hands.
September, 1834: Work completed on tide lock.
Cost: $10,105.30

C. RIVER LOCKS

Edward's Ferry River Lock: Section No. 51
September 2, 1835: Contract let to Michael Byrne.
October, 1835: Work commenced on outlet lock.
November, 1838: Work completed on outlet lock.
Cost: $19,174.08

Shenandoah River Lock: Section No. 109
July–August, 1832: Contract let to Littlejohn and Co.
September, 1832: Work commenced on outlet lock.
June, 1833: Work completed on outlet lock.
Cost: $12,544.00

Shepherdstown River Lock: Section No. 133
May 20, 1833: Contract let to John Cameron.
July, 1833: Work commenced on outlet lock.
January, 1835: Work completed on outlet lock.
Cost: $15,244.41

D. GUARD LOCKS

Guard Lock No. 1: Section G–H
The water from the pool behind Dam No. 1 was let into the canal by means of a feeder and guard lock. These structures had been part of the Potomac Company's Little Falls Skirting Canal and were adapted for use by the Chesapeake and Ohio Canal at a cost of $3,197.82.

Guard Lock No. 2: Section No. 34
March 14, 1829: Contract let to Holdsworth and Isherwood.
June, 1829: Work commenced on guard lock.
November, 1830: Work completed on guard lock.
Cost: $7,338.99

Guard Lock No. 3: Section No. 112
August 18, 1832: Contract let to Fries and McDonnell.
August, 1832: Work commenced on guard lock.
August–September, 1833: Work completed on guard lock.
Cost: $7,120.75

Guard Lock No. 4: Section No. 156
March 4, 1833: Contract let to Joseph Hollman.
April, 1833: Construction commenced on guard lock.
April, 1834: Construction completed on guard lock.
Cost: $8,720.81

Guard Lock No. 5: Section No. 202
August 25, 1832: Contract let to Michael Byrne and Co.
March, 1833: Work commenced on guard lock.
January, 1835: Work completed on guard lock.
Cost: $8,428.31

Guard Lock No. 6: Section No. 258
September 14, 1836: Contract let to George Weaver.
October, 1836: Work commenced on guard lock.
September–October, 1838: Work completed on guard lock.
Cost: $46,548.58 (includes Dam No. 6 abutments)

Guard Lock No. 8: Section No. 367
September 29, 1837: Contract let to William P. Sterritt and William Lockwood.
May, 1838: Work commenced on guard lock.
December 28, 1839: Contract abandoned.
February 27, 1840: Contract relet to William P. Sterritt.
February, 1840: Work recommenced on guard lock.
Early 1842: Work suspended.
November, 1847: Contract let to Hunter, Harris and Co. to finish canal;
 Subcontract to William Lockwood in December, 1847.
April–May, 1848: Work recommenced on guard lock.
April–May, 1850: Work completed on guard lock.
Cost: $79,992.99 (includes Dam No. 8; 1842 assessment)

E. AQUEDUCTS

Aqueduct No. 1 [Seneca Aqueduct]: Section No. 35
October 25, 1828: Contract let to Holdsworth and Isherwood.
July, 1829: Work commenced on aqueduct.
March–April, 1832: Work completed on aqueduct.
Cost: $24,340.25

Aqueduct No. 2 [Monocacy Aqueduct]: Section No. 73
August 20, 1828: Contract let to Hovey and Legg; on October 31, Hitchcock was substituted for Legg.
March, 1829: Work commenced on aqueduct.
December, 1829: Contract abandoned.
December 9, 1829: Contract relet to Asher P. Osborn.
August 7, 1830: Contract assigned to Byrne and LeBaron.
May, 1833: Work completed on aqueduct.
Cost: $128,859.23

Aqueduct No. 3 [Catoctin Aqueduct]: Section No. 91
February 25, 1832: Contract let to Tracy and Douglas.
April, 1832: Construction commenced on aqueduct.
February, 1834: Construction completed on aqueduct.
Cost: $33,325.92

Aqueduct No. 4 [Antietam Aqueduct]: Section No. 126
June 5, 1832: Contract let to Gibson, Noonan, Midler and Fresh and Co.
October, 1832: Work commenced on aqueduct.
April, 1835: Work completed on aqueduct.
Cost: $24,337.33

Aqueduct No. 5 [Conococheague Aqueduct]: Section No. 188
August 25, 1832: Contract let to Michael Byrne and Co.
February, 1833: Work commenced on aqueduct.
October–November, 1835: Work completed on aqueduct.
Cost: $43,283.78

Aqueduct No. 6 [Licking Creek Aqueduct]: Section No. 222
July 3, 1835: Contract let to Richard Holdsworth.
September, 1835: Work commenced on aqueduct.
February 24, 1837: Contract reassigned to Enos Childs after death of Holdsworth.
October 25, 1837: Contract abandoned.
November 8, 1837: Contract reassigned to Enos Childs.
May, 1838: Work completed on aqueduct.
Cost: $48,023.45

Aqueduct No. 7 [Tonoloway Aqueduct]: Section No. 235
July 3, 1835: Contract let to Robert Brown.
September, 1835: Work commenced on aqueduct.
June, 1839: Work completed on aqueduct.
Cost: $48,423.10

Aqueduct No. 8 [Sideling Hill Creek Aqueduct]: Section No. 263
April 1, 1837: Contract let to John Cameron.
April, 1837: Work commenced on aqueduct.
May–June, 1840: Work completed on aqueduct to the point that a final estimate was paid.
November, 1847: Hunter, Harris and Co. let subcontract to Gonder, Brayton and Co.; subcontract assigned to Fraser and Co.
Spring, 1850: Finishing touches put on aqueduct.
Cost: $39,050.07 (1840 final estimate)

Aqueduct No. 9 [Fifteen Mile Creek Aqueduct]: Section No. 271
September 29, 1837: Contract let to William Pratt.
May 23, 1838: Contract relet to Enos Childs.
September, 1838: Work commenced on aqueduct.
December 28, 1839: Contract abandoned.
July 23, 1840: Contract let to George S. marsh.
July, 1840: Work recommenced on aqueduct.
April, 1842: Contract abandoned.
November, 1847: Hunter, Harris and Co. let a subcontract to Gonder, Brayton and Co.; subcontract to Thomas Bell.
March–April, 1848: Construction recommenced on aqueduct.
Summer, 1850: Construction completed on aqueduct.
Cost: $28,119.51 (1842 assessment)

Aqueduct No. 10 [Town Creek Aqueduct]: Section No. 323
September 29, 1837: Contract let to Frederick Pratt.
April, 1838: Work commenced on aqueduct.
November 14, 1838: Contract abandoned.
November, 1847: Hunter, Harris and Co. recommence work on aqueduct.
Summer, 1850: Construction completed on aqueduct.
Cost: $3,747.89 (1838 assessment)

Aqueduct No. 11 [Evitts Creek Aqueduct]: Section No. 360
September 29, 1837: Contract let to George G. Johnson.
February, 1838: Work commenced on aqueduct.
December 28, 1839: Contract abandoned.
January 23, 1840: Modified contract relet to George G. Johnson.
October, 1841: Work completed on aqueduct to the point that a final estimate was paid.
November, 1847: Contract let to Hunter, Harris and Co.
Spring, 1850: Finishing touches put on aqueduct.
Cost: $45,986.00 (1841 assessment)

F.   DAMS

Dam No. 1: Section No. 1
December 10, 1828: Contract let to Dibble, Beaumont and McCord.
June, 1829: Construction commenced on dam.
May 19, 1830: Contract terminated when dam was completed to Snake Island.
March 11, 1831: Contract relet to Samuel Goodrich to finish dam to Virginia shore.
Spring, 1831: Work recommenced on dam.
Spring, 1831: Contract abandoned.
June, 1831: Work recommenced on dam under Superintendent John Y. Young and company hands.
April, 1832: Work completed on dam from Snake Island to Virginia shore.
Cost: $37,091.30

Dam No. 2: Section No. 34
December 10, 1828: Contract let to Dibble, Beaumont and McCord.
July, 1829: Construction commenced on dam.
May 19, 1830: Contract terminated.
August 7, 1830: Contract relet to Obediah Gordon; he was aided by Elias Gumaer.
August, 1830: Work recommenced on dam.
October, 1831: Work completed on dam.
Cost: $26,978.95

Dam No. 3: Section No. 109
Dam No. 3 was neither constructed nor owned by the Chesapeake and Ohio Canal Company. It was built by the United States Government to supply water power to the musket factory of the United States Amory at Harpers Ferry. Two dams, built in 1799 and 1809, preceded the government dam used by the canal company.
July, 1820: Contract let to John Lowstetter.
1821: Work completed on government dam.

Dam No. 4: Section No. 156
June 7, 1832: Contract let to Joseph Hollman.
September, 1832: Work commenced on dam.
June, 1835: Work completed on dam.
Cost: $50,803.17

Dam No. 5: Section No. 202
August 25, 1832: Contract let to Byrnes and Co.
March, 1833: Work commenced on dam.
December, 1834: Work completed on dam.
Cost: $47,088.67

Dam No. 6: Section No. 258
September 14, 1836: Contract let to Joseph Hollman and George Reynolds; contract for abutments let to George Weaver.
October, 1836: Construction commenced on abutments.
March, 1837: Construction commenced on dam.
August–September, 1838: Construction completed on abutments.
September 7, 1838: Contract for dam abandoned.
September, 1838: Work recommenced on dam with company hands under Superintendent John R. Young.
February, 1839: Work completed on dam.
Cost: $102,390.75 (including abutments and guard lock)

Dam No. 8: Section No. 367
September 29, 1837: Contract let to William P. Sterritt and William lockwood.
May, 1835: Construction commenced on dam.
December 28, 1839: Contract abandoned.
February 27, 1840: Contract relet to William P. Sterritt.
February, 1840: Work recommenced on dam.
Early 1842: Work suspended.
November, 1847: Contract let to Hunter, Harris and Co. to finish canal; subcontract for Dam No. 8 let to William Lockwood in December, 1847.
April–May, 1848: Work recommenced on dam.
April–May, 1850: Work completed on dam.
Cost: $72,992.99 (includes Guard Lock No. 8; 1842 assessment)

G. LOCKHOUSES

Lockhouses for Locks Nos. 1–4: Section A
Canal company records are not clear about the lockhouses in Georgetown, but they appear to indicate that there were two or three structures serving this purpose. A canal company ledger covering the period 1828–1841 seems to indicate that there were at least two lockhouses on Section A. There are no dates, contractors or cost estimates for these houses; thus, it might be deduced that the canal company adapted existing structures for use as lockhouses in Georgetown. Locust–post fences were built around these two structures in the spring of 1831 by James Hook, at a cost of $174.90.

The same ledger indicates that a lockhouse (other canal documents identify this structure as Lockhouse No. 2) was located on Section A between Locks Nos. 2 and 3. The work done on this structure was done in the spring of 1830 and of 1831 at a cost of $120.02. Because the average cost of a lockhouse was over $700, it can be assumed that this lockhouse was also an existing structure adopted for use by a lock tender. Most of this work was ascribed to Michael Corcoran.

Lockhouses for Locks Nos. 5–6: Section 1
(Canal company records identify these as Lockhouses Nos. 3–4, respectively)
December 11, 1828: Contract for Lockhouse No. 4 let to Thomas and Munroe.
Spring, 1829: Contract for Lockhouse No. 3 let and contract for Lockhouse No. 4 relet to Richard Grosline.
May 1829: Work commenced on lockhouses.
September 1829: Work completed on lockhouses.
Cost: $1,432.03

Lockhouse for Lock No. 7: Section No. 4
(Canal company records identify this as Lockhouse No. 5)
March 28, 1829: Contract let to James O'Brien
May 1829: Work commenced on lockhouse.
July 1829: Work completed on lockhouse.
Cost: $720.00
Lockhouse for Lock No. 8: Section No. 7 (Canal company records identify this as Lockhouse No. 6)
Spring, 1829: Contract let to Thornhill and McKennie.
June, 1829: Work commenced on lockhouse.
May, 1830: Work completed on lockhouse.
Cost: $785.75

Lockhouse for Locks Nos. 9–10: Section No. 8
(Canal company records identify this as Lockhouse No. 7)
August 20, 1828: Contract let to Henry B. Richards.
December, 1828: Work commenced on lockhouse.
Spring, 1829: Contract abandoned.
Spring, 1830: Contract relet to W. W. Fenlon and Co.
April, 1830: Work recommenced on lockhouse.
May, 1830: Work completed on lockhouse.
Cost: $774.73

Lockhouse for Lock No. 11: Section No. 8
(Canal company records identify this as Lockhouse No. 8)
September 11, 1828: Contract let to Morgan Kavenaugh and Co.
May, 1829: Work commenced on lockhouse.
March, 1830: Work completed on lockhouse.
Cost: $789.25

Lockhouse for Locks Nos. 12–14: Section No. 9
December 11, 1828: Contract let to J. W. Maynard.
Spring, 1829: Contract relet to Thornhill and McKennie.
June, 1829: Work commenced on lockhouse.

May, 1830: Work completed on lockhouse.
Cost: $836.74

Lockhouse for Locks No. 15–16: Section No. 17
(Canal company records identify this as Lockhouse No. 10)
December 11, 1828: Contract let to J. W. Maynard.
Summer, 1829: Contract relet to Pine, Crown and Darlington.
Spring, 1830: Contract relet to Robert Warfield.
June, 1830: Work commenced on lockhouse.
June, 1831: Work completed on lockhouse.
Cost: $818.25

Lockhouse for Lock No. 16: Section No. 17
(Canal company records identify this as house to Lock No. 16)
June 7, 1837: Board authorized Superintendent John Y. Young to build lockhouse.
CA. spring, 1838: Work commenced on lockhouse with company hands.
April, 1839: Work completed on lockhouse.
Cost: $892.16

Lockhouse for Locks Nos. 17–18: Section No. 18
(Canal company records identify this as Lockhouse No. 11)
December 11, 1828: Contract let to J. W. Maynard.
December 2, 1829: Contract relet to Pine, Crown and Darlington.
December, 1839: Work commenced on lockhouse.
August, 1830: Work completed on lockhouse.
Cost $749.00

Lockhouse for Locks Nos. 19–20: Section No. 18
(Canal company records identify this as Lockhouse No. 12)
December 11, 1828: Contract let to J. W. Maynard.
December 2, 1829: Contract relet to Pine, Crown and Darlington.
December, 1829: Work commenced on lockhouse.
March, 1831: Work completed on lockhouse.
Cost: $739.00
Soon after its completion, Lockhouse No. 12 was enlarged, remodeled and named Crommelin House.

Lockhouse for Lock No. 21: Section No. 23
(Canal company records identify this as Lockhouse No. 13)
December 2, 1829: Contract let to Pine, Crown and Darlington.
Spring, 1831: Contract relet to Henry B. Richards.
May, 1831: Work commenced on lockhouse.
August, 1832: Work completed on lockhouse.
Cost: &765.00

Lockhouse for Lock No. 22: Section No. 29
(Canal company records identify this as Lockhouse No. 14)
December 11, 1828: Contract let to Wines, Brackett and Wines; company later reorganized under Ruben Brackett.

October, 1829: Work commenced on lockhouse.
April, 1830: Work completed on lockhouse.
Cost: $853.20

Lockhouse for Lock No. 23 and Guard Lock No. 2: Section No. 34
(Canal company records identify this as Lockhouse No. 15)
November, 1829: Contract let to Charles Shepherd.
Summer, 1830: Contract relet to Thomas and Munroe.
Fall, 1830: Contract relet to Mathias Duffie (contract let to Obediah Gordon to build basement).
October, 1830: Work commenced on lockhouse.
Cost: $958.49
Soon after its completion, Lockhouse No. 15 was enlarged, remodeled and named Rushville House.

Lockhouse for Lock No. 24: Section No. 35
(Canal company records identify this as Lockhouse No. 16)
December 11, 1828: Contract let to Holdsworth and Isherwood.
November, 1829: Work commenced on lockhouse.
April, 1830: Work completed on lockhouse.
Cost: $1,066.25

Lockhouse for Lock No. 25: Section No. 51
(Canal company records identify this as Lockhouse No. 17)
December 11, 1828: Contract let to Thomas and Munroe.
November, 1829: Work commenced on lockhouse.
March, 1830: Work completed on lockhouse.
Cost: $903.00

Lockhouse for Lock No. 26: Section No. 68
(Canal company records identify this as Lockhouse No. 18)
December 11, 1828: Contract let to Thomas and Munroe.
June, 1829: Work commenced on lockhouse.
January, 1830: Work completed on lockhouse.
Cost: $849.00

Lockhouse for Lock No. 27: Section No. 72
(Canal company records identify this as Lockhouse No. 19)
December 11, 1828: Contract let to Thomas and Munroe.
June, 1829: Work commenced on lockhouse.
June, 1830: Work completed on lockhouse.
Cost: $893.25

Lockhouse for Lock No. 28: Section No. 87
(Canal company records identify this as house to Lock No. 28)
May 21, 1836: Contract let to Michael Foley.
June, 1836: Work commenced on lockhouse.
May, 1837: Work completed on lockhouse.
Cost: $983.16

Lockhouse for Lock No. 29: Section No. 89
(Canal company records identify this as house to Lock No. 29)
May 21, 1836: Contract let to Michael Foley.
June, 1836: Work commenced on lockhouse.
May, 1837: Work completed on lockhouse.
Cost: $947.98

Lockhouse for Lock No. 30: Section No. 98
(Canal company records identify this as house to Lock No. 30)
August 16, 1836: Board authorized Superintendent William S. Elgin to purchase a house and Lot No. 3 in Berlin (now Brunswick) for use as the lockhouse at Lock No. 30; selling price – $1,050; owner – Robert Kemble.
September 26, 1836: Board authorized Elgin to pay Kemble additional sum for repairs recently made to the house.

Lockhouse for Lock No. 31: Section No. 104
(Canal company records identify this as Lockhouse No. 23)
May 24, 1833: Contract let to Peter G. Mathias.
May, 1833: Work commenced on lockhouse.
August, 1833: Work completed on lockhouse.
Cost: $1,031.40

Lockhouse for Lock No. 32: Section No. 108
(Canal company records identify this as house to Lock No. 32)
August 24, 1836: Contract let to Jonah Hood.
September, 1836: Work commenced on lockhouse.
April, 1837: Work completed on lockhouse.
Cost: $1,169.45

Lockhouse for Lock No. 33: Section No. 109
(Canal company records identify this as house to Lock No. 33)
Spring, 1837: Contract let to James A Foster.
May, 1837: Work commenced on lockhouse.
July, 1837: Work completed on lockhouse.
Cost: $1,035.60

Lockhouse for Lock No. 34: Section No. 111
(Canal company records identify this as house to Lock No. 34)
May 21, 1836: Contract let to Michael Foley.
June, 1836: Work commenced on lockhouse.
October, 1836: Work completed on lockhouse.
Cost: $999.62

Lockhouse for Locks No. 35–36 and Guard Lock No. 3: Section No. 112
(Canal company records identify this as house to Locks 35 and 36 and Guard Lock No. 3)
May 21, 1836: Contract let to Jonah Hood.
August, 1836: Work commenced on lockhouse.
April, 1837: Work completed on lockhouse.
Cost: $1,074.25

Lockhouse for Lock No. 37: Section No. 122
(Canal company records identify this as house to Lock 37)
Spring, 1836: Contract let to James and Baker.
May 21, 1836: Contract relet to John D. Grove.
August, 1836: Work commenced on lockhouse.
July, 1837: Work completed on lockhouse.
Cost $981.25

Lockhouse for Lock No. 38: Section No. 133
(Canal company records identify this as house to Lock 38)
July 24, 1837: Contract let to James A. Foster.
September, 1837: Work commenced on lockhouse.
September, 1838: Work completed on lockhouse.
Cost: $1,530.34

Lockhouse for Lock No. 39: Section No. 135
(Canal company records identify this as house to Lock 39)
Spring, 1836: Contract let to Jams and Baker.
May 21, 1836: Contract relet to John D. Grove.
August, 1836: Work commenced on lockhouse.
July, 1837: Work completed on lockhouse.
Cost: $1,259.73

Lockhouse for Lock No. 40: Section No. 146
(Canal company records identify this as house to Lock 40)
Spring, 1836: Contract let to James and Baker.
May 21, 1836: Contract relet to John D. Grove.
October, 1836: Work commenced on lockhouse.
July, 1837: Work completed on lockhouse.
Cost: $1,029.18

Lockhouse for Guard Lock No. 4: Section No. 156
(Canal company records identify this as house to Guard Lock No. 4)
Spring, 1836: Contract let to James and Baker.
May 21, 1836: Contract relet to John D. Grove.
December, 1836: Work commenced on lockhouse.
July, 1837: Work completed on lockhouse.
Cost: $1,056.14

Lockhouse for Locks Nos. 41–62: Section No. 173
(Canal company records identify this as house to Locks 41 and 42)
Spring, 1836: Contract let to James and Baker.
May 21, 1836: Contract relet to John D. Grove.
August, 1836: Work commenced on lockhouse.
July, 1837: Work completed on lockhouse.
Cost: $1,005.92

Lockhouse for Lock No. 43: Section No. 173
(Canal company records identify this as house to Lock 43)

Spring, 1836: Contract let to James and Baker.
May 21, 1836: Contract relet to John D. Grove.
August, 1836: Work commenced on lockhouse.
July, 1837: Work completed on lockhouse.
Cost: $980.74

Lockhouse for Lock No. 44: Section No. 187
(Canal company records identify this as house for Lock No. 44)
Spring, 1835— Contract let to Joseph Hollman.
June, 1845: Board authorized Superintendent John G. Stone to build lockhouse.
Summer–fall, 1845: Lockhouse built by company hands under supervision of Stone.
Cost: Approximately $300

Lockhouse for Guard Lock No. 5: Section No. 202
(Canal company records identify this as house to Guard Lock No. 5)
Spring, 1837: Contract let to George Fagen.
Summer, 1837: Work commenced on lockhouse.
June, 1837: Work completed on lockhouse.
Cost: $1,058.50

Lockhouse for Locks Nos. 45–46: Section No. 203
(Canal company records identify this as house to Lock 49)
Spring, 1837: Contract let to Jesse Schofield.
Summer, 1837: Work commenced on lockhouse.
June, 1839: Work completed on lockhouse.
Cost: $1,109.80

Lockhouse for Locks Nos. 47–50: Section No. 206
(Canal company records identify this as house to Lock 49)
Spring, 1837: Contract let to Jesse Schofield.
August, 1837: Work commenced on lockhouse.
February, 1839: Work completed on lockhouse.
Cost: $1,447.50

Lockhouse for Locks Nos. 51–52: Section No. 233
(Canal company records identify this as house to Lock 51)
July 25, 1837: Contract let to Jesse Schofield.
September, 1837: Work commenced on lockhouse.
December 26, 1838: Contract abandoned.
May 15, 1839: Contract relet to John W. Beideman.
June, 1839: Work recommenced on lockhouse.
July, 1840: Work completed on lockhouse.
Cost: $1,016.60

Lockhouse for Lock No. 53: Section No. 253
(Canal company records identify this as house to Lock 53)
July 24, 1837: Contract let to Jessie Schofield.
December 26, 1838: Contract abandoned.
May 15, 1839: Contract relet to John W. Beideman.

July, 1839: Work commenced on lockhouse.
July, 1840: Work completed on lockhouse.
Cost: $975.00

Lockhouse for Locks No. 54–55 and Guard Lock No. 6: Section No. 259
(Canal company records identify this as house at Dam No. 6)
Canal company records appear to indicate that a temporary shanty was built near Guard Lock No. 6 by company hands during the fall of 1840 to house the lock tender for Locks Nos. 54–55 and Guard Lock No. 6. It is also possible that a nearby building may have been adapted for use as a lockhouse. The sum of $30 was expended on December 31, 1842 for this purpose.
While the canal company records are not clear, company engineers apparently built a larger structure to serve as a lockhouse for these locks during 1849–1850. There is no indication that any work was done on the lockhouse, and the contract was declared abandoned on May 11, 1839.
Canal company records indicate that a contract for the construction of a lockhouse at Lock No. 54 was let to Henry Smith on March 23, 1836. There is no indication that any work was done on the lockhouse, and the contract was declared abandoned on May 11, 1839.

Lockhouses for Locks No. 56–75
(Canal company records identify these as Lockhouses at the following locks: Nos. 56, 57, 58, 59, 60, 61, 62, 66, 67, 68, 70, 72, 73, 75 and Guard Lock No. 8)
When work resumed on the "fifty–mile" section of the canal on November 18, 1847, Hunter, Harris and Co. subcontracted for the construction of these lockhouses. Canal company records do not indicate the names of the subcontractors, the dates of construction, or the building costs. The records indicate that not all of these lockhouses were completed by October 10, 1850, when the canal was formally opened to navigation. It may be assumed that they were completed during the following year.

H. STOP LOCKS (STOP GATES)

Stop Lock: Section C
August 5, 1835: Contract let to William Easby.
August, 1835: Work commenced on stop lock.
March–April, 1837: Work completed on stop lock.
Cost: $4,375.36

Stop Gate: Section No. 38
Resident Engineer Charles B. Fisk apparently directed the construction of this stop gate between March, 1835 and March, 1836. Company laborers were used for the work.
Cost: $122.43

Stop Gate: Section No. 156
July 29, 1836: Board authorized George W. Rodger, a company employee, to build the structure.
December, 1837: Work commenced on stop gate.
April, 1839: Work completed on stop gate.
Cost: $5,375.48

Stop Gate: Section No. 195
November 12, 1834: Contract let to Eli and J. S. Stake.

November, 1834: Work commenced on stop gate.
May, 1835: Work completed on stop gate.
Cost: $585.12

Stop Gate: Section No. 209
June 25, 1838: Contract let to Philip Gormley.
July, 1838: Work commenced on stop gate.
June, 1839: Work completed on stop gate.
Cost: $4,399.98

Stop Gate: Section No. 213
June 7, 1837: Contract let to William Brown.
June, 1837: Work commenced on stop gate.
July, 1838: Work completed on stop gate.
Cost: $2,490.70

Stop Gate: Section No. 217
September 29, 1837: Contract let to Timothy Cunningham.
June, 1838: Work commenced on stop gate.
February, 1839: Work completed on stop gate.
Cost: $3,720.20 (including adjacent waste weir)

Stop Gate: Section No. 228
September 28, 1838: Contract let to John Bain.
October, 1838: Work commenced on stop gate.
June, 1839: Work completed on stop gate.
Cost: $2,439.29

I.   FEEDERS

Rocky Run Feeder: Section No. 9
Spring, 1830: Contract let to John Seale.
June, 1830: Work commenced and completed on feeder.
Cost: $198.60

Great Falls Feeder: Section No. 18
June 4, 1830: Contract let to Bargy and Guy.
May, 1830: Work commenced on feeder.
April, 1831: Work completed on feeder.
Cost: $2,110.45

Tuscarora Feeder: Section No. 78
February 6, 1833 – Contract let to Stephen Sands.
February, 1833: Work commenced on feeder.
November, 1833: Work completed on feeder.
Cost: $3,151.69

J. MISCELLANEOUS STRUCTURES

Paw Paw Tunnel: Sections Nos. 309–310
March 15, 1836: Contract let to Lee Montgomery.
June, 1836: Work commenced on tunnel.
November, 1841: Work suspended on tunnel.
November, 1848: Contract let to Hunter, Harris and Co. to complete the canal; subcontract to finish tunnel let to McCulloch and Day.
1850: Work completed on tunnel (except for brick lining which was completed after the canal was opened to navigation).
Cost: $616,478.65 (includes adjoining deep cuts; 1841 assessment)

Broad Run Trunk: Section No. 53
(Canal company records identify this structure as Culvert No 44½)
October 1, 1829: Contract let to Albert Hovey.
Winter, 1829: Contract abandoned.
Summer, 1830: Contract relet to James Costigan.
October, 1830: Work commenced on culvert.
March, 1831: Contract abandoned.
March 11, 1831: Contract relet to Bargey and Roach.
November, 1831: Contract recommenced on culvert.
August, 1832: Contract abandoned.
Fall, 1832: Contract relet to Thomas Walter.
December, 1832: Work recommenced on culvert.
May, 1833: Work completed on culvert.
Cost: $[not provided]
Note: Culvert No 44½ was washed out in a flood of 1846, and was replaced by a wooden trunk as a temporary expedient. By 1856, the structure had deteriorated to a point where maintenance was no longer feasible. At this time, it was decided to rebuild the structure as a wooden trunk; and aside from routine repairs, no major work appears to have been done on the structure between 1857 and 1924.

Rock Creek Basin: Section A
(Including mole, basin, causeway and waste weir)
December 10, 1828: Contract let to Dibble, Beaumont and McCord.
May, 1829: Work commenced on basin and related structures.
October, 1831: Work completed on basin and related structures.
Cost: $69,567.20

Towpath for Big Slackwater: Sections Nos. 157–166
July 29, 1836: Contract let to Joseph Hollman.
August 17, 1836: John D. Grove became partner of Hollman.
September, 1836: Work commenced on towpath.
December, 1838: Work completed on towpath.
Cost: $31,416.36

Towpath for Little Slackwater: Section No. 203
June 12, 1837: Contract let to John Seale.
November, 1837: Work commenced on towpath.

April, 1839: Work completed on towpath.
Cost $8,204.40

APPENDIX A

PRESIDENT JOHN QUINCY ADAMS'S REMINISCENCES
OF CANAL GROUND-BREAKING CEREMONIES, ON JULY 4, 1828.

"4th, Independence Day. Chesapeake and Ohio Canal commenced. Between seven and eight this morning, I went with my son John to the Union Hotel, at Georgetown, where were assembling the President and Directors of the Chesapeake and Ohio Canal Company; the Mayors and Committees of the corporations of Washington, Georgetown, and Alexandria; the heads of Departments, foreign Ministers, and a few other invited persons. About eight o'clock a procession was formed, preceded by a band of music, to the wharf, where we embarked in the steamboat *Surprise*; followed by two others, we proceeded to the entrance of the Potomac Canal, and up that in canal-boats to its head—near which, just within the bounds of the State of Maryland, was the spot selected for breaking the ground. The President of the Chesapeake and Ohio Canal Company, with a very short address, delivered to me the spade, with which I broke the ground, addressing the surrounding auditory, consisting perhaps of two thousand persons. It happened that at the first stroke of the spade it met immediately under the surface a large stump of a tree; after repeating the stroke three or four times without making any impression, I threw off my coat, and, resuming the spade, raised a shovelful of the earth, at which a general shout burst forth from the surrounding multitude, and I completed my address, which occupied about fifteen minutes. The President and Directors of the Canal, the Mayors and Committees of the three Corporations, the heads of Departments, members of Congress, and others, followed, and shoveled up a wheelbarrow-full of earth. Mr. Gales, the Mayor of Washington, read also a short address, and was answered extemporaneously by Andrew Stewart, the Director of the Company from Pennsylvania. After a short repose under a tent on the banks of the canal, we returned by the canal-boats to the landing, and thence in the steamboat, where, as we re-descended the Potomac, the company partook of a light collation upon the deck. I was asked for a toast, and gave, 'The Chesapeake and Ohio Canal: perseverance.' Mr. Mercer and Mr. Rush also gave toasts.

"About half-past two I was landed by Davidson's wharf, where my carriage was waiting, and, after taking Mr. Rush home, I returned to mine. The Marshals of the day escorted me home on horseback, came in and took a glass of wine, and took leave with my thanks for their attentions. The day was uncommonly cool for the season, with a fresh breeze, and towards evening there was a gentle shower. The exertion of speaking in the open air made me hoarse, and with the anxiety, more oppressive than it should have been, to get well through the day, exhausted and fatigued me, so that I was disqualified for thought or action the remainder of the day. As has happened to me whenever I have had a part to perform in the presence of multitudes, I got through awkwardly, but without gross and palpable failure. The incident that chiefly relieved me was the obstacle of the stump, which met and resisted the spade, and my casting off my coat to overcome the resistance. It struck the eye and fancy of the spectators more than all the flowers of rhetoric in my speech, and diverted their attention from the stammering and hesitation of a deficient memory. Mr. Vaughan, Chevalier Bangeman Huygens, Barons Krudener and Stackelberg, and several other members of the Corps Diplomatique were present, and thought it, perhaps, a strange part for a President of the United States to perform.

Governor Kent, of Maryland, was there, as one of the directors of the company, and compared the ceremony to that said to be annually observed in China."[1]

---

[1] Excerpted from Memoirs of John Quincy Adams, Vol. 8, 49–50.

APPENDIX B

DESCRIPTION OF THE SEAL OF THE CHESAPEAKE & OHIO CANAL COMPANY, SEPTEMBER 3, 1828:

"In diameter two inches and seven twentieths of an inch, its surface quartered and having in one quarter a Loom in operation with a weaver seated at it; in another quarter a Man ploughing with a single horse; and in a third quarter two boats underway, one drawn by a horse, the other impelled by steam, & on the fourth quarter a ship under full sail; the said devices being designed to denote Agriculture, Manufactures, Internal and External Commerce. Over the seal as a Crest two clasped hands with the motto, "Esto Perpetua", illustrative of the union of the Eastern and Western waters, to be accomplished by the Chesapeake & Ohio Canal; and below a Mountain, perforated by a Tunnel, with the motto "Perseverando", indicating the manner of effecting this Union, and the long continued labor which it may require. Around the quartering of the field, are the words "Chesapeake & Ohio Canal Company."[1]

---

[1] *Proceedings of the President and Board of Directors*, A, 63.

APPENDIX C

LIST OF CONTRACTORS FOR 34 SECTIONS
BETWEEN LITTLE FALLS AND SENECA FALLS, AUGUST 20, 1828[1]

Section	Contractor	Section	Contractor
1	A. B. Hovey & Co.	18	Daniel Renner
2	Daniel Bussard	19	Joseph H. Bradley
3	Daniel Bussard	20	James C. Lackland
4	John W. Baker	21	Thomas Crown
5	Daniel Bussard	22	John Farqurharson & Co.
6	Wathen and Underwood	23	Henry Smith
7	Clark & Clements	24	William Scott
8	W. W. Fenlon & Co.	25	Arnold T. Winsor
9	Daniel Bussard	26	Callen & Clements
10	Daniel Bussard	27	James O'Reilly
11	David Bussard	28	Washburn, Gustin & Bond
12	George Ketchum	29	Rubin Bracket & Co.
13	Thomas B. Tripp	30	H. W. Campbell
14	W. W. Fenlon & Co.	31	H. W. Campbell
15	Parmencies Asams	32	A. B. Hovey & Co.
16	Luke Hitchcock	33	A. H. Millard
17	Henry Smith	34	H. W. Campbell

---

[1] *Proceedings of the President and Board of Directors*, A, 41–41.

APPENDIX D

CONTRACTORS FOR SECTIONS BETWEEN SENECA FALLS AND POINT OF ROCKS AND FOR MASONRY WORK BETWEEN LITTLE FALLS AND POINT OF ROCKS, OCTOBER 25, 1828:[1]

Section	Contractor	Section	Contractor
35	Knapp & Co.	60	McIntosh & Co.
36	Knapp & Co.	61	Richard Cromwell
37	Knapp & Co.	62	Richard Cromwell
38	Knapp & Co.	63	Darrow & Whitmore
39	Crown & Lanham	64	Darrow & Whitmore
40	Thomas Crown	65	McIntosh & Bennett
41	Plater & Helm	66	A. H. Millerd
42	Plater & Helm	67	R. Brackett & Co.
43	Plater & Helm	68	R. Brackett & Co.
44	Plater & Helm	69	R. Brackett & Co.
45	Plater & Helm	70	R. Brackett & Co.
46	Plater & Helm	71	T. McIntosh & Co.
47	Thomas Crown	72	( )
48	Thomas Crown	73	J. Hurd & Co.
49	Higgins & Owens	74	Donley & Co.
50	Higgins & Owens	75	McIntosh & Bennett
51	Higgins & Owens	76	McIntosh & Bennett
52	Higgins & Owens	77	Donley & Co.
53	( )	78	J. Hurd & Co.
54	J. Costigan	79	J. Hurd & Co.
55	Garey Hickman	80	J. Hurd & Co.
56	T. Gatton & Co.	81	J. Hurd & Co.
57	H. W. Campbell	82	J. Hurd & Co.
58	T. H. McCubbin	83	J. Hurd & Co.
59	W. A. Nichols & Co.	84	Walter B. Kemp
Lock	Contractor	Lock	Contractor
5	Bennett & Brackett	17	Kenny & Roberts
6	Bennett & Brackett	18	J. & J. Maynard
7	Brackett & Hovey	19	J. & J. Maynard
8	Brackett & Hovey	20	J. & J. Maynard
9	W. W. Fenlon & Co.	21	Holdsworth & Isherwood
10	Hale & Nichols	22	Kenny & Roberts
11	Kavenaugh & Knox	23	Kenny & Roberts
12	J. & J. Maynard	24	Holdsworth & Isherwood
13	Patrick Donnelly	25	Lafferty & Boland
14	Patrick Donnelly	26	Amos Johnson
15	J. & J. Maynard	27	Lafferty & Boland
16	J. & J. Maynard		
AQUEDUCT NO. 1		Holdsworth & Isherwood	
CULVERTS NOS.	10–12, 17	W. W. Fenlon & Co.	

---

[1] *Proceedings of the President and Board of Directors*, A, 93–98

APPENDIX E

LIST OF ENGINEERS APPOINTED ON THE FIRST DIVISION OF THE CHESAPEAKE & OHIO CANAL, NOVEMBER 22, 1828[1]

The distribution of the engineers on the first division of the canal was as follows:

(a) to the first residency, covering the line from the eastern termination of the canal through Section No. 6, were assigned Thomas F. Purcell, resident engineer, Charles D. Ward, assistant engineer, Peter Von Smith, rodman, and Randolph Coyle, volunteer rodman;

(b) to the second residency, covering Sections Nos. 7–18, were assigned Daniel Van Slyke, resident engineer, Herman Boye, assistant engineer, and James Mears, Jr., rodman;

(c) to the third residency, covering Sections Nos. 19–38, were assigned W. M. C. Fairfax, resident engineer, William Beckwith, assistant engineer, R. J. Bowie, rodman, and Thomas H. DeWitt, volunteer rodman;

(d) to the fourth residency, covering Sections Nos. 39–64, were assigned Erastus Hurd, resident engineer, Charles B. Fisk, assistant engineer, and L. G. Davis, rodman; and

(e) to the fifth residency, covering Sections Nos. 65–84, were assigned Alfred Cruger, resident engineer, Charles Ellet, assistant engineer, and William Wallack, rodman.

---

[1] *Proceedings of the President and Board of Directors*, A, 107–115.

APPENDIX F

LIST OF CONTRACTORS FOR WORK ON CANAL
BETWEEN ROCK CREEK AND LITTLE FALLS, DECEMBER 10, 1828[1]

Section	Contractor
A	Issac McCord & Co.
B	John Baker
C	B. J. Forrest & Co.
D	B. J. Forrest & Co.
E	B. J. Forrest & Co.
F	B. J. Forrest & Co.
G	Hewes, Lewis & Hewes
H	Hewes, Lewis & Hewes

Dam	Contractor
1	Issac McCord & Co.
2	Issac McCord & Co.

Bridge	Contractor
1	Issac McCord & Co.
2	Issac McCord & Co.

Lock	Contractor
1	Issac McCord & Co.
2*	Issac McCord & Co.
3*	Issac McCord & Co.
4*	Issac McCord & Co.

* with bridges

Culvert	Contractor
E	B. S. Forrest & Co.
F	B. S. Forrest & Co.
G	B. S. Forrest & Co.
H	B. S. Forrest & Co.
I	B. S. Forrest & Co.
K	Hewes, Lewis & Hewes
L	Hewes, Lewis & Hewes

Pier, Waster Weir and Tide Lock at Rock Creek Basin—Isaac McCord & Co.

---

[1] *Proceedings of the President and Board of Directors*, A, 127.

APPENDIX G

LIST OF CONTRACTORS FOR LOCKHOUSES, DECEMBER 11, 1828[1]

House	Contractor
4	Thomas & Munroe
7	Richards & Kavenaugh
8	M. Kavenaugh & Co.
9	J. W. Maynard
10	J. W. Maynard
11	J. W. Maynard
12	J. W. Maynard
14	Wines, Bracker & Wines
16	Holdsworth & Isherwood
17	Thomas & Munroe
18	Thomas & Munroe
19	Thomas & Munroe

---

[1] *Proceedings of the President and Board of Diredctor*, A, 129.

APPENDIX H

LIST OF CONTRACTORS FOR RELET LOCKS, MARCH 14, 1829[1]

Lock	Contractor
5	A. Knapp & Co.
6	A. Knapp & Co.
7	Fenlon & Bosteder
8	A. Knapp & Co.
12	Fenlon & Bosteder
15	A. Knapp & Co.
16	A. Knapp & Co.
17	A. Knapp & Co.
18	A. Knapp & Co.
19	Fenlon & Bosteder
20	A. Knapp & Co.
22	F. C. Clopper
23	Holdsworth & Isherwood
26	A. Knapp & Co.

---

[1] *Proceedings of the President and Board of Directors*, A, 178.

APPENDIX I

LIST OF LOCK TENDERS AND LOCATION OF LOCKHOUSES FROM LITTLE FALLS TO SENECA FALLS, AUGUST 7, 1830[1]

Lock	Lockhouse	Section	Lock Keeper
5	3	1	Mr. Whalen
6	4	1	William Connor
7	5	4	Robert Brooke
8	6	7	Solomon Drew
9 & 10	7	8	Thomas Burgess
11	8	8	Mr. Edmonston
12, 13 & 14	9	9	Charles L. Sears
15 & 16	10	17	(No name given)
17 & 18	11	18	William Roberts
19 & 20	12	18	William Roberts
21	13	23	Mr. Fuller
22	14	29	Mr. Wright
23	15	34	Lewis Sewell

---

[1] *Proceedings of the President and Board of Directors*, B, 157-159. Later on November 20, W. W. Fenlon was selected as lock-keeper of Locks Nos. 19 and 20 with general supervision of Locks Nos. 15-18.

APPENDIX J

LIST OF CONTRACTORS FOR SECTIONS FROM
POINT OF ROCKS TO HARPERS FERRY, MARCH 14, 1832[1]

Section	Contractor	Section	Contractor
90	Williams & Dawes	102	Offutt & Stone
91	Kemp G. Carter	103	Judson C. Pumphoy
92	Fred Bryan	104	L. F. & J. Pumphrey
93	Hawley & Campbell	105	L. F. & J. Pumphrey
94	O'Neill & Lanaghan	106	Pat McLaughlin
95	Ennis, Grimes & Ennis	107	Andrew Clements
96	Bers & Hyde	108	James Collan
97	Zach & Siatton	109	T. & S. McCoy
98	Watkins & Gatton	110	Bernard Collins
99	Lemuel Offutt	111	H. A. & J. Stewart
100	T. S. & G. M. Watkins	112	Henry Smith
101	Stephen Sands		

---

[1] Ledger A, 1828–1841, 370–414.

APPENDIX K

LIST OF CONTRACTORS FOR SECTIONS NOS. 113–117
(DAMS NOS. 3–4), JUNE 2, 1832.[1]

Section	Contractor	Section	Contractor
113	John Noonan	136	Stephen Sands
114	J. & B. Gorman	137	Stephen Sands
115	William Harte	138	Frink, Hubbard & Co.
116	Samuel Miller	139	Frink, Hubbard & Co.
117	Morris & Nurray	140	J. P. & J. Dougherty
118	James & Fresh	141	Joshua Jamison
119	Sullivan & Mahorney	142	Josephus Beall
120	Sherlock & Gene	143	Gatton & Watkins
121	Dolan & Harford	144	A. & T. N. Clements
122	William Pollock	145	A. & T. N. Clements
123	Tenning Dodge	146	G. M. & R. W. Watkins
124	John Noonan	147	John Stocksdale
125	Sherlock & Gene	148	Enos Childs
126	William Eldridge & Co.	149	Josephus Beall
127	Stephan Sands	150	Offutt & Maccubbins
128	Stephan Sands	151	Offutt & Maccubbins
129	Z. & E. M. Gatton	152	Offutt & Maccubbins
130	Z. & E. M. Gatton	153	Seale & Curran
131	Gatton & Watkins	154	Gorman, Conolly &
132	Gatton & Watkins	155	Kennedy & O'Neill
133	Simon Dwyer	156	Kennedy & O'Neill
134	Seale & Curran	157	Thomas Heunessey
135	Charles H. McCann		

---

[1] Ledger A, 1828–1841, 416–504.

APPENDIX L

LIST OF MASONRY STRUCTURES AND DIFFICULT SECTIONS BETWEEN DAM NO. 5 AND THE CACAPON RIVER LET FOR CONTRACT, JULY 3, 1835[1]

Aqueduct	Contractor
6	Richard Holdsworth
7	Robert Brown

Lock	Contractor	Lock	Contractor
45	W. Morrow	49	Daniel K. Cahoon
46	I. C. Lissig	50	Daniel K. Cahoon
47	Daniel K. Cahoon	51	Robert Brown
48	Daniel K. Cahoon	52	Robert Brown
		53	Patrick McGinley

Section	Contractor	Section	Contractor
203	John Seale	226	James Lonergan
204	John Seale	229	R. W. Watkins
205	David Lyles	230	R. W. Watkins
206	David Lyles	235	Samuel S. Piddle
207	Thomas M. McCubbin	236	James Ryan
209	Michael McMahon	237	Samuel S. Piddle
222	Lee Montgomery	243	Daniel C. Cahoon
225	Anthony Loftus	244	Daniel K. Cahoon
247	John Gorman	252	Bernard Gorman
248	John Gorman	255	Thomas Barr

Culvert	Contractor	Culvert	Contractor
137	John Lambie	173	Michael Smith
138	David Lyles	174	Michael Smith
139	David Lyles	175	Michael Smith
140	James J. McElhery	176	James Ryan
141	Daniel K. Cahoon	177	E. H. Fielding
142	James J. McElhery	178	E. H. Fielding
143	James J. McElhery	179	E. H. Fielding
158	Lee Montgomery	180	E. H. Fielding
159	Lee Montgomery	181	E. H. Fielding
163	Anthony Loftus	182	E. H. Fielding
164	James Lonergan	189	Daniel K. Cahoon
165	James Lonergan	190	John Gorman
166	James Lonergan	191	John Gorman
167	James Lonergan	192	William Brown
168	Michael Smith	193	William Brown
169	Michael Smith	194	John Lambie
170	Michael Smith	195	Daniel K. Cahoon
171	R. M. Watkins	196	John Lambie
172	Michael Smith	197	Daniel K. Cahoon

---

[1] *Proceedings of the President and Board of Directors*, D, 360–362.

APPENDIX M

LIST OF CONTRACTORS FOR SECTIONS BETWEEN DAM NO. 5 AND THE CACAPON RIVER, FEBRUARY 10, 1836[1]

Section	Contractor	Section	Contractor
210	George Young	233	P. McGirk
211	P. Driskell	234	M. Mulhollon
212	John Moore	238	W. Story
213	G. S. Marsh	239	W. Story
214	G. S. Marsh	240	S. Nichols
215	G. S. Marsh	241	G. Magruder
216	G. S. Marsh	242	W. Blakely
217	G. M. Watkins	245	G. W. Higgins
218	John Moore	246	E. M. Gatton
219	G. S. Marsh	249	Patrick Crowley
220	G. S. Marsh	250	Patrick Crowley
221	G. S. Marsh	251	Patrick Crowley
223	Lee Montgomery	253	Patrick Crowley
224	G. M. Watkins	254	T. Gealey
227	Jonah Hood	256	J. O. Hearn
228	Jonah Hood	257	J. Hynes
232	P. McGirk	258	Henry Smith

---

[1] *Proceedings of the President and Board of Directors*, E, 18–19.

APPENDIX N

LIST OF CONTRACTORS FOR 54 SECTIONS AND 4 LOCKS
BETWEEN DAM NO. 6 AND CUMBERLAND, SEPTEMBER 27, 1837[1]

Section	Contractor	Section	Contractor
262	John O'Neill	320	Casper Dull
269	John O'Neill	321	E. Y. Bright
270	George D. Jorman	322	Nahum Starr
271	John Bevans	323	Wells Hatch
272	John Kirkwood	329	Robert McCoy
273	Martin Phelan	335	George W. Henry
274	J. Ferguson	336	Isaiah Frost
275	Zenus Barnum	341	George W. Henry
276	Zenus Barnum	342	Anson Bangs
278	Peter Bargey	343	Anson Bangs
279	Joseph Miller	344	R. Worthington
280	George Grier	347	W. P. Sterritt
281	Harvey Hackley	348	W. P. Sterritt
292	Robert L. Patterson	349	George Grier
293	Robert L. Patterson	350	George W. Johnson
294	Harvey Hackley	351	George G. Johnson
297	R. H. Bangs	352	Dennis Dougherty
312	Bernard O'Friel	353	Patrick Driskell
313	John Waldron	354	Henry McCurdy
317	George Murray	355	Henry McCurdy
318	Patrick McEvoy	356	Patrick Hagan
319	E. M. Gatton	357	W. P. Sterritt

Section	Contractor	Section	Contractor
358	George Grier	363	Simon Nicholls
359	Henry McCurdy	364	Clark Burnbam
360	Thomas M. McCubbin	365	Charles Murray
361	John Dougherty	366	H. Devine
362	Simon Nicholls	367	H. Devine

Lock	Contractor	Lock	Contractor
68	Robert McCoy	74	George G. Johnson
73	George G. Johnson	75	George G. Johnson

---

[1] *Proceedings of the President and Board of Directors*, E, 317–319.

APPENDIX O

LIST OF CONTRACTORS FOR MASONRY WORK BETWEEN DAM NO. 6
AND CUMBERLAND, SEPTEMBER 29, 1837[1]

Aqueducts	Contractor
9	Frederick Pratt
10	Frederick Pratt
11	George G. Johnson

Lock	Contractors	Lock	Contractors
56	John Cameron	63	Michael Byrne
57	W. C. Steedman	64	Michael Byrne
58	W. C. Steedman	65	Michael Byrne
59	Edward H. Fielding	66	Michael Byrne
60	Michael Byrne	69	William Pratt
61	Michael Byrne	70	William Pratt
62	Michael Byrne	71	William Pratt
		72	G. W. Henry

Dam No. 8 and Guard lock No. 8—Sterritt & Lockwood

---

[1] *Proceedings of the President and Board of Directors*, E, 320–321.

APPENDIX P

LIST OF CONTRACTORS FOR AQUEDUCT NO. 9 AND 17 SECTIONS LET UNDER APRIL 2 ORDER OF THE BOARD, MAY 23, 1838[1]

AQUEDUCT NO. 9—Enos Childs

Section	Contractor
270	John O. Hearn
272	Enos Childs
274	Patrick Gormly
279	S. A. Leckey
294	McLean Moore
297	J. S. Thompson
317	Selah Chamberlain
318	Patrick Hagan
319	Wells Hatch
342	Patrick Crowley
344	J. Dilley
351	J. Harris
353	George Hoblitzell
356	George Hoblitzell
363	William Story
364	L. Gatton
365	Edward Doyle

---

[1] *Proceedings of the President and Board of Directors*, E,

APPENDIX Q

LIST OF CONTRACTORS FOR LOCKS NOS. 57–67 AND CULVERTS NOS. 204, 210, 219–220, 225, AND 229 LET UNDER APRIL 2 ORDER OF THE BOARD, MAY 24, 1838[1]

Lock	Contractor
57–58	James Wherry
59–66	Michael Byrne
67	J. Lobdell

Culvert	Contractor
204	C. B. Ford
210	John Reiley
219	Everitt & Dilley
220	Everitt & Dilley
225	G. W. Henry
229	John Reiley

---

[1] *Proceedings of the President and Board of Directors*, E, 425. At a later unspecified time, Lock No. 68 was let to J. N. Nesbett.

APPENDIX R

LIST OF SUBCONTRACTORS FOR SECTIONS BETWEEN DAM NO. 6 AND CUMBERLAND, APRIL 11, 1848[1]

Section	Contractor	Section	Contractor
260	Ignatius Renner	315	John Kelley
261	Ignatius Renner	316	Andrew McMahon
264	William Whitman	321	Dr. Fitzpatrick
269	William Whitman	324–328	Everitt & Dilley
272	Thomas Bell	329	John Eggert
277	William Whitman	330–332	Fraser & Co.
282–291	Ritner & Co.	337–338	John Waldron
295–296	Henry Gallagher	339–342	W. W. Buel & Co.
298–299	Buel & Watt	345	John McManus
311–312	McCullough & Day	346	John McQuard
313	Thomas Sims	347–348	Sterritt & Humber
314	John Eggert	351–352	Sterritt & Humber

---

[1] *Twentieth Annual Report* (1848), C & O Co., Appendix D, 17–18.

APPENDIX S

LIST OF CONTRACTORS FOR CULVERTS BETWEEN DAM NO. 6 AND CUMBERLAND, APRIL 11, 1848[1]

Culvert	Section	Contractor
202	262	Moyal, Randal & Co.
204	277	Moyal, Randal & Co.
206	283	Ritner & Co.
207	285	Ritner & Co.
208	291	Ritner & Co.
210	296	Henry Gallagher
211	313	R. Sims & Co.
212	316	R. Sims & Co.
215	322	Sterrtt & Co.
216	330	Bruce & Haughey
217	331	Bruce & Haughey
218	332	Bruce & Haughey
221	337	Bruce & Haughey
223	339	Bruce & Haughey
224	340	Bruce & Haughey
228	342	Bruce & Haughey
230	345	Bruce & Haughey
231	346	Bruce & Haughey

---

[1] *Twentieth Annual Report* (1848), C & O Co., Appendix D, 12.

HISTORIC RESOURCE STUDY
CHESAPEAKE & OHIO CANAL NHP

6.
FLOODS ON THE C & O CANAL 1829–1936

BY HARLAN D. UNRAU
HISTORIAN, C&O CANAL RESTORATION TEAM, SENECA
DENVER SERVICE CENTER
1976

CONTENTS

I.	INTRODUCTION	277
II.	THE FLOODS, 1829–1889	277
	AUGUST 1829	277
	SEPTEMBER 1829	277
	FEBRUARY 1831	278
	JANUARY 1832	278
	JANUARY 1834	278
	JUNE 1836	279
	APRIL 1843	282
	AUGUST 1843	283
	SEPTEMBER 1843	283
	MARCH 1846	287
	JULY 1846	288
	OCTOBER 1847	289
	APRIL 1852	290
	AUGUST 1855	295
	WINTER 1855–56	295
	FEBRUARY–MAY 1857	295
	APRIL 1859	296
	SEPTEMBER 1859	296
	NOVEMBER 1860	296
	APRIL 1861	297
	JULY 1861	298
	APRIL–MAY 1862	298
	JUNE–JULY 1862	300
	APRIL 1864	300
	MARCH 1865	301
	OCTOBER 1866	301
	SPRING 1868	301
	SEPTEMBER 1870	302
	AUGUST 1872	303
	FEBRUARY 1873	303
	AUGUST 1873	303
	APRIL 1874	304
	JULY–AUGUST 1875	304
	NOVEMBER 1877	304
	JUNE 1884	308
	APRIL–MAY 1886	308
	MAY–JUNE 1889	311
III.	THE FLOODS, 1897–1936	317
	1897, 1902, 1907, 1914	317
	MARCH 1924	317
	MARCH 1936	318

IV.	CONCLUSION		322
III.	APPENDIXES		323
	A.	DESCRIPTION OF NOVEMBER 1877 FLOOD AT CUMBERLAND	323
	B.	DESCRIPTION OF NOVEMBER 1877 FLOOD IN WASHINGTON COUNTY	324

I. INTRODUCTION

An effort has been made in this chapter to examine the major water and ice freshets that struck the Chesapeake & Ohio Canal from 1828 to 1936. The focus for this chapter has been an examination of the causes and extent of the freshets, as well as the damage inflicted on the canal by them and the consequent repairs effected on the waterway. Although some portion of the canal was adversely affected by high water virtually every year, this chapter consist of descriptions of those floods which were considered as significant in the company records and in contemporary newspaper accounts.

II: THE FLOODS 1829-1889

AUGUST 1829

The first recorded instance when a freshet affected the construction of the Chesapeake & Ohio Canal occurred in August 1829. Early that month, high water caused by heavy rains in the Potomac Valley did considerable damage to the embankment and locks of the old Potomac Company skirting canal still operating around Little Falls. As the locks and canal were no longer operable, the Chesapeake & Ohio Canal directors learned that persons passing the locks at Great Falls were refusing to pay any tolls. In an effort to restore quickly the commercial usefulness of a canal around Little Falls, the board established a committee headed by Walter Smith to rush the construction of the nearby section of the new canal. Isaac Leach and Company, the contractor on Section F, agreed to complete his works by October 1, 1829, if he were paid more. Goodrich and Company, the contractor for Sections G and H, agreed to a similar modification in its contract. Accordingly, Smith was able to report to the board on August 12 that he had arranged "to expedite the completion of that part of the Canal alongside of the old Canal and which was carried away in many places."[1]

Although there is no map showing the locations of Sections F, G and H, documentary evidence appears to indicate that they were the westernmost sections of the eight constructed between Rock Creek and Little Falls. As such they probably included the feeder portion extending out to the river at High Island. The sketchy evidence suggests that the old canal washed out between High Island and present Lock No. 5, because the skirting canal turned inland between those two points and the distance between the canal and the river was narrowest in that distance. In this case, the probable solution was to enlarge the old canal below present Lock No. 5 and bypass the feeder washout by completing the new channel above the lock. Regardless of what actually was done, documentary evidence indicates that the work required no more land than was contained in the 180-foot wide strip of Potomac Company land in that vicinity.[2]

SEPTEMBER 1829

A freshet occurred in the Potomac during September 1829. The principal damage to the canal works under construction was at Locks Nos. 21 and 23 where the pits were filled with water. As the contracts that had been let for the locks did not contain provisions for additional allowances to

---

[1] *Proceedings of the President and Board of Directors*, A, 320–321, 325.
[2] Steven H. Lewis, *Stabilization Study: Little Falls Skirting Canal, Maryland and District of Columbia*, (NPS Mss., 1966), 13–14.

cover bailing out flood water, Holdsworth and Isherwood, the contractors for the locks, requested, unsuccessfully, such aid.[3]

FEBRUARY 1831

A heavy freshet struck the newly-completed portion of the canal between Georgetown and Seneca in mid-February 1831 just six weeks before its formal opening to navigation. The flood, which was described as "extraordinary," did little or no damage to the canal where the water had "been admitted or retained in the Canal to an elevation as great as that in the river." The only level on the waterway to be damaged was that "immediately below the Seneca Guard Lock" where "a disaster of some moment" had occurred. The most significant damage was to the culvert below the guard lock which was broken apart by the force of the water.[4]

JANUARY 1832

In January 1832 a heavy ice freshet struck the canal, concentrating most of its fury on the Dam No. 1 complex. According to canal officials, the "accumulation of ice" was "unparalleled" as it reached in some places the height of forty feet above tidewater. During the afternoon of January 10, the ice carried away the guard gate on the Little Falls feeder. A temporary guard gate was installed immediately, but the ice again forced open the gate that night. At the same time, the ice "was flushed over the towpath into the canal at the powder mill on the Little Falls branch. The Little Falls Bridge, which carried a public road over the canal and which was high enough to allow passengers to remain on the top deck of packets using the waterway, was destroyed. At the Peak of the freshet, the water in the canal was near the top of the banks and the ice was several feet higher, but the prism, with one exception, was not damaged. Just as canal officials were preparing to cut away the towpath near the waste weir below Lock No. 5 to prevent further damage, the ice bored a channel through the canal embankments near where the Little Falls Bridge had stood.[5]

When the ice freshet subsided, canal officials found that Dam No. 1 had received extensive damage. The completed portion of the dam between the Maryland shore and Snake Island was nearly destroyed, and the partially-completed section of the dam between Snake Island and the Virginia shore was in need of heavy repairs. Later on July 5, the board authorized canal Superintendent J. Y. Young to repair the structure. The part of the dam between Snake Island and the Maryland shore was "to be rebuilt after the manner of its late construction." This work entailed the reconstruction of the 855-foot arched dam built of loose rubble stone and brush held in place by wood cribbing. The partially-finished portion of the dam between the island and the Virginia shore was "to be restored by the use of stone and brush" prior to its completion. Along with these repairs, the board also directed Young "immediately hang up the new Gate at Guard Gate No. 1"[6]

JANUARY 1834

In mid-January 1834 a heavy ice freshet struck the Potomac Valley centering primarily on that portion of the canal between Shepherdstown and Four Locks. At its peak on January 14, the ice

---

[3] Holdsworth and Isherwood to President and Directors, September 24, 1829, Ltrs. Recd., C & O Co.
[4] ..VanSlyke to Mercer, February 24, 1831, Ltrs. Recd., C & O Co.
[5] .Purcell to Mercer, January 11, 1832, and Lockland to President and Directors, May 10, 1832, Ltrs. Recd., C & O Co.
[6] .*Proceedings of the President and Board of Directors*, C, 182-184.

caused the Potomac River to rise 16 feet in about 12 hours. The ice was "piled" to a height of about 30 feet and 4 miles in length above Dam No. 4. Two bridges across the river near Williamsport were carried away, but there was no reported damage either to the canal trunk or to Dam Nos. 4 and 5, which were both only partially completed. At Dam No. 4, Joseph Hollman, the contractor, lost his boats and some loose lumber. However, the dam, which was then constructed to a height of 21 feet and which was only partly planked on its top, was not injured. Optimistically, Engineer Thomas F. Purcell noted that:

> It is impossible that these dams can ever again be exposed to so severe a trial, as that to which they were subjected by the ice freshet of yesterday; and they stand uninjured, a striking refutation of the position assumed as the result of experience on the works made by the State of Pennsylvania, that dams across rivers, to supply canals with water, were insecure & could not be made to stand.[7]

JUNE 1836

During the spring of 1836, the Potomac Valley experienced "an almost unprecedented season of wet weather." In early June, six days of continuous rain swelled the courses of the Potomac's tributaries and caused the highest freshet in the river since 1810.[8] On the completed portion of the canal, the most extensive damage occurred at Dam No. 4 and Harpers Ferry and from Seneca to Little Falls. Considerable injury was inflicted on the canal embankments still under construction below the Cacapon River.[9]

The course of the 1836 freshet is interesting to follow through the canal company papers and local newspapers as it was the most severe flood to strike the Potomac Valley since the commencement of construction on the canal. In its early stages, fears were aroused concerning the durability of the canal works and the wisdom of building it along the banks of the river. But when navigation was restored along the line within three weeks, the early doubts disappeared as canal officials became even more obsessed with the idea that the canal was immune from all but periodic minor injury from even the heaviest freshets of the river.

On June 1, Superintendent J. Y. Young of the Georgetown Division reported to the board the sudden 3-foot rise in the Potomac below Seneca was largely the result of the heavy inflow of water from the swollen Shenandoah at Harpers Ferry. At that point, the Potomac above the town had risen very little. While little damage had as yet been reported on his division, he noted that the outer side of the heavy embankment on Section No. 11 between Locks Nos. 14 and 15 had slipped. Accordingly, he had ordered his hands to withdraw the water from that level of the canal to ease the pressure on the remaining embankment.[10]

---

[7] Purcell to Ingle, January 15, 1834, Ltrs. Recd., C & O Co.
[8] .The only major flood to strike the Potomac Valley in the years 1800–28 occurred in Washington County on November 10, 1810. The flood centered around Williamsport where the Potomac and Conococheague Creek rose to unprecedented heights inundating much of the town and the surrounding countryside. A bridge that had just been built across the creek at the town was swept away as were Towson's Warehouse and quantities of tar and coal. The flood caused little, if any, damage to the Potomac Company works. As this flood was the highest-known freshet to hit the valley in the years prior to the construction of the Chesapeake & Ohio Canal, company engineers generally attempted to construct the waterway above its high-water levels. Thus, they apparently were convinced that they had taken the necessary precautions to protect the new canal from the ravages of the river. John Thomas Scharf, *History of Western Maryland* (2 Vol., Philadelphia, 1882), Vol. II, 1201.
[9] *Alexandria Gazette*, June 8, 1836.
[10] Young to Ingle, June 1, 1836, Ltrs. Recd., C & O Co.

That the Potomac continued its sudden rise was attested to by Superintendent Young's report to company officials the following day. By that time water was passing over the towpath below Lock Nos. 5, 7 and 8, and it had completely covered the abutments of Dam No. 1. The deterioration of the embankment on Section No. 11 had increased and new reports indicated that the slippage had extended to Section No. 10.[11]

On June 3 the *Alexandria Gazette* reported that the "uncommonly high" water had destroyed part of the Potomac Bridge. About 20 or 30 yards beyond the draw, on the Virginia side, the structure had been swept away. Despite the high water, the works at the Potomac Aqueduct, then under construction, were all safe.[12]

As the swollen Shenandoah continued to pour its water into the Potomac, the Harpers Ferry vicinity suffered extensive flooding. By June 3 the lower portion of the town was inundated, and residents living near the banks of the river were moving to higher ground.[13]

After a personal examination of his division, Superintendent Young reported on June 4 concerning the damage between Georgetown and Seneca. Over this 22-mile distance there were six extensive breaches in the waterway. On Section E (just below Little Falls), 5 (above Lock No. 7), 18 (near Crommelin House), and 23 (near Lock No. 22), water had passed from the canal through common earth embankments. In addition, two large breaches had developed when water ran over the Muddy Branch Culvert and the culvert next above it. The six breaches averaged from 100 to 150 feet in length and from 4 to 10 feet below the bottom of the prism. The water from the river passed over the embankments into the canal on Sections G (near Guard Lock No. 1), 7 (near Lock No. 8), 22 (below Lock No. 21), 29 (near Lock No. 22), and 34 (near Lock No. 23). At Section G the canal embankment was not injured, but at the remaining points the top of the embankments was cut away from 1 to 5 feet in depth and from 200 to 400 yards in length, leaving them in "an uneven ragged state." The earth removed from the embankments was deposited in the trunk, thereby creating large sand and gravel bars. With the exception of some dry masonry walls, he was certain that all the masonry works were secure.[14]

Along with his report on the damage done to the Georgetown Division, Young informed the board concerning his efforts to repair the canal. He already had his hands making temporary dams around the breaches to force the water through the various nearby waste weirs. In addition, he had sent several messengers out into the surrounding countryside to recruit additional workers and carts to haul materials and to collect provisions. He estimated that 20 men and 12 carts would be needed to repair each large breach and 10 men to remove each deposit from the canal trunk. The repairs would take two weeks after which the navigation could be restored. Mr. McNear, an experienced workman in Georgetown who had a force of carts and hands on the city streets, had been hired to make the repairs on Section E.[15]

Although the damage done to the canal between Harpers Ferry and Seneca was not so extensive as that on the Georgetown Division, there were several places over this distance that were hard-hit.[16] At Harpers Ferry the feeder was filled with sand, gravel and earth as a result of

---

[11] *Ibid*, June 2, 1836, Ltrs. Recd., C & O Co.

[12] *Alexandria Gazette*, June 3, 1836.

[13] *Ibid*, June 9, 1836.

[4] Young to Ingle, June 4, 1836, Ltrs. Recd., C & O Co. Later on July 28, Young modified this latter assertion in his report by informing the directors that the stone portion of Dam No. 1 between Snake Island and the Maryland shore had been severely damaged. The tumbling waste between the mouth of the Little Falls Feeder and Guard Gate No. 1 was also injured. The cost or repairing these structures, together with added protection walls and embankments, was estimated to be $1,500. Young to Board of Directors, July 28, 1836, Ltrs. Recd., C & O Co.

[15] Young to Ingle, June 4, 1836, Ltrs. Recd., C & O Co.

[16] Ingle to Elgin, June 4, 1836, Ltrs. Sent, C & O Co.

several breaks in the levels above it and of the washing of the embankments at Lock Nos. 35 and 36. A series of breaches in the canal embankments occurred between Edwards Ferry and Seneca, the most serious of which took place on Section No. 40 (some 2½ miles above Seneca Creek). At various points on the 38-mile distance between Dams Nos. 3 and 2, the high water had washed badly the surface of the towpath and left it in a ragged condition.[17]

Because of the limited damage to his division of the canal between Harpers Ferry and Seneca, Superintendent W. S. Elgin was able to report on June 10 that his portion of the waterway was ready for the readmittance of water. All the breaches had been repaired and the embankments raised enough to admit 4½ feet of water.[18]

Above Harpers Ferry the only significant damage to the completed portion of the canal occurred at Dam No. 4. A serious breach of undetermined extent took place requiring several weeks of repair.[19]

On the portion of the canal between the Cacapon River and Dam No. 5, then under construction, there were two points where the high water damaged the canal works. On Section Nos. 247 (below Lock No. 53) and 252 (between Locks Nos. 53 and 54), the earthen embankments were heavily washed as the level of the river reached the height of the top of the canal. On the former, 1,700 cubic yards of material were washed away, while on the latter 4,100 cubic yards were swept away. It was estimated that it would require the labor of 20 horses and carts and 15 hands for two months to repair the damage on Section No. 252 alone. The embankment material on Section No. 247 was replaced with earth brought to the canal from a point 1/3 of a mile distant at a cost of nearly $500, while the material for the embankment on section No. 252 was brought from a point less than ¼ of a mile distant at a cost of nearly $950. As the losses in both cases put the respective contractors in desperate financial straits, the canal company agreed to pay for the repairs although it was not bound to do so by the provisions of the contracts.[20]

Repairs to the completed portion of the waterway proceeded at a rapid pace. On June 20, Superintendent Young reported that navigation had been restored from Georgetown to Harpers Ferry. Several weeks later on July 6, Superintendent George W. Rogers informed the board that the line between Harpers Ferry and Dam No. 5 was ready for the admission of water.[21]

Despite the damage to the canal from the freshet, canal officials were relieved that the injuries were not as great as had first been feared.[22] The optimism that this realization produced was evident in the comments of President George C. Washington to the company stockholders in June 1836:

> No interruption of any consequence to the navigation has occurred, until the recent freshet, which raised the waters of the Potomac to an unprecedented height, and carried off some of our embankments. Great apprehension was entertained of extensive and serious injury, but we are happy to state that the damage is not so great as we had feared. Had the board ever doubted the expediency of the location adopted by Mr. Fisk, those doubts would have been wholly dissipated by the results of the recent freshet, as the chief injury sustained by the canal has been at points where it approximates too closely the

---

[17] Elgin to Washington, June 10 & 13, 1836, Ltrs. Recd., C & O Co.

[18] *Ibid*, June 10, 1836, Ltrs. Recd., C & O Co.

[19] *Alexandria Gazette*, June 8, 1836, and Elgin to Washington, June 13, 1836, Ltrs. Recd., C & O Co. No details concerning the breach at Dam No. 4 could be found in the company records. See John F. Luzader, *Dam No. 4, Historic Structure Survey* (NPS Mss, 1964), 17.

[20] Gorman to President and Directors, June 15, 1836, Ltrs. Recd., C & O Co.; Fisk to Bender, June 20, 1836, Ltrs. Sent, Chief Engineer; and *Proceedings of the President and Board of Directors*, E, 89.

[21] *Proceedings of the President and Board of Directors*, E, 77, 89.

[22] *Alexandria Gazette*, June 13, 1836.

river line. The new locations have been made with the view of placing the canal above any rise of the river, and consequently, its entire security. The economy of such locations is evident, both in the permanency of the work, and the assurance of an uninterrupted navigation...The strength of the masonry, and its admirable construction, were fully tested by the recent freshet; and not withstanding the immense pressure on the aqueducts and other masonry, none have been injured.[23]

APRIL 1843

In mid-April 1843 the highest freshet since the commencement of the canal struck the Potomac Valley. Occasioned by the rapid melting of heavy snow in the western Maryland mountains, the flood caused destruction to the waterway primarily between Edwards Ferry and Georgetown. On April 18 and 19 the high water in the river ran over all the "low levels" on the Georgetown Division, opening one or more breaches on each of them. In most cases the water passed into the canal at the high or upper end of the levels and out by the breaches below. Precautionary measures were taken by cutting the embankments at points where the least damage would take place.[24]

Although the damage west of Edwards Ferry was not as severe, the canal between Dams Nos. 4 and 6 was washed in many places by the flood waters which covered portions of this distance by as much as three feet.[25] Four miles below Williamsport, the top of the bank and berm sides of a culvert were "carried away to the bottom of the canal."[26] Embankments at several other nearby culverts were washed down also. At its peak, the flood water rose to a height of "six inches over the abutment of Dam No. 5," causing three breaches in the level below. The towpath at the dam was "washed away to within 2 ft. of bottom, about 200 ft. in length."[27]

When the freshet subsided, Chief Engineer Fisk surveyed the damage to the canal and estimated that it would cost $20,000 to place the waterway below the Cacapon River in the condition that it had been before the freshet. To merely restore navigation, it would take two weeks to repair the Georgetown Level and that portion of the canal above Edwards Ferry, while it would require three weeks to repair the line between Little Falls and Edwards Ferry. The total cost of the immediate repairs needed was estimated to be $10,000.[28]

As the financial condition of the company was desperate, canal officials negotiated a $10,000 loan from three banks in the District of Columbia in May to pay for the immediate repairs. The loan, which was secured by two-thirds of the tolls and water rents collected by the company until the loan was paid, was acquired as follows: Farmer's and Mechanic's Bank of Georgetown, $5,000; Bank of Metropolis, $2,500; and Bank of Washington, $2,500.[29]

Portions of the canal were reopened to navigation on May 2, and the entire waterway on May 6. Later in July, traffic was suspended for 22 days while work was undertaken to remove the sand bars in the canal prism that had been left in the wake of the freshet.[30]

---

[23] *Eighth Annual Report* (1836), C & O Co., 8.
[24] Young to Turner, April 19, 1843, Ltrs. Recd., C & O Co.
[25] Fisk to Coale, September, 17, 1843, Ltrs. Recd., C & O Co.
[26] Stone to Fisk, April 20, 1843, Ltrs. Recd., Chief Engineer.
[27] Ibid, April 20, 1843, Ltrs. Recd., Chief Engineer.
[28] Fisk to Ingle, April 20, 1843, Ltrs. Recd., C & O Co.
[29] *Proceedings of the President and Board of Directors*, G, 25–26; and *Fifteenth Annual Report* (1843), C & O Co., 3–4.
[30] *Sixteenth Annual Report* (1844), 21, 40–41.

AUGUST 1843

Extraordinary heavy rains struck several parts of the Potomac Valley in August 1843 causing several streams passing under the canal "to rise to a height unprecedented within the memory of man." The two streams where the heaviest flooding occurred were Tonoloway Creek at Hancock and the Monocacy River. The water of the later overflowed the canal and caused high water to plague the canal all the way down to Edwards Ferry. The flooding at the two areas caused extensive washing of the towpath and heavy erosion of the canal embankments, but no serious breaches were reported.[31]

SEPTEMBER 1843

After several days of heavy rain throughout the Potomac Valley in mid-September 1843, a flood of greater proportions than the April freshet struck the canal. Damage was extensive all along the line from Georgetown to Dam No. 6, then the western termination of the canal, but the lower portions of the waterway suffered most. As the embankments damaged by the April freshet had not yet been raised to their full height and completed, navigation was now suspended for one month and repairs totaling $30,000 in addition to the amount still unexpended from the April $20,000 estimate were made to restore the waterway to the condition that it had been in before the spring freshet.[32]

On September 19 and 21, Superintendent Young reported on the damage to the canal on his division from Georgetown to Lock No. 26. The Georgetown level had suffered two large breaches—one near Pointers and the other opposite the Alexandria Aqueduct quarry. The estimated cost of repairing the two breaches was $2,500. From the Alexandria Aqueduct to Dam No. 1 the canal banks had been washed considerably, particularly above the Powder Magazine. Near the dam there was another serious breach and the banks were washed badly. About one-third of the Lockhouse at Lock No. 6 had been carried away, and he assumed that it would go entirely. Above Lock No. 7 there were two breaks, and the embankment below Lock No. 8 was heavily injured where the river overflowed it. The damage on the levels between Lock Nos. 6, 7 and 8 was similar to those caused by previous floods but was far more extensive. On the "log wall" level between Locks Nos. 14 and 15, there was a considerable slide on the riverside of the towpath embankment. Below Great Falls the river reached the top of the high embankment walls and washed out the filling, and the water poured into the canal below Lock No. 16. Taking immediate precautionary measures to prevent the loss of the heavy embankment, Young had cut the banks, thereby minimizing the damage to that level. Above Lock No. 20 there was a breach, and the banks above Lock No. 21 were severely washed. There were two breaches and a similar wash just below Lock No. 22. Between this lock and the Seneca Feeder, there were two breaches at Long Acre, and the whole bank was nearly carried away for a distance of 300 yards in length at the point of rocks just below Lock No. 23. It was the most damaged level on the canal below Seneca except for that at Georgetown, and he feared that it would be difficult to procure the needed materials for its repair. From Guard Lock No. 2 to Great Falls, the canal had been covered with water from 2 to 6 feet deep, the marks of which he had directed to be made permanent all along the line.

Between Seneca and Edwards ferry there were two spots where the freshet had inflicted heavy damage on the canal. About two-thirds of the barrel of the Beaver Dam Culvert was washed away on its riverside along with about 200 feet of embankment on each side of the canal. Although he had cut the embankment to protect the culvert, the water at Edwards Ferry had cov-

---

[31] *Sixteenth Annual Report* (1844), 40.
[32] Fisk to Coale, September 17, 1843, Ltrs. Recd., C & O Co.

ered the canal to a depth of 4 or 5 feet. In addition there were three breaches in the canal banks between Locks Nos. 25 and 26. The banks in many places above Seneca had been torn by the water flowing over the towpath, but no masonry works, other than the Beaver Dam Culvert, has been damaged.

Young estimated that the cost of repairs to his division would total more than $9,000. From Georgetown to Lock No. 8 the repairs would cost $4,000, from Lock No. 8 to Seneca $3,000, and from Seneca to Edwards Ferry $2,300. However, these estimates did not include the raising of the towpath where it was "washed off at a point above high water in the canal," nor did it include the masonry repairs on the Beaver Dam Culvert.

Above Edwards Ferry the canal also suffered damage, although it was not as extensive as the lower portion of the line. The high water caused "east berm corner" of the Little Monocacy Culvert to settle. The abutment was almost entirely undermined and the "upper wall & all the paving" were gone as that the water stood "nearly 4 feet under the culvert." Part of the abutment wall at the upper berm corner had also fallen down.[33]

From Point of Rocks to Dam No. 4, the damage was double to that inflicted on the waterway by the April freshet. At Harpers Ferry the water was 2 to 3 feet higher than in April and at Taylor's Landing it was 2½ feet higher. The embankments adjacent to the Shenandoah River Lock were washed severely, and one of the gates of the lock was torn out. One of the company's house boats near Harpers Ferry was washed over the towpath and lost along with a large supply of tools and provisions. The high water passed around the abutments of Dam No. 4, causing a breach and a severe washing of the adjacent embankment.[34]

Between Dams Nos. 4 and 5 there were numerous breaks in the canal, but none were very serious in extent and none were below the bottom of the trunk. Most of the damage on this distance resulted from the towpath being washed into either the river or the canal, and in the latter case forming bars that needed to be removed.

The canal above Dam No. 5 experienced about the same amount of damage as it had earlier in April despite the fact that the height of the water was generally at least three feet lower. Some of the sheeting on Dam No. 5 was washed off. There were two serious breaks between Hancock and Dam No. 6, one at Roundtop Cement Mill and the other just below Lock No. 53. The embankments below Dam No. 6 had been strengthened with an outer layer of stone rip-rap the previous summer, and this work was credited with protecting the towpath and the canal trunk below from further injury. Had all the breaks caused by the April freshet been repaired in such a manner on the portions of the line, Superintendent John G. Stone of the Third Division reported that "the damage would have been but a trifling in comparison to what they are now."[35]

After receiving the reports of damage all along the canal, Chief Engineer Fisk informed company president James M. Coale on September 17 that the total cost of repairs would be about $30,000 and that navigation would be suspended for 30 days. This sum would be in addition to the unexpended portion of the $20,000 estimate of repairs from the April freshet. However, he urged the president not to be merely satisfied with repairs but to order further precautionary work to protect the waterway from even higher freshets in the future.[36]

As soon as the flood waters subsided below Little Falls, the residents of Georgetown pressed canal officials to repair the Georgetown Level immediately. Many of the citizenry were alarmed because the water had poured over the canal banks and inundated sections of the town,

---

[33] Elgin to Fisk, October 1, 1843, and Eldridge to Fisk, October 18, 1843, Ltrs. Recd., Chief Engineer.
[34] Elgin to Coale, September 23, 1843, Ltrs. Recd., C & O Co.
[35] Stone to Fisk, September 19 and October 23, 1843, Ltrs. Recd., Chief Engineer.
[36] Fisk to Coale, September 17, 1843, Ltrs. Recd., C & O Co. As the company funds were low, the banks in Frederick granted a substantial loan for the emergency repairs.

thereby increasing the chances of an outbreak of cholera. The milling interests were also interested in a prompt restoration of their water supply. Accordingly, canal officials determined to commence repairs on the Georgetown to Little Falls section of the waterway on September 19 and to construct an undetermined number of badly needed waste weirs in the area to prevent future disasters.[37] To fund these repairs the Georgetown millers loaned the sum of $3,000 to the company, and the loans pledged the water rents of the company in the District of Columbia as collateral.[38]

Repairs all along the line of the canal were commenced as soon as the high water subsided. Superintendent Young informed the board on September 21 that he already had a large force working at the Beaver Dam Culvert. It was his intention to raise the embankments below Edwards Ferry only "above the water mark" in order to restore navigation within thirty days. After the canal was reopened for trade, the embankments could be raised by crews working from boats.[39]

Repair crews were also at work on the canal upstream within several days. Superintendent Stone informed the board on September 19 that his repair force was on the job above Dam No. 4. As they would have to boat material some distance until the canal navigation was restored, the work would take longer than it had in April.[40] By September 26 Superintendent Elgin reported that he had two large repair crews working on his division: one at Harpers Ferry consisting of 70 men and 17 horses and carts, and one at Crowley's consisting of 144 men and 34 horses and carts.[41] The canal was repaired to the extent that navigation was restored from Edwards Ferry to Dam No. 6 on October 17 and from Georgetown to Edwards Ferry on November 8.[42]

Despite the resumption of navigation, the canal was still not in the operating condition that it had been before the April freshet. Further, the devastating floods of 1843 had called into question the security of the entire waterway and its capability of withstanding future freshets. Accordingly, canal officials carefully examined their work during the winter of 1843-44 and determined to commence a program of thorough repair and long-range improvements during the next year.

Examples of thorough repair were such efforts as those at the Little Monocacy Culvert and at the Shenandoah River Lock. At the former, a new foundation and new abutment walls were constructed to not only repair the flood damage but also to give the structure additional strength to withstand future freshets.[43]

At the Shenandoah River Locks, the board determined to raise the river end of the structure and to elevate the adjacent canal embankment. This work was an effort to prevent future breaches in an area that had experienced serious injuries and to protect the line below from the repeated damage inflicted upon it by water overflowing the banks at this spot. The repairs on this portion of the waterway were completed during the spring of 1845.[44]

---

[37] Ingle to Coale, September 18, 1843, Ltrs. Recd., C & O Co.
[38] *Proceedings of the President and Board of Directors*, G, 113-114.
[39] Young to Coale, September 21, 1843, Ltrs. Recd., C & O Co.
[40] Stone to Fisk, September 19, 1843, Ltrs. Recd., Chief Engineer.
[41] Elgin to Fisk, September 26, 1843, Ltrs. Recd., Chief Engineer.
[42] *Niles' Register*, LXV (October 14, 1843), 112; *Proceedings of the Stockholders*, C, 230-232; and *Sixteenth Annual Report* (1844), 40-41. During the completion of repairs below Edwards Ferry, the navigation was reopened for light boats along the river between the river locks at Seneca and Edwards Ferry for some 15 days to bypass the heavy breach at the Beaver Dam Culvert.
[43] Eldridge to Fisk, October 18, 1843, and Elgin to Fisk, November 28, 1843, Ltrs. Recd., Chief Engineer.
[44] *Seventeenth Annual Report* (1845), C & O Co., 17-18.

The most extensive long-range improvements to be made on the canal were those on the Georgetown Level. After an examination of the area by Chief Engineer Fisk in the spring of 1844, the stockholders were informed on June 3 that:

> It appears that the length of the level, including that part of the feeder from the Potomac lying below the guard gates, which is connected with it, is 4 2/3 miles. Of this distance, three-fifths of a mile below the guard gates is usually overflowed by heavy freshets. This occurred twice last year, viz: in April and September. At the last-mentioned freshet, the water ran over the towpath in places to the depth of four feet. Whenever such an inundation from the river takes place, breaches must inevitably occur lower down, by which the surplus water which has entered the canal returns to its natural channel. Such breaches, owing to the great height of the canal, upon that part of it, above the level of the river, are generally very heavy. As a protection against these river freshets it will be necessary, as soon as adequate means (for which we are now negotiating) can be obtained, to raise the part of the towpath liable to overflow, and also the feeder bank below the guard gates, at least one foot above the highest water mark hitherto known in the Potomac; or, in other words, about one foot higher than the rise of the last September freshet. This, with a tumbling waste 500 feet long on the towpath side of the canal, near the fourth milestone, and some few other repairs of minor importance, it is thought would oppose an effectual barrier against the inroads of the river at all times hereafter, and would amply compensate the Company for the cost of the outlay, in the savings from breaches, in the course of three or four years. The repairs of the breaches on this level in 1842 was $2,242 and in 1843, $4,053. The proposed improvements, if they had been constructed in time, would have saved all this expense. The entire cost of making them is estimated by the Chief Engineer at about $9,000, including the reconstruction of the bridge over the canal [just east of the Market] in Georgetown, which is imperatively called for...[45]

After the report was considered, the company agreed to the Chief Engineer's recommendations provided that the Corporation of Georgetown would make available a $10,000 loan upon a pledge of the company's water rents in the District of Columbia.[46] When Georgetown demanded "a deed of Mortgage" on canal company property for the security of the loan, the board rejected the loan offer and the negotiations for the loan were terminated.[47] Accordingly, the board, aware of the financial limitations of the company authorized the construction of a tumbling waste that in the opinion of President Coale and Chief Engineer Fisk "may be necessary to secure the said portion of the canal from damage by the usual river freshets & overflow from the Falls Branch." The directors also authorized the construction of such improvements "as may be necessary" to the security of this level, with the funding for such projects to come from company finances.[48]

On November 4, 1844, the improvements to the Georgetown Level began when a contract for the waste weir and spillway at Falls Branch was awarded to Roberts and Cleveland.[49] The improvements continued through the winter and into the following spring. The progress of the work was described by President Coale on January 15, 1845:

---

[45] *Sixteenth Annual Report* (1844), 17–18.
[46] *Proceedings of the President and Board of Directors*, C & O Co., 154, 163.
[47] "A Resolution to Authorize a Loan of Money to the Chesapeake & Ohio Canal Company". August 3, 1844, *Ordinances of the Corporation of Georgetown* (Georgetown, 1846), 13–14, and *Proceedings of the President and Board of Directors*, G, 190, 196.
[48] *Proceedings of the President and Board of Directors*, G, 196–197.
[49] *Ibid*, G, 201.

The Board have caused some improvements to be made on that part of the line, and have contracted for others, which are now in progress, and will be completed during the winter. The improvements finished are, the tightening of the Little Falls feeder, by which that level is supplied with water, and the raising of the guard banks of the canal at such points as are most exposed to the overflow of the river. The improvement in progress is the construction of a tumbling waste, two hundred and fifty feet long in the clear which is thought will hereafter furnish a sufficient security against breaches on that portion of the Canal in ordinary freshets. The Board have only been deterred from making this improvement ...by the limited extent of their means...[50]

On April 30, 1845, the improvements on the Georgetown Level were completed when the board passed a final estimate for the tumbling waste, a structure which cost $1,908.75.[51]

MARCH 1846

The first of two major floods in 1846 struck the Potomac Valley in March. The water rose to within 4 feet of the September 1843 flood, but the breaches were "not generally of a serious nature." The heaviest damage was inflicted on the line between Dams Nos. 4 and 5. About 80 feet of Dam No. 4 was carried away by the swollen river. The gates of Locks Nos. 41–44 were either broken or washed out, and some 50 to 60 feet of the sheeting on Dam No. 5 was swept off.

As soon as the flood waters subsided, the few minor breaches in the canal banks between the two dams were repaired. The damage at Dam No. 4 did not interrupt navigation for long as there was a plentiful supply of water in the river during the normally dry summer months, and the remaining portion of the dam was able to divert a sufficient quantity of water into the canal for operating purposes. Restoration work on the dam was still in progress in early July when another heavy freshet occurred.

The damage caused to Locks Nos. 41–44 by the freshet and the frequent breaking of the lock-gates during the day-to-day operations of the canal brought about a slight modification in the construction of the gates. In accordance with instructions issued by Chief Engineer Fisk the new gates had cast iron frames with arms that were framed "with a shoulder of 2 inches on the upper side." This improvement, it was thought, would prevent the "breaking of the tendons of the arms."

At Dam No. 5 improvements were commenced to prevent the structure and the canal below it from suffering more extensive damage in future floods. It was estimated that if the river had risen one foot higher at the dam, the entire length of the towpath down to Lock No. 44, which was rebuilt the previous year, would have been carried away. Accordingly, operations were begun to raise the towpath below the dam and protect it with stone. Plans were made also to raise the coping of Guard Lock No. 5 some three feet and to install a new set of gates of appropriate size. In this manner it was hoped that the structure would "effectually keep out the water of the highest freshet." As was the case with Dam No. 4, these repairs and improvements were still in progress when another freshet struck the canal in early July.[52]

---

[50] *Seventeenth Annual Report* (1845), 17–18.
[51] *Proceedings of the President and Board of Directors*, G, 248.
[52] *Nineteenth Annual Report* (1847), C & O Co., 6–7; *Niles' Register*, LXX (March 28, 1846), 64; and Stone to Fisk, March 21, 1846, Ltrs. Recd., Chief Engineer.

JULY 1846

The second major freshet of 1846 struck the canal in July. At its peak the height of the flood waters was 3½ feet lower than that of the September 1843 freshet below Seneca and 14 inches lower at Harpers Ferry. Farther up the river from Williamsport to Dam No. 4 the water was higher than it had been in the 1843 freshet. Despite the height of the water, the flood did only about one-fourth as much damage as had the 1843 freshet, due mainly to the improvements that had been made to the line during the succeeding years.

A review of the damage inflicted upon the canal by the freshet demonstrates the value of the improvements that had been made since 1843. One breach occurred in the Rock Creek Basin, and about 10 others were reported on the line from Georgetown to the Monocacy River. The line from Lock No. 8 to Seneca sustained little damage owing to the embankments that had been raised in many places where less freshets had overflowed the banks in previous years. The tumbling waste that had been built at Falls Branch in 1844–45 was credited with saving the Georgetown Level from damage. While none of the masonry works on this portion of the canal were heavily damaged, several locks near Georgetown suffered from the high water and required renovation or considerable repairs.

The only serious problem below the Monocacy was at Broad Run where the high water entirely destroyed the two-arch (16-foot span each) culvert. The arches and the abutments were carried away entirely, and the whole width of the canal for a distance of about 70 feet at the culvert was washed out.

The 18-mile section of the canal from the Monocacy to Harpers Ferry was uninjured primarily because of the improvements that had been made at the Shenandoah River Lock. About the only serious damage to be reported above Harpers Ferry was at Dam No. 4 and the level below it. The repairs on the dam from the March freshet, which were nearly completed, were washed away, and the breach in the structure was widened. The guard bank at the dam suffered $1,000 in damage as it was not high enough to keep the river out of the company works. The damage below the dam resulted primarily from the fact that the stop plank was not put in the stop lock early enough to prevent an overflow of the canal banks.[53]

After surveying the damage, Chief Engineer Fisk and Superintendent Elgin on July 8 informed President Coale that it would cost about $8,000 to restore the canal for navigation purposes. Trade could be resumed in three weeks because many of the breaks had occurred near places where materials were conveniently located for repairs. The only two problems spots were at the Rock Creek Basin and the Broad Run Culvert. At the former, a narrow bank could be put in quickly so that the water could be admitted before more extreme work was undertaken. At the latter, a temporary wooden tank costing in excess of $2,000 would be thrown over new wing walls that were to be constructed of stone salvaged from the wrecked culvert so that navigation could be resumed quickly. While these temporary repairs would permit an early resumption of boat navigation, the two officials recommended that an additional $10,000 be expended over the next several months "on work rendered necessary by the late freshets and on the breach in the dam."[54]

Despite a shortage of laborers for the repair crews, the job of restoring the canal to operating condition began as soon as the high waters subsided. Navigation was resumed by August 1, but the major repairs at Dam No. 4 continued until June 1847. Because of the depressed condition of the company's finances, nothing was done to renovate the deteriorating locks near Georgetown

---

[53] Fisk to Coale, July 6 and 8, 1846, and Elgin to Coale, July 2 and 8, 1846, Ltrs. Recd., C & O Co., and Coale to Fisk, July 5, 1846, Ltrs. Recd., Chief Engineer.
[54] Fisk to Coale, July 8, 1846, and Elgin to Coale, July 8 and August 18, 1846, Ltrs. Recd., C & O Co.

or to reconstruct the Broad Run Culvert. All told the company had spent $21,327.76 by June 1847 to repair the damage caused by the freshets of March and July 1846.[55]

OCTOBER 1847

In October 1847 a major flood struck the eastern United States causing particularly heavy damage in Ohio, Pennsylvania, Virginia and Maryland. In Ohio the Ohio and Erie and the Miami and Erie Canals were considerably damaged, while in Pennsylvania the Main Line Canal in the Juniata Valley was severely injured. The James River and Kanawha Canal in Virginia was damaged also by the raging flood waters. While the railroads in all of these states were disrupted by the high water, the Baltimore & Ohio Railroad appears to have suffered most, particularly on its 40-mile route between Baltimore and Washington.[56]

The Potomac Valley was not spared from the full effects of the storm as the river surpassed all previous high water marks. John Thomas Scharf one of the most well-known Maryland historians described the flood as a "fearful freshet" in which "bridges were swept away, gardens washed out, and buildings damaged."[57] While the Chesapeake & Ohio suffered less damage in proportion to its length and resumed navigation earlier than did the other canals in the surrounding states, it nevertheless experienced considerable damage that curtailed its operations for more than two months and cost $48,201.56 to repair.[58]

The Potomac River began rising on October 7 and alarm soon spread throughout the valley. The following day Superintendent Elgin at Harpers Ferry reported that the river was already near the height of the highest freshet in 1846 and from all appearances he was certain that it would soon be "the highest water ever known in this River."[59] Later the same day Superintendent Stone at Clear Spring observed that the water was "20 inches higher than it ever has been since I have been on the canal" and the water was still rising. He noted that new gates had been placed in Guard Lock No. 5 only ten days before, which was fortunate for the company as the old gates would not have withstood the freshet.[60] By October 9 Elgin was informing canal officials that "we have had the highest freshet in the Potomac that I have ever seen" and that the canal at Harpers Ferry was still submerged under water.[61] On the 9th Superintendent John Lambie at Georgetown also notified the board that the water, which had been rising for 3½ days, was 12 to 15 inches higher than the previous high water mark set by the September 1843 freshet and still rising.[62]

Although there were numerous breaches in the canal banks all along the canal, the most critical damage to the waterway was concentrated in the following areas: Lock No. 7 to Widewater; the levels above Great Falls; Point of Rocks to Dam No. 4; and the vicinity of Dam No. 5. On the Georgetown Division there were two large breaches, one above Lock No. 7 and the other at the high wall near Widewater. At the latter, more than 200 feet of the wall had collapsed. There was some damage done to the Georgetown Level, and there were a series of minor breaches on every level above Great Falls.[63]

---

[55] *Nineteenth Annual Report* (1847), 6, 8.
[56] *Niles' Register*, LXXIII (October 16, 1847), 112, and *Twentieth Annual Report* (1848), C & O Co., 11–12.
[57] Scharf, *History of Western Maryland*, Vol. I, 560.
[58] *Twentieth Annual Report* (1848), 11–12, 28, and *Niles' Register*, LXXIII (October 16, 1847), 112.
[59] Elgin to Coale, October 8, 1847, Ltrs. Recd., C & O Co.
[60] Elgin to Coale, October 8, 1947, Ltrs Recd., C & O Co.
[61] Stone to Coale, October 9, 1847, Ltrs. Recd., C & O Co
[62] Lambie to Coale, October 9, 1847, Ltrs. Recd., C & O Co.
[63] *Ibid.*

Farther up the valley there were between 8 to 10 large breaches on the line from Point of Rocks to Dam No. 4. At the dam itself, the damage was much greater than that caused by the 1843 floods and the flood waters rose three feet above the previous high water mark. The entire cross guard bank between the stop lock and the dam abutment was carried away, thereby allowing the river to run around the Maryland abutment and the guard lock. The main guard bank had also been damaged, causing Superintendent Elgin to conclude that it would cost more than $5,000 to restore the area. There was a heavy breach about one-half mile below the dam where the water that was running around the dam abutment was re-entering the river. Accordingly, efforts were made, even before the flood waters subsided, to stop the water from running around the dam abutment.[64]

Above Dam No. 4 there was no serious damage done at any one place, but there were injuries to almost every level. The towpath was washed in many places and there were numerous small breaches in it. The only damage to the masonry occurred where the water carried away the berm end of a culvert and about 30 perches of the Virginia abutment of Dam No. 5 at which point the water had risen to 3½ feet above any freshet since 1828. The culvert would require repairs before the readmission of the water, but the work on the abutment could be postponed. Some of the older lock gates were broken, but they could be mended to handle the boat traffic until the winter. The rest of the season this portion of the canal would have only 3 to 3½ feet of water and it would take until the following spring to have the banks fully restored to their proper height.[65]

Once the damage had been assessed, company officials reported that navigation would be restored in one month at a cost of $20,000. With the aid of various banks, repair work was begun immediately. Additional work crews and horses were hired and a company agent was dispatched to Baltimore to purchase tools as there was a shortage of such items in some parts of the valley. New freshets in November and December delayed the repairs so that the navigation was not re-opened until mid-December below Harpers Ferry and the full canal to Dam No. 6 was not ready for operations until February 15, 1848. By that time $48,201.56 had been spent to restore the waterway.[66]

APRIL 1852

The worst flood in the history of the Potomac to that date, devastated the entire line in April 1852. The flood was as great a surprise to the canal board as it was a disaster to the waterway itself. In 1849–50 the directors, with the aid of $200,000 of repair bonds from the State of Virginia, had renovated the canal from Georgetown to Dam No. 6, raising the embankments at the most exposed places above the level of the highest freshets in the history of the valley.[67] They based their

---

[64] Elgin to Fisk, October 10, 1847, Ltrs. Recd., C & O Co.
[65] Stone to Coale, October 10 and 12, 1847, Ltrs. Recd., C & O Co.
[66] Ibid, and *Twentieth Annual Report* (1848), 11–12, 28. As had been the case after earlier floods, the company attempted to make some improvements that would protect the canal from damage by even higher freshets. Such was the case at Dam No. 5 where in January and February 1848 the Virginia abutment was not only repaired but operations were commenced also to raise it. The work on this improvement included 87 perches of masonry, 1900 perches of dry wall, and 9,700 cubic yards of embankment and its total cost was $6,790.50. Stone to Fisk, and Stone to Coale, December 27, 1848, Ltrs. Recd., C & O Co.
[67] *Proceedings of the President and Board of Directors*, H, 127, 251–257, and *Twenty-Second Annual Report* (1850), 7–9. This renovation effort was not performed as a result of any one particular flood but rather as a response to the general disrepair of the canal caused by the series of floods in the 1840s, the temporary stop-gap measures taken to resume navigation after each freshet, and the lack of thorough annual maintenance work by the financially-strapped company. As such the major 1849–50 renovation effort will be con-

action on the levels attained in the flood of 1847, which had been the worst since 1784 when operations on the Potomac Company Canals were commenced. The precautions proved to be in vain for in April 1852, six consecutive days of heavy rain caused the river to rise six feet higher at most point below Cumberland than the levels attained in 1847. At Great Falls it reached the unprecedented height of 64 feet. Had the crest been only two or three feet lower, the waterway might have escaped serious injury. As it was, by the time the work of restoration was completed the cost of repairs amounted to nearly $100,000[68] The canal itself was weakened by the disaster but the effect on its trade and its financial condition was even more serious, as company officials admitted later to stockholders in June 1855:

> The disaster occasioned by the flood in the spring of 1852, was very detrimental to the interests of the company, in causing not only a large debt, and heavy expenses in repairing the canal, and the loss of three or four months revenues during the suspension of navigation that year, but had a still more unfavorable influence by the loss of confidence in the stability and reliability of the work as a means of transportation.[69]

The first intimation of the approaching disaster occurred at Cumberland on April 18 after a heavy thunderstorm and two days of pouring rain. Both Wills Creek and the Potomac overflowed their banks, the latter rising higher than it ever had since 1816. The water passed into the canal basin around the outlet locks and flooded Ward's boat yard and the wharves and warehouses around Shriver's Basin. The water broke through a wall separating Bruce's and Brengle's warehouses on Canal Street and a considerable portion of the town was inundated, including the tracks of the Baltimore & Ohio Railroad.[70]

That same day the Potomac overflowed its banks at Williamsport causing widespread flooding and destruction. The water covered the towpath to a depth of 12 feet and several company houses and canal boats were swept down the river. According to reports in the *Alexandria Gazette*

> Car loads of flour, stacks of grain, shanties, trees, logs and timber were seen whirling through the angry waters in rapid succession. The mill of Messrs. Van Lear was submerged nearly to the roof, and their loss in flour and wheat is from $5,000 to $10,000.[71]

The following day, Superintendent Elgin voiced his fears that the continuing rain was bringing the highest freshet ever seen in the Potomac Valley. The water had risen 3½ feet since dawn, and at mid-morning it was rising one foot per hour.[72]

By the 21st, Superintendent Elgin had examined the canal from Harpers Ferry to the Monocacy River. He found that the canal had been considerably injured with several large breaches between Dam No. 3 and Point of Rocks. It appeared that the canal suffered most wherever there was a curve in its passage through the narrow passes over this distance. At Harpers Ferry the Government Dam had been submerged in water up to fifteen feet in depth (some 5 to 6 feet higher than in 1847) and the river had broken through the embankments around the Maryland

---

sidered as one of the highlights of the company maintenance efforts in a later chapter of this Historic Resource Study.
[68] *Twenty-Fourth Annual Report* (1852), C & O Co., 3–4; *Twenty-Fifth Annual Report* (1853), C & O Co., 3; and *Alexandria Gazette*, April 22, 1852.
[69] *Twenty-Seventh Annual Report* (1855), C & O Co.
[70] William Harrison Lowdermilk, *History of Cumberland, Maryland* (Washington, D.C., 1878), 375.
[71] *Alexandria Gazette*, April 23 and 27, 1852.
[72] Elgin to Ringgold, April 19, 1852, Ltrs. Recd., C & O Co.

abutment. In returning to the river channel, the water passed over and through the towpath above Lock No. 34 causing damage greater than that done by the 1847 freshet. The level above Lock No. 33 also had experienced more extensive damage and several warehouses and a number of canal boats in the vicinity of the lock had been swept away. From Point of Rocks to the Monocacy River, he found the damage quite light compared to what he had expected and generally less than in 1847. In his opinion $6,000 would be needed to restore the 20 miles below Dam No. 3 for the readmission of 4 to 5 feet of water for navigation.[73]

On the 22nd reports began reaching canal officials concerning the heavy drainage to the canal between Georgetown and Great Falls. Along the canal in Georgetown many of the wharves and warehouses with their stores of flour, lumber, coal and firewood were destroyed. Both the Little Falls Bridge and the Long Bridge were washed away.[74] On the Georgetown Level there were four large breaks in the canal banks—a 300-foot cut at the waste weir near the site of the Little Falls Bridge a 70-foot breach about 600 yards below Gillhouses', and two smaller breaks just below Lock No. 5. Between Lock No. 5 and Widewater there were two breaches—a 30-foot cut at the Powder Magazine and a 100-yard break commencing at Lock No. 7 and extending to the small culvert next above it. On the Widewater level there were two serious breaks in the log wall at the lower end of Bear Island where the high embankment connected the island with the mainland. The most critical of these occurred at the same location as the large break in the 1847 freshet. It was 500 feet long, of which 200 feet were swept out to the bottom of the canal. The remaining 300 feet were so badly damaged the removal down to the foundation was necessary. It was estimated that it would take up to $10,000 and two months to repair this one break alone. About 100 yards above this break there was a 75-foot cut, and because of continuing water seepage there was fear that the two breaches would unite. Some 8½ miles above Great Falls there were two small breaks that were close to each other—one 20 feet long and the other 40 feet. There was a breach, 130 feet wide and 8 feet deep, in the embankment of the berm side of Guard Lock No. 2. Another breach, 30 feet wide and 6 feet deep, took place across the towpath about 60 feet west of the guard lock. All told, the lower 22 miles of the canal suffered the most destruction from the floods as they had many times before.[75]

Between April 22 and 29 various reports of the damage caused by the flood above Harpers Ferry reached company officials. From Dam No. 3 to Dam No. 4 the damage was generally similar to that experienced in 1847, the most critical breach occurring at the latter site where the river broke over the guard bank and around the Maryland abutment. The canal embankments were washed heavily at a few points between Dams Nos. 4 and 5, but the damage was generally less than in 1847. There were numerous small breaches in the canal embankments between Dams Nos. 5 and 6 but none were serious. Nearly all the filling in Dam No. 5 was washed out. At Dam No. 6 the river broke through the earthen embankment around the Virginia abutment, making a deep breach about 2 feet in length which was sufficient to pass all the water of the normal flow of the river.

From the Cacapon to Town Creek there were eight levels which had been injured. On each of these, there was generally one and in some cases two or three small openings in the towpath near the head of the level through which the water passed into the canal and a breach at the lower end where the water passed through the embankment back in the river. At some points the towpath was left in a ragged state, and at a few places the prism was partially filled by silt deposits. The most serious breach on this section of the waterway was on the lower end of the level

---

[73] Elgin to Ringgold, April 21, 1852, (two letters), Ltrs. Recd., C & O Co.
[74] *Alexandria Gazette*, April 22, 1852.
[75] Page to Ringgold, April 22, 1852, Ltrs. Recd., C & O Co.; Elgin to Fisk, April 25, 1852, Ltrs. Recd., Chief Engineer; and *Alexandria Gazette*, April 23 and 26, 1852.

near a waste weir just above Lock No. 66 where some 10,000 cubic yards of embankment had been washed out, thus submerging the upper end of the Paw Paw Tunnel Lock. Here the drainage was partially attributable to a berm bank that had been built near the waste weir on Section No. 312 causing a revised curve in the line. A second trouble spot was just below the Town Creek Aqueduct where a culvert had given way, causing a cut through both canal banks some 40 feet wide and down to about 3 feet above the bottom of the prism. On the 21 miles from Town Creek to Cumberland there was no damage to the canal banks or to the masonry.[76]

After reviewing the wreckage to the canal, Engineer and General Superintendent Fisk reported that it would cost $80,000 to repair the line. Of this sum, $25,000 was needed for the 22 miles below Seneca alone. It would take about 10 weeks before navigation could be resumed in early August. In repairing the waterway he recommended that the breaches at the head of the levels be closed first "as we may have another freshet before the opening at the foot of the levels can be repaired." Hoping to dispel some of the gloom that pervaded the company, he noted that:]

> It is proper that I should state that if the late freshet had been no higher than that of 1847, which did damage to an amount not less than $50,000, the canal, in consequence of work done since to guard against freshet of that height, would have sustained very little injury, and the navigation would have been interrupted for but a very short time thereby. The canal may therefore be considered as having been placed in a condition almost entirely safe against all freshets, except such, judging from the past, as may occur not oftener than every 50 years.[77]

A large force was soon put to work on the repairs, and company officials commenced efforts to secure loans from local banks and town along the line to finance the restoration. By June 16 the company had received $77k900 in pledges from Corporations of Georgetown and Alexandria, banks in the District cities and Cumberland, water renters in Georgetown, and individuals in Cumberland. In addition, William W. Corcoran and George Washington Riggs promised to provide the company with a personal loan of $5,000 if it was needed to complete the work.[78] The loans were advanced to the company on the pledge of its future revenue subject to existing priorities.[79]

LOANS TO REPAIR 1852 FLOOD DAMAGE[80]

Corporation of Georgetown	$30,000
Corporation of Alexandria	10,000
Bank of the Metropolis	10,000
Patriotic Bank	5,000
Bank of Commerce, Georgetown	2,500

---

[76] Dungan to Brengle, April 22, 1852, and Fisk to Board of Directors, April 29, 1852, Ltrs. Recd., C & O Co., Fisk to Dungan, April 23, 1852, Ltrs. Sent, Chief Engineer, Stone to Fisk, June 13, 14 and 19, 1852, Ltrs. Recd., Chief Engineer and *Alexandria Gazette*, April 27, 1852.

[77] Fisk to Board of Directors, April 29, 1852, Ltrs. Recd., C & O Co. Also see Fisk to Dungan, April 23, 1852, Ltrs. Sent, Chief Engineer.

[78] Ringgold to Chairman, Committee of Georgetown Corporation, June 16, 1852, and Grason to Corcoran, July 19, 1852, Ltrs. Sent, C & O Co.; Dangerfield to Ringgold, May 10, 1852, Ltrs. Recd., C & O Co.; and *An Ordinance Providing Aid Towards the Repairs of the Chesapeake & Ohio Canal*, May 7, 1852, in *Ordinances of the Corporation of Georgetown* (Georgetown, 1852), 9-10. A statistical breakdown of the loans may be seen on the above table.

[79] *Twenty-Fourth Annual Report* (1852), C & O Co., 4.

[80] Ringgold to Chairman, Committee of Georgetown Corporation, June 16, 1852, Ltrs. Sent, C & O Co.

Far Branch Bank, Alexandria	5,000
Bank of the Old Dominion	5,000
Exchange Bank	5,000
Water Renters, Georgetown	2,000
Individuals and Bank Loan, Cumberland	3,400
	$77,900

While the repairs were in progress, Chief Engineer Fisk successfully urged the board not only to effect the repairs but also to make additional improvements at five locations where more than half of the entire flood damage had occurred. The five points were located below Great Falls, and Seneca Falls and at Dams Nos. 3, 4 and 6. The purpose of the improvements, which would push the total cost of repairing the waterway to nearly $100,000, was to make these points covering a distance of less than six miles of the waterway "safe against a freshet as high as the recent one."[81]

Good progress was made on the restoration of the waterway, and navigation was resumed in late July.[82] The repairs and the more permanent improvements, not all of which were completed when the water was readmitted to the canal, cost $100,000.[83] Among the additional improvements that were made was "the substitution of a heavy wall of masonry for the embankment carried away at Dam No. 6"[84] and the construction of a new guard bank from Guard Lock No. 3 to Lock No. 36 that was several feet higher than the 1852 freshet.[85] The guard bank below Great Falls, Dam No. 2, and Dam No. 4 had also been raised to heights exceeding that of the flood. New waste weirs were built on all the canal levels that were subject to overflow by high water in the river, and some of the older wastes were extended in length to accommodate more water. The cross-section of a portion of Dam No. 5 was changed so as to "free it from the effects of reaction during freshets, by which it has heretofore been very much injured."[86]

At the annual meeting of the company stockholders on June 6, 1853, Engineer and General Superintendent Thomas L. Patterson attempted to present an optimistic view of the repairs effected after the freshet. Among other comments, he observed that:

> It is the subject of congratulation ...that a freshet six feet higher than any ever known attempted to be guarded against, should have done, comparatively, so little damage, cannot fail to give well founded confidence in the security of the Canal, when it is considered, that the points where two thirds of the damage was sustained, have been rendered secure against even a higher freshet...It is not probable ...that the navigation would be obstructed for more than a few days by any freshet not higher than that of last year.[87]

Nevertheless, the disaster not only weakened the canal but also had a detrimental effect on its trade and it financial condition. In fact the flood repairs caused a financial panic among the company officials, forcing them to suspend payment of the semi-annual interest on the construction loans which had been issued for repairs to the canal below Dam No. 6 in 1849.[88]

---

[81] Fisk to President and Directors, June 5, 1852, Ltrs. Recd., C & O Co., and *Twenty-Fourth Annual Report* (1852), 13.
[82] Ringgold to O'Neal, December 16, 1852, Ltrs. Sent, C & O Co.
[83] *Twenty-Fifth Annual Report* (1853), C & O Co., 3.
[84] *Ibid*, 8-9. The stone was quarried in Morgan County, Virginia, and transported to the canal on the Baltimore & Ohio Railroad.
[85] Fisk to Elgin, May 5, 1852, Ltrs. Sent, C & O Co. The work comprised 1,083 perches of stone wall.
[86] *Twenty-Fifth Annual Report* (1853), 8-9.
[87] *Ibid*.
[88] Frederick *Examiner*, June 30, 1852.

AUGUST 1855

On the night of August 1, 1855, a flash flood struck the canal in the vicinity of Dam No. 4 washing out a road culvert and causing a partial suspension of navigation for three or four weeks.[89]

WINTER 1855–56

During the winter of 1855–56, several ice freshets swept down the Potomac, causing some damage to the rubble stone dams at Little Falls and Seneca Falls and the masonry dam at Cumberland. Accordingly, the two lower dams were repaired and a temporary plank structure was put at Dam No. 8 to prevent it from further injury while permanent restoration work was underway.[90]

FEBRUARY–MAY 1857

Periodic droughts in the dry summer months coupled with the almost continual leaking of Dams Nos. 4 and 5 had curtailed boat navigation on the canal since the 1830s. When another drought in August 1856 brought a renewal of complaints of low water in the canal below the two dams, the company determined to put an end to the nuisance permanently by replacing them with mew tight masonry dams. Contracts were let for Dam No. 4 in October 1856 and for Dam No. 5 in January 1857.[91]

No sooner were the new dams contracted for than a series of four successive freshets roared down the valley between February and May 1857, suspending navigation for more than three months. In February the severe winter weather suddenly warmed, causing "an Ice Freshet such as had not for very many years, if ever, occurred before." Dams Nos. 4 and 5, which had been decaying for some years, gave way, the former being badly damaged and the latter having 500 feet totally swept off its foundation from the Virginia abutment to the more recently repaired portal on the Maryland side. During the next two months a large force completed the repairs on Dam No. 4, which consisted of building temporary cribs to close the gap, filling them with stone, and covering them with wooden sheeting. On April 12 just as the repair crews were preparing to fill the temporary cribs at Dam No. 5, a second freshet occurred, carrying away the short crib connecting the main crib and the old dam. This work previously had been thought to be secure, but the foundation proved to be defective. Repairs on Dam No. 5 had again reached an advanced stage and were within a few days of completion on May 4, when the river rose for a third time and poured over the dam. Although workmen waged a four-day struggle to save the structure, the torrent carried off some 200 feet of the repairs that had been made and weakened what was left. At Dam No. 4 about sixty feet of the old structure were swept away. The repairs were promptly resumed in the hope that navigation could be restored by June 1, but a fourth freshet in mid-May delayed repairs on Dam No. 5 for several days and tore a hole in Dam No. 4. Finally in mid-June boat navigation was resumes, and the construction of the masonry dams commenced in earnest.[92]

The disasters of 1857 all but wrecked the company financially. It had never been in better than a precarious condition since the completion of the waterway. Debts had continued to pile up during the previous decade to add to the already staggering burden of acceptance, balances due,

---

[89] Washington *Evening Star*, August 2 and 7, 1855, and *Twenty-Eighth Annual Report* (1856), C&O Co., 8.
[90] Stake to Board of Directors, June 11, 1856, Ltrs. Recd., C & O Co.
[91] *Twenty-Eighth Annual Report* (1856), 3–4; *Twenty-Ninth Annual Report* (1857), C & O Co., 9, 11; and *Proceedings of the President and Board of Directors*, I, 298–299, 316.
[92] Washington *Evening Star*, May 7, 1857; *Twenty-Ninth Annual Report* (1857), 12–13; and *Thirtieth Annual Report* (1858), C & O Co., 3–4, 59–63.

scrip, state loan and the repair bills after the floods of 1847 and 1852. Thus, company officials felt compelled to offer to the stockholders the following explanation for their actions during the disastrous spring of 1857:

> These repeated frustrations of the confident hopes of the restoration of navigation at the periods indicated, involving as each did a large additional expenditure for further efforts at repair, have severely taxed the patience and feelings of the Board, as well as of all those parties anxiously awaiting the event, but it was plain that no course remained other than to continue to labor—to wait patiently till the Destroyer had passed, and then to survey calmly and carefully the ravages which marked his desolating course, and lose no time from vigorous efforts to blot out those ravages in useless regrets and complainings.[93]

APRIL 1859

A high freshet struck the canal in the vicinity of Williamsport in April 1859. The flood greatly damaged the partially completed new masonry Dam No. 4. As the old dam just upstream from the new construction site was still in place, timber falling over it hit the uncompleted masonry dam, knocking out a great deal of stone work.[94]

SEPTEMBER 1859

A sudden freshet in the Potomac in Williamsport County again struck the canal in September 1859, causing considerable damage to the partially-built new masonry Dam No. 4 and to the level below Shepherdstown. The high water seriously injured the new 175-foot masonry portion of the Virginia abutment of the dam, removing parts of both the front and the back of the structure. A temporary crib was erected in front of the damaged portion of the dam and a contract was let to Lewis Stanhope on October 28 to construct a permanent crib at that point and fill the space between the old and new dams with stone. These repairs progressed slowly as they were interrupted by two periods of high water in March and April 1860.[95]

NOVEMBER 1860

Heavy rains over the Potomac Valley in November 1860 caused the river to rise rapidly. The river reached its peak at Williamsport where its height was measured at 29 feet above normal. The curbing at Dam No. 6 was injured, and a 25-foot section of the masonry abutment on the Virginia side of Dam No. 5 was swept away. Except for a blunder on the part of the Superintendent of the Antietam Division in failing to put a stop plank in the stop lock near Dam No. 4, damage from the high water would not have been great. However, considerable destruction was done to the guard lock and towpath below the dam, and the Marsh Run Culvert was washed out. Some sections of the canal were filled with silt deposits and debris. On the Georgetown Division the only reported damage occurred at Lock No. 21 where the walls had partially collapsed.[96]

---

[93] *Twenty-Ninth Annual Report* (1857), 12–13.
[94] *Thirty-First Annual Report* (1859), C & O Co., 6.
[95] *Thirty-Second Annual Report* (1860), C & O Co., 7, 16–17, and Stone to President and Directors, Sept. 28, 1859, Stone to Ringgold, March 22, 1860, and Stake to Ringgold, April 10, 1860, Ltrs. Recd., C & O Co.
[96] *Thirty-Third Annual Report* (1861), C & O Co., 3, 8–9; Charleton to Board of Directors, November 7, 1860, Fitzpatrick to Ringgold, November 6, 1860, and Stake to Board of Directors, November 13, 1860,

The canal navigation was shut down for three weeks while temporary repairs were made. When the canal was drained for the winter in late December, more permanent repairs were made to restore the canal to its operating condition before the freshet. General Superintendent A. K. Stake turned his men to Lock No. 21, giving it a new foundation, replacing the lost masonry and strengthening its supporting embankments. The guard lock and towpath below Dam No. 4 were restored, the wooden trunk over Marsh Run was replaced by a stone culvert, the missing masonry in the Virginia abutment of Dam No. 5 was filled with stone from a nearby quarry, and the curbing at Dam No. 6 was reinforced. Debris and silt deposits were removed from the trunk all along the line. As a result of these efforts, the company looked forward to a prosperous boating season in 1861 despite the looming clouds of the Civil War.[97]

APRIL 1861

Torrential rains drenched the entire watershed of the Potomac Valley beginning on April 12, 1861. The following day H. D. Carleton, the company's agent at Cumberland, reported that "the Potomac is very high. A measurement showed that the river stage was within ten inches of being as high as it had been in the previous November. All that he saw satisfied Carleton that the canal would suffer considerable damage unless the river had crested.[98]

Reports in the Washington *Evening Star* of the same date voiced similar fears for the lower portion of the canal. Already the water had passed over the towpath of the Cabin John Level and there was a break in the canal embankments on the Eight Mile Level above Seneca which would interrupt navigation for at least two weeks.[99]

The Potomac continued to surge upward. Upon the upper portion of the canal, it reached a height only exceeded by the great flood of 1852. At Georgetown most of the wharves along the waterway were soon flooded. Measures were taken at once by General Superintendent Stake to repair the damage. After checking with his division superintendent, Stake discovered that destruction to canal property had been "very much aggravated by the unprotected condition of the embankments near the feeder at Dam No. 4." A number of washes and breaches had occurred on the Cumberland, Hancock, Williamsport and Antietam Divisions, while additional cribbing was required at Dam No. 5. At South Branch the steam pumps were out of order and covered with mud and debris. Damage to the Monocacy and Georgetown Divisions was not as significant as had been feared.[100]

Two factors retarded the work of the repair crews. One of these, the straightened financial condition of the company, was to be expected. The other, the secession of Virginia from the Union on April 17, was not. Upon adoption of the Seneca Ordinance by the Virginia Convention, Confederate militia converged on Harpers Ferry, eager to seize the arms and machinery at the United States Armory and Arsenal. Unable to capture their objective before it was fired by the retreating Federal troops, the Rebel army used the area as a concentration point where untrained

---

Ltrs. Recd., C & O Co.; and Edwin C. Bearss, *War Comes to the Chesapeake & Ohio Canal*, " West Virginia History" , XXIX (April, 1968), 153.
[97] Ringgold to Colston, December 15, 1860, Ltrs. Sent, C & O Co., and *Thirty-Third Annual Report* (1861), 9–10, 14.
[98] *Thirty-Third Annual Report* (1861), 10, and Carleton to Ringgold, April 13, 1861, Ltrs. Recd., C&O Co.
[99] Washington *Evening Star*, April 13, 1861.
[100] *Thirty-Third Annual Report* (1861), 10; Washington *Evening Star*, April 15 and 17, 1861; Bearss, *War Comes to the Canal*, 154; and Lowe to Spates, June 7, 1862, Ltrs. Recd., C & O Co.

volunteers were organized into a fighting force by Colonel Thomas J. Jackson. Troops were sent across the Potomac into Maryland, occupying Point of Rocks and Maryland Heights.[101]

Despite the presence of the Confederates around Harpers Ferry, progress in effecting repairs of the flood damage was reported by the division superintendent. Water was back in the entire line by May 14, but the activities of the Virginia militia at Harpers Ferry, Point of Rocks and Alexandria made the coal shippers hesitant to use the waterway until the military situation was clarified.[102]

JULY 1861

Heavy rains at the beginning of July 1861 caused new damage to the canal. Although Union advances in the Potomac Valley had compelled the Confederates to pull back from the river, the repair crews did not want to take any chances. General Superintendent Stake complained that the Rebels seemed determined to oppose any navigation on the canal, and it was "impolitic if not dangerous to attempt repairs." Consequently, the repair of sections that could be attended to without risk would be pushed.

Work was to be commenced on July 8, and Stake estimated that it would require eight to ten days to restore navigation. As the regular work crews that resided along the line of the canal had left, the company would be forced to transport men, supplies and provisions into the areas needing repairs. Stake's fears that the canal would be subjected to damage by marauding soldiers as long as the Union and Confederate armies confronted each other along the Potomac were heightened as he prepared to send the repair crews when he was warned of a threat by the Rebels to "below down Dam No. 6." At the same time a Union officer warned that no repairs should be made to Dam No. 1. If the warning was not heeded, he would have his men destroy the dam. The hazards of repairing the canal were increased by the almost daily habit of roving Confederate bands shooting across the Potomac toward the canal at numerous points along the river.[103]

Despite the hindrances to the work crews, all of the repairs on the canal were finished by July 20, except those at Edwards Ferry, a culvert three miles above Paw Paw Tunnel, and the Oldtown Deep Cut. While the last repairs were underway, the U. S. Government dispatched a company of troops to Hancock to protect the waterway from Williamsport to Cumberland. The repairs at Edwards Ferry were completed quickly thereafter, but it took an 80-man crew with 20 horses and carts some 25 days to restore navigation at the large breach near the aforementioned culvert and the heavy rock slide at the Oldtown Deep Cut. On august 26 water was readmitted to this section, and the canal was again operable from Cumberland to Georgetown.[104]

APRIL–MAY 1862

During the last week of April 1862 torrential rains drenched the Potomac Valley. The river and its tributaries rose rapidly, and heavy damage was caused before the river crested at Dam No. 4. Two residents of Williamsport complained bitterly that this was the

---

[101] *The War of the Rebellion: A Compilation of the Official Records of the Union and Confederate Armies* (Washington, 1880–1900), Series I, Vol. II, 809–810.
[102] Spates to Ringgold, May 6 and 13, 1861, Ltrs. Recd., C & O Co., and *Thirty-Fourth Annual Report* (1862), C & O Co., 3.
[103] Stake to Spates, July 6, 1861, Ltrs. Recd., C & O Co.
[104] Spates to Ringgold, July 20 and 24, August 1, 13 and 25, 1861, Ltrs. Recd., C & O Co. Available documentation does not provide information relative to the precise identification of the culvert. It is likely, however, that it was located in the vicinity where Little Cacapon River empties into the Potomac.

7th high water within the last 18 months. After every high water, we have had the unwelcome and astonishing news that the plank at the stop lock at Dam No. 4 had either not been put in, or if put in had gone out. Invariably has this been the case for the last 18 months or two years. The last high water proves that with all the sad experience for that length of time with a cost of not less than $50,000 to the canal but no improvement has been made, for the report is now that several of the plank gave way, and the rushing water has done its usual work of in some places filling up and others sweeping away the embankment.[105]

Company officials estimated that it would take two weeks to restore navigation. However, critics led by A. C. Greene, a company director and an agent for the Borden Mining Company, observed that the time lost would be closer to one month. Such disasters, it was charged, had cost the canal its flour trade, two-thirds of which had been taken over by the Baltimore & Ohio Railroad. Millers had complained that no reliance could be placed on the canal for ten days at a time, and they had been compelled to seek a more reliable mode of transportation than the canal.[106]

When the full report of the damage caused by the freshet reached Cumberland, Greene exploded:

> The concurrence of circumstances against the resumption of canal trade this spring are positively infernal. Not only is the Canal deprived of revenue, but the trade itself is imperiled by the untoward events. I have great fears that the largest and most important buyers of coal will despair of getting anything from us this year.

At the time of the difficulties there were at Dam No. 4 some 1,800 tons of coal afloat and enroute to Georgetown. Greene trusted that every effort would be made to restore navigation as soon as possible, as much depended on the boatmen's ability to deliver the coal in early May.[107]

Accordingly, the superintendents of the Williamsport and Antietam Divisions pushed their repair crews hard to shore up the damaged embankments and clear out the obstructions. Continued rains added to their difficulties, but by May 8 water was readmitted to these divisions from the feeders at Dams Nos. 3 and 4, and the entire canal was again open to navigation.[108]

Traffic on the canal increased rapidly, but on the night of May 14 heavy rains fell on the upper reaches of the Potomac's watershed, causing a rapid rise on the river above Dam No. 5. The work programmed to repair the damage inflicted on the dam by General Jackson's Confederates in December 1861 had not been completed, and considerable damage was done to that structure by the high water. The news dismayed the Cumberland coal shippers, and President Spates rushed to the scene of the latest disaster. Encouraged by his presence, the work crews were able to effect temporary repairs and prevent any interruption to navigation at this critical period.[109]

On June 2 President Spates informed the company stockholders that:

> The frequent and heavy rains for some months past have kept the river very high and several breaches in the banks of the Canal have caused interruptions to the navigation, which have, however, been repaired as soon as circumstances would admit, and the Canal may now be deemed in fair navigable condition, but for the want of adequate means to make

---

[105] Embey and Son to Dellinger, April 26, 1862, Ltrs. Recd., C & O Co.
[106] Greene to Ringgold, April 26, 1862, Ltrs. Recd., C & O Co.
[107] Ibid, April 29, 1862, Ltrs. Recd., C & O Co.
[108] Spates to Ringgold, May 2, 1862, Ltrs. Recd., C & O Co.
[109] Greene to Ringgold, May 15, 1862, Ltrs. Recd., C & O Co.

durable improvements and repairs at Dam No. 5; the guard lock at Dam No. 4, and some other points requiring considerable expenditures, we cannot be assured of uninterrupted navigation...[110]

JUNE JULY 1862

Heavy rains in the first days of June 1862 caused the Potomac River to reach flood stage. On June 2 a break occurred in the canal near the Antietam Ironworks. The break was so sudden that a work scow was swept through the breach and smashed. First reports indicated that it would take six to eight days to repair the break, but President Spates urged the division superintendent to turn out as large a force as possible, including available boatmen, and to institute round-the-clock working parties.[111]

On the night of June 4 the railroad bridge at Harpers Ferry was swept away, thus severing the Potomac Valley line of the Baltimore & Ohio Railroad.[112] The following day the rains ceased and the river fell.

A. C. Greene on June 12 and 21 urged President Spates to rush the repairs on the Antietam Division because the damage to the Baltimore & Ohio and Confederate demolitions at Martinsburg had cut off all transportation of coal from Cumberland to the District cities. It was imperative that coal shipments be resumed as soon as possible on the canal so that demands could be met. Flood damage to the Pennsylvania rail network could be expected to throw upon the Cumberland coalfields a heavy demand and it was of great importance that the waterway be ready to grasp the opportunity. He trusted that attention was also being given to Dam No. 5 where, unless a close check was kept on the pool, there would be insufficient water for navigation now that the rains had ceased.[113]

By late June construction crews had a new railroad bridge in operation across the Potomac at Harpers Ferry and the canal above that town was being watered. However, full navigation on the waterway was not restored, because work had dragged at Dam No. 5 and the pool backed up by that structure was too low to supply water to the sections of the waterway between Dams Nos. 4 and 5. A heavy rain on the night of July 1 eased this problem but created another, as "a good amount of sand was washed back into the canal at Dam No. 4," and a breach was opened in the canal embankments above Hancock.[114]

Work on getting a suitable depth of water in the canal throughout its length continued to drag. However, President Spates reported on July 24 that the breach above Hancock had been repaired and that work on Dam No. 5 was also progressing satisfactorily. Boats laden with coal were now able for the first time since July 2 to make the run from Cumberland to Georgetown.[115]

APRIL 1864

Heavy rains in scattered parts of the Potomac Valley in early April 1864 caused some flood damage to the canal, particularly on the Monocacy and Williamsport Divisions. On the former, a heavy earth and rock slide occurred near the Marble Quarry about one mile below Lock No. 26.

---

[110] *Thirty-Fourth Annual Report* (1862), 6.
[111] Benton to Ringgold, June 3, 1862, and Spates to Ringgold, June 4, 1862, Ltrs. Recd., C & O Co.
[112] *War of the Rebellion*, Series I, Vol. XII, pt. 3, 304, 323, 342, 361 and 362
[113] Greene to Ringgold, June 12 and 21, 1862, Ltrs. Recd., C & O Co. and Edwin C. Bearss, *1862 Brings Hard Times to the Chesapeake & Ohio Canal*," West Virginia History," Vol. XXX (January, 1969), 445.
[114] *Thirty-Fifth Annual Report* (1862), 8, and Greene to Ringgold, July 2, 1862, and Benton to Ringgold, July 2, 1862, Ltrs. Recd., C & O Co.
[115] Apates to Ringgold, July 24, 1862, Ltrs. Recd., C & O Co.

The level was drained and the rock blasted into powder and removed with wheelbarrows. Although the high water had covered most of the towpath from Seneca creek to Lock No. 26, the canal banks were not washed badly "to stop navigation." As a number of lock gates and balance beams had been broken, a large quantity of timber was purchased at Orleans and Harpers Ferry for repairs. Since the damage was generally light, the division was "in good boating order" within a week.[116]

On the Williamsport Division the only damage suffered by the canal was the number of sand bars washed into the trunk by the high water. Although the flood waters had covered the towpath on the slackwater behind Dam No. 4 for an unheard of 15 days, the banks had not been significantly washed. Accordingly, the division was ready for navigation within five days.[117]

MARCH 1865

In March 1865 the Potomac Valley was struck by a heavy flood caused by the simultaneous breaking up of the ice flows in the river and considerable downpours of rain. The canal banks and the towpath were washed in many places, but, with the exception of some logs being removed from the cribs on the Virginia side of Dam No. 5, there were no serious breaches or injuries to the masonry work. After quick remedial repairs, the canal was ready for navigation about March 20.[118]

OCTOBER 1866

When the Civil War ended in spring 1865, the company resumed operations to complete the new masonry Dam No. 5. By the fall of 1866 one section of sixty feet of masonry was completed and a coffer dam was prepared for a second section of equal length, which was expected to be completed before freezing temperatures arrived. However, a severe freshet in October 1866 carried off the coffer dam and partially injured the completed 60-foot masonry section. The continued high water in the river and lateness of the season prevented the resumption of the work until the spring and summer of 1867.

Optimistically, the board of directors reported to the company stockholders in June 1867 that:

> The Canal, it is believed, is now in better condition, and more durable than at any former period, and in evidence of it, but slight damages have been sustained by several unusually heavy floods in the river during the past two years [March 1865 and October 1866], and in no previous years has the navigation been so regular or as briefly interrupted from breaches or other casualties, or repaired in less time, or at less cost.[119]

SPRING 1868

Two heavy freshets struck the canal during the spring of 1868 causing extensive damage. The first of three, an ice freshet which cannot be precisely dated due to the limitations of the available documentation, wrecked particular havoc on Dam Nos. 1 and 2 and the Rock Creek Basin. While

---

[116] George W. Spates to Alfred Spates, April 16 and 19, 1864, Ltrs. Recd., C & O Co.
[117] Masters to Ringgold, April 13, 1864, Ltrs. Recd., C & O Co.
[118] *Thirty-Seventh Annual Report* (1865), C & O Co., 3; Masters to Board of Directors, March 2, 1865, Ltrs. Recd., C & O Co.; and *Hagerstown Mail*, February 25, 1865.
[119] *Thirty-Ninth Annual Report* (1867), C & O Co., 5–6.

Dam No. 1 and the basin were heavily injured, the chief damage to the canal works was experienced at Dam No. 2 where one-half of the structure was torn away entirely. Repairs to these structures continued until mid-July, but canal workmen effected temporary works at these points to permit the entire length of the waterway to be opened for navigation about April 1.[120]

The canal continued to operate until May 15 when a sudden rise in the river overflowed the waterway "in some places for a great distance, damaging culverts and towpath in many places, to such an extent, as to delay navigation for eight or ten days." Available documentation does not offer more detailed information on the specific sites of major damage or on the repairs effected.[121]

SEPTEMBER 1870

A major freshet, known generally as the "Shenandoah Flood of 1870," struck the Potomac Valley below Harpers Ferry on September 30 and suspended navigation on the canal until mid-October. The most significant damage to the waterway occurred between Sandy Hook and Lock No. 33 at Harpers Ferry. Here a breach 850 feet in length was opened in the canal embankment, and the "sea wall" which supported the towpath was greatly undermined. The surface of the towpath between Harpers Ferry and the Monocacy River was severely washed. On the Nine-Mile Level south of the Monocacy, there were five small breaches and the towpath as well as the berm bank was considerably cut down by washing from the river. The Eight-Mile Level between Edwards Ferry and Seneca suffered three serious breaches on the towpath and two on the berm banks.

The Georgetown Division below Seneca also received great damage. The towpath from Seneca Creek to Great Falls was heavily washed, and a considerable breach was opened in the canal bank about three-fourths of a mile below Seneca. One-fourth of a mile below Great Falls there was a breach 86 feet long and 36 feet deep. Near Seven Locks, some five miles below Great Falls, there were two breaches. The towpath near the Cabin John Culvert was cut down three feet in height for a distance of 800 feet by the rampaging water. There was a 176-foot breach in the canal just above Little Falls, and at Lock No. 5 the towpath was washed off to a depth of three feet below its normal grade for nearly 1,760 yards. The guard bank at Dam No. 1 lost nearly six feet of its height for a distance of 450 feet. The towpath near the Chain Bridge was reduced some two feet in height for nearly 1,000 feet. Three miles west of Georgetown the height of the freshet made it necessary for canal officials to cut the embankments in order to protect the high banks and walls of the waterway in the vicinity of the town. This preventative measure, however, created a breach of some 360 feet in length which "cut out some 12 feet below bottom."

Aside from the devastation visited upon the canal prism, the flood damaged ten locks to a greater or lesser degree. The following points of injury were specifically cited by company officials: Lock No. 16, one gate and three balance beams broken and washed away; Lock No. 20, two balance beams broken; Lock No. 22, one gate and three balance beams broken; Lock No. 25, one balance beam broken; Lock No. 27, coping removed and filing behind embankment walls washed out; Lock No. 29, one gate swept away; Lock No. 30, flume destroyed; Lock No. 31, chamber filled with eight feet of sand; Lock No. 32, coping and filling behind both chamber side walls washed away; and Lock No. 33, coping and filing behind chamber walls on towpath side heavily damaged.

As it was late in the boating season, the canal company was anxious to have the waterway repaired as quickly as possible. Accordingly, a large number of laborers were recruited, and by October 9, 1.080 men and 200 horses and carts were working day and night between Harpers

---

[120] Mans to President and Directors, July 11, 1868, Ltrs. Recd., C & O Co.
[121] *Fortieth Annual Report* (1868), C & O Co., 7.

Ferry and Georgetown. The workers were paid $2 per day plus board, and the price paid for the use of the horses and carts was $3 per day each.

In preparing the canal for the readmission of the water, the work force repaired the canal embankments, replaced the missing coping, gates and wall backing at the locks, and restored the surface of the towpath to its operating grade. In addition, the men relaid the masonry "sea wall" between Sandy Hook and Lock No. 33 and restored the guard bank at Dam No. 2. Altogether the men repaired breaches and raised the towpath and berm banks of the canal trunk for a total length of 4,218 feet with an average height of seven feet and an average width of twelve feet. The canal was ready for the readmission of water on October 11 and navigation was restored four days later. After the resumption of boating, many of the workers stayed on the line to complete the more lengthy repairs.[122]

AUGUST 1872

Heavy rain on the night of August 29, 1872, in Washington, D.C., caused Rock Creek to rise suddenly. The rush of water from the creek caused eight boats that were moored in the Rock Creek Basin either to be thrust on top of the dam at the mouth of the creek or to be broken and sunk. Five of the barges, three of which were loaded with stone, were sent down crashing on top of the dam. Of the remaining three, one, which was loaded with stone, was broken in half, and two were sunk. The following day the five boats that were left perched on the dam by the high water were removed without serious injury occurring either to the dam or to the boats. On August 31, the water was drawn off the creek to permit the salvage of the broken and sunken barges.[123]

FEBRUARY 1873

A heavy ice freshet along the entire length of the river, from Cumberland to Georgetown, in February 1873 raised fears among canal officials that the company dams would be greatly damaged. When the ice had passed off it was found that none of the "permanent" dams had suffered serious injury. However, President Arthur P. Gorman reported to the directors that the freshet has "nearly demolished Dams Nos. 1 & 2 which are merely dikes of loose stone." The dams would require "extensive repairs to enable us to keep up a proper supply of water from Seneca to Georgetown."[124] Apparently, repair crews had raised the dams to such a height as would provide sufficient water for the canal's operation as the entire length of the waterway was opened for navigation in April.[125]

AUGUST 1873

The freshet of August 1873, taking place in the middle of five years of almost unprecedented profits for the company, showed the precarious nature of the canal's prosperity. A flash flood following fourteen days of rain so swelled the smaller tributaries of the Potomac that the culverts under the canal were not able to pass the miniature rivers. Many of them were washed out by the

---

[122] Clarke to Board of Directors, September 30, 1870, Ltrs. Recd., C & O Co. Apparently, some of the repairs were never fully completed. For instance, Chief Engineer William A. Hutton reported on August 1, 1872, that as the damage to the guard bank below Lock No. 6 caused by the Shenandoah Flood of 1870 had not been fully repaired it " should be made up to its full height without delay." *Report of W. R. Hutton, Chief Engineer, As to Condition of Chesapeake & Ohio Canal* (Annapolis, 1872), 22.

[123] Mans to Gorman, August 30, September 3, 1872, Ltrs. Recd., C & O Co.

[124] Gorman to Board of Directors, March 10, 1873, Ltrs. Recd., C & O Co.

[125] *Forty-Fifth Annual Report* (1873), C & O Co., 10–11.

torrents. The total destruction was the greatest experienced by the canal from natural causes since 1852, and it was the first time that the canal was damaged so severely by the numerous mountain streams that passed under it to the river.

The most serious damages sustained by the waterway occurred on the Antietam and Monocacy Divisions. On the former, in addition to the flood damage, two breaches were opened in the canal banks that were caused by leaks in the limestone region which had existed since the trunk was constructed. The leaks had given similar trouble in the past, and the heavy rains had weakened the banks to such an extent that they gave way to the undermining leaks.

Within a few hours after the flash flood, several hundred additional men were recruited to repair the damage. The Baltimore & Ohio Railroad aided the canal company by providing extra trains to transport the men and the necessary materials to the damaged parts of the work. Repairs were delayed and in some cases undone by a succession of storms which struck them while in an exposed stage of construction. However, the damage was so far repaired as to pass boats on August 26 less than one month since the flood had suspended the navigation. All told, the company spent nearly $25,000 to repair the flood damage and lost some $50,000 in revenue from tolls.[126]

APRIL 1874

During the month of April 1874 heavy rains in the Potomac Valley caused a greater rise in the river than had occurred for many years. The water entirely submerged the canal below Dams Nos. 4 and 5 and at various points on the Monocacy Division. However, the system of general improvements on the canal directed by Chief Engineer Hutton since 1871 had made the waterway's embankments so "solid" and "permanent" that the high water passed off without doing serious injury. Navigation was delayed for several days to effect minor unspecified repairs.[127]

JULY–AUGUST 1875

Continuous rains in July and August 1875 caused considerable damage to the canal. Although no serious breach occurred to suspend the navigation, the banks of the waterway were washed severely and the trunk filled with sand silt. A portion of the dam at the mouth of Rock Creek was destroyed, and one boat loaded with coal was swept over it and sunk in the Potomac. The dam was reconstructed, and a steam dredge was used to clean out the prism from Georgetown to Seneca. Navigation was continued while the repairs were in progress. All told, the company spent some $3,000 on the flood repairs. Again the company officials, as they had the previous year, credited their general improvement program "that no greater loss was sustained by the unprecedented rains of July & August."[128]

NOVEMBER 1877

Following five days of heavy rain, another great flood swept down the Potomac Valley on November 24, 1877. This one was the worst in 150 years of the recorded history of the region. In its wake it left the canal almost a total wreck and brought trade to an end for the season. The crest of the flood was generally two feet higher than the previous record established in 1852, but at South Branch the freshet's peak was six feet higher. At Great Falls, the water ran over the high guard

---

[126] Gorman to Board of Directors, September 10, 1873, Ltrs. Recd., C & O Co.; *Proceedings of the President and Board of Directors*, M, 124–127; and *Forty-Sixth Annual Report* (1877), C & O Co., 4, 28.

[127] Gorman to Board of Directors, April 15, 1874, Ltrs. Recd., C & O Co., and *Proceedings of the President and Board of Directors*, M, 154–157.

[128] Gorman to Board of Directors, September 14, 1875, Ltrs. Recd., C & O Co.

bank, the top of which was about 70 feet above the usual low water mark of the river. Damage was scattered all along the line, but the middle section, because of the extremely high rise of the Antietam and the Conococheague, suffered the most. All along the line, quantities of repair materials, stores and cargoes were lost.[129]

Within two weeks after the flood waters subsided, the canal board had received numerous reports of the extensive damage inflicted on the waterway. On the line extending from Cumberland to Hancock, there were fifteen breaks in the canal banks, the towpath was virtually destroyed, and many of the locks were injured. Of the fifteen breaks, the most serious occurred at Hancock where there was a 70 to 80-foot-long breach extending down to the bottom of the canal. Both of the abutments at Dam No. 6 were slightly damaged, but the injuries were not so great as had been feared. Some of the shorter levels were filled with silt and debris from one to three feet in depth, and many boats had been grounded or sunk during the storm.[130]

From Hancock to Lock No. 41 at the head of Big Slackwater, the canal banks suffered innumerable washes. As had been the case above Hancock, some of the shorter levels were filled with silt and debris. The most serious damage to this part of the line occurred at Dam No. 5 where both abutments were heavily injured and on the Seven mile Level near Williamsport, where the embankment was washed away entirely for a considerable distance. All told, President Gorman informed the board that it would cost $38,850 to repair the 96-mile section of canal from Cumberland to Big Slackwater.[131]

The greatest single point of destruction took place at Dam No. 4, the 720-foot-wide and 22-foot-high structure that company officials had considered to be one of the most substantial masonry dams in the nation when it was completed in 1861. It had given way even before the flood waters reached their crest. Nearly 200 feet in length near the center of the dam had been swept away, thus permitting the entire flow of the river to pass through the aperture. Officials were shocked by the destruction here as the dam had been "thoroughly sheathed and backed." As the water had risen, it had swept over the entire guard bank (1¼ miles long and 19 feet height), causing extensive damage to it. At the lower end of the bank, the rushing water had carried away that portion of the bank between the stop lock and the dam abutment. It was estimated that it would cost $37,000 to repair the dam, its abutments, and the guard bank.[132]

From Dam No. 4 to the mouth of Seneca Creek, a distance of 67 miles, the canal was utterly devastated. In many places, the towpath and the retaining walls were damaged badly, and the canal was filled with mud and debris. There were several breaks in the embankments in the vicinity of Antietam Creek, which had risen eight to ten feet above its previous high-water mark. At Harpers Ferry, where the river had risen to a height of 26 feet above its ordinary height, the guard bank at the feeder was washed away entirely for a distance of one-half mile. The guard lock and the feeder were entirely filled with mud, gravel and sand. Locks Nos. 32 and 33 were almost totally destroyed, the stone work being torn up and washed out except for the heavy retaining

---

[129] *Fiftieth Annual Report* (1878), C & O Co., 3, 9. The flood in the Potomac Valley was part of an extended storm system that struck all along the East Coast of the United States, inflicting heavy losses in property and causing numerous deaths in its wake. It was in this storm that the U. S. steamer " Huron" was lost on the North Carolina coast with about 100 of her officers and crew. Scharf, *History of Western Maryland*, Vol. II, 1202.

[130] *Proceedings of the President and Board of Directors*, N, 11–12; and *Baltimore Sun*, November 30, 1877. In his *History of Western Maryland*, Scharf describes the situation at Cumberland during the flood, a copy of which may be seen in Appendix A.

[131] *Proceedings of the President and Board of Directors*, N, 11–12, and *Baltimore Sun*, November 30, 1877. In his *History of Washington County*, Scharf describes the course of events at Williamsport and throughout Washington County during the flood, a copy of which may be seen in Appendix B.

[132] *Proceedings of the President and Board of Directors*, N, 12–14.

walls at the former and the inner facings of the latter. The gates of both locks were carried away and washed down the canal for more than a mile. Above Lock No. 33 the heavy embankments were washed away down to the bottom of the trunk for a distance of 100 yards, and below it the towpath and "sea wall" were wholly destroyed for more than 2,000 feet. The company shops at Sandy Hook were carried away, along with 12,000 feet of lumber. Between Sandy Hook and the Monocacy River there was "scarcely a vestige of the towpath, and large sections of the bank" were "washed bodily out into the river." The damage to the canal on the 20-mile stretch from the Monocacy to Seneca was less severe than any other portion of the waterway. All told, it was estimated that it would cost $92,518 to repair the canal from Dam No. 4 to Seneca (exclusive of Dam No. 4 itself).[133]

On the 22 miles below Seneca the canal was also hard-hit by the flood. Four canal boats were swept into the river along with numerous small houses and sheds along this part of the line. Lock No. 23 was severely damaged as its wing walls were carried away and its main walls partially collapsed. This level was seriously injured; its towpath and berm banks were washed, its retaining walls were destroyed, and it prism was filled with mud. Between Lock No. 23 and Little Falls there were a great number of breaks, and much of the masonry and towpath were battered. One part of the most serious breaks occurred at the "Log Wall," a large portion of the wall being swept away. At Lock No. 5 there were a great many breaks, and much of the masonry and towpath were bettered. Below the lock the towpath was considerably washed all the way to Chain bridge, and there was a large break below the bridge. The towpath had been cut for a distance of 80 feet in length above Edes Mill so as to prevent a more serious break and possibly great property loss at Georgetown, but in passing out the trunk the water carried out a large portion of the towpath embankment and puddling of the prism. It was estimated that it would cost $32,000 to repair the 22-mile section of the canal above Georgetown, thereby making the total amount of estimated repairs on the canal to be $200,368.[134]

The work of restoration began immediately. Repairs began on the Georgetown Level on November 26 so that the Georgetown millers would have their necessary supply of water. Under the direction of Stephen Gambrill, a large force of hands had the water restored to that level by December 20. In early December Superintendent Fletchall was placed in charge of a large crew assigned to the repair of the canal between Locks No. 5 and 23, with Assistant Superintendent J. R. Mans on the work near Seneca. Superintendent J. J. Moore was instructed to supply 200 laborers and as many stone masons and horses and carts as were needed to repair the guard banks at Dams Nos. 3 and 4. Superintendent Stanhope, an experienced dam builder, was given charge over that portion of the canal between Dams Nos. 4 and 6, and by December 12 he already had a large number of men "employed getting logs to construct cribs" for Dam No. 4. In addition he was ordered to hire sixty men to repair Dam nos. 5 and 6. Asa Williams, the collector at Cumberland, was charged with repairing the canal from the Cacapon River to Cumberland, and he soon had 100 men at work on the line. As an economy measure the company suspended all lock-keepers, collectors and other officials, but most of them probably found employment directing and making repairs.[135]

All winter long the work continued as rapidly as possible. Aided in part by mild temperatures and the absence of high water and ice flows, the repairs progressed faster than had been ex-

---

[133] *Baltimore Sun*, November 29, 1877; *Proceedings of the President and Board of Directors*, N, 12–13; Scharf, *History of Western Maryland*, Vol. II, 1201–1202; and *Report of the Standing Committee . . . in the Chesapeake & Ohio Canal Investigation* (Annapolis, 1889), 223.
[134] Washington *Evening Star*, November 26, 1877; *Baltimore Sun*, November 29, 1877; and *Proceedings of the President and Board of Directors*. N, 13–14. All the records and books in the Georgetown Collectors Office were destroyed by the flood. Fawcett to Moore, March 2, 1878, Ltrs. Recd., C & O Co.
[135] *Proceedings of the President and Board of Directors*, N, p.114 and *Fiftieth Annual Report* (1878), 9–10.

pected. All available company resources were used, augmented by loans totaling $70,000 from various banks in Washington, Baltimore and Cumberland, loans of $10,000 each from the Maryland, American, Consolidation and Borden Coal Companies and a personal loan of $5,000 from President Gorman.[136]

In addition to these loans President Gorman went to the state legislature for help. By the terms of an earlier court decision, *Commonwealth of Virginia vs. Chesapeake & Ohio Canal Company*, the right of the company to issue bonds for repairs on a pledge of its revenues was recognized as legally unrestricted. To insure a market for the bonds, however, it was deemed necessary to limit the right to a sum that might be reasonably repaid.[137] Upon the request of the canal company, the legislature passed an act in February 1878, specifically waiving the state's prior lien on canal property for repair bonds up to $500,000 in amount. The additional pledge of property for the repayment of the bonds was considered necessary to strengthen the market value of the issue. At first the directors authorized the sale of only $125,000 of the bonds to pay for the repair costs, for these obligations were not subject to cancellation before maturity.[138]

By April 10, 1878, it was reported that the repairs had been substantially completed and that navigation would be resumed on the 15th, only one month later than usual. Although the repairs to the masonry at Dam No. 4 could not be carried out until the stone was quarried, a temporary crib work had been built that would keep up the navigation for the coming season. Much of the canal had been reexcavated, and the "sea wall" at the Shenandoah River Lock had been replaced. At many points the towpath had been rebuilt, and all of the numerous lock gates that had been swept away were replaced. Since all of the towpath bridges on the canal had been lost, they too had been reconstructed. Many of the injured locks still needed to be renovated, but temporary repairs had been made to make them serve their purpose for one more boating season. Much still needed to be done to strengthen the embankments and improve the towpath surface, but the waterway was in good enough condition to resume the navigation.[139]

The magnificent effort already had cost the company $153,923.70 by April 30, and the total cost of all permanent repairs had been revised upward to between $225,000 and $250,000. Yet President Gorman was pleased to report on May 15 that the "canal is now in as good condition, or better than it has been for many years past." He allowed that "the embankments and masonry, while in fair condition are not as substantial as they were prior to the flood" and that "much remains to be done to strengthen and complete the work. However, this could "be more economically done during the current year with the regular and a few extra repair hands."[140]

The flood repairs continued into the year 1879. By January 1, the expenditures for such work totaled $199,190.46. Later on June 2, the stockholders were informed that all the repairs had been completed except for the breach at Dam No. 4. Not only had "the work been placed in as good a condition as it was prior to the damage," but at several points where the greatest destruction had occurred such as at Harpers Ferry, "extensive improvements have been made by raising

---

[136] *Proceedings of the President and Board of Directors*, N, 17–20, 68; *Fiftieth Annual Report* (1878), 11; and Gorman to Board of Directors, May 15, 1878, Ltrs. Recd., C & O Co.

[137] *Baltimore Sun*, January 28, 1878.

[138] *Laws Made and Passed by the General Assembly of the State of Maryland* (Annapolis, 1878), Ch. 58; *Proceedings of the President and Board of Directors*, N, 20–23, 26–27, 300; and *Proceedings of the Stockholders*, E, 302–303.

[139] *Proceedings of the President and Board of Directors*, N, 17–20, 66–68 and *Fiftieth Annual Report* (1878), 10.

[140] *Proceedings of the President and Board of Directors*, N, p.23, and *Fiftieth Annual Report* (1878), pp.10–11.

the towpath and constructing high retaining walls so as to prevent damage from like freshets hereafter."[141]

Finally on June 7, 1880, the board of directors was able to report to the stockholders that every part of the canal "which was damaged by the flood of November, 1877, has been thoroughly repaired and strengthened." The canal was "now unquestionably in better condition than it has been at any time since 1860," and its navigation was "now more reliable than it has been at any time since it was constructed." All told, the repairs had cost the company $238,500.21, and had left it saddled with a debt of $196,463.96.[142]

JUNE 1884

The canal company was subjected to heavy financial losses occasioned in June 1884 by one of the heaviest freshets that ever struck Washington County. The waterway from Hancock to Harpers Ferry sustained extensive damage, but available documentation does not specify the particular points of injury or the repairs effected. Additional hands were employed to make the necessary repairs, and the waterway was reopened to trade within one week.[143]

APRIL–MAY 1886

Three freshets within a period of six weeks in April and May of 1886 left the canal in a fearful state of disrepair and the company finances in a precarious position bordering on bankruptcy. On April 1, a flood swept down the entire length of the upper Potomac Valley, tearing a great hole in Dam No. 6, and generally wreaking havoc along the waterway. Four days later, another freshet widened the gap in the dam and added to the destruction of the canal proper.[144]

After the flood waters subsided, the board ordered that a complete report of the damage and recommended repairs be made by Stephen Gambrill, the company treasurer, and G. W. Smith, a well-known Potomac Valley civil engineer. On April 22, the two men reported to the board concerning the damage they had found, some of the repairs that were already underway, and recommendations for the reconstruction of Dam No. 6. On the Georgetown Level there were two extensive sand bars in the canal prism near Chain Bridge that were already being removed with a steam dredge by George Latchford and his 12-man crew. The slope walls of Locks Nos. 1–4 had been heavily washed. At the upper end of the level above Lock No. 5 the towpath was washed away almost entirely for a distance of 200 yards, with much of the sand, gravel, and dirt now filling that portion of the trunk. Just above Lock No. 6 there was a break in the towpath 44 feet long and 12 feet deep, and the towpath surface on this level was washed severely for a distance of one-half mile. There were 26 men and 6 carts repairing the damage on this level. On the Cabin John Level the tumbling waste was half gone and the towpath badly damaged. Fourteen men were reconstructing the portion of the waste that had been swept away and bringing the towpath up to its operating grade. The level above Great Falls was damaged severely; there was a large leak at the waste weir, nearly all of the towpath on the level was carried away to a depth of from three to five feet, and there were two small breaks in the embankments extending down to the bottom of the trunk. Thirty men and nine carts were at work on these repairs under the direc-

---

[141] *Fifty-First Annual Report* (1879), C & O Co., 9.
[142] *Fifty-Second Annual Report* (1880), C & O Co., 8 and 10. On March 18, 1879, a contract was let to Lewis Stanhope to reconstruct Dam No. 4, and operations were completed on October 10. *Report on Committee on Construction of Dam No. 4*, September 27, 1879, Ltrs. Recd., C & O Co.
[143] *Proceedings of the President and Board of Directors*, N, 272-273.
[144] *Fifty-Ninth Annual Report* (1887), C & O Co., 5-6; Washington *Evening Star*, April 2, 1886; and Thomas J. C. Williams, *History of Frederick County, Maryland* (2 Vols., Frederick, 1910), Vol. I, 395.

tion of Superintendent Elgin. Lock No. 21 had been undermined and its walls endangered. On the Three-Mile Level above Lock No. 21 there was a break on the towpath near the culvert thirty feet long and extending to the bottom of the trunk. The culvert was somewhat damaged, and the towpath near Lock No. 22 was washed away. On these repairs Elgin had 100 men at work under the direction of Lockkeeper Pennifield. The towpath below Seneca was considerably washed.

The towpath on the Eight- and Nine-Mile Levels above Seneca were washed severely in many places, and repairs were proceeding with a work crew of eighteen men under the direction of Messrs. Collier and Reneberger. From the Monocacy River to Harpers Ferry, the towpath was torn and battered in many places. On the Four Mile Level above Harpers Ferry there were heavy washes on the towpath, two small breaches, and several sand bars. Forty men and sixteen carts were at work on this section under Mr. Drenner. A serious 50-foot break near the tumbling wash on the Mountain Lock Level had taken place, and the canal for a distance of 120 yards was filled to a depth of two feet with sand, silt and debris. There were two more fills at Shepherdstown and at a point just below the river lock, both of which were 150 yards in length and 2 feet in depth. Just above the river lock the canal was filled with silt to a depth of three feet for a distance of 150 yards, and the towpath on the One-Mile Level was damaged seriously. On the Five-Mile Level above Lock No. 39 there were four specific problem areas: a break 40 feet long and several feet below the canal bottom; a fill 180 feet long and 2 feet deep; a small break at the foot of Lock no. 41; and the severe washing of the towpath face all along the level. Eighty men and 32 carts were at work on this section under the superintendence of Mr. Morrow. On the level above Lock No. 40 there was a break just above the lock some 40 feet long and extending to the bottom of the trunk, a sand bar 100 yards long and two feet deep, and three fills each 300 yards long and 3 feet deep. In addition, the entire length of the towpath on this level was washed to a depth of one to two feet. Sixty-four men and nineteen carts under the direction of Mr. Burgan were at work on these repairs.

From the head of Big Slackwater to Williamsport the towpath was considerably damaged in many places and there were two small breaks. Making these repairs were twenty-two men and one cart. On the Williamsport Level (above Lock No. 44) there was a break some 30 feet long and extending 3 feet below the bottom of the canal at Cruger's Warehouse. The towpath was torn up badly near Miller's Bend for a distance of over one mile, the trunk was filled with deposits from one to three feet deep, and a waste weir was washed out. On the Two-Mile Level below Four Locks the towpath was damaged greatly and there were several leaks. Forty-three men and eighteen carts under Mr. Masters were at work on these repairs. Damages to the Fourteen-Mile Level above Four Locks included heavy washes along the towpath at Little Pool and two breaks at that point, one of 40 feet in length at its foot and one of smaller extent at its head. On the Hancock Level (above Lock No. 52) the upper portion was filled to a depth of several feet for a considerable distance, much of the towpath surface was swept away, and two breaks were found near the Round Top Cement Mill, one of which was nearly 60 feet long and several feet below the bottom of the trunk. The Four Mile Level from Sir Johns Run to Dam No. 6 suffered greater damage than it had in 1877. Among its significant injuries were the following: the towpath on its upper portion for a distance of one mile was almost entirely washed away; similar damages were inflicted on the level's lower one-quarter mile; the trunk was filled to an average depth of two feet for almost half its length; and the berm bank and the balance of the towpath were damaged in many places. A crew of 62 men and 22 carts under the superintendence of Mr. Sterling was handling the repairs from Little Pool to Sir Johns Run.

The damage at Dam No. 6 was so extensive as to require a total reconstruction of the structure at a cost of $50,000, although outside estimates had ranged as high as $119,000. Some 175 feet of the 475-foot structure had been carried away, and the remaining 183 feet on the Virginia side of the river was almost a total wreck. The 117 feet still standing on the Maryland side, which had been partially rebuilt in 1884, was rotten, its timber above the waterline almost entirely gone, and its stone held in place only by the sheathing. If the dam were rebuilt as recommended, it should be made with sawed white oak and not hewn timber as had been done on the old structure. It should also be filled with broken stone instead of the field stone or the smoothly-worn rock excavated from the river bottom, both of which had been used on the old structure and both of which had been the cause of so much leakage through it.

Part of the chamber walls of Locks Nos. 56 and 57 had yielded, and the lower towpath wing walls and hollow quoins of Lock No. 56 had settled. On the Tunnel Level the embankments were washed badly, and there was a heavy land slide on the berm side. There was also a large slide in the cut below the Tunnel, and the One-Mile Level below Paw Paw Tunnel was heavily washed. Twelve men under Mr. Kelly were effecting repairs in this vicinity. At the head of the Four-Mile Level near Lock No. 61 a waste weir was swept away, and the towpath was carried out to a depth of two to four feet. On the Seven-Mile Bottom above Lock No. 71 one-half mile of the towpath was carried away to a depth of two to four feet. There was a break in the canal banks at Burns Hollow some 40 feet in length and 3 feet in depth. The towpath was damaged, and there was a considerable fill in the prism. A force of 50 men and 20 carts under Messrs. Hottenhouser and Young were at work making these repairs.[145]

On May 9 a third flood struck the Potomac Valley, causing further destruction to the canal and retarding the repairs that were in progress. The most significant damage resulting from this freshet occurred at Dam No. 6 where an additional 62 feet were added to the gaping hole in the structure.[146]

To meet the costs of the restoration of the canal after the floods of 1886, the company began to sell the remaining repair bonds of 1878 without restraint. On April 22, it ordered the firm of Robert T. Baldwin, or his assignees, Robert A. Garrett and Sons, to exercise the option to purchase $71,000 of the bonds at 80.[147] This transaction, along with an earlier sale of $189,000 of the bonds at 86 to the same firm in September 1885, ultimately gave control of the bonds to the Baltimore & Ohio Railroad.[148] John Hambleton and Company bought $75,000 of the bonds in August 1887 at 78, and the final sale, at the end of the year, was for $38,000 at 76.[149] By that time a total of $498,000 of the bonds had been sold.[150]

The bonds were particularly desirable, for they carried a preferred mortgage on the physical property of the canal. By the mid-1880s the administration of the canal under its present management was believed by many to be of short duration. In the reorganization that would follow its bankruptcy, the waterway would probably be sold. Hence the bonds were a good investment. Railroad companies, particularly the Baltimore & Ohio and the West Virginia Central, eyed the canal right of way as a possible roadbed, and thus were especially interested for the control of the 1878 bonds could force the sale of the canal in the bankruptcy proceedings. Accordingly, the two railroad companies and their agents began buying up the bonds, but when the West Virginia interests discovered that the Baltimore & Ohio already possessed a majority they suspended their purchases.[151]

The canal was repaired so that the waterway was again in limited operation by early June, although much of the more substantial masonry work was postponed until the coming winter

---

[145] *Proceedings of the President and Board of Directors*, N, 329–332. Also see *Fifty-Eighth Annual Report* (1886), C & O Co., 15–17, 23–26.
[146] *Fifty-Ninth Annual Report* (1887), 25.
[147] *Proceedings of the President and board of Directors*, N, 332–333.
[148] Ibid., N, 317–319, and Washington *Evening Star*, June 6, 1889.
[149] *Proceedings of the President and Board of Directors*, N, 338–339, 344, 348–349.
[150] *Fifty-Ninth Annual Report* (1887), 6.
[151] Washington *Evening Star*, June 6, 1889.

months. The most complex repair work was at Dam No. 6. After considering the plans and specifications for the total reconstruction of the dam submitted by Robert M. Martin, the Water Engineer of the City of Baltimore, it was determined that the structure should merely be repaired by company laborers under the supervision of canal engineers. The operations on the dam were completed in the latter part of the summer at a cost of nearly $45,000.[152]

MAY–JUNE 1889

Between May 30 and June 1, 1889, a titanic flood swept the Potomac, the crest of which was higher than any ever before recorded in the history of the valley. On the upper Potomac in Maryland, there were 50 lives lost and more than $2,000,000 worth of property was destroyed. The devastation left in the wake of the flood was described graphically in *Appletons' Annual Cyclopedia and Register* (1889):

> There was not a mountain or rivulet in the western part of the State which was not transformed into a freshet. Scores of villages, some of them containing important manufactories, were inundated, and thousands of acres of farm lands were laid waste. The loss by ruined bridges, washouts and land slides of the Western Division of the Baltimore & Ohio road reached more than half a million dollars.... The Western Maryland Railroad and its connecting lines, the Baltimore and Harrisburg and the Cumberland Valley roads were extensively damaged by washouts and destruction of bridges over a length of about sixty miles. Hundreds of square miles in the vicinity of Hagerstown and Shippensburg and in the Cumberland valley were submerged and many thousand cattle drowned. The overflow of the Monocacy and its branches at the mountain town of Frederick was the cause of widespread havoc in the city and the surrounding farming region. The water rose thirty feet above its level at the railroad bridge, and most of the city was submerged. The loss in Frederick County was about $300,000. At Williamsport the railroads were entirely washed away, and the new iron bridge over the Potomac totally destroyed....On the Shenandoah and Potomac near Harpers Ferry hundreds of houses were swept away by the wrath of the waters, which came roaring down through the narrow gorges forty feet in height....Along the South Mountains in Washington and Allegheny counties the havoc was great and the loss of life considerable, and $100,000 worth of property was swept away at Point of Rocks. All the bridges of Frederick County...were destroyed.[153]

The flood began with a disturbance that was described as a cyclone which entered the valley near Martinsburg, West Virginia, and crossed the river a few miles above Williamsport before crossing back into West Virginia at Falling Waters.[154] It was followed by heavy rains which swelled the Potomac until it poured over its banks. At Cumberland the water rose both in the main river and in Wills Creek until it completely submerged the land between them. At Hancock, it reached a point three feet above previous records set in 1877. At Williamsport, the crest was 44-1/3 feet above the low-water mark, 7½ feet above 1877 levels. The junction of the Potomac and the Conococheague was described as a huge lake, and Aqueduct No. 5 was out of sight. At Harpers Ferry, it rose to the height of 34 feet above the low-water stage and 21 feet above the towpath. At its peak, the water was 2.8 feet above the Baltimore & Ohio rails on the Harpers Ferry Bridge and

---

[152] *Proceedings of the President and Board of Directors*, N, 335–336, 338.
[153] *Appletons' Annual Cyclopedia and Register of Important Events of the Year 1889* (New York, 1890), 531–532.
[154] Washington *Evening Star*, June 1, 1889.

6.8 feet higher than the 1877 freshet. Just below Harpers Ferry at Sandy Hook, the water reached a point 8 feet higher than the railroad tracks which were 17 feet above the canal itself.[155]

On the lower portion of the canal the river also reached new heights. At Great Falls, the river rose 16 feet above the top surface of the coping on the dam and 4 feet higher than in the 1877 freshet. At Chain Bridge where strong southeasterly winds made the tides unusually high, it was 43.3 feet above tide level. Further down the canal, the river reached 19.5 feet and 13.3 feet at the Potomac Aqueduct and Easby's Wharf in Georgetown respectively. At the latter location, the crest was three feet above the level of the 1877 flood. In the District of Columbia the river remained within 3 feet of its maximum height for a period of 24 hours and within 6 feet of it for about 30 hours.[156]

The damage caused by the rampaging river was fully as impressive as the record heights established by the flood. The canal below Harpers Ferry was especially hard-hit. It was reported to be:

> One of the peculiarities of the freshet of 1889 was that the stone-work of the walls, &c., is more generally involved than on any previous occasion of the kind. The telephone wires have been swept away ...and every bridge for which the canal company is responsible is down.[157]

The flood waters carried away canal boats, teams and cargoes, destroying 176 barges or depositing them crazily along both sides of the valley.[158] The swirling current also damaged mills, warehouses and wharf facilities along the canal and at Georgetown.[159]

Within ten days the canal board received extensive reports on the damage done to the waterway by Superintendent Ed Mulvaney and J. P. Biser. The two men noted that Rock Creek Dam had been destroyed. Its wing walls had been washed out, and a hole 125 feet wide had been torn in its center. The 15-foot-high, 5-foot-wide protecting wall from the dam to a point 700 feet up Rock Creek was largely decimated. The mole and the towpath at the basin were washed badly, and the basin itself was filled with some 1,200 cubic yards of deposit. The steam dredge and all the scows on the Georgetown Level were gone. One-half mile above the Georgetown Tidelock, there was a breach in the canal banks 125 feet long and 11 feet below the bottom of the trunk. Opposite to Little Falls Church there was a break 200 feet long and 12 feet below the canal bottom; below Chain Bridge there was a break 600 feet long and 4 feet below the canal bottom. From the latter westward for 1,000 feet the towpath was deeply washed. At Chain Bridge there was a break 100 feet long and 12 feet deep, and from the bridge to Lock No. 5 the towpath was

---

[155] Sanderlin, *The Great National Project*, 256; U.S. Congress, House, Committee on Public Lands, *Chesapeake & Ohio Canal Report*, H. Doc. 687, 81st Congress, 2nd Session, 1950, 56; and U.S. Geological Survey, *The Potomac River Basin* (Washington, 1907), 181–182. Numerous newspaper accounts also tell the story of the flood. Among the most important are Cumberland *Evening Times*, May 30, June 1, 1889; Frederick *Examiner*, June 5, 1889; and Hagerstown *Mail*, June 7, 1889.

[156] U.S. Geological Survey, *Potomac River Basin*, 181–182, and Washington *Evening Star*, June 1, 1889. At its maximum height, the mean velocity of the water in the river at the Potomac Aqueduct was 12.4 feet per second. It was estimated that the discharge of the river at Chain Bridge reached a peak of 470,000 second-feet and that the discharge of Rock Creek reached a peak of nearly 25,000 second-feet.

[157] Cumberland *Evening Times*, June 11, 1889, quoted in Sanderlin, *The Great National Project*, 257.

[158] Washington *Evening Star*, June 1 and 3, 1889, and *Report of Ed Mulvaney and S. D. Young to Board of Public Works*, Washington County, May 13, 1890, C & O Canal Company Records, Receivership Papers, Washington County (MD) Courthouse. Of the 176 boats, 156 were loaded with coal, 11 with lime and stone and 9 with grain.

[159] Washington *Evening Star*, June 1 and 3, 1889.

washed to a depth of 2½ feet. At Lock No. 5 220 feet of coping was carried away, and the entire backing behind the lock walls was ripped out. The flume was washed out as wide and deep as the canal itself and the gates damaged. The guard bank, the feeder, and the feeder gates were badly injured. The height of Dam No. 1 had been reduced by 18 inches. Near Lock No. 5 the waybill office was swept away and the lockhouse partially damaged.

The towpath between Locks Nos. 5 and 7 was heavily washed, and Locks Nos. 6–8 were nearly destroyed, their lockhouses washed out, and their gates carried away. Cabin John Culvert was damaged, but the majority of the Seven Locks area was unhurt. On the "Log Wall Level" there was a break near the clubhouse 150 feet long and 30 feet deep, and the 60-foot-high retaining wall on the river side had been carried away. Some 300 yards above this break at the mouth of Widewater there was a break 500 feet long, 80 feet wide, and 32 feet deep, and the 60-foot-high retaining wall was gone. To repair this one breach it was estimated that 160,000 cartloads of material would be required for filling. Just above this break were three separate breaches: one 325 feet long, 40 feet wide and 6 feet below the canal bottom; one 180 feet long and 30 feet deep; one 80 feet long and 20 feet deep; and one 310 feet long and 10 feet deep. The Log Wall Bridge was gone, and the 20-foot-wall supporting the towpath was washed away for the distance of 1,000 yards.

At Locks Nos. 15 and 16 the stone lockhouses were swept away, as were the coping, backing, gates and flume of the two locks. The stop lock above Lock No. 16 had been wrecked and its embankment damaged. Locks Nos. 17–19 were considerably injured along with their flumes, and the lockhouse at Lock No. 17 was gone while that at Lock No. 18 was partially standing. Nearly every house between the canal and the river from Chain Bridge to Great Falls had been swept away; the only structure still standing in that area was the Sycamore Island Clubhouse.

The damage to the canal at Great Falls included a break 50 feet long and 3 feet below the bottom. Some 300 yards above this spot, there were two large breaks—one 250 feet long and the other 300 feet long and 8 feet deep. More than 2 feet were washed off the towpath for a distance of 2 miles.

Locks Nos. 23 and 24 were badly washed, and approximately 3,000 perches of stone in Dam No. 2 had been swept away. Opposite to the Seneca Red Stone Quarry just above Seneca Creek there was a break in the towpath and berm 150 feet long and 4 feet below the bottom. In the vicinity of Horse Pen Culvert there were two large deposits of mud and debris in the trunk, one of 5,000 cubic yards and the other of 1,200.

At Edwards Ferry the pivot bridge and the company carpenter shop were gone and a loaded barge was lying across Lock No. 25. Just above the ferry another road bridge was swept away. Near the Haunted House there was a break 20 feet long and 4 feet deep. The east end of Aqueduct No. 2 had a break 40 feet long, and the horse dredge at that location had been carried away. There were heavy bars in the levels between Locks Nos. 24 and 25, 25 and 26, and 27 and 28.

From Point of Rocks to Weverton, the locks and lockhouses were slightly damaged and numerous bars were filling the prism. Lock No. 31 was nearly destroyed and just above it there was a 50-foot-wide break. The towpath from Weverton to Sandy Hook was badly damaged. At Sandy Hook the entire cluster of company buildings—carpenter shop, blacksmith shop, sheds, cart houses, storehouses and dwelling house—were carried away along with a number of lock gates, carts and tools. Lock No. 32 was carried away except for its chamber walls, and its flume was washed out. From the Lock to above the Harpers Ferry Bridge the towpath and heavy river walls were destroyed for the distance of one mile, the river and canal being one body of water for the majority of this length. The Shenandoah River Lock was totally destroyed. The company boarding house, the lockhouse and the storehouse near Lock No. 33 were all carried away. Locks

Nos. 34–36 were all badly injured, and the entire towpath between Locks Nos. 33–36 was washed out. Guard Lock No. 3 was filled with stone and gravel, and the guard banks at Dam No. 3 were badly damaged. Above Lock No. 36 there was a break 125 feet long and 8 feet below the bottom.

The chamber of Lock No. 37 was filled with mud, and a large culvert nearby was entirely gone. In addition there were many washes and bars between Lock No. 36 and the Shepherdstown River Lock. The carpenter shop with its stores of lumber and lock gates at Shepherdstown was swept away. Above Shepherdstown the face and top of Lock No. 39 were damaged, and there was a 50-foot-long break on the level between Locks Nos. 39 and 40.

At Lock No. 40 the gates were gone, the backing was washed out, the chamber was filled with 3 feet of mud, and the recently-built lockhouse was swept away. On the same level the company boarding house and other buildings were gone. There was a break on the feeder level below Dam No. 4 some 60 feet long and 8 feet below the bottom. At Guard Lock No. 4, the gates were gone, the backing was washed out, the chamber was filled with mud, and the new lockhouse was swept away. The stop lock and the nearby lockhouse were entirely gone. In the protection banks between the stop lock and the Dam No. 4 feeder, there were 10 breaks totaling 1,260 feet in length, 37 feet in width, and 11 feet in depth. The gates and lockhouse at Lock No. 42 were destroyed. In the vicinity of Opequon Creek midway between Locks Nos. 42 and 43 there was a break 75 feet long and the towpath was washed 2½ feet for the distance of one mile. All along this level there were heavy deposits of sand in the trunk.

On the level below Lock No. 44 the towpath was damaged and there was considerable filling in the canal. The towpath on nearly all of the Williamsport Level was badly washed, and the towpath bank at the town had a slip on its river side about 100 feet long and 20 feet wide. Almost one-half of the slope had been carried away, and the banks were cracked for several hundred feet above the slip. Much of the town had been under water including the canal basin and Aqueduct No. 5, but the company works generally had survived.

Lock No. 45 received considerable damage, and between Locks Nos. 46 and 47 the towpath was washed from 1 to 4 feet for the distance of one mile. Much material was deposited in the canal trunk on this level. Between Four Locks and Hancock the towpath was washed to depths up to 4 feet for the distance of several miles. Below Aqueduct No. 6 there was a 100-foot-long break. There was a breach 100 feet long and 6 feet below the bottom in the vicinity of Fort Frederick, and below Big Pool there was a similar 100-foot-long break. On the Hancock Level the towpath was badly washed for half its length. Lock No. 53 was damaged badly and its adjacent lockhouse washed away. On the level above the lock the towpath was nearly swept away. The sheathing was torn from the old part of Dam No. 6 for a considerable distance, and about 100 feet of the cribs on the new dam just below it were gone. The gates of Lock No. 55 and Guard Lock No. 6 were injured severely.

At Sideling Hill Creek the towpath was carried away for a mile and deposited in the canal. There was a 60-foot-long break in the towpath near Aqueduct No. 8 and another 50-foot break at Lock No. 56. The towpath on the Little Orleans Level was damaged greatly, and there was a 100-foot break below Aqueduct No. 9. Above Little Orleans the towpath was washed badly, and the trunk was filled for 200 yards by slips from the mountain side and by 4 large trees. When the obstruction was cleared, thousands of cubic yards of additional material would slide down. Below Paw Paw Tunnel virtually 3 miles of the towpath has been washed into the canal. Between the tunnel and Town Creek there were two 100-foot breaks in the towpath. The wooden trunk and culvert at Aqueduct No. 10 were gone.

Above Town Creek there was little significant damage to the waterway except for three breaks and some heavy silt deposits in the prism. Near Kelly's Road Culvert (some 4 miles above Lock No. 71) there was a 60-foot breach, and the canal was filled with mud. On the level above

Lock No. 75 there were two smaller cuts in the banks. There was no significant damage reported at Cumberland.[160]

Preliminary reports estimated the damage to the canal at from $500,000 to $1,000,000.[161] These early estimates were soon reduced officially to $250,000 or $300,000 in a special report to the Washington County Court by President Stephen Gambrill on June 13.[162] However, when the canal company admitted that it could not raise the necessary funds for the restoration of the waterway the stage was set for the canal to go into a receivership with the Baltimore & Ohio Railroad emerging as the majority owner of both the 1878 and the 1844 bonds, thereby giving it control of the preferred mortgages on the physical property and the revenues of the canal.

While a final determination was pending in the Washington County Court on the precise nature of the receivership, a contract was let on June 20 to George W. Cissell, Arthur B. Crossley, Robert B. Tenney, W. H. Burr and F. L. Moore to restore the Georgetown Level. Fearful of the ruinous economic consequences to their businesses if their source of water was not quickly restored, these four millers agreed to advance $16,000 to the company for the repairs, the loan to be repaid out of rents under existing water leases.[163] Among the terms of the contract were the following:

> The said parties of the first part [the Georgetown millers] do covenant and agree with the party of the second part [the C&O Co.], that they will rebuild and put in good condition and repair all that part of the canal ... which lies between Lock No. 4 and Lock No. 5 including the Feeder Lock & Gate, and the Feeder itself ...rebuild the guard bank at said Feeder, to its original height and width, rebuild the tow-path, with good material with banks properly sloped on either side and worked up in the bottom, whenever there is new work on said banks, so that a perfect connection may be formed between said new & old work, having along the center of said bank, whenever made from the bottom of the breaks and washouts to the top of said towpath a core of not less than six feet in width made of good clay; the sides of said towpath next to the water of said Canal to be paved with large flat stones closely laid together whenever the breaks and washes go through the banks of the Canal, and the side next to the river to be well rip rapped with stones wherever the breaks and washes so through the banks of the Canal; and generally to restore said part of said canal to the condition in which it was before the freshets of May & June, 1889, that is to say, with sufficient water to float loaded boats to the coal wharves.
>
> The parties of the first part covenant and agree that whenever it shall be necessary they will rebuild and make watertight, with good cement and stone all culverts along said level.[164]

The repairs were effected by August 1, and water was readmitted into the Georgetown Level to provide the mills with their necessary supply of water.[165]

Similar work was done locally on the Williamsport and Cumberland Levels while the courts determined the legal framework of the receivership. On March 3, 1890, the Washington

---

[160] Baltimore *Sun*, June 11, 1889; Washington *Evening Star*, June 1 and 3, 1889; *Proceedings of the president and Board of Directors*, N, 415; and *Report of Mulvaney and Young to Board of Public Works*, May 13, 1890, Receivership Papers.

[161] Washington *Evening Star*, June 3 and 4, 1889.

[162] *Special Report to the President and Directors*, June 13, 1889, in Circuit Court for Washington County, *George S. Brown, et. al. vs. Chesapeake & Ohio Canal Company* (Equity No. 4191), 9.

[163] Washington *Evening Star*, June 4, 4 & 8, 1889.

[164] *Proceedings of the President and Board of Directors*, N, 415–418.

[165] *Ibid.*, N, 418–419.

County Court appointed receivers, and on June 9, these individuals filed optimistic estimates that the total cost of restoration would be $268,698, including the repairs already effected.[166]

Following the legal proceedings, the Baltimore & Ohio Railroad undertook the restoration of the waterway. The actual work of repair, which commenced in the autumn of 1890, took much longer and was more expensive than had been anticipated. At least part of the additional cost of the work was due to the delay in beginning repairs as "it was found that the eighteen months during which the canal was practically abandoned and dried out had added much to the damage caused by the flood of 1889, and had also weakened the canal at points untouched by the flood."[167] Water was not readmitted into the entire length of the canal until August 1891, and traffic did not begin to move on the waterway until September 1. However, repairs continued to be made until the spring of 1893 when the trustees announced that the "canal is now in better condition as a waterway than ever before in its history." The canal had a 6-foot depth throughout its length, and "as a consequence the average loading of the boats was heavier during the last boating season [1893] than ever before." The total cost of the restoration of the canal was $430,764.43, all of which had to be borrowed from outside sources.[168]

ESTIMATES OF COSTS OF REPAIRS OF 1889 FLOOD DAMAGE	
From Cumberland to Dam No. 6	$10,988.00
Repair to Dam No. 6	10,850.00
From Dam No. 6 to Lock No. 44	6,140.00
From Lock No. 44 to Dam No. 4	2,688.00
From Dam No. 4 to Lock No. 36	37,116.00
From Lock No. 36 to Lock No.32	22,503.00
From Lock No. 32 to Lock No. 20	9,511.00
From Lock No. 20 to Lock No. 15	8,694.00
From Lock No. 15 to Lock No. 14	37,057.00
From Lock No. 14 to D. C. Line	4,638.00
	$150,185.00
20% Contingencies	30,033.00
Cost of lumber, carpenters work, lock houses, repairing locks, flumes, waste weirs, lock gates and other wooden structures	45,000.00
Repairs to canal in District of Columbia	15,000.00
Repairs to Cumberland wharf	1,000.00
Repairs to telephone line	7,500.00
Contingencies	20,000.00
	$268,698.00

---

[166] 2nd Report of Receivers, June 9, 1890, in *Brown et al. vs. Chesapeake & Ohio Canal Company*, 111–133. A copy of the breakdown of the cost of restoring the waterway may be seen on page 45.
[167] Report of Trustees, January 30, 1894, in *the State of Maryland vs. John K. Cowen et al., Trustees*, June 17, 1896, *Maryland Reports* (1896), LXXXIII, 552–553.
[168] Ibid.

III: THE FLOODS: 1897–1936

1897, 1902, 1907, 1914

In his *The Great National Project,* Walter S. Sanderlin writes that after 1889 freshets occurred with depressing regularity, the most serious ones in 1897, 1902, 1907 and 1914." Using George Nicolson, the General Manager and Superintendent of the canal from 1891 to 1938, as his source, Sanderlin further elaborates that:

> The work of repair and restoration went on unceasingly. As soon as the rough spots from one freshet were smoothed out, another would bring in new bars, cause new breaches and wash the towpath again. None of the floods, however, was so disastrous that the railroad hesitated to repair the damage, and none approached the proportions of the freshets of 1877 and 1889.[169]

MARCH 1924

On March 29, 1924, the first major flood in 35 years swept down the Potomac Valley and wrecked the canal. Melting snow and heavy rains caused the Potomac and its tributaries, especially the Shenandoah, to rise and overflow their banks. For the first time in the history of the valley, newspaper editorials placed partial blame for the flood on the heavy timber cutting that had greatly denuded the Allegheny Mountain watershed in western Maryland. A brief cold snap, highlighted by a 10-inch snowfall in the upper valley, momentarily halted the rise of the Potomac on March 30, and even reversed it. The next day the river rose again, but by that time the threat of a major disaster similar to that of 1889 was past, as much of the run-off had occurred. A survey of the damage in the valley revealed that the flood was not nearly so serious as had been feared. The freshet, which centered its destruction primarily in the upper reaches of the valley, was of short duration and caused comparatively slight damage outside the canal.[170]

Heavy rains at Cumberland on March 29 swelled the Potomac River and Wills Creek so that the two mounted at a rate of 30 inches an hour to levels approaching the record crest of 1889. The water continued to rise until nearly one-half of the city was under 15 to 20 feet of water by the following day. Just east of the Western Maryland Railroad station the river crumbled away the embankment separating it from the canal and washed away some $50,000 worth of timber from the Cessna Lumber Company southward toward the canal basin in Shantytown. The wharves at the basin were partially destroyed, and the canal banks greatly washed. When the flood waters began to fall much of the town, along with the canal, were left lying under a deposit of mud up to 2 feet deep. All told, Cumberland, the worst-hit town in the valley, suffered a property loss of some $3,000,000.[171]

---

[169] Sanderlin, *The Great National Project,* 276.
[170] Frank Moore Colby and Herbert Treadwell Wade, eds., *The New International Year Book* (New York, 1925), 249. Local newspaper accounts also described the general nature and extent of the flood, among the most important of which were the Hagerstown *Daily Mail,* March 29 & 31, 1924, and the Hagerstown *Morning Herald,* April 1 & 3, 1924.
[171] *The Washington Post,* March 30 & 31, 1924, Washington *Evening Star,* March 29, 30 & 31, 1924. The Baltimore & Ohio and the Western Maryland Railroads suffered extensive losses to their lines in Cumberland and in the region to the west. All of the railroad bridges across the Potomac between Cumberland and Westernport were swept away. Some 26 miles of track belonging to the Baltimore & Ohio were uprooted while the Western Maryland lost 40 carloads of freight. Many of the mines in the Georges Creek coal region were forced to close.

Tremendous damage also occurred at Hancock where the canal and three-fourths of the town was wholly or partially submerged by the water. All the railroad and canal bridges in the vicinity were destroyed, and the canal banks and masonry were badly washed.[172]

At Williamsport the river reached a point 28 feet above normal, seven feet below the peak of the 1889 flood. Although no major injuries were inflicted on Dams Nos. 4 and 5, the Potomac Edison Company's substations at both points were put out of commission as was the main plant at Williamsport. The water covered the entire length of the canal trunk on the Williamsport Division, obliterating the banks and tearing the masonry.[173]

Despite the high water, the lower valley communities escaped serious damage. However, the canal was not so fortunate as many miles of its banks and its masonry were badly washed, particularly below the Shenandoah and the Monocacy, both of which rose some 20 feet above normal. At Little Falls the crashing waves of the river reached a height of 20 feet, opening a 50-foot-long and 12-foot-deep gap in the canal banks at Dam No. 1 and causing one breach below the dam and another at Guard Lock No. 1. At Washington, the river crested 8 feet above the normal high tide level, but there was no flooding in the city.[174]

The flood of 1924 provided the opportunity for the Baltimore & Ohio Railroad to relieve itself of the expense of operating the canal. The receivers made no effort to restore the canal beyond the Georgetown Level. So that the Georgetown millers could quickly have their necessary supply of water restored, a contract was let to the Vang Construction Company on April 1 to repair the 50-foot cut at Dam No. 1, while canal workmen closed the breaches below the dam and at the guard lock.[175]

Aside from these repairs, the receivers authorized enough restoration work in the years 1924-26 to protect what was left of the waterway and to enable them to assert that the canal could quickly be put into navigable condition if sufficient business was presented to warrant the effort.[176] The canal was left a wreck, but technically a going concern in which the water rents received from the Georgetown manufacturers paid the expenses of the small operating staff. The court accepted the position of the receivers, and ruled that the canal had not forfeited its rights by non-operation, but that the other aspect of its business, the maintenance of a canal for navigation purposes, was merely suspended temporarily in the absence of remunerative business.

MARCH 1936

A sudden thaw in the wintry temperatures throughout the eastern United States from Maryland to the Canadian border in mid-March 1936 led to the heaviest flood in the recorded history of the Potomac Valley. While the loss of life was comparatively slight, numerous buildings, roads and bridges were destroyed. The Potomac not only flooded its upper reaches to epic proportions, but for the first time in living memory, it went out of its banks along its southern border and caused extensive damage almost down to the Atlantic.[177]

The flood surpassed all previous high-water marks in the Potomac Valley. In Georgetown the river crested seven inches higher than it had in 1889 and at Little Falls it was one foot higher. At Seneca the crest was nine inches higher than in 1889. The flood covered the canal at Point of Rocks to a depth of 17 feet for a period of 54 hours, both of which statistics exceeded those of

---

[172] Washington *Evening Star*, March 31, 1924.
[173] *Ibid.*
[174] *The Washington Post*, April 1, 1924; Washington *Evening Star*, March 31 and April 2, 1924; Colby and Wade, *New International Year Book*, 249; and Frederick *Post*, April 1 & 2, 1924.
[175] Washington *Evening Star*, April 2, 1924.
[176] Reports of Trustees for 1924, 1925 and 1926m Receivership Papers.
[177] Frank H. Vizetelly, ed., *The New International Year Book* (New York, 1937), 432.

1889. At Harpers Ferry the water rose to an elevation of 21 feet above the towpath, a similar height to that attained in 1889. The canal at Shepherdstown was inundated for 62 hours, and at its peak the flood reached an elevation of 22 feet above the towpath, a height exceeding the 1889 figure by five feet. In the vicinity of Four Locks, the river rose 10 feet above its 1889 crest. At Hancock the river covered the towpath to a depth of some 7 to 8 feet for a period of 24 hours, while the peak of the flood at Cumberland covered the canal with 3 to 4 feet of water for 12 hours.[178]

The heavy flood wrecked havoc on the now-deserted canal and left it in the dilapidated condition in which it was found when the federal government acquired it two years later. A survey of the flood damage follows:

1. On the Georgetown Level, the banks washed and the prism was heavily silted.
2. Much of Dam No. 1 was destroyed down to its foundation, and the feeder was filled with trees, debris and silt.
3. There is no available documentation relative to the damage between Lock No. 5 and Seneca Creek.
4. There were two breaks on the Eight Mile Level above Lock No. 24, one of which was just above Aqueduct No. 1 and the other near the Beaver Dam Culvert.
5. The abutments of the bridge across the canal at Noland's Ferry were washed into the trunk.
6. The company house and all outbuildings at Point of Rocks were swept away.
7. The bridge across Lock No. 30 at Brunswick was washed out.
8. There was a small washout at Sandy Hook. The blacksmith shop at that place was entirely gone, and the carpenter shop was partially destroyed. The machinery had been saved out of the latter shop.
9. The level between Locks, Nos. 32 and 33 was utterly devastated. The guard wall, bank and towpath for 200 to 300 feet below the Harpers Ferry Bridge was badly washed, and there was much torn stonework lying in the trunk.
10. At Lock no. 33, the brick lockhouse which had withstood the 1889 flood was destroyed. The lock chamber walls were heavily damaged, the filling around the lock was washed out, and the gates were swept away.
11. The towpath between Locks Nos. 33 and 34 was not badly damaged, but the trunk was filled with mud, debris and gravel. At Lock No. 34 the gates were washed out and the brick lockhouse was destroyed. Below the lock the guard bank was heavily washed.
12. The level between Locks Nos. 34 and 35 was heavily damaged. A considerable portion of Dam No. 3 was gone. At the feeder there were two breaches in the guard bank, the largest of which was 40 feet long and 25 feet deep. The top of the guard bank was badly washed, and many perches of stone from the wall next to the river and the breaks in the guard bank had been deposited in the feeder. The towpath was left in a ragged condition for several hundred feet below the dam. The section of the canal between Lock No. 34 and Dam No. 3 was filled with rock, mud and debris.
13. Little damage was inflicted on the canal from Lock No. 36 to Shepherdstown, except for some injuries to the lock gates. However, all the river bridges at Shepherdstown were washed out, and the bridge over the canal there was carried

---

[178] House Document 687, 56, 58 and Index to Correspondence, Office of Trustees.

downstream and lodged in the river lock. The upper gates of the river lock were still good, but one of the lower ones had been washed out. The lockhouse at Lock No. 38 was partially destroyed when a heavy drift knocked in its northwest corner.

14. Between Shepherdstown and Dam No. 4 all the buildings along the line of the canal were swept away, including the lockhouse at Lock No. 40.

15. Dam No. 4 received serious damage during the flood. Earlier on February 27 an ice drift had carried away a section of the dam near the Maryland abutment. The March flood widened the break, and when the water subsided it was found that the gap started at a point about 45 feet from the Maryland abutment and averaged 55 feet in width. The guard bank at the dam was little damaged, but the cross bank at the nearby stop lock was more seriously affected. Both approaches to Guard Lock No. 4 were destroyed. The lockhouse at Lock No. 41, which had withstood the 1889 freshet, was swept away.

16. Extensive damage was caused by the flood at Williamsport. The carpenter shop was pushed down across the flume at Lock No. 44, and its floor had dropped out. The nearby corn shed had collapsed. All canal buildings, except for one old company house, were gone. The lockhouse at Lock No. 44 had been under water to within three feet of its eaves, but it was still standing. Just below the town, the house at Lock No. 43 and the Falling Waters Bridge were gone.

17. Between Williamsport and Dam No. 5 there were no washouts, and the former company house on this level survived the storm. There was a large quantity of sand in the trunk at Miller's Bend, and the bridge at Dam no. 5 was swept away.

18. From Dam No. 5 to Big Pool there was considerable damage to the canal. The mule crossover bridge at Lock No. 46 was knocked into the trunk below. At Lock No. 47 the lockhouse, which had withstood the 1889 freshet, was destroyed.

19. At Big Pool there were three large breaks in the embankments: one was 4 feet deep and 10 feet long near the railroad bridge; a second was from 1 to 5 feet deep from the waste way to the foot of the pool; and a third extended for a length of 35 feet and a depth of 10 feet around the stop lock.

20. The wooden trunk that had been placed on Aqueduct No. 6 in the 1870s was nearly gone.

21. The canal was heavily damaged in the vicinity of Round Top Cement Mill. There was one breach about 30 feet long and 3 to 4 feet below the bottom. Nearly two feet was washed off the towpath for a considerable distance.

22. Approximately, one-half of Dam No, 6 was gone, while the sheeting of the remaining half was carried away. The lockhouses at Locks Nos. 53 and 55 were destroyed.

23. The mule [s/b pedestrian?] bridge near Aqueduct No. 8 [Sideling Hill] was carried away, as was the berm side of the aqueduct itself.

24. From Aqueduct No. 8 to Town Creek, the lockhouses at Locks Nos. 58, 59, 60, 61 and 67, which had survived the 1889 freshet, were gone. The top of the towpath near the railroad bridge above Paw Paw Tunnel was washed off to a depth of two feet for a distance of 100 yards. The trunk on this section was filled with a sand bar three feet deep and 250 feet long. Some of the masonry on Aqueduct No. 10 was torn off and carried away.

25. From Town Creek to Lock No. 72, there was considerable damage. The lockhouse at Lock No. 68 was undermined, and the chamber of Lock No. 71 and a

nearby waste weir were clogged with debris. There were two large breaks; one was 30 feet long and 8 feet below the trunk bottom, while the other was 25 feet long and 4 feet deep. The top of the towpath at Spring Gap was badly washed. The approach to the Patterson Creek Bridge was washed away to a depth of six feet for a distance of 25 feet. The pump house just below Lock No. 72 had bulged out toward the canal.

26. Between Lock No. 75 and Cumberland, there were three heavy washes of the towpath in the vicinity of Wiley Ford Bridge, covering a total of 350 feet and varying from two to three feet in depth. There was one small break, some 20 feet wide and 2 feet below the bottom, at the head of Dougherty's Widewater. The lockhouse at Lock No. 75 lost much of its foundation, and a combined culvert-waste weir 1½ miles below Evitts Creek was choked with debris. The old stop lock below the Cumberland Basin was undermined by a 15-foot-wide and 3-foot-deep washout on its towpath side. The concrete slab below Dam No. 8 was partially removed.[179]

Some repairs were effected on the canal after the flood waters subsided. The loose stone and rubble dam at Little Falls was restored so that the Georgetown business interests would have their necessary water supply. In addition the banks of the Georgetown Level were renovated, and trees, debris and mud were removed from the Little Falls Feeder. All told, these repairs were completed by early December at a cost of $25,460.05.[180]

In the spring of 1936 the Potomac Edison Company was requested by the canal trustees to let a contract and to supervise the work of repairing Dam No. 4.[181] The firm of Sanderson and Porter commenced the work on July 13. Among the repairs that were effected was the use of 595 cubic yards of "High-Early Strength" cement to close the break and the construction of a concrete cap-piece with a curved top over the entire dam. The latter project, which required 730 cubic yards of cement, was built to provide "a stream-lined effect" that would "discharge flood waters faster and back up flood waters less than the old angular ice-guards."[182]

---

[179] Wine to Nicolson, March 19 and April 10, 1936, Burgan to Nicolson, March 21, 24 & 30, 1936, Shivas to Nicolson, March 22, 1936, Everitts to Nicolson, March 25, 1936, Fisher to Nicolson, March 25, 1936, Sterling to Nicolson, [ca. March 30, 1936], and Anonymous Report to [Nicolson], [ca. April 1, 1936], Ltrs. Recd., Office of Trustees; Nicolson to Horton, December 19, 1936, and Nicolson to Preston, December 4, 1936, Ltrs. Sent, Office of Trustees; and Martin J. Umer, *Report on 1936 Repairs and Improvements at Dam No. 4, December 10, 1936* (Misc. Mss., Office of Trustees).

[180] Nicolson to Preston, December 4, 1936, Ltrs. Sent, Office of Trustees.

[181] The cause of the break in the dam was attributed to two theories. One theory was that the break started at the bottom of the dam. This idea was supported by the fact that the greatest amount of leakage had been at the section which failed for years and some subsidence at this point had been apparent. The second theory, which held that the break started at the top of the dam, was supported by three facts: a floating tree had been seen carrying away part of the structure's crest; the February drift ice had removed some of the timber ice guards; and the solid rock ledge under the dam showed no signs of scarring or undermining. Since the masonry had been laid with soft lime mortar and the interior consisted of weaker rubble masonry, it was determined that the second theory was more plausible. Umer, *Report on 1936 Repairs and Improvements at Dam No. 4*, (Misc. Mss., Office of Trustees).

[182] *Ibid.*

IV. CONCLUSION

One of the principal reasons for the collapse of the canal was the recurrence of great floods which repeatedly wrecked the waterway. The forces of nature were continually at work tearing down the physical fabric of the waterway and interfering with its trade. Despite the fact that most of the canal was in the flood plain of the Potomac, approximately 90 percent of it was built above the normal annual high-water level of the river. Yet a heavy rain or a small freshet at any time was likely to wash sand bars into the waterway, cause land or rock slides, undermine culverts, and cause breaches in the embankments. The canal company was never able to cope effectively with these natural occurrences. The most careful and expensive preparations would be undone in several days by a freak storm or by an abnormal rise in the river caused by melting snow, thawing ice, or heavy rain.

The worst of all the destructive forces of nature were the periodic Floods in the Potomac Valley. As the area became deforested and more and more ground was cleared for cultivation and settlement, the run-off became greater and swifter. Simultaneously, the Potomac was filling up as a result of the silt deposits in its bed, and the canal and the railroads were encroaching on the river channel at many points, particularly at the narrow passes of the stream. As a result of these developments, the major floods in the valley occurred more frequently, reached increasingly higher levels, and caused greater destructiveness. This emerging pattern can be seen in the substantial freshets of 1836, 1843, 1846, 1847, 1852, 1857, 1861, 1862, 1865, 1866, 1868, 1870, 1873, 1877, 1886 and 1889.Repairs and improvements to the waterway based on the experience of earlier disasters proved insufficient to withstand the ever higher crests that swept down the river. Particularly was this true at those places along the canal that proved to be most susceptible to the ravages of the river—Dam No. 6, Dam No. 5, Williamsport, Dam No. 4, Shepherdstown, Harpers Ferry, Sandy Hook, Point of Rocks, Edwards Ferry, Dam No. 2, Great Falls, Widewater, Dam No. 1 and Rock Creek Basin. On top of everything else, the floods were completely irregular and unpredictable.

The great floods of 1877, 1886 and 1889 occurred at a most inopportune time. The canal company was hard pressed financially; it was meeting the most severe competition in its history from the railroads; and it faced the necessity of undertaking an extensive program of improvements. The floods struck the waterway a heavy blow on all three points. They reduced company income and increased expenses, rendered its transportation services highly irregular and unreliable, and forced the suspension of the program of improvements. The canal never recovered.

APPENDIX A

DESCRIPTION OF NOVEMBER 1877 FLOOD AT CUMBERLAND

"The effects of the storm of the 22nd, 23rd and 24th of November, 1877, were more severe in Cumberland than ever before known, except perhaps in 1810....The one great point of interest and occasion of alarm, however, was the canal-bank at the foot of Canal Street. About an hour after the great rise in Will's Creek water was noticed trickling through the bank, and at once measures were taken to stop the leak, but little success attended the efforts at first. Finally, after a short consultation, it was decided to use a different method to secure the bank, which proved successful and allayed the growing excitement of the people. The extent of the averted disaster may be imagined when it is known that the surface of the water, which was within a few inches of the top of the bank, was nearly on a level with the pavement in front of the Ocean City Hotel. The west side of Will's Creek was inundated by the waters of the Potomac, which was higher than ever before known. In South Cumberland many houses were inundated with from six inches to three feet of water...The Baltimore and Ohio Railroad sustained great damages, their wires being torn down for miles, trestles washed out and bridges destroyed, which caused a delay of trains for several days. The Cumberland and Pennsylvania also suffered heavy loss. A number of trestles between Ocean and Westernport were washed out, and the tracks badly damaged in some places. The business of the inundated portion of Cumberland was suspended until the waters subsided."[1]

---

[1] Excerpted from Scharf, *History of Western Maryland*, Vol. II, 1390.

APPENDIX B

DESCRIPTION OF NOVEMBER 1877 FLOOD IN WASHINGTON COUNTY

The water in the Potomac during the great flood of 1852, according to a mark at Embrey's warehouse in Williamsport, was three-quarters of an inch higher than the flood of 1877 reached, but this mark is not looked upon as accurate, and according to all other marks the water rose higher in the latter year than in the former. Along the entire line of the river great damage was done; not only fencing, grain, hay, fodder, stock and lumber being swept away, but several houses, and quite a number of stables, hog-pens, chicken-coops and different sorts of outhouses were seen passing down the river at Williamsport and other points. Many visitors from Hagerstown and the surrounding country were in Williamsport on Sunday, viewing the surging river and watching the debris brought down with the flood. At Embrey's and Cushwa's warehouse the damage was but slight, but Mr. S. Culbertson, on the west side of the Conococheague, lost between forty and sixty thousand feet of lumber.

At the junction of the Conococheague and the Potomac there was a vast lake, covering canal, aqueduct and everything except the tops of the trees. Ardinger's mill was in the middle of the Conococheague, and the water was pouring into the windows of the upper story, leaving but a few feet of the stone walls visible between the waters and the eaves of the roof. The stone bridge at this point and the aqueduct on the canal were submerged, but not materially injured. The most serious damage near Williamsport was the injury done to the Cumberland Valley Railroad Bridge. The superstructure of this costly work went about five o'clock on Sunday afternoon. Its danger was appreciated, and six car-loads of coal, railroad and pig iron were sent out from Hagerstown to hold down the capping of the bridge and track. T. J. Nill, the agent there, accompanied the train, and it was run to the Virginia side, which was in greatest danger, and there stationed. But a slight space remained between the surface of the stream and the track on the bridge, so that its destruction by the heavy bodies coming down the stream was inevitable. Three canal-boats in turn, which had broken loose from Williamsport, struck the bridge. Two passed under and went down the stream, while the other blocked the stream. Then came an immense float of drift-wood, which cut off a large willow tree as with a knife, and, striking the bridge with a concussion which sounded like a discharge of artillery, and was heard in Williamsport, bore off with it the whole superstructure save only that which spanned the canal, and the canal-boat which was held in suspense was thus released and went down the stream with the moving mass. At this juncture it was Mr. Nill's good fortune to escape in a manner that may be termed miraculous. He was the last upon the bridge, some fifteen or twenty men having just left it, when he saw the impending danger and started in a run for the Maryland side. The first concussion knocked his feet from under him and he fell; but recovering just as the portion of the bridge behind him was swept away, and whilst that upon which he ran was coiling up and moving under his feet, he succeeded in reaching the shore uninjured, and almost at the instant the bridge disappeared. The leading officials of the road, President Kennedy, General Superintendent Lull and General Agent Boyd were all present on the bridge a few minutes before it went down, with fifteen or twenty other persons. A little engine had been trying to haul out the canal-boat that had lodged to the Virginia shore, but without effect. Col. Kennedy and Col. Lull had walked off towards the Maryland side, leaving Gen. Boyd and Mr. Nill. The former started a few minutes before the latter, and was about fifty yards ahead of him when he saw the drift approaching and started in the manner above described.

Only a small portion of the fine "Dam No. 4," the best on the river, having cost almost a half-million dollars, was washed away. This dam was between the Cumberland Valley bridge and the Shepherdstown bridge, one span of which was washed away. This span was one of four, each one hundred and fifty feet long, and was secured and made fast some distance below. A canalboat loaded with coal, belonging to George McCann, was the first to strike this bridge, and was followed by two others, which were empty, belonging to Lawson Poffenberger and Mr. Boyer.

These were the first boats to strike the Harper's Ferry iron bridge, which was supposed for some time to have been in great danger, but withstood the terrific shocks and pressure brought against it in a wonderful manner, it having been struck by no less than fifteen canal-boats, besides the Powell's Bend bridge, houses, logs and all kind of floating missiles. Mr. Ways, agent of the Baltimore and Ohio Railroad Company, stated that but a single span of the bridge—that over the current—was affected, and that only in the bending of some of the irons.

The damage to the canal was very great, causing the suspension of its operation for the season. The locks at Harper's Ferry and several other locks were washed out and greatly damaged. From Sandy Hook past Harper's Ferry, a distance of four miles, the tow-path was wholly destroyed.

In places the bed of the canal was filled with mud, and all the locks were choked up with accumulations of various kinds. The canal company's buildings were all of them either damaged or washed away, and the total injury to the property of the company amounted to five hundred thousand dollars. The only fatal disaster in Washington County was the drowning of Charles Little, of Hancock, which took place Saturday evening below Dam No. 4, below Williamsport. Mr. Little, who was a boatman, was proceeding up the canal. When the water got deep on the towpath his driver refused to go any further. Mr. Little got on one of the mules to drive. In a short time the current was too strong, the mules were swept down in the flood, and Mr. Little was drowned. The two mules scrambled to the bank, some distance below, and were saved.

At Powell's Bend, opposite Falling Waters, the dwelling-house of Andrew Pope, a well known farmer of that neighborhood, was taken up, carried away, and deposited upon the land of one of his neighbors. David Straw, of the same vicinity, lost a corn-crib. Mrs. Louisa Davis, another neighbor, lost seventy-five barrels of corn, a buggy, sleigh and other articles. The house of John Snyder, a small building, was carried away, as also was a small house owned by John H. Gattrell, and occupied by a man named Price. Mr. Gattrell's saw-mill was also injured, and was moved four inches. Everything between the canal and the river, from Williamsport to Hancock, that could be carried off by the storm was swept away, and the canal and railroad were greatly damaged. The upper part of Hancock was under water, and along the flats and slopes beyond that town many houses were swept away. All the bridges between Hancock and Indian Spring on the turnpike were carried off or rendered impassable. The Antietam rose to a point higher than was ever before known. Bridges were destroyed all along the line of the creek—among them the one at the Forks, midway between Leitersburg and Waynesboro, Pa., and the one at the Little Antietam, near Hartle's. Among the numerous losses suffered along this stream were the washing away of Mr. Walter's stable, the partial destruction of Fisby M. Stouffer's saw-mill, and the washing away of outhouses, fences, etc. The substantial bridge over the Antietam on the National road was not injured, but the other bridge, built by the county over this stream at Funkstown, was materially damaged. At Rose's paper-mill, an old frame structure sixty feet long, used as a bleach-house, was washed away.

At the Roxbury mill the whole dam was swept away and the stone bridge injured. A portion of the dam at Myer's mill was also destroyed. The Antietam Iron Works, at which every preparation had been made by the Messrs. Ahl for starting work, were damaged to the extent of several thousand dollars, about eight hundred tons of coke having been washed away. The Conococheague, like the Antietam, rose to a higher point than had ever been reached before, but except the damage done at Williamsport no great loss was suffered, the principal injury being the washing away of fences and fodder, and the submerging of the lower stories of buildings.[2]

---

[2] Excerpted from Scharf, *History of Western Maryland*, Vol. II, 1201-1202.

HISTORIC RESOURCE STUDY
CHESAPEAKE & OHIO CANAL NHP

7.

BOATS AND NAVIGATION REGULATIONS ON THE C & O CANAL

BY HARLAN D. UNRAU
HISTORIAN, C&O CANAL RESTORATION TEAM, SENECA
DENVER SERVICE CENTER
1976

CONTENTS

I.	BOATS ON THE CHESAPEAKE & OHIO CANAL: 1830–1924	331
	A. C&O CANAL BOATS: 1830–1850	331
	1. SEARCH FOR A SUITABLE BOAT	331
	2. TYPE OF BOATS THAT NAVIGATED THE CANAL	336
	3. FORMAL COMMENCEMENT AND OPERATION OF PACKET SERVICE	337
	4. RENEWED INTEREST IN STEAM NAVIGATION	341
	5. PROVISIONS FOR THE REPAIR OF BOATS	345
	B. C&O CANAL BOATS: 1851–1889	346
	1. GENERAL DESCRIPTIVE MATERIAL	346
	2. TOPICS OF SPECIAL CONCERN	356
	C. C&O CANAL BOATS: 1889–1924	361
	1. GENERAL DESCRIPTIVE MATERIAL	361
	2. GOVERNMENT OWNED COAL BARGES DURING WORLD WAR I	363
II.	REGULATIONS FOR NAVIGATING THE CHESAPEAKE & OHIO CANAL: 1830–1924	364
	A. REGULATIONS FOR 1830–1835	364
	B. REGULATIONS FOR 1835–1850	372
	C. REGULATIONS FOR 1851–1889	377
	D. REGULATIONS FOR 1889–1924	398
APPENDIXES		399
	A. SIDE VIEW AND PLAN OF THE *SWIFT*	399
	B. EXPERIMENTAL RESULTS OF THE *SWIFT*, JULY 9, 1830	400
	C. SIDE VIEW AND PLAN OF THE *LORD DUNDAS* IRON TWIN BOAT	403
	D. PLAN AND DRAWING OF THE *CYCLOPS*	404
	E. DRAWINGS OF AN IRON STEAMBOAT	405
	F. DRAWINGS OF A CANAL STEAMER	406
	G. SPECIFICATION OF A LIGHT IRON PASSAGE BOAT	407
	H. JOURNAL OF EXPERIMENTS ON THE NAVIGATION OF THE CHESAPEAKE & DELAWARE CANAL BY STEAMBOAT *LEWIS*, SEPTEMBER 22, 1883	411

I.	EXTRACT FROM AN ACT OF THE GENERAL ASSEMBLY OF MARYLAND DECEMBER 1831	420
J.	ACT OF CONGRESS APPROVED JULY 14, 1882	422
K.	DRAWINGS OF CHESAPEAKE & OHIO CANAL FREIGHTER	423
L.	ACCOUNT OF LIFE ON A CHESAPEAKE & OHIO CANAL BOAT	424

I. BOATS ON THE CHESAPEAKE & OHIO CANAL: 1830–1924

A. BOATS ON THE CHESAPEAKE & OHIO CANAL: 1830–1850

1. SEARCH FOR A SUITABLE BOAT DESIGN

The first reference to boats in the canal company records occurred on June 26, 1828, about one week before the groundbreaking ceremonies. On that date, the canal board determined that a boat

> be provided with suitable furniture and awnings to facilitate the survey and location of the line of the proposed canal, and for the use of the President and Directors and the Chief Engineer and his Assistants in the execution and superintendence of the said canal

Walter Smith, one of the directors, was authorized to contract for such a boat and to provide for its safekeeping and maintenance.[1]

At the first annual meeting of the company stockholders in June 1829, President Mercer implied that the board had agreed upon the minimum dimensions for the canal boats. The general plan of the boats was to be similar to that used for the craft on the Erie and the Ohio and Erie Canals. They were to be at least 13½ feet wide and have a draft of 3 feet. The prow of the boats was to be rectangular, and the sides and the bottom of the boat were to conform accordingly, thus making the cross-section of the vessel 40.5 square feet. The rate of traveling speed was to be approximately 2½ miles per hour.

Beyond these practical considerations, Mercer voiced the dreams of the board that

> Should the confident hope inspired by intelligence, recently received from the canals of Europe, as well as of the United States, be confirmed, and it be found practicable to substitute, on this canal, the application of steam, for animal labor, as its propelling power, its...surface will favor alike economy of transportation and the comfort of the traveler...Boats of elevated cabins and double decks, propelled by steam; well countervail, by a velocity of seven or eight miles an hour, the transient suspension of their motion by the locks; and by supplying the wants of every description of passengers, will afford at the same time, cheap accommodation to the needy and multiplied enjoyments to the rich.[2]

The canal company records are silent on the subject of boats until February 3, 1830, when Chief Engineer Benjamin Wright submitted his recommendations for a boat design to President Charles F. Mercer. Wright suggested that the boats should be 90 feet long and 14 ½ feet wide, as this would be the maximum size of craft that could take advantage of the canal's lock chambers (100 feet long and 15 feet wide). The boats should have a draft of 5 feet to take advantage of the 6-foot depth of the waterway. Such a boat would displace water equal to 5,460 cubic feet or 152 tons and 820 pounds. Since the boats would weigh approximately 22 tons and 820 pounds when they were empty, the design would permit the boats to carry a maximum cargo of 130 tons. When the canal was in full operation, he was certain that the draft of the boats could be increased slightly so that they could carry cargoes of up to 150 tons. Despite the fact that he submitted a sketch (no

---

[1] *Proceedings of the President and Board of Directors*, A, 7. It is probable that the packet *Charles F. Mercer*, completed two years later, was the boat acquired pursuant to this action of the board. On September 21, 1830, William Easby, a well-known boat builder in Washington, sent a bill for the construction of the *Charles F. Mercer* to the company the details of which may be seen on page 8. Easby to Mercer, September 21, 1830, Ltrs. Recd., C&O Co.
[2] *First Annual Report* (1829), C&O Co., 12–18, 16.

332   Chesapeake & Ohio Canal Historic Resource Study
                                       Unrau: 7. Boats & Navigation Regulations

longer extant) to accompany his recommended boat design, Wright concluded that he did not wish to be misunderstood that he approved of this design as the most economical for use on the canal. On the contrary, he was convinced that boats carrying from 50 to 70 tons would be the best size for canal navigation, a notion no doubt emanating from his experiences on the Erie and Chesapeake and Delaware Canals.

Wright went on to discuss the design and velocity of passenger boats. Such craft would not vary much in their cross sections from that of the cargo-carrying boats. However they should be built lighter and have 6 to 8 inches more keel. They should be built so as not to draw more than 10 inches of water exclusive of the keel, and they should have sharper bows and cleaner runs in the stern. Four horses could pull these packets at a speed of 7 miles per hour, or three horses could pull them at a velocity of 6 miles per hour. Passage through a lock for such a boat should average between 2 to 3 minutes. While a small steam engine could be placed in the boats with a wheel in the stern to increase the velocity, he was certain that this was not practicable since the engine would take up considerable space and would create too much heat in warm weather for the comfort of the passengers.[3]

On February 5 the board ordered Clerk John P. Ingle to advertise for a boat design "suited to the navigation of the Canal both with and without steam power." Proposals were also to be solicited for constructing the boats and a suitable steam engine.[4]

Within three weeks the Baltimore firm of Alexander Cummins and Andrew Armstrong made an offer to build boats and steam engines for the canal company. Cummins and Armstrong recently had constructed two boats having dimensions of 90 feet in length, 15 feet beam, 3 feet hold, and 8 to 10 inches draft for the Citizen's Canal Line between Baltimore and Philadelphia. As the boats were still at their plant, they invited the company officials to make a personal inspection of their craft.[5]

Apparently, the canal officials were not interested in the offer of Cummins and Armstrong because the company records reveal no further communication relative to their proposal. Later on March 13, the directors authorized President Mercer to request Commodore John Rodgers to submit a plan for a canal boat.[6]

By early October 1830 the board was anxious to complete its search for an acceptable boat design as the canal between Little Falls and Seneca Falls was about to be opened for navigation. One boat (of undetermined description) traversed this entire distance on an experimental run on October 1.[7] Three days later the board, having heard that a passenger boat called the *Swift* had been constructed on the Forth and Clyde Canal in Scotland which was faster and yet less injurious to the canal banks than the boats commonly in use, appointed Phineas Janney, one of the direc-

---

[3] Wright to Mercer, February 3, 1830, Ltrs. Recd., C&O Co.
[4] *Proceedings of the President and Board of Directors*, B, p.23.
[5] Cummins and Armstrong to Ingle, February 25, 1830, Ltrs. Recd., C&O Co.
[6] *Proceedings of the President and Board of Directors*, B, 43. Born at Lower Susquehanna Ferry (now Havre de Grace), Maryland in 1773, Rodgers was the son of a Scottish emigrant who served as an officer in the Maryland militia during the Revolution. After spending eleven years in the merchant service, President John Adams appointed him second lieutenant on board the *Constellation* on March 8, 1798, during the naval war with France. He participated in the wars with the Barbary pirates from 1802 to 1806, and as a result of a war-scare growing out of the affair involving the *Chesapeake* and the *Leopard*, he was placed in command of the New York flotilla and naval station in July 1807. In the War of 1812 he was the ranking officer in active service, and he took part in cruises extending to the east coast of Spain and in the defense of Washington and Baltimore. In 1815 President James Madison appointed him to head the newly created Board of Navy Commissioners, authorized by Congress to administer the navy material. Six years later he became the senior officer of the navy and in 1823 he served for a time as secretary of the navy *ad interim*. He remained a commissioner until 1837 when he resigned because of ill health, partly the result of a cholera attack. *Dictionary of American Biography*, Vol. XVI, 75–77. There is no record of whether Rodgers submitted the requested sketch. If it was sent to the board, the drawing and other pertinent material is no longer extant.
[7] Van Slyke to Board of Directors, October 2, 1830, Ltrs. Recd., C&O Co.

tors, to determine if this were true. Should he find the rumor to be correct, he was to obtain drawings and specifications of the boat so that it could be built for use on the canal.[8]

Upon examination of the available information on the *Swift*, Janney found that the boat was 60 feet long, 8 feet 6 inches wide, twin built, and fitted to carry 50 to 60 passengers. The width of its center trough (extending longitudinally down the middle of the boat) was 2 feet 6 inches at the low, 22 inches at amidships, and 3 feet 6 inches at the stern. It was gig-built, light timbered, and weighed about 2,700 pounds.

Janney also acquired a copy of the book *Remarks on Canal Navigation* (1831) by William Fairbairn, a Scottish engineer involved with Thomas Grahame in experiments testing the seaworthiness of the *Swift* on its maiden voyage between Glasgow and Edinburgh on July 7–9, 1830. According to Fairbairn, the *Swift* averaged 6 to 12 miles per hour on its 113-mile journey. Furthermore, it appeared that

> when she moved through the water, at the rate of six or seven miles per hour, there was a great swell or wave constantly in her front, and she was followed by a strong surge or wave, bearing against the bank of the canal. At these times, the hauling rope was tight, and the horses appeared to be distressed. But as the speed was increased, the wave or swelling of water in her front sunk down; and when the speed came to be about nine miles per hour, the swell entirely disappeared; the waters in her front became smooth and level; the hauling rope slackened; and the horses seemed easy, and little or no surge was to be seen on the banks behind the vessel.
>
> There appears, therefore, no reason to fear, that the banks of canals can ever be hurt, by increasing the speed of boats to the utmost attainable height. . .[9]

The results of Janney's research on the *Swift* apparently impressed the company officials. In the *Third Annual Report* of the company in June 1831, President Mercer quoted extensively from Fairbairn's observations, and in a special report to Congress relative to the progress of the canal submitted on April 17, 1834, Mercer again devoted considerable space to the experiments made on British canals.[10]

While Janney was conducting his study of the Scottish experiments, the canal between Locks Nos. 5 and 23 rapidly became a busy thoroughfare. By mid-November 1830, it was reported that numerous boats had passed over this distance.[11] The following month it was reported that 45 boats passed through Locks Nos. 17–20 in one day.[12] While there is no available information concerning the physical description of these boats, it can be assumed that they were of various types and sizes.

During this period the directors undertook an experiment to see how quickly a boat could pass through the locks. It was found that the fastest passage through a lock took 2½ minutes, while the average time was slightly less than 3 minutes. The boat used for the experiment was 75 feet long and 11 feet 8 inches wide.[13]

---

[8] *Proceedings of the President and Board of Directors*, B, 194–195.
9 William Fairbairn, *Remarks on Canal Navigation* (London, 1831), 25–27, 88. A copy of the side view and plan of the *Swift* may be seen in Appendix A, and a copy of the experimental results during the trip of the *Swift* may be seen in Appendix B.
10 *Third Annual Report* (1831), C&O Co., in *Proceedings of the Stockholders*, A, 152–159, and U. S., Congress, House, Committee on Roads and Canals, Chesapeake and Ohio Canal, H. Rept. 414, 23 Cong., 1st Sess., 1834, 377–378.
11 *Second Annual Report* (1830), C&O Co., 32.
12 *Frederick Town Herald*, January 15, 1831.
13 *Niles' Register*, Vol. XXXIX (November 27, 1830), 8.

Early in the spring of 1831 the canal navigation was opened one mile below Lock No. 5 and within two months it was further extended another mile, thus permitting navigation within several hundred yards of the boundary of Georgetown. Soon a "passage boat" was carrying United States mail daily between Georgetown and Seneca "in connection with two lines of public stages, which pass over to Leesburg, in Virginia, crossing the Potomac, at Edward's Ferry."[14]

Sometime during the spring of 1831 a packet service was begun on the canal between Little Falls and Seneca Falls. In May two articles appeared in the *National Intelligencer* and *Niles' Register* describing the packet boat and the trip up the canal to Great Falls as follows:

> It is not easy to imagine a more delightful excursion for pleasure at this season of the year, than that in the canal packet boat to the falls, or even to Seneca. The boat is very handsomely fitted and furnished for the service it is employed in....The hands at some of the locks are not as dexterous in the management of them, perhaps, as longer practice will make them. The passenger who is not on his guard, may chance thus to get a jolt or two; but as this involves no danger he will not regard it. The bridges over the canal are few; and a moderate inclination of the body enables those who stand on the roof, (or deck), of the boat to pass under them; whilst those who remain in the cabin are as much at ease and as comfortable as if they were in their parlors or drawing rooms at home. The packet-boat is drawn by three horses, at the rate of six miles an hour whilst in motion. The passage of the locks of course causes some detention, but we made the whole passage to the falls, with about seventy persons on board, in less than four hours.[15]

At the third annual meeting of the stockholders in June 1831 the General Committee was authorized to "enquire into the practicability and expediency of introducing a steam boat navigation" on the canal and on the Potomac River.[16] While the canal company records do not indicate the reasons that this decision was made, similar experiments were already underway on other American canals and Fairbairn's book on canal navigation probably was a factor as he described four experimental steam-powered canal boats either already operating or under construction for use on the Forth and Clyde Canal. His descriptions of the four models were as follows:

TWIN STEAM BOAT
Whole length—68 feet
Breadth on beam—11 feet, 6 inches
Depth—4 feet, 6 inches
Width of tunnel or wheel-trough—3 feet, 10 inches. This wheel-trough extends longitudinally down the middle of the boat;—it is made wider at each end, in order to facilitate the supply and escapement of water from the paddle wheel.
Depth of tunnel—3 feet, 6 inches
Steam engine—10 horses' power, which it is intended shall give from 50 to 60 strokes, or thereabouts, per minute.
Diameter of paddle wheel—9 feet
Whole weight, including engine, paddle-wheel, & c.—7 tons, 16 cwt.
Draft of water—16 inches.

---

[14] *Third Annual Report* (1831), C&O Co., 5.
[15] Washington *National Intelligencer* quoted in *Niles' Register*, Vol. XL (May 21, 1831), 206.
[16] *Third Annual Report* (1831), in *Proceedings of the Stockholders*, A, 179.

CYCLOPS
Whole length—68 feet
Breadth on beam—15 feet, 6 inches
Depth—about 7 feet, 3 inches from the keel to the deck
Weight, including engine, boiler, fittings, & c.—about 38 tons
Steam engine—14 horses' power
Plan—American, based on steam boat plying Mississippi River at New Orleans
Draft of water—4 feet, 6 inches aft and 1 ½ inches forward (when lightly loaded)

IRON STEAM BOAT
Whole length—68 feet
Breadth on beam—15 feet
Depth from keel to deck—8 feet
Steam engine—24 horses' power, having two cylinders on the locomotive principle: paddle wheels, each 11 feet diameter, and 3 feet wide
Weight, including paddle wheels, engine, & c.—22 tons, 12 cwt., 9 lbs.
Carrying cargo—50 tons
Draft of water—3 feet, 9 inches
Material—strong iron ribs and plate sheeting about 1/4 inch thick

CANAL STEAMER
Whole length—88 feet
Breadth of beam—20 feet
Depth from keel to deck—9 feet
Steam engine (high pressure)—60 horses' power, having two cylinders as per plan
Paddle-wheels—12 feet diameter each and 4 feet wide
Whole weight, including steam engine, paddle wheels, rigging, stores, & c.—46 tons, 4 cwt., 3 qrs.
Carrying cargo—116 tons
Draft of water—4 feet, 6 inches.[17]

Although the stockholders' General Committee investigated the possibilities of introducing steam navigation on the waterway, the directors disapproved of the idea. On July 16, 1831, the board adopted regulations for the navigation of the canal which specifically excluded the use of steam boats on the waterway by stating that "every boat or float, navigating the Canal after the 15th day of August next, shall be propelled by a towing line drawn by men or horses."[18]

BILL FOR CONSTRUCTING THE *CHARLES F. MERCER*

Labor, 588 days work	$747.30
Lumber, knees, etc.	441.00
Hardware	125.00
Painting	219.00
Smiths bills	48.94
Freight of timber in from Alexandria	12.00

---

[17] Fairbairn, *Remarks on Canal Navigation*, 31, 89–93. Copies of drawings of the four boats may be seen in Appendices C, D, E, and E-1 respectively.
[18] *Proceedings of the President and Board of Directors*, B, 410.

Sundries	12.45
Superintendence	147.00
	$1,752.69

The *Charles F. Mercer* was later leased to W. W. Fenlon to use as a packet. Fenlon was appointed lock tender at Locks Nos. 19–20, and he later operated Crommelin House as a tavern-hotel for tourists.19

2. TYPE OF BOATS THAT NAVIGATED CANAL

There are no drawings, specifications, or detailed descriptions of the early boats that plied the canal. However, a general picture of the various craft can be gathered from the regulations established by the board, numerous complaints of violations of those rules, and, in a few cases, brief newspaper and periodical account.

According to the regulations for navigating the canal adopted by the board on July 16, 1831, all boats or floats were to be propelled by a towing line drawn by men or horses. They were to be furnished with strapping or snubbing lines for passage through the locks without damaging them. Iron shod or sharp-pointed setting poles were not to be used in navigation. Boats traveling at night were required to have a light on the bow and rafts, gondolas, or scows were to have the light at the forward end of the bow. Square-headed or sharp-covered boats, such as scows and gondolas, were to have a semicircular platform firmly fastened upon each end so as to save other craft and the canal prism and masonry from injury by contact with the corners. The rudders on the boat were to be constructed in such a manner that they would not interfere with or cut the towing rope of a passing boat. No raft or tow of timber was to consist of more than eight cribs; if they were comprised of more than one crib, they were to be joined so that they could conform to the curvatures of the canal banks and could glide past them without rubbing.[20]

In addition to the by-laws concerning the design and operation of the boats on the canal, the directors classified the craft into four general categories. These boat classifications were as follows:

1. Packet boats—designed for passenger transportation only
2. Freight boats—designed for passage and freight
3. Scows—large, flat-bottomed boats having broad square ends
4. Gondolas—long, narrow, flat-bottomed boats with a high prow and stern.[21]

Despite the passage of the regulations and the lengthy search of the board to find suitable designs for boats, the quality of the boats operating on the canal quickly became a point of particular grievance to the company officials. No one appeared to be willing or able to undertake to fulfill the directors' dreams of steamers and double-decked packets plying the waterway at speeds up to 8 miles per hour.[22] In fact, the boatmen were reluctant to meet even the minimum requirements of the regulations. Complaints were frequently made of iron-shod boats, leaky scows, drifting rafts, and sunken wrecks obstructing navigation.[23] By the enforcement of the regulations, the provision of drydocks, the assessment of fines, and by other devices the company sought to drive undesir-

---

[19] *Proceedings of the President and Board of Directors*, B, 455; C, p.7.
[20] *Ibid*, B, 410–419.
[21] *Ibid*.
[22] *First Annual Report* (1829), 16.
[23] *Proceedings of the President and Board of Directors*, C, 30, and Young to Ingle, October 25, 1838, and Stone to Ringgold, June 6, 1847.

able craft off the waterway and to encourage the construction of new and larger boats. In this they were partly successful, assisted by the growing demands of the trade, as the size of the boats increased steadily. The directors also levied a rate discrimination of 100 percent against rafts in April 1835.[24]

By the spring of 1835 larger and better-built boats were plying the canal. On April 11, 1835, the Williamsport *Banner* reported that the "first regularly formed boat, which has entered the canal at its head (Dam No. 5)," had arrived in the basin there. Named the *Lady Washington*, it had a capacity of some 800 barrels of flour. The boat was a "handsomely decorated and 'trim built' craft, with a cabin roof of white with red hangings painted upon it."[25]

In May 1835 the canal company determined to solicit plans for building boats and scows that were needed on the canal. One of the results of this effort was a specification for scows, which appears in the company records of 1836.[26] Nevertheless, the lumber trade and the incidental trade of the farmers, who built their own craft designed to last for only one trip (usually to be sold at Georgetown for firewood), made the struggle for better boats a never ending one.[27]

SPECIFICATION FOR A SCOW

Length 80 ft., breadth at bottom 13 ½, at top 14 ft., depth 40 inches from out to out sides 7 ½ inches thick at bottom 4 ½ at top and not exceeding two pieces in depth or two in length of yellow heart pine.

18 floor timbers, 4 x 6 inches white oak
2 head pieces 10 by 10 inches white oak
3 Kelsons 6 x 8 inches white oak
3 deck stringers 6 by 8 inches white oak supported by stanchions
18 knees on each side 6 inches by 8 of white oak
Deck and bottom of 2 inch yellow pine

Plates of iron 4 in. by 3/8 on the rakes each plate 9 feet in length
The rake 6 feet measured horizontally
The deck to raise in the center 3 inches
5 inch spikes—3 to be used at each end of each plank
and 2 at each intermediate support
The four angles of the boat to be well braced
A sufficient pump."

The whole to be done in a workmanlike manner and to be completed and delivered in the basin of Rock Creek on or before the day of 1836.

3. FORMAL COMMENCEMENT AND OPERATION OF PACKET SERVICE

Although packet service had been commenced on the canal in the spring of 1831, it was not until July of that year that formal authority was granted for such an operation. On July 1, 1831, permis-

---

[24] *Proceedings of the President and Board of Directors*, D. 284–285.
[25] Williamsport *Banner*, April 11, 1835.
[26] *Proceedings of the President and Board of Directors*, D, 307–308, 320–321. A copy of this specification may be seen on the following page.
[27] Walter S. Sanderlin, *The Great National Project: A History of the Chesapeake and Ohio Canal* (Baltimore 1946), 187–188.

sion was granted to the proprietors of the packet boats, *George Washington* and *Tyber*, to navigate the canal subject to the charges and regulations of the company.[28] As part of the regulations for navigating the canal passed by the board on July 16 Rule 27 made the following stipulations for packet service:

> No boat shall be used as a Packet Boat on said Canal, unless specially licensed therefore, which license shall give to the said Boat the privilege of carrying passengers to and from any point on said Canal, between the Basin at Georgetown (water was not admitted into the canal through Georgetown to Rock Creek Basin until September 19) and Rushville: and the owner or master of said Packet Boat shall pay for every trip up or down between said Basin and Rushville, or any intermediate points, the sum of one dollar and fifty cents, which sum shall be paid weekly to such Collector as may be authorized to receive the same, and on any failure to pay the said sum, or fraudulent return by the owner, master, or other person having charge of the said Boat, of the number of voyages made in the week by said Boat, its license shall be forfeited.[29]

Ten days later the board authorized Clerk Ingle to grant licenses to W. W. Fenlon, L. M. Offutt, and Charles Embrey, the owners or operators of the packet boats *Charles Fenton Mercer*, *George Washington* and *Lafayette*, respectively. At the same time, the Collector of Tolls at Little Falls was authorized to collect tolls from all packets plying the waterway.[30]

Advertisements in Georgetown newspapers indicate that great efforts were made by the packet proprietors to commence an active excursion business. One such advertisement inserted in the *Columbian Gazette* by L. M. Offutt noted that the *George Washington* made daily runs from Frederick Street Bridge in Georgetown to Great Falls, leaving the former at 8:00 a. m. and returning "at, or before sunset." The fare was 50 cents per passenger for a round trip, and the excursion included dinner at Crommelin House.

An advertisement inserted in the same newspaper by Thomas Thorpe the agent for the *Lafayette,* informed the readers that the packet would accommodate 100 people without crowding and afforded room for twenty couples "in a cotillion at a time." The boat made runs between Georgetown and Great Falls for the fare of $1.00 per passenger. Dinner could be purchased on board, the excursion parties could provide their own food, or dinner could be eaten at Crommelin House.[31]

Although there are few eye-witness accounts of the packet trips to Great Falls by passengers or crew, one such glimpse does appear in the writings of Edward Thomas Cole, an Englishman who visited the Potomac Valley during the summer of 1832. Describing his excursion up the canal on one of the daily packets, he wrote that

> the traveling was most delightful. I was the only passenger, and there was a neat, well-furnished cabin about 50 feet long by 14 broad. We were drawn by three horses at the rate of five miles an hour, a huge negro riding on the beast, and driving the other horses before him with a long whip, which he flourished and cracked most adroitly.[32]

---

[28] *Proceedings of the President and Board of Directors*, B, 402.
[29] *Ibid,* B, 416–417.
[30] *Ibid,* B, 434.
[31] Georgetown *Columbian Gazette*, July 3, 21, 1832.
[32] Edward Thomas Cole, *A Subaltern's Furlough: Descriptive of Scenes in Various Parts of the United States, Upper and Lower Canada, New Brunswick, and Nova Scotia, During the Summer and Autumn of 1832* (London, 1833), 115–116.

There are no records indicating the number of passengers actually carried on the packets, but there is evidence that the packet trade was generally unprofitable. On September 16, 1831, the toll on packet boats was reduced to $1.00 per trip as a means of encouraging the languishing service.[33] The following summer on July 3, the *Columbian Gazette* reported that the *Lafayette* would be sold at public auction after July 4.[34] On July 21 the last advertisement, which was greatly reduced in size compared to earlier entries, appeared in the *Columbian Gazette* for the *George Washington*.[35] Only the *Charles F. Mercer* appears to have continued operating as a packet, but as there is no available documentation on its service it is impossible to assess its profitability.[36]

After a period of time in which the packet service on the canal nearly came to an end, William Easby on April 27, 1833, sent a proposal to the company for the construction of a sheet-iron packet. The proposal was referred to Directors John J. Abert and William Gunton, and they promptly requested information from the Chesapeake and Delaware Canal Company, which was experimenting with such a boat on its waterway.[37] Apparently, the directors were satisfied with the experimental results on the Chesapeake and Delaware, because, when Easby submitted a second proposal to the board on September 13 to build a sheet-iron packet, Gunton and Walter Smith, a fellow director, were authorized to negotiate a contract for its construction.[38] Another reason for their acceptance of Easby's proposal at this time was the fact that water would be admitted to the canal between Dams Nos. 2 and 3 by November 1, and they were anxious to have a packet service established between Georgetown and Harpers Ferry by the spring of 1834.[39]

While Easby was building the packet at his boatyard in Washington, company officials made the necessary arrangements for the passenger service. On November 22 Gunton and Smith were authorized to purchase the furnishing for the boat, and President John H. Eaton was requested to engage the necessary drivers and horses to propel the craft.[40] In March 1834 the packet, which was named *The President*, was delivered to the company at a cost of $1,400.[41]

Although there are no extant drawings or plans of this packet, it is possible that Easby was influenced by the design of a light iron passage boat used for experiments on the Forth and Clyde Canal by Sir John Benjamin MacNeill in the spring of 1833.[42] While the assertion cannot be proved, it can be documented that MacNeill's work was widely-read by canal men in America and that the Chesapeake and Ohio officials gave great prominence to his observations on the most effective design and velocity of canal boats.[43]

After several months of operation, the canal company, which was rapidly approaching bankruptcy, determined to sell the packet and six horses to James B. Wager for $1,600 and to grant him toll-free privileges on the canal until December.[44] Apparently, the sale was never made because on June 16, 1835, the directors ordered that the "Iron Boat belonging to the Company be

---

[33] *Proceedings of the President and Board of Directors.*
[34] Georgetown *Columbian Gazette*, July 3, 1832. On January 12, 1833, the canal company purchased the *Lafayette* for $300 and fitted it for the accommodation of hands employed under the Superintendent of the Canal. *Proceedings of the President and Board of Directors*, C, 263, 264, 278.
[35] Georgetown *Columbian Gazette*, July 21, 1832.
[36] Ingle to Offutt, March 22, 1834, Ltrs. Sent, C&O Co.
[37] *Proceedings of the President and Board of Directors*, C, 331, 336.
[38] *Ibid*, C, 426.
[39] *Ibid*, D, 3.
[40] *Ibid*, D, 20.
[41] *Ibid*, D, 55, and Ingle to Offutt, March 22, 1834, Ltrs. Sent, C&O Co. Approximately 2 ½ tons of iron were used in the construction of the packet.
[42] Sir John Benjamin MacNeill, *Canal Navigation, On the Resistance of Water to the Passage of Boats Upon Canals and Other Bodies of Water* (London, 1833). A copy of the specification used to construct the light iron boat may be seen in Appendix F.
[43] House Report 414, 318–378.
[44] *Proceedings of the President and Board of Directors*, D, 109.

put in order for use; and, that $50 be advanced to William Easby on that account."[45] After being refitted, the iron packet failed to turn a profit and on December 11, 1836, the board ordered that it be sold at a price of not less than $200. In turn, the vessel was offered to Easby for $300, but when he demurred, it was recommended that it be sold to Hugh Smith who would melt the sheet iron and produce lock gate castings for the company.[46]

Despite the unprofitability of a regular passenger service, the canal company continued to promote such an operation by periodically taking government officials on well-publicized excursions from Georgetown to Great Falls, Seneca and Harpers Ferry. These trips were usually taken on the *Charles F. Mercer*, which apparently by this time had been reacquired from W. W. Fenlon. One such occasion took place in early August 1835 when President Andrew Jackson and a company of fifty people were the guests of the canal board. The party left Georgetown at 8:30 a.m., the U. S. Marine Band serenading the group on board. After reaching Seneca, the party ate dinner on the boat—a "sumptuous" meal consisting of "a great variety of good things, embracing an abundance of the choicest luxuries of the season, and a generous supply of capital wines and beverages. After dinner the guests retired on deck, and as they approached Georgetown the ladies honored the men "with their company in the pleasing amusements of the dance."[47] A similar junket was taken in the spring of 1836 when the directors sponsored a trip for a number of Congressmen from Georgetown to Harpers Ferry at a cost of more than $1,700.[48]

During the summer of 1835 the canal company made another attempt to commence a packet operation on the waterway. A committee was formed to study the matter on July 2, and the following day it submitted to the directors the form of a contract which it proposed be used to enter into an agreement with a private company for the operation of a packet service. The directors adopted the recommendation and authorized the committee to negotiate such a contract for one year.[49] On September 11 an agreement was made with O. M. Linthicum, president of the recently organized Georgetown Canal Packet Company, to operate daily packets between Georgetown and Harpers Ferry for one year free of tolls.[50]

The packet service appears to have prospered under the new arrangement. On October 10 a new contract was signed with the packet company extending the service to Shepherdstown.[51] With the coming of cooler weather, Linthicum on October 30 requested and received permission to reduce the number of trips from one per day to three per week until March 1, 1836.[52] Despite its success, the packet company reported that it was forced to operate on a "strict economy" in order to turn a profit.[53]

During the summer of 1836 packet service was extended from Shepherdstown to Williamsport by a new packet company operated by Joseph Hollman, the contractor for Dam No. 4. On June 20 an agreement was signed granting Hollman the same privileges that had been pro-

---

[45] *Ibid,* D, 339.
[46] *Ibid,* E, 180, and Ingle to Smith, December 16, 1836, Ltrs. Sent, C&O Co.
[47] *Niles' Register,* Vol. XLVIII (August 15, 1835), 431.
[48] *Proceedings of the President and Board of Directors,* E, 43, 63, 181.
[49] *Ibid,* D, 358.
[50] *Ibid,* D, 398.
[51] *Ibid,* D, 410–411.
[52] *Ibid,* D, 419.
[53] Linthicum to Board of Directors, June 29, 1836, Ltrs. Recd., C & O Co. The profit margin was so stringent that even the officers of the packet company were denied free passage. Thus, when the lockkeepers of the canal company began to abuse their privileges and demand free passage on the packets while on private business, Linthicum complained to the directors that his profits were strained severely by such practices. Accordingly, the board on July 6 ordered that the lockkeepers could not obtain free passage on the packets unless they had papers from their divisional superintendent that they were on official company business. *Proceedings of the President and Board of Directors,* E, 87.

vided in the contract with the Georgetown Packet Company. The agreement was to extend until the end of the calendar year.[54]

The canal company became dissatisfied with the quality of the boats employed by the Georgetown Packet Company during the summer of 1836. On October 14 when the packet company applied to the board for an extension of its one-year contract the request was referred to a special committee consisting of President George C. Washington and Directors Thomas Carbery and Phineas Janney. These men were authorized "to make arrangements for the employment of boats better suited for the purposes of packets, than those heretofore used by this Packet Company are."[55]

When negotiations broke down over the matter of improving the quality of the packet boats, the Georgetown Packet Company on January 14, 1837, requested an extension of its privilege to navigate the canal free of tolls until another company could be formed to operate the packet service on the waterway, but there is no record of any response from the company.[56] More than two years later on November 2, 1839, the board granted permission to A. Himrickhouse to navigate the canal free of toll for the period of one year with a passenger boat carrying the U. S. Mail.[57]

4. RENEWED INTEREST IN STEAM NAVIGATION

Although the canal board earlier had rejected the use of steamboats on the waterway, the widespread publicity given to experiments with steam navigation on the Chesapeake and Delaware Canal in September 1833 by Alexander Dallas Bache, professor of Natural Philosophy and Chemistry at the University of Pennsylvania, brought forth renewed interest in the introduction of steam navigation on the Chesapeake and Ohio. Using a canal boat that had originally plied upon the Schuylkill and had a reputation for "quickness," and a steam engine and accessories supplied by the firm of Rush & Muhlenburg, the Chesapeake and Delaware Canal Company carried on a series of experiments under the direction of Bache to test the validity of Fairbairn's assertions in his *Remarks on Canal Navigation*. Bache described the dimensions of the experimental steamboat as follows:

> A canal boat, which had originally plied upon the Schuylkill, and been noted as a quick boat, was altered, under the direction of the President of the Chesapeake and Delaware Canal Company, (Robt. M. Lewis, Esq.) so as to increase the length, and to give greater sharpness to the bow, as well as to reduce the bottom to a regular and gently swelling curved surface, from the stem and stern, without any internal flexures. The length of the boat was thus made eighty feet, the length of the false bow, in the direction of the axis of the boat, being seven and a half feet; the width of the boat was ten feet; the draught, when light, twelve inches, and with a load of forty tons, fourteen inches, exclusive of the keel. The alterations were made under the direction of Mr. James Rush, of the firm of Rush and Muhlenburg, and the engine, paddle wheels, & c. put in under his charge; from him I obtained the details just given, and those which follow, in relation to the boat and engine.
>
> The engine was the result of an exchange, which enabled the experiment to be made with economy; it proved, however, to be much too small for the purposes in view. The diameter of the cylinder was eight and a half inches, and the length of stroke two and a half feet, the pressure of the steam with which it was supplied was about 140 lbs.; 150

---

[54] *Proceedings of the President and Board of Directors*, B, 77.
[55] *Ibid*, E, 152.
[56] *Ibid*, E, 292.
[57] *Ibid*, F, 115.

lbs. to the square inch, on the safety valve, being the maximum pressure. The steam was cut off at half stroke and the escape steam served to heat, in part, the water, which was thrown into the boiler. The nominal power of the engine was ten horses; but with a mean effective pressure, during the stroke, of 80 lbs. per square inch, an estimate probably not far from the truth if the pressure within the boiler was correctly stated, and supposing thirty-five double strokes to be made in a minute, the power would be more than double the nominal amount. The boiler was a vertical cylinder, six feet in length, and three feet in interior diameter, containing one hundred and twenty draught tubes from an inch and a half to two inches in diameter, and thirty inches in length, the tubes uniting above in a wide chimney. It appeared by the experiments that this boiler was competent to keep up a supply of steam for about thirty-five double strokes of the engine per minute. The paddle wheels were placed at the sides of the boat, and between one-third and one-half of the length of the boat from the bow; the wheels were eight feet two inches in exterior diameter, and four and a half feet wide; the buckets were six inches deep, and made of cast iron. The weight of the boiler was stated to be 2214 lbs., and of the wheels about one ton.[58]

Three conditions were tested during the September trials: use of the steamboat alone, use of the steamboat in towing light passenger barges, and use of the steamboat in towing heavily laden freight vessels. While care was taken to obtain accurate figures concerning the speed and engine capabilities of the boat, the greatest interest was in observing the effects of high-speed travel on the canal banks. Bache observed that the wake from passenger barges being towed by horses was at least three times as great as that produced by the steamboat. In using the steamboat alone, the wave created by the bow was disposed of by the paddle wheels; in towing barges, the barges themselves effectively disposed of the remaining swell created by the towboat. Speeds of up to 7 and 8 miles per hour were "attained by even this imperfect model" steamboat, which used an engine too small and weak for the vessel on which it was mounted. The speeds compared favorably with those produced by the work of eight horses. Bache concluded that the experiments "go far to remove, entirely" any doubts concerning the advantageous application of steam on the larger canals and that steam power may be substituted for horse towing with great savings to the canal, particularly at high velocity.[59]

Within six months after the publication of Bache's report the Chesapeake and Ohio directors received three proposals for the building of steam packet boats to ply the canal. On June 20, 1834, the firm of Phillips and Delin submitted a model of such a vessel, but after a quick review of the proposal, the directors voted to table the matter temporarily.[60] Later on December 3, the board received two proposals to build steamboats for canal navigation from Jacob Morgan and A. H. Brown, the latter apparently having had some experience in the development of steam navigation on the Farmington Canal in Connecticut.[61] After President Washington had obtained favorable information from the Farmington Canal Company concerning the results of steamboat navigation on its waterway, the board passed the following resolution on January 13, 1835:

---

[58] *Experiments Made on the Navigation of the Chesapeake and Delaware Canal by Steam*, Reported by A. D. Backe (Philadelphia, 1834), 2.
[59] *Ibid*, 2–13. A copy of the text of Backe's observations and conclusions on the various experiments may be seen in Appendix G. Also see Ralph D. Gray, *The National Waterway: A History of the Chesapeake and Delaware Canal, 1769–1965* (Urbana, 1967), 85–87.
[60] *Proceedings of the President and Board of Directors*, D, 110–112.
[61] *Ibid*, D, 198.

that for the purpose of encouraging the use of Steam as a moving power upon the Canal, the right to navigate the same for one year free of tolls will be granted to the first Steam Packet Boat which shall within twelve months from this date be placed upon the Canal and run daily at a speed not less than eight miles per hour, without injury to the Banks of the Canal, and shall in all other respects conform to the regulations for navigating the same.

The resolution was ordered to be published in the *National Intelligencer*.[62]

Near the end of January, Asa Waters sent to the board a proposal to put a steamboat on the canal according to the terms of the published resolution. Several days later, however, Waters requested that the directors modify their propositions by designating a specific day on which they would make their choice from the various steamboats built for the canal navigation.[63] Accordingly, the board modified its resolution

to grant the free use of the Canal for one year, to the best Steam Packet Boat which shall be upon the Canal on the 1st day of August next, the speed of which shall not be less than 8 miles per hour, without injury to the Banks of the Canal. In deciding upon the Boat, which may be entitled to the privilege hereby granted, its capacity and suitableness for the purposes of a Packet Boat will be considered, as well as its speed.

All steamboats with a velocity of 8 miles per hour would be able to navigate the canal free of tolls until August 1 provided that they did not injure the canal banks.[64]

There is no documentation in the company records to indicate subsequent developments relative to the introduction of steam power on the waterway during the remainder of 1835 and 1836. The financial difficulties of the company, the growing nationwide economic malaise, and the poor agricultural harvests in the Potomac Valley during these years undoubtedly all played a part in preventing the introduction of steam power on the canal. The next discussion of the subject occurred in February 1837 when the board considered the use of steam power to tow barges through Big Slackwater above Dam No. 4. However, the continual cost of repair, which they felt such an operation would necessitate, induced the directors to build a permanent towpath along the pool "which, in the end, it is believed, will be found decidedly the most economical improvement."[65]

Experiments with the English-built iron screw-propelled steamer *Robert F. Stockton* on the Delaware and Raritan Canal in the spring of 1839 again excited the interest of the board in introducing steam navigation to their waterway. In 1836 John Ericson, a Swedish engineer living in England, had invented and patented the screw propeller, which revolutionized navigation. In 1837 he had built a steam vessel having twin screw propellers, which on trial towed the American packet-ship *Toronto* at the speed of five miles per hour on the Thames River. At the order of Robert F. Stockton, the president of the Delaware and Raritan Canal Company and the son of a signer of the Declaration of Independence, Ericson in 1838 constructed the iron screw-steamer which crossed the Atlantic under canvas in 1839 to be used on the waterway to tow 60-ton coal

---

[62] *Ibid*, D, 220.
[63] *Ibid*, D, 228–229.
[64] *Ibid*, D, 229. Two weeks later on February 18, the board adopted new regulations for navigating the canal. The new rules, which specifically allowed the introduction of steam power on the canal. *Ibid*, D, 240.
[65] Washington to Veazey, February 4, 1837, Ltrs. Sent, C&O Co.

barges from Bordentown, New Jersey to New York City. Thus, the steamboat became "the first screw-propeller ship operated for utilitarian purposes on American waters."[66]

The board authorized the president to obtain such information on the *Robert F. Stockton* as he could relative to its dimensions, speed, and cost.[67] However, the approaching collapse of the company finances again thwarted any serious initiatives to inaugurate steam power on the canal.

During the spring of 1842 the board granted permission to William Easby to operate a "newly invented steam passenger boat, of his own construction" free from tolls until January 1, 1844. The only two conditions to the agreement were that he pay the usual tolls for the transportation of freight and that the canal banks were not to suffer from abrasion. In June the company stockholders were told that the boat was nearly completed and would soon be ready for service. President Michael C. Sprigg voiced the hope that during the summer or early fall "a safe, pleasant, and cheap mode of conveyance will be afforded to those who may desire to pass between Hancock and the District, or to the intermediate places."[68]

In December 1842 the board again consulted with Ericson as to the estimated cost of transporting coal from Cumberland to Washington on screw-propelled steamboats.[69] In reply, he stated that his repeated trials with sixteen propeller-driven steamboats (probably on the Delaware and Raritan Canal) had shown that the most economical mode of conveyance was that of towing one freight barge with a steamer, both vessels carrying approximately the same amount of goods. Accordingly, the basis for his estimate was 200 tons of coal nearly equally divided on the two boats–a safe supposition since the steam machinery and propellers weighed seven tons and the consumption of fuel for a round-trip would be twelve tons. The cost for the two vessels would be $4,000–$2,000 for the steam machinery and $1,000 for each boat. The monthly expenses for such an operation would be:

Wear and tear and interest on capital	$88
Wages and maintenance of crews	220
Fuel consumption—48 tons of coal	
(24 mooring days at 2 tons per day) at $1 per ton	48
Oil, lamp, and tallow for machinery	10
	$366

As five years' experience had shown that the most economical speed was three miles per hour he calculated only four round-trips carrying 200 tons per trip each month. Thus, the cost of transportation would amount to less than 46 cents per ton.[70]

In the spring of 1843 the board again attempted to take steps to stimulate steam navigation on the canal. On May 3 a resolution was passed

---

[66] Appletons' *Cyclopedia of American Biography, Vol. II*, 364; Crawford Clark Madeira, Jr., *The Delaware and Raritan Canal* (East Orange, 1941), 40–41; and Richard F. Veit, *The Old Canals of New Jersey* (Little Falls, 1963), 71. The steamboat operated on the Delaware and Raritan Canal for 25 years.
[67] *Proceedings of the President and Board of Directors*, F, 67.
[68] *Fourteenth Annual Report* (1842), C&O Co., 5.
[69] Ericson had come to the United States in November 1839, and in 1841, he had furnished to the U. S. Navy the designs for the screw warship *Princeton*, the first vessel having its propelling machinery below the water-line out of the reach of enemy gunners. During the construction of the *Princeton*, he built and furnished numerous steam propelled vessels for carrying freight on the American Rivers and canals. Appletons' *Cyclopedia of American Biography, Vol. II*, 364.
[70] Ericson to Board of Directors, December 30, 1842, in *Sixteenth Annual Report* (1844), C&O Co., 26–27.

That any one packet boat propelled by steam in such manner as in the opinion of the President & Ch. Engineer shall not be injurious to the Canal shall pass over the Canal free till the 1st day of January 1845.

The only condition was that the operations of the steamboats would pay the ordinary tolls on all freight with the exception of the passengers and their luggage.[71]

From the available documentation it does not appear that regular steam navigation was commenced on the canal until the late 1840s. On October 2 of that year Samuel W. Dewey was granted permission to run a line of steam packets for passenger service toll-free for a two-year period provided that the operation was begun within one year and that the boats would obey the designated speed limits.[72] In December 1849 the board authorized Lemuel Williams to operate steamboats on the canal for the purpose of towing freight boats. The steam tugs and their necessary fuel were to be toll-free so long as they did not weaken the canal banks. The tugboats were to be constructed upon a plan similar to the *Virginia* on which the directors recently had taken an experimental cruise.[73] By May 1850 N. S. Denny & Co. was operating a fleet of steam tugboats on the canal – a development which posed problems for the company as some of the bridges over the waterway did not permit the 12 ½ foot clearance required for the passage of the tugs.[74]

5. PROVISIONS FOR THE REPAIR OF BOATS

Soon after the first portion of the canal was opened to navigation between Little Falls and Seneca Falls, the canal company began to discuss ways in which it could encourage the repair of boats on the waterway. After considerable debate, the board in July 1831 submitted the question of building a drydock along the canal for this purpose to a committee headed by the noted military engineer John J. Abert.[75] The following month the committee reported its conclusion that the construction of a drydock was "inexpedient," and the board took no further action.

While the company records indicate little about the subject, it is apparent that the problem of repairing boats continued to keep the question of building drydocks before the board. On May 30, 1833, it was determined that the resident engineers select a suitable spot on each residency for a drydock and recommend a plan for their construction.[76]

While the locations of these drydocks and their construction plans could not be found, the physical remains of one on the berm side of the canal next to Lock No. 35 provides a general picture of their plan of design and method of operation. Several masonry supports in an elongated pit paralleled the lock. At the upper end, it was connected with the canal, and at its lower end there was a waste structure. When a boat floated in over the supports, the water could be drained through the waste structure.[77]

No mention of drydocks was found in the canal records again until October 1847. At that time the board authorized John Moore, the lock tender at Georgetown, to build such a structure near Lock No. 1 under the direction of the chief engineer. Moore was to operate the drydock at "the pleasure of the board" with 30 days' notice required for the abrogation of the lease.[78]

---

[71] *Proceedings of the President and Board of Directors*, G, 31.
[72] *Ibid*, H, 83.
[73] *Ibid*, H, 319.
[74] *Ibid*, H, 353.
[75] *Ibid*, B, 29.
[76] *Ibid*, C, 361.
[77] John P. Miele, *"The Chesapeake and Ohio Canal: A Physical History"* (NPS Mss., 1968), 120.
[78] *Proceedings of the President and Board of Directors*, H, 81–82.

During the following month, permission was granted to Owen Ardinger to construct a drydock on the berm side of the canal near Williamsport. Accordingly, the company president was authorized henceforth to allow qualified persons to build drydocks on the berm side of the waterway. The construction of the drydocks was to be monitored by the chief engineer or the division superintendent.[79]

B. BOATS ON THE CHESAPEAKE & OHIO CANAL: 1851–1889

Research on the canal boats during the period 1851–1889 has turned up much interesting information. For the purposes of clarity, the data has been divided into two sections – general descriptive material and topics of special concern to the canal company such as the promotion of steamers and packets on the waterway and the steps taken to keep the boats in repair.

1. GENERAL DESCRIPTIVE MATERIAL

a. First Boats on the Completed Waterway

Following the ceremonies at Cumberland on October 10, 1850, formally opening the canal to navigation, a procession of boats proceeded down the canal. The distinguished visitors, canal company officials, and prominent citizens embarked on the canal packet *Jenny Lind* and the canal boat *C. B. Fisk*, both of which had been fitted specially for the occasion. Behind these boats was another barge on which rode the Eckhart Light Artillery with a battery of two field pieces. At the rear of the procession were five coal boats – the *Southampton, Elizabeth, Ohio,* and *Delaware* belonging to the Merchants' Line of McKaig and Agnew of Cumberland, and the *Freeman Rawdon* belonging to Ward's Cumberland Line, a New York based company. The coal boats were loaded with some 411 tons of coal destined for Georgetown and Alexandria and some 80 tons destined for Williamsport. This towage was reported to exceed the total amount of coal carried on the Lehigh Navigation Canal during its first year of operation, and canal officials congratulated themselves for this accomplishment.[80] After stopping at a spring ten miles east of Cumberland and partaking of a large dinner on board the *Jenny Lind* and the *C. B. Fisk*, the party returned to Cumberland while the coal boats continued on their way to the East.

Of the five boats, the *Elizabeth* went only to Williamsport, the *Southampton* and the *Freeman Rawdon* reached Alexandria, and the *Delaware* and the *Ohio* got stuck above Dam No. 6, because of the low level of water in the canal. The latter drew 4 feet with their load, instead of 3½, which would have passed. The *Freeman Rawdon* won the race with the *Southampton*, reaching Washington about 6 p. m., on October 17. Horses and mules were requisitioned along the way to maintain the speed, and the boats arrived within a short time of each other.

At the same time that these boats were descending the waterway, a number of barges commenced the journey up the canal from the District cities. Ten empty boats were launched from Georgetown and two loaded vessels embarked from Alexandria and proceeded to Cumberland as quickly as the water would permit.[81]

---

[79] *Ibid,* H, 112.
[80] Frederick *Examiner,* October 23, 1850.
[81] *Georgetown Advocate,* October 15, 19, 22, 1850; *Report to the Stockholders on the Completion of the Chesapeake and Ohio Canal to Cumberland* (Frederick, 1851), 137; and Elgin to Coale, October 18, 1850, and Fisk to Coale, October 20, 1850, Ltrs. Recd., C&O Co.

b. Regulations Established Governing the Classification and Construction of Boats

Upon the completion of the canal to Cumberland, the board issued a new set of regulations to govern the classification and equipment of the boats plying the waterway. These rules were largely a confirmation of the existing regulations, modified and brought up to date by the lessons of the first revisions. The new rules went into effect on April 1, 1851.

> The regulations divided the boats on the canal into seven categories:
> Class A—"Decked boats of substantial build, carrying one hundred tons and upwards"
> Class B—"Boats of similar construction, carrying less than one hundred tons"
> Class C—"Boats not decked, of substantial build, carrying one hundred tons and upwards"
> Class D—"Boats of similar construction, carrying less than one hundred tons"
> Class E—"Long boats and scows, decked or not decked, of substantial build"
> Class F—"Gondolas and other floats designed for temporary use"
> Packets—"Boats used chiefly for the transportation of passengers"

The new set of regulations also established standards relative to the form, equipment, fixtures, and condition of the boats navigating the canal. These requirements, beginning with number 13, were as follows:[82]

> 13. No boat or float of any kind, except gondolas passing along the Canal for the first time and rafts, shall navigate or be moved on the Canal, unless the bow of said boat or float be firmly and permanently constructed, and so curved, that the versed sine or depth of the curve shall not be less than one fourth of the cord or width of the boat or float. PENALTY for a violation of this regulation, *five* dollars.
>
> 14. No boat or float, strapped or faced with iron on the front part of the stem, or other prominent part or parts of the bow or sides thereof, shall navigate, or be moved on the Canal, unless there shall be suspended, and thoroughly secured in front of the stem or other prominent part or parts of the bow or on its sides,–in such manner as effectually to prevent such iron facing strap or straps thereof from striking upon or against any lock, lock gate, guard gate, bridge or other work or device appertaining to the Canal,–a good and sufficient fender or fenders, composed of rope or rope yarn, at least six inches in diameter,–PENALTY for a violation of this regulation, *five* dollars.
>
> 15. No boat shall navigate or be moved on the Canal, without a guard or plate of iron, firmly attached to the keel and extending back under the rudder, or some other permanent device, that shall cover and secure the opening between the keel or stern post and the rudder, so as effectually to prevent the tow-rope of any other boat or float from entering said opening. PENALTY for a violation of this regulation, *five* dollars.
>
> 16. No boat, except scows and gondolas shall navigate or be moved on the Canal, without a knife or sharp metallic instrument, so affixed upon its bow, as to cut apart any tow-rope, which otherwise might pass over such bow. PENALTY for a violation of this regulation, *five* dollars.

---

[82] *By-Laws, Rules, and Regulations: In Force on the Chesapeake and Ohio Canal, 1st April 1851* (Baltimore, 1894), 4–9.

17. No boat or float shall navigate or be moved on the Canal, without two good and sufficient snubbing lines. PENALTY for violation of this regulation, *five* dollars.

18. No boat shall navigate or be moved on the Canal, at night, without a conspicuous light on its bow; and no raft shall navigate or be moved on the Canal, at night, without a conspicuous light on the forward end of the same; and every raft moored or tied up, shall, at all times during the night, have a conspicuous light at each end of each tow, near the outer corners thereof. PENALTY for a violation of either of the provisions of this regulation, *five* dollars.

19. No boat or float shall navigate the Canal, that shall be in a leaky condition, and that cannot safely be used for the purposes of navigation.

20. No boat, except a gondola, shall navigate the Canal, which has not its name, and its hailing place corresponding with its boat's register then in force, and the letter or name of its class and the number of the said boat's register distinctly painted, in letters and figures of at least four inches in height, on both sides of said boat,–and on some permanent part thereof, so high above the water that they may be plainly seen from either bank of the Canal. PENALTY for a violation of this regulation, *five* dollars.

21. No boat, except those belonging to class F., shall navigate the Canal, unless distinctly marked on each side–at the bow, stern and amidships–so as to show accurately the draft of such boat in feet and inches, at the bow, stern and amidships–when empty, and when partially or fully loaded–and every owner or master of such boat who shall neglect or refuse to comply with this regulation, and every owner or master of a boat that is erroneously or falsely marked at the bow, stern or amidships, shall be subject be a PENALTY of *ten* dollars.

22. No raft or tow of timber or plank, on the Canal, shall exceed in length ninety feet–and no raft or tow of timber or plank shall approach any other raft or tow of timber or plank, nearer than thirty rods, unless for the purpose of passing, or be moored nearer than thirty rods to any other raft or tow of timber or plank previously moored. The first and leading crib in every raft or tow of timber or plank shall have the outer edge of the forward end of every outside stick or plank rounded. And no transverse stick or plank shall extend within one inch of the outer edge of the outside stick or plank of such crib. Every violation, of either of the provisions of this regulation, shall subject the owner, person or persons having charge of such tow or raft, to a PENALTY of *five* dollars.

23. Each and every time, *on different days*, that any boat or float shall be found navigating the Canal in violation of any of the provisions of the 13th, 14th, 15th, 16th, 17th, 18th, 19th, 20th, 21st and 22nd regulations, or that any raft shall be found lying by and moored at night, without lights, as required by the 18th regulation, shall be considered a distinct offence.

24. Each Superintendent, Collector, acting Collector, Inspector, or Lock-keeper, on the Canal, is hereby authorized to determine whether the requirements of the 13th, 14th, 15th, 16th, 17th, 18th, 19th, 20th, 21st and 22nd regulations, are fully complied with, in the case of any boat or float, the owner or master of which is applying for a way-bill for the said boat or float, or for a permit for it to navigate the Canal, or having obtained a way-

bill or a permit, is proceeding with the said boat or float on its voyage;–and each and every of them, if such requirements are not fully complied with, are hereby authorized and required not to issue such way-bill or permit, or, if the boat or float, having obtained a way-bill or permit is on its voyage, to detain the said boat or float and stop its further progress, until all the requirements aforesaid are complied with, and all penalties incurred in consequence of their not having been, are satisfied and paid. Provided however, that the owner or master of any boat, considered unsafe and unfit for use, under the 19th regulation, by either of the above mentioned officers of the Company, shall have the right to call upon an experienced boat builder or master, who with another to be appointed by the said officer,—and a third to be selected by the two thus appointed, in case of a disagreement,—may make a survey of the boat or float aforesaid,—and upon the decision of a majority of the three being made and communicated in writing to the said officer, if adverse to his opinion, a way-bill or permit, as the case may be, shall be granted, or the boat or float allowed to proceed on its voyage, but otherwise not.[83]

c. First Registration of Boats under the New Regulations

Throughout the first year of operation on the completed waterway, a total of 223 boats were registered under the new regulations.[84] The breakdown of this total by classification was as follows:

Class A	9
Class B	49
Class C	108
Class D	41
Class E	10
Class F	6
Packets	1

Although it has been generally assumed that the canal boats for this period had fairly standard dimensions, the 1851 registration books detailing the dimensions of the vessels into classes of craft on the canal were as follows:

Class A—length (minimum of 76 feet, 9 inches; maximum of 92 feet); width (minimum of 14 feet; maximum of 14 feet, 6 inches); draft when empty (minimum of 10 inches; maximum of 14 inches); draft when loaded (minimum of 4 feet; maximum of 6 feet).

Class B—length (minimum of 70 feet; maximum of 90 feet); width (minimum of 11 feet, 9 inches; maximum of 14 feet, 7 inches); draft when empty (minimum of 10 inches; maximum of 18 inches); draft when loaded (minimum of 3 feet; maximum of 4 feet, 6 inches).

Class C—length (minimum of 86 feet; maximum of 92 feet); width (minimum of 13 feet, 6 inches; maximum of 14 feet, 7 inches); draft when empty (minimum of 8 inches; maximum of 18 inches); draft when loaded (minimum of 4 feet; maximum of 6 feet).

---

[83] By-Laws, Rules and Regulations; In Force on the Chesapeake and Ohio Canal, 1st April 1851 (Baltimore, 1894), 4–9.

[84] This total includes the cancellation and reregistration of 16 boats for various reasons, thus making the actual number of boats plying the canal at 207. It is estimated that about 140 of these boats were new, the majority of which were Class A or C involved in the carrying of coal.

Class D—length (minimum of 66 feet, 7 inches; maximum of 90 feet); width (minimum of 10 feet, 8 inches; maximum of 14 feet, 6 inches); draft when empty (minimum of 6 inches; maximum of 4 feet, 2 inches).

Class E—length (minimum of 58 feet, 10 inches; maximum of 85 feet, 4 inches); width (minimum of 13 feet, 4 inches; maximum of 14 feet, 6 inches); draft when empty (minimum of 10 inches; maximum of 12 inches); draft when loaded (minimum of 2 feet, 9 inches; maximum of 4 feet, 6 inches.

Class F—length (minimum of 71 feet, 4 inches; maximum of 85 feet); width (minimum of 9 feet, 1 inch; maximum of 14 feet, 6 inches); draft when empty (minimum of 1½ inches; maximum of 6 inches); draft when loaded (minimum of 10 inches; maximum of 3 feet, 6 inches).[85]

d. Capacity of Early Boats on the Completed Waterway

In April 1851 the first general descriptions of the boats on the canal appears in the company records. As some of the levels only had a depth of five feet of water, the boats were drawing an average of 4 feet, thereby permitting the largest boats to carry from 100 to 110 tons (of 2,240 pounds) of coal. Within a month the draft of the boats was to be increased to 4 feet, 3 inches, and by 1852 the average draft was expected to be 4 feet, 6 inches, thus allowing the largest boats to carry cargoes of up to 120 tons. The average cost of the canal boats was estimated at $1,200.[86]

At the end of the first boating season following the completion of the canal to Cumberland, the company reported to the Maryland Secretary of State concerning the state of the navigation. Among other items, the company clerk noted that the number of boats navigating the canal was 205 of which about 140 were engaged in the coal trade. The majority of these boats were "new and built expressly for coal transportation." They were generally capable of transporting upwards of 100 tons, and when the level of the water in the canal would permit the average tonnage of the boats would increase to more than 120.[87]

e. Increase of Boats on the Canal

Trade began on the completed waterway with a severe shortage of boats. During the boating season of 1851 the company reported that the inadequate number of boats was hurting the prospects of an extended coal business. The board observed wistfully that

> we cannot but repeat the hope, that from the high rates of transportation paid, and the constant occupation which may be given, strong inducements will exist with capitalists to engage in boating; and that before the close of the present year, a much larger number may be added.[88]

In the succeeding years, the number of boats navigating the canal continued to increase. By the end of the 1852 boating season, 237 boats were registered for transportation on the waterway. Of this total, about 61 were new and 160 were engaged in the coal trade and the majority were capa-

---

[85] Record of Boat Registrations, 1851–74, C&O Co.
[86] Ringgold to Barnes, April 23, 1851, Ltrs. Sent, C&O Co., and *Twenty-Third Annual Report* (1851), C&O Co., 5, 8.
[87] Ringgold to O'Neal, December 26, 1851, Ltrs. Sent, C&O Co.
[88] *Twenty-Third Annual Report* (1851), 8.

ble of carrying between 100 and 130 tons. The coal boats averaged two full round trips on the waterway per month.[89]

In May 1854 it was reported that 290 boats were registered for navigation on the canal, of which about 200 were engaged in the coal trade. Although few boats had been added on the canal during the previous year, the board reported that the prospects for boat-building during the present boating season were encouraging.[90]

The following year in June the company stockholders were informed that 323 boats were registered for service on the canal. About 200 were engaged in the coal trade with capacities ranging from 110 to 125 tons each.[91]

During the next year 20 new boats were put into service on the canal, thus bringing the total registered to 343. However, it was observed by company officials that this figure did not represent the actual number of boats in "active and efficient service." Many boats had decayed or had become otherwise unserviceable and had been withdrawn from the canal. Others, which had required repairs, had not been put into active service because the severe winter had prevented their refitting. Thus, only about 250 boats were in active service. Since the board asserted that it was powerless to increase the number of boats, it depended on "individual enterprise" to supply "these means of transportation."[92]

There was a tremendous increase in boat-building along the canal beginning in the winter of 1856–57 and continuing through the summer of 1858. The surge was primarily the result of the company's decision to replace with substantial masonry structures Dams Nos. 4 and 5, which had been unable to supply adequate amounts of water to the canal for years because of chronic leaking. More than 100 new boats were ready for the spring boating season in 1857. During the next twelve months the board observed that new boats were "multiplying daily, one single gentleman having already invested in building boats near $100,000, and intending to build at his own yard 5 new boats monthly" throughout the summer of 1858. Furthermore, others were operating on a smaller scale all along the canal "actively engaged in building new boats." Optimistically the directors noted that

> steady, enterprising, and valuable men of small means along the entire line, who could procure horses and equipments for the boats,—a class of men of the highest value to the successful development of the energies which have too long lain hidden in the bosom of this work, but which were and are beginning to be aroused,—were in anxious inquiry for Boats, by the conduct of which they would enrich themselves, and the builders, with unerring certainty, the navigation being regular and uninterrupted.[93]

In the spirit of expansion, the board purchased a number of boats from the recently-enlarged Erie Canal during the winter of 1857–58 to engage in the Cumberland coal trade.[94]

f. Description of Ante-Bellum Canal Boats

Few descriptions of the physical make-up of the boats plying the canal after 1850 have survived. However, there is one account written by an unemployed New England man who, during the

---

[89] Ringgold to Eachus, April 22 and November 9, 1852, and Ringgold to O'Neal, December 16, 1852, Ltrs. Sent, C&O Co., and *Twenty-Fourth Annual Report* (1852), C&O Co., 12.
[90] Ringgold to Eachus, May 10, 1854, Ltrs. Sent, C&O Co.
[91] *Twenty-Seventh Annual Report* (1855), C&O Co., 14.
[92] *Twenty-Eighth Annual Report* (1856), C&O Co. 8–9
[93] *Twenty-Ninth Annual Report* (1857), C&O Co, 12, 19.
[94] Ringgold to Shaw, May 29, 1858, Ltrs. Sent, C&O Co.

summer of 1850, made a round-trip voyage on the canal from Cumberland to Georgetown and on to Alexandria and return. In an anonymous manuscript, which has been edited by Ella E. Clark and Thomas F. Hahn and printed under the title *Life On The Chesapeake & Ohio Canal 1859* (1975), the writer made some interesting observations on the canal boats [See Appendix K].

g. Canal Boats during the Civil War

During the Civil War, great destruction was wrought upon the canal and its trade. The boats received their share of damage as the federal government seized about 100 for the defense of Washington and boat-burning and mule-stealing became regular practices along the canal.

In March and April 1862, during the panic accompanying the specter of the Merrimac running wild on the Potomac and bombarding Washington, the government seized the boats and took some 60 of them to Georgetown where they were held for use in case of emergency. About 36 of these vessels were moved down the river for possible use in heading off a Southern attack coming up the Potomac, and 8 of them were filled with stone and sunk to block the channel of the river. The remaining 40 boats were used by officers of the Union army to transport government stores from various points on the canal to Alexandria.[95]

When the shipment of the government stores to Alexandria was completed in April, the 40 canal boats were released to their owners. The remaining 60 boats that were held in Georgetown and those taken down the river remained in government hands for a longer period, and many of them were never returned to the canal. Thus, the board announced in June that the number of boats "now serviceable for the coal trade, inclusive of some recently built, and others now building was about 150."[96] Later, however, in October 1862 and in June and July 1863 more of the boats were seized by the government for briefer periods during General Robert E. Lee's two invasions of Maryland.[97]

Boat-burning and mule-stealing became regular occurrences by June 1863. A number of boats were destroyed on the Williamsport and Hancock Divisions during Lee's second invasion of Maryland during that summer.[98] In 1864, other raids by Early, Mosby, and White, in July, August, and September, respectively, caused widespread damage to the canal and its boats, some 60 of which were burned during Early's raid alone.[99] By this time, even the threat or rumor of a raid was sufficient to send the boatmen scurrying for shelter.[100]

h. Resurgence of Navigation on the Canal

In the years following the Civil War, the canal was gradually restored and commerce, sparked by the heavy demand for the Cumberland coal, soon improved over pre-war levels. By June 1870, 395 boats were engaged in the coal trade.[101] In fact the commerce on the canal prospered to such a degree in the early 1870s that one of the officers of the Maryland Free Stone Company, the firm that operated the Seneca Quarries, complained in June 1871 that the Georgetown level was so clogged with boats as to stop "navigation almost entirely." On the morning of June 14 he had counted ten tiers of boats three abreast, twenty tiers two abreast, and two tiers four abreast.[102]

---

[95] Greene to Ringgold, March 24, April 11 and 16, 1862, Ltrs. Recd., C&O Co.
[96] *Thirty-Fourth Annual Report* (1864), C&O Co., 3–6.
[97] Washington *Evening Star*, July 15, 1863.
[98] *Proceedings of the President and Board of Directors*, K, 366.
[99] Ibid, K, 385, 398, 429, and Walter S. Sanderlin, *"The Vicissitudes of the Chesapeake and Ohio Canal During the Civil War,"* Journal of Southern History, Vol. XI (February, 1945).
[100] Greene to Spates, September 29, 1864, and Spates to Ringgold, October 16, 1864, Ltrs. Recd., C&O Co.
[101] Clarke to Weber, June 20, 1870, Ltrs. Sent, C&O Co.
[102] Hayden to Clark, June 14, 1871, Ltrs. Recd., C&O Co.

During the winter of 1871–72, 60 new boats were built along the canal, thus bringing the carrying capacity of the boats plying the waterway to 1,000,000 tons of coal in an 8-month boating season of uninterrupted navigation.[103] The great increase of the coal trade was demonstrated in an October 1872 Cumberland *News* article comparing the volume of traffic on the waterway for the current boating season up to October 16 with that of the corresponding period of the 1867 season as follows:

	Boats Cleared	Tons Shipped	Ave. Tonnage of ( )
1872	6,351	697, 036.15	109.24
1867	3,346	361,501.08	108.10 ½
Increase	3,005	335,535.07	1.13 ½ [104]

The following winter in February 1873 the Williamsport *Pilot* reported that there were 400 boats in constant operation on the canal during the boating season, requiring employment of 2,000 mules.[105] In 1873 canal officials reported that the coal companies built 91 new boats at Cumberland and put them into service, increasing the number of vessels navigating the canal to about 500 with an average capacity of 112 tons.[106] One boat passed over the entire line in 1873 carrying 131 tons of coal.[107] The following year the stockholders were informed that 79 boats were built in Cumberland alone and that the average annual tonnage of the vessels plying the waterway had risen to 113½ as a result of the continuing improvements along the line.[108]

During the years 1873–74, the canal company surveyed the condition of the boats on the waterway and reregistered them on a new list. As this reregistration coincides with the peak years of the canal trade, it is interesting to look at its listings closely. Its value is enhanced by the fact that it is the last register of boats extant in the company records that indicates the classification and dimensions of each vessel.

According to the 1873–74 register, there were 539 boats operating on the canal. The boats were divided into the following classifications as established by the 1851 regulations:

Class A	110
Class B	56
Class C	358
Class D	14
Class E	1

The register listed the dimensions of the boats, which indicated the great disparity in the sizes of the vessels. The dimensions of the various classes of craft were as follows:

Class A—length (minimum of 89 feet; maximum of 92 feet); width (minimum of 14 feet; maximum of 14 feet, 6 inches); draft when empty (minimum of 11 inches; maximum of 18 inches); draft when loaded (minimum of 4 feet, 6 inches; maximum of 4 feet, 9 inches).

---

[103] *Forty-Fourth Annual Report* (1872), C&O Co., 8.
[104] Cumberland *News*, October 18, 1872, in Arthur P. Gorman Collection, University of North Carolina, Chapel Hill.
[105] Williamsport *Pilot*, February 8, 1873. The mules consumed some 25,000 barrels of corn, 3,840 bushels of oats, and several thousands tons of hay that year at a cost of nearly $60,000.
[106] *Forty-Sixth Annual Report* (1874), C&O Co., 14.
[107] *Proceedings of the President and Board of Directors*, M, 114.
[108] *Forty-Seventh Annual Report* (1875), C&O Co., 9–37.

Class B—length (minimum of 50 feet; maximum of 90 feet); width (minimum of 13 feet, 4 inches; maximum of 14 feet, 6 inches); draft when empty (minimum of 10 inches; maximum of 18 inches); draft when loaded (minimum of 2 feet, 6 inches; maximum of 4 feet, 9 inches).

Class C—length (minimum of 88 feet; maximum of 96 feet); width (minimum of 14 feet; maximum of 14 feet, 6 inches); draft when empty (minimum of 10 inches; maximum of 18 inches); draft when loaded (minimum of 4 feet, 6 inches; maximum of 4 feet, 9 inches).

Class D—length (minimum of 75 feet; maximum of 90 feet); width (minimum of 14 feet; maximum of 14 feet, 6 inches); draft when empty (minimum of 8 inches; maximum of 14 inches); draft when loaded (minimum of 3 feet; maximum of 4 feet, 6 inches).

The one boat in Class E was 90 feet in length, 14 feet, 2 inches in width, and had a draft of 1 foot when empty and 2 feet, 6 inches when loaded.

Two boats in Class C were described as scows, one of which was 59 feet in length and the other 65 feet. Both were 14 feet wide and had a draft of 9 inches when empty. One had a draft of 2 feet, 6 inches when loaded and the other 3 feet, 6 inches.

The ownership of the boat demonstrates the tremendous influence of the coal trade on the canal commerce. While almost all the boats registered in 1851 had been owned by individual owners, nearly one-fourth of the boats on the 1873–74 list were owned by the coal companies. The companies who owned boats were as follows:

	Class A	Class B	Class C	Class D	Scows
American Coal Co.	24	8	46		
Consolidated Coal Co.	18	10	27		
Borden Mining Co.	1				
Maryland Free Stone Co.				9	
Washington Blue Stone Co.			1		2
Potomac Cement Co.			1		109

i. Declining Years of the Canal Trade

In the latter 1870s trade on the canal declined appreciably. From a peak of 973,805 tons carried on the waterway in 1875, the total tonnage was reduced to 662,508 three years later. Thus, it is not surprising to find that the register of boats for that year listed a total of only 391 vessels as operating on the waterway. Reflecting the fact that about 95 percent of the trade consisted of the movement of coal was the register's listing 283 boats as employed by the coal companies. The breakdown of this figure was as follows:

CUMBERLAND COAL COMPANIES
American Coal Company   62 boats
Borden Company   49 boats

---

109 Record of Boat Registrations, 1851 – 74, C & O Co. Many of the remaining boats that were individually owned were employed by the coal companies.

Consolidated Coal Company	39 boats
Maryland Coal Company	38 boats
New Central Coal Company	44 boats
Hampshire Coal Company	28 boats
Blaen Avon Coal Company	14 boats

WILLIAMSPORT COAL COMPANIES

| Steffy & Findlay Company | 5 boats |
| Embrey & Cushwa Company | 4 boats |

Of the remaining 108 boats on the canal, 8 were listed as grain boats, 1 as a brick boat, and 1 as a limestone boat. The other 91 were classified as "outside boats" presumably for the use of general trade.

The 1878 register of boats is a valuable document as it is the only extant list that gives the name of the firm that built the boats and the year in which they were built. The names of the boat builders, almost all of which were based in Cumberland, were as follows:

Doener and Bender	76 boats
Weld and Sheridan	52 boats
William Young	62 boats
Frederick Mertens	141 boats
B. Mitchell	2 boats
Consolidation Coal Company	39 boats
R. & M. Coulehan	11 boats
Issac Gruber	7 boats
Unnamed (Built at Tidewater)	1 boat

The breakdown of the boats by the year in which they were built is as follows:

1868	6 boats
1869	23 boats
1870	32 boats
1871	82 boats (including 4 rebuilt)
1872	67 boats (including 5 rebuilt)
1873	58 boats (including 2 rebuilt)
1874	80 boats (including 1 rebuilt)
1875	25 boats (including 2 rebuilt)
1876	13 boats
1877	5 boats

Sixteen of the boats were listed as steamers.[110]

The years between 1878 and 1889 were a time of declining trade and financial stress for the canal company. Although the average tonnage carried per boat rose to 114 during the 1880 boating season as a result of improvements to the waterway after the 1877 flood, the total amount of goods passing up and down the waterway continued to decline. The series of heavy floods in

---

[110] Register of Boats Employed on the Canal, January 1, 1878, C&O Co.

the 1880s climaxed by the titanic freshet in 1889 marked the final phase of canal operations before it went into a receivership.[111]

2. TOPICS OF SPECIAL CONCERN

a. Promotion of Steam Packet Service

The promotion of steam packet service became a topic of special concern to the canal company after the completion of the waterway to Cumberland. On July 9, 1851, the directors granted permission to W. R. L. Ward, the operator of the New York-based Cumberland Line, to run a steam packet boat on the canal free of tolls. The conditions that Ward accepted as his part of the bargain were: (1) the General Superintendent would monitor the craft for signs of damage to the canal resulting from the speed of the boat and would accordingly prescribe the rate of speed of the vessel; (2) all articles carried on the boat, other than its fixtures and furniture, would be subject to the established toll rates; and (3) company packages and officers would be transported on the regular trips of the vessel free of charge.[112]

Some two months later on September 22 the board authorized the firm of Reeside and Lynn to run two or three packets on the canal between Georgetown and Harpers Ferry free of toll for a period of two years. If the firm desired, the board determined to extend the privilege to Williamsport. Although Ward strenuously objected to the agreement with Reeside and Lynn, the directors were convinced that competing packets would reduce the cost of passenger service and thus promote the packet business.[113]

The packet service provided by Reeside and Lynn apparently did not survive because there is no information on their subsequent affairs. Accordingly, the board restored competition to the Ward passenger service on June 4, 1853, by granting permission to Volney Pursell to run the steam packet Congress on the canal free of toll subject to the same terms that had been given to Ward.[114]

In 1855 the canal board created some controversy by attempting to regulate the sale of liquor on the Congress. On April 5 the sale of all intoxicating beverages was prohibited. The following month the prohibition was modified "to extend only to persons employed on the canal." In September a complaint from Captain Montgomery C. Meigs stating that "disorder was frequently produced among (his) laborers employed on the Washington Aqueduct in consequence of their obtaining liquor from the packet boat Congress" led the directors to ban entirely the sale of liquor on the vessel. If the order was not complied with immediately, the Congress would be refused permission to navigate the canal.[115]

The company records reveal little about the status of the steam packet service between 1855 and 1858. The only two references to packet that could be found reported serious accidents. On July 14, 1855, a packet collided with a freight boat and sunk.[116] Some three years later on June 4, 1858, two packets owned by John Moore and W. H. Ritter collided causing extensive damage to both vessels.[117]

Other than these two references the company records reveal little about the operation of packet service on the canal until March 1859. At that time W. H. Ritter and B. F. Wells were

---

[111] *Fifty-Second Annual Report* (1880), C&O Co., 14–15.
[112] *Proceedings of the President and Board of Directors*, H, 466.
[113] *Ibid*, H, 476–477.
[114] *Ibid*, I, 27.
[115] *Ibid*, I, 169, 204.
[116] *Ibid*, I, 193.
[117] *Ibid*, K, 32.

given permission to run steam packets on the canal between Georgetown and Harpers Ferry free of toll. The boats were to operate on alternate days, and they were to yield the right-of-way to passing freight boats.[118]

The board permitted the licensing of a steamboat for the transportation of both passengers and freight for the first time in April 1860. The boat *Flying Cloud*, owned by John Moore, was to operate subject to the conditions "heretofore imposed on packet boats." Later in June 1862 Moore received a new license for the *Flying Cloud* to transport passengers and light freight, provided the boat did not exceed a speed of five miles per hour and that it paid the regular tolls.[119]

Disturbed by the findings that the propelling of the steam packets were causing damage to the canal banks, the board revised its policies relative to packet boats on several occasions in 1860. On August 15 the directors determined to prohibit the passage of steam packets on the canal after September 1. However, a petition signed by numerous parties in Georgetown and all along the canal caused them to modify their stand. On September 6, the directors agreed to the continuation of steam packet service provided that "such boats shall not draw more than three feet of water, shall not be propelled at a greater speed than four miles per hour, shall have no preference over freight boats in passing the locks, and shall be subject to the payment of tolls provided by the existing toll rates." In October an exception was made for the *Antelope* which was permitted to travel at a rate of 5 miles per hour.[120]

During the months immediately following the end of the Civil War, there was renewed interest in the establishment of steam packet service on the canal. In July John Moore received permission to operate the *George Washington* for the conveyance of passengers and light freight at the rate of 4 cents per mile for the boat and the regular tolls on the freight. The boat was not to receive any other privileges, and its maximum speed was not to exceed 5 miles per hour. Similar authorization was given to Charles H. Merrill and W. H. Ritter to operate the steam packet *Minnesota* between Georgetown and Harpers Ferry in April 1866. A third packet, operated by John Weinlrod for the transportation of freight and passengers, was authorized by the board in September 1865, but as it was propeller-driven its speed was limited to a maximum of 4 miles per hour.[121] In the winter of 1865–66, the company commissioned the construction of a steam excursion board, called the *Washington*, for the use of the president and directors. The expense of such an undertaking appears to have triggered some controversy because one company official wrote that "from my experience in Canal traveling, I incline to think, after the novelty is over, there will be no great desire for many excursions by the Prest. & directors. In this fast age canal travel has in a measure become obsolete."[122] Such a forecast was fulfilled in the case of the regular steam packets because there was no passenger service on the canal by the spring of 1867.[123] Evidence that the packet service was losing out to the Baltimore & Ohio could be seen in the company decision in August 1871 to refit a former passenger steamer lying "idle and decaying" at Cumberland as a boarding boat for the canal repair crews.[124]

From a cursory review of the canal company records, it appears that there was no further regular packet service on the canal after this period. In the 1870s Howard A. Garrett, the operator

---

[118] *Ibid*, K, 90–91, 93. Ritter operated a horse-drawn packet for more than a month before his new steam packet was ready, thus causing irritation to Wells who had his steam packet *Antelope* ready for operation when the contracts were signed.
[119] *Ibid*, K, pp.167–168, 299.
[120] *Ibid*, K, 208–209, 213–214, 216, and Ringgold to Soper, August 25, 1860, and Ringgold to Dodge, August 27, 1860, Ltrs. Sent, C&O Co.
[121] *Proceedings of the President and Board of Directors*, K, 434, 448, 483.
[122] Greene to Ringgold, December 1, 1865, Ltrs. Recd., C&O Co., and *Proceedings of the President and Board of Directors*, K, 461, 520.
[123] Ringgold to Newson, May 21, 1867, Ltrs. Sent, C&O Co.
[124] *Proceedings of the President and Board of Directors*, L, 435–436.

of Great Falls Tavern, took "pleasure parties" from Georgetown to his hotel several times a week, but he borrowed the canal paymaster's boat to do so.[125] In August 1878 Edwin Reeside contracted to carry the U. S. Mail from Washington to Point of Rocks on a steam packet for a period of three years, but there is no evidence that passenger service was connected with his operation.[126]

b. Steam-Operated Freight Boats

One of the dreams of the canal's founders was the introduction of steam-operated freight boats on the waterway that would not injure its banks. In October 1857 J. L. Cathcart of Washington informed the board that he had constructed a steam propeller for the transportation of coal which would not cause abrasion to the canal prism. Although the board refused his request to let the boat operate at half-toll, it did encourage him to experiment with the vessel on the canal.[127] Again in April 1862 the directors granted permission to J. E. Reeside to use steam-propelled boats for the transportation of coal at the established toll rates provided the experiment would not damage the canal banks.[128] Apparent from the company records that neither of these two experiments was successful.

In April 1871 Chief Engineer William R. Hutton submitted to the board a new scheme for steam navigation on the canal devised by John W. Duval, a blacksmith and wheelwright in Georgetown. Under this plan, the boat would carry "two wheels which can be raised & lowered." The one near the stern would serve as a guide wheel to keep the boat on a wooden rail which would run along the side of the canal on short posts. The other wheel would serve as a driving wheel, "working on a cranked axle" and "revolved by a small steam engine." To avoid being lifted off the track and to procure the required degree of traction, the wheels would be kept down "by the pressure of steam in a piston working in a cylinder connection with the boiler."[129]

During the 1870s the number of steamers plying the canal increased slowly. In 1873 one steamer was built to navigate the canal, and three more were constructed the following year. The 1875 boating season saw at least five new steam-driven coal boats were introduced on the canal. Among the most successful of these was the *Ludlow Patten* built by William Young and employed by the Borden Coal Company. It was the first coal boat to leave Cumberland for Georgetown at the commencement of the canal navigation that year. At the end of the season the company officials recommended it as the most efficient and seaworthy steam-propelled coal boat to navigate the canal to date.[130]

In the winter and spring of 1875–76 the canal board took further steps to encourage the use of steamboats in the canal trade. H. Ashton Ramsay, a builder of iron ships and marine engines and boilers in Baltimore, was commissioned to build a model "iron screw steamer" which the directors chose to name the *Maryland*. The boat, which entered service on the canal some time in June, had an iron hull, two decks, and a skylight.[131]

The number of steamers on the canal continued to mount as four were built in 1876 and three more in 1877, making a total of sixteen by 1878. The register of boats in the latter year listed the owners, builders, and employers of the steamers as follows:

---

[125] Garrett to Gorman, April 22, 1874, Ltrs. Recd., C&O Co.
[126] Reeside to President and Board of Directors, August 11, 1878, Ltrs. Recd., C&O Co.
[127] *Proceedings of the President and Board of Directors*, I, 385–386.
[128] *Ibid,* K, 287–288.
[129] Hutton to Clarke, April 20, 1871, Ltrs. Recd., C&O Co.
[130] Webber to Fawcett, April 1, 1875, and Pearce to Fawcett, February 26, 1876, Ltrs. Recd., C&O Co.
[131] Hutton to Gorman, January 26, March 29, May 24, 26, June 28, July 11, August 24, 30, 1876, Ltrs. Recd., C&O Co.

Owners	Cowden and Sons	1
	John Gorman	1
	William G. Hassett & Bro.	2
	Weld & Sheridan	5
	Benjamin Mitchell	1
	Patrick Ganly	1
	Paul & Sinclair	1
	Doener & Bender	4
Builders	William Young	4
	Weld & Sheridan	6
	R. & M. Coulehan	2
	Doener & Bender	4
Employers	Borden Coal Company	4
	Maryland Coal Company	7
	New Central Coal Company	1
	General Trade	4[132]

The number of steamboats carrying coal on the canal increased to 19 by 1879. In that year the steamers made a total of 272 trips on the waterway transporting 26,428.19 tons. Thus, the average number of trips for each steamer during the boating season was about 14 while the average tonnage carried per trip was 97.16.[133] Regular steamboat operation continued thereafter until 1889.

STEAMERS—1879

	TONS	CWT	TRIPS
Star 1	1,678	4	17
Star 2	1,515	16	16
Star 3	1,958	17	20
Star 4	1,642	11	17
Star 5	1,793	19	18
Star 6	1,427	9	15
Star 7	788	6	8
H. G. Wagner	815	15	8
Arcturus	2,058	14	22
A. Lovell	1,897	11	19
New Era 1,	469	14	15
Regulus	1,839	0	19
Antares	669	18	7
F. L. Moore	1,554	18	16
L. Patton	1,048	6	11
T. Venners	1,086	6	11
Hancock	693	14	7
H. J. Weld	662	2	7
T. H. Paul	1,827	19	19
	26,428	219	272

---

[132] Register of Boats Employed On the Canal, January 1, 1878, C&O Co.
[133] *Fifty-Second Annual Report* (1880), C&O Co., 28. A summary of the number of trips and total tonnage carried by each steamer may be seen on the following page. During the same year, the total number of trips, the total tonnage, and the average tonnage per trip for coal boats pulled by animal-power was 4,425; 496,475.03; and 112.17 respectively.

c. Double Boats

Faced with the growing competition of the Baltimore & Ohio Railroad, the canal company began a series of improvements to the waterway to increase its carrying capacity. In 1875 the board announced its intention of doubling the length of the locks so that "double boats" transporting up to 250 tons could ply the waterway. The "double boats," which in reality were two canal boats fastened together, would reduce the cost of freight by nearly 50 percent at little increase of power. Thus, the boat owners and operators would receive a better margin of profit, the cost of transportation would favorably compete with that of the railroad, and the company could charge tolls that would produce enough revenue to cancel its debts. Various experiments were undertaken, including one by the Maryland Coal Company, to test the ability of the mules to pull two boats, but the dreams of the company were soon dashed by the major floods of 1877, 1886, and 1889, and the accompanying financial reverses.[134]

d. Provisions for Repair of Canal Boats

During the period 1851 to 1889 the canal company made greater provision for the repair of the craft plying the waterway than it had in earlier years. At various times the board established committees to examine all the boats being loaded to see if they were fit for navigation.[135] At other times the directors ordered the re-registration of all the boats on the canal, a process which meant that the boats would have to be examined and their dimensions taken before receiving a new license to navigate the canal.[136] If the boats did not meet the standards established by the company regulations they had to be repaired in the drydocks along the canal or in the small boat yards along the canal such as those at Georgetown, Weverton, and Hancock.[137] When the boats required a major refitting the task of rebuilding was usually done at the larger boat yards in Cumberland. In addition, vessels that were damaged in accidents on the canal were generally taken to the nearest drydock for repairs.

After the completion of the canal to Cumberland, the board made provision for the construction and lease of drydocks along the waterway. The forms were to be executed by the parties then holding grants from the company as well as for those who would apply for such privileges in the future. The authority to grant permission for the building of such structures was given to the chief engineer subject to the approval of the directors.[138]

During the 1851–89 period, there were at least six drydocks built along the line of the canal. Their locations and dates were as follows:

1. Locks Nos. 45–46—On September 14, 1854, Lewis G. Stanhope was granted permission to construct a drydock at Locks Nos. 45–46.[139]

2. Lock No. 30—Thomas Hassett was given permission on September 7, 1855, to build a drydock near Lock No. 47. Later in March 1864, the board granted him a 10-year "privilege" to continue the operation of this drydock.[140]

---

[134] *Forty-Seventh Annual Report* (1875), C&O Co., 16–17; *Fifty-Second Annual Report* (1880), C&O Co., 15–16; and Grason to Gorman, June 12, 1877, Ltrs. Recd., C&O Co.
[135] Mulvany to Gorman, June 28, 1872, and Resley to Gorman, March 7, 1873, Ltrs. Recd., C&O Co.
[136] The registration process was ordered by the board on at least five occasions during the period from 1851 to 1889.
[137] Mitchell to President and Directors, October 29, 1875, and Moore to Gorman, August 31, 1878, Ltrs. Recd., C&O Co.
[138] *Proceedings of the President and Board of Directors*, H, 434.
[139] *Proceedings of the President and Board of Directors*, K, 480.
[140] *Ibid*, K, 375.

3. Lock No. 44—On May 5, 1862, Charles Embrey & Son were granted the right to build a drydock above Lock No. 44 under the direction of the Superintendent of the Williamsport Division. The drydock was located on private property at the mouth of a ravine which had been depositing sediment into the canal for years. Accordingly, they were permitted to run a trunk under the canal to carry off the water from the ravine as well as the drydock.[141]

4. Lock No. 14—On April 29, 1864, John Ellis was given permission to construct a drydock above Lock No. 14 under the supervision of the Superintendent of the Georgetown Division.[142]

5. Edward's Ferry Basin—In November 1872 the board directed the Superintendent of the Monocacy Division to build a drydock at Edward's Ferry for a sum not to exceed $100. After its construction, the drydock was rented to Colonel E. V. White of White's Ferry.[143]

6. Lock No. 10—A letter from Richard M. Minnis to the canal president on November 10, 1875, refers to the operation of a drydock "in the rear" of Lock No. 10. There is no other information in the company records relative to its construction.[144]

C. BOATS ON THE CHESAPEAKE & OHIO CANAL 1889-1924

1. GENERAL DESCRIPTIVE MATERIAL

There is little documentary information on the boats plying the canal during the receivership period. In 1902 the Canal Towage Company was organized to provide economy and regularity in the runs of the waterway. Sponsored by the Consolidation Coal Company and the canal receivers, this company supplied the boats, teams, and equipment, and established a regular schedule for the boatmen to follow. It also cut freight rates and controlled the distribution of cargoes. Boats were numbered instead of named, and they became more uniform and utilitarian. Traffic on the canal became regularized on a time-table basis.[145]

In a National Park Service report prepared in 1939-40 by Thomas C. Vint, Chief of Planning of the Branch of Plans and Design, the methods used to build the boats for the Canal Towage Company were described. All of the barges

> were built in Cumberland by local boatwrights who were so familiar through experience with the job that they used no plans or drawings. Their only guides were a set of sheet-metal templates for the big uprights at the end of the boats. These timbers established the curves at bow and stern and the planking at these points was 1½" oak, steamed and bent to fit. The rest of the structure was of straight lumber, generally Georgia pine. The seven longitudinal heels were three 6" by 6" members and 4" x 6" members. The bottom plank-

---

[141] *Ibid*, K, 291-292.
[142] *Ibid*, K, 391.
[143] White to President and Directors, November 21, 1872, Ltrs. Recd., C&O Co.
[144] Minnis to Gorman, November 10, 1875, Ltrs. Recd., C&O Co.
[145] *Washington Evening Star*, July 11, 1905.

ing nailed transversely under the keels was of 3" lumber, dressed to an even thickness, and the inner planking which constituted the floor of the cargo holds, was of 2" stuff.[146]

In an interview with National Park Service officials in January 1939, George L. Nicholson, the general manager of the canal from 1891 to 1938, elaborated on the average dimensions of the boats during the receivership period. The barges were 14 feet, 6 inches in the beam and 93 feet in total length. The straight sides of the boats were 85 feet long to the points where they tapered to the bow and stern. Their hulls were 7 feet deep and their draft when fully loaded was 5 feet, 3 inches.

The boats had a cabin, 12 feet by 14 feet, on the stern, under which was a 3-foot space which was filled with coal. In the center of the boat there was another cabin, about 6 feet by 6 feet, called the hay house, where the hay was kept and where the crew slept. The mules, usually 4 or 5 (2 large and 3 smaller ones), were kept in the bow of the boat. The tow rope was 9/16-inch Plymouth rope and generally about 225 feet long. The boats usually carried some 115 gross tons. After the 1889 flood no packet or passenger boats operated on the canal, and there were few motorboats most of which were privately-owned pleasure craft.[147]

One other source, that of a field survey made by the *Monthly Labor Review* in 1921, gives some general details relative to the physical make-up of the canal boats during the receivership period and the procedures used to operate them. While the dimensions given in this report differ somewhat from those provided by Nicholson, the report nevertheless provides a clearer picture of the compartments on deck. The report states:

> The average size of the cabins on the boats of the Chesapeake & Ohio Canal was 10 by 12 feet. All cabins had two bunks, one set into the inner wall of the main cabin and the other located in the so-called stateroom, which was partitioned off from the main cabin by a diagonal wall. These bunks were 36 inches wide, sufficient space for one person but ordinarily occupied by two. In addition to the cabin bunks, the feed box extending across the deck at the center of the boat was ordinarily used for sleeping purposes. This box was 4 feet wide and 4 feet high....

Relative to the operation of the canal boats, it was noted that two procedures were involved– driving the mules and steering the boat. The mules were harnessed tandem to two long ropes or "lines" attached to the bow of the boat. From two to five mules were used in "spells," two or three mules being stabled in the fore cabin at rest while the other pulled the boat. The boat hands took turns at driving, either walking beside the mules or riding the leader.

Steering the boat was accomplished by means of the "stick." This controlled the rudder and could be guided by the pilot sitting or standing against it. As there was virtually no current to change the direction of the boat, the operation was simple unless the boat was heavily loaded.[148]

---

[146] Thomas O. Vint, *Outline Report of Architectural Work on the Restoration of the Chesapeake and Ohio Canal for Recreational Use, Georgetown D. C. To Seneca, Md.* (NPS Mss., (1939–40)), 13–14. Much of Vint's research on the boat was gathered from measurements he made in the late 1930s of the only surviving canal boat then stuck in the mud near Hancock. A copy of the drawings of this boat from Vint's report may be seen in Appendix J.

[147] Statement of George L. Nicholson, January 25, 1939, Misc. NPS Mss. An account of a trip down the canal in a privately-owned motorboat may be seen in John P. Cowan, *Sometub's Cruise on the C&O Canal* (Pittsburgh, 1916), 5–44.

[148] Ethel M. Springer, "Canal Boat Children," Children's Bureau, U. S. Department of Agriculture, reprinted from *Monthly Labor Review* (Washington, 1923), 5–9.

2. GOVERNMENT-OWNED COAL BARGES DURING WORLD WAR I

During the spring of 1918 the Washington *Evening Star* and several citizens' groups in the Potomac Valley advocated government control of the canal as a means of increasing coal shipments to Washington and thereby relieving congestion on the railroads. The proposal was endorsed by an Inland Waterways Commission survey ordered by William Gibbs McAdoo, who had been appointed as director general of the railroads and coastwise and intercoastal shipping when they were temporarily nationalized on January 1, 1918. The commission entered into an agreement with the Canal Towage Company to increase the delivery of coal to the boats and to facilitate the unloading of the coal at Washington and at government stations along the Potomac River. Later the government entered into a contract with the company guaranteeing it against loss in operation. It was determined that the government would supply ten new coal barges to supplement the 80 vessels then employed by the company in the coal trade.

The ten government coal barges were constructed at Elizabeth City, North Carolina. The vessels were towed from that place by way of Albemarle Sound to Norfolk and from thence up Chesapeake Bay and the Potomac. Five of the boats arrived in Washington in late September and the remaining five in early October. There is no information on the dimensions, capacity, or physical description of these boats.[149]

---

[149] Washington *Evening Star*, September 26, 1918.

II. REGULATIONS FOR NAVIGATING THE
CHESAPEAKE & OHIO CANAL: 1830–1924

A. REGULATIONS 1830–1835

Just prior to the opening of the canal between Little Falls and Seneca Falls in November 1830, the board determined to adopt a "system of rules for the government of toll collectors and the protection of their works, as well as for the regulation of boats." Accordingly, the directors authorized Clerk Ingle to write to Silas Conduct, president of the Morris Canal and Banking Company that operated the Morris Canal, Edward Everett, a Massachusetts legislator active in the promotion of his state's canals, Gideon Tomlinson, Governor of the State of Connecticut, Horatio Seymour, a New York State Canal Commissioner, and Samuel Fleuding, treasurer of the Delaware and Hudson Canal Company. Ingle was to request from these men copies of laws passed by their States relative to police powers on their canals and of regulations passed by the various canal companies under their jurisdiction.[150]

After receiving the replies to these inquiries, the board immediately noticed that its company charter contained "no express provision" giving it the authority to establish by-laws, rules and regulations for the preservation of the works on the canal, and the policing of its navigation. Apparently, the framers of the company charter had overlooked this important item as all the other canal companies had such a provision in their charters authorizing them to pass and enforce regulations "in subordination to the Constitution and laws of the United States, and of the several States in which they exist, and are required to act."[151] Thus, the directors on October 19 authorized President Mercer to present memorials to the Maryland General Assembly and the U. S. Congress requesting the enactment of such laws "as shall be calculated to establish a suitable police on the Chesapeake & Ohio Canal, and to protect from injury the rights and interests of the Company in their works and other property."[152] Despite the entreaties of Mercer neither legislative body enacted the proposed legislation that year.

Through the winter months of 1830–31, President Mercer drafted several regulations "for registering all the boats as they may enter the Canal at Seneca" and "for prohibiting the use of poles pointed with iron, in navigating the Canal." On March 25, 1831, the board adopted these rules with some modifications and ordered them to be printed.[153]

On April 2, 1831, Daniel Van Slyke, the newly-appointed Superintendent of the Canal, reported to President Mercer that the canal had been thronged with boats since it was opened to navigation on March 19. Canal officials had experienced great difficulty in preserving order among the boatmen "who in striving to push forward for a preference in passing the several locks are sometimes disposed to injure each others boats as a means of carrying their point." Such an incident had taken place at one of the locks on Section

---
[150] Ingle to Conduct, *Ibid.* to Everett, *Ibid.* to Tomlinson, *Ibid.* to Seymour, and *Ibid.* to Fleuding, October 5, 1830, Ltrs. Sent, C&O Co.
[151] *Third Annual Report* (1831), in *Proceedings of the Stockholders*, A, 173.
[152] *Proceedings of the President and Board of Directors*, B, 206.
[153] *Ibid*, B, 290.

No. 9 (Locks Nos. 12, 13, or 14) the previous week when a "strongly constructed boat ran her bow against a gondola loaded with flour, and so much injured her as to render it necessary to transship the load." Since fifteen or twenty boats frequently arrived at a lock within thirty minutes, it was important that the board, formulate and publish regulations governing the lock tender and the order in which boats would be permitted to pass the locks.[154]

The board responded to this request on May 6 by authorizing Mercer "to prepare and cause to be published, a code of, regulations for the government of the lock keepers, boat-men, packet owners, and others having business on the canal."[155] On July 16 he submitted a draft of the regulations for navigating the canal, and after making some amendments, the board adopted them and ordered them to be printed for distribution.[156]

Included in the regulations was a stipulation that all craft on the waterway must be propelled by a towing line drawn by men and horses. Other provisions required that care be taken at all times to prevent injury to the canal and to those navigating it. The regulations prohibited the use of iron-tipped poles and forbade the operation of pointed boats and craft with iron-shod corners. Traffic was to keep to the right in passing, and a system of preference was established to facilitate navigation boats had the right of way over rafts, descending boats over ascending craft, packets over freight boats at all times, and packets carrying the mail over all others. Vessels traveling at night were required to have a light on the bow. Due notice must be given upon approaching a lock to permit the tender to open the gates, and only if the latter failed to do his duty was the boatmen to lock his own craft through. Boats were to tie up only on the berm side of the canal to prevent interference with traffic on the towpath. All craft must be registered and plainly marked on both sides with name, number, and marks denoting the draft of the vessel.[157]

The text of the "Regulations for Navigating the Chesapeake & Ohio Canal" was as follows:[158]

July 16, 1831
REGULATIONS FOR NAVIGATING THE CHESAPEAKE & OHIO CANAL

1st   Every Boat or Float, navigating the Canal after the 15th day of August next, shall be propelled by a towing line drawn by men or horses, and shall be moreover furnished with strapping or snubbing lines for passing through the locks of the Canal without injury to the same.

2nd   No Boat or Float shall, under any circumstances, use any iron shod or sharp pointed setting pole on the Canal.

3rd   No Boat or Float shall forcibly strike, or violently rub against any other boat, or against the banks, locks, aqueducts, inside walls, or wastes, or bridges of the Canal.

---

[154] Van Slyke to Mercer, April 2, 1831, Ltrs. Recd., C&O Co.
[155] *Proceedings of the President and Board of Directors*, B, 314.
[156] *Ibid*, B, 410
[157] *Ibid*, B, 410–419.
[158] *Ibid*.

4th   No Boat or Float shall be permitted to pass along the Canal at night, unless with a conspicuous light on its bow; in case of rafts, gondolas, or scows, such light shall be at the forward end thereof.

5th   No Boat or Float shall unnecessarily lie by, or be moored opposite to any waste, or within 150 yards of any Lock, or in any short basin or pool between two locks

6th   When any owner, master, or other person having charge of any boat or float, designs to leave the same, for any time, in any other part of the Canal, he shall give notice of such intention to the Lock-keeper, in whose district the boat or float is to remain, and before he leaves his boat or float, he shall moor it along the berm, or side of the Canal opposite the towing path; and there, so secure it, as that it may, under no circumstances, lie across the Canal so as to obstruct, impede, or delay the passage of any other boat or float, along the same. And so, in like manner, when a boat or float, shall stop for the night, or lie by on account of high winds, or for any other transient or accidental cause, the owner, master, or other person having charge thereof, shall moor it securely against the berm of the Canal, or side opposite the towing path. Under no circumstances whatever, shall any boat or other floating thing, lie fastened to, or moored along the tow path of the Canal; nor shall the owner, master, or other person or persons, having charge thereof, encamp upon the towpath, or drive stakes into the top or slopes thereof, or place stones thereon, or kindle fires upon the same; or in any way or manner, obstruct or incommode the free and common use of the Canal by day or night.

7th   Any boat or float left unmoored in the Canal, without any information thereof having been given by its owner or master, or other person having charge thereof, to the Lock-keeper of the District, in which such boat or float may be found, shall be considered as abandoned by the owner, master, or other person having had charge of the same; and if sunk in the Canal, or found floating loosely thereon, shall, by the Lock-keeper aforesaid, or some person duly authorized by him, be removed from the Canal as a nuisance, and the cost of removing the same, shall be chargeable to the owner of such boat or float; and in no case, shall the Lock-keeper be required to make sale thereof, or be held accountable for preserving the same, from farther injury by reason of the neglect of the owner.

8th   No carcass, or dead animal, or putrid substance of any kind, be thrown into the Canal, or into any basin or feeder connected therewith.

9th   Square headed or sharp covered boats, such as scows and gondolas, shall each have a semicircular platform, firmly fastened upon each end thereof, so as to save other boats or floats, and the banks and locks of the Canal, from injury by contact with either of the corners thereof; and no such boat, without such provision, shall, after the first day of October next, be allowed to enter the Canal, or to pass through any lock upon the same.

10th Every Boat or Float shall have its rudder so constructed, as not to catch, interfere with, or cut the tow-rope of a passing boat.

11th No raft or tow of timber passing on the Canal, shall consist of more than eight cribs, and when consisting of more than one, they shall be so united, as to conform readily to the curvatures of the Canal banks, and to glide by the same without rubbing against them.

12th   All Boats or Floats descending the Canal, shall have a right to keep the towpath side thereof.
13th   When any Boat or Float ascending the Canal, shall be about to meet another, it shall be the duty of the owner, master, or other person navigating or having charge thereof, to turn from the towing-path, so as to allow room for the descending boat to pass with ease; provided, however, that Packets or Boats, constructed exclusively for the conveyance of passengers, shall, until otherwise ordered, have the right to keep the towing-path side, both in ascending and descending the Canal. A boat authorized to carry the United States Mail, shall have preference of all others. All boats shall have preference to rafts.
14th   When the owner, master, or other person having charge of any Boat or Float, shall perceive, or be told, or apprised by sounding a horn or by any other signal, that a packet boat, following him can, from its speed, pass him, and is desirous to do so, he shall turn his boat from the tow-path side of the Canal, and give way to the swifter moving boat to pass by, unless he be at such time within 150 yards of some Lock, in which case, if entitled to no preference, on any other score, the hinder shall wait, till the other shall pass the Lock: and all rafts shall, in like manner, give place to freight boats.
15th   The passing of one boat by another, shall be effected by checking the boat bound by the preceding rules, to give way, as soon as she has opened a passage for the other, so as that the tow-line may sink to the bottom of the Canal, the boat entitled to pass shall float over the tow-line.
16th   No Boat or Float, unless specially licensed to travel with greater speed, shall move on the Canal where its banks are not of rock on both sides, or not paved or walled on both sides, so as to guard them from abrasion, with a velocity exceeding four miles an hour.
17th   In case of any breach or leak through the Canal banks, or of the apprehension of one, the several boats or floats, which may be near the place of danger, shall take such position in the Canal, as the Superintendent, or Officer, or Engineer, or Lock-keeper of the Company, or other person charged to repair or guard against such breach or leak may direct.
18th   In all cases, boats engaged in repairing the Canal, shall have preference of all other boats, if their use at the time require it.
19th   In approaching a Lock, the boat which first arrives within 150 yards thereof, not being in any lock shall have a preference, and if several boats arrive at or near the same time, within that distance of any lock, they shall have a right to pass in the order of their arrival within that distance; provided, that if two boats, at or very near the same moment, approach from above, and below, within such distance of any lock, the descending boat shall have the preference if the lock be at such time, full of water; if empty, the ascending boat; and one boat having passed from above through a lock, another boat from below shall have liberty to pass up, before another boat be admitted from above, and vice versa, except, that packet boats shall have preference of freight boats, and a boat carrying the United States Mail, of all others.
20th   The preference granted to packet boats, by the preceding regulations, shall not extend to such as are less than 60 feet long.

21st All boats arriving within 150 yards of any lock, shall have preference of such parts of rafts as shall remain, after one or more cribs or parts of the same raft shall have already passed through any lock.

22nd Every owner, master, or other person having charge of any boat, in approaching a lock, by night, shall, for ten minutes, if necessary, give signal of his approach, by blowing a horn or knocking at the Lock-keeper's door, and if in that time, or after such knocking, the Lock-keeper shall not appear or answer, such owner, master, or other person, may proceed to let himself through the Lock, taking care to close the head-gates of the lock after passing, and to leave the paddle gates of the culverts as he found them: and no person, other than the Lock-keeper, or one acting under his authority, or with his consent shall open or shut any guard or lock gate, or handle or turn any paddle gate, but under the circumstances above stated; and at all times, for any damage to the Canal or its works, resulting from the violation of this rule, the offender shall be held personally responsible.

23rd Every Boat or Float which shall not avail itself of the first title it acquires to pass through any lock, shall lose its preference, thereat, till all the boats awaiting a passage through the same, in the same direction, shall have passed.

24th In approaching a Lock, the owner, master, or other person having charge of any boat or float, shall slacken his speed, at such distance therefrom as the Lock-tender or any person, acting by his authority, shall direct; and take care to enter the Lock without injury thereto.

25th In passing the Lock he shall fasten the bow and stern snubbing lines of his boat, to the strapping posts, on the proper side of the lock, until the lock is filled or emptied as the case may be, and in all other respects, he shall use his strapping ropes according to the instructions of the Lock-keeper, and tow his boat into or out of the lock, at such time, and in such manner as the Lock-keeper may direct. He shall especially make use of all possible diligence to go out of the lock, when the gates shall have been opened for his departure, so as to occasion no unnecessary delay to other boats, waiting to pass the same lock, or any other lock in charge of the same Lock-keeper.

26th Every breach or violation of any of the preceding regulations, by the owner, master, or other person having charge of any Boat or Float, shall be reported by the Lock-keeper, or any other person having cognizance thereof, to the Register at Rushville, or to the Collector at or near Georgetown, or to the Superintendent of the Canal, or to some other Officer of the Company, together with the number of the Boat, and the name of the owner, master, or person having charge of the same for the time being; and from the occurrence of such breach or violation of any of the said Rules, such boat shall be excluded from the navigation of the Canal, until it otherwise be adjudged and ordered by the President and Directors of the Chesapeake & Ohio Canal Company.

27th No Boat shall be used as a Packet Boat on said Canal, unless specially licensed therefore, which license shall give to the said Boat the privilege of carrying passengers to and from any point on said Canal, between the Basin at Georgetown and Rushville: and the owner or master of said Packet Boat shall pay for every trip up or down between said Basin and Rushville: or any intermediate points, the sum of one dollar and fifty cents, which sum shall be paid weekly to such Collector as may be authorized to receive the same, and on any failure to pay the said sum, or fraudulent return by the owner, master, or other person having charge of the said Boat, of the number of voyages made in the week by said Boat, its license shall be forfeited.

28th The tolls upon laden boats shall remain as heretofore, until otherwise ordered.

29th After the 1st day of August next, there shall be charged, for every empty freight boat, passing the Guard lock at Rushville, with a view of descending the Canal, the sum of one dollar, and, the same for every empty boat entering the Canal at the old locks below the Little Falls, or passing by the same up the new Canal. The same sum shall be paid for every boat having cargo, the toll upon which shall not amount to one dollar.

30th There shall be a book kept by the Register at Rushville, in which shall be entered the number, owner's name, and place of abode, length, breadth, and draft of water, of every Boat or Float navigating the Canal, except such Boat or Float as shall enter the Canal from above Seneca, without designing to return.

31st Preparatory to numbering the boats, a classification of them shall be made under the following denominations: Packet Boats, or Boats designed for passengers exclusively, Freight boats, Boats for passage and freight, Scows and Gondolas. The boats of each class or denomination, shall be numbered as they arrive at the Guard Lock, from 1 upwards.

32nd The number of each boat shall correspond with the number by which it is entered in the Register, and be inscribed on both sides of the boat, in figures not less than three inches long, near the stern thereof, so high above water that, as the boat navigates the Canal, the number may at all times be plainly discerned from either bank.

33rd On numbering and entering each boat, the Register shall issue, according to such printed form as may be prescribed, to the owner, master, or other person having charge thereof, a certificate, to be called the Boat's Register, which shall contain the number and description of the boat, and shall correspond with the entry thereof.

34th After the 15th day of August next, no Boat required to be numbered by the preceding regulations, shall be permitted to enter the Canal, or to pass through any Lock thereof, which has not been duly numbered and registered, or of which the owner, master, or other person having charge thereof, shall refuse to show the Boat's Register to any District Lock-keeper who may demand sight thereof: Provided, That any boat ascending the Canal for the first time, need not be so numbered until it shall have reached Rushville; but in lieu of a register, such boat shall be provided with a certificate from the Collector at or near Georgetown, or from the first District Lock-keeper, by whose lock it may pass, that it is on its first voyage up or down the Canal.

35th No owner, master, or other person shall alter the number of any boat, without the express permission in writing of the Register; and, on the sale or transfer of any boat from one owner to another, notice thereof shall be given when the boat next enters the Guard Lock at Rushville, to the Register, by whom a Record of such sale or transfer shall be made in the Register opposite to the number and description of the boat.

36th On the destruction or accidental loss of any Boat which has been numbered and registered, the number of such boat may be given to any boat not hitherto numbered and registered, and a new certificate issued to the owner thereof, if requested.

37th On satisfactory proof to the Register, that the certificate of any boat's register has been unintentionally destroyed, or accidentally lost, he shall renew the name, on application of the owner, master, or other person having charge of such boat.

38th Every Boat or Float duly registered, which, in descending the Potomac to Rushville, is not provided with wooden pointed setting poles, shall be entitled to receive of the Register, in exchange for its iron shod poles, an equal number of wooden pointed setting poles, for its voyage down and up the Canal, and shall have its iron shod poles returned, on delivering up those which it had received in exchange therefore; and for any poles so supplied, and which may have been lost, the Register shall demand and receive the cost thereof. No Boat or Float shall be permitted to enter the Canal, until she shall have delivered up all iron shod poles which she may have on board.[159]

At the same time the Board adopted a set of rules to govern the toll collectors along the canal in the execution of their duties. These regulations were as follows:

Whenever a descending Boat or Float applies for admission into the Canal, through the Guard Lock at Rushville, the Register and Lock-keeper thereat shall see that such boat or float is equipped as the general regulations respecting the navigation of the Canal require, and if not registered, shall see that such boat or float, if designed for a regular trader, is duly numbered and registered before it proceeds on its voyage. Having discharged this duty, the Register shall next inspect the cargo, and make out and sign a faithful list thereof, to be called a way bill, according to such printed form as may be supplied to him. This way bill he shall deliver to the owner, master, or other person having charge of such boat or float, before he enters the Guard Lock. The several way bills shall be numbered in the order in which they are issued. Of every such way bill, he shall at the same time make a brief entry in a book to be kept by him for that purpose, and ruled in columns, according to such stated forms as he may be instructed to use; which columns shall comprehend the number and date of the way bill, the number and class of the boat or float, the contents of her cargo, her destination, and the name of the owner, master or other person having charge thereof.

The owner, master or other person, in proceeding to his destination, shall deliver up this way bill to the Collector at or near Georgetown, if the destination of the boat or float be to or below the same; if to a point above, to the District Lock-keeper next above the part of the Canal to which his cargo is destined; and shall pay to the Collector, or to such District Lock-keeper, as the case may be, the toll chargeable on such boat.

Every such way bill shall be forwarded to the Company's Office in Washington, at the end of the month in which it is received, accompanied by an account of the tolls received thereon, the amount of which shall be forthwith deposited in Bank to the credit of the Company.

If any boat within this Canal shall proceed from one place to another thereon, above the Collector's office in Georgetown, and below Rushville, this owner, master or other person having charge thereof, shall receive a permit to proceed to his destination, from the first District Lock-keeper by whose lock he first passes, and shall pay his toll to the District Lock-keeper by whose house he last passes. Forms of such permits shall be supplied the Lock-keepers, and shall be filled up with the supposed tonnage of the boat,

---

[159] *Ibid.*

and the distance between it place of departure and destination, and the amount of toll chargeable thereon.

Every owner, master or other person having charge of any boat or float which may offer to pass any lock, may be required by the District Lock-keeper, or his assistant, to produce the boat's register and way bill or permit, or if his boat shall have commenced her voyage below Rushville, the state the place or places at which he took in his cargo, if he has any, and his destination, and shall pay a toll thereon according to the distance he has navigated the Canal.

Every owner, master or person having charge of any boat or float, who shall refuse either to show any Lock-keeper demanding sight thereof, his register, bill of lading, or permit, or being without either to state from whence he began his voyage, or took in, or increased his cargo, shall be refused a passage through the Lock at which such demand is made.

Each Lock-keeper shall monthly report the date of passage, number or description, owner's name, destination and cargo, of every boat or float which shall pass through his Lock without the bill of lading, and shall render in his monthly accounts and deposit in Bank to the credit of the Company, such sums as he may collect as tolls thereon.[160]

Less than one week later on July 22 the board ordered that the canal "between the Seneca feeder and the wooden lock next above the foundry and the bridges and road ways within that distance" be officially "declared open and free for trade and passing, subject to the Regulations of the Company."[161]

It is apparent from a perusal of the canal company records that there was widespread disregard of the new regulations on the canal by the boatmen. By November the directors had received numerous reports that the trunk was obstructed in various places by sunken or broken gondolas, boats, and lumber and that many of the boatmen were still propelling their boats with poles. Accordingly, the board directed Superintendent Van Slyke to require that the lock-keepers strictly enforce the regulations governing the use of poles and the design of the boats. The company engineers were authorized also to report any infringement of the company's navigation rules. Henceforth, the use of poles, except for passing the locks, would be prohibited entirely.[162]

As the company was experiencing great difficulty in enforcing its navigation by-laws, the board in early December reported the matter to the General Committee of the Stockholders. After some deliberation, the committee on December 6 determined to repeat the earlier attempt to obtain authority to establish a system of police for the preservation of the canal. Accordingly, memorials were sent to the Maryland General Assembly and the U. S. Congress requesting that the charter be amended to provide for such a police authority.[163]

This time the canal company was successful in obtaining from these two bodies laws amending the canal charter to provide for the desired police authority. During the 1831 December session, the Maryland General Assembly passed a bill providing for the following: (1) any person found guilty of injuring, impairing, or destroying any of the property or works of the company was to be taken before a local justice of the peace and was to be made subject to a fine not exceeding $50 payable to the company or he was to be indicted by a county court and, upon conviction, punished by incarceration or fine or both; (2) the company was empowered to pass by-laws for the exercise of the powers vested in it by its charter provided the regulations did not prevent

---

[160] *Ibid,* B, 419–421.
[161] *Ibid,* B, 432.
[162] *Ibid,* C, 30.
[163] *Proceedings of the Stockholders,* A, 194.

the proprietors through whose land the canal passed from having convenient access to the canal or from crossing the waterway according to agreements already made with the company (violations of the by-laws were to be punished by $5 fines); and (3) the company was given authority to prescribe the physical dimensions and equipment of the boats using the canal and to order offending boats to leave the waterway through any of the outlet locks.[164] An Act of Congress passed on July 14, 1832, gave the assent of the United States to the Maryland act.[165]

During the years 1832–33, the canal board passed various resolutions relative to the navigation rules on the canal. While they all consisted of changes in the regulations adopted earlier, their general intent was to promote the efficiency of navigation and the preservation of the canal. On March 24, 1832, it was determined that no boat cargoes could be deposited nearer than eight feet to the margin of the Rock Creek Basin and that no sand could be deposited on either side of the basin below Lock No. 1. It was decided also to discourage the accumulation of commodities on the margin of the basin by requiring that the same rate of toll, which was paid on the goods for admission into the basin, be paid each day after the first day of unloading.[166]

On June 4, 1833, the board took steps to force the lock tenders to enforce the company regulations more stringently. After this date, they would be held responsible for any damage done to the locks under their care by boats "violently" entering the chambers or by boatmen using iron-pointed poles, unless in each case of damage the number, description, and captain of the boat was reported to the Collector in Georgetown before the craft returned through the lock. The lock-keepers would be held responsible for any injury done to the lock gates or masonry unless they made a similar report. If the lock tenders failed to provide such information, the cost of repairing the damage would be deducted from their wages the following month. To make this provision effective, the canal superintendent was to certify that the locks were in good order each month before the salaries of the lock keepers were paid.[167]

In late June 1833 the board decided to have the lock tenders enforce its earlier prohibition from navigation of all square-headed or sharp-covered scows that did not have a semicircular platform firmly fastened upon each end. For an undetermined reason, gondolas were excepted from this rule, although they had been included under it since 1831.[168]

B.   REGULATIONS FOR 1835–1850

As the canal was about to be opened to navigation as far west as Dam No. 5, the directors felt that a revised code of regulations should be adopted to govern navigation on the waterway. Accordingly, an updated set of by-laws was approved on February 18, 1835, to supersede the regulations approved in July 1831 and their subsequent amendments. The only significant change was in Rule 1, which now made provision for the operation of steam boats on the canal. These revised by-laws were to continue in effect until 1851 when a new code was drawn up after the canal was completed to Cumberland.

The 1835 rules for navigation were as follows:

February 18, 1835

---

[164] *Laws Made and Passed by the General Assembly of the State of Maryland* (Annapolis, 1831), Ch. 297. A copy of excerpts from this law may be seen in Appendix H.
[165] Act of Congress, July 14, 1832. A copy of this act may be seen in Appendix I.
[166] *Proceedings of the President and Board of Directors*, C, 112.
[167] *Ibid*, C, 368–369.
[168] *Ibid*, C, 392.

BY-LAWS, RULES, AND REGULATIONS FOR NAVIGATING THE CHESAPEAKE & OHIO CANAL

1st Every boat or float navigating the Canal, and not specially licensed to move by paddle wheels, shall be propelled by a towing line, drawn by men or horses, and all boats and floats shall be moreover, furnished with strapping or snubbing lines for passing through the locks of the Canal, without injury to the same.

2nd No boat or float shall, under any circumstance, use any iron-shod or sharp pointed settling pole on the Canal; nor shall they be allowed to pass any lock till all such have been deposited with the lock keeper, whose duty it shall be safely to keep the same, and return them to the master of such boat upon her return.

3rd Square headed or sharp cornered boats, such as scows and gondolas, shall each have a semicircular platform, firmly fastened upon each end thereof, so as to save other boats or floats, and the banks and locks of the Canal, from injury by contact with either of the corners thereof; and every boat or float shall have its rudder so constructed as not to catch, interfere with, or cut the tow-rope of a passing boat.

All boats or floats not conforming to these three rules, shall be proceeded against as provided for by the act of Maryland, hereto annexed. (Appended act–Extract from an act of the General Assembly of Maryland, entitled "An act further to amend the act incorporating the Chesapeake & Ohio Canal Company," passed at the December session, 1831.)

4th Every boat, gondola, and scow, navigating the Canal, must be named or numbered, and such name or number must be inscribed, by the direction and at the expense of those who are interested in her, with oil paint, in letters or figures, not less than three inches long, on both sides of such boat, gondola, or scow, and on some permanent part thereof, so high above water that it may be plainly seen from either bank of the Canal; and such name, together with the description of boat, (i.e. whether packet boat, freight boat, gondola, or scow,) must be inserted in her register, or license, and way-bills, or permit, and be entered in the records and returns of the collectors: provided, however that, in the first voyage down, if the owners or master shall have found it inconvenient to have had such name inscribed, the boat may be permitted to pass, designating her in her way-bill, &c. as a new boat; but after arriving at her destination, she shall not be permitted to return until her name has been inscribed as above directed; and provided, also, that, where the same name or number shall have been given to two or more boats of the same description, the one which has been most recently so named or brought on to the Canal shall be required to have the name so altered, or a number added thereto, as to easily distinguish it from the previous one.

5th No raft or tow of timber passing on the Canal shall consist of more than eight cribs, and when consisting of more than one, they shall be so united as to conform readily to the curvatures of the Canal banks, and to glide by the same without rubbing against them.

6th No boat or float shall forcibly strike or violently rub against any other boat, or against the banks, locks, aqueducts, inside walls, or wastes, or bridges of the Canal.

7th   No boat or float shall be permitted to pass along the Canal at night, unless with a conspicuous light on its bow; in case of rafts, gondolas, or scows, such lights shall be at the forward end thereof.

8th   No boat or float shall unnecessarily lie by or be moored opposite to any waste, or within one hundred and fifty yards of any lock, or in any short basin or pool between two locks.

9th   When any owner, master, or other person having charge of any boat or float, designs to leave the same for any time in any other part of the Canal, he shall give notice of such intention to the nearest lock-keeper; and, before he leaves his boat or float, he shall moor it along the berm or side of the Canal opposite the towing-path, and there so secure it that no part of it shall be more than one-third of the width of the Canal from the berm-bank; and, in like manner, when a boat or float shall stop for the night, or lie by on account of high winds, or for any other transient or accidental cause, the owner, master, or other person having charge thereof, shall moor it securely along the berm side of the Canal.

10th   Under no circumstances whatever shall any boat, or other floating thing, lie fastened to or moored along the tow-path of the Canal; nor shall the owner, master, or other person or persons having charge thereof, encamp upon the tow-path, or drive stakes into the top or slopes thereof, or place stones thereon, or kindle fires upon the same, or in any way or manner obstruct or incommode the free and common use of the Canal by day or night

11th   No carcass, or dead animal, or putrid substance of any kind, shall be thrown into the Canal, or into any basin or feeder connected therewith, or be put upon or left on either bank of the Canal, or upon any part of the Canal property, so as to be offensive to travelers or others; and in the event of such being left, it shall be the duty of the lock-keeper nearest thereto to have it forthwith removed, and to endeavor to obtain such evidence as may lead to the conviction of the offender.

12th   Whenever any superintendent or lock-keeper shall find any boat or float moored or fastened in any manner to the tow-path side of the Canal, or so moored or fastened in the Canal, or to the berm side thereof, that any part of such boat or float shall be more than one-third of the width of the then water surface of the Canal from the berm-bank, he shall forthwith direct the person or persons in charge of it to prevent its continuing so to lie. And if the person or persons in charge of such boat or float shall refuse or neglect to remove the same, he or they shall be proceeded against according to law; but if no person be found on board, or near at hand, in charge of such boat or float, the superintendent or lock-keeper shall cause it to be removed, and secured as near to the nearest lock-house as conveniently may be; and when the person claiming to be the master or owner thereof, or to be acting in behalf of the master or owner, shall apply for the repossession of it, it shall be delivered to him; but if he do not at the same time pay the expense of so removing and securing it, a prosecution shall ensue for the violation of these by-laws.

13th   Whenever a superintendent or lock-keeper shall find any boat, float, or other substance, floating loose upon, or sunk in the Canal, or any of its basins, ponds, or feeders, the owner of which is unknown, or, if known, neglects or refuses, after reasonable notice, to remove the same, such superintendent or lock-keeper shall cause it to be broken up and removed from the Canal.

14th   All boats and floats descending the Canal shall have the right to keep the tow-path side thereof; and when any ascending boat or float is about to meet a descending one, it shall be the duty of the owner, master, or other person navigating or having charge thereof, to turn from the towing-path, so as to allow room for the descending boat to pass with ease; provided, however, that licensed packet boats shall, until otherwise ordered, have the right to keep the towing-path side, both in ascending and descending the Canal, with this exception: that when two such licensed packet boats meet, the ascending one shall lose its right to the towing-path side for the time occupied in passing such other packet boat.

15th Rafts shall, in all cases, give place for boats of all descriptions to pass between them and the towing-path; and in like manner all boats moved by steam power, or any other means than by a towing line, whether they be packet boats or not, shall in all cases give place for boats or floats moved by a towing line to pass between them and the tow-path

16th When the owner, master, or other person having charge of any boat or float, shall perceive, or be told, or apprized by sounding a horn, or by any other signal, that a packet or other boat following him can, from its speed, pass him, and is desirous to do so, he shall turn his boat from the tow-path side of the Canal, and give way to the swifter moving boat to pass by, unless at the time of such signal he be within three hundred yards of the next lock ahead of him.

17th The passing of one boat by another shall be effected by checking the boat bound by the preceding rules to give way, as soon as she has opened a passage for the other, so as that the tow-line may sink to the bottom of the Canal, and boat entitled to pass may float over it.

18th In case of any breach or leak through the Canal banks, or of the apprehension of one, the several boats or floats, which may be near the place of danger, shall take such position in the Canal, as the superintendent, or officer, or engineer, or lockkeeper of the company, or other person charged to repair or guard against such breach or leak, may direct.

19th In all cases, boats engaged in repairing the Canal shall have preference of all other boats, if their use at the time require it.

20th If several boats are approaching a lock at the same time, from the same direction, the one which first arrives within one hundred and fifty yards thereof shall be entitled to pass through it first, and the others in the order of their arrival, within said distance of one hundred and fifty yards; provided, however, that if there be one or more packet boats among them, such packet boars shall be passed in preference to all others, except the one that may be in the lock at the time when such packet or packets arrive within the one hundred and fifty yards; and after such packet or packets shall have passed, the others will resume the order of their passing as before. In like manner, freight boats, gondolas, and scows, shall have a preference over rafts, and such parts of rafts, as remain after one or more cribs of the same raft shall have passed.

21st In all the short levels, to wit, between locks 1 and 4, between locks 9 and 14, between locks 15 and 20, between locks 35 and 36, and between locks 41 and 43, all freight boats, gondolas, scows, or rafts, passing in the same direction with a packet boat or boats, shall give way for such packet or packets to enter the lock at the end of such level, except the freight boat or other craft that may be in such lock at the time when the gates of the lock at the other end of the level are opening to pass such packet out; in which case such freight boat or other craft shall be passed through the lock it may have so entered, and wait in the next level (if it be one of the short ones above referred to) till such packet or packets shall have passed her.

22nd The preference granted to packet boats by any of the preceding rules shall not extend to such as are less than sixty feet long; and no boat shall be deemed to be a packet, within the meaning of these rules, until she shall have obtained a license as such, signed by the President and Clerk of the Company, nor after such license shall have been annulled by a vote of the President and Directors, at some legal meeting of the Board.

23rd If two or more licensed packets approach a lock at the same time, from the same direction, the one which first arrives within one hundred and fifty yards of the same shall pass first, and the other or others in the order of their arrival within that distance. And in this and the three preceding rules, no distinction shall be made whether the boats be moved by a towing line, steam power, or other means.

24th If boats or other craft are approaching a lock from above and below at the same time, the descending one, which, by the foregoing rules, would have the right to pass, were they all bound in the same direction, shall be passed first, whatever may be the distance at which she is first discovered, if the lock be full of water, and it is the opinion of the lock-keeper, judging from her speed, that the water cannot be drawn off before she will have reached the lock, and, in like manner, the ascending one shall be passed first, if the lock be empty, and it is the opinion of the lock-keeper that it cannot be filled before such ascending one will have reached it.

25th No boat or float shall pass in any degree the walls of a lock, above or below its gates, until directed by the lock-keeper so to do; nor shall it take or keep a position, contrary to the orders of the lock-keeper, so as to prevent another from freely passing out or in. The Seneca aqueduct must be considered as forming part of the walls of the lock with which its connected, so far as relates to this rule.

26th In all questions as to a boat or float being in a lock, it shall be held that if any part of it shall have passed the extreme end of the walls of such lock, in its regular turn, and with the consent of the lock-keeper, then it is in the lock, within the meaning of the foregoing rules, but not otherwise. In like manner, a boat or float shall be considered as within one hundred and fifty yards of a lock, if the bow of it shall have passed the mark indicating that distance, but not otherwise.

27th In all cases when there are several boats, or other craft, waiting near a lock to pass in both directions, so soon as one of them shall have been passed down, agreeable to the foregoing rules, the ascending one, entitled to enter, shall be passed up, if ready, and if not, then the next in order that is ready, before another from above shall be passed down; and in like manner, if an ascending boat, or other craft, shall have passed first, a descending one, if ready, shall be passed down before another shall pass up.

28th Every boat or float which shall not avail itself of the first title it acquires to pass through any lock, shall lose its preference thereat, till all those have passed which were, at the time of such neglect, awaiting a passage through the same, in the same direction.

29th It is made the duty of every lock-keeper to remove into his lock-house before going to bed, the cranks, or handles, by which the paddle gates of every lock in his charge are turned, so that no person but himself, or one acting under his authority, can turn any such gates. And it is further hereby made the duty of every lock-keeper, at any hour of the night, upon being apprized of the wish of any boat or

30th boats to pass, either by the blowing of a horn, knocking at his door, or other signal, to rise and pass such boat or boats, or have it done by some one acting under his authority.

30th Every owner, master, or other person having charge of any boat or float which may offer to pass any lock, by night or by day, may be required by the lock-keeper or his assistant to produce the boat's register and way-bill or permit; and if such owner, master, or other person having charge, shall refuse either to show to the lock-keeper demanding sight thereof his register, bill of lading, or permit, or, being without either, to state from whence he began his voyage, or took in or increased his cargo, he shall be refused a passage through the lock at which such demand is made.

31st In approaching a lock, the owner, master, or other person having charge of any boat or float, shall slacken his speed, at such distance therefrom as the lock-keeper, or any person acting by his authority, shall direct; and take care to enter the lock without injury thereto.

32nd In passing the lock he shall fasten the bow and stern snubbing lines of his boat, to the strapping posts, on the proper side of the lock, until the lock is filled or emptied, as the case may be; and in all other respects he shall use his strapping ropes according to the instructions of the lock-keeper, and tow his boat into or out of the lock, at such time, and in such manner, as the lock-keeper may direct. He shall especially make use of all possible diligence to go out of the lock, when the gates shall have been opened for his departure, so as to occasion no unnecessary delay to other boats waiting to pass the same lock, or any other lock in charge of the same lock-keeper.

33rd No cart, wagon, or wheel carriage of any description, shall travel upon, or be permitted to use, the towpath bank, or berm-bank of the Canal, except in crossing them, in the shortest convenient direction, at some authorized ferry.

34th It is hereby made the duty of every lock-keeper to note, or bear in mind, every breach or violation of any of the preceding rules, so as to be able to give testimony in the case, whenever legally required to do so; and also to report all such breaches and violations to the superintendent.

35th All rules and regulations heretofore made, so far as they conflict with the foregoing rules, regulations, or by-laws, are hereby repealed.

Enacted by the President and Directors of the Chesapeake & Ohio Canal Company, at a meeting of the Board, this 18th day of February 1835.[169]

Between 1835 and 1850 the company records show virtually no changes in these regulations. However, a federal law passed in February 1839 did affect the boats on the canal. From that time all boats weighing in excess of five tons were to be licensed by the Collector of the Port of Georgetown.[170]

C. REGULATIONS FOR 1851–1889

After the completion of the waterway to Cumberland in 1850, the company prepared to

---

[169] *Ibid,* D, 240–252.
[170] *Ibid,* F, 25.

enter a new phase of its existence. Among other activities, the directors issued a new set of resolutions to govern navigation on the canal.[171] These rules were largely a confirmation of the existing regulations, modified and brought up to date by the lessons of the first revisions. The regulations were printed on sheet paper to be posted in all of the offices of the collectors and lock-keepers along the line. They were also published in pamphlet form with other regulations concerning the administration of the company for the canal officials located on the line of the canal.[172]

The new regulations, which went into effect on April 1, 1851, were as follows:

DEFINITIONS and EXPLANATIONS
of certain terms and words used in these regulations.

1. The term "float" as used in these regulations, shall be construed to embrace every boat, vessel, scow, gondola, raft or floating thing, navigated or moved on the Canal, by, or under the direction and charge of any person or persons; and the term "master," as so used, shall be construed to apply to every person having for the time, the charge, control, or direction of any such float.

2. The term "manifest," as used in these regulations, shall be construed to mean a just and true statement and account or bill of all the property constituting the lading of any boat or float, at the time of its clearance, made out in such form, and containing such information in relation to the said lading, as shall from time to time be prescribed and required by the Company,—signed by the consignor or consignors of said lading, and by the master of the said boat or float, and also verified by the oath of the said master.

3. The term "way-bill," as used in these regulations, shall be construed to mean a certificate made out and signed by someone of the Collectors or acting Collectors on the Canal, that the boat or float named therein, has been duly and properly CLEARED for a voyage on the Canal, and containing a statement and account of the property on board of such boat or float at the time and place of clearance,—and the term "permit," as so used, shall be construed to mean a certificate, given in certain cases, under these regulations,—signed by a Collector, acting Collector or Lock-keeper, stating that the boat or float named therein, has permission to pass on the Canal for the distance specified therein, without a way-bill.

4. The term "boat's register," as used in these regulations, shall be construed to mean a register signed by the Clerk of the Company, containing the name or names of the owner or owners of the boat or float; and his or their respective places of abode; its class and hailing place; and also, its length, breadth, light draft, and draft with a maximum load,—and authorizing the said boat or float to navigate the Canal, under and in conformity with the rules and regulations of the Company.

5. The words "first offence," "second offence," and "subsequent offence," in the 48th and 58th regulations, shall be construed as meaning the first, second, or subsequent, as the case may be, like offence, of the person, at the time, master of the boat or float referred to in those regulations, respectively, during the whole period, *he may have been employed as a master of a boat or float navigating the Canal*—although during that period, he may, at different times, have been master of several different boats or floats: and the said words, in the 73rd, 74th, 80th, 81st, 82nd, 83rd, 84th and 86th regulations, shall be

---

[171] *Proceedings of the President and Board of Directors*, H, 407–414, 431–434.
[172] Ringgold to Bryan, February 21, 1851, Ltrs. Sent, C&O Co.

construed as meaning the first, second, or subsequent, as the case may be, like offence, of the owner or owners, or of the master of the boat or float referred to in these regulations, respectively, during the period that the said boat or float may have been the property of the said owner or owners, and been commanded by the said master.

In regard to the DRAFT *and* SPEED *of Boats and Floats.*

25. No boat drawing more water, than shall from time to time be prescribed by the Canal Board or by the General Superintendent, shall navigate the Canal; and it shall be the duty of every Collector, acting Collector, Superintendent and Inspector, to cause every boat found, at any point on the Canal, violating this regulation, to be forthwith so far unloaded as to bring it within the prescribed limit: and in every case where a boat is so unloaded, the fact shall be entered on its way-bill or permit by the said Collector, acting Collector, Superintendent or Inspector, with a statement of the portion of its cargo taken off, and if by reason of any subsequent addition to its cargo the draft of such boat shall be found to exceed that prescribed as aforesaid, its master or owner shall be subject to a PENALTY of *ten* dollars, to be imposed and collected by any and every Superintendent, Collector, acting Collector and Inspector, who shall at different times and places detect such overdraft;—and it shall be the duty of every such officer, to gauge any boat or float, whose draft, he has reason to believe, is not correctly shown by the marks on its bow, stern and amidships, required by the 21st regulation. If the owner or master of any boat or float, shall refuse or not permit the said boat or float to be thus gauged, he shall be subject to a PENALTY of *twenty* dollars.

26. No boat or float, except Packet boats, licensed as such, shall move on the Canal faster than at the rate of four miles an hour. PENALTY for a violation of this regulation, *five* dollars.

27. No Packet boat shall move on the Canal faster than at the rate prescribed in its license. PENALTY for a violation of this regulation, *five* dollars.

PASSING *of one Boat or Float, by another,*
whether moving in the same or in opposite directions.

28. Whenever any boat or float shall approach within the distance of fifty feet of any other boat or float, which shall, at the time, be moving in the same direction and at a less speed than at the rate of four miles per hour, it shall be the duty of the forward boat or float, except at points where there is not sufficient width for boats to pass, or within one hundred and fifty yards of a lock or of the tunnel, to turn from the towing path and give to the rear boat or float every practicable facility for passing; and to stop whenever it shall be necessary, until the rear boat or float shall have passed. *PENALTY* for a violation of this regulation, *five* dollars.

29. Whenever any boat or float shall meet with any other boat or float, it shall be the duty of the master of the descending boat or float to turn out to the tow-path side, and of the ascending boat or float to turn out to the berm side, so that the former, where the Canal does not exceed fifty feet in width on its surface, shall be wholly on the tow-path side, and the latter, wholly on the berm side of the center of the Canal; and along those parts of the Canal that exceed fifty feet in width on its surface, and in the slack water above Guard locks No. 4 and 5, the ascending boat or float shall turn out sufficiently from the tow-path to allow the descending boat or float to pass with ease and safety between it and the tow-path; *Provided,* however, that licensed packet boats, ascending the

Canal, meeting descending boats or floats *that are not licensed packet boats*, shall have the right to keep the towing path side, in passing;—and *provided,* also, that rafts shall, in all cases, whether descending or ascending, the Canal, give place for boats and every other description of floats to pass, between them and the tow-path. PENALTY for a violation of either of the provisions of this regulation, *five* dollars.

30. Whenever any boats or floats moving in opposite directions, approach a place in the Canal which is less than thirty feet wide on its surface, or which will not safely permit their passing, it shall be the duty of the master of the boat or float ascending the Canal, to stop at such distance from such narrow place as may be convenient for the descending boat or float to pass through such narrow place, and there to wait until such passage is effected: *Provided,* however that a descending boat or float, *that is not a licensed packet boat* which is about thus to meet an ascending licensed packet boat, shall stop and give place for the said licensed packet boat, first to pass through the said narrow place;- and, *provided,* also, that descending rafts shall, in all such cases, stop and give place for boats and every other description of ascending floats first to pass through the same. PENALTY for a violation of either of the above provisions of this regulation, *five* dollars. *Regulations in regard to the order in which boats or floats, moving in opposite directions, shall pass through the Tunnel, will be, from time to time, presented by the Canal Board or General Superintendent, and shall be complied with, under a* PENALTY *of ten dollars, for each violation of either of their provisions.*

31. Whenever two boats or floats moving in opposite directions, approach each other, in the vicinity of a raft, in such manner that they would, if both should continue their headway, meet by the side of such raft, the boat or float which is going in the same direction as the raft, shall stop until the boat or float going in the opposite direction shall pass such raft. PENALTY for a violation of this regulation, *five* dollars.

32. The passing of one boat or float by another, whether moving in the same or in opposite directions, shall be effected in the manner usual upon Canals,–and so that the boat or float entitled by these regulations to a passage next the tow-path, and the horses or mules by which it is towed, shall pass, with ease and safety and without detention, over the tow line of the other. PENALTY for a violation of this regulation, *five* dollars.

Order *in which Boats and Floats*
SHALL PASS THROUGH *Locks.*

33. Any descending boat or float which has arrived within one hundred and fifty yards of a lock, the upper gates of which are open,–or any ascending boat or float which has arrived within one hundred and fifty yards of a lock, the lower gates of which are open, shall be permitted to pass such lock before any boat or float not on the same level; *Provided,* however, that no ascending raft, the upper end of which has not already passed the lower gates of the lock, shall thus be permitted to pass, while a licensed packet boat is awaiting a passage in the opposite direction.

34. If two or more boats or floats are awaiting a passage in the same direction through any lock, they shall be permitted to pass such lock in the order in which they arrived within one hundred and fifty yards of it; *Provided,* however, that no boat or float that is not a licensed packet boat, the bow of which has not already passed the extreme end of the walls of the lock, shall thus be permitted to pass, while a licensed packet boat is awaiting a passage in the same direction.

35. In all the short levels; to wit, between locks 1 and 4, between locks 9 and 11, between locks 12 and 14, between locks 15 and 20, between locks 35 and 36, between

locks 41 and 42, between locks 45 and 46, between locks 47 and 50, between locks 54 and 55, between locks 63 1/3 and 66, and between locks 73 and 75, all freight boats or other craft, passing in the same direction with a packet boat or boats, shall give way for such packet or packets to enter the lock at the end of such level, except the freight boat or other craft, the bow of which has already passed the extreme end of the walls of such lock, at the time when the gates of the lock at the other end of the level are opening to pass such packet out; in which case, such freight boat or other craft shall be passed through the said lock, and wait in the next level, (if it be one of the short ones above referred to,) till such packet or packets shall have passed it.

36. Every boat or float which shall not promptly avail itself of the preference it may have over other boats or floats to pass through any lock, shall lose such preference, till all those have passed which were, at the time of such neglect, awaiting a passage through the lock, in the same direction.

37. The General Superintendent of the Canal may, however, whenever and for such length of time, as in his opinion it may be advisable and necessary, with a view to the saving of water upon any part of the Canal, suspend the four preceding regulations and temporarily prescribe such other, in lieu thereof, during such period of suspension, as he may deem necessary.

38. All questions that shall arise among the masters or persons in charge of two or more boats or floats, at any lock, as to which, under these regulations, shall be first entitled to pass, shall be determined by the lock-keeper, or any other agent having at the time charge of such lock, and such boats or floats shall be passed in the order in which such lock-keeper or other agent shall direct.

RELATIVE TO the PASSING OF BOATS
AND FLOATS THROUGH LOCKS

39. No boat or float shall enter any lock without the permission of the lock-keeper, or other agent at the time having charge of such lock, nor take or keep a position contrary to the orders of the lock-keeper, or said agent, so as to prevent another boat or float from freely passing out or in. The Seneca aqueduct will be considered as forming part of the walls of the lock with which it is connected, so far as relates to this rule. And no master of any such boat or float, or person assisting him in the management thereof, shall open either of the large gates of a lock, or either of its paddle gates, without the permission of the lock-keeper. PENALTY for a violation of either of the provisions of this regulation, *five* dollars.

40. It shall be the duty of every lock-keeper, at any hour of the day or night, upon being apprized of the wish of the master of any boat or float to pass such boat or float through the lock of which he has charge, either by the blowing of a horn, knocking at his door, or other signal, to pass such boat or float, if entitled to a passage under these regulations, or have it done by some one acting under his authority.

41. Every master of any boat or float who may desire a passage, for such boat or float, through any lock, may be required by the lock-keeper, or his assistant, to produce the boat's register and way-bill or permit; and if such master shall refuse to show to the lock-keeper, demanding sight thereof, said register and way-bill, or permit, or either of them, a passage, for such boat or float, through the lock shall be refused. PENALTY for every such refusal, although the register and way-bill, or permit, may be subsequently shown to the lock-keeper or his assistant, and the boat passed.–*five* dollars.

42. Every master of any boat or float who may desire with such boat or float to pass any lock, who shall be without a register and way-bill or permit, or without either, shall be refused a passage for such boat or float through the said lock, until such register and way-bill or permit, or either, as the case may be, shall have been obtained at the place or places prescribed by these regulations.

43. In approaching a lock, the master of any boat or float, shall slacken its speed, at such distance therefrom as the lock-keeper, or any person acting by his authority, shall direct; and, if such boat or float is ascending the Canal, it shall enter the lock, without striking or running against the upper gates of the lock,–or if descending the Canal, without striking or running against the lower gates. PENALTY for a violation of either of the provisions of this regulation. *five* dollars.

44. The snubbing lines of every boat or float, while passing a lock, shall be secured to the snubbing post alongside of the lock, and be used in such manner as the lock-keeper or his assistant may direct; and the boat shall be towed into and out of the lock, at such times, and in such manner, as the lock-keeper may direct;–*Provided*, however, that the use of the snubbing lines while passing a lock, may be dispensed with, if there is attached to the boat or float any device or contrivance that will, in the opinion of the lock-keeper, if properly used, prevent the lock, its gates and fixtures from being injured,–in which case the said device or contrivance shall be used as the lock-keeper or his assistant may direct. PENALTY for a violation of either of the provisions of this regulation, *five* dollars.

45. There shall be no unreasonable or unnecessary delay of a boat or float in a lock, or in entering or leaving a lock; and every boat or float which shall not be towed into a lock or out of it, when other boats or floats are in waiting to pass said lock, shall be considered as having violated this regulation. PENALTY for a violation of this regulation, *five* dollars.

46. Any master, or person for the time, in charge of any boat or float, who shall enter, or permit any other person or persons to enter, any lock, with such boat or float, when *forbid* by the lock-keeper or his assistant; or if such boat or float has entered any lock, who shall pass, or permit any other person or persons to pass, with the same, through such lock, when *forbid* by the lock-keeper or his assistant; or of which is thus forbidden, to be immediately withdrawn from the lock, shall be subject to a PENALTY of *twenty* dollars.

AT WHAT PLACES *Boats and Floats may*
STOP, LIE BY OR BE MOORED.

47. No boat or float shall unnecessarily stop, lie by, or be moored, within twenty rods of any waste or waste-weir, except in a basin,–or in the Tunnel, or in any aqueduct, or in any lock, or in any part of the Canal where the width of water surface, when the Canal is full, is less than forty feet,–or within twenty rods of any lock, except in a basin,–or in either of the short levels between locks No. 1 and 4, between locks No. 9 and 10, between locks No. 12 and 14, between locks No. 15 and 20, between locks No. 35 and 36, between locks No. 41 and 42, between locks No. 45 and 46, between locks No 47 and 50, between locks No. 51 and 52, between locks No. 54 and 55, between locks No. 63 1/3 and 66, and between locks No. 73 and 75. PENALTY for violating this regulation, by stopping, lying by or mooring in the Tunnel or in any lock or aqueduct, *twenty* dollars,–or if at any of the other places above enumerated, *five* dollars.

48. Under no circumstances whatever shall any boat or float, or other floating thing, lie fastened to or be moored along the tow-path of the Canal, nor shall the owner, master, or other person or persons having charge thereof, encamp upon the tow-path, or drive stakes into the top or slopes thereof, or place stones or kindle fires thereon, feed their horses or mules upon the tow-path, or in any way or manner obstruct or incommode the free and common use of the Canal and its tow-path by day or night. PENALTY for a violation of this regulation–for the first offence *five* dollars, and for any subsequent offence, *twenty* dollars.

49. No person or persons shall, without the permission in writing, of a Superintendent, Collector, acting Collector or Inspector, moor a boat or float in the Canal for a longer period than four days, unless in a basin, or where the Canal has a width at water surface, when full, of not less than sixty feet: In Georgetown no boat or float shall be moored in the Canal except in a basin, for a longer period than is reasonable for discharging or taking in the load of such boat or float, without a written permission from the Superintendent, or in his absence of the Collector or Inspector:–And in all cases, when moored for the purpose of loading or unloading, or of stopping for the night, or for feeding their horses or mules or for any cause whatever,–every boat and float shall be so secured along the berm side of the Canal, in places permitted by the preceding regulations– that no part of them shall be more than one-third of the width of the Canal from the berm bank. PENALTY for a violation of either of the provisions of this regulation, *ten* dollars.

50. It shall be the duty of every Collector, acting Collector or Inspector, and if there be no Collector, acting Collector or Inspector present, of every Superintendent, wherever in the opinion of such officer it shall be necessary, to assign berths as far as practicable to all boats when loading, unloading or stopping at any landing place on the Canal and in its basins. And every master, owner or person having charge of a boat, who shall refuse or neglect promptly to comply with directions given by a Collector, Inspector or Superintendent, in this regard, or any person or persons other than those in charge of said boat, who shall forcibly remove or attempt to remove the same from the berth assigned it by either of said officers, without his permission, shall be subject to a PENALTY of not less than *five* nor more than *twenty* dollars,–at the discretion of the Collector, acting Collector, Inspector or Superintendent aforesaid.

Relative to Boats and Floats, when there is a BREACH *or* LEAK,
or SUSPENSION OF THE NAVIGATION, *&c, or where* REPAIRS *are making.*

51. In case of any breach or leak through the Canal banks, or of the apprehension of a breach, or in case of a suspension of the navigation, upon any part of the Canal, from any cause,–or when the Canal is filling with water,–the Superintendent, Collector or lock-keeper, or other person charged to repair or guard against such breach or leak,–or to restore the navigation,–or to attend to such filling of the Canal with water,–shall have the right to direct the boats or floats which may be near such breach, leak or place of suspension of navigation,–or which in his opinion may obstruct the filling of the Canal with water, to lie in such places and to be moved backward or forward on the Canal as he shall think most advisable and proper, and a refusal or neglect to comply promptly with his directions in this respect, shall be considered a violation of this regulation. PENALTY for a violation of this regulation, *ten* dollars.

52. In all cases, boats engaged in repairing the Canal shall have preference of all other boats or floats in passing along the line of the Canal, or through its guard and lift locks, if in the opinion of the person or persons in charge of those boats, their use, at the

time, require such preference,—and any person or persons who shall prevent, in any case, any such boat, from having such preference, shall be considered as having violated this regulation. PENALTY for a violation of this regulation, *five* dollars.

MISCELLANEOUS PROVISIONS *in relation to Boats and Floats.*

53. No boat or float shall, under any circumstances, except in the Rock Creek, Wills Creek and North Branch basins, and along the slack water above Dams No. 4 and 5.—use any iron or metallic-shod or sharp-pointed setting pole on the Canal,—and except at the places above named, no such pole shall be kept on deck or within convenient reach of those managing the said boat or float. PENALTY for a violation of either of the provisions of this regulation, *five* dollars.

54. No boat or float shall forcibly strike or violently rub against the banks, inside walls, wastes, waste-weirs, bridges, stop-locks, aqueducts, or tunnel of the Canal, or against any of its stop, guard or lift locks; and every boat or float shall be conducted into, through and out of every guard or lift lock on the Canal, in a careful manner, so as to do no injury to such lock, its gates or any of its fixtures. PENALTY for a violation of either of the provisions of this regulation, *five* dollars.

55. The master of any boat or float who shall, at any time, with such boat or float, either carelessly or by design, strike, rub, or run against any other boat or float, in such manner as to sink, disable or injure such boat or float, or force it with violence against the bank or side of the Canal, shall,—if such other boat or float is, at the time, moving on the Canal or lying by, as the case may be, in strict conformity with these regulations,—be subject to a PENALTY of not less than *five*, nor more than *twenty* dollars, at the discretion of the Superintendent in charge of the portion of the Canal on which the offence is committed.

56. Whenever a boat or float, or several boats or floats, are stopped at any place on the Canal, awaiting a passage through a lock, or in consequence of a breach or leak in the Canal, or any interruption to the navigation from any cause, no boat or float, subsequently arriving at such place, shall pass by, or shall lie alongside of any one of those that previously arrived. The master of any boat or float, who shall violate either of the provisions of this regulation, shall be subject to a PENALTY of *five* dollars.

57. The horse or horses, mule or mules, of any boat or float navigating the Canal, shall not pass over a tow-path bridge faster than in a walk,—nor shall they be passed into or out of any boat or float over or upon the walls or sides of any lock or aqueduct. PENALTY for a violation of this regulation, *three* dollars.

58. No hay, straw, manure or litter of any kind shall be discharged or thrown, from any boat or float, into the Canal, or upon either of its banks or any of its works.—PENALTY for a violation of this regulation, for the first offence, *five* dollars, and for any subsequent offence, *ten* dollars.

Miscellaneous Provisions to
GUARD AGAINST INTERRUPTION TO THE NAVIGATION *and* INJURY TO THE CANAL.

59. The FERRY BOAT, at an authorized ferry on the Canal, when not in actual use, shall be secured, at each end, in either the tow-path or berm ferry recess, in such manner, that no part or either end of it, shall project into the Canal, outside of such re-

cess; and such boat shall not be used for the purpose of crossing the Canal at any other place, or lie by or be moored, except in one of the said recesses. For each violation of either of the above provisions of this regulation, the owner or owners of such ferry boat,—if the offence is committed by him or them, or by a person or persons in his or their employ, or with his or their consent and permission,—shall be subject to a PENALTY of *five* dollars; but if any other person or persons without the authority of the said owner or owners, shall use the said ferry boat, at any place not permitted by this regulation, or shall cause any part or either end of it, to project outside of the recess in the manner above prohibited, he or they shall be subject to a PENALTY of *ten* dollars.

60. The PIVOT OR MOVEABLE BRIDGES that have been constructed at several of the locks on the Canal, shall be under the charge and control of the lock-keepers, respectively, at those locks, and shall be attended to and kept by the said lock-keepers, in such manner as will best promote public convenience, in the case of bridges constructed for the accommodation of public roads,—or the convenience of the person or persons for whose use they were intended, in the case of bridges constructed for the accommodation of individuals,—and, at the same time, in each case, to prevent interruption to the navigation of the Canal,—and any person or persons, who shall move or turn either one of the aforesaid bridges, when forbid by the lock-keeper in charge thereof,—or any person or persons, not entitled to use the same, who shall move or turn either one of the said bridges intended for the use of individuals, shall be subject to a PENALTY *five* dollars.

61. Whenever a Superintendent, Collector or Lock-keeper shall find any boat, float, raft, timber or other substance floating loose upon or sunk in the Canal or any of its basins, ponds, feeders or other works,—the owner of which is unknown, or if known, does not reside within the County in which the said boat, float, raft, timber or other substance is floating or sunk, or if known and a resident of the County, shall neglect, after notice, forthwith to remove the same,—such Superintendent, Collector or Lock-keeper shall cause the same to be broken up and removed from the said Canal, its basins, ponds, feeders or other works—and the materials of the broken boat, float, raft, timber or other substance so broken up and removed, shall be forfeited to and become the property of the Canal Company.

62. No persons, or persons shall place on the towing path or berm bank, or in the Canal or any of its feeders or basins, or on any of the banks of its feeders or basins, logs, timber or other materials, without the permission in writing of a Superintendent; and every violation of this regulation shall subject such person or persons to a PENALTY of *ten* dollars.

63. No person or persons shall, without the permission in writing of a Superintendent, roll or draw, from or into the Canal, its feeders or basins, over the side of any lock or aqueduct, or over any structure of masonry or timber, or over the side of any embankment,—except at regularly established landing places or wharves, any log, timber or other material; and every violation of this regulation shall subject every such person or persons to a PENALTY of *ten* dollars.

64. No person or persons shall drive a cart, wagon or wheel carriage of any description, nor lead or drive any horse, mule, ox or other animal, except for the purpose of towing boats or floats, upon the tow-path or berm bank of the Canal, except in crossing them, in the shortest convenient direction, at some authorized ferry nor shall any person or persons, except an officer or agent of the Company, ride any horse or mule, along or upon the tow-path in the Tunnel, or along or upon the tow-path in the Deep Cuts adjoining the Tunnel, that is not, at the time, employed in towing some boat or float. PEN-

ALTY for a violation of this regulation, for the first offence, *five* dollars,–and for any subsequent offence, *ten* dollars.

65. Any person who shall put or leave, or cause to be put or left, any disabled animal or any carcass, dead animal, or putrid substance of any kind, into the Canal, or into any basin or feeder connected therewith, or upon either bank of the Canal, or upon any part of the Canal property, shall pay the expense of removing the same and, in addition, be subject to a PENALTY of *ten* dollars.

66. Any person or persons, who shall throw or place, or cause to be thrown or placed, stones, gravel, earth, or any other substance or materials whatever, into the Canal, its feeders, basins, or other works, or upon the tow-path of the Canal, shall pay the expense of removing the same and, in addition, be subject to a PENALTY of not less than *five*, nor more than *twenty* dollars, at the discretion of the Superintendent in charge of the portion of the Canal on which the offence is committed.

67. Any person or persons, who shall *carelessly or neglectfully*, by any means whatever, injure, impair, break or destroy any part of the Canal or any part of its feeders, dams, locks, aqueducts, wastes, waste-weirs, culverts, walls, embankments, bridges, buildings or other works of the said Canal, such person or persons shall each of them pay a FINE of *five* dollars,–and any one or more of them shall also be liable to pay a sum *equal to the damage sustained by said Company by such injury.*

68. Any person or persons, who shall *willfully or maliciously*, open or close any waste gate, or any gate or wicket of any lock on the Canal or on any of its feeders, or shall, willfully or maliciously, by any means whatever, injure, impair, break or destroy any part of the Canal, or any part of its feeders, dams, locks, aqueducts, wastes, waste-weirs, culverts, walls, embankments, bridges, buildings or other works, of the said Canal, such person or persons, so offending, shall for every such offence, forfeit and pay to the said Canal Company at FINE of *twenty* dollars,–and any one or more of them shall also be liable to pay a sum equal to the damage sustained by said Company by such injury;– *and as, by law, every such offender will be subject to indictment in the Court of the County in which the offence shall be committed, and upon conviction, to imprisonment for a term not exceeding six months, in the discretion of the Court,*–it is hereby made the duty of any Superintendent or Collector on the Canal, who shall know from his own observation, or have good cause to believe, that such offence has been committed, to do whatever may be necessary to bring the same to the notice of the Grand Jury of the County.

INSPECTORS *to be regarded as* ASSISTANTS OF THE COLLECTORS

69. The Inspector or Inspectors at any place on the Canal, will be considered, under these regulations, as an assistant or as assistants of the Collector at that place, and every act done by such Inspector or Inspectors,–under special or general directions from such Collector, given for the purpose of carrying into effect and enforcing these regulations, so far as it is the duty of the said Collector to carry into effect and to enforce the same,–shall be considered and regarded, under these regulations, as the act of the said Collector.

Which Lock-keepers are also ACTING COLLECTORS.

70. The Lock-keepers at tide lock B., at locks No. 5, No. 21, No. 23, and the Se-

neca guard lock adjoining, at lock No. 25, and Edward's Ferry outlet lock, at locks No. 26, No. 28 and No. 30, at lock No. 36 and Guard lock adjoining, at lock No. 37, at lock No. 38 and Shepherdstown outlet lock, at locks No. 40, No. 42, No. 46, No. 51, No. 54 and Guard lock No. 6, at locks No. 57, No. 60, No. 66, No. 70, and No. 75, shall also be acting Collectors, under these regulations, and as such shall perform the duties required of acting Collectors by these regulations; and in the performance of these duties, they shall have all the right, control and authority, that they would have, and may do all the acts, that they might do, were they Collectors.

ARRANGEMENT *of Cargoes consisting of*
ARTICLES PAYING DIFFERENT RATES OF TOLL

71. Where any boat, scow or other craft, navigating the Canal, shall be laden with articles paying different rates of toll, or with articles some of which shall be chargeable with toll by weight, and others by measure or count, it shall be the duty of the master or owner, so to arrange the said lading that the several Collectors, acting Collectors, and Inspectors on the Canal, can conveniently examine and inspect the same. And if not so arranged, the master or owner shall, at his own expense, on the request of any Collector, acting Collector, or Inspector, unload in whole or in part the said cargo, so as to furnish all the necessary information for the purposes of imposing tolls or detecting or preventing frauds. And in case of the neglect or refusal of any master or owner to comply with this regulation, the whole cargo of such boat, scow or craft, shall be charged with toll at the rate of those articles on board paying the highest rate of toll.

In regard to WAY-BILLS, PERMITS AND MANIFESTS.

72. No boat or float shall be permitted to pass on the Canal, unless the master thereof shall first have obtained a way-bill therefore, for the voyage then making or about to be made, from the proper Collector or acting Collector of tolls on said Canal, except in the cases hereinafter particularly specified.

73. The way-bill for each voyage shall be obtained from the Collector or acting Collector, whose office is kept nearest to the place at which the voyage is commenced, provided there be such an office within one mile of such place. If there be no such office within one mile of the place at which the voyage is commenced, the way-bill for such voyage shall be obtained from the Collector or acting Collector at whose office the boat or float shall first arrive in the course of the voyage; and such boat or float shall be permitted to proceed from the place where the voyage was commenced to such office, and no further, without a way-bill; *provided,* however, that if there be any lock or locks through which such boat or float must pass on its way to the said office, a permit must be obtained from the keeper of the lock first arrived at, allowing the boat or float to proceed, as above without a way-bill; which permit must be delivered over and surrendered to the Collector or acting Collector from whom the way-bill is obtained,–and unless such permit shall have been obtained, or, if obtained, unless it is delivered as above, such Collector or acting Collector shall refuse to make out a way-bill for the said boat or float, and shall stop the further passage of the same, until a PENALTY of *five* dollars for the first offence, or *twenty* dollars for any subsequent offence, shall have been paid by the owner or master for the violation of this regulation.

74. If there be no Collector or acting Collector, whose office is within one mile of the place where the voyage is commenced,–nor within one mile of the place where the

same shall terminate,–nor at any intermediate place,–the master of the boat or float shall, within ten days after the termination of such voyage, exhibit a manifest, verified by his oath, of the lading transported on board of such boat or float, at any time during such voyage, to the Collector or acting Collector whose office shall be nearest to the place where such voyage terminated, or, if more convenient, to the one whose office shall be nearest to the place where the voyage commenced, and shall pay to such Collector or acting Collector the tolls due on such boat or float and lading; *provided*, however, that if there be any lock or locks through which the said boat or float shall pass on its voyage, a manifest shall be exhibited to the keeper of the first lock passed through, by the master, of the lading then on board of his boat or float, and a permit be obtained from the said Lock-keeper allowing the boat to proceed on such voyage; which permit shall be delivered to the Collector or acting Collector aforesaid, at the time of delivering the manifest and paying the tolls as above required, and every master who shall neglect to obtain such permit, or, if obtained to deliver over the same to the said Collector or acting Collector, shall be liable to a PENALTY for a *first* offence of *five* dollars, and of *twenty* dollars for any subsequent offence, or if he shall neglect to exhibit such manifest, under oath, to the Collector or acting Collector and to pay such tolls, within the period above limited,–he shall be liable to a PENALTY of *twenty-five* dollars.

75. Every master of a boat or float applying to any Collector or acting Collector for a way-bill, shall exhibit to him a manifest of the cargo on board of such boat or float,–containing first the name of each place on the Canal where any portion of such property was shipped, and the place for which it is intended to be cleared, specifying the portion shipped at each of such places, and the portion intended to be cleared to each place, second a statement of the weight of all articles of such property on which toll is to be charged by weight, of the number of articles on which toll is to be charged by number, and of the feet of each article on which toll is to be charged by the foot; and third, a specification of the weight, number or quantity of each article or of the articles on which one rate of toll is to be charged, and which is to be transported to one place; separately from other articles on which a different rate of toll is to be charged or which is to be transported to a different place.

76. If any property or lading shall be received on board of any boat or float, during any voyage, after such boat or float shall have proceeded one mile from the place at which the way-bill was obtained, or shall have proceeded one mile from the place at which, as hereinafter provided,–an addition or endorsement shall have been made to, or upon the said way-bill by any Collector or acting Collector, a manifest thereof, to be called manifest No. 2, or No. 3, &c., as the case may be, conforming in all respects to the requirements hereinbefore stated, in regard to the making out of manifests, shall be exhibited to the Collector or acting Collector, whose office shall be next in order, in the course of the voyage, to the place where such property or lading was received on board,–and until the said manifest No. 2 or No. 3, &c., as the case may be, shall have been thus exhibited, and a statement of the property or lading taken on board of the boat or float, since its way-bill was obtained, or the last preceding addition, made thereto by some Collector or acting Collector, shall have been added to the said way-bill by such Collector or acting Collector,–the said boat or float shall not proceed on its voyage, under a PENALTY of *twenty-five* dollars.

77. Every master of a boat or float navigating the Canal, who shall deliver any article mentioned in its manifest or way-bill at a place beyond that to which such article shall have been cleared, and shall not promptly report the fact to the Collector or acting

Collector, whose office is nearest to the place where such article is delivered, and pay the toll thereon, shall be subject to a PENALTY of *twenty-five* dollars.

78. If in unloading any boat or float, it shall be discovered that the cargo, in consequence of any unintentional error, exceeds the quantity stated in its manifest or manifests, it shall be the duty of the master of such boat or float, immediately to report such excess, and pay the lawful toll thereon, to the Collector or acting Collector at the place where such error may be discovered, if there be any such at the place; and if there be no Collector or acting Collector at such place, to the next Collector or acting Collector, at or near whose office the boat shall arrive after the discovery of such error, under a PENALTY of *twenty-five* dollars.

79. Every master of any boat or float shall exhibit its way-bill and manifest or manifests,–*first*, to the Collector or acting Collector, whose office shall be next in order, in the course of the voyage to the place where the way-bill was obtained;–*second*, to the Collector or acting Collector at the place where an portion of the cargo shall be unloaded, or any additional cargo received; and if there be no Collector or acting Collector at such place, to the Collector or acting Collector whose office shall be next in order in the course of the voyage; and *third*, to every other Collector or acting Collector who shall demand that said way-bill and manifest or manifests shall be exhibited to him. PENALTY for a violation of either of the provisions of this regulation for which a penalty is not provided by some other of these regulations, *twenty-five* dollars.

80. No boat or float shall proceed, upon the Chesapeake & Ohio Canal, beyond the place to which it shall be cleared, named in its way-bill or permit, under a PENALTY of *five* dollars for the first offence, and *twenty* dollars for any subsequent offence.

81. Upon the arrival of any boat or float, in the course of its voyage, at a place where a portion only of its cargo is to be unloaded, such portion of the cargo shall not be unloaded, until the master of the said boat or float shall have exhibited its way-bill and manifest or manifests to the Collector or acting Collector, at or within one mile of such place, and shall have paid the toll that may then be due thereon,–nor after such portion of the cargo is unloaded, shall the said boat or boat proceed on its voyage until the said Collector or acting Collector shall have endorsed on the way-bill, what portion of the cargo has thus been unloaded–but if there be no Collector or acting Collector at or within one mile of the place, such portion of the cargo may be unloaded, if the toll thereon shall have been previously paid,–but in that case, the master of the boat or float shall report the fact to the Collector or acting Collector whose office shall be next in order in the course of the voyage, and exhibit to him such evidence as shall satisfy him, that such portion of the cargo has been unloaded,–and until this shall have been done, and the said Collector or acting Collector shall have endorsed upon the way-bill what portion of the cargo has been thus unloaded, the said boat or float shall not proceed on its voyage. PENALTY for a violation of either of the provisions of this regulation, for the first offence, *five* dollars, and for any subsequent offence, *twenty* dollars.

82. Upon the arrival of any boat or float at its destination, or at a place where its master desires with such boat or float to leave the Chesapeake & Ohio Canal and enter upon any other Canal or the Potomac river,–the said master shall exhibit his manifest or manifests, and shall deliver his way-bill, to the Collector or acting Collector, if there be one, whose office is at or within one mile of such place,–and shall pay to him the toll that may then be due on the said boat or float and its cargo, before any portion of the cargo shall be unloaded, or before the said boat or float shall thus leave the Chesapeake & Ohio Canal and enter upon any other Canal or the Potomac river. PENALTY for a violation of

this regulation, for the first offence, *five* dollars, for the second offence, *twenty-five* dollars, and for any subsequent offence, *fifty* dollars.

83. If there be no Collector or acting Collector, whose office is at or within one mile of the place to which a boat or float is cleared, or at which its master desires, with it, to leave the Chesapeake & Ohio Canal and enter upon any other Canal or the Potomac river, the said master shall exhibit his manifest or manifests, and deliver his way-bill,–and shall pay the tolls that may then be due on his boat or float and its cargo, for the voyage then making, to the last Collector or acting Collector whose office shall be passed by the boat or float, in the order of the voyage,–and shall thereupon receive a permit from such Collector or acting Collector, to proceed to the place to which the boat or float is cleared,–and until such permit is given, the boat or float shall not proceed on its voyage under a PENALTY of *twenty-five* dollars for the first offence, and of *fifty* dollars for any subsequent offence. And the said permit shall be returned and delivered, by the said master, to the Collector or acting Collector from whom it was obtained, within ten days after the said boat or float arrives at its destination, upon the Chesapeake & Ohio Canal, or leaves the said Canal as aforesaid; or whenever the said boat or float shall next again pass the office of the said Collector or acting Collector, if within the said ten days,–under a PENALTY, for the first offence, of *five* and of *ten* dollars for any subsequent offence.

84. A permit, instead of a way-bill, shall be issued by a Collector or acting Collector to any boat or float, provided the voyage for which such permit is issued, shall not extend to, nor within a mile of any place on the Canal where there is a Collector's or acting Collector's office,–but not until a manifest shall have been exhibited to him of the cargo then on board of the said boat or float, nor until all the tolls chargeable on the said boat or float for such voyage shall have been paid,–and the said permit shall be returned and delivered, by the master, to the Collector or acting Collector from whom it was obtained, within ten days after the said boat or float shall have arrived at its destination upon the Chesapeake & Ohio Canal, or shall have left the said Canal as aforesaid,–or whenever the said boat or float shall next again pass the office of the said Collector or acting Collector, if within the said ten days,–under a PENALTY, for the first offence, of *five* dollars, and of *ten* dollars for every subsequent offence.

85. In all cases in which permits are given, by any Collector or acting Collector, for a boat or float to proceed beyond the office of such Collector or acting Collector, the master of such boat or float shall, whenever any addition is made to its cargo after the permit is obtained, note the same upon the permit, in such manner and with such particularity, that the toll chargeable thereon can be accurately ascertained, and shall pay the toll on such addition, to the Collector or acting Collector from whom the permit was obtained, upon returning and delivering to him the said permit, as above required–which endorsement by him upon the permit he shall verify by his oath–under a PENALTY of *twenty-five* dollars for a violation of either of the provisions of this regulation.

86. Boats and floats, regularly and constantly employed in the transportation, upon the Canal, of articles or property of but one description, in each direction, between two points or places not exceeding ten miles apart,–and between which points or places there is not more than one Collector's or acting Collector's office, may, at the discretion of the Collector or acting Collector, be allowed thus to navigate the Canal without a permit for each voyage,–but, in lieu thereof, with a permit for such period, not exceeding one month, as the Collector or acting Collector may think most advisable;–and in such case each cargo of the said boat or float shall be subject to inspection, the same as though a permit for each voyage, were given;–and at the expiration of the period for which the permit was obtained, the owner or master of the said boat or float shall deliver, to the said

Collector or acting Collector, a statement of the number of voyages made during such period, and a manifest of the cargo of the said boat or float carried each voyage, both of which shall be verified by the oath of the said owner or master,–and shall pay the tolls that may then be due on the said boat, and its cargoes,–and until such permit, statement, and manifest shall have been delivered and the said tolls paid,–the said boat or float shall not be permitted to navigate the Canal,–and unless such delivery and payment shall be made within two days after the expiration of the said period, the said owner or master shall be subject to a PENALTY of *twenty-five* dollars, for the first offence, and of *fifty* dollars for every subsequent offence.

87. In every case in which the manifest or manifests and the way-bill of any boat or float shall, under these regulations, be exhibited, or the way bill delivered to any Collector or acting Collector;–the said Collector or acting Collector, shall make such examinations and comparisons of the said manifest or manifests, way-bill and cargo as may be sufficient to satisfy him whether the said cargo has been accurately entered in the said way-bill,–and if it has not been, he shall make the necessary corrections in the way-bill; and if such boat or float, not having arrived at its destination, shall proceed on its voyage, or unload any portion of its cargo,–or having arrived at its destination, shall unload the whole or any portion of its cargo, before such examinations and comparisons are made, the owner or master of the boat or float shall be subject to the same penalty as if the said manifest or manifests and way-bill had never been exhibited or delivered to the aforesaid Collector or acting Collector.

88. Whenever a difference shall arise between a Collector or acting Collector and the master of any boat or float, as to the amount of tolls chargeable on the lading of such boat or float, the Collector or acting Collector shall detain the boat or float, and the articles in regard to which the difference has arisen, and shall weigh, count or measure the said articles, as the case may require;–and if it shall be ascertained that the weight, number or quantity of the said articles exceeds the amount stated in the manifest or manifests of the boat or float, the Collector or acting Collector shall charge toll according to the weight, number or quantity thus ascertained, and the master shall pay to the Collector or acting Collector the expense of such weighing, counting or measuring,–and for such expense the said articles, and the boat or float containing them, as well as the master and the owner of the said boat or float shall severally be liable.

89. If the master of any boat or float shall, upon any voyage of such boat or float, use, or attempt to use for that voyage, a way-bill or permit given for any preceding voyage, or the way-bill or permit of any other boat or float,–or a false way-bill or permit,–or shall exhibit to any Collector or acting Collector a false manifest, he shall be subject to a PENALTY of FIFTY dollars.

In regard to the PAYMENT OF TOLLS, PENALTIES, *&c.*

90. The full amount of toll chargeable on any boat or float, and on each and every article of property which shall be on board thereof, or constitute any float, at the time application is made to any Collector or acting Collector for a way-bill, and on each and every article which would enter into the way-bill, shall be paid to such Collector or acting Collector, before he shall issue a way-bill for such boat or float, in all cases in which he shall know, or have reason to believe, that the owner or owners, or the master of the said boat or float,–has or have, either as the owner or owners of the said boat or float, or of any other boat or float,–or as the master of the said boat or float, or any other boat or float,–within one year immediately preceding, rendered himself or themselves liable for

any penalty under these regulations, exceeding five dollars, in amount, for any single offence,–but otherwise the said Collector or acting Collector may, at his discretion, issue a way-bill and allow the said boat or float to proceed to its destination and pay the tolls, at the place or places, in such cases, designated and required by these regulations:– *provided*, however, that in no case, shall a new way-bill be issued, by any Collector or acting Collector, for any boat or float,–until all arrearages of tolls and all penalties and expenses of the kind mentioned in the 88th regulation, so far as known to him, for which such boat or float is liable, shall be paid.

91. And, in like manner, shall no endorsement on the way-bill of any boat or float be made by any Collector or acting Collector, of the addition to the cargo of any boat or float, while on its voyage, until the tolls thereon have been paid,–unless in such cases, as the Collector or acting Collector would be permitted, by the last regulation, to issue a way-bill,–if a way-bill was applied for, instead of an endorsement upon the way-bill, by the owner or master of such boat or float.

92. Upon the arrival of any boat or float at the place where the toll, upon the said boat or float and its cargo, or any part of its cargo, must, under these regulations, be paid, when not paid in advance; or where any balance, due on the said toll, arising from an error in any previous calculation of it or from any other cause, must be paid,–if such payment be refused or not promptly made, any Collector or acting Collector of tolls, in the employment of the Company, may seize such boat or float, or the produce or other articles composing or which had composed, in whole or in part, the cargo of said boat or float, wherever found, and sell the same, or so much thereof as he may deem expedient, at auction, for cash; and the proceeds, of such sale or sales, shall be applied to the payment of the amount due the Company, as aforesaid, and all the expenses of seizure and sale; and the balance, if any, shall be paid over to the person or persons who had charge or possession of the property that may be thus sold, at the time of the seizure thereof.

LIABILITY OF PERSONS AND PROPERTY FOR THE PAYMENT OF TOLLS, PENALTIES, &c.

93. The person or persons specified in the boat's register of any boat or float, as the owner or owners thereof, shall in all cases be deemed in law the true owner or owners thereof, and to all intents and purposes he or they shall be liable as such, and the said boat or float be subject to execution, as his or their property, as regards the collection and enforcement of tolls and penalties, under these regulations.

94. The master, and the owner or part owner of any boat or float, on the Canal, and likewise the boat or float itself, shall severally be liable for the payment of all penalties and forfeitures incurred, and all damages which may accrue, in consequence of the violation of any of the provisions of these regulations, by the master or the owner or part owner thereof, or by any boatman, or other person assisting in the navigation or management of such boat or float at the time of such violation; and also for the payment of tolls chargeable on the said boat or float or chargeable on any property transported on boat thereof; and every such boat or float may, at the discretion of the General Superintendent, or any Collector or acting Collector of tolls or Superintendent, be prevented from navigating said Canal until such penalty, forfeiture, damages, toll, and costs accrued in prosecuting therefore, shall be duly paid.

CANAL OFFICERS MUST ENFORCE THESE REGULATIONS

95. Superintendents, Collectors, acting Collectors, Inspectors and Lock-keepers, are hereby required on every violation of the above regulations, known to them, or brought to their notice, to make an entry of the nature of every offence, the names of the offenders, the time and place where the offence was committed, and the names of witnesses: And it is further strictly enjoined on each of the above officers, to carry these regulations into full effect.

AUTHORITY OF CANAL OFFICERS TO SUE FOR PENALTIES

1st—SUPERINTENDENTS.

96. Each Superintendent of repairs upon the Canal, is hereby authorized, to prosecute in the name of the Chesapeake & Ohio Canal Company, for any penalty incurred by the violation of any or either of the following regulations,–to wit– Nos. 13, 14, 15, 16, 17, 18, 19, 20, 21, 22, 25, 26, 27, 28, 29, 30, 31, 32, 39, 41, 43, 44, 45, 46, 47, 48, 49, 50, 51, 52, 53, 54, 55, 56, 57, 58, 59, 60, 62, 63, 64, 65, 66, 67, 68, 80 and 89; and shall prosecute for all such penalties whenever such Superintendent shall know from his own observation, or have good cause to believe, that any of the said penalties have been incurred.

2nd—COLLECTORS.

97. Each Collector upon the Canal, is hereby authorized, to prosecute in the name of the Chesapeake & Ohio Canal Company, for any penalty incurred by the violation of any or either of the following regulations,–to wit–Nos. 7, 8, 9, 10, 11, 13, 14, 15, 16, 17, 18, 19, 20, 21, 22, 25, 47, 48, 49, 50, 51, 53, 54, 55, 56, 57, 58, 64, 65, 73, 74, 76, 77, 78, 79, 80, 81, 82, 83, 84, 85, 86, 87, 88 and 89; and shall prosecute for all such penalties whenever such Collector shall know from his own observation, or have good cause to believe, that any of the said penalties have been incurred.

3rd—ACTING COLLECTORS.

98. Each acting Collector upon the Canal is hereby authorized, to prosecute in the name of the Chesapeake & Ohio Canal Company, for any penalty incurred by the violation of any or either of the following regulations,–to wit– Nos. 10, 11, 13, 14, 15, 16, 17, 18, 19, 20, 21, 22, 25, 49, 50, 73, 74, 76, 77, 78, 79, 80, 81, 82, 83, 84, 85, 86, 87, 88 and 89; and shall prosecute for all such penalties whenever such acting Collector shall know from his own observation, or have good cause to believe, that any of the said penalties have been incurred.

4th—LOCK-KEEPERS

99. Each Lock-keeper upon the Canal, is hereby authorized, to prosecute in the name of the Chesapeake & Ohio Canal Company, for any penalty incurred by the violation of any or either of the following regulations,–to wit–Nos. 10, 13, 14, 15, 16, 17, 18, 19, 20, 21, 22, 26, 27, 28, 29, 30, 31, 32, 39, 41, 43, 44, 45, 46, 47, 48, 49, 51, 52, 53, 54, 55, 56, 57, 58, 60 and 89; and shall prosecute for all such penalties whenever such Lock-keeper shall

know from his own observation, or have good cause to believe, that any of the said penalties have been incurred.

100. These by-laws, rules, and regulations, shall take effect and be in full force and operation, from and after the 1st day of April 1851 inclusive; and all existing by-laws, rules, and regulations, so far as they conflict therewith, shall, from and after said time, be held and considered as, and are hereby, repealed.

101. These by-laws, rules, and regulations, certified to by the Clerk of the Chesapeake & Ohio Canal Company, shall be printed, and a copy thereof shall be set up for public inspection, for at least ten days prior to the 1st day of April 1851, at some one of the Collector's offices, or some one of the lock-houses, on the said Canal, in each County in the State of Maryland, through which the Canal passes,–and also at the Collector's office, at Georgetown, in the District of Columbia.[173]

In June 1851 President Samuel Sprigg reported satisfaction with the operation of the new regulations in spite of the opposition of some of the unruly boatmen. The rules already had brought "beneficial results" in the preservation of the works of the company," thus "producing a degree of order and regularity on the part of those navigating the canal, which has heretofore not existed." Company officials were certain that

all well-disposed persons engaged in navigating the canal, regard these regulations as wholesome and necessary, acting both as a protection to the works of the company, insuring more regularity, and less frequent interruptions to the navigation of the canal, and, at the same time, preventing collisions with some of the boatmen, who have hitherto been disorderly.[174]

The regulations established in 1851 remained in effect until 1889 with some periodic modifications or additions. The changes were made whenever the board felt that circumstances warranted a revision. Among the most significant changes in the regulations were the following:

    1. April 3, 1856—The privileges granted to packet boats in Regulations Nos. 30 and 34 were revised insofar as they applied to descending boats loaded and under headway. All such boats were henceforth to be upon an equal footing with packets relative to all cases referred to in the aforementioned rules.[175]

    2. April 15, 1858—The board adopted an order directing that when passing, all ascending freight boats take the towpath side of the canal and all descending boats take the berm side. After only three weeks, this new directive was rescinded on May 5.[176]

    2A. May 7, 1858—The board directed that all boats ascending and descending the canal between Georgetown and Cumberland be required to prepay

---

[173] *By-Laws, Rules, and Regulations; In Force on the Chesapeake & Ohio Canal, 1st April 1851* 3–4, 9–33.
[174] *Twenty-Third Annual Report* (1851), C&O Co., 3–4. During the first three months in which the rules were in effect, the amount of fines had totaled $60.
[175] *Proceedings of the President and Board of Directors*, I, 251–252.
[176] *Ibid*, K, 14, 19.

their boat tolls.[177]

3. May 3, 1859—Approximately one year before this date the board had ordered that boats could not operate on the canal on Sundays. Under considerable pressure by the boatmen and other company officials, the order was repealed on this date, thereby reopening the canal to traffic seven days a week. [178]

4. November 4, 1860—The board determined to suspend that portion of Regulation No. 47 that applied to the short levels between Locks Nos. 1–4 in Georgetown. Boats were to be permitted to load or to unload cargoes in those levels provided that they did not interfere with the free navigation of the canal.[179]

5. November 14, 1860—A new rule was passed regulating the payment of tolls when a boat did not pass any locks. The rule, which was to take effect immediately, was as follows:

> Any boat or float navigating the Canal where there is no lock to pass to its destination, and the owner or other person having charge of the same, shall refuse to pay the toll, when such payment shall be demanded by the proper officers, shall on the requisition of said officer tie up the same at such place as said officer shall direct, and so remain until the tolls due thereon shall be paid, and on refusal of such owner, or other person having charge of the boat or float, or the removal of said boat or float after being tied up until the tolls and fines thereon be paid, shall be subject to a penalty for the first offence of $20, and for each subsequent offence by the same party of $50.[180]

6. October 12, 1869—April 15, 1873—During this period, the canal company again experimented with a Sabbath law–adopting and repealing the order prohibiting Sunday runs on several occasions. In October 1866 the board received a memorial from Charles Embrey and other boatmen from the vicinity of Williamsport asking that the Sunday trade be suspended on the waterway. The board rejected the request because the Sunday law passed in 1858 had proven to be a failure. After a one-year trial, the directors had repealed that law "at the instance both of parties navigating the Canal and of residents near the Canal, complaining of riots and depredations committed by boatmen congregating together."[181]

Nothing more was done about the question of Sunday navigation until September 8, 1869, when representatives of the Sabbath Association of Maryland appeared before the board and submitted a number of petitions favoring the suspension of the Sabbath trade. The board appointed a committee headed by President Josiah Gordon to study the matter and to make a recommendation. On October 12 the directors, after having received the committee's report urging the passage of a Sunday prohibition, divided evenly by a 3 to 3 vote on a motion to table the subject. President Gordon cast a negative vote against the motion after which the following order was adopted:

---

[177] Ringgold to Hollingsworth and Shaw, May 7, 1858, Ltrs. Sent, C&O Co.
[178] *Proceedings of the President and Board of Directors*, K, 104.
[179] Ibid, K, 227.
[180] Ibid, K, 227–228.
[181] Ibid, K, 518.

that from and after the first day of November 1869 no trade or traffic will be allowed on the Chesapeake & Ohio Canal on the Sabbath day, and that the Lockkeepers be required to close their Locks at 12 o'clock on Saturday night, and open them at 12 o'clock on Sunday night.[182]

Beginning in the spring of 1870 the canal board experienced great difficulty in enforcing the Sunday rule. Because of widespread disregard for the law, the board on May 6 voted to remit the fines imposed during the months of March and April "except ten dollars on each boat." Since the fine for breaking the Sabbath law was only $5, this action by the board indicates that many of the boatmen were disobeying the law on a frequent basis. The defiant behavior on the part of some of the unruly boatmen caused the board to rescind the Sunday law on October 12, 1870. However an order prohibiting Sunday navigation was put into effect again on August 1, 1871, only to be repealed on August 16.[183]

After this series of events, the stockholders took up the question of Sunday navigation at their annual meeting in June 1872. They passed a resolution to have the Sunday law strictly enforced on the canal, and the board dutifully issued such a directive in September. Following a number of incidents arising from the renewed prohibition, the problem was referred to Walter S. Cox, the company counsel. It was his opinion that the canal was "declared to be a public highway" and he could not "see why the Company would have any more control over its use on Sunday than a Turnpike Company would over the use of its road." Thereafter, the company officials "indefinitely postponed" the consideration of a Sunday prohibition on canal trade, the earlier directive was repealed, and the question was never seriously discussed again.[184]

   7. SPRING 1870—Prior to the commencement of the 1870 boating season Chief Engineer Hutton sent a circular to the superintendents on the line, urging them to enforce strictly all the regulations for the navigation of the waterway. In the circular he announced one change in the by-laws. That section of Regulation No. 57, which prohibited the changing of mule teams while a boat was in a lock chamber, was to be suspended providing that such an action did not cause delays in the navigation.[185]

   8. May 23, 1870—As the number of boats plying the canal increased, the Georgetown Level became particularly crowded. Accordingly, the board, under the authority of Regulation No. 50 of the By-Laws, drew up additional rules to govern the navigation and the loading and unloading procedures on this section of the waterway. The new regulations were as follows:

> Boats consigned to points on this level will, on arriving, take position at the upper end of the line of waiting boats, and retain the same until notified by the Harbor Master to proceed to their respective places of discharge, but no boat shall lie nearer above the Alexandria Aqueduct than one hundred yards.

---

[182] *Ibid,* L, 193, 196, 209–210.
[183] *Ibid,* L, 317, 369, 422, 435–436, and Anon. To Gordon, May 19, 1870, Ltrs. Recd., C&O Co.
[184] *Proceedings of the President and Board of Directors,* L, 57, 105–106.
[185] Circular to Superintendents, (Spring), 1870, Ltrs. Sent, C&O Co.

Superintendents of Coal Wharves and other Consignees shall notify the Harbor Master what boats they wish to unload, and shall promptly discharge the same on their arrival at the wharf.

Boats shall not lie two or more abreast, at any point on this level, without express permission of the Harbor Master or Superintendent. When in position they must be moored close to the bank or wall, both head and stern.

No boat shall attempt to pass another moving in the same direction, below the upper end of the line of waiting boats.

When boats moving in opposite directions approach the wharf next above Frederick street bridge, while a boat is lying at that wharf, it shall be the duty of the Master of the ascending boat to stop below the bridge until the descending boat shall have passed.[186]

9. April 10, 1872– The great increase in canal trade during the early 1870s resulted in frequent and lengthy delays at the Paw Paw Tunnel while the boats awaited their turn to enter the narrow passage. There were two proposals, for the solution of this problem one for a system of signals to show when the boats might enter and the other for the assignment of a watchman to direct traffic.[187] On March 22, 1871, Chief Engineer Hutton submitted to the board recommendations for regulations to govern the navigation through the tunnel, and the directors adopted these proposed rules with little modification on April 10, 1872.[188] The new regulations were as follows:

1st A watchman will be stationed at the west end of the tunnel, both night and day.
2nd No ascending boat shall enter the tunnel at the East end when a flag is shown at the west end in daytime, or a light at night.
3rd When there are no signals shows at the west end of the tunnel, ascending boats have the right to enter at the east end and pass through.
4th All descending boats shall enter the tunnel at the west end and pass through or stop, as the watchman shall direct.
5th It shall be the duty of the Watchman, when ascending boats have been waiting at the east end of the tunnel two hours, to stop the descending boats at the west end and remove his signal and give the ascending boat or boats the right to pass through.
6th When the descending boats have been waiting at the west end of the tunnel, one and a half hours, it shall be the duty of the Watchman to show his signals and give the descending boats the right to pass through.
7th When from any cause of detention a large number of boats may have collected at the tunnel, they shall pass through in sections, as the watchman shall direct.
8th If from any cause boats meet in the tunnel or create a jam, they shall move or pull, as the watchman shall direct.

---

[186] "Regulations for the Georgetown Level," May 23, 1870, broadside in Ltrs. Recd., C&O Co.
[187] Report for the Year 1870 (Frederick, 1871), 7–8.
[188] Hutton to Clarke, March 22, 1871, Ltrs. Recd., C&O Co.

Penalty for a violation of either of the provisions of these regulations, Ten Dollars.[189]

D. REGULATIONS FOR 1889–1924

There is no available information regarding the regulations for navigating the canal during the receivership period. It is presumed that most or all of the regulations of the 1851–1889 period remained in effect.

---

[189] *Proceedings of the President and Board of Directors*, M, 9.

APPENDIX A

SIDE VIEW AND PLAN OF THE *SWIFT*.[1]

Is a side view and plan of the experimental Boat "*Swift*;" her dimensions are as under:

Whole length, 60 feet.
Breadth on beam, 8 feet 6 inches.
Width of centre trough (extending longitudinally down the middle of the boat) 2 feet 6 inches at the bow, 22 inches at midship, and 3 feet 6 inches at the stern.

The *Swift* is gig-built, light timbered, and weighs about 27 cwt.

[IMAGE NOT INCLUDED]

---

[1] William Fairbain, *Remarks on canal navigation, illustrative of the advantages of the use of steam, as a moving power on canal: etc.* (Longman, Rees, Orme, Brown and Green, 1831), 88 and Plate I.

APPENDIX B

EXPERIMENTAL RESULTS OF THE *SWIFT*, JULY 9, 1830[2]

Note of a series of experiments, made on the Forth of Clyde Canal,
with Mr. Graham's Twin Boat *Swift*, Friday, July 9, 1830

All trips:
One mile in length; canal's average width 63 feet.and average depth 9 ft.9in.

No. of experiments	Weight of boat and cargo	Draught of water, in inches			No. of horses	Time		Miles per hour	Force of traction in lbs	Remarks
	Cwr.qrs.lbs.	Bow	Stern	Mean		Min	Sec			
1	116 1 14	14½	16½	15½	2	14	28	4.14	54.40	Against the wind, light breeze
2	116 1 14	14½	16½	15½	2	14	15	4.21	34.00	With the wind
3	116 1 14	14½	16½	15½	2	9	45	6.15	128.70	Against the wind; a ripple was observed rising at the bows and extending to the banks on each side of the canal.
4	116 1 14	14½	16½	15½	2	9	35	6.26	93.80	With the wind, ripple the same.
5	116 1 14	14½	16½	15½	2	8	35	7.50	207.50	Against the wind, with a slight surge at stern.
6	116 1 14	15½	16½	16	2	7	50	7.65	202.35	With the wind, surge the same.
7	116 1 14	16	16	16	2	7	29	8.01	264.30	Against the wind, the surge a little increased.
8	116 1 14	16	16	16	2	6	28	9.27	272.20	With the wind, surge the same.
9	116 1 14	14½	15½	15	2	7	22	8.14	266.50	No sensible difference in surge.
10	116 1 14	14½	15½	15	2	7	35	7.91	243.20	Wind nearly subsided, surge the same.
11	116 1 14	14½	15½	15	2	7	6	8.45	328.00	Rather more surge at stern.
12	116 1 14	14½	15½	15	2	7	17	8.23	298.00	Rather more surge at stern.
13*	116 1 14	14½	15½	15	4	4	52	12.32	410.00	Surge decreased.
14	61 2 7	7	9	8	4	4	16	14.06	352.06	In this experiment the surge was greatly diminished, a rippling wave only seen at the stern, and not the least surge in front of the boat.

Temperature 50°   *The mercury stood fixed in this experiment at 410 pounds

---

[2] House Project 414, 377–378.

Note of experiments, made with the Twin Boat
on the Monkland Canal, on the 12th of July, 1830

All trips: ¼ mile in length; canal's average width 40 ft. and average depth 5 ft. 4 in.

No. of experiments	Weight of boat and cargo	Draught of water, in inches			No. of horses	Time		Miles per hour	Force of traction in lbs	Remarks
	Cwr.qrs.lbs.	Bow	Stern	Mean		Min	Sec			
1	108 2 21	14½	16	15½	3	3	5	4.86	72.0	With the wind and no surge
2	108 2 24	14½	16	15¼	3	3	7	4.81	92.0	Against the wind, no surge.
3	108 2 24	14½	16	15¼	3	2	23	6.29	191.3	With the wind, a slight surge.
4	108 2 24	14½	16	15¼	3	2	26	6.16	219.3	Rather more wind ahead, with a slight surge at stern.
5	108 2 21	14½	16	15¼	3	2	11	6.87	389.0	With the wind, same swell.
6	108 2 24	14½	16	15¼	3	1	57	7.69	368.1	Against the wind, a swell in front and stern, rolling over the banks of the canal.
7	108 2 24	14½	16	15¼	3	1	21	11.11	420.0	With the wind, no surge.

8	108 2 24	14½	16	15¼	3	1	14	12.16	446.9	No surge, wind subsided.
9	108 2 24	14½	16	15¼	3	1	12	12.50	439.3	No wind and no surge.
10	57 2 9	The draught not measured			3	1	9	13.04	390.0	Light breeze ahead, no surge; a part of the cargo removed from the boat.

APPENDIX C

SIDE VIEW AND PLAN OF THE *LORD DUNDAS* IRON TWIN BOAT.

Represents a side view and plan of the "*Lord Dundas*" Iron Twin Boat; it will not be necessary here to give the dimensions, as a detached account of her length, breadth, weight, &c. is given in the 6th page of this work: suffice it to observe, that she is constructed of exceedingly light material, the plates or sheeting of the iron ribs being under 1/16 of an inch in thickness, and her whole weight, exclusive of the steam engine, paddle-wheel, &c. not exceeding two and a half tons.[3]

[IMAGE NOT INCLUDED]

---

[3] William Fairbain, *Remarks on canal navigation, illustrative of the advantages of the use of steam, as a moving power on canal: etc.* (Longman, Rees, Orme, Brown and Green, 1831), 88 and Plate I.

APPENDIX D

PLAN AND DRAWING OF THE *CYCLOPS* [4]

Conveys nearly a correct representation of the *Cyclops* now plying on the Forth and Clyde Canal, to Alloa, on the Firth of Forth: this vessel has a fourteen horses' power steam engine, placed in the position A, near the stern; it gives motion to the paddle-wheel, by the connecting rod B: the boiler C is fixed on the opposite side of the engine, and is so arranged as to give room for the man to fire, and space for a sufficient quantity of coal to last the voyage. This boat is built on the American plan, and works, with great steadiness in the canal, at four miles an hour; her dimensions are as follow:

>Whole length, 68 feet.
>Breadth on beam, 15 feet 6 inches.
>Depth, about 7 feet 3 inches from the keel to the deck.
>Weight, including engine, boiler, fittings, &c. about 38 tons.

On examining the side view of the *Cyclops*, it will be seen that her water lines are shown,

First, as represented by the line a, when light; that is, with no cargo except a sufficient quantity of water in the boiler, and two tons of coals on board, when her draught was 4 feet 6 inches, aft, and 1 ½ inch forward.

Second, by the line b, with a cargo of 20 tons 3 qrs. 17lbs. her draught being, in this instance, 4 feet aft, and 2 feet 6 inches forward. The loading on this occasion was improperly disposed.

Third, by the line c, with a cargo of 29 tons 3 cwt. 3 qrs. 17 lbs. her draught, in this case, being 3 feet 9 inches aft, and 3 feet 6 inches forward.

It has already been remarked by Mr. Grahame, that a cargo, or not a cargo, makes little difference to the *Cyclops*, as her speed is neither increased, nor much diminished by the change; this, no doubt, is owing to the weight of the engine, boiler, paddle-wheel, &c. raising the bow, and bearing down the stern, when she is light, and sinking the paddle-wheel to a depth that must rather churn the water, than produce an effective impulse, as may be seen by the variation of the water lines a, b, c, which sufficiently illustrates this part of the subject.

[IMAGE NOT INCLUDED]

---

[4] William Fairbain, *Remarks on canal navigation, illustrative of the advantages of the use of steam, as a moving power on canal: etc.* (Longman, Rees, Orme, Brown and Green, 1831), 89-90 and Plate III.

APPENDIX E

DRAWINGS OF AN IRON STEAMBOAT [5]

Represents a side view and plan of the improved iron steam boat, now building for the Forth and Clyde Canal Company: this vessel is intended for the double purpose, of navigating the canal, and the adjoining coasts; the following are her dimensions:

> Whole length, 68 feet.
> Breadth on beam, 15 feet
> Depth from the keel to the deck, 8 feet.
> Steam engine 24 horses' power, having two cylinders on the locomotive principle: paddle wheels, each 11 feet diameter, and 3 feet wide.

Computed weight of boat, paddle-wheels, engine, &c.

	Tons.	Cwt.	Qrs.	Lbs.
Boat,	10	5	2	0
Engine,	6	2	0	0
Machinery,	2	18	2	9
Rigging; stores, &c.	_3	_6	_0	_0
Total weight,	22	12	0	9

This vessel will contain a cargo of 50 tons, on a draught of water of about 3 feet 9 inches; she will be constructed of the best material, with strong iron ribs, and plate sheeting about ¼ inch thick. The same objection may be urged against this boat as the *Cyclops*, so far as respects her water lines, which, from the position of the steam engine, paddle-wheels, &c. must cause her to hang much by the stern; this objection is of no moment, as vessels of this description seldom sail without some loading; and, at all times, there is the power to trim the cargo, so as to give her the proper bearing in the water. I therefore deem the weight of machinery at the stern of less consequence, than the loss of power and inconvenience of conveying the motion from the engine (if placed nearer the bows) to the wheels, in that position: besides, placing the engine nearer the middle of the hold, would in a great measure destroy valuable stowage, and materially limit her carrying capacity.

---

[5] William Fairbain, *Remarks on canal navigation, illustrative of the advantages of the use of steam, as a moving power on canal: etc.* (Longman, Rees, Orme, Brown and Green, 1831), 90-91 and Plate IV.

APPENDIX F

DRAWINGS OF CANAL STEAMER[6]

Is a side view and plan of a Canal Steamer, calculated for sea voyages, and a direct communication with the internal parts of the country, through canals constructed for the admission of such vessels: it will be seen, that a part of the side of the boat is supposed to be cut out, for the purpose of representing a sectional view of her steam engine, paddle-wheels, boiler, &c. A slight glance at the plate will show, that the wheels are advanced nearer midship; that considerable care is taken to occupy as little space as possible in the vessel; that the whole machinery is exceedingly compact, and takes up no more of the vessel's stowage than 21 feet in length, including space for firing, and room to stop and start the engine. The paddle-wheels are placed in the position H, to obviate the apprehended danger and difficulty of working them advantageously at sea, and also, to retain them as near the stern as possible, on account of saving the vessel's bearings, and allowing a free discharge from the wheels when her portcullises are down, which would always be the case in passing through the canal.

The dimensions are as under, viz:

Whole length, 88 feet
Breadth on beam, 20 feet
Depth from the keel to the deck, 9 feet.
Steam engine (high pressure) 60 horses' power, having two cylinders as per plan.
Paddle-wheels, 12 feet diameter each, and 4 feet wide.

Computed Weight.

	Tons.	Cwt.	Qrs.	Lbs.
Boat, composed of strong- ribbed iron and plates, 1/16 inch thick	21	14	3	0
Steam-engine, boiler, &c.	12	10	0	0
Paddle-wheels, &c.	3	10	0	0
Riggs, stores, &c.	8	10	0	0
Total weight Tons.	46	4	3	0

Carrying power, draught of water, &c. will be:

	Burthen Tons.	Drought of Water, Feet.	In.
When light, including engines and coals under forecastle, equal to cargo of	10	2	0
With a cargo of	48	3	0
With a cargo of	92	4	0
With a cargo of	116	4	6

So that a full cargo of 116 tons would give a draught of water, four feet six inches, which I apprehend is not too much for most canals communicating with the different sea ports on the coast.

---

6   William Fairbain, *Remarks on canal navigation, illustrative of the advantages of the use of steam, as a moving power on canal: etc.* (Longman, Rees, Orme, Brown and Green, 1831), 92–93 and Plate V.

APPENDIX G

SPECIFICATIONS OF A LIGHT IRON PASSAGE BOAT

Specification of a light iron passage boat, such as ply on the summit level of the Forth and Clyde Canal, between Port Dundas and Windford, and such as was used in the experiments detailed in the foregoing paper.

	Feet
Extreme length,	70
Extreme breadth	5 ½

The iron of the very best manufacture.

The body plates, in particular, must be free from rust, cracks, blisters, and roughness of every description. The whole of the iron must be coated with linseed oil, previous to its being used. And the boat must be built under cover, so that the work may be kept dry until the boat is finished.

Although not shown on the plan, the said boat (plate IV.) has a hollow keel, so as to prevent the lodgement of water beneath the floor, between the ribs. The stem and stern shall consist of bars of iron, six inches in breadth and a quarter of an inch thick, which are hammered flat at the lower part to the breadth and thickness of the keel-plate, to which they are scarfed and secured with clench rivets.

As stated above, the keel-plates are formed hollow, and consist of hoop iron, six inches in breadth, and one-eighth of an inch in thickness. To which a wood keel, of Memel plank, fifty feet in length, nine inches in depth, three inches in thickness next the bottom of the boat, and an inch and a half at the lower edge, tapered off to nothing at each end, must be secured to the keel-plates with glands an inch and a half in breadth, and a quarter of an inch thick, sunk flush into the keel, and screwed inside at the distance of three and a half inches apart.

The ribs shall consist of T and angle iron, and placed alternately at the distance of twelve inches from each other, and extending from gunwale to gunwale, after being bent to suit the curved form of the vessel, two rows of holes are punched on the flat side of the angle and T ribs to secure the body plate, and holes at convenient distances are punched through the upright flange to secure the false ribs for the inside lining.

The body plates must consist of the best double-rolled No. 16 sheet-iron, two and a half lbs. per superficial foot, and these sheets are in lengths of eight and ten feet. The first range of bottom plates, which join the hollow keel, eight feet in length and twenty-four inches in breadth; the next two ranges on each side, which form the bilge, ten feet in length by twelve inches in breadth; and the range next gunwale, ten feet in length by eighteen inches in breadth. Particular attention is requisite, both with the view to the strength and appearance of the boat, that the whole of the body plates be run in fair sheer lines from stem to stern, and that the lower edge of each succeeding length or range of plates cover the upper edge of their accompanying ones three quarters of an inch, so that the boat in every respect may have the appearance of being clencher built.

The butts, or end joints of the plates, must be kept smooth, and meet on the centre of the T rib, and the joints of each succeeding plate be so shifted as to meet on the T rib nearest the centre of its accompanying ones. It must, however, be expressly understood, that, previous to any of the plates being riveted, thin stripe of cotton cloth, dipped in white-lead paint, be put in between the overlaps of the edge joint, and between the ribs and the end joints, so as to prevent leakage and corrosion. The whole end and edge joints must be secured with countersunk rivets, made from a three-sixteenth of an inch bore, placed at the distance of three-fourths of an inch from centre to centre, and made from the best charcoal rivet iron; the rivets, except those for securing the end joints, must be placed two inches distant from each other; and the whole, as stated above, be countersunk, and kept as smooth as possible.

Plates, six inches in breadth and one-eighth of an inch in thickness, to be placed on each side along the bilge, over the body plates, where they are most exposed to injury when taking on board and landing passengers, which will extend from the round of the entry, at the bow, to the commencement of the run or exit, at the stern; and is secured to the ribs and body plates with countersunk rivets, placed at the distance of three inches apart; but before they are secured, both the bilge plates and body plates must be properly coated with white-lead paint, and a ply of sheathing, dipped in the same, put in between.

One and a quarter inch of angle bars extend from stem to stern, to form the gunwale, to which welts or wood mouldings are secured; and another, of the same dimensions, to be placed seven inches below the gunwale, to which the wood belting, three inches thick, and four inches deep round off, is to be secured.

The boat is framed and moulded, and in every respect formed exactly and agreeably to the plan, and the work must be done in a substantial and workmanlike manner.

*Specification of the Carpenter and Joiner Work
of such a Light Iron Canal Passage Boat*

The length of the boat, as specified, at seventy feet in length, five feet six inches in breadth, and two feet six inches in depth. It is divided in the following manner, viz

        Fore deck   4 feet in length.
        Fore sheets   According to the number of the travellers intended
        Space for steerage cabin and principal cabin, &c.
        After sheets for.[?]
        After deck   4 feet.

The false ribs for securing the inside lining consist of willow timber, one inch in breadth, and seven-eighths of an inch in deepness, which must be free from knots and shakes, so that they may bend easily after being stoved to the curved form of the boat, to which they are secured with nails, riveted to the upright flange of the ribs.

The sea-crofts, fore and aft, must extend from the stem and stern to the end of the cabins, and be four inches in breadth, and two inches in thickness, of the best Memel plank; which is kept flush with the gunwale inside, and secured with three-eights of an inch rivets, one throughout each rib.

Two timber heads on each side, near the bow and stern, are laced in the most convenient situation for mooring the boat, and secured with glands fixed with clenched rivets, so that the timber heads may be taken out and replaced, when found necessary; to consist of solid oak timber, five inches in breadth, two inch thick, one foot in length below the gunwale, and seven inches above.

The beams which support the deck, fore and aft, consist of oak plank two inches thick, three inches deep in the centre, and two inches deep at each end, with a curve of half an inch to the foot in length; and they are secured with a sheet-iron plate the to gunwale, angle iron, and sea-croft.

The gunwale or covering boards should consist of the best Memel fir plank, one inch in thickness, which extends from stem to stern; the cover is secured to the gunwale flange and wele, that forms a moulding round the same.

The ends and divisions of the cabins should consist of Memel plank, two and a half inches in breadth, and one inch and three-fourths thick, which will form diagonal frames, for the purpose of strengthening the boat, so as to resist external pressures. The said frames must be lined at the ends of the cabins outside, with the best half-inch American yellow pine plank. The framing in the inside of the cabins may be lined as may be approved of.

The sleepers, for support of the flooring, should be two inches deep, by one inch and a quarter thick, placed and fitted to each alternate rib, and fixed to the upright flange with rivet nails. The flooring should consist of the best yellow pine plank, one inch thick, and not to exceed six inches in breath, which must be properly cleaned, ploughed, and feathered.

The height of the cabins, from the top of the floor to the lower part of the beams, six feet at the centre, and the heights of the sides above the level of the floor will be five feet under the beams; consequently, the beams will have a curve of twelve inches.

The standards or stancheons of the sides of the cabins should consist of the best white American oak, one inch thick, and one a and a half broad at the gunwale, and one inch in breadth at the top of the cabin, and placed at each alternate rib, to which it is secured; the distance being twenty-four inches from centre to centre. The top gunwale, for the support of the roof, to be made of the best Memel fir or red pine, free of blemish or knots, and extend the whole length of the cabin, two and a half inches deep outside; the upper edge is bevelled to suit the curve of the beams, and two inches in thickness, mitered to fit the tenure of the standard, having a projection for a head, and thickness of outside lining.

The beams, as stated above, to have a curve of twelve inches, to consist of the best clean ash timber, an inch and a half in breadth, by one inch in depth, the lower part rounded to a half circle, and is placed at the distance of two feet from centre to centre, dove-tailed and secured to he gunwale with screw-nails; and a framing of iron wire gauze, well painted, shall be made to connect them, so that the top may form one solid connected form from end to end.

A stringer extends the whole length of the cabins, in the centre, to support the roof, which is let in, and bound to the diagonal frames, the upper edge kept flush with the top of the curve, consisting of clean solid white Quebec oak timber, three inches in depth by an inch and a half thick; into which the beams are let nearly in the whole depth, and made exactly for the top covering.

The space outside of the cabin, fore and aft, must be lined from the floor to the gunwale with five-eights of an inch red pine boards, and seated in the usual form; the tops seven-eights of an inch thick, with round supports and cross bearers, with two front rails, two and a half inches in breadth, beaded, and let in flush with the bottom and top of the supports or feet.

In order that the boat may be kept as light as possible in the fittings-up, there should be no inside lining of wood from the floor up; consequently, the whole seatings in the cabins must have fronts supported with brackets; these brackets to be secured to a stringer, fixed to the sides of the boat the whole lengths of the cabin, three inches in breadth, by an inch and a quarter thick, to which the brackets are let in flush, and nailed to it and the floor. The seats in the principal cabin to be sixteen inches in height, so as to allow cushions two inches thick and eighteen inches in breadth; the back to be one inch lower than the front, which is considered an improvement as a comfortable seat; the seats in the principal cabin may consist of cane, light wood, or lacing, as may be approved of; the fronts consisting of the best American yellow pine five-eights boards. The seats in the steerage, eighteen inches in height, by fourteen inches in breadth, and fixed with brackets in the same manner as the principal cabin, and be seven-eights of an inch in thickness.

The outside lining between the gunwale and top of the cabins should consist of the best yellow pine half-inch boards, well seasoned, free of knots, sound, and properly cleaned, ploughed, and feathered. The first board will extend the whole length of the cabins, eights inches in breadth, nearly joined to the coverings boards; thin fitters being fitted between the standards or stauncheons, and laid in white-lead paint, so as to be water-tight, and fixed to the side standards with springs.

The space between the standards being twenty-four inches from centre to centre, it is proposed that light windows, or patent gauze wire, shall be place in every alternate space, so as the passengers may have a view of the country without being under the necessity of removing to the outside. These windows and frames should be made as light as possible, and made to slide or fold, as may be considered most convenient.

The inside lining, from the seats up, and between the windows, should consist of oil-cloth, fixed and finished with heads and facings.

The top or cover of the cabins to consist of oil-cloth, which must be perfectly water-tight, and fixed to the beams, top gunwales, and ends of the cabin, with a moulding. It will be necessary to have a thin sheet of plate-iron for the funnels, so as to prevent any danger from the heat of the stoves during the winter.

The outside doors should consist of red pine plank, one inch and a quarter thick, bound and pannelled, to be hung with neat light bats and bands, have good five-inch rimmed locks, brass mounted, to open out in two halves, and to have small brass slip bolts at top and bottom. The doors in the divisions to have check locks, and hung with five inch edge hinges.

The inside doors should consist of the best yellow pine plank, one and one-eighth inch thick, and twenty-two inches in breadth, and finished with facings.

That the whole of the inside, previous to the joiner work being commenced should have two coats of good lead-color paint; and the whole of the iron-work on the outside, as well as the wood-work in the outside and inside, should have three coats of paint of different colors, and finished in a sufficient and workmanlike manner.

House Report 414, 367–37

APPENDIX H

Journal of the Experiments on the Navigation of the Chesapeake and Delaware Canal by the Steam-boat Lewis, September 22nd, 1853.

FIRST EXPERIMENT

The steam-boat towing one of the barges, for passengers, used upon the canal.

Length of barge 90 feet, breadth of beam 19 feet, draught, when light 23 inches, including the keel, which is 11 inches; draught, with the ordinary number of passengers, 55 inches.* Awning of the barge up.

The barge 15 feet in rear of the steam-boat.

Twenty-eight persons in the steam-boat; seven in the barge.

Points at
which the
observations
were made

Middle of
Delaware
bridge

Middle of
Delaware
bridge

26 2/3

26 2/3

- Ratio of velocity of boat to velocity of wheel.

Mean rate of boats, wind in favour	6.56 miles	Relative rates
Mean rate of boats, wind adverse	4.63 miles	1.417 to 1
Mean	5.59 miles	
Greatest rate of boats, wind in favour	6.96 miles.	Relative rates
Greatest rate of boats, wind adverse	4.88 miles.	1.426 to 1
Mean ratio of velocity of boat to velocity of wheel, wind in favour,		.63
Mean ratio of velocity of boat to velocity of wheel, wind adverse		.46
Mean		.55

SECOND EXPERIMENT

The steam-boat, with thirteen persons on board.

Points at which the observations were made	Time of Observation			RPM	Remarks	Width of Waterway	Dist. Bet. Sta	Time bet. Stations		Rate/ Hr.	Ratio*
	H.	M.	S.			Yds	Yds	M.	S.	Miles	
					Steam-boat alone						
Post 300 yds W of Del. Lock	9	12	35	39	Wind as in 1st exp't						
Post 300 yds E of Del. Bridge	9	14	35	39	Faster than boat and in favour	26 2/3	471	2	00	8.03	.71
Middle of Delaware bridge	9	16	00		Steam shut off, in part, for 20 seconds	26 2/3	302				
Post 300 yds W of Del bridge	9	17	32	37½	More wash than in first exp't but still harmless	56	302				
Mile post No. 1	9	19	20	37½		59	385	1	48	7.29	.67
Mile post No. 2	9	26	30	39		59	1770	7	10	8.42	.77
Mile post No. 3	9	34	09	37½		55	1768	7	39	7.88	.72
Mile post No. 4	9	41	50	37½		176	1755	7	41	7.79	.71
Post 300 yds E of Penna. lock	9	43	30		Pass Penna lock, wind slower than boat just at a point opposite the bow	44		1	40		
Post 300 yds W of Penna. lock	9	58	08			275		15	22		
Mile post No. 5	10	00	50	39		190		2	42		

| Mile post No. 6 | 10 | 08 | 13 | 37½ | was measured upon a stick, and found to be about 1 inch. Canal 9 to 10 feet deep; pond 800 ft. wide. Exp't not precise. | 132 | 1764 | 7 | 23 | 8.14 | .73 |

After passing mile post No. 6 a sloop was attached by tow lines to the steam-boat; the burthen of the sloop was forty-four tons, the actual load being fifty tons of anthracite, and the draught sixty-two inches exclusive of the keel. The helmsman of both the steam-boat and the sloop, not understanding the management of their respective vessels, in the new circumstances in which they were placed, there was so much sheering in one direction and another, that it was deemed expedient to cast off the tow lines, on the approach of the passenger barge which appeared in sight. The speed was estimated differently at from three to four miles per hour, but the checks, which it constantly met with, rendered any accuracy of estimate out of the question. The passenger barge, towed by *eleven* horses, now passed, and the steam-boat followed; part of the experiment, which follows, was made in the shallower end of a former mill-pond, and the other through about one quarter of a mile of the deep cut.

Points at which observations were made	Time of observation			RPM	Remarks	Width Waterway	Dist. Bet. Sta.	Time bet. Stations		Rate/ Hr.	Ratio*
	H.	M.	S.		Steam-boat alone	Yds	Yds	M.	S.	Miles	
Mile post No. 7	10	34	52	37	From the bottom of the	210					
Mile post No. 8	10	42	57	36	Depression to the top of the swell created by the barge, was, at the lowest, 3.5 feet; the same height for the swell of the boat was 1 foot, at the most.	26 2/3	1736	8	05	7.41	.70
					Mean					7.85	.71

Chesapeake & Ohio Canal Historic Resource Study
Unrau: 7. Boats & Navigation Regulations

Points at which observations were made	Time of observation			RPM	Remarks	Width Waterway	Dist. Bet. Sta.	Time bet. Stations		Rate/ Hr.	Ratio*
	H.	M.	S.			Yds	Yds	M.	S.	Miles	
					Steam-boat alone						
Mile post No. 7	11	23	30	37½	Light wind ahead	270					
Mile post No. 6	11	31	42	35	Wind strengthens	132	1769	8	12	7.36	.70
Mile post No. 5	11	39	53	37½		190	1764	8	11	7.35	.68
Post 300 yds W of Penna lock	11	43	52	37½		275		3	59		
Pennsylvania lock	11	50	20		In lock and going 300 yds			6	28		
Post 307 yds E of Penna. Lock	11	52	18	33		44		1	58		
Mile post No. 4	11	54	10	34½		176		1	52		
Mile post No. 3	12	02	20			55	1755	8	10	7.33	.3
Mile post No. 2	12	10	18	35½		59	1768	7	58	7.56	.74
Mile post No. 1	12	17	55			59	1770	7	35	7.92	.77
Post 300 yds W of Del bridge	12	19	40			56	385	1	45	7.50	
Middle of Delaware bridge	12	21	05		Steam slack	26 2/3	302	1	24		
Post 300 yds E of Del bridge	12	22	57	34½		26 2/3	302	1	52		
Post 300 yds W of Del bridge	12	25	15	33			471	2	18	6.98	.70
					Mean					7.43	.72

Mean velocity of steam-boat, wind in favour 7.85 miles per hour   Relative rates
Mean velocity of steam-boat, wind adverse 7.43 miles per hour   1.055 to 1
                    Mean   7.64
Greatest vel. of steam-boat, wind in favor 8.42 miles per hour   Relative rates
Greatest vel. of steam-boat, wind adverse 7.92 miles per hour   1.068 to 1
Mean ratio of velocity of boat to velocity of wheel, wind in favour, .71
Mean ratio of velocity of boat to velocity of wheel, wind adverse,   .72

THIRD EXPERIMENT

Steam-boat towing a freight barge of twenty-five tons burthen, loaded with from fifteen to eighteen tons of merchandise, and drawing two and a half feet of water.

Wind very light, in favour of the boat.

Points at which observations were made	Time of observation			RPM	Remarks	Width Waterway	Dist. Bet. Sta.	Time bet. Stations		Rate/ Hr.	Ratio*
	H.	M.	S.			Yds	Yds	M.	S.	Miles	
Post 300 yds W of Delaware lock	12	40	34	34	Towing a freight barge						
Post 300 yds E of Delaware bridge	12	43	31	34		26 2/3	471	2	57	5.44	.55
Middle of Delaware bridge	12	45	25		Steam slacked for 20 sec	26 2/3					
Post 300 yds W of Delaware bridge	12	47	18	34½		56					
Mile post No. 1	12	49	22	35		59	385	2	04	6.36	.62
					Mean					5.95	.58

The passenger barge from the west appearing in sight, the freight barge was disengaged, and the boat put about. At the first part of this experiment there was a difficulty encountered similar to that noticed in the case of the attempt to tow the sloop, but less in degree; it resulted from the inexperience of the helmsman of the barge, and as soon as he had been directed how to steer, and followed the directions, there was no further trouble from this source.

FOURTH EXPERIMENT

Steam-boat alone, returning in rear of the passenger barge drawn by seven horses.
Light wind ahead.

Points at which observations were made	Time of observation			RPM	Remarks	Width Waterway	Dist. Bet. Sta.	Time bet. Stations		Rate/ Hr.	Ratio*
	H.	M.	S.			Yds	Yds	M.	S.	Miles	
Mile post No. 1	12	58	45		Steam-boat alone	59					

Post 300 yds W of Delaware bridge	1	00	40		56	385	1	55	6.84	
Delaware bridge	1	02	00		26 2/3	302	1	20	7.74	
Post 300 yds E of Delaware bridge	1	03	32		26 2/3	302	1	32	6.63	

The barge had seven horses, which of course were fatigued, for which circumstance allowance must be made; there was, however, no point of time in which the steam-boat could not have passed the barge after it had come up to it and, in fact, during part of the last 500 yards, and after passing the 500 yards post the steam was slackened occasionally, to keep from running too close to the barge.

Summary of the Average Results

Mean velocity	Mile per Hour	Mean Ratio*	Remarks	Avg. RPM
Steam boat alone	7.64	.71	A mile in 7 min and 7/8	36.9
With passenger barge in tow	5.59	.55		34.7
With freight barge in tow	5.95	.58	No exp't against the wind	35.1

*Mean Ratio of velocity of boat to velocity of water.

In these experiments, at the highest rate of motion obtained, there was no swell produced in the straight parts of the canal, which would have been likely to injure the banks although not specially protected. The wave from the bow of the boat, owing to the peculiar form of that part, fell in with the wheels, and was disposed of by them; while the lean form of the stern brought together the waves produced by the wheels, which, therefore, spread very little, if at all, in a lateral direction, that is, towards the banks, being directed towards the tow-path only in parts of the curved portions of the canal. When the barge was in tow, and with the more rapid rate then assumed, nearly seven miles per hour, there was no perceptible swell behind the barge, the swell from the wheels not appearing after meeting the bow of the barge. There was no obvious change in the character of the swell at low and high velocities, but the experiments did not permit numerical accuracy upon this point.

At the time when the heights of the wave from the barge and from the steam-boat are noted in the remarks, the barge was so far before the boat that the latter was free from any effect produced by the swell of the former. It was in the deep cut, and the bow of the barge was elevated, and the stern depressed, mounting an inclined plane, while, besides the wave which preceded the bow, a destructive surge followed sweeping above the stoning of the banks of the tow-path. The wave from the steam-boat was included within the limits comprising only a portion of the cover of the banks, and did not break with the violence necessary to carry away the soil and pebbles from behind the stones.

The boat suffered no sensible retardation in passing into the deep cut, for, in the latter part of the second experiment, with thirty-six and thirty-seven revolutions, the speed was about seven and a half miles per hour, while in the wider portions, with thirty-seven and a half, the speed was about seven miles and three-quarters. The same conclusion is to be drawn by comparing these results with those obtained in the Schuylkill; in fact, the average speed with a given number of revolutions upon the canal, rather exceeds that with the same number upon the river.

he want in power of the engine prevented the experiments from being conclusive in relation to towing, with high rates of motion, though they seem to indicate greater advantages from towing, at rapid rates, than in moving with the boat alone. That the speeds attained by even this imperfect model, compare with those which the labour of eight horses is capable of producing, appears by the annexed memorandum received from the captain of one of the passenger barges which passes daily through the canal on the line from Philadelphia to Baltimore.

		Min	Sec		MPH
From the 11th to the 10th mile post		9	40		6.02
10th	9th	10	00		6.00
9th	8th	9	00		6.67
8th	7th	8	40		6.92
7th	6th	7	55		7.58
6th	5th	7	20		8.18
5th	4th	13	50	Includes lockage	
4th	3rd	8	38		7.02
3rd	2nd	8	20		7.20
2nd	1st	7	20		8.18
1st	0th	8	58		6.69

The average speed is about nine minutes to the mile, and two hours are required to pass the canal."

While then it would seem to be an easy matter to exceed the average speed, which is attainable in towing by horses, the swell produced by one and by the other mode of conveyance are not comparable with each other.

A review of the experiments leads me to the conclusion indicated in the commencement of this article, namely, that steam power may be substituted for the present method of towing by horses on large canals, with great advantage to the canal, particularly at high velocities.

There was no opportunity on this occasion to examine into the cost of this mode of transportation, by ascertaining the amount of fuel consumed in the different trips; this point was investigated, and a further trial in towing heavy vessels was made by Caleb Newbold, Esq. As the results will serve to render my statements more full, I subjoin them.

	Hrs	Min	MPH
1st Expt Steamboat alone, St. Georges to Delaware City (4.25 miles)	0	33	7.75
2nd Exp't Steamboat alone, Delaware City to Chesapeake	1	55	6.91
3rd Exp't Steamboat alone, Chesapeake to Delaware City	1	50	7.23

"In both of the last experiments the steam was slackened off repeatedly to accommodate vessels; the time given is exclusive of six minutes for lockage. The most rapid rates of motion were one mile in six minutes and twenty seconds, (9.48 miles per hour,) and one mile in six minutes and thirty seconds (9.23 miles per hour.) The greatest number of revolutions made in one minute by the wheels was forty-two. 575 lbs of *pine wood*, of fair good quality, (about one-fifth of a cord,) were consumed in keeping up the steam for one hour and fifty minutes.

"4th. Experiment." Delaware City to St. Georges, towing the schooner *William and George*, of 45½ tons burthen, empty, fifty-six minutes, (rate 4.5 miles per hour.)

"5th. Experiment. St. Georges to Delaware City, towing the sloop *Martha and Elizabeth*, of 59 tons, clump built, heavily laden; drawing six feet of water; one hour and two minutes, (rate 4.1 miles per hour.) Part of the way there was a fair wind, and part of the way a strong side wind, which, owing to the want of keel of the steam-boat, pressed it somewhat on the tow path. The vessel is one of the heaviest *towers* of her class. No difficulty in steering, nor any embarrassment from *sheering*."

Experiments Made On the Navigation of the Chesapeake and Delaware Canal By Steam, Reported by A. D. Bache (Philadelphia, 1834), 4-13.

APPENDIX I

EXTRACT FROM AN ACT OF THE GENERAL ASSEMBLY OF MARYLAND, DECEMBER 1831

Extract from an act of the General Assembly of Maryland, entitled "An act further to amend the act incorporating the Chesapeake & Ohio Canal Company," passed at the December session, 1831.

Be it enacted by the General Assembly of Maryland, That if any person or persons shall willfully, by any means whatever, injure, impair, or destroy, any part of the Chesapeake & Ohio Canal, or any part of its feeders, dams, locks, aqueducts, culverts, walls, embankments, bridges, buildings, or other works now constructed, or which may hereafter be constructed, by the Chesapeake & Ohio Canal Company, under the several acts incorporating the said Canal Company, or amendatory thereof, or supplementary thereto, such person or persons so offending shall each of them, for every such offence, forfeit and pay to the said Canal Company a sum not *exceeding* fifty dollars, *recoverable* by action of debt before any justice of the peace in and for the county wherein the offence shall be committed, reserving to the parties the right of appeal from the decision of the said justice of the peace to the county court in the county in which judgment may be had; or every such offender shall be subject to indictment in the court of the county in which the offence shall be committed, and, upon conviction of such offence, shall be punished by fine or imprisonment, or both, in the discretion of the court.

    2. *And be it enacted*, That the President and Directors of the Chesapeake & Ohio Canal Company, or a majority of them, acting in behalf of the said Company, shall be, and they are hereby, authorized and empowered, from time to time, to pass all by-laws which may be necessary for the exercise of the powers vested in said Company by the several acts incorporating the same, or amendatory thereof, or supplementary thereto: *Provided, always*, That such by-laws shall not be contrary to the laws of this State, or of the United States, or of the States in which they operate, and that the said Company shall not be authorized, by any such by-laws or regulations, to prevent the proprietor or proprietors of any lands through which the said canal, dams, basins, feeders, or other appurtenant works may be constructed, from joining or connecting with the said works any fence or wall which shall not be found to injure the work aforesaid; nor to prohibit the aforesaid proprietor or proprietors from having access to the said Canal and its appurtenant works, at the most convenient place and from crossing and recrossing the same at their discretion, in any of the modes hitherto agreed upon by the said Company; *Provided*, in doing so, they do not impede the navigation, or injure the said works. And if any person or persons shall willfully offend against any such by-laws, after a copy thereof shall have been set up for public inspection at each of the toll-houses on the canal, such person or persons, so offending, shall each of them, for every such offence, forfeit and pay to the said Company the sum of five dollars, to be recovered in the name of the said Company before any justice of the peace for the county wherein the offence may be committed.

    3. *And be it enacted*, That the said President and Directors or a majority of them, acting in behalf of the Chesapeake & Ohio Canal Company, may prescribe the form, dimensions, and equipment of the boats and floats to be used upon the canal, with a view to prevent accidental injury to them, or to the works of the canal, in passing each other, or in passing by or through any of the works; and if the owner, captain, or other person, having charge of any boat or float, shall negligently violate, or refuse to comply with any such regulation, the President and Directors may require the owner, captain, or other person having charge thereof, to withdraw his said boat or float from the canal, by some one of the outlets thereof; or, in the event of his failure to do so, on

reasonable notice, may order the same to be broken up and removed from the canal, or any of its basins, ponds, feeders, or other works, and in like manner may be broken up and removed from the canal, or any of its basins, ponds, or feeders, any boat or float, or other substance, floating loose upon, or sunk therein, the owner of which is unknown, or, if known, neglects or refuses, after reasonable notice to remove the same; and the materials of the broken boat, float, or other substance, so broken up and removed, shall be the property of the Canal Company, and be applied to defray the cost of breaking up and removing such nuisance.

APPENDIX J

Act of Congress, approved July 14, 1852

Be it enacted by the Senate and House of Representatives of the United States of America in Congress assembled, That the assent of the United States be, and the same is hereby, given to an act of the General Assembly of Maryland, entitled "An act further to amend the act incorporating the Chesapeake and Ohio Canal Company," which passed the General Assembly of Maryland at December session one thousand and eight hundred and thirty-one: *Provided,* That nothing therein contained shall be construed to impair any right possessed by the said company to the passage of said act, nor to authorize any individual to obstruct the said canal, along the berm bank, or other land for the construction and use thereof, nor to prevent Superintendent, or officers of said company, from up and down the said canal....

APPENDIX K

DRAWINGS OF CHESAPEAKE & OHIO CANAL FREIGHTER

Vint, *Outline Report of Architectural Work*, 70

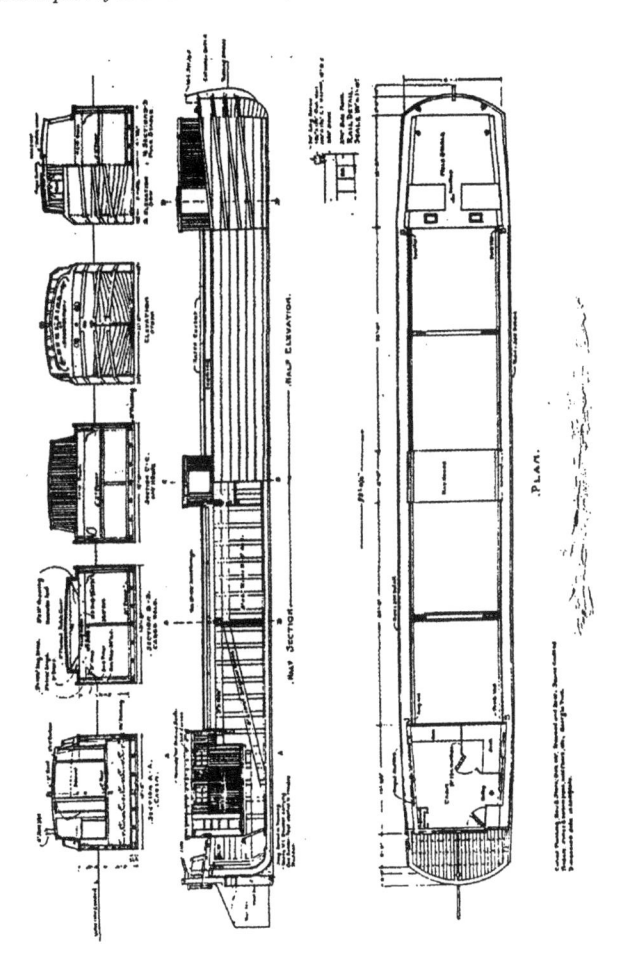

APPENDIX L

ACCOUNT OF LIFE ON A CHESAPEAKE & OHIO CANAL BOAT

There were two kinds of boats on the canal, one of very primitive shape, being nearly the shape of an oblong box with great square ends. These boats would carry large loads but were slow sailors, as the water made a great resistance to the flat end in front and did not leave the boat easily at the stern. There were very few of these boats left and those that were painted at all were covered with a coat of coal tar. The other boats had their ends molded and formed the same as a ship, making as fine lines as was consistent with the load they were to carry and the slow speed they sailed. All the new boats were built at Cumberland where they had a miniature ship yard employing the various mechanics as ship carpenters, smiths, painter and caulkers to be found in large shipyards.

A boat is divided into three compartments; the center was left open except for a narrow walk around the edge and formed the hold where the freight is stored. Over this were placed removable hatches making a watertight covering. At each end of the boat is a cabin with a roof raised about three feet above the deck. The front one is used for a stable and the rear one is divided into a stateroom with berths and cooking galley. The cabin was not so wide as the boat above the deck leaving foot ways, on each side. Behind the rear cabin was the tiller deck from which the cabin stairs went down, and under it a kind of cockpit, about four feet high, where Pic and his boy slept and no place could suit them better as it was the hottest and least ventilated part of the boat.

When the boat was loaded, the water came within a foot of the deck, but when it was light it just skimmed over the water not drawing more than one or two feet and would be almost unmanageable outside of the canal as it had no keel to prevent it from drifting with the wind. There were some three or four hundred boats on the canal and [they] were of all ages and in every stage of repair from those that were bright and shiny to those that you could not tell what was the color of the last coat of paint. A hundred or more of these boats were brought from the Erie Canal, when that was enlarged, by the canal companies who now own nearly all the boats, the boatmen furnishing teams and outfit, receiving so much a ton for hauling the coal, paying their own expenses and the toll on the empty boat back to Cumberland. The cost of a new boat was from twelve to fifteen hundred dollars.

I was not long on board before I was given a lesson in boat steering, Pic keeping watch with a hand ready to grasp the tiller if by some mischance the boat should get the advantage of me and try to run ashore. Boat steering is very simple; you stand with one arm over the tiller and sight across the bow of the boat; then pull or push according to the direction you wish it to go, but it requires constant attention and the steersman has to be constantly on the watch for the slightest deviation from the direct line and immediately overcome it by moving the rudder. This soon becomes instinctive, like steering a bicycle, and requires but little exertion but sometimes, by carelessness or otherwise, and you often feel that it was mere wantonness on the part of the boat, it will take a start for one side and, do the best you can it will hardly escape striking the bank, when over it will go to the other side and just miss grounding there, back and forth it will go half a dozen times before you get it calmed down to straight ahead then perhaps for miles it will not deviate a foot from the right direction. This erratic steering reduces the speed of the boat and adds to the pull of the mules, besides, there was the danger of running the boat aground or in some places of bumping a hole in the bottom on a ledge.

The connection between the mules and the boat is the tow-line, a strong rope three fourths of an inch in diameter and near a hundred feet long, which was fastened to an eye bolt on one side near the middle of the boat, and as this was near the pivot point on which the boat turned and drew nearly straight ahead, it had but little effect on the steering.

In canal language the mules were geared together and not harnessed. The mule gearing was of the simplest description possible consisting of a bridle and breastplate with a strap around the body to keep it in place. The traces were chains that hooked into rings on the mule in the rear with spread sticks between each mule and one where the chains came together at the towline. When we had all four mules hitched tandem they formed a straight line between two long chains that were nearly as rigid as wooden poles, the spread sticks keeping the chains a sufficient distance apart as not to chafe them. It took no little power to start a boat loaded with one hundred and twenty tons of coal drawing five feet of water for a standstill and get it up to speed of two miles per hour. A quick pull of a hundred horses would have little effect except to break the towline, yet a boy ten years old could start the boat by making a long steady pull; after awhile he would feel it yield and perhaps in three or five minutes could make a single step, then another until the boat would move at a slow but steady speed according to the strength of the boy. In the same way the well trained mule could draw the tow-line tight and make an easy pull leaning against their breastplates until the boat began to move, then step after step until the boat was up to speed and all day they seemed to be resting on their breastplates and stopping only to keep from falling forward.

At night, or when we stopped to feed, the boat was hauled up to the shore and made fast, the mules ungeared and the feed trough brought out. This was about a yard long and large enough to hold two buckets of corn in the ear and had but two legs, a tree, post or fence serving for the others, being fastened to it by a rope which passed through two holes in the back. This made the trough a fixture that could not be tipped over or run away with.

We are sailing on and on making from a mile and three fourths to two miles an hour according to the number of mules in use at a time; occasionally we meet a boat going up the canal some of whose crews saluted Capt. Coss or Pic but most of them passed silently by. Some of the boats were drawn by a single mule others had what was once a horse, still others had two or more, but none had a better team than ours. We saw very few boats going in our direction either on the down or return trip except when we tied up to the bank, for the rate of speed was so near the same in all of the boats that the time spent in passing a lock would keep them separate until they came to the next and only on long levels could one gain enough to pass another. We were tied up to no particular hours and lived in Arcadian simplicity. We rose with the early morning light, fed the mules, and when they had eaten their breakfast a pair was hitched up and we started on our day's journey driving them about four hours when they were changed for the other pair; at the end of the next four hours they were again changed, and so on making four shifts and sailing from sixteen to eighteen hours a day, the Capt. Pic and myself taking turns at the rudder while the two boys changed off from time to time and occasionally Pic and myself would drive for an hour or two, walking for exercise; the boys usually rode the rear mule.[7]

---

[7] Excerpt from: Ella B. Clark and Thomas F. Hahn, eds., *Life on the Chesapeake & Ohio Canal: 1859* (New York, 1975), 12–15

HISTORIC RESOURCE STUDY
CHESAPEAKE & OHIO CANAL NHP

8.
COMMERCE ON THE C & O CANAL 1830–1924

BY HARLAN D. UNRAU
HISTORIAN, C&O CANAL RESTORATION TEAM, SENECA
DENVER SERVICE CENTER
1976

CONTENTS

I.	COMMERCE ON THE C & O CANAL: 1830–1850	431
	A. TARRIFS OF TOLL: 1830–1850	431
	B. ANALYSIS OF CANAL TRADE DURING THE CONSTRUCTION YEARS: 1830–1850	437
	C. ENCOURAGEMENT OF TRADE ON THE CANAL: 1830-1850	452
	D. COMPETITION WITH THE B&O RAILROAD: 1830–1850	453
II.	COMMERCE ON THE C & O CANAL: 1851–1889	457
	A. TARRIFS OF TOLL: 1851–1889	457
	B. IRREGULAR UPWARD COURSE OF CANAL TRADE: 1851–1860	463
	C. DECLINING TRADE ON THE CANAL DURING THE CIVIL WAR 1861-1865	471
	D. RESURGENCE OF THE CANAL TRADE IN THE POSTWAR ERA: 1866-1869	475
	E. THE GOLDEN YEARS OF CANAL TRADE, 1870–1875	478
	F. DECLINING YEARS OF THE CANAL TRADE: 1876–1889	486
III.	COMMERCE ON THE C & O CANAL: 1891-1924	496
	A. RESUMPTION OF TRADE: 1891–1894	496
	B. CORPORATE DEVICES TO OPERATE THE CANAL	497
	C. EVALUATION OF CANAL TRADE: 1891–1924	498
	D. POSSIBILITY OF TRADE AFTER 1924	499
APPENDIXES		501
	A. ASCENDING AND DESCENDING TRADE: 1831–1850	501
	B. ASCENDING TRADE: 1851–1878	513
	C. DESCENDING TRADE: 1851–1878	517
	D. TOLLS COLLECTED 1830–1850	521
	E. TOLLS COLLECTED 1851–1889	522
	F. TOLLS COLLECTED 1891–1924	523
	G. CANAL TRADE 1850–1876	524
	H. CANAL TRADE 1850–1876	525
	I. CUMBERLAND COAL TRADE: 1872 & 1874	526
	J. CUMBERLAND COAL TRADE: 1872 & 1874	527
	K. CUMBERLAND COAL TRADE: 1877	528
	L. CUMBERLAND COAL TRADE:1879–1888	529
	M. CUMBERLAND COAL TRADE: 1870–1888	533
	N. CUMBERLAND COAL TRADE: 1879–1889	534

I. COMMERCE ON THE CHESAPEAKE & OHIO CANAL: 1830-1850

The commerce on the canal during the years 1830 to 1850 was almost wholly the transportation of agricultural produce, the least majority of which descended the waterway from the fertile farmlands of Montgomery, Frederick and Washington Counties. As long as this continued, the company was barely able to meet expenses, and all hopes of the promoters had to be expressed in terms of future prospects. The canal board preferred to point to the great lumber and coal resources of the upper valley and the valuable trade to and from the West, which would boost the canal's profits once the waterway was completed to Cumberland. When comparisons had to be made with other canals, the directors used the successful Erie and British waterways as the measure of the future prospects of their canal. In the second annual report to the stockholders in June 1830, President Charles B. Mercer voiced these sentiments:

> Two commodities alone, coal and iron, the transportation of which supplies the chief source of revenue to the most profitable Canals of Scotland and England, are found in inexhaustible quantities near the very line of the latter Canal (Chesapeake & Ohio), while they have not yet been discovered, to any very great extent, if at all, on the Erie Canal of New York. The mineral productions of a country whose surface is comparatively flat and unbroken, cannot be expected to rival, in variety or quantity, those of a region so diversified by mountains and valleys, as the country watered by the Potomac, the Youghiogheny and their tributary streams; some of which, like the Shenandoah and the Monongahela, surpass, themselves, in the actual length of their practical navigation.[1]

Nevertheless the company did not ignore the river trade, keeping the Potomac Company's locks and canals in repair and operation until its own works were completed.[2]

A. TARIFFS OF TOLL, 1830-1850

On October 10, 1830, some three weeks before the canal between Lock Nos. 5 and 23 were opened to navigation, the board fixed the tariffs of tolls at the same rate as the Potomac Company had charged at Great Falls.[3] These tolls were as follows:

ARTICLE	UNIT	TOLL
Domestic spirits	Hogshead	1/6
Tobacco	Hogshead	1/0
Linseed oil	Cask	1/3
Wheat, peas, beans, flax seed	Bushel	0/½
Corn	Bushel	0/¼
Flour	Barrel	0/3
Beef	Barrel	0/4

---

[1] *Second Annual Report* (1830), C & O Canal Co., 15.
[2] *Proceedings of the President and Board of Directors*, A, 312–313, 342, B, 30.
[3] *Ibid*, B, 194. As early as August 21, 1828, the canal board had voted to continue the tariff of tolls previously established by the Potomac Company on all of the locks and skirting canals that were still in operation. The only modifications in those rates were those made to help the contractors building the Chesapeake & Ohio. On August 21, it was determined that granite stone could be taken through the Little Falls locks at 3 cents per perch. After much pressure from the contractors, the board on August 30 decided to allow all building materials and provisions to pass the old Potomac Company locks and canals free of charge. *Ibid*, A, 44–45, 54.

Pork	Barrel	0/6
Hemp, flax, potash	Ton	2/6
Mfd. Iron; copper, lead, etc. (ores)	Ton	2/0
Iron ores and stone	Ton	0/5
Lime	Bushel	1/3
Coal	Chaldron	0/5
Staves (hhds. And bbls.)	Hundred	0/2¼, 0/1½
Plank	Hundred feet	0/10
Timber	Hundred feet	0/5½
Packaged goods	Hundred weight	0/1½
Boats	Each (except empties returned)	2/6[4]

Although a committee was appointed to consider a modification of the tariffs of tolls on December 21, 1831, little was done until the spring of 1834 when the canal was opened to Harpers Ferry.[5] April 4, the board established the first comprehensive rates of tolls. These rates were as follows:

ARTICLE	UNIT, per ton of	Toll, per mile	
		1st 15 mi.	there-after
Tobacco	2 hogsheads	2¢	
Wheat, corn, meal, rye chop, flax seed, clover seed	40 bushels	2¢	
Oats	80 bushels	2¢	
Mill Offal	100 bushels	2¢	
Flour	10 bushels	2¢	
Potatoes	35 bushels	2¢	
Salt	35 bushels	2¢	
Apples	12 bushels	2¢	
Cider, ale, beer	8 barrels	2¢	
Whiskey, pork	7 barrels or 2 hogsheads	2¢	
Hammered, Rolled iron	2,240 pounds	2¢	2¢
Steel, lead, other metals	2,240 pounds	2¢	2¢
Bacon	2,240 pounds	2¢	2¢
Slaughtered hogs, other meat	2,240 pounds	1½¢	1½¢
Livestock	30 sheep, 15 hogs or 3 cattle	2¢	2¢
Shad, herring	600 shad or 4,000 herring	2¢	1¢
Oysters	4,000 or 28 bushels	2¢	1½¢
Salted or pickled beef, pork, fish	7½ barrels	2¢	1½¢
Ale, beer, cider	8 barrels or 2 hogsheads	2¢	2¢
Whisky, Domestic spirits	8 barrels or 2 hogsheads	2¢	2¢
Wine, Foreign spirits	8 barrels or 2 hogsheads	2¢	2¢

---

[4] U.S. Congress, Senate, *Documents Relating to the Chesapeake & Ohio Canal*, S. Doc. 610, 26th Congress, 1st Session, 1840, 80–81, 105–106.

[5] *Ibid*, C, 17, and *Niles' Register*, Vol. XLVI (April 19, 1834), 119. The only two changes in the toll schedule recorded between 1831 and 1834 occurred in October 1831. The toll on stone was set at 1 cent a perch per mile, while the rate on empty freight boats or scows ascending the canal was put at 5 cents a mile.

Salt	45 bushels, fine or 38 bushels, coarse	1½¢	1½¢
Plaster (stone)	2,240 pounds	1½¢	1¢
Plaster (ground)	28 bushels	1½¢	1¢
Grind Stones, Mill Stones	15 cubic feet	2¢	2¢
French Burrs (in blocks)	15 cubic feet	1½¢	1½¢
Bricks, tiles, roofing slates	500 bricks or tiles, 800 slates	1¢	1¢
Coal	28 bushels	1¢	½¢
Hay, straw	2,240 pounds	2¢	1¢
Pig, cast and bar iron	2,240 pounds	2¢	2¢
All other articles	2,240 pounds	2¢	2¢

In addition to these rates for articles, tolls were also levied on the boats that plied the canal. Boats or scows, either empty or having cargos on which tolls amounted to less than 5 cents per mile, were to be charged at the rate of 5 cents per mile for the first 15 miles and 3 cents per mile for any additional distance. Boats used principally for passenger transportation were to pay 10 cents per mile for the first 15 miles and 8 cents per mile thereafter. The tolls on the packets included the toll on the passengers and their baggage, but all other merchandise was to be charged the established rates.

These toll rates applied to both the use of the canal and that of the river from Dam No. 1 to Dam No. 3. For the privilege of navigating the river above Harpers Ferry, the old Potomac Company tolls were to be charged.[6]

The year 1835 saw a revised list of changes put into effect. On January 28 the board extended the 1834 rate of tolls to that portion of the canal between Harpers Ferry and Dam No. 5.[7] Shortly thereafter a committee was appointed to revise the tariff of tolls, and their recommendations were adopted with some modifications by the directors on April 23. [8]The new toll rates, which were to take effect on July 1, were as follows:

ARTICLE	UNIT, Per ton of	Toll, per mile	
		1st 15 mi.	Thereafter
Wheat, Rye, Barley, Buckwheat, Indian Corn	40 bushels	2¢	1½¢
Flour	10½ barrels	2¢	1½¢
Corn Meal	45 bushels	2¢	1½¢
Bran, Shorts, Mill Offal	100 bushels	2¢	1½¢
Oats, Corn on Ear	80 bushels	2¢	2¢
Tobacco, unmanufactured	2½ hogsheads	2¢	1½¢
Flax, Seed, Grass Seeds	40 bushels	2¢	2¢
Dried Apples, Peaches	45 bushels	2¢	2¢
Apples, Peaches, not dried	40 bushels or 14 barrels	2¢	2¢
Potatoes, Turnips	40 bushels	1½¢	1½¢
Hemp, Flax	2,240 pounds	2¢	2¢
Hay, Straw	2,240 pounds	2¢	1¢
Firewood (in boats)	Cord of 128 cu. Ft.	1½¢	½¢

---

[6] *Proceedings of the President and Board of Directors*, D, 67–69.

[7] *Ibid*, D, 226.

[8] *Ibid*, D, 279, 284.

Bark (in boats)	Cord of 128 cu. Ft.	2¢	¾¢
Wood, Bark (in rafts)	Cord of 128 cu. Ft	4¢	1½¢
Boards, Plank (in boats)	1,000 feet b.m.	2¢	1¢
Plaster	28 bushels	1½¢	1¢
Fish	7 barrels	2¢	1¢
Wood	Coed of 128 cu. Ft.	2¢	½¢
Bark (tanners)	Cord of 128 cu. Ft.	3¢	1¢
Lumber, Plank (in boats)	1,000 feet b.m.	2¢	1¢
Lumber, Square timber (in boats)	70 cubic feet	2¢	1¢
Shingles (in boats)	3,000 cubic feet	2¢	1¢
Staves and Headings (in boats)	1,000 cubic feet	2¢	1¢
Barrels, Hogsheads (in boats)	500 cubic feet	2¢	1¢
Above five items if in rafts		2¢	2¢
Charcoal and Coke	56 bushels	2¢	1¢

In addition to these rates, tolls were to be charged on various types of boats. Packet or pleasure boats used chiefly for the transportation of people were to pay 8 cents per mile for the first 15 miles and 4 cents per mile thereafter. This rate included the baggage of the passengers, but all other articles on these boats would be charged the established tolls. All other vessels plying the waterway–freight boats, gondolas, scows–were to pay, in addition to the established tolls, 4 cents per mile for the first 15 miles and 2 cents per mile thereafter.[9]

The 1835 toll rates were the first to require ratification by commissioners appointed by the State of Maryland. The commission had been established pursuant to a resolution passed by the General Assembly during the 1834 December Session "regulating the tolls of the Chesapeake & Ohio Canal Company and of the Baltimore and Susquehanna Rail Road Companies'." Accordingly, the new rates were submitted to the commissioners who quickly approved them.[10]

Several weeks before the new rates were to take effect, John P. Smart, who owned a mill in Virginia, complained against the company policy of charging for the use of the Potomac between his mill and Guard Lock No. 2. After discussing the matter, the board on June 15 determined that after July 1 no tolls would be charged for the use of the river. The only two exceptions to this ruling were: (1) the improved 3½-mile pool where slackwater navigation in the Potomac bed was technically a part of the canal above Dam No. 4 and (2) instances where boats using the river passed guard or river locks through which they could enter the canal. In the case of the latter, the same toll would be charged for the use of the river as was established for the use of the corresponding portion of the canal. If the navigation of the waterway was ever suspended, no tolls were to be charged for boats using the river opposite the obstructed portion of the canal.[11]

Another major revision in the tariff of tolls occurred on March 15, 1841 when the directors raised the charges on the major agricultural products and provisions to a flat 2 cents a ton per mile. The tariff on coal and lime remained at 1 cent a ton per mile. The new rates, which were to take effect on April 30, were as follows:

ARTICLE	UNIT, Per ton of	Toll, per mile	
		1st 15 mi.	Thereafter
Wheat, Rye, Barley, Buckwheat,	40 bushels	2¢	1½¢

---

[9] Ibid, D, 284–286.

[10] Ibid, D, 287.

[11] Ingle to O'Reilly et al., June 26, 1835, Ltrs. Sent, C & O Co., and *Proceedings of the President and Board of Directors*, D, 333–334.

Indian Corn			
Flour	10½ barrels	2¢	1½¢
Corn Meal	45 bushels	2¢	1½¢
Bran, Shorts, Mill Offal	100 bushels	2¢	1½¢
Tobacco (unmanufactured)	2½ hogsheads	2¢	1½¢
Potatoes, Turnips	40 bushels	2¢	2¢
Hay, Straw	2,240 pounds	2¢	2¢
Mineral Coal	28 bushels	1¢	½¢
Lime	28 bushels	1¢	½¢
Timber, Round or square (in boats)	50 cubic feet	1¢	½¢
Shingles, Plasterer's Laths (in boats)	3,000 shingles or 5,000 laths	2¢	1¢
Staves, Headings (in boats)	1,000 barrels or 500 hogsheads	2¢	1¢
Hoop Poles (in boats)	1,000 barrels or 500 hogsheads	2¢	1¢
Fence Rails, Posts (in boats)	1,000 barrels or 500 hogsheads	1¢	½¢
Above 5 items in rafts	Double the rate for those in boats		
Charcoal and Coke	56 bushels	2¢	1¢
Stone (rough)	Perch of 25 cu. Ft.	1¢	½¢
Limestone	Perch of 25 cu. Ft.	1/3¢	1/3¢
Marble, Other stone (wrought or cut)	15 cubic feet	2¢	2¢
Iron Ore, Other metallic ore	2,240 pounds	½¢	½¢
Pig, Scrap iron	2,240 pounds	1¢	1¢
Iron castings	2,240 pounds	1½¢	1½¢

With the exception of these changes, the tariff approved in 1835 was to remain in effect.[12]

In an effort to spur trade, the directors reduced the tolls on plaster and coal in April 1842. The rate for plaster was reduced from 2 cents a ton per mile to 1½ cents a ton per mile for the first 20 miles and to 1 cent a ton per mile for the remaining distance. The charges on coal were reduced from 1 cent to 2/3 cent a ton per mile. The toll on coal was lowered as a result of the lower rates on coal on the Pennsylvania canals and the relatively cheap price of coal from Richmond, Virginia, that had recently appeared for sale in the District cities.[13]

In May 1843 the canal board received a series of reports concerning the advantages to trade on the waterway that would be gained by a reduction of the 1841 modifications back to the approximate levels of 1835. A major stimulus to such a reduction was the increasing competition of the Baltimore & Ohio Railroad, which had been completed to Cumberland in 1842. Accordingly, a revised tariff of tolls was approved by the board and the Maryland commissioners. The new rates, which went into effect on June 20, were as follows:

ARTICLE	UNIT, Per ton of	Toll, per mile	
		1st 20 mi.	Thereafter
Flour	10 barrels	2¢	1½¢
Wheat, Rye, Barley, Buckwheat	40 bushels	2¢	1½¢
Flax Seeds, Grass Seeds	40 bushels	2¢	1½¢
Indian Corn	40 bushels	1½¢	1½¢
Corn Meal	45 bushels	2¢	1½¢
Dried Apples, Peaches	45 bushels	2¢	1½¢

---

[12] *Proceedings of the President and Board of Directors*, F, 295-296.
[13] *Fourteenth Annual Report* (1842), C & O Co., 5.

Apples, Peaches (not dried)	40 bushels or 14 barrels	2¢	1½¢
Tobacco (unmanufactured)	2½ hogsheads	2¢	1½¢
Hemp, Flax	2,240 pounds	2¢	1½¢
Bacon	2,240 pounds	2¢	1½¢
Hammered, Rolled Iron, Steel, Lead, Metals	2,240 pounds	2¢	1½¢
Marble, Stone (wrought or cut)	15 cubic feet	2¢	1½¢
Grind Stones, Mill Stones	15 cubic feet	2¢	1½¢
Livestock	30 sheep, 15 hogs or 3 cattle	2¢	1½¢
Pleasure Carriages, Horses	2 2-wheeled, 1 4-wheeled, or 2 horses	2¢	1½¢
Window Glass	2,800 feet	2¢	1½¢
Furniture	100 cubic feet of space occupied	2¢	1½¢
Ale, Beer, Cider, Whiskey, Domestic Spirits	8 barrels or 2 hogsheads	2¢	1½¢
Wine, Foreign Spirits	220 gallons	2¢	1½¢
Salted, Pickled Beef, Pork, Fish	8 Barrels	2¢	1½¢
Oysters	4,000 or 28 Bushels	2¢	1½¢
Potatoes, Turnips	40 bushels	1½¢	1½¢
Bran, Shorts, Mill Offal	100 bushels	1½¢	1½¢
Slaughtered Hogs, Meats	2,240 pounds	1½¢	1½¢
Iron Castings, Bloom Iron	2,240 pounds	1½¢	1½¢
French Burrs (in blocks)	15 cubic feet	1½¢	1½¢
Oats, Corn in ear	80 bushels	2¢	1¢
Hay, Straw	2,240 pounds	2¢	1¢
Shad, Herrings	600 shad or 4,000 Herrings	2¢	1¢
Salt	45 bushels (fine) or 32 bushels (coarse)	1½¢	1¢
Plaster	2,240 pounds (stone) or 28 bushels (ground)	Free	Free
Bricks, Tiles, Roofing Slates	500 Bricks or tiles, or 800 Slates	1¢	1¢
Carts, Wagons, Plows	2 carts, 1 wagon or 10 ploughs	1¢	1¢
Ice	2,240 pounds	1¢	1¢
Pig, Scrap Iron	2,240 pounds	1¢	1¢
Lime	28 bushels	1¢	½¢
Timber (round or square), in Boats	70 cubic feet	1¢	½¢
Fence Rails, Posts, in Boats	100 Rails or posts	1¢	½¢
Rough Stone (except Limestone)	Perch of 25 cubic feet	1¢	½¢
Bark, in Boats	Cord of 128 cubic feet	1¢	¾¢
Boards and Plank, in Boats	1,000 feet, B.M.	1¢	¾¢
Shingles, Plasterer's Laths, in Boats	3,000 shingles or 5,000 laths	1¢	¾¢
Staves and Heading, in Boats	1,000 barrels or 500 Hogsheads	1¢	¾¢
Hoop poles, in Boats	1,000	1¢	¾¢
Charcoal, Coke	56 bushels	1¢	¾¢

Firewood, in Boats	Cord of 128 cubic feet	1¢	¼¢
Iron Ore, Metallic Ores	2,240 pounds	½¢	½¢
Mineral Coal	28 bushels	½¢	½¢
Limestone	Perch of 25 cubic feet	¼¢	¼¢
Dry Goods, Groceries, Crockery, Glassware, Sundries	8 barrels, 4 Tierces, 2 hogsheads or 40 cubic feet in bundles, bales, crates or boxes	2¢	1½¢

In addition to these rates, packets and pleasure boats used chiefly for the transportation of passengers were to be charged 8 cents per mile for the first 20 miles and 4 cents for any additional miles, the toll covering all passengers and their customary baggage. Freight boats, gondolas and scows were to pay 4 cents per mile for the first 20 miles and 2 cents per mile thereafter. Timber, fence rails, posts, bark, boards, plank, shingles, lath, staves and heading, hoop-poles and firewood, when transported in rafts, were to pay double the rates as when carried in boats.[14]

The tariff of tolls, which took effect on June 20, 1843, remained in effect with some slight modifications (which will be cited later in this chapter) until after the canal was opened to Cumberland in October 1850.

B. ANALYSIS OF CANAL TRADE DURING THE CONSTRUCTION YEARS, 1830-1850

The agricultural nature of canal trade, which was indicated by the toll schedules and testified to by the company officials, was also demonstrated by the annual analysis of trade on the waterway as well as by newspaper and periodical accounts. Throughout the 20-year period from the opening of the canal between Little Falls and Seneca Falls in November 1830 until its final completion to Cumberland in October 1850 the chief articles transported were flour, wheat, corn and other agricultural products. Lumber, lime, stone and some coal were also shipped in varying quantities. Although consistent and detailed listings did not begin until 1842, by which time the canal had already reached Dam No. 6, the extant company records and other accounts are sufficient to establish the fact that the canal was heavily dependent on the agricultural production of the Potomac Valley for its trade during the construction period.[15]

Trade grew slowly before the canal was completed to Cumberland in 1850. After the initial enthusiasm of 1831, the total business on the canal decreased the following year and remained stationary until 1837. Beginning in 1838 the pace of trade increased annually, doubling within four years to over 60,000 tons in 1841. Thereafter commerce leveled off and fluctuated irregularly about the new level. In the four years prior to the completion of the canal, business on the waterway again increased to 71,440 tons in 1847, 86,436 tons in 1848, 102,041 tons in 1849 and 101,950 tons in 1850. During the late 1840s, the ascending trade accounted for some 16 to 23 percent of the annual commerce on the waterway, while the descending trade comprised some 77 to 84 percent.[16]

---

[14] *Fifteenth Annual Report* (1843), C & O Co., 13-14.

[15] For a copy of the available listings of ascending and descending trade on the canal from 1831 to 1850, see Appendix A. It is interesting to note that in 1851 the company destroyed waybills and toll returns for the period prior to 1847, inasmuch as the accounts were closed and the papers were "of no value for future reference." *Proceedings of the President and Board of Directors*, H, 449.

[16] See Appendices A and D.

1831

Almost as soon as the canal was opened to navigation between Locks Nos. 5 and 23, numerous boats, filled with agricultural produce, began plying the waterway. The Frederick *Town Herald* reported on January 15, 1831:

> Very recently forty-five boats passed through the locks (Nos. 15–20) of the 17th and 18th sections in one day, laden with more than 6,000 barrels of flour, part of which descended by the Shenandoah, from Port Republic, a point within 20 miles of Stanton, the geographical center of Virginia; and another from Williamsport, in Maryland, 100 miles above the District of Columbia; and wood, for fuel, has already been brought down the canal a distance of 16 miles, from above the Great Falls of the Potomac.[17]

Within ten days after the canal was watered to within a few hundred yards above the Georgetown boundary in March 1831 some 30,000 barrels of flour "with much other merchandise" had descended the waterway.[18] According to various accounts, the original reason for the heavy movement of flour from Seneca to Georgetown was that the cost for its transportation had dropped from $1 to 30 cents a barrel by January 13 and to 7 cents a barrel, including tolls, by early April.[19] From March 21 to May 14, it was reported that 83,106 barrels of flour descended the canal, and from June 1 to the close of navigation in November the total was 71,172.[20]

An analysis of the ascending and descending trade from June 1 until the close of navigation in November demonstrates the almost total dependence of the canal on the agricultural produce of the Potomac Valley during its first full year of operation. Among the major products brought down the canal during this 6-month period were the following:

Flour	71,172 barrels
Bran, Shorts, etc.	10,003 bushels
Wheat	4,745 bushels
Corn	2,145 bushels
Hemp and Flax	5,240 pounds
Hogs	5,000 pounds
Lard and butter	2,460 pounds
Bacon	1,700 pounds
Whiskey	1,472 barrels
Leather	7,790 pounds
Coal	906 bushels

On the other hand, the only products listed for the ascending trade were:

Fish	183 barrels
Salt	901 bushels
Plaster	51½ tons

---

[17] Frederick *Town Herald*, January 15, 1831.

[18] *Niles' Register*, Vol. XL (April 9, 1831), 95.

[19] Lee to Mercer, Jan. 13, 1831, Ltrs. Recd., C & O Co., and *Niles' Register*, Vol. XL (April 9, 1831), 91.

[20] *Niles' Register*, Vol. XL (July 2, 1831), 307, and *Fourth Annual Report* (1832), C & O Co., Appendix B, 20 ff.

The heavy dependence of the canal upon its descending agricultural trade for revenue would remain a consistent factor in the commerce of the waterway until its completion to Cumberland in 1850.[21]

1832

The year 1832 witnessed a continuation of the heavy transportation of flour down the waterway that for the year was $32,992.66, a sum that would not be reached again until 1838.[22] Moreover, the board was encouraged by a report that the proprietor of a Georgetown lumber mill was preparing 10,000 cords of wood above Great Falls to be taken down the canal. It was predicted that this shipment of wood on the waterway would be the harbinger of a new flourishing trade.[23] During the month between February 12 when the navigation was resumed and March 10, 27,638 barrels and 194 half barrels of flour had been unloaded in Georgetown.[24] By May 31 the total number of barrels of flour received at Rock Creek Basin had risen to 91,224.[25]

The listings for the ascending and descending trade on the canal again showed the large volume of agricultural produce traveling down the canal and the relatively light commerce moving up the waterway. The principal products descending the canal between February 12 and May 31 (the only extant records for the year) were as follows:

Flour	91,224 bushels
Bacon	82,500 pounds
Bran, Shorts, etc.	9,002 bushels
Lard and butter	11,121 pounds
Hemp and Flax	8,900 pounds
Wheat	8,093 bushels
Corn	1,745 bushels
Whiskey	1,631 barrels
Rye and Chop	1,281 bushels
Stone	5,377 perches

Again, as in 1831, only three articles were listed for the ascending trade:

Fish	1,023 barrels
Salt	705 bushels
Plaster	305 ¾ tons

Although the statistics for the ascending trade show that they accounted for a very small proportion of the total commerce, there was some encouragement in that the amounts of fish and plaster shipped up the canal increased six-fold while that of salt decreased by some 20 percent.[26] All

---

[21] *Fourth Annual Report* (1832), Appendix B, 20 ff.
[22] *Report to the Stockholders on the Completion of the Chesapeake & Ohio Canal to Cumberland* (Frederick, 1851), Appendix K, 152.
[23] *Proceeding of the Stockholders*, A, 177.
[24] *Niles' Register*, Vol. XLII (March 31, 1832), 82.
[25] *Fourth Annual Report* (1832), Appendix B, 20 ff
[26] Ibid.

told, the initial enthusiasm of 1831 declined somewhat as the total amount of tolls collected fell some $8,000 to $24,986.02.[27]

1833

There are no statistics available concerning the amount of articles carried in the ascending or descending trade on the canal for the year 1833. However, according to the Georgetown *Gazette* on May 24, 1833, there was a brisk trade on the waterway:

> It is with real pleasure we announce that the canal and locks, as far as the eye can reach from Georgetown towards Crommelin, is literally covered with boats as close as they can stow, filled with flour and other produce. Not less then 15,000 barrels passed through the locks into the basin yesterday, more than 150 boats it is said, were above the town, coming down.[28]

Despite this early report of optimism, the canal trade for the entire year was greatly reduced as evidenced by the decline in tolls from $24,976.02 in 1832 to $16,663.49 in 1833.[29] This decline in trade was due partially to the obstruction of the Potomac navigation by the works above Harpers Ferry, but, more importantly, it was the result of a poor wheat crop in the valley. Recognizing the intimate relationship between canal trade and local agricultural prosperity, the board warned the stockholders in June 1833 that:

> The revenue of the canal, like the commerce of the District of Columbia, will be ever subject to such fluctuation, till its tonnage rests on a foundation less mutable, than the wheat crops of the upper country, a single agricultural product, subject to annual variations of quality as well as quantity, with the change of the seasons.

In the minds of the company officials such problems would be solved when the canal reached the rich coalfields and vast timberlands of western Maryland.[30]

1834

There are no statistics available concerning the amount of commodities carried on the ascending or descending trade of the canal for 1834. However, the amount of tolls collected rose from $16,663.49 in 1833 to $20,131.62 in 1834, indicating some improvement in commerce but still well below the peak year of 1831 when $32,992.66 had been collected. The increase of trade in 1834 can be partially attributed to the formal opening of the canal to Harpers Ferry in November 1833, thus permitting the waterway to tap the commerce of the Shenandoah Valley. Despite the slight improvement in trade the directors were disappointed as they had expected a great increase of trade once the canal reached Harpers Ferry.[31]

---

[27] *Report to the Stockholders on the Completion of the Canal*, Appendix K, 152.
[28] Georgetown *Gazette*, May 24, 1833.
[29] *Report to the Stockholders on the Completion of the Canal*, Appendix K, 152.
[30] *Fifth Annual Report* (1833), C & O Co., 10–11. There are no statistics available for the amount of articles carried in the ascending or descending trade of the canal from 1833 to 1841.
[31] *Sixth Annual Report* (1834), C & O Co., 3–5; *Report to the Stockholders on the Completion of the Canal*, Appendix K, 152; and *Niles' Register*, Vol. XLV (November 23, 1833), 199.

1835

The year 1835 witnessed both encouraging and discouraging prospects for the canal trade. In April the waterway was opened to Dam No. 5, and it was reported that the Williamsport Basin was crowded "with boats, arks, &c. laden with coal and flour."[32] By mid-April it was observed that business on the canal was thriving, the first boat having arrived at Rock Creek Basin loaded with 359 barrels.[33] In late April it was noted that the canal was in excellent navigable order all the way to Dam No. 5 and already sixty boats had passed through Lock No. 43 on their way down the canal.[34]

The canal board exhibited a new mood of optimism at the annual stockholders' meeting in June when it discussed the increasing prospects for trade. They noted that the

> evidence of increasing trade are daily multiplying, and from sources which have heretofore, been alien to us. Already have the agricultural products and manufactured iron of Pennsylvania been brought to the canal at Williamsport, as the readiest and cheapest mode of conveyance to ports for transshipment to Eastern markets.

Coal properties in Allegany County were already rising in price in anticipation of the canal reaching Cumberland. When the waterway reached Cacapon River, it would be able to tap one of the heaviest timbered areas on the Potomac. In addition to these sources of descending trade was the prospect of the increasing demand for fish, gypsum and salt in the upper valley that would boost the ascending trade.[35]

Despite these encouraging prospects, the increase in trade was limited by a poor grain harvest in the Potomac Valley. Accordingly, the total amount of tolls collected rose only by some $6,400 to $26,568.15, still well below the peak year of 1831.[36]

1836

Trade on the canal during 1836 rose slightly as the amount of tolls collected increased to $28,769.33.[37] When navigation opened in spring the descending flour trade was brisk. In the first week of April, 8,106 barrels of flour descended the canal and the average daily tolls were reported to be $800.[38] However, the worst grain harvest in the Potomac Valley in many years that summer again curtailed the growth of commerce on the waterway. In a special report to Governor Thomas W. Veazey on February 4, 1837, President George C. Washington wrote:

> The unprecedented failure of the agricultural products of the two years, 1835 and 1836, especially so the last has had a corresponding influence on the revenue of the canal derived from tolls. Until the final completion of the canal to Cumberland, when the vast and inexhaustible resources of that mineral region are brought into action, its chief reliance for revenue is to be derived from the products of the rich agricultural country bordering the Potomac and its tributaries.[39]

---

[32] *Niles' Register*, Vol. XLVIII (April 11, 1835), 89.
[33] *Ibid*, Vol. XLVIII (April 18, 1835), 113.
[34] *Ibid*, Vol. XLVIII (April 25, 1835), 134.
[35] *Seventh Annual Report* (1835), C & O Co., 10.
[36] *Report to the Stockholders on the Completion of the Canal*, Appendix K, 152.
[37] *Ibid*, and *Eighth Annual Report* (1836), C & O Co., 8.
[38] *Niles' Register* Vol. L (April 16, 1836), 113.
[39] Washington to Veazey, Feb. 4, 1837, Ltrs. Sent, C & O Co.. Also see *Ninth Annual Report* (1837), C & O Co., 10.

1837

The directors looked forward to a more profitable year of trade on the canal in 1837. The river locks at Edward's Ferry and opposite the mouth of Goose Creek were completed during the summer, this giving canal officials the hope that they could tap the trade of Loudoun County, Virginia, which bordered the Potomac for some 40 miles.[40] However, another poor grain harvest in the valley curtailed canal commerce for the third consecutive year; and the tolls collected fell some $2,000 to $26,702.49.[41] Accordingly, President Washington again informed Governor Veazey on December 23 that there had been no material change in the toll receipts of the company since the previous year:

> their increase being as yet chiefly dependent on agricultural products, which for the past two years have failed to a lamentable degree throughout the whole extent of country bordering on the Potomac and its tributaries. These, and the various other articles for transportation on the canal, are considered as only auxiliary to the main source of revenue to be derived from the mineral regions of Maryland and Virginia...[42]

1838

The year marked an upswing in canal trade as the result of an "unusually fine" and "abundant harvest" of grain crops throughout the Potomac Valley. The tolls collected by the company increased by over $8,000 to $34,958.55. Thus, commerce on the waterway showed a healthy upsurge of activity despite the nationwide economic dislocation caused by the Panic of 1837.[43]

1839

The company officials looked forward to a prosperous business year on the canal in 1839. The section of the waterway between Dams No. 5 and 6 was opened to navigation in the spring. It was expected that this opening would produce a significant rise in both the ascending and descending trade since the new section connected with the National Road at Hancock. Furthermore, coal could be brought down the river to Dam No. 6 from where it could be loaded on to canal barges and taken down to the District cities.[44]

During the early spring there was both good and bad news relative to the expansion of canal trade. In late April it was reported that already

> several boats, freighted with potatoes, fish, salt and other merchandise, from the District (of Columbia) have passed through this one hundred and thirty seven miles of canal, to points on the river above the 6th dam.

At the same time it was observed that the water in the river was at such an unusually low level between Cumberland and Hancock that

---

[40] *Ninth Annual Report* (1837), 4.
[41] *Report to the Stockholders on the Completion of the Canal*, Appendix K, 152.
[42] *Tenth Annual Report* (1838), C & O Co., 7.
[43] *Report to the Stockholders on the Completion of the Canal*, Appendix K, 152, and *Tenth Annual Report* (1838), 12-13.
[44] *Tenth Annual Report* (1838), 13.

out of the seven coal boats which have left Cumberland lately, during a small rise in the river, but three reached the canal, the others being lost.[45]

The board of directors informed the stockholders in June of the encouraging trade prospects of the canal. The amount of tolls collected was up over 25 percent over the previous year, and improvements could be seen in the number and size of the boats plying the waterway. New sources of trade were being developed which would enhance the canal revenues. Nevertheless, the company would be unable to show a profit until the canal reached the main source from which its prosperity was to be derived–the coal and iron of Allegany County.[46]

A series of serious breaches in the canal banks between Harpers Ferry and Shepherdstown in November hampered canal trade in the waning months of the year and led to widespread discussion in the Potomac Valley newspapers on the unreliability of the waterway as an effective transportation line. The Williamsport *Banner* reported in mid-November that during the interruption in navigation considerable quantities of flour and produce had been arriving at the basin there, which were destined for Baltimore and Washington as soon as the breach was repaired.[47] The following week the Georgetown *Advocate* informed its readers that when the canal had been rewatered between Dams Nos. 3 and 4 after the breach had been repaired it had given way again. Thus, the agricultural produce, which had accumulated at Williamsport, would not be able to reach the District cities before ice closed the canal for the winter.[48]

Despite the loss of revenue from these breaches, the canal trade had its best year to date. The tolls collected amounted to $47,865.94, a sum exceeding the previous year's high by nearly $13,000.[49]

1840

The year 1840 marked a downturn in the volume of canal trade. The navigation was again disrupted for a long period in mid-summer by breaches in the lime sink areas at Prather's Neck and at a point four miles below Hancock. Consequently, the amount of tolls collected decreased some $4,000 to $43,808.02.[50]

1841

The year 1841 saw a slight increase in trade on the canal, although a portion of the increased revenues from tolls could be attributed to the new tariff which went into effect on May 1 raising the charges of the major agricultural products and provisions to a flat 2 cents a ton per mile. This rate increase, which had been prompted by similar increases by the Baltimore & Ohio Railroad, compensated for the relatively light grain harvests during the summer and the lingering sluggishness in the national economy. The total amount of tolls collected for the year amounted to $57,012.29, or an increase of more than $13,000 over the previous year.[51]

---

[45] Washington *National Intelligencer*, Vol. LVI (April 27, 1839), 131–132.
[46] *Eleventh Annual Report* (1839), C & O Co., 7.
[47] Williamsport *Banner* quoted in *Niles' Register*, Vol. LVII (November 16, 1839), 180.
[48] Georgetown *Advocate* quoted in *Niles' Register*, Vol. LVII (November 23, 1839), 201.
[49] *Report to the Stockholders on the Completion of the Canal*, Appendix K, 152
[50] *Twelfth Annual Report* (1840), C & O Co., 8, and *Report to the Stockholders on the Completion of the Canal*, Appendix K, 152
[51] *Seventeenth Annual Report* (1845), C & O Co., 19–20, and *Report to the Stockholders on the Completion of the Canal*, Appendix K, 152

1842

Because of another light grain harvest in the valley and the continuing economic problems of the nation, canal trade declined slightly in 1842 as the amount of tolls collected dipped approximately $1,000 to $56,005.80. A secondary and yet significant cause of the slump in trade was the continuing effort of the Baltimore & Ohio to monopolize the flour trade.[52] The listings for the ascending and descending trade on the canal, the first such yearly statistics available since those of 1832, reveal that the canal remained heavily dependent on the transportation of agricultural products for its revenues, although coal and lumber made up a greater proportion of the downstream trade than they had in 1832. The principal articles of the descending trade were as follows:

Flour	151,966 barrels
Wheat	214,569 bushels
Corn and Oats	59,199 bushels
Mill Offal	46,472 bushels
Coal	111,293 bushels
Lumber	916,184 feet, board measure

On the other hand, the only two articles listed for the ascending trade were:

Plaster	3,206 tons
Salted fish	5,294 barrels[53]

1843

The forecast of a good grain harvest throughout the Potomac Valley in 1843 led company officials to predict a banner year for canal trade with estimates of toll revenues ranging as high as $80,000. However, the failure of the harvest to reach its expectations, the lowering of the tariff of tolls on most agricultural products in response to the Baltimore & Ohio's lower rates, and the suspension of navigation for more than six weeks following two heavy floods in April and September combined to reduce toll revenues nearly 20 percent from the previous year to $44,540.51.[54]

An analysis of the descending and ascending trade for the year shows little deviation from the previously established patterns. The principal articles in the descending trade were:

Flour	156,242 barrels
Wheat	142,785 bushels
Corn	167,326 bushels
Oats	38,930 bushels
Corn Meal	18,942 bushels
Mill Offal	49,642 bushels
Pork	50,324 pounds
Lumber	500,000 feet, board measure

---

[52] *Fourteenth Annual Report* (1842). C & O Co., 4 and *Report to the Stockholders on the Completion of the Canal*, Appendix K, 152.
[53] *Fifteenth Annual Report* (1843), C & O Co., 11.
[54] *Fourteenth Annual Report* (1842), 4; *Fifteenth Annual Report* (1843), 13–14; *Sixteenth Annual Report* (1844), C & O Co., 39–44; and *Proceedings of the Stockholders*, C, 230–232.

The only three articles listed for the ascending trade were:

Salted Fish	3,533 barrels
Salt	1,240 tons
Plaster	4,259 tons[55]

1844

Canal officials looked forward to a promising year for the canal trade in 1844. Large quantities of flour and other agricultural produce had accumulated in warehouses all along the line during the one-month suspension of navigation following the mid-September 1843 flood, and it was expected that considerable revenue would be made when these articles were shipped downstream the following spring. It was also felt that the trade of the canal would be enhanced by the spring of the Potomac Aqueduct and the Alexandria Canal to navigation in December 1843.[56]

The volume of commerce on the canal did increase by nearly 20 percent for the year with the amount of tolls collected raising some $8,000 to $52,674.24. The descending trade again reflected the canal's heavy dependence on the agricultural production and the timber resources of the valley, the principal articles being:

Flour	172,796 barrels
Wheat	199,620 bushels
Corn	173,023 bushels
Oats	39,000 bushels
Bran, Mill Offal	76,683 bushels
Corn Meal	15,631 bushels
Lumber	1,000,000 feet, board measure

As in previous years, the only three articles listed as passing up the canal in quantity were:

Salted Fish	2,075 barrels
Salt	1,295 tons
Plaster	4,838 tons[57]

From the record it is apparent that one of the most significant factors in the increase of commerce on the canal during 1844 was the expansion of the descending flour trade. The total number of barrels for this product increased by more than 16,000 over that of 1843. Canal officials attributed this increase to the fact that the farmers and millers of the southwestern counties of Pennsylvania had found that the canal afforded them the cheapest and most convenient transportation line to the eastern markets and had consequently adopted it.[58]

Arrivals and Departures of Boats from Georgetown January 1843 to May 1844:[59]

---

[55] *Proceedings of the Stockholders*, C, 305, 385.
[56] *Proceedings of the Stockholders*, C, 232–233.
[57] *Seventeenth Annual Report* (1845), C & O Co., 32–33, and *Report to the Stockholders on the Completion of the Canal*, Appendix K, 152.
[58] *Seventeenth Annual Report* (1845), 20–21.
[59] *Proceedings of the Stockholders*, C, 379.

Boat Arrivals and Departures	1843	1844
January	31	48
February	3	12
March	247	665
April	152	98
May	371	391
June	365	
July	146	
August	191	
September	91	
October	70	
November	459	
December	355	
	2,484	1,214
Total in first 5 months of 1843:		-804
	Increase:	410

1845

The year 1845 saw a slight decrease of trade on the canal, as the revenue collected from the toll charges declined some $800 to $51,810.70. It is interesting to note that this decline in traffic on the canal took place despite optimistic reports in the Williamsport *Banner* that trade was very heavy during the year. On November 1 the *Banner* reported that

> the trade of that part of the Canal, which is completed, never before was so brisk. Immense quantities of flour, grain and other kinds of produce have been collected in our town, and are now ready for transportation to the District Cities. This, we understand too, is the case at other points along the line of the Canal. Within the last week or two, an unusually large number of boats has passed down the Canal.[60]

Flour	170,464 barrels
Wheat	299,607 bushels
Corn	126,799 bushels
Oats	35,464 bushels
Mill Offal	38,575 bushels
Corn Meal	16,327 bushels
Pork	15,250 pounds
Lumber	508,083 feet, board measure
Stone	12,060 perches

The ascending trade, the records for which were the most complete to date, apparently improved somewhat over the totals for the previous year. The principal products transported up the canal were:

---

[60] *Niles' Register*, Vol. LXIX (November 8, 1845), 147.

Salted Fish	4,569 barrels
Salt	1,265 tons
Plaster	4,721 tons
Lumber	820,000 feet, board measure
Potatoes	2,511 bushels
Bricks	118,225 units
Wheat	1,708 bushels
Oysters	1,351 bushels[61]

1846

Trade on the canal in 1845 showed a slight improvement over that of 1845 as the revenue from tolls rose some $1,500 to $53,357.24. For the first time since the opening of navigation, the company kept separate statistics relative to the tolls for the ascending and descending trade. The total of the former was $6,078.81 while that of the latter was $47,278.38.[62]

Traffic on the canal was heavy during the first four months of the year, the $10,058.64 collected in tolls for April being the highest total for any month in the history of the waterway. The upturn in canal business was primarily the result of a bumper harvest in the Potomac Valley the previous year and the continuing increase in trade from the southwestern counties of Pennsylvania.[63]

The expansion of trade in the early months of the year was sustained until July when a major flood struck the valley, wrecking destruction on the summer grain crops and suspending navigation for a considerable period. Despite the problems posed by the flood, the canal flour trade increased by over 25 percent to 234,539 barrels, the largest quantity ever transported in one year on the waterway. However, the number of bushels of corn and corn meal carried down the canal were considerably reduced, the totals for the former being 126,799 in 1845 and 30,005 in 1846 while those of the latter were 16,327 and 8,437 respectively. Canal officials attributed much of this as a result of the greater demand for these products in Baltimore than in the District cities. The shipping industry in Baltimore had reached unprecedented heights within the past year, as evidenced by the fact that the Baltimore shippers had even imported corn from New York to fill their cargo needs for exportation to Europe.[64]

All told the ascending trade comprised the equivalent of 10.986 tons while the amount of descending trade was 49,161 tons. The principal articles moving up the canal were:

Salted Fish	3,475 barrels
Plaster	3,839 tons
Lumber	1,061,855 feet, board measure
Coal	1,003 tons
Potatoes	1,526 bushels

---

[61] *Seventeenth Annual Report* (1845), C & O Co., 38-39, and *Report to the Stockholders on the Completion of the Canal*, Appendix K, 152. The reason that more complete records for canal trade are available for the period from 1845 on is that on August 13, 1845, the board ordered the company clerk to keep 'a book in which he shall make a regular monthly entry of the articles transported on the Canal – designating where they are loaded, where unloaded and the quantity of each kind, under their respective heads, -- the said entries to be made from the 1st of January 1845." *Proceedings of the President and Board of Directors*, G, 293.

[62] *Report to the Stockholders on the Completion of the Canal*, Appendix K, 152.

[63] *Eighteenth Annual Report* (1846), 22.

[64] *Nineteenth Annual Report* (1847), C & O Co., 7-8.

Bricks	440,996 units
Bacon	5,700 pounds
Lard and Butter	64,960 pounds

The principal articles in the descending trade were:

Flour	234,539 barrels
Wheat	264,115 bushels
Corn	30,005 bushels
Oats	30,047 bushels
Mill Offal	63,486 bushels
Bacon and Pork	27,047 pounds
Lumber	2,851,541 feet, board measure
Bricks	17,500 units
Shingles, Staves, Laths, etc.	297,025 units[65]

1847

The early months of 1847 appeared to auger a banner year for canal trade. The amount of tolls collected through May 31 was $30,331.85 or $7,295.80 more than the corresponding period for the previous year. The corn trade, which had declined in 1846, was again active, as 16,351 bushels, or five times the quantity shipped for that entire year, had already passed down the canal by June 1. Accordingly, company officials informed the stockholders that unless there was a poor grain harvest in northwestern Virginia, western Maryland and southwestern Pennsylvania, there was "just cause to expect that our revenues this year will much exceed the receipts of any former year."[66]

  The expectations of the company officials were again thwarted by the highest flood in the history of the Potomac Valley in early October. The consequent damage to the canal and the surrounding countryside severely affected the overall statistics for the canal trade. The ascending trade increased by nearly 2,000 tons to 12,809, and the descending trade increased by some 9,000 tons to 58,631. However, there was not a corresponding increase in the revenue from tolls as the average distance of transportation was less in 1847 than in 1846 and a large portion of the tonnage increase comprised articles on which small rates of toll were charged. In actual fact, the ascending tolls amounted to $6,774.80 while the descending tolls were $45,665.55. The combined total of the revenues collected from tolls was $52,440.35, a decrease of some $900 from 1846.[67]

The principal articles in the ascending trade were:

Salted Fish	3,723 barrels
Plaster	3,829 tons
Lumber	770,300 feet, board measure
Coal	1,687 tons
Potatoes	1,112 bushels

---

[65] *Eighteenth Annual Report* (1846).
[66] *Nineteenth Annual Report* (1847), 10, 48.
[67] *Proceedings of the Stockholders*, D, 122–123, and *Report to the Stockholders on the Completion of the Canal*, Appendix K, 152.

Bricks	178,000 units
Mill Offal	3,362 bushels
Iron Ore	3,009 tons
Bacon	9,300 pounds

The bulk of the descending trade consisted of the following articles:

Flour	176,789 barrels
Wheat	235,212 bushels
Corn	238,216 bushels
Oats	32,035 bushels
Corn Meal	17,958 bushels
Mill Offal	87,644 bushels
Bacon and Pork	26,965 pounds
Lumber	1,583,600 feet, board measure
Nails	11,892 kegs
Bricks	45,500 units
Shingles, Staves, Laths, Hoop Poles	955,525 units[68]

1848

The year 1848 saw an increase of trade over the totals of 1847 of 14,996 tons and $1,705.86 in revenues from tolls. The ascending tonnage increased to 16,439 while that of the descending trade rose to 69,997. The ascending tolls increased to $8,405.40 while those of the descending trade rose to $45,740.81, providing a total revenue of $54,146.21. A significant portion of the increased tonnage of the descending trade was the increase in the amount of flour transported totaling 40,332 barrels over the quantity shipped in 1847. The increase in the revenue did not attain a corresponding ratio with the enlarged tonnage as the average distance of transportation was less than in 1848 and the greater portion of the increase of tonnage consisted of articles on which small rates of toll were charged.[69]

The principal products of the ascending trade were:

Salted Fish	3,477 barrels
Salt	2,133 tons
Plaster	7,310 tons
Lumber	1,391,000 feet, board measure
Iron Ore	2,575 tons
Oysters	4,700 bushels
Bricks	22,000 units

The primary articles of the descending trade were:

Flour	217,112 barrels
Wheat	220,025 bushels

---

[68] *Proceedings of the Stockholders*, D, 122–123.
[69] *Twenty-First Annual Report* (1849), C & O Co., 14.

Corn	144,103 bushels
Oats	12,959 bushels
Mill Offal	77,553 bushels
Limestone	10,030 perches
Lumber	2,080,600 feet, board measure
Bricks	10,000 units
Shingles, Staves, Laths, Hoop Poles	993,100 units[70]

1849

The year 1849 witnessed a significant rise in canal trade both in tonnage carried and toll revenues collected. The ascending tonnage increased from 16,439 in 1848 to 20,778, while that of the descending tonnage rose from 69,997 to 81,263. The combined totals of the ascending and descending trade amounted to 102,041 tons, an increase of 15,601 tons over the tonnage of 1848. The tolls collected from the ascending trade were $9,188.84 while those from the descending trade were $52,634.33, thus providing the company with $61,823.17 in toll revenues. This sum, which was some $7,600 over the 1848 total, was the largest amount ever collected in a single year to date by the company.[71]

The principal products of the ascending trade were:

Salted Fish	3,995 barrels
Salt	2,019 tons
Plaster	6,599 tons
Coal	1,236 tons
Coke	2,854 tons
Lumber	1,617,000 feet, board measure
Iron Ore	4,025 tons
Bricks	42,000 units

The major articles in the descending trade of the canal were:

Flour	236,620 bushels
Wheat	240,073 bushels
Corn	244,281 bushels
Oats	13,200 bushels
Mill Offal	45,423 bushels
Apples	12,970 bushels
Stone (rough)	17,750 perches
Lumber	1,560,956 feet, board measure
Bricks	39,000 units
Shingles, Staves, Laths, Hoop Poles	783,800 units[72]

---

[70] *Twenty-First Annual Report* (1849), 32–33.

[71] *Twenty-Second Annual Report* (1850), C & O Co., 10–11, 23.

[72] *Ibid,* 23–24.

1850

Trade on the canal in 1850 showed little change from the previous year despite the continuance of agricultural prosperity in the valley and the formal opening of navigation to Cumberland on October 10. The repairs to the waterway below Dam No. 6 had restored the capacity of the canal to its original intended dimensions, thereby allowing the boats to carry heavier cargoes. During the spring, a single boat had descended the canal from Dam No. 4 to Georgetown with 1,110 barrels of flour (equivalent to 105 tons of 2,240 pounds), making it the largest cargo to pass down the canal since the heavy floods of the mid-1840s had battered the waterway.[73]

The trade statistics for the year show mixed results when compared with those of 1849. The ascending tonnage increased by nearly 2,500 tons to 23,261, while the descending tonnage was reduced by nearly the same amount to 78,689. Thus, the aggregate trade on the waterway was 91 tons less than 1849.

While the tonnage was somewhat lower than the previous year, the amount of tolls collected increased some $2,600 to $64,442.03. The amount of toll revenue for the ascending trade rose some $400 over the 1849 totals to $9,628.21 while that of the descending trade increased by nearly $2,200 to $54,813.81. The increase in the descending trade tolls was primarily the result of the shipment of 7,171 tons of coal down the canal from Cumberland after October 10. Consequently, the company officials informed the stockholders in February 1851 of the bright future prospects of the coal trade on the revenues of the company:

> As the Canal is now opened to the coal region the future annual statements of the Company will present much larger results.
>
> The prospect of a large and augmenting coal trade by the Canal is of the most flattering character. An immense amount of capital has been invested in the coal mines, principally by parties residing in New York and Boston, who will consequently have a strong and direct interest in introducing the Cumberland coal into the markets of these two great and thriving cities where such vast quantities may be consumed, and railroads connecting the mines with the Basins of the Canal at Cumberland have already been constructed at a considerable cost, which are capable of bringing down about a million of tons per annum. The capacity of these connections may be increased to any desirable extent. The only present subject of regret is the want of a due supply of Cars for the connecting railroads, and of Boats for the canal. These deficiencies, from present indications, will soon be remedied. A number of Boats were constructed during the past winter, and all the Boat yards are now busily engaged in increasing the supply. But the preparations for the commencement of the trade, limited as they appeared, were more advanced upon this canal than upon other similar improvements, at the time of their completion. More coal started down the Chesapeake & Ohio Canal on the first day of the opening, than was transported on the Lehigh navigation, upon which the Anthracite coal trade of Pennsylvania was *commenced* on the year 1820 during the first *year* of its operations. In that year only 365 tons were carried down from the Lehigh mines to Philadelphia, and we are informed in a history of the Lehigh Coal and Navigation Company published by the order of the Board of Managers of the Company in 1840, that "this quantity completely stocked the market and was with difficulty disposed of during the year." The quantity of coal which started down the Chesapeake & Ohio Canal from Cumberland on the 10th of October last, the day of the opening of the navigation, was 491 tons. The whole quantity that passed down from the 10th of October to the 21st of December 1850 was 7,171 tons. The

---

[73] *Ibid*, 9–10.

whole quantity transported on the Schuylkill navigation in 1825, the first year of its operation, was only 6,500 tons, and this was the whole quantity sent down from the Schuylkill coal region during that year. In the year 1849 there were sent to market from that region 3,203,462 tons of coal, and it was scarcely sufficient to supply the demand. When the Lehigh navigation was opened the use of coal was comparatively unknown in the United States. Now it is one of the common necessaries of life in the cities of the Atlantic, and its consumption for Steam vessels, Railroad Locomotives and manufacturing purposes, is large and constantly increasing. The Cumberland coal, therefore, whatever quantities of it may be thrown into the markets, will not have to labor under the disadvantages which attended the first introduction of the Anthracite, and its superiority to the latter will, we believe, at once give it the command of the markets. If sold at reasonable rates, the consumption will only be limited by the extent of the supply.

The principal products in the ascending trade were as follows:

Fish, Salted and Fresh	758 tons
Groceries	643 tons
Salt	1,607 tons
Lumber, Laths, Palings, Shingles, Hoop-Poles	1,249 tons
Ore	7,455 tons
Coal	1,783 tons
Coke	2,205 tons
Plaster	5,334 tons

The principal articles in the descending trade were as follows:

Flour	27,120 tons
Wheat	5,318 tons
Corn	1,726 tons
Lumber, Laths, Palings, Shingles, Stoves, Hoop-Poles	2,765 tons
Iron, Pig and Scrap	1,196 tons
Coal	7,956 tons
Wood	4,275 tons
Stone, rough (perches)	13,303 tons
Limestone	10,234 tons[74]

C. ENCOURAGEMENT OF TRADE ON THE CANAL: 1830–1850

On the whole, the problem of developing business for the canal was not clearly or fully recognized during the period until 1850. The directors tended to look upon their work as a magnificent enterprise to which trade would naturally be attracted. They conceived their task to be mainly the construction and maintenance of the waterway. Thus the efforts of the board to increase canal trade were haphazard.

---

[74] *Report to the Stockholders on the Completion of the Canal*, Appendix A, 6–7; C, pp.141–143; & K, 153. In 1850 the company began a new system of calculating its ascending and descending trade in terms of tons rather than the various kinds of units that had been used from 1830 to 1849.

In March 1833 the board refused the request of the Alexandria Canal Company to transport stone for the construction of the Potomac Aqueduct toll-free on the canal even though it was widely recognized that the completion of the structure would provide a valuable outlet market for the waterway.[75] As was seen in the preceding chapter, the board sought to encourage the development of passenger travel, packet service, boat-building and steamboat passage, but they did nothing to establish and operate a freight line for the company. Throughout the period, the company spent large sums on dredges, ice-breakers and repair gangs to keep the canal open for navigation, but forbade its employees to have any connections with individuals or businesses operating boats on the canal.[76] Despite the heavy dependence of the canal on the descending flour trade, the directors generally placed their hopes for the continuing expansion of this business in "the proper encouragement on the part of purchasers or commission merchants" in Georgetown.[77] They manipulated the toll tariffs of 1841 and 1843 so as to compete with the Baltimore & Ohio Railroad for business, but made little effort to control all the charges of transportation, such as freights and wharfage.[78] Recognizing the intimate relationship between canal trade and local agricultural prosperity, the board on October 10, 1848, reduced charges on bones and bone dust for fertilizers, in cooperation with the Virginia Society for the Advancement of Agriculture, in order to help increase the productively of the soil and thus indirectly stimulate trade.[79] Later, on March 1, 1849, the toll rates were reduced to ¼ cent a ton per mile on guano, ashes, plaster of paris, pondrel, resats, lime, chemical salts and oyster shells for the same purpose, but at the same time the directors refused to have any connection with the business of transporting these products.[80]

Throughout the 1830s and 1840s while the canal board was pursuing this uneven approach to the stimulation of trade, it frequently cited the value to the State of New York of the Erie Canal in terms of the trade it produced for the state as much as the profits earned by the canal itself. Subsequently after 1850 the Chesapeake & Ohio Canal Company reversed itself on most of these points and took a more active approach to the stimulation of trade.

D. COMPETITION WITH THE B & O RAILROAD, 1830–1850

Two factors tended to discourage the growth of trade between 1830 and 1850. One was the interruptions to navigation due to breaches and floods, both of which subjects [are] covered elsewhere in this Historic Resource Study. The other was the competition of the Baltimore & Ohio Railroad for the flour and coal trade, the two main present and prospective sources of canal revenue.

The struggle for the lucrative Shenandoah flour trade at Harpers Ferry involved considerable maneuvering between the canal and the railroad.[81] Until May 1, 1841, the charges by rail from Harpers Ferry to Baltimore, a distance of 82 miles, were 34 cents a barrel plus 3 cents for

---

[75] *Proceedings of the President and Board of Directors*, C, 299. Aside from the short-sightedness of the directors, this decision also reflected the opposition of the Georgetown merchants who feared the loss of trade to Alexandria with the completion of the Potomac Aqueduct.

[76] *Ibid*, B, 410–419; D, 240–252, 440.

[77] *Nineteenth Annual Report* (1847), 7–8.

[78] *Proceedings of the President and Board of Directors*, F, 295–296; H, 163; and *Fifteenth Annual Report* (1843), 13–14.

[79] *Proceedings of the President and Board of Directors*, M, 214.

[80] *Ibid*, H, 238–239.

[81] It is interesting to note that the canal directors had scoffed at the threat of the railroad to its flour trade in the early 1830s. In June 1832, the stockholders had been told: The spectacle which has recently been presented, of a single horse of moderate size and strength, drawing 512 barrels of flour, in a heavy boat with apparent ease, a distance of 22 miles, through twenty-three locks, in a single day, is calculated, of itself, to countervail the numerous theories of utility of railroads, by which the public mind has been perplexed. *Fourth Annual Report* (1832), 18.

receiving and delivery fees. On May 10 the railroad raised the rate to 50 cents a barrel, including handling. It then petitioned the state legislature to compel the canal company to raise its toll to a "profitable rate," and the canal obliged by raising its charges without awaiting the action of the General Assembly. Within a month, on June 3, the railroad reduced its rates to 34 cents a barrel, including handling. As the charges from Frederick to Baltimore at the time were said to be 30 cents, the additional charge for the 21 miles from Frederick to Harpers Ferry was only 4 cents. Between June and December 1841, the flour trade on the canal from Harpers Ferry fell off 4,411 barrels as compared to the 1840 figures:

	1840	1841
June	6,362	2,695
July	2,649	702
August	1,889	747
September	777	1,821
October	1,331	2,239
November	1,298	1,661
December	933	963
	15,239	10,828

A large amount of this decrease was attributed to the actions of the railroad company.[82]

In October 1844 the railroad again reduced its rates on the transportation of flour by 25 percent. Within the month, the citizens of Alexandria complained of the loss of the Harpers Ferry flour trade to the Baltimore millers. They sent two of their representatives, Robert H. Miller and Thomas M. McCubbin, to urge the canal board to consider some remedial action.[83] At the same time, the railroad accused the canal company of charging so little for the toll on flour that it could not make a profit and therefore of cheating the railroad and the City of Baltimore.[84]

The canal company sought to settle the unrest in the District cities and to answer the charges of the railroad by devoting a large portion of their annual reports of 1845, 1846 and 1847 to the problem. The tolls that the canal had charged on flour throughout this period were as follows:

1835–1842: 2 cents a barrel per mile for the first 15 miles and 1 ½ cents thereafter.
1842–1843: 2 cents a barrel per mile flat rate.
1843–1847: 2 cents a barrel per mile for the first 20 miles and 1 ½ cents thereafter.

These tolls were much higher than that charged for the transportation of flour on the New York canals and the Susquehanna and Tidewater canal. Despite the high rates, however, the volume of the flour trade on the canal had increased each year irregardless [of] the attempts of the railroad to lure away the flour trade at Harpers Ferry. The number of barrels transported on the canal from 1842 to 1846 had grown as follows:

---

[82] Elgin to Ingle, Dec. 23, 1841, Ltrs. Recd., C & O Co. In July 1841 the railroad also attempted to lure the plaster trade away from the canal by reducing its charges from $2.40 to $2.00 per ton from Baltimore to Harpers Ferry. Later the railroad permitted all plaster that was to be transferred to the Winchester and Potomac Railroad to pass over its line free of any toll.
[83] *Resolutions Adopted by Citizens of Alexandria, October 14, 1844*, Ltrs. Recd., C & O Co.
[84] *Eighteenth Annual Report* (1846), 14–19.

1842	151,966 barrels
1843	156,242 barrels
1844	172,464 barrels
1845	170,464 barrels
1846	234,539 barrels

The canal board attributed much of this increase to the fact that the farmers of the southwestern Pennsylvania counties had begun to use the waterway as the cheapest outlet for their products to the eastern markets. The directors used these statistics to back up their argument that the railroad was totally unable to compete with the canal upon equal terms in the transportation of heavy freight. As a consequence, they saw little reason for reducing the charges on the item from which they gained the largest portion of their revenue.[85]

The struggle for the Cumberland coal trade, which began in the 1840s ultimately proved to be the decisive factor in the course of canal trade and prosperity. From December 1843 until March 1845, the railroad and the canal cooperated in the handling of the lucrative business. According to their agreement the railroad which had reached Cumberland in 1842, undertook to carry all the coal offered for shipment via the waterway over its own tracks to the western terminus of the canal at Dam No. 6. The coal was to be carried by the Baltimore & Ohio at the special rate of 2 cents a ton per mile providing the trade did not interfere with the general business of the railroad and did not require a considerable increase in the amount of rail equipment on the line.[86]

Canal officials looked forward to the operation of this arrangement in the spring of 1884. Anxious to gain increased revenues from the coal trade, the board established a toll on its transportation of 7/10 cent a ton per mile, the same rate as charged on the Schuylkill Navigation Canal in Pennsylvania. However, by June 1 only 549 tons of coal had been transported on the canal below Dam No. 6. The tardiness of the coal operators to take advantage of the new agreement was attributed "to the expectation of the usual spring freshets, by which means they have heretofore been in the habit of bringing down their coal from Cumberland to Dam No. 6 by the natural channel of the river." During the late spring and early summer, the coal companies began to transport larger quantities of coal from the Georges Creek mines to Cumberland and soon the railroad was delivering the product to the canal at Dam No. 6. In mid-June it was reported that five boats were active in the canal coal trade and that the canal company revenues derived from the commerce amounted to $250 per week. The future prospects of the coal trade looked even more promising when it was announced that the firm of Atkinson and Templemen had contracted with the federal government for the delivery of 40,000 tons of coal to the District of Columbia.[87] By the end of the year, some 40,000 tons of coal had been delivered to the canal basin at Cumberland by the railroad.[88]

The passage of the canal bill by the Maryland General Assembly in March 1845 whereby the company was permitted to issue $1,700,000 of preferred construction bonds on the mortgage of its revenues in order to finance the construction of the remaining 50 miles of the waterway to Cumberland brought an abrupt end to this arrangement.[89] The railroad and its ally, the City of

---

[85] *Seventeenth Annual Report* (1845), 21–21; *Eighteenth Annual Report* (1846), 14–19; and *Nineteenth Annual Report* (1847), 7–8.

[86] *Proceedings of the President and Board of Directors*, G, 97–100, 15; *Proceedings of the Stockholders*, C, 192–302; McLane to Coale, Sept. 17, 1843, Ltrs, Recd., C & O Co.; *Seventeenth Annual Report* (1845), 5–7, 24–26; and *Special Report of the President and Directors of the Chesapeake & Ohio Canal Company, to the Stockholders, on the Subject of Completing the Canal to Cumberland*, Nov. 16, 1843 (Washington, 1843), 1–59.

[87] *Proceedings of the Stockholders*, C, 306–307, 315–316; and *Niles' Register*, Vol. LXVI (June 22, 1844), 272.

[88] *Seventeenth Annual Report* (1845), 6.

[89] *Niles' Register*, Vol. LXVIII (March 8, 1845), 16 and *Ibid,* Vol. LXVIII (March 15, 1845), 23–24.

Baltimore, began a large-scale assault on the trade of its competitor, which threatened to deprive the latter of all possible chance of success, even before it was completed.

The City of Baltimore aided the efforts of the railroad by passing a city ordinance in April 1845 awarding the railroad to run its trains into the city with coal, iron ore, &c. The ordinance also permitted the railroad to lay tracks to a new depot on the south side of Baltimore Harbor where vessels could dock free of charges, which had been in effect up to this time. The city council also urged the railroad to lower the price of bringing the coal and iron ore from western Maryland to Baltimore "to a mere nominal sum" to defy the competition of the canal.[90]

The railroad abruptly terminated its agreement for the transportation of coal from Cumberland to Dam No. 6. The rates were raised to 4 cents a ton per mile for coal and 6 cents for iron. The excuse given by railroad President Louis McLane for the action was, curiously enough, that the amount of business was "so inconsiderable as scarcely to authorize a longer continuance of our preparation for its accommodation at present rates." Besides the railroad was making plans for a more extensive trade to Baltimore, which was more important to his company.[91] The canal company refused to recognize the abrogation as an act in good faith, but, other than sending a resolution to that effect to the railroad, made no sustained protest.[92] President Coale observed in the reply to McLane that whether:

> The reasons given in your letter are sufficient to authorize a departure from the arrangement entered into between the two Companies in Sept. 1843, & whether the interests of "the public generally" will be subserved by the imposition of a prohibitory tariff between Cumberland and Dam No. 6, are questions upon which I think impartial men will differ with you.[93]

The action of the railroad totally stopped the transportation of coal from Cumberland to Dam No. 6. In June 1845 the canal stockholders were informed that the coal trade had not materialized as expected due to the discriminatory rate charges of the railroad.[94]

The following year the directors reported that no coal had been transshipped to the canal at Dam No. 6 by the railroad during the preceding year.[95]

After several years, the canal board determined to take steps to compete with the railroad for the Cumberland coal trade. On March 1, 1849 the toll on coal was reduced from 7/10 cent a ton per mile to ½ cent a ton per mile for the first twenty miles and to 4/10 cent a ton per mile thereafter. However, the board could do little else until the waterway was completed to Cumberland.[96]

---

[90] *Niles' Register*, Vol. LXVIII (April 12, 1845), 85.
[91] McLane to Coale, May 7, 1845, Ltrs. Recd., C & O Co.
[92] *Proceedings of the President and Board of Directors*, G, 252–253.
[93] Coale to McLane, May 9, 1845, Ltrs. Sent, C & O Co.
[94] *Seventeenth Annual Report* (1845), 21–22.
[95] *Eighteenth Annual Report* (1846), 12.
[96] *Proceedings of the President and Board of Directors*, H, 239.

II. COMMERCE ON THE CHESAPEAKE & OHIO CANAL: 1851-1889

A. TARIFFS OF TOLL, 1851-1889

Upon the completion of the canal to Cumberland, the board took under consideration revision of the existing toll rates. As coal soon became the principal article of trade, the charges on that product became the chief source of canal revenue. The directors offered to fix the toll on coal and coke at 2 mills a ton per mile, if the owners of the Maryland Mining Company, the Washington Coal Company, the Allegany Company and the Frostburg Coal Company would guarantee to ship 300,000 tons in 1851 and 600,000 tons in 1852 via the canal.[97] When the coal companies indicated that they were unable to make the necessary guarantees, the board made another offer to reduce the toll on coal and coke to the same level provided the coal companies would promise to ship 500,000 tons between July 1, 1851 and July 1, 1852.[98] Again the companies were unable to take advantage of the offer, and the toll remained at ¼ cent a ton per mile.[99] Other preliminary modifications of the existing charges, adopted on February 28, 1851, affected a variety of agricultural and non-farm products:

- Hogs Slaughtered, Bacon & Other Meats–2 cents a ton per mile.
- Whisky and Other Domestic Spirits; Fish, fresh and salted–2 cents a ton per mile for the first 20 miles and 1 cent a ton per mile thereafter.
- Salt–1 cent a ton per mile for the first 20 miles and ¾ cent a ton per mile thereafter.
- Fire Brick–1 cent a ton per mile for the first 20 miles and ½ cent a ton per mile thereafter.
- Bricks and Ice–1 cent a ton per mile for the first 20 miles and ¼ cent a ton per mile thereafter.
- Sand, Gravel, Clay, Earth and Paving Stones–¼ cent a ton per mile.[100]

These early rate changes continued the downward trend of tolls on the 1840s and anticipated the general reductions, which were incorporated in the revised list. The new permanent schedule went into effect on July 1, 1851. It divided all articles transported on the canal into six classes. Reductions below the series established in 1835 ranged from 25 to 75 percent, the greatest decrease being that in the toll on coal. The classes and their charges were as follows:

Class I (at a rate of 2 cents a ton per mile for the first 20 miles, and 1 cent a ton per mile thereafter).

1. Ale, beer, cider per ton of 8 barrels or 2 hogsheads.
2. Beef, pork (salted and pickled) per ton of 8 barrels.
3. Dried apples, peaches per ton of 45 bushels.
4. Fresh apples, peaches per ton of 40 bushels or 14 barrels.
5. Barley, buckwheat, corn, flax, grain, seeds, rye, wheat per ton of 40 bushels.
6. Corn on the ear per ton of 80 bushels.

---

[97] *Proceedings of the President and Board of Directors*, H, 387-388.
[98] *Ibid*, H, 404.
[99] *Proceedings of the Stockholders*, D, 412 - 413.
[100] *Proceedings of the President and Board of Directors*, H, 423-424.

7. Corn meal per ton of 45 bushels or 10 barrels.
8. Dry goods, groceries, glass, and crockery ware per ton of 8 barrels or 2 hogsheads in bundles, bales, crates or boxes of 40 cubic feet.
9. Flour per ton of 10 barrels.
10. Fish (salted and fresh) per ton of 3 barrels salted, 600 shad or 4,000 herring.
11. Furniture, empty carts per ton of 100 cubic feet or space occupied.
12. Grindstones, millstones, marble, cut and wrought stone per ton of 15 cubic feet.
13. Hemp, flax per ton of 2,240 pounds.
14. Slaughtered hogs, bacon, and other meats per ton of 2,240 pounds.
15. Iron hammered and rolled steel, lead, other metals per ton of 2,240 pounds.
16. Livestock per ton of 30 sheep, 15 hogs, or 3 cattle.
17. Nails per ton of 20 kegs.
18. Pleasure carriages, horses per ton of 2 2-wheeled, 1 4-wheeled, 2 horses, or 2 buggies and 1 horse cart.
19. Tobacco unmanufactured per ton of 2 hogsheads.
20. Wine, foreign spirits per ton of 220 gallons.
21. Window glass per ton of 2,800 feet.
22. Whisky, domestic spirits per ton of 8 barrels or 2 hogsheads.
23. Sundries per ton ascertained by measurement.

Class II. (at a rate of 1 cent per ton per mile).

24. Bran, shorts, mill offal per ton of 100 bushels
25. Carts, wagons, ploughs per ton of 2 carts, 1 wagon, or 10 ploughs.
26. Boards, plank in boats per ton of 1,000 feet, board measure.
27. Shingles, laths per ton of 3,000 shingles or 5,000 laths.
28. Staves, heading per ton of 1,000 barrels or 500 Hogsheads.
29. Hoop-poles per ton of 1,000 barrels or 750 hogsheads.
30. Charcoal per ton of 56 bushels.
31. Hay, straw per ton of 2,240 pounds.
32. Potatoes, turnips per ton of 40 bushels.
33. Oats per ton of 70 bushels.
34. Oysters per ton of 28 bushels or 4,000.
35. Slate for roofing, tiles per ton of 800 slated and 500 tiles.

Class III (at a rate of 1 cent a ton per mile for the first 20 miles and ¾ cent a ton per mile thereafter).

36. Salt per ton of 45 bushels fine, 32 bushels coarse or 10 sacks.

Class IV (at a rate of 1 cent a ton per mile for the first 20 miles and ½ cent a ton per mile thereafter).

37. Fire bricks per ton of 500 bricks.
38. Iron castings, bloom, railroad iron per ton of 2,240 pounds
39. Lime, cement per ton of 28 bushels or 7 barrels.
40. Rough stone other than prepared limestone per ton of 25 cubic feet.
41. Rails, fence posts in boats per ton of 180 rails or posts.
42. Timber round or square per ton of 70 cubic feet.

Class V. (at a rate of 1 cent a ton per mile for the first 20 miles and ¼ cent a ton per mile thereafter).

43. Bricks per ton of 500 bricks.
44. Ice per ton of 2,240 pounds.
45. Iron (pig and scrap) per ton of 2,240 pounds.
46. Bark in boats per cord of 128 cubic feet or ground bark per ton of 2,240 pounds.
47. Firewood in boats per chord of 128 cubic feet.

Class VI. (at a rate of ¼ cent a ton per mile).

48. Mineral coal per ton of 2,240 pounds or 28 bushels.
49. Coke per ton of 2,240 pounds.
50. Ore, iron, metals per ton of 2,240 pounds.
51. Ashes, bone dust, guano, plaster of paris, powdered lime for manure, oyster shells, manures per ton of 2,240 pounds.
52. Sand, gravel, clay, earth, paving stones per ton of 2,240 pounds.
53. Limestone per perch of 25 cubic feet.

Packet boats, pleasure boats, or boats used chiefly for the transportation of persons including all passengers and their customary baggage (all other articles to be charged at established rates)–8 cents per mile for the first 20 miles and 4 cents per mile thereafter.

Freight boats, gondolas, scows, and other craft–4 cents per mile for the first 20 miles and 2 cents per mile thereafter.

Timber, fence rails, posts, boards, plank, shingles, laths, staves, heading, hoop-poles, and firewood when transported in rafts pay double the tolls as when carried in boats.

Toll charged for 1 mile when distance less than 1 mile; over 1 mile, fraction rounded off to nearest whole mile.[101]

There appeared to be general satisfaction with the new toll rates. At their annual meeting in June 1852 the stockholders were informed that the tariff

has had a beneficial effect, not only in maintaining the trade already established upon the canal; but in opening new sources from which produce is drawn; in conciliating the good feelings of the transporters; and in increasing the revenues of the Company, by the augmented transportation upon the canal.[102]

There were some modifications of these schedules in the course of the first decade. In an effort to encourage boat-building and indirectly to stimulate the lagging coal trade, the company again offered in 1852 to reduce the toll on coal and coke to 2 mills a ton per mile as soon as 100 new

---

[101] *Ibid,* H, 449–453.
[102] *Twenty-Fourth Annual Report* (1852), C & O Co. 7.

first-class boats were registered.[103] This condition was not fulfilled, however and the charges remained the same.

On January 8, 1857, a Committee on Revision of Toll made some recommendations to the board concerning some slight changes within and between toll classifications. Accordingly, the directors adopted new rates, which were to take effect on July 1. The changes (which follow) shifted salt from Class III to Class IV rates, corn and fish from Class I to Class II, and wood products from Class II to Class V:

> Corn on the ear - 1¢ a ton per mile
> Fish, salted and fresh (per ton of 8 barrels salted, 800 shad or 5,000 herring) - 1¢ a ton per mile
> Salt (per ton of 45 bushels fine, 32 bushels coarse, or 10 sacks) - 1¢ a ton per mile for the first 20 miles and ½¢ a ton per mile thereafter
> Boards, planks, shingles, laths, staves, headings, hoop-poles, - (in boats) 1¢ a ton per mile for the first 20 miles and ¼¢ a ton per mile thereafter
> Limestone (per perch of 25 cubic feet) - ¼¢ a perch per mile up to 64 miles and 16¢ a perch for all distances thereafter
> Lime and Cement (per ton of 28 bushels or 7 barrels) - 1¢ a ton per mile for the first 20 miles and ½¢ a ton per mile thereafter for distances up to 80 miles; 50¢ per ton for all distances thereafter.[104]

There were two changes in the toll rates between 1857 and the outbreak of the Civil War. In June 1858 the board lowered the rates on railroad iron from Class IV to Class V,[105] in an effort to stimulate trade on the eve of the Civil War, the board on September 1, 1860, reduced rates on all commodities in Class I to the level of those in Class II.[106]

After 1860 there were no comprehensive changes made in the tariff of tolls. With several exceptions, all the revisions were those in the toll on coal, the product which produced up to 95 percent of the canal's annual revenues. The toll changes on products other than coal were:

1. Leather and hides–On August 10, 1869 the toll on these articles was reduced to $1.15 per ton for the entire 184 miles. The rate was proportioned for shorter distances.[107]
2. Ice–On March 24, 1870 the board reduced the toll on ice to 30 cents per ton for the entire 185 miles. Shorter distances were to be charged proportionately.[108]
3. Stone–On June 3, 1870 the rate on all stone transported on the canal was set at ¼ cent a ton per mile.[109]
4. Grain and Flour–On May 17, 1876 the toll on these products was reduced to ¾ cent a ton per mile from points between Williamsport and Weverton to Washington. This action was taken to aid canal shippers in their competition with the Baltimore & Ohio Railroad for the agricultural trade of the Potomac Valley.[110]

---

[103] *Proceedings of the President and Board of Directors*, H, 570.
[104] *Ibid*, I, 333.
[105] *Ibid*, K, p.35.
[106] *Ibid*, K, 209, and Ringgold to Soper, August 25, 1860, Ltrs. Sent, C & O Co.
[107] *Proceedings of the President and Board of Directors*, L, 185.
[108] *Ibid*, L, 294.
[109] *Ibid*, L, 321.
[110] *Ibid*, M, 255, 258.

Between 1863 an 1889 there were some nineteen revisions in the toll on coal. The rate of ¼ cent a ton per mile established in 1851 was equal to about 46 cents for the 185 miles from Cumberland to Georgetown. The following list details the changes made in this rate:

1. April 10, 1863: The board raised the toll on coal to 5/16 cent a ton per mile until November 1. The additional revenue from this temporary rate hike was to compensate for the interruption of trade and the damage to the canal caused by the Civil War.[111]

2. April 15, 1864: The toll on coal was increased to 3/8 cent a ton per mile after May 1.[112]

3. July 28, 1864: On the recommendation of the Board of Public Works of the State of Maryland, the board increased the toll on coal to ½ cent a ton per mile after August 1.[113]

4. September 5, 1866: The toll on coal was reduced to 4 mills a ton per mile after September 15.[114]

5. February 15, 1867: The toll on coal and coke was further reduced to 3 4/5 mills a ton per mile after March 1.[115]

6. March 26, 1868: At the urging of an Allegany County citizens committee, the board reduced the rate on coal to ¼ cent a ton per mile after April 1. The directors were forced to make this reduction because of the depressed coal trade, the high rates charged for wharfage at Cumberland and Georgetown, and the declining market value of coal in the District cities. Although the Board of Public Works failed to ratify this action, the canal company began to charge the lower rate in an effort to prevent the loss of its coal trade to the Baltimore & Ohio Railroad.[116]

7. February 13, 1873: The toll on coal was raised 5 cents per ton to a total of 51 cents for the entire distance from Cumberland to Georgetown. The additional revenue from this action was needed to finance the program of improvements on the waterway.[117]

8. April 6, 1875: The board reduced the toll on coal to 43 cents per ton plus 5 cents for wharfage at Cumberland. For the first time the board adopted a system of rebates amounting to 5 to 10 cents per ton on the published rates for coal companies shipping large quantities of coal on the canal. This action was taken to maintain the position of the canal in the coal trade vis-à-vis the railroad.[118]

---

[111] *Ibid*, K, 329 – 330
[112] *Ibid*, K, 382.
[113] *Thirty-Seventh Annual Report* (1865), C & O Co., 6.
[114] *Proceedings of the President and Board of Directors*, K, 511.
[115] *Ibid*, L, 10.
[116] *Fortieth Annual Report* (1868), C & O Co., 5–6, and *Forty-Fifth Annual Report* (1873), C & O Co., 23 24.
[117] *Proceedings of the President and Board of Directors*, M, 94; *Forty-Fifth Annual Report* (1873), 10–11; and *Cumberland Times*, May 31, 1873, in Arthur Pue Gorman Collection, University of North Carolina, Chapel Hill.
[118] Cumberland *Daily Times*, March 20, 1875, in Gorman Collection, and *Forty-Seventh Annual Report* (1875). C & O Co., 39–44.

9. April 18, 1876: The nationwide depression reached the canal in 1876 and forced the directors to reduce the toll on coal to 41 cents per ton (plus 5 cents wharfage). The rebate system of 5 to 10 cents per ton remained in effect for large shippers.[119]

10. April 10, 1877: The year 1877 promised little improvement in canal trade or revenue since the country was still in the grip of the depression and a rate war between the canal and the railroad was in the offing. Accordingly, the board reduced the toll on the coal to 33 cents per ton (plus 3 cents wharfage). The rebate system of 5 to 10 cents per ton for large shippers remained in effect.[120]

11. August 21, 1877: To keep in competition with the railroad, the board further reduced the tolls on coal to 22 cents per ton (plus 3 cents for wharfage) after September 1. Because the rates were so ruinously low already, the rebate system was withdrawn.[121]

12. April 10, 1878: Prospects for a marked recovery appeared to be slight as business remained generally depressed and coal prices continued their deflationary tendency. However, the state legislature came to the aid of the canal in 1878 by passing an act curbing the competitive practices of the Baltimore & Ohio Railroad. On the strength of this act the canal board raised tolls from 22 cents to 36 cents per ton from Cumberland to Georgetown and wharfage charges from 3 cents to 4 cents. At the same time, the board restored the rebate system for large shippers.[122]

13. April 14, 1880: The efforts of the canal company to come to terms with its competitors involved both force and compromise. In 1880 it voluntarily cooperated with the Baltimore & Ohio and the Pennsylvania Railroad Company to fix charges on the coal trade at profitable levels. This arrangement enabled the board to raise the toll on coal to 51 cents per ton from Cumberland to Georgetown (plus 4 cents wharfage). The rebate system remained in effect for large coal shippers.[123]

14. June 13, 1883: In the face of renewed bitter competition among the coal carriers, Messrs. Winship, Martens, Agnew and Hassett petitioned the board to reduce the rate on coal. Accordingly, the toll on coal was lowered to 36 cents per ton (plus 4 cents wharfage). The rebate system was maintained for large shippers as a further hedge against the inroads of the Railroad on the canal coal trade.[124]

15. April 10, 1884: Upon the petition of a large delegation of Cumberland boat owners and captains and coal shippers, the board reduced the toll on coal to 33 cents per ton from Cumberland to Georgetown (plus 3 cents wharfage). At the same time, the rebate system was repealed.[125]

---

[119] *Proceedings of the President and Board of Directors*, M, 255.

[120] "Draft of Resolution," 1877, Ltrs. Sent, C & O Co.; *Proceedings of the President and Board of Directors*, M, 296; and Gorman to Garrett, April 10, 1877, Ltrs. Sent, Gorman Collection.

[121] *Proceedings of the President and Board of Directors*, N, 4.

[122] *Fiftieth Annual Report* (1878), C & O Co., 11–12, and *Proceedings of the President and Board of Directors*, N, 20.

[123] *Proceedings of the President and Board of Directors*, N, 101–102.

[124] *Ibid*, N, 220.

[125] *Ibid*, N, 251.

16. February 6, 1885: In the face of the continuing cutthroat competition of the Baltimore & Ohio Railroad, the board reduced the toll on coal to 22 cents per ton (plus 4 cents wharfage).[126]

17. March 4, 1887: The board raised the toll on coal to 36 cents per ton from Cumberland to Georgetown (plus 4 cents wharfage).[127]

18. April 27, 1887: Following the protests of the large Cumberland coal companies to the board's action on March 4, a revised set of tolls was established on coal. For the first time the directors made a distinction in toll charges between coal destined for the District cities in which there would be less rivalry and that which was intended for transshipment to other Eastern markets. The board fixed the rate for the latter at 30 cents per ton (plus 4 cents for wharfage) from Cumberland to Georgetown while locally-consumed coal paid 36 cents per ton (plus 4 cents wharfage).[128]

19. February 14, 1888: The board raised the toll on coal destined for the District cities to 40 cents per ton (plus 4 cents wharfage) in order to produce increased revenue. At the same time, it left the rate on coal for the coastwise trade at the same level as the previous year.[129]

B. IRREGULAR UPWARD COURSE OF CANAL TRADE, 1851–1860

When the canal was completed to Cumberland, canal officials, as well as many Potomac Valley residents, eagerly anticipated a new era of prosperity. At the ceremonies in Cumberland formally opening the canal to navigation on October 10, 1850, William Price, a long-time promoter of the waterway, voiced the expectation by observing:

> The capacity of the canal is practically unlimited. All the coal companies have their railroads and other means of shipment upon the canal, completed. With such a staple and such an avenue to market, what is to limit the emoluments of the work? Coal, however, is but one item of its trade. And when we look to the agricultural products of Western Maryland, and of the contiguous portions of Virginia and Pennsylvania, and after all this, add to the account, the ascending trade, consisting of the merchandize for the supply of the territory already indicated, and a share of that destined for the west, it is no exaggeration to say, that, the work will in due time pay off its own debt and leave the state in possession of a permanent fund, adequate to all her financial wants.[130]

Several weeks later the publishers of the Frederick *Examiner* commented that

> we earnestly hope and feel persuaded, these expectations will be more than realized. If so, it will not be long before Maryland can hold her head proudly up and say - I am out of

---

[126] *Ibid*, N, 308.
[127] Ibid, N, 356.
[128] Ibid, N, 360.
[129] Ibid, N, 372, and *Sixty-First Annual Report* (1889), C & O Co., 7.
[130] Cumberland *Civilian* quoted in *Report to the Stockholders on the Completion of the Canal*, 131.

debt, and prosperity is before me. I now take rank with the proudest of the Sister States of this glorious confederacy.[131]

Total Tonnage and Toll Revenue

The glowing expectations of rapid commercial growth and immediate economic prosperity were not realized in the 1850s. During this period the canal trade followed an irregularly upward course. Tonnage doubled between 1850 and 1851, soaring to 203,893 tons. Thereafter it moved to new peaks in cycles of two- and three-year duration. The following list illustrates this point:

	TONNAGE	TOLLS
1851	203,893	$110,504.43
1852	167,595	92,248.90
1853	270,705	145,100.54
1854	235,923	119,306.03
1855	283,252	138,675.84
1856	287.836	153,051.56
1857	196,525	94,802.37
1858	353,588	171,085.97
1859	359,716	189,134.57
1860	344,532	[132]182,343.86

Ascending and Descending Trade

A breakdown of the total tonnage into the two categories of ascending and descending trade reveals that the amount of articles transported up the canal during the 1850s varied between some 2 and 10 percent of the total canal business. Accordingly, the tonnage moving down the waterway varied between some 90 to 98 percent of the aggregate commerce on the canal. The following list illustrates this point:

	ASCENDING	DESCENDING	TOTAL
1851	22,951	180,942	203,893
1852	16,226	151,369	167,595
1853	21,495	249,210	270,705
1854	18,724	217,199	235,923
1855	24,839	287,836	283,252
1856	15,028	272,808	287,836
1857	21,152	175,373	196,525
1858	29,396	324,192	353,588
1859	8,630	351,086	359,716
1860	9,999	334,533	[133]344,532

Principal Articles of Ascending and Descending Trade

---

[131] Frederick *Examiner*, October 23, 1850.
[132] See Appendices R and G.
[133] See Appendices B and C.

An examination of the ascending and descending trade statistics provides an interesting study of the principal articles transported on the canal in each of these categories. The chief items in the ascending trade throughout the decade were fish (salt and fresh), groceries, salt, lumber, plaster, ore and manures. The main articles transported in the descending commerce were coal, coke, pig iron, lumber, flour, wheat, corn and offal. The following list amplifies this subject:

ASCENDING TRADE								
	FISH	GROCERIES	SALT	LUMBER	PLASTER	ORE	MANURES	TOTAL
1851	1,335	642	2,263	1,534	6,560	5,239	1,079	22,951
1852	455	402	2,851	1,484	5,489	2,715	1,325	16,226
1853	1,387	658	2,433	1,983	6,390	5,074	1,410	21,495
1854	1,054	543	1,852	1,494	3,298	5,220	3,302	18,724
1855	981	473	2,342	1,748	3,774	3,721	3,031	24,839
1856	960	356	1,762	1,679	2,276	3,903	2,297	15,028
1857	490	195	1,539	1,366	2,136	3,069	1,300	21,152
1858	217	178	1,945	884	2,813	190	1,504	29,396
1859	248	220	1,556	947	2,735	0	1,739	8,630
1860	322	74	1,385	853	2,741	0	1,898	[134]9,999

DESCENDING TRADE								
	FLOUR	WHEAT	CORN	OF-FAL	LUM-BER	PIG IRON	COAL	COKE	TOTAL
1851	27,761	6,861	5,783	994	2,736	910	82,690	1,161	180,942
1852	26,755	9,805	4,755	832	2,640	1,650	63,289	2,346	151,369
1853	25,602	9,906	8,327	1,131	3,606	2,418	151,959	4,593	249,210
1854	15,643	5,417	2,618	538	2,588	201	145,319	3,633	217,199
1855	14,240	6,986	628	388	3,051	2,505	188,029	3,060	258,413
1856	14,853	9,017	6,893	425	3,209	2,541	205,568	3,110	287,836
1857	10,967	3,750	5,592	288	1,847	1,212	125,526	2,045	175,373
1858	11,007	4,402	6,275	549	2,669	933	254,684	0	324,192
1859	12,106	5,531	4,931	391	2,810	967	300,743	0	351,086
1860	11,087	5,452	3,048	518	2,593	96	283,249	[135]0	344,533

Factors Influencing the Expansion of Canal Trade

Despite the overall expansion of canal trade during the 1850s the fluctuations experienced in its development were discouraging at best. There were three principal causes for the indifferent course of canal prosperity during the decade: (1) the frequent interruptions of navigation due to floods, breaches and droughts; (2) the disappointing volume of coal shipped via the canal during the early 1850s; and (3) the poor agricultural harvests in the Potomac Valley. Throughout the decade these problems were exacerbated by the competition of the Baltimore & Ohio Railroad.

The irregular course of canal fortunes was largely the result of the unreliability of the canal as a carrier. In 1851, the first full year of operation of the entire canal, there were slight interruptions to the trade as a result of breaches and low water.[136] During the first six weeks of the boating season in 1852 the canal trade flourished as 37,621 tons of goods passed over the water-

---

[134] See Appendix B.
[135] See Appendix C.
[136] *Twenty-Fourth Annual Report* (1852), 6.

way. However, the highest flood in the history of the canal struck the valley in April and navigation was not restored until the end of July. Several breaches in the canal embankments occurred in August and September interrupting navigation for another month.[137] During the period from June 1853 to June 1854 the progress of the canal trade was checked considerably by an obstruction at Dam No. 5.[138] A severe drought between Cumberland and Dam No. 6 during the summer months of 1854 suspended the coal trade for eight weeks.[139] Navigation was again suspended for nearly four weeks in August 1855 when a road culvert was undermined and carried away following a heavy rain.[140] A heavy ice freshet in the spring of 1857 caused extensive damage to Dams Nos. 4 and 4, suspending traffic on the canal for several months.[141] Rock slides in the deep cut below Paw Paw Tunnel in November 1857 and the spring of 1858 stopped navigation for more than two months.[142] Two freshets in April and September 1859 caused serious breaches in Dam No. 4, thus limiting the extent of boat traffic that season.[143]

The volume of coal shipped via the canal proved to be disappointing in the early years of the decade. At the inaugural ceremonies at Cumberland on October 10, 1850, President James M. Coale stated:

> The canal commences its operations under flattering auspices. The circumstances which surround and attend the opening [of] navigation, are of the most favorable character. Unlike other works, constructed with a view principally to the coal trade, it is not required to await the slow process of preliminary preparations...The coal mines have been opened, the laborers have been gathered, facilities of connection with the canal basin, have been constructed, and the coal trade of Allegany is already considerably advanced. Little more is necessary, than for it to turn to its appropriate channel - the canal - and go on increasing.[144]

This theme was amplified in a report to the stockholders in February 1851 in which it was stated that the canal was "destined to be the carrier of the coal and iron and other articles of heavy burden" in the Potomac Valley. The coal mines west of Cumberland were connected with the canal basin at Cumberland by two railroad lines, one belonging to the Maryland Mining Company extending into Braddock's Run Valley and the other to the Mount Savage Iron Company passing through Jenning's Run Valley. These two lines were considered to be capable of bringing more than 1,000,000 tons of coal to the canal annually. Projects were underway to increase the means of transportation between the mines and the canal and it was expected that within several years the coal trade would produce prosperity to the waterway.[145]

The canal board announced in February 1851 that the coal trade promised to be a profitable one that year. During the fall and winter of 1850 and 1851 the canal directors observed that the price of Cumberland coal had greatly increased after the opening of the entire length of the canal. Large sales of coal had recently been negotiated by the Allegany County coal companies.

---

[137] *Twenty-Fifth Annual Report* (1853), C& O Co., 3–4, and Ringgold to O'Neal, Dec. 16, 1852, Ltrs. Sent, C & O Co.
[138] *Twenty-Sixth Annual Report* (1854), C & O Co., 7–8.
[139] *Twenty-Seventh Annual Report* (1855), C & O Co., 5–6.
[140] *Proceedings of the Stockholders*, E, 6–7.
[141] *Ibid*, E, 59
[142] *Ibid*, E, 62–63.
[143] Thirty-Second Annual Report (1860), C & O Co., 7, 16–17.
[144] Cumberland *Civilian* quoted in *Report to the Stockholders on the Completion of the Canal*, 135.
[145] *Report to the Stockholders on the Completion of the Canal* (1851), 121, 126–127.

A heavy concentration of capital, primarily from the Eastern seaboard, had been invested in the western Maryland coal industry.[146]

However, the promising coal trade did not materialize as expected. By June the directors reported to the stockholders that the canal trade

> during the present season compares very favorably with any former year, in the leading articles of transportation (flour, wheat, corn and coal); but we regret to say in the article of coal, there has so far, been less transported, than we were induced to expect from the representatives of the various mining companies..

Although 20,319 tons of coal had been transported on the canal between January 1 and May 31 compared to 807 tons over the same period the previous year, the amount was well below the figure for which the directors had hoped. The reasons for the faltering coal trade were attributed to (1) the shortage of boats of which there were only 140, (2) the efforts of the coal companies to pressure the board into lowering the rate on coal to 25 cents a ton before committing the transportation of their product to the waterway, and (3) the competition of the Baltimore & Ohio Railroad.[147]

During the last six months of 1851 the coal trade increased, making a total of 82,799 tons for the year. Some 65 new boats were put on the canal during this period, increasing the number of craft on the waterway to 205 of which about 140 were involved in the transportation of coal. The board rejected all pressures to reduce its tolls on coal–(1/4 cent a ton per mile–aggregate toll 46¼ cents a ton from Cumberland to Georgetown)–stating that its rates were the lowest on any American waterway.

For its part, the Baltimore & Ohio was attempting to undercut the canal's attempt to attract the Cumberland coal trade by reducing its charges on transporting coal from the latter city to tidewater from $2.57 per ton in October 1850 to $1.75 by the spring of 1852. When these figures were compared with the canal's tolls on coal and on the boats (4 cents per mile for the first 20 miles, 2 cents per mile thereafter, making a total of $4.10), the railroad had a decided advantage. Thus, the amount of coal shipped over the railroad in 1851 was 174,701 tons or more than double that of the canal.[148]

The directors looked forward to a banner year in the coal trade in 1852 as executives of the Cumberland mining concerns indicated that they intended to ship 300,000 tons on the waterway. However, the heavy flood in April ended these expectations, and the coal companies made arrangements to ship their product on the railroad. As a result, the amount of coal transported on the canal declined to 65,719 tons while that on the railroad increased to 268,459 tons.[149]

Despite the disappointment in the development of the coal trade the directors continued to exude optimism in their reports to the stockholders. In June 1853 the board observed that the mining companies in Allegany County were rapidly extending their operations in working the mines and providing railroad cars, canal boats and sea vessels to transport their coal to the eastern seaboard and to foreign markets. Thus, within three years, the board expected the canal coal trade to reach its long-predicted potential.[150]

Within a year this optimistic forecast was partially negated by a two-month strike at the mines in the spring of 1854. Moreover, a series of breaches, droughts and freshets convinced

---

[146] *Ibid*, 126–127.

[147] *Twenty-Third Annual Report* (1851), 7 – 8.

[148] *Proceedings of the stockholders*, D, 431–432, and Ringgold to O'Neal, Dec. 26, 1851, Ltrs. Sent, C & O Co.

[149] Ringgold to O'Neal, Dec. 16, 1852, Ltrs. Sent, C & O Co., and *Twenty-Fifth Annual Report* (1853), 3–4.

[150] *Twenty-Fifth Annual Report* (1853), 7–8.

many of the mine operators of the unreliability of the canal as a carrier and accordingly transferred their business to the railroad. The tonnage of coal carried over the two lines from 1853 to 1856 demonstrates the pace at which the railroad was outdistancing the canal for the Cumberland coal trade:

	B. & O. RR.	C. & O. Canal	TOTAL
1853	376,219	157,760	533,979
1854	503,836	155,845	659,681
1855	478,486	183,786	662,272
1856	502,330	204,120	706,450[151]

Gradually, the canal directors lost their earlier optimism and their reports to the stockholders became both more realistic and more desperate. In 1855 they complained that the shortage of coal boats and the interruptions to navigation had placed the waterway at a great disadvantage with the railroad in the competition for the coal trade. Moreover,

> On the completion of the canal to Cumberland, with a view of establishing the coal trade as early as practicable on a solid basis, the toll upon coal was put at a lower rate than that charged upon any other work, with assurances from those representing the coal interests, that an early, large and yearly increasing transportation of coal could be relied upon; these promises have been delusive. Although the rate of toll remains still at this low rate, which at the time it was fixed, was regarded only as a temporary measure, to aid in establishing the trade so firmly that it would in a short period admit of higher rates being charged, it has been without effect; and until the trade can be so established, it is not deemed advisable to advance the rates.[152]

The following year the directors pointedly stated that the success of the company was "dependent upon the coal trade from the Allegany region, and until this be developed to a much greater extent than it has yet been, we cannot anticipate any material amendment of its finances." What particularly alarmed the directors was that the railroad had nearly doubled its coal tonnage since 1852 despite raising its freight prices from $1.75 to $2.75 per ton from Cumberland to Baltimore. At the same time the canal's coal tonnage had risen slightly although its toll and freight charges had declined to $1.81 per ton from Cumberland to tidewater. The only explanation for such a course of events was the unreliability of the canal navigation.[153]

After the flood of 1857 drove the canal's coal trade to a six-year low, the demand for coal in the District cities in 1858–60 produced a sharp increase in the tonnage on the canal. The total amount of coal carried on the railroad and the canal during this period was as follows:

	B. & O. RR.	C. & O. Canal	TOTAL
1857	465,912	116,574	582,486
1858	395,405	254,251	649,656
1859	426,512	297,842	724,354

---

[151] *Twenty-Sixth Annual Report* (1854), 7–8; *Twenty-Seventh Annual Report* (1855), 5–6, 10, 13–14 & Appendix H.
[152] *Twenty-Seventh Annual Report* (1855), 13.
[153] *Twenty-Eighth Annual Report* (1856), in *Proceedings of the Stockholders*, E, 7–8, 14–15, 21–22, and *Twenty-Ninth Annual Report* (1857), C & O Co., 7–9.

| 1860 | 493,031 | 295,878 | 788,909[154] |

Poor crops in the Potomac Valley and the competition of the Baltimore & Ohio Railroad were all responsible for the irregular trade on the canal during the 1850s. During the middle years of the decade droughts during the summer growing season resulted in severe wheat, corn and grain crop losses to valley farmers. Thus, the canal's descending trade in flour, wheat and corn–the three staples of its agricultural commerce–declined by almost half in 1854 and 1855:

	Flour	Wheat	Corn
1851	25,761	6,861	5,783
1852	26,755	9,805	4,755
1853	25,602	9,966	8,327
1854	15,643	5,417	2,618
1855	14,240	6,986	628

The canal did not regain its pre-1854 totals in the descending agricultural trade during the remainder of the decade as the railroad reduced its rates on these articles to accommodate Baltimore's burgeoning milling industry, the majority of which products were designed for foreign export. The irregular course of the descending agricultural trade from 1856 to 1860 was as follows:

	Flour	Wheat	Corn
1856	14,853	9,017	6,893
1857	10,967	3,750	5,592
1858	11,007	4,402	6,275
1859	12,106	5,531	4,931
1860	11,087	5,452	3,048[155]

Efforts to Stimulate Trade during the 1850s

During the first decade after the completion of the canal to Cumberland, the board tried various ways of stimulating commerce. In 1851 they granted permission to the G. L. Thompson Company and others for the construction of basins on the towpath side of the Georgetown Level to encourage the development of transfer facilities there. This decision, which aided private parties "to ascertain the best and most convenient mode of handling and unloading or transshipping coal upon its arrival at tidewater," was made subject to five conditions:

1. The quantity of water used was not to exceed the amount used in the normal locking from the canal into the river and back
2. The works constructed were to be substantial, permanent, and watertight.
3. Moveable bridges were to be built across the entrance to the basins so that navigation on the canal would not be interrupted by the absence of a continuous towpath. When boats entered or exited from the basins, they were not to interrupt canal traffic for more than four minutes.

---

[154] See Appendix H.
[155] *Twenty-Seventh Annual Report* (1855), 10, 13–14; *Twenty-Eighth Annual Report* (1856), in *Proceedings of the Stockholders*, E, 7; and Appendix C.

4. All plans for the basins were to be approved by the chief engineer.
5. If the agreement were violated or if the basins were abandoned, the works were to be removed and the towpath restored at the expense of the owner.

As the first sites for these experimental basins, the directors allowed the interested parties to use the College Run vicinity and several small pieces of ground above the Potomac Aqueduct.[156]

Following the decline of trade in the middle of the decade, the directors initiated a series of changes to stimulate business on the waterway in 1856. They requested the Alexandria Canal Company to keep its locks open later in the evening, until 8 p.m.[157] Packets were deprived of their right-of-way over loaded freight boats descending the canal in order to reduce the delays in the passage of trade on the canal.[158]

The late spring of 1856 saw the successful completion of a major undertaking along the banks of the canal in western Georgetown, which was designed to improve the shipping facilities. After nearly four years of agitation by Georgetown business leaders and negotiations between property owners and the canal company, the towpath between Frederick (present day 34th) and Warren (present day 37th) Streets was changed from the southern to the northern side of the canal. A new towpath bridge was constructed across the canal above the aqueduct near Warren Street over which the mules and drivers could pass from the upper to the lower towpath. This move left the lower bank free fro the construction of sorely-needed unloading facilities, including basins, wharves and railway chutes connecting directly with the riverfront.[159]

To augment the small coal trade the canal company in June 1856 directed the Baltimore & Ohio Railroad to permit the construction of a spur from Cumberland Coal and Iron Company's railroad across the tracks of the former to a projected wharf on the canal. This procedure had been provided for in a contract between the two companies in 1851 by which the canal company permitted the railroad to effect a connection at Cumberland with the western section of its main line. In return, the railroad agreed to allow its tracks to be crossed by other railroads seeking to reach the canal basin at Cumberland from the mines in the Frostburg, Georges Creek and Savage River districts of western Maryland, when so requested by the canal directors.[160]

The board also considered several proposals for the improvement of the canal itself to facilitate the expansion of trade. Among the most important of these were plans for raising the Georgetown bridges to accommodate the larger vessels on the waterway, the installation of a steam pump near the mouth of the South Branch (the original site for feeder Dam No. 7, which had never been built), for the repair or replacement of Dams Nos. 1–5, all of which were leaking badly, and for the renovation of the Washington branch.[161] Because of financial difficulties, natural disasters and the Civil War, most of these projects were delayed or forgotten. The raising of the Georgetown bridges was not completed until 1867. A steam pump was erected at the mouth of South Branch in 1856, but it failed to relieve entirely the summer water shortages on the canal

---

[156] *Proceedings of the President and Board of Directors*, H, 416–429. Agreements were made with Alexander C. Ray in August 1855, James R. Wilson in June 1858 and W. A. Bradley in June 1859 to build such basins in Georgetown for the unloading of coal. *Ibid,* I, 194–195; K, 39, 111.
[157] *Ibid,* I, 248.
[158] *Ibid,* I, 251–252.
[159] *Proceedings of the President and Board of Directors*, I, p.252, and *Proceedings of the Stockholders*, E, 11–12.
[160] *Proceedings of the President and Board of Directors*, I, pp.267–268. The Baltimore and Ohio had agreed to this arrangement in 1851 because the approval of the canal company to its line in Cumberland was necessary in view of the decision of the Maryland Court of Appeals in 1832 sustaining the claim of the canal company to the right of prior location of its waterway in the Potomac Valley.
[161] *Proceedings of the President and Board of Directors*, H, 453; *Proceedings of the Stockholders*, D, 411; *Twenty-Fourth Annual Report* (1852), 4–6; *Twenty-sixth Annual Report* (1854), 5–6; and *Twenty-Seventh Annual Report* (1855), 4–5, 7.

between Cumberland and Dam No. 6. Some fruitless efforts were made to tighten Dams Nos. 1–3, and Dams Nos. 4 and 5 were replaced by masonry structures in the late 1860s. The Washington branch was never restored, but instead deteriorated into a cesspool of filth.

C. DECLINING TRADE ON THE CANAL DURING THE CIVIL WAR 1861–1865

The outbreak of the Civil War in April 1861 came at a time when the fortunes of the waterway appeared to be approaching their lowest point. As a result of the secession of Virginia, the canal found itself on the border between the Union and the Confederacy, in the path of the marauding armies. During the first two or three years of the conflict, its trade was greatly reduced and its works alternately occupied and/or destroyed by the opposing forces. Furthermore, the war adversely affected the canal trade by destroying or curtailing its markets and damaging many mills along its course. The condition of the company and its properties materially deteriorated from even their gloomy pre-war status. Only toward the end of the war when interference with navigation declined did its trade and financial status improve.[162]

The hostilities had an adverse effect on the canal trade through the destruction of its markets outside the Potomac Valley as well as through the damage to the mills along its course. The existence of a state of war reduced the coastal trade, which had created some of the demand for canal coal. As part of the Union's Southern blockade policy, the Treasury Department announced in April 1862 that henceforth the coastwise shipment of coal would be restricted to the region north of the mouth of the Delaware River. This was a heavy blow to the fortunes of the canal as two of the better markets for its coal were South America and the British West Indies.[163] In the area above the mouth of the Delaware, the Cumberland coal faced severe competition from the Pennsylvania Broad Top coal, on which the Pennsylvania Central Railroad already had reduced its charges by 30 cents per ton.[164] The institution of the Potomac blockade by federal forces also handicapped the coastal trade of canal coal from the port of Georgetown.[165] The subsequent releasing of the shipping restrictions were welcomed in April 1862 when the Treasury modified its prohibition to read "ports north of Cape St. Rogue, South America, and west of that longitude."[166] The canal officers were further heartened when the blockade of the Potomac was withdrawn in the same month when fears of a Southern invasion up the river had subsided.[167]

The effect of the war on some of the mills along the canal can be seen in the experiences of the Potomac Cotton Foundry in Georgetown and Jacob Miller's above Antietam Creek. The former, a large cotton factory and a user of water power from the canal, was cut off from its supply of raw material and forced to close down in 1861. The reasons given for the shut-down were high wages, high prices, scarcity of raw cotton, lack of markets for finished goods and ruined credit.[168] The latter was caught in the ebb and flow of military operations and forced to stop operations in the fall of 1862. The mill was occupied by troops in the spring of that year, and after that it was idled because of the lack of water power from the damaged canal from July 1 to 12, for twelve days in August, and from September 14 on. During the last period of suspension, the mill

---

[162] Walter S. Sanderlin, *The Great National Project: A History of the Chesapeake & Ohio Canal* (Baltimore, 1946), 212–222. A more complete treatment of the canal during the Civil War will be the subject of a later chapter in this Historic Resource Study.
[163] Washington *National Intelligencer*, Apr. 21, 1862, and *Forty-Fifth Annual Report* (1873), C & O Co., 16.
[164] Greene to Ringgold, Apr. 11, 1862, Ltrs. Recd., C & O Co.
[165] Washington *Evening Star*, May 2, 1861.
[166] Washington *National Intelligencer*, Apr. 21, 1862
[167] Ibid.
[168] Williamson and Company to President and Directors, June 20, 1861, Ltrs. Recd., C & O Co.

was again occupied by troops, first as a hospital after the Battle of Antietam and then as a picket's rendezvous. When the soldiers moved out, they left the mill a wreck, taking everything moveable with them and destroying what they could not carry off.[169]

The effect of the restrictions and destructions of the war on the business of the canal was almost disastrous. Military operations resulted in the virtual extinction of canal trade from late April to early August 1861, causing the company president to report that there was "comparatively no business on the canal before September."[170] The lack of trade can be graphically seen when the tolls received for this period are compared with those of the previous year:

	1860	1861
May	$19,214.19	$657.36
June	18,529.60	206.27
July	23,051.10	16.94
August[171]	23,005.02	2,444.07

September and October, generally the most active months for the canal, showed only a slight revival but they were still well below prewar levels:

	1860	1861
September	$33,084.04	$10,509.22
October[172]	32,547.54	17,793.22

All told the year 1861 was a disaster when its total trade was compared with that of the previous year. The total tonnage and tolls for the two years were as follows:

	1860	1861
ASCENDING	9,999 tons	3,250 tons
DESCENDING	334,533 tons	144,814 tons
TOTAL	344,532 tons	148,064 tons
TOLLS[173]	$182,343.86	$70,566.99

From a business standpoint, the following year 1862 was on the whole even worse. Although there was no single month as poor as May, June or July 1861, between the seizure of the canal boats in the spring and the rebel raids in the summer and fall, no month witnessed a satisfactory amount of business. Up until May 31 only 25,259 tons of coal had been [shipped and the tolls] collected were only $18,449.86, both of which statistics did not comprise one prosperous month of trade.[174] So complete was the severance of trade that in August an agent of one of the coal companies and a director of the canal wrote, "There has been no real through navigation on the canal this year."[175] The invasion of Lee in September and October ruined the trade on the canal

---

[169] Miller to President and Directors, May 1, 1863, Ltrs. Recd., C & O Co.
[170] *Thirty-Fourth Annual Report* (1862), C & O Co., 3.
[171] *Thirty-Third Annual Report* (1861), C & O Co., Appendix C, 14, and *Thirty-Fourth Annual Report* (1862), C & O Co., Appendix B, 9.
[172] Ibid.
[173] *Thirty-Fourth Annual Report* (1862), C & O Co., 8.
[174] Ibid, 3–6.
[175] Greene to Ringgold, Aug. 11, 1862, Ltrs. Recd., C & O Co.

for these months and the tolls fell to $5,282.48 and $538.78 respectively.[176] The total tonnage carried on the waterway for the year was 126,793 (ascending 2,603; descending 124,190) and the total tolls collected were $63,985.85 both of which figures were the lowest since the canal had been completed to Cumberland.[177]

There was a revival of trade on the canal in 1863 as military movements in the area caused fewer interruptions to the navigation than in the two proceeding years. The canal's recovery, however, was set back by rebel activity from mid-June to late August during the Gettysburg campaign of the Army of Northern Virginia. July of that year was the worst single month of canal navigation since July 1861 as a mere $480.06 in tolls were collected.[178] Besides this interference, there were no other major interruptions and the ascending tonnage rose by more than 10 percent to 2,936 tons, the descending tonnage more than doubled to 262,911 and the total tonnage increased to 265,847. The revenue from tolls for the [year] rose by more than $90,000 to $154,928.26. Had it not been for the interruptions of the Gettysburg campaign, the toll revenues would have superceded the total of any previous year.[179]

An active trade began on the canal in the spring of 1864, giving promise of the best year in the waterway's history. The coal trade was so prosperous that the company was confident enough to raise the toll on coal from 3/8 cent to ½ cent a ton per mile in July. However, Early's raid that month, followed by Mosby's and White's incursions in August and September, severely curtailed the volume of commerce on the canal for the normally most profitable months of the year. The month of August saw no through navigation at all, and the $398.80 in tolls collected gave the canal its new low for a single month since July 1861.[180] Nevertheless, the business on the canal for the year was the best to date as the total tonnage rose to 290,772 tons and the amount of tolls received increased to $225,897.34.[181]

Canal officials looked forward to a banner year in trade in 1865 because of the lessening of tensions in the Potomac Valley and the quantity of products at Cumberland ready to be shipped. Although heavy ice on the western levels delayed the commencement of navigation until April and a partial suspension in coal shipments reduced the tonnage in May and June by nearly one-half, commerce was active for the rest of the year with only several minor interruptions. The problems in the coal market were the result of the high rates previously paid for mining and transportation, which the coal companies were unable to continue, and the miners and transporters were unwilling to reduce. Up until May 31 the amount of coal shipped was only 61,677 tons compared to 101,390 tons for the same period in 1864. Nevertheless, the brisk business, which followed the settlement of the controversy more than made up for the loss as the total tonnage of coal in 1865 reached a high of 340,736 tons, compared with 260,368 tons the previous year. All told the total tonnage and the tolls collected reached new highs of 372,335 tons and $346,165.47, respectively.[182]

Perhaps the most severe set-back in business experienced by the canal due at least in part to the irregularity of navigation during the war was the loss of more than half of its share of the flour trade. Complaining that they could not rely on the canal for even a 10-day period, many of the valley mill operators turned to the more dependable railroad.[183] Despite the determined effort

---

[176] *Thirty-Fifth Annual Report* (1863), C & O Co., 6.
[177] See Appendices B, C and E.
[178] *Thirty-Sixth Annual Report* (1864), C & O Co., Appendix B, 10.
[179] *Ibid,* 3, 8.
[180] Washington *Evening Star*, Aug. 22, Sept. 13, 1864 and *Thirty-Seventh Annual Report* (1865), C & O Co., 6, 10.
[181] *Thirty-Seventh Annual Report* (1865), C & O Co., 3.
[182] *Thirty-Seventh Annual Report* (1865), 3, 6–7; Hagerstown *Mail*, Feb. 25, 1865; and Ringgold to Greene, Dec. 1, 1865, Ltrs. Sent, C & O Co.
[183] Embry and Son to Dellinger, April 26, 1862, Ltrs. Recd., C & O Co.

of the railroad to lure the flour trade away from the canal in the 1840s, the flour trade had continued to be one of the larger though erratic sources of canal revenue. From 14,880 tons in 1843, it rose to 25,761 tons in 1851 and fell to 11,087 tons in 1860. In 1861 it dropped to 7,067 tons, and after a slight recovery in 1862 (7,340 tons) and 1863 (8,566 tons), it declined to 5,962 tons and 5,383 tons in 1864 and 1865, respectively.[184]

Despite the troubles in the early years, the canal was an important transportation agency during the war. Between raids and repairs the canal provided invaluable service for the Union, hauling troops and supplies, particularly coal, which the government hoarded.[185] The amount of coal transported on the waterway during the hostilities were as follows:

1861	119,893 tons
1862	94,819 tons
1863	229,416 tons
1864	260,368 tons
1865[186]	340,736 tons

The canal provided the sole direct link between Washington and Harpers Ferry for the transportation of men and materials to that important post, as well as other points in the Potomac Valley.

Summary of Canal Trade during the Civil War

The bleakness of the early years of the conflict was largely reversed toward the end of the struggle. Despite continuing raids and occupation, business on the canal began to revive in 1863 and improved steadily until the end of the war. The trade statistics for the war period were:

	ASCENDING	DESCENDING	TOTAL
1861	3,250	144,814	148,064
1862	2,603	124,190	126,793
1863	2,936	262,911	265,847
1864	1,891	288,881	290,772
1865[187]	2,707	369,628	372,335

The principal products of the ascending and descending trade were:

ASCENDING						
	FISH	FLOUR	SALT	LUMBER	PLASTER	MANURES
1861	139	674	604	143	856	643
1862	162	33	478	131	274	1,029
1863	200	21	535	102	574	632
1864	110	49	545	207	382	477
1865	104	100	498	543	664	647

---

[184] *Sixteenth Annual Report* (1844), Appendix No. 11, 46; *Twenty-Fourth Annual Report* (1852), Appendix B, 26; *Twenty-Third Annual Report* (1861), Appendix C, 16; *Thirty-Fourth Annual Report* (1862), Appendix B, 11; *Thirty-Seventh Annual Report* (1865), Appendix B, 12; and *Thirty-Eighth Annual Report* (1866), Appendix C, 15.
[185] Washington *National Intelligencer*, Mar. 10, 1862, and Washington *Evening Star*, Sept. 12, 1862.
[186] See Appendix C.
[187] See Appendix B & C.

DESCENDING					
	FLOUR	WHEAT	CORN	MILL OFFAL	LIMESTONE
1861	7,067	4,286	1,941	520	642
1862	7,340	6,640	1,027	534	1,936
1863	8,566	9,014	1,789	395	4,650
1864	5,962	6,168	1,914	254	4,727
1865	5,383	5,700	775	250	6,386

DESCENDING CONTINUED[188]					
	LUMBER	ROUGH STONE	LIME, CEMENT	COAL	WOOD
1861	1,994	2,852	467	119,893	3,773
1862	1,693	760	49	94,819	8,025
1863	1,403	19	794	229,416	4,513
1864	1,248	390	601	260,368	3,888
1865	1,216	2,900	1,004	340,736	3,971

The improvement in business was paralleled by increasing revenues. The general inflationary tendency of prices toward the end of the war also permitted the toll on coal to be raised from ¼ cent a ton per mile to 5/16 cent a ton in April 1863, to 3/8 cent a ton in April 1864 and finally to ½ cent a ton in July 1864.[189] Annual revenues during the war soared from lows of $70,566.99 in 1861 and $63,985.85 in 1862 to $154,928.26 in 1863, $225,897.34 in 1864, and $346,165.47 in 1865.[190]

D. RESURGENCE OF THE CANAL TRADE IN THE POSTWAR ERA: 1866–1869

Factors Influencing the Development of Trade

The canal emerged from the war on both a somber note and a hopeful one. The waterway itself had suffered great physical damage from the activities of the opposing armies. Furthermore, the federal government continued to occupy the Potomac Aqueduct and a portion of the Rock Creek Mole until 1868 to the detriment of the canal's business.[191] On the other hand, the company's finances had improved as a result of the revival of trade after 1863. Bankruptcy no longer threatened the immediate operation of the waterway, and the improved commercial and financial status of the company made it possible to undertake necessary and long-delayed repairs and improvements.

The physical condition of the canal in 1865 was much worse than it had been before the war. Despite growing trade and revenues and some increase in repair expenditures toward the end of the conflict, the waterway had been largely neglected. In addition to the destruction of its works in the war it had not received the attention required for normal maintenance. Only the most necessary repairs had been made, and then usually in a hasty and slip-shod fashion.[192] The general state of deterioration of the canal was described as follows to the stockholders in June 1869:

---

[188] See Appendix C.
[189] *Proceedings of the President and Board of Directors*, K, 329, 382, 395.
[190] See Appendix G.
[191] *Proceedings of the President and Board of Directors*, K, 511; L, 56; Moore to Ringgold, May 28, 1866; and Godey to Ringgold, Jan. 10, 1866, Ltrs. Recd., C & O Co.
[192] Manning to President and Directors, May 31, 1866, Ltrs. Recd., C & O Co.

During the last ten years little or nothing had been done toward repairing and improving lock-houses, culverts, aqueducts, locks, lock-gates and waste weirs of the Company; many of them had become entirely unfit for use and were becoming worthless, rendering it absolutely essential to the requirements of the Company to have them repaired ...[193]

The restoration and improvement of the canal began almost immediately after the conclusion of the war.[194] Construction of the masonry dams replacing the old structures at Dam Nos. 4 and 5 were resumed and were completed by the end of the decade. The company finally came to an agreement with the corporate authorities of Georgetown concerning the manner of raising the bridges over the canal, and the new structures were completed in 1867 by Duvall and Company at a cost of $31,000.[195] Rock Creek was dredged, the tumbling dam at its mouth was restored, and the outlet lock repaired in 1867 by the firm of Deeter and Maynard at a cost of $9,000 in anticipation of the resumption of trade through Georgetown.[196]

While the main concern of the board during the postwar era was to restore the canal to a good navigable condition, it also took several steps to stimulate commerce. In January 1866 the directors ordered the removal of coal unloading platforms, built by the Cumberland Coal and Iron Company and the Borden Mining Company, which extended 10 feet over the berm of the prism and hence restricted navigation in Georgetown.[197] To encourage the expansion of the coal trade, company ground at strategic points along the canal was rented to the Cumberland shippers for use as coal yards and storage facilities.[198] Because of the seven-fold growth of the trade in rough stone during the period, permission was granted in February 1869 to the Maryland Free Stone Mining and Manufacturing Company for the construction of a wharf on Rock Creek below K Street.[199] As the expanding coal trade necessitated greater loading facilities at Cumberland, the board in February 1869 made provision for the construction of a new wharf, an adjacent water course, and a new railroad line from the Mount Savage Railroad to the wharf.[200]

The postwar years also had their difficulties. Heavy freshets occurred in the Potomac Valley in 1866 and 1868, the former sweeping away 60 feet of the temporary coffer Dam No. 5 and the latter carrying off one-half of Dam No. 1.[201] The end of the war also brought a decline in trade as the demand for coal lessened from the wartime peaks. At the same time wage disputes occurred between the miners and the coal companies, interfering with the coal trade in April 1866.[202] In the face of the deflationary tendency of coal prices and the decreasing demand for that product, the board reduced the tolls by some 24 percent to 3.8 mills per ton (or from 92 cents to 62.29 cents per ton from Cumberland to Georgetown) in September 1866, and back to ¼ cent a ton per mile (or 46¼ cents per ton from Cumberland to Georgetown) in March 1868. Had the company not made these reductions, it would have lost its share of the Cumberland coal trade, which varied between 31 and 39 percent of the total during the period, to the Baltimore & Ohio

---

[193] *Forty-First Annual Report* (1869), C & O Co., 4–5.
[194] Manning to President and Directors, Feb. 1, May 31, 1866, Ltrs. Recd., C & O Co.
[195] *Thirty-Ninth Annual Report* (1867), 5.
[196] *Thirty-Eighth Annual Report* (1866), 4–5; *Thirty-Ninth Annual Report* (1867), 5.; *Proceedings of the President and Board of Directors*, K, 491–492; and *Fortieth Annual Report* (1868), C & O Co., 4–5.
[197] *Proceedings of the President and Board of Directors*, K, 471, 479.
[198] Ringgold to Hassett, Nov. 15, 1867, Ltrs. Sent, C & O Co.
[199] *Proceedings of the President and Board of Directors*, L, 139.
[200] Spates to President and Directors of Baltimore and Ohio Railroad Company, Feb. 5, 1869, Ltrs. Sent, C & O Co.
[201] *Thirty-Ninth Annual Report* (1867), 5 and Mans to President and Directors, July 11, 1868, Ltrs. Recd., C & O Co.
[202] *Thirty-Eighth Annual Report* (1866), 3, 5; *Thirty-Ninth Annual Report* (1867), 3; Manning to Ringgold, Apr. 22, 1866, and Greene to Ringgold, April 27, 1866, Ltrs. Recd., C & O Co.

whose rate-cutting practices were causing great concern to canal officials.[203] The interference of local political influence by the state Democratic Party machine also returned after the war with no less than four changes in canal administration occurring between 1865 and 1870.

Total Tonnage and Toll Revenues

Despite unsettled trade conditions, political interference, and the appropriation of large amounts for the restoration and improvement of the waterway, the financial condition of the company continued to improve. As a result of the statewide industrial and commercial boom, canal trade recovered quickly from each setback, rising to a new high each year and nearly doubling over the 4-year period. The total tonnage and receipts from toll collections for the period were:

	TONNAGE	TOLLS
1866	383,408	$355,660.76
1867	521,402	374,932.75
1868	552,987	276,978.71
1869[204]	723,938	368,483.42

Ascending and Descending Trade

A breakdown of the total tonnage into the two categories of ascending and descending trade reveals that the amount of articles transported up the canal during the postwar years comprised less than 2 percent of the total canal trade. Accordingly, the tonnage moving down the waterway amounted to more than 98 percent of the aggregate commerce on the canal. The following list illustrates this point:

	ASCENDING	DESCENDING	TOTAL
1866	6,658	376,750	383,408
1867	10,160	511,242	521,402
1868	10,479	541,508	552,987
1869[205]	14,238	709,700	723,938

Principal Articles of Ascending and Descending Trade

An examination of the principal articles in the ascending and descending trade of the postwar years provides an interesting study. The chief items in the ascending trade throughout the period were fish (salted and fresh), flour, salt, lumber, ore, plaster and manures. The most important of these products was ore, which made up nearly 40 percent of the ascending trade of the 4-year period. The primary articles of the descending trade were flour, wheat, corn, lumber, pig and scrap iron, bricks, rough stone, lime cement, coal, bark, wood and limestone. The most important of these articles was coal, which comprised between 89 and 95 percent of the annual total tonnage. The following list illustrates these facts:

ASCENDING TRADE

---

[203] *Hagerstown Mail*, Mar. 1, 1867; *Proceedings of the President and Board of Directors*, K, 511; L, 82, 89; *Thirty-Ninth Annual Report* (1867), 6; and *Fortieth Annual Report* (1868), 5–6.
[204] See Appendices F and G.
[205] See Appendices B and C.

	FISH	FLOUR	SALT	LUMBER	ORE	PLASTER	MANURES	TOTAL
1866	172	361	873	607	2,478	682	1,062	6,658
1867	277	128	794	705	5,067	1,328	959	10,160
1868	240	131	1,362	975	2,618	1,181	1,845	10,479
1869	297	158	1,280	1,923	7,000	792	1,476	14,238[206]

DESCENDING TRADE						
	FLOUR	WHEAT	CORN	LUMBER	PIG & SCRAP IRON	BRICKS	ROUGH STONE
1866	2,620	4,946	6,307	1,852	612	240	589
1867	3,058	9,510	10,794	3,051	1,785	404	2,970
1868	2,120	9,164	5,502	2,936	2,225	3,057	4,503
1869	2,220	15,147	2,339	1,097	3,782	1,145	4,161

DESCENDING TRADE CONTINUED						
	LIME CEMENT	COAL	BARK	WOOD	LIME STONE	TOTAL
1866	2,080	344,160	1,115	2,900	7,845	376,750
1867	3,143	458,009	705	1,931	10,091	511,242
1868	1,975	484,849	900	2,016	16,148	541,508
1869	1,985	661,828	1,104	2,492	11,204	709,700[207]

E.   THE GOLDEN YEARS OF CANAL TRADE, 1870–1875

Factors Influencing the Development of Trade

The burgeoning industrial and commercial expansion of the state and nation in the early 1870s provided the most stable and prosperous period in the history of the waterway. The company enjoyed unprecedented financial profits, and for the first time the waterway gave promise of fulfilling the hopes of its promoters. The canal board continued the program of restoration and improvement, fostered the growth of trade to record levels, and continued payments on the long-term debts of the company.

Despite the repairs already made, there was still much to be done. Chief Engineer William R. Hutton recommended a thorough overhauling of the canal at an estimated cost of $78,000 in 1871, including repairs to locks, aqueducts, culverts and the prism itself.[208] By 1874, many of the canal's masonry structures had been repaired, the waterway had regained its full prism, and the strength of its banks had so increased that an April flood which completely submerged the canal on the levels below Dams Nos. 4 and 5 did no appreciable damage.[209] The extent of canal improvements was at least partially reflected in the increased tonnage carried by the freight boats. The annual average rose from 109½ tons in 1872 to 112 in 1873 and to 113½ tons in 1874.[210]

---

[206] See Appendix B
[207] See Appendix C.
[208] *Report by W. R. Hutton, Chief Engineer, As to Condition of Chesapeake & Ohio Canal* (Annapolis, 1872), 3–30.
[209] *Forty-Sixth Annual Report* (1874), C & O Co., 11–12, and *Proceedings of the President and Board of Directors*, M, 154–155.
[210] *Forty-Seventh Annual Report* (1875), C & O Co., 8–9.

Trade continued to improve somewhat irregularly in the first two years of the decade. From a total of 723,938 tons in 1869, commerce on the waterway fell off by nearly 9 percent to 661,772 tons in 1870, but soared by more than 46 percent to a record peak of 968,827 tons in 1871.[211] The Shenandoah flood in October 1870, a strike of boatmen and dock laborers at Cumberland in 1871, and a four-month drought in the same year, which reduced the average tonnage of boats from 110–115 to 85–90 tons, did not appreciably interfere with the expanding prosperity of the waterway.[212] Business was so active in 1871 and 1872 that canal shippers found it difficult to obtain enough coasting vessels to load coal at Georgetown. Stocks piled up on wharves forcing a deliberate curtailment of shipments over the canal.[213]

The method of expediting trade on the Georgetown level soon became the major obstacle to the continued growth of business. Uploading and transfer facilities were unable to handle the increasing tonnage, which was brought to them. Nearly all the shipments from Cumberland were carried as far down as the Potomac Aqueduct, and two-thirds of them were unloaded on the overburdened wharves in Georgetown. As a result, boats experienced annoying and costly delays as they lined up in the canal to await their turn to unload and canal employees began to complain that it was almost impossible to maintain order.[214] [The Georgetown] level posed other problems in that the canal was not wide enough to accommodate the ordinary traffic to and from the Rock Creek Basin and the Potomac Aqueduct and the clamoring boatmen awaiting access to the coal wharves. Particularly serious was the congestion on the waterway between the aqueduct and Market Street where the coal boats waiting in line got in the way of the grain boats heading for the large flour mills in that vicinity.[215] In June it was reported that the large number of boats on the level had nearly stopped navigation as there was at one time "ten tiers of boats three abreast–20 tiers two abreast" and in several instances "4 boats abreast."[216] President James C. Clarke summarized conditions in the following words in December 1871:

> As it is now, it is not infrequently the case that from sixty to eighty boats have to lie along the Canal bank singly, so as to allow sufficient room in the Canal for boats to pass in opposite directions. Often a string of loaded boats from half a mile to a mile in length is seen lying above the Collector's Office in Georgetown, waiting their turn to get to the wharves to discharge their cargoes.[217]

At the same time the tremendous increase in the number of boats arriving at Georgetown brought to a head another problem that had plagued the canal company. Private wharf owners, allowed to operate unregulated along the banks of the canal in Georgetown, were extracting exorbitant wharfage fees from canal boats. This practice represented a direct threat to the attempts by the company to regulate freight rates effectively.[218]

Accordingly, the board determined to build a new outlet above Georgetown because it would reduce the congestion by discharging boats above the city while at the same time freeing

---

[211] See Appendix
[212] *Proceedings of the President and Board of Directors*, L, 365, 426–427; and *Report of the President for the Year 1871* (1871), C & O Co., 5.
[213] *Report for the Year 1871* (1871), 5 and *Proceedings of the President and Board of Directors*, M, 14.
[214] Hutton to Clarke, Mar. 31, 1871, Ltrs. Recd., C & O Co.
[215] *Forty-Second Annual Report* (1870), C & O Co., 35-36.
[216] Hayden to Clarke, June 14, 1871, Ltrs. Recd., C & O Co.
[217] *Proceedings of the Stockholders*, E, 187-188.
[218] Cumberland *Daily News*, Mar. 2, 1875, in Gorman Collection.

canal boats from the grip of private wharf owners. The outlet would give canal boats access to the Potomac, where they would be towed to any number of river points below Georgetown.[219]

In response to the board's decision to build an outlet, H. H. Dodge, a local politician and president of the Potomac Lock and Dock Company, advised the directors that he would construct an outlet lock and lease it to the company for a sum sufficient to assure a fair return on his investment. Dodge's proposal was accepted by the board, and on May 10, 1872, a contract for the construction of the outlet was signed.[220] When the board realized that an outlet lock capable of lowering canal boats between the waterway and the river would require more water than was often available on the Georgetown Level, they shifted their plans. Upon the recommendation of Chief Engineer Hutton, the directors ordered that instead of an outlet lock, an inclined plane similar to those on the Monkland Canal in Scotland and on the Morris Canal in New Jersey be constructed. The desired change was made in the contract with the Potomac Lock and Dock Company, and the construction of the incline was begun during the spring of 1875.[221]

With the help of the canal improvements and despite periodic interruptions to the navigation, trade continued at a high level between 1872 and 1875. At first it fell off slightly from the record peak of 1871 because the suspension of operations in the Pennsylvania mines that year had created an unusual demand for Cumberland coal which could not be expected to continue when the mines reopened.[222] But the canal trade quickly recovered and in 1875 reached an all-time high. Company statistics show a decline to 973,805 tons in 1875.[223] In the latter year, the canal achieved its highest monthly tonnage total in May when more than 121,000 tons of coal were shipped.[224]

During this period the board discovered a new source of business in the gas coal trade. As several large companies in western Pennsylvania indicated their interest in sending large shipments of this product to Washington via the Pittsburgh and Connellsville Railroad and the canal, the board granted rebates to encourage the development of this new trade. In 1874 the drawback was 5 cents a ton for 50,000 tons or more, and in 1875 it was 5 cents a ton for 100,000 tons or more and 6 cents for 200,000 tons or more. The gas coal trade rose rapidly from an average of less than 3,000 tons in 1870-72 to nearly 16,000 tons in 1873 and to more than 65,000 tons in 1874. However, it declined almost as rapidly as it had developed, decreasing by some 40,000 tons alone in 1875, because of the excessive amount of sulfur in the West Virginia gas coal and the strict inspection standards in the District of Columbia. For the remainder of the decade an annual average of some 22,000 tons of Youghiogheny gas coal passed down the waterway.[225]

It is interesting to note that commerce flourished on the canal during the period from 1872 to 1875 despite a score of incidents that disrupted trade for brief periods. A shortage [of] coasting vessels in the spring of 1872 led to the piling up of coal on the Georgetown and Alexandria wharves and thus to a curtailment of the coal trade.[226] A severe drought in the Potomac Valley during August, September and October followed by an early winter in 1872, which forced the

---

[219] Harold Skramstad, "The Georgetown Canal Incline" Technology and Culture, Chapt. X, Oct. 1969, 550–551.
[220] Proceedings of the Stockholders, E, 187, 198–199, 215–222, and Proceedings of the President and Board of Directors, M, 19–24.
[221] Skranstad, Georgetown Canal Incline, 552 – 554, and Dodge to Gorman, June 29, 1876, William R. Hutton Papers, Museum of History and Technology, Smithsonian Institution.
[222] Cumberland News, July 1872, in Gorman Collection.
[223] See Appendix.
[224] Weber to Gorman, June 1, 1875, Ltrs. Recd., C & O Co.
[225] Proceedings of the President and Board of Directors, M, 151–152, 206; Bartol to Gorman, April 3, 1878, Ltrs Recd., C & O Co.; Forty-Fifth Annual Report (1873), 16–17; Forty-Seventh Annual Report (1875), 9–10; and Fiftieth Annual Report (1878), C & O Co., 24.
[226] Forty-Fourth Annual Report (1872), C & O Co., 9.

canal to close on December1, hampered operations for the year.[227] A fire in the Borden Mining Company shaft in the Cumberland coal fields in March, strikes by the Boatmen's Benevolent Society in Cumberland and by the western Maryland miners in March and April protesting a 5-cent per ton rate increase on coal as well as a reduction in boating charge and a decrease in the shipments of the Consolidation Coal Company which generally accounted for one-fourth of the canal coal trade hindered the progress of commerce in 1873.[228]

A late-summer drought at Cumberland followed by a flash food in September 1873, which caused the greatest destruction to the canal from natural causes since 1852, suspended navigation for nearly one month.[229] Also in November 1873 an epidemic stripped the boats of their crews for a brief period and was responsible for the loss of many canal mules.[230] In March and April of 1874 heavy rains forced the swollen river to overflow the canal banks below Dams Nos. 4 and 5 and on the Monocacy Division.[231] Trainmen on the Cumberland and Pennsylvania Railroad went on strike in August 1874, briefly stopping that vital link in the transportation between the coal mines and the canal. At about the same time, the Boatmen's Benevolent Society, which had grown to an active membership of 324 and which controlled 374 boats, again struck, demanding $1.35 a ton freight rates from Cumberland to Georgetown. Canal traffic was virtually stopped for one month before the company, fearing that the mining companies would turn their shipments over to the Baltimore & Ohio, employed police and strike-breakers to bring the boatmen to terms.[232] The commerce on the canal in 1875 was affected by the nationwide economic depression which had grown steadily worse since 1873, unsettled freight rates and heavy ice on the Potomac until March thus causing large amounts of coal to be piled up at Georgetown and Alexandria.[233]

Both the coal companies and the canal board undertook to encourage the increasing trade. The former added numerous new boats to the canal during the period, thus increasing the number of vessels plying the waterway to 539 with an average capacity of 112 tons by 1874.[234] In 1878, sixteen steamers were operating on the canal realizing for the first time the great dream of the canal's founders.[235]

The canal company, as its part, helped to speed the flow of navigation by abolishing the sporadically enforced Sabbath Law prohibiting Sunday runs and adopting rules for the [movement] of traffic on the Georgetown Level and at the Paw Paw Tunnel.[236] Amid reports of the continuing congestion at the Georgetown Tidelock, the directors tried to rush the construction of the inclined plane.[237] When the financial stringency in the nation postponed even the commencement of this work, the board purchased a steam dredge for $10,000 in 1873 and cleaned out the Rock Creek Basin, removing nearly 58,000 tons of sand and mud within two years.[238] The additional

---

[227] *Proceedings of the President and Board of Directors*, M, 53–54, 62, 68–69, and *Forty-Fifth Annual Report* (1873) 3
[228] President, Boatmen's Benevolent Society to Gorman, Jan. 1, 1873, Ltrs. Recd., C & O Co.; Williamsport *Pilot*, Jan. 11, 1873, in Gorman Collection; *Forty-Fifth Annual Report* (1873), 3; and *Report of President to Board of Directors*, May 13, 1873, Ltrs. Recd., C & O Co.
[229] *Proceedings of the President and Board of Directors*, M, 124, 127; and *Forty-Sixth Annual Report* (1874), p.11
[230] Williamsport *Pilot*, Dec. 21, 1872, in Gorman Collection.
[231] *Report of President to Board of Directors*, March and April 1874, Ltrs. Recd., C & O Co.
[232] *Proceedings of the President and Board of Directors*, M, 173, 176–177, 180–185; and Cumberland *Times*, Jan. 23, 1875, in Gorman Collection.
[233] *Forty-Seventh Annual Report* (1875), 19–21.
[234] Record of Boat Registrations, 1851 – 74, C & O Co.
[235] Register of Boats Employed on the Canal, January 1, 1878, C & O Co.
[236] *Report for the Year 1870* (1870), 7–8 and *Proceedings of the President and Board of Directors*, M, 57, 106.
[237] Morgan to Gorman, May 1, 1875, Ltrs. Recd., C & O Co.
[238] *Proceedings of the President and Board of Directors*, M, 133, 163; *Forty-Sixth Annual Report* (1874), 12; and *Forty-Seventh Annual Report* (1875), 8.

room in the basin came none too soon for in July 1874 it was reported that because of a large breach on the Alexandria Canal 840 boats had been locked from the basin into the river in one month.[239] Permission was granted to some of the Cumberland coal operators, such as the Baltimore and Borden Coal Company, the New Central Coal Company and the Georges Creek and Cumberland Coal Company, to enlarge and improve their basins and wharves in Georgetown to accommodate the growing coal trade.[240] Arrangements were made with the Consolidation Coal Company for increased accommodations at its wharf in Cumberland.[241] To promote the continued expansion of trade in both agricultural produce and coal, the canal company sought to facilitate the construction of the Cumberland Valley Railroad, a short line which ultimately extended from Harrisburg, Pennsylvania to Winchester, Virginia crossing the canal at Powell's Bend just below Williamsport, and the Western Maryland Railroad, which was to connect Baltimore with the canal at Big Pool.[242] Over the winter of 1874–75, the company leased the Lynn-owned Potomac Wharf at Cumberland for a period of two years, thus putting it in a position to reduce the exorbitant wharf charges in that town.[243]

Mounting Profits

As trade increased, company income and profits also mounted. Receipts from tolls collected, Ascending and Descending, during the 1870 to 1875 period were as follows:

1870	$342,644.40
1871	485,019.65
1872	459,654.59
1873	482,528.57
1874	500,416.24
1875[244]	458,534.66

The income rose accordingly from some $109,000 in 1870 to a peak of over $290,000 in 1874.[245] The board applied the excess of revenues over current expenses to the task of restoration and improvement and to the payment of the back interest on the repair bonds of 1849 and the preferred construction bonds of 1844. Of the $200,000 repair bonds, $199,000 had been paid off with interest by 1873. By December 1875 the board had paid off 19 coupons, representing 9½ years interest, amounting to $902,457.66.[246] The financial condition and reputation of the canal rose perceptibly throughout the period.

Program Of Improvements Recommended As Answer To Railroad Competition

---

[239] *Proceedings of the President and Board of Directors*, M, 173.
[240] Hutton to Gorman, July 18, Aug. 19, 1876; Fletcher to Gorman, Feb. 5, 1875; and *Report of President*, to Board of Directors, Jun. 16, 1874, Ltrs. Recd., C & O Co.; *Proceedings of the President and Board of Directors*, M, 216–217; *Forty-Fourth Annual Report* (1872), 7–8; and *Forty-Seventh Annual Report* (1875), 3–4, 8–9.
[241] *Ibid,* M, 160, 168–170.
[242] *Forty-Fifth Annual Report* (1873), 16–17; *Forty-Sixth Annual Report* (1874), 18; and *Proceedings of the President and Board of Directors*, M, 469–470.
[243] *Forty-Seventh Annual Report* (1875), 19–21.
[244] See Appendix
[245] Sanderlin, *The Great National Project*, 309.
[246] *Forty-Fifth Annual Report* (1873), 8, and *Forty-Eighth Annual Report* (1876), 10.

Despite the prosperity of the canal and the substantial improvements already made, President Arthur P. Gorman recommended in 1875 the continuation of the general program to modernize the canal as a carrier and establish more firmly its future as a transportation line. The Baltimore & Ohio was in the process of completing its third rail line between Baltimore and Cumberland, and it would soon be able to transport coal for less than 1 cent a ton per mile. This together with the superior facilities of the Port of Baltimore, as compared with those at Georgetown and Alexandria, for the purpose of transshipment to northern ports, would soon force the canal to make corresponding reductions in cost and improved facilities. Moreover, within the past four years, another competing line had been built to the Cumberland coal fields by the Pennsylvania Railroad Company. As the owner of the Pennsylvania canal system, the railroad was contemplating the enlargement of its waterways to within 80 miles of the Allegany County mines and the construction of a line to connect the coal fields with their canal system. When this transportation line would be completed, much of the coal trade of the canal and Baltimore & Ohio would be diverted from Maryland to Philadelphia and New York.[247]

To enable the Chesapeake and Ohio to [meet] this challenge by the railroads, Gorman proposed that four necessary improvements be made to the canal. They were: (1) the restoration of the prism so that the average tonnage of the boats could be increased to 120 tons; (2) the control of the amount of terminal charges by the canal company; (3) the procurement of such control as to enable the canal company to fix and maintain a uniform rate of freight charges and (4) the enlargement of the locks so as to increase the capacity of double boats to 250 tons.[248]

Competition with the Baltimore & Ohio Railroad for the Canal Trade

The insistence on continued efforts to improve the canal's position as a transportation line was not premature, even in the peak year of 1875. The threat of a rate war among the competing coal carriers was always present although there had been none for some years. Since 1870, new markets for the Cumberland coal had opened in South America, the West Indies, and the trans-Atlantic trade, thus allowing each of the coal carriers to expand their tonnage without overt competitive tactics. Between 1870 and 1872 the total output of the Cumberland mines had grown from 1,717,075 tons to 2,355,471 tons, an increase abetted by the high price of English coal and the widespread recognition that the Maryland soft coal was superior to other kinds for the generation of steam.[249] Accordingly, the coal tonnage on the canal had risen at an irregular pace from 604,137 tons in 1870 to 850,339 tons in 1871 and to 816,103 tons in 1872.[250] Canal officials were pleased with the promise of a growing coal trade, and their optimism for the future growth of the trade was shown by their decision in February 1873 to increase the rate on coal some 5 cents to a total of 51 cents per ton from Cumberland to Georgetown in order to finance the program of canal improvements. Thus, the cost of transporting a ton of coal over the entire length of the canal was $2.18½ (including tolls, 51 cents; wharfage at Cumberland, 5 cents; freight charges, $1.35; wharfage at Georgetown, 25 cents; commission, 2½ cents). This compared favorably with the sum of $2.73, which it cost to transport a ton of coal over the Baltimore & Ohio Railroad from Cumberland to Baltimore.[251] As a result of the nationwide depression, the total amount of the Cumberland coal trade and the volume of coal shipped via the Baltimore & Ohio and the Penn-

---

[247] *Forty-Seventh Annual Report* (1875), 14–15.
[248] *Ibid,* 16–17.
[249] *Forty-Fifth Annual Report* (1873), 16–17.
[250] See Appendix H; Williamsport *Pilot,* Dec. 21, 1872, and Cumberland *News,* Oct. 18, 1872, in Gorman Collection; and *Proceedings of the President and Board of Directors,* L, 391.
[251] Cumberland *Times,* May 31, 1873, in Gorman Collection, and *Forty-Fifth Annual Report* (1873), 25–26.

sylvania Railroads fell off as early as 1874. However, the canal's trade continued to improve as the following statistics indicate:

	C&O Co.	B&O RR	Pa. RR Co.	TOTAL
1870	604,137	1,112,938	------	1,717,075
1871	850,339	1,494,814	------	2,345,153
1872	816,103	1,517,347	22,021	2,355,471
1873	778,802	1,780,710	114,589	2,674,101
1874	767,064	1,576,160	67,671	2,410,895
1875	879,838	1,302,237	160,698	2,342,773[252]

To compensate for its losses and to regain its share of the coal trade [lost to the] canal since 1850, the Baltimore & Ohio triggered a rate war by reducing its charges on coal to $2.45 per ton early in 1875.[253] Although this still left the canal with a slight advantage, of 3½ cents per ton to tidewater, the fact that coal shipped by railroad sold for between 15 and 20 cents more per ton than that transported by water, together with the greater efficiency of the railroad, made it mandatory for the board to lower its rates. Accordingly, the directors on January 13, 1875, ordered a general reduction of charges, including tolls, wharfage and freights in order to maintain its position in the trade. Over-all charges were reduced 22 cents: tolls, 8 cents; freight, 10 cents; and wharfage, 4 cents. Rebates of 5 to 10 cents per ton were also made available to large shippers.[254] The board was put under pressure to lower the rates still further by up to 10 cents per ton by three citizen's groups in Cumberland, Hancock and Sharpsburg but the requests were turned down.[255] As a result of the cutbacks, coal tonnage on the waterway increased greatly in 1875 to 879,838 tons from 778,802 tons in 1873 and 767,064 tons in 1974, but the canal revenues from tolls declined from $500,416.24 in the peak year of 1874 to $458,534.66 in 1875.[256]

Total Tonnage and Toll Revenues

The total tonnage and toll revenues for the 1870–75 period were:

	TONNAGE	TOLLS
1870	661,772	$342,644.40
1871	968,827	485,019.65
1872	923,581	459,654.59
1873	845,248	482,528.57
1874	909,959	500,416.24
1875[257]	973,805	458,534.66

---

[252] See Appendix H, and *Proceedings of the President and Board of Directors*, M, 210–202.

[253] Cumberland *Daily Times*, March 20, 1875, in Gorman Collection.

[254] *Proceedings of the President and Board of Directors*, M, 210–211; *Forty-Seventh Annual Report* (1875), 19–21; and Cumberland *Times*, Mar. 1873, in Gorman Collection. Coal shipped by railroad sold at a better price, because it tended to be less broken than that shipped by canal.

[255] Petitions to the President and Directors of the Chesapeake & Ohio Canal Company, March 3, 1875, Ltrs. Recd., C & O Co.

[256] See Appendices E and G.

[257] See Appendix G.

Ascending and Descending Trade

A breakdown of the total tonnage into the two categories of ascending and descending trade reveals that the amount of articles transported up the canal during the 1870-75 period comprised between some 1-2 percent of the total canal trade. Accordingly, the tonnage moving down the waterway amounted to some 98-99 percent of the aggregate commerce on the canal. The following list illustrates this point:

	ASCENDING	DESCENDING	TOTAL
1870	12,719	649,053	661,772
1871	18,552	950,275	968,827
1872	20,060	903,521	923,581
1873	16,271	828,977	845,248
1874	13,978	895,981	909,959
1875	10,338	963,467	973,805[258]

Principal Articles of Ascending and Descending Trade

An examination of the principal articles in the ascending and descending trade of the 1870-75 period provides some insight into the cargos that were passing over the waterway during its peak years. The chief items in the ascending trade throughout the period were hay, salt, lumber, ore, plaster, manures and sand. The most important of these articles was ore, which made up nearly 47 percent of the ascending trade of the 6-year period. The primary products of the descending trade were flour, wheat, corn, lumber, pig and scrap iron, bricks, rough stone, lime cement, coal, wood and limestone. The most important of these articles was coal, which comprised between some 89 and 96 percent of the annual descending trade and between some 87 and 92 percent of the yearly total tonnage. The following list illustrates these facts:

ASCENDING TRADE[259]							
	HAY	SALT	LUMBER	ORE	PLASTER	MANURES	SAND	TOTAL
1870	4	1,296	933	5,801	879	913	867	12,719
1871	45	2,043	1,929	8,960	943	1,780	672	18,552
1872	1,418	1,014	1,028	11,090	379	1,482	1,484	20,060
1873	690	1,906	1,147	8,458	1,610	418	414	16,271
1874	235	1,157	627	6,380	1,883	1,552	694	13,978
1875	77	1,194	443	2,560	2,075	1,633	295	5,443

---

[258] See Appendices B and C.
[259] See Appendix B.

DESCENDING TRADE[260]					
	FLOUR	WHEAT	CORN	LUMBER	PIG, SCRAP IRON	BRICKS
1870	1,845	11,710	2,929	968	1,833	4,073
1871	2,025	14,369	5,005	2,410	4,247	23,840
1872	980	8,416	3,844	1,761	3,730	12,308
1873	1,744	8,569	3,285	1,582	1,874	4,086
1874	1,526	9,780	5,312	1,102	3,053	1,303
1875	1,000	8,894	3,553	1,270	669	2,456

DESCENDING TRADE CONTINUED					
	ROUGH STONE	LIME	COAL	WOOD	LIME STONE	TOTAL
1870	4,133	608	696,707	2,289	10,451	649,053
1871	15,177	9,473	848,199	3,635	14,145	950,275
1872	31,243	4,970	814,335	2,499	12,916	903,521
1873	15,994	4,700	796,717	4,336	12,868	828,977
1874	12,146	5,602	836,996	1,349	13,666	895,981
1875	11,462	7,596	904,898	1,077	14,559	933,533

F.   THE DECLINING YEARS OF CANAL TRADE, 1876–1889

Factors Influencing the Development of Canal Trade

In 1876 the great nationwide depression, which had affected many parts of the country since the Panic of 1873, finally reached the canal. Trade fell off sharply to 709,130 tons (of which the coal trade consisted of 654,409 tons), and the revenue from tolls plummeted to $290,274.39. That part of the trade which was retained was kept only by lowering the rates of tolls and wharfage from 51 cents to 46 cents per ton from Cumberland to Georgetown in April as a direct response to the Baltimore & Ohio's reduction of its charges from $2.30 per ton to $2.02 per ton to Baltimore.[261] In addition to this reduction, the board adopted a system of drawbacks on published rates for coal companies shipping large quantities of coal via the canal, and rebates were quickly granted to the Consolidation Coal Company and the Maryland Mining Company.[262] Gorman succinctly identified the causes of the downturn in company affairs when he noted in June 1876:

> The continued depression in all branches of industry has so lessened the demand for coal as to seriously affect our business. The depression has also induced the shippers of coal from other regions and transportation lines leading to tidewater, to reduce the price of coal at commercial centers, so that (a) large reduction in prices was necessary in Cumberland coal.[263]

In an effort to compete with other carriers for the declining trade, the board authorized the president to reduce tolls on all commodities at competing points on the canal to whatever rates were

---
[260] See Appendix C.
[261] *Proceedings of the President and Board of Directors*, M, 255; *Forty-Eighth Annual Report* (1876), C & O Co., 10; Cumberland *Civilian*, Apr. 29, 1877, in Gorman Collection.
[262] *Proceedings of the President and Board of Directors*, M, 246.
[263] *Forty-Eighth Annual Report* (1876), C & O Co., 10.

necessary to retain the trade. As the Baltimore & Ohio had reduced its charges on flour by 4 cents a bushel from Harpers Ferry to Baltimore, President Gorman lowered the toll on flour from 1 cent to ¾ cent a ton per mile from all competing points between Williamsport and Weverton.[264] In an attempt to reduce the cost of canal coal and to stimulate trade, Gorman secured the passage of a law by the Maryland General Assembly to compel the Cumberland and Pennsylvania Railroad, which carried most of the coal from western Maryland mines to the canal at Cumberland, to reduce its charges from 3 cents to 2 cents a ton per mile.[265] The railroad resisted the move, however, and the reduction did not take effect until the Maryland Court of Appeals upheld the validity of the law in May 1877.[266] The board directed surveys to be made up the north branch of the Potomac in December 1876 with the view of establishing a direct connection between the canal basin at Cumberland and the coal fields either by extending the canal to the mouth of the Savage River or construction a new rail line to the vicinity around George's Creek, the Savage River and Laurel Run.[267]

Despite all efforts to stimulate trade, reduce charges and provide direct connections with the mines, the coal trade, as well as the total trade, on the waterway continued to drop as the production of the Cumberland region declined markedly. This dismal state of affairs was summarized in the June 1877 annual report to the stockholders:

> The business from the Maryland coal region during the year (1876) has proved one of the most unsatisfactory in its history. The decrease in the number of tons of coal shipped from this region to tidewater amounts to 507,692 tons, equal to a decrease of twenty-one (21) percent, as compared with 1875.[268]

The decrease in trade and the reduction [in] tolls caused canal revenues from that source to fall some $268,000 from the 1875 level to $290,274.39. Company profits also fell some $149,000 from the 1875 figures to $67,144.40.[269] Most of the canal improvements, which had been projected or were in progress, were suspended. The company, however, did lease for 25 years at a cost of $15,000 a year the Georgetown Incline Plane, which was finally completed in June 1876.[270] Ironically, by the time the incline was put into operation, the decline of commerce had relieved the canal of the immediate need for it. The directors authorized the payment of only one coupon (that for July 1864) on the construction bonds in 1876.[271]

1877

Trade on the canal faced even more critical challenges in 1877 as the nation remained in the grip of the depression and a rate war among the transportation lines was in the offing. The Baltimore & Ohio reduced its charges 22 cents below the published rate of $2.03 for 1876. Canal officials

---

[264] *Proceedings of the President and Board of Directors*, M, 255, 258, and Cockrell and Engle to Gorman, Jan. 26, and Mar. 9, 1877, Ltrs. Recd., C & O Co.

[265] Sanderlin, *The Great National Project*, 239.

[266] *Forty-Ninth Annual Report* (1877), C & O Co., p.3, and *Proceedings of the President and Board of Directors*, M, 296.

[267] *Proceedings of the President and Board of Directors*, M, 283, and Hamill, Bannon and Farrands to Gorman, Jan. 9, 1877, Ltrs. Recd., C & O Co. The committee that carried out the study recommended the construction of a direct rail line connection.

[268] *Forty-Ninth Annual Report* (1877), 3.

[269] *Ibid*, 4.

[270] *Ibid*, 9.

[271] *Proceedings of the President and Board of Directors*, M, 281. This coupon was the last ever paid.

were informed that the railroad had offered rebates of 18 to 20 cents in 1876.[272] The desperate situation of the canal was graphically described in November of that year by a holder of some canal construction bonds living in Philadelphia. In a letter to the company, he observed:

> From what I see in the Cumberland papers I should judge that the canal will before long be available only as a nice swimming place for ducks and geese, & possibly a source of motive power to grist mills. It would seem that the Balt. & Ohio R.R. is going to gobble up all your business...[273]

The distressing news came to them in the spring of 1877 when officials of the American Coal, Maryland Coal and the Borden Mining Companies informed them that the railroad was offering similar private drawbacks of up to 20 cents per ton to those who were willing to guarantee a shipment of 35,000 tons for the year.[274] Although the Cumberland and Pennsylvania Railroad finally reduced its charges to 2 cents a ton per mile, the competition of the Baltimore & Ohio Railroad interests and the Pennsylvania Clearfield anthracite coal was so great that the canal board decided on April 10 that it would be impossible to make any profit on the coal trade that year, and that the important thing was to hold the trade which the waterway already had.[275] Thereupon the board, charging that the railroad had violated its earlier agreement with the canal to provide for uniform and moderate rates, plunged into the thick of the rate war.[276] It reduced tolls twice in the course of the year from 41 cents per ton to 33 cents on April 10 and to 22 cents on August 21.[277]

The troubles of the canal in 1877 were complicated by a boatmen's strike from June 21 to August 20. Trade came to a virtual standstill during this period as the striking boatmen hindered traffic all along the line and tied up their barges on the first level west of Seneca to await some redress from their grievances. By the time that the strike ended, many of the canal shippers had made other arrangements with the railroad for the transportation of their business for the rest of the year.[278]

The last of the series of misfortunes, which befell the canal in 1877, occurred on November 24 when the worst flood in 150 years of the recorded history of the region swept down the Potomac Valley. The canal was left almost a total wreck and trade was brought to an end for the season. In all there had been only 161 days of navigation during the year, and the total trade on the waterway had fallen to 627,913 tons (of which 603,096 tons was coal) and the toll revenues to $187,756.66.[279] Despite the decline in trade on the canal, the board took some pride in the fact that the waterway carried only 102,707 tons of coal less than did the Baltimore & Ohio. Statistical charts relative to the coal company shipments and the destination of the coal cargoes may be seen on the following tables:

---

[272] *Proceedings of the President and Board of Directors*, M, 293–294.

[273] Harris to Fawcett, Nov. 23, 1876, Ltrs. Recd., C & O Co.

[274] Borden to Gorman, Mar. 26, 1877; Lloyd to Gorman, Mar. 28, 1877; and Loveridge to Gorman, Apr. 7, 1877, Ltrs. Recd., C & O Co.

[275] *Proceedings of the President and Board of Directors*, M, 293–296.

[276] Gorman to Garrett, Mar. 31, 1877, in *Ibid*, M, 295–296. An excellent summary of the canal – railroad rate war may be found in the New York *Herald*, Apr. 6, 1877, and the New York *Times*, Apr. 20, 1877.

[277] *Ibid*, N, 4; *Fiftieth Annual Report* (1878), C & O Co., 6; and Gorman to Garrett, Apr. 10, 1877, Ltrs. Sent, in Gorman Collection.

[278] Stanhope to Gorman, July 1, 1877, Ltrs. Recd., C & O Co., and *Fiftieth Annual Report* (1878), 3, 6.

[279] *Fiftieth Annual Report* (1878), 3–4, 9–10.

POINTS TO WHICH COAL WAS SHIPPED - 1877	
	TONNAGE
Georgetown	563,907.04
Williamsport	36,272.06
Hancock	881.03
Harpers Ferry	764.16
Shepherdstown	515.10
Berlin (Brunswick)	326.08
Knoxville	117.01
Mercerville	112.09
Sharpsburg	103.16
Seneca	73.02
Two Locks	22.19
Total[280]	603,096.14

CUMBERLAND COAL TRADE — 1877					
Company	To B&O Railroad	To C&O Canal	To Pa. Railroad	Local	Total
Consolidation Coal Co.	201,390	125,633	352	21,010	348,385
New Central Coal Co.	64,688	128,055	152,312	983	346,038
Georges Creek Coal & Iron Co.	120,683			870	121,553
Maryland Coal Co.	18,350	101,193		1,000	120,543
American Coal Co.	24,816	92,043	25	550	117,434
Borden Mining & Coal Co.	5,986	71,526	18,052	2,343	97,907
Atlantic & Georges Coal Co.	92,736			3,475	96,211
Hampshire & Baltimore Coal Co.	55,360	34,966		1,190	91,516
Potomac Coal Co.	63,399			260	63,659
Canton Coal Co.	48,812		60	224	49,096
Franklin Mines	45,220				45,220
Piedmont Coal & Iron Co.	35,123		83	500	35,706
Blaen Avon Mining Co.	560	31,580		1,629	33,769
Union Mining Co.	880			2,360	3,240
Georges Creek Mining Co.	1,725				1,725
Canton Mine	1,212				1,212
Georges Creek Valley Mine	1,122				1,122
TOTALS[281]	782,065	584,996	170,884	36,394	1,574,339

When the canal reopened for trade on April 15, 1878 prospects for a recovery appeared to be slight. Business remained generally depressed, and coal prices continued their deflationary tendency. The price of a ton of coal on board vessels at Georgetown, which had been $4.65 in 1872, fell to $2.60 in 1878. The tolls, which had amounted to 12 percent of the value of coal transported on the canal in 1872, totaled 15½ percent of its value by early 1879, thus preventing canal officials from raising rates.[282] Under these conditions trade remained slow, and revenues had little opportunity to rise. In an effort to end the ruinous rate war, the canal company enlisted the assistance of the Maryland General Assembly to bring the Baltimore & Ohio to accept a compromise. The legislature came to the aid of the canal as hostility toward the railroad had been growing in

---

[280] *Fiftieth Annual Report* (1878), 24.

[281] *Fiftieth Annual Report* (1878)

[282] *Fifty-Second Annual Report* (1880), 6–7.

the state since the local elections in 1875 during which the railroad had cast off its allegiance to the Democratic Party, dominated by Gorman.[283] In 1878 it passed an act curbing the competitive practices of the Baltimore & Ohio Railroad.[284] On the strength of this act the two companies reached a toll rate agreement whereby the railroad lowered its rates west of Cumberland and promised not to increase its charges east of that town while the canal raised its tolls on coal from 22 cents to 40 cents a ton from Cumberland to Georgetown.[285] As a result of this agreement and an increase of some 105,000 tons in the total coal production of the western Maryland mines, trade on the canal increased slightly to 662,508 tons (of which 630,290 tons were coal) and toll revenues increased greatly to $282,181.18.[286]

Attempts to Improve Canal as Coal Carrier

Meanwhile the company turned to other means of improving its position as a carrier. At least four courses of action were possible: (1) to secure an independent connection with the coal fields; (2) to gain control of freight rates on the canal; (3) to reduce operating expenses; and (4) to make further agreements with its competitors. All four ways were tried during 1879 and 1880.

The object of securing an independent connection with the coal fields was to reduce the cost of transportation for the coal companies and to [rid] the canal of its dependence on the Baltimore & Ohio and its subsidiaries. The company made arrangements with the owners of the Davis mine in West Virginia in 1879 for the transportation of coal from that mine.[287] It sought to facilitate the construction of two independent railroad connections with the canal at Cumberland by invoking the agreement of 1881 to compel the Baltimore & Ohio to permit the railroads to cross its tracks. Among these were the Georges Creek and Cumberland Railroad, which proposed to build a line all the way down the Potomac to the coal basin, and the Pennsylvania Railroad. Two other roads, the West Virginia Central and Pittsburgh and the Potomac and Piedmont, agreed to build short feeder lines to the Baltimore & Ohio tracks on the promise of special rates from the canal for coal shipped over it.[288]

The purpose of gaining control of freight rates on the canal was to reduce the profits of the various agencies involved in canal transportation so as to [help] the company to reduce overall charges while maintaining a profitable rate of tolls. In this regard, the company achieved success in an assault on the owners of the wharves at Cumberland and Georgetown. The wharf owners, who had invested some $300,000 in their facilities, received handsome annual returns, which had reached a peak of $344,000 in 1874.[289] At the same time, their charges were so high that they forced the canal board to reduce its rates on the coal trade in order to compete with the railroads for business. The low rate of tolls, on the other hand, did not produce enough revenue to pay anything on the great investment of capital in the company. The board dredged to Rock Creek Basin and made improvements to the tidelock and incline in order to make the river bank available for wharf facilities, thus seeking to force wharfage fees at Georgetown down to a fair level. At Cumberland, the company renewed its lease of the Potomac Wharf from the Consolidation Coal Company and cut rates until others were forced to reduce theirs.[290] On January 1, 1879 it purchased the Basin Wharf, the largest such facility at Cumberland, from William Walsh and Thomas J.

---

[283] Frederick *Examiner*, Feb. 27, and Mar. 3, 1878.
[284] *Acts of the General Assembly of the State of Maryland* (Annapolis, 1878), Ch. 155.
[285] *Fiftieth Annual Report* (1878), 11–12, and *Proceedings of the President and Board of Directors*, N, 20, 24.
[286] *Fifty-First Annual Report* (1879), C & O Co., 5–6.
[287] *Fifty-Second Annual Report* (1880), C & O Co., 12.
[288] Ibid, 12–13, and *Proceedings of the President and Board of Directors*, N, 99–100, 102–103, 112
[289] Cumberland *Daily News*, Mar. 2, 1875, and Anon. Report, h. d. in Gorman Collection.
[290] Graham to Gorman, Jan. 5, and Feb. 28, 1877, and Hicks to Gorman, Apr. 20, 1877, Ltrs. Recd., C & O Co.

McKaig for $100,000, and thereby secured a permanent control over wharfage at the western terminus of the canal.[291]

The company attempted to reduce its own operating expenses by initiating cost-savings improvements that would permit a lower toll rate but which would still leave the canal a profit. One improvement completed and in operation by October 1879, was the installation of a 3-station telephone line, the longest single circuit in existence at the time, along the waterway so located as to be within easy reach of any point on the canal.[292] The telephone system provided for more effective communication both for canal employees as well as shippers and permitted the company to reduce its maintenance staff, thus providing for an annual savings of nearly $12,000. Another proposed improvement was the lengthening of at least 27 locks by 10 feet each, but only 14 had been extended by 1882, thereby denying to the coal shippers the anticipated advantages of operating larger boats.[293]

The efforts of the canal company to come to terms with its competitors resulted in a compromise settlement with the Baltimore & Ohio and the Pennsylvania Railroad Companies in April 1880. It voluntarily cooperated with the two rail lines to fix charges on the coal trade at profitable levels. The arrangement attracted the attention of the West Virginia coal operators located west of Piedmont, thus opening up a new source for the canal trade. The contract enabled the board to raise canal tolls on coal to 51 cents per ton from Cumberland to Georgetown.[294]

Hindrances to Canal Trade

The attempts of the board to improve the position of the canal as a transportation line were hindered by many obstructions. A miner's strike from September 4 to October 8, 1879, followed by a serious drought, which limited the carrying capacity of the boats to 80 tons, caused an estimated loss of 100,000 tons of commerce that year.[295] In 1880 there were several short strikes in the mines and coal feeder railways. An 8-week strike of boatmen led by those employed by the Borden Mining Company interfered with navigation from late June to late August, causing a drop in trade from an average of 21,374 tons to 13,--- tons a week.[296] Hardly was the strike settled, than the river lock at Rock Creek Basin gave way and was abandoned.[297] In the same year Daniel K. Stewart, a holder of some of the repair bonds of 1878 that had been issued to repair the flood damage to the canal, challenged the right of the company to sell the bonds to raise funds for lengthening the locks.[298] After the company had won a doubtful victory in the Stewart case, Governor Hamilton, a political foe of President Gorman, expressed his doubts about the legality of using the bonds for that purpose, thereby ruining the market for the bonds and bringing the improvements to a halt.[299] Meanwhile the Georges Creek and Cumberland Railroad was having trouble securing the necessary permission to cross the Baltimore & Ohio tracks to the canal basin, thus depriving the waterway of its much-needed independent connection with the mine fields as late as 1881.[300] Another severe drought in August and September of the same year so reduced the water in the river and in the canal that boats having a 4½ foot draft, could be passed only in fleets

---

[291] *Fifty-First Annual Report* (1879), 10.
[292] *Proceedings of the President and Board of Directors*, N, 94–97, and *Fifty-Second Annual Report* (1880), 11.
[293] *Proceedings of the Stockholders*, E, 353–355.
[294] *Proceedings of the President and Board of Directors*, N, 101–102, and *Fifty-Second Annual Report* (1880), 12.
[295] *Fifty-Second Annual Report* (1880), C & O Co., 6.
[296] *Proceedings of the President and Board of Directors*, N, 117–118.
[297] *Proceedings of the President and Board of Directors*, N, 119, and *Fifty-Third Annual Report* (1881, 8.
[298] *Fifty-Second Annual Report* (1880), C & O Co., 10.
[299] *Fifty-Fourth Annual Report* (1882), C & O Co., 21
[300] *Proceedings of the President and Board of Directors*, N, 148–149, and *Fifty-Fourth Annual Report* (1882), 7.

every six or eight days by means of collecting the water at the upstream dams and then passing it through the canal along with the boats down to the lower levels.[301] Finally in 1882 another lengthy strike occurred among the coal miners lasting from April until August during which there was little trade on the canal. By the time the miners agreed to resume their work, there were only three months of active navigation remaining and many of the boatmen had left the canal and disposed of their crews and stock. The lack of trade also ended any hopes by the board to further the program of canal improvements and of lengthening the locks (14 of which had been completed).[302]

During the decade from 1879 to 1888, the canal went into a period of decline from which it never emerged. Under the continuing depressed state of trade, there was little the officials could do to put the waterway back on its feet, and it became scarcely possible to keep the canal in shape for navigation. The dilemma faced by the board was that the canal could not be maintained or improved unless additional funds were spent on it and these funds could not be raised unless the canal was improved so as to keep pace with the increasing facilities of the competing railroads.[303] Thus, the last decade of its independent existence was one of trade stagnation, financial depression, physical deterioration, political interference and outside intrigue.

The business on the waterway by this time was almost totally dependent on the demand for coal. In view of the continued depression in industry, this demand remained relatively stagnant during the early years of the decade. The competition of the great railroad lines, which had reduced the cost of its services by making improvements in its equipment whereby one locomotive could haul three times the number of cars as before, also acted to keep the coal shipments on the canal at a minimum.[304] In 1884 the canal's business was curtailed by the efforts of the leading Cumberland coal companies to force the board to lower its charges by arguing that such a course of action was needed because of the decline in popularity of Cumberland coal, the growing demand for anthracite, the greater handling and breakage of canal-shipped coal, the obsolescence of the port at Georgetown, and the dependence of the canal on the coal trade.[305] The general paralysis of business, continuing freight wars between the railroads, and strikes in the coal fields led to the suspension of navigation for four of the first six months of 1885.[306] A prolonged general strike by the miners beginning in March 1886 had a similar effect that year.[307] Natural disasters continued to plague the canal as a heavy freshet struck Washington County in July 1884 and three floods in April and May 1886 virtually destroyed Dam No. 6.[308]

The Coal Trade: 1879–1888

The general stagnation of the canal's trade was clearly reflected in the annual canal tonnage and toll revenue figures from 1879 to 1888. The statistics are as follows:

---

[301] *Fifty-Fourth Annual Report* (1882), C & O Co. 15
[302] *Fifty-Fourth Annual Report* (1882), 9 and *Fifty-Fifth Annual Report* (1883) C & O Co. 7–8.
[303] *Fifty-Eighth Annual Report* (1886), C & O Co. 5.
[304] *Fifty-Eighth Annual Report* (1886), C & O Co. 6–7.
[305] *Proceedings of the President and Board of Directors*, N, 260, and Borden to Gorman, Apr. 1, 1878, Loveridge to Gorman, Apr. 1, 1878, Loveridge to Gorman, Apr. 15, 1878 and Reppelier to Gorman, Apr. 19, 27, 1878, Ltrs. Recd., C & O Co.
[306] *Fifty-Seventh Annual Report* (1885), C & O Co. 6–7
[307] *Proceedings of the President and Board of Directors*, N, 328
[308] *Ibid*, N, 273, 329–331, and *Fifty-Ninth Annual Report* (1887), C & O Co. 5–6.

	COAL TONNAGE	TOLLS
1879	522,904	$234,976.52
1880	615,423	361,757.68
1881	521,189	284,435.59
1882	316,648	143,730.76
1883	708,465	284,234.00
1884	378,352	135,693.59
1885	398,012	106,940.39
1886	295,415	81,718.73
1887	277,688	110,667.83
1888[309]	286,813	121,218.25

Canal revenues declined irregularly in the face of the bitter competition among the coal carriers. The directors lowered canal tolls from 51 cents in 1880 to 36 cents in June 1883, to 33 cents in April 1884, and finally to 22 cents in February 1885 in order to offset the reductions in charges by the railroads and to stimulate trade.[310] In 1885 the Baltimore & Ohio was carrying coal to deep water docks at Locust Point in Baltimore Harbor for $1,30 a ton and frequently for as low as $1.00 a ton whereas as late as 1865 it had charged $5.58 a ton. This reduction in charges had been made possible by the use of steel tracks, heavy locomotives and enlarged cars. On the other hand, the capacity of the canal boats–112 tons–was the same as it had been in 1852 and the number of men and mules required to operate the boats was the same as it had been in 1852 and the number of men and mules required to operate the boats was the same as it had been since 1830.[311]

The decline in revenue made the financial position of the debt-ridden, outdated canal, very precarious. If the interest on the repair bonds went unpaid for more than two years, the bondholders could obtain a foreclosure according to the decision of the U. S. Circuit Court in 1886. On the other hand, if the canal's income were used to pay this interest, the company would not have the funds to make the improvements necessary to enable the waterway to compete with the low freight charges of the railroads and thereby to obtain the money to repay the loans.[312]

To resolve this financial dilemma as well as it was able, the company resorted to several devices. First, it cut the ordinary expenses of operation by reducing salaries, discharging laborers and abolishing staff offices between 1882 and 1884.[313] Second, the company applied its economy measures to the work of maintenance and improvement, authorizing only the most essential repairs to the waterway and suspending work on the comprehensive program of improvements laid down by the Gorman administration in the early 1870s.[314]

About the only hopeful sign in the otherwise bleak records of the 1880s was the completion of the Piedmont and Cumberland Railroad in 1886. An independent connection with the West Virginia coal fields had at last been realized, as this railroad had built its line down the Potomac Valley to the south of the Baltimore & Ohio. This course of action had been taken to circumvent the necessity of obtaining a permit from that road to cross its tracks to reach the Cumberland basin.[315] The ill-fated Cumberland and Georges Creek Railroad had been blocked this

---

[309] See Appendix E and N. After 1878, the company only maintained tonnage statistics for the coal trade.
[310] *Proceedings of the President and Board of Directors*, N, 220, 251 and 308.
[311] *Fifty-Eighth Annual Report* (1886), 9.
[312] *Ibid*, 8–10.
[313] *Proceedings of the President and Board of Directors*, N, 189–190, 214, 246, 257–258, 267–268, 274 and 276.
[314] *Fifty-Seventh Annual Report* (1885), 5–6, 9–10.
[315] *Fifty-Ninth Annual Report* (1887), 11.

way for many years, and as late as April 1888, was still urging the canal company to compel the Baltimore & Ohio to permit the crossing it wished.[316] The Piedmont and Cumberland Railroad approached the basin from the other direction and easily gained the consent of the canal board to build its tracks across the waterway to a connection with the basin wharf.[317]

The canal company received considerably less benefit from the completion of the two feeder lines to the Baltimore & Ohio, although their completion had been encouraged by the board's promise in 1880 to grant special rates for coal shipped over it from these lines. In 1882 the West Virginia Central and Pittsburgh Railroad was completed from a point near Bloomington on the Baltimore & Ohio trunk to Fairfax Stone at the Elk Garden coal fields some 13 miles distant. Soon 800 tons of coal were being shipped over this line per day, and it was expected by the canal board to become one of the largest carriers of the Cumberland coal.[318] At about the same time the Potomac and Piedmont Railroad completed its line from a point between Piedmont and Bloomington up the North Branch some 11 miles to the Big Vein at the Elk Garden coal fields.[319] Both these lines undoubtedly contributed to the increase of the canal trade to over 707,000 tons in 1883, but the freight wars, miners' strikes and general stagnation of business caused their contribution to the canal's coal trade to decline markedly after that.

One other bright spot in the otherwise bleak coal trade during the 1880s was the emergence of Williamsport as an important coal shipping point. The amount of coal shipped to that town increased sharply in 1883 from a previous annual average tonnage of 37,000 tons to nearly 63,000 tons. The two coal companies whose shipments accounted for much of this increase were the Consolidation Coal Company and the National Coal Company. In 1884 more than 76,000 tons of coal were shipped to that town. Despite the continuing decline in the overall coal trade on the canal, the amount transported to Williamsport remained at a high level, falling somewhat to 55,000 and 53,000 tons in 1885 and 1886 but then rising to more than 72,000 tons in 1888.[320]

The financial condition of the company improved somewhat in 1887 and 1888. Coal tonnage declined but slightly from 295,415 tons in 1886 to 277,688 tons in 1887 and 286,183 tons in 1888. On the strength of higher tolls, revenues from that source actually increased from $81,718.73 in 1886 to $110,667.83 in 1887 and $121,218.27 in 1888.[321] For the first time the board made a distinction in toll charges between coal destined for the District cities market in which there would be less rivalry and that which was intended for transshipment to Eastern markets. The directors fixed the rate for the latter at 30 cents a ton from Cumberland to Georgetown while locally consumed coal paid 36 cents a ton in 1887 and 44 cents a ton in 1888.[322] This strategy to top the coastwise coal trade came to naught because of a great shortage of coasting vessels at Georgetown. The shippers at that port had been outmaneuvered by their counterparts at Philadelphia, Newport News and Norfolk in contracting for the available coasting ships. The canal directors estimated that this problem had deprived them of 100,000 tons of coal trade.[323]

Even had the canal been able to reach tonnage expectations, the tolls and the quantity of trade still would have been too low to produce revenues or profits on the scale of those in the prosperous early 1870s. The company continued to have insufficient funds for the ordinary expenses of operating the waterway and for the payment of interest on the repair bonds.[324]

---

[316] *Proceedings of the President and Board of Directors*, N, 376.
[317] *Ibid*, N, 345-346.
[318] *Fifty-Fourth Annual Report* (1882), 9-10.
[319] *Ibid*.
[320] *Fifty-Sixth Annual Report* (1884), 16-17 and Appendix L.
[321] See Appendix R.
[322] *Proceedings of the President and Board of Directors*, N, 360, 372.
[323] *Sixty-First Annual Report* (1889), C & O Co., 7.
[324] *Ibid*, N, 392.

End of the Canal as an Independent Carrier

The year 1889 witnessed a series of problems that ended the independent existence of the canal. A large break in the limestone region above Shepherdstown on March 24 delayed navigation for ten days. This was followed on April 2 by a heavy rock slide at the deep cut near the lower end of Paw Paw Tunnel that suspended navigation of 16 days. As a result, only 55,887 tons of coal (producing $20,500.34 in toll revenue) had been transported by May 30, when the highest flood in the history of the valley swept down the Potomac and left the canal a total wreck.[325] Because of the extensive destruction to the waterway, navigation was suspended for more than two years.

---

[325] *Sixty-Second Annual Report* (1890), in Receivership Papers, Washington County Courthouse, Hagerstown

III: COMMERCE ON THE
CHESAPEAKE & OHIO CANAL: 1891–1924

A. RESUMPTION OF TRADE: 1891–1894

After the canal had been left idle in disrepair for more than a year after the titanic flood of 1889, an effort was made to ascertain if there was any reason to repair the waterway. As part of this program, the Cumberland coal companies were approached as to their interest in shipping coal on the canal if it was restored. In response, four companies indicated that they would ship a total of 450,000 tons of coal annually for a period of four years after the canal was reopened. The companies and their promised shipments were as follows:

Consolidation Coal Company	200,000
Georges Creek Coal & Iron Company	150,000
Barton & Georges Creek Valley Company	50,000
Big Vein Coal Company	50,000
	450,000

The promises were made on the condition that: (1) the tolls from Cumberland to Georgetown would not exceed 40 cents per ton with a rebate of 10 cents per ton for coal shipped in the coastwise trade; (2) the wharfage and shipping charges at Cumberland would not exceed 4 cents per ton; and (3) boat freight from Cumberland to Georgetown would not exceed 65 cents. If the railroads raised their rates, the canal would also be allowed to do so, but if the canal navigation was interrupted the coal companies would reduce their shipments proportionately. Some of the companies, which had formerly made heavy coal shipments on the canal, such as the West Virginia Central and Pittsburgh Railroad, refused to make any promises.[326]

When the canal was reopened for business on September 1891, commerce recovered quickly, but was unable to expand beyond the low averages of the 1880s. The prolonged suspension of navigation had caused many boatmen to leave the valley or turn to other occupations, and the port facilities at Georgetown had deteriorated. While the rate of tolls established for the coal trade was that which the Cumberland coal companies had urged in June 1890, the charges were not likely to divert much of the trade from the Baltimore & Ohio to the waterway. Moreover, the low toll charges did not attract enough business to meet expenses. Thus, the canal never operated at profitable levels after 1891.[327]

The coal tonnages on the waterway in the first three years after navigation resumed never reached the totals promised by the Cumberland coal companies in June 1890. The totals for this period were:

	COAL TONNAGE	TOLL REVENUES
1891	50,533.14	
1892	265,799.08	$135,979.89
1893[328]	336,295.11	130,923.35

---

[326] *Fourth Report of District Receivers*, June 25, 1890, Receivership Papers.
[327] Report of Trustees, Jan. 30, 1894, in *Chesapeake & Ohio Canal Company vs. Western Maryland Railway Company*, Jan. 18, 1904, Maryland Court of Appeals, 109–112.
[328] Hagerstown *Daily Herald* and *Torch Light*, June 21, 1894, Receivership Papers.

B. CORPORATE DEVICES TO OPERATE THE CANAL

To enable the canal to show a profit as a court order had required, the railroad company resorted to a shadow corporation in January 1894 for the operation of the waterway. The trustees organized the Chesapeake & Ohio Transportation Company as a corporation under the Maryland laws. In return for the latter's guarantee to keep the canal in navigable condition, the transportation company agreed to provide the necessary boats to carry the trade offered and guaranteed an annual profit of $100,000. The trustees retained the right to let similar contracts to other companies if the need arose.[329]

In 1902 the receivers and the Consolidation Coal Company took another step towards the improvement of service and the efficiency of navigation by organizing the Canal Towage Company. The primary function of this enterprise was to provide economy and regularity to the operation of the waterway. To accomplish this the company supplied the boats, teams and equipment and established a regular schedule of runs. It also cut the freight rates and controlled the distribution of cargoes. For all practical purposes, this concern drove the last remaining independent boatmen off the canal since they could not compete with the company and its sponsors.[330] A comparison of receipts and expenses of independent boatmen before the organization of the Canal Towage Company and the boats operated by that company clearly demonstrates the relative disadvantage of the independent boatmen. A copy of this balance sheet follows:

TOTAL COAL TONNAGES & TOLL REVENUES COLLECTED: 1894–1924[331]			
BALANCE SHEET (PER TRIP)			
INDEPENDENT BOATMEN		CANAL TOWAGE COMPANY	
Receipts		Receipts	
90 tons @ 65¢ a ton	= $58.50	90 tons @ 45¢ a ton	= $40.50
Expenses		Expenses	
Boat Rent	$15.00	Way Bills	$4.80
Mule Hire	16.00	Feed	5.00
Way Bills	4.80		$9.80
Feed	5.00		
	$40.80		
Profit	$17.70	Profit	$30.70

There are few statistics relative to the progress of canal trade from 1894 to 1924. The available figures show the steady decline of the waterway as a coal carrier and transportation agency. The coal tonnage and toll revenues for this period are:

	COAL TONNAGE	TOLLS
1894	Unavailable	$117,622.29
1895	Unavailable	116,728.40
1896–1905	Unavailable	Unavailable
1906	Unavailable	59,840.01
1907	(approx.) 203,000	64,425.92

---

[329] Report of Trustees, Apr. 6, 1901, in *Chesapeake & Ohio Canal Company vs. Western Maryland Railway Company*, 114–116, 129.
[330] Sanderlin, *The Great National Project*, 269–270, and Washington *Evening Star*, July 11, 1905.
[331] Sanderlin, *The Great National Project*, 270.

1908	(approx.) 190,000	62,094.16
1909	183,694	59,105.66
1910	170,444	52,965.37
1911	166,463	43,924.73
1912	172,556	41,644.24
1913	176,491	41,407.71
1914	171,062	42,236.97
1915	173,997	41,271.46
1916	158,036	38,956.77
1917	151,667	40,545.74
1918	138,087	71,404.43
1919	133,529	47,346.95
1920	127,871	62,102.38
1921	66,477	42,017.33
1922	Unavailable	3,435.18
1923	56,404	31,899.32
1924[332]	Unavailable	1,215.60

C. EVALUATION OF CANAL TRADE: 1891–1924

The chief articles in the canal trade during the receivership period were coal and West Virginia limestone. Lesser amounts of wood, bark, lumber, pulpwood, railroad ties, sand and flour were transported on the waterway.[333] Of these commodities, the most important was coal, which accounted for almost the entire business on the waterway. In fact there apparently were no statistics kept for the trade other than those for coal. Most of the coal mined during this period came from the Georges Creek region near Frostburg between Piedmont and Cumberland.[334] The Consolidation Coal Company, owned by the Baltimore & Ohio, supplied over 99 percent of the business. The former transported the coal from its mines to its own wharf at the canal basin in Cumberland over the Cumberland and Pennsylvania Railroad, also owned by the Baltimore & Ohio. It shipped the coal down the canal in its own fleet of boats, operated by the Canal Towage Company. Thus, in effect, the trade on the waterway in the receivership period was limited primarily to that supplied by the Baltimore & Ohio interests for consumption in the local market.

During World War I the canal carried coal for the government proving grounds at Indian Head, Maryland, some 30 miles down the Potomac from Washington. The canal was nationalized on January 1, 1918, and placed under the Inland Waterways Commission, which operated the railroads and the coastwise and intercoastal shipping during the war emergency. The commission entered into an agreement with the Canal Towage Company to increase the delivery of coal to the boats and to facilitate the unloading of the coal at Washington and at government stations along the Potomac River. For the first time tugs regularly hauled canal boats with their coal cargoes up and down the river below tidewater. It is interesting to note that the war brought a revival of

---
[332] See Appendix
[333] Chesapeake & Ohio Canal Company Papers, 1891–1923, Duke University Library, Durham, North Carolina. Also see, Waybills (Manifests of Whole Cargo) Issued at Georgetown, 1893–1919, and Daily Reports of Boats and Cargos Arriving and Clearing and Daily Exhibits of Business Transacted, May–July and September, 1923, Chesapeake & Ohio Canal Company Records, Record Group 79, National Archives.
[334] Interview of George L. Nicholson, January 25, 1939, Misc. NPS Mss.

many of the same problems that had plagued canal trade during the Civil War–strikes, increasing wages for the boatmen and lock tenders, and draft-related manpower shortages.[335]

At no time during the receivership period did the amount of trade on the canal justify the continued operation of the waterway. In fact, the commerce continued to decline despite the growth of the Washington metropolitan area and the demands of the world war. Among the most important reasons for this decline were:

1. Lack of aggressive leadership.
2. Obsolescence of the waterway as a transportation line, of Georgetown as a port, and of the Potomac River as a channel for competitive trade.
3. Irregularity of navigation.
4. Competition of the Baltimore & Ohio Railroad.
5. Interference of navigation by the freshets of 1897, 1902, 1907 and 1914, and by occasional breaches, particularly in the lime sinks of the upper valley.[336]

The steady decline in the canal trade during the receivership period was also a reflection of the fact that the Cumberland coal region, which had often been described as inexhaustible, was almost worked out. The production of the Maryland coal reached a peak in 1907 with 5,532,628 tons, but after that the trend went downward to 4,065,239 tons in 1920 and 3,078,353 tons in 1926. Along with the reduction in coal production went a disastrous decline in the price of the coal and hence its overall value. In 1920 coal sold for $4.63 per ton at the mines, thereby making the net value of the Maryland coal $18,822,057, whereas six years later the price had decreased to $2.21 per ton, thus reducing the value of the entire Maryland coal production to $6,800,000. The miners' strike of 1922, which was a response to the steady trend downward of employment in the western Maryland mines from the peak year in 1912 when some 6,162 had worked there, was further evidence of the declining productivity of the mines. The strike itself was a virtual death-blow to the coal fields and the canal alike.[337]

D. POSSIBILITY OF TRADE AFTER 1924

The flood in the spring of 1924 provided the opportunity for the railroad to relieve itself of the expense of operating the canal. The receivers made little effort to restore the canal beyond the Georgetown Level. They authorized only enough repairs to protect what was left of the wrecked waterway and to enable them to assert that the canal could quickly be put into navigable condition if sufficient business was presented to warrant the effort. The canal was left a wreck, but technically arousing concern in which the water rents received from the Georgetown mills paid the expenses of a skeleton operating staff. For a brief period in 1928–29 the trustees considered opening the canal between Cumberland and Williamsport, and in the latter year even had studies made of the cost of such a resumption and of the amount of coal that would be needed to be shipped to justify the necessary expenditures for restoration. However, negotiations with the Cumberland coal companies

---

[335] Washington *Evening Star*, September 26, 1918.
[336] Sanderlin, *The Great National Project*, 272.
[337] Bureau of Business and Economic Research, University of Maryland, *Coal in the Maryland Economy: 1736–1965* (College Park, 1953), 2–5.

proved futile, and efforts to resume navigation on the canal ceased with the onset of the Great Depression.[338]

---

[338] Report of Trustees, 1922, 1923 and 1924; 1925 and 1926; 1927; 1928; 1930 and 1931, in Receivership Papers.

APPENDIX A

ASCENDING AND DESCENDING TRADE: 1831–1850

1831

ASCENDING		
ARTICLE	UNIT	TOTAL
Fish	Barrels	183
Salt	Barrels	901
Plaster	Tons	51½
Sundries	Variety of articles	
DESCENDING		
Tobacco	Hogsheads	30
Wheat	Bushels	4,745
Flour	Barrels	71,172
Bran, Shorts, etc.	Bushels	10,003
Rye and Chop	Bushels	446
Corn	Bushels	2,145
Corn Meal	Bushels	300
Flax and Seed	Bushels	0
Oil	Barrels	1
Hemp, Flax	Pounds	5,240
Whiskey	Barrels	1,472
Hogs	Pounds	5,000
Bacon	Pounds	1,700
Lard and Butter	Pounds	2,460
Leather	Pounds	7,790
Cement	Barrels	6
Stone	Perches	32
Coal	Bushels	906
Iron-Pig, Bar & Castings	Tons	74
Wood	Cord	0
Sundries	6,000 stand of arms[1]	

1832

(Statistics available only for February 12 to May 31)

ASCENDING		
ARTICLE	UNIT	TOTAL
Fish	Barrels	1,023
Salt	Bushels	705
Plaster	Tons	305¾

---

[1] *Fourth Annual Report* (1832), Appendix B, 20ff.

Sundries	Variety of articles	
DESCENDING		
Tobacco	Hogsheads	0
Wheat	Bushels	8,093
Flour	Barrels	91,224
Bran, Shorts	Bushels	9,002
Rye and Chop	Bushels	1,281
Corn	Bushels	1,745
Corn Meal	Bushels	0
Flax, Seed	Bushels	Oats 50 Flax 10
Oil	Barrels	2
Hemp, Flax	Pounds	8,900
Whisky	Barrels	1,631
Hogs	Pounds	9,058
Bacon	Pounds	82,500
Lard and Butter	Pounds	11,121
Leather	Pounds	0
Cement	Bushels	15
Stone	Perches	5,377
Coal	Bushels	300
Iron-Pig, Bar and Castings	Tons	21
Wood	Cords	1,407
Sundries[2]		0

[Transcribers Note: There are no entries for 1833 to 1841, see footnote 30, page 11]

1842

ASCENDING ARTICLE	UNIT	TOTAL
Salted Fish	Barrels	5,294
Plaster	Tons	3,206
Sundries	Large quantities of salt, fresh fish, lumber, laths Shingles and groceries	
DESCENDING		
Wheat	Bushels	214,569
Flour	Barrels	151,966
Corn and Oats	Bushels	59,199
Mill Offal	Bushels	46,472
Coal	Bushels	111,293
Lumber	Feet, B.M.	916,184

[2] *Fourth Annual Report* (1832), Appendix B, 20ff.

Wood	Cords	4,279
Whisky	Barrels	1,772
Pig Iron	Tons	710
Limestone	Perches	2,933
Sundries	Large quantities of apples, butter, lard, pork, lime, cement, barrel and hogshead staves.[3]	

1843

ASCENDING ARTICLE	UNIT	TOTAL
Salted Fish	Barrels	3,533
Salt	Tons	1,240
Plaster	Tons	4,259
Sundries	Quantities of fish in bulk, lumber and groceries.	
DESCENDING		
Wheat	Bushels	142,785
Flour	Barrels	156,242
Corn	Bushels	167,326
Oats	Bushels	38,930
Corn Meal	Bushels	18,942
Mill Offal	Bushels	49,672
Whisky	Barrels	3,398
Limestone	Perches	2,897
Iron Ore	Tons	411
Bituminous Coal	Tons	2,108
Wood and Bark	Cords	5,435
Pork	Pounds	50,324
Lumber	Feet, B.M.	500,000
Sundries	Hay, Straw, Fence Rails, Fruit[4]	

1844

ASCENDING ARTICLE	UNIT	TOTAL
Salted Fish	Barrels	2,075
Salt	Tons	1,295
Plaster	Tons	4,838

---

[3] *Fifteenth Annual Report* (1843), 11.
[4] *Sixteenth Annual Report* (1844), 46.

Sundries	Considerable quantities of fruit, potatoes, turnips, hay, straw, shingles, laths, coopers' stuff and groceries	
DESCENDING		
Wheat	Bushels	199,620
Flour	Barrels	172,796
Whiskey	Barrels	4,811
Corn	Bushels	173,023
Oats	Bushels	39,000
Corn Meal	Bushels	15,631
Bran, Mill Offal	Bushels	76,683
Wood	Cords	6,802
Lime	Tons	1,118
Limestone	Perches	6,127
Coal	Tons	4,871
Pig Iron	Tons	443
Lumber	Feet, B.M.	Approx. 1,000,000
Sundries	Considerable quantities of fruit, potatoes, turnips, hay straw, shingles, laths, coopers' stuff and groceries.[5]	

1845

ASCENDING		
ARTICLE	UNIT	TOTAL
Salted Fish	Barrels	4,569
Salt	Tons	1,265
Plaster	Tons	4,721
Lumber	Feet, B.M.	820,000
Shad & Herring (fresh)	Tons	635
Coal	Tons	332
Flour	Barrels	102
Whiskey	Barrels	141
Lime	Tons	21
Potatoes	Bushels	2,511
Iron	Tons	54
Bricks	Number	118,225
Wheat	Bushels	1,708
Flax, Seed	Bushels	21
Oysters	Bushels	1,351
Oats	Bushels	80
Apples	Bushels	22

---

[5] *Seventeenth Annual Report* (1845), 32–33.

Sundries	Tons	589
DESCENDING		
Wheat	Bushels	299,607
Flour	Barrels	170,464
Corn	Bushels	126,799
Oats	Bushels	35,464
Corn Meal	Bushels	16,327
Mill Offal	Bushels	38,575
Whiskey	Barrels	5,396
Apples	Bushels	2,685
Lime	Tons	1,115
Limestone	Perches	2,996
Pork	Pounds	15,250
Bacon	Pounds	547
Lard and Butter	Pounds	5,771
Coal, Bituminous	Tons	2,376
Iron	Tons	515
Wood	Cords	5,411
Flax, Seed	Bushels	2,577
Cement	Tons	42
Lumber	Feet, B.M.	508,083
Potatoes	Bushels	1,115
Stone	Perches	12,060[6]

1846

ASCENDING ARTICLE	UNIT	TOTAL
Salted Fish	Barrels	3,475
Salt	Tons	950
Plaster	Tons	3,839
Lumber	Feet, B.M.	1,061,855
Shad & Herrings (fresh)	Tons	406
Coal	Tons	1,003
Flour	Barrels	133
Whiskey	Barrels	20
Lime	Tons	41
Potatoes	Bushels	1,526
Iron	Tons	361
Bricks	Number	440,946
Flax, Seed	Bushels	19
Oysters	Bushels	598
Corn	Bushels	677

---

[6] *Eighteenth Annual Report* (1846), 38–39.

Mill Offal	Bushels	707
Wood, Bark	Cords	90
Cement	Tons	17
Iron Ore	Tons	410
Bacon	Pounds	5,700
Lard and Butter	Pounds	64,960
Nails	Kegs	128
Tobacco	Hogsheads	52
Rails	Rails	887
Sundries	Tons	1,265

Equivalent to 10,986 tons.

1846 (Continued)

DESCENDING	UNITS	TOTAL
Wheat	Bushels	264,115
Flour	Barrels	234,539
Corn	Bushels	30,005
Oats	Bushels	30,047
Rye	Bushels	501
Corn Meal	Bushels	8,437
Mill Offal	Bushels	63,486
Apples	Bushels	8,158
Whiskey	Barrels	1,952
Lime	Tons	958
Limestone	Perches	3,316
Stone	Perches	117
Bacon and Pork	Pounds	27,047
Lard and Butter	Pounds	4,257
Bituminous Coal	Tons	1,952
Iron	Tons	376
Iron Ore	Tons	298
Wood	Cords	4,999
Bark	Tons	286
Lumber	Feet, B.M.	2,851,541
Flax, Seed	Bushels	393
Potatoes	Bushels	3,021
Nails	Kegs	4,739
Cement	Barrels	1,105
Hay	Tons	109
Bricks	Number	17,500
Rails	Number	7,378
Shingles, Staves, Laths	Number	297,025
Tobacco	Hogsheads	92
Sundries	Tons	362[7]

---

[7] *Nineteenth Annual Report* (1847), 21–22.

Descending: Equivalent to 49,161 tons
Ascending: Equivalent to 10,986 tons
Total: 60,147 tons

1847

ASCENDING		
ARTICLE	UNIT	TOTAL
Salted Fish	Barrels	3,732
Salt	Tons	988
Plaster	Tons	3,829
Lumber	Feet, B.M.	770,300
Shad, Herring (fresh)	Tons	626
Coal	Tons	1,687
Flour	Barrels	115
Whiskey	Barrels	11
Lime	Tons	19
Potatoes	Bushels	1,112
Iron	Tons	104
Bricks	Tons	178,000
Flax, Seeds	Bushels	112
Oysters	Bushels	919
Corn Meal	Bushels	464
Mill Offal	Bushels	3,362
Wood, Bark	Cords	72
Iron Ore	Tons	3,009
Bacon	Pounds	9,300
Nails	Kegs	202
Round Timber	Tons	212
Dry Goods, Groceries Sundries	Tons	924

Equivalent to 12,809 tons

1847 (Continued)

DESCENDING	UNITS	TOTAL
Wheat	Bushels	235,212
Flour	Barrels	176,789
Corn	Bushels	238,216
Oats	Bushels	32,035
Rye	Bushels	5,108
Corn Meal	Bushels	17,958
Mill Offal	Bushels	87,644
Apples	Bushels	1,833
Whiskey	Barrels	1,867
Lime	Tons	1,180
Limestone	Perches	5,499

Wrought Stone	Perches	5,656
Bacon, Pork	Pounds	26,965
Butter, Lard	Pounds	2,843
Coal	Tons	2,170
Iron	Tons	1,078
Wood	Cords	5,450
Bark	Cords	954
Lumber	Feet, B. M.	1,583,600
Flax, Seeds	Bushels	1,197
Potatoes	Bushels	2,459
Nails	Kegs	11,892
Cement	Barrels	2,800
Hay	Tons	195
Bricks	Tons	45,500
Round Timber	Tons	107
Shingles, Staves, Laths, Hoop-Poles	Tons	955,525
Tobacco	Hogsheads	103
Sundries	Tons	526[8]

Descending: Equivalent to 58,631 tons
Ascending: Equivalent to 12,809 tons
Total: 71,440 tons

1848

ASCENDING		
ARTICLE	UNIT	TOTAL
Salted Fish	Barrels	3,477
Salt	Tons	2,133
Plaster	Tons	7,310
Coal	Tons	880
Shad, Herring (fresh)	Tons	535
Lumber	Feet, B.M.	1,391,000
Lime	Tons	61
Iron	Tons	41
Iron Ore	Tons	2,575
Flour	Barrels	155
Potatoes	Bushels	856
Corn Meal	Bushels	59
Mill Offal	Bushels	278
Oysters	Bushels	4,700
Bricks	Number	22,000
Dry Goods, Groceries, Sundries	Tons	1,010

Equivalent to 16,439 tons

---

[8] *Twentieth Annual Report* (1848), 25, 26.

1848 (Continued)

DESCENDING	UNITS	TOTAL
Wheat	Bushels	220,025
Flour	Barrels	217,112
Corn	Bushels	144,103
Corn Meal	Bushels	7,266
Rye	Bushels	360
Oats	Bushels	12,959
Mill Offal	Bushels	77,553
Flax, Seed	Bushels	852
Potatoes	Bushels	2,135
Apples	Bushels	7,776
Whiskey	Barrels	2,213
Cement	Barrels	1,744
Limestone	Perches	10,030
Rough Stone	Perches	8,879
Lime	Tons	1,366
Coal	Tons	3,284
Iron	Tons	559
Iron Ore	Tons	63
Hay	Tons	95
Nails	Kegs	8,358
Tobacco	Hogsheads	38
Wood	Cords	6,904
Bark	Cords	1,364
Lumber	Feet, B.M.	2,080,600
Shingles, Staves, Laths, Hoop-Poles	Number	993,100
Rails	Number	5,425
Round Timber	Tons	227
Bricks	Number	10,000
Sundries	Tons	685[9]

Descending: Equivalent to 69,997 tons
Ascending: Equivalent to 16,439 tons
Total: 86,436 tons

1849

ASCENDING ARTICLE	UNIT	TOTAL
Salted Fish	Barrels	3,995
Salt	Tons	2,019
Plaster	Tons	6,599

---

[9] *Twenty-First Annual Report* (1849), 32–33.

Coal	Tons	1,236
Coke	Tons	2,854
Shad and Herring	Tons	434
Lime and Cement	Tons	140
Iron Ore	Tons	4,025
Manures	Tons	324
Bricks	Number	42,000
Lumber	Feet, B.M.	1,617,000
Dry Goods, Groceries, Sundries	Tons	946

Equivalent to 20,778 tons

1849 (Continued)

DESCENDING	UNITS	TOTAL
Wheat	Bushels	240,073
Flour	Barrels	236,620
Corn	Bushels	244,281
Corn Meal	Bushels	7,225
Rye	Bushels	1,795
Oats	Bushels	13,200
Mill Offal	Bushels	45,423
Flax, Seed	Bushels	1,643
Potatoes	Bushels	1,440
Apples	Bushels	12,970
Whiskey	Barrels	2,674
Cement	Barrels	1,382
Limestone	Perches	8,662
Stone (rough)	Perches	17,750
Lime	Tons	723
Coal, Bituminous	Tons	5,224
Iron	Tons	1,351
Hay	Tons	147
Tobacco	Hogsheads	200
Nails	Kegs	3,682
Wood	Cords	5,083
Bark	Cords	1,076
Lumber	Feet, B.M.	1,560,956
Shingles, Staves, Laths, Hoop-Poles	Number	783,800
Rails	Number	3,906
Bricks	Number	39,000
Manures	Tons	324
Sundries	Tons	747[10]

Descending: Equivalent to 81,263 tons

---

[10] *Twenty-Second Annual Report* (1850), 23–24.

Ascending: Equivalent to 20,778 tons
Total: 102,041 tons

1850

ASCENDING		
ARTICLE	UNIT	TOTAL
Ale, Beer, Cider	Tons	11
Liquors, Wines	Tons	45
Fish, Salted & Fresh	Tons	758
Flour, Meal, Grains, Seeds	Tons	89
Bacon, Meats	Tons	15
Furniture, Empty Barrels	Tons	238
Horses, Livestock	Tons	1
Wrought Stone	Tons	56
Hardware, Nails, Wrought Iron	Tons	85
Tar, Pitch, Rosin	Tons	18
Dry Goods	Tons	66
Groceries	Tons	643
Mill Offal	Tons	18
Potatoes, Turnips	Tons	142
Wagons, Carts, Plows	Tons	5
Iron Castings, Bloom Iron	Tons	43
Oysters	Tons	61
Salt	Tons	1,607
Lumber, Laths, Palings, Shingles, Hoop-Poles	Tons	1,249
Pig and Scrap Iron	Tons	157
Slates, Tiles	Tons	65
Bricks	Tons	61
Lime, Cement	Tons	121
Rough Stone	Perches	19
Rails, Posts, Timber	Tons	12
Ore	Tons	7,455
Coal	Tons	1,783
Coke	Tons	2,205
Wood	Cords	85
Plaster	Tons	5,334
Manures	Tons	561
Sundries	Tons	253
		23,261

1850 (Continued)

DESCENDING	UNITS	TOTAL
Flour	Tons	27,120
Corn Meal, Chop	Tons	72

Wheat	Tons	5,318
Corn	Tons	1,726
Rye, Grain, Seeds	Tons	18
Apples, Fruit	Tons	80
Ale, Beer, Cider, Vinegar	Tons	4
Whiskey	Tons	412
Tobacco	Tons	28
Flax, Hemp, Sumac	Tons	1
Bacon, Meats	Tons	11
Butter, Lard	Tons	21
Furniture, Empty Barrels	Tons	54
Wrought Mill, Grindstones	Tons	3
Nails	Tons	601
Livestock	Tons	2
Mill Offal	Tons	720
Potatoes, Turnips	Tons	24
Bloom, Cast Iron	Tons	65
Hay, Straw	Tons	233
Oats	Tons	166
Lumber, Laths, Palings, Staves, Hoop-Poles	Tons	2,765
Pig, Scrap Iron	Tons	1,196
Bricks	Tons	15
Rough Stone	Perches	13,303
Lime, Cement	Tons	982
Rails, Posts, Timber	Tons	108
Coal	Tons	7,956
Bark	Cords	711
Wood	Cords	4,275
Manures	Tons	339
Limestone	Perches	10,234
Sundries[11]	Tons	126

Descending: Equivalent to 78,689 tons
Ascending: Equivalent to 23,261 tons
Total: 101,950 t

---

[11] *Report to the Stockholders on the Completion of the Canal* (1851), 141–142

APPENDIX B

ASCENDING TRADE: 1851–1878

		1851	1852	1853	1854	1855	1856	1857	1858	1859	1860	1861
1	Ale, Beer, Cider	33	4	0	8	3	0	0	0	0	0	0
2	Liquors, Wines	214	84	62	52	55	58	28	71	36	17	22
3	Fish, salt & fresh	1,335	455	1,387	1,054	981	960	490	217	248	322	139
4	Flour, meal, grains, seeds	204	137	99	316	613	252	362	244	508	942	674
5	Bacon, meats	28	14	17	16	25	8	8	0	0	0	0
6	Furniture, empty barrels	268	270	326	145	201	161	177	82	43	48	69
7	Horses, livestock	2	0	0	0	0	0	0	0	0	0	0
8	Wrought stone	164	38	34	2	14	0	5	398	41	0	0
9	Hardware, wrought iron, nails	171	199	132	49	65	82	32	29	4	0	0
10	Tar, pitch, rosin	27	26		14	14	12	0	0	4	3	0
11	Dry goods	199	80	79	97	0	0	0	0	0	0	0
12	Groceries	642	402	658	543	473	356	195	178	220	74	58
13	Mill offal	2	0	0	0	37	10	8	0	0	0	0
14	Potatoes, turnips	45	48	63	40	45	19	10	38	37	7	0
15	Wagons, carts, plows	18	5	23	19	11	0	3	0	0	0	0
16	Iron castings, bloom iron	65	8	28	43	47	140	22	0	11	67	15
17	Oysters	63	53	53	9	58	16	18	39	38	6	0
18	Hay, straw, oats	10	41	0	4	11	0	0	16	0	0	7
19	Salt	2,263	2,851	2,433	1,852	2,342	1,762	1,539	1,945	1,556	1,385	604
20	Lumber, laths, palings, etc.	1,534	1,484	1,983	1,494	1,748	1,679	1,366	884	947	853	143

		1851	1852	1853	1854	1855	1856	1857	1858	1859	1860	1861
21	Pig and scrap iron	295	51	48	309	20	151	584	0	0	0	0
22	Slates, tiles	0	0	0	0	0	0	0	0	0	0	0
23	Bricks	167	46	435	72	4,629	138	4,827	2,833	40	455	0
24	Lime, cement	130	18	156	51	436	37	2,050	8,344	59	758	0
25	Rough stone (perches)	119	0	0	20	110	0	0	1,433	0	95	0
26	Rails, posts, timber	144	20	0	9	0	27	0	0	0	0	0
27	Ore	5,239	2,715	5,074	5,220	3,721	3,903	3,069	190	0	0	0
28	Coal	109	206	238	467	241	135	183	670	326	235	0
29	Coke	955	0	0	145	160	0	340	0	0	0	0
30	Bark (cords)	0	0	0	0	0	0	0	0	0	0	0
31	Wood (cords)	32	75	140	0	50	0	50	0	0	0	0
32	Plaster	6,567	5,489	6,390	3,298	3,774	2,276	2,136	2,813	2,735	2,241	856
33	Manures	1,079	1,325	1,410	3,302	3,031	2,297	1,300	1,504	1,739	1,898	643
34	Sand	630	0	0	0	1,831	527	2,323	7,365	0	417	0
35	Hides	0	0	0	0	0	0	0	0	0	0	0
36	Ashes	0	0	0	0	0	0	0	0	0	0	0
37	Timber	0	0	0	0	0	0	0	0	0	0	0
38	Sundries	198	82	227	74	93	22	27	103	38	76	20
39	TOTAL	22,951	16,226	21,495	18,724	24,839	15,028	21,152	29,396	8,630	9,899	3,250

ASCENDING TRADE: 1851–1878 (Continued)

		1862	1863	1864	1865	1866	1867	1868	1869	1870	1871	1872
1	Ale, Beer, Cider	0	0	0	0	0	0	2	57	18	22	9
2	Liquors, Wines	8	20	0	0	0	0	0	0	0	0	0
3	Fish, salt & fresh	162	200	110	104	172	277	240	297	169	305	250
4	Flour, meal, grains, seeds	33	21	49	100	361	128	131	158	122	149	209
5	Bacon, meats	0	0	0	0	0	0	50	15	28	14	5
6	Furniture, empty barrels	118	39	17	47	100	139	173	91	184	523	270
7	Horses, livestock	0	0	0	0	0	0	0	0	3	1	0
8	Wrought stone	0	0	0	0	0	0	2	24	5	84	90
9	Hardware, wrought iron, nails	0	0	0	0	0	0	20	0	24	21	164
10	Tar, pitch, rosin	0	0	0	0	0	0	17	0	8	28	2

11	Dry goods	0	0	0	0	0	0	315	193	266	258	223
12	Groceries	166	46	5	0	0	0	21	0	0	0	17
13	Mill offal	0	0	0	0	0	0	8	24	8	46	23
14	Potatoes, turnips	9	46	0	0	0	0	6	4	4	0	0
15	Wagons, carts, plows	0	0	0	0	0	0	172	97	41	34	17
16	Iron castings, bloom iron	0	38	0	0	0	0	24	479	115	27	7
17	Oysters	0	0	0	0	0	0	10	0	3	4	9
18	Hay, straw, oats	0	0	0	0	0	0	0	6	4	45	1,418
19	Salt	478	535	545	498	873	794	1,362	1,280	1,296	2,043	1,014
20	Lumber, laths, palings, etc.	131	102	207	543	607	705	975	1,923	933	1,929	1,028
21	Pig and scrap iron	0	354	0	0	0	0	40	0	0	6	18
22	Slates, tiles	0	0	0	0	0	0	0	0	0	0	0
23	Bricks	0	50	24	0	6	146	28	18	96	201	67
24	Lime, cement	81	25	19	0	51	50	126	90	43	49	34
25	Rough stone (perches)	0	0	0	0	0	0	0	4	0	3	0
26	Rails, posts, timber	0	0	0	0	0	0	19	8	9	37	2
27	Ore	0	0	0	0	2,478	5,067	2,618	7,000	5,801	8,960	11,090
28	Coal	61	80	10	0	90	147	120	262	177	192	233
29	Coke	0	0	0	0	0	0	0	11	0	0	0
		1862	1863	1864	1865	1866	1867	1868	1869	1870	1871	1872
30	Bark (cords)	0	0	0	0	0	0	0	0	0	0	2
31	Wood (cords)	0	0	0	0	0	0	171	298	0	0	70
32	Plaster	274	574	382	664	682	1,328	1,181	792	879	943	379
33	Manures	1,029	632	477	647	1,062	959	1,845	1,476	913	1,780	1,482
34	Sand	0	80	0	0	0	0	234	1,164	867	672	1,484
35	Hides	0	0	0	0	0	234	396	345	528	2	0
36	Ashes	0	0	0	0	0	0	113	91	0	99	428
37	Timber	0	0	0	0	0	0	30	4	153	22	3
38	Sundries & Ice	53	94	46	104	166	186	30	29	22	53	13
39	TOTAL	2,603	2,936	1,891	2,707	6,648	10,160	10,479	14,238	12,719	18,552	20,060

ASCENDING TRADE: 1851–1878 (Continued)

		1873	1874	1875	1876	1877	1878
1	Ale, Beer, Cider	22	3	3	7		
2	Liquors, Wines	0	0	0	0	0	0
3	Fish, salt & fresh	245	149	51	44	54	13
4	Flour, meal, grains, seeds	126	90	475	235		
5	Bacon, meats	1	6	5	5		
6	Furniture, empty barrels	255	260	283	221		

7	Horses, livestock	0	0	2	4		
8	Wrought stone	3	0	8	3		
9	Hardware, wrought iron, nails	1	1	7	13		
10	Tar, pitch, rosin	0	43	1	0		
11	Dry goods	236	169	169	97		
12	Groceries	0	0	0	0		
13	Mill offal	20	6	31	4		
14	Potatoes, turnips	0	0	0	0		
15	Wagons, carts, plows	13	6	10	16		
16	Iron castings, bloom iron	0	4	0	0		
17	Oysters	6	9	6	2		
18	Hay, straw, oats	690	235	77	364		
19	Salt	1,906	1,157	1,164	790	711	791
20	Lumber, laths, palings, etc.	1,147	627	443	347		
21	Pig and scrap iron	23	10	0	2		
22	Slates, tiles	0	5	52	1		
23	Bricks	162	149	14	46		
24	Lime, cement	47	29	121	157		
25	Rough stone (perches)	0	30	9	14		
26	Rails, posts, timber	50	29	25	65		
27	Ore	8,458	6,380	2,560	0		
28	Coal	280	295	241	530		
29	Coke	0	0	0	12		
30	Bark (cords)	0	0	4	0		
		1873	1874	1875	1876	1877	1878
31	Wood (cords)	0	25	55	64		
32	Plaster	1,610	1,883	2,075	2,484	4,975	3,446
33	Manures	418	1,552	1,633	1,981	1,219	2,511
34	Sand	414	694	295	4		
35	Ice & Hides	0	75	416	26		
36	Corn, (in ear)	119	31	20	2		
37	Apples, Melons, etc.	0	14	51	6		
38	Sundries	19	12	32	162		
39	TOTAL	16,271	13,978	10,338	7,711	6,959	6,761[12]

---

[12] Annual Reports, Statements of Articles Transported, 1850–78, C & O Co

APPENDIX C

DESCENDING TRADE: 1851-1878

		1851	1852	1853	1854	1855	1856	1857	1858	1859	1860
1	Flour	25,761	26,755	25,602	15,643	14,240	14,853	10,967	11,007	12,106	11,087
2	Corn Meal, Chop	317	199	204	136	33	41	95	68	79	31
3	Wheat	6,861	9,805	9,966	5,417	6,986	9,017	3,750	4,402	5,531	5,452
4	Corn	5,783	4,755	8,327	2,618	628	6,893	5,592	6,275	4,931	3,048
5	Rye, grains, seeds	111	98	111	39	12	58	10	329	79	35
6	Apples, fruit	29	99	68	18	55	615	71	20	5	0
7	Ale, beer, cider, vinegar	4	16	0	0	0	0	0	0	0	0
8	Whiskey	432	450	326	250	133	242	248	293	160	51
9	Tobacco	44	25	56	11	2	3	0	3	12	11
10	Flax, hemp. Sumac	14	13	14	10	1	0	0	25	24	0
11	Bacon, meats	84	25	96	13	77	66	0	29	0	0
12	Butter, lard	12	21	31	17	18	0	0	0	0	0
13	Furniture, empty barrels	297	199	349	297	295	414	82	92	99	150
14	Wrought mill, grindstones	1	0	3	1	3	120	0	0	0	0
15	Wrought iron, hardware	25	7	4	4	11	0	0	0	742	0
16	Nails	645	108	159	56	0	0	00	0	0	0
17	Livestock	8	0	0	10	6	0	0	0	0	0
18	Mill offal	994	832	1,131	533	388	425	288	549	391	518
19	Potatoes, turnips	114	27	66	71	2	0	21	22	12	12
20	Bloom, cast iron	4	8	94	68	9	43	8	561	0	1,266
21	Hay, straw	276	143	470	318	226	104	137	102	253	227
22	Oats	262	116	113	77	77	158	160	228	261	205
23	Lumber, laths, palings,	2,736	2,640	3,606	2,588	3,051	3,209	1,847	2.669	2,810	0

14	Wrought mill, grindstones	0	0	0	0	0	0	0	0	0
15	Wrought iron, hardware	0	0	0	0	0	0	0	0	0
16	Nails	0	0	0	0	0	0	0	0	0
17	Livestock	0	0	0	0	0	0	0	5	1
18	Mill offal	520	534	395	254	250	228	217	211	205
19	Potatoes, turnips	0	0	7	53	0	0	0	64	0
20	Bloom, cast iron	0	0	0	0	0	17	0	46	0
21	Hay, straw	236	175	165	417	265	221	35	42	12
22	Oats	205	40	44	623	87	162	162	92	99
23	Lumber, laths, palings,	1,994	1,693	1,403	1,248	1,216		3051	2,936	1,097
24	Charcoal	0	0	0	0	0	0	0	101	26
25	Pig, scrap iron	50	0	1,103	237	292	612	1,785	2,225	3,782
26	Bricks	72	499	87	378	0	340	404	3,057	1,145
27	Rough stone (perches)	2,852	760	19	390	2,900	589	2,970	4,503	4,161
28	Lime, cement	467	49	794	601	1,004	2,080	3,143	1,975	1,985
29	Rails, posts, timber	35	15	80	93	0	0	0	131	54
		1861	1862	1863	1864	1865	1866	1867	1868	1869
30	Ore	0	0	0	0	0	108	0	2,236	360
31	Coal	119,893	94,819	229,416	260,368	340,736	344,160	458,009	484,849	661,828
32	Coke	0	0	0	0	0	359	0	0	0
33	Bark (cords)	97	335	647	837	544	1,115	705	980	1,104
34	Wood (cords)	3,773	8,025	4,513	3,888	3,971	2,900	1,931	2,016	2,492
35	Manures	70	0	0	0	0	0	0	48	1
36	Limestone (perches)	642	1,936	4,650	4,727	6,386	7,845	10,091	16,148	11,204
37	Sand	416	0	0	315	0	0	4,208	2,265	40
38	Sundries & Ice	53	182	74	120	50	28	90	552	190
39	Descending TOTAL	144,814	124,190	262,911	288,881	369,628	376,750	511,242	541,508	709,700
	Ascending TOTAL	8,250	2,603	2,936	1,891	2,707	6,658	10,160	10,479	14,238
	Aggregate TOTAL	148,064	126,793	265,847	290,772	372,335	383,408	521,402	552,987	723,938

DESCENDING TRADE: 1851–1878 (Continued)

		1870	1871	1872	1873	1874	1875	1876	1877	1878
1	Flour	1,845	2,025	980	1,744	1,526	1,000	734	519	634
2	Corn Meal & Chop	299	108	177	4	4	19	291		
3	Wheat	11,710	14,369	8,416	8,569	9,780	8,894	11,754	10,048	14,005
4	Corn	2,929	5,005	3,844	3,285	5,312	3,553	6,723	5,382	2,489
5	Rye, grains, seeds	58	62	197	67	107	73	166		
6	Apples, fruit	102	74	135	46	24	56	11		
7	Ale, beer, cider, vinegar	13	5	31	4	39	10	6		
8	Whiskey	17	14	2	0	0	0	0		
9	Tobacco	0	2	0	0	0	0	0		

10	Flax, hemp. Sumac	81	158	136	11	111	289	208	
11	Bacon & other meats	0	10	5	1	6	0	1	
12	Butter, lard	2	5	0	0	0	0	0	
13	Furniture, empty barrels	22	76	79	57	41	147	32	
14	Wrought mill, grindstones	20	252	361	0	1,601	700	0	.
15	Wrought iron, hardware	1	4	59	0	5	2	1	
16	Nails	2	0	0	0	0	0	0	
17	Livestock	0	3	9	1	5	30	19	
18	Mill offal	254	239	75	390	233	70	157	
19	Potatoes, turnips	8	23	6	0	0	0	31	
20	Iron, bloom and cast	3	10	27	20	4	14	17	
21	Hay, straw	67	220	235	192	215	153	127	
22	Oats	196	109	27	74	67	25	52	
23	Lumber, laths, palings,	968	2,410	1,761	1,582	1,102	1,270	1,696	353	1,665
24	Charcoal, Ice, Fire Clay	74	1,200	1,850	26	0	39	0	
25	Iron, pig & scrap	1,833	4,247	3,730	1,874	3,053	669	172	
26	Sand		245	751			142		
27	Bricks	4,073	23,840	12,308	4,086	1,303	2,456	0	
28	Rough stone (perches)	4,133	15,177	31,243	15,994	12,146	11,462	6,416	4,357	1,364
29	Lime, cement	608	9,473	4,970	4,700	5,602	7,596	1,533	4,478	12,151
		1870	1871	1872	1873	1874	1875	1876	1877	1878
30	Rails, posts, timber	0	75	618	237	87	319	1,751	
31	Wagons, Coke, Ice	0	1	0	0	60	2.965	438	
32	Coal	696,707	848.199	814,335	796,717	836,996	904,898	654,409	623,096	630,292
33	Plaster, Coal Anthracite	0	70	102	10		152		
34	Bark (cords)	161	4,501	1,370	434	275	462	0	
35	Wood (cords)	2,289	3,635	2,499	4,336	1,349	1,077	292	
36	Manures	0	30	51	145	1,198	44	1,008	
37	Limestone (perches)	10,451	14,145	12,916	12,868	13,666	14,559	28	
38	Leather or Ore	82	4	64	200	0	253	13,191	
39	Sundries	25	250	42		55	69	90	
40	Descending TOTAL	649,053	950,275	903,521	864,359	895,981	963,467	701,419	
	Ascending TOTAL	12,719	18,552	20,060	16,271	13,978	10,338	7,711	6,959	6,761
	Aggregate TOTAL	661,772	968,827	923,581	880,630	909,959	973,805	709,130	

APPENDIX D

TOLLS COLLECTED 1830–1850

TOLLS COLLECTED ON POTOMAC RIVER AND POTOMAC COMPANY WORKS

JUNE 1828 TO OCTOBER 31, 1830	$33,281.26
OCTOBER 31, 1830 TO DECEMBER 31, 1830	142.61
TOTAL	$33,423.87

TOLLS COLLECTED ON CHESAPEAKE & OHIO CANAL

	ASCENDING	DESCENDING	TOTAL
1830			$2,044.36
1831			32,992.66
1832			24,976.02
1833			16,663.49
1834			20,131.62
1835			26,568.15
1836			28,769.33
1837			26,702.49
1838			34,958.55
1839			47,865.94
1840			43,808.02
1841			57,012.29
1842			56,005.80
1843			44,540.51
1844			52,674.24
1845			51,810.70
1846[13]	$6,078.81	$47,278.38	53,357.19
1847	6,774.80	45,665.55	52,440.35
1848	8,405.40	45,740.81	54,146.21
1849	9,188.84	52,634.33	61,823.17
1850[14]	9,628.21	54,813.81	64,442.02
			$853,733.11

---

[13] Prior to 1846, the tolls from the ascending and descending trade were not kept separately.
[14] *Report to the Stockholders on the Completion of the Canal*, Appendix K, 152.

APPENDIX E

TOLLS COLLECTED 1851-1889

	ASCENDING	DESCENDING	TOTAL
1851	$14,499.67	$96,004.76	$110,504.43
1852	10,846.14	81,402.76	92,248.90
1853	15,430.73	129,669.81	145,100.54
1854	12,906.48	106,399.55	119,306.03
1855	15,528.17	123,147.67	138,675.84
1856	14,306.70	138,744.66	153,051.36
1857	8,664.16	86,138.21	94,802.37
1858			171,084.91
1859			189,134.57
1860			182,343.86
1861	5,234.27	65,332.72	70,566.99
1862			63,985.85
1863			154,928.26
1864	10,690.09	215,207.25	225,897.34
1865	14,531.52	331,633.95	346,165.47
1866	15,085.78	340,574.98	355,660.76
1867	20,541.44	354,391.31	374,932.75
1868	21,717.54	255,261.17	276,978.71
1869			368,483.42
1870			342,644.40
1871	37,029.86	447,989.79	485,019.65
1872	34,646.37	424,988.22	459,654.59
1873			482,528.57
1874	33,690.82	466,725.42	500,416.24
1875			458,534.66
1876			290,274.39
1877	13,272.57	174,484.09	187,756.66
1878	14,861.98	267,319.20	282,181.18
1879	12,640.22	222,330.30	234,970.52
1880			361,757.68
1881	12,446.01	271,989.58	284,435.59
1882	7,511.84	136,218.92	143,730.76
1883	15,975.03	269,058.97	284,234.00
1884	8,249.06	127,444.53	135,693.59
1885	9,561.14	97,379.25	106,940.39
1886	7,057.92	74,660.81	81,718.73
1887			110,667.83
1888	6,609.17	114,609.08	121,218.25
1889[15]			20,500.34

---

[15] Annual Reports

APPENDIX F

TOLLS COLLECTED 1891–1924

1891	
1892	$135,979.89
1893	130,923.35
1894	117,622.29
1895	116,728.40
1896–1905[16]	
1906	59,840.01
1907	64,425.92
1908	62,094.16
1909	59,105.66
1910	52,965.37
1911	77,527.55
1912	41,644.24
1913	41,407.71
1914	42,236.97
1915	41,271.46
1916	38,956.77
1917	40,545.74
1918	71,404.43
1919	47,346.95
1920	62,102.38
1921	42,017.33
1922	3,435.18
1923	31,899.32
1924[17]	1,215.60

---

[16] No statistics available on tolls received.
[17] Tolls are given after deduction for rebates.
Source: Reports of Trustees, Sanderlin, *The Great National Project*, 308.

APPENDIX G:

CANAL TRADE 1850–1876

	TOTAL TON-NAGE	ASCEND-ING TONNAGE	DESCEND-ING TONNAGE	AVERAGE DISTANCE OF ARTICLES TRANSPORT-ED	AVERAGE TOLL PAID PER MILE	TOTAL TOLLS
1850	101,950	23,261	78,689	56 Miles	1.128	$34,442
1851	203,893	22,951	180,942	102.20	0.542	110,504.43
1852	167,595	16,226	151,369	102.50	0.554	92,248.90
1853	270,705	21,495	249,210	127.67	0.536	145,100.54
1854	235,923	18,724	217,199	132.00	0.557	119,306.03
1855	283,252	24,839	258,413	137.00	0.489	138,675.84
1856	287,836	15,028	272,808	147.50	0.566	153,051.36
1857	196,525	21,152	175,373	132.50	0.482	94,802.37
1858	353,588	29,396	324,192	133.50	0.484	171,084.91
1859	359,716	8,630	351,086	163.50	0.315	189,134.57
1860	344,532	9,999	334,533	160.00	0.315	182,343.86
1861	148,064	8,250	144,814	147.25	0.310	70,566.99
1862	126,793	2,603	124,190	147.00	0.343	63,985.85
1863	265,847	2,936	262,911	166.00	0.350	154,928.26
1864	290,772	1,891	288,881	165.00	0.452	225,897.37
1865	372,335	2,707	369,628	171.00	0.554	346,165.47
1866	383,408	6,658	376,750	169.00	0.550	355,660.76
1867	521,402	10,160	511,242	167.00	0.430	374,932.75
1868	552,987	10,479	541,508	163.00	0.320	276,978.71
1869	723,938	14,238	709,700	163.00	0.320	368,483.42
1870	661,772	12,719	649,053	161.00	0.320	342,644.40
1871	968,827	18,552	950,275	161.00	0.310	485,019.65
1872	923,581	20,060	903,521	162.00	0.307	459,654.59
1873	880,630	16,271	864,359	163.00	0.337	482,528.57
1874	909,959	13,978	895,981	165.00	0.333	500,416.24
1875	973,805	10,338	963,464	164.00	0.287	458,534.66
1876	709,130	7,711	701,419	163.00	0.239	[18]290,274.39

---

[18] Statements of Articles Transported, 1850–76, C & O Co.

APPENDIX H:

CUMBERLAND COAL TRADE: 1842–1877

	FROSTBURG REGION	PIEDMONT REGION	VIA B&O R.R.	VIA C&O CANAL	VIA PA. R.R.	TOTAL
1842	1,708		1,708			1,708
1843	10,082		10,082			10,082
1844	14,890		14,890			14,890
1845	24,653		24,653			24,653
1846	29,995		29,995			29,795
1847	52,940		52,940			52,940
1848	79,571		79,571			79,571
1849	142,449		142,449			142,449
1850	196,848		192,806	4,042		196,848
1851	257,679		174,701	82,978		257,679
1852	334,178		268,459	65,719		334,178
1853	460,254	73,725	376,219	157,760		533,979
1854	478,378	181,303	503,836	155,845		659,681
1855	369,457	292,915	478,486	183,786		662,272
1856	394,475	311,975	502,330	204,120		706,450
1857	278,490	303,996	465,912	116,574		582,486
1858	368,278	281,378	395,405	254,251		649,656
1859	418,680	305,674	426,512	297,842		724,354
1860	447,047	341,862	493,031	295,878		788,909
1861	147,460	122,214	172,075	97,599		269,674
1862	211,425	106,109	218,950	98,684		317,634
1863	445,675	302,670	531,553	216,792		748,345
1864	613,444	44,552	399,354	258,642		657,996
1865	832,150	71,345	560,293	343,202		903,495
1866	988,467	90,964	736,153	343,178		1,079,331
1867	1,121,290	72,532	735,669	458,153		1,193,822
1868	1,241,785	88,658	848,118	482,325		1,330,443
1869	1,798,945	83,724	1,230,518	653,151		1,882,669
1870	1,628,052	89,023[19]	1,112,938	604,137		1,717,075
1871	2,167,482	177,681	1,494,814	850,339		2,345,153
1872	2,148,666	206,805	1,517,347	816,103	22,021	2,355,471
1873	2,492,716	181,375	1,745,429	778,802	114,589	2,674,101
1874	2,243,754	166,636	1,576,160	767,064	67,671	2,410,895
1875	2,188,436	154,337	1,392,237	879,838	160,698	2,342,773
1876	1,718,853	116,228	1,032,285	632,440	131,866	1,835,081
1877	1,574,339		818,459[20]	584,996	170,884	1,574,339
	27,323,253	4,167,523[21]	20,739,908	10,683,240	667,729	32,090,877

[19] From 1870, this figure includes coal mined in West Virginia

[20] This figure includes 36,394 tons used on the line of the Cumberland and Pennsylvania Railroad and its branches and at Cumberland and Piedmont. Also, 94,362 tons were used by the B & O Railroad in its locomotive rolling mills, etc.

APPENDIX I:

CUMBERLAND COAL TRADE: 1872, 1873, 1874 & 1875

SHIPMENTS BY CUMBERLAND COAL COMPANIES

	1872[22]	1873[23]	1874[24]	1875[25]
Firebricks	459	19		39
Lumber	208	268		382
Other Articles	97	46		34
American Coal Company	127,740	129,387	122,649	122,612
Borden Company	107,436	109,788	111,443	182,092
Consolidated Coal Company	215,804	96,244	135,619	171,905
George's Creek Coal & Iron Co.	40,751	40,667	38,624	24,223
Hampshire & Baltimore Coal Co.	41,218	54,043	52,908	53,645
Maryland Company	60,632	110,663	157,104	195,890
New Central Company	145,976	156,340	100,179	93,036
Keystone Coal Company			4,849	
Blaen Avon Company			35,916	34,074
Atlantic Coal Company			12,060	1,413
Individuals	64,988	100,703		
Gas Coal Company			65,642	25,904
TOTAL	805,309	797,838	836,997	905,249

---

[21] Of this sum, 35,149 tons of coal were shipped to the canal via Piedmont and the B & O Railroad.
[22] *Forty-Fifth Annual Report* (1873), Table M
[23] *Forty-Sixth Annual Report* (1874), Table H
[24] *Forty-Seventh Annual Report* (1875), Table H
[25] *Forty-Eighth Annual Report* (1876), Table H

APPENDIX J:

CUMBERLAND COAL TRADE: 1872, 1873, 1874 & 1875

POINTS TO WHICH COAL SHIPMENTS WERE MADE

	1872[26]	1873[27]	1874[28]	1875[29]
Georgetown	786,951	763,403	794,241	858,673
Point of Rocks & Knoxville	589	598	304	417
Harpers Ferry	507	534	1,013	782
Antietam	10,043	4,371	6,204	1,451
Shepherdstown	3,011	3,186	2,301	1,337
Williamsport	9,599	22,367	29,395	39,435
Hancock	1,789	1,701	1,345	1,180
Berlin (Brunswick)	243	209	318	106
Monocacy & Other Points	487			227
Oldtown & Sharpsburg	331	211	167	244
Mercerville & Falling Waters	327	343	710	211
Four Locks (and Two Locks)	481	724	549	450
White's & Conrad's Ferry		185	328	271
Noland's Ferry			117	
TOTAL	814,358	797,838	836,997	904,784

---

[26] *Forty-Fifth Annual Report* (1873), Table M
[27] *Forty-Sixth Annual Report* (1874), Table H
[28] *Forty-Seventh Annual Report* (1875), Table H
[29] *Forty-Eighth Annual Report* (1876), Table H

APPENDIX K:

CUMBERLAND COAL TRADE: 1877
GENERAL COAL SHIPMENTS–1877

	TONNAGE
Fire Bricks	827.17
Lumber	291.00
Other Articles	171.10
American Company	92,044.05
Borden Company	70,542.12
Consolidated Coal Company	125,183.04
New Central Company	127,068.14
Maryland Company	99,796.13
Hampshire and Baltimore Coal Company	34,132.18
Blaen Avon Company	31,647.04
Gas Coal	22,681.04
TOTAL[30]	603,096.14

---

[30] *Fiftieth Annual Report* (1878), 24.

APPENDIX L:

CUMBERLAND COAL TRADE: 1879-1888
DESTINATIONS OF COAL SHIPMENTS

TO: Georgetown	1879	1880	1881	1882	1883	1884	1885	1886	1887	1888
American Coal Company	67,805	87,276	39,201	37,717	89,516	31,385	1,141			
Borden Mining Company	83,551	98,918	104,497	37,866	71,194	49,393	68,057	44,836	28,942	17,279
Blaen Avon Coal Co.	35,129	43,694	23,817	7,012	58,185	306	232	426		
Consolidation Coal Co.	111,232	132,133	137,093	59,891	109,871	90,133	71,757	66,458	78,136	73,371
Georges Creek Coal	14,284	38,116	37,324	14,654	92,541	62,876	93,189	67,938	84,831	106,183
Gas Coal Company	22,584		3,067	17,623						
Hampshire & Balt. Coal	15,145	3,138	14,335							
Keystone Coal Company	1,745		561	404						
Maryland Coal Company	43,274	88,204	41,093	38,068	121,916	25,739	71,754	46,852	2,561	
New Central Coal Co.	90,243	67,722	60,986	33,366	32,716	468	352			
"Gas," Sinclair Company		6,561	8,731							
Gaston Coal Company		3,947	4,288	4,001	3,926	780	3,199	2,208		
Despard Coal Company		1,485	1,548	1,501	1,482	1,528	2,061	1,841	227	
Elk Garden Company		350							6,773	
Piedmont Coal & Iron		5,755	926	474						
Buffalo Valley Company				2,252						
Cumberland & Elk Lick				3,487						
National Coal Company				3,295	13,731	4,905	219			

WV Central & Pittsburgh			12,013	12,213	20,422				
Pennsylvania Gas Co.					16,907	16,274	13,876	4146	
Rafferty Gas Company					7,386	4,137			
Bigley "Gas" Company						4,909	8,841	776	
Youghiogheny Gas Co.						3,478	3,869	3,806	
Beverly Gas Company							1,138	225	
Charles Garden Company									14,491
TOTALS	484,996	577,305	477,423	273,833	639,799	296,316	339,690	239,518	201,472	211,325

TO: Williamsport	1879	1880	1881	1882	1883	1884	1885	1886	1887	1888
Borden Mining & Coal Co.	16,824	1,302	413	117	336	111			114	111
Blaen Avon Coal Company	781	1,253	112		159					
Consolidation Coal Company	14,987	25,812	35,378	36,279	54,504	56,387	45,042	47,278	62,160	51,264
Gas Coal Co.	217		316							
Hampshire & Balt. Coal Co.	220									
Maryland Coal Co.	2,728	3,832	1,784							
New Central Coal Co.			104							
Cumberland & Elk Lick Co.		339		365						
Gas Coal Co.		344		227						
Piedmont Coal & Iron Co.				2,991						
American Coal Co.					116	4,424	4,599	5,603	1,916	
Georges Creek Coal					452		5,192	443	439	225

& Iron Co.									
Newburgh & Orrel Gas Co.		118			228	105			
National Coal Co.					7,152	15,397	645		
Elk Garden Co.									8,474	20,502
TOTALS	35,760	33,003	38,109	39,981	62,951	78,425	55,479	53,325	73,105	72,104

TO: Hancock	1879	1880	1881	1882	1883	1884	1885	1886	1887	1888
Borden Mining & Coal Co.	308	228	542		110			104	310	1,258
Blaen Avon Coal Co.	338	59	62		105	230				
Consolidation Coal Co.	772	438	757		667	225	545	328	159	112
Keystone Coal Company		84								
American Coal Co.			117	427	317	543	620	624	114	
Maryland Coal Co.			98	218						
Cumberland & Elk Lick Co.				117						
New Central Coal Co.				125						
National Coal Co.			115	115	113	320	113			
Piedmont Coal & Iron Co.				90						
Georges Creek Coal & Iron Co.					109	118	552	519	950	
Elk Garden Co.									518	652
TOTALS	1,418	811	1,577	1,095	1,424	1,438	1,832	1,576	2,053	2,023
TO: Harpers Ferry	1879	1880	1881	1882	1883	1884	1885	1886	1887	1888
Consolidation Coal Co.	331	222	180							
Piedmont Coal & Iron Co.		329								
Hampshire & Balt. Coal Co.	432									
Borden Mining & Coal Co.					81			24		
George's Creek Coal & Iron Co									121	
American Coal Co.							333		225	112
TOTALS	763	552	180	0	81	0	333	24	346	112
TO: Shepherdstown	1879	1880	1881	1882	1883	1884	1885	1886	1887	1888
Blaen Avon Coal Company	52	327				216				
Consolidation Coal Company	423	1550	2,180	540	559	561	458	535	431	565
Piedmont Coal & Iron Co.		215								
Maryland Coal Company	108	108								
Borden Mining & Coal Co.			99							

New Central Coal Company		227	110						
American Coal Company				215	1,686	2,297	113		
National Coal Company				226	337	102		102	
Elk Garden Company								99	236
Georges Creek Coal & Iron Co.					114		111	180	.334
Keystone Coal Company					210				
TOTALS	584	2,429	2,390	982	2,583	3,502	572	750	711	1,136
TO: Four Locks	1879	1880	1881	1882	1883	1884	1885	1886	1887	1888
Borden Mining & Coal Co.	333									
Consolidation Coal Co.	93									
New Central Coal Co.	113									
TOTALS	540	0	0	0	0	0	0	0	0	0
TO: Conrad's Ferry	1879	1880	1881	1882	1883	1884	1885	1886	1887	1888
Blaen Avon Coal Co.	315									
Maryland Coal Co.	101									
TOTALS	416	0	0	0	0	0	0	0	0	0
TO: Berlin (Brunswick)	1879	1880	1881	1882	1883	1884	1885	1886	1887	1888
Consolidation Coal Co.	182	325	303	180						
Big Vein (Pa.)			92							
Piedmont Coal & Iron Co.			109							
National Coal Co.					105	118				
TOTALS	182	325	505	180	105	118	0	0	0	0
TO: White's Ferry	1879	1880	1881	1882	1883	1884	1885	1886	1887	1888
Blaen Avon Coal Co.		305	646		207					
National Coal Co.				227	267	341				
TOTALS	0	305	646	227	474	341	0	0	0	0
TO: Knoxville	1879	1880	1881	1882	1883	1884	1885	1886	1887	1888
New Central Coal Co.		116	355	112						
Consolidation Coal Co.		123		118						
Piedmont Coal & Iron Co.		110		116						
TOTALS	0	350	355	347	0	0	0	0	0	0
TO: Point of Rocks	1879	1880	1881	1882	1883	1884	1885	1886	1887	1888
Blaen Avon Coal Co.					106			220		
National Coal Co.						101	103			
George's Creek Coal Co										110
TOTALS[31]	0	0	0	0	106	101	103	220	0	110

---

[31] Data derived from *Fifty-Second, Fifty-Third, Fifty-Fourth, Fifty-Fifth, Fifty-Sixth, Fifty-Seventh, Fifty-Eighth, Fifty-Ninth, Sixtieth* and *Sixty-First Annual Reports.*

APPENDIX M:

CUMBERLAND COAL TRADE: 1870–1888
NUMBER OF BOATS CLEARED WITH COAL FROM PORT OF CUMBERLAND

	BOATS	TONNAGE	AVERAGE PER BOAT
1870	5,537	606,707	109
1871	7,801	848,200	108
1872	7,412	814,365	109
1873	7,126	797,838	112
1874	7,378	836,997	113
1875	7,995	904,898	113
1876	5,700	654,409	114
1877	5,380	603,096	112
1878	5,525	630,293	114
1879	4,627	522,904	113
1880	5,464	615,423	112
1881	4,667	521,189	111
1882	2,803	316,648	113
1883	6,283	707,466	112
1884	3,378	378,352	112
1885	3,559	398,012	111
1886	2,699	295,415	109
1887	2,538	277,688	109
1888	2,518	286,813	114[32]

---

[32] *Sixty-First Annual Report* (1889), 23

APPENDIX N:

CUMBERLAND COAL TRADE: 1879–1889

COAL TONNAGE TOTALS: 1879–1889

	TONNAGE
1879	522,904
1880	615,423
1881	521,189
1882	316,648
1883	707,468
1884	378,352
1885	398,012
1886	295,415
1887	277,688
1888	286,183
1889[33]	57,079

NOTE: The canal company kept statistics only for the coal tonnage after 1878.

---

[33] SOURCE: Annual Reports, Sanderlin, *The Great National Project*, 308.

HISTORIC RESOURCE STUDY
CHESAPEAKE & OHIO CANAL NHP

9.
MANAGEMENT OF MAINTENANCE OPERATIONS ON THE C & O CANAL 1830–1924

BY HARLAN D. UNRAU
HISTORIAN, C&O CANAL RESTORATION TEAM, SENECA
DENVER SERVICE CENTER
1976

CONTENTS

I.	FIRST PROVISIONS FOR MANAGEMENT OF CANAL MAINTENANCE: 1830	539
II.	FIRST FORMAL DEVELOPMENT OF GUIDELINES FOR MANAGEMENT OF CANAL MAINTENANCE: 1831	540
III.	ESTABLISHMENT OF NEW MANAGEMENT DIVISIONS TO ACCOMMODATE WESTWARD EXPANSION OF THE CANAL: 2833–1839	545
IV.	POLITICAL INFLUENCE AND THE MANAGEMENT OF CANAL MAINTENANCE: 1840–1841	546
V.	FLUCTUATION IN MANAGEMENT OF CANAL MAINTENANCE	548
VI.	ADOPTION OF NEW BY-LAWS AND ORGANIZATIONAL ALIGNMENT TO MANAGE MAINTENANCE ON THE COMPLETED CANAL: 1850–1851	550
VII.	POLITICAL INFLUENCE DISRUPTS EFFICIENCY OF MANAGEMENT OF CANAL MAINTENANCE	556
VIII.	MANAGEMENT OF CANAL MAINTENANCE UNDER THE HEGEMONY OF THE STATE DEMOCRATIC PARTY: 1867–1889	568
IX.	MANAGEMENT OF CANAL MAINTENANCE DURING THE RECEIVERSHIP PERIOD: 1889–1934	585
X.	RESUMPTION OF REGULAR MAINTENANCE PERFORMED BY CANAL COMPANY CREWS	587

	APPENDIXES	589
A.	PROPERTY ON AND ABOUT THE 2ND DIVISION HOUSEBOAT, AUGUST 1870	589
B.	TOOLS, BOATS, AND MATERIALS ON THE SENECA DIVISION, AUGUST 1870	590
C.	REPORT ON CANAL TELEPHONE LINE, SEPTEMBER 27, 1879	591
D.	REPORT ON CANAL TELEPHONE LINE, NOVEMBER 1, 1879	592
E.	EMPLOYEES JULY 1, 1839	595
F.	OFFICERS FEBRUARY 1, 1840	599

G.	OFFICERS, ENGINEERS, AND AGENTS APRIL 2, 1841	602
H.	OFFICERS JUNE 1, 1841	604
I.	OFFICERS, ENGINEERS, AND AGENTS JANUARY 1, 1842	607
J.	OFFICERS MAY 31, 1842	609
K.	OFFICERS MAY 31, 1845	611
L.	OFFICERS DECEMBER 31, 1846	614
M.	OFFICERS DECEMBER 31, 1848	617
N.	OFFICERS DECEMBER 31, 1850	620
O.	PRESIDENTS, DIRECTORS, AND CHIEF OFFICERS FROM JUNE 1828 TO FEBRUARY 27, 1851	623
P.	LIST OF CANAL POSITIONS, APRIL 1884	625
Q.	LIST OF CANAL POSITIONS, FEBRUARY 1885	629

I. FIRST PROVISIONS FOR MANAGEMENT OF CANAL MAINTENANCE ACTIVITIES: 1830

In November 1830 the first portion of the canal between Dams Nos. 1 and 2 was opened to navigation.[1] On October 1 the management of the operation and maintenance of this stretch of the canal, as well as the superintendence of the construction of the line between the tidelock at Georgetown and Dam No. 1 and between Seneca and Point of Rocks was divided into two residencies, each in the charge of an engineer.[2] The 1st Residency stretched from the eastern terminus of the waterway to Section No. 40 (about 2½ miles above Seneca) and the 2nd Residency covered the remainder of the canal to Section No. 84 at Point of Rocks. Thomas Purcell, the resident engineer of the 1st Residency, had his headquarters near Dam No. 2, while Daniel Van Slyke, the resident engineer of the 2nd Residency had his office near Aqueduct No. 2. In addition to his other duties, Van Slyke was named as the first superintendent of the canal with supervisory responsibility over all the newly-designated lock tenders between Dams Nos. 1 and 2.[3]

The responsibilities of the superintendent and the lock-keepers during the early period of navigation apparently were never formally spelled out. The only description of their duties appears in the form of an order in the *Proceedings of the President and Board of Directors* on November 20, 1830:

> That each Lock-Keeper be supplied with such tools as may be necessary for the preservation and repair of that portion of the Canal under his care: that receipts be taken from the Lock-Keepers for the tools delivered to them, to be filed with the Clerk of the Company; and that the Superintendent make monthly report to the Board of the condition of all such tools and the condition of the Lock-Keeper's houses and other property of the Company under his inspection: And it was further ordered, that an inventory be made of all tools etc. now belonging to the Company, from which to supply the Lock-Keepers as far as practicable.[4]

---

[1] *Second Annual Report* (1830), C & O Co., 32, and *Third Annual Report* (1831), C & O Co., 4–5.

[2] Benjamin Wright, the chief engineer of the canal company since its formation in 1828, resigned his position on October 1, primarily because the legal difficulties with the Baltimore and Ohio Railroad would prevent active engineering operations above Point of Rocks for an indefinite period. His position was abolished and was replaced by the two residencies. As part of the reorganization, the former 1st and 2nd Residencies were combined into the new 1st Residency while the former 3rd, 4th and 5th Residencies were united into the new 2nd Residency. The reorganization was ordered by the board of directors as a means of reducing the engineering staff and company payroll costs pending a final resolution of the legal conflict with the railroad. *Proceedings of the President and Board of Directors*, B, 171–173.

[3] *Proceedings of the President and Board of Directors*, B, 173–174.

[4] *Ibid,* B, 225. While there is little information on the specific maintenance duties of the lock tenders, there is some indication that the navigable portion of the waterway was divided into "lock-keeper districts." For instance, the directors on July 1, 1831, extended the "authority of the District Lock-keeper at Rushville" so "as to enable him to regulate under the authority of the Superintendent, at the levels between Locks Nos. 21 and 22." *Ibid,* B, 397.

II: FIRST FORMAL DEVELOPMENT OF GUIDELINES
        FOR MANAGEMENT OF CANAL MAINTENANCE ACTIVITIES: 1831

The absence of formally defined regulations for the navigation and the management of the line of the canal soon presented serious problems to Superintendent Van Slyke and the lock tenders. On April 2, 1831, Van Slyke reported to the directors on the chaotic state of operations on the waterway:

> The canal has been so thronged with boats since the opening of the navigation on the 19th March last that it is with great difficulty we have been able to preserve order among the Boatmen, who in striving to push forward for a preference in passing the several locks are sometimes disposed to injure each others boats as a means of carrying their point....It would seem important that some rule be adopted by the Board to govern the Lock Keepers, so that the boats may pass the locks by turn as they arrive, as it frequently occurs that fifteen or twenty boats arrive at a lock within half an hour. Hence the contention for tight of preference, which I believe would be allayed if it was known that they must be permitted to pass only by turn as they arrive.[5]

After discussing the remarks by Van Slyke, the directors on May 6 authorized President Charles F. Mercer "to prepare and cause to be published, a code of Regulations for the government of the lock-keepers, boat-men, packet owners and others having business on the Canal."[6] On July 16 the board amended and approved the "Regulations for Navigating the Chesapeake & Ohio Canal," the "Rules for the Collection of Tolls on the Chesapeake & Ohio Canal," and the "Distribution of the Chesapeake & Ohio Canal for the Purposes of Navigation, Inspection, and Repairs, into Lock-keepers Districts," all of which Mercer had submitted[7] The latter set of regulations not only defined the location of the lock-tenders' districts but it also provided the first formally-written description of their duties as follows:

DISTRIBUTION OF THE CHESAPEAKE & OHIO CANAL,
FOR THE PURPOSES OF NAVIGATION, INSPECTION,
AND REPAIRS, INTO LOCK KEEPERS DISTRICTS.

> The first Lock-keeper's District shall extend from the eastern termination of the Canal in Washington, to the waste weir next above the old locks at the Little Falls of Potomac, and shall include the basin between Georgetown and Washington, as well as those locks.
> The second Lock-keeper's District shall extend from the first, as high up as to include the waste weir next above the United States powder magazine, and shall also include the dam and feeder at the Little Falls.
> The third Lock-keeper's District shall extend from the second, to the lower end of the external slope of protection wall next above the culvert over Cabin John Run.
> The fourth Lock-keeper's District shall extend from the third district, to the first culvert above his dwelling house.
> The fifth Lock-keeper's District shall extend from the fourth, to the waste weir through the berm of the canal next below the entrance of the Rocky Run Feeder.

---

[5] Van Slyke to Mercer, April 2, 1831, Ltrs. Recd., C & O Co.
[6] *Proceedings of the President and Board of Directors*, B, 314.
[7] *Ibid*, B, 410–428.

The sixth Lock-keeper's District shall extend from the fifth, to the lower end of the first high vertical protection wall above, and shall embrace Rock Run Dam and Feeder.

The seventh Lock-keeper's District shall extend from the sixth to the lower end of the first external slope or protection wall above the Great Falls of Potomac.

The eighth Lock-keeper's District shall extend from the seventh, to the first high bluff above the culvert over Watt's branch.

The ninth Lock-keeper's District shall extend from the eighth, to the lower end of the first external slope or protection wall above the culvert over Muddy Branch.

The tenth Lock-keeper's District shall extend from the ninth, to the upper end of the external slope or protection wall next above the Seneca Aqueduct.

The Lock-keeper of the First District will have charge of the Tide lock, the four lift locks next above the same, and the locks at the Little Falls, with three assistants, one of whom shall live at the lock house near the old locks and attend the same.

The Lock-keeper of the second District will have charge of two locks, with one assistant, who shall live at the lock house, which he himself does not occupy.

The Lock-keeper of the fifth District will have charge of three locks, with one assistant, who shall live at the lock house which he himself does not occupy.

The Lock-keeper of the sixth District will have charge of three locks, with one assistant.

The Lock-keeper of the seventh District will have charge of six locks, with two assistants, one of whom shall live at the lowest lock house on the District, and the other at the lock house next to his own.

The Lock-keeper of the tenth District will have charge of the Seneca Guard, and two lift locks, and be required to keep one assistant till the Canal above Seneca be brought into use, and after that, two assistants; one of whom shall live at the lock house near the Seneca Aqueduct.

The Several District Lock-keepers, and their assistants, will have charge of all the Company's works and property of every description within, or appertaining to the part of the Canal within their respective districts, and will be held responsible for the due care and preservation thereof, from all damages, trespasses, and injuries, and for keeping in order the grounds, fences, &c. about their locks and houses.

The District lock-keepers will appoint, and pay their own assistants; they will themselves be appointed by the President of the Company, on his nomination, approved by the Board of Directors, and will be removable at his discretion, or that of any two Directors of the Board, in the absence of the President.

All orders will be given them, either by, or through the President of the Company, the Superintendent of repairs, or some equally authorized officer, or engineer of the Company, and they will be held responsible for the prompt, diligent, and faithful execution thereof.

Their ordinary standing duties will be as follows:

To attend constantly and diligently by day and night, to the filling and emptying of the lock or locks, within their respective districts, and the passage of all boats or floats, through the same, according the general regulations of the President and Directors, and to such further or particular instructions as they may hereafter receive, in relation thereto.

They shall never absent themselves from their districts, but by special leave of the President of the Company, or of the Superintendent of repairs, except in cases of unavoidable necessity and in cases of this description they shall always leave some safe and trusty substitute to supply their places until their return.

The District Lock-keepers, are constituted inspectors of the Canal, and it various appurtenances, and of the Company's grounds and property within their respective districts. As such, they are required personally to examine or ascertain, by their assistants, the actual condition of all the works and property of the Company within their respective districts, once at least in every week; and when practicable, once at least every other day. In doing so, they shall carefully examine the several locks, aqueducts, culverts, waste weirs, bridges, dams, embankments, slopes, and walls committed to their care; and once every month they shall report in writing, to the Board, through the Superintendent of repairs, the condition of the same, and the number of visits they have made; if any damage or injury has been sustained by any of the said works since the last monthly report, the nature, extent, and scope thereof, and of any to be apprehended, the grounds of such apprehension.

If a District Lock-keeper shall, at any time, discover, that any of the works on the Canal, within his district, are out of repair, he shall immediately report the fact in person or by express, which, for that purpose, he is authorized to hire, to the Superintendent of repairs, and if from the nature of the repairs required, or of the damage apprehended, time be not allowed without farther injury to the Canal or its appurtenances, to wait the orders of the Superintendent, the Lock-keeper shall consider himself empowered, and he is required, at the cost of the Company, to take immediate steps, in the absence of the Superintendent, to repair the injury which has happened, or to prevent that which is apprehended. Of all expenses so incurred by him, for the benefit of the Company, he shall keep a fair account, a copy of which, he shall hand over to the Superintendent, as soon as his presence shall enable him to take charge of such repairs, the Superintendent shall repay to the Lock-keeper, the sums so expended. All such accounts shall be settled as soon as practicable, after they arise, and, at least, once in every month.

No Lock-keeper shall be entitled to receive his monthly pay, who shall have an unsettled account with the Company.

The District Lock-keepers shall be bound, if required, to provide by themselves, or their assistants, accommodation and subsistence, at a reasonable rate, not to exceed a given sum per week, for the Superintendent, and such hands or laborers as may be engaged in such repairs, or on any improvements upon, or alterations of the Canal.

Each Lock-keeper and Lock-keeper's assistant shall be furnished with 2 wheelborrows, 3 shovels, a pick and a crow-bar, to be used in the improvement and repair of the Canal, whensoever required, and shall be held responsible for the good order and safe keeping of the same; and each District Lock-keeper, in his monthly return to the board, shall state the number and condition of the tools within his District.

In addition to his monthly pay, each District Lock-keeper, shall be entitled to an enclosed lot, near his house.

Every Lock-keeper shall be at liberty, subject to the restraints and regulations of the existing laws, to accommodate the boatmen, and other travelers at his lock house, provided that under no circumstances whatever, shall any Lock-keeper, or his assistant, be allowed to sell or to supply on any terms, to any boatmen, traveler, or other person, any spirituous, or intoxicating liquor, or to allow the use or consumption of any such liquor within or upon his premises, unless particularly authorized so to do by the President and Directors of the Company; and for any violation of this rule, the offender shall be immediately discharged from the service of the Company.

In like manner any District or Assistant Lock-keeper, who shall at any time be found in a state of intoxication, shall be forthwith discharged.

Every District Lock-keeper, and his assistant, shall afford to the boatmen and all other persons navigating the canal, every aid and accommodation in his power, while he duly enforces the regulations for the protection of the Canal and its works–he shall instruct the boatmen how to navigate the Canal, to the best advantage, and especially to what part of their boat they should attach their tow or tracking line; how to track it with most comfort to themselves, and especially the manner of entering and passing out of the locks, and the use of their bow and stern strapping or snubbing ropes.

Every District Lock-keeper having reason to suspect a boat or float to have increased her cargo subsequent to the date of her waybill, is authorized to call upon the owner, master, or other person having charge of said boat or float for a sight of his waybill, to compare with the actual cargo of such boat, and if any augmentation of such cargo shall appear to have been made, subsequently to the date of the permit or waybill, to endorse a notice hereof, on such waybill, for the information of the Collector, and the other Lock-keepers.

All boats or floats left by their owners, or such persons as may have had charge thereof, either sunk in the canal or loosely floating thereupon, and all floating logs, planks or branches of trees, as well as other nuisances within the Canal, the Lock-keeper of the district within which the same may be, shall promptly cause to be removed or abated.

Every District Lock-keeper is required to pay particular attention to the orders regulating the height of water in the several levels between the locks of his district; and the Lock-keepers of the eighth and ninth districts, may be required to receive their orders through the Lock-keepers of the seventh or of the tenth district; and in like manner those of the second, third, and fourth, through the Lock-keepers of the first or fifth district.

In all cases, where practicable, the various levels shall be regulated by the use of the wastes and feeders of the Canal, reserving the side culverts and paddle gates of the locks for their appropriate use – that of filling and emptying the locks when required by the passage of boats.

Each District Lock-keeper shall see that obvious and suitable marks, by description stones or boards, be kept up, above and below each lock, to denote where a boat approaching the same, shall slacken its speed or await its turn for entering the Lock, if other boats have a right to precede it.

No Lock-keeper is authorized to practice himself, or to countenance others, in resisting, by violence, except in self-defense, any outrageous or disorderly conduct on the canal, but he shall take, at the cost of the Company, prompt measures to suppress and punish the same, by the judicial tribunals having cognizance thereof.[8]

Although there was no mention of repair work crews in the company regulations, such laborers were hired on an "as-needed basis" and placed under the direction of the superintendent. One of the earliest extant payrolls in the canal company records indicates that during the period from February 1 to March 1, 1832, 137 laborers were making improvements and repairing breaches, embankments and culverts on the navigable portion of the canal preparatory to its opening for boats in the spring. The number of days worked by the men varied from 1 to 26¼ days during that month at wages varying between 25 cents and $1 a day. Some 233½ "man-days" of work were performed by the hands boarded by the company on its "boarding-house' boat. The men who

---

[8] *Ibid*, B, 422 - 428. On July 22, 1831, the canal from Dam No. 1 to Dam No. 2 was declared "open and free for trade and passing, subject to the Regulations of the Company." Water was not admitted into the canal all the way to the Georgetown tidelock until September 19, 1831. *Ibid,* B, 432, C, 5.

were boarded at the expense of the company received 40 cents or less per day, while the remainder of the men who supplied their own board and lodging were paid 65 cents or more per day.[9]

On March 24 Superintendent James C. Lackland, who had replaced the sickly Van Slyke on July 1, 1831, was authorized by the directors to perform two duties to upgrade the effectiveness of the regular maintenance activities on the canal. The two assignments were as follows:

> That the Superintendent do examine the several lock-keepers with a view to ascertain those that are acquainted with the extent of their respective districts and the various duties required of them, by the printed or other regulations, and orders of the President and Directors; and that he report to the President of the Company, the name of every lock-keeper, whom he shall find, upon examination, to be ignorant of his duty or in any way negligent or remiss in its performance; that he especially instruct the said lock-keepers to inspect, as required, the embankments on both sides of the Canal, within their respective districts in order to ascertain whether any leak exists or is threatened in any part thereof; whether any muskrats have made lodgments therein, and if any, the entrance of their habitations; and that he instruct them in their daily or weekly inspections, and take special care in his own, to pass thro' the several viaducts or culverts of the canal within their district and under his superintendence . . . or . . . by looking thro' the same, whether any leak exists thereon, and that, where any such leaks are discovered, they be promptly stopped, or effectual measures be taken to prevent their enlargement. . . .
>
> That a reward of 25 cents be paid by the superintendent, and charged by him in his periodical settlement of accounts, for every muskrat, which he shall have satisfactory evidence has been killed on the Canal, in the embankments thereof or on the river side adjacent thereto.[10]

Preventive maintenance became an issue in June 1833 when the board ordered Superintendent William H. Bryan to inform the lock-keepers that they were to enforce rigidly the regulations prohibiting the navigation of iron-pointed scows and the use of iron-pointed poles.[11] In the future, each tender would be responsible for the damage done to his locks by such boats and poles unless it could be proven that an effort had been made to enforce the regulations or that violations had been reported immediately to the Collector at Georgetown. Unless such efforts could be proven, the cost of repairs to the locks could be deducted from the monthly wages of the lock-keepers. To give effect to this provision, the superintendent was directed to certify that the locks were in good order each month before the tenders were paid.[12]

---

[9] *Miscellaneous Accounts and Other Records Concerning Construction and Maintenance, 1828–1882*, C & O Co. There is no documentary information on the "boarding House" boat. However, the board purchased the *Lafayette* from Charles Embrey of Williamsport for $300 in January 1833. The *Lafayette* was fitted for the accommodation of hands employed by the canal superintendent. *Proceedings of the President and Board of Directors*, C, 263–264, 278.

[10] Ibid, B, 393, 454, C, 111–112. A similar effort to pay bounties for muskrats killed along the canal was revived for a short period in 1870.

[11] On June 1, 1832m John Y. Young was appointed as superintendent of the canal at a salary of $750 per year in place of Lackland who was retiring because of ill health. Sometime early in 1833, William H. Bryan superseded Young as superintendent. *Proceedings of the President and Board of Directors*, C, 139, 154, 357.

[12] Ibid, C, 368–369, 392. Later in June 1836, the board directed the superintendent to notify the lock tenders that they would be held responsible for all damages to their districts which resulted from the neglect of duty. Ibid, E, 69.

III. ESTABLISHMENT OF NEW MANAGEMENT DIVISIONS TO ACCOMMODATE WESTWARD EXPANSION OF CANAL: 1833–1839.

In October 1833 the board took steps to provide for the supervision of the new section of the Canal between Dams Nos. 2 and 3 which was to be watered later in the month. Charles B. Fisk, who had been employed as an engineer on the waterway since September 30, 1828, was appointed as the superintendent for the division at a salary of $500 in addition to his pay as an engineer.[13]

The years between 1834 and 1835 witnessed significant progress in the construction of the waterway and the consequent realignment of management responsibilities for the maintenance of the canal. After Tidelock B was completed in September 1834, the First Lock-Keeper's District was extended to include the entire portion of the canal works from that lock the Little Falls. This stretch of the canal was placed under the responsibility of the tender at Locks Nos. 1–4 who was also serving as the Collector of Tolls at Georgetown. He was to employ assistant lock tenders to operate the locks and to make the necessary inspections and repairs of the line.[14]

In December 1834 the canal between Dams Nos. 3 and 4 was completed and watered. To provide for the supervision of this line of the canal the board extended the authority of Fisk's superintendence to include the newly-opened portions. His first duties were to appoint temporary lock-keepers and to erect shanties in which they could live.[15]

The canal between Dams Nos. 4 and 5 was opened to navigation by early July 1835 when the board of directors proceeded up the canal in their iron 0packet to examine the status of the completed and projected portions of the waterway. While they were in Williamsport on July 13, the directors appointed George W. Rodgers as the assistant engineer and superintendent of the canal from Harpers Ferry to Dam No. 5 at a salary of $1,000 per year. At the same time, the portion of the canal below Dam No. 3 was divided into two superintendencies. John Y. Young was to oversee the waterway from Georgetown to Edwards Ferry, while William S. Elgin was to be responsible for the line between Edwards ferry and Dam No. 3.[16]

In April 1839 the section of the canal between Dams Nos. 5 and 6 was completed and watered. This section of the waterway was established as the fourth division with John G. Stone as superintendent. At this time new salary scales were adopted whereby Young and Elgin received an annual salary of $1,000 while Rogers and Stone were paid $1,200.[17]

---

[13] *Ibid,* C, 436, D, 1.
[14] *Ibid,* D, 181.
[15] *Ibid,* D, 199.
[16] *Ibid,* D, 366, E, 161.
[17] *Ibid,* F, 38, and *Twelfth Annual Report* (1840), C & O Co., 38–39. In April 1837 Fisk had been promoted to Chief Engineer with supervisory responsibilities over both the construction engineers and the division superintendents.

IV. POLITICAL INFLUENCE AND THE MANAGEMENT OF CANAL MAINTENANCE ACTIVITIES: 1840-1841

A disputed contest in Maryland state politics erupted in 1837 and 1838 between the rising Democrats and the entrenched Whig coalition that had been in power, with a few exceptions, for many years. The political unrest resulted in constitutional amendments providing for the popular election of the governor and the Senate and abolition of the Governor's Council. The electoral reforms paved the way for the election of William Grason as the first Democratic governor in 1838. The momentum gained by the Democrats in his election enabled them to win a majority in the House of Delegates the following year.[18]

The new Grason administration in Annapolis soon took steps to apply the Jacksonian-inspired spoils system to the operation of the canal. In the first large turnover of company employees, many long-time and reliable Whig-appointed officials were dismissed or voluntarily retired under pressure and were replaced by generally less-experienced and more politically motivated Democrats. In June 1839, the respected George C. Washington, who had been president of the company since 1834 and had done much to promote additional subscriptions to canal stock by the state legislature, was replaced by Francis Thomas, Jr., who had been a Democratic Congressman since 1831 from Frederick County and was destined to succeed Grason as governor of the State in 1841.[19] Following an abortive attempt to move the company headquarters to Baltimore in June 1839, the board of directors ordered it removal to Frederick in June 1840.[20] Among the canal officials who were fired or resigned between May and November 1840 were the following:

> May 7—Joseph Hollman replaces John G. Stone as Superintendent of 4th Division.
> May 7—William Mathews replaces William H, Bryan as Commissioner.
> July 9—John D. Grove replaces George W. Rodgers as Superintendent of 3rd Division.
> July 9—John P. Ingle resigns as Clerk and is replaced by Thomas Turner.
> Sep. 17—William O'Neale replaces William S. Elgin as Superintendent of 2nd Division.
> Sep. 26—Chief Engineer and Principal Assistant Engineer positions combined and filled by Ellwood Morris; Charles B. Fisk fired.
> Nov. 14—Samuel Lyles replaces Robert Barnard as Treasurer and Accountant.
> Nov. 14—Edward Shriver replaces Thomas Fillebroun, Jr., as Assistant Clerk.
> Nov. 14—Ezra Houck appointed Collector General to supervise all toll collectors.[21]

The wholesale changes attracted considerable public notice as the ousted officials carried into the newspapers their opposition to the directorate and other observers expressed their opinions on the separations. In commenting on the resignation of Clerk John P. Ingle, the *National Intelligencer* observed:

---

[18] Richard Walsh and William Lloyd Fox, eds., *Maryland: A History, 1632-1974* (Baltimore, 1974), 279-280.

[19] *Proceedings of the Stockholders*, E, 347-348; *Proceedings of the President and Board of Directors*, F, 75-76; *Niles' Register*, (LVIII (July 4, 1840), 278-281; and *Biographical Directory of the American Congress, 1774-1971* (Washington, 1971), 1805, 1886. Under the direction of Thomas, it was determined to continue construction of the hard-pressed waterway on the basis of the unrestricted issuance of scrip. The decision was highly unpopular with the fiscal conservatism of the Whig-appointed officials and thus played a role in some of the resignations.

[20] *Proceedings of the President and Board of Directors*, F, 76, 82, 234.

[21] *Proceedings of the President and Board of Directors*, F, 246–247, 256–257, 259–260, and Ingle to Stone, May 7, 1840, Ingle to Bryan, May 7, 1840, Turner to Schnebly, August 12, 1840, and Turner to Elgin and to O'Neale, September 17, 1840, Ltrs. Sent, C & O Co.

> The company will miss the services of Mr. Ingle much, especially if it is intended, as some suppose, to force also the other experienced officers of the company out of its service.[22]

After the Whigs won a majority of seats in the House of Delegates in the 1840 elections, the new legislature demanded explanations of the canal board's conduct of company affairs.[23] Following the release of a report by President Thomas to Governor Grason in which it was admitted that some canal officials had been removed for "political opinion's sake," the stockholders met on April 2, 1841, to oust the directorate. A special stockholder's committee reported that from all available evidence it was:

> satisfied that very valuable and faithful officers have been removed from the service of the Company, and, in some cases, men not competent to perform the duties have been appointed in their places, to the serious injury of the best interests of the Company.[24]

As the controlling stockholder, the State of Maryland on April 2 replaced the Thomas-led board with a predominantly Whig directorate headed by Michael S. Sprigg who had held a variety of company offices in previous years.[25] The new board proceeded to reinstate as many of the old officials as were still available and to reform canal affairs. Among the returning officials were William S. Elgin, George W. Rodgers, and John C. Stone as Superintendents of the 2nd, 3rd, and 4th Divisions, respectively, and Charles B. Fisk as Chief Engineer, along with ten of his former assistants.[26] A resolution was adopted forbidding company officials from interfering in politics, and a copy of the resolution was sent to every one of the nearly 60 permanent canal employees.[27]

---

[22] Washington *National Intelligencer* quoted in *Niles' Register*, LVIII (July 18, 1840), 308.
[23] *Proceedings of the President and Board of Directors*, F, 279, 284.
[24] *Proceedings of the Stockholders*, B, 417–419.
[25] *Proceedings of the President and Board of Directors*, F, 301–302.
[26] Turner to O'Neale, Elgin, Hollman, Stone, Grove, and Rodgers, April 15, 1841, Ltrs. Sent, C & O Co. and Morris to Sprigg, April 7, 1841, and Fisk to President and Directors, April 29, 1841, Ltrs. Recd., C & O Co.
[27] *Proceedings of the President and Board of Directors*, F, 315.

V. FLUCTUATIONS IN MANAGEMENT OF CANAL MAINTENANCE
ACTIVITIES DUE TO DESPERATE COMPANY FINANCES: 1842–1850

By 1842 the financial condition of the canal company was desperate and construction between Dam No. 6 and Cumberland had cone to a halt.[28] Accordingly, steps were taken to reduce the number of canal employees and management positions and the company's overhead costs to operate and maintain the waterway. One scheme that was attempted in December 1842 by Superintendent Young was in an effort to reduce repair costs on the 1st Division was that of contracting for the hire of Negro slave work gangs.[29] In June 1843 the board of directors instructed Young to reside at Seneca and to function as the tender at Lock No. 23 and Guard Lock No. 2 in addition to his supervisory duties.[30]

Upon the recommendation of Chief Engineer Fisk, the board of directors on May 25, 1844, reduced the number of divisions on the navigable portion of the canal from four to three. The new divisional alignment was as follows:

1st Division—Eastern terminus to Edwards Ferry River Lock—32 miles—John Y. Young, Superintendent
2nd Division—Lock No. 25 to 500 feet above head of Guard Lock No. 4—54.8 miles—William S. Elgin, Superintendent.
3rd Division—Point 500 feet above head of Guard Lock No. 4 to current western terminus at Dam No. 6—48.5 miles—John G. Stone, Superintendent.

The superintendents, each of whom received an annual salary of $800, were directly responsible for the supervision of the collectors, lock tenders and repair crews on their divisions.[31]

Another reduction in the number of divisions was made in June 1845 following the resignation of Superintendent Young. At first, the directors agreed to reduce the length of the 1st Division only to cover the distance from the eastern terminus to and including the Little Falls Feeder and Guard Lock No. 1. John Moore, the newly appointed superintendent of this division, would receive $60 per year. The canal from Guard Lock No. 1 to the Edwards Ferry River Lock would be added to the 2nd Division under Elgin for which increased responsibility he would receive an additional annual stipend of $300. When Moore declined the offered position "at the compensation fixed," the entire 1st and 2nd Divisions were combined under Elgin for which service he was to be paid $1,200 per year.[32] This arrangement, according to the report of President James M. Coale, reduced the operating expenses of the waterway and provided for more "efficient attention to the canal and its works."[33]

A special committee of the stockholders issued a report in July 1846 on the inadequacies of the system of managing the operation and maintenance of the canal. Recently, there had been numerous complaints about the incompetency and neglect of some of the lock-keepers that was contributing to the detention of trade and the necessity for costly repairs at various places. The committee conceded that the 135-mile length of the canal was difficult to supervise. It noted the widely-held belief that many grievances were kept quiet because the local people tended to frown on informers. As the board was far away from the canal and only met monthly, the investigations

---

[28] *Niles' Register*, LVX (September 9, 1843), 19 and I*bid*, LXII (March 26, 1842), 52.
[29] *Proceedings of the President and Board of Directors*, F, 513.
[30] *Ibid*, G, 44. At the same time, Superintendent George W. Rodgers was ordered to reside in Williamsport "or at some other more central part of his division, but upon the line of the canal."
[31] *Ibid*, G, 165 and *Seventeenth Annual Report* (1845), C & O Co., 9–10.
[32] *Proceedings of the President and Board of Directors*, G, 244–245, 249.
[33] *Seventeenth Annual Report* (1845), 4.

of reported problems often took place long after the fact and allowed the tender to cover their actions. Moreover, the lock-keepers generally refused to cooperate with or respect the superintendents who had little authority to enforce their orders. To alleviate these problems, the committee recommended that the tenders be made directly responsible to the superintendents who would in turn be held accountable for all negligence and dereliction of duty. The number of divisional superintendents should be increased to three, and they should be placed under the direction of the chief engineer who would assume the title of general superintendent.[34]

Some portions of the committee's report were adopted by the board in December 1846 when Chief Engineer Fisk was ordered to lay the canal out into three divisions. In February 1847 the directors approved Fisk's divisional boundaries as follows:

> 1st Division—Tidelock B at the mouth of Tyber Creek in Washington to and including the Dam No. 2 complex.
> 2nd Division—Dam No. 2 complex to near and above Guard Lock No. 4.
> 3rd Division—Near and above Guard Lock No. 4 to Dam No. 6.

John Lambie, a highly-recommended citizen of Washington County was appointed as Superintendent of the 1st Division at an annual salary of $700, while Elgin and Stone were retained on the 2nd and 3rd Divisions, respectively, each at annual salaries of $900.[35]

President Coale explained the recent changes in canal management to the stockholders in June 1847 by observing:

> The past year...has been one of peculiar trial to the Company and of labor and anxiety to the subordinate officers on the several divisions of the line. In no former year in the recollection of any one connected with the Company have so many freshets occurred and of such general magnitude. Admonished by its results, and with a view of guarding the Canal against injury by every reasonable precaution which it is in our power to provide, the Board...laid off the line into three divisions, in such a manner as in their opinion would be best calculated to insure the utmost amount of personal supervision on the part of the Superintendents...[36]

---

[34] *Proceedings of the Stockholders*, C, 592–594.
[35] *Proceedings of the President and Board of Directors*, G, 475–477, H, 1–2. In August 1847 the company headquarters was moved back to Frederick from Cumberland where it had been located for several years. This more central location would be more convenient and accessible to all portions of the navigable portion of the canal, and thus would provide for more efficient management of the line. *Ibid,* H, 18–19, 67, 69.
[36] *Nineteenth Annual Report* (1847), C & O Co., 6–7.

VI. ADOPTION OF NEW BY-LAWS AND ORGANIZATIONAL ALIGNMENT TO MANAGE MAINTENANCE ON THE COMPLETED CANAL: 1850–1851

The construction of the canal between Dam No. 6 and Cumberland was completed in the fall of 1850. On October 10 festive ceremonies were held at Cumberland to formally open trade on the waterway to that city. From that date until the winter weather closed the canal to navigation for the season, the recently-completed portion of the waterway was designated as the 4th Division. Fifteen en ers were appointed to operate the locks on the division, but no superintendent was named.³⁷ d

In November 1850 the board of directors adopted a six-division alignment for the "superintendence of the repairs" which was to take effect on January 1, 1851. The names and boundaries of the divisions, which were laid out by Chief Engineer Fisk, were as follows:

1st—Georgetown Division—Eastern terminus to Seneca Feeder, inclusive.
2nd—Monocacy Division—Above Seneca Feeder to Dam No. 3 Feeder, inclusive.
3rd—Antietam Division—Above Dam No. 3 Feeder to point 500 feet above Guard Lock No. 4.
4th—Williamsport Division—Point 500 feet above Guard Lock No. 4 to first stop lock below Licking Creek.
5th—Hancock Division—Above first stop lock below Licking Creek to Lock No. 59.
6th—Cumberland Division—Above Lock No. 59 to western terminus at Cumberland.[38]

On April 1, 1851, new "by-laws, rules, and regulations" for the officers of the company were put into effect by the board. According to the by-laws, the officers connected with the management and preservation of the canal and the collection of tolls were as follows:

1. General Superintendent
2. Superintendent of Repairs
3. Lock-keepers
4. Collectors
5. Acting Collectors
6. Inspectors

The by-laws included general regulations and position descriptions for the officers which remained in effect with slight modifications until 1889 when the canal went into a receivership:

GENERAL REGULATIONS

103. They shall give their personal and constant attention to the duties of their respective offices, and shall not be directly or indirectly concerned in any store, shop, or other trading establishment for the purchase or sale of spirits, produce, merchandise, or property of any description, on or near the line of the Canal, or have directly or indirectly an interest

---

[37] *Report to the Stockholders on the Completion of the Chesapeake & Ohio Canal to Cumberland* (Frederick, 1851), 140.
[38] *Proceedings of the President and Board of Directors*, H, 391–391. Later, the following individuals were named as the division superintendents: John Lambie, Georgetown; William S, Elgin, Monocacy; Levin Benton, Antietam; John G. Stone, Williamsport; Overton G. Lowe, Hancock; and Henry M. Dungan, Cumberland.

in any boat running upon the Canal, or have any other employment or occupation without the special permission of the President and Directors; under the penalty of being dismissed from service.

104. It shall be their duty to preserve and take care of all books, papers, vouchers, maps, documents, instruments, tools, and other property of the Company, which may come into their possession; and every such officer or agent, leaving the service of the Company, shall surrender up and deliver over to his successor, or other person duly authorized to receive the same, all the books, papers, vouchers, maps, documents and instruments pertaining to his office and all other things whatever, the property of the Company, which may be in his control.

105. No officer of the Canal shall either directly or indirectly be interested in any contract for labor, materials, provisions, implements, or other thing connected with the construction, improvements, repairs or expenses of the Canal or its appurtenant works; and no officer shall either directly or indirectly derive any benefit from the annual expenditures on the Canal beyond his established compensation.

GENERAL SUPERINTENDENT

106. The General Superintendent shall have the general management and direction of all repairs and improvements of the Canal, that may, that from time to time, be required. He shall give general directions and instructions to the Superintendents of repairs, in regard to the manner of making and carrying on the ordinary repairs, and special directions and instructions in regard to all those not of an ordinary character, and in regard to all improvements.

107. He shall, so far as practicable, personally examine all breaches,—particularly those that will take more than one week for their repair,—and shall give special directions and instructions to the Superintendents of repairs in regard to the manner in which they shall be repaired.

108. He shall, as often as practicable, examine the accounts of the Superintendents of repairs, to ascertain whether economy is observed in the doing of the work entrusted to their management; and may, if he think it advisable, at any time, require that their accounts and vouchers for disbursements shall be transmitted through him, to the Canal office.

109. He may, if he think it advisable, require that all reports and returns made by any or all of the Superintendents of repairs to the office of the Company, shall be transmitted through hi8n; and in like manner that all communications to them, from the office of the Company, shall be transmitted through him.

110. He may, if he deem it necessary, suspend any Superintendent or Lock-keeper and fill the vacancy thereby created, until the next meeting of the President and Directors, at which time, he shall report to the said President and Directors, such suspension and temporary appointment, with his reasons therefore and the facts of the case.

111. In the case of the death, resignation or removal of any Superintendent or Lockkeeper, he shall nominate for appointment by the President and Directors, some suitable person to fill the vacancy; and, if he deem it necessary, may temporarily fill the vacancy until such appointment is made.

112. He shall personally inspect and examine the Canal and all its structures, every six months, and, also, after any high fresh in the Potomac that does serious injury to the Canal; and shall, after every such inspection and examination, make a full report thereof to the President and Directors.

113. He shall, in his semi-annual reports, required by the last regulation, sum up and classify the expenses and cost of maintenance of the Canal, during the six months next preceding, shall give a condensed account of the operations in his department since the last preceding semi-annual report, and shall recommend whatever he may think necessary to promote the interest of the Company so far as it is dependent upon the condition in which the Canal is kept.

114. He shall, from time to time, make such other reports, and shall perform such other duties as the President and Directors may require and prescribe.

SUPERINTENDENTS OF REPAIRS

115. It shall be the duty of each Superintendent of repairs, under general or special directions and instructions from the General Superintendent, to superintend and direct the repairs and improvements of the Canal on his division, and to do every thing in his power to preserve said Canal, and the works connected therewith, from injury, and to keep them in a good state and condition; for which purpose he shall be allowed such bosses or foremen, removable at his pleasure, each with such force of laborers, and governed by such regulations, as the General Superintendent may prescribe; and he is particularly charged with the duty of seeing that the bosses or foremen and laborers under his charge shall be diligent and faithful in the performance of their respective duties to the Company.

116. He shall have charge of all the boats, horses, tools, implements, and other personal property of the Company on his division, and shall cause all such property, not in use, to be kept in a place of safety; and at the close of each quarter shall return, through the General Superintendent, to the office of the Company, to be placed on file, an inventory of all such property under his charge.

117. He shall purchase, under such regulations as the General Superintendent may deem proper and prescribe, provisions, materials, implements and tools, needed for the execution and prosecution of the work under his charge.

118. He shall visit the whole length of his division as often as the General Superintendent may require; and shall keep the General Superintendent constantly informed, of the state and condition of the line under his charge, and of all other matters under his superintendence; and at the close of each quarter, and oftener if required, he shall make report to the General Superintendent, of the state and condition of the Canal under his charge, and its appurtenant works, as also of the houses and enclosures of the lock-keepers; including in such report what injuries the Canal has sustained since the last preceding report and the

cases thereof; what measures he may have taken or may think necessary to guard against similar injuries in future; what depredations or encroachments may have been committed on the Canal or its works or other property of the Company; and such other information as he may consider important to its interests.

119. On the occurrence, on his division, of any breach in the Canal, or other injury to its works, suspending the navigation, he shall immediately proceed to the same, remain thereat, and superintend the repairs thereof, until the navigation shall be restored. He shall, also, as soon as practicable, and from time to time as he may be able, report to the General Superintendent, in writing, the occurrence of such breach or injury, with the place, time, causes, extent, and descriptions thereof, the means adopted or proposed to be adopted by him for repairing the same, the time which will probably be occupied by such repairs, their probable cost, and all other information in his power relative to that subject, which may be useful or interesting. He shall also apprise the several Collectors of such breach or other injury, and of the time at which the navigation will probably be restored; and shall send similar information to the office of the Company.

120. He shall superintend and direct the Lock-keepers, on his division, in the performance of their duties, and report the misconduct of any Lock-keeper to the General Superintendent.

121. He shall by the 20th of each month send, in such form as shall be prescribed, through the General Superintendent, to the Clerk of the Company, an estimate of the probable amount of the expenses of the month, on his division, for repairs and maintenance of the Canal.

122. He shall, by the 20th of each month, send to the Treasurer of the Company, his account of payments for the preceding month accompanied by the requisite vouchers.

123. He shall, under no circumstances whatever, take a receipt for labor done, services performed, or materials, provisions, implements, or tools purchased for the Company, unless the money for the same shall have been actually paid.

124. He shall, by the 10th of each month, send to the Clerk of the Company, through the General Superintendent, a statement of the fines imposed on his division, during the preceding month. In this statement shall be fully and particularly given and set forth, in each case, the name or names of the person or persons on whom the fine was imposed; the nature of the offence; by whom the fine was imposed; and whether the same has been paid or not; and if the offence was committed by the owner or master of any boat or float, or by any person employed thereon or assisting in the management thereof, the name of such boat or float shall also be given.

125. He shall, at the close of each month, obtain from the acting Collectors on his division, and from such Collectors as he may be instructed to do, accurate returns of all way-bills and permits *issued* and *received* by them during the month,—also, the way-bills and permits *received*,—and shall transmit the said returns and the said way-bills and permits *received*, to the Clerk of the Company, by the 10th of the succeeding month.

126. The money that he shall receive under the 135th, 154th and 155th regulations, for fines imposed and tolls collected,—also that he may himself receive for fines imposed, shall be held in such manner or deposited in such place to the credit of the Company, as may be from time to time directed and prescribed.

127. The Superintendent of repairs shall perform such other duties in addition to those already enumerated, as the President and Directors or General Superintendent shall from time to time assign to them.

LOCK-KEEPERS

128. It shall be the duty of all lock-keepers to make a daily and particular inspection of the locks under their charge, and of any other works which they may be directed, by order of the General Superintendent or of the Superintendent of repairs on whose division they are, to attend to; and to prevent by all lawful means within their power, any injury to said locks or other works, from carelessness of boatmen or from malicious or disorderly persons.

129. They shall use their utmost exertions to keep the said locks or other works in the best possible order, and in case of any accident or injury to them, or to the Canal in the vicinity of their stations, requiring immediate attention, they shall take the necessary measures to remedy the same and to prevent further injury; and in the meantime to send the earliest intelligence thereof to the Superintendent of repairs on that part of the Canal.

130. It shall be their duty, at all hours, by night as well as by day, unless otherwise ordered by the General Superintendent or Superintendent of repairs on that part of the Canal, to pass all boats and floats presenting themselves at their locks, and entitled to pass the same under the regulations of the Company.

131. They shall not permit the boatmen to pass their boats or floats through any lock, except in the presence and under the direction of the keeper thereof or his assistant.

132. The Lock-keepers shall not absent themselves from their locks, on any occasion, without leave from the Superintendent of repairs on that part of the Canal. They shall reside in the houses provided for them, at their respective stations; and shall be charged with the care and preservation of their respective houses and of the enclosures attached thereto; and also any property of the Company that may be put in their keeping by the General Superintendent or the Superintendent of repairs on that part of the Canal; and for any injury to the said house or enclosures or the said property, if occasioned by their neglect or carelessness, they shall be, respectively, liable.

133. Lock-keepers, when repairs are making in the neighborhood of their locks, at points where, and at times when, there is difficulty in obtaining board and lodging for those persons employed upon such repairs, shall afford such accommodation, in the way of boarding and lodging, the whole or in part of the said persons, at fair and usual rates, as in the opinion of the Superintendent of repairs of that part of the Canal, he can reasonably and with propriety be asked and required to afford.

134. Although, under these regulations, the Lock-keepers are, in many cases, authorized to impose fines; yet, except in cases of emergency, it is desired that they should forthwith report each violation of a regulation to the Superintendent of repairs on that part of the Canal, with all the facts in the case, in order that the fine may be imposed by the said Superintendent; and that such other measures in relation to the said violation may be taken as in the judgment of the said Superintendent may be thought necessary.

135. All fines imposed by Lock-keepers shall be forthwith reported to the Superintendent of repairs on that part of the Canal; and all monies received by them for fines imposed by them shall be immediately paid over to the said Superintendent.

136. Any Lock-keeper who shall knowingly permit a boat to pass his lock in violation of any provision of these regulations; or who shall himself neglect or refuse to comply promptly, with any one of such of these regulations as prescribes his duties, either towards the Company or those engaged in boating on the Canal, shall be forthwith suspended from duty by the Superintendent of repairs on that part of the Canal, on his becoming cognizant of the facts; and a report of the case shall be immediately made to the General Superintendent, by the said Superintendent, for his action thereon; and in the meantime the said Superintendent may appoint some person to fill, temporarily, the vacancy thus created.

137. Every Lock-keeper shall perform such other duties connected with the Canal, as the General Superintendent may from time to time require of him.[39]

In June 1851 the stockholders were informed about the early operation of the management of the canal under the new divisional alignment and the by-laws by President Sprigg as follows:

In conformity to the recommendation contained in a resolution passed at your last meeting, the board have appointed Charles B. Fisk, Esq., general superintendent of the canal, and has conferred upon him such authority over the subordinate officers on the line of the canal, as will, it is believed, give an efficient organization to this important branch of the service. In this connection, we would also state, that we have adopted a system of by-laws, rules, and regulations for the government, and prescribing the duties of the various officers connected with the management and preservation of the canal, and the collection of tolls. We have every reason to believe, as far as we can judge, from the short period which has elapsed since the by-laws of the company went into operation on the first of April last, that very beneficial results have, and will attend them; in the preservation of the works of the company, in securing a proper vigilance and subordination on the part of the officers on the line of the canal, and producing a degree of order and regularity on the part of those navigating the canal, which has heretofore not existed...[40]

---

[39] *By-Laws, Rules, and Regulations; In Force on the Chesapeake & Ohio Canal, 1st April 1851* (Baltimore, 1894), 33–39. Since the duties of the collectors, acting collectors, and inspectors pertain more directly to the regulation of trade on the canal, their positions descriptions may be found in Chapter XII of this study.

[40] *Twenty-Third Annual Report* (1851), C & O Co., 3–4. In June 1851 it was determined to move the company headquarters from Frederick to the Washington City Hall. After the new office was established, the books and papers of the company were "simplified and arranged with such order and method, as have not before existed," thus affording efficient reference to the affairs of the company and eliminating many of its earlier cumbersome management difficulties. *Proceedings of the President and Board of Directors*, H, 448–449, and *Twenty-Fourth Annual Report* (1852), C & O Co., 19.

VII. POLITICAL INFLUENCE DISRUPTS EFFICIENCY OF MANAGEMENT OF CANAL MAINTENANCE: 1852–1867

Hard on the heels of the destruction wrought by the April 1852 flood there was an equally devastating assault on the fortunes of the canal by political interference in its management and operation. In 1851 the Democrats had capitalized on the reapportioned legislative structure provided by the new constitution adopted that year to win decisive control over the General Assembly for the first time. At the annual meeting in June 1852, the controlling stockholder, the State of Maryland, acting through its representatives appointed a new administration for the company headed by ex-Democratic Governor William Grason as president. The dominance of the state in company affairs meant, in effect, that the political party in power in Maryland also controlled the selection of the canal board and indirectly the many subordinates on the line, thereby making the canal positions objects of party patronage. Canal positions had been used for party purposes once before in the early 1840s at which time there had been two successive sweeps of office, as the Democrats installed its political friends in 1840 and the Whigs promptly reinstated the older officials when they returned to power the following year. Thereafter, there had been no large-scale interference until 1851, primarily because the Whigs had maintained majorities in the General Assembly for most of this period while the Democrats had controlled the governorship except for an interlude in 1844–47. Now that the Democrats controlled both the executive and legislative branches of the state government, the Grason administration proceeded to revive the spoils system in the management of the canal, reaching all the way down to the lock-tenders and the repair crew bosses in the thoroughness of its sweep.[41]

As had been the case in the early 1840s many of the older and experienced canal officials were replaced by generally less competent political appointees. All of the division superintendents were fired with the exception of John Lambie of the Georgetown Division. The new superintendents were as follows:

    Monocacy Division—William O'Neal, Jr.
    Antietam Division—Charles Clarke
    Williamsport Division—Benjamin F. Hollman
    Hancock Division—James Condy
    Cumberland Division—William P. Sterritt

In addition, the collectors at Williamsport and Cumberland were relieved of their jobs while the collector at Georgetown resigned. Perhaps, the most significant resignation was that of General Superintendent Fisk, who had served the company for some 24 years in a variety of engineering positions. In his stead, the board appointed Thomas L. Patterson at an annual salary of $1,800.[42]

Thereafter, more or less complete reorganizations reflecting the unsettled conditions in Maryland politics, occurred regularly until 1867 when the Democrats emerged as the dominant party of the state. As new boards succeeded the old ones, they promptly replaced their political enemies with party favorites. There was little or no concern for the welfare of the canal. The serious effects which the continued political interference had on the operation and the maintenance of the canal was later graphically described by a group of disgruntled bondholders in 1881:

> In such way money was raised for completion of the Canal in 1850 [repair bonds of 1844], more than thirty years ago. And for two or three years the interest on the Bonds

---

[41] Walsh and Fox, *Maryland*, 280, 295–297, 301, and Sanderlin, *Great National Project*, 208–209.
[42] *Proceedings of the President and Board of Directors*, H, 537–541, 550–552, 556.

was promptly and punctually paid: a fact which was calculated to allay any anxiety that may have prevailed in the premises, and to appreciate the value of the Bonds on the markets.

The canal was thus under a stable, anti-political, and very able management, no changes having been made in its executives for seven years. But about this time the state made a change in the canal management, giving it into the hands of a political administration instead of the stable business control which had lifted it from the lowest stages of depression in 1840–1, 2 and 3, to completion and apparent prosperity in 1850.

Therefore [after 1850] as the State administration changed, so did the management of the canal, until about 1870, when it was ascertained that during the twenty years preceding there had been a dozen different administrations and executive heads in the management of this once popular and magnificent State Work. As an inevitable consequence of this too much-management the canal became a magnificent failure; transportation was uncertain; the big ditch was gradually filling up; the culverts were dilapidated; interest on the bonds was unpaid and largely in arrears; and the bonds themselves sunk in the market to a point below sale or quotation. . . . the State. . . by virtue of her ownership of five Eights of the Capital Stock, has had . . . the Exclusive Management, and has absolutely shaped and controlled the policy of the Company.

Administrating its affairs by officers chosen by her; changing those officers with every change of her politics; removing one year officials who had just begun to be familiar with the duties and responsibilities of their position . . . it is no wonder this Enterprise has languished. . . . Without a fixed and Stable policy; without a Corps of trained and Experienced officers; without Judicious and systematic Economy, paralyzed by perpetual Changes in its administration; the victim of abuses, Mismanagement and lavish Expenditures; its power and influence Constantly used in the Service of [the] political organization which, for the time, appointed its officers and regulated its direction. . . [43]

In the autumn of 1853 the Democratic candidate for Governor, T. Watkins Ligon, was elected to replace the outgoing Democrat, Enoch Louis Lowe, while the Whigs recaptured both houses of the state legislature. As a result of these political developments, Samuel Hambleton was installed as the new canal president in June 1854 in place of Grason. The new board instituted several changes in the management of the line during the following year. In June 1855 the new management policies were explained to the stockholders:

Rigid rules were prescribed for the conduct of the superintendents upon the line of the canal. Weekly reports were required of them upon their respective divisions, which have since been regularly made to the office at this place [Washington]. Monthly reports were also enforced from the general superintendent; the good results of both which requirements have been manifested.

The Board deeming the continuance of the office of Engineer of the Company, at a salary of $1,800 per annum, an unnecessary expense, as no repairs or construction requiring scientific plans and estimates were within the present means of the Company, abolished this office and substituted that of General Superintendent, with a salary of $1,200 per annum, in its stead. The good results of this policy have been manifested to the Board. They secured the services of Mr. A. K. Stake upon the canal, whose practical

---

[43] "Memorial of Certain Bondholders of the Chesapeake & Ohio Canal Company to the Board of Public Works of Maryland," *Fifty-Third Annual Meeting* (1881), and *Proceedings of the Stockholders*, E, 340–341, 343.

knowledge of the canal, having been engaged upon it in various capacities for many years; his untiring energy in the service of the Company, passing twice a month over the greater part of the line, and his regular monthly reports in writing of its condition, were found to be far preferable to the results of the former office of Engineer. A rigid system of economy was ordered and enforced.[44]

As part of the effort to reduce operating costs, the board recommended that the division superintendents sell the house boats which were used to lodge the repair crews and make arrangements for "room and board" for the men at lockhouses or private dwellings along the waterway. When it was found that such arrangements were difficult to make, the directors withdrew the recommendation.[45]

On June 30, 1855, the Hambleton board ordered a small reorganization of personnel. The following officers and individuals were involved:

DIVISION SUPERINTENDENTS
Antietam—Charles Clarke replaced by Levin Benton
Williamsport—Henry Artz replaced by Lewis G. Stanhope
Hancock—James Condy replaced by Denton Jacques
Cumberland—Asahel William replaced by Lloyd Lowe

COLLECTOR OF TOLLS
Williamsport—Charles Embry replaced by Ellie Stake
Hancock—David E. Price replaced by Henry Wells.[46]

Next the Hambleton board turned its attention to a reorganization of the company office. The separate offices of clerk and treasurer were combined, and an assistant clerk was hired in the place of an accountant whose office had been combined formerly with that of treasurer. These changes reportedly contributed to the efficient management of the company and provided an annual savings of $300 in overhead expenses.

The stockholders were informed in June 1856 concerning the beneficial results of the newly-created office of clerk and treasurer held by W. S. Ringgold:

> As the affairs of the Company are now necessarily managed by a President and Board of Directors who meet monthly, much of the responsibility devolves upon this confidential officer, in the intermediate periods of meeting; great familiarity with the past records and affairs of the Company, with its present condition and resources; with the routine of duty and reports from superintendents and employees on the line of the canal; prompt intelligent and vigorous action is required, in the absence of the President and Directors, and other reasons readily suggesting themselves, will show the high qualities required on this officer.
>
> The insuring to the Company increased usefulness and devotion in this office on the part of the present Clerk and Treasurer, alone swayed the Board in the change of organization above mentioned.

The stockholders were also told of the valuable service of General Superintendent Stake:

---

[44] *Twenty-Seventh Annual Report* (1855), C & O Co., 3–4.
[45] *Proceedings of the President and Board of Directors*, I, 103–104.
[46] *Proceedings of the President and Board of Directors*, I, 181.

I [Hambleton] feel it a duty to bear testimony to the great energy and devotion of the general Superintendent of the canal to the duties of his station; his great familiarity with every department of the work, resulting from his long previous business connections with it;—his industry and known intelligence;—his special weekly personal attendance on the line to his duties;—his regular and accurate reports, have all been a source of great satisfaction to the Board for the past two years.[47]

As a result of the statewide elections in the autumn of 1855, the American Party, which was the offspring of the nativist Know Nothing Movement, gained control of the House of Delegates and had sufficient strength, with the cooperation from a few of the sympathetic Whig holdovers, to organize the Senate as well.[48] The victorious Americans proceeded to remove the Hambleton board in June 1856 and replace it with a new set of directors headed by William P. Maulsby as president. Within a month the new board ordered a thorough reorganization of both the management of the line and the company office. The six divisions were reduced to four, and the general superintendent and the division superintendents were replaced by new appointees. Moreover, the authority of the general superintendent was diminished to the extent that the division superintendents were made directly responsible to the directors. The boundaries and superintendents of the four new divisions were:

> Georgetown Division: Eastern terminus to Conrad's Ferry; James P. Wade, Superintendent.
> Monocacy Division: Conrad's Ferry to Dam No. 4; Charles Clarke, Superintendent
> Hancock Division: Dam No. 4 to Dam No.6; Denton Oliver, Superintendent
> Cumberland Division: Dam No. 6 to Dam No. 8; Richard M. Sprigg, Superintendent
> Dewalt Stottlemeyer was named as the new general superintendent.[49]

President Maulsby presented the rationale for this reorganization to the annual meeting of the stockholders in June 1857. According to his report, when the board had been selected in the previous June

> it adopted the conclusion that the true policy . . . was to reduce, as far as possible, the number of officers on the line of the Canal, and to require from those remaining increased activity and attention. . . It was thought that the entire time and attention of the six Division Superintendents had not been occupied, and perhaps could not be profitably occupied, in the discharge of their official duties, and it was deemed wise, so to apportion the number to the duties to be discharged, as to leave to the incumbents no unoccupied time. Accordingly the Board determined to reduce the number from six to four, reserving for the future action a further reduction, if experience should demonstrate its propriety.

Maulsby went on to cite the reasons for diminishing the authority of the general superintendent and making the division superintendents directly responsible to the board by observing that the

> several grades of officers, and consequent degrees of responsibility each to the other, actually interfered with, rather than promoted, the prompt and efficient making such repairs

---

[47] *Twenty-Eighth Annual Report* (1856), C & O Co., 11–12.
[48] Walsh and Fox, *Maryland*, 314–315.
[49] *Proceedings of the President and Board of Directors*, I, 277–283.

as are constantly needed to keep the Canal in order, and which to be effectual must be, when needed, quickly done.—The work actually done on the line is by, and under the immediate supervision of, the Bosses. These being responsible to, must wait form in theory at least, and too frequently in practice when not really necessary, the directions of the Division Superintendent. The Division Superintendent, being responsible to the General Superintendent, and not amenable for a failure to make repairs, except such as, and when, ordered by the General Superintendent, might wait for the directions of that officer; and thus it did occur that the whole trade on the Canal, at a period not remote, was suspended for several days because of the breaking of the beam of a Lock-gate, which might have been repaired in a few hours; (the means being offered by a gentleman residing adjacent to the spot,) but was not done until the employees of the several grades could meet and consult each other, and obtain the authority, professed at all events to be, deemed requisite. This circumstance is mentioned but as an instance illustrating too general a habit. The members of the Board saw, on their own inspection, that repairs were not made with the promptness which they deemed due to the interests dependent on the Chesapeake & Ohio Canal, and in their attempts to trace out the cause they found themselves involved in a maze of uncertainty, the ultimate responsibility generally resting where a charge of manifest negligence could not well be sustained against the individual officer, altho' the interests mentioned were not the less sorely suffering; and by the way of relieving the difficulty, to an extent at least, they abolished the office of General Superintendent, thus making the Division Superintendent responsible directly to the Board. An incidental result of this action has been a saving to the Company of Three Thousand Two Hundred and Fifty Dollars—Two Division Superintendents at $900.00 each, and the General Superintendent at $1200.00 for salary and $250.00 an allowance made by a former board for his traveling expenses—although the primary object in this reduction of officers was, not a reduction of expenses, but a promotion of efficiency. So well satisfied had the Board been with the effect of its action in this respect, that whatever change shall hereafter be made should, in its opinion, consist in further reduction of the number of Superintendents, and if need be an increase of salaries to those retained, rather than in an increase in the number of officers. A regulation heretofore adopted prohibits any Superintendent from engaging in or attending to any other occupation whatever; and although the present Board has earnestly striven to enforce it, and although it believes that it has succeeded to some greater extent than was the case prior to its efforts, yet it thinks with regret that the success has not been perfect, and that efforts to that end should not be surceased until they shall have attained perfect success. The mighty interests, connected with and dependent ou the management of the Canal, demand that each individual, who shall consent to take on himself a part of so weighty a responsibility, shall surrender to the duty each mental and physical energy with which he may be endowed, and that a dereliction of duty in this regard can hardly be too harshly characterized.

Maulsby concluded his remarks on the new management apparatus of the company by describing the changes in the central office:

> The Board felt itself constrained by the supposed requirement of the intent of the Charter of the Company to rescind the action of its Predecessors, and to separate the discharge of the duties of Treasurer from those of the Clerk, and accordingly elected Samuel M. Magraw Esq., Treasurer, and re-elected W. S. Ringgold Esq., Clerk. It was at the same time felt that the change could not with propriety be accomplished at an increased cost to the Company, in its then and now financial condition, and accordingly the salaries lately paid

to the Clerk and Treasurer, and a subordinate Clerk—$2800.00—were divided, and $1400.00 fixed as the salary of each officer, Clerk and Treasurer. In this connection the Board asks leave to say, that such increase in the net revenues of the Company at no distant period is anticipated, as will justify the payment to the Clerk of a salary better apportioned to the labor, skill and devotion which the invaluable officer now occupying that position, daily brings to the complete discharge of the duties imposed upon him.[50]

In the hotly-contested statewide elections in the fall of 1857 the American Party maintained its control of the state legislature and its nominee for Governor, Thomas H. Hicks, won the statehouse.[51] On March 18, 1858, the canal company stockholders met and, at the direction of the Hicks administration, elected a new board of directors headed by Lawrence J. Brengle as president.[52] The new board quickly set to work reorganizing the management of the company. The office of engineer was abolished and replaced by the office of engineer and general manager with an annual salary of $1,500. John G. Stone, a former division superintendent, was appointed to fill the position. The old six-division alignment was restored and most of the former superintendents were returned to their positions:

> Georgetown Division: Eastern terminus to Seneca Feeder; Horace Benton, Superintendent
> Monocacy Division: Seneca Feeder to Dam No. 3 Feeder; Silas Browning, Superintendent
> Antietam Division: Dam No. 3 Feeder to Guard Lock No. 4; Levin Benton, Superintendent
> Williamsport Division: Guard Lock No. 4 to Guard Lock No. 5; Andrew M. Stake, Superintendent
> Hancock Division: Guard Lock No. 5 to foot of Lock No. 58; Lewis G. Stanhope, Superintendent
> Cumberland Division: Lock No. 58 to Western Terminus; Lloyd Lowe, Superintendent.

The board approved the following resolution relative to the duties and performance of the division superintendents and the general superintendent:

> That it shall be the duty of the division Superintendents to devote their whole time, and give their undivided attention to the care and management of their respective divisions; and that it be the duty of the General Superintendent to see that they comply with the provisions of this order.

Among other personnel changes were the appointment of three new collectors at Williamsport, Hancock and Cumberland, and a new Inspector of Cargos at Georgetown, and 44 new lock tenders. The old office of treasurer and accountant was reestablished and given to Henry W. Hoff-

---

[50] *Twenty-Ninth Annual Report* (1857), C & O Co., 3–5.
[51] Walsh and Fox, *Maryland*, 324–326.
[52] Since the election of a new board was usually held at the annual meeting of stockholders in June, Maulsby complained that the election was illegal and that his board should be entitled to hold office until June. He submitted the question to the company counsel for a legal opinion but was overruled. Angered by his abrupt dismissal, Maulsby locked the vault containing the books and papers of the company and locked the door to his office and took the possession of the keys. *Proceedings of the President and Board of Directors*, K, 1–4.

man, an American Party Congressman from Western Maryland who had just been defeated in his bid for reelection.[53]

In June 1858 President Brengle reported to the stockholders concerning the recent changes in the management of the canal:

> The [Maulsby] board immediately preceding the present board, on assuming the direction of the affairs of the Company, proceeded at once to change the organization which had existed on the line of the Canal since its completion to Cumberland, by removing, in the first place the General Superintendent and all six division Superintendents, who were all experienced, well tried men, and had long been connected with the Canal; then, reduced the Superintendencies from six to four, and appointed a General Superintendent and four division Superintendents, to these responsible positions, who, with a single exception, had hitherto never been connected with the Canal, and as we are informed, had no experience or knowledge of such duties as pertained to their stations.
>
> In a few months thereafter, the office of General Superintendent was abolished, thus leaving the whole line of the Canal of 186 miles under the direction of four division Superintendents, without experience themselves, without the immediate direction and control of an experienced head, and with no general system of management. To this mistaken policy chiefly, we think, can be attributed the disasters which have occurred [at Dams Nos. 4–5].
>
> The present board, believing that past experience justified the course, have restored the former organization of the line of the Canal, by establishing six divisions; and with two exceptions have appointed the former experienced Superintendents of divisions. We have also appointed John G. Stone, Esq., Engineer and General Superintendent, who was long connected with the canal in former years; and it is believed from his experience, energy and capacity, that he will render very efficient services in this station.
>
> With this organization on the line of the Canal, it is confidently hoped that renewed energy, vigor and economy, will be experienced in the management of the work, and that it will result in a more reliable, and less interrupted navigation of the Canal, than has existed for the past two years.[54]

Capitalizing on the collapse of the American Party and utilizing the heightened negrophobia following John Brown's Raid on Harpers Ferry, the Democrats secured control of the Maryland General Assembly in the November 1859 elections.[55] At a special meeting of the canal stockholders in May 1860 a new board of directors was selected with James Fitzpatrick as president. The following day ex-American Party Congressman Hoffman resigned from his position as treasurer and accountant and was replaced by John M. Miller.

A committee composed of the president and three of the newly-elected directors was asked to review the management system of the canal and to make recommendations for its improvement. In its report on May 16 the committee observed:

> that in their judgment the existing arrangement of six superintendents having control and management has proved utterly inefficient and unworthy of further reliance. Therefore they would respectfully recommend that the entire line of the canal be divided into sixteen supervisorships in distance regulated as nearly as possible to the condition of the ca-

---

[53] *Ibid,* K, 1–10, 13–16, 18–19.
[54] *Thirteenth-Annual Report* (1858), C & O Co., 3–4.
[55] Walsh and Fox, *Maryland,* 329–330.

nal at the several points along its entire length; and that on each of such divisions one supervisor be employed at fifty dollars per month, and that each supervisor shall be subject to, and under the control of the President and Directors...and the General Superintendent in the employment of the Company....[56]

The canal board quickly adopted the recommendations contained in the report with several accompanying amendments. The number of supervisorships was increased to eighteen and the salaries of the supervisors were raised to $55 per month. The directors then proceeded to fire and abolish the positions of the six division superintendents and their repair crews bosses, after which the eighteen supervisors were appointed to districts whose boundaries were determined by General Superintendent Stake:

Isaac R. Maus—Tidelock B to Magazine
Joshua W. Offutt—Magazine to Lock No. 22
George W. Spates—Lock No. 22 to Edwards Ferry
John A. Dade—Edwards Ferry to Monocacy Basin
John Short—Monocacy Basin to Berlin
John T. O'Bryne—Berlin to Dam No. 3
P. C. Savin—Dam No. 3 to Aqueduct No. 4
Lawson Puffenberger—Aqueduct No. 4 to Lock No. 40
George W. Grove—Lock No. 40 to Guard Lock No. 4
W. P. McCardell—Guard Lock No. 4 to Lock No. 44
Thomas Charlton—Lock No. 44 to Lock No 45 (including dam and feeder)
Emanuel Tice—Lock No. 45 to Aqueduct No. 6
B. B. Boatman—Aqueduct No. 6 to Lock No. 53
Lawrence Murray—Lock No. 53 to Dam No, 6
John McLaughlin—Dam No. 6 to Lock No. 61
Frederick Kasekamp—Lock No. 61 to Lock No. 67
Thomas Sammon—Lock No. 67 to Lock No. 73
David Wineow—Lock No. 73 to Cumberland

Among the other personnel changes were the appointment of new employees to fill the following positions: inspector of cargos at Georgetown; watch at Paw Paw Tunnel; collectors at Georgetown, Williamsport, Hancock and Cumberland; 47 lock tenders; superintendent of boats at Georgetown; and paymaster.[57]

President Fitzpatrick offered a lengthy rationale for the new system of management to the stockholders at their annual meeting in June, 1860:

---

[56] *Proceedings of the President and Board of Directors*, K, 177-178, 183. Under the Brengle administration, the canal company had experienced such desperate financial problems that it had been forced to pay the lock tenders and repair crews with certificates of indebtedness. So serious was the financial condition of the company that even President Brengle went unpaid for a period of months. *Ibid*, K, 147-148, 219.

[57] *Ibid*, K, 182-186, 192-195, and *Thirty-Second Annual Report* (1860), C & O Co., 16-19. Before the eighteen new supervisors began their work on June 1, General Superintendent Stake provided them with general instructions which required them
> to devote their entire time and attention to the Canal, to prevent breaches or other interruptions, if possible, to repair them promptly, assist each other promptly, carry out the By-Laws, send information about interruptions to the different Collector's Offices, and pay strict attention to the portion of Canal under their charge, rtc.

The present Board of Directors, deeply impressed with the magnitude of the trust confided to their charge, and anxious to realize the just expectations of all persons connected in interest with the prosperity of the Canal, to prevent in future those disastrous interruptions of its navigation, which have prostrated the business of important portions of the State, and to restore confidence to all great interests involved in its fate, gave their earliest attention, at their very first meeting, to the whole system of management heretofore adopted on it, and made such alterations, as in their judgment, will remove evils that have been so deeply felt and so justly complained of.

They have reduced the management to a rigid, responsible, practical and economical system. They have abolished the offices of Division Superintendents, which they considered were disbursing agents, and substituted for them, eighteen Bosses or Supervisors, each of whom will have charge of a certain number of miles, ranging in extent according to the condition of the work, as some parts of the Canal require more vigilance and labor to repair and preserve it in navigable order for five miles, than other parts will be for fifteen. The Board retained the office of General Superintendent, and that officer, who is familiar with the condition and wants of every mile of the Canal, will assign their respective divisions to the eighteen Supervisors, but no distance will exceed fifteen miles. Under the old system of Superintendents, there were sixteen Bosses, who received liberal pay and who really discharged all the valuable and responsible duties on their respective divisions. By abolishing the Superintendents and elevating the Bosses to power and direct responsibility, the valuable part of the old system is developed into the most efficient usefulness.

The Board entertains well grounded confidence, that the operation of this system, which went into effect on the first instant [June], will prove beneficial to the work and to all persons interested in its prosperity. By it the entire Canal is placed under the daily personal examination of vigilant officers who have been selected with reference to their industry and fitness, and whose duty it will be to take charge of the men employed under them, labor with them, and give their whole time and undivided attention to that part of the work allotted to their respective care and supervision. Each of them will be immediately responsible to the Board for the condition of his division, the whole of which he can examine every day in person, and prevent, by timely attention, those breaks which have so frequently occurred from neglect and the absence of that watchfulness, which should guard every portion of a work, upon the uninterrupted navigation of which the welfare of so many depends. It will be strongly impressed upon them, that negligence, incompetency or dereliction of duty, will be promptly visited with the forfeiture of their places, and that no man will remain in the service, who will not give practical proofs of his competency and fidelity in the discharge of the duties, which, by accepting the position, he assumed to perform. The interests involved are too numerous and important to admit the idea of retaining men in places who are not willing and able to labor skillfully and untiringly to establish and maintain its prosperity and usefulness on a permanent basis.

While this alteration is confidently expected to introduce vigor and promptness in the working of the Canal, no additional expense had been incurred in its adoption.

Six Superintendents received each $900 per year,	$5,400
Sixteen Bosses under them received each $450 per year	$7,200
	$12,600
Eighteen Supervisors will now receive $660 per year	$11,880
Showing difference in favor of the new system of:	$720

To this must be added the salary of a paymaster [James Condy], whose duty will be to pass over the entire line monthly and pay off all the employees of the Company and take their receipts in person. The Board considers the appointment of a paymaster indispensable to the perfection and accuracy of the system they are endeavoring to inaugurate. For many and obvious reasons the paying department of the service should be distinct and separate from those who control the labor and provide the necessary supplies of various materials. The Supervisors will have but one duty to perform—the preserve their respective divisions in navigable and good repair, and from that, nothing but unavoidable casualties will excuse them.[58]

The statewide elections in the fall of 1861 were held under the cloud of the Civil War. The Union Party, in its own right but fortified by the presence of the Federal military, won large majorities in both houses of the General Assembly as well as the governorship with Augustus W. Bradford as candidate. The election was significant in that it virtually ended any hope for pro-Southern elements to gain control in the state.[59]

The state Unionist forces lost little time in reorganizing the management machinery and personnel of the canal company. On January 30, 1862, Alfred Spates, a rising Allegany County Democrat who had been elected as president of the company the previous year, was reconfirmed in his office.[60] At a board meeting on February 12 the directors abolished the fourteen supervisorships and determined to restore the former six division management system. The new divisions and superintendents were:

> Georgetown Division: Tidelock B to Lock No. 23 (inclusive); Horace Benton, Superintendent
> Monocacy Division: Lock No. 23 to Guard Lock No. 3 (inclusive); John Caneron, Superintendent
> Antietam Division: Guard Lock No. 3 to Guard Lock No. 4 (inclusive); Levin Benton, Superintendent
> Williamsport Division: Guard Lock No. 4 to Guard Lock No. 5 (inclusive); Jacob B. Masters, Superintendent
> Hancock Division: Guard Lock No. 5 to Guard Lock No. 6 (inclusive); Thomas Hassett, Superintendent
> Cumberland Division: Guard Lock No. 6 to Guard Lock No. 8 (inclusive); Lloyd Lowe, Superintendent

Other changes were also made in the management and personnel of the company. The office of treasurer and accountant was abolished and replaced by the combination of the offices of clerk and treasurer into one position and an assistant clerk. The four collectors at Georgetown, Williamsport, Hancock and Cumberland were replaced, and 21 new lock tenders were appointed.[61]

---

[58] *Thirty-Second Annual Report* (1860), 3–5. Later in December 1860, the supervisorships of John Short, George W. Grove, Emanuel Trice and Thomas Sammon were abolished and incorporated into the fourteen remaining subdivisions. *Proceedings of the President and Board of Directors*, K, 232.
[59] Walsh and Fox, *Maryland*, 354–355.
[60] *Proceedings of the President and Board of Directors*, K, 250–253. Immediately following the election of Spates, General Superintendent Stake had resigned his position. Ringgold to Stake, July 10, 1861, Ltrs. Sent, C & O Co.
[61] . *Proceedings of the President and Board of Directors*, K, 272–277, 282. Apparently the position of general superintendent was not filled; thus, the division superintendents were directly responsible to the board.

President Spates notified the stockholders in June 1862 that the former system of management had been restored to the canal. His justification for the reorganization was as follows:

> Two years ago a change was made in the supervision of the line of the canal, by the appointment of eighteen supervisors and a paymaster, in place of six superintendents of divisions as had previously existed (with occasional change in the number,) since the canal was opened for navigation. It was supposed that this would be more efficient and less expensive than the former system. After a brief trial it was found otherwise, and that a divided responsibility, want of regularity and system, without satisfactory checks and responsibility for payments made, rendered the change not only less efficient and satisfactory, but more expensive. The present Board have therefore restored the former system of management by the appointment of six experienced and efficient superintendents of divisions, who will make the disbursements on the line of the Canal under proper regulations, and thus dispense with a paymaster. Some other changes in the emphasis of the Company have been made, without detriment to the efficiency of the service, and by these various reforms, effecting an annual reduction in the expenses of the Company of about $8,000.[62]

After receiving reports that some superintendents were neglecting their duties, the board established a new policy to govern their conduct. In December 1862 the following order was approved and distributed to each superintendent:

> That the several Supts. of the Canal be required to conform themselves strictly to the rules and regulations of the Company, that said Supts. be required to pass over the entire length of their respective divisions at least once a week, and to report to the Clerk of the Company, and also to the Collectors of Tolls at Georgetown and Cumberland, whenever any interruptions of the navigation shall occur, and how long such interruption will continue; that they also be required to make monthly reports to the Board of the conditions of their respective divisions, and that any carelessness on their part in the performance of these duties will be deemed cause for their removal from office.[63]

In the elections held in the fall of 1864, the Unionist coalition, dominated by its Radical wing since 1862, maintained control of the state legislature. Nevertheless, the emergence of a powerful Conservative force within the coalition was manifested by the election of Thomas Swann as governor. Encouraged by the gubernatorial victory, the Conservatives began a campaign to wrest control of the Unionist movement from the Radicals. With the collapse of the Confederacy in April 1865, the Radicals were left in a state of disarray as support for the war, which had been a cohesive core for the Union Party, was now gone and could no longer be used to submerge divisive issues in the coalition.[64]

At the annual meeting of the stockholders in July 1865 the Swann administration pushed through the election of Jacob Snively as company president in place of Alfred Spates.[65] The new president and directors appear to have made few alterations in the system of management of the

---

[62] *Thirty-Fourth Annual Report* (1862), C & O Co., 5.
[63] *Proceedings of the President and Board of Directors*, K, 315. In April 1864 the board authorized salary increases for the division superintendents, repair crew bosses and lock tenders. The superintendents' annual pay was set at $1,000, while the monthly wages of the bosses were put at $45. In October 1864 the superintendent of the Georgetown Division was authorized to hire a harbor master for the regulation of boats in Georgetown at a monthly salary of $45. *Ibid,* K, 383, 402.
[64] Walsh and Fox, *Maryland*, 381-382.
[65] *Proceedings of the President and Board of Directors*, K, 431.

canal. One change that was made was the reestablishment of the position of engineer and general superintendent in December 1865. To this position the directors named Charles P. Manning, a noted civil engineer who had earlier been employed to examine and report on the condition of the canal and the repairs and improvements needed to restore it to its prewar operating condition.[66] In November 1866 John Cameron was removed as superintendent of the Georgetown Division and replaced by Isaac R. Maus.[67]

---

[66] *Proceedings of the President and Board of Directors*, K, 465. Later in September 1866, the board dispensed with the services of Manning and again abolished the position. Ringgold to Manning, September 10, 1866, Ltrs. Recd., C & O Co.
[67] *Proceedings of the President and Board of Directors*, K, 526.

VIII.: MANAGEMENT OF CANAL MAINTENANCE ACTIVITIES UNDER THE HEGEMONY OF THE STATE DEMOCATIC PARTY: 1867–1889

By 1867 Maryland's period of "Self-Reconstruction" has come to an end and a more stable party alignment had emerged. In that year the ascendant Democrats pushed through the adoption of a state constitution and captured control of the governorship and the state legislature. Out of the political flux of the previous fifteen years, the Democrats—now augmented by Conservative Unionists, new voters, and returning veterans—became the dominant party in Maryland and would remain so into the twentieth century. Hence the canal management was no longer subject to the political whims resulting from the frequent shifts of power in Annapolis but was solely an instrument of Democratic patronage in Western Maryland.[68]

In August 1867, several months prior to the November elections, the company stockholders elected Alfred Spates, a long-time Democrat, to a second term as canal president as support for Jacob Snively, who had replaced Spates in 1865, had evaporated along with the Unionist cause. The new Spates administration made few changes in the overall machinery or personnel in the management of the waterway. The only significant change occurred in July 1868 when the number of divisions was increased from six to seven by the creation of a new Seneca Division out of portions of the Georgetown and Monocacy Divisions as follows:

> Georgetown Division: Tidelock B to Lock No. 21 (inclusive)
> Seneca Division: Lock No. 21 to Lock No. 26 (inclusive)
> Monocacy Division: Lock No. 26 to Dam No. 3 (inclusive)

George W. Spates and Amos Thomas were appointed as the new superintendents of the Seneca and Monocacy Divisions, respectively.[69]

Following reports of financial embezzlement and other fiscal irregularities on the part of President Alfred Spates and Superintendent George W. Spates, the stockholders elected Josiah Gordon to the company presidency in June 1869. Upon the recommendation of Arthur Pue Gorman, a rising political star in the emerging Democratic machine in Annapolis who was serving his first year in office both as a member of the canal board and the House of Delegates, the directors employed William R. Hutton, a well-known civil engineer, to serve as the canal's engineer and general superintendent and Sydney I. Wailes as paymaster. The latter was hired to breakup the reported corrupt system of money management that had been perpetrated by several division superintendents under the Spates presidency. An investigation revealed how the former officials had embezzled large sums of company funds for their own purposes:

> The time of the laborers and mechanics, under the system of working on the Canal, was kept by the bosses, and returned to the Superintendents. The Superintendents then returned it upon their abstracts to the Board, and received the amount from the Treasurer, which they professed to pay, according to their return. But we found, by comparing the

---

[68] Walsh and Fox, *Maryland*, 389–392. There are numerous references in the canal company records to the use of the waterway as a tool of Democratic patronage in Western Maryland. Among these are the following: Gilleace to Clarke, October 13, 1871, Blackford to Clarke, December 20, 1871, Hill to Gorman, August 9, 1872, Duvall, Gannon & Duvall to Fawcett, June 5, 1873, Shay to President and Directors, October 8, 1873, Michael to President and Directors, November 25, 1873, Hawkin to Gorman, February 15, 1875, Biser to Fawcett, August 6, 1875, Prettyman to Gorman, November 7, 1876, Pope to Fawcett, December 8, 1876, Polk to Gorman, March 16, 1877 and Peter to Fawcett, April 10, 1878, Ltrs. Recd., C & O Co.

[69] *Proceedings of the President and Board of Directors*, L, 104. Earlier in May the board had replaced the harbor master at Georgetown and the tender at Locks Nos. 1–4 with its own appointees. *Ibid*, L, 94.

bosses' time books and the abstracts of the Superintendents, that there were very large discrepancies between them, and that a great deal more money had been drawn by two of the Superintendents than had been returned by the bosses, or paid to the laborers under their charge. These two Superintendents have ceased to be officers of the Company.

Although the salaries of Hutton and Wailes added considerably to the expenses of the company, the activities of both men in streamlining the management of the canal more than paid for their employment. In fact, the savings on the Seneca Division alone were enough to pay the salaries of both men. All told, it was announced in June 1870 that the new management polices reduced the bills of expenses submitted by the superintendents by some $8,757 over the sums of the preceding year.[70]

The Gorman-dominated board was also responsible for two other decisions that had a significant impact on the management of the waterway. In July 1869 the company office was moved to Annapolis, thereby signifying the close affiliation of the company's affairs with the political interests of the state Democratic machine.[71]

On May 4, 1870, Engineer Hutton submitted a plan for the complete reorganization of the line that he claimed would save the cost-conscious board nearly $12,000 in annual salary expenses. According to the proposed plan, the seven divisions would be reduced to five as follows:

1st Division: Tidelock B to and including Dam No. 2 and Guard Lock—23.4 miles
2nd Division: Dam No. 2 to Dam No. 3 and Lock No. 35—40.2 miles
3rd Division: Lock No. 35 to upper end of Big Slackwater at tail of Lock No. 41—26.6 miles
4th Division: Lock no 41 to Lock No. 55 and Dam No. 6—45.2 miles
5th Division: Dam No. 6 to Dam No. 8—50.4 miles

The number of bosses and repair crews on each division was to be as follows:

1st Division: Two bosses and sets of hands
2nd Division: Three bosses and sets of hands
3rd Division: Three bosses and sets of hands
4th Division: Four bosses and sets of hands, the bosses on leaky sections to have a larger number of hands
5th Division: Three bosses and twenty men as at present.

The number of hands to be employed under each boss was not to be maintained at a fixed standard, but rather was to vary according to the work needs. One carpenter shop would be required on each division, with the exception of the fifth which would have two, and each shop would employ from 2 to 4 carpenters. The proposed plan would save the annual salaries of the following positions:

2 Superintendents	$2,000
3 Bosses	$1,620
2 (or 3) Horses	$600
Estimated 12 men @ $260	$4,320

---

[70] *Forty-Second Annual Report* (1870), C & O Co., 8, 15, and *Proceedings of the President and Board of Directors*, L, 180.
[71] *Proceedings of the President and Board of Directors*, L, 167–168, 182.

3 Cooks at $216	$648
3 Carpenters (estimated @ $750)	$2,250
	$11,938

Additional savings would also be made in the costs for fuel and lights, the maintenance of houses and work scows, and the expense of furniture. As the lock tenders were being overworked because of the increasing canal traffic, they were to receive higher wages so that they could hire one assistant for each lock under their jurisdiction.[72]

The canal board enthusiastically adopted the Hutton report, but before it could be put into effect a new board headed by James C. Clarke as president was installed in June 1870.[73] The following month the new directors voted to implement the Hutton plan on August 1. The superintendents of the divisions were appointed as follows:

1st Division (Georgetown)—Isaac R. Maus
2nd Division (Monocacy)—Amos Thomas
3rd Division (Antietam)—John Shay
4th Division (Hancock)—Denton Jacques
5th Division (Cumberland)—Edward Mulvaney

The offices of general superintendent and paymaster were abolished, and President Clarke assumed the responsibilities of those jobs, for which he was placed under a $50,000 bond for the faithful discharge" of the "trusts committed to him." In October it was determined to move the company office from Annapolis to Hagerstown so that the directors would be more accessible to the employees on the line of the waterway. All of the changes were made, according to Clarke in his report to the stockholders in June 1871, "to introduce more system, and greater discipline in the service than heretofore existed" and to secure "greater economy by holding to a more rigid accountability the officers and employees in [the] discharge of their duties."[74]

Two property inventories survive from the 1870 reorganization which indicates the quantity and types of tools, supplies and provisions that were kept aboard a repair crew's house-boat on the former Seneca Division and those that were under the immediate control of the division's superintendent. The house-boat inventory was made because the vessel was transferred from the former Seneca Division to the Georgetown Division to enable Superintendent Maus to house his men while working in the Georgetown area. Up to this time, repair crews had been housed at a local tavern while working in Georgetown at a cost to the company exceeding the 50 cents per day charged the laborers by the canal directors for their room and board. The property inventory of the Seneca Division was made because almost all of its length was transferred to the new Monocacy Division in the reorganization.[75]

---

[72] *Forty-Second Annual Report* (1870), 48–50.

[73] The Hutton recommendation relative to the salary increases for the lock tenders was put into effect on May 6. Each tender of a single lock was to be paid $50 per month, while each lock keeper of two locks was to receive $75 per month. The single lock tenders were to hire one assistant and the double lock-keepers were to employ two assistants subject to the approval of the division superintendent. *Proceedings of the President and Board of Directors*, L, 314–315.

[74] *Forty-Third Annual Report* (1871), C & O Co., 8; *Forty-Fourth Annual Report* (1872), C & O Co., 10–11; and *Proceedings of the President and Board of Directors*, L, 338–339, 349, 369, 393.

[75] Hutton to Clarke, August 3, 1870, Ltrs. Recd., C & O Co. The inventories may be seen in Appendices A and B. A cursory look at the company ledgers during the 1870s indicates that the company usually made a profit from the collection of the 50-cent daily charge from each laborer for room and board. For instance, the company realized a net gain of $1,144.32 from January to July 1870 between the amount collected and

The Clarke administration took a number of steps to up-grade the quality of the repair-maintenance work on the canal as well as the productive capacity of the work crews. In June 1871 the wages of journeymen carpenters were increased by 25 cents a day to a total daily rate of $2.50.[76] Two months later, a decaying packet boat lying idle at Cumberland was refurbished and converted into a repair crew house-boat.[77] With trade reaching record levels every year, the additional revenues were used to employ increasing numbers of workers to make the long-deferred repairs and improvements during the winter months. An example of the growing number of winter repairmen can be seen in a report by Superintendent Maus detailing the work activities on the Georgetown Division from November 1871 to March 1872:

> A gang of (6) six men under Boss Mason John Brannon commenced cutting stone at Great Falls on 1st November, 1871, and worked up to Feb. 2nd 1872.
>
> A gang of (5) men under Boss Mason John Brannon commenced repairing and rebuilding Locks 7, 10, 11, 13, 14, 15, 16, 18, 19, 20 and 21 on Jan. 8th 1872, and worked up to February 21st 1872 laying 1351 feet of new stone with cement.
>
> A gang of (17) seventeen masons under Boss John Brannon commenced putting up Feeder Wall Feb. 20th 1872, and worked up to March 4th 1872. Length of wall 400 feet, 3 feet thick and from 9 to 15 feet high layed in cement.
>
> A gang of (4) four man under Boss Mason John Brannon commenced repairing walls on Towpath and Berm side of Canal in Georgetown and worked from March 5, 1872 up to March 9th 1872.
>
> A gang of (6) six men under Boss Quarryman Levi Barnes commenced to quarry stone at High Island Feb. 20, 1872, and worked up to March 4th getting out stone.
>
> I placed a work on 1st December, 1871, (5) five Carpenters and (2) two helpers under Boss Carpenter John Collins and have accomplished the following work viz: Repaired Locks 7, 10, 11, 13, 14, 15, 18, 19, 20 & 21. Built Bridge near Lock 15 on Log wall Level, 3 stanks and one Crib in Feeder, and laying Truck with Lumber from Quarry to high Island, taking up truck put in (2) two new flumes one at Lock 5 and one at Lock 6.
>
> Built (2) two Bridges at the foot of Market house East and West span in Georgetown, and put up railings on Towpath side under Bridges at Market House and Aqueduct.
>
> I placed at work on Jan. 2nd 1872 a gang of (9) nine men under Boss William Matthews, who have done the following work—Building stank at Head of Feeder, removing dressed stone to Locks, worked on Crib to Feeder, puddle culvert below Chain Bridge, repaired Wall at Jennys Mill, puddling Trunk at Thompson & Edmonston's Mill, cutting bushes on Berm Bank from Lock 5 to Lock 8, removed mud & stone from Lock 5 to stop Lock, making stank and pumping out Lock 6, worked on Feeder and cleaning out Bottom of Canal in Georgetown Level.
>
> I placed at work on Jan. 2nd 1872, a gang of (8) eight men under Boss John C. Myers, who have done the following work viz: Tearing down Lock 15, attending Masons at Locks 7, 10, 11, 13, 14, 15. Tearing down Lock 14, removing mud and stone from

---

that spent. In January 1872 the net profit was $476.32 and in September 1875 the profit was $558.45. Apparently, the carpenters and others who worked in the company shops along the line rented their own quarters except when they were on special assignments at various points along the line. On those occasions, they boarded on the company house-boats or in lock houses or other company structures and paid 50 cents per say for room and board. *Monthly Statements of Receipts and Expenditures for Boarding Employees on the Canal Line, 1872–1877,* C & O Co.

[76] *Proceedings of the President and Board of Directors,* L, 411.
[77] *Ibid,* L, 435–436.

Lock 8 to Lock 15. Worked at Feeder from Feb. 20th up to March 4th. Also removed mud & stone out of Bottom of Canal on Georgetown Level.

I placed at work on Jan. 2nd 1872, a gang of (9) nine men who have accomplished the following work—Tearing down and attending Masons at Lock 15, 16, 18, 19, 20 & 21. Cut the Bushes on Berm Bank of Canal at Lock 20. Cutting to Lock 20, removed mud and stone from out of Bottom of Canal at Lock 20 to Lock 23. Worked on Feeder from Feb. 20th to March 4th, removed mud and stone out of Bottom of Canal on Georgetown Level. This gang under Boss I. G. Fields.

I placed at work on Feb. 13th 1872, under Bosses Cammack, Kendle & Connel (104) one hundred & four men who were wheeling stone, wheeling sand, carrying cement, mixing cement and cleaning out the Bottom of [the] Canal, removing mud and stone out of Georgetown Level. Working off and on to March 11, 1872.

We have on hand (6) six new lock gates and 3 old ones that have been repaired which I consider almost as good as new. There has been more work accomplished on this Division this past winter, than has been done any season for the past ten (10) years; the Division is in a great deal better condition now than it has ever been for that space of time.[78]

In June 1872 Arthur Pue Gorman, who had served both as a member of the canal board and the House of Delegates since 1869, was elected as president of the canal company. Almost immediately Gorman moved the canal office from Frederick to Annapolis. However, there was no reorganization of the canal management or significant turnover of personnel until the latter end of his ten-year presidency.[79] One of the earliest surveying registers of canal employees that list the positions, number of workers, and salaries by division from Georgetown to Cumberland is that for March 1873. The register is as follows:

GEORGETOWN DIVISION		
Superintendent	I. R. Maus	$83.33 per month
Collector	W. W. Blunt	125.00 per month
Assistant Clerk	C. Stewart	75.00 per month
Inspector	Hughes	75.00 per month
Harbor Master	James S. Kemp	75.00 per month
Lock-keepers (18)		
Boss Carpenter		70.00 per month
Carpenter (5 men)		2.50–3.00 per day
Boss Mason		5.00 per day
Masons (3 men)		2.50–4.00 per day
Blacksmith		60 per month
Helper		1.50 per day
Boss of Laborers		47.50 per month

---

[78] *Ibid*, L, 561–564.
[79] Frederick *Examiner*, June 5, 1872, and *Proceedings of the President and Board of Directors*, M, 32, 34, 113, 171, 223, 265, N, 1, 49, 87, 108, 192.

Laborers (14 men)		1.50 per day
Cook		20.00 per month
Boss of Laborers (2 men)		47.50 per month
Assistant		1.58 1/3 per day
Laborers (24 men)		1.50 per day
Level Walker		46.50 per month
Cook		20.00 per month
MONOCACY DIVISION		
Superintendent	D. T. Lakin	$83.33 per month
Collector	George T. Pope	75.00 per month
Assistant Clerk	Joseph Holland	60.00 per month
Lock-keepers (12)		
Boss Carpenter		2.50 per day
Carpenters (3 men)		2.25 per day
Boss Mason		4.00 per day
Masons (5 men)		1.50–4.00 per day
Blacksmith		2.25 per day
Boss of Laborers		47.50 per month
Laborers (11 men)		1.50 per day
Cooks (2 women)		20.00 per month
Assistant cook		1.50 per day
Boss of Laborers		47.50 per month
Laborers (19 men)		1.50 per day
Cook		20.00 per month
Boss of Laborers		47.50 per month
Laborers (24 men)		1.50 per day
Cook		20.00 per month
ANTIETAM DIVISION		
Superintendent	John Shay	$83.33 per month
Lock-keepers (6)		
Carpenters (2 men)		2.25 & 2.50 per day
Blacksmiths (2 men)		2.25 per day

Boss		45.00 per month
Level Walker		1.50 per day
Laborers (9 men)		1.40 per day
Cook		20.00 per month
Boss		45.00 per month
Level Walker		1.50 per day
Laborers (5 men)		1.50 per day
Cook		20.00 per month
Boss		45.00 per month
Level Walker		1.50 per day
Laborers (7 men)		1.50 per day
Cook		20.00 per month
Mason		3.50 per day
HANCOCK DIVISION		
Superintendent	Denton Jacques	$83.33 per month
Collector	H. Blackman	35.00 per month
Collector	J. V. L. Ensminger	35.00 per month
Lock-keepers (11)		
Carpenters (4 men)		2.00–2.50 per day
Blacksmith		2.00 per day
Masons (3 men)		3.00–3.50 per day
Stone Cutter		3.50 per day
Tender		1.50 per day
Boss		45.00 per month
Laborers (32 men)		1.50 per day
Cook		18.00 per month
Boss		45.00 per month
Laborers (11 men)		.96–1.50 per day
Cook		18.00 per month
Boss		45.00 per month
Laborers (10 men)		1.50 per day
Cook		18.00 per month

Boy		16.00 per month
Boss		45.00 per month
Laborers (9 men)		1.50 per day
Cook		18.00 per month
Horse Hire (26 mules & drivers)		189.25 per month
CUMBERLAND DIVISION		
Superintendent	Edward Mulvaney	$83.33 per month
Collector	William Weber	125.00 per month
Assistant Collector	John M. Resley	100.00 per month
Inspector	C. V. Hammond	75.00 per month
Assistant Inspector	Phoebe A. Neil	16.67 per month
Lock-keepers (20)		
Boss Carpenter		75.00 per month
Carpenters (5 men)		2.25–2.35 per day
Boss		45.00 per month
Laborers (10 men)		1.50 per day
Cook		18.00 per month
Boss		45.00 per month
Laborers (6 men)		1.50 per day
Boss		45.00 per month
Laborers (8 men)		1.50 per day
Cook		18.00 per month[80]

As the canal company had been operating with a five-division alignment since 1870, a group of 29 citizens addressed a memorial to the Gorman board in May 1873 requesting the reestablishment of the Williamsport Division as the sixth superintendency. The memorial contained seven reasons for such an action:

    (1) Most previous boards maintained the division
    (2) Williamsport was centrally located on the canal line
    (3) Williamsport was an historic canal-centered town
    (4) Williamsport had fostered the canal in its early years and had extended credit to the company during the financially-troubled years.
    (5) The coming connection of the Western Maryland Railroad with Williamsport would increase the commercial prospects of the town
    (6) The great lengths of the present divisions

---

[80] Payrolls, March 1873–July 1874, C & O Co.

(7) The danger of the slackwaters behind Dams Nos. 4 and 5 required closer attention.

In conclusion, the memorial mentioned the increasingly important political considerations underlying the request:

> But, we respectfully submit, there are other reasons deemed equally as important by the entire party to which, we, in common with the entire management of the Canal belong. So long as the President and Directors of the Company are appointed solely from the dominant political party in the State, so long will that party be held politically responsible for its management. The President and Directors being appointed with equal reference to their political affiliations and their known competency and integrity, the masses of the party naturally expect the principle to be carried out with regard to the patronage and subordinate places. And we beg to remind your honorable Board, in no spirit of captious fault-finding that the failure to fully recognize this principle has placed the supremacy of our party in this county [Washington] in jeopardy, and threatens us now with impending defeat. Recognizing the importance, at this time, of this view of the matter, and to evince our unity and harmony in the accomplishment of what we believe to be off essential importance to the good management of the Canal and the success of our political party, we have laid all individual preferences aside and agreed to recommend Jonathan Spillman for the position of Superintendent, believing that he is in every way competent, and that he will give unbounded satisfaction to the Company and the people of Williamsport.

The memorial was referred to a special committee which recommended that the management of the canal did not require a new Williamsport Division; thus, the proposal was rejected at that time.[81]

During the years 1875 and 1876 disputes arose over the wages paid by the company to the repair crews, and further conflicts developed over how much should be deducted from the worker's pay to cover the cost of room and board. In 1875 thirteen crew bosses sent a petition to the directors asking for a pay increase. The petition is interesting in that it describes some of the conditions under which the repairs crews operated:

> Our pay remains the same that it was when the present system for managing the Canal was inaugurated and when we take into consideration the increase of labor and responsibility consequent upon the increased trade upon the Canal we feel confident you cannot fail to see the justice of our prayer. We would further set forth that we receive one third less pay than others occupying similar positions under other corporations or public works. In consequence of the regulations established we are prohibited from engaging in any other business; we are therefore dependent upon this above for the support of our families, and when you take into consideration the increase in cost of living compared with the past you will discover that we are rending service for less pay than formerly. This too when some of us flatter ourselves that by a constant and undivided attention to our duty we have contributed much to the present financial prosperity of this great work. We would further submit that we are in the discharge of our duty constantly exposed to contagious and malarial diseases entailing upon us great physical suffering as well as pecuniary loss. In conclusion permit us to say that we are all deeply impressed with the

---

[81] Memorial, variously signed, to President and Directors of the Chesapeake & Ohio Canal Company, May 31, 1873, Ltrs. Recd., C & O Co.

great responsibility of our position and feel a deep interest in this great work under your charge and knowing you to be gentlemen of enlarged and liberal views, we ask nothing but justice and right at your hands.[82]

In May 1876 trouble erupted near Sharpsburg when Superintendent Samuel Mc Graw of the Antietam Division ordered his men to repair a breach in the canal. Those workers with carts refused to go to the site of the break until they were assured of receiving $3.50 per day. The common laborers joined in the short-lived sit-down strike until McGraw agreed to pay them $1.50 plus room and board per day. Similar wage increases soon spread throughout the entire length of the canal.[83]

The question of what amount should be deducted from the wages of canal employees for room and board also arose in May 1876. Up to this time the company had deducted 50 cents per day from the pay of workers to pay for the cost of food and housing in "house-boats," lockhouses, or company-owned structures along the line. Such arrangements were not provided for the carpenters and blacksmiths who worked in the company shops at such locations as Lock No. 5, Great Falls, Edwards ferry, Sandy Hook, Williamsport and Cumberland. These men had to provide for their own room and board (which averaged 75 cents a day) with the exception of those periods when they were assigned to projects along the canal. The problem was complicated by the fact that the company deducted 50 cents a day from the workers' wages even though at times the company was forced to board its hands in private homes at 75 cents per day. Thus there was considerable dissatisfaction by both canal officials and employees with the company's system of providing for room and board. Before the problem could be resolved, however, the declining fortunes of the canal would eliminate the need for discussions about the adoption of a more equitable system of providing for the men.[84]

In November 1877 the most disastrous flood in the history of the canal up to that time struck the canal, reaching levels from two to six feet higher than the worst previous flood in 1852. On December 1 all the company employees, including the collectors and lock tenders, who were not engaged on the repairs were relieved from duty so that expenditures were restricted to the actual cost of repairs and office expenses. The line of the canal was also reduced to three divisions as follows:

> 1st Division—Eastern terminus to and including Dam No. 2—John T. Fletchall, Superintendent; Isaac Maus, assistant superintendent
>
> 2nd Division—Dam No. 2 to upper end of slackwater at Dam No. 4—J. J. Moore, Superintendent; Samuel Mc Graw, assistant superintendent
>
> 3rd Division—Head of Dam No. 4 slackwater to western terminus—L. G. Stanhope, Superintendent.[85]

---

[82] Memorial, variously signed, to Board of Directors of Chesapeake & Ohio Canal Company, 1875, Ltrs. Recd., C & O Co. Apparently, the board paid little attention to the petition.

[83] Mc Graw to Gorman, May 17, 1876, Ltrs. Recd., C & O Co. Up to this time, the laborers had received $1.50 per day out of which 50 cents was deducted for room and board.

[84] Fletchall to Gorman, May 27, 1876, Ltrs. Recd., C & O Co.

[85] *Fifteenth Annual Report* (1878), C & O Co., 9–10. Paymaster Stephen Gambrill was placed in charge of the repairs on the Georgetown Level; Fletchall was given immediate supervision over the repairs from Lock No. 5 to Dam No. 2; Moore was instructed to employ 200 laborers and as many horses and carts as he could at Dams No. 3 and 4; Stanhope was ordered to rebuild Dam No. 4 and hire 60 men to repair Dams No. 5 and 6; and Cumberland collector A. Willison was authorized to employ 100 men to repair the canal from Dam No. 6 to Cumberland. Gorman to Board of Directors, December 12, 1877, Ltrs. Recd., C & O Co.

After the canal was restored to navigation in the spring of 1878, the old seven-division management system was reestablished. The positions, number of employees, and salaries that were adopted at this time were as follows:

> "The salaries of officers and pay of employees are: President, $2,500; Treasurer, $2,000; Engineer, $2,400; Paymaster, $1,500; Collector at Cumberland, $1,500; Collector at Georgetown, $1,500; Collectors at Williamsport and Hancock, each $25 per month; assistant clerk to Treasurer, $1,200; Inspector of cargoes at Georgetown, $900; Directors, while in season, $4 per day; seven division Superintendents, each $1,000 per annum; 17 bosses, each $45 per month; average of 20 laborers to each division at $1 per day and board; 15 smiths, $2.25 per day; about 3 carpenters to each division at from $4 to $2.25 per day; lock-keepers, $60 per month for double and $40 for single locks.[86]

During the late 1870s the Gorman board sought for ways to reduce its operating expenses by introducing various improvements. One improvement, completed and in operation by October 1879 was the installation of a telephone line along the waterway built by company hands under the supervision by Telephone Engineer J. Frank Morrison at a cost of nearly $15,000. There were 43 stations so located as to be within easy reach of any point on the canal. The telephone system, which was the longest single circuit then in existence, enabled the canal company to reduce operating costs by providing fast communication of information relative to breaches and canal traffic problems. Such information had been carried formerly on foot or by horseback or mail.[87]

In his annual report to the stockholders in June 1880 President Gorman announced that the telephone system had proven successful in facilitating canal repairs and enabling the company to concentrate its regular work at several locations along the waterway. Such developments had reduced the cost of labor and lessened the need for seven division superintendents. Accordingly, the number of divisions had been reduced to two:

> 1st Division—Eastern terminus to Lock No, 39—J. J. Moore, superintendent
> 2nd Division—Lock No. 39 to Western terminus—Lewis G. Stanhope, superintendent

It was calculated that this reorganization would save the company some $12,000 annually in overhead expenses.[88]

By 1880 Gorman had used his position as canal president to secure his hold of the Democratic Party in Maryland and win election to the United States Senate. Some critics, such as ex-canal president Alfred Spates, accused Gorman of relegating the real needs of the canal to a level of concern secondary to his effort of employing his position—one of great political influence in Western Maryland and hence Annapolis—as a vehicle to achieve his personal political ambitions. Such charges were summarized in an article in the Cumberland *Civilian* on March 3, 1878:

---

[86] Frederick *Citizen*, 1878, in Alfred Spates Papers, University of Virginia Library, Charlottesville. The precise date of the article, which had been clipped from the newspaper, could not be determined.
[87] *Proceedings of the President and Board of Directors*, N, 92–97, and *In the Circuit Court of the United States for District of Maryland: In Equity Daniel K. Stewart vs. Chesapeake & Ohio Canal Company and others* (Baltimore, [1878]), 106, 328–329, 333–334. Two descriptions of the telephone system may be seen in Appendices C and D.
[88] *Fifty-Second Annual Report* (1880), C & O Co., 11.

These charges allege that under the present management the canal has been for several years past in bad condition; that previous to 1872 boats carried from 130 to 135 tons of coal, and now carry no more than 110 to 120. That the prism has filled up as to make it almost impossible for boars to pass in many places; three guagers are employed to do the work of one; two men are employed as collectors at Cumberland at an expense of $2,700, while one of them offers to do all the work for $1,500; that an officer of the company here employed a large number of men solely to make use of them for political purposes in the Democratic primaries, so as to defeat certain men who were objectionable to the President of the company, and that for their political services they were paid by the canal company; that officers of the company bought votes, and thus aided in defeating the Democratic candidate; that certain officials were appointed solely in consideration of their promise to render certain services at Annapolis at the bid of the President and Directors of the canal company; that a contingent of $6,000 in the hands of these officials was expended in such a way as to demand investigation; that some of the officials of the canal company are receiving pay for two offices; and that Directors who are forbidden by the charter to receive more than the amount of their expenses are getting salaries, and that the pay of others has been doubled; that expensive excursions are of frequent occurrence, on which occasions an elegant boat with costly appointments is used, and unnecessary expenses incurred....[89]

Gorman replied to the charges by denying the specific allegations of wrongdoing while at the same time admitting that political considerations had been involved in filling canal jobs. In commenting on the Gorman years as president of the canal company, his biographer, John R. Lambert, commented:

The canal reflected the political complexion of the state. Maryland was the largest stockholder and as such chose its governing officials. The board of public works was composed of the governor, the comptroller, and the treasurer, all of whom had strong party affiliations that dictated their choice of the president and directors of the canal. In the same way, the lesser appointments in the company's service were also made, for the most part, from members of the dominant party. It [the system] had always existed.

According to Gorman, the system was justified because:

In the ranks of either of the political parties, which divide the intelligence of the country not less than its votes, it is always easy to find honest and capable men who are fitted, intellectually and morally, for the most important trusts, and have no great unwillingness to accept them.[90]

In August 1882 Gorman retired as president of the canal company to devote full time to his political career. A secondary reason for his departure was the decline in the fortunes of the canal as a result of trade stagnation, financial depression, stiff competition, and physical deterioration. Following the reign of Gorman, there was a succession of short administrations by political appointees, all of whom owed their positions to him. The administrations were as follows: Lewis C.

---

[89] Cumberland *Civilian*, March 3, 1878, in Spates Papers.
[90] Quoted in John R. Lambert, *Arthur Pue Gorman* (Baton Rouge, 1953), 71–72.

Smith, (August 1882); L. Victor Baughman (December 1884); and Stephen Gambrill (January 1888).[91]

To resolve the financial dilemma as well as it was able, the canal company resorted to several devices. First, it cut the ordinary expenses of operation whenever and wherever possible. Second, the board applied its economy measures to the work of maintenance and improvement by authorizing only the most essential repairs to the waterway and suspending work on the comprehensive program of improvements laid down by the Gorman administration in the mid-1880s.

During a miner's strike in the spring of 1882 trade on the canal was virtually suspended. The board reduced the pay of the lock tenders from $40 to $20 per month and that of the bosses and horsemen from $45 and $25 to $25 and $15 per month, respectively. The salaries were not restored to the pre-strike levels until May 1883.[92]

Further steps were taken to reduce operating expenses during the winter of 1883–84. Effective January 1, the pay of the lock tenders was reduced by 50 percent. Moreover, 65 employees on the 1st Division and 40 on the 2nd Division were laid off. Many of the men were rehired in the early spring to help get the canal ready for the new boating season.[93]

Still unable to meet its expenses, the board on April 24, 1884, ordered a 50 percent reduction in the number of its laborers. Accordingly, the following cuts were made:

DIVISION NO. 1			
J. Shipley	Boss Carpenter	From Self & 3 men	to Self & 1 man
M. Lynch	Boss Carpenter	From Self & 2 men	to Self & 1 man
J. P. Biser	Boss Carpenter	From Self & 7 men	to Self & 3 man
G. G. Latchford	Boss	From Self & 14 men	to Self & 4 men
Connell	Boss	From Self & 15 men	to Self & 6 men
Scraggs	Boss	From Self & 20 men	to Self & 10 men
Riley	Boss	From Self & 17 men	to Self & 10 men
Elgin	Boss	From Self & 13 men	to Self & 6 men
Boteter	Boss	From Self & 15 men	to Self & 6 men
Allen	Boss	From Self & 18 men	to Self & 10 men
Drenner	Boss	From Self & 15 men	to Self & 6 men
Marrow	Boss	From Self & 12 men	to Self & 6 men
		From 12 Bosses & 141 men	to 12 Bosses & 69 men
DIVISION NO. 2			
S. D. Young	Boss Carpenter	From Self & 5 men	to Self & 1 man
J. W. Burgess	Boss Carpenter	From Self & 3 men	to --------------
S. Troup	Boss Carpenter	From Self & 3 man	to Self & 1 man
Kelly	Boss	From Self & 12 men	to Self & 4 men
Sprigg	Boss	From Self & 12 men	to Self & 4 men
Hittenhouser	Boss	From Self & 7 men	to Self & 4 men
Masters	Boss	From Self & 8 men	to Self & 4 men
S. Sterling	Boss	--------------	----------
J. F. Sterling	Boss	From Self & 14 men	to Self & 6 men

---

[91] Sanderlin, *Great National Project*, 247–248, and *Proceedings of the President and Board of Directors*, N, 197–198, 298–299, 301, 323–324, 350, 370.
[92] *Proceedings of the President and Board of Directors*, N, 189–190, 214.
[93] Ibid, N, 246, and *Fifty-Sixth Annual Report* (1884), C & O Co., 17.

Hughes	Boss	From Self & 9 men	to Self & 6 men
Burgan	Boss	From Self & 16 men	to Self & 8 men
		From 10 Bosses & 89 men	to 9 Bosses & 38 men

In addition, one gang of hands at the Basin Wharf in Cumberland was to be dismissed to provide a savings of 25 percent in its operating costs.[94]

Faced with increasing debts and a continuing decline in trade revenues, the board in June 1884 ordered 20 to 25 percent cuts in pay and personnel. The following reductions were made:

DIVISION NO. 1			
J. J. Moore	Superintendent	From $125	to $100 per month
J. Isaccs	Assist. Superintendent	From $100	to $80 per month
William Snowden	Collector	From $125	to $100 per month
W. Jarboe	Clerk	From $100	to $75 per month
36 Lock-keepers		From $40	to $30 per month
4 Lock-keepers		From $45	to $35 per month
1 Lock-keeper		From $50	to $40 per month
1 Lock-keeper		From $65	to $55 per month
Richard Clark	Helper at Outlet	From $30 per month	to dismissal
James Vaughan	Mason	From $1.75 per day	to dismissal
E. Elias	Assist. Carpenter	From $1.75 per day	to dismissal
D. Reed	Assist. Carpenter	From $1.75 per day	to dismissal
William Danner	Assist. Carpenter	From $1.75 per day	to dismissal
Joseph Elgin	Assist. Carpenter	From $1.75 per day	to dismissal
G. G. Latchford	Boss of Dredge	From $70	to $35 per month
A. W. Latchford	Engineer & Watchman	From $2	to $1 per day
Average Monthly Force (12 men)		From $1.10 per day	to dismissal
W. H. Riley	Boss	From $55 per month	to dismissal
Average Monthly Force (10 men)		From $1.10 per day	to dismissal
Cannell	Boss	From 8 men to 4 men at $1.10 per day	
C. F. Elgin	Boss	From 10 men to 4 men at $1.10 per day	
Scaggs	Boss	From 12 men to 4 men at $1.10 per day	
R. H. Botter	Boss	From 6 men to 4 men at $1.10 per day	
William Allen	Boss	From 12 men to 4 men at $1.10 per day	
Silas Duncan	Boss	From 8 men to 4 men at $1.10 per day	
James Marrow	Boss	From 7 men to 4 men at $1.10 per day	
DIVISION MO. 2			
Lewis G. Stanhope	Superintendent	From $125	to $100 per month
A. Willison	Collector	From $150	to $125 per month
John Edwards	Assist. Collector	From $100	to $75 per month
J. Ranahan	Guager	From $50	to $30 per month
E. J. Neill	Inspector	From $40	to $30 per month
J. Spielman	Collector	From $50	to $40 per month

---

[94] *Proceedings of the President and Board of Directors*, N, 257–258, and *Fifty-Sixth Annual Report* (1884), 19–20.

28 Lock-keepers		From $40	to $30 per month
4 Lock-keepers		From $65	to $55 per month
2 Lock-keepers		From $50	to $40 per month
H. Tedrick	Packet	From $50	to $35 per month
Carpenter		From $1.75 per day	to dismissal
Blacksmith		From $1.75 per day	to dismissal[95]

Additional drastic cuts were made in the staff of the central office at Annapolis in July. The offices of general superintendent, assistant superintendent and engineer were abolished, and President Smith assumed the duties of general superintendent. The number of employees at Annapolis was reduced to five—president, treasurer, accountant, clerk, messenger—and their salaries were reduced by 20 percent.[96]

At the annual meeting of the stockholders in June 1885 L. Victor Baughman, who had been elected as president of the canal company in the previous December, announced that the reduction of salaries and wages, the discharge of unnecessary employees, and the consolidation of offices had resulted in a savings of $26,473.57 in operating expenditures. However, the company was still unable to meet its monthly payroll and had fallen behind several months in its payments to the workers. Most of the company laborers were continuing to perform their jobs despite the backlog in wages, although some workers in Washington County had left their places of employment. Henceforth the two superintendents, J. P. Biser and Edward Mulvaney, would make monthly trips over their divisions and submit written reports to the president concerning the work that needed to be done.[97]

Owing to the limited means of the company, Superintendents Biser and Mulvaney were ordered to dispense with the services of the entire canal labor force in January and February 1886. Only those employees who were needed to police company property were to stay on the payroll and then at reduced salaries.[98]

AMOUNTS DUE TO UNPAID LABORERS AND OTHER PERSONS 1883–1889	
1883	$ 2,088.54
1884	$ 2,803.94
1885	$ 174.46
1886	$ 589.45
1887	$ 4,686.48
1888	$21,609.98
1889	$26,554.06
	$58,509.91*

* Amount unpaid as of Nov. 1, 1889, Register of amounts Due Labor, 1883–1889, C & O Co.

---

[95] *Proceedings of the President and Board of Directors*, N, 267–268.
[96] *Ibid*, N, 274. In addition, the position of assistant collector at Georgetown was abolished, and all of the carpenters on Division No. 1 were consolidated under the supervision of J. J. Biser.
[97] *Fifty-Seventh Annual Report* (1885), C & O Co., 6–7, 9. See the following page for a list of the "Amounts Due to Unpaid Laborers and Other Persons, 1883–1889."
[98] *Fifty-Eighth Annual Report* (1886), C & O Co., 11–12.

President Baughman reported to the stockholders at their annual meeting in January 1887 on the results of the cost-saving policies of his administration and the prospects of the company for the coming year. Among his comments were the following statements:

> It will be observed that in the first year of our management a saving of over thirty thousand dollars on the running expenses of the canal was effected over the expenditures of the year 1884. A still further reduction of nearly twenty-three thousand dollars was effected this year over the year 1885, thus making the reduction for 1886 nearly fifty-three thousand dollars less than it cost to run the canal in 1884....We feel assured by an enforced system of economy we will be able to make still further reductions during the year 1887.
> The present administration does not propose to take advantage of honest labor by employing men in various positions when there is no prospect of obtaining the means by which they are to be remunerated.
> We have endeavored to carry out the pledges made to the people of Maryland when we assumed charge of the affairs of this Company two years ago, at which time we gave our assurance that a strict business management would be inaugurated, and that under no circumstances should this great work be prostrated for political purposes.[99]

An article appeared in the Baltimore *Sun* on August 20, 1887, describing in considerable detail the company provisions for room and board for its workers. In light of the desperate financial condition of the company and its numerous cost-cutting polices relative to labor, the article appears to be self-serving. Nevertheless, it is the most exhaustive treatment of the living and working conditions of the canal maintenance crews that is available:

> The number of employees of the Canal Company is about 275, of whom 125 are laborers who live in houses on land or in boats owned by the company, their quarters are fitted up with berths, wash stands, dining tables and other conveniences, and are noted for cleanliness. The laborers are paid $1.10 per day and are charged forty cents daily for board. Good cooks prepare and serve the food, which consists of beef, pork, bacon, vegetables, butter, bread, coffee and sugar. Each berth has a comfortable mattress and clean sheets and plenty of blankets. It was a wise act on the part of President Baughman to provide the men with good food and quarters, as they are in better condition physically than formerly, and, being satisfied, work harder. The cooks, of whom there are about twenty, are the only women in the laborers' houses. They have separate apartments, and manage to preside over their stoves and tables in a manner that commands respect. The men eat breakfast between six and seven o'clock, go to work at seven, take an hour for dinner at midday, and quit work at six o'clock. Then they wash, and spend the evening smoking, singing, telling jokes, and having a good time generally. The company's boats are towed to any point where work is required....
> Carpenters, bosses and miscellaneous workmen make up the remainder of the list of employees.[100]

In his last annual report to the stockholders in January 1888 just before Stephen Gambrill, the son-in-law of Senator Gorman, was elected to replace him, President Baughman recited the accomplishments of his three year administration. Although somewhat exaggerated, the report indi-

---

[99] *Fifty-Ninth Annual Report* (1887), C & O Co., 11–12.
[100] Baltimore *Sun*, August 20, 1887, in Spates Papers.

cates his concern for the achievement of the most efficient management system possible for the canal in light of the deteriorating company finances:

> Impressed with the belief that the proper administration of its affairs demanded a total divorce of its management from all political entanglements, we distinctly asserted in our letter of acceptance three years ago that the canal should, during our term, be conducted solely on business principles.
>
> With that end in view, useless offices were abolished, the number of employees decreased, expenses were curtailed, a close personal supervision was given to every branch and department, and no effort was left unused to secure an increase of tonnage and to stimulate the development of trade. As a consequence there is not today, and there has not been during our term, a single supernumerary or extra hand in the service of the company; there has not been, and there is not now, a single instance where a saving could have been effected in any way consistent with maintaining the efficiency of the works that have been overlooked, and every available ton of freight which the capacity of the boats was equal to was secured for transportation. Politics and political matters were kept studiously out of the business and the management of the canal, and we can say, without the fear of a successful denial from any source whatsoever, that the canal has not in any shape or form been used in the interest of or against any political party during our incumbency of the office of president.[101]

---

[101] *Sixtieth Annual Report* (1888), C & O Co. 5–6.

IX.: MANAGEMENT OF CANAL MAINTENANCE ACTIVITIES DURING THE RECEIVERSHIP PERIOD: 1889-1924

Following the titanic flood of 1889, the canal company admitted that it was unable to raise funds to repair its works and that it was bankrupt. As the majority owner of both the 1878 and 1844 bonds, the Baltimore & Ohio Railroad held preferred mortgages on the physical property and the revenues of the canal. On December 31, 1889, it petitioned the Circuit Court of Washington County for the appointment of receivers under the mortgage of 1844. On March 3, 1890, receivers were appointed to restore and operate the canal.[102]

The receivers soon took steps to restore the navigation of the canal. H. C. Winship, a long-time employee of the canal company, was hired as general manager, while H. D. Whitcomb, a former general engineer for the Chesapeake & Ohio Railroad Company and one of the commissioners for the construction of the levees on the Mississippi River, was employed as chief engineer. By the spring of 1891 some 1,000 laborers were involved in the repairs.[103]

At the same time the receivers commenced a review of the overall maintenance and operating needs of the waterway. The assessment led to the preparation of a list of the estimated number and types of positions required to manage the canal:

1	General Superintendent and Manager	$3,000
1	Assistant Superintendent, 1st Division	1,200
1	Assistant Superintendent, 2nd Division	1,200
1	Collector at Cumberland	1,000
1	Clerk at Cumberland	600
2	Boss Carpenters (@ $60 per month)	1,440
1	Assistant Carpenter (@ $35 per month)	420
40	Laborers (250 days @ $1.10 per day)	11,000
3	Boss Carpenters (10 months @ $60 per month)	1,800
7	Assistant Carpenters (10 months @ $39 per month)	2,730
10	Section Bosses (10 months @ $60 per month)	6,000
10	Section Bosses (2 months @ $15 per month)	300
80	Laborers (250 days @ $1.10 per day)	22,000
11	Level Walkers (300 days @ $1.10 per day)	3,630
15	Horses Owned by Bosses & Others (@ $15 per month)	2,700
1	Collector at Hancock (@ $30 per month)	360
1	Collector at Williamsport (@ $40 per month)	480
59	Lock-Keepers (10 months @ $20 per month)	11,800
6	Lock-Keepers, Outlets and Bridges (10 months @ $30 per month)	1,800
2	Lock-Keepers, Waybills & Feeders (10 months @ $40 per month)	800
1	Lock-Keeper, Feeder (10 months @ $25 per month)	250
3	Lock-Keepers and Inspectors (10 months @ $35 per month)	1,050
1	Collector at Georgetown	1,200
1	Clerk at Georgetown	720
1	General Bookkeeper and Cashier at Company Office	1,500
		$78,980

---

[102] Sanderlin, *Great National Project*, 263–266.
[103] Petition of Trustees, April 25, 1891, Receivership Papers, Washington County Courthouse, Hagerstown, Maryland

In addition, a list of other estimated maintenance and operating costs was compiled as follows:

Cumberland Wharf	$5,000.00
Trimming Cargoes	2,606.50
Operating Territory within District of Columbia including Georgetown Incline	5,000.00
Material for Repairs (gates, houses, flumes, wasteways, trunk bridges, scows, boats, wheelbarrows, shovels, picks, iron	14,020.00
	[104]$28,626.50

It is not known how closely this estimate was followed in subsequent years as the receivers established a management system for the maintenance and operation of the canal. The payrolls for this period, which are listed as existing in the Chesapeake & Ohio Canal records at the National Archives, have been lost. As a result, there is no accurate method of determining the composition of the employees on the line. However, a cursory examination of the annual expenditures by the trustees during the receivership period indicates a close correlation between those figures and the listed cost estimates in 1890.[105]

Because of the unavailability of payroll lists and detailed annual reports for the period little is known about the men who managed the canal during the receivership. The only individual for whom there is some information is George L. Nicholson, who served as general manager and superintendent of the waterway from the early 1890s until 1938 when the canal was sold to the federal government.[106] Another man long associated with the canal during this period was Samuel Sidney Connell, who served as section boss from Lock No. 22 to Brunswick from the early 1900s to 1924.[107]

---

[104] "Estimated Cost of Operating Canal," filed June 9, 1890, Receivership Papers.
[105] Reports of Trustees, 1891–1924, Receivership Papers.
[106] Sanderlin, *Great National Project*, 186–187.
[107] Jane Chinn Sween, "A History of Dawsonville and Seneca, Montgomery County, Maryland" (Mss. Maryland Historical Society, 1967), 69. Connell lived in a company house beside the Seneca basin during his tenure from the early 1900s to 1933. The structure was torn down after his death in the latter year.

X. RESUMPTION OF REGULAR MAINTENANCE ACTIVITIES PERFORMED BY CANAL COMPANY CREWS

A review of the canal company records indicates that virtually throughout the operating history of the canal regular maintenance activities were performed by work crews headed by bosses who were generally under the immediate supervision of the division superintendents. During the winter months from mid-December to mid-March the canal was usually closed to navigation. It was during this period that the crews removed siltation deposits and other obstructions from the canal trunk, made major repairs to the masonry locks, aqueducts and culverts, and restored the towpath to grade. Repairs or improvements were made to the lockhouses and the company shops and offices along the waterway. The wooden gates and the wicket rods in the locks and the waste weirs were replaced by new ones built in the company carpenter shops at various points along the canal. Such items as the woodwork in the composite locks also were overhauled during the winter. The winter months were also the time when long-range improvements, such as the lengthening of some of the locks in the 1870s and 1880s, were accomplished. Sometimes when a break occurred at an aqueduct or a culvert during the navigation season, a temporary wooden trunk would be thrown over the "trouble-spot" until more extensive repairs could be made in the winter.

During the boating season which usually lasted from mid-March to mid-December, the company crews were kept busy with a variety of duties. Some of their more frequent activities included clearing deposits and debris from the culvert barrels, strengthening the towpath and berm embankment protection walls, and making minor repairs as needed on the canal structures. Aside from these duties, the crews were kept busy repairing breaches in the canal banks, replacing lock gates that had been damaged by boats, and raising sunken hulls. The crews also performed the necessary restoration work to the canal after the frequent spring and fall freshets which struck the Potomac Valley. When major floods occurred additional hands were often recruited in the towns and villages along the canal to supplement the regular work crews. One of the most frequent problems to face the canal company during the summer months was that of an inadequate supply of water. As this situation was generally caused by the low level of the Potomac and leaks in the dams, the crews often spent much time tightening the structures in an effort to raise the level of the pool of water backed up behind them.

APPENDIX A

PROPERTY ON AND ABOUT THE HOUSEBOAT ON THE 2ND DIVISION, AUGUST 1870

An inventory of property belonging to the Chesapeake & Ohio Canal Company on and about the house boat on the 2nd division J. Y. Fletchall Superintendent [August 1, 1870].

J. Y. Fletchall Superintendent [August 1, 1870][1]
2 wheel barrows old sag ½ worn
6 wheelbarrows very good (new)
2 wheelbarrows for stone new & good
3 crow Bars
4 picks
6 shovels old ¾ worn
1 cart & gear
1 tool box in good order
1 feed box in good order
1 small house for provisions
1 stable for horse in very bad order
1 scow in good order
The House Boat in fair condition—a few repairs needed
13 mattresses more than half worn out
13 sheets half worn
13 Bolsters half worn
13 pr Blankets in all, (1 pr.) for each bed or bunk
2 Lamps
1 Boat Lamp
1 Cooking Stove & Fixtures say ½ worn

17 saucers & 13 cups for Table
1 pepper box, 2 oil cans
21 plates, 2 white dishes 1 Brown dish
1 stew pan, 2 Molasses mugs
1 Pitcher, 3 tin pans
1 Kitchen Lamp, 1 Tea Pot, 1 Sifter
1 Coffee mill, 1 Wash bowl
1 Jug, 4 Buckets (wood), 3 tin cups
1 office Stove half worn, 2 chairs
2 Benches for table, 1 long table & one small table for office
1 Stove in Scow & pipe 2/3rds worn
1 Block & fall in good order
1 Tow line new—some old rope of little use
4 spalding hammers—! Grind Stone ½ worn
2 Sledges, 1 shovel
3 Wash basins, 2 stools
6 Table spoons & 6 Tea spoons
½ doz. Tin plates, 10 knives & forks very bad
2 Looking Glasses
1 Small flat boat
1 new arc and 2 old (of no use)

---

[1] Ltrs. Recd., C & O Co.

APPENDIX B

TOOLS, BOATS, AND MATERIALS
ON THE SENECA DIVISION 1870

A list of tools, boats, and materials belonging to the Chesapeake & Ohio Canal Company on the "Seneca Division"

Delivered to A. Thomas as follows [August 1, 1870][2]

One small flat, 10 pr blankets—8 blankets—10 bed ticks, 7 pillow ticks, 10 pillow slips—26 sheets—2 table cloths, 5 towels, 2 curtain mosquito bar, 15 knives, 8 forks, 8 tea spoons, 7 table spoons, 6 buckets, 6 tin cups, 29 plates, 22 cups and 15 saucers, 3 molasses cans, 2 sugar bowls, 1 bowl, 2 milk pots—2 coffee mils, 3 jugs, 1 pitcher, 3 boxes—2 trays—1 polling pin—2 oil cans—tin lantern—dish pan—4 tin plated—2 coffee pots—1 cooking stove & fixtures—2 lamps—1 clock—3 tables—3 chairs—6 benches—4 stools—office stove—Bow lamp—wash pan—3 Sad irons—Bed Stead in office—oil cloth—3 axes—1 hatchet, 2 wash tubs—1 grind stone—2 striking hammers—1 set blocks & rope, 4 cross bars, 2 pinch bars—1 lamping bar, 15 shovels—6 picks—8 wheel barrows—3 spawling hammers—2 sledges—1 tool chest—2 locks—1 water keg—390 rails—62 post 1 hand made scoop in good repair—1 old stove.

1 Dirt scow, 1 large flat, 1 house boat, 2 pumps—want repairing—1 blanket, 1 towel—3 knives—2 butcher knives, 4 forks—6 spoons—1 canister—2 dish pans—1 tin bucket, 2 coffee pots—2 lamps, 2 pans—1 shovel, nearly worn out.

13 Heel posts—11 tow posts—2 marking sticks, 19 beams—146 arms—3 pieces 4x5 yellow pine—250 ft. I in. oak—200 ft. 1 in. pine—100 ft. ¾ in. oak—150 ft 3 in. oak—50 ft 1½ in. oak—1 piece 6x10—5 trussels—400 ft 2 in. white pine, lock & key—work bench—2 bench screws 1 cross cut saw—1 boring machine—7 augers—1 Canal stamp—2 bars iron 1 wrench—2 axes—2 crow bars set shear polls & rig—½ bbl. Pitch—bale oakum, 2 timber jacks and 4 rollers—1 cant hook—1 ladder—one grab hook—1 grind stone—2 buckets, 1 cup—22 bolts—5 new pivots—1 old pivot—3 new pots—5 old pots—4 new frames & paddles—1 frame—200 old bolts—T.C.L.s & taps—3½ keys, spikes, 40 nails—1 oil can, 1 brush, 2 hoes—3 sets cast gears—3 jumper drills, 1 churn drill, 5 hand drills—1 scraper—about 1500 old railing iron—2 old shovels—3 house casts, 1 stone truck—1 ring mall about 1000 ft., old lumber, 7 wheel barrows—2 new stone barrows—2 old stone barrows—1 old grout box—3 old barrows worth nothing—3 pumps nearly worn out.

---

[2] Ltrs. Recd., C & O Co.

APPENDIX C

REPORT ON CANAL TELEPHONE LINE, SEPTEMBER 27, 1879[3]

The undersigned committee appointed at the last meeting of the Board of Directors held in Annapolis to examine and inspect the "Telephone" recently constructed under your direction by Mr. Morrison, from Georgetown to Cumberland, and also to examine and inspect the re-building of Dam No. 4 which was washed away by the floods in the Potomac in the year 1877, beg leave to submit the following report:

In company with Mr. Morrison we examined a large portion of the "Telephone" line constructed by him, and now in use, and find the number of poles to the mile to be thirty (30) of good solid chestnut timber, twenty five (25) feet high of an average size of six (6) inches at the upper end, well set in the embankment, on straits four and one half (4½) feet deep and on curves five (5) feet in clay driven foundations except in crossings over Railroads, or county Bridges or other obstructions, in the way of the line where they range from thirty five (35) to forty and forty-five (40–45) feet in height in order to clear the line from all possible contact with such obstructions. At Big Slack Water the line changes from the towpath to the berm side of the Canal and instead of using poles, which was impossible owing to the change from the towpath to the berm side, the wire is strung on iron arms or brackets, securely fastened in the rock on the berm side of the canal, a distance of four (4) miles, and then recrosses to the towpath. The wire used in its construction is galvanized No. 9 gauge regular standard Telegraph wire fulfilling all the Electrical conditions of first class material, placed on the poles by screw glass insulators, or brackets, secured to poles by six (6) inch spikes. All line wire points firmly soldered at the ends in the most approved manner. The instruments are connected with the main line by No. 14 gauge copper wire passing through hard rubber tubes through the wall of the Telephone building and soldered to the line wire and side. The entire line is worked by five (5) cells gravity battery placed at each Telegraph Station, ten (10) additional cells of the same character at terminal points. The Telephone is a carbon transmitter "Edison's Patent."

The simple and easy method of communication by telephone adapts it peculiarly well to canal transportation service, and the facilities afforded to work and transportation on the canal must and will very soon dispense with a number of superintendents and other employees necessary under the present management. We have at different places along the line, test the method of communication between different points or stations, and find the line in good working order. Mr. Morrison, who constructed the line, under your direction, accompanied us for the purpose of explaining the manner of operating the line, and to him we are indebted for so much instructing information on the subject.

At the big tunnel an additional line is constructed over the hill from the first lock, east end of tunnel to the watch box at the west end of the tunnel, affording additional facilities for the passage of boats through the tunnel.

---

[3] *Proceedings of the President and Board of Directors*, N, pp. 92–93.

APPENDIX D

REPORT ON TELEPHONE LINE, NOVEMBER 1, 1879[4]

Under instructions from your Board during the year 1878, I made a complete survey of the Chesapeake & Ohio Canal, for the purpose of constructing a Telegraph line and establishing stations at proper points for the transaction of the company's business and to expedite the making of repairs when necessary.

In January of the current year, I reported to you that if the line of poles put up by the Superintendents of Divisions on the Canal could be used, that the cost of putting up the wire including line wire insulation etc. would be in round numbers about $14,000.

From time to time poles have been erected on which it was proposed to place the wires. In March of the current year however, under your direction I made an inspection of the poles and condition of the work and found that the poles already up were too light for the purpose for which they were intended. It was therefore deemed expedient to supply entirely new poles which would not only carry wires to provide for the addition of other wires from time to time as the wants of the company might require. I also found that the dense growth of timber along the canal necessitated the employment of gangs of men other than those engaged in construction to open the way for the building of the line. I began work on the 12th day and completed and put the line in service through its entire length on the first of October. Although it was not until the 31st of the same month that the line was cleared of trees and overhanging brush and placed in perfect condition. The original plan for a Telegraph line was abandoned because of the cost of skilled Telegraph operators and telephones were put in, in which are now being successfully worked by the Locktenders and other canal employees. Every assistance was rendered by the officers and employees of the canal company to expedite the work, men and materials were promptly supplied and in little over five months a line was constructed which from the difficulties to be overcome would ordinarily have taken at least double that time. In many places the only foot hold we could obtain for the poles was by drilling into the solid rock. In spite of this, and other difficulties, the work was completed in the short time above mentioned. The canal company is now in passion of one of the best telegraph lines.

The following description of the work material and equipment will give you a proper understanding of the character of the line. The poles are Chestnut timber not less than six inches at the top, twenty five feet high on the plains with from thirty to forty five feet high at crossings and other places when required.

The average depth in the ground is four & one half feet, except in curves and strains when from five to six feet set was given them. They are set in driven clay and every precaution taken to prevent them caving in on curves. White oak brackets fastened to the poles with six inch spikes support the glass insulators upon which the line wore is securely fastened with tie wire of its own gauge. The line wires are No. nine galvanized wire and stood all the standard tests for conducting tensile strength &c. The equivalent consists of Forty Eight "Edison Universal telephones," comprising Transmitter, Desk Pony, Crown Receiver Switch Key, Signal Bell and Relay. The Battery consists of four hundred cells of "Calland Gravity Battery" distributed as follows:

Georgetown	35 cells
Woods Lock	25 cells
Dam No. 4	15 cells
Dam No. 6	25 cells

---

[4] *Proceedings of the President and Board of Directors*, N, pp. 93–97.

| Cumberland | 24 cells |

The remaining stations thirty eight in number have 195 cells distributed Five cells to each station where telephones are placed. The telephones are set up in the watch boxes and Lock keepers houses and connected to the outside line wire by No. four gauge insulated copper wire. Where the wires pass through the walls of these buildings hard rubber tubing is inserted through which they are passed to insure perfect insulation. All the wires and instruments are protected by lightning arresters connected to heavy copper plates which are buried in the damp earth at a proper depth to insure perfect ground connection. All the materials, and all the work, is of the very best description, and all the appliances which modern science has furnished has been applied to make the service as nearly perfect as possible.

Portions of the line have been in service since the middle of September and the entire line since the first of October. The officers of the canal report the service entirely satisfactory. In addition to the main line from the collector's office at Georgetown to the collector's office at Cumberland, I built and equipped two short auxiliary lines, one from the Consolidation Coal Company Wharf at Georgetown to Lock No. five a distance of six and one half miles, to be used for the purpose of regulating boats on the Georgetown level. The other over the Tunnel at Paw Paw, to be used for the purpose of regulating boats passing through the Tunnel.

The total number of poles used in the construction was
5,273 Twenty five feet long
   24 Forty five feet long
   13 Forty feet long
   55 Thirty feet long
and three hundred poles twenty five feet long, span, distributed at different points along the line for repairs making a total of 5,665 poles.
69,300 lbs. of wire was used, including the wire for the auxiliary lines and tie wires.
7,500 screw glass insulators with 6,000 brackets.

The telephones are placed at the following named places:
Collectors office at Cumberland
Bodigan's Lock
Crawfis' Lock
Twiggs Lock
Darkey's Lock
West end of Tunnel
East end of Tunnel, Lock 66-1/3
Bells Lock
Ashkettes Lock
Dam No. 6
Murrays Lock
Brewers Lock
Ticis Lock
Sterlings' Shanty
Sir Johns Run
Williamsport
Hughes' Shanty
Moravey's Lock, Big Slack Water
Guard Lock Dam No. 4

Burgans Shanty
Deloney's Lock
Marrows Shanty
Shepherdstown
Drennans House Boat
Zimmermans Lock
Strippeys Lock
Harpers Ferry
Superintendent Moore's Office
McKernan's Lock
Berlin
Maumons Lock
Woods Lock, Head of nine mile level
Whites Ferry
Lock at head of Eight mile level
Seneca Feeder Lock
Great Falls
Moon's Lock
Outlet Lock
Browning's Shanty
Collector's Office, Georgetown
Winship's Office, Consolidation Coal Cos. Office
Dam No. 5

At Georgetown (Collector's Office) and the station at the east end of the Tunnel two extra telephones were placed to work the auxiliary lines, making a total of Forty six telephones inserted. We have two span telephones on hand to be placed subject to order making a total of Forty Eight telephones.

For ordinary working the line is divided into three sections by switches placed at the following named points:

>
> Dam No. 6
> Dam No. 4
> Woods Lock (head of nine mile level)

Three switches are so arranged that by a simple movement the whole line can be thrown together making a continuous circuit from Georgetown to Cumberland. To keep the line and instruments in order I recommend the employment of three line Repairers, who have been and are now employed in that capacity.

APPENDIX E

EMPLOYEES JULY 1, 1839

List of persons in the employment of the Chesapeake and Ohio Canal Company on the 1st July, 1839, with the compensation of each.[5]

Robert Barnard, treasurer and accountant, Washington, per annum	$1,400.00	
John P. Ingle, clerk, Washington	1,800.00	
Thomas Fillebrown, jr., assistant clerk	1,000.00	
William E. Howard, assistant clerk	1,000.00	
George Costin, messenger	250.00	
		$5,450.00
C. B. Fisk, Chief Engineer, entire line of canal	$5,000.00	
John A, Byers, principal assistant, between	2,000.00	
Elwood Morris, principal assistant, Dam No. 6	2,000.00	
Charles H. Randolph, principal assistant	2,000.00	
Joshua Gore, principal assistant, Cumberland	2,000.00	
Israel Dickinson, assistant, Cumberland	1,200.00	
Henry M. Dungan, assistant, Cumberland	1,200.00	
Samuel H. Williams, assistant, Cumberland	1,200.00	
Thomas L. Patterson, assistant, Cumberland	1,200.00	
Clement W. Coote, assistant, Cumberland	1,000.00	
Robert P. Dodge, assistant, Cumberland	800.00	
J. A. Sorecki, draughtsman $3 per day, Cumberland	1,277.50	
William H. Bryan, rodman, Cumberland	780.00	
Fitzhugh Coyle, rodman, Cumberland	720.00	
Benjamin T. Brannan, rodman, Cumberland	540.00	
James R. Young, rodman, Cumberland	540.00	
John T. Cox, rodman, Cumberland	540.00	
Thomas Gore, rodman, Cumberland	540.00	
John Buchanan, rodman, Cumberland	540.00	
John C. Howard, vol. Rodman, Cumberland	360.00	
Charles E. Weaver, rodman, Cumberland	360.00	
Fenton M. Henderson, rodman, Cumberland	360.00	
William T. Winsor, vol. rodmen, duty as chainman	360.00	
A. S. Bender, rodman, duty as chainman	360.00	
		$26,877.50
Daniel Pierce, axeman, $26 per month, Cumberland	$312.00	
John Ogleton, axeman, $26 per month, Cumberland	312.00	
John Doyle, chain and axeman, Cumberland	396.00	
George Stump, $20 per month and found, Cumberland	396.00	
Abel T. Crabtree, equal, per year, Cumberland	396.00	
John H. Sargent, equal, per year, Cumberland	396.00	
		$2,208.00

---

[5] *Twelfth Annual Report* (1840), pp. 36–39.

William, (negro) $15 per month, Cumberland	$336.00	
David Knode, chainman, $20 per month and found, No. 6	396.00	
Robert Gates, axeman, $17 per month and found, Cumberland	360.00	
Samuel Chase, axeman, $17 per month and found, Cumberland	360.00	
John Eberts, axeman, $1 per day, Sundays included	360.00	
Thomas Maxwell, $1 per day, Sundays included	365.00	
William Jones, $1 per day, Sundays included	365.00	
		$2,542.00
Alex. B. McFarland, superintendent of masonry, Cumberland	$1,800.50	
*William Anderson, superintendent of masonry, Cumberland	681.50	
*Duncan Grant, superintendent of masonry, Cumberland	681.50	
*William Challoner, superintendent of masonry, Cumberland	681.50	
*Daniel Logan, superintendent of masonry, Cumberland	681.50	
*William Hurd, superintendent of masonry, Cumberland	681.50	
*James Turnbull, superintendent of masonry, Cumberland	681.50	
*James Ellis, superintendent of masonry, Cumberland	681.50	
♣Joseph Knode, superintendent of masonry, Cumberland	547.50	
♣Frederick C. R. Maus, superintendent of masonry, Cumberland	547.50	
♣James Thompson, superintendent of masonry, Cumberland	547.50	
♣Morgan Snively, superintendent of masonry, Cumberland	547.50	
♣Thomas Snyder, superintendent of masonry, Cumberland	547.50	
♣Lewis Bartlett, superintendent of masonry, Cumberland	547.50	
♣James M. Cushing, superintendent of masonry, Cumberland	547.50	
♣Reuben Hurle, Jr., superintendent of masonry, Cumberland	547.50	
♣George Young, superintendent of masonry, Cumberland	730.00	
		$11,680.50
Jas. Hilton, lock-keeper—Lock B, Washington	50.00	
Jas. O. Reiley, lock-keeper tide-locks, & locks 1, 2, 3 & 4, Georgetown	1,200.00	
Thos. B. Offut, lock-keeper, Lock No. 5 & Guard-lock No. 1	250.00	
J. Whelan, lock-keeper, Lock No. 6	150.00	
M. Hart, lock-keeper, Lock No. 7	150.00	
L. Barret, lock-keeper, Lock No. 8	150.00	
J. Y. Young, lock-keeper, Lock No. 9 & 10	200.00	
William Burgess, lock-keeper, Lock No. 11	150.00	
Fred. Metts, lock-keeper, Lock No. 12, 13 and 14	250.00	
Hez. Metts, lock-keeper, Lock No. 15 and 16	276.00	
Jos. Caldwell, lock-keeper, Lock No. 17 and 18	276.00	
Daniel Collins, lock-keeper, Lock No. 19 and 20 Crom.	200.00	
R. C. Field, lock-keeper, Lock No. 21	150.00	

* Assistant superintendents of masonry, who are paid at the rate of $2 per day in the winter months, and $2.25 the rest of the year, Sundays exclusive.
♣ Superintendents of sections at $1.50 per day, Sunday's inclusive, with the exception of George Young, who receives $2 per day, he being connected with the superintendence of Dam No. 8, in addition to his other duties.

M. F. Harris, lock-keeper, Lock No. 22	150.00	
		$3,602.00
W. H. Hammondtree, lock-keeper, Lock No. 23 & Guard Lock No. 2	$200.00	
C. H. Shanks, lock-keeper, Lock No. 24	150.00	
Asa Aud, lock-keeper, Lock No. 25, & Edwards Ferry outlet lock	250.00	
James Fitch, lock-keeper, Lock No. 26	150.00	
Thomas Waller, lock-keeper, Lock No. 27	150.00	
P. McGaughan, collector, Point of Rocks	300.00	
James Davis, lock-keeper, Lock No. 28	150.00	
William Waller, lock-keeper, Lock No. 29	175.00	
William Kuhn, lock-keeper, Lock No. 30, Berlin	100.00	
A. B. Ward, lock-keeper, Lock No. 31	175.00	
J. B. Shope, lock-keeper, Lock No. 32	175.00	
W. S. Elgin, lock-keeper & collector, Lock No. 33 & H. Ferry outlet L	300.00	
John Crowley, lock-keeper, Lock No. 34	175.00	
William McKay, lock-keeper, Lock 35, 36, Guard-lock No. 3, H. Ferry	300.00	
J. Kercheval, lock-keeper, Lock No. 37	150.00	
G. W. Hughes, lock-keeper, Lock No. 38 & river lock, Shepherdstown	200.00	
Joseph Gwyn, lock-keeper, Lock No. 39	150.00	
A. McCoy, lock-keeper, Lock No. 40	150.00	
L. R. Shaw, lock-keeper, Guard Lock No. 4, Dam No. 4	150.00	
Henry Boyd, lock-keeper, Lock No. 41 and 42	200.00	
M. Crisman, lock-keeper, Lock No. 43	150.00	
William Irwin, collector, Williamsport basin	400.00	
Jacob Morten, lock-keeper, Guard Lock No. 5	150.00	
		$4,450.00
Philip Trammel, lock-keeper, Locks Nos. 45 and 46	200.00	
Daniel Brewer, lock-keeper, Locks Nos. 47, 48, 49 and 50	300.00	
Henry Rowland, lock-keeper, Lock No. 51 and 52	200.00	
Vacant, lock-keeper, Lock Mo. 53	150.00	
Vacant, lock-keeper, Guard Lock, Dam No. 6	150.00	
		$1,000.00
J. Y. Young, superintendent from Georgetown basin to Edward's ferry	$1,000.00	
William S. Elgin, superintendent, from thence to Harpers Ferry Falls	1,000.00	
George W. Rogers, superintendent, from Harpers Ferry to Dam No. 5	1,200.00	
John G. Stone, superintendent, from thence to Dam No. 6	1,200.00	
		$4,400.00
		$62,210.00
Western Survey party, (temporarily engaged)		
Jno. S. McColloh, acting assistant, entered service May 19, 1839, at		

$66 2/3 per month		
Richard S. McColloh, rodman, entered service, June 8, 1839, at $45 per month		
John Widener, chainman, entered service, May 24, at $1 per day, Sundays inclusive		
John Paw, chainman, entered service, May 22, at $1 per day, Sundays inclusive		
Samuel Davis, axeman, entered service June 2, 1839, at $1 per day		
Thomas Taylor, axeman, entered service, May 22, 1839 at $1 per day, Sundays inclusive		
The cost of the "Western Survey" last year was $1,029.37, viz:		
Pay of F. Coyle, acting assistant, (while engaged on the "Western Survey") 3 2/3 months, at the rate of $60 2/3 per month	$244.44	
J. S. McColloh and R. S. McColloh, volunteer rodmen, 3 5/6 months, at $30 per month	230.00	
Pay of hands and board	498.87	
Contingencies	56.06	
	$1,029.37	
President and Directors		
Francis Thomas, President, $3,000 per annum		
John J. Abert	Directors—$4 per day to each director during the time which he shall be actually engaged in the duties of his office, provided that such compensation does not exceed, in any one year, the sum of $300.	
Phineas Janney		
Thomas Perry		
James Carroll		
Jacob G. Davies		
Joseph White		
Summary of annual expenses, as before stated, exclusive of President and Directors		
At the office in Washington	$5,450.00	
Engineers, axemen and chainmen	31,627.50	
Superintendents of masonry and sections	11,680.50	
Superintendents on the line finished	4,400.00	
Lock-keepers and collectors	9,052.00	
	$62,210.00	
The pay of the party now temporarily employed in the survey of the Western section, is at the rate of $2,800 per annum		

APPENDIX F

OFFICERS FEBRUARY 1, 1840

List of the officers of the Chesapeake and Ohio Canal Company, in service on the 1st day of February, 1840, with the rate of compensation paid to each.[6]

Francis Thomas, President (compensation per annum)	$3,000.00
Jacob G. Davies, Robert P. Dunlop, Washington Duval, Phineas Janey, John W. Maury, Joseph White — *Directors*—$4 per day to each, during the time he shall be actually engaged in the duties of his office, provided the pay of each director shall not exceed 300 dollars per annum.	1,800.00
John P. Ingle, clerk	1,800.00
Robert Barnard, treasurer and accountant	1,400.00
Thomas Fillebrown, Jr., clerk	1,000.00
William E. Howard, assistant clerk	1,000.00
George Costin, messenger	250.00
Maximum compensation if each director shall receive $300	$9,250.00
John Y. Young, superintendent 1st Division canal	$800.00
William S. Elgin, superintendent 2nd Division	800.00
George W. Rogers, superintendent 3rd Division	800.00
John G. Stone, superintendent 4th Division	800.00
Jas. O. Reiley, collector and keeper Locks Nos. 1,2,3,4	1,200.00
P. McGaughanm collector, Point of Rocks	300.00
William Irwin, collector, Williamsport	400.00
Arthur Blackwell, collector, Hancock	400.00
John P. Hilton, keeper of tide-lock B	50.00
Thomas B. Offut, keeper, Lock No. 5, and guard lock	250.00
James Dalzell, keeper, Lock No. 6	150.00
Michael Hart, keeper, Lock No. 7	150.00
Levi Barrett, keeper, Lock No. 8	150.00
John Y. Young, keeper, Lock No. 9 and 10	200.00
Weston Burgess, keeper, Lock No. 11	150.00
Frederick Metts, keeper, Lock No. 12, 13 and 14	250.00
Hezekiah Metts, keeper, Lock No. 15 and 16	276.00
Joseph Caldwell, keeper, Lock No. 17 and 18	276.00
Daniel Collins, keeper, Lock No. 19 and 20	200.00
R. C. Fields, keeper, Lock No. 21	150.00
M. F. Harris, keeper, Lock No. 22	150.00
W. H. Hammondtree, keeper, Lock No. 23 and guard	200.00
Charles H. Shanks, keeper, Lock No. 24	150.00
Asa Aud, keeper, Lock No. 25 and outlet	250.00

---

[6] *Twelfth Annual Report* (1840), pp. 34–36.

James Fitch, keeper, Lock No. 26	150.00
Thomas Walter, keeper, Lock No. 27	150.00
James Davis, keeper, Lock No. 28	150.00
William Walter, keeper, Lock No. 29	175.00
William Kuhn, keeper, Lock No. 30	100.00
A. B. Ward, keeper, Lock No. 31, &c	175.00
J. B. Shope, keeper, Lock No. 32	175.00
W. S. Elgin, keeper, Lock No. 33 and collector	300.00
John Crowley, collector, Lock No. 34	175.00
William McKay, keeper, Lock No. 35, 36 and guard	300.00
John Kercheval, keeper, Lock No. 37	150.00
George Hughes, keeper, Lock No. 38 and outlet	200.00
Joseph Gwyn, keeper, Lock No. 39	150.00
Andrew McCoy, keeper, Lock No. 40	150.00
Levi R. Shaw, keeper, Guard Lock No. 4	150.00
Henry Boyd, keeper, Locks No. 41 and 42	200.00
Michael Chrisman, keeper, Lock No. 43	150.00
Joseph Hollman, keeper, Lock No. 44, water power	
Jacob Motter, keeper, Guard Lock No. 5	150.00
Phillip Trammell, keeper, Locks No. 45 and 46	200.00
Daniel Brewer, keeper, Locks No. 47, 48, 49 and 50	300.00
Upton Rowland, keeper, Locks No. 51 and 52umberland	200.00
H. Connwe, keeper, Lock No. 53	150.00
John Roberts, temporary, Guard Lock No. 6	456.00
Superintendents, collectors, and lock-keepers	$12,958.00
Charles B. Fisk, Chief Engineer	$4,000.00
Elwood Morris, principal assistant	2,000.00
Joshua Gore, principal assistant	2,000.00
Israel Dickinson, assistant	1,200.00
Hugh M. Dungan, assistant	1,200.00
Samuel H. William, assistant	1,200.00
Thomas L. Patterson, assistant	1,200.00
R. S. McColloh, rodman	540.00
Benjamin F. Branan, rodman	540.00
James R. Young, rodman	540.00
Fenton M. Henderson, rodman	540.00
, axeman	365.00
, axeman	365.00
, axeman	365.00
, axeman	365.00
A. B. McFarland, superintendent of masonry	681.50
D. Logan, superintendent of masonry	681.50
Joseph Knode, superintendent of sections	547.50
Morgan Snively, superintendent of sections	547.50
Thomas Snyder, superintendent of sections	547.50

James M. Cushing, superintendent of sections	547.50
George Young, superintendent of sections	730.00
Wm. H. Brayan, commissioner and clerk in the office of the Chief Engineer	1,000.00
Engineers, commissioners, &c.	$21,703.00

Summary of yearly compensation.	
The President, and Clerks, (if the directors receive the maximum of their compensation)	$9,250.00
The superintendents, collectors, and lock-keepers	12,958.00
The engineers and commissioner	21,703.00
	$43,911.00

Note: There are a few other officers in the service of the company at this time, but as their term of service will expire on the 1st of March next, they are not entered on this list.

APPENDIX G

OFFICERS, ENGINEERS, AND AGENTS APRIL 2, 1841

List of the officers, engineers, and agents in employ of the Chesapeake & Ohio Canal Company, on the 2nd day of April, 1841, the day on which the present Board of President and Directors were elected, with the rate of compensation paid to each annually.[7]

Francis Thomas, (president) compensation per annum		$3,000
Dr. William Tyler,	Directors—$4 per day to each, during the time he shall be actually engaged in the duties of his office, provided the pay of each director shall not exceed 300 dollars per annum.	1,800
Jacob Markell,		
John McPherson,		
Robert P. Dunlop,		
James Swan,		
William Lucas		
Thomas Turner, clerk		1,800
Edward Shriver, assistant clerk		1,000
Ezra Kouck, collector general of tolls		1,000
Samuel Tyler, treasurer and accountant		1,400
Albert Maybury, messenger		200
		10,200
Elwood Morris, chief engineer 1st Division canal		$4,000
Henry M. Dungan, assistant engineer		1,200
Thomas L. Patterson, assistant engineer		1,200
Jacob C. Schnebly, rodman		540
Benjamin F. Brennan, rodman		540
Two chain and axeman		730
Samuel M. Semmes, commissioner		1,000
		9,210
John Y. Young, superintendent 1st division		$800
William O'Neale, superintendent 2nd division		800
John D. Grove, superintendent 3rd division		800
Joseph Hololman, superintendent 4th division		800
Benjanin F, Mackall, collector of tolls at Georgetown		800
P. McGaughan, collector of tolls at Point of Rocks		800
William McKepler, collector of tolls at Williamsport		400
Arthur Blackwell, collector of tolls at Hancock		400
John Hilton, keeper of Lock B		50
James O'Riley, keeper of locks Nos. 1, 2, 3 and 4		500
Thomas B. O'Offutt, keeper of lock No. 5 and guard lock		250
James Dalzell, keeper of lock No. 6		150
Michael Hart, keeper of lock No. 7		150
Levi Barrett, keeper of lock No. 8		150
Osbourn Crawford, keeper of locks No. 9 and 10		200
Wilton Burgess, keeper of Lock No. 11		150

---

[7] *Fourteenth Annual Report* (1842), pp. 24–25.

Frederick Metts, keeper of locks No. 12, 13 and 14	250
Hezekiah Metts, keeper of locks No. 15 and 16	276
William H. Henderson, keeper of locks Nos. 17 and 18	276
D. Collins, keeper of locks Nos. 19 and 20	$200
Robert C. Fields, keeper of lock No. 21	150
John Fields, keeper of lock No. 22	150
William H. Hammontru, keeper of lock No. 23 and guard lock	200
Charles H. Shanks, keeper of lock No. 24	150
Asa Aud, keeper of lock No. 25 and outlet	250
James Fitch, keeper of lock No. 26	150
Thomas Walter, keeper of lock No. 27	150
James Davis, keeper of lock No. 28	150
John Walter, keeper of lock No. 29	175
W. Kuhn, keeper of lock No. 30	100
Dennis Harrison, keeper of lock No. 31, &c.	175
A. W. Jones, keeper of lock No. 32	175
W. S. Elgin, keeper of lock No. 33 and collector of tolls	300
John Crowley, keeper of lock No. 34	175
William McKay, keeper of locks Nos. 35, 36 and guard	300
John Kerchwell, keeper of lock No. 37	150
George Hughes, keeper of lock No. 38 and outlet	200
Joseph Gwyn, keeper of lock No. 39	150
Andrew McKoy, keeper of lock No. 40	150
Levi R. Shaw, keeper of guard lock No. 4	150
Henry Boyd, keeper of locks Nos. 41 and 42	200
Michael Crisman, keeper of lock No. 43	150
Joseph Hollman, keeper of lock No. 44—water power granted	
Jacob Motter, keeper of guard lock No. 5	150
John Herbert, keeper of locks Nos. 45 and 46	200
Daniel Brewer, keeper of locks Nos. 47, 48, 49 and 50	300
Upton Rowland, keeper of locks No. 51 and 52	200
H. Conner, keeper of lock No. 53	150
Thomas Fleming, keeper of guard lock No. 6	175
Superintendents, collectors and lock-keepers	12,777
Summary	
The President, and Clerks, ($300 each Director)	$10,200
Engineers, rodmen, axemen and commissioners	9,210
Superintendents, collectors and lock-keepers	12,777
Total	32,187

THO. TURNER,
Clerk of the Chesapeake and Ohio Canal Company.

APPENDIX H

OFFICERS JUNE 1, 1841

List of the officers of the Chesapeake & Ohio Canal Company, in service on the 1st day of June, 1841, with the rate of compensation paid to each annually.[8]

Michael C. Sprigg, (president) compensation per annum	$3,000
James M. Coale	
John P. Ingle	
Frisby Tilghman	
John T. Dale	1,800
Daniel Burkhart	
John O. Wharton	
Directors—$4 per day to each, during the time he shall be actually engaged in the duties of his office, provided the pay of each director shall not exceed 300 dollars per annum.	
Thomas Turner, clerk	1,800
Robert Barnard, treasurer and accountant	1,400
Ezra Houck, collector general of tolls	1,000
Albert Mayberry, messenger	200
	$9,200
John Y. Young, superintendent 1st division canal	$800
William S. Elgin, superintendent 2nd division canal	800
George W. Rodgers, superintendent 3rd division canal	800
John G. Stone, superintendent 4th division canal	800
Benjamin F. Mackall, collector at Georgetown	800
Henry Jamison, collector at Point of Rocks	200
Elie Stake, collector at Williamsport	300
Arthur Blackwell, collector at Hancock	300
John B. Hilton, keeper of Lock B	50
James O'Riley, keeper of locks Nos. 1, 2, 3 and 4	500
Thomas B. O'Offutt, keeper of lock No. 5 and guard lock	250
James Dalzell, keeper of lock No. 6	150
Michael Hart, keeper of lock No. 7	150
Levi Barrett, keeper of lock No. 8	150
Osbourn Crawford, keeper of locks No. 9 and 10	200
Wilton Burgess, keeper of Lock No. 11	150
Frederick Metts, keeper of locks No. 12, 13 and 14	250
Hezekiah Metts, keeper of locks No. 15 and 16	276
William H. Henderson, keeper of locks Nos. 17 and 18	276
Daniel Collins, keeper of locks Nos. 19 and 20	200
Robert C. Fields, keeper of lock No. 21	150
John Fields, keeper of lock No. 22	150
W. H. Hammontree, keeper of lock No. 23 and guard lock	200
Charles H. Shanks, keeper of lock No. 24	150
Asa Aud, keeper of lock No. 25 and outlet	250

---

[8] *Thirteenth Annual Report* (1841), pp. 85–87.

James Fitch, keeper of lock No. 26	150
Thomas Walter, keeper of lock No. 27	150
James Davis, keeper of lock No. 28	150
John Walter, keeper of lock No. 29	175
William Kuhn, keeper of lock No. 30	100
Dennis Harrison, keeper of lock No. 31, &c.	175
A. W. Jones, keeper of lock No. 32	175
William S. Elgin, keeper of lock No. 33 and collector	300
John Crowley, keeper of lock No. 34	175
William McKay, keeper of locks Nos. 35, 36 and guard	300
John Kerchwell, keeper of lock No. 37	150
George Hughes, keeper of lock No. 38 and outlet	200
Joseph Gwyn, keeper of lock No. 39	150
Andrew McKoy, keeper of lock No. 40	150
Levi R. Shaw, keeper of guard lock No. 4	150
Henry Boyd, keeper of locks Nos. 41 and 42	200
Michael Crisman, keeper of lock No. 43	150
Joseph Hollman, keeper of lock No. 44—water power granted	
Jacob Motter, keeper of guard lock No. 5	150
John Herbert, keeper of locks Nos. 45 and 46	200
Daniel Brewer, keeper of locks Nos. 47, 48, 49 and 50	300
Upton Rowland, keeper of locks No. 51 and 52	200
H. Conner, keeper of lock No. 53	150
Thomas Fleming, keeper of guard lock No. 6	456
Superintendents, collectors and lock-keepers	$12,758
Charles B. Fisk, chief engineer	$3,000
John A. Byers, assistant	1,100
Charles H. Randolph, assistant	1,100
Henry M. Dungan, assistant	1,100
Samuel H. Williams, assistant	1,100
Thomas L. Patterson, assistant	1,100
Thomas Gore, rodman	500
Fenton M. Henderson, rodman	500
Jacob L. Schnebly, rodman	500
John J. Buchanan, Jr., rodman	500
William J. Bryan, rodman	500
Axeman	300
Axeman	300
Axeman	300
Axeman	300
Axeman	300
Axeman	300
Axeman	300
Axeman	300
Samuel M. Semmes, commissioner	1,100

	$14,000

Summary of yearly compensation

The President, directors and Clerks, (if the directors receive the maximum of their compensation)		$9,200
The superintendents, collectors and lock-keepers		12,758
The engineers and commissioner		14,400
	Total	$36,358

Or thus:

The president, directors and clerks (if the directors receive the maximum of their compensation)		$9,200
4 superintendents	$3,200	
45 collectors and lock-keepers	9,558	
		12,758
1 chief engineer	3,000	
5 assistant engineers	5,500	
5 rodmen	2,500	
8 axemen	2,400	
		13,400
1 commissioner		1,000
		$36,358

APPENDIX I

OFFICERS, ENGINEERS, AND AGENTS JANUARY 1, 1842

List of the officers, engineers, and agents in the service of the Chesapeake & Ohio Canal Company, on the 1st day of January, 1842, with the rate of compensation paid to each annually.[9]

Francis Thomas, President		$1,000
James M. Coale,	Director —$4 per day to each, during the time he shall be actually engaged in the duties of his office, provided the pay of each director shall not exceed 300 dollars per annum.	1,800
Frisby Tilghman,		
J. P. Ingle,		
J. R. Dall,		
J. O. Wharton,		
D. Burkhart,		
Thomas Turner, clerk and superintendent of tolls		1,500
Robert Barnard, treasurer and accountant		1,200
	Total	5,500
Charles B. Fisk, chief engineer		$3,000.00
John A. Byers, assistant engineer		1,100.00
Charles H. Randolph, assistant engineer		1,100.00
Henry M. Dungan, assistant engineer		1,100.00
Samuel H. Williams, assistant engineer		1,100.00
Thomas L. Patterson, assistant engineer		1,100.00
Thomas Gove, rodman		500.00
Jacob C. Schnebly, rodman		500.00
John Buchanan, Jr., rodman		500.00
William H. Bryan, rodman		500.00
R. Lorman Ross, rodman		360.00
four axemen		1,110.00
Morgan Snively, superintendent at tunnel, and axeman, $1.50 per day		547.50
Amauel M. Semmes, commissioner		200.00
		12,717.50
John Y. Young, superintendent 1st division		$700
William S. Elgin, superintendent 2nd division		700
George W. Rodgers, superintendent 3rd division		700
John G. Stone, superintendent 4th division		700
Benjanin F, Mackall, collector of tolls at Georgetown		600
Henry Jamison, collector of tolls at Point of Rocks		200
Eli Stake, collector of tolls at Williamsport		300
Arthur Blackwell, collector of tolls at Hancock		300
John Hilton, keeper of Lock B, at Washington		50
James O'Riley, keeper of locks Nos. 1, 2, 3 and 4		600
Thomas B. Offutt, keeper of lock No. 5 and guard lock		250
James Dalzell, keeper of lock No. 6		150
Michael Hart, keeper of lock No. 7		150

---

[9] *Fourteenth Annual Report* (1842), pp. 25–27.

Levi Barrett, keeper of lock No. 8	150
Osbourn Crawford, keeper of locks No. 9 and 10	200
Wilton Burgess, keeper of Lock No. 11	150
Frederick Metts, keeper of locks No. 12, 13 and 14	250
Hezekiah Metts, keeper of locks No. 15 and 16	$276
William H. Henderson, keeper of locks Nos. 17 and 18	276
Daniel Collins, keeper of locks Nos. 19 and 20	200
Robert C. Fields, keeper of lock No. 21	150
John Fields, keeper of lock No. 22	150
William H. Hammontree, keeper of lock No. 23 and guard lock	200
Charles H. Shanks, keeper of lock No. 24	150
Asa Aud, keeper of lock No. 25 and outlet	250
James Fitch, keeper of lock No. 26	150
Thomas Walter, keeper of lock No. 27	150
James Davis, keeper of lock No. 28	150
John Walter, keeper of lock No. 29	175
Dennis Harrison, keeper of lock No. 30	175
Wm. Kuhn, keeper of lock No. 31	100
A. W. Jones, keeper of lock No. 32	175
W. S. Elgin, keeper of lock No. 33 and collector of tolls	300
John Crowley, keeper of lock No. 34	175
William McKay, keeper of locks Nos. 35, 36 and guard	300
John Kerchwell, keeper of lock No. 37	150
George Hughes, keeper of lock No. 38 and outlet	200
Joseph Gwyn, keeper of lock No. 39	150
Andrew McKoy, keeper of lock No. 40	150
Levi R. Shaw, keeper of guard lock No. 4	150
Henry Boyd, keeper of locks Nos. 41 and 42	200
Michael Crisman, keeper of lock No. 43	150
Joseph Hollman, keeper of lock No. 44—water power granted	
Jacob Motter, keeper of guard lock No. 5	150
John Herbert, keeper of locks Nos. 45 and 46	200
Daniel Brewer, keeper of locks Nos. 47, 48, 49 and 50	300
Upton Rowland, keeper of locks No. 51 and 52	200
H. Conner, keeper of lock No. 53	150
Thomas Fleming, keeper of guard lock No. 6	175
Total, Superintendents, collectors and lock-keepers	11,977
Summary	
The President, Directors, and Clerks, ($300 each Director)	$5,500.00
Engineers, rodmen, axemen and commissioners	12,717.50
Superintendents, and lock-keepers, and collectors	11,977.00
Total	$30,194.50

THO. TURNER,
Clerk of the Chesapeake and Ohio Canal Company.

APPENDIX J

OFFICERS MAY 31, 1842

List of the officers in the service of the Chesapeake & Ohio Canal Company, on the 31st day of May, 1842, with the rate of compensation paid to each annually.[10]

Michael C. Sprigg, President	$1,000
James M. Coale, Frisby Tilghman, John R. Dall, John O. Wharton, Daniel Burkhart, John P. Ingle — *Directors*—$4 per day to each, during the time he shall be actually engaged in the duties of his office, provided the pay of each director shall not exceed 300 dollars per annum.	1,800
Thomas Turner, clerk and superintendent of tolls	1,500
Robert Barnard, treasurer and accountant	1,200
Total	5,500
Charles B. Fisk, chief engineer	$2,000
Henry M. Dungan, assistant engineer	1,100
Total	3,100
John Y. Young, superintendent 1st division	$700
William S. Elgin, superintendent 2nd division	700
George W. Rodgers, superintendent 3rd division	700
John G. Stone, superintendent 4th division	700
Total	2,800
Benjanin F, Mackall, collector of tolls at Georgetown	600
Henry Jamison, collector of tolls at Point of Rocks	200
William S. Elgin, collector of tolls, Harpers Ferry	300
Elie Stake, collector of tolls, Williamsport	300
Arthur Blackwell, collector of tolls at Hancock	300
Total	1,700
John Hilton, keeper of Lock B, at Washington	50
James O'Riley, keeper of locks Nos. 1, 2, 3 and 4, Georgetown	600
Thomas B. Offutt, keeper of lock No. 5 and guard lock	250
James Dalzell, keeper of lock No. 6	150
Michael Hart, keeper of lock No. 7	150
Levi Barrett, keeper of lock No. 8	150
Osbourn Crawford, keeper of locks No. 9 and 10	200
Wilton Burgess, keeper of Lock No. 11	150
Frederick Metts, keeper of locks No. 12, 13 and 14	250
Hezekiah Metts, keeper of locks No. 15 and 16	276
William H. Henderson, keeper of locks Nos. 17 and 18	276
Daniel Collins, keeper of locks Nos. 19 and 20	200
Robert C. Fields, keeper of lock No. 21	150
John Fields, keeper of lock No. 22	150

---

[10] *Fourteenth Annual Report* (1842), pp. 25–27.

William H. Hammontree, keeper of lock No. 23 and guard lock	200
Charles H. Shanks, keeper of lock No. 24	150
Asa Aud, keeper of lock No. 25 and outlet	250
James Fitch, keeper of lock No. 26	150
Thomas Walter, keeper of lock No. 27	$150
James Davis, keeper of lock No. 28	150
John Walter, keeper of lock No. 29	175
Dennis Harrison, keeper of lock No. 30	175
William. Kuhn, keeper of lock No. 31	100
A. W. Jones, keeper of lock No. 32	175
John Crowley, keeper of lock No. 34	175
William McKay, keeper of locks Nos. 35, 36 and guard	300
John Kerchwell, keeper of lock No. 37	150
George Hughes, keeper of lock No. 38 and outlet	200
Joseph Gwyn, keeper of lock No. 39	150
Andrew McKoy, keeper of lock No. 40	150
Levi R. Shaw, keeper of guard lock No. 4	150
Henry Boyd, keeper of locks Nos. 41 and 42	200
Michael Crisman, keeper of lock No. 43	150
Joseph Hollman, keeper of lock No. 44—water power granted	
Jacob Motter, keeper of guard lock No. 5	150
John Herbert, keeper of locks Nos. 45 and 46	200
Daniel Brewer, keeper of locks Nos. 47, 48, 49 and 50	300
Upton Rowland, keeper of locks No. 51 and 52	200
H. Conner, keeper of lock No. 53	150
Thomas Fleming, keeper of guard lock No. 6	175
Total	$7,477
Total	$20,577
RECAPITULATION	
President, Directors, clerks, and treasurer	$5,500.00
Engineer and assistant	3,100
Superintendents	2,800
Collectors of tolls	1,700
Lock-keepers	7,477
Total	20,577

THO. TURNER,
Clerk of the Chesapeake and Ohio Canal Company
Canal Office, Frederick, May 31, 1842.

Note. The aggregate pay for the directors for the year ending 31st May, 1842, was $924.

Chesapeake & Ohio Canal Historic Resource Study
Unrau: 9. Managing Maintenance 1830–1924

APPENDIX K

OFFICERS MAY 31, 1845

Schedule of officers in the service of the Chesapeake & Ohio Canal Company in the year ending 31st May, 1845, and the compensation to which they have been severally entitled.[11]

		Name of officer, &c.		Amount	
1st		In the office at Frederick, viz:			
		James M. Coale, President, per annum		$1,000	
		D. Burkhart, attendance as director	$136		
		William Darne, attendance as director	112		
		J. P. Ingle, attendance as director	192		
		William Price, attendance as director	64		
		F. Tilghman, attendance as director	160		
		J. O. Wharton, attendance as director	136		
				800	
		Thomas Turner, clerk, per annum		1,500	
		Robert Barnard, treasurer and accountant		1,200	
		William Price, standing counsel		250	
		C. B. Fisk, chief engineer		2,000	
					$6,750
2nd		First superintendency, viz:			
		J. Y. Young, superintendent		800	
		B. F. Mackall, collector		600	
		John Moore, keeper locks 1 to 4, and tide		600	
		Frederick Metz, keeper lock 5 and guard		250	
		James Dalzell, keeper lock 6		150	
		James Wilburn, keeper lock 7		150	
		Levi Barrett, keeper lock 8		150	
		O. S. Crawford, keeper locks 9 and 10		200	
		W. Burgess, keeper lock 11		150	
		Asa Tarman, keeper locks 12, 13 and 14		150	
		Hezekiah Metz, keeper lock 15	12.50		
		William Nevitt, keeper lock 15	137.50		
				150	
		Thomas Brewer, keeper lock 16		150	
		W. W. Henderson, keeper locks 17 and 18	138.00		
		Horrace Benton, keeper locks 17 and 18	138.00		
				276	
		Daniel Collins, keeper locks 19 and 20		200	
		R. C. Fields, keeper lock 21		150	
		John Fields, keeper lock 22		150	
		J. Y. Young, keeper lock 23 and guard		200	
		John Wells, keeper lock 24		150	

---

[11] *Seventeenth Annual Report* (1845), pp. 9–10.

	Asa Aud, keeper Edwards Ferry outlet		50	
				4,776
3rd	Second superintendency			
	W. S. Elgin, superintendent		800	
	L. C. Belt, Point of Rocks, collector		50	
	W. S. Elgin, Harpers Ferry, collector		100	
	Asa Aud, keeper lock 25		200	
	James Fitch, keeper lock 26		150	
	Thomas Walter, keeper lock 27		150	
	E. Davis, keeper lock 28	125.00		
	John Plummer, keeper lock 28	25.00		
			150	
	John Walter, keeper lock 29		175	
	William Kuhn, keeper lock 30		150	
	D. Harrison, keeper lock 31		150	
	A. W. Jones, keeper lock 32		175	
	W. S. Elgin, keeper lock 33 and Shenandoah		200	
	John Crowley, keeper lock 34		175	
	John Kercheval, keeper locks 35 and guard, &c.		250	
	J. L. Jordon, keeper lock 37		150	
	George Hughes, keeper lock 38 and outlet	83.33		
	Edward Hayes, keeper lock 38 and outlet	116.67		
			200	
	Joseph Gwyn, keeper lock 39		150	
	Andrew McKoy, keeper lock 40		150	
	L. R. Shaw, keeper guard lock 4		150	
	M. Newman, bridge and ferry tender, Noland's Ferry		150	
				3,825
4th	Third superintendency, viz:			
	John G. Stone, superintendent		800	
	Eli Stake, Williamsport, collector		300	
	Arthur Blackwell, Hancock, collector		300	
	Henry Boyd, keeper locks 41 and 42		200	
	Isaac Dodd, keeper lock 43		150	
	Joseph Hollman, keeper lock 44, (water power)			
	Jacob Motter, keeper guard 5		150	
	John Herbert, keeper locks 45 and 46	100.00	200	
	Henry Harsh, keeper locks 45 and 46	100.00		
			200	
	Daniel Brewer, keeper locks 47 to 50		300	
	Upton Rowland, keeper locks 51 and 52		200	
	Hugh Conner, keeper lock 53		150	
	James Finney, keeper guard 6		200	
				2,950
				18,301

	RECAPITULATION			
	President, directors, and clerks at Frederick			$4,750
	Chief Engineer			2,000
	Superintendents			2,400
	Collectors			2,400
	Lock-keepers			7,801
	Total			18,301

THO. TURNER, *Clerk.*

APPENDIX L

OFFICERS DECEMBER 31, 1846

Showing the Officers in the service of the Chesapeake & Ohio Canal Company in the year ending 31st December, 1846, and the compensation to which they have been severally entitled for same period.[12]

1st	James M. Coale, president		$3,000.00	
	Daniel Burkhart, Director	$176.00		
	R. W. Bowie, Director	196.00		
	John P. Ingle, Director	196.00		
	William Price, Director	192.00		
	Frisby Tilghman, Director	170.00		
	John O. Wharton, Director	176.00		
			1,106.00	
2nd	Thomas Turner, Clerk, to 20th Dec.	$1,120		
	Walter S. Ringgold, since	30		
			1,150.00	
	F. B. Sappington, Assistant Clerk, to 1st July		366.66	
	Robert Barnard, Treasures, to February	117.20		
	Philemon Chew, Treasurer, to 15th April	200.00		
	L. J. Brengle, since,	800.55		
			1,117.75	
	William Price, standing counsel		250.00	
	C. B. Fisk, Chief Engineer		2,500.00	
				5,384.41
				$9,490.41
3rd	First superintendency			
	William S. Elgin, superintendent		400.00	
	C. Hogmire, collector to 1st April	$350		
	W. H. Bryne, since	250		
			600.00	
	John Moore, keeper of locks 1 to 4		600.00	
	Frederick Metz, keeper lock 5, &c.		200.00	
	James Delzell, keeper lock 6		150.00	
	James Wilburn, keeper lock 7		150.00	
	Levi Barrett, keeper lock 8		150.00	
	O. Crawford, keeper locks 9 and 10		200.00	
	W. H. Burgess, keeper lock 11		150.00	
	Asa Tarman, keeper lock 15		175.00	
	William Nevett, keeper locks 12, 13 and 14		250.00	
	Thomas Brewer, keeper lock 16		175.00	
	Horace Benton, keeper locks 17 and 18		225.00	
	Daniel Collins, keeper locks 19 and 20		200.00	

---

[12] *Nineteenth Annual Report* (1847), pp. 19–20.

	H. Conner, keeper lock 53		150.00		
	James Phinney, keeper guard lock 6		200.00		
				1,550.00	
					2.950.00
					$20,590.41

RECAPITULATION

President, Directors, Standing Counsel, Clerks and Chief Engineer	$9,490.41
Superintendents	2,000.00
Collectors	1,350.00
Lock-keepers	7,750.00
	$20,590.41

L. J. BRENGLE, *Treasurer.*
Office Chesapeake and Ohio Canal Co.,
Cumberland, January 6, 1847

APPENDIX M

OFFICERS DECEMBER 31, 1848

Statement showing the Officers in the service of the Chesapeake & Ohio Canal Company in the year ending 31st December, 1848, and the compensation to which they have been severally entitled for same period.[13]

1st	James M. Coale, President, salary at $1,000 to 1st August		$586.07	
	Since at $2,000		827.85	
				$1,413.92
	William A, Bradley, Director		132.00	
	George Schley, Director		132.00	
	Samuel P. Smith, Director		264.00	
	Henry Daingerfield, Director		72.00	
	William Cost Johnson, Director		84.00	
	John Pickell, Director		96.00	
				780.00
	George Schley, Standing Counsel		200.00	
	Walter S. Ringgold, Chief Clerk, at $1,000		1,000.00	
	Walter S. Ringgold, Sec. to Stockholders at $100		100.00	
	Lawrence J. Brengle, Treasurer, at $1000		1,000.00	
	F. B. Sappington, Asst. Clerk to 21st July at $500	254.18		
	F. D. Tormey, Asst. Clerk from 7th Aug. at $500	200.10		
			454.28	
				2754.28
				4948.20
2nd	First Superintendency			
	John Lambie, Superintendent			700.00
	William H. Bryan, Collector at Georgetown		800.00	
	John Page, Inspector of Cargoes, Georgetown		300.00	
				1100.00
	John Moore, Keeper of Locks 1 to 4		600.00	
	Frederick Metz, Keeper of Lock 5, &c.		200.00	
	James Delzell, Keeper of Lock 6		150.00	
	James Wilburn, Keeper of Lock 7		150.00	
	Levi Barrett, Keeper of Lock 8		150.00	
	John Lambie, Keeper of Locks 9 and 10		200.00	
	W. H. Burgess, Keeper of Lock 11		150.00	
	John T. Harrison, Keeper of Locks 12, 13 and 14		250.00	

---

[13] *Twenty-First Annual Report* (1849), pp. 30–31.

	Rebecca Tarman, Keeper of Lock 15		175.00		
	Mary A. Brewer, Keeper of Lock 16		175.00		
	William D. Howser, Keeper of Locks 17 and 18		225.00		
	Daniel Collins, Keeper of Locks 19 and 20		200.00		
	Samuel Fisher, Keeper of Lock 21		150.00		
	John Fields, Keeper of Lock 22		150.00		
	Edward L. Trail, Keeper of Lock 23		200.00		
				3125.00	
					4925.00
3rd	Second superintendency				
	William S. Elgin, superintendent			900.00	
	Lloyd C. Belt, collector at Point of Rocks	$50.00			
	William S. Elgin, collector at Harpers Ferry	100.00			
				150.00	
	John Wells, Keeper of Lock 24		150.00		
	Asa Aud, No. 25th to the 1st of June	$111.11			
	George W. Bozzell, since	138.89			
				250.00	
	James Fitch, Keeper of Lock 26		150.00		
	Thomas Walter, Keeper of Lock 27		150.00		
	Galen Benton, No. 28th to 1st August	$87.50			
	William Watkins, since	62.50			
				150.00	
	John Walter, Keeper of Lock 29		175.00		
	William Kuhn, Keeper of Lock 30		150.00		
	Dennis Harrison, Keeper of Lock 31		150.00		
	A. W. Jones, Keeper of Lock 32		175.00		
	William S. Elgin, Keeper of Lock 33, &c.		200.00		
	John Crowley, Keeper of Lock 34 &c.		175.00		
	John Kercheval, Keeper of Lock 35, &c.		250.00		
	John L. Jordan, Keeper of Lock 37		150.00		
	Edward Hays, Keeper of Lock 38, &c.		200.00		
	Joseph Gwynn, Keeper of Lock 39		150.00		
	Andrew McCoy, Keeper of Lock 40		150.00		
	John Buchanan, Dam 4		150.00		
	W. Watkins, ferry to the 5th of May		51.26		
				2,976.26	
					4,026.26
4th	Third superintendency				
	John G. Stone, superintendent			800.00	
	Eli Stake, collector at Williamsport		300.00		
	Arthur Blackwell, collector at Hancock		300.00		
				600.00	
	A. K. Stake, Keeper of locks 41 & 42 to 1st July	$100.00			

L. Stanhope, since	100.00			
		200.00		
Isaac Dodd, Keeper of Lock 43		150.00		
J. Hollman, Keeper of Lock 44 (water power)				
C. Myers, Keeper of Locks 45 and 46		200.00		
Jacob Morter, Guard Lock 5		150.00		
Daniel Brewer, Keeper of Locks 47,48,49 & 50		300.00		
Upton Rowland, No. 51 and 52 to 1st April	$50.00			
J. Miller, since	150.00			
		200.00		
Sarah Conner, Keeper of Lock 53		150.00		
J. Doyle, Guard Lock 6		200.00		
			1,550.00	
				2.950.00
				16,849.46

RECAPITULATION	
President, Directors, Standing Counsel, Clerks and Treasurer	$4,948.20
Superintendents	2,400.00
Collectors	1,850.00
Lock-keepers	7,651.26
	16,849.46

L. J. BRENGLE, *Treasurer.*
Office Chesapeake and Ohio Canal Company,
Frederick, January 10th, 1849

APPENDIX N

OFFICERS DECEMBER 31, 1850

Statement showing the Officers in the service of the Chesapeake & Ohio Canal Company, in the year ending 31st December, 1850, and the compensation to which they have been severally entitled for same period.[14]

1st	James M. Coale, President			$2,000.00
2nd	William A, Bradley, Director		$68.00	
	Henry Daingerfield, Director		64.00	
	John Pickell, Director		116.00	
	Wm. Cost Johnson, Director		32.00	
	George Schley, Director		116.00	
	Samuel P. Smith		184.00	
				580.00
3rd	George Schley, Standing Counsel		200.00	
	W. S. Ringgold, Chief Clerk		1,400.00	
	W. S. Ringgold, Sec. to Stockholders		100.00	
	L. J. Brengle, Treasurer		1,400.00	
				3,100.00
				5,680.00
4th	First Superintendency			
	John Lambie, Superintendent			900.00
	William H. Bryan, Collector at Georgetown		800.00	
	John Page, Inspector of Cargoes, Georgetown		300.00	
				1,100.00
	Thomas Sampson, Lock B		50.00	
	John Moore, Locks 1 to 4		600.00	
	Frederick Metz, Lock 5 to 10th March	$55.56		
	Hy. L. Thomas, Lock 5 since	144.44		
			200.00	
	James Delzell, Lock 6		150.00	
	W. Duly, from 8th March, Lock 7		121.77	
	Levi Barrett, Lock 8		150.00	
	John Lambie, to 15th Dec., Locks 9 and 10	$191.17		
	Charles Resenthral, since	8.83		
			200.00	
	W. H. Burgess, Lock 11		150.00	
	John T. Harrison, Locks 12, 13 and 14		250.00	
	John L. Trammel, Lock 15, one month	$14.58		
	Richard Collins, from 8th March to 15th June	47.28		
	John Minnes, from 1st Augusr	72.91		

---

[4] *Report to the Stockholders on the Completion of the Chesapeake & Ohio Canal to Cumberland* (Frederick, 1851), pp. 139–140.

			134.77		
	Joseph Nevitt, Lock 16, one month	$14.58			
	Lucy A. Metts, from 10th March	140.98			
			155.56		
	Wm D. Houser, Locks 17 and 18		225.00		
	Daniel Collins, Locks 19 and 20		200.00		
	Samuel Fisher, Lock 21		150.00		
	John Fields, Lock 22		150.00		
	Edward L. Trail, Lock 23		100.00		
				2,987.10	
					4,987.10
5th	Second superintendency, viz:				
	Wm S. Elgin, Superintendent			900.00	
	Lloyd C. Belt, collector at Point of Rocks		$50.00		
	Wm S. Elgin, collector at Harpers Ferry		100.00		
				150.00	
	John Wells, Keeper of Lock 24		150.00		
	George W. Bozzell, Keeper of Lock 25		250.00		
	James Fitch, Keeper of Lock 26		150.00		
	Thomas Walter, Keeper of Lock 27		150.00		
	William Watkins, Keeper of Lock 28		150.00		
			850.00	1,050.00	10,667.10
	John Walter, Keeper of Lock 29		175.00		
	William Kuhn, Keeper of Lock 30		150.00		
	Dennis Harrison, Keeper of Lock 31		150.00		
	A. W. Jones, Keeper of Lock 32		175.00		
	Wm. S. Elgin, Keeper of Lock 33, &c.		200.00		
	John Crowley, Keeper of Lock 34 &c.		175.00		
	John Kercheval, Keeper of Lock 35, &c.		250.00		
	John L. Jordan, Keeper of Lock 37		150.00		
	Edward Hays, Keeper of Lock 38, &c.		200.00		
	Joseph Gwynn, Keeper of Lock 39		150.00		
	Andrew McCoy, Keeper of Lock 40		150.00		
	Thomas Wilson, Dam 4		150.00		
				2,925.00	
					3,975.10
6th	Third superintendency, viz:				
	John Stone, Superintendent			800.00	
	Eli Stake, collector at Williamsport		300.00		
	Arthur Blackwell, collector at Hancock		300.00		
				600.00	
	L. Stanhope, Keeper of locks 41 & 42		200.00		
	Isaac Dodd, Keeper of Lock 43		150.00		
	J. Buchanan, Keeper of Lock 44		150.00		
	Jacob Morter, Guard Lock 5		150.00		
	C. Myers, Keeper of Locks 45 and 46		200.00		

Treasurer's Office Chesapeake and Ohio Canal Company,
Frederick, January 1st, 1851
L. J. BRENGLE, *Treasurer and Accountant*

APPENDIX O

PRESIDENTS, DIRECTORS, AND CHIEF OFFICERS
FROM JUNE 1828 TO FEBRUARY 27, 1851

A list of the Presidents, Directors, and chief officers, of the Chesapeake & Ohio Canal Company, from its organization in June, 1828, to February 27th, 1851.[15]

Presidents	Period of Service		In Office		
	From	To	years	mo's	days
Charles Fenton Mercer	June 21, 1828	June 6, 1833	4	11	15
John H. Eaton	June 6, 1833	June 27, 1834	1	00	21
George C. Washington	June 27, 1834	June 3, 1839	4	11	7
Francis Thomas	June 3, 1839	April 2, 1841	1	10	00
Michael C. Sprigg	April 2, 1841	Dec. 3, 1842	1	8	00
Wm. Gibbs McNeill	Dec. 3, 1842	Aug. 17, 1843	0	8	14
James M. Coale	Aug. 17, 1843	Feb. 27, 1851	7	6	10
Directors					
Joseph Kent	June 21, 1828	June 11, 1831	2	11	21
Phineas Janney	June 21, 1828	June 2, 1840	11	11	12
Walter Smith	June 21, 1828	June 3, 1839	10	11	13
Peter Lenox	June 21, 1828	June 6, 1833	4	11	16
Andrew Stewart	June 21, 1828	June 6, 1833	4	11	16
Frederick May	June 21, 1828	June 11, 1831	2	11	21
William Price	June 11, 1831	June 27, 1834	3	00	16
John J. Abert	June 11, 1831	Dec. 21, 1839	8	6	10
William Gunton	June 6, 1833	June 3, 1839	5	11	28
Richard H. Henderson	June 6, 1833	June 3, 1839	5	11	28
George Bender	June 27, 1834	April 29, 1835	0	10	2
M. St. Clair Clarke	June 15, 1835	June 22, 1836	1	00	7
Thomas Carbery	June 22, 1836	July 16, 1838	2	00	24
John Hoye	July 16, 1838	June 3, 1839	0	10	18
Thomas Perry	June 3, 1839	Dec. 21, 1839	0	6	18
James Carroll	June 3, 1839	Dec. 21, 1839	0	6	18
Jacob G. Davies	June 3, 1839	June 2, 1840	1	00	00
Joseph White	June 3, 1839	June 2, 1840	1	00	00
Robert P. Dunlop	Dec. 21, 1839	April 2, 1841	1	3	12
Washington Duvall	Dec. 21, 1839	June 2, 1840	0	5	12
John W. Maury	Dec. 21, 1839	June 2, 1840	0	5	12
Frederick A. Schley	June 2, 1840	Declined	0	00	00
James Swan	June 2, 1840	April 2, 1841	0	10	00
John McPherson	June 2, 1840	April 2, 1841	0	10	00
William Lucas	June 2, 1840	April 2, 1841	0	10	00

[15] *Report to the Stockholders on the Completion of the Chesapeake and Ohio Canal to Cumberland* (Frederick, 1851), pp. 149–150

William Tyler	June 2, 1840	April 2, 1841	0	10	00
Jacob Markell	July 22, 1840	April 2, 1841	0	9	11
Frisby Tilghman	April 2, 1841	June 7, 1847	6	2	5
John R. Dall	April 2, 1841	Aug. 5, 1842	1	4	3
John O. Wharton	April 2, 1841	June 24, 1847	6	2	22
Daniel Burkhart	April 2, 1841	June 24, 1847	6	2	22
James M. Coale	April 2, 1841	Aug. 17, 1843	2	4	15
John P. Ingle	April 2, 1841	June 24, 1847	6	2	22
William Price	Aug. 5, 1842	June 24, 1847	4	10	19
William Darne	June 4, 1844	July 23, 1845	1	1	19
Robert W. Bowie	July 23, 1845	June 7, 1847	1	10	15
William A. Bradley	June 24, 1847				
Henry Daingerfield	June 24, 1847				
Wm. Cost Johnson	June 24, 1847				
John Pickell	June 24, 1847				
George Schley	June 24, 1847				
Samuel P. Smith	June 24, 1847				
Chief Engineers					
Benjamin Wright	June 23, 1828	Nov. 13, 1830	2	4	20
Charles B. Fisk	April 12, 1837	Sept. 26, 1840	3	5	14
Elwood Morris	Sept. 26, 1840	April 13, 1841	0	6	17
Charles B. Fisk	April 13, 1841				
Clerks					
Asa Rogers	June 28, 1828	Declined	0	00	00
John P. Ingle	July 5, 1828	July 9, 1840	12	00	4
Thomas Turner	July 9, 1840	Dec. 20, 1846	6	5	11
Walter S. Ringgold	Dec. 20, 1846				
Treasurers					
Clement Smith	July 5, 1828	July 7, 1834	6	00	2
Robert Barnard	July 18, 1834	Nov. 14, 1840	6	3	27
Samuel Tyler	Nov. 14, 1840	April 13, 1841	0	5	00
Robert Barnard	April 14, 1841	June 4, 1841	0	1	20
M. C. Cramer	June 4, 1841	Aug. 6, 1841	0	2	2
Ezra Houck	Aug. 6, 1841	Sep. 15, 1841	0	1	9
Joseph Schell	Sept. 16, 1841	Dec. 22, 1841	0	3	6
Robert Barnard	Dec. 22, 1841	Feb. 13, 1846	4	1	21
Philemon Chew	Feb. 13, 1846	April 14, 1846	0	2	1
Lawrence J. Brengle	April 15, 1846				

APPENDIX P

LIST OF CANAL POSITIONS, APRIL 1884[16]

Division No. 1		
Superintendent	J. J. Moore	$125 per month
Collector	William Snowden	$125 per month
Assistant Collector	William Jarboe	$100 per month
Clerk	J. B. North	$50 per month
Harbor Master	Frank Fishe	$50 per month
Assistant Superintendent	Joseph Isaacs	$100 per month
42 Lock-Keepers		$40–$65 per month
Superintendent, telephone		$50 per month
Chief Engineer, Georgetown Incline		$100 per month
Assistant Engineer, Georgetown Incline		$72 per month
Helpers (4)		$40–$50 per month
Boss Carpenter (3)		$65 per month
Carpenters (8)		$1.75 per day
Smith		$1.75–$2 per day
Caulker		$1.75 per day
Laborer		$1.10 per day
Boss		$55 per month
Laborers (23)		$1.10 per day
Level Walker		$40 per month
Mason		$2.50 per day
Cook		$20 per month
Boss of Dredge		$70 per month
Engineer		$2 per day
Dipper Tender		$1.50 per day
Fireman (2)		$1.50 per day
Deck Hand		$1.15 per day
Laborers (16)		$1.10 per day
Cook		$20 per month
Boss		$55 per month
Laborers (8)		$1.10 per day
Level Walkers (2)		$1.10 per day
Cook		66-2/3 cents per day
Boss		$55 per month
Laborers (7)		$1.10 per day

---

[16] Payrolls, April 1884–February 1885, C & O Co.

Cook		$20 per month
Boss		$55 per month
Laborers (13)		$1.10 per day
Cook (2)		$.66 2/3–$1.10 per day
Boss		$55 per month
Laborers (7)		$1.10 per day
Cook		$20 per month
Boss		$55 per month
Laborers (15)		$1.10 per day
Cook		$20 per month
Boss		$55 per month
Laborers (9)		$1.10 per day
Cook		$20 per month
Boss		$55 per month
Laborers (8)		$1.10 per day
Cook		$20 per month
Horse Hire		$509
Total Payroll per month—$6,222.06		
Total Collected for Room and Board—$918.79		
Division No. 2		
Superintendent	Lewis G. Stanhope	$125 per month
Collector	A. Willison	$150–$50 per month
Collector	J. Spielman	$150–$50 per month
Clerk	E. Edwards	$100 per month
Gauger	John Ranahan	$50 per month
Inspector	E. Null	$40 per month
35 Lock-Keeper		$40–$65 per month
Telephone		$50 per month
Steam Packet		$25–$30 per month
Assistant Engineer		$38 per month
Boss Carpenter (3)		$65 per month
Carpenters (9)		$1.10–$2 per day
Masons (3)		$1.75–$2.65 per day
Boss		$55 per month

Laborers (6)		$1.10 per day
Cook		$20 per month
Laborers on Mud Machine		$1.10 per day
Boss		$55 per month
Laborers (9)		$1.10 per day
Cook		$20 per month
Boss		$55 per month
Laborers (7)		$1.10 per day
Cook		$20 per month
Boss		$55 per month
Laborers (5)		$1.10 per day
Cook		$20 per month
Boss		$55 per month
Level Walkers		$1.10 per day
Laborers (5)		$1.10 per day
Cook		$20 per month
Boss		$55 per month
Level Walkers (2)		$1.10 per day
Laborers (6)		$1.10 per day
Cook		$20 per month
Boss		$55 per month
Laborers (7)		$1.10 per month
Cook		$20 per month
Boss		$55 per month
Level Walkers (2)		$1.10 per day
Laborers (1)		$1.10 per day
Cook		$20 per month
Horses (19)		$388.75
Teams (2)		
Total Payroll per month—$5,713.15		
Total Collected for Room and Board—$629.53		
BASIN WHARF (INCLUDED IN DIVISION NO. 2 PAYROLL		
Clerk		$100 per month
Boss		$50 per month
Trimmer		$50 per month
Watchman		$50 per month

Hostler		$35 per month
Carpenters 92)		$1.50 per day
Laborers (3)		$1.10 per day
Dumpers (5)		$1.65 per day
Trimmers (7)		$1.65 per day
Driver		$1.50 per day
Total Payroll per month—$373.30		

APPENDIX Q

LIST OF CANAL POSITIONS, FEBRUARY 1885[17]

Division No. 1		
Superintendent	J. P. Biser	$60 per month
Collector	William Snowden	$50 per month
Clerk	J. B. North	$20 per month
Harbor Master	Frank Fisher	$50 per month
40 Lock-Keepers		$15–$40 per month
1 Assistant Lock Keeper		$15 per month
Captain—Packet		$35 per month
Telephone		$50 per month
Engineer, Georgetown Incline		$47.50 per month
Assistant Engineer, Georgetown Incline		$35 per month
Helpers		$25 per month
Cook		$20 per month
Boss Carpenter (3)		$65 per month
Laborers (2)		$1.10 per day
Carpenters (2)		$1.50–$1.75 per day
Boss, Dredge		$22.50 per month
Engineer		$1.10 per day
Cook		$20 per month
Boss		$55 per month
Laborers (6)		$1.10 per day
Level Walker		$40 per month
Cook		$20 per month
Quarryman		$25 per ½ month
Laborers (11)		$1.10 per day
Cook		$10 per month
Boss		$55 per month
Laborers (23)		$1.10 per day
Masons (2)		$2.50 per day
Cook		$20 per month
Boss		$55 per month
Laborers (5)		$1.10 per day
Cook		$20 per month

---

[17] Payroll, April 1884–February 1885, C & O Co.

Boss		$55 per month
Laborers (6)		$1.10 per day
Cook (2)		$20 per month
Boss		$55 per month
Laborers (12)		$1.10 per day
Cook		$20 per month
Boss		$55 per month
Laborers (6)		$1.10 per day
Cook		$20 per month
Boss		$55 per month
Laborers (6)		$1.10 per day
Mason		$2.50 per day
Cook		$20 per month
Boss		$55 per month
Laborer		$1.10 per day
Cook		$20 per month
Horse Hire		$281.50
Total Payroll per month—$2,672.92		
Total Collected for Room and Board—$530.40		
Division No. 2		
Superintendent	Edward Mulvany	$65 per month
Collector	A. Willison	$62.50 per month
Assistant Collector	John L. Edwards	$37.50 per month
34 Lock-Keeper		$15–$27.50 per month
Telephone		$50 per month
Engineer, Pump		$38 per month
Boss Carpenter (3)		$65 per month
Carpenters (3)		$1.10–$1.75 per day
Blacksmith		$1.90 per day
Mason		$2.40 per day
Boss		$55 per month
Laborers (4)		$1.10 per day
Cook		$20 per month

Boss		$55 per month
Laborers (4)		$1.10 per day
Cook		$20 per month
Boss		$55 per month
Laborers (5)		$1.10 per day
Cook		$20 per month
Boss		$55 per month
Laborers		$1.10 per day
Cook		$20 per month
Boss		$55 per month
Laborers (12)		$1.10 per day
Cook		$20 per month
Boss		$55 per month
Laborers (9)		$1.10 per day
Cook		$20 per month
Horse Hire		$237
Total Payroll per month—$2,413.21		
Total Collected for Room and Board—$236.80		
BASIN WHARF (INCLUDED IN DIVISION NO. 2 PAYROLL)		
Boss		$25 per month
Watchman		$50 per month
Hostler		$30 per month

HISTORIC RESOURCE STUDY
CHESAPEAKE & OHIO CANAL NHP

10.
THE ECONOMIC IMPACT ON THE POTOMAC VALLEY OF THE C & O CANAL: 1828–1924

BY HARLAN D. UNRAU
HISTORIAN, C&O CANAL RESTORATION TEAM, SENECA
DENVER SERVICE CENTER
1976

Chesapeake & Ohio Canal Historic Resource Study
Unrau: 10. Economic Impact

CONTENTS

I.	IMPACT OF THE WESTWARD PROGRESS OF THE CANAL AND RAILROAD	637
II.	IMPACT OF THE CONSTRUCTION OF THE CANAL AND RAILROAD	639
III.	IMPACT OF THE ENLARGED PROJECT THROUGH THE ADDITION OF BRANCH LINES AND CONNECTING TRADE LINKS	646
IV.	IMPACT OF THE OPERATION OF THE CANAL AND RAILROAD	652

	A.	NEW INHABITANTS	652
	B.	ECONOMICAL TRANSPORTATION AND AGRICULTURAL DIVERSIFICATION	652
	C.	SALE OF WATER POWER	654
	D.	COAL TRADE	657
	E.	GROWTH OF RELATED INDUSTRIES	658
	F.	COMPETITION BETWEEN THE CANAL AND RAILROAD	661

V.	IMPACT ON THE DEVELOPMENT OF TOWNS	664

	A.	GEORGETOWN	664
	B.	GREAT FALLS (CROMMELIN)	665
	C.	SENECA (RUSHVILLE)	666
	D.	POINT OF ROCKS	667
	E.	BRUNSWICK (BERLIN)	667
	F.	KNOXVILLE	668
	G.	WEVERTON	668
	H.	SANDY HOOK	669
	I.	HARPERS FERRY	670
	J.	SHEPHERDSTOWN	670
	K.	WILLIAMSPORT	671
	L.	HANCOCK	674
	M.	CUMBERLAND	675
	N.	SUMMARY	680

VI.	IMPACT ON THE POPULATION	681

APPENDIXES		683

	A.	WATER POWER LEASES FOR GEORGETOWN MILLS: 1839–1900	683
	B.	WATER POWER LEASES BETWEEN GEORGETOWN AND LITTLE FALLS: 1839–1900	691
	C.	WAREHOUSES ALONG THE C&O CANAL: 1850–1890	694

D.	COAL YARDS AND WHARVES USING CANAL WATERPOWER TO SHIP COAL: 1856–1880	699
E.	COAL YARDS AND WHARVES NOT USING WATERPOWER TO SHIP COAL: 1856–1880	700
F.	CHIEF RETAIL COAL DEALERS NEAR THE CANAL IN GEORGETOWN: 1860–1880	701

I. IMPACT OF THE WESTWARD PROGRESS OF THE CANAL AND RAILROAD

On July 4, 1828, groundbreaking ceremonies were held to commence the construction of two transportation lines that were designed to link the East and the West—the Chesapeake & Ohio Canal and the Baltimore & Ohio Railroad. During the next quarter century both works were extended gradually up the Potomac Valley to Cumberland and beyond. Prior to January 1832 both lines were confined to the area east of the Catoctin Mountains by the existence of injunctions prohibiting land acquisition above that point.[1] In October 1830, the waterway was opened between Dams Nos. 1 and 2, and in September 1831, navigation was commenced between the Georgetown tidelocks and Little Falls.[2] The railroad reached Frederick in December 1831 and Point of Rocks in April 1832.[3] Thus at the time of the settlement of the legal controversy between the two rival companies in January 1832, both projects had nearly completed their works below the Catoctin Range, a distance of some 48 miles from Georgetown by canal and some 69 miles from Baltimore by rail. By the terms of a compromise approved on May 9, 1833, the joint construction of the two transportation lines through the narrow passes of the river between Pont of Rocks and Harpers Ferry was undertaken. The latter town was reached by the canal in November 1833 and the railroad in December 1834.[4]

Above Harpers Ferry the canal and railroad followed separate paths up the Potomac Valley. The railroad abandoned the Maryland side of the river and pursued a more direct course through the rugged and sparsely settled terrain of Western Virginia, free of the competition with the canal for the right-of-way, to a point just below Cumberland. Only for brief intervals did it return to the Potomac Valley prior to recrossing the river into Maryland. The canal followed the winding river to Cumberland remaining entirely within the immediate narrow confines of the valley on the Maryland side of the stream. Hence the canal, much of which was in the flood plain of the river, followed a more difficult and circuitous route.[5]

Since work on the canal above Harpers Ferry was in progress even before the completion of the joint construction above Point of Rocks, the 22.2-mile section between Dams Nos. 3 and 4 was opened in April 1834; six months after the waterway reached the Ferry.[6] By slackwater navigation in the pool formed by Dam No. 4, Williamsport could be reached, a total distance of about 100 miles from tidewater.[7]

In April 1835 the 22.3-mile section between Dams Nos. 4 and 5 was completed.[8]

Because of the financial and labor problems together with increasingly more difficult terrain to overcome, the waterway was not finished to Dam No. 6 near the mouth of the Cacapon River, some 135 miles above Georgetown, until April 1839.[9] By the time of the suspension of work in 1842, a considerable amount of excavation had been accomplished on the remaining fifty

---

[1] *Second Annual Report* (1830), C & O Co., 9.
[2] *Proceedings of the President and Board of Directors*, B, 194, and C, 5. Also see Van Slyke to Mercer, Apr. 2, 1831, Ltrs. Recd., C & O Co. and *Niles' Register*. Vol. XL (Apr. 9, 1831), 91.
[3] Edward Hungerford, *The Story of the Baltimore & Ohio Railroad, 1827–1927*, (2 Vol., New York, 1928), Vol. I, 116–117.
[4] *Proceedings of Stockholders*, A, 170–174; *Proceedings of the President and Board of Directors*, C, 341–342 and D, 3; *Niles' Register*, Vol. XIV (Oct. 5, 1833), 84; *Ibid.* Vol. XLV (Nov. 23, 1833), 199; and Milton Reizenstein, *The Economic History of the Baltimore & Ohio Railroad, 1827–1857* (Baltimore, 1897), 29–32.
[5] Walter S. Sanderlin, *A Study of the History of the Potomac Valley*, (Washington, 1950), 87.
[6] *Sixth Annual Report* (1834) C & O Co., 4.
[7] Fredericksburg *Arena*, Oct. 6, 1835, quoted in *Niles' Register*, Vol. XLIX (Oct. 24, 1835), 127.
[8] *Niles' Register*, Vol. XLVIII (Apr. 11, 1835), 89.
[9] *Ibid,* Vol. LVI (Apr. 27, 1839), 131–132.

miles to Cumberland, but the work was to idle until November 1847 while numerous attempts were made to secure finances for the continuation of the work.[10]

In the meantime, the Baltimore & Ohio had pushed its railroad rapidly westward, paying little heed to one of its original sponsors, the State of Maryland, or to the needs and desires of the citizens of Western Maryland. The route chosen by the Baltimore railroad promoters in their race for the Cumberland coal trade and the Ohio Valley did carry tracks close to the Potomac River on the Virginia side opposite Hancock, but this provided little consolation to the inhabitants on the northern side of the river. Hagerstown and Williamsport, two of the most important towns in Washington County were completely ignored, although the former was eventually connected with the main line by a spur track from Weverton in December 1867.[11]

In this manner, the Baltimore & Ohio arrived at Cumberland in November 1842, eight years ahead of the canal, and continued westward.[12] The canal was formally opened as far as Cumberland on October 10, 1850, amid fanfare and enthusiastic celebrations.[13]

However, the Baltimore & Ohio continued to push its lines westward, reaching Piedmont in July 1851 and Fairmont in June 1852. On January 10, 1853, the railroad completed the connection of its eastern and western sections at Cumberland and opened its lines all the way to Wheeling on the Ohio River, some 379 miles from Baltimore. Thus, less than three years after the canal reached Cumberland, it was further outdistanced by its rival line for the lucrative east-west trade markets.[14]

---

[10] *Ibid,* Vol. LXIV (July 29, 1843), 342–343; *Ibid,* Vol. LXV (Aug. 12, 1843), 372–373; and *Twentieth Annual Report* (1848), C & O Co., 3–8.
[11] Hungerford, *The Story of the Baltimore & Ohio Railroad,* Vol. I, 70–72.
[12] William H. Lowdermilk, *History of Cumberland* (Washington, 1878), 351–352.
[13] Cumberland *Civilian,* reprinted in *Proceedings of the Stockholders,* D, 390–395.
[4] Lowdermilk, *History of Cumberland,* 376, Reizenstein, *Economic History of the Baltimore & Ohio,* 85.

II. IMPACT OF CONSTRUCTION OF THE CANAL AND RAILROAD

The Potomac Valley reflected the influence of the westward progress of the canal and railroad at almost every stage of construction. The farmer and other property holders benefited in many ways. Those fortunate enough to own land in the paths chosen by the two companies profited immediately from the sale of their property to the internal improvements companies.

From the first year of construction, the canal company was forced to pay exorbitant sums for the purchase of its right-of-way. While some of the landholders, on the route over which the canal was to pass, readily granted the company the title required, many others obstructed the work and refused to surrender their property voluntarily, in the hope of realizing great profits from forced sales. In the latter instances, condemnation proceedings were resorted to. These increasingly became the rule as construction moved up the river and as the speculation fever of the landowners rose.[15]

Among those who resisted the condemnation efforts of the canal company were those who held out for the highest possible price and those who would not sell for any price. The former included those who resisted the verdict of the juries, called for new trials and generally tried to secure higher prices by delaying tactics, which raised their nuisance value.[16]

The second group usually had other motives in the background. Charles Carroll, for example, brushed aside all offers for the purchase of land on Dougheregan Manor, his 10,000-acre estate in Frederick County. He was one of the founders of the Baltimore & Ohio Railroad, which at that time was locked in a struggle with the canal company for the right-of-way in the Potomac Valley.[17]

After the legal controversy was settled in January 1832, the canal company continued to face large land prices as the waterway entered Washington County, near Harpers Ferry. The first land condemned was that of Gerard B. Wager, a bitter opponent of the canal company. The damages awarded were very high, and the verdict provided a discouraging precedent for the directors who had hoped for more favorable settlements in the county. The determination of the local landholders to exact full satisfaction was further strengthened by the award of the utmost damages obtainable in the condemnation of land owned by Casper Wever, an official of the railroad and enemy of the canal project. Even some of the friends of the canal participated in the onslaught that followed. The more impatient proprietors resorted to injunctions to enforce prompt payment of their awards.[18]

In 1835 and 1836 juries in both Washington and Allegany counties continued to exact full satisfaction for land purchased by the canal company between Dams No. 5 and 6. Although the company won a victory in one appeal to the courts and the juries were severely censured, the hoped-for relief proved illusory. Land costs averaged $2,290 a mile, more than double the estimate of $1,000 made in 1834, ranging all the way from 2½ to 25 times the estimated costs. In a letter to the board, Commissioner George Bender described the situation as follows:

> I commenced my efforts to obtain there land with a strong hope of compromising and did in fact compromise with eight of the proprietors who has thus signed, and two others who had not before a simple jury was carried to the ground, viz. with Wade, Harvey, Brawles, Mrs. Jacques, Stottlemeyer, A. Snyder, Lespand, R. Summers, N. Summers and Michael Smith; but from these persons it had become necessary by the new line to acquire 191½

---

[15] *Proceedings of the Stockholders*, A, 41–41, and Walter S. Sanderlin, *The Great National Project: A History of the Chesapeake & Ohio Canal* (Baltimore, 1946), 79.
[16] *Proceedings of the Stockholders*, A, 42.
[17] Carroll to Mercer, Feb. 26, 1829, Ltrs. Recd., C & O Co.
[18] Sanderlin, *The Great National Project*, 91.

acres at the aggregate sum of $7,372 instead of 108¾ acres at the aggregate sum of $5,575 as estimated by Mr. Cruger (in 1834). In other words, for the 41,664 feet length of canal through their estates, I had to pay $705.70 per mile. These compromises, however it must be borne in mind, consisted in large proportion of land of little or no value for cultivation and when I attempted to compromise for the more valuable portions of the line, yet confined myself at all within the limits of Mr. Cruger's estimate, I found myself entirely baffled. In some case the owners were minors, or their titles were not perfect, or there were claims for loss of mill power and etc., so that it became necessary to resort to the linguistics of juries as prescribed by the charter of the company.

Bender then noted the results of the jury awards:

	1834 Estimate	Cost
Heir of Dan Smith	$1,000	$2,300
J. Charles, Jr.	100	2,500
Sam Prather	1,000	2,960
Prather Heirs	500	1,287
Tobias Johnson	1,150	10,600
Otto	225	1,775
Linn	400	1,575
Peter Miller (per agreement)	150	1,200
J. Chambers	625	2,350
Widow Bevans	575	1,000

The commissioner concluded his report by stating that:

So long as the value of the land taken is to be judged of by the neighbors and friends of the land proprietor brought together a jury against a company of strangers as they are taught to consider, so long will the expense attending the acquisitions be much greater than has been heretofore anticipated.[19]

Previous to this series of condemnations, some proprietors in Allegany County had been willing to compromise, if only to avoid paying the lawyers fees. The prices up to that time approximated the estimates of the engineers. Thereafter, the prospects for windfall profits were so promising that landowners were willing to pay legal cost to gain the larger damages.[20]

Potomac Valley residents also benefited from the increase in the value of the property not required by the canal and railroad. For instance, property values in Cumberland increased from $931,118 to $2,124,400 in 1860.[21]

This effect extended far beyond the immediate neighborhood of the new transportation facilities and was perhaps the most widely bared benefit of their construction. The cause of the increase in land values was the advantage, which these commercial arteries brought of cheap and easy access to the principal markets for their products and the major sources of their necessities.[22]

Another effect on the valley was the immigration of many persons seeking employment on the internal improvement projects. These people brought with them their families, their cus-

---

[19] Bender to President and Directors, May 31, 1836, Ltrs. Recd., C & O Co.
[20] Price to Washington, Oct. 25, 1836, Ltrs. Recd., C & O Co.
[21] Lowdermilk, *History of Cumberland*, 351, 388.
[22] Sanderlin, *A Study of the History of the Potomac Valley*, 89.

toms and their beliefs; sometimes, quite alien to the valley. The Catholic Irish were particularly disturbing to the established local communities comprised primarily of Protestant German and Scotch Irish stock, more so than the relatively fewer Dutch, German, Welsh and English immigrants. The presence of large numbers of persons in crowded and filthy temporary quarters also brought health problems to the valley. Minor epidemics among the Irish during the "summer season" were not unusual in the valley, and there were two major scares in 1832 and 1833 over the spread of cholera from the workers to the local inhabitants along the waterway. In addition, the presence of so many rough and trouble unassimilated laborers in a limited area saved the question of the maintenance of order. Drunken brawls accompanying all-night drinking bouts disturbed the valley, and clashes between the Irish factions in the mid-1830s terrified the citizens in the neighboring towns. The later disputes between the workers and the canal company and between the various nationalities employed on the lines, which erupted into violence on several occasions and put the inhabitants of the area into the difficult positions of militia arbiters and innocent victims. The groundswell of racial bitterness produced by these antagonistic events laid the foundation for the early rise of political nativism in Western Maryland during the 1830s.[23]

The inhabitants of the Potomac Valley were able to take an active part in the process of the construction. When agricultural workers were not pressing, many inhabitants took employment on the line of the worker. Because of the need for large numbers of workers and the relatively small pool of labor in the valley, the rate of wages remained at a high level throughout the construction firms and receive contract to build the various canal structures. The farmers found a ready market, relatively free of shipping costs and widespread competition, for their surplus food and drink. Lumber, the principal value of which previously had been as a local building product and as fuel, found a more profitable use in construction. Stone, which like lumber had heretofore been limited to local use, received a good price as ballast and building material, or, in the case of limestone, as a valuable ingredient in hydraulic cement.[24]

The last important way in which the Potomac Valley was influenced by the construction of the canal was in financial affairs. The valley prospered directly from the existence of the sizeable payrolls of the transportation companies, most of which was spent in the immediate neighborhood. The alternating cycles of boom business circles in the valley rose and fell with the employment and fortunes of the internal improvement companies. When the canal was nearly completed from Georgetown to Seneca, the *National Intelligencer* reported on June 29, 1830:

> The execution of this great National work has progressed with a rapidity as astonishing as it is unparalleled in the history of works of this description. A short time only has yet elapsed since the necessity existed of rousing public sentiment to proper appreciation of the importance of this great enterprise by essay after essay, and of diverting the national energy to its accomplishment by convention after convention. But now, only have the moral obstacles to its progress been removed, the root of prejudice eradicated, and the rock of error blown away, but physical obstructions, far more difficult than any one can appreciate who has not seen them, have been overcome, and, under the plastic hand of man, made subservient to the great interests of commercial intercourse.[25]

---

[23] See Chapter VII of this study for more information on the canal's labor force and its effect on the Potomac Valley.
[24] *Proceedings of the President and Board of Directors*, A, 288; C, 357–361; Knapp, Ford and Chapman to President and Directors, Mar. 26, 1829, Ltrs. Recd., C & O Co. For more information on this subject also see Chapter VIII of this study.
[25] Washington, *National Intelligencer*, June 29, 1830.

On January 15, 1831, the Frederick *Town Herald* noted the enthusiasm with which Virginia and Maryland agricultural and lumber interests were using the first stretch of the waterway to be opened:

> The operations on this great work still continue, we are informed, with great vigor. As late as the 18th of December, the weekly returns of effective laborers gave 2,205 men and 379 horses...Very recently forty-five boats passed through the locks of the 17th and 18th sections in one day, laden with more than 6,000 barrels of flour, part of which descended by the Shenandoah, from Port Republic, a point within 20 miles of Stanton, the geographical center of Virginia; and another from Williamsport, in Maryland, 100 miles above the District of Columbia; and wood, for fuel, has already been brought down the canal a distance of 16 miles, from above the great falls of Potomac.[26]

Some five months later, on June 4, 1831, the same newspaper glowingly detailed the economic impact of the canal and railroad on the growth of business activity in Frederick:

> From the returns . . . we learn that during the quarter ending on the 12th ult. One thousand and ninety-three barrels of flour have been inspected in this city. The increased inspection has been caused by the demand for the laborers engaged on the public works in this vicinity – and if our natural advantages for the establishment of manufactories, especially on the Monocacy, were improved, the markets for the products of our farmers would be greatly extended. As Mr. Jefferson said: "The manufactures should be seated alongside the agriculturalist."[27]

In February 1835 when the canal company was attempting to lobby the Maryland legislature for additional pledges to its stock in an effort to keep construction of the waterway moving, *Niles' Register* reported on the beneficial effects that an affirmative decision would have on the trade of Cumberland and the commerce of the state itself as follows:

> For then a very heavy business must need be transacted on the canal, the town (Cumberland) just named becoming a great place of deposit between the east and west, whether commodities are proceeding to or from Pittsburgh or Wheeling; and especially from the former when the Monongahela shall be opened for navigation, as it will be, sooner or later.[28]

When work on the canal was suspended in early 1836 pending a further loan from the State of Maryland, the optimistic prospects for Cumberland changed to pessimism and depression:

> The stoppage of the work on the Chesapeake & Ohio Canal has caused a very considerable panic in Cumberland. Two hours after the arrival of the news, the price of produce came down at least 10 percent. Business still continues to be dull; our principal streets presenting an unusual barrenness; the merchant is idle; and the mechanic slow in the transaction of his business; the speculator is cut to the quick, and those who engaged to pay high rents on account of the prospects of the canal, have been suddenly and seriously

---

[26] Frederick, *Town Herald*, Jan. 15, 1831.
[27] Frederick, *Town Herald*, June 4, 1831.
[28] *Niles' Register*, Vol. XLVII (Feb. 21, 1835), 428.

disappointed. Indeed, the citizens of the town generally, and the farmers for many miles around, have great cause to regret this temporary suspension.[29]

After the canal was completed to Dam No. 6 in the spring of 1839, the *National Intelligencer* noted the prospects for the improvement in canal trade and the need for completing the waterway to Cumberland:

> We may now expect a great increase to the trade of the canal, because the portion in use connects with the national road at Hancock.
>
> Owing to the unusual low stage of the water at this season of the year, the river navigation between Cumberland and the point to which the canal is finished is very dangerous; so much so, that out of seven coal boats which left Cumberland lately, during a small rise in the river, but three reached the canal, the others being lost. This fact shows how important the completion of the canal is to the people of Maryland, as well as the advantages which the people of this district (District cities) may reasonably anticipate, upon the accomplishment of that event.[30]

When the Maryland legislature failed to authorize another appropriation for the completion of the canal to Cumberland before it adjourned in the spring of 1842 *Niles' Register* observed:

> The unfortunate disagreement between the two houses of the legislature of Maryland, in relation to amendments to the bill for completing this stupendous work to the coal and iron regions of Allegany County, which alone can bring the work into profitable operation, will have the inevitable effect of suspending all operations, for the year, and leave the unfinished work to certain dilapidation, with the contracts subject to expensive litigation, and the state saddled with the interest accruing upon seven million of dollars invested in the undertaking. . . So disastrous are likely to be the consequences of the upper counties of the state, that large meetings are convened and calls are making the Governor to convene an extra session of the legislature with the view of adopting a measure that would not only divert the catastrophe, but bring to our aid the vast resources that are now almost within our grasp.[31]

During the five-year suspension of work on the canal from 1842 to 1847, there were several unsuccessful attempts to negotiate new loans for the recommencement of construction. When one such attempt was first reported in July 1843, *Niles' Register* commented that "This is glorious news for Maryland."[32]

Later, in December 1843, after it was reported that an offer had been made to complete the canal for $1,300,000, *Niles' Register* noted that the waterway when finished, "will place Maryland in the very focus of the most prosperous and productive trade."[33]

In late 1845 when work was resumed briefly under a new contract, *Niles' Register* informed its readers:

> The subcontractors with apparatus and corps of laborers are now strewed all along the line from Dam No. 6 to Cumberland. Day is dawning again after a long gloomy night.

---

[29] *Ibid,* Vol. XLIX (Feb. 20, 1836), 426.
[30] *Ibid,* Vol. LVI (Apr. 27, 1839), 131–132.
[31] *Ibid,* Vol. LXII (Mar. 26, 1842), 52.
[32] *Ibid,* Vol. LXIV (July 15, 1843), 320.
[33] *Ibid,* Vol. LXV (Dec. 30, 1843), 276–277.

> The Williamsport *Banner* of the 1st inst. says the trade of that part of the Canal, which is completed, never before was so brisk. Immense quantities of flour, grain and other kinds of produce have been collected in our town, and are now ready for transportation to the District Cities. Thus, we understand too, is the case at other points along the line of the Canal. Within the last week or two, an unusually large number of boats have passed down the Canal.[34]

After lengthy negotiations, construction on the last portion of the canal was finally resumed in November 1847 under a contract with Messrs. Hunter, Harris and Thompson. Again business circles in the Potomac Valley and the surrounding region expressed their renewed faith in the future economic growth of the area, for example:

> Immense beds of the best coal exist at Cumberland; and Washington, Georgetown and [35] Alexandria will doubtless be highly benefited by the commerce in this article, as soon as they can ascend by this Canal to the primitive and exhaustless formations. In seventeen of the counties of Virginia and Maryland situated on the borders or vicinity of this canal, with a population of 232,784 persons, there have been raised in one year 14,425,134 bushels of grain, being nearly 62 bushels to each inhabitant. With about one seventy-third part of the population of the Union, according to the census of 1840, these seventeen counties produce one forty-second part of the grain raised in the United States.

The sufficiency or scarcity of money in the valley was also related in part to the level of activity on the transportation projects and the financial policies of their works both the railroad and the canal resorted to the issuance of their own paper money at various times. The Chesapeake & Ohio first issued scrip, amounting to some $90,000 in $5, $10, and $20 notes payable in one year at four percent interest in April 1834 to enable work to continue until the anticipated returns from the sale of Maryland bonds could be realized. The first experience was uneventful because the proceeds of the bond sale were more than sufficient to redeem the notes by September 1835. In fact, it was very popular throughout the valley, for it prevented a work stoppage.[36]

In the currency famine following the panic of 1837, both the railroad and canal had occasion to resume the issuance of paper money. The anticipation of the proceeds from the sale of additional Maryland bonds again provided the necessary excuse for the action. Accordingly, the canal company on June 7 determined to issue scrip amounting to $50,000 in notes of denominations between 50 cents and $5, the size of the notes being accounted for by the fact that there were almost no notes in the valley of less than $5 value.[37]

Once more the decision was at first a popular one in the valley. Joseph Shriver, the president of the Cumberland Bank of Allegany County informed canal officials on June 29, 1837, that his institution approved of the company's plan to put small notes into circulation and requested several hundred dollars' worth as there was an urgent call for them.[38]

Two weeks alter on July 12, Shriver again requested $200 to $300 of company notes as those "already recently have been paid out and the demand for them continues as great as ever." Unless the company notes were placed in the hands of the Cumberland citizenry as quickly as

---

[34] *Ibid*, Vol. LXIX (Nov. 8, 1845), 147.
[35] *Ibid*, Vol. LXIV (Nov. 1, 1848), 286.
[36] *Proceedings of the President and Board of Directors*, D, 408, and *Niles' Register*, Vol. XLVI (Apr. 26, 1834), 133, and Vol. XLVII (May 3, 1834), 149.
[37] *Proceedings of the President and Board of Directors*, E, 268–269.
[38] Shriver to Ingle, June 29, 1837, Ltrs. Recd., C & O Co.

possible, other notes would begin flowing into the town "from all quarters to supply the amount of change" and reduce the demand for the canal notes.[39]

Even in Baltimore public sentiment was in favor of the canal company decision to issue scrip. According to the President George C. Washington on August 13, 1837, an article in the Baltimore *Gazette* on the previous day, compliments the directors for their "spirit and foresight on assuring that we have nearly a million in circulation, when in fact we have not $50,000." The demand for corporate notes was so great in the north that it was estimated that arrangements could be made "for the reception in New York alone for a quarter of a million of our small notes, without obligation to pay interest." Similar results were predicted for canal scrip in both Philadelphia and Baltimore. Already corporate issues of small notes had supplanted entirely the market for individual notes in the latter city.[40]

The popularity of the corporate scrip and the failure of the expected sales of the State bonds to materialize, forced the canal and railroad enterprises to enlarge their issues. From the limited issue of notes of small denominations only, which had been a temporary expedient to fill a gap in the local monetary picture, the two companies proceeded to large-scale emissions of notes. In August and September 1837 the canal company authorized the printing of $260,000 worth of $5, $10 and $20 notes, payable at six months after date and bearing an interest rate of six percent.[41]

At the same time the unfavorable condition of the market, which was indicated by the lack of sales, made the security behind the notes the subject of doubt. Discounting of notes became frequent; even the Baltimore & Ohio's notes, which had been issued to pay employees' salary, were discounted 20 percent in Cumberland and 25 percent in Baltimore as late as 1842, on the eve of its completion to the former town.[42]

Indirectly, the Potomac Valley was affected by the impact of the heavy cost of the railroad and canal projects on the finances and credit of the State and local banks. Taxes, property values, the condition of local currency and the state of business health itself were all dependent in part on the State and upon the larger banks in Baltimore and the eastern part of the state.[43]

---

[39] *Ibid*, July 12, 1837, Ltrs. Recd., C & O Co.
[40] Washington to Ingle, Aug. 13, 1837, Ltrs. Recd., C & O Co.
[41] *Proceedings of the President and Board of Directors*, E, 298–299, 317, 426. Ultimately, the following notes were issued: 6,000 sheets of two $5 notes, one $10 note and one $20 note = $240,000 and 500 sheets of two $5 notes, one $10 note, and one $20 note = $20,000. The form of the notes was as follows: $20 note—the $20 note of the Bank of Montgomery County with the exception of the margin on the ends for which was substituted the ends of the Urganna Banking Company $20 note; $10 note—the $1 note of the Philadelphia Loan Company with the end margin of the $10 note of the Bank of the State of Arkansas; and $5 note—the $10 note of the Bank of Rochester with the end margin of the $50 note of the Columbia Bank and Bridge Company. Ingle to Underwood, Bald Co., Aug. 1837, Ltrs. Recd., C & O Co.
[42] Lowdermilk, *History of Cumberland*, 350. Ironically, shinplasters circulated by the Good Intent Stage Company were still redeemed at face value.
[43] Sanderlin, *A Study of the History of the Potomac Valley*, 93. For instance, state stocks fell to 64 percent of par value in March 1844 after the state legislature refused to pass a bill providing for the completion of the canal to Cumberland. When the bill had been under consideration and had a chance of passage, the state stocks had sold at 82 percent of par value in Baltimore. Coale to Ward, Mar. 14, 1844, Ltrs. Recd., C & O Co.

III. IMPACT OF ENLARGED PROJECTS THROUGH THE ADDITION OF BRANCH LINES AND CONNECTING TRADE LINKS

The canal was not "complete" when it reached Cumberland. Unlike the Baltimore & Ohio however, the canal was unable to extend its waterway over the mountains to the Ohio River. Nevertheless much work was done during the late 1820s and early 1830s in surveying the route, securing land titles, and making detailed plans for the proposed middle and western sections of the canal between Cumberland and Pittsburgh.[44]

The project was dropped and lay dormant for some forty years before it was revived in the early 1870s during the most prosperous years of the canal trade. At that time, it was estimated that the canal could be extended to the Ohio River at a cost of between $24,000,000 and $28,000,000.[45]

With the decline of the coal trade, the bitter competition of the railroad and the deterioration of the waterway itself during the following decade, the project was not seriously considered again.[46]

In addition to the ambitious planning for the extension of the main line of the Chesapeake & Ohio to Pittsburgh, several branches were considered by the directors and by other interested promoters. Among these were a number of feeders in the Potomac Valley and three extensions from the eastern terminus of the waterway, all of which would have the effect of binding the valley more closely together and of expanding the benefits on the main line.

At various times almost every major tributary of the Potomac River was considered as the site of a possible feeder. One projected branch up the Monocacy River to Frederick was frequently discussed in 1829. In February of that year the Canal directors agreed to build a feeder to supply water from the Monocacy River to a canal to be built by the newly incorporated Frederick County Canal Company connecting the town of Frederick with the Chesapeake & Ohio.[47]

At about the same time, the board recommended that a connection between the Monocacy and the Susquehanna might be effected, thus providing an inland waterway to New York.[48]

Dr. John Martineau and Frederick authorized a survey of the proposed Monocacy improvement during the summer and fall of 1829 and estimated the cost of the 24-mile waterway at $296,389.[49]

The citizens of Frederick soon lost interest in the waterway however, and turned again to the railroad. The canal directors, who had looked upon the branch primarily as a feeder for that part of their own canal above Dam No. 2, were greatly disappointed by this lack of cooperation. Seeking ways of utilizing its waterway above the Seneca Dam while the railroad injunction was still in effect above Point of Rocks, the Canal board again considered the Monocacy River as a

---

[44] "Reports and Letters from the Engineers Employed in the Revised Location of the Western Section of the Chesapeake & Ohio Canal," in *First Annual Report* (1829) C & O Co., 104 ff. and William Archer, "Communication from Wm. Archer, esq., to the Stockholders of the Chesapeake & Ohio Canal, On the Subject of the Location of the tunnel through the Allegany Mountain", (Washington, 1835), 1–7.

[45] Records Concerning Proposed Extension of the Canal, ca. 1874, C & O Co., U. S. Congress, House, *Letter of the Secretary of War on the Extension of the Chesapeake & Ohio Canal*, Exec. Doc. 20, 43rd Congress, 1st Session, April 14, 1874, 5–9; and U. S., Congress, House, *Letter of the Secretary of War, Transmitting the Report of Engineer Merrill on the Chesapeake & Ohio Extension*, Exec. Doc. 137, 44th Congress, 1st Session, Mar. 2, 1876, 2–3.

[46] The subject of the western extension of the canal was speculatively revived during World War Two and in the late 1920s and early 1930s. The cost of the project was estimated at $219,000,000 in 1930 and $242,000,000 in 1934. Washington *Star*, Jul. 17, 1927, Oct. 25, 1929, May 4, 1930 and Sep. 30, 1934.

[47] *Proceedings of the President and Board of Directors*, A, 164.

[48] *Proceedings of the Stockholders*, A, 53.

[49] Frederick *Examiner*, quoted in *Niles' Register*, Vol. XXXVII (July 4, 1829), 302, and *Niles' Register*, Vol. XXXVIII (Mar. 20, 1830), 69.

feeder in 1831, along with the Little Monocacy, Tuscarora Creek, Broad Run, Abraham's Branch and other streams below that town.[50]

The board of directors also showed some interest in the development of the Shenandoah River trade and detailed plans were drawn up to make that river navigable in February 1832.[51] However, the strained financial condition of the company made it impossible to undertake any major work on that river. As its resources neared exhaustion, the improvement of any tributaries of the Potomac by the canal company in the immediate future was impracticable. In 1831, the company waived its rights to those branches in order to encourage the organization of state corporations to make the branches navigable and serve as connectors to the canal. Company officials were especially eager to see such enterprises improve the Monocacy and Antietam and Conococheague Creeks.[52]

Later in November 1838 the canal directors appealed in vain to the Virginia legislature for aid to connect the Chesapeake & Ohio with the South Branch, Cacapon and Shenandoah Rivers and make improvements on them for navigation purposes.[53]

In March 1839, the board gave its assent to acts of the Maryland and Virginia General Assemblies incorporating the Union Company and the Union Potomac Company to construct a canal or slackwater navigation on the North Branch of the Potomac from the proposed terminus of the Chesapeake & Ohio at Cumberland to the north of the Savage River, but the project was never undertaken because of the extended delay of the main line in reaching that town.[54]

There were three projects for independent canals to tap the trade of the main stem at its eastern terminus, two of which were ultimately carried to completion and put into operation. The Maryland ("Cross-Cut") Canal, which would have connected Baltimore with the main stem, was under consideration until 1839 and again briefly in the a870s, but it was never built because of its prohibitive cost, the rapid westward construction of the railroad and the various competing political rivalries in Maryland and between Baltimore and the District Cities.[55]

However, the Washington City and the Alexandria Canals were finished, and the latter became an important outlet for the trade of the Chesapeake & Ohio.

The Washington City Canal, which had been built between 1810–1815, was a 2¼-mile waterway connecting the Potomac and Anacostia Rivers. It extended from the mouth of Tiber Creek to the foot of present New Jersey Avenue at the Eastern Branch, with the second line following the course of James Creek from a junction with the first route near the present intersection of New Jersey Avenue and E Street, S.E., to the Anacostia River east of Greenleaf Point (present day grounds of the War College).[56]

The organization of the Chesapeake & Ohio Canal Company revived interest in the already deteriorating city canal as a means by which the trade of the former could be brought to Washington. The city and the Chesapeake & Ohio reached a compromise in September 1828 by which the latter agreed to extend its waterway from Rock Creek Basin to a basin, which the city undertook to construct at the mouth of Tiber Creek.[57] The extension of the Chesapeake & Ohio was completed in 1837 at a cost of $310,000, of which Congress appropriated $150,000, and its

---

[50] *Proceedings of the Stockholders*, A, 132 and *Proceedings of the President and Board of Directors, B, 384–385; C, 35.*
[51] Stewart to Mercer, Feb. 10, 1832, Ltrs. Recd., C & O Co.
[52] *Proceedings of the Stockholders*, A, 190–192.
[53] *Proceedings of the President and Board of Directors*, E, 521.
[54] *Ibid*, F, 31–33.
[55] Sanderlin, *The Great National Project*, 171–175.
[56] Wilhelmus Bryan, *A History of the National Capital* (2 Vol., New York, 1914–1916), Vol. I, 499–501; and Sanderlin, *The Great National Project*, 175–177.
[57] *Proceedings of the Stockholders*, A, 23–24.

operation as a toll-free public highway was placed under the control of a commission appointed by the city council.[58]

Although the Washington City Canal remained one of the possible outlets for the trade of the Potomac Valley until the 1880s, it was seldom used for a variety of reasons. Among those were the following:

1. The tide consistently filled the channel, requiring continual dredging operations.
2. In the early years, the trade on the main canal and the demand of the city markets were not great enough to provide much business for it.
3. By the time the Chesapeake & Ohio was completed to Cumberland, the canal boats had become so large that navigation under the low Georgetown bridges was virtually impossible; hence, trade with both Georgetown and Washington declined as boats crossed the Potomac Aqueduct to reach tidewater at Alexandria.
4. In 1871, four years after Georgetown bridges were raise, Congress took over the direction of city affairs, and the city canal was neglected as Congress was not interested in the commercial development of the city as much as it was in its role as the National Capital.[59]

The most important of the proposed extensions of the Chesapeake & Ohio was the canal to Alexandria built between 1831 and 1843 at a cost of $1,250,000. To obtain a reasonable proportion of the anticipated increased commerce from the Chesapeake & Ohio, local merchants took the lead in the formulation of the Alexandria Canal Company to construct a tidewater canal along the south bank of the Potomac from an aqueduct across the river above Georgetown. The major undertaking in the project was the Potomac Aqueduct, a structure over 1,500 feet long, 30 feet wide and 5 feet deep. Eight stone piers rising from the bed of the river and two stone abutments on the north and south banks carried the wooden trunk, in excess of 1,000 feet, across the river and some 30 feet above tide. The company over-came the hostility of Georgetown, whose merchants saw the project as a threat to their monopoly of the valley trade, and surmounted the failure of the Chesapeake & Ohio to build the northern abutment of the aqueduct as was required of it by an agreement.[60]

By 1850 the Alexandria branch had become the primary outlet of the Chesapeake & Ohio to the river, for the Georgetown bridges were too low for many of the canal boats and Rock Creek Basin was often greatly filled in and generally out of repair. From 1867, when the Georgetown bridges were raised, to 1887, when Congress purchased the Potomac Aqueduct and converted it to a bridge, Alexandria had to share the coal trade on the canal, which gradually declined until it became negligible.[61]

Aside from the independent canal connection at its eastern terminus, the Chesapeake & Ohio encouraged and facilitated other connecting trade links with its main stem. The company constructed three river locks to provide direct boat communication between the Virginia side of the river and the canal. The three locations were: Edwards Ferry, built in 1835–38, to tap the rich agricultural commerce of Loudoun County; near Sandy Hook just below Harpers Ferry, built in 1832–33, to connect with the Shenandoah River trade; and across from Shepherdstown, built in

---

[58] Ibid, A, 224–225; and Bryan, *A History of the National Capital* Vol. II, 110.
[59] Sanderlin, *The Great National Project*, 178–179; Bryan, *A History of the National Capital* Vol. II, 265–266, 576, 626; and *Proceedings of the Stockholders*, E, 185.
[60] *Niles' Register*, Vol. XL (July 9, 1831), 328; Ibid, Vol. XLVIII (June 1835), 241; Washington *National Intelligencer*, Dec. 1843; Sanderlin, *The Great National Project*, 179–182; and Washington D.C., Georgetown, and Alexandria Collection, Holland Loan, Library of Congress.
[61] *Proceeding of the President and Board of Directors*, N, 362, and Sanderlin, *The great National Project*, 182.

1833–35, to procure the business of that town and the surrounding hinterland of Jefferson County. The guard locks at each of the canal dams across the Potomac permitted boats to enter and exit the canal and cross the river in the slackwater pools behind the dams. In addition, the canal company encouraged the operation of ferries or constructed bridges across its waterway at points where established trade routes were already located between the Maryland and Virginia sides of the river.[62]

During the 1870s the Chesapeake & Ohio Canal Company sought to promote the continued expansion of trade in both agricultural produce and coal by facilitating the construction of the Cumberland Valley Railroad and the Western Maryland Railroad where those lines touched upon the canal's rights. This policy had the effect of both expanding the economic benefits of the canal and knitting the valley more closely together. Completed in 1874, the Cumberland Valley Railroad was a short line extending from Harrisburg to Winchester, crossing the canal just below Williamsport at Powell's Bens. At that point the canal directors agreed to allow the construction of wharf facilities for loading and unloading of coal, lumber, and agricultural produce.[63] The Western Maryland Railroad, completed in December 1873, provided a connection between the canal at Big Pool just above Williamsport and Baltimore. It was anticipated that the waterway would carry most of the railroad's coal business from Cumberland to the western terminus at Big Pool.[64]

The canal company also encouraged the construction of railroad spur lines between the Cumberland Basin and the coal fields west of the city. By January 1877 there were four such existing rail lines as follows:

1. The Baltimore & Ohio passed through the town westward up the North Branch to Piedmont where it connected with the southern portion of the Cumberland coal region. As the decision of the Maryland Court of Appeals in 1832 had sustained the claim of the canal company to the prior location of its waterway in the valley, the railroad needed the approval of the canal board for its proposed route through the town. Accordingly, on February 14, 1851, the two companies signed a contract whereby the route of the railroad was approved and tracks were constructed to the canal basin between Hay's and Shriver's Mills. Since any railroad from the coal fields in the Frostburg, Georges Creek and Savage River districts would have to cross the Baltimore & Ohio to reach the canal, the canal company required it to permit its tracks to be crossed by other railroads seeking to reach the canal basin, when so requested by the canal directors.[65]
2. The Cumberland and Piedmont Railroad was the result of a consolidation of various railways running from Cumberland to all the coal mines west of that town. Terminating at Piedmont, where it connected with the Baltimore & Ohio, this railroad carried all the coal mined in Western Maryland that passed to the canal, the Baltimore & Ohio, and the Pennsylvania Railroad.[66]
3. The Cumberland and Pennsylvania Railroad, which had taken over the lines of the Mount Savage Railway, ran from the coal basin in Cumberland through the narrows of Wills Creek to the Mount Savage Coal mines. From there it extended over the mountains

---

[62] *Proceedings of the President and Board of Directors*, C, 242–243. Also see Chapter IX of this study for more information on this subject.
[63] *Proceedings of the President and Board of Directors*, L, 469–470, and *Forty-Fifth Annual Report* (1873), C & O Co., 16 –17.,
[64] Hood to Gorman, Mar. 11, 1876, Ltrs. Recd., C & O Co. and *Forty-Sixth Annual Report* (1876), 18. The anticipated coal trade was never fully realized as the Western Maryland Railroad failed to obtain adequate terminal facilities in Baltimore.
[65] Hamill, Brannon and Farmands to President and Directors, Jan. 9, 1877, Ltrs. Recd., C & O Co., and Sanderlin, *The Great National Project*, 245.
[66] Hamill, Brannon and Farmands to President and Directors, Jan. 9, 1877, Ltrs. Recd., C & O Co.

where it connected with Georges Creek Railroad, thus offering a continuous line from Cumberland to Piedmont.[67]

4. The Pittsburgh and Connellsville Railroad, which had at one time been controlled by the Baltimore & Ohio, extended from the canal basin through the narrows of Will's Creek up to the Pennsylvania State Line and on to Pittsburgh.[68]

During the period 1878 to 1880, the canal company attempted to secure an independent connection with the coal fields in order to reduce the cost of transportation for the coal companies and to free the waterway of its dependence as a coal carrier on the aforementioned railroads. It sought to facilitate the construction of no less than four independent railroad companies with the canal basin at Cumberland by invoking the agreement of 1851 to compel the Baltimore & Ohio to permit the roads to cross its tracks. Among these were the following:

1. The Georges Creek and Cumberland Railroad, organized and incorporated in 1879, built its line from the center of the Georges Creek coal field to Cumberland, a distance of 24 miles. There it connected with the canal basin and the Baltimore & Ohio.[69]
2. Two railroad companies, the Bloomington and Fairfax and the Potomac and Piedmont, agreed in 1880 to build short feeder lines to the Baltimore & Ohio Railroad on the promise of special rates from the canal for coal shipped over it.[70]
3. In 1880 the canal board invoked the agreement of 1851 at the request of the Pennsylvania Railroad to compel the Baltimore & Ohio to permit the former road to cross its tracks in order to enter Cumberland and connect with the basin.[71]

In 1886 and 1887 an independent connection with the West Virginia coal fields was realized with the completion of the Piedmont and Cumberland Railway, a subsidiary of the West Virginia Central and Pittsburgh Railroad Company. This railroad built its line down the Potomac Valley to the south of the Baltimore & Ohio, and therefore was not balked in its efforts to reach the canal by the refusal of that company to permit a crossing of its tracks. Approaching Cumberland basin from the west, the Piedmont and Cumberland quickly gained the consent of the waterway to a connection with the basin wharf.[72]

Like the canal company, the Baltimore & Ohio constructed branch railroads that played a role in knitting the Potomac Valley more closely together as well as expanding the economic benefits of its main line. Among these branches were the following:

1. On December 1, 1867, the Washington County Railroad was opened for the 24-mile distance from Weverton on the main stem to Hagerstown
2. In 1868 the Metropolitan Branch was opened, making a direct connection between Washington, D. C., and Point of Rocks and thus shortening by some 54 miles. The previous circuitous rail route between the national capital and the west.
3. The 28-mile Winchester and Potomac Railroad between Winchester and Harpers Ferry, which had been opened for service in 1836, was taken over by the Baltimore & Ohio in

---

[67] *Ibid.*
[68] *Ibid.*
[69] *Fifty-Second Annual Report* (1880), C & O Co., 12, and John Thomas Scharf, *A History of Western Maryland* (2 Vol. Philadelphia, 1882), Vol. II, 1430–1431.
[70] *Fifty-Second Annual Report* (1880), C & O Co., 13, and *Proceedings of the President and the Board of Directors*, N, 99–100, 112.
[71] *Proceedings of the President and the Board of Directors*, N, 114–115.
[72] *Fifty-Ninth Annual Report* (1887), C & O Co., 11, and *Proceedings of the President and Board of Directors*, N, 345–346.

1848. Between 1866 and 1870 it was extended some 20 miles to the Shenandoah Valley town of Strasburg where it made connection with the Strasburg and Harrisonburg Branch of the Virginia Midland.
4. In 1871 a branch railroad was built from Cumberland to Pittsburgh, which for years had been regarded as the exclusive province of the Pennsylvania Railroad.[73]

As has already been mentioned, the effect of the branch lines to the main stem of the Chesapeake & Ohio Canal and the Baltimore & Ohio Railroad was to knit the Potomac Valley more closely together and to expand the economic benefits of the principal lines. The operation of this new transportation network completed the revolution in the life of the valley begun by the Ohio Company in 1749, the Potomac Company in 1785, and the National Road in 1806 and advanced during the period of the construction of the canal and the railroad. The essentially isolated, agricultural pattern of life was modified to accommodate an expanded commercial, mining and limited industrial development.[74]

The principal influence of the canal and railroad transportation systems, in their operation, was as a basis for all trade and communication in the valley. Evan the local road networks in some areas were keyed to the two main lines. For example, it was reported in the Washington *Star* on June 10, 1889, that the closing of the canal by the recent titanic flood had taken away in Montgomery County,

> the means of transportation from a belt of county averaging 10 miles on the side of the canal, and which at present has no outlet except by wagon over inferior roads to stations on the Metropolitan Branch of the Baltimore & Ohio Railroad . . . while the uncertainty of future transportation has caused almost panic among the landowners. . . Another indirect loss, in case the canal is not restored or a railroad built on its bed, is the change in roads, which will be necessary. The canal is the objective point of many roads in this county. These will have to be changed or closed, and new roads laid out to enable people to get to market.[75]

There was a marked shift of trade from the historic north-south route following the natural contour of the valley to an east-west direction based upon the two new transportation systems. This was accompanied by a decline in the prominence of numerous ferries across the Potomac as well as other remnants of local provincial trade arteries. In their early operating years both companies were interested both in local and through trade, but the railroad gradually concentrated on the latter and thus out distanced its rival work as a carrier.[76]

---

[73] Hungerford, *The Story of the Baltimore & Ohio*, Vol. I, 70–72, 113–119.
[74] Sanderlin, *A Study of the History of the Potomac Valley*, 94.
[75] *Washington Star*, June 10, 1889.
[76] Sanderlin, *A Study of the History of the Potomac Valley*, 94–95

IV. IMPACT OF THE OPERATION OF CANAL AND RAILROAD

A. NEW INHABITANTS

The operation of the canal and the railroad had a significant impact on the socio-economic development of the Potomac Valley. A new type of inhabitant was brought to the valley, even as the construction period had drawn a new group of people to the hitherto largely isolated, agricultural valley dotted with small Protestant Scotch-Irish and German communities. The canaller—including lock keepers, maintenance crews, and boatmen—who generally lived in close proximity to the canal were the most pronounced of the new type during the operating period. Their life was a hard one, irregular and unpredictable, and their independent habits fitted their lifestyle. Highly individualistic, yet definitely feeling themselves to be a group apart from the mainstream of valley society, the canallers usually shunned the towns, because it cost too much to buy provisions and they felt out of place even while wintering along the line of the waterway, they had their own settlements on the fringes of the towns or often quite far from them. As a rule, their coarse behavior, disrespect for authority, and lack of civilized ways made them the cause of unease among the farmers and townsfolk. Yet the purchasing power they brought into the valley economy and the services they performed made them an indispensable part of its existence, however grudgingly this fact might be conceded.[77]

The impact of the canallers on the valley economy was amply demonstrated in an article in the Williamsport *Pilot* on February 8, 1873:

> The Chesapeake & Ohio Canal employs 400 boats constantly during the boating season. These boats require 2,000 head of mules, and give employment to 2,000 persons directly and 2,000 indirectly. The mules consume at least 25,000 barrels of corn, 3,840 bushels of oats, and 500 tons of hay. This provender, which is mainly purchased along the line of canal, costs in the aggregate $60,000. The wages of employees, other than hands on repairs, amounts to the sum of $156,800. These figures are rough estimates, based on the lowest prices for everything, and will be found in the main, lower than the actual figures would make them. And from them some idea may be formed of the real worth of this work to the people of Maryland.[78]

B. ECONOMICAL TRANSPORTATION AND AGRICULTURAL DIVERSIFICATION

To the basic agricultural existence of the Potomac Valley, the waterway and railroad provided the stimulus of a cheap and easier access to the markets of the District Cities and Baltimore. An indication of the immediate impact on the agriculture of the valley appeared in *Niles' Register* on April 9, 1831 noting that upon the completion of the canal between Little Falls and Dam No. 2 the shipping costs to Georgetown for a barrel of flour had fallen from $1 to 30 to 50 cents and eventually to 7 cents, including tolls. During the last ten days of March some 30,000 barrels of flour "with much other merchandise" had descended the waterway, providing the canal company with nearly $3,000 in toll revenues.[79]

When the canal reached Harpers Ferry in November 1833, it had a similar effect on the cost of transporting flour and wheat. Formerly, it had cost between 85 cents and $1 to send a bar-

---
[77] Sanderlin, *A Study of the History of the Potomac Valley*, 95.
[78] Williamsport *Pilot*, Feb. 8, 1873, in Arthur Pue Gorman Collection, University of North Carolina Library, Chapel Hill, NC.
[79] *Niles' Register*, Vol. XL (April 9, 1831), 91, 95, and Lee to Mercer, Jan. 13, 1831, Ltrs. Recd., C & O Co.

rel of flour to Georgetown by wagon, but the opening of the waterway resulted in a reduction of this cost to 40 cents. In a similar manner, the canal allowed a reduction of 12 cents per bushel for the transportation of wheat from the Ferry to the District Cities.[80]

The three principal agricultural products carried on the canal were flour, corn and wheat. The flour trade via the waterway started at 151,966 barrels in 1842 and exceeded 200,000 barrels each year from 1848 to 1853, reaching a peak of nearly 280,000 barrels in 1850. The rapid increase in the flour trade resulted from the westward progress of the canal into the rich grain-growing areas of the upper Potomac Valley and from the fact that the farmers and millers of Franklin, Fulton, Bedford and Somerset Counties of southwestern Pennsylvania began using the waterway in 1884 as their principal means of transport since it afforded "them the cheapest and most convenient mode of transportation to market."[81]

A severe drought in the valley during the mid-1850s reduced the canal's flour trade by some 50 percent.[82]

During the late 1850s and the Civil War years, the railroad began virtually to monopolize the valley flour trade, and the canal never carried more than 24,000 barrels of flour after 1867.[83]

Flour shipments on the Baltimore & Ohio increased from 146,936 barrels in 1832, to 294,385 in 1842, and to 774,410 barrels in 1862,[84]

Large quantities of wheat and corn were also shipped on the canal. The former averaged about 225,000 bushels a year between 1842 and 1849, 275,000 bushels a year between 1850 and 1850, and nearly 415,000 a year between 1866 and 1878, reaching a peak of 605,880 bushels in 1869. The latter averaged about 145,000 bushels a year between 1842 and 1849, 170,000 bushels a year between 1850 and 1860, and nearly 100,000 bushels a year between 1866 and 1878, reaching a peak of 431,760 bushels in 1867.[85]

The stimulus that the canal provided to increase agricultural production in the Potomac Valley by offering economical transportation of produce to market was underscored by Victor Cushwa, a leading Williamsport merchant and canal shipper, in two newspaper articles in the late 1880s. On December 30, 1887, he observed in the Hagerstown *Mail* that:

> When our canal was flourishing, until recent years, our farmers within its reach frequently got more for their grain, hay, potatoes, etc. than they commanded in Baltimore or other eastern markets, thereby appreciating real-estate, private and public wealth.[86]

After the canal had been wrecked by the titanic flood of 1889, Cushwa noted in the Baltimore *Sun* of December 26, 1889, that:

> The failure on the part of the management to repair and operate the canal has brought upon our people the most disastrous results. Lose of business, labor and property amounting to hundreds of thousands of dollars, and the depreciation still going on, are matter that go down deep into the recesses of the heart, and most seriously affect the prosperity of the people of Western Maryland, to so many of whom the canal was the only market

---

[80] Millard Kessler Bushong, *Historic Jefferson County* (Boyre, 1972), 122.
[81] *Proceedings of the Stockholders*, C, 461, and Sanderlin, *The Great National Project*, 306–307.
[82] *Twenty-Seventh Annual Report* (1855), C & O Co., 13–14.
[83] Enbrey to Somnto Dellinger, Apr. 26, 1862, Ltrs. Recd., C & O Co., and Sanderlin, *The Great National Project*, 30 – 33.
[84] Reizenstein, *The Economic History of the Baltimore & Ohio Railroad*, 74–75.
[85] Sanderlin, *The Great National Project*, 306–307, and Sanderlin, *A Study of the History of the Potomac Valley*, 96. Shipments of grain on the railroad increased from 14,120 bushels in 1832 to nearly 200,000 bushels in 1852. Reizenstein, *The Economic History of the Baltimore & Ohio Railroad*, 75.
[86] Hagerstown *Mail*, Dec. 30, 1887, in Spates Papers.

and sole artery of trade. Our own fertile county of Washington, noted for its fine farms and thrifty farmers, is skirted by the canal a distance of 77 miles out of the 185 miles, the canal's entire length. The farmers of our sister counties in Pennsylvania (Franklin and Fulton), notwithstanding that many of them were favored with shipping facilities by nearby railroads, found better markets on the line of the canal, and hauled to it from miles inland the products of the farm, returning with coal, plaster, lumber, etc., benefited by the exchange. We would here answer a question often asked: "How can the canal create a better market than the railroads?" Simply because the canal is a consumer of farm produce as well as carrier of it. The boatmen are liberal buyers of every product of the farm...[87]

The canal played a role in stimulating the diversification of agricultural production in the Potomac Valley aside from merely providing a transportation route for the marketing of farm produce. One such example occurred in 1848 and 1849 when the canal board reduced the charges on fertilizers, in cooperation with the Virginia Society for the Advancement of Agriculture, in order to help increase the productivity of the soil. This policy was of particular importance to Montgomery County, where the once fertile land had been worn out by successive tobacco crops. Thus, the county, earlier known for its large tobacco plantations began to face a serious decline in its agricultural production by the late 1830s and early 1840s and significant numbers of people emigrated to the West and the South during that period. In 1845, the Society of Friends, in conjunction with the efforts of the Virginia Society for the Advancement of Agriculture, introduced Chincha Island Peruvian Guano in the country. The new fertilizer soon came into widespread use, the worn out lands were restored, and new crops of revels and grasses were grown. After the Civil War, it was estimated that the county farmers spent $15 million per year on fertilizer as the county quickly became one of the richest agricultural centers in the State, producing from 18 to 50 bushels of wheat and 30 to 60 bushels of corn per acre and providing enough produce for the operation of 30 mills.[88]

C. SALE OF WATER POWER

In addition to the stimulus to agricultural production, the canal and railroad promoted milling and manufacturing in an attempt to develop other sources of trade. The canal board saw a twofold advantage in the sale of surplus water from the canal to mills and manufactories along its banks: The financial return from the sale of the water and the added business, which industrial establishments would bring. The continued financial straits of the company forced the canal directors to give increasing attention only to the first advantage. On May 26, 1835, the *National Intelligencer* urged the company officials to give the surplus water away in return for the benefits of increased trade from the factories:

> The Chesapeake & Ohio Canal Company can furnish as much water power in the District of Columbia, as will propel every machine now in operation in the state of Rhode Island, but which must lie dormant for years, if the price at which the water is now held shall not be materially reduced. Would not the canal company be infinitely more benefited by giving the water without charge to such establishments, at the termination of the canal, and derive their income from the increased business on it, than by holding it at an ordinary

---

[87] *Baltimore Sun*, Dec. 26, 1889, in Spates Papers.
[88] *Proceedings of the President and Board of Directors*, H, 214, 239; Thomas Hulings Stockton Boyd, *The History of Montgomery County, Maryland* (Baltimore,1879), 107–110; and Scharf, *A History of Western Maryland*, Vol. I, 672.

price for revenue, prevent its occupation? Capital and manufacturing skill can only be brought here by liberal encouragement.[89]

The desperate finances of the company, however, prevented such ideas from receiving serious consideration. The early promoters of the canal also thought that small; manufacturing villages would spring up all along the line, at every lock at which waste and flume power would be available. This idea persisted among the company officials as late as 1874 despite the obvious failure of earlier expectations and reports from other canal authorities telling them to expect sales only near towns.[90]

In the beginning, the canal company did not possess the right to dispose of its surplus water by sale to manufactures as its charter granted the undertaking rights to only that water which was essential for purposes of navigation.[91] During the winter of 1828–29, the board petitioned for the necessary grant of authority from the parties to the charter, but only gradually did the directors overcome the opposition of the valley inhabitants, some of whom attempted to construe the old Potomac Company charter and its modification in the Chesapeake & Ohio charter as giving them the sole right to use the surplus water of the river in proceedings before the Supreme Court.[92] Virginia, whose citizens had the least to lose, gave the necessary authority in February 1829.[93] Under pressure from the local proprietors on the Maryland side of the river who viewed the company request as an infringement of their own rights, the state legislators in Annapolis continued to refuse to grant the petition. After a second unsuccessful attempt during the winter of 1829–30, the stockholders were informed that despite another rejection;

> It is not possible that the people of Maryland will long hazard a transfer to the shores of Virginia, of every manufacturing village, to which a judicious use of the surplus water of the Potomac might give rise; or that both states will permit a source of common improvement so fruitful of good, to remain unprofitable to either bank of the Potomac.[94]

Finally on March 22, 1833, the Maryland General Assembly assented in return for the consent of the Chesapeake & Ohio to the extension of the railroad between Point of Rocks and Harpers Ferry.[95]

After a lengthy delay, Congress gave its approval for the sale of water power in the District of Columbia in March 1837.[96]

The only restriction on the power received under their acts was the stipulation of the Maryland laws that no water could be sold within the state for the manufacture of grain—a prohibition, designed to exclude competition with the Baltimore millers, that would hinder full realization of the program to encourage industrial development until its repeal in the early 1870s.[97]

---

[89] Washington *National Intelligencer*, May 26, 1835.
[90] *Proceedings of the Stockholders*, A, 151; Allen to Starbach, Jan. 1, 1835. Ltrs. Recd., C & O Co.; and *Forty-Sixth Annual Report* (1874), C & O Co., 19.
[91] Washington to Stewart, Jan. 20, 1836, Ltrs. Sent, C & O Co.
[92] *Proceedings of the Stockholders*, A, 31, 44–45.
[93] *Act of the Virginia Assembly*, Feb. 27, 1829, and *Proceedings of the Stockholders*, A, 213. Pennsylvania had given is approval for the sale of surplus water in its act of incorporation in Feb. 1828
[94] *Proceedings of the Stockholders*, A, 151.
[95] *Ibid*, A, 287, and *Laws made and Passed by the General Assembly of the State of Maryland* (Annapolis, 1832), Ch. 291
[96] *Congressional Globe*, Vol. IV, 110 and Vol. V. 114 & 217.
[97] *Forty-Sixth Annual Report* (1874), 19. In 1835 the Canal Co. sold rights to water power at Williamsport and Weverton, since both were within the state of Maryland, the Canal Co. did not have to await the consent of Congress.

During the struggle to acquire the legal authority to sell surplus canal water, the company also faced difficulty in establishing a clean title to the surplus water from Dam No. 1, the most valuable source of potential water power on the line. The claims of John K. Smith under the Potomac Company, which had first been raised in 1816, had been inherited by Colonel Amos Binney, a Boston capitalist. After the Colonel's death, his son Amos, a zoologist and paleontologist who took over the family's real estate and business ventures, took his claim into court after failing to come to an understanding with the canal directors over his claim to 300 acres of land at Little Falls encompassing all of the water power at that location. After a series of cases and appeals, the canal company won most of its points and compromised the few remaining ones in an out-of–court settlement in March 1836. Thus it was ready to take full advantage of its rights when Congress consented to the sale of surplus water the following year.[98]

In preparation for exercising its new authority, the company appointed a committee on Water Power, consisting of President George C. Washington and Directors Phineas Janney, Walter Smith and Thomas Carberry.[99]

The committee studied carefully the procedures on other canal and water-works where water was sold to manufactories, particularly the development at Paterson, New Jersey, Lowell and Fall River, Massachusetts and Richmond, Virginia.[100]

The committee modeled its own rules after the review of those works and provided a gradual scale of increasing rents and for the location and control of water gauges. The grants were to be made for 20 years at an annual rate of $2 per inch for the succeeding ten years. The leases could be renewed indefinitely for 30-year periods provided application was made within 20 days of expiration and a bonus of $2.50 per inch was paid for the first renewal and $3 per inch for each subsequent renewal. After the renewal of the lease, the annual rental rate would be $3.[101]

On May 10, 1837, the canal board voted to advertise that water power and sites for manufacturing concerns were for sale in the District of Columbia.[102] The national economic downturn in the aftermath of the Panic of 1837 retarded the development of manufactories along the line of the canal for several years, but by 1839–40 several leases for water power in Georgetown had been negotiated. During March 1839 the company finally adopted a standard form of agreement, which was thereafter followed in executing water leases.[103] According to available evidence, the first permanent lease of water from the canal for manufacturing purposes in Georgetown was made to George Bomford retroactive to January 1, 1839. The company granted him 400 square inches of water annually for use at his brick flour mill.[104]

While water power rights were granted over the next fifty years at various places along the canal, including Weverton, Williamsport and Hancock, the most important development was at Georgetown. Here the greatest opportunity was available for the establishment of industries because of (1) the nearness to markets, labor supply and capital, (2) the location of Dam No. 1 at

---

[98] *Proceedings of the Stockholders*, A, 423–431; *Dictionary of American Biography*, Vol. I, 279–280; *Amos Binney vs. Chesapeake & Ohio Canal Company* in Chancery Court, Sep. 1829, Ltrs. Recd., C & O Co.; Chesapeake & Ohio Canal Company vs. Binney & Cranch, C. C. 68; and Binney vs. Chesapeake & Ohio Canal Company, 8 peter, 201.
[99] *Proceedings of the President and Board of Directors*, B, 216–217.
[100] *Form for Water Power Leases*, Aug. 1832, and Allen to Starbuck, Jan. 1, 1835, Ltrs. Recd., C & O Co., *Proceedings of the President and Board of Directors*, C, 35; E, 255.
[101] *Conditions for Letting Water Power in the District of Columbia*, Mar. 23, 1837, Ltrs. Recd., C & O Co. and *Proceedings of the President and Board of Directors*, I, 159.
[102] *Proceedings of the Stockholders*, B, 113, and *Proceedings of the President and Board of Directors*, E, 255. Pending the granting of full authority to the canal company to sell surplus water, the company had made several temporary agreements prior to 1837 for the sale of waste water in the Georgetown vicinity. Bomford's flour mill had begun to use water from the canal as early as 1835. At about the same time two agreements were made with Leckie and Nourse. In 1836 Mason's foundry commenced the use of canal water. *Ibid,* E. 253–255; F. 116.
[103] *Proceedings of the President and Board of Directors*, F, 31, 34.
[104] *Ibid,* F, 63–64.

Little Falls, (3) the large dimensions of the feeder and the Georgetown Level, (4) absence of restrictions on the use of the water, and (5) the fact that the town was a long-established port city and trade center and the site of various warehousing, merchandising and manufacturing concerns.[105]

Millers, founders and textile manufactures soon became the chief users of water power in Georgetown.[106]

D. COAL TRADE

The Cumberland coal fields, lying west of the city of Cumberland in a basin (known as Frostburg or George's Creek Barge) some five miles and twenty-five miles long between the Great Savage Mountain on the northwest and Dan's Mountain on the southeast, provided the greatest opportunity for the canal and railroad to promote economic diversification of the valley. Both lines were actually aware of the commercial promise of the mining areas and for more than half a century vigorously exploited the trade. In 1842, the year in which the Baltimore & Ohio reached Cumberland, only 1,708 tons of coal was transported over its line. The quantity of Cumberland coal carried by the railroad had grown to 192,806 tons by 1850, the year the canal reached that town. In that year, during which the canal managed to ship 4,042 tons of coal, the Cumberland coal mining operations were conducted by the following companies: Maryland Mining, Washington Coal, New York Mining, Allegany Mining, Frostburg Coal, Mount Savage Iron, George's Creek Coal and Iron, Border Mining, Parker Mining, Cumberland Coal and Iron, Wither's Mining and Aston Mining.[107] By the late 1870s the Cumberland coal fields comprised 44,132 acres of land. The aggregate depth of the coal formation was 1,100 feet and there were three principal veins: the Big Vein, measuring fourteen feet; the Four-Foot Vein; and the Six-Foot Vein. Fifteen mining companies were conducting operations in the fields: Borden Mining, Consolidation Coal, Blaem Aveon Coal, Hampshire and Baltimore, George's Creek Coal and Iron, New Central Coal, Maryland Coal, American Coal, Atlantic and G. C. Coal, Piedmont Coal and Iron, Swanton Mining, Potomac Coal, Maryland Union Coal, Davis' Brothers Virginia Mines and Union Mining.[108]

All told, the total coal trade of the canal and railroad between 1842 and 1877 was nearly 32,000,000 tons. During that 36-year period, the canal carried 10,683,240 tons and the railroad 20,739,908 tons, the former reaching it peak in 1875 when it shipped 904,898 tons and the latter achieving its peak in 1873 when it transported 1,780,710 tons. In 1872 the Pennsylvania Railroad Company made an independent connection to the coal fields, and from that year until 1877 it shipped 667,729 tons. During 1873, the peak year of shipments from Cumberland mines, 2,674,101 tons of coal was transported by the three lines: the Baltimore & Ohio, 1,780,710 tons; the Chesapeake & Ohio, 778,802 tons; and the Pennsylvania Railroad, 114,589 tons. It is fair to conclude that from the 1850s to the 1880s the prosperity of the Baltimore & Ohio and the Chesapeake & Ohio depended to a large extent upon the coal trade from this region since it accounted

---

[105] Rogers W. Young, *The Chesapeake & Ohio Canal and the Antebellum Commerce of Old Georgetown*, National Park Service, Manuscript, 1940, 1–6.
[106] *Ibid*, 58–93, 149–176. In Appendix I of his study, Rogers listed the details of the "Water Leases for Mills on the Chesapeake & Ohio Canal in the Limits of Georgetown, D.C., 1839–1900" and the "Water Power Leases for Mills on the Canal between Georgetown and the Little Falls of the Potomac, 1840–1900." Copies of Young's lists may be seen in Appendix A and B of this chapter.
[107] *Report to the Stockholders on the completion of the Chesapeake & Ohio Canal Company to Cumberland* (Frederick, 1851), 126–127.
[108] Scharf, *A History of Western Maryland*, Vol. II, 1434–1441, and C. J. Orrick, *The Mineral Resources and Manufacturing Facilities of the City of Cumberland, MD* (Cumberland, 1975), 8–11.

for between 45 and 55 percent of the annual total tonnage transportation of the railroad and between 85 and 95 percent of the total tonnage of the waterway.[109]

At the same time, the coal trade had a significant economic impact on the general prosperity of the valley. Such a point was made by Victor Cushwa on December 30, 1887, when he described the beneficial results of the coal trade on the standard-of-living in Washington County:

> The direct revenue of canals or other public or private works . . .may not be enormous or even medium, but the indirect revenue is sometimes almost beyond computation when the great reduction in coal [price] alone is considered, thereby cheapening merchandise of all kinds in our county, the benefits of which independent transportation is the chief factor, the indirect benefits are almost incalculable. People are too apt to look only at the direct interest of public as also private enterprise. Too eager to keep in constant sight the almighty dollar and its direct profit, losing sight of the indirect and general good.[110]

E. GROWTH OF RELATED INDUSTRIES

The operation of the two transportation lines, especially of the canal, provided many related activities, which supported countless families in the Potomac Valley. Shipbuilding and repair became quite a profitable occupation. At the peak of the canal trade in the early 1870s, there were eight principal firms involved in the construction and maintenance of boats:

> Doener and Bender (Cumberland)
> Weld and Sheridan (Cumberland)
> William Young (Cumberland)
> Frederick Mentens (Cumberland)
> Benjamin Mitchell (Hancock)
> Consolidation Coal Co. (Cumberland)
> R. and M. Coulehan (Cumberland)
> Isaac Gruber (Cumberland)[111]

In addition, there were at least seven dry docks built along the waterway for repair of boats:

> Lock No. 10—Ca. 1875
> Lock No. 14—Ca. 1864
> Edwards Ferry Basin—Ca. 1872
> Lock No. 30—Ca. 1855
> Lock No. 35—Ca. 1900
> Lock No. 44—Ca. 1862
> Lock No. 45—Ca. 1854[112]

Shipping lines also became an important source of profit as a result of the canal trade. By the late 1850s packets of the New York and Washington Steam Ship line were putting in weekly calls at the Georgetown wharves.[113] More important was the development of coastwise and foreign trade, chiefly in coal [that] had been found to be particularly suited for New England textile mills,

---

[109] *Fiftieth Annual Report* (1878), C & O Co., 26–27 and *Fiftieth Annual Report* (1876), B & O Co., 36–37.
[110] Hagerstown *Mail*, Dec. 30, 1887, in Spates Papers.
[111] See Chapter XI of this study for more information on this subject.
[112] See Chapter XI of this study for more information on this subject.
[113] Mary Mitchell, *Divided Town* (Banre, 1968), 3.

steamship bunkering and iron smeltering. Hence, much of the capital invested in the Maryland coal region before the Civil War was supplied by eastern or English businessmen, such as Evastus Corning, William H, Aspinwall, August Belmont, Edward Cunard and the Borden family of Fall River, Massachusetts, with special manufacturing or transportation interests, particularly in the Northeastern United States.[114] During the late 1850s several shipping lines were formed to transport the coal from the canal wharves at Georgetown and Alexandria down the Potomac River, through the Chesapeake Bay, and up the Atlantic Coast to New York, Boston and other New England seaports. After a slow-down in the amount of coal shipped on these lines during the Civil War, the coastwise trade from the District Cities reemerged with new vigor in 1867 and remained heavy for nearly a decade. In the late 1870s a decline in the production of Cumberland coal and stiff competition from the Baltimore & Ohio drew off much of the coastwise coal trade from the District Cities.[115]

To a lesser extent, Cumberland coal descending the canal to Georgetown and Alexandria was shipped to foreign markets. From the late 1850s to the mid-1870s shipping lines transported coal to the British West Indies and ports on the northern coast of South America where there were English naval and commercial interests.[116]

In the 1840s and 1850s flour became a principal element of the coastline and foreign trade originating at Georgetown. That product, some of which passed down the canal from the upper Potomac Valley and much of which was produced in the Georgetown flour mills using canal water power, was shipped via coasting vessels to the populous cities of New York and Boston and to a lesser extent via steamship line to foreign ports. The coastwise and foreign shipment of flour from Georgetown was short-lived, however, as the Baltimore & Ohio Railroad acquired between one-half and two-thirds of the descending canal trade during the Civil War. Thereafter, the port of Baltimore became the central focus of the coastwise and foreign shipment of flour from the Potomac Valley and the flour produced at Georgetown was used primarily to meet the local needs of the District Cities.[117] Many individuals made a comfortable living from the operation of grocery and feed stores along the waterway, supplying the boatmen with their necessary provisions for themselves, their families and their mules. Available evidence indicates that a conspicuous exception to this trend was the flour milling operations of Abraham Herr after 1862. When his large industrial holdings on Virginias Island at Harpers Ferry were destroyed during the fighting in 1861 and 1862, Herr moved to Georgetown and purchased the Columbia Flouring mill on the south line of the canal. He left the mill in the day-to-day superintendence of his head miller, Welch, and moved to Baltimore, where he initiated his own enterprise as a commission merchant miller on Smith's Wharf. From there he exported flour milled in Georgetown to markets in the West Indies and Brazil. At that time the Latin American markets wanted a high grade flour made from wheat with a relatively low moisture and high gluten content, such as would stand passage by sea through the tropics. The wheat from the upper Potomac Valley which descended the canal met such a description, and Herr, who was equipped to produce high grade flour and had an office in a port-city where flour constituted 70 percent of the exports to Brazil and over 50 percent of the shipments to other South American countries, continued to prosper. After the peace at Appomattox, Welch bought the Columbia Mill from Herr, who in turn bought the old cotton factory built along the canal in 1844. He converted this mill, which had been closed since 1861, into an-

---

[114] Katherine A. Harvey, *The Civil War and the Maryland Coal Trade*, 'Maryland Historical Magazine", Vol. LXIII (Dec., 1967), 361-362.
[115] Young, *Antebellum Commerce of Old Georgetown*, 167-168, 176.
[116] Washington, *National Intelligencer*, Apr. 21, 1862, and *Forty-Fifth Annual Report* (1873) C & O Co., 16.
[117] Young, *Antebellum Commerce of Old Georgetown*, 176; Embrey and Son to Dellinger, April 26, 1862, Ltrs. Recd., C & O Co.; Reizenstein, *An Economic History of the Baltimore & Ohio*, 82-83 and Sanderlin, *The Great National Project*, 217-218.

other large and prosperous flour mill, which ultimately became the Wilkins-Rogers Company, manufacturing *Washington Flour*.[118]

At least 27 grocery and feed stores were built along the canal at the following locations:

Lock No. 6	ca. 1873	Lock No. 28	ca. 1864
Lock No. 10	ca. 1873	Lock No. 29	ca. 1864
Lock No. 13	ca. 1871	Lock No. 30	ca. 1863
Seven Locks	ca. 1873	Lock No. 33	ca. 1859
Lock No. 20	ca. 1851, 1869	Lock No. 37	ca. 1876
Lock No. 22	ca. 1870	Lock No. 39	ca. 1866
Guard Lock No. 2	ca. 1870	Lock No. 41	ca. 1877
Lock No. 23	ca. 1883	Lock No. 46	ca. 1865
Lock No. 24	ca. 1873	Williamsport	ca. 1866
Edwards Ferry	ca. 1864–65	Lock No. 50	ca. 1865
Lock No. 25	ca. 1872	Lock No. 51	ca. 1866
Conrad's Ferry	ca. 1863	Lock No. 52	ca. 1865
Lock No. 27	ca. 1866	Dam No. 6	ca. 1865
		Oldtown	ca. 1859

In addition, a number of concerns in the vicinity of the eastern and western terminuses of the canal in Georgetown and Cumberland, respectively, catered to the grocery and mule-provender needs of the boat.[119]

Because the Baltimore & Ohio Railroad concentrated on the through east-west trade, it provided fewer opportunities for profitable sideline businesses in the Potomac Valley than did the canal. However, warehouses and wharf owners fared equally well from the trade and transfer business of both railway and waterway.[120] In fact the transfer business was perhaps the principal related benefit from the existence of the transportation lines. For instance, the canal directors reported that:

> in 1874 the boatmen received for their services $1,070,000, the wharf owners $344,000, while the canal company received from tolls on coal and boats but $428,000 for maintaining and operating a work which cost over $11,000,000, being but $84,000 more than was received by the wharf owners on their investment of about $300,000.[121]

The handsome return on the relatively small capital outlay of the Georgetown and Cumberland wharf owners disturbed the canal board. At the same time that the private owners were making large profits, their rates were so high (8 cents per ton of coal at Cumberland and 25 cents per ton at Georgetown) that they forced the canal directors to reduce their charges on the coal trade in order to compete with the railroads for business.[122]

---

[118] Mitchell, *Divided Town*, 158–161.
[119] See Chapter XVI of this study for more information on this.
[120] See Appendix C for a "List of Warehouses along the Chesapeake & Ohio Canal: 1850–1890."
[121] Anonymous newspaper article in Gorman Collection. See 126 A.
[122] Cumberland *Times*, May 31, 1873, and Washington *Daily News*, March 2, 1875, in Gorman Collection. In Appendix II of this report is a list of the Georgetown coal yards and wharves using water power from the canal to unload and ship coal as well as those not using water power to ship coal during the period 1856 to 1880. This data may be seen in Appendices D and E of this chapter.

Accordingly the board dredged the Rock Creek Basin and repaired the outlet lock in order to make the river bank available for wharf facilities, and these actions soon forced the average cost of wharfage to be reduced by 10 cents per ton at Georgetown.[123]

On the other hand, at Cumberland the canal company leased two-thirds of the Potomac Wharf from Consolidated Coal Company in March 1875 and cut rates until the private wharf owners were forced to cut theirs.[124]

Later in July 1878, the company followed the example of the Baltimore & Ohio Railroad, which had earlier secured its own wharf facilities at the town, by purchasing the Basin Wharf property from Welsh and McKaig for $86,000. Since it was the largest wharf on the canal basin, the canal company secured permanent control over wharfage at that end of the canal.[125]

F. COMPETITION BETWEEN THE CANAL AND RAILROAD

Perhaps the most direct advantage to the citizens of the Potomac Valley from the operation of the two transportation lines was the limited commercial competition which developed. There were at least four focal points of the rivalry which were of sufficient importance to merit attention.

In the earliest days, the struggle for the lions' share of the valley trade occurred at Point of Rocks, this was the location where the railroad first entered the immediate confines of the valley and hence where the two lines first met on confrontation. The railroad completed its line to Point of Rocks in April 1832, three months after the settlement of controversy over the legal right-of-way of the two works. On the other hand, the canal was not opened above Dam No. 2 until November 1833 because of its need to reach the Harpers Ferry feeder to provide water for the 40 mile section between Seneca and the Ferry. Within months of the arrival of the railroad at Point of Rocks, several warehouses and other facilities were built at the town for the transfer to the rail line of agricultural produce, lime, timber and stone brought down the river from the upper valley and across the stream from Loudoun County, Virginia. When the canal reached the town, it attempted to acquire its share of this trade for shipment to the District Cities. Even after the canal and railroad extended their lines westward, the town remained an important transfer point and a place where the two lines competed for business.[126]

The rivalry over the Shenandoah wheat and flour trade at Harpers Ferry during the early 1840s was a renewal of the difficulties which had occurred during the preceding decade when the railroad attempted to block the canal's access to the Virginia side of the river at that strategic point.[127] Beginning in 1840, merchants engaged in the flour trade in Baltimore petitioned the railroad executives stating that the low rates charged for the shipment of flour on the canal (2 cents a barrel per mile for the first 15 miles, and 1½ cents a barrel per mile thereafter) were diverting that product from their city to the District of Columbia. Since the flour trade constituted a key portion of the Baltimore economy, the railroad quickly took steps to acquire a dominant share of the developing Shenandoah wheat and flour trade. Until May 1, 1841, the charges by rail from Harpers Ferry to Baltimore were 34 cents a ton plus 3 cents for handling (a ton amounted to 10½ to 11 barrels). On May 1, the railroad raised the rate to 50 cents, including handling, and sent a petition to the canal company to raise its toll to a "profitable rate." Soon the canal board raised its toll on

---

[123] Sanderlin, *The Great National Project*, 245–246.
[124] *Proceedings of the President and Board of Directors*, M, 291; Cumberland *Times*, March 20, 1875, in Gorman Collection; and Tilghman to Gorman, May 17 and June 14, 1875, Hall to Gorman, Jan. 15, 1876, Graham to Gorman, Jan. 5, and Feb. 28, 1877, and Hicks to Gorman, Apr. 20, 1877, Ltrs. Recd., C & O Co.
[125] *Proceedings of the President and Board of Directors*, N, 56 –57.
[126] Reizenstein, *An Economic History of the Baltimore & Ohio*, 26–27, and *Niles' Register*, Vol. XLV (Nov. 23, 1833), 199.
[127] Sanderlin, *The Great National Project*, 193–195.

flour to a flat rate of 2 cents a barrel per mile. Within a month, on June 3, 1841, the railroad reduced its rates to 34 cents a ton, including handling. It was reported that the charges from Frederick to Baltimore were 30 cents, thus making the additional charge for the 21 miles from Frederick to Harpers Ferry a mere 4 cents. As a result, the flour trade on the canal from the Ferry fell off by over 4,400 barrels as compared with the previous year. A large amount of this decrease was attributed to the maneuvering of the railroad company.[128]

Again, in 1844, leading citizens in Alexandria complained of the loss of the flour trade to the Baltimore millers.[129]

In 1845 the Baltimore & Ohio intensified its efforts to win the flour trade from the canal. Its board of directors resolved "to reduce charges only along that portion of the road that was adjacent to the Chesapeake & Ohio Canal to a minimum which would at least pay the expenses of transportation." At the same time the railroad sought to place obstacles in the way of the transfer of canal trade across the river at Harpers Ferry. It continued to charge at the rate of 20 cents a ton per mile for goods shipped one-quarter mile over the viaduct, although it had agreed to a maximum rate of 8 cents. It refused to allow the use of its own cars, and those of the Winchester and Potomac Railroad were forced to pay a high fee to participate in the trade. Delay was a common occurrence in the landing of what little business that was transacted at the Ferry.[130]

Competition for the Shenandoah wheat and flour trade, as well as that of Washington County, led to a short rate war in 1876 from which the local farmers profited. In the wake of the Panic of 1873 which struck the Potomac and Shenandoah Valleys with full force in 1876, the railroad attempted to hold its share of the declining trade by reducing its charges on grain by 4 cents per bushel from that point to Baltimore. In an effort to compete with the railroad, the canal lowered the toll on grain and flour from 1 cent a ton per mile to ¾ cent a ton per mile from all points between Williamsport and Weverton to Georgetown.[131]

The struggle for the Cumberland coal trade, which began in the late 1840s, not only proved to be the decisive factor in the course of canal trade and prosperity but also served as a boon to the Allegany County coal companies. From December 1873 until March 1845, the railroad and the canal cooperated in the handling of the lucrative business. According to their agreement the railroad, which had reached Cumberland in November 1842, undertook to carry all the coal offered for shipment via the waterway over its own tracks to the western terminus of the canal navigation at Dam No. 6 at the special rate of 2 cents a ton per mile.[132]

When the state legislature passed the bill providing for the completion of the waterway to Cumberland in March 1845, the railroad and its ally, the City of Baltimore, began an all-out assault on the trade of its arch competitor. The Baltimore City Council approved an ordinance to allow the railroad to run its tracks into the city to a new depot on the south side of the harbor where vessels could dock free of port charges. The city authorities also encouraged the railroad to lower its charges on coal shipments. According to *Niles' Register* on April 12, 1845, such actions would encourage the coal and iron companies and the western county people to keep up the spirit of a competition, which however ruinous to canals and railroads, would enable them to get their material wealth and products to markets, for a mere song, the very thing for them.[133]

---

[128] Elgin to Ingle, Dec. 23, 1841, Ltrs. Recd., C & O Co. and Reizenstein, *An Economic History of the Baltimore & Ohio*, 82–83.
[129] Maccubin to Turner, Nov. 6, 1844, Ltrs. Recd., C & O Co.
[130] Reizenstein, *An Economic History of the Baltimore & Ohio*, 83, and Elgin to Coale, Nov. 2, 1845, Ltrs. Recd., C & O Co.
[131] Cockrell and Engle to Gorman, Jan. 26 and Mar. 8, 1877, Ltrs. Recd., C & O Co., and *Proceedings of the President and Board of Directors*, M, 255, 258.
[132] *Niles' Register*, Vol. LXVI (June 22, 1844), 272; *Proceedings of the Stockholders*. C, 243–245; and McLane to Coale, Sep. 17, 1843, Ltrs. Recd., C & O Co.
[133] *Niles' Register*, Vol. LXVIII (Apr. 12, 1845), 85

One month later, the Baltimore & Ohio abruptly terminated its arrangement for the transportation of coal from Cumberland to Dam No. 6, doubling its rates to 4 cents a ton per mile.[134]

Competition for the declining Cumberland coal trade in the aftermath of the Panic of 1873 proved to be a boon to the Allegany coal companies as both of the transportation lines slashed their rates in an effort to retain their share of the commerce. Until 1876 the canal and the railroad had a general understanding to charge moderate rates on coal that were published and applied to all shippers. In that year, however, the railroad began to offer rebates of up to 20 cents per ton to some shippers. After the canal company announced its 1877 rates, which were 33 cents a ton per mile or 8 cents less than the 1876 price, the railroad lowered its charges 22 cents below the published rates for 1876 to $1.81 per ton from Cumberland to Baltimore. At the same time, it offered "Kickbacks" of up to 20 cents per ton to any coal company that would transfer its entire trade from the canal to the railway. As a result, the canal board lowered its toll on coal to 22 cents a ton per mile in August 1877.[135]

The rate war between the two lines subsided between 1878 and 1882, but the battle resumed during the last seven years of the independent existence of the waterway.[136] By 1885 the railroad was carrying coal to deep-water docks in the Port of Baltimore for $1.30 a ton, and there were reports that rebates to the coal companies often lowered the cost to $1.00 a ton.[137] Accordingly, the debt-ridden canal was forced to lower its tolls from 51 cents a ton per mile to 36 cents in June 1883, to 33 cents in April 1884 and to 22 cents in February 1885.[138]

---

[134] McLane to Coale, May 7, 1845, Ltrs. Recd., C & O Co., and Coale to McLane, May 9, 1845, Ltrs. Sent, C & O Co.
[135] *Proceedings of the President and Board of Directors*, M, 293–296, and N, 4; New York *Herald*, Apr. 6, 1877; and New York *Times*, Apr. 20, 1877 in Gorman collection; and Lloyd to Gorman, Mar. 28, 1877, Loveridge to Gorman, Apr. 7, 1877, and Garrett to Gorman, May 19, 1877, Ltrs. Recd., C & O Co.
[136] *Fifty-First Annual Report* (1879), C & O Co., 6.
[137] Reizenstein, *An Economic History of the Baltimore & Ohio*.
[138] Sanderlin, *The Great National Project*, 314

V. IMPACT ON THE DEVELOPMENT OF TOWNS

One of the best ways to demonstrate the impact of the canal upon the Potomac Valley would be to examine its effect upon the towns in the area. As the waterway advanced up the valley, it promoted the development of many towns, which depended largely upon it for a livelihood. In some cases the influence was temporary, lasting only for a brief interval until the head of navigation moved westward. Several towns flourished to a greater or lesser extent as long as the canal was in regular operation. At least one town—Cumberland—took on a permanent position of socio-economic importance in the life of the valley.

A. GEORGETOWN

Founded near the head of tidewater on the Maryland shore of the Potomac River in 1751, Georgetown gradually became a colonial port of some importance. Shipping quickly became the chief industry of the town, as foreign and domestic vessels deposited manufactured good and wines as well as sugar, molasses and rum from the West Indies. In turn, the ships
Founded near the head of tidewater on the Maryland shore of the Potomac River in 1751, Georgetown gradually became a colonial port of some importance. Shipping quickly became the chief industry of the town, as foreign and domestic vessels deposited manufactured good and wines as well as sugar, molasses and rum from the West Indies. In turn, the ships sailed away with large quantities of Maryland and Virginia flour and tobacco, the latter being the chief commodity marketed at Georgetown until the early 1830s. From 1804 to 1835, a thriving coastwise grocery trade flourished in Georgetown. Nevertheless, commercial enterprise and foreign exports began declining in the 1820s as Washington, the seat of national government, expanded and drained off much of Georgetown's trade and capital investment, and Alexandria emerged as the deep-water seaport for the foreign commerce of the District Cities.[139]

The coming of the Chesapeake & Ohio Canal aided in stemming the gradual decline of the old port's commercial importance and its disappearing coastwise and foreign trade. From the mid-1830s until the outbreak of the Civil War, the developing waterway contributed to a momentary revival of both the coastwise and foreign trade of Georgetown. The renewed coastwise trade in wheat, flour and agricultural produce, which began in the mid-1830s served to replace Georgetown's early coastwise commerce in groceries and merchandise. The renewed foreign trade with the West Indies involving mainly farm and forest products, which replaced the earlier exports of tobacco and flour, was short-lived in the face of competition from Alexandria's rising deep-water commerce.[140] Within Georgetown, the great tobacco and grocery warehouses of the 1820s were replaced by new flour and cotton [mills] using water power from the canal, and coal wharves for the transshipment of the Cumberland coal. Primarily because of the waterway's commerce, by 1856 Georgetown had numerous brick storehouses lining M Street, five flour mills on the canal, a 2,560-spindle, 84-boom factory of the Pioneer Cotton Company, several lumber and coal yards at the east and west ends of the water front, and thirty-three brick warehouses fronting south on K Street.[141]

Indicative, however, of the small economic gains arising from this transition, is the fact that Georgetown's population grew by only 292 inhabitants from 8,441 in 1830 to 8,733 in 1860, while during the same period the population of Washington was more than tripling from 18,826 to 61,122.[142] The economic benefit brought to Georgetown by the canal during the antebellum

---

[139] Young, *Antebellum Commerce of Old Georgetown*, 1–6.
[140] Richard Plummer Jackson, *The Chronicles of Georgetown, D.C.* (Washington, 1878), 49.
[141] Mitchell, *Divided Town*, 2–3, and Constance Green, *Washington*, (2 Vols., Princeton, 1963), Vol. I, 157
[142] Green, *Washington*, 21.

period served to compensate the old port for the loss of its former trade and business, and for the increasing surrender of its foreign commerce to Alexandria. While the new enterprises in Georgetown did little more than replace the old, had it not been for this new business, largely produced by the canal, Georgetown's commercial life probably would have disappeared during the mid-1830s.[143]

During the post-Civil War years, the foreign export and coastwise trade of Georgetown began to revive as a result of the burgeoning canal commerce. This revival was shorn by a growth in population of the town to 11,384 in 1840—the last year in which population figures are available for the town as its separate government was abolished by Congress in 1871 and it became part of the District of Columbia. Although the foreign trade of Georgetown remained negligible for the remainder of the 19th Century, a heavy coastwise trade in coal shipments began in 1867 and continued until the late 1870s when the canal's coal business went into a tailspin as a result of national depression, railroad competition and declining production in the coal field.[144]

B. GREAT FALLS (CROMMELIN)

The canal company directors anticipated that a small community would develop at Great Falls on the strength of the canal trade, the attraction of the area for leisure activities by Washington and Georgetown residents, and the possibility of water-powered manufactories along the canal banks. Accordingly, the board approved the following resolution on June 10, 1831:

> Whereas, the Chesapeake & Ohio Canal Company are indebted to the confidence, liberty and enterprise of the Messrs Crommelin of Amsterdam, for the facilities afforded by their loan to the cities of the District of Columbia, for the payment of one million and a half of stock subscribed to the construction of the canal; be it therefore resolved, that in all orders and proceedings of the Board, the grounds belong to the Company and the Buildings erected thereon, at or near the Great Falls of the Potomac, be hereafter named "Crommelin".[145]

The projected development at Great Falls, however, never reached an advanced stage of development. Aside from the tavern facilities in Crommelin House, the expectations for Great Falls amounted to little more than the construction of several canal company maintenance shops, a mule stable and feed house, a grocery store, a horse stable and buggy shed, and a few residential dwellings. The known structures, along with their approximate dates and location were as follows:

> Lock "Shanty"—ca. 1899—located at northwest corner of Lock No. 20. Stable and Feed House—ca. 1900—located at northwestern edge of towpath, abutting the spillway at Lock No. 20 (ca. 1913—buildings removed to site on towpath 350 feet north of Lock No. 20). Carpenter Shop—ca. 1830—located about 1,000 feet north of the tavern on the berm bank of the canal (destroyed by fire and replaced by new shop between 1893 and 1896).
> Collier Dwelling—ca. 1859—located about 350 feet north of the tavern on the slope of the hill just beyond the northeast corner of the old gatehouse of the Washington Aqueduct (ca. 1875 moved to site about 250 feet north of the tavern and occupied by

---

[143] Young, *Antebellum Commerce of Old Georgetown*, 176.
[144] Young, *Antebellum Commerce of Old Georgetown*, 167–168, and Green, *Washington*, 21. See Appendix of this study for a "List of the Chief Retail Coal Dealers Near the Chesapeake & Ohio Canal in Georgetown: 1860-1880" and Appendix G for a "Diagram of Georgetown Showing C & O Canal and Riverfront Development: 1830-1900."
[145] *Proceedings of the President and Board of Directors*, B, 382–383.

Richard Collier, a canal employee, who resided in the house until about 1896 when it was razed by the canal company). Canal Company Residence—ca. 1850—located above the southern edge of Conduit Road and at a point about one-quarter mile northeast of tavern (destroyed by fire in 1889). Garrett Stone—ca, 1869—located on western edge of towpath near northern end of Lock No. 20 (ca. 1879 larger two story building containing a storeroom, office, saloon and living quarters erected on same site; structure razed by canal company ca. 1910).

Two Frame Dwellings and Log Cabin—ca. 1873—1884—located along the berm bank of the canal immediately to the south of the tavern (built by Howard A. Garnett for residential purposes). Buggy Shed and Stable—ca. 1890—located on the berm bank of the canal some 50 and 75 feet northeast of Lock No. 19 (razed ca. 1913).[146]

C.   SENECA (RUSHVILLE)

Seneca, the first western terminus of the waterway, also held the spotlight briefly in the early 1830s. The canal directors anticipated that a small community would develop between Dam No. 2 and the mouth of Seneca Creek for the following reasons: (1) the growth of canal trade; (2) the expected emergence of the area to serve as an outlet for the large grain production of the surrounding region; (3) the large pool formed by the dam which would provide an opportunity for the canal to tap the trade of upper Fairfax County and lower Loudoun County in Virginia; (4) the timber resources of the surrounding region; (5) the further development of operations at the already famous red sandstone quarries; and (6) the possibility of water-powered manufactories along the banks of Seneca Creek and the canal. Accordingly, the directors on June 10, 1831, passed a resolution naming the site Rushville, in honor of Richard Rush, the former Secretary of the Treasury who had negotiated the loan from the Dutch capitalists, enabling the District Cities to pay their subscriptions to the canal stock.[147]

As the canal advanced westward, the spotlight moved with the construction and the hopes for the development at Seneca were never fully realized. The nearby red sandstone quarry, which had been in use prior to the American Revolution, continued to be operated until about 1900. Built during the late 1830s, the stone mill near the quarry was used to cut and dress the stone, the power for such work being supplied by water from the canal. At its peak in the post-Civil War era, the mill employed some 100 men, and the stone was shipped to Georgetown and Washington where it was used in the popular "brownstone" architecture of the period. Several warehouses were built along the canal in the 1870s to store wheat and flour produced in the surrounding region preparatory to shipment down the waterway to the District Cities. Throughout the history of the canal period, gristmills were in operation on Seneca Creek about ½ mile from the waterway—the last mill being operated by the Tschiffely family from 1900 to 1931.[148]

---

[146] Rogers W. Young, *A Preliminary Historical Study on the Area Along the Maryland Shore of the Potomac at great Falls during the Heyday of the Chesapeake & Ohio Canal: 1858–1880*, (NPS Manuscript, 1939), 19–26, 35–40. A number of buildings were also constructed at Great Falls relating to the Washington Aqueduct project. Among these were the old gatehouse, several temporary construction sheds and shanties, a brick and stone residence, a garage, and several frame dwellings. *Ibid,* 30 –34.
[147] *Proceedings of the President and Board of Directors*, B, 382–383.
[148] Jane Chinn Sween, *A History of Dawsonville and Seneca, Montgomery County, Maryland* (Md. Hist. Soc. Mass., 1967), 69–70, and *Proceedings of the President and Board of Directors*, L, 454, 467, and M, 5.

D. POINT OF ROCKS

A flourishing commercial enterprise sprang up at Point of Rocks in the early 1830s under the joint impact of the Baltimore & Ohio Railroad and the Chesapeake & Ohio Canal. As the western terminus of the railroad during the legal controversy with the canal over the right-of-way between an important exchange point where freight was collected from the surrounding area on both sides of the Potomac for shipment to Baltimore. Later in November 1833 when the canal was opened to navigation from Seneca to Harpers Ferry, Point of Rocks became an important exchange point between the two transportation lines as well as a center from which the canal tapped the agricultural commerce of upper Loudoun County, Virginia.

A contemporary description of the community appeared in the Frederick *Times* in November 1833, shortly after the canal was opened to Harpers Ferry:

> The Point of Rocks is now the point of attraction, and really presents, as we are told, an animating scene. Railroad cars and canal boats, constantly arriving, interchanging passengers and cargoes and then departing—the bustle of a little village suddenly arisen, as it were, out of the earth and actually doing business of a commercial emporium—its inhabitants hardly yet acquainted with each other, and very often outnumbered by the transient strangers who throng thither in pursuit of business and pleasure—the very novelty itself, of two great public enterprises so long at war with each other, just going into harmonious operation upon the spot which may be called the battle ground; and that spot too so lately unknown save to the wild foxes of the mountains—in a word, the noblest exhibitions of art and nature contending for mastery, are the rich reward of those who may find it convenient to make an excursion upon the canal via the Point of Rocks.[149]

But the prosperity of the village was only temporary, and it declined rapidly as the canal was opened to Dam No. 4 by the spring of 1834 and the railroad was completed to Harpers Ferry by December 1834. Despite its declining prosperity, Point of Rocks was laid out in regular lots in 1835 by H. G. O'Neal for Charles Johnson. Depending largely on the canal and railroad for its livelihood, the town remained a small hamlet at the eastern foot of Catoctin Mountain, reaching a population figure of 290 in 1880.[150]

E. BRUNSWICK (BERLIN)

The town of Berlin was originally laid out in 1870 by Leonard Smith. In early times, the town had a flour mill and considerable trade with the surrounding countryside. When the canal and railroad reached Berlin, they brought a temporary increase in economic and commercial activity. The increased prosperity declined as both works pushed westward, although Berlin continued to profit as a result of its location on the canal and railroad. The town served as a profitable conduit for trade between the two transportation lines and Loudoun County as it was a widely-used Potomac River crossing point at first by the use of a ferry and after 1858 by a bridge. In December 1874 Berlin was described by the Cumberland *Times* as "a small village of Frederick County, containing sixty voters" whose principal business was "the mill of Messrs. Jordan, Graham and Wenner, which is run by the water from (the) canal." By 1880 the population of the town had increased to 217, and within another decade the population had grown to 300. When the Baltimore & Ohio

---

[149] Frederick *Times*, quoted in *Niles' Register*, Vol. XLV (Nov. 23, 1833), 199
[150] Schoaf, *History of Western Maryland*, Vol. I, 369–370 and Thomas John Chew Williams, *History of Frederick County, Maryland* (2 Vol., Frederick, 1910), Vol. I, 321–322.

built its railroad yards at Berlin in 1890, the town and its population grew rapidly. Because of its rising importance as a railroad center, the name of the town was changed to Brunswick in order to avoid confusion with another town in Maryland by the same name.[151]

F.   KNOXVILLE

Knoxville was another little valley community, which prospered for a brief period in the 1830s and 1840s as a result of the increased trade, brought by the canal and railroad. On September 12 and 19, 1849, the Frederick *Examiner* described the town as a flourishing community with bright prospects for economic development as a result of its close proximity to Weverton and the two transportation lines:

> there are a number of improvements now in progress at this place and in contemplation that must render it in a few years a place of very great importance . . . There is a large hotel erecting and several other buildings in contemplation. The Messrs. Barken and Co., from Baltimore, a wealthy company, have secured the most valuable mines of iron [that] are on the Shenandoah and Potomac Mines above this place, and have lately made a purchase of Col. Richard Johnson, adjoining Knoxville, of some twenty acres of land lying immediately between the Railway and Canal and was purchased at a reduced price, considering the very favorable location. The Company are now erecting a large furnace, storehouse and intend putting up between twenty and thirty other buildings for their workmen. This Company have several other furnaces in operation, but have selected this location believing it the most desirable as they can manufacture iron here at from five to seven dollars cheaper than at any other location in Maryland . . The advantages are so manifest that they must and will command the attention of Iron masters and manufactures. Messrs. Barker and Co. . . intend to extend their operations to a valley Mill foundry and Nail Factory.

These expectations were not fulfilled, however, and the town declined steadily after this time. In 1880 it had a population of 265.[152]

G.   WEVERTON

Weverton was named after Casper W. Wever, a celebrated engineer connected with the Baltimore & Ohio Railroad, who had been associated formerly with the construction and laying out of the National Road, the first bridge at Harpers Ferry, and Pennsylvania Avenue in Washington, D. C. Attracted by the possibility of utilizing the water power of the Potomac River at this point and of taking advantage of the railroad and the canal to transport finished goods to Baltimore and the District Cities, he formed the Weverton Manufacturing Company and purchased 500 acres of land in 1834 on which he intended to build a manufacturing town similar to that at Lowell, Massachusetts. Along with the land, he purchased the rights to the water power of the river from his acreage to Harpers Ferry, some 3 miles distant. The fall of water in that stretch of the river was ap-

---

[151] Williams, *History of Frederick County*, Vol. I, 39, 238–239; Cumberland *Times*, Dec. 1, 1874, in Gorman Collection; David H. Brown, *Bridges at Berlin* (c. Burs. Artz Library Mss., Frederick, 1953), 1, 3; John R. Miele, *A Physical History of the Chesapeake & Ohio Canal* (NPS Mss., 1968) 131–133; and Scharf, *History of Western Maryland*, Vol. I, 369–370.
[152] Frederick *Examiner*, Sept. 12 and 19, 1849, quoted in Williams, *History of Frederick County*, Vol. I, 274, and Scharf, *History of Western Maryland*, Vol. I, 369–370.

proximately fifteen feet—estimates to amount to 200,000 horsepower, which was sufficient to turn 3,000 spindles—and it was his intention to furnish the water power at an annual rental.

When his projected plans were delayed by the economic depression in the late 1830s, Wever attempted to broaden the financial base of the new community by forming a joint stock company in 1847. The leaders in this new venture were George Jacobs of Waynesboro, Pennsylvania, as president, Martin Kinsell of Chestnut Hill, Pennsylvania and Captain Hezekiah Boteler, Edward Garrott, Lewis Bell, John Gray and Barton Boteler as directors.

In May 1847 the first sale of lots was advertised. Twenty-six plots were sold at an average price of $75, amounting to $1,800 for less than an acre of land. A contract was made with Joseph P. Shannan to construct a dam across the river for $25,000, the work to be supervised by Charles B. Fisk, the chief engineer of the canal. Lots were offered at a nominal price for factory sites and free to any church, all with the proviso that no liquor should be sold.

In 1849 Joseph G. Chapman of Charles County, Maryland, succeeded Jacobs as president of the company and James M. Buchanan was elected counsel, Barton Boteler, Treasurer, William Loughridge general agent, and Casper W, Wever, secretary. Soon thereafter, three large manufactories were built at the town—a large cotton mill by the Potomac Company, a rifle factory by the Henderson Steel and Manufacturing Company, and a marble work by William Loughridge. A number of boarding houses for the workers also were constructed.

A series of articles in Frederick newspapers in July and September 1849 described in glowing terms the success of the venture at Weverton and its bright prospects for the future. The development was compared with the successful experimental "textile city" at
Lowell, Massachusetts, which had been in operation since the late 1820s, as well as other new industrial developments in the United States.

All the high expectations for a great manufacturing center perished soon thereafter with Wever's untimely death in late 1849. The recently built factories were closed down and the property of the joint stock company was advertised at public sale by Samuel B. Preston, a local constable, to satisfy the claims of Jarvis Spencer and Joseph I. Merrick. Later in 1852, the major freshet that struck the Potomac Valley did considerable damage to the Weverton works.

In the aftermath of the Civil War, at least one mill was opened for operation. During the spring of 1886 the canal company made provision to transfer power for a mill owned by Merrill and Grafton.

After the devastating flood in 1877 the canal company purchased the cotton mill and the file factory. The mill, which had never been put into operation, was torn down, and the file factory was sold to Chapman and Stewart. By 1880 much of the property in the little village of 100 persons was for sale at low prices. Jasper Kandell had become the owner of all the water rights, but apparently only one mill was in operation—a flour mill owned by David Rinehart.[153]

H.   SANDY HOOK

Situated on the Maryland side of the Potomac River just below Harpers Ferry, the village of Sandy Hook flourished under the influence of the railroad and canal. Receiving its name from a quicksand pool in which a teamster lost his team on the road to Frederick, the settlement had two houses in 1830. As a result of the growing trade induced by the two transportation lines, the village continued to grow until it had 373 inhabitants in 1880. This growth was enhanced by the canal company's decision to construct the Shenandoah River Lock in 1832–33 to permit boats de-

---

[153] Scharf, *History of Western Maryland*, Vol. I, 369–370; Vol. II, 1284–1285; Williams, *History of Frederick County*, Vol. I, 271–174; Frederick *Citizen*, July 13, 1849, and Frederick *Examiner*, Sept. 12 & 19, 1849, quoted in *Ibid*; *Proceedings of the President and Board of Directors*, K, 490; and Rothbury to Coale, Oct. 17, 1850, and Masning to president and Directors, Apr. 12, 1866, Ltrs. Recd., C & O Co.

scending the Shenandoah River to cross the Potomac and enter the canal near the village. The company also built a number of shops there for the maintenance of the canal. According to the Baltimore *Gazette* on November 30, 1874, a large force of workers were employed at the company shops producing new lock gates and other articles for use on the waterway. Included in the canal company building complex were a carpenter shop, blacksmith shop, cart house, tool shed, storehouse and dwelling house as well as several warehouses for the storage of repair materials for the canal.[154]

I.   HARPERS FERRY

Harpers Ferry succeeded Point of Rocks as a commercial emporium. Because of its location at the mouth of the Shenandoah River, it served as both the outlet for the trade of that valley and as the point of deposit for that of the upper Potomac. Its commercial position was not solely dependent on the railroad or the canal, nor was it of recent development. First settled in 1733 by Peter Stephens, Harpers Ferry already had a long history as a depot for North-South and East-West trade. Thus its increased prosperity under the influence of the coming of the canal in November 1833 and the arrival of the railroad in December 1834 was better grounded and more permanent than that of most of the valley settlements. During the years from 1830 to 1850, the population of Harpers Ferry increased from 1,379 to 1,747. On the eve of the Civil War, the industries on Virginius Island included two cotton factories, a sawmill, a flour mill, a carriage factory and an ironwork. The nine large brick buildings of Hall's Rifle Works supplemented the other thriving manufactories along the river. The most important industry, however, was the United States Armory and Arsenal, established by Congress in 1796.[155]

J.   SHEPHERDSTOWN

Shepherdstown, which had been settled by Pennsylvania Germans as early as 1730, received economic stimulus from the canal as the site of lime mills supplying the major portion of the cement to the canal contractors during the early years of construction. After the canal was completed to Dam No. 4 in the spring of 1834, it carried a large amount of the town's trade.

As one of the oldest towns in the Potomac Valley, Shepherdstown took an active interest in the economic development of the region through the promotion of internal improvements. The town of 1,326 inhabitants gave its full support to the canal project and subscribed $20,000 of Canal Co. stock.

Sometime before construction was commenced on the canal, Henry Boteler and George Reynolds operated a flour mill, known as Potomac Mill, about 240 yards upstream from Pack Horse Ford, the historic Potomac River crossing just below Shepherdstown. The mill was powered by water impounded by a dam across the Potomac, commonly called Boteler's Dam. One of the most urgent problems that arose in connection with the construction of the canal was the procurement of an adequate supply of hydraulic lime. In January 1828 Robert Leckie, the inspector or masonry on the canal, undertook to locate a source of cement lime that would be both readily available and of adequate durability. Such a source was found on the Virginia side of the river in the vicinity of Potomac Mill, and after some negotiations, the canal company persuaded the two proprietors to convert a portion of their mill to the manufacture of cement. Kilns were erected nearby, and extensive experiments were conducted in order to develop a durable water lime. Al-

---

[154] Baltimore, *Gazette*, Nov. 30, 1874, in Spates Paper; Scharf, *History of Western Maryland*, Vol. II, 1284–1285; and Baltimore *Sun*, June 11, 1889.
[155] Bushong, *Historic Jefferson County*, 85, 126–127, 139, and Sanderlin, *The Great National Project*, 165.

though the mill was not extensively used by the canal company after 1837, it continued to play an important role in the economic activity of the region served by the canal until 1861 when it was destroyed by Federal troops. Rebuilt after the Civil War, the mill continued to operate until the turn of the 20th century.

Closely associated with the mill in its connection with the canal was the dam that provided the power for its operation. The impoundment formed a slackwater pool that occasioned the construction of a river lock in 1833–35 to provide access to the canal from the river. This made possible the tapping of an extensive Virginia trade, which was an important source of business for the canal. Barges were loaded on the Virginia (West Virginia) side, floated across the river, and entered the canal via the river lock. When the dam was destroyed in 1889, the slackwater was eliminated and the lock was filled in and incorporated into the towpath bank of the canal.[156]

K. WILLIAMSPORT

Above Harpers Ferry the most promising site for industrial and commercial development along the canal was Williamsport. At this town, which was founded by General Otho H. Williams in 1786 at the junction of the Conococheague Creek and the Potomac River, conditions were favorable to the establishment of mills and manufactories utilizing water power. Dam No. 5, located only eight miles above the town, fed a relatively short stretch of the canal, thus making available ample surplus water. Williamsport might also become the channel for the trade of Hagerstown with the Eastern Markets via the canal.

Because of its location, Williamsport was actively interested in the development of transportation in the Potomac Valley. During the first three decades of the 18th century, the trade of Williamsport was largely with the District Cities by means of river boats. In September 1827 a group of citizens meeting in Williamsport formed an association to support the construction of a canal in the expectation that such a transportation line would enhance the commercial prospects, of the town.[157]

When the canal reached Williamsport in April 1835, the town took on new life. *Niles' Register* observed:

> We learn from the Williamsport *Banner* that the water was let into the canal below that place on the 1st inst. and it was expected that, in a few days, the canal would be navigable the whole distance from Dam No. 5, above Williamsport, to Washington City. The *Banner* says: 'The basin at the foot of Potomac St. has been for upwards of a week past, crowded with boats, arks, etc. laden with coal and flour, and that the busy, bustling appearance which the arrival of the boats has given to that part of town, in the vicinity of the canal, is truly gratifying, and brings to mind the wharves of a commercial city.'[158]

On April 11, the Williamsport *Banner* reported:

> Wednesday and Thursday last, the 8th and 9th instant, were busy days with us on the canal. The water was let into the level next below Williamsport, and the numerous vessels

---

[156] John F. Luzader, *Historic Sites, Shepherdstown, West Virginia* (NPS Mss., 1963), 1- 4; Miele, *Physical History*, 139–143; Sanderlin, *The Great National Project*, 81; Boteler to Mercer, Jan. 14 and 22, 1828, in U. S. Congress, House, Committee on Roads and Canals, *Chesapeake & Ohio Canal*, H. Rpt. 141, 20th Congress, 1st Session, 1828, 38–39, McFarland to Ingle, May 29, 1829, and McFarland to Leckie, July 23, 1829, Ltrs. Recd., C & O Co.; and Ingle to Boteler to Reynolds, Apr. 22, 1830, Ltrs. Sent, C & O Co.
[157] Scharf, *History of Western Maryland*, Vol. II, 1223, 1230 and Sanderlin, *The Great National Project*, 166.
[158] *Niles' Register*, Vol. XLVIII (Apr. 11, 1835), 89.

> which had, within the previous few days, been literally wedged in our basins and canal, forming as complete a bridge of boats as ever crossed the Rhine, thronged and pressed to the lock, eager for passage below. As fast as balance beam and valve key could be plied, were they passed on amid the shouts of a number of our citizens, who had assembled to witness the novel sight. Of the number of vessels, which were admitted, we have not been duly informed; but our estimate, and we speak, we are sure, much within the number, is from fifty to sixty. . .
>
> It was a glorious sight to see the numerous boats as they lay in the basin at night, each illuminated by a glowing coal fire, which cast a long level rule of light across the water; and the silence of night was not unpleasantly interrupted by the cries of the hoarse boatmen, as they were disturbed from their moorings by new arrivals, and driven to close contact with their neighbors; we heard diverse remonstrances, boisterous and uncouth against "scrounging," to make use of the navigator's expressive, however inelegant term.[159]

The increase in commercial activity did not turn out to be of a temporary nature and Williamsport settled down to become perhaps the outstanding canal town along the route of the canal. On May 26, 1835, the *National Intelligencer* reported on the continuing developments at the town:

> From Williamsport . . . we learn that that town has quite a lively appearance, from the bustle of business, present and prospective. Among other circumstances, consequent on the extension of the Canal thus far, we learn that two considerable iron-master in the neighborhood of Chambersburg, in Pennsylvania, have agreed to send, each, five thousand tons of bar-iron and castings to Williamsport, this year, for transportation down the Canal, to be forwarded to New York, Massachusetts, etc. The advantage of this arrangement to them is, that the same wagons, which bring down the iron, can load back with coal from the Canal. For the purposes of this branch of business, a very large warehouse is now building on the margin of the basin of the Canal at Williamsport. We understand, further, that the officers of the company, on a late visit up the line of the Canal, made a disposition of water power to individuals at three different places in the vicinity of Williamsport.[160]

Furthermore, the economic development of Williamsport was enhanced by the Baltimore & Ohio Railroad's decision to build its line west of Harpers Ferry on the Virginia side of the river. Thus, the rich flour and grain trade of Hagerstown and the Cumberland Valley was diverted to Georgetown through Williamsport via the canal, whereas previously most of it had gone to Baltimore via the National Road.[161]

Through the years, Williamsport, which grew from population of 859 in 1830 to 1,503 in 1880, depended on the canal for a large portion of its economic activity. The Williamsport *Pilot* observed on August 24, 1872, that:

> There are 48 boats owned by citizens of this town, not counting the immediate vicinity. These 48 boats upon an average carry 5,000 tons of coal per trip. Allow each boat 20 trips per season and you have in round numbers 100,000 tons of coal carried to market by our boatmen. The toll upon this coal at 46 cents per ton would amount to $46,000. Add to

---

[159] Williamsport, *Banner*, Apr. 11, 1835, quoted in Niles' Register, Vol. XLVIII (Apr. 25, 1835), 135.
[160] Washington, *National Intelligencer*, May 26, 1835.
[161] Thomas John Chew Williams, *History of Washington County, Maryland*, (2 Vols. Hagerstown, 1906), Vol. I, 196.

this the toll on each boat for each trip, $8.16, and you have $7,833.60 more, in all the sum of $53,833.60 earned by our boatmen during the course of a boating season for the company. Of course this is simply the coal trade, and does not include the local trade from this port, or have any reference to tolls collected here. The amount of flour, grain, etc., shipped from, and the amount of lumber, hoop poles, plasters, phosphate, etc. received here, is considerable.[162]

Later that same year on December 21 the *Pilot* again discussed the heavy reliance of Williamsport on the canal trade for its general prosperity. Reporting on the town's coal trade for the 1872 boating season, the newspaper noted that:

> The report is exclusive of a considerable amount of coal, the toll upon which was paid here, but which was not delivered exactly at the wharf at this place. . . The horse disease, low water, and the early close of navigation by the ice, rendered the season not only unprofitable to boatmen but made shipments much shorter than they would otherwise have been. The coal shipped by Mr. Cushwa was for the sole use and consumption of the Western Maryland Railroad Company (whose line was then being completed to Big Pool), and a great deal of it is on the wharf here yet awaiting wagon transportation to Hagerstown. That received by Messrs. Embrey and Steffey, respectively, was to supply not only the local demand, but manufactories of various kinds in Pennsylvania and those portions of Maryland lying along the line of the W. M. Railroad.

Victor Cushwa	4,234,.03	Tons cut
O. Embrey and Son	3,725.06	
E. P. Steffey	1,544.16	
Total	9,504.05	

The value of this coal at $4.50 per ton, which is about the average, is $38,018.20[163]

The canal company's efforts in the early 1870s to promote the continued expansion of trade in both agricultural produce and coal by facilitating the construction of the Cumberland Valley Railroad and the Western Maryland Railroad, where those lines touched upon the canal's rights, were an added economic stimulus to Williamsport. Completed to the town on December 17, 1873, the Western Maryland ultimately provided a connection between the canal at Big Pool (above Williamsport) and Baltimore. The Cumberland Valley, which was opened to Martinsburg in 1874, ultimately provided a link between Harrisburg and Winchester, crossing the canal at Powell's Bend one mile below Williamsport. As a result of the new lines, it was estimated that the coal trade of Williamsport increased to the point that one-half of the town's population was involved in the shipment, unloading and transfer of coal. According to the Washington *Evening Star* on July 11, 1902, business on the canal at Williamsport was:

> flourishing, there being a continuous string of boats to and from Cumberland. About 50 boats are unloaded there every month, carrying over 5,000 tons of coal. Large consignments of coal are also being shipped to Powell's Bend, 1 mile below, where it is transferred to the Cumberland Valley RR. New machines for unloading boats in use on wharves at Williamsport greatly facilitate business, about 3 times as many being

---

[162] Williamsport, *Pilot*, Aug. 24, 1872, in Gorman Collection.
[163] Williamsport, *Pilot*, Dec. 21, 1872, in Gorman Collection.

unloaded as before. Shippers are full up with orders for coal, which is shipped over the Western Maryland railroad.[164]

L. HANCOCK

Above Williamsport, the next major objective of the canal was Hancock, a small village of 367 inhabitants in 1830. Located on the National Road, the town was 100 miles from Baltimore and 39 miles from Cumberland. Because of its location, it acted as a center for the local trade of western Washington County, eastern Allegany County and the Cacapon Valley as well as a conduit for the East-West trade.[165]

The canal company looked to Hancock as a prospective point where contact could be made with the turnpike from the west. Here it was hoped that the canal might secure some of the wagon traffic from as far west as the Ohio River. As early as October 4, 1834, *Niles' Register* observed that when the canal would be opened to Dam No. 5 during the following spring:

> it will then be opened for navigation 110 miles; and, as the Dam No. 5 backs water of the Potomac up to Hancock, the navigation of the canal will be connected with the business on the national road, and Hancock becomes a temporary place of deposit between the east and west, whether from or to Washington, by the canal, or from or to Baltimore by the railroad, after its junction with the canal, either at Harpers Ferry or the Point of Rocks, as shall appear most expedient—and no doubt, canal boats will be fitted to receive the bodies of loaded wagons, as the railroad cars now receive them. There is much convenience, as well as safety, in this proceeding. The western merchant, at Baltimore or at Wheeling, personally inspects the stowage of his merchandise, if he pleases, and according to his own judgment of the manner in which it should be packed—with a confidence that it will not be changed until its arrival at the place of its destination . . .[166]

Canal officials began making plans to exploit the trade potential of Hancock in March 1835 when the canal was completed to Dam No. 5 as evidenced in a letter written by President George C. Washington:

> By the middle of March we shall have an unobstructed navigation of 110 miles, ready to receive the spring trade of the whole valley of the Potomac. Our upper dam (Dam No. 5), makes a backwater navigation of about ten miles, being within two miles of the Cumberland Road. At this point the water merchants of Wheeling etc. propose immediately to connect their lines of transportation and such by this means will be the saving, that they believe they can successfully compete with Pennsa (Pennsylvania) Canal. The lumber of the Cacapon region will also at this point, be brought into the canal, and we understand preparations are making at Cumberland to forward a quantity of coal.[167]

However, the anticipated business did not develop as expected, primarily because the canal did not reach Hancock until April 1839 at which time the national economy was still in the throes of depression. By that date the Baltimore & Ohio was speeding its construction westward, and the

---

[164] Washington, *Evening Star*, July 11, 1902. Also see Baltimore *Evening Sun*, Aug. 12, 1937; Scharf, *History of Western Maryland*, Vol. II, 1005–1008 and 1230–1231; *Forty-Fifth Annual Report* (1873), C & O Co., 16–17; and Sanderlin, *The Great National Project*, 230–232.
[165] Scharf, *History of Western Maryland*, Vol. II, 1252, and Williams, *History of Washington County*, Vol. I, 196.
[166] *Niles' Register*, Vol. XLVII (Oct. 4, 1834), 65.
[167] Washington to Colston, Jan. 31, 1835, Ltrs. Sent, C & O Co.

Pennsylvania Main Line Canal had consolidated its hold on much of the anticipated trade of the southwestern portions of its state.[168]

Nevertheless, Hancock did benefit from the canal and served as a center of local trade. By 1880 the town had grown to a population of 931 and had a number of stores, several grain and flour warehouses, and several boat yards, all of which were directly affiliated with the canal trade. The major business enterprise was the Round Top Cement Company located west of town and owned by Robert Bridges and Charles W. Henderson. Originally established in 1837 by George Shafer to supply the canal company with water lime, the cement works were purchased by Bridges and Henderson in 1963 and employed 120 men by 1880. After the cement was placed in barrels, most of it was run across the Potomac by cable to a company warehouse before it was transferred to the Baltimore & Ohio Railroad via switches that connected with the main line. The canal, which provided the water power necessary to run the mill, was used also as a medium for shipping the cement and for receiving the coal required to operate the kilns.[169]

M. CUMBERLAND

The town of Cumberland at the mouth of Wills Creek is perhaps the greatest accomplishment of the Potomac trade route. Founded by the Ohio Company in 1749, it served as a natural canter for the business and commerce of the upper valley and for the trans-mountain trade. In the aftermath of the Seven Years' War, fur traders and a few settlers began to move into the Allegheny and Trans-Allegheny region. Because of its location on the Potomac Valley route to the west, Cumberland was involved in every major effort to develop and improve transportation in the upper valley during the next century. The improvements on the river undertaken by the Potomac Company after 1785 ended at Cumberland. Construction of the federally-sponsored National Road began at Cumberland in 1811 and the pike was completed to Wheeling on the Ohio River in 1818, thereby making the town an important point in the East-West trade.[170]

The completion of the railroad and the canal to Cumberland on November 1, 1842, and October 10, 1850, respectively, brought to the town a dependable means of transportation to the eastern markets and large transfer business in coal from mines in the Georges Creek region and farther west. During the decade from 1840 to 1850, the population of the town nearly tripled from 2,384 to 6,105. William H. Lowdermilk, a noted historian of Cumberland, has written concerning the significance of the railroad to that town:

> No other event has ever transpired in the history of the place, which created so much pleasurable excitement. Business was entirely suspended, and men, women and children gathered about the terminus of the road to witness the arrival of the trains. From the mountain tops, and valley, throughout the adjoining country, the people came in crowds, and the town was in a fever of excitement for many days.
>
> The opening of this road proved the inauguration of a new era in the history of the town. This was made the point of exchange for passengers and merchandise between the East and West. Hotels were erected for the accommodation of travelers, and large warehouses, along the railroad tracks, for the storing of goods, which were to be trans-shipped from cars to wagons for the West, and from wagons to cars for the East. The facilities thus furnished for rapid transportation induced many persons to make the journey across the mountains, and the stage companies were compelled to build new coaches and

---

[168] Miele, *Physical History*, 153 and *Niles' Register*, Vol. LVI (Apr. 17, 1839), 131–132.
[169] Scharf, *History of Western Maryland*, Vol. II, 1252 and 1256.
[170] Miele, *Physical History*, 160 –161; Sanderlin, *The Great National Project*, 166–167; and Kenneth P. Bailey, *Thomas Cresap:Maryland Frontiersman* (Boston, 1944), 94.

to erect large stables. Every morning and evening upon the arrival of the cars, long lines of stages drew up in front of the hotels. Inside they carried nine passengers, and outside one on the seat with the driver. In the "boot" and on the roof was placed the baggage. When all were loaded, at a given signal, a dozen whips would crack, a dozen four-horse teams would take the road, and dash through the streets at a brisk trot, which would be kept up until Frostburg was reached, in less than two hours. Here horses were exchanged, and up the mountain grade they went, on their way to Wheeling.

In a little while after the completion of the railroad to Cumberland, the National Road became a thoroughfare such as the country has never before or since seen, for a like distance. On every mile of the road were to be seen stages, carriages and heavy freight wagons, carrying tons of merchandise piled up under their canvas-covered bows, drawn by six powerful horses. In addition to these, great droves of cattle, hogs, sheep, etc. were daily on the road. Taverns were to be found every few miles with jolly landlords, who knew all the teamsters, drivers and guards. These were "good old times" and the "pike boys" still living look back to them with many a sigh of regret.[171]

When the canal was formally opened to through navigation all the way to Cumberland on October 10, 1850, it was the occasion for elaborate ceremonies and jubilant celebration. Among the speeches was one given by William Price, a long-time canal promoter from the town:

> It was natural, perhaps, that things should be precisely as they have been, both with the enterprise itself, and with the individuals whose fortunes have been connected with it. The uncommon magnitude, and the uncommon finish of the work, may be regarded as cause sufficient for all the alternations and disappointments attending its history. The reasoning of men, from their experience upon works of different dimensions and character, might have been expected to lead to disappointment when applied to a work like this.
>
> Go view those magnificent aqueducts, locks and culverts, of hewn stone—those huge embankments, on which you may journey for days down the river; go view the great tunnel passing three fifths of a mile through rock, and arched with brick, its eastern portal opening upon a through-cut almost equal in magnitude to the tunnel itself. Look at the vessels lying in that basin ready to commence the work of transportation, and large enough to navigate the Atlantic, -- look at all these things, then think how soon the fortunes of individuals embarked in the prosecution of such an enterprise would be swallowed up, leaving upon it but little more impression than the bubbles which now float upon its waters. It will not be deemed out of place, if I here express the hope, that, those whose losses have been gains of the company, should not in the hour of its prosperity be forgotten.
>
> It has been greatly decried and greatly misunderstood, but it is a magnificent work, whatever may be said to the contrary. Of its probable revenues now that it is completed, I se no reason to distrust the opinions heretofore entertained by it s friends. And why should it not be as profitable as, from the first, it was expected to be? The same great coal deposits which originally induced its projection, and which have animated the hopes of its friends, during all the trials and vicissitudes of its history still lie in these mountains waiting an avenue to market. Its quality has in no wise deteriorated and is known to be such as to give it a preference over every other description of coal on this side of the Atlantic. The capacity of the coal companies have their railroads and other means of shipment upon the canal, completed. With such a staple and such an avenue to market, that is

---

[171] Lowdermilk, *A History of Cumberland*, 349, 351–351, 371.

to limit the emoluments of the work? Coal, however is but one item of its trade. And when we look to the agricultural products of western Maryland, and of the contiguous portions of Virginia and Pennsylvania, and after all this, add to the account, the ascending trade, consisting of the merchandise for the supply of the territory already indicated, and a share of that destined for the west, it is no exaggeration to say, that the work will in due time pay off its own debt and leave the state in possession of a permanent fund, adequate to all her financial wants.

The opening of yonder gates to let through the first boat carrying freight from Cumberland to tide water, signals a happy epoch in the financial condition of the state. It is the turning point in history of the canal, and marks the precious moment of time, when this great work ceases forever to be a burden upon the tax-payers of Maryland, and begins to reimburse those who have so long and so patiently borne the charge of its construction. Such an event is cause of congratulations to the people of the whole state.[172]

With the arrival of the canal, Cumberland again experienced greater prosperity based on the increased trade and transfer business developed by the waterway and from the related activities associated with its operation. The boom proved to be short-lived in its extreme form, however, for on January 10, 1853, the Baltimore & Ohio Railroad was opened for travel between Cumberland and Wheeling, and two great excursion trains passed over the road, from Baltimore to the Western terminus. The effect was soon felt in Cumberland, as most of the stage lines were taken off, and the great business of transferring merchandise at this point was largely diminished.[173]

Thereafter the city settled down to a robust prosperity based primarily on the coal trade of the railroad and the canal and on its location at the western terminus of the waterway. Estimates of property values available for Cumberland in 1842 and 1860 show an increase from $931,118 to $2,124,000 and population statistics indicate that the city grew from 6,105 in 1850 to 7,302 in 1860, 1870, and 10,693 in 1880.[174]

Cumberland secured a large amount of trade from the canal-related economic activities and from the boatmen between runs and during the winter. The economic impact of the canal on the livelihood of the town is revealed in a series of local newspaper articles in the 1870s during which time the waterway was facing increasing competition for its share of the coal trade from the railroad. On May 24, 1873, the Cumberland *Times* reported:

> The shipments of coal by canal for the current season show a remarkable falling off from those of last year. By Mr. Slack's tables we find that the shipments to May 10th inst. over his road to the canal amount to 112,099.03 tons, against 136,887.08 tons to a corresponding period last year, showing a decrease for the present season of 24,758.05 tons; while the shipments by the same route to the Baltimore & Ohio Railroad amount to 474,290.02 tons against 414,705.01 tons to a corresponding period last year, showing an increase of 59,585.01 tons in favor of the railroad to a corresponding period last year. This estimate does not include companies that habitually ship by railroad alone, but puts the matter in the best light for the Canal Board.
>
> For our city and for the large number of people who depend upon a successful canal season for a living, this is a poor showing, and the prospects for the future is far from reassuring. .

---

[172] *Report to the Stockholders on the Completion of the Canal to Cumberland*, 130–132.
[173] Lowdermilk, *A History of Cumberland*, 376.
[174] *Ibid,* 381, 388, 492, and James Walter Thomas and Thomas John Crew Williams, *History of Allegany County, Maryland* (@ Vols., Cumberland, 1923), Vol. I, 124.

Canal shipments are what our people here are interested in. It matters but little to them how many hoppers go daily rolling by upon the railroad; they derive no benefit therefrom, but with canal shipments the case is different. Every additional ton of coal shipped by this route, adds its proportion to the prosperity of the city. Many boatmen live here; boats are built in our yards; feed and forage for stock are sold by our dealers, and our grocers derive a busy trade in canal supplies when the season is good...[175]

A similar theme was noted by the Cumberland *Alleganian and Times* in three separate articles in April and May 1877. On April 30 the newspaper observed that:

The canal is the only present surety for Allegany's prosperity, and when its stability is endangered every citizen of the county has a bounden duty in its protection. Cumberland is probably more deeply interested in its success than any other section of the county, because she has more property dependent on it outside of the coal companies; but all of Allegany is deeply concerned...There are Eastern interests which demand Cumberland coal for its qualities; and their demands are sufficient to keep the railroad busy. There are other interests, which prefer our coal, while it can compete with other regions; but when the price is higher, they will take the other. This latter class is what we would lose if the canal should be closed, while the Baltimore company would charge its own price on the former. The canal is now in efficient working order throughout, and the tolls are lower than the Baltimore road. The canal terminates here, and its trade is local. Destroy its local traffic and it perishes. The Baltimore road is almost national, and our trade is not essential to its success. It can hedge us about. It can forgo profits on coal until it crushes us...[176]

On May 5, 1877, the newspaper printed a detailed analysis of the economic impact of the canal on the city:

The principal income of this region is from the coal trade. When shipments are large, our businessmen feel the good results; when they are small, our trade interest lag. The coal shipped through Cumberland is beneficial to this region only to the extent of the cost of production, which benefits Cumberland only secondarily. It is the amount shipped by canal that results immediately to our benefit...Hypothetically, we will assume there are 30 boats leaving this port daily, carrying 115 tons each, at 80 cents per ton, making 180 boats per week, which would be a gross receipt of $20,700 per week, employing 600 men and an equal number of mules. At lest two-thirds of this money is disbursed in Cumberland, giving over $16,000 per week, or $70,000 per month. Aside from this, there are over 200 men employed here on the canal in various kinds of work—loading coal, repairing boats, cleaning basin, etc., which increases the receipts by not less than $10,000 per month. Thus...it is reasonable to conclude that the people of Cumberland receive from this source not less than $80,000 per month. Can we afford to lose this trade?[177]

On May 15, 1877, the same newspaper observed:

---

[175] Cumberland, *Times*, May 24, 1873, in Gorman Collection.
[176] Cumberland, *Alleganian and Times*, Apr. 30, 1877, in Gorman Collection.
[177] Cumberland, *Alleganian and Times*, May 5, 1877, in Gorman Collection.

> We have hundreds in Cumberland dependent on coal shipments by canal where Baltimore has 10 by rail. Five hundred canal captains have their all invested in their boats, and 2,000 men are subject to the captains. Our boat builders have tens of thousands dependent upon the employment of these men. Our businessmen derive one half their profits from the proceedings of the canal, and our landlords would get nothing for their houses if we lose our canal trade. The miner would decrease in his product were the canal out of the way; for the Baltimore road would have the monopoly of the trade, and would desire no more coal produced than its capacity would admit of carrying...
>
> As further proof of the fact that the town could not rely on the Baltimore & Ohio, the article noted that the railroad-owned Cumberland Rolling Mill had just laid off 300 man and 100 boys.[178]

By the time that the canal began to fall into decline in the late 1870s, Cumberland had developed an independent and permanent basis of economic prosperity and continued as an important industrial and commercial canter. The economic diversification of the city during this period can be seen from a list of its principal business concerns:

1. Steel Rail Mill and Merchant Bar Mill owned and operated by the Baltimore & Ohio Railroad. The Baltimore *American* of May 7, 1877, reported on the positive economic impact of the railroads Rollin Mill on the growth of Cumberland:

    > In the fiscal year 1873–74, the Baltimore & Ohio Company employed an average of 853 man per month in the rolling mill in the second great city of Maryland, Cumberland. The total wages paid during the year at that mill amounted to $432,858.55; 16,284 tons of metal were consumed at that mill, nearly all of which was purchased in the State of Maryland, and which was made at the furnaces in Washington, Frederick, Allegany and Baltimore counties. During that year the consumption of coal alone at the mill reached 100,000 tons, and there were large expenditures for other supplies...[179]

2. Bowery Blast Furnace owned and operated by the Cumberland Coal and Iron Company.
3. Five Frederick Companies
    a. Union Mining and Manufacturing Company at Mt. Savage.
    b. Savage Mountain Firebrick Manufacturing Co. at Frostburg.
    c. Globe Fireclay Manufacturing Co. at Bridgeport.
    d. Savage Firebrick Manufacturing Co. at Keystone Junction.
    e. Reese, Lemon and Co. at Ellerslie.
4. Two iron foundries and machine shops
5. Mills of Cumberland Cast Steel Works
6. Cumberland Cotton Factory
7. Cumberland Hydraulic Cement Manufacturing Company
8. Three steam tanneries in the city and two in the vicinity
9. Car, locomotive works, and machine shops of the Cumberland and Pennsylvania Railroad Company at Mt. Savage

---

[178] Cumberland, *Alleganian and Times*, May 14, 1877, in Gorman Collection. At the same time, the Baltimore (insert 225A)

[179] Baltimore, *American*, May 7, 1877, in Gorman Collection.

10. Several large flour mills
11. Steam furniture works of K. H. Butler (Largest furniture plant in the state)
12. Numerous other factories including planning and saw mills and sash and door factories[180]

N. SUMMARY

Of the towns mentioned as receiving a definite stimulus from the operation of the canal or the railroad, only one achieved a permanent status as a result of these influences. Cumberland survived and prospered as the second largest city in the State into the 20th century. Projected communities such as Crommelin and Rushville never got off the ground. Towns such as Brunswick, Knoxville, Weverton and Williamsport which drew so heavily from the canal for their support declined with the fortunes of the waterway. Point of Rocks, Harpers Ferry and Hancock which were primarily exchange points in the valley trade, declined as through traffic replaced local business or survived on a lower level of economic activity and importance.[181]

---

[180] Orrick, *Mineral Resources and Manufacturing Facilities of Cumberland*, 7–31.
[181] Sanderlin, *A Study of the History of the Potomac Valley*, 102.

VI. IMPACT ON THE POPULATION

The expanded transportation facilities and related activities of the canal and railroad played a part in the growth of population in Western Maryland. The statistics for the four counties through which the canal passed were as follows:

	1820	1830	1840	1850	1860	1870	1880
Montgomery	16,400	19,816	15,456	15,860	18,322	20,563	24,759
Frederick	40,459	45,789	36,405	40,987	46,591	47,572	50,482
Washington	23,075	25,269	28,850	30,848	31,417	35,712	38,561
Allegany	8,654	10,609	15,690	22,769	28,348	38,536	43,802[182]

During this period the total population of the four Western Maryland counties in relation to the overall population of the state was as follows:

	State	Western	% of State
1820	407,350	88,588	21.7
1830	447,040	101,482	22.7
1840	470,019	96,401	20.5
1850	583,034	110,464	18.9
1860	687,049	124,678	18.1
1870	780,894	141,383	18.1
1880	934,632	169,779*	18.2[183]

The percentage of change in the population of the Western Maryland counties in comparison with that of the population in the State as a whole during this period was as follows:

	Western	State
1820–30	+12.7%	+8.9%
1830–40	-5.0%	+4.9%
1840–50	+12.7%	+19.4%
1850–60	+11.4%	+15.1%
1860–70	+11.8%	+12.0%
1870–80	+16.7%	+16.4%

---

[182] Scharf, *A History of Western Maryland*, Vol. I, 369–370, 654–656, Vol. II, 974, 1554, and Boyd, *History of Montgomery County*, 107. In 1836 Carroll County was established out of the eastern portion of Frederick and the western portion of Baltimore County, and in 1872 the western portion of Allegany County became Garret County. The latter had a population of 12,175 in 1880.

[183] Scharf, *A History of Western Maryland*, Vol. II, 1554. * The population of Garrett County is figured in this statistic.

Chesapeake & Ohio Canal Historic Resource Study
Unrau: 10. Economic Impact

APPENDIX A

WATER POWER LEASES FOR MILLS ON THE C&O CANAL IN GEORGETOWN: 1839–1900

LEASE NO. 1

Lessee	Type of Mill	Location	Sq. in. of Water leased	Actual date of lease	Effective Date	Date of Expiration
George Buford, Washington	Flour, to 1843 burned, 1844; rebuilt 1845, cotton from 1845—sold to Wilson, 1850	South of the canal, sw corner of the market space and Potomac St.	400	May 7, 1846	Jan. 1, 1838	Jan. 1, 1886, mill sold to Thomas Wilson, 1850
Thomas Wilson, Baltimore, MD. Sublet to A. Pryor Williams and Co.	Cotton: 1860 to 1861		300	Transferred Renewed May 1, 1860	Jan. 1, 1860	Jan. 1 1859 Jan. 1, 1870 Mill closed 1861 Sold to A.H. Herr, 1865
Superior to 300 A.H. Herr Georgetown	Herr converted it from cotton to flour; And flour milling "Pioneer Mill" began in 1867, 140' x 50' in size		300	Assignment Approved on Nov. 9, 1865	Jan. 1865	Jan. 1, 1879
Superior to 330 G. A. Herr Austin Herr (Herr & Cissell)	Flour		300	Transferred	Sep. 30, 1836	1900

LEASE NO. 2

Lessee	Type of Mill	Location	Sq. in. of Water leased	Actual date of lease	Effective Date	Date of Expiration
Joseph Hocks Of Georgetown			Surplus water of Rock Creek Basin		Feb. 27, 1840	Feb. 27, 1860 Abandoned in 1840. forfeited on Sep. 5, 1844

LEASE NO. 3

Lessee	Type of Mill	Location	Sq. in. of Water leased	Actual date of lease	Effective Date	Date of Expiration
Nathaniel and A.P. Scaver (or Seaver)	Bark Mill	N. side of Water St., between Potomac and Market St., near rear Hotshot	50		Mar. 4, 1840	Withheld and suspended by Apr. 1847
V. Turner, Trustee For Mrs. A. Robinson (Estate of Wm. Robinson)	Remodeled as a flour mill, 1845	Practically the same site as Seever's mill	125	Renewed and 75 inches added	Apr. 13, 1847	Apr. 1, 1860 transferred to Coor & Schroder & Co.
Leased from Robinson: Gerald Wilson	Flour	Adjacent	125	July 1, 1861 Sublet to Wilson		July 1, 1857
L. Benjamin Darkey and John Shoemaker, Georgetown	Flour and grist	Known as the "Rivers De Mill" under Shoemaker	125	Apr. 11, 1867	Apr. 1, 1860	Apr. 1, 1880 transferred to Shoemaker & Co. 1880 bought by Shoemaker & Co. 1864

LEASE NO. 4

Lessee	Type of Mill	Location	Sq. in. of Water leased	Actual date of lease	Effective Date	Date of Expiration
Thomas Brown	Bakery	N.E. Corner of Water and Lingan Streets	50		July 1, 1840	July 1, 1880
Successor to Brown: John Hutton	Flour and grist		50	July 6, 1860 Renewed	July 1, 1860	July 1, 1880 Transferred to Fenny in 1872
Successor to John Hutton	Flour and grist		50	Transferred Renewed Apr 14, 1837	Jan. 12, 1872 Jul 1, 1880	July 1, 1880 July 1, 1900

LEASE NO. 5

Lessee	Type of Mill	Location	Sq. in. of Water leased	Actual date of lease	Effective Date	Date of Expiration
Thomas J. Davis	Flour, built in 1841	N. side of Water St., between Lingan and Fayette St. and near the N.W. corner of Water & Fayette Sts.	500		Sep 1, 1841	Sep 1, 1861 Sold to Boyd & Taylor
Successor to Davis Boyd & Taylor	Flour		500		Mar 9, 1854 Bought by Boyd & Taylor	Sep 1, 1881 Assigned 1860 to Boyce, Thomas and

Successor to Boyd & Taylor: Alfred H. Herr and James S. Welsh	Flour, corn and plaster	Called the "Columbia Mill"; a 4 story brick structure, size 128' x 60'	500	Aug 1, 1862 Also assigned by Herr to Welsh	Sep 1, 1861	Sep 1, 1881 Assigned to Welch on Apr 1, 1862
Successor of Herr and Welsh: Jim S. Voigh			500	Aug 1, 1862	Sep 1, 1861	Transferred to Proctor 1879
Successor of Voigh: Richard Proctor	Flour		500	Transferred	Sep 30, 1879	Transferred to Herr, 1880
Successor to Proctor: Austin Herr of Herr and Cissell	Flour		500	Transfer renewed	Jun 30, 1880 Sep 1, 1881	Sep 1, 1881 Sep 1, 1901

LEASE NO. 6

Lessee	Type of Mill	Location	Sq. in. of Water leased	Actual date of lease	Effective Date	Date of Expiration
R. E. Duvall, Georgetown		N. side of Water St. between Fayette and Lingan. Between Brown's Bakery and Davis' Mill			Apr. 13, 1843	1848

LEASE NO. 7

Lessee	Type of Mill	Location	Sq. in. of Water leased	Actual date of lease	Effective Date	Date of Expiration
Miller and Duvall	Saw	S.W. Corner of Water and Fayette Streets	50		1844	1843 Sold to Rynax 1843
Successor to Miller and Duvall: John Rynax	Iron foundry		50		Jun 1846	1882
Successor to Rynax: Mark Young	Grist		50	1862	1862	Dec 31, 1880

LEASE NO. 8

Lessee	Type of Mill	Location	Sq. in. of Water leased	Actual date of lease	Effective Date	Date of Expiration
Successor to 108 of Hungford Alexander Ray, Washington, D.C.	Flour and grist	N.W. corner of Water and Potomac Streets	100	Assigned to A. Ray May 1, 1860 Renewal to A. Ray; Reassigned to A. Ross Ray & Bro.	Jan 1, 1839	Jan 1, 1859 Reassigned to A. Ross Ray & Brother by 1849 Jun 1, 1879
Andrew Abes May Washington, D.C.	Flour and grist	N.W. corner of Water and Potomac Streets; known as the "Arlington Mill"	150		Aug 14, 1845	Apr 1, 1880
And Albert May Firm of A. Ross Ray and Brother			400	May 1, 1880	Apr 1, 1860	Apr 1, 1880
Successor of A. Ross Ray and Brother: A. Ross Ray and Brother	Flour		500	Renewed	Apr 1, 1880	Apr 1, 1900 Transferred Sep 30 1885 to G.W. Cissell
Successor of A Ross Ray and Brother: G.W. Cissell & Co	Flour		500	Transferred	Sep 30, 1885	1900

LEASE NO. 9

Lessee	Type of Mill	Location	Sq. in. of Water leased	Actual date of lease	Effective Date	Date of Expiration
Wm. P. McConnell and Co., Georgetown			25	Granted for 2 years. Not renewable	Oct. 2, 1847	Oct 2, 1849 Transferred to Morrow & Co., 1848
Successor to McConnell Company: Wm. Morrow and Company	Tannery		50	Transferred and increased to 50 inches	May 8, 1848	Tannery burned in Dec. 1849

LEASE NO. 10

Lessee	Type of Mill	Location	Sq. in. of Water leased	Actual date of lease	Effective Date	Date of Expiration
Thomas P. Morgan			Surplus water of Rock Creek Basin		Dec 21, 1849	Jan 20, 1880 Transferred to Morgan and Rhinehart, 1860
Successor to Morgan: Morgan and Rhinehart					Jan 20 1860	Jan 20, 1880

LEASE NO. 11

Lessee	Type of Mill	Location	Sq. in. of Water leased	Actual date of lease	Effective Date	Date of Expiration
William A. Bradley, Of Washington	Iron Foundry	N. E. Corner of Water and Fayette	100		July 1, 1851	Apr 1, 1880 Transferred Jun 30, 1859 to Elms and Bradley
Successor to Bradley: James Elms and William A. Bradley, Washington, Firm of Elms & Bradley	Flour		150	May 1, 1860, Renewed and increased to 150 inches	Apr 1, 1860	Apr 1, 1880 Mill burned 1879 This firm failed Dec 31, 1880

LEASE NO. 12

Lessee	Type of Mill	Location	Sq. in. of Water leased	Actual date of lease	Effective Date	Date of Expiration
William C. Duvall	Cracker Bakery until 1857, when remodeled into flour mill	N. Side of Water Street, between Market and Frederick; near Frederick			About 1857	Apr 1, 1860 Renewed to Davidson, 1860
Successor to Duvall: John Davidson, Georgetown	Flour and grist	"The Model Mill"	200	May 1, 1860, renewed	Apr 1, 1860	Apr 1, 1880, Transferred to Tenney and Son, 1872
Successor of John Davidson: William H. Tenney and Son	Flour and grist		200	Transferred Renewed Apr 14, 1887	Jan 12, 1872 Apr 1, 1880	Apr 1, 1880 Apr 1, 1900

LEASE NO. 13

Lessee	Type of Mill	Location	Sq. in. of Water leased	Actual date of lease	Effective Date	Date of Expiration
William H. Edes	Flour	70 Water Street	50	May 1, 1860, Permission from Nov 10, 1859 to transfer 50 inches from Little Falls	Apr 1, 1860	Apr 1, 1880 Transferred to Gartrell and Cissell, 1863
Successor to Edes: Cartwell and Cissell	Flour	Cherry Street near Potomac Street	50 50	Transferred Renewed	Jan 1, 1863 Apr 1, 1880	Apr 1, 1880 1900

LEASE NO. 14

Lessee	Type of Mill	Location	Sq. in. of Water leased	Actual date of lease	Effective Date	Date of Expiration
George Hill Jr., Washington	Paper, "Potomac Paper Mill"	N.E. Corner of Water and Potomac Streets. A warehouse until 1864	200 200 400 417	Jan 21, 1864 200 additional inches granted Jan 1, 1863 by decision of U.S. Supreme Court Order of Feb. 1863 Increased to total of 417 square inches	Jul 1, 1864	July 21, 1884 Firm failed Jan 1, 1885

LEASE NO. 15

Lessee	Type of Mill	Location	Sq. in. of Water leased	Actual date of lease	Effective Date	Date of Expiration
D. L. Shoemaker	Flour	Water, corner of High	96		1867	1880

LEASE NO. 16[1]

Lessee	Type of Mill	Location	Sq. in. of Water leased	Actual date of lease	Effective Date	Date of Expiration
Beall and Shoemaker	Flour	73 Water Street	125		1872	1880

---

[1] Young, *Antebellum Commerce of Old Georgetown*, 200–204

APPENDIX B

WATER POWER LEASES FOR MILLS ON THE C&O CANAL
BETWEEN GEORGETOWN AND LITTLE FALLS: 1840–1900

LEASE NO. 1

Lessee	Type of Mill	Location	Sq. in. of Water leased	Actual date of lease	Effective Date	Date of Expiration
Farmers and Merchants Bank of Georgetown	Flour and grist	At "Old Locks", 2½ miles west of Georgetown	120 Perpetual grant by C&O Co. for cleaning old canal	Soon after Sep 11, 1839	Apr 1, 1840	Apr 1, 1860 Assigned by Feb 27 1881 to Edes
Successor of Farmers and Merchants Bank: William A. Edes	Flour and grist		120 50 170	Abandoned by Feb 27, 1851 after Edes purchased the mill from the bank	Feb 22, 1851 Lease increased 50 inches	Apr 1, 1880
Successor to Edes: David L. Shoemaker, Georgetown, Firm of D. L. Shoemaker and Brother	Flour and grist	"The Lock Mill"	200	May 1, 1860	Apr 1, 1860	Apr 1, 1880
Successor to D. L. Shoemaker and Brother: David F. Robinson, Georgetown	Flour and Grist		200	Mar 1, 1880	Apr 1, 1880	Apr 1, 1900

LEASE NO. 2

Lessee	Type of Mill	Location	Sq. in. of Water leased	Actual date of lease	Effective Date	Date of Expiration
James H. Mason, Executer of Gen. John Mason, Deceased	Iron Foundry	One half mile west of Georgetown	100	Apr 20, 1854	Feb 1, 1840	Apr 1, 1880
Successor to Mason: David L. Shoemaker and Francis D. Shoemaker, Corporation	Flour and grist	Foundry site "Foundry Mill"	100	May 1, 1860	Feb 1, 1860	Feb 1, 1880, transferred to Peall and Shoemaker, 1877
Successor to D. L. Shoemaker and Brother: 1.Peall and Shoemaker 2.David F. Robinson	Flour and grist	Foundry site Foundry site	100 100	Transferred Sep 22, 1880	Jan 1, 1877 Feb 1, 1880	Feb 1, 1880 Feb 1, 1900[2]

	Firm	Location	Tenure
1.	M. L. Williams	Market Space at the canal	1862–1864
2.	E. S. Barrett	Congress Street near the canal	1862–1864
3.	Dickson and King	Corner of Greene and Water Streets	1862–1879
4.	Charles Myers	42 Water Street	1862–1864
5.	H. Barron and Son	49 Greene Street	1862–1866
6.	James A. Donnelly	105 Water Street	1863–1865
7.	J. C. Hieston and Company And Hayfield and Hieston	Corner of Jefferson Street and the canal And corner of Greene St. and the canal	1863–1886
8.	William R. Snow and Co.	79 Water and 107 Water St.	1864–1867[3]

LEGEND   Symbols   [MAP FROM YOUNG]
Location of former streets, bridges and structures
Location of former railways, chutes and wharves for unloading and shipping coal
Towpath, 1831–1858
Towpath, 1855–1884

Mills Using Water Power
1. Flour and cotton, 1833–1866
2. Use Unidentified, 1840
3. Bark and flour, 1840–1882

---

[2] Young, *Antebellum Commerce of Old Georgetown*, 205–207
[3] Young, *Antebellum Commerce of Old Georgetown*, 25.

4. Bakery and flour, 1840–1900
5. Flour, 1841–1901
6. Use unidentified, 1843–1848
7. Saw, iron foundry and grist, 1844–1880
8. Flour, 1847–1900
9. Tannery, location unidentified, 1848–1849
10. Use unidentified, 1849–1880
11. Iron foundry and flour, 1831–1880
12. Bakery and flour, 1857–1880
13. –13A. Flour, 1880–1900
14. Paper, 1884–1885
15. Flour, 1887–1880
16. Flour, 1872–1880

Coal Wharves Using Water Power
a. "Upper Coal Wharf", 1806–1880
b. "Ray's Docks", 1858–1880
c. W. A. Bradley, 1859–1860

Coal Wharves Not Using Water Power
a. American Coal Company, location unidentified, 1857–1880
b. James R. Wilson, 1857–1887
c. Morgan and Rhinehart, 1857–1867
d. Allen H. Sherman, 1857–1867
e. Aetna and Midland Coal Companies, 1858–1861
f. John F. Agnew, 1854–1886
g. Consolidation Coal Company, 1834–1880
h. New Hope Mine, 1866
i. Cumberland Coal and Iron Co., 1867–1873
j. Hampshire and Baltimore Coal Co., location unidentified, 1869–1873
k. Henry C. Winship, 1872–1875
l. Merodith, Gilmore & Co., 1875–1886

Key to Georgetown Street Names in the Appendices

Old	Modern
Greene	29
Washington	30
Jefferson	Jefferson
Congress	31
High	Wisconsin Avenue
Cherry	Grace
Potomac	Potomac (partially closed)
Market	33 (partially closed)
Frederick	34 (partially closed)
Fayette	35 (partially closed)
Lingan	36 (partially closed)
Water	K[4]

---

[4] Map, Legend, and Key from Young, *Antebellum Commerce of Old Georgetown*,

APPENDIX C

WAREHOUSES ALONG THE C&O CANAL: 1850-1890

LOGWALL OR WIDEWATER AREA (LOCKS NOS. 14-15)

In August 1861 John Pettibone was granted permission to build icehouses on the berm side of the canal near the Logwall just off the property of the company. The purpose of the structures was to provide facilities for the transportation of ice down the waterway to Georgetown. Nearly a year later in August 1862, the canal board authorized President Alfred Spates to execute an agreement with Baylis Kidder, granting them the privilege to cut ice in the Logwall vicinity for a 10-year period at an annual rental of $50.[5]

LOCK NO. 22

A list of the canal company's improved and unimproved real estate holdings along the waterway in 1890 indicates that three warehouses were standing near the lock at that time. The list provides the following information on the structures:

> Warehouse of W. L. Thrasher—lease expires 1897—$5 rent per annum.
> Warehouse of Upton Darby and Co.—rent unknown.
> Warehouse of George Pennifield—carried away by 1889 flood—lease expires 1897—$36 rent per annum[6]

LOCK NO. 24

At least two warehouses were built in the vicinity of Lock No. 24 in the early 1870's. On October 1871, the canal company granted a lease to John Darby and Son for "as much land as may be necessary to erect a warehouse on (the) berm side of (the) canal at Mouth of Seneca." The following year on March 5 the company directors approved a fifteen-year rent-free lease to James H. Gassaway, American Dawson, Samuel Dyson and others for "the right and privilege to erect a warehouse near the Mouth of Seneca." The structure was to be used for the purpose of "Freighting grain" from that point.[7]

The list of the canal company's improved real estate holdings in 1890 indicates that two storehouses or granaries were located near Lock No. 24. One was leased to William A. West for $36 per year, while the other tenant was listed as unknown. The West lease was to expire in 1893.[8]

---

[5] *Proceedings of the President and Board of Directors*, K, 257, 270.
[6] *Real Estate, improved and unimproved. From the Records in Canal Co.'s office at Hagerstown and Information Obtained Orally from other Reliable sources*, 1890, Receivership Papers, Washington County Courthouse, Hagerstown, Maryland. The Thrasher warehouse was built apparently sometime in 1883, because an application by the Thrasher brothers to build a warehouse near Lock No. 22 was made in June of that year. *Proceedings of the President and Board of Directors*, N, 218.
[7] *Proceedings of the President and Board of Directors*, M, 5.
[8] *Real Estate, Improved and Unimproved*, 1890, Receivership Papers.

LOCK NO. 25

Canal company records indicate that a warehouse was being operated by James C. Young in 1859. There is no readily available information as to the dates of construction and early tenants of the warehouse.[9]

On October 5, 1861, the canal board approved the following resolution:

> That B. R. Poole be permitted to build a warehouse on the land of the Company at Lock 25, under the direction of the supervisor, on the usual terms of such grants and paying therefore an annual rent of $12 provided, that the company shall be exempt from any claim for damages, arising from any source.[10]

Nearly three years later on July 28, 1864, Charles F. Elgin requested permission to build a warehouse at Edwards Ferry for shipping granite. Although it is difficult to prove, this request may have been the warehouse used by the Potomac Red Sand Stone Company for which the canal company was receiving $625 in rent per year in 1890.[11]

According to a statement in the Montgomery County Circuit Court on May 28, 1872, there existed at Edwards Ferry a warehouse:

> partly built on the Canal Company's property by Geo(rge) W. Spates, and that a carpenter's shop belonging to the Canal Company stands nearby, where a lot of ground belonging to Spates is used for storing lumber. The agreement allows Spates to let (the) warehouse stand for ten years and Spates agrees to allow (the) Canal Co. to continue to use Spates' land for (the) Carpenter Shop.[12]

Aside from the aforementioned Potomac Red Sand Stone Company's operations, the list of the canal company's real estate holdings in 1890 indicates that a granary warehouse was located on the berm side of the canal near Lock No. 25. Its annual rental was unknown, and its tenants were not given.[13]

LOCK NO. 26

Sometime during 1864 Daniel S. White built and occupied a warehouse on the berm of the canal just above the lock and adjacent to the road leading to the ferry landing (then known as Conrad's Ferry). The two-story warehouse was 70 feet long paralleling the canal and 23 feet in width. There were chutes on the canal side through which the grain was poured into canal barges. White paid $36 a year for the lease of the warehouse, but by 1890 the lessee and rental fees were listed as unknown. The structure was razed by the National Park Service in 1962, but the foundation, built of Seneca red sandstone, remains to indicate its location.[14]

---

[9] *Proceedings of the President and Board of Directors*, K, 87, 97.
[10] Ibid, K, 222.
[11] Ibid, K, 393, and *Real Estate, Improved and Unimproved*, 1890, Receivership Papers.
[12] Land Records, Liber., 52, EBP 10-p. 4 –5, Montgomery County Circuit Court, Clerk's Office, Rockville, Md.
[13] *Real Estate, Improved and Unimproved*, 1890, Receivership Papers
[4] Miele, *Physical History*, 119; John F. Luzader, *Historic Structures Survey Report, Warehouse-Granary White's Ferry* (NPS Mss., 1962), 1–3; and *Proceedings of the President and Board of* Directors, K, 410. See 264–265 for drawings describing the operation of this structure.

MOUTH OF MONOCACY, NOLAND'S FERRY, POINT OF ROCKS

In November 1865 Otho W. Trundle was granted permission to build warehouses at the basin at the mouth of the Monocacy River, Noland's ferry and Point of Rocks. The warehouses were all to be built under the direction of the Superintendent of the Monocacy Division. The other stipulations in the agreement were: (a) the annual rental for each building would be $36; (b) the buildings should not be placed so as to interfere with the navigation of the waterway; and (c) no liquor was to be sold on any of the premises.[15]

LOCK NO. 28

The real estate list of 1890 refers to a warehouse near Lock No. 28. It was leased to J. G. Waters at $36 per year. No other information has been found relative to this structure.[16]

LOCK NO. 29

On March 24, 1864, the board of directors granted permission to George P. Remberg to construct a "warehouse on the lands of the Company on the berm side of the Canal near Lock No. 29." In 1890 the tenants and annual rental for the warehouse were listed as unknown.[17]

LOCK NO. 42

A canal company document in 1877 indicates that Charles Dellinger had leased a stone storehouse and a wood hay shed near Lock No. 42 for an undetermined period. The storehouse, which was used for the storage and shipment of "grain, corn and store goods", fronted on the berm side of the lock and was 30 feet wide and 20 feet long. The hay shed adjoined the storehouse and was 30 feet wide and 18 feet back. In 1877 Charles Dellinger died and his son Daniel took over the lease. In 1890 he was still leasing the "storehouse and granary" for an annual rent of $36.[18]

MERCERSVILLE

A warehouse and loading dock, Known as Harris' Warehouse and later as Boyer's Warehouse, stood at Mercersville about 1 ½ miles above Lock No. 40 during the operation of the canal. The remains of the dock on the berm side of the canal are all that remain of this site, now known as Taylor's Landing.[19]

WILLIAMSPORT

There were at least three warehouses along the canal in Williamsport during the operating years of the waterway. Near Lock No. 44 were two warehouses leased to F. H. Darby and Sons and Charles Embrey and Sons. Both firms were involved in the coal and grain trade. On the basin just east of Aqueduct No. 5 was the warehouse operated by Victor Cushwa for his profitable coal and

---

[15] *Proceedings of the President and Board of* Directors, K, 458–459.
[16] *Real Estate, Improved and Unimproved*, 1890, Receivership Papers.
[17] *Proceedings of the President and Board of* Directors, K, 374, and *Real Estate, Improved and Unimproved*, 1890, Receivership Papers.
[18] Miele, *Physical History*, 121.
[19] Dellinger to Gorman, May 1, 1877, Ltrs. Recd., C & O Co. and *Real Estate, Improved and Unimproved*, 1890, Receivership Papers.

grain transportation business. Although Cushwa had established his concern prior to the 1870's, he signed a 50-year lease for his warehouse in 1879 at an annual rental of $100 for the first five years and $120 thereafter.

GUARD LOCK NO. 5

In 1890 a warehouse was operated by Abram Roth near the guard lock. The date of construction and other information relative to the warehouse is not available.[20]

LOCKS NOS. 47–50 (FOUR LOCKS)

The board granted permission to Denton Jacques on April 19, 1863, to lease company land near Lock No. 49 for the purpose of building warehouses. He was given a 10-year lease to a plot of ground 100 by 125 feet on the berm side and a plot 10 by 15 feet wide on the towpath side. The rental fee was set at $10 per year. At the end of the lease he was to be given an additional 10-year lease at an undetermined rent, provided none of the structures would interfere with the free use of the canal and that no liquor would be sold on the property.

On June 1, 1866, William J. Hassett was authorized to build a warehouse and establish a coal yard on the canal berm at Lock No. 50. The warehouse and coal yard, which he was to rent at $36 per year, were to be constructed under the direction of the engineer and general superintendent of the canal.

In 1890 there were two warehouses listed on canal property at Four Locks. A store, warehouse and hay shed were operated by Snyder and Fennser, and a warehouse near Charles' Mill on the canal berm was rented to the operator of the mill.[21]

MCCOY'S FERRY

In 1890 the company records listed a warehouse as being operated by Frank Winter on the berm side of the canal just above McCoy's Ferry.[22]

HANCOCK

Just above Lock No. 52 in Hancock were located the Cohills Sumac Mills. This manufacturing concern, for which construction data is unavailable, consisted of several warehouses, a flour mill and store rooms. In 1890 the operation was listed as being leased to S. Rhinehart, who was paying an annual rent of $100 for water power.[23]

LOCK NO. 67

In 1890 a store and warehouse at the lock were listed as being rented to M. H. Russell for $36 per year, the lease to expire in 1898. No other information relative to the construction of these buildings is available.[24]

---

[20] *Real Estate, Improved and Unimproved*, 1890, Receivership Papers.
[21] Ibid, and *Proceedings of the President and Board of Directors*, K, 327, 494..
[22] *Real Estate, Improved and Unimproved*, 1890, Receivership Papers.
[23] Ibid.
[24] Ibid.

LOCK NO. 70

Near Lock No. 70 were a warehouse, storehouse and icehouse according to the 1890 company list. No other information is available on these structures.[25]

LOCK NO. 71

Near Lock No. 71 was a warehouse which according the 1890 company list was unoccupied. No other information is available on this structure.[26]

---

[25] *Ibid.*
[26] *Ibid.*

APPENDIX D

COAL YARDS AND WHARVES USING WATER POWER FROM THE CHESAPEAKE AND OHIO CANAL TO UNLOAD AND SHIP COAL: 1856–1880[27]

Lessee	Location	Water used	Actual date of grant	Effective Date	Date of Expiration
Swanton Coal and Iron Company	East of the Alexandria Aqueduct, at the S.E. corner of Water and Lingen Streets in the river front	Water supplied gratis to unload canal boats if quantity did not exceed that required to lock boat into river and back to canal	Oct. 12, 1855	Spring, 1836	March, 1858 Acquired by Borden Mining Company, 1858
Successor to the Swanton Company: Borden Mining Co. John R. Masters, Agent Beginning in 1872	Same as Swanton Company known as the "Upper Coal Wharf"	Same as Swanton Company until 1873, when annual rental changed		Mar 1853	Free grant to 1873 Rental to 1880
Longcoming Coal and Transportation Co., Washington, Alexander Ray, Agent, Georgetown. The MD and New Central Coal Companies were also shipping over Ray's Docks by 1869, and S.P.S. Hutson by 1870. Central transferred to Agnew in 1876.	Immediately west of Market Street, extending to river front wharf near the S. W. corner of Water and Market Streets. Known as "Ray's Docks" and "Lower Coal Wharf"	Same as in Grant A until 1873, when annual rental charged	Aug 5, 1855	Fall, 1858	Free grant to 1873 Rental to 1880
William A. Bradley	N.W. corner of Water and Fayette Streets, extending southward to riverfront wharf near S.E. corner of Water and Fayette Streets	Same as in Grant A, until 1860		June 7, 1859	1860

---

[27] Young, *Antebellum Commerce of Old Georgetown*, 208–212.

APPENDIX E

LIST OF COAL YARDS AND WHARVES IN GEORGETOWN SHIPPING COAL WITHOUT THE USE OF WATER POWER: 1856–1880[28]

Lessee	Location	Effective Date	Date of Expiration
American Coal Company		Aug 18, 1857	1880
James R. Wilson	Western end of Rock Creek Mole, adjoining Georgetown	Soon after Sep 3, 1857	Sep, 1867
Morgan and Rhinehart	On berm of the Rock Creek Basin at Georgetown	Sep 7, 1857	June, 1867
Allen M. Sherman	S.E. end of Rock Creek Mole, adjoining Georgetown	Oct. 1, 1857	Oct 1, 1867
Aetna Coal Company and Midland Coal Company, James R. Wilson, Agent, Georgetown	Between Market and Frederick Streets, extending southward to riverfront wharf between the same streets	Soon after Jun 30, 1858	1861
John P. Agnew, from 1876, agent of the New Central Coal Company	Foot of Frederick Street on the riverfront	1864	Through 1866
Consolidation Coal Company, Henry I. Weld, agent	On Linthicum's Wharf at the foot of Market Street on the riverfront	Nov 10, 1884	Through 1880
New Hope Mine J.H.T. McPherson, agent	Foot of Market Street on the riverfront	1866	1868
Cumberland Coal and Iron Company	Near and east of the Alexandria Aqueduct, on the riverfront between Lingan and Fayette Streets	1867	1878
Hampshire and Baltimore Coal Company		1869	Through 1878
Henry C. Winship	At the S.E. corner of the intersection of Market Street with the canal	1872	1875
Meredith Gilmor and Company	Foot of 30 Street on the riverfront	1875	1886

---

[28] Young, *Antebellum Commerce of Old Georgetown*, 203–204.

APPENDIX F

THE CHIEF RETAIL COAL DEALERS NEAR THE
CHESAPEAKE AND OHIO CANAL IN GEORGETOWN: 1860-1880[29]

1	M. L. Williams	Market Space at the Canal	1862-1964
2	E. B. Barrett	Congress St. near the canal	1862-1864
3	Dickson and King	Corner of Greene and Water Sts.	1862-1879
4	Charles Myers	41 Water St.	1862-1864
5	H Barron and Son	49 Greene St.	1862-1866
6	James A. Donnelly	105 Water St.	1863-1865
7	J. C. Hieston & Co. and Mayfield & Hieston	Corner of Jefferston St. and the canal; and corner of Greene St. and the canal	1863-1886
8	William R. Snow & Co.	79 Water St. and 107 Water St.	1864-1867

MILLS USING WATER POWER

1. Flour and cotton, 1839-1900
2. Use unidentified, 1840
3. Bark and flour, 1840-1882
4. Bakery and flour, 1840-1900
5. Flour, 1841-1901
6. Use unidentified, 1843-1848
7. Saw, iron foundry, and grist, 1844-1880
8. Flour, 1847-1900
9. Tannery, location unidentified, 1848-1849
10. Use unidentified, 1849-1880
11. Iron foundry and flour, 1857-1900
12. Bakery and flour, 1857-1900
13. -13A.   Flour, 1860-1900
14. Paper, 1864-1885
15. Flour, 1867-1880
16. Flour, 1872-1880

COAL WHARVES USING WATER POWER

A. "Upper Coal Wharf," 1856-1880
B. "Ray's Docks," 1858-1880
C. W. A. Bradley, 1859-1860

COAL WHARVES NOT USING WATER POWER

A. American Coal Company, location unidentified, 1857-1880
B. James B. Wilson, 1857-1867

---

[29] Source: Young, Rogers W. "The Chesapeake and Ohio Canal and the Antebellum Commerce of Old Georgetown." Branch of Historic Sites. National Park Service, January 1940.

- C. Morgan and Rinehart, 1857–1867
- D. Allen M. Sherman, 157–1867
- E. Aetna and Midland Coal Companies, 1858–1861
- F. John P. Agnew, 1864–1886
- G. Consolidation Coal Company, 1864–1880
- H. New Hope Mine, 1866
- I. Cumberland Coal and Iron Co., 1887–1878
- J. Hampshire and Baltimore Coal Co., location unidentified, 1869–1878
- K. Henry C. Winship, 1872–1875
- L. Meredith, Gilmore & Co., 1875–1886

HISTORIC RESOURCE STUDY
CHESAPEAKE & OHIO CANAL NHP

11.
THE C & O CANAL DURING THE CIVIL WAR: 1861–1865

BY HARLAN D. UNRAU
HISTORIAN, C&O CANAL RESTORATION TEAM, SENECA
DENVER SERVICE CENTER
1976

CONTENTS

INTRODUCTION		707
I.	THE CANAL PRIOR TO THE OUTBREAK OF THE WAR	709
II.	WAR COMES TO THE CANAL: 1861	710
III.	THE CANAL REACHES ITS LOWEST EBB: 1862	724
IV.	COMMERCE ON THE CANAL EXPERIENCES A REVIVAL: 1863	743
V.	THE CANAL TRADE EXPANSION CONTINUES: 1864	754
VI.	PEACE COMES TO THE CANAL: 1865	767
VII.	THE CANAL IN THE AFTERMATH OF THE CIVIL WAR	770
APPENDIXES		777
A.	DISCOVERY AND DEVELOPMENT OF GOLD VEINS NEAR GREAT FALLS	777
B.	STATEMENT OF BOATS NAMES AND OWNERS HELD BY THE U.S. GOVERNMENT APRIL 17, 1861	779

INTRODUCTION

A study of the Civil War experiences of the Chesapeake & Ohio Canal Company indicates a continuation of the ups and downs which had characterized the history of the waterway since the 1830s. The immediate effects were almost all negative. During the early war years the canal failed to share in the general prosperity which came to the northern states. One reason for its failure to secure much of the increased trade was that it was not a through route to the transmontane west, thereby limiting its portion of the heavy east-west traffic. Also, its geographical location was unfortunate because its entire line was on the border between the Union and the Confederacy, in the path of the contending armies. Consequently its trade was greatly reduced and its works alternately occupied and/or destroyed by the opposing forces. The resulting irregularity of its services as a carrier argued against large-scale use of it by the government or by private shippers. Furthermore the financial straits in which the company continually labored were a serious obstacle to the progress of the canal.

The only direct advantage derived from the war was the large demand for coal. Of the 15½ million tons of coal mined in the United States in 1860, nearly 60 percent was Pennsylvania anthracite while the remainder came from the Appalachian fields of Maryland and Virginia (including West Virginia). A specialized "super-coal," Maryland's product was particularly suited for New England textile mills and for steamship bunkering, and it had been used successfully for smelting iron. Thus, with Virginia coal no longer available to the northeastern market, Maryland's contribution became increasingly important to the Union cause. Yet the company had to wait over two years before its carrier was sufficiently clear of the battle zone to permit long periods of uninterrupted navigation.[1]

In the long run, the war both encouraged and discouraged hopes for improved business prospects. The year 1863 marked a definite financial turning point in canal affairs as profits rose sharply to levels well above those of the prewar years. For a decade after the war, the net income of the company rose measurably with a regularity hitherto unknown to the disaster-ridden canal. It should be noted, however, that during the conflict a sizeable portion of the increased profits were the result of the neglect of the physical condition of the canal and of rising toll rates during the inflationary period, rather than by a marked increase in trade.

In other important ways, the war record was even less bright. Markets were affected differently. The lucrative flour trade, which was already passing to the Baltimore & Ohio in 1860, was finally and definitely lost as a result of the unreliability of canal navigation during the war. The coal trade, on the other hand, improved steadily toward the end of the conflict, and by 1865 it had become, for all practical purposes, the sole support of the canal company. Accounting for more than 90 percent of the trade on the waterway, the traffic in coal came to bear a great weight in canal affairs. When technological improvements later enabled the railroad to compete more successfully for the trade, the Allegany County coal companies forced toll reductions which deprived the canal of its profits before the trade was lost.

The physical condition of the waterway deteriorated greatly during the hostilities. Years passed before the masonry structures were properly repaired and the trunk restored to its original dimensions. As a result of the suspension of improvements, the canal was becoming outmoded and incapable of meeting the demands of an enlarged business. When improvements became unavoidable during the next fifteen years, the company found itself without the tremendous sums required. At best, the prosperity of the latter war years merely arrested the inevitable decline of

---

[1] Katherine A. Harvey, "The Civil War and the Maryland Coal Trade," *Maryland Historical Magazine*, LXII (December, 1967), 361–362.

the canal. At worst, the war indirectly hastened the end, while causing much incidental anguish to those who depended on it for a livelihood.[2]

---

[2] Walter S. Sanderlin, "The Vicissitudes of the Chesapeake & Ohio Canal During the Civil War," *Journal of Southern History*, XI (February, 1945), 51–53, 66–67.

I. THE CANAL PRIOR TO THE OUTBREAK OF WAR

The year 1860 had not been profitable for the Chesapeake & Ohio Canal Company. Political influence from the Maryland legislature had brought about the wholesale turnover of employees and the reorganization of the administration of the company in May and June.[3] The canal had not been opened to navigation until mid-May. Business had then been brisk until November, when heavy rains over the Potomac Valley caused the rivers to rise rapidly. Dams Nos. 5 and 6 were injured, while considerable destruction was done to Guard Lock No. 4 and the towpath below Dam No. 4. The Marsh Run Culvert was washed out, several sections of the trunk were filled with silt and debris, and the walls of Lock No. 21 partially collapsed. The canal was shut down for three weeks while temporary repairs were made thus preventing the movement of coal from Cumberland to the District cities when such trade could be expected to be at its height. Income from the tolls which had totaled $32,547.54 in October fell to $15,951.47 for the final two months of the year, and the annual trade statistics showed a decline of more than 17,000 tons of coal from the 1859 totals.[4]

When the canal was drained for the winter in late December, more permanent repairs were made to restore the canal to its operating condition before the freshet. As a result of these efforts, company officials looked forward to a "prosperous boating season" in 1861 despite the looming clouds of war.[5] Nevertheless, the approaching conflict was the cause of some anxiety and mixed emotions to the canal directorate as evidenced by the following communication from President Lawrence J. Brengle to Clerk Walter S. Ringgold on New Year's Day:

> We are in great excitement here [company headquarters at Frederick] with regard to the National Crisis, and don't know what to do that will be of any advantage to arrest the difficulty. We are much divided in sentiment on the subject. I still hope there is conversation enough in the country yet to save it.[6]

Water was readmitted to the canal in the second week of March 1861, and during the following month there were heavy shipments of coal from the Allegany County mines. In March income from the tolls was $16,768.25, while during the first ten days of April $12,581.01 was collected.[7]

On April 12 torrential rains drenched the entire watershed of the Potomac Valley, causing a disaster that dashed the company's hopes of a profitable year.[8] The Potomac continued to surge upward. Upon the portion of the canal, it reached a height only exceeded by the 1852 flood. Considerable destruction was caused to canal property as a result of "the unprotected condition of the embankments near the feeder at Dam No. 4." A number of washes and breaches occurred on the Cumberland, Hancock, Williamsport, and Antietam Divisions while damage to the Monocacy and Georgetown Divisions was less severe than had been feared.[9]

---

[3] *Proceedings of the President and Board of Directors*, K, 183-183, 192-195.
[4] *Thirty-Third Annual Report* (1861), C&O Co. pp.3, 8-9, 14, and Charleton to Board of Directors, November 7, 1860, Fitzpatrick to Ringgold, November 6, 1860, and Stake to Board of Directors, November 13, 1860, Ltrs. Recd., C&O Co.
[5] Ringgold to Colston, December 15, 1860, Ltrs. Recd., C&O Co., *Thirty-Third Annual Report* (1861),9-10, 14; and *Proceedings of the President and Board of Directors*, K, 240, 244.
[6] Brengle to Ringgold, January 1, 1861, Ltrs. Recd., C&O Co.
[7] *Thirty-Third Annual Report* (1861), 10, and *Thirty-Fourth Annual Report* (1862), C&O Co.,3, 9.
[8] Carleton to Ringgold, April 13, 1861, Ltrs. Recd., C&O Co.
[9] *Thirty-Third Annual Report* (1861), 10, and Washington *Evening Star*, April 15, 17, 1861

II. WAR COMES TO THE CANAL: 1861

As the repair crews prepared to restore the waterway, they were hindered by two factors—the desperate financial condition of the company and the withdrawal of Virginia from the Union on April 17, thus insuring that the Potomac Valley and the canal would feel the full impact of the grim struggle about to engulf the United States. Upon the adoption of the Secession Ordinance by the Virginia Convention, Confederate militia converged on Harpers Ferry, eager to seize the arms and machinery at the Unite States Armory and Arsenal. Unable to capture their objective before it was fired by the retreating Federal troops, the Rebel army used the area as a concentration point where untrained volunteers were organized into a fighting force by Colonel Thomas J. Jackson. Troops were sent across the Potomac into Maryland, occupying the strategic locations at Point of Rocks and Maryland Heights.[10]

Despite the presence of the Confederates around Point of Rocks and Harpers Ferry, progress in effecting repairs of the flood damage was reported by the division superintendents. Water was back in the entire line by May 14, but the activities of the Virginia militia around Harpers Ferry and Alexandria made the coal shippers hesitant to use the waterway until the military situation was clarified.[11] Although the canal records do not indicate how many boats were detained by the Rebels between Point of Rocks and Harpers Ferry, it was reported that a boat owned by Thomas McKaig had been held up at the latter town by a detachment of Confederate soldiers while its load of salt was removed.[12]

The coal operators were further alarmed by reports during the period of repairs that small bands of Confederate pickets were gathering near the Potomac Aqueduct. In an effort to drive the pickets away, small bodies of Federal troops commenced frequent forays across the Potomac at night in late April and early May. Finally on May 23 the United States Government occupied the aqueduct, and on the following day Union troops occupied the Virginia shore opposite Washington. As the towpath of the aqueduct proved to be inadequate for the military exigencies, it was later determined to shut the water off from the structure and convert its trunk into a double-track wagon road by overlaying the floor with 4 inch planks. By December 5, the bridge over the aqueduct was under construction, and on December 16, the water was drawn off to permit the erection of long wooden inclines on trestles to form connections with the roads on either side. A dam was placed across the Georgetown entrance of the aqueduct by December 23, thus closing the structure to the trade of the canal.[13]

By late spring the Cumberland coal trade had virtually been halted. On June 1, the Pottsville *Miners' Journal* announced that the trade "appears to be entirely suspended for the present by Railroad as well as Canal. The dislodgement of the Rebels from Harper's Ferry, which will soon take place, will re-open the trade by Railroad from Cumberland again, but not by Canal."

---

[10] *The War of the Rebellion: A Compilation of the Official Records of the Union and Confederate Armies* (Washington, 1880–1900), Series I, Vol. II,809–810.
[11] Spates to Ringgold, May 6, 13, 1861, Ltrs. Recd., C&O Co., and *Thirty-Fourth Annual Report* (1862), 3.
[12] *Proceedings of the President and Board of Directors*, K, 290.
[13] Washington *Evening Star*, May 2, 24, December 5, 16, 23, 1861; Maj. Gen. J. G. Barnard (Brevet), *A Report on the Defenses of Washington to the Chief of Engineers, U.S. Army* (Washington, 1871),79–80. The long wooden incline on the Georgetown side of the aqueduct extended over the canal and connected present-day 36th Street with the abutment. Commission of Fine Arts and Historic American Buildings Survey, *Georgetown Architecture—The Waterfront* (Washington, 1968), 151. Prior to the construction of the bridge over the aqueduct, an alternative proposal of building a boat bridge was studied seriously. However, the idea was given up because of the depth and powerful currents of the river in the vicinity and the frequency of floods and icing.

Meanwhile the competing Pennsylvania Broad Top Coal was "coming into demand to supply its place."[14]

The annual meeting of the company stockholders was held at Frederick on June 4. The fears and uncertainties of the period were reported as follows:

> The general condition of the canal for navigation at this time is believed to be better than it has been for some years past, and a fair business for the season could be done, but for the political agitations of the country, by which business has been prostrated, transportation rendered uncertain and precarious, and subject to frequent delays, if not seizures by the contending parties on the banks of the Potomac, and unless there be an early removal of the seat of war, it is feared that a general suspension of the transportation on the Canal, will occur.[15]

During the second week of June, Brigadier General Joseph E. Johnston, who had replaced Jackson as commander at Harpers Ferry in May, received news that a Union column under Major General George B. McClellan advancing eastward along the Baltimore & Ohio Railroad had occupied Cumberland on the 10th. Shortly thereafter, he learned from his scouts that Major General Robert Patterson, the federal commander of the recently-created Department of Pennsylvania with headquarters at Chambersburg, was closing in on Williamsport with 14,000 troops. Sensing that his position at Harpers Ferry was a trap for his command, Johnston on June 15 pulled troops out of that vicinity and fell back to Winchester.[16]

Before evacuating Harpers Ferry, Johnston had his demolition teams sabotage the canal. These groups wreaked considerable havoc on the waterway from Harpers Ferry to Dam No. 5. On the evening of June 8 word was received in Williamsport that some rebel soldiers were attempting to put "a blast into Dam No. 5, to blow it up." The Clearspring Guards proceeded to the dam and drove off the Virginians after a brief skirmish. Later in the night, the Confederates returned and planted a cannon to defend their men while at work on the dam. One blast was ignited which destroyed a small portion of one of the stone-filled cribs, but no serious damage took place. The next morning a small band of Unionists armed with Minnie muskets left Williamsport and aided the Clearspring Guards in repossessing the dam. During the following week, a series of skirmishes took place at the dam as each side attempted to drive the other out of the area.[17]

On June 13 canal president Alfred Spates reported that the canal was badly injured above Harpers Ferry. Gates at four of the locks were destroyed, and a number of boats had been burned. Based on the damage that he had seen, he complained that he felt "very sad at the destruction committed."[18]

The Washington *Evening Star* on June 14 reported that the Virginians were making a concerted effort to destroy Dam No. 4. According to the account, the rebels were

> engaged every night, with dark lanterns, drilling holes in the solid rock on which Dam No. 4 rests, on the Virginia side, in order to blow up the same. Should they make successive heavy blasts the dam must give way. The work is superintended by Redmond Broun,

---

[4] Pottsville *Miners' Journal*, June 1, 1861, quoted in Harvey, "Civil War and Maryland Coal Trade," p. 365.
[15] *Thirty-Third Annual Report* (1861), 4.
[16] Edwin C. Bearss, "War Comes to the Chesapeake & Ohio Canal," *West Virginia History*, XXIX (April 1968),155–156. Patterson's troops occupied Williamsport but made no effort to cross the Potomac at that time.
[17] Washington *Evening Star*, June 11, 14, 1861.
[18] Spates to Ringgold, June 13, 1861, Ltrs. Recd., C&O Co.

an Irishman who superintended its construction. He has two sons among the Confederate troops.

Heavy firing was reported at the dam as a company of 45 Sharpshooters from Boonsboro had gone to assist the Sharpsburg Company in an attempt to drive the Confederates away. Already four Virginians had been wounded badly during the skirmishing.[19]

The presence of Southern troops on the Virginia side of the Potomac made it unsafe to attempt any repairs. What especially worried General Superintendent A.K. Stake was that it was difficult to secure planks to repair the stop lock at Dam No. 4. Unless this was done promptly, the canal below that point would be subjected to extensive damage by a freshet. The discouraged engineer reported to company officials on June 26 that

> Nothing but soldiers, baggage, wagons, camps, guns, pistols and swords, meets our gaze here [Williamsport]. Wherever we go they have pretty nearly eaten up everything we have. I hope they will get away soon.[20]

Because of the straightened finances of the canal company President Spates on July 1 urged Clerk Ringgold to see if he could collect in advance from the Georgetown millers $1,000 of their water rents.[21] Of this sum $500 would be allocated for the repair of the stop lock at Dam No. 4. Once completed, this would enable the boatmen to bring down a number of stranded coal boats. The captains were reportedly willing to pay their tolls in cash on their arrival in Georgetown. Repairs to the canal in the Harpers Ferry area were progressing rapidly, but Dam No.1 was leaking so badly that it would take a good force ten days to tighten it.[22]

While the company was attempting to collect advances from the Georgetown millers on their water rents, it received word from several enterprises that the war had forced them to cease operations. One such message came on July 9 from Williamson & Co. which had leased the Pioneer Cotton Factory in Georgetown on January 1, 1861. With the outbreak of hostilities in April, inflationary wages and expenses, the scarcity and high price of cotton, and a drastic reduction of sales even at prices below production costs had ruined the company's credit. As a result, the plant had been closed and all hands had been discharged. Until the conflict ended and the factory was back in operation, the company requested that it be relieved of its water rents.[23]

A Cumberland minister also described the depressing effect of the outbreak of hostilities upon the interests of Western Maryland and his town. Among other observations, he wrote that

> Her great thoroughfare, the Baltimore & Ohio Railroad, was interrupted and her Canal closed. Trade from Virginia was withdrawn. Every industry was stopped or curtailed; stores were closed and marked "for rent;" real estate sank rapidly in value. Merchants without customers slept at their counters, or sat at the doors of their places of business. Tradesmen and laborers, out of employment, lounged idly about the streets. The railroad workshops were silent and operations in the mining regions almost entirely ceased. Then commenced a deep, painful feeling of insecurity and an undefined dread of the horrors of war. Panic makers multiplied and infested society, startling rumors were constantly float-

---

[19] Washington *Evening Star*, June 14, 1861.
[20] Stake to Spates, June 26, 1861, Ltrs. Recd., C&O Co.
[21] In fiscal year 1861, the company had collected $5,202.24 in water rents.
[22] Spates to Ringgold, July 1, 1861, Ltrs. Recd., C&O Co.
[23] Williamson and Co. to President and Directors, June 20, 1861, Ltrs. Recd., C&O Co., and *Proceedings of the President and Board of Directors*, K, 254. Desperate for revenue, the canal company refused to grant the request of Williamson & Co. on July 9.

ing about of secret plots and dark conspiracies against the peace of the community and private individuals.[24]

It was July 2 before the Union troops crossed the Potomac at Williamsport. In the campaign that ensued, Johnston, the Confederate commander, took his army eastward out of the Shenandoah Valley and combined with the force under Pierre G. T. Beauregard to maul the Federals in the war's first major battle at Manassas on July 21. During the maneuvering in the weeks before the battle, marauding bands of Confederates made several forays against the canal, one of which took place at Great Falls, Maryland, on July 7. In the day-long fire fight, the Confederates nearly succeeded in driving out the Eighth Battalion of the District of Columbia Volunteers that was protecting that strategic position.[25]

Heavy rains at the beginning of July caused additional damage to the canal. Although Union advances in the Potomac Valley had compelled the Confederates to pull back from the river, the repair crews did not wish to take any chances. General Superintendent Stake complained that the Rebels seemed determined to oppose any navigation on the canal, and it was "impolitic if not dangerous to attempt repairs." Only those sections that could be attended to without risk would be pushed. Work was to be commenced on July 8, and Stake estimated that it would require eight to ten days to restore navigation. As the regular work crews that resided along the line of the canal had left, the company would be forced to transport men, supplies, and provisions into the areas needing repairs. Stake's fears that the canal would be subjected to damage by marauding soldiers as long as the Union and Confederate armies confronted each other in the Potomac Valley were heightened as he organized the work crews when he was warned of a threat by the Rebels to "blow down Dam No. 6." At the same time a Union officer warned that no repairs should be made to Dam No.1. If the warning was not heeded, he would have his men tear down the dam. Almost daily roving Confederate bands were in the habit of shooting across the Potomac toward the canal at numerous points along the river.[26]

Despite the hindrances to the work crews, all of the repairs on the canal were finished by July 20, the day before the Battle of First Manassas, except those at Edwards Ferry, a culvert three miles above Paw Paw Tunnel, and the Oldtown Deep Cut. While the last repairs were underway, General Robert Patterson dispatched a company of troops to Hancock to protect the waterway from Williamsport to Cumberland. The repairs at Edwards Ferry were completed soon thereafter, but it took an 80-man crew with 20 horses and carts some 25 days to restore navigation at the large breach near the aforementioned culvert and the heavy rock slide at the Oldtown Deep Cut. When an inspection of the repairs by President Spates revealed that the pool behind Dam No. 5 was so low that the canal could not be navigated, a crew was put to work tightening the dam. Finally on August 26 the canal was again navigable from Cumberland to Georgetown. To affect the repairs, Spates had been forced to borrow $1,000 from the Merchant's Bank in Baltimore and $1,000 from the Cumberland Bank of Allegany County.[27]

With the canal again open for its entire length, trade improved rapidly led by the loaded coal barges that had been stranded below Dam No. 6. Tolls which had fallen to $657.36 in May, $206.27 in June and $16.94 in July zoomed upward to $2,444.07 in August and $10,509.17 in September. During the three-week period after August 26, 10,628 tons of coal, in 96 boats, were

---

[24] Will H. Lowdermilk, *History of Cumberland* (Washington, 1878), 396–397.
[25] *O. R.*, Series I, Vol. II, 123.
[26] Stakes to Spates, July 6, 1861, Ltrs. Recd., C&O Co.
[27] Spates to Ringgold, July 20, 24, August 1, 13, 25, 1861, Ltrs. Recd., C&O Co. General Superintendent Stake, frustrated by the effect of the war on the canal, resigned his position effective August 1. Ringgold to Stake, July 10, 1861, Ltrs. Recd., C&O Co.

shipped from Cumberland to the District cities.[28]

The rise in trade was encouraged by several factors. First, to keep the Confederates from interfering with boating on the upper divisions of the canal, President Spates, who was a friend of one of the aides of General Robert E. Lee, made an agreement with them.[29] Second, President Abraham Lincoln on July 20 approved a communication from Secretary of War Simon Cameron to Representative Francis Thomas, a former president of the canal company in 1839-41, authorizing the organization of four regiments of loyal citizens

> on both sides of the Potomac River from the Monocacy to the west boundary of Maryland, for the protection of the canal and of property and persons of loyal citizens.[30]

Third, as the Potomac divided the territory held by the Union and Confederate forces in the weeks following the Battle of First Manassas, Federals reporting to Brigadier General Charles P. Stone watched the river from Great Falls to the Monocacy River, while units under General Banks held the line of the river from the Monocacy to Shepherdstown. By mid-August, Stone's main force was camped at Poolesville, while Edward's Ferry, Conrad's Ferry and Seneca were held by strong detachments and a string of pickets stretched down to Great Falls. With his division encamped near Hyattstown, Banks assigned the 2nd Massachusetts to occupy Harpers Ferry and hold the Virginia bridgehead, and posted the 13th Massachusetts at Sharpsburg, the 1st Maryland Infantry at Williamsport, the 28th New York at Berlin, and the 28th Pennsylvania at Point of Rocks. The primary mission of the Federal forces was to observe "the enemy across the Potomac and protect the Chesapeake & Ohio Canal.[31]

Fourth, heavy rains in early August caused the Potomac and its tributaries to swell. With the river at near flood stage, there was little immediate danger of a Confederate thrust into Maryland as the unseasonably high water level prevented fording of wagons and artillery.[32]

As a result of these factors, canal traffic proceeded with little interruption until mid-October. To be sure there were several incidents along the canal during this period, but none had a serious affect on the operation of the waterway. On August 16 and several days following there were reports that a company of Confederates had shot at canal boats near Edwards and Conrad's Ferries from positions across the river. A canal boatman was mortally wounded by Rebel fire at Shepherdstown on September 9. During the skirmish at that town, the Federals destroyed the Potomac Mill which had passed into the ownership of Alexander R. Boteler, a former Congressman elected by the American Party from the Harper's Ferry District who was now a member of the Confederate Congress and a colonel on the staff of General Jackson.[33] The bridge across the Po-

---

[28] Carleton to Ringgold, September 14, 1861, Ltrs. Recd., C&O Co., and *Thirty-Fourth Annual Report* (1862), 9. In comparison, the toll collections for the same months in 1860 had been as follows: May—$19,214.19; June—$18,529.60; July—$23,051.10; and August—$28,005.02. *Thirty-Third Annual Report* (1861), C&O Co., 14.

[29] Spates to Ringgold, August 13, 1861, Ltrs. Recd., C&O Co. The terms of the agreement were never made public.

[30] *O. R.*, Series III, Vol. I, 338–339, and Roy P. Basler, ed., *The Collected Works of Abraham Lincoln* (8 Vols., New Brunswick, 1953), IV, 455.

[31] *O. R.*, Series I, Vol. V, 560, 565, 567, 569, 574. One of the regiments from which picket details were sent to the Great Falls area was the 71st Pennsylvania. Most sources agree that members of this regiment, known informally as the "First California Regiment," were the first to discover free samples of gold near the falls during this period. For more information on this topic, see Appendix A. of this chapter.

[32] *Ibid*, 565, 573

[33] Ezra J. Warner and W. Buck Yearns, *Biographical Register of the Confederate Congress* (Baton Rouge, 1975), 25–26; Hagerstown *Mail*, January 18, 1867; and Misc. Mss., Alexander R. Boteler Papers, Duke

tomac was also wrecked by the Union troops in the hope that such an action would deprive the Rebels of easy access into Maryland.[34]

Six days later, on September 15, a severe skirmish erupted at Harpers Ferry following sporadic clashes on the 13th and 14th between a strong Rebel force attempting to retake the town and northern troops under Colonel John W. Geary. Placing his left behind the railroad embankment southeast of the abutment of the burned Y-bridge and his right along the canal towpath near Lock No. 35, Geary drove the Confederates back in the direction of Bolivar Heights after a two-hour fire-fight.[35]

The increase in canal trade and the apparent inability of the Confederates to mount an offensive across the Potomac into Maryland contributed to the optimism of businessmen along the canal. Hence several new enterprises were commenced along the waterway in early October. John Pettibone was granted permission to build ice houses on the berm of the canal near the "logwall" to facilitate the transportation of that item to Washington.[36] B. R. Poole was authorized to build a warehouse on the land of the canal company near Lock No. 25 for an annual rental fee of $12.[37]

Despite the trade increase, however, the company was forced to admit by October 1 that its means were inadequate to operate and maintain the canal properly. Accordingly, the board passed the following resolution:

> Whereas on the 6th of Feby. last, the Board adopted a resolution "that the Company will continue to receive the Certificates of tolls in payment of tolls so far as their means and financial ability will admit, and Whereas, in consequence of suspension of business on the canal for some months past, owing in a great measure to the belligerent operations on the Potomac, the means of the Company are inadequate to the proper repair and maintenance of the Canal, therefore it is,
> Resolved, that from and after this day, all tolls accruing on the Canal be required to be collected in cash, until otherwise ordered.[38]

There was a marked increase in military activity along the canal in mid-October. Union soldiers under Colonel Geary crossed the Potomac, pushed through Harpers Ferry, and occupied Bolivar heights. Once a picket line was formed, fatigue parties began removing and boating to the Maryland side hundreds of bushels of wheat stored in the flour mill on Virginius Island. By the evening of the 15th, the Union men had completed their task, but before they could be withdrawn across the Potomac the next morning, a strong force of Confederates led by Lieutenant Colonel Turner Ashby advanced and drove in Geary's picket line. A sharp fight ensued in which the Yankees defeated Ashby's troops, and under the cover of darkness on the night of October 16 the Federals evacuated their bridgehead and recrossed the Potomac.[39]

The bloody Battle of Ball's Bluff occurred on October 21. A 1,700-man brigade led by

---

University Library, Durham, North Carolina. Later in 1864, Federal troops crossed the river at Boteler's Ford and marched toward the Shenandoah Valley to destroy its usefulness for the Confederacy. On the way, Boteler's home ("Fountain Rock") near Shepherdstown was burned. Shepherdstown *Register*, July 16 and August 21, 1924, in Boteler Papers.

[34] John F. Luzader, *Historic Sites: Shepherdstown, West Virginia* (NPS Mss., 1962), 21
[35] *O. R.*, Series I, Vol. V, 197–199, 569, 594.
[36] *Proceedings of the President and Board of Directors*, K, 257. Later on July 29, 1862, the firm of Bayliss and Kidder was granted the privilege of cutting ice on the "logwall" for ten years at an annual rent of $50., *Ibid,* K, 270.
[37] *Ibid,* K, 222.
[38] *Ibid,* K, 258
[39] *O. R.*, Series I, Vol. V, 239–342.

President Lincoln's close friend, Colonel Edward Baker, had crossed the Potomac at Harrison's Island using a number of flatboats, one of which had been moored in the canal about one mile away. After occupying Ball's Bluff as part of a general reconnaissance campaign ordered from Washington, the Federals were assailed by a 1,700-man Confederate force under Brigadier General Nathan G. Evans and routed. The withdrawal became a disaster as the Union troops fell back to the crest of the bluff and then attempted to escape. Baker was killed along with 49 of his men, 158 were injured, and 714 missing, many of whom drowned, compared to only 155 casualties for the Confederates.[40]

Two days after the debacle at Ball's Bluff, on October 23, a small pitched battle broke out at the mouth of South Branch. The fight was triggered when the Confederates attempted to blow up the abutment of the South Branch Bridge. Some six companies of Federal troops, whose strength was diminished by a raging epidemic of measles, were required to drive the Rebels off and restore order.[41]

The Union success at South Branch forestalled the intent of the Confederates to destroy Dam No. 6. Earlier on October 20, Colonel Angus W. McDonald, headquartered at Romney, had issued the following order:

> Col. E. H. McDonald will take all the mounted men of his command, except those upon scout service, and with them, together with Captain Sheets' Co. of the Cavalry Regt., repair to the mouth of Big Capon, in the County of Morgan, and then proceed to destroy Dam No. 6, by digging around the abutment a sufficient ditch on the Va. shore to drain the Dam, and by such other means as may suggest to him as best to effect the destruction, confining his operations to the Va. shore. The necessary implements will be provided to accompany you. Having effected all you can towards the destruction of the Dam you will proceed to destroy the water stations of the B & Ohio R.R. as far up the South Branch, or as many as you can convenient with a speedy return to this point with your command. Arriving there you will proceed to destroy the abutments of the Bridge thereof. On your arrival at Dam No. 6, and every 12 hours after, you will dispatch a courier to report your progress to Head Quarters [at Romney, Virginia]. Upon your return you will report in writing your action under this order.[42]

The repercussions resulting from the disaster at Ball's Bluff sapped the enthusiasm of Generals Banks and Stone for operations designed to wrestle the initiative from the Confederates. In early November there would be elections in Maryland, and the States Rights Party, composed of pro-Southern elements, was making a bid to gain control of the Border State. A responsive War Department ordered the Union commanders to give furloughs to soldiers of the Maryland Volunteers so that they might return home and add their weight to the polls. General Banks was also directed to send detachments of men to various points to protect Union voters from intimidation by "disunionists" and to arrest any such persons who had just returned from Virginia. If necessary he was authorized to suspend the writ of *habeas corpus*. As expected under such circumstances, the generally peaceful election swept Augustus W. Bradford, a conservative Unionist, to victory as Governor by a margin of 57,502 to 26,070 over his States Rights opponent, Benjamin C. Howard

---

[40] E. B. Long, *The Civil War Day by Day: An Almanac, 1861–1865* (Garden City, 1971), 129–130, and *O. R.*, Series I, Vol. V, 327–329.
[41] Smith to Ringgold, October 23, 1861, Ltrs. Recd., C&O Co.
[42] This copy of the orders was found in an anonymous pamphlet, *To the People of Maryland: The Canal and its Management Vindicated* (n. d.) Rare Book Division, Library of Congress. The orders were taken from the personal baggage of Col. Angus W. McDonald by Brigadier General B. F. Kelley at the capture of Romney.

and Unionists gained healthy majorities of 68 to 6 and 13 to 8 in the House of Delegates and the Senate respectively.[43]

The setback suffered by the troops led by Colonel Ashby at Bolivar Heights on October 16 had far-reaching repercussions. Influential citizens of Jefferson County, Virginia, led by Representative Alexander R. Boteler of Shepherdstown, began to urge President Jefferson Davis to appoint a battle-tested commander to lead the recruits in that area. On October 24, Boteler warned Davis that the "enemy along the canal has been re-enforced." The previous day he had watched a Union fatigue party construct a raft at Dam No. 4, and he had seen a number of loaded coal barges pass down the waterway.[44] The barrage of letters caused Davis to act, and on November 5 he issued orders for Major General Thomas J. Jackson, who had acquired the nickname "Stonewall" at the Battle of First Manassas, to proceed to Winchester and assume command of the newly-created Valley District.[45]

Meanwhile, trade on the canal had continued to be heavy during the month of October. Up until the 26th, 154 boats carrying 27,313 tons of coal had cleared the Cumberland mole. Of these, 78 had discharged their cargoes at points above Georgetown, principally Sandy Hook just below Harpers Ferry where a large Federal supply depot was located.[46]

Heavy downpours in early November caused the Potomac to crest at the highest levels since the devastating flood in 1852. However, little serious damage was inflicted on the canal except at the Harpers Ferry bridge abutment, where part of the stone wall on the towpath side had been washed into the canal and a portion of the high wall on the berm side had been undermined, and at the Round Top Cement Mill above Hancock, where a major break had occurred. On the Monocacy Division repairs were slowed, when the Union troops took possession of the company scow, wheelbarrows, and tools. The icebreaker had also been appropriated by the Federals to transport artillery and had been damaged. In making the repairs, money was the biggest problem because the superintendents, in most cases, were out of cash, credit, and provisions. Workers on the Antietam Division, complaining that they had not been paid for over a month, walked off their jobs in early December.[47]

Despite some of the military's actions that tended to hinder the repairs, Union soldiers in the vicinity of the canal also aided in its restoration. On November 10, Brigadier General Stone informed President Spates that during the flood he had sent large parties of his men to protect the canal. Without such efforts, much of the embankment would have been "permanently injured." The troops

> carefully watched the towpath, and as soon as the water receded from it, commenced refacing. 90 men being employed in my division the first day & more since.
>
> Three breaches were promptly stopped. One large one near Seneca, in front of Genl. Banks' Division was repaired, but gave way again & is, I believe, made whole even more, by men from Genl. Banks' division.[48]

---

[43] Richard Walsh and William Lloyd Fox, eds., *Maryland: A History, 1632–1974* (Baltimore, 1974), 354–355; *Secret Correspondence Illustrating the Condition of Affairs in Maryland* (Baltimore, 1863), 30–39; *O. R.*, Series I, Vol. V, 628–29, 641, 645–647, 651–652; and Hagerstown *Herald & Torch*, November 13, 1861.
[44] *O. R.*, Series I, Vol. V, 898–899, 919.
[45] *O. R.*, Series I, Vol. V, 938.
[46] Carleton to Ringgold, October 26, 1861, Ltrs. Recd., C&O Co.
[47] Murray to Ringgold, November 5, 14, 1861, Byrns to Spates, November 6, 1861, Jones to Ringgold, November 11, 1861, and Boatman to Ringgold, December 2, 1861, Ltrs. Recd., C&O Co.
[48] Stone to Spates, November 10, 1861, Alfred Spates Papers, Alderman Library, University of Virginia, Charlottesville.

Although the repairs to the canal were underway, the Confederates were convinced that the waterway would not be reopened until spring. The Winchester *Republican* expressed these sentiments when it reported on November 15 that:

> The Chesapeake & Ohio Canal has been damaged by the recent freshet as to render it entirely worthless for purposes of navigation, nor could it be repaired, were every facility afforded, before spring. We conversed with a gentleman who walked across the dry bed of the canal at Hancock a few days since. He reports that it is broken at many points, and that the Yankees had abandoned all hope of having it in running order again this winter. The Canal closed, and the Potomac blockaded, the infidels will have to rely exclusively upon the Washington & Baltimore Rail Road for fuel and supplies of all kinds.[49]

As a result of the flood and the lengthy period of repairs, revenue from tolls fell from $17,793.22 in October to $3,245.56 in November. Liquid assets of the canal company were non-existent. In an effort to secure funds, the collectors at Georgetown and Cumberland were instructed not to pass any boats whose owners refused to pay their tolls in cash.[50] The financial condition of the company was so poor by late November that it was forced to suspend payment of interest due on its debts to various banks.[51]

On November 24 just as the entire length of the canal was about to be opened for navigation, President Spates sent a letter to Major General George B. McClellan, calling attention to the strategic value of the canal to the Northern armies and asking for increased protection of the waterway by Federal troops. The communication read as follows:

> It is the desire and intention of the Directors of the canal to keep it open for navigation as long as the season will admit and if the water is moderate in its temperature this may be done with no large expenditure throughout the entire season. It will offer great facilities to this community in the transportation of coal from the mining regions of Alleghany and may also be of material advantage to the U. State in facilitating the transportation of supplies for the army not only through the course of the canal, but in connection with the Baltimore & Ohio Railroad from the west to Cumberland and thence by canal to Washington. To accomplish this it is desirable and essential that proper protection of the works and facilities for transportation should be given by the United States. Hitherto for some months past detention has arisen by the military restrictions which have been imposed upon the boats navigating the canal;—They have not been allowed to run during the night and have been unnecessarily detained during the day so as to prolong their voyages nearly double the usual time required. It is in this view that I take the liberty of addressing you and earnestly request that you will give such orders as you may deem requisite to give ample protection to the canal and proper facilities for transportation upon it, and also that property of the company consisting of boats, houses & c. which are essential to the proper conduct of the canal and which have been used by the military authorities be directed to be returned to the officers of the company.[52]

---

[49] Winchester *Republican*, November 15, 1861, in Boteler Papers.
[50] . Spates to Ringgold, November 3, 1861, Ltrs. Recd., C&O Co. On November 12, the canal board relaxed its policy to permit the "several Mining Companies and others engaged in the transportation of coal...at established rates" to pay their tolls at the end of the month. *Proceedings of the President and Board of Directors*, K, 262.
[51] Reed to Ringgold, November 26, 1861, Ltrs. Recd., C&O Co.
[52] Spates to McClellan, November 24, 1861, Ltrs. Sent, C&O Co. The following day Spates wrote a similar letter to Quartermaster General Montgomery C. Meigs. Spates to Meigs, November 25, 1861, Ltrs Sent,

By the beginning of December, the canal was again open to navigation for its entire length. During the first two weeks of the month, 87 boats carrying 7,613 tons of coal, 633 tons of lumber, cord wood, and cooperage, and 89 tons of hay and oats left Cumberland. More than one-half of the boats were slated to discharge their cargoes at the Sandy Hook government supply depot.[53]

Meanwhile General Stonewall Jackson, while waiting for reinforcements to move against the Union force at Romney, had determined to impede reconstruction of the Baltimore & Ohio Railroad and to stop boating on the canal. When the Confederates had reoccupied the line of the railroad from Harpers Ferry to Cumberland after the Battle of First Manassas, the federal government had imposed heavy duty on the waterway as a line of supply. At Cumberland the Baltimore & Ohio relayed to the canal large quantities of supplies for the Army of the Potomac and Washington's civilian population.[54] Since October numerous reports had been reaching Richmond that troops and munitions were being sent up the canal for use in probable thrusts against the valuable agricultural region in the Shenandoah Valley. The failure of his generals to destroy the Baltimore & Ohio Railroad and the Chesapeake & Ohio Canal had caused Jefferson Davis to complain that such a default had left the foe "in possession of great advantages for that operation."[55] In early December word reached Jackson that large numbers of empty coal boats were passing up the canal to Cumberland, and he recognized that the reopened canal would be "of great service to the Federal Army at Washington." Since the Cumberland coal fields were an important source of that product and the farm lands served by the canal supplied flour, wheat, and corn, Jackson decided "to cut off western supplies by breaking Dam No. 5."[56]

Sending his militia troops in a feint toward Williamsport, Jackson marched his main force to the vicinity of Dam No. 5 on December 7. That afternoon a Rebel force of about 400 infantry and 200 horse soldiers commanded by Captain William McLaughlin appeared on the Virginia shore of the dam. Throwing their three 10-pounder Parrotts, one 12-pounder Sawyer, and two 6-pounder smoothbores into battery, the cannoneers of the Rockbridge Virginia Artillery "commenced throwing shells and shot at the dam and houses on the Maryland shore." A barn was set on fire and all the houses within range, including the lock-tender's residence, were riddled, but the projectiles failed to do any damage to the crib and rubble dam. The bombardment continued until dusk. The only Union troops at the dam were a company of the 13th Massachusetts, which had been assigned to guard the river from Harpers Ferry to Oldtown, on picket and several companies of the 12th Indiana, which had been posted at Sharpsburg, Williamsport and Dams Nos. 4 and 5 since October 13. As all the Federals were armed with short-range smoothbore muskets, their weapons were useless against the Rebel gunners. That night Colonel Samuel H. Leonard of the 13th Massachusetts dispatched a canal boat to Cumberland, and the craft quickly returned with Company G, 13th Massachusetts, which was armed with long-ranged Enfield rifle-muskets. The

---

C&O Co.
[53] Carleton to Ringgold, December 9, 13, 1861, Ltrs. Recd., C&O CO.
[54] Festus P. Summers, *The Baltimore & Ohio Railroad in the Civil War* (New York, 1939), 100–109.
[55] *O. R.*, Series I, Vol. V, 946
[56] *O. R.*, Series I, Vol. V, 390, and Walter S. Sanderlin, *The Great National Project: A History of the Chesapeake & Ohio Canal* (Baltimore, 1946), 207. Originally, Jackson had considered destroying both Dams Nos. 4 and 5, but he opted against the former because the new masonry Dam No. 4, considered by some to be "the strongest of its kind in the country," had been completed in the spring of 1861. On the other hand, construction of a new masonry Dam No. 5 to replace the old leaking log-cribbed, rock-filled structure was proceeding more slowly and was still only partially completed. Aside from the fact that Dam No. 5 was more vulnerable, it also had the advantage of being farther removed from the Frederick region, where General Banks had camped his division in early December. John Miele, "The Chesapeake & Ohio Canal: A Physical History" (NPS Mss., 1964), 46–47, and O. R., Series I, Vol. V, 676–677.

newcomers were posted in the woods on the Maryland shore and ordered not to fire until given word.[57]

Early on the morning of December 8, the Confederate artillerists reopened their concentrated fire on the dam. Emboldened by the slight resistance of the previous day, they advanced their gun to the brink of the river and fearlessly exposed their position. Following the order of Colonel Leonard, the newly-arrived men from Company G, 13th Massachusetts, opened fire from their hiding places along the river. Within a few minutes, the Rebel artillerists abandoned their guns and fled to less dangerous ground along with the cavalry and infantry. Without sufficient numbers of men and a supporting battery, Leonard was unable to cross the Potomac to take possession of the fieldpieces, thus enabling the Confederates to withdraw their six guns at nightfall.[58]

On December 9 the Confederates opened a scathing small-arms fire on the Federals. Covered by the Southern fire, a Confederate fatigue party worked its way down to the southern abutment of the dam. Using entrenching tools, they began digging a ditch around the end of the abutment, into which they hoped to divert sufficient water from the Potomac to erode the ground from the abutment and eventually cause it to topple and the dam with it. The Confederates worked until dark, protected by the stone abutment from the fire of the Union sharpshooters. By the time that they were recalled, water was pouring through the ditch.[59]

Satisfied that his efforts to destroy Dam No. 5 were successful, McLaughlin recalled his troops and returned to Winchester. However, the level of the Potomac was falling rapidly, and the water passing through the Confederate ditch soon diminished to a trickle and then ceased. On the 14th, Jackson reported:

> I have made two attempts to prevent navigation on the canal, but have not thus far succeeded. The only good results that I am aware of having been effected was the capture of 1 captain, 2 corporals, and 5 privates of the Twelfth Indiana Regiment, and damaging this end of Dam No. 5, and killed 1 of the enemy. On our part 2 men are supposed to be mortally wounded. The injury done to Dam No. 5 is not sufficient to admit the passage of water on the Virginia side.[60]

Two days after the action at Dam No. 5, on December 11, Union Brigadier General Stone assumed "military supervision of the Chesapeake & Ohio Canal" in compliance with Special Order No. 322, issued at the command of Major General McClellan:

> The Secretary of War directs that the Chesapeake & Ohio Canal be placed under the military supervision of Brigadier General C. P. Stone, Volunteer Service. The immediate superintendence of the canal will be under the President of the Company, Alfred Spates, Esq. The officers of the canal, serving under him shall be in all respects, satisfactory to the military authority. The receipts of the canal will be applied to meet current expenditure on account of its operations, and any excess or deficit in the income will be placed to the account of the Canal Company. The President of the Canal Company will furnish General Stone with an account current of the monetary affairs of the company, monthly. General Stone will give military protection to the canal property and such aid as is con-

---

[57] Washington *Evening Star*, December 10, 1861; Charles E. Davis, *Three Years in the Army: The Story of the Thirteenth Massachusetts Volunteers from July 16, 1861 to August 1, 1864* (Boston, 1864), 16–17; Ted Perry, ed., *Civil War Letters of Edwin Rice* (Boston, 1975), 18, 20; Baltimore *Evening Sun*, August 11, 1937; and Harold R. Mannakee, *Maryland in the Civil War* (Baltimore, 1961), 64–64.
[58] Washington *Evening Star*, December 10, 1861.
[59] Ibid.
[60] *O. R.*, Series I, Vol. V, 365.

sistent with the good of the service in keeping it in repair. Should the execution of this last provision extend beyond the limits of General Stone's command, his requisition on the proper commanders will be promptly complied with.[61]

Accordingly, all officers commanding pickets between Great Falls and the Monocacy River were ordered (and all officers of pickets along the rest of the canal were requested) to "give all aid and assistance in their power, consistent with the good of the service, to the Canal Co. authorities in the preservation & improvement of the canal."[62]

Before making another attempt to destroy Dam No. 5, Jackson circulated reports that he planned to attack the Federal forces at Romney with some 7,000 men. While the Union commanders prepared to head off such an attack, Jackson completed preparations to oversee personally the destruction of Dam No. 5. By the time that he left Winchester on December 16 at the head of the Stonewall Brigade, his scouts had collected and secreted a number of small boats to be used in crossing the Potomac. After sending a brigade of militia to feign an attack against Williamsport via Falling Waters, the Stonewall Brigade, which had been reinforced by Colonel Ashby's cavalry south of Martinsburg, took position on the hills overlooking Dam No. 5 at dusk on the 17th. That night a fatigue party led by Captain R. T. Colston of Company E, 2nd Virginia, who was familiar with the area and the structure of the dam, moved out. Colston and his men crept half way across the dam and slid down into the icy water to begin hacking away at the dam's cribs. Their muffled blows went undetected by Union sentinels on the north bank until nearly daybreak. At the first alarm, the Federals opened fire on the workmen, but they soon saw that the Rebels had piled up stone in the middle of the dam to form a crude but effective breastwork.[63]

As additional protection for Colston's fatigue party, Jackson had placed two guns on a hill commanding the dam. The cannoneers promptly put their pieces into action, shelling a brick house on the Maryland side of the river from which Yankee sharpshooters were harassing the workmen. The Federals soon scattered, but a section of the 1st Pennsylvania Artillery quickly galloped into view, threw their two 10-poundrt Parrotts into battery, and forced the Rebel artillerists to desert their guns. The deadly Union artillery and rifle fire compelled Colton's fatigue party to drop their tools and take cover because the demolition team in going to and from the barricade across the dam had to run a deadly gauntlet.[64]

General Banks took steps to cope with this threat to the canal. As there was the possibility that the Confederate forces which had occupied Falling Waters might move against Dam No. 4, he directed Colonel John R. Kenly of the 1st Maryland Infantry, camped four miles west of Frederick, to be prepared to march his regiment to either Dam No. 4 or No. 5 "as necessity may require or as the movements of the enemy may dictate." When it became obvious that Dam No. 5 was the Rebels' objective, Kenly pushed his column forward and established his command post at

---

[61] Special Order No. 322, December 6, 1861, in Spates Papers.
[62] General Order No. 33, December 12, 1861, in Spates Papers. Stone immediately requested from Spates information on four topics of vital concern to the operation of the waterway, (1) a list of canal company employees including their duties, stations, and salaries; (2) an estimate of the number and type of ice boats needed on each division to keep the canal open during the winter; (3) an estimate of the number of animals needed for full-scale operations; and (4) a list of stations where boats should be able to stop and discharge cargo in order to eliminate the current system that placed restrictions on the movement of goods on the waterway. Stone to Spates, December 11, 1861, in Spates Papers. Spates was given a pass so that he could travel on the towpath at any time with a servant and two horses. Pass issued by A. P. Banks, December 16, 1861, in Spates Papers.
[63] O. R., Series I, Vol. V, 395–396, 688, and Bearss, "War Comes to the Canal," pp170–171.
[64] O. R., Series I, Vol. V, 390, 397, and Washington Evening Star, December 21, 1861.

Four Locks on the 19th.[65]

At the same time, Banks deployed four infantry regiments with eight field pieces along the Potomac between Shepherdstown and Hancock. Two regiments, the 5th Connecticut and the 29th Pennsylvania, and a section of guns from Battery F, 4th U. S. Artillery, were called up from the reserve to reinforce the units charged with the defense of the canal.[66]

Colston's fatigue party, reinforced by companies from the 27th and 33rd Virginia, continued their demolition work in the bitterly cold water during the nights of the 18th and 19th. Union artillery and sharpshooters shelled the Virginia shore and the dam, scattering the fatigue party and killing and maiming several of them. Nevertheless, they continued their efforts, under the cover of Rebel gunners, until mid-afternoon of the 20th. By that time, a breach had been opened that Jackson believed to be of sufficient size to cripple the canal, and the Confederates pulled back.[67]

After the retirement of Jackson's troops, Union patrols crossed the Potomac and visited the site of the Confederate encampment. There they picked up numerous blankets and entrenching tools and burned a mill that the foe had been using. Upon inspecting the dam, Colonel Leonard found that damage was not extensive, and working parties were organized to assist canal hands with its repair.[68]

On December 21 canal navigation was resumed both above and below Dam No. 5. During the day, two guns were rushed to Little Georgetown, where some Rebel infantry appeared on the south bank of the Potomac. Although the Confederates withdrew after a few shots, the troops guarding Dam No. 4 were reinforced with the 29th Pennsylvania and the 5th Connecticut was ordered to Hancock.[69]

The canal was still open New Year's Day 1862, and, according to President Spates, the "waterway, despite the recent activities of the Confederates is in good order and things look very well all over the line."[70] Despite the Confederate attempts to destroy Dam No. 5, the heavy December traffic in coal caused the toll collections to rise sharply to $6,345.14 for the month.[71]

Nevertheless, 1861 had been a disastrous year for the canal company as well as for the Western Maryland coal industry. The trade statistics on the waterway for the year compared with those of 1860 demonstrate the drastic decline in traffic and revenue:

	TOTAL TONNAGE	COAL TONNAGE	TOLLS
1860	344,532	283,249	$182,343.86
1861	144,814	119,893	70,566.99

The statistics of the aggregate Cumberland coal trade for the year also reveal the dependence of the Allegany County interests on the through transportation of the canal and the Baltimore &

---

[65] *O. R.*, Series I, Vol. V, 397, and Bearss, "War Comes to the Canal," p. 172. Some of Kenly's men occupied Fort Frederick and "knocked a hole in the wall through which to point a gun for taking pot shots at the Confederates across the Potomac." John Thomas Scharff, *History of Western Maryland* (2 vols., Philadelphia, 1882) Vol. I, 217.

[66] *O. R.*, Series I, Vol. V, 368, and Washington *Evening Star*, December 21, 1861.

[67] *O. R.,* Series I, Vol. V, 390, and Bearss, "War Comes to the Canal," p. 174.

[68] *O. R.*, Series I, Vol. V, 390, 398, and Washington *Evening Star*, December 21, 1861.

[69] *O. R.*, Series I, Vol. V, 399–400, and Bearss, "War Comes to the Canal.' P. 175. Apparently, Jackson, who was back in Winchester by the 21st, was deceived by the over-optimistic stories of his subordinates, because he reported on Christmas Eve, "There is reason to believe that the recent breaks in Dam No. 5 will destroy any vestige of hope that might have been entertained of supplying Washington with Cumberland coal by the Chesapeake & Ohio Canal." O. R., Series I, Vol. V, 390

[70] Spates to Ringgold, January 1, 1862, Ltrs. Recd., C&O Co.

[71] *Thirty-Fourth Annual Report* (1862), 9.

Ohio Railroad. The shipments of the various coal companies fell from 789,000 tons in 1860, which was an all-time high up to that date, to slightly less than 270,000 tons in 1861, an amount almost exactly that shipped in 1851 when the trade was just opening on the newly-completed canal.[72]

At the annual meeting of the stockholders in June 1862, President Alfred Spates commented on the dismal ramifications of the canal operations during 1861:

> The last annual report [June 1861] anticipated to some extent the unfavorable operations of the Canal for the past year, owing to the belligerent movements then in progress on the Potomac, and although the direct damages done to the Canal and its works by the military were not very great, yet, its business results were even more disastrous than was expected. This was caused by the damages arising from the proximity of the contending forces on the river, the restrictions imposed upon the transportation by the military authorities, and the frequent detentions of the boats, by which the time usually required to complete their voyages was nearly doubled.
>
> The Canal was opened for navigation about the 15th of March, 1861, with an active business for one month, which was then interrupted by a freshet in the river, causing considerable injury to the Canal and the suspension of navigation for a month, which time was required to complete the repairs. When navigation was again restored, active hostilities had commenced, and there was comparatively no business on the Canal before September. Between this [date] and ... December, there were occasional interruptions by breaches in the Canal.
>
> The diminished revenues of the Company have prevented any improvements on the Canal, and indeed have been altogether insufficient to keep it in proper condition, and this has resulted in an increased indebtedness for services and materials, in addition to the numerous and large claims of that class previously existing.
>
> It will be observed that the expenses for ordinary repairs, &c., have been unusually small, but this has been the consequence of the limited means of the Company, which were not adequate to the repairs actually required for the security of the Canal, and the proper maintenance of the navigation.

As a result of the depredations of nature and man, 1861 was the worst year financially that the company had experienced since 1848, two years before the canal was completed to Cumberland.[73]

---

[72] Harvey, "Civil War and the Maryland Coal Trade," 364–365.
[73] *Thirty-Fourth Annual Report* (1862), 3–5.

III. THE CANAL REACHES ITS LOWEST EBB: 1862

Under the direction of the military authorities, canal company officials attempted to keep the waterway open during the winter of 1861-1862 for the first time since the waterway had been completed to Cumberland in 1850. Icebreakers were employed in the fight to keep the canal operating as the military was anxious to transport supplies to its troops preparatory to the coming spring offensive and the canal officials were eager to make up for the loss of trade during the previous year. A cold snap in early January closed the canal, but the weather soon moderated and by the 15th it was again open and ice-free as far west as Hancock. Despite the resumption of trade, income from tolls fell to $954.19 for the month.[74]

At the beginning of the new year, General Jackson made a final effort to interrupt traffic on the canal. Reports reaching Jackson led him to conclude that the reinforced Federals might converge on Martinsburg and then push on toward his base at Winchester. To counter such a movement, the Confederates took the field on January 1 and marched from Winchester toward the Potomac. After a long march through bitter winter weather, the Rebels occupied Bath on the 4th after the Federal garrison was scattered and fled across the Potomac in boats.[75] Here Jackson was reinforced by Colonel Ashby, who had been engaged since December 30 in a vain effort to reopen the breach at Dam No. 5 by placing a rifled gun on the Virginia side and firing shots at it.[76] On the morning of the 5th, the Confederates advanced on Hancock, but after a two-day bombardment of the town, Jackson ordered his gunners to cease fire and withdraw to Romney when it was learned that more Union troops were being sent into the fray. Cold weather now put a stop to military operations along the canal.[77]

After the canal navigation was closed, Major General Banks ordered the canal officials to make repairs on the waterway with the aid of his men. If the division superintendents did not commence the work immediately, the military would oversee the work entirely. The government would pay the repair crews so that the men would not have to be concerned about getting paid.[78]

Political influence brought about a wholesale turnover of employees during the period from February to April 1862. Alfred Spates was reelected president, but the administration of the line was reorganized. Six new superintendencies were formed and new collectors and lock tenders were appointed. Although these appointments were the last during the war years, some of the new officials soon proved to be less than efficient employees.[79]

In late February Major General Nathaniel P. Banks' advance guard crossed the Potomac and occupied Harpers Ferry. A pontoon bridge could keep this force supplied, but the Federals' plan called for large-scale operations and he restoration of through traffic on the Baltimore and Ohio Railroad. Among the proposed plans for such an undertaking was that advanced by President Lincoln to bridge the river at Sandy Hook with canal boats, while a Philadelphia engineering firm rebuilt the railroad bridge at Harpers Ferry. A number of canal boats on the Monocacy and Antietam Divisions were appropriated by the military for the project. However when McClellan visited the area on February 27, he determined that the banks were too steep for the projected boat bridge, and plans for it were scrapped.[80]

---

[74] Carleton to Spates, January 8, 1862, and Spates to Ringgold, January 15, 1862, Ltrs. Recd., C&O Co.; *Thirty-Fourth Annual Report* (1862), 9; *Thirty-Fifth Annual Report* (1863), C&O Co., 8; and Washington *National Intelligencer*, March 10, 1862.

[75] O. R., Series I, Vol. V, 391-392.

[76] Washington *Evening Star*, January 1, 1862.

[77] O. R., Series I, Vol. V, 391-392, and Washington *Evening Star*, January 7, 1862.

[78] Leonard to Link, February 6, 1862, and Banks to Spates, March 6, 1862, in Spates Papers.

[79] *Proceedings of the President and Board of Directors*, K, 272-274, 276-277, 282.

[80] O. R., Series I, Vol. V, 49, 730, and Lincoln to McClellan, February 8, 1862, in Basler, *Collected Works*

With the arrival of warmer weather, the canal, whose westernmost sections had been closed during much of February, was again opened to navigation from Cumberland to Georgetown by March 1. Coal stockpiles in the District cities had been depleted during the severe winter, and would have to be replenished from the Allegany County coal mines. Since it was assumed that the powerful army organized by McClellan would seize and hold the initiative during the coming year, canal officials were optimistic that the waterway would escape being a scene of active military operations and would consequently have a banner year in trade.[81]

Reports submitted by the division superintendents in early March indicated that the canal was generally in good navigable condition. However, the company's carpenter and blacksmith shops on the Monocacy Division had been robbed and a number of tools were missing. One of the company scows had been located, but it had been seized by the army and was being used as a ferry on the river.[82] On the Cumberland Division it was reported that the towpath and berm banks along some sections had been injured by government wagons passing over them. The railings on the aqueducts had been removed to allow military vehicles to pass.[83]

The naval engagement at Hampton Roads, Virginia, in which the Confederate ironclad *Merrimac* destroyed two Union warships—*Cumberland* and *Congress*—on March 8, had repercussions which affected the canal. News of this defeat frightened and panicked officials in Washington. President Lincoln was so distressed

> that he could not deliberate or be satisfied with the opinions of non-professional men, but ordered his carriage and drove to the navy yard to see and consult with Admiral [John] Dahlgren [the officer in charge of the Washington Navy Yard] and other naval officers, who might be there.[84]

Perhaps the most gloomy assessment of the battle was rendered by Secretary of War Edwin M. Stanton:

> The Merrimac...would destroy every vessel in the service, could lay every city on the coast under contribution, could take Fortress Monroe; McClellan's mistaken purpose to advance by the Peninsula must be abandoned, and Burnside would inevitably be captured. Likely the first movement of the Merrimac would be to come up the Potomac and disperse Congress, destroy the Capitol and public buildings; or she might go to New York or Boston and destroy those cities, or levy from them sufficient to carry on the war.[85]

Knowing that the Union ironclad *Monitor* was en route to Hampton Roads from New York Harbor, Secretary of the Navy Gideon Welles attempted to reassure them that the *Merrimac*, if she tried to ascend the Potomac, could not pass Kettle Bottom Shoals. Rejecting the optimistic report by Welles, Stanton, with Lincoln's concurrence ordered on March 9 Quartermaster General Montgomery C. Meigs and Admiral Dahlgren to seize 50 or 60 canal boats and other craft. The barges would be filled with stone and gravel, moved down the river, and sunk at Kettle Bottom Shoals or at some other point in the channel to prevent the *Merrimac* from ascending the Poto-

---

of Lincoln, V, 130
[81] Edwin C. Bearss, "1862 Brings Hard Times To the Chesapeake & Ohio Canal," *West Virginia History*, XXX (January, 1969), 436
[82] George W. Spates to Alfred Spates, March 8, 1862, Ltrs. Recd., C&O Co.
[83] Lowe to Ringgold, March 8, 1862, Ltrs. Recd., C&O Co.
[84] *Diary of Gideon Wells* (3 vols., Boston, 1911), Vol. I, 61–62
[85] *Ibid*, 63.

mac. That afternoon all unemployed boats on the Georgetown Division were taken to the Washington Navy Yard, where a large fatigue party began loading them with gravel. By nightfall, eight were ready to cast off, and a similar number would be ready to sail by dawn.[86]

On the evening of March 10, news reached Washington that in a battle on the previous day; the *Monitor* had forced the *Merrimac* to retire to the Confederate navy yard at Norfolk. On the basis of this report, Welles succeeded in getting Lincoln to forbid the sinking of any of the 60 canal boats that had been loaded with gravel and sent down to Kettle Bottom Shoals as long as the *Monitor* could keep the *Merrimac* from entering the Potomac.[87]

Meanwhile, Commander Wyman had been making soundings on the river, and he concluded that the best points to obstruct the Potomac were at Smith's Point and Mattawoman Muds. Accordingly, orders were issued to move the gravel-loaded canal boats to Smith's Point.[88]

After the crisis atmosphere subsided, the military continued to rush boats down the canal. On March 10, some 103 canal barges, most of which were empty, passed through Williamsport under the charge of army officers. Of this fleet of boats, 37 had come from Cumberland and the rest from unknown points.[89] None of them had any way bills.

Several weeks later, President Lincoln, Secretary Stanton, and other officials passed down the Potomac on board a steamer for Fortress Monroe. When the long line of canal boats moored near the Maryland shore attracted attention, the President jokingly exclaimed:

> that is Stanton's navy. That is the fleet concerning which he and Mr. Welles became so excited in my room. Welles was incensed and opposed the scheme, and it has proved that Neptune was right. Stanton's navy is as useless as the paps of a man to a suckling child. They may be some show to amuse the child, but they are good for nothing for service.[90]

After detaining the 103 boats for more than a month, the Federals found a need for about 50 of them in late April. Commander Wyman had ascended the Rappahannock to Fredericksburg with his squadron, while at the same time Major General Irwin McDowell had commenced an overland advance from Aquia Creek to Fredericksburg. As his troops pushed forward, they repaired the Rappahannock, Fredericksburg, and Potomac Railroad, which had been wrecked by the withdrawing Rebels. Forty canal boats were convoyed down the Potomac and up the Rappahannock to Fredericksburg to bridge the latter river.[91]

By late March 1862 the tide of the war had turned momentarily in favor of the Union. Banks' troops had occupied Winchester, and Stonewall Jackson's columns had been forced to withdraw up the Shenandoah Valley to Mount Jackson. McClellan's Army of the Potomac had occupied the fortified Confederate camp at Centreville and then marched to Alexandria from where it had embarked aboard ship for Fortress Monroe. These Union gains in the eastern theater of the war removed the canal for the time being from the sphere of active military operations.[92]

With the threat of invasion lifted, canal company official hoped that full-scale navigation could be resumed. The Cumberland coal companies alerted their people to be ready to resume shipments. Although there was a shortage of boats as a result of the military's actions, it was forecast that with "uninterrupted navigation" there would be enough vessels to earn a large revenue. To take advantage of the trade opportunities, appeals were sent to McClellan and other mili-

---

[86] Bearss, "1862 Brings Hard Times," 437–438.
[87] *Diary of Gideon Welles*, Vol. I, 63–66.
[88] Bearss, "1862 Brings Hard Times," 438.
[89] Wolfe to Ringgold, March 10, 1862, Ltrs. Recd., C & O Co.
[90] *Diary of Gideon Welles*, Vol. I, 67.
[91] O. R., Series I, Vol. XII, 3, 94, 98, 105, 121, 207.
[92] Bearss, "1862 Brings Hard Times," 438–439.

tary and civil officials, asking for the prompt release of the seized boats that were so vital to the economic life of the canal.[93]

The issue of disloyalty and labor difficulties with the boatmen soon arose to cloud the prospects for a profitable trade. As Maryland was a Border State with a strong pro-Southern element, Unionist authorities suspected Democrats of being disloyal and throughout the war many such individuals lost their jobs or were imprisoned. One of the canal company's most capable division superintendents, B. B. Boatman of the Antietam Division, was fired for disloyalty, because at the previous November election he had refused to write his name on the back of his ballot. On April 4 he sent a letter to the canal board protesting the charges against him:

> I have been identified in interest with it, since it has been a canal, now removed, from my position, I suppose, because of my attention to the business relating to it upon the day of election, instead of subjecting myself to the contemptible position of a serf, by unauthorized and unconstitutional act, of requiring each voter to endorse his name on the back of the ticket. I have never concealed my political views, been an open and avowed Democrat, and now, even in this day of bickering and clamor, challenge any man, to allege one charge against me, in word or act disloyal. [I] have spent much of my time laboring on this work, not receiving my monthly dues, always hoping in its prosperity, and that finally [I] would receive the compensation.[94]

Although no charges of disloyalty were proven against Boatman, the canal company refused to reinstate him.

The company representatives in Cumberland were distressed by rumors that the boatmen were planning to strike. While the coal companies were willing to pay higher rates, the demands of the boatmen, which ranged between $1.50 and $1.75 a mile per ton, were such that they would cause the price of Cumberland coal to rise to a point where it would be unable to compete with coal from the Pennsylvania mines. Already, the Pennsylvania Railroad Company had reduced its hauling charge on Broad Top Coal by 30 cents a ton per mile.[95]

The dispute with the boatmen was resolved on April 11, when the canal directors agreed to permit an increase in the toll on coal from 1/4 to 5/16 of a cent per ton mile.[96] As soon as this compromise was reached, a large number of boats were loaded with coal to begin the spring coal navigation. However, the small number of boats available for the canal trade was alarming. As many of the canal boats that had been taken over by the government were lying idle at Georgetown, President Spates prevailed upon Governor Augustus W. Bradford of Maryland to intervene on the company's behalf and get the Federal authorities to release the desperately-needed barges. The situation was urgent since the lack of boats would soon ruin the canal company and the laborers of Allegany County, some of whom had been out of work for nearly a year. In the meantime the Pennsylvania interests had moved "heaven and earth to maintain themselves on the ground they were enabled to occupy" by the disasters that had befallen the canal. It was reported that the Pennsylvania Railroad Company was prepared to reduce its coal-hauling charges still further to exclude the waterway "from market another year when an attempt to regain it on our part will be almost impossible." As a result, the "very existence of the canal" was "trembling in the

---

[93] Ringgold to Greene, March 24, 1862, Ltrs. Sent, C & O Co., and Greene to Ringgold, April 1, 1862, Ltrs. Recd., C & O Co.
[94] Boatman to Board of Directors, April 4, 1862, Ltrs. Recd., C&O Co. Boatman claimed the canal company owed him $1,000 in back pay and that he would be willing to settle for two-thirds of the amount if he received the rest immediately.
[95] Greene to Ringgold, April 7, 1862, ltrs. Recd., C & O Co.
[96] *Thirty-Fifth Annual Report* (1863), 5

balance." It would be impossible for the boatmen to replace in 1862 the 100 boats held by the government.[97]

On April 15 Governor Bradford contacted Quartermaster General Montgomery C. Meigs on behalf of the canal company. That same day Meigs sent a memorandum to President Lincoln recommending that the War Department

> take immediately all necessary measures to have all boats, scows, and other property used in repairing and navigating the Canal restored to their rightful owners. If boats have been used for the uses of the Army or Navy and cannot be restored, they are forthwith to be paid for, so that trade on the Canal may be revived.

Lincoln submitted the memorandum to Secretary Stanton with the following comment:

> I do not sign the within, because I do not know but there is a good reason, known to the Secretary of War, why the course indicated should not be taken. But if no such reason is known, I think that course should be adopted.[98]

The communication by Governor Bradford was effective, because on April 16 Stanton promised canal officials that he would issue an order within 24 hours for the restoration of the government-held canal boats to the company. The company was to receive compensation for those boats that had been destroyed or injured. Some 36 boats had been sent down the Potomac to the Rappahannock and they would be returned as soon as possible. Six or eight of the boats had been sunk with stone, and if practicable, they were to be raised from the river bottom and returned to the company. Twenty-four boats at Georgetown were to be released at once. About 40 boats which had been released earlier and which had been taken again by Army officers for the transportation of government stores from various points on the canal to Alexandria were to be unloaded and released immediately. There was also hope for the restoration of the Potomac Aqueduct to canal purposes.[99]

Secretary Stanton saw that a General Order was issued by Lorenzo Thomas, Adjutant General of the United States. General Order No. 44 dated April 21, 1862, directed that

> All the lock-houses, boats, scows and other property belonging to the Chesapeake and Ohio Canal Company, on the line of said canal, now held, used or occupied by the United States officers or troops, will be forthwith given up and restored to the President of the said company. All officers of the Army will respect Alfred Spates, Esq., as President of the said company, and are hereby prohibited from interfering in any manner with him in the management of the canal; but are directed to give such aid and assistance as is consistent with the good of the service, in keeping it in repair, and removing all restrictions which have been imposed upon the boats navigating the said canal. The President of the said Canal Company is authorized to give all passes that may be required to be used on the canal, subject to the approval of the Commander of the District.[100]

---

[97] Greene to Ringgold, April 11, 1862, ltrs. Recd., C & O Co.
[98] Lincoln to Stanton, April 15, 1862, in Basler, *Collected Works of Lincoln*, Vol. V, 191.
[99] Ringgold to Greene, April 16, 1862, Ltrs. Sent, C & O Co. A copy of the "Statement of Boats & Names of Owners &c.—Held by the U.S. Government from Books of the Quartermaster, U.S.A., Washington, D.C., April 17, 1861 [1862]," may be seen in Appendix B.
[100] General Order No. 44, April 21, 1862, in Ltrs. Recd., C & O Co.

On the same day that the order was issued, the *National Intelligencer* reported that:

> The canal continues in fine order, and boats with flour, grain, wood, and limestone arrive hourly. Our information tonight justifies the belief that on Monday next we shall welcome the first boats from Cumberland bringing large cargoes of coal; and, as the Aqueduct is now changed to a bridge, Georgetown must have the full benefit of the trade.[101]

Several weeks earlier, the board, in an effort to stimulate the coal trade, had granted permission to J. E. Reeside to experiment with steam-propelled boats in the transportation of coal.[102]

Meanwhile, Superintendent Jacob Masters of the Williamsport Division had reported in early April that while there was plenty of water for navigation, it would be wise to repair the damage done to Dam No. 5 by the Confederates in December 1861. The repairs, which could be undertaken as soon as the stage of the Potomac fell, were to be made either by building upon the foundations of the old crib, which were still standing, or by closing the space between the new masonry dam and the abutments of the old.[103] The canal board authorized Masters to commence the project at an opportune time and allocated the necessary funds.[104]

Despite the shortage of boats, traffic on the canal quickly increased. Tolls collected for April reached $4,637, a figure five times the March total.[105] During the last week of April, however, the canal was damaged heavily as torrential rains drenched the Potomac Valley, causing the river to rise rapidly and crest at Dam No. 4. Two residents of Williamsport complained that this was the

> 7th high water within the last 18 months. After every high water, we have had the unwelcome and astonishing news that the planks at the stop lock [at] Dam No. 4 had either not been put in, or if put in had gone out. Invariably has this been the case for the last 18 months or two years. The last high water proves that with all the sad experiences for that length of time with a cost of not less than $50,000 to the canal but no improvement has been made, for the report is now that several of the plank gave way, and the rushing water has done its usual work of in some places filling up and others sweeping away its embankment.

The two Williamsport residents went on to castigate the canal board for its inefficient and shortsighted repair policy:

> It is said the Repair can be made in two weeks but if the two weeks prove to be such weeks as it generally takes at that point, four instead of two will come nearer the time. Now the question is can there be no remedy for this intolerable evil, will the Board remain quiet and let this state of things continue until the canal for the want of means to keep up these continued repairs fail & become entirely worthless. We hope not. We hope and pray that your Honbl. Board will appoint a committee to investigate this matter, and see if some means cannot be devised that will effectually resist the weight of water at said stop lock which has proved as destructive to canal interest for the last two years. We say emphatically it can be done and at little cost. We have said that the canal has lost $50,000

---

[101] Washington *National Intelligencer*, April 21, 1862.
[102] *Proceedings of the President and Board of Directors*, K, 287–288.
[103] Masters to Board of Directors, April 8, 1862, Ltrs. Recd., C & O Co.
[104] *Thirty-Fifth Annual Report* (1863), 4. The cost of repairs to Dam No. 5 totaled $3,338.58 for 1862.
[105] *Ibid*, 8.

by the continued disasters by the giving away of the Stop Lock. The basis of our calculation is this. 7 times the level's damaged that required $2,000 to make full repair, $14,000—average the loss of toll each time, 12 days @ $500 per day, $42,000—add $14,000 cost of repair—and we have $56,000 to the company at this point.

Furthermore, it was charged that such disasters had cost the canal its flour trade, two-thirds of which had been taken over by the Baltimore and Ohio Railroad during the preceding decade. Millers had complained that they could not rely on the canal for ten days at a time, and they had been compelled to find a more reliable channel of transportation.[106]

When news of the damage caused by the freshet reached Cumberland, A. C. Greene, one of the canal directors and an agent of the Borden Mining Company, exploded:

> The concurrence of circumstances against the resumption of canal trade this spring are positively infernal. Not only is the canal deprived of revenue, but the trade itself is imperiled by the untoward events. I have great fears that the largest and most important buyers of coal will despair of getting anything from us this year.

Already the Broad Top Company of Pennsylvania was "straining everything to retain" its foothold in the District cities' coal market that it had secured the previous year. At the time of the difficulties he had some 1,800 tons of coal en route to Georgetown, and nearly 7,000 tons ready for loading at the Cumberland wharves. Greene trusted that every effort would be made to restore navigation as soon as possible, as much depended on the boatmen's ability to deliver the coal in early May. As the Baltimore and Ohio was still out of operation, the canal was the sole outlet to market for the Cumberland coal.[107]

The superintendents of the Williamsport and Antietam Divisions pushed the repair crews hard to shore up the battered embankments and clear out the obstructions. Continued rains added to their difficulties, but by May 8 water was readmitted to these divisions from the feeders at Dam Nos. 3 and 4, and the entire canal was again open to navigation.[108]

Traffic on the canal increased rapidly, but on the night of May 14 heavy rains fell on the upper reaches of the Potomac's watershed, causing a rapid rise on the river above Dam No. 5. The work programs to repair the damage inflicted on the dam by the Confederates in December 1861 had not been completed, and the high water caused considerable damage to that structure. Encouraged by the presence of President Spates who had rushed to the scene of the latest disaster, the work crews were able to effect temporary repairs and prevent any interruption to navigation at this critical period.[109]

In May 1862 General Stonewall Jackson launched his famous lightning like offensive in the Shenandoah Valley. Following defeats at McDowell, Front Royal, and Winchester, the battle-weary Federals fled toward the Potomac. Thus the shifting tide of war in the Shenandoah at a time when there was heavy traffic on the canal again threatened commerce on the waterway.[110]

---

[106] Embrey and Son to Dellinger and Greene to Ringgold, April 26, 1862, Ltrs. Recd., C&O Co. The railroad had made a determined effort to win the flour trade away from the canal in the 1840s. Nevertheless, the flour trade continued to be one of the larger though erratic sources of revenue. From 14,880 tons in 1843, it rose to 25,761 tons in 1851 and fell to 11,087 tons in 1860. In 1861 it had dropped to 7,067 tons, and after a slight recovery to 7,340 tons in 1862 and 8,566 in 1863, it declined to 5,962 tons and 5,383 tons in 1864 and 1865 respectively, Sanderlin, *Great National Project*, 217.
[107] Greene to Ringgold, April 29, 1862, Ltrs. Recd., C & O Co.
[108] Spates to Ringgold, May 2, 1862, Ltrs. Recd., C & O Co.
[109] Greene to Ringgold, May 15, 1862, Ltrs. Recd., C & O Co.
[110] Bearss, "1862 Brings Hard Times," 442–443.

In May 26 most of the Union troop crossed to the Maryland side of the river at Williamsport. The soldiers and their wagons crossed the river on a ferry and marched over the bridge spanning the canal. One brigade, however, recrossed the Potomac at Jameson's Ferry, three miles above Dam No. 4. The recent rains had swollen the river and made the crossings a laborious effort.

Rebel cavalry units hounded the rear guard of the Union army as far as Martinsburg, where on the 27th; they captured a large amount of supplies. The next day, two squadrons of the 2nd Virginia Cavalry made a forced reconnaissance to within one mile of the Potomac, but Union batteries, emplaced near the canal at Williamsport went into action and forced the Confederates to withdraw. On the 29th, several Confederate forces in the area united under Brigadier General Charles W. Winder and carried out Jackson's instructions to attack with artillery the Federal troops of Brigadier General Rufus Saxton posted on Bolivar Heights covering the approaches to Harpers Ferry. However, word soon reached Jackson that a strong Union column under Major General James Shields was advancing westward from the Manassas area toward the Blue Ridge, while a powerful force under Major General John C. Fremont was approaching across the mountains from South Branch. As the two Federal divisions would sever his line of communications, Jackson pulled his men back from Bolivar Heights and retired rapidly up the Shenandoah Valley before the jaws of the trap snapped shut.[111]

Following the Confederate withdrawal, the Union armies quickly reestablished control of the south bank of the Potomac. By June 4th, the Federals were again in possession of Martinsburg, Charles Town, and Winchester. A survey showed that the Confederates had done little damage to the Baltimore and Ohio during their brief stay in the area, and it was predicted that through trains would again be running east and west out of Martinsburg within one week.[112]

The company stockholders were informed by President Spates at their annual meeting on June 2 that the heavy spring rains and the shortage of boats had retarded business activity on the waterway since the resumption of navigation in mid-April. The entire trade up to May 31 did not comprise one full month of normal operations. All told, only 25,259 tons of coal had been shipped from Cumberland, yielding a meager $18,449.86 in toll revenues.[113]

Heavy rains in early June which caused the Potomac to flood hampered the Union army's efforts to cross and recross the river. On the night of June 4 the railroad bridge at Harpers Ferry was swept away along with lesser important railroad bridges and trestles in the area, thus severing the line of the Baltimore and Ohio. Until the river crested and fell, it would be impossible for the Union trains and remaining columns to cross. To aid in the crossing, a steam tug was sent up the canal from Georgetown and placed in the river at Harpers Ferry. On the 5th the rains ceased and the river began to recede and by the evening of June 8 the last of the Federal wagons got back over to the Maryland side of the Potomac at Williamsport.[114]

The June flood also caused extensive damage to the canal. On June 2, two days before the Harpers Ferry Bridge was destroyed, a break occurred in the waterway near the Antietam Ironworks. The break was so sudden that a work scow was swept through the breach and smashed. First reports indicated that it would take about one week to repair the break, but President Spates urged the division superintendent to turn out as large a force as possible including available boatmen, and to institute round-the-clock working parties.[115]

---

[111] O. R, Series I, Vol. XII, pt. 1, 530–535, 606–607, 626–640, 707, 730, 738, pt. 3, 530.
[112] *Ibid*, Series I, Vol. XII, pt. 1, 539–541, 813–814.
[113] *Thirty-Fourth Annual Report* (1862), 5–6.
[114] O. R., Series I, Vol. XII, pt. 1, 540–542, pt. 3, 304, 323, 342, 361–362.
[115] Benton to Ringgold, June 3, 1862, and Spates to Ringgold, June 4, 1862, Ltrs. Recd., C & O Co.

In a letter on June 12, A. C. Greene urged President Spates to rush the repairs on the Antietam Division, because the flood damage to the Baltimore and Ohio and Confederate demolitions at Martinsburg had cut off all transportation of coal to the District Cities. It was imperative that coal shipments be resumed quickly on the canal so that demand could be met. As flooding had damaged the Pennsylvania rail network, there was the prospect of a heavy demand for Cumberland coal and it was of great importance that the waterway be ready to grasp the opportunity.[116]

When there still was no through navigation on the canal by June 21, Greene complained that "it is 1000 pities" that "we are in no condition to meet this call for coal." He trusted that repairs were being pushed on the Antietam Division and that attention was also being given to Dam No. 5. Unless a close check was kept on the pool above that structure, there would be insufficient water for navigation during the dry summer months.[117]

By the end of June, construction crews had a new railroad bridge in operation across the Potomac at Harpers Ferry. However, the canal above Dam No. 3 was still dry. As a result, the receipts from tolls, which had amounted to $11,607.72 in May, had fallen to $3,813.61 in June.[118]

On the evening of June 28, water was admitted to the canal above Harpers Ferry, and it was predicted that boats would start arriving at Cumberland by July 2. However, as work had dragged on at Dam No. 5, the pool behind that structure was too low to supply water to the sections of the canal between Dam Nos. 4 and 5, thereby delaying navigation.[119] A heavy rain during the night of July 1 eased the low-water problem but created another by washing a "good amount of sand" back into the canal at Dam No. 4.[120]

Meanwhile, the canal company was continuing to receive distressing news of the effect of the war on the mills along the waterway. On June 26, the board was informed that the Columbia Mills in Georgetown, which had not been in operation for some eighteen months, had been sold by Boyce and Taylor to Herr and Welch. Despite the dismal outlook, the company negotiated a 20-year water lease to the new company.[121]

Work on getting a suitable depth of water in the canal throughout its entire length continued to drag during the summer months. The division superintendents and their crews appeared to be more inefficient than at any time in the previous history of the canal. By July 24 a troublesome breach above Hancock had been repaired, and work on Dam No. 5 had progressed to the point that boats laden with coal were now able for the first time since July 2 to make the run from Cumberland to Georgetown. Accordingly, toll collections for July showed an increase over June of nearly 50 percent to $7,130.73.[122]

More trouble befell the canal on August 4 when a leak in Dam No. 6 caused an "utter failure" of navigation at that point. Superintendent Lowe reported that same day that one of the leaks had been located, and that the water in the pool was slowly rising. Because of the severe drought, it would have been helpful if the steam pump at the South Branch, which had been vandalized by a Confederate band the previous winter, had been repaired, but no funds were available for such work. Lowe, one of the most efficient superintendents, commenced the construction of a crib to prevent the bank at the dam from washing, and navigation was commenced the following day.[123]

---

[116] Greene to Ringgold, June 12, 1862, Ltrs. Recd., C & O Co.
[117] *Ibid*, June 21, 1862, Ltrs. Recd., C & O Co.
[118] *Thirty-Fifth Annual Report* (1863), 8.
[119] Greene to Ringgold, July 2, 1862, Ltrs. Recd., C & O Co.
[120] Benton to Ringgold, July 2, 1862, Ltrs. Recd., C & O Co.
[121] *Proceedings of the President and Board of Directors*, K, 290–291, 298–299, 305.
[122] Spates to Ringgold, July 24, 1862, Ltrs. Recd., C & O Co., and *Thirty-Fifth Annual Report* (1863), 8.
[123] Greene to Ringgold, August 4, 1862, and Spates to Ringgold, August 26, 1862, Ltrs. Recd., C & O Co.

It was reported that the first boats in a week arrived at Cumberland on August 6. Nevertheless, canal officials were distressed that no rain had fallen in the Potomac Valley for nearly a month. As the drought continued to worsen, it was feared that low water would soon terminate through navigation on the canal. If no rain came, Greene hoped that there would soon be a big "battle with substantial victory on our side."[124]

Canal officials, including Clerk Ringgold and Director Greene, soon became irritated with the inefficiency and mismanagement of the canal by the division superintendents. On August 8, Ringgold observed:

> The frequent interruption in the navigation of the canal is very discouraging and from mismanagement or some other cause, has been worse this season than at any former period. Unless some remedy can be speedily adopted, I apprehend the most unfavorable results.[125]

Angered by reports that navigation had been delayed again by sand bars near Point of Rocks, Greene wrote on August 11:

> There has been no real through navigation on the Canal this year—that is no boat, I believe, has been able to make a round trip without detention. Whatever may be the excuse for the troubles above Harpers Ferry, there can certainly be none whatever, for neglecting the removal of sand bars from the section at Point of Rocks until this time. That work most surely could have been done while the canal was idle from the damage at Dam No. 4 and the Supt. Of that division [Monocacy] is to blame for putting off attention to his work that length of time.

Greene was further incensed by the fact that the work at Dam No, 6 had been delayed by a lack of hands. As there were about 80 canal boats tied up in the vicinity, he was convinced that at least a dozen boatmen could be found who were willing to work on the dam for cash wages. Unless there was a speedy reform in the company management, Greene threatened to resign as he had no "idea of being disgraced by such mismanagement."[126]

The following day Greene reported to Ringgold that he had received word that the boats, after being detained while the bars were removed, had started arriving at Georgetown. At the same time, there were rumors that a lack of water at Dam No. 4 had stopped through navigation. As no word of confirmation had been received from Superintendent Masters, Greene had informed the coal shippers to ignore the rumors. Several railroad passengers were now overheard to say that below Harpers Ferry, where the canal was visible from the trains, there was no water in the ditch. While these stories circulated, the coal operators were compelled to keep an "expensive force in idleness expecting the arrival of boats hourly." The Baltimore and Ohio had likewise kept locomotives and cars standing by "at large expense" expecting the boats. All this was taking place because division superintendents were ignoring orders of the directors to report any stoppages which occurred in their jurisdictions. Such mismanagement as had been witnessed that summer demanded an investigation, and he recommended that all the division superintendents be summoned to Washington for questioning.[127]

---

[124] Greene to Ringgold, August 6, 1862, Ltrs. Recd., C & O Co.
[125] Ringgold to Greene, August 8, 1862, Ltrs. Sent, C & O Co.
[126] Greene to Ringgold, August 11, 1862, Ltrs. Recd., C & O Co.
[127] Ibid, August 12, 1862, Ltrs. Recd., C & O Co.

The military also was becoming irritated with the inefficiency of several division superintendents and the pro-Southern sympathies of some canal employees. The post commander at Point of Rocks, Captain R. C. Bomford, complained on August 28 that Superintendent George Spates of the Monocacy Division was derelict in his duties. The entrance and chamber of Guard Lock No. 3 had been allowed to fill in with sediment, thus causing delays to heavily-loaded barges passing down the canal. The locks on the division were deteriorating badly, and the waste weirs were not fit for use. The towpath bridge across McGill's Ford just above Point of Rocks was so unsafe that every team that passed over it was in danger of being drowned. The towpath, especially at the high embankment at Callico Rocks, was in such disrepair that a rise in the water level of 2 or 3 inches above normal would cause a breach. The carpenters on the division had been kept busy at menial labor instead of repairing bridges and other structures. Moreover, Spates had employed two lock-keepers and one crew boss who were reportedly disloyal. The only way to weed out treason and inefficiency on the Monocacy Division, Bomford asserted, was for the company to fire George Spates and replace him with "a loyal man" so that "we can feel safe in passing him through our lines."[128]

After reviewing the communications from Bomford, the board instructed Clerk Ringgold to request further information from the officer. On September 4, Ringgold drafted the following reply to Bomford on behalf of the board:

> It is the earnest desire as it is the duty of this Board to see that no disloyal person is employed in any part of the work under their charge.
>
> You make a distinct charge of your own personal knowledge against one so employed. We must have his name, not strike in the dark, and we call upon you as an officer and citizen to furnish the name without delay. You must be quite aware that to suppress the name under such circumstances will be conniving at the offence. If there are others whose names have been furnished to you with such information as will justify you in making distinct charges we desire to have those names and also the witnesses on whose statements the charge is based.[129]

Before Bomford could answer the board's request for further information, the canal was once again to become a theater of active military operations. During the last week of June and on July 1, General Robert E. Lee, who had taken charge of the Army of Northern Virginia on June 1, had turned on and attacked McClellan's Army of the Potomac, then closing in on Richmond from the southeast. After compelling McClellan to retreat to the cover of a fortified camp at Harrison's Landing on the James River, Lee sent Jackson with three divisions to Orange, Virginia, to watch Major General John Pope's newly-constituted Army of Virginia. Following the defeat of Banks' corps of Pope's army at Cedar Mountain on August 9 by Jackson, Lee moved his forces to join the victorious Confederate divisions and set the stage for another Union defeat at the Battle of Second Manassas on August 29–30. The bluecoats fell back into the formidable defenses covering the approaches to Washington, and several days later, on September 2, the exposed Union force at Winchester under Brigadier General Julius White fell back to Harpers Ferry.[130]

News of the Confederate offensive had important repercussions for the belligerents, as well as the canal company. When President Lincoln on August 4 ordered a draft of 300,000 militia to serve for nine months, the company appealed to Secretary Stanton to obtain exemptions for

---

[128] Bomford to Board of Directors, August 28, 1862, Ltrs. Recd., C & O Co.
[129] Ringgold to Bomford, September 4, 1862, Ltrs. Recd., C & O Co., and *Proceedings of the President and Board of Directors*, K, 309.
[130] O. R., Series I, Vol. XII, pt. 3, 811.

its employees and the boatmen as the draft would have serious effects on the business operations of the canal.[131]

More ominous for the canal company was Lee's determination on September 3 to carry the war north of the Potomac. The Army of Northern Virginia was put in motion toward Loudoun County. On the morning of the 4th, a Confederate battery unlimbered its guns on Ball's Bluff and fired several volleys at a passing canal boat. General McClellan, who had been charged with repelling the Rebel invasion of Maryland, advised his superiors at the War Department that shelling canal boats "is an old amusement of the rebels; it is probably a pretty strong proof that they do not intend to cross at Edwards Ferry."[132]

At Leesburg, Lee's lead division, under Major General D. H. Hill, made preparations for the offensive across the Potomac. One brigade was dispatched to the river across from Berlin to attack with artillery any Baltimore and Ohio trains that might be passing. With two brigades deployed in line of battle, Hill approached the river at White's Ford. This crossing of the Potomac and the nearby Monocacy Aqueduct were guarded by men of the 1st Potomac Home Guard Regiment and the 87th Ohio. The Union pickets quickly fled, and by nightfall Hill's combat-ready veterans had established a bridgehead almost without firing a shot.[133]

Before allowing his troops to bivouac, Hill charged a detail with the task of stopping traffic on the canal and taking measures to make it easier for the main body of troops to cross the ditch. Near the Monocacy Aqueduct, the trunk could be crossed by a few pivot bridges and under passed by the White's Ford Culvert. Since these structures would turn into bottlenecks for the Army of Northern Virginia, General Hill had a fatigue party wreck the Little Monocacy Culvert and drain the Seven-Mile Level. The berm and towpath banks were cut down, the prism corduroyed, and the artillery and trains started rolling across. The next morning, on the 5th, Stonewall Jackson's corps forded the Potomac, crossed the canal, and pushed for Frederick.[134]

Meanwhile, the men from Hill's division charged with wrecking key canal structures in the area were at work. Thomas Walter, the tender at Lock No. 27 who had worked for the canal company for 30 year and was one of the men believed by Captain Bomford to be disloyal to the Union cause, pled with General Hill not to destroy the aqueduct or the lock. If the Confederates intended to stop navigation on the waterway, he informed the general that it would be easier to cut down the banks than blow up the masonry structures. General Hill disagreed, and for awhile the discussion between the officer and the lock tender became so heated that bystanders feared that Walter would be arrested.[135]

After consulting with his chiefs of ordnance and engineers, Hill learned that in the division there were not enough tools or spare powder to insure the destruction of the Monocacy Aqueduct, so he ordered his demolition team to concentrate on Lock No. 27. A hole was drilled into the masonry of the lock and a small charge of powder was detonated, causing slight damage to the structure. Having breached the Little Monocacy Culvert, cut down the banks at several points, and burned several canal boats trapped on the Seven-Mile Level, Hill recalled his troops on the evening of September 5 and proceeded toward Frederick to join Jackson. During the next several

---

[131] Ringgold to Stanton, August 21, 1862, Ltrs. Sent, C & O Co. Events were to calm the anxieties of the canal officials, because the draft was never put into effect. Long, *Civil War, Day by Day*, 247.
[132] O. R., Series I, Vol. XIX, pt. 2, 175.
[133] *Ibid*, pt. 1, 1019, pt. 2, 144–145.
[134] *Ibid*, pt. 1, 952.
[135] Petition to Board of Directors, October 14, 1862, Ltrs. Recd., C&O Co. When the canal company later moved to discharge Walter for collaborating with the enemy, a petition was sent to the directors from his neighbors asking that no disciplinary action be taken against him because of his successful effort to save the Monocacy Aqueduct from destruction..

days, other units of Lee's Army of Northern Virginia crossed the Potomac and canal at White's Ford.[136]

On September 9 at Frederick, Lee divided his army into three major units and commenced operations to move against the strong Union force under Colonel Dixon Miles that was holding the Harpers Ferry–Martinsburg area. By eliminating Miles' command, Lee would be able to supply his army via the Shenandoah Valley. Accordingly, Jackson moved out with his corps, crossed South Mountain, passed through Boonsboro, turned southwestward, and struck for the Potomac. Major General Lafayette McLaws with two divisions advanced across Pleasant Valley, and took position on Maryland Heights which commanded Harpers Ferry on the north. The division under Major General John G. Walker was to destroy the Monocacy Aqueduct, recross the Potomac at Cheek's Ford, and occupy Loudoun Heights. With the remainder of his troops, Lee would cover Jackson's column, taking position to hold the South Mountain gaps.[137]

Reaching the Monocacy Aqueduct just before midnight on September 9, Walker's division quickly drove off the thin line of Union pickets holding the aqueduct. Fatigue parties were organized, tools were passed out, and men put to work drilling holes for placing charges to wreck each of the seven arches of this aqueduct. After several hours, Walker's chief engineer reported little progress, complaining that the drills were extremely dull while the masonry was of "extraordinary solidity and massiveness." To demolish the aqueduct would take days not hours. As this would ruin Lee's plan for the attack against Harpers Ferry, the fatigue parties were recalled.[138]

That same night a Union force moved into the area, took possession of the aqueduct, and placed artillery to command the approaches to that structure as well as Cheek's Ford. Surprised by the Union advance, Walker determined to recross the Potomac farther upstream at Point of Rocks on the night of September 10. The crossing was carried out with much difficulty, owing to the destruction of the pivot bridge over the canal at Lock No. 28 and the steepness of the river banks.[139]

The Confederate invasion of Maryland had a disastrous effect on the operations of the canal and its ability to carry provisions and coal to the Union armies and the civilian population of the District cities. The Washington *Evening Star* reported on September 12:

> Canal navigation is suspended beyond a point twenty miles from here—that is, at Seneca Dam. From that point up, for from thirty to forty miles, there is no water in the canal, the Confederate forces having drawn it off a week ago, by blowing up a culvert, when they first crossed into Maryland—hence supplies for the army cannot be sent up by canal further than Seneca.
>
> This suspension of navigation with the up country of course cuts off arrivals of flour and grain from the fine grain-growing country in Maryland and Virginia lying near the Potomac. The market here, therefore, is very unsettled, and the stock of flour on hand is held at considerably higher figures by wholesale dealers. The only sales since the suspension is of high grades extra, in small lots, at from $7 to $8, according to quality, mostly at the intermediate rate of $7.50. The government contract closed last week was taken at rates considerably below these figures.

---

[136] Spates to Ringgold, September 13, 1862, Ltrs. Recd., C&O Co. In this letter, Spates wrote that the damage could be repaired in two or three weeks with an adequate force and the necessary funds. He had made arrangements with a gentleman to put a large force of horses, carts, and hands to work on the repairs, but since the Rebels were holding the river at Point of Rocks nothing could be done
[137] Bearss, "1862 Brings Hard Times," 450.
[138] O. R., Series I, Vol. XIX, pt. 1, 912–913.
[139] *Ibid.*

There is a fair stock of wheat in millers' hands, and they are buying the limited quantity brought by wagons at rates ranging from $1.35 to $1.40, for red. Any considerable lots of good red would command $1.37 to $1.40, and prime $1.40 to $1.45 per bushel.

In corm, nothing doing, there being no arrivals: Prices have advanced from 2 to 5 cents this week, and good white would fetch from 70 to 75 cents per bushel. Oats are more active, with further supplies from Baltimore, fetching from 45 to 50 cents for good new, but for heavy old oats 60 cts. are paid. Some of the very light new oats sell as low as 35 to 40 cents per bushel measure.

The coal trade from Cumberland is of course entirely cut off, perhaps for the season. A fair supply had already been bought forward.

The harbor of Georgetown looks very active, with numerous steamers moving about, as well as other vessels, mostly in government trade.

Hay in bales sells at $20 per ton, an advance of $1 within a week.[140]

Meanwhile, Lee's forces were converging on the Union troops holding Martinsburg and Harpers Ferry. On the 11th, Jackson's columns passed through Williamsport and crossed the canal and the Potomac at Light's Ford, and on the 12th forced General White's troops to evacuate Martinsburg and retire to Harpers Ferry. After closing in and investing the 11,000-man Union garrison at Harpers Ferry for two days, the Confederates accepted the surrender of the surrounded Federals on September 15. Meanwhile, McClellan's bluecoats had forced the Southern forces to abandon Turner's and Fox's Gaps on South Mountain, and General Lee fell back behind Antietam Creek, thus setting the stage for the bloody Battle of Antietam fought on September 17.[141]

Shortly after the fighting began, General McClellan dispatched Captain Charles H. Russell with his company of the 1st Maryland Cavalry to Williamsport to burn the pivot bridge across the canal at Lock No. 44 and to destroy the Conococheague Aqueduct in an effort to cut one of Lee's avenues of retreat. With the aid of some Pennsylvania militiamen who were holding the town, Russell's men destroyed the pivot bridge, organized demolition teams, and burned eleven boats, nine of which were loaded with coal, that had been forced to tie up at Williamsport. Unable to materially damage the sturdy masonry of the aqueduct, Russell's troops returned to the battlefield and the Pennsylvanians withdrew to Hagerstown. By the end of the fighting in the area, some of the coal from the fired boats was still smoking, and a group of local citizens extinguished the fires, salvaging what coal remained.[142]

On the day following the bloody event at Antietam, the two armies lay exhausted in their positions. Then under the cover of darkness on the 19th, the Confederates retired across the Potomac into Virginia at Boteler's Ford near Shepherdstown. Three brigades formed the rear guard and remained in line on the Maryland side until the crossing was accomplished.[143]

When McClellan learned of the Confederate withdrawal, he sent Major General Fitz John Porter's V Corps to pursue Lee's battered army. When Porter reached the river, he found that the Rebels were holding the southern bank and defending the fords with 44 artillery pieces. Determining to clear the fords and, if possible, cross the Potomac and capture the guns, a strong force of skirmishers advanced and took position along the embankment of the towpath side of the canal, from which the water had been withdrawn earlier, and along the river bank. Covered by the

---

[140] Washington *Evening Star*, September 12, 1862.
[141] Bearss, "1862 brings Hard Times", 451.
[142] Miller to Ringgold, October 3, 1862, Greene to Ringgold, December 2, 1862, and Masters to Board of Directors, February 8, 1864, Ltrs. Recd., C & O Co.
[143] O. R., Series I, Vol. XIX, 986.

fire of the sharpshooters and a heavy artillery barrage, the Federals stormed across the Potomac at Boteler's Ford, scaled the heights beyond, and captured five cannon. The next day, the Confederates under Jackson counter-attacked and drove the Union troops back through Shepherdstown and across the Potomac. Most of the retreating men used the ford while some walked across the river on the top of the Potomac Mills dam. As the Union armies fled across the river, a large contingent of the Rebel line advanced to the river bank, where some took cover in the burned-out Potomac Mill. A steady fire was maintained, inflicting a number of casualties upon the retiring enemy. Once across the river, the Federals deployed a line behind the canal embankment until they were relieved on the 21st. The Rebels remained on the field until nightfall, when upon being relieved by cavalry units, they marched to rejoin the main body.[144]

Meanwhile, the Confederate cavalry leader, Major General James E. B. "Jeb" Stuart, had been ordered by General Lee to take several cavalry and infantry units and recross the Potomac into Maryland at Williamsport, thus creating a useful diversion by exposing McClellan's flank. Under the cover of darkness on the 19th some of the troops forded the Potomac above the town, while a contingent crossed the river at Williamsport and put to flight some Union pickets. A working party was organized and quickly opened a good road under the Conococheague Aqueduct. By passing under the canal, the confederates moved out and took position on the ridges beyond Williamsport before daybreak. On the 20th, the Rebels attempted to expand their bridgehead, but after encountering a heavy force of Union cavalry converging on the town, they withdrew at dark across the Potomac. During their one-day occupation of Williamsport, the Southern cavalry burned one canal boat, *Independence*, and the gates of Lock 44, and wrecked Lockhouse No. 44.[145]

Following the Confederate withdrawal from Williamsport into Virginia, Superintendent Masters reported to Clerk Ringgold on September 22:

> We have been cut off from the outside world until yesterday so that we had no opportunity to send or receive anything by mail since the 6th of Sept. The damage done the canal at this place [Williamsport] by the recent military operations will amount to $2,000 beside the loss of eleven canal boats burnt…If necessary the damage here can be repaired in a week's time; the most serious is the burning of the lock gates.[146]

Immediately following the Battle of Antietam and the Confederate withdrawal into Virginia, General McClellan proposed to establish a supply depot for his army near Harpers Ferry. Consequently, it would be vital to reopen for trade as soon as possible the canal and the railroad. On September 21, McClellan's chief quartermaster, Lieutenant Colonel Rufus Ingalls, wrote Quartermaster General Meigs requesting that orders be issued for the repair of the waterway. When it was reported that repairs could not be commenced as long as the Confederates occupied portions of the southern bank of the Potomac and kept the canal under artillery fire, McClellan promised full protection to the repair crews and to the boats, once the waterway was reopened. As soon as navigation was resumed, all the small steamers plying the canal were to be sent to Harpers Ferry.[147]

---

[144] *Ibid,* 338–340, 344–349, 351–352, 830–833, 912–913, 957, 982, 986, 989–990, 1001–1004. For a more complete study of the fighting in the aftermath of the Battle of Antietam, see John F. Luzader, "Historic Sites, Shepherdstown, W. Va." (NPS Mss., 1963), 4–19.
[145] Masters to Board of Directors, February 8, 1864, Ltrs. Recd., C & O Co., and Bearss, "1862 brings Hard Times", 452.
[146] Masters to Ringgold, September 22, 1862, Ltrs. Recd., C & O Co.
[147] O. R., Series I, Vol. XIX, pt. 2, 339–340, 342–343.

By late September, Lee's Army of Northern Virginia had pulled back into the Winchester area, thus enabling the canal repairs to proceed without hindrance. The Washington *Evening Star* reported on the 26th that:

> There is some hope now that the Chesapeake and Ohio Canal may be rendered navigable again for the fall trade. It is found that the damage done it by the Confederate forces was not so great as had been apprehended ... therefore the repairs may be easily made if the line is kept free of the enemy.[148]

McClellan, on September 30, ordered the formation of large fatigue parties to assist canal officials in effecting repairs. On October 1, a 65-man detail reported to Superintendent George W. Spates of the Monocacy Division. The soldiers were put to work closing the breach at the Little Monocacy Culvert, thus freeing the regular division repair crews to patch the masonry at Lock No. 27. The military detail was enlarged to a force of 150 on October 7, and Spates reported on the 14th that his division was again ready for navigation.[149]

During the first week of October, President Spates inspected the canal from Williamsport to Cumberland. He was to see that initial reports of heavy damage to the Antietam and Williamsport Divisions had been exaggerated. Except for the actions of the Maryland and Pennsylvania troops, there would have been little destruction at Williamsport. On the Antietam Division, the only damage done by the invaders was the burning of the gates at Guard Locks Nos. 3 and 4. Although the Confederates had burned all the railroad bridges between Sir Johns Run and South Branch, there was no damage to the canal above Williamsport. Of more immediate concern was the drought in the Potomac Valley that had reduced the depth of the river at Cumberland to three feet.[150]

Early in October the Confederates staged two raids designed to harass McClellan's build-up and wreak havoc on the Union supply lines. Col. John D. Imboden and 900 men left their base at Camp Lee in Hardy County, and after surprising a Union patrol at Hanging Rock, they attacked the entrenched camp manned by Company K, 54th Pennsylvania, at the mouth of Little Cacapon on the 4th. After forcing the Federals to surrender, the Baltimore and Ohio Bridge across the Little Cacapon was burned, along with the encampment. A cavalry battalion was sent across the Potomac to cut off the escape of the Federals posted at the Paw Paw Railroad Tunnel. Moving down the canal towpath, the Rebel horsemen forced the encampment of Company B, 54th Pennsylvania, located some 500 yards from Paw Paw Tunnel to surrender. While the Confederates were destroying the captured camp and equipment, they learned that the guard at their base camp near Cacapon Bridge had been scattered by Union cavalry. This news caused Imboden to abandon his plans to destroy the railroad bridge across South branch and withdraw from the area.[151]

In the early morning hours of October 10, General "Jeb" Stuart crossed the Potomac at McCoy's Ferry with 1,800 horse soldiers and four guns. The sixteen Union pickets in the area were driven in so rapidly that they were cut off from their reserve and were unable to report the attack. Informed that the Confederates were fording the river by a long-time local resident, Launcelot Jacques, Captain Thomas Logan immediately moved his troops camped at Green Springs Furnace to mount, but Stuart's horsemen had already pushed northward toward Chambersburg.

---

[148] Washington *Evening Star*, September 26, 1862.
[149] Spates to Ringgold, September 30, October 6, 14, 1862, Ltrs. Recd., C & O Co., and *Proceedings of the President and Board of Directors*, K, 310–311.
[150] Spates to Ringgold, October 6, 1862, Ltrs. Recd., C & O Co. Also see, Benton to Ringgold, October 18, 1862, Ltrs. Recd., C & O Co. On October 9, the canal company requested an army detail to help repair the Williamsport Division. *Proceedings of the President and Board of Directors*, K, 310–311.
[151] O. R., Series I, Vol. XIX, pt. 2, 16–25, 631.

As the Rebel objective was to destroy the machine shops and depot at that town, they did not attempt to damage the canal. After committing their destructive acts at Chambersburg on the 11th, the Rebels turned back toward Virginia and determined to cross the canal and Potomac at White's Ford before the Union troops, numbering between 4,000 and 5,000, at Poolesville and Mouth of Monocacy could intercept them.[152] Although a battalion of the 99th Pennsylvania was posted on a precipitous quarry bluff overlooking the crossing, the bluecoats, after receiving word of the Confederate advance, quickly abandoned their position and marched eastward down the towpath to Weedon's Ford, thus permitting the Rebels a secure crossing of the river.[153]

While Stuart's Chambersburg Raid increased the growing dissatisfaction of government officials with the performance of General McClellan, the canal suffered no damage at the hands of the Rebel raiders. On October 14, water was readmitted to the Monocacy Division. Although the damage inflicted on the canal by the Confederates during their Antietam Campaign had been repaired, there would be no through navigation on the canal until the drought was broken.[154]

Heavy rains during the latter part of October caused the Potomac to rise. However, the high water caused a serious breach at Dam No. 5 on November 4, because the new masonry dam was still only partially completed as a result of the recent military activities in the valley. Thus, there was not enough water in the pool to induce a sufficient depth of water on the Williamsport Division to float heavily laden boats.[155]

The canal trade was hampered further during the final days of October when McClellan, goaded by President Lincoln and Secretary Stanton put his Army of the Potomac into motion. Beginning on the 26th, the Federals crossed the Potomac at Berlin, White's Ford, and Edwards Ferry on pontoon bridges which had been sent up the canal from Washington. To facilitate the movement of this ponderous army, Union engineers threw four bridges across the canal that was so low that they stopped all traffic on the waterway. This news caused the Cumberland coal companies to withdraw the boats that had pulled into the basin ready to load. Large numbers of miners, concluding that canal navigation was over for the season left Allegany County and headed for Pennsylvania.[156]

It was November 2 before the entire Army of the Potomac had crossed the river into Virginia. For the next three days, the army continued to be supplied from the big depots that had been established at Berlin and Harpers Ferry. Brigadier General George Stoneman's division, which had crossed the river on October 27 and occupied Leesburg, was supplied by canal boats sent from Washington to the Edwards Ferry River Locks where they crossed the Potomac and passed up Goose Creek to the turnpike where a depot had been established. By November 5, the Union army was in contact with the Manassas Gap Railroad and henceforth it used that line to transport its rations, munitions, clothing and fodder.[157]

Canal company officials and boatmen alike laid plans to resume navigation as soon as the low bridges at Berlin were dismantled on November 12. That evening a fleet of 36 boats, loaded

---

[152] *Ibid*, 36–37, 52–53, and Hassett to Ringgold, October 14, 1862, Ltrs. Recd., C & O Co.
[153] O. R., Series I, Vol. XIX, pt. 2, 50, and Bearss, "1862 Brings Hard Times", 456–457.
[154] Bearss, "1862 Brings Hard Times", 457.
[155] *Proceedings of the President and Board of Directors*, K, 313, and Greene to Ringgold, November 4, 1862, Ltrs. Recd., C & O Co.
[156] Greene to Ringgold, November 13, 1862, Ltrs. Recd., C & O Co., and O. R., Series I, Vol. XIX, pt. 2, 494, 499. It is interesting to note that on October 25, the day before the Federals began this operation, McClellan had his Assistant Adjutant General send a letter to President Spates promising that the Army of the Potomac would discontinue activities that hampered canal operations. Williams to Spates, October 25, 1862, in Spates Papers.
[157] O. R., Series I, Vol. XIX, pt. 2, 494, 531, 544.

with bridge materials, started down the canal. The next morning, 40 additional boats with the remainder of the pontoons, stringers, and sleepers proceeded to Washington.[158]

At the same time, company official took steps to close the critical breach at Dam No. 5. The board had grown increasingly dissatisfied with Superintendent Masters for "his neglect and inattention to his duties" and "his want of action ... in the maintenance of his division" which had "contributed much to the loss of revenue and of business upon the canal."[159] Accordingly, the directors assigned the job of repairing the dam to Superintendent Hassett of the Hancock Division. By the 17th, the leak had been repaired, the water behind the dam had been raised several feet, and there was sufficient water along the entire canal for the first time in a month.[160]

Just as the company, boat captains, and shippers were preparing to capitalize on the improved situation along the Potomac, a small-scale raid by some Virginia cavalry caused some anxious moments. On the evening of November 24, a small Confederate band slipped across the Potomac at Conrad's Ferry, swept into Poolesville where they captured 16 Federals and a telegraph operator, and quickly recrossed the river at White's Ford. Despite fears that the raiders would cut the canal, it was found that no damage had been done.[161]

Even with all these difficulties, commerce on the canal showed a great increase in November as toll revenues rose to $6,084.10 from $538.78 the previous month.[162] President Spates was so encouraged by this turn of events that he boasted the "canal has not been in better order for 10 years than now with a few exceptions." One of the main exceptions was the run-down condition of the Georgetown Division. Superintendent Horace Benton had neglected the division, especially the needed repairs at Lock No. 3.[163]

In early December 1862 the U. S. Treasury Department took cognizance of the fact that the canal provided the government with an established route of communication along the boundary between the North and South. Accordingly, upon the recommendation of President Spates and the authorization by military authorities who conducted "loyalty investigations," six canal employees were appointed to act as revenue agents at $2 a day. These men and their revenue-collecting offices were: George W. Spates at Poolesville; Levi Benton at Sharpsburg; John Warner at Shepherds Landing; Joseph F. Farrow at Williamsport; Thomas Hassett at Four Locks; and A. C. Blackman at Hancock. Four other individuals who were not employed by the company were appointed as revenue agents at Point of Rocks, Harpers Ferry, Dam No. 5, and Cumberland.[164]

President Spates and Director Greene remained in Cumberland to expedite the shipment of all the coal they could in the final weeks of the boating season. As a hard freeze was expected in the mountains at any time and there were too few boats available for the amount of coal to be shipped, competition for the boats was keen with boatmen able to demand higher freight rates of up to $2.50 per ton from the shippers.[165]

Several icebreakers were outfitted to keep the Cumberland and Williamsport Divisions open as long as possible. On the 20th Spates reported that he had spent the past two weeks "doing all in my power by hard work & otherwise to keep the canal open."[166] As a result, the receipts

---

[158] *Ibid,* Series I, Vol. XXI, 148–149.
[159] Greene to Ringgold, November 13, 1862, Ltrs. Recd., C & O Co.
[160] Spates to Ringgold, November 17, 1862, Ltrs. Recd., C & O Co.
[161] O. R., Series I, Vol. XXI, 12, and Spates to Ringgold, November 26, 1862, Ltrs. Recd., C & O Co.
[162] *Thirty-Fifth Annual Report* (1863), 8.
[163] Spates to Ringgold, December 1, 1862, Ltrs. Recd., C & O Co.
[164] *Ibid.*
[165] Greene to Ringgold, December 2, 5, 1862, Ltrs. Recd., C & O Co.
[166] Spates to Ringgold, December 2, 5, 9, 12, 20, 1862, and Masters to Board of Directors, December 30, 1862, Ltrs. Recd., C & O Co.

from tolls for December had been $9,245.14, or more than 30 percent greater than November.[167] Hence navigation continued until February 1, 1863.[168]

During the month of December, the canal board continued to receive reports about the inefficiency and dereliction of duty on the part of several division superintendents. The most remarkable charges were those against Superintendent George W. Spates of the Monocacy Division who was accused of remaining at his home near the mouth of the Monocacy River from August 13 to October 21 "transacting his farming affairs & hauling coal from the canal." Moreover, he had refused to reimburse the military for work scows borrowed for use by his repair crews, and he had failed to replace tools that had been burned by the Rebels. During his absence from the line, his workers had gone unpaid.[169]

Upset by such charges of willful misconduct, the directors issued an order to all the division superintendents on December 11:

> That the several Supts. of the Canal be required to conform themselves strictly to the rules and regulations of the Company, that said regulations be strictly conferred on all parties connected with the canal, and that said Supts. be required to pass over the entire length of their respective divisions at least once a week, and to report to the Clerk of the Company, and also to the Collectors of tolls at Georgetown and Cumberland, whenever any interruptions of the navigation shall occur, and how long such interruption will continue; that they also be required to make monthly reports to the Board of the condition of their respective divisions, and that and carelessness on their part in the performance of these duties will be deemed cause for their removal from office.[170]

All told, the year 1862 was even more disastrous financially for the canal company than 1861. The aggregate tonnage on the canal declined more than 12 percent from 144,814 tons in 1861 to 126,793 tons in 1862. Toll revenues plummeted nearly 10 percent from $70,566.99 in 1861 to $63,985.85 in 1862. Receipts from all sources for 1862 amounted to $72,624.95 while expenditures were $231,711.68. As a result of the seizure of canal boats by the Federals in March, the Confederate invasion of Maryland in September, several major freshets, and the inefficiency of some division superintendents, the canal company reached its lowest ebb during the war in 1862.[171]

The equally distressing statistics of the aggregate Cumberland coal trade in 1862 were summarized in the Pottsville *Miners' Journal* of January 10, 1863:

> Since the war broke out the trade from this Region has been almost entirely suspended. The Railroad only carried Coal in the months of May, June, July, August and September—and the trade on the Canal was interrupted entirely in the months of May and October, and only partially resumed in the other months....

In spite of its handicaps, the Cumberland region shipped about 318,000 tons in 1862, an increase of roughly 48,000 tons over the previous year.[172]

---

[167] *Thirty-Fifth Annual Report* (1863), 8.
[168] Bearss, "1862 Brings Hard Times" 462.
[169] Chambers to Board of Directors, December 10, 1862, Ltrs. Recd., C & O Co.
[170] *Proceedings of the President and Board of Directors*, K, 315.
[171] Sanderlin, *The Great National Project*, 307, 309.
[172] Pottsville *Miners' Journal*, January 10, 1863, quoted in Harvey, "Civil War and the Maryland Coal Trade." 371.

IV. COMMERCE ON THE CANAL EXPERIENCES A REVIVAL: 1863

With the use of icebreakers and the help of the comparatively mild January weather, the canal remained open to navigation until February 1, 1863. It was during this time that a debate was carried on in the military, the War Department, and the Congress over what measures should be adopted to protect the canal and the railroad from further depredations by the Southern armies. One proposal that received some attention was that of Colonel Gabriel E. Porter who recommended that adequate protection could be accorded both transportation lines by establishing camps of instruction at strategic points between New Creek and Harpers Ferry. He emphasized the fact that concentrating troops in this area would provide training under actual war conditions, thereby resulting in appreciable savings to the Federal Treasury because officers could serve in the dual role of instructor and commander. Although the War Department rejected the proposal, Congress became sufficiently interested in Porter's plan to entertain a resolution offered by Representative Francis Thomas of Maryland on January 12:

> That the Committee on Military Affairs be instructed to inquire into the expediency of providing for the establishment of camps of military instruction at suitable points on or near the Baltimore & Ohio Railroad, as an effectual means of protecting the Chesapeake & Ohio Canal and the Baltimore & Ohio Railroad, so that those public improvements may be safely used for the transportation of coal for the use of steam vessels of the United States Navy, and of supplies for the United States Army, while operating in Eastern Virginia, or on our Atlantic front.

The peak of interest in the proposal was reached in this resolution, and the problem of protecting the strategic canal and railroad was given back to the War Department.[173]

On February 1, the water was withdrawn from the trunk so that necessary repairs could be made. During the month of February it was reported that the tender of Locks Nos. 1-4 in Georgetown had left his job without notice, and, consequently, the directors appointed Samuel Smart to that important position at the eastern terminus of the canal. About March 1 the canal was reopened to boat traffic and the pace of trade quickly picked up.[174]

With the apparent course of the war changing in favor of the North, Congress in early March finally authorized an appropriation of $13,000 for the raising of the Georgetown bridges over the canal to facilitate the expansion of trade. The bridges, which originally had been planned

---

[173] *Congressional Globe*, January 12, 1863, and Summers, *Baltimore & Ohio in Civil War*, 155–157. Later in 1863 and 1864, blockhouses were built at strategic points along the Potomac to guard the river fords. The blockhouses were

> barns constructed out of the largest and longest logs that could be obtained, each barn being from forty to fifty feet square and ten to twelve feet in height. They were timbered on the top to keep the shells out and were notched through the sides for the purpose of shooting through above the earthworks. In building them, stone was first piled around the proposed foundation, about four feet high, then a deep ditch, four or five feet wide, is dug around the stone pile, the earth from the ditch being thrown upon the stones to a height of six or seven feet to protect the inmates of the house from shot and shell. The whole is surrounded with an abattis. . . and the entrance to the building was made in a zigzag fashion

Summers, *Baltimore & Ohio in Civil War*, 157–158.
[174] *Proceedings of the President and Board of Directors*, K, 318, 322–324.

and constructed according to the practice prevailing on the Erie Canal in the late 1820s, allowed a clearance of only 8 feet above the normal level of water in the canal. By 1850, the barges had become so large that they could pass fully loaded under the bridges but could not return empty until the water level in the canal was lowered. As a result, long delays which hampered trade to and from Rock Creek Basin soon forced much of the business on the waterway to pass over the Potomac Aqueduct and down the Alexandria Canal to the river at that city, from where it was taken to Washington by barge. To reopen the route through Georgetown, eight bridges and the market-house in Georgetown and one bridge over the basin needed to be raised to allow at least a 12-foot clearance. The board considered this improvement in the early 1850s, but after 1854 the matter was dropped as far as independent action by the canal company was concerned. Appeals to Congress for financial assistance failed to pass during the remainder of the decade.[175] The closing of the Potomac Aqueduct in 1861 seriously inconvenienced canal trade, and, after political pressure by canal, Georgetown, and Maryland authorities, Congress passed the appropriation.[176]

Although canal officials soon met with the corporate authorities of Georgetown to discuss the most expedient plans for raising the bridges, the actual work did not get under way until April 1865.[177] Nevertheless, the Georgetown authorities responded to the authorization by passing two ordinances. First, it was determined on April 4 that the canal president should submit his plans for altering the bridges and market-house to them for approval before the work commenced. Second, on August 8 plans were approved for a new market-house to be constructed on the site of the present building which was to extend to within eight feet of the north bank of the canal.[178]

In late March President Spates sent two communications to Brigadier General Benjamin S. Roberts, then in command of the Union troops along the canal, complaining that the Federals were not complying with McClellan's General Order No. 44 issued on April 21, 1862. In response, Roberts justified the military's activities on the grounds that the canal company was employing suspected "disloyalists" and that the waterway was being used to secret[e] supplies and information to the Confederates. His lengthy accusations were as follows:

> On entering upon my duties...and before I issued my General Order No. 2, I was informed by many reliable persons that a large contraband trade was carried on between Maryland and Virginia and information constantly passing to the Confederate Army, by means of small boats and skiffs along the river and canal on the lines where trade with Virginia is forbidden by a recent law of Congress. In order to carry into effect that law and the regulations of the Treasury and War Dept. intended for that purpose, I deemed it a military necessity to seize the boats and other water craft as designated in Part IV of that order. It had been stated to me that many boats used in this contraband trade belonged to the Chesapeake & Ohio Canal Co. and were hidden away under culverts and bridges along the canal and river, and rented by the captains, and agents of the Company to speculate in this atrocious traffic and to give encouragement and carry supplies to Dis-

---

[175] Sanderlin, *The Great National Project*, 206–207, and Constance McLaughlin Green, *Washington Village and Capital, 1800–1878* (2 Vols., Princeton, 1962), Vol. I, 265.
[176] *Proceedings of the President and Board of Directors*, K, 325.
[177] Ibid, 422.
[178] *Ordinances of the Corporation of Georgetown, from January, 1863, to January, 1864* (Washington, 1864), 25, 44–45. Later on January 9, 1864 an ordinance was passed changing the plan of the market-house to include a second story on the north end of the building. On February 20, 1864, a resolution was approved providing that a basement be constructed under the entire building. *Ordinances of the Corporation of Georgetown* (Washington, [1871]), 3–4, 15. The plans and specifications for the new market-house were approved on May 7, and a contract was let to John A. Rheem of Washington on June 4. Later on July 2, the plans for the basement were dropped. *Ibid*, 30, 33, 39.

loyalists and Rebels in Virginia. It was my first duty, under the state of things as thus represented, to seize all and every kind of skiff or boat that could be taken by secessionists from their place of concealment by night or day by force, or that could be rented of unfaithful employees of the Company without its knowledge.

It was not of course my intention in any manner to interfere with proper commerce and trade along the canal, or to embarrass in any degree its lawful business, known to me to be of great importance to the Federal Government. But if the Company has in its employment agents or persons who disregard the laws of Congress and the regulations of the Treasury Department and the Army, it must suffer the consequences; as I cannot permit boats or skiffs to be kept within the lines of my command that can be used in any manner, with or without the assent of the Company or its agents, to aid the enemies of the Federal Government.

When the company was ready to repair the abutment of Dam No. 5, the commandant at North Mountain would release the boats captured near the dam to aid in the restoration work. However, it was hoped that the company would

> consent willingly to any transient and slight inconveniences the exigencies of the crisis may impose on them. All truly loyal and good citizens are expected to make such sacrifices, and the more willingly, as they are intended for the permanent and great good of the public.[179]

As the prospects for canal trade were greatly improve in the spring of 1863, the board received several petitions from parties at Cumberland and Hancock, urging an increase in the toll on coal of 1/8 of a cent per ton mile. The petitions argued that such a decision would increase the revenue of the company and enable it to improve its desperate financial condition. Moreover, the general inflationary tendency of prices during the war years had witnessed increased freight rates on the railroads and canals of the North, and, consequently, the Cumberland coal shippers would not be hurt.[180]

On April 10, the canal board met to consider the two petitions. After some discussion, the directors approved the following resolution:

> That in consequence of the interruption of trade and of injuries received by the canal within the two years last past, it is absolutely necessary to make a temporary increase in the rates of toll on coal; and upon full consideration, the said toll is hereby increased 1/16

---

[179] Roberts to Spates, March 28, 1863, in Spates Papers. According to Mary Mitchell in her study of Georgetown during the Civil War, the only underground activities carried out in that town were initiated by small local tradesmen, laborers and citizens of obscure origins. Her research in Old Capitol Prison records revealed that "time and again, drovers, brewers and boatmen, who gave Georgetown as their residence, were incarcerated for blockade running, smuggling and disloyalty, denied *habeas corpus*, and released only after the interrogation of the prison authorities had extracted all possible information from them." The most sensational case concerned a drug ring of apparently large proportions. The local anchorman was John Crumbaugh, a former cattle drover from Loudoun County, Virginia, who had been a butcher in the Georgetown market-house until 1861 when he purchased a wood and fuel business on the canal wharf at the foot of 33rd Street. He then bought a home on N Street and used its cellar as a way station between drug wholesalers, his canal boats, and a Virginia contact. In February 1863 he was caught with $14,000 worth of quinine, morphine and nitrate of silver concealed in apple and potato crates. He was sent to the Old Capitol Prison and died there in 1864. Mary Mitchell, *Divided Town* (Barre, 1968), 122–123.

[180] Petitions, variously signed, to President and Directors, April 6, 1863, Ltrs. Recd., C & O Co.

of a cent (making 5/16 of a cent) per ton per mile, to take effect on all cargoes shipped on or after the first day of May next, and to continue to the first day of November next, after which date the rate will be 4/16 ct, of a ton per mile, as it now is.[181]

The rise in trade and canal revenue triggered a petition from a number of canal employees, asking for a general wage increase to compensate for the rising inflation of the war years. This request was tabled immediately by the directors as it would further drain the company finances at a time when they were attempting to place the operation of the waterway on a more firm footing.[182]

Just as canal navigation was increasing, the canal company began to feel the effects of the Federal Draft Act that President Lincoln had signed on March 3. This, the first effective Federal draft, imposed liability on all male citizens between the ages of 20 and 45 with the exception of the physically or mentally unfit, men with certain types of dependents, those convicted of a felony, and various high federal and state officials. Draft quotas for each district would be set by the President on the basis of population and the number of men already in the service from each district. A drafted man could hire another as a substitute or purchase his way out for $300.[183]

In mid-April the canal board received word that two lock tenders, M. Burris and I. Edelin, had been drafted. As they were both poor men with large families, neither of them was financially able to procure a substitute. Accordingly, a canal official had loaned Edelin $100 for that purpose, while Burris borrowed a similar sum. By this time, the company owed each man over $200, and unless the board could do something soon, the men would "be compelled to dispose of their claims at a great sacrifice."[184]

The quickened pace of trade activity during April and May 1863 produced a sense of optimism along the canal and local entrepreneurs quickly took steps to participate in the new-found prosperity. On April 19, Denton Jacques rented for 10 years at an annual fee of $10 two parcels of land near Lock No. 49 about 100 by 125 feet on the berm side and 10 by 15 feet on the towpath side on which he intended to build several warehouses.[185] The firm of Bridges and Henderson, which had recently purchased the Round Top Cement Mill above Hancock, commenced negotiations in early May with canal officials to obtain free passage on the waterway to ship needed supplies between Hancock and the mill.[186] George Hill, Jr., obtained a 20-year lease on a large parcel of ground belonging to the company just west of the Potomac Aqueduct on which he planned to construct a mill. To run his new enterprise, he negotiated a 20-year lease for 200 inches of water power from the canal company.[187]

At the same time, the improving trade gave rise to at least one proposal to provide the canal with an outlet to the Potomac just west of the Potomac Aqueduct and thus avoid the costly delays of boating through Georgetown. On May 7, T. S. Kidwell offered

> to take the whole front of the Canal from Shoemakers Mill to within 200 feet of a right line drawn from the West line of the Aqueduct upon a lease reviewable forever, at $500 per annum, with the privilege reserved to this Company [Chesapeake & Ohio] of dropping loaded boats from the Canal into the river by mechanical contrivances, at any point along said line.

---

[181] *Proceedings of the President and Board of Directors*, K, 329–330.
[182] Petitions, variously signed, to President and Directors, April 6, 1863, Ltrs. Recd., C & O Co.
[183] Long, *Civil War Day by Day*, 325.
[184] White to Board of Directors, April 10, 1863, Ltrs. Recd., C & O Co.
[185] *Proceedings of the President and Board of Directors*, K, 327.
[186] Hassett to Ringgold, May 4, 1863, Ltrs. Recd., C & O Co.
[187] *Proceedings of the President and Board of Directors*, K, 335–336.

After considering the proposal, the board determined that it was not "expedient or proper" to pursue the matter further at that time.[188]

Despite the economic upturn along the canal, the directors continued to receive reports of the long-term ill effects of the previous two years of hostilities on the mills along the waterway. One such report arrived in early May from Jacob Miller who owned a sawmill near Sharpsburg. Soldiers had taken his mill on January 19, 1862, and had prevented his sawing until May 14. After that, the water was out of the canal from July 1 to 12, for nearly two weeks in August, and again from September 14 on. Following the Battle of Antietam, soldiers used the mill as a hospital and then as a pickets' rendezvous. When the soldiers moved out, they carried the doors, windows, partitions, garners, flooring, weatherboarding, chimney stove, and other movable things with them. Even his post and board fence had been cut down and burned. By then it was too late in the year to resume operation, even if the repair materials had been available.[189]

On May 20, Captain E. S. Allen of the Quartermaster's Office informed the canal board that the tidelock at Georgetown was deteriorating and needed immediate repairs. Irked by the continued military occupation of the Rock Creek Basin, the directors authorized Clerk Ringgold to send the following cryptic reply:

> they [the board] have given directions to the Superintendent to make the Lock effective as early as can be done, but inasmuch as it may require repairs beyond the available means of the Company, and as it is and has been used for sometime past almost exclusively for the United States, and the injury has arisen in some degree from their agents, and further that the U. States have made free use of the Canal, without payment of tolls, I would suggest whether it would not be proper that they should contribute to the repairs of the Lock in question.[190]

At the 35th annual meeting of the company stockholders held on June 1, President Spates reported on the upsurge of canal trade in the spring of 1863. Since January1, 83,396 tons of coal had been transported on the waterway, compared to 94,819 tons for the entire year of 1862. With the help of the rate increase in April, revenue from tolls for the first five months of 1863 was $56,615.14, or nearly 90 percent of the $63,985.85 that had been collected during the entire previous year. Although there was still a deficiency in the number of boats needed for the growing trade, it was thought that the rising freight rates would encourage boat-building. Already, there were a number of new boats being built in Cumberland.[191]

After frustrating two Federal attempts to penetrate the strong defensive positions at Fredericksburg and march on Richmond, the Confederates on June 3 again undertook a strategic offensive. This effort was designed to carry the war to the North and relieve pressure on Vicksburg and Chattanooga by making the Federals withdraw strength from those areas to counter Lee's threat to the rich Cumberland Valley. By June 8 Lee had concentrated most of his Army of Northern Virginia near Culpeper. During the northward movement of the Confederates, General Joseph Hooker, who had been named commander of the Army of the Potomac on January 26, ordered reconnaissance operations that resulted in the Battles of Franklin's Crossing on June 5 and Brandy Station on June 9. After the Rebels had driven Union troops out of their positions at Berryville and Martinsburg, the 9,000-man 2nd Division at Winchester was routed by Confederate

---

[188] *Ibid*, K, 334.
[189] Miller to President and Directors, May 1, 1863, Ltre. Recd., C & O Co.; Ringgold to Benton, May 29, 1863, Ltrs. Sent, C & O Co.; and *Proceedings of the President and Board of Directors*, K, 324–325, 340.
[190] Ringgold to Allen, May 29, 1863. Ltrs. Recd., C & O Co.
[191] *Thirty-Fifth Annual Report* (1863), 5.

infantry and cavalry on June 14. On the 15th, Southern troops under Major General R. E. Rhodes crossed the Potomac at Williamsport, and after a short skirmish, drove off the small defending force. The next day, while most of the men were resting, bathing, and washing their clothes, a fatigue party made attempts to blow up the Conococheague Aqueduct and wreck the other nearby canal structures. Three days later, on the 18th, the remainder of Lee's army crossed into Maryland at Boteler's Ford near Shepherdstown. After moving his army into Maryland, Lee concentrated it at Hagerstown, six miles from the Potomac and 74 from Harrisburg, Pennsylvania, his principal objective.[192]

During the period in which the Army of Northern Virginia was proceeding northward, the canal was the scene of active military operations. At daybreak on June 10, some 250 Virginia cavalry under Major John S. Mosby crossed the Potomac at Muddy Branch to attack Company I, Sixth Michigan Cavalry, on duty near Lock No. 24. Dashing up the towpath, Mosby's Raiders drove in the patrols and chased the retreating Federals to within three miles of Poolesville. The Rebels quickly withdrew after capturing some 17 prisoners and 20 horses. After burning the Union tents, stores, and equipment at Seneca, they proceeded down the towpath and recrossed the river at Muddy Branch.[193]

A daring raid was launched on the 17th by Lieutenant-Colonel Elijah V. White with 125 men against a small Federal company under Captain Samuel C. Means stationed at Point of Rocks. Crossing the river near Catoctin Creek, he sent a company of 70 men toward Frederick, while he took the remainder down the canal towpath, routed Means' company, and captured and burned three wagons and eighteen train cars. After cutting the telegraph wires and tearing up some railroad tracks, he recrossed the river with 53 of the 100 prisoners he had captured, all without the loss of any of his men.[194]

A third raid was launched against the Cumberland Division of the canal between Paw Paw Tunnel and the "Narrows" several days before June 20. Although the only available information on the raid appears in a letter from Superintendent Lowe to Clerk Ringgold on that date, it is apparent that the Rebels intended to disrupt canal navigation. One or two lock gates were damaged, and the waterway was cut just below Lock No. 67 and between Locks No. 71 and 72 in a high embankment. Fortunately for the canal company, both breaches were made in slate material which did not wash easily. Thus, all the damage could be repaired in 10 working days with sufficient hands at a cost of about $600.[195]

After a series of engagements between Northern units and remnants of Lee's troops at Aldie, Middleburg, and Upperville in the Loudoun Valley, Lee ordered his main army to proceed from Hagerstown toward Pennsylvania on June 22. Upon learning of the Confederate movement, Hooker on the 25th directed his troops to cross the Potomac into Maryland at Edwards Ferry on a pontoon bridge, the materials for which had been brought up the canal from Washington. Using

---

[192] O. R., Series I, Vol. XXVII, pt. 2, 549–550; Glenn Tucker, *High Tide at Gettysburg* (New York, 1958), 27–39; Clifford Dowdey, *Death of a Nation* (New York, 1958), 37–41;and Mark Mayo Boatner III, *The Civil War Dictionary* (New York, 1959), 331–332. At the time that the Confederates crossed the river at Shepherdstown, Major General Edward E. Johnson took up headquarters at Ferry Hill Plantation, the house being owned by the father of Henry Kyd Douglas who was a member of his staff. Wilbur Sturdevant Nye, *Here Come the Rebels!* (Baton Rouge, 1965), 147.
[193] O. R., Series I, Vol. XXVII, 786–788, and John S, Mosby, *Mosby's War Reminiscences - Stuart's Cavalry Campaigns* (New York, 1958), 158–162.
[194] O. R., Series I, Vol. XXVII, pt. 2, 768–771.
[195] Lowe to Ringgold, June 20, 1863, Ltrs. Recd., C&O Co.

the canal towpath and nearby roads, the Army of the Potomac had proceeded to Frederick by the 28th where it interposed itself between Lee's columns and Washington.[196]

Meanwhile, General "Jeb" Stewart had commenced his famous Gettysburg Raid with three brigades on June 24 in an effort to circle around Hooker' rear and flank and connect with the Confederate columns marching toward Harrisburg. As the Potomac was two feet above its normal level on the night of June 27 when Stewart determined to cross the river at Rowser's Ford, a short distance below Dam No. 2, he ordered his caissons and limber chests to be emptied and his cavalrymen to carry the artillery shells and powder bags across in their arms. Then the guns and caissons were dragged into the water and, completely submerged at times, towed through nearly a mile of water to the Maryland shore below Seneca Creek.[197]

Regarding the canal as of strategic value to Hooker, Stuart seized possession of the waterway from Lock No. 23 to the Seneca Aqueduct and ordered his lead company to establish vedettes beyond the canal. To facilitate the crossing of the waterway, a passing barge was commandeered and turned crosswise to serve as an improvised bridge. Twenty dismounted men crossed over to the berm side of the canal and established an outpost, while the remainder of the Rebel forces crossed the waterway over the pivot bridge at Lock No. 23, which the Federals had failed to destroy prior to pulling out of the area. During the night, twelve barges blundered into the vicinity and were promptly commandeered. All were carrying freight except two with loads of Union soldiers, both white and black, en route to Washington. The Confederates found a valuable supply of grain on the boats. The prisoners were marched off toward Rockville, eight miles to the northeast. Before proceeding to Rockville to interdict the main supply route and line of communications for the Union army, Stuart had nine of the canal boats burned both above and below the Seneca Aqueduct, including one in its trunk that damaged the wooden railing. The gates of Lock No. 23 and Guard Lock No. 2 were destroyed and the towpath embankment breached, thereby draining the Monocacy Division of water and causing the other three boats to sink.[198]

On June 30, Superintendent Spates of the Monocacy Division reported that his jurisdiction was again in good boating order. The burned and sunken hulls at Seneca had been moved to one side of the canal and would be removed from the trunk as soon as possible. The lock gates had been replaced and the towpath embankment repaired. In addition, his crews had replaced the gates at Locks Nos.13 and 16 and the pivot bridges at Lock No. 13 and Great Falls, which had been destroyed by the Federals charged with guarding the line of the Potomac. The only remaining problem on his division was the pivot bridges at Lock No. 25 which the Army of the Potomac had used to cross the canal at Edwards Ferry on its way to Pennsylvania. The bridge had been damaged to the extent that it no longer turned on its pivot. Boats were passing in either direction between Seneca and Harpers Ferry in the employ of the federal government.[199]

Following the momentous Battle of Gettysburg, July 1-3, the Confederates commenced a retreat toward Virginia. A severe storm made the Potomac unfordable when Lee's advance guard reached Williamsport on July 6. Here Union cavalry under Major General John Buford attacked

---

[196] Roger S. Cohen, "The Civil War in the Poolesville, Maryland, Area" (MD. Hist. Soc. Mss., 1961), 11.
[197] O. R., Series I, Vol. XXVII, pt. 2, 693, and Nye, *Here Come the Rebels*, 316.
[198] O. R., Series I, Vol. XXVII, pt. 2, 694; Nye, *Here Come the Rebels*, 316–317; Jane Chinn Sween, "A History of Dawsonville and Seneca, Montgomery County, Maryland," (Md. Hist. Soc. Mss., 1967), 70–71; and Spates to President and Directors, June 30, 1863, Ltrs. Recd., C & O Co. Although C. E. Detmold, the owner of four of the boats that were burned, later requested that he be relieved from the payment of tolls, the board on January 23, 1864, determined that the "payment of tolls be required on the cargoes of all boats to the points where such cargoes were transported and destroyed." *Proceedings of the President and Board of Directors*, K, 366.
[199] Spates to President and Directors, June 30, 1863, Ltrs. Recd., C & O Co.

the Rebel force under Brigadier General John Daniel Imboden but were repulsed.[200] The rest of Lee's army reached Hagerstown on July 7 and entrenched to await replacement of the pontoon bridge at Falling Waters that had been destroyed by Federal cavalry. Confederate engineers quickly began taking canal boats and pieces of houses and lumber to reconstruct the bridges. Following several more skirmishes between Union cavalry and the retreating Rebels in the vicinity of McCoy's Ferry, Clear Spring, and Williamsport on the 8th and the 10th, Lee determined to commence the river crossing before the pontoon bridges were completed as the level of the Potomac had receded to a fordable level. On the 10th, small Rebel contingents began crossing the river in canal boats and hastily-constructed hulls "at the rate of three teams an hour," but the bulk of Lee's army withdrew across the river on the night of July 13-14 over the pontoon bridge that had been finished that morning.[201] During the crossing, Major General Henry Heth staged a rearguard action at Falling Waters in which he lost two guns and 500 prisoners to the advancing Federals.[202] With the entire Confederate force on the Virginia side of the river by the early afternoon of the 14th, the pontoon bridge was cut loose to allow the river's current to carry it downstream and dash it against the banks. That same afternoon, the Northern army crossed the river into Virginia over a pontoon bridge thrown across the Potomac at Harpers Ferry.[203]

After both armies had crossed back into Virginia, canal officials surveyed the condition of the waterway and commenced plans for the restoration of navigation. Superintendent Masters informed canal officials on July 19 that the damage wrought by the Confederates and the late rains on his Williamsport Division would require three weeks of repairs before navigation could be restored.[204] Henry S. Miller, the collector at Williamsport, reported on July 22 that he was forwarding the toll permits that he had received for the month of June:

> The cause of delay in these permits was an anxiety to have them there in good season - hence when the Rebels came into our place, I gave my permits to a man from our country, who expected to reach Washington, but was arrested, yet was successful in concealing my papers. He has just returned & I hasten them on. Please send me black waybills & return sheets. The Rebs tore in pieces every paper they could find about my office, but, I had all books and papers of importance concealed. We expect to see the boats running in about 2 weeks if the Johnny Rebs do not return. This morning we see their pickets again on the opposite side of the river. I am fearful we are not entirely clear here yet.[205]

After traveling down the canal from Cumberland to Williamsport, Greene observed on July 25 that navigation had been restored as far down the waterway as Dam No. 5. Provided the Rebel pickets did not reappear on the Virginia shore, the Williamsport Division might be reopened as early as August 1. For more than a week, repair crews had been at work removing sandbars mending the towpath, and patching the Conococheague Aqueduct. He remarked that "It is really wonderful that a month's hostile occupancy of the canal should have resulted in as little damage" for he had heard that the Antietam Division was unharmed. Thus, he was "charmed with the appearance of the work" and was encouraged that the Rebel pickets had disappeared. The one bad break on the Cumberland Division had been repaired, and he was pleased to note that a local farmer had prevented another by cutting a waste weir.[206]

---

[200] O. R., Series I, Vol. XXVII, pt. 2, 299, 433–436.
[201] *Ibid,* 275, 280, 301–303.
[202] *Ibid,* 639–642.
[203] *Ibid,* 301, and J. Warren Gilbert, *The Blue and the Gray* ([Gettysburg], 1922), 121.
[204] Masters to Ringgold, July 19, 1863, Ltrs. Recd., C & O Co.
[205] Miller to Ringgold, July 22, 1863, Ltrs. Recd., C & O Co.
[206] Greene to Ringgold, July 25, 1863, Ltrs. Recd., C & O Co.

Because of his full-scale operations to repair the Williamsport Division, Superintendent Masters did not submit a full report to the board until August 4. The chief damage to his division had occurred at the Conococheague Aqueduct where the Rebels had torn "down to the bottom of the canal the 4 corners" of the structure—an "aggregate space of 74 feet." All the coping and railing had been thrown into the creek and partially destroyed. A hole had been made in one of the arches "nearly the width of the aqueduct & 6 or 10 feet wide." The four gates at Lock No. 44 were burned, and the two upper courses of the lock walls had been torn up and thrown into the chamber. Four roads had been made through the canal banks on the division through which the Confederate troops had passed. The aqueduct would be rebuilt "with masonry as high as the water mark or as far as the stone on hand." The repairs would be completed by August 8 at a total cost of nearly $5,000.[207]

Despite the resumption of navigation in the second week of August 1863, the operation of the waterway was disrupted repeatedly by Rebel guerilla raids in which large numbers of mules and quantities of provisions were stolen from the boatmen. A bitter Greene complained to Clerk Ringgold on September 2 that "the canal is again practically closed by the neglect of the Government to afford the boatmen protection." As a result, numerous boats which arrived at Cumberland were refusing "to load and tie up their boat being unwilling and, in fact, unable to risk the loss of, in many cases, everything they have." Although the military authorities had promised to "secure" the canal, a large number of boats "have since been disabled by the loss of their teams and have stopped." He concluded his remarks by observing:

> I think it would meet the unanimous approbation of this whole community [Cumberland] if Mosby or White or whoever leads these incursions should ride into Washington some fine night and carry off with them to parts unknown, Gen. Halleck, Sec. Stanton, and everybody else whose duty it was to prevent these shameful raids - - even for their own sakes. If we could only have some heavy rains to raise the river enough to render it unfordable, we might hope to do some business, but our old-fashioned drought is upon us with no prospect of a let-up until winter.[208]

During the month of August, President Spates sent at least four letters to various Union commanders, complaining that the Federal troops along the canal were not effectively protecting it from the Rebel raids and were, in fact, hindering navigation by seizing horses and mules from the boatmen and damaging canal company property. As a result of the correspondence, additional cavalry units were sent from Washington in late August to guard the canal between Georgetown and the Monocacy River, and the commanders at Harpers Ferry and Hagerstown were ordered to have their troops secure the line of the canal in their areas. Copies of General Orders No. 44, which had been issued on April 21, 1862, were sent to all the officers stationed along the river with instructions not to interfere with navigation on the waterway.[209]

On September 1, the military authorities arrested a number of Marylanders and confined them at Fort McHenry, charged with having communicated with the enemy or having provided information to the Rebel forces during the Gettysburg campaign. Among those incarcerated were President Spates and William Broun, the contractor building the Virginia abutment at the new masonry Dam No. 5. In the case of Spates, the reason for his confinement was a boast that he had visited General Lee during the campaign. William H. Hoffman, to whom the conversation was

---

[207] Masters to President and Directors, August 4, 1863, Ltrs. Recd., C & O Co.
[208] Greene to Ringgold, September 2, 1863, Ltrs. Recd., C & O Co.
[209] Hentzelman to Spates, August 13, 22, 1863, Tucker to Spates, August 24, 1863, and Freeman to Spates, August 31, 1863, Spates Papers.

addressed, had passed the information to the military authorities. The men were to be held at the prison facility in Baltimore pending their appearance before a military tribunal on the charges of disloyalty.[210]

The canal board on September 10 appointed Lawrence Brengle as company president *ad interim* during the confinement of Spates. At the same time, Brengle and Director Joseph H. Bradley were ordered to proceed to Baltimore in an effort to procure the release of Spates and Broun.[211]

On the 15th, Brengle informed Ringgold concerning the results of the visit to Ft. McHenry. During a conversation with Spates, the confined president had acknowledged that he, in company with Davis Raman, had visited the headquarters of General Lee at Hagerstown during the recent campaign. However, he had not conversed with Lee but with Charles Marshall, one of the General's aides with whom he had been "intimate" in Baltimore before the outbreak of the war.[212] His visit to Marshall had been made so as to prevent his arrest by Confederate soldiers as he passed along the waterway and "to secure the interest of the canal as far as possible." Because the two canal representatives were unable to affect the release of Spates, Director Bradley intended to meet with Secretary Stanton, who was considered to be more sympathetic to the case. Although the charges against Spates were not conclusive, his enemies along the canal were "striving to keep him in the Fort." The charges against Broun were only rumors, and his release was expected within several days.[213]

Spates was still confined at Fort McHenry on September 24, when the board received a letter from him urging the adoption of certain measures to serve the interests of the company.[214] Sometime after that date, he was transferred to the prison at Fort Lafayette in New York. Finally on January 25, 1864, after further intercession on his behalf by company officials, he was released by special order from Secretary Stanton.[215]

Despite the uncertainties caused by Rebel raids and the disarray in the canal leadership, business on the waterway continued to improve after its reopening in mid-August. Evidence of the resurgence of trade was manifested by the new enterprises that were commenced along the line. On September 24, Mortimer Osborn was granted permission to install a counter and shelves in a room of Lockhouse No. 30 for the purpose of selling dry goods and groceries to the passing boatmen.[216] On the same day, George W. Case, the tender at Locks Nos. 19-20, was authorized to establish a tavern at Crommelin House.[217] When it was discovered that the company did not own the tract of land adjoining the Potomac Aqueduct that had been rented earlier to George Hill, Jr.,

---

[210] Fickey to Ringgold, September 1, 3, 1863, Ltrs. Recd., C & O Co.; Washington *Evening Star*, September 2, 1863; and Stake to Brengle, September 17, 1863, Ltrs. Recd. C & O Co. This was the second time that Spates was placed under arrest for disloyalty. Although no information could be found concerning his first arrest, it is presumed that it occurred in the aftermath of the Antietam Campaign in 1862.
[211] *Proceedings of the President and Board of Directors*, K, 349-350, and Middletown *Valley Register*, September 18, 1863.
[212] Spates was a native of Montgomery County, having owned a 287-acre farm, which he called "Contention," along the old road between Washington and Rockville. By 1846 he was living in Baltimore, where he remained until 1853 when he moved to Cumberland to assume the position of Deputy Clerk of the Circuit Court of Allegany County, Cumberland *Alleganian*, June 24, 1876; Cumberland *Daily News*, June 24, 1876; Rockville *Advocate*, June 29, 1876; Rockville *Sentinel*, June 30, 1876; Baltimore *Gazette*, June 28, 1876; Cumberland *Civilian*, June 25, 1876; Card, Lodge No. 48, Independent Order of the Odd Fellows, February 1, 1853; and "Alfred Spates Qualification as Deputy Clerk," March 11, 1853, in Spates Papers.
[213] Brengle to Ringgold, September 15, 1863, Ltrs. Recd., C & O Co.
[214] *Proceedings of the President and Board of Directors*, K, 351.
[215] Greene to Ringgold, January 25, 1864, Ltrs. Recd., C & O Co.
[216] *Proceedings of the President and Board of Directors*, K, 351.
[217] *Ibid*, K, 352.

the company executed a 20-year lease for 200 inches of water power with him for use at his mill located at the corner of Potomac and Water streets in Georgetown which would soon commence operation.[218] On December 17, Daniel L. White was granted permission to construct a storehouse on the berm side of the canal at Conrad's Ferry.[219]

During this period, the canal company continued to face the problem of inefficiency on the part of some of its division superintendents and of disloyalty charges against others. On September 14, Horace Benton, who had allowed the Georgetown Division to deteriorate, was fired and replaced by John Cameron, a long-time company employee.[220] Later on December 17, the board received an anonymous note charging Superintendent George W. Spates of the Monocacy Division with disloyalty and recommending Alex Dent as his replacement. Although generally dissatisfied with the performance of Spates, the directors took no action on the communication.[221]

All told, the year 1863 witnessed a tremendous revival in the overall Cumberland coal trade as its aggregate production increased to more than 748,000 tons, only a little less than the amount shipped in 1860 and 430,000 tons more than was shipped in 1862. One of the reasons for the increased orders in the Maryland field was that the Broad Top mines were closed for three months in 1863 as the result of the Gettysburg Campaign and a two-month miners' strike.[222]

The canal shared in the revival of trade as the total tonnage carried on the waterway soared to 265,847 tons, a sum that nearly equaled the combined tonnages of 1861 and 1862. The coal tonnage rose to 229,416 tons, more than double the 94,819 tons that had been transported in 1862. The tolls received from the trade increased to $154,928.26, compared with the sum of $134,552.84 collected during the previous two years combined.[223]

In June 1864 the stockholders were informed about the progress of canal trade during 1863 as follows:

> The business of the Canal for the past year has been much better than that of the two preceding years; there was less interruption to the trade from military movements and other casualties to which it had been subjected, but for the invasion of June last, which in a great measure suspended business for two months of the most active period of the year, the revenues of the Company would have exceeded those of any former year.
>
> The damages sustained by this invasion required an expenditure of about $15,000 to restore the navigation and the loss of revenue for two months, which would probably have been not less than $50,000. With this exception there was but little interruption to the navigation during the season of business which commenced about the 15th of March and continued till near the end of December.[224]

---

[218] *Ibid*, K, 358, and Ringgold to Hill, November 27, 1863, Ltrs. Sent, C & O Co.
[219] *Proceedings of the President and Board of Directors*, K, 361.
[220] *Ibid*, K, 349.
[221] *Ibid*, K, 361.
[222] Harvey, "Civil War and Maryland Coal Trade", 371.
[223] Sanderlin, *The Great National Project*, 307.
[224] *Thirty-Sixth Annual Report* (1864), C & O Co., 3.

V. THE CANAL TRADE EXPANSION CONTINUES: 1864

The canal was closed by ice from late December 1863 to early February 1864. At that time, the water was withdrawn to remove obstructions in the prism and make repairs in the banks and masonry structures along the waterway. Navigation was to resume in early March, and the canal board looked forward to even a more prosperous year than the previous one.[225]

While the repairs were underway, the canal board confronted a number of issues that were symptomatic of the greatly expanding commerce on the waterway. On February 18, Edward M. Linthicum, a long-time prominent Georgetown merchant, submitted a proposal to the directors for the construction of an inclined plane just west of the Potomac Aqueduct "to pass boats from the canal to the river." Such a structure would alleviate the growing congestion of the traffic through Georgetown and in the Rock Creek Basin. The board was interested in the idea and determined to visit the Morris Canal in New Jersey in April to observe the world-famous inclined planes operating on that canal. The clerk and the treasurer were directed to procure a topographical survey plat of the company land on the river side of the canal between the aqueduct and the Foundry property.[226]

On April 14, President Spates, together with Directors Albert, Brengle, and Watson and the Maryland Commissioners of Public Works proceeded to Newark, New Jersey. Here they were met by W. H. Talcott, the engineer in charge of the works on the Morris Canal who gave them a tour of the canal and a "verbal explanation" of the operation of the inclined planes. Greatly impressed by what they saw, the directors returned to Washington very enthusiastic about the construction of an inclined plane above Georgetown. However, the uncertainties of the war and a shortage of expendable cash prevented the immediate building of the plane.[227]

The canal board determined on February 18 to terminate the leases of those parties renting company land west of the tidelock and tumbling dam at the mouth of Rock Creek. The company was anxious to reacquire use of this land so that it could be relet to interests who would install improvements for the transfer of coal to river boats. The current tenants, William H. Godey, Walter Godey, Solomon Stover, Dickson & King, and J. L. Sims, were notified that they were to vacate the property by March 31. At a public meeting on March 15, the property was advertised for new one-year rentals to begin April 1. All the lots were rented to M. P. McPherson, an agent of Edward Mayer of New York, for an annual sum of $3,760. As he intended to erect the necessary improvements to facilitate the transfer of coal to river boats, the board quickly extended the one-year agreement on the condition that the new operation would be a successful venture. As the current tenants possessed leases to the properties that had not expired, they refused to relinquish their claims to the land. Unable to force the tenants off the lots, the board on April 11 resorted to negotiating equitable arrangements with the lessees in order to turn possession of the property over to the Mayer coal interests as early as possible.[228]

As the boating season approached, the board received more applications for the construction of feed stores and warehouses along the canal to accommodate the growing trade. On February 18 the directors forwarded to Superintendent Spates of the Monocacy Division three such requests from M. E. Alexander, L. Roderick, and George P. Ramsberg to build structures near Lock No. 29. Upon the recommendation of Spates, M. E. Alexander was granted permission on March

---

[225] *Thirty-Sixth Annual Report* 1864), 6.
[226] *Proceedings of the President and Board of Directors*, K, 370–371.
[227] *Ibid*, K, 379. On September 8, 1864, the board paid $75 to W. C. Smith, a civil engineer, for conducting a survey and drawing plans for the outlet locks to be built at the same location as the proposed site of the inclined planes. *Ibid*, K, 398. Ultimately, the controversy would be settled in the early 1870s when it was determined to build the Georgetown Incline Plane.
[228] *Ibid*, K, 369, 376–378, 381–382.

24 to build a store house on the canal berm near the lock to sell feed and provisions to the boatmen. At the same time, George P. Ramsberg was authorized to build a warehouse on the company land on the canal berm in the vicinity of the lock.[229]

Although the canal was reopened to navigation in early March, little trade passes down the waterway for several weeks. On March 14 Superintendent Lloyd Lowe of the Cumberland Division reported:

> The canal has been navigable ten days. No boats been loaded. Two or three that was loaded last December has started down. The Boatmen are holding back for an increase on freight. They are having trouble to get hands. I found it necessary last month to advance the pay of Laborers, and will have to continue it to obtain old hands...[230]

Three days later the Washington *National Republican* published an article that elaborated on the labor unrest as follows:

> nearly all the miners and boatmen have struck for higher wages. The company [Cumberland Coal and Iron Company] refuse to accede to these demands from the fact that to do so would necessarily carry up the price of coal to such a high rate that there would be comparatively little demand for it, especially when brought in competition with a superior coal selling at about the same price. There is very little coal at the mines now, hence this strike is the more unfortunate. If the miners insist upon their demand for increased wages, it is said that the company will discharge the hands and employ others. In such an event, resistance is threatened, but as some of Gen. Sigel's forces are near at hand, it will not amount to much.[231]

The strike was short-lived for on March 18 Greene wrote from Cumberland that

> We shall have a season of great trouble, I fear, in our business. The boatmen have gone to work at two dolls freight 'for the present.' I do not doubt they will make a demand for more, later in the season. The miners are concocting a strike for $.25 a ton additional! So we go. These demands cannot be granted and I have hardly a hope of avoiding serious suspension of business.[232]

Shortly after commencement of navigation, the board on March 24 took further steps to facilitate the growing coal trade. On that date Edward Lynch proposed to erect a platform and two derricks on the towpath near the Foundry above Georgetown that were to be used for loading and unloading coal. As the structure would eliminate some of the congestion in Georgetown, the board quickly approved the idea. To make room for the new facility, it was decided to change the towpath by passing it from the south side under the canal trunk, through the culvert above the Foundry and on to the road on the north bank. The road was to be repaired and made secure, and a 3-to-4-foot high post & rail fence was to be built along the wall of the north side of the waterway.[233]

---

[229] *Ibid*, K, 370, 373–374.
[230] Lowe to Ringgold, March 14, 1864, Ltrs. Recd., C & O Co.
[231] Washington *National Republican*, March 17, 1864, quoted in Harvey, "Civil War and Maryland Coal Trade," 372–373.
[232] Greene to Ringgold, March 18, 1864, Ltrs. Recd., C & O Co.
[233] *Proceedings of the President and Board of Directors*, K, 374–375, 387.

The canal was in full operation by late March with fifteen to twenty boats leaving Cumberland every day. However, repairs on the towpath and other structures were still underway. Included in the repairs were the replacement of the gates at Lock No. 72 and the substitution of a causeway for the bridge across the canal opposite the mouth of Patterson Creek, both of which had been burned by Confederate cavalry raiders under Brigadier General Thomas L. Rosser during a sweep of the Patterson Valley in January and February.[234] Among other projects, the company carpenters were put to work building new gates for use in case of an emergency. Because of the war, labor for the work crews was scarce throughout the Potomac Valley, particularly in Montgomery County. The maintenance of the waterway was hindered also by the government's use of some of its scows for the purpose of "moving and building block houses at the different fords on the river in order that the canal may be strongly-guarded this coming season." Company officials continued to face the demands of its employees for higher wages as a result of the wartime inflation.[235]

Heavy rains in scattered parts of the Potomac Valley in early April caused some flood damage to the canal, particularly on the Monocacy and Williamsport Divisions. On the former, a heavy earth and rock slide occurred near the Marble Quarry about one mile below Lock No. 26. The level was drained and the rock blasted into powder and removed with wheelbarrows. Although the high water had covered most of the towpath from Seneca Creek to Lock No. 26, the canal banks were not washed badly. As a number of lock gates and balance beams had been broken, a large quantity of timber was purchased at Orleans and Harpers Ferry with which to build replacements. Since the damage was generally light, the division was reopened for boat traffic within a week.[236]

On the Williamsport Division the only damage suffered by the canal was the number of sand bars washed into the trunk by the flood waters. Although the high water had covered the towpath on the slackwater behind Dam No. 4 for an unheard-of 15 days, the banks had not been washed significantly. Accordingly, the division was ready for navigation within five days.[237]

The board made two significant decisions on April 15 that reflected the rising inflation of the period. After May 1 the toll on the coal would be increased from 5/16 to 3/8 of a cent a ton per mile.[238] At the same time, a new set of wage increases for the company employees would take effect. The pay raises would be as follows:

Collector of Tolls, Georgetown	$900 (annual)
Division Superintendents	$1,000 (annual)
Lock-Keepers at Locks Nos. 6–62, 67–72, 75	Present pay plus $5 per mo.
Lock-Keeper at Locks Nos. 63 1/3–66	$600 (annual)
Lock-Keeper at Locks Nos. 73–74	$500 (annual)
Lock-Keeper at Guard Lock No. 8	$400 (annual)
Repair Crew Bosses	$45 (monthly)[239]

The increasing trade on the canal during the spring of 1864 was reflected in the growing number of business activities along the waterway. The old Robinson Mill in Georgetown, which had been closed because of the war-induced cutbacks in demand, was purchased in early April by Benja-

---

[234] Lowe to Ringgold, February 3, March 24, 1864, Ltrs. Recd., C & O Co.
[235] Spates to President and Directors, March 31, 1864, Ltrs. Recd., C & O Co.
[236] Spates to A. Spates, April 16, 19, 1864, Ltrs. Recd., C & O Co.
[237] Masters to Ringgold, April 13, 1864, Ltrs. Recd., C & O Co.
[238] *Proceedings of the President and Board of Directors*, K, 382.
[239] *Ibid.* K, 383.

min Darby and George Shoemaker, Jr., and quickly put back into operation.[240] On May 12 the firm of McVeirs and Jones was granted permission to erect a store on the berm side of the canal at Edwards Ferry to sell groceries and feed to the passing boatmen.[241] That same day the board responded to the inquiry of J. Phillip Roman by authorizing him to build a steam packet and to commence passenger service on the waterway. As an inducement for such an undertaking, the directors agreed to permit the boat to navigate the canal free of tolls and to pay him an annual sum of $200 as long as the vessel was well-maintained.[242] To aid in the repair of the growing number of boats on the waterway, John Ellis was permitted on June 2 to commence construction of a dry dock above Lock No. 14.[243]

The canal company stockholders were informed at their annual meeting on June 6 that navigation on the waterway was proceeding at a brisk pace. Although there had been brief interruptions from high water in April, no material injuries had been inflicted on the canal by the frequent and unusual rising of the river during the spring. The rising price of coal in 1863–64 had allowed the company to raise its toll on that product. It was believed that the

> advanced rates will not injuriously affect the coal interest, will materially increase the revenues of the Company, enable them to keep the Canal in good condition, make permanent improvements upon it, insure to a greater extent than heretofore, uninterrupted navigation, and to materially reduce during the present year, pressing and meritorious pecuniary obligations, which have been an incubus upon its revenues, and greatly restricted essential improvements during the past three years.

Many new boats had been built during the past year, and it was predicted that the higher coal prices would encourage the construction of more vessels. Up until May 31, 101,390 tons of coal had been shipped on the waterway, producing $74,988.58 in toll receipts.[244]

During the month of July, more requests from local valley residents reached the canal board, asking for permission to build warehouses and grocery and feed stores along the waterway to take advantage of the increasing commerce passing over the line. On July 7 Greenbury Foot was authorized to build a feed store near Lock No. 28.[245] That same day a request from Daniel F. Roderick to construct a grain warehouse near Lock No. 29 was referred to Superintendent Spates for comment.[246] Later on the 28th, another proposal from Charles F. Elgin to build a warehouse at Edwards Ferry for shipping granite from the nearby quarry was submitted to Spates for a recommendation.[247]

Before any action could be taken on these proposals, the canal again became the scene of active military activities. In late June, Lieutenant General Jubal A. Early was sent to clear Union forces from the Shenandoah Valley. Having accomplished this objective, Early, with 14,000 men, was directed to cross the Potomac and march toward Washington in an effort to relieve the Northern siege of Petersburg, rail head of the roads leading to Richmond and an important industrial center of the waning Confederacy, begun on June 19.[248] He was also to destroy the canal and the Baltimore & Ohio Railroad..

---

[240] *Ibid*, K, 375, 380–381.
[241] *Ibid*, K, 380, 385.
[242] *Ibid*, K, 387.
[243] *Ibid*, K, 391.
[244] *Thirty-Sixth Annual Report* (1864), 5–6.
[245] *Proceedings of the President and Board of Directors*, K, 393.
[246] *Ibid*.
[247] *Ibid*.
[248] Frank E. Vandiver, *Jubal's Raid: General Early's Famous Attack on Washington in 1864* (New York,

At the same time that Early was preparing to cross into Maryland, a band of guerrillas under Mosby forded the river near Lock No. 28, about one mile above Point of Rocks, on July 4. At the lock, the Confederates attacked a canal excursion boat with a number of Treasury Department officials aboard who were traveling from Harpers Ferry to Washington. All valuables were taken, several passengers were taken prisoner, and the boat was set on fire. The Rebels proceeded to Point of Rocks where they took many private possessions, burned a warehouse, robbed several stores, and burned military equipment left behind by a retreating Federal detachment. After raiding Poolesville where they committed further depredations, the raiders recrossed the river below Point of Rocks.[249]

Early reached the vicinity of the Potomac River near Harpers Ferry on July 4 and prepared to cross into Maryland. Fighting broke out at South Branch Bridge, Patterson's Creek Bridge, and Frankford, West Virginia, and a portion of the Confederate cavalry occupied Shepherdstown. As they retreated before the Rebels, Union troops under Major General Franz Sigel burned the bridge at Lock No. 38.

During the night of the 4th, the Union forces evacuated Harpers Ferry and took position on Maryland Heights after burning the railroad and pontoon bridges across the river. After finding Harpers Ferry too difficult to take because of the Northern guns commanding the town from Maryland Heights, Early began crossing the Potomac into Maryland at Boteler's Ford near Shepherdstown on the 5th. As a result, skirmishes were fought at Keedysville, Noland's Ferry, Point of Rocks, and Solomon's Gap. A portion of his men were sent to encamp near Antietam Furnace from where working parties were dispatched to destroy the Antietam Aqueduct and the nearby canal locks and burn as many boats as possible during the night. Early himself participated in the burning of several canal barges near the aqueduct.[250] On the 6th, Early's Confederates captured Hagerstown and skirmished at Sir John's Run and Big Cacapon Bridge, West Virginia, and Antietam Creek, Maryland. The following day saw fighting at Middletown, Brownsville, and Catoctin. After encounters at Antietam, Frederick and Sandy Hook on the 8th, miscellaneous Federal units gathered under Major General Lew Wallace in an effort to halt the move on Washington. On the 9th, 6,000 bluecoats stood directly in the way of the Confederate advance on Washington. Early's 10,000 infantry moved toward to the Monocacy River several miles southeast of Frederick. After a stiff fight, the Federals were routed and the way to Washington was clear. Skirmishes took place at Rockville and Gunpowder Bridge on the 10th. The Confederates reached Silver Spring the following day, and fighting ensued in the Northern outskirts of the Northern capital, particularly at Fort Stevens. Seeing Federal troops moving into the massive fortifications of the city, Early commenced a withdrawal toward the Potomac on the 13th, and after several fire fights at Rockville and Poolesville he crossed his infantry and artillery at Conrad's Ferry and his cavalry at Edwards Ferry. To delay pursuit, the Confederate rear guard burned the towpath bridge across the Edwards Ferry River Locks.[251]

During the 10-day period that Early was advancing on Washington, a number of Confedcrate raiding parties were sent out to wreak as much havoc against the canal as possible. As a result, lock gates, bridges, and canal boats were burned in addition to the extensive damage to the Antietam Aqueduct. The principal damage to the canal occurred on the Monocacy, Antietam, and

---

1960), 59–88.
[249] Mantz to Smith, July 5, 1864, in William E. Bain, ed., *B & O in the Civil War from the Papers of Wm. Prescott Smith* (Denver, 1966), 99–100.
[250] *Ibid*, 88, and Frank E. Vandiver, ed., *War Memories: Jubal Anderson Early* (Bloomington, 1960), 383–385.
[251] *A Memoir of the Last Year of the War for Independence in the Confederate States of America* (Lynchburg, 1867), 54–62; Long, *Civil War Day by Day*, pp.533–539; O. R., Series I, Vol. XXXVII, pt. 1,pp. 169–358; and Vandiver, *Jubal's Raid*, 89–121, 148–174.

Williamsport Divisions, while no injuries to canal structures were reported between Georgetown and Seneca and between South Branch and Hancock.[252]

On the Monocacy Division, the damage was concentrated on the portion of the line between Locks Nos. 24 and 29. The gates of Lock No. 24 were destroyed, while those at Lock No. 25 were "thrown down, [the] beams cut off, [and] one gate cut in two." The bridge at the Edwards Ferry River Locks was burned and thrown into the waterway. The gates at Lock No. 26, near White's Ford where Early's troops had crossed the river back into Virginia, were thrown down and burned. One of the lock chamber's walls was torn down for some 30 feet in length and from 2 to 4 feet in depth. The gates of Lock No. 29 were taken down and cut. None of the other masonry structures on the division were damaged, but many tools and wheelbarrows had been taken. Two boats had been burned—the packet *Flying Cloud* and the new ice breaker scow. Attempts had been made to burn the repair crew's houseboat, but Mrs. Null, the cook, had defended it successfully. A large force of laborers, carpenters, and masons was soon at work on the repairs, and it was expected that the division would be ready for navigation by August 1.[253]

The Antietam Division suffered considerable damage. Four lock gates and between 35 and 41 canal boats were burned. The most critical damage occurred at the Antietam Aqueduct where most of the masonry on the berm and towpath parapets was destroyed. A portion of two of the arches was also torn out. As the entire countryside was in such a state of panic, workers, particularly masons were difficult to find until the end of July. Finally, on the 28th, the directors ordered Superintendent John Cameron of the Georgetown Division to proceed to the aqueduct "as early as practicable" to superintend the repairs.[254]

Considerably less injury was inflicted on the Williamsport Division. Nine boats, one of which was loaded, were burned, and six lock gates were cut at the heel posts. The railing was torn off the Conococheague Aqueduct, and the lock shanty at Williamsport was burned. The small bridge at Four Locks was also destroyed. While none of the damage was critical enough to interrupt travel for more than several days, the leaks in Dam No. 5, coupled with a summer drought, were so serious that the water on the division was too shallow to pass loaded barges. The repair crews had scattered during the raids, so it would be some time before the cam could be tightened.[255]

The Cumberland Division received some damage, primarily in the vicinity of Lock No. 68. The bridge over the lock was burned, and the masonry and gates partially damaged. Fourteen boats were captured in the vicinity of the lock and after the horses and mules were unhitched, the craft, most of which were loaded with coal, were set on fire. The Patterson Creek railroad bridge was burned as was the temporary bridge over the canal at that point. Even more serious to the operation of this division was the continuing drought which prevented the passage of boats drawing more than four feet of water.[256]

The Confederate raids had a devastating impact on canal trade and the economic fortunes of the towns along its line. Aware of what damage guerillas could do to their mule teams and boats, the boatmen at Georgetown balked at leaving the security of the town. From the Potomac Aqueduct west to Chain Bridge, their barges formed a solid chain. With no grain the mills were

---

[252] Washington *National Intelligencer*, July 15, 1864.
[253] Spates to Ringgold, July 16, 1864, and Spates to President and Directors, July 25, 1864, Ltrs. Recd., C & O Co. Also see John S. Mosby, *Mosby and His Men* (New York, 1867), 210–223.
[254] Benton to Ringgold, July 20, 1864, Ltrs. Recd., C & O Co., and *Proceedings of the President and Board of Directors*, K, 392–393.
[255] Masters to Ringgold and Miller to Ringgold, July 18, 1864, Ltrs. Recd., C & O Co.
[256] Lowe to Ringgold, July 25, 1864, Ltrs. Recd., C & O Co.

closed, and with no coal or flour the coasting vessels were idled. It was reported that "Georgetown was like Sunday on Tuesday."[257]

In view of the needed repairs and the rising price of coal, the board on July 25 ordered an increase in the toll on that product. The rate, which was to take effect on August 1, would be raised from 3/8 of a cent to ½ cent a ton per mile.[258]

The directors also became embroiled in a controversy with the Treasury Department at this time over the payment of a 2½ percent federal tax on the gross receipts of the revenues of the company. Congress had passed a bill on June 30 imposing such a tax on canals and other corporations to help finance the war effort. In July and August, canal officials resisted the claim, insisting that by Section 9 of the Act of the General Assembly of the State of Virginia incorporating the canal which was approved by Section 1 of the Act of Congress on March 3, 1825, the waterway was tax exempt. Refuting such an allegation, Assistant Assessor R. B. Ferguson informed Clerk Ringgold on August 27:

> Section 9 of the act of incorporation by the General Assembly of Virginia declares that said canal shall 'be forever exempt from the payment of any tax imposition or assessment whatsoever." This I understand to apply only so far as the State of Virginia is concerned. Section 1 of the Act of Congress above referred to ratifies and confirms the act of incorporation by the State of Virginia only so far as the District of Columbia is concerned; or in other words, the general provisions of the incorporating act is thereby extended over that part of the Ches. & Ohio Canal in the District of Columbia. I do not understand this section of the Act of Congress to say or to mean that the Ches. & Ohio Canal shall 'be forever exempt from the payment of any tax, imposition or assessment whatsoever.'[259]

Near the end of July, the canal again became the scene of military hostilities. After routing the Federals under General George Crook at the Second Battle of Kernstown, Virginia, on July 24, Early's Confederates in the northern Shenandoah followed the retreating bluecoats in a heavy rain to Bunker Hill, north of Winchester. Fighting erupted at Bunker Hill, Martinsburg, and Williamsport on the 25th, and the Union troops crossed the Potomac at Boteler's Ford on the 26th and encamped near Hagerstown, leaving guards at all the Potomac River fords between Antietam Creek and Hancock.[260]

As Early carried out an operation to destroy portions of the Baltimore & Ohio Railroad in the northern Shenandoah, changes were made in the Union command along the Potomac better to oppose the new Rebel threat. On the 29th Early's cavalry under Brigadier General John McCausland crossed the Potomac at McCoy's Ferry. Marching directly on Clear Spring, the Rebels drove a 400-man Federal cavalry unit five miles back toward Hagerstown before proceeding to Mercersburg, Pennsylvania. The following day saw the firing of Chambersburg and further skirmishing at Emmitsburg, Monocacy Junction, and Shepherdstown.

Entering Hancock early on the morning of the 31st, the Rebels under McCausland demanded a ransom of $30,000 and 5,000 cooked rations from the town. Although this demand could not be met, the citizens collected all the money they could raise and delivered it to the Rebel commander. Among the funds handed over to the invaders were "large sums of script, bonds,

---

[257] Washington *Evening Star*, July 9, 1864, and Washington *Daily Intelligencer*, July 22, 1864.
[258] *Proceedings of the President and Board of Directors*, K, 395.
[259] Ferguson to Ringgold, August 27, 1864, Ltrs. Recd., C & O Co.
[260] O. R., Series I, Vol. XXXVII, pt. 1, 326–331, and Long, *Civil War Day by Day*, 545–546.

and acceptances of the [canal] company" that were taken from Jacob Snively, the collector at the town.[261]

Federal cavalry under Averell pursuing the Confederates attacked them at Hancock later in the day. The Rebels pulled out to the northwest toward Cumberland. Here on August 1 the Confederates staged an assault on the Union lines stretched along the heights two miles east of the city near Folck's Mill overlooking the valley of Evitts Creek.[262]

During the night the Rebels abandoned the field and on August 2 they proceeded down the Oldtown Road toward the Deep Cut. Here the 153d Ohio, after destroying Cresap's Bridge over the canal, had taken position on Alum Hill. While Confederate artillery softened the Federals, several Virginia battalions marched toward a section of the canal that had been left unguarded by the bluecoats. Wrecking a nearby building, the Rebels used the timbers to bridge the waterway. Crossing the canal, the Rebels quickly turned the Ohioans' flank and forced them to flee across the Potomac. On the south side of the river some of the Union soldiers were posted behind the railroad embankment while others boarded an ironclad train that had been brought down from Cumberland. The train, consisting of four armored cars with three guns on each, was soon knocked out by the Confederate artillery, and the Ohioans were forced to surrender.[263]

Meanwhile, the Confederates had begun to sense trouble as more Federals were moving into the area. Moreover, Major General Philip H. Sheridan had been named commander of the Army of the Shenandoah on August 1 with the specific task of ridding the Valley of Early and all Confederates. Thus, while the Ohioans were surrendering at Oldtown, Early's cavalry were fighting a rear-guard action at Hancock as they recrossed the Potomac. After a day of rest on the 3rd, Early's men skirmished at Antietam Ford, Maryland, on the 4th, as they remained a bane of the Federal forces in Virginia.[264] The following day skirmishing broke out at Keedysville, Williamsport, and Hagerstown as Confederate units once more entered Maryland in a brief foray. Following a period of maneuvering on the Shenandoah as Sheridan attempted to destroy the Confederate guerillas under Early and Mosby, Early advanced toward the Potomac in late August but found all the fords between Shepherdstown and Williamsport well guarded.[265]

The Confederate raids into Maryland and the Federal attempts to quash the guerilla movements took their toll on the trade of the waterway. The Washington newspapers reported on the dismal fortunes of the canal during this period. On August 9 the *Chronicle* observed that the damage done to the waterway and to the boats along its line would "keep back over a hundred thousand tons of coal from the Washington market this season." Although repairs had commenced on the Antietam Aqueduct, Rebel forces in the vicinity had driven the crews away by firing across the river.[266]

The *Evening Star* of August 22 gave even a darker picture of the effect of the military activities on the canal. The plight of the waterway was described as follows:

> Business upon the canal amounts to nothing comparatively. All that was received since the 1st of August by the canal was wood from farms within 20 miles of town. Ice from Middleton's ice-houses, 12 miles distant [at Widewater], and a few hundred bushels of grain from points on the canal, the most distant of which is Berlin, 55 miles. The total number of arrivals was 20, an average of one daily up to last Saturday.

---

[261] *Proceedings of the President and Board of Directors*, K, 398–399.
[262] O. R., Series I, Vol. XXXVII, pt. 1, 188–189, 354–355.
[263] *Ibid*, and Lowe to Ringgold, August 25, 1864, Ltrs. Recd., C & O Co.
[264] Long, *Civil War Day by Day*, 549–551.
[265] Joel J. Williamson, *Mosby's Rangers* (New York, 1896), 220–222.
[266] Washington *Chronicle*, August 9, 1864.

> The prospect of reopening of the coal trade this season is regarded by the agents of the companies as very unpromising.[267]

As there was no through navigation at all during the month of August, only $398.80 in tolls was collected giving the canal its new low for a single month since July 1861.[268]

As a result of effective Federal cavalry operations the Potomac Valley was quiet by early September, and the scene of small military skirmishes and raids moved well back into the Shenandoah Valley. On the 8th the board, taking cognizance of the return of calm to the valley, commenced to place the canal back into operation. The directors determined

> That the payment of toll be required on such boats as were destroyed by burning, only for the distance which the cargo was transported, and that the several Supts. be directed to deliver such coal as has been removed from the canal, as far as practicable, to the several owners thereof.[269]

The prospects for reopening the canal to boat traffic were more encouraging by mid-September than they had been for nearly two months. In an article on the 13th, the Washington *Evening News* reported that:

> The news from the western divisions of the canal is cheering. The repairs are progressing rapidly, and it is hoped that the empty boats which are lying at Georgetown, about fifty in number, will be able to go through to Cumberland before the close of the week, and that next week the coal trade will be reopened, and all the docks be as noisy as ever, with the busy beavers employed in receiving the cargoes for shipment at the wharves.
>
> Up to this date [during the month of September] the arrivals by the canal were an even dozen. Of these, three were rafts bringing iron from Cabin John Bridge; six were boats laden with wood from points within twenty miles of town; two boats laden with grain and flour, and one with hay, all from landings within forty-five miles of town. In the same time there were twenty-one departures, three of these boats, venturing to try to pass through to Cumberland; the others were bound for nearer landings.
>
> Of these five only carried cargoes, principally dry goods, groceries, lumber and fertilizers. The resumption of trade through to Cumberland will restore to Georgetown the appearance of life which was visible just before the rebel raid which suspended the trade by this route.[270]

Encouraged by these developments, the representatives of the Allegany County coal companies met in mid-September to agree upon joint action with reference to the demands of the miners and boatmen for higher rates. The result of the conference was that the demands of both groups were met. The price for mining was fixed at $1 per ton and that for transportation was set at $3 per ton.[271]

---

[267] Washington *Evening Star*, August 22, 1864.
[268] *Thirty-Seventh Annual Report* (1865), C & O Co., Appendix B, 10.
[269] *Proceedings of the President and Board of Directors*, K, 398.
[270] Washington *Evening Times*, September 13, 1864.
[271] Cumberland *Alleganian*, September 21, 1864, quoted in Harvey, *Civil War and Maryland Coal Trade*, 376.

Meanwhile, the repair crews which had commenced work shortly after the Confederate withdrawal had the canal ready for navigation by September 20. However, the repairs and clean-up details continued at their jobs until the end of the month. Superintendent Benton of the Antietam Division reported on October 1 that he had just completed the removal of 24 loaded coal boats that had been burned and sunk between Dams Nos. 3 and 4. Moreover, four new lock gates had been installed at Lock No. 37, and the Antietam Aqueduct had been completed with the aid of Superintendent Cameron of the Georgetown Division.[272]

Superintendent Masters of the Williamsport Division informed canal officials on October 3 that he had commenced repairs as soon as the Rebels had left the country. Considerable damage had been done to the upper portion of the Conococheague Aqueduct during the last raid. However, the major problem on the division was the leaks in Dam No.5 which had resulted in a shortage of water for passing loaded boats down to Dam No. 4. After some boats were partially unloaded at Guard Lock No. 5 on September 30 to allow them to proceed down the canal, a rain storm on October 1 had raised the level of water behind the dam. Repair crews were at work tightening the structure and hopefully would succeed in patching the leaks before the water level fell again.[273]

Periodic night forays across the Potomac by Confederate guerilla units under Mosby and White continued to hamper canal operations during September and October. Known as "Mosby's Rangers," and "White's Battalion" or the "Loudoun Rangers," these roving bands numbering some 400 men spread fear among the boatmen along the canal as they staged a series of lightning raids into Maryland to steal horses and mules, burn barges, destroy Baltimore & Ohio trains, and cut the telegraph wires leading from Washington.[274] On September 29, the company officials received word from A. C. Greene at Cumberland that the

> Rebs are stealing the horses from the Boats clear to Cumbd. Two boats have been robbed within ten miles of Cumbd. and last night a gang of McNeill's men crossed at Black Oak bottom, passed over Will's Mountain into the valley of Georges Creek and swept the coal mines of their horses. The American Co. lost sixteen.

Greene went on to complain that the Union army commander at Cumberland was doing nothing to counter the tactics of the guerrillas:

> In the meantime Gen. Kelly sits in Cumbd. surrounded by thousands of men but takes no steps to prevent or to punish their maraudings. I wish you would impress upon [Secretary of War] Stanton the facts and the consequences resulting from them. The canal trade is paralyzed by reason of them.[275]

The most notorious raid occurred on the night of October 14 when some 80 of Mosby's men under Captain William Chapman crossed the Potomac at White's Ford, four miles below the mouth of the Monocacy River. Moving up the towpath, the marauders burned some ten canal boats loaded with freight after stealing about 20 horses and mules from the boatmen. They also wreaked havoc on the Noland's Ferry Bridge by tearing loose its superstructure and throwing the debris into the canal. The Rebel band then passed through Licksville to Adamstown, cutting the telegraph wires along the route. After fighting off a Union cavalry unit near Point of Rocks, the

---

[272] Benton to President and Directors, October 1, 1864, Ltrs. Recd., C & O Co.
[273] Masters to President and Directors, October 3, 1864, Ltrs. Recd., C & O Co.
[274] Williamson, *Mosby's Rangers*, 249–250.
[275] Greene to Spates, September 29, 1864, Ltrs. Recd., C & O Co.

Rebels reached the canal only to find a detachment of Federal infantry tearing up the bridge across the waterway and throwing the timber into the prism. Quickly routing them, Chapman had his men relay the bridge and recross the river at Cheek's Ford. The Confederate unit reached the Virginia shore in safety without having any injuries throughout the entire operation.[276]

Two days after the raid, on the 16th, Superintendent Spates of the Monocacy Division informed canal officials of the consequences of the foray. Many boatmen between Dams Nos. 2 and 3 were refusing to move their vessels as there were no Union guards between Muddy Branch and Nolands Ferry. Unless Federals were posted along the river between those two locations, navigation on that stretch of the canal would stop.[277]

Two weeks later, on the 30th, Superintendent Spates informed the directors that the canal was functioning very well. Federal army units had been placed along the river from Muddy Branch to Nolands Ferry, and the boatmen were making every effort to use the remaining balance of the season to the best advantage. However, there were several problems on his division. The bridge over the canal at Nolands Ferry that had been destroyed by the Rebels had not been replaced. As the military was no longer using the ferry at that location, he had ordered his crews to gather up the timbers and put them in a secure place until the ferry was reopened and the bridge was needed. The feed store at Lock No. 28 was being utilized as a picket station by Northern troops, thus depriving the owner of its use. The Baltimore & Ohio Railroad had placed a stationary engine along the berm side of the canal at Sandy Hook to pump a considerable quantity of water from that portion of the trunk to supply a heavy trade on their line. This action, which he had not approved, was reducing the level of the water in the canal to such an extent that some loaded boats were scraping the bottom.[278]

The normal functioning of the canal during the remainder of the boating season was reflected in the expanding business ventures along the line. Consideration was given to a request by Cyrus Dellinger on November 10 to erect a feed store at Williamsport to cater to the needs of the passing boatmen.[279] On December 9 the directors granted permission to Dan S. White to occupy and use the warehouse that he had constructed at Conrad's Ferry prior to the summer Confederate raids for the receipt, storage, and transportation of coal on the waterway.[280]

Perhaps the most ambitious project to be undertaken at this time was the decision of the Consolidation Coal Company to install new hoisting machinery and make other improvements for the transshipment of coal at the Linthicum-owned wharf in Georgetown. As water from the canal would be needed to operate the new hoisting apparatus, the directors determined to allow the coal company

> to take so much water from the canal, not exceeding the quantity necessary to pass a loaded boat into the river and back again as may be needed to make their experiment with the pneumatic cylinder in transferring coal from the canal to the river.

The water was to be leased from the canal company on terms similar to those that had been granted earlier to William Ray and the Swanton Coal Company for the installation of unloading machinery.[281]

---

[276] Williamson, *Mosby's Rangers*, 264–267, and Spates to Ringgold, October 16, 1864, Ltrs. Recd., C & O Co.
[277] Spates to Ringgold, October 16, 1864, Ltrs. Recd., C & O Co.
[278] Spates to President and Board of Directors, October 30, 1864, Ltrs. Recd., C & O Co.
[279] *Proceedings of the President and Board of Directors*, K, 406.
[280] *Ibid*, K, 410.
[281] *Ibid*, K, 406–407.

Despite the quickened pace of business activity on the canal, there were still numerous reports of discouraging developments along the waterway. On November 10 the directors were informed by W. C. Smith, a civil engineer who was under contract to the company, that he had measured recently the amount of water used by various mills and coal wharves at Georgetown. He had found that most of the establishments were using large amounts of water in excess of the quantities allowed by their leases. Accordingly, the Superintendent of the Georgetown Division was authorized to install new water gauges that were approved by Smith at each of the mills. The cost of the new devices was to be paid by the mill owners. Henceforth the canal company would initiate action against those millers who continued to disregard their leases.[282]

On the same day that the board received word of the water problem, it was notified of other events along the line that were related to the military situation in the Potomac Valley. Superintendent Spates of the Monocacy Division reported that he had been robbed recently of $50 by several Union soldiers while carrying out his duties.[283] George Hardy, the tender of the important Harpers Ferry locks, Nos. 35–36, had been drafted into the Federal army, and his wife and children were operating the locks in his absence.[284] Obadiah Barger, an old man who had tended Locks Nos. 45–46 for a number of years until Susan Newcomer was appointed to the position in September 1864, complained that she had never worked at the locks but instead had assigned her job to an inexperienced youth without informing the division superintendent. As he was an aged man who could not support himself in another occupation, he requested and received his old lock-tender job back.[285]

More discouraging news arrived from Superintendent Spates on November 30. Although the Monocacy Division was operating, the locks, waste weirs, and flumes were showing signs of considerable decay. The feeder outside Guard Lock No. 3 was almost filled with sediment and there were large sand bars inside the feeder for some 200 yards. The Union soldiers stationed along the canal had filled up the towpath and berm sides of several culverts, and when he had ordered his repair crews to clear the culvert barrels the soldiers had prevented the work. The family of the lock-keeper at Lock No. 33 was "much annoyed and almost driven from the lock by the offensive odor arising from the embalming of dead bodies" in a nearby company-owned house that had been rented to the embalming parties by Messrs. Robias and Rogers, its tenants. Allen M. Benson, the keeper at Lock No. 27 had been fired "for disobedience of orders and for destroying and threatening to destroy the Company's property."[286]

After the canal was closed by ice in early December, President Spates began to press the military for the removal of obstructions in the culverts. Accordingly, Brigadier General E. B. Tyler informed Spates on December 21 that orders had been issued to open all the culverts that had been closed by the military. As he fully appreciated "the importance of the canal to both the Government and the public," Tyler promised that he would not permit his men "to interrupt its workings."[287]

Despite the Confederate raids and the lingering uneasiness of the military situation in the Potomac Valley, the year 1864 was a profitable one for the Cumberland coal trade and the canal company. Writing in the *Merchants' Magazine and Commercial Review* in May 1865, concerning the rising demand for coal to support the Northern war effort, C. B. Conant stated that

---

[282] Ibid, K, 407, 419, 422–423.
[283] Ibid, K, 405.
[284] Ibid.
[285] Barger to Brengle, Spates, and Watson (three letters), November 4, 1864, Ltrs. Recd., C & O Co.
[286] Spates to President and Directors, November 30, 1864, Ltrs. Recd., C & O Co.
[287] Tyler to Spates, December 21, 1864, in Spates Papers.

more coal was demanded [in 1864] by private manufacturers and carriers engaged in making and transporting arms, munitions, and supplies for Government.

The federal government itself increased its consumption of coal by 200,000 tons in 1861 to 1,000,000 tons in 1864.[288]

The prosperous year also saw an increase in the coal trade statistics on the canal. The total tonnage on the line rose by nearly 10 percent over the 1863 figure to 290,772 tons. The amount of coal shipped over the canal increases by some 12 percent over the total for the previous year to 260,368 tons. The rise in trade, as well as the increase in tolls on coal, enabled the company to realize a 32 percent increase in revenue from tolls over the previous year's totals to $225, 897.34. All told, the year 1864 saw the highest total tonnage carried on the waterway since 1860, and it was the third best year in that respect in the history of the company. In terms of the revenue derived from the tolls, it was the most profitable in the history of the canal to date.[289]

At the annual meeting of the stockholders held on June 5, 1865, President Spates reported on the progress of the waterway during 1864. He observed that

> We have the satisfaction to state that the business of the Company for the past year has been more prosperous than any preceding year since its organization; that the condition of the Canal has been better than for many years previously; and that the transportation upon it was more regular and less interrupted, until the invasion of the enemy in July last, when material damages were sustained, and the navigation was suspended for three months of the most active and profitable portion of the year. The cost of repairs from the destruction of the works did not exceed $12,000, but it was estimated that the revenues of the Company were diminished by the casualty to the extent of $200,000, and about eighty boats were destroyed, thus reducing the means of transportation after the resumption of navigation.[290]

---

[288] C. B. Conant, "Coal Fever: The Price and Prospects of Anthracite Coal," *Merchants' Magazine and Commercial Review*, (May 1865), 359.
[289] Sanderlin, *The Great National Project*, 307.
[290] *Thirty-Seventh Annual Report* (1865), 3.

VI. PEACE COMES TO THE CANAL: 1865

The extreme severity of the 1864–65 winter closed the canal to navigation earlier than usual in December and precluded the commencement of repairs until spring. The Potomac River and the canal were still frozen in late February arousing fears that the spring coal trade would be hindered, and even worse, that an ice freshet might sweep down the valley when warmer weather broke up the ice. The Hagerstown *Mail* reported on February 25 that:

> It has been hoped that there would be a speedy reopening of the navigation to Cumberland, and some of the dealers have expected to receive supplies of coal by the 1st of March; but this is considered by the superintendent of the canal as an impossibility. The ice on the western levels is very thick and bank high. A sudden freshet is dreaded, and not without reason, for such a freshet, bringing down the ice, would be very dangerous to the lower sections, and might so damage the canal as to delay navigation for a considerable length of time. It is ordered by the Canal Commissioners that the water shall be drawn off at this terminus on the 22d instant, and the workmen will proceed at once to repair damages, which will probably require ten days to complete the work. After which the route will be opened as soon as possible, and the coal and produce trade will be resumed. The quantity of supplies at the western depots will require a large number of boats for transportation.[291]

Not only were the Potomac Valley residents concerned about the weather, but they were also alarmed by two daring Confederate raids at Cumberland and Edwards Ferry in late February. On the night of February 21–22, some 65 men, known as McNeill's Rangers, crossed the Potomac near Brady's Mills and entered Cumberland while approximately 8,000 Federals were encamped in the city. After destroying the office of the military telegraph, the Rebels captured Generals Kelly and Crook while they were sleeping and took them, along with their horses, down the canal towpath to Wiley's Ford, where they crossed the river into Virginia. A Federal cavalry company pursued the guerrillas to Romney, where a skirmish occurred, but the prisoners were already on their way to Richmond.[292] Relative to the foray at Edwards Ferry, the New York *Times* reported on February 26:

> A night or two ago a squad of White's guerrillas crossed the Potomac River, in the neighborhood of Edward's Ferry, and drove in our pickets. They shot three men of the First Delaware Cavalry, who are on duty there, and carried off a number of horses. A part of the gang visited a store in the neighborhood, and took from it all the articles they could carry off. They then retired across the river into Virginia, not however, without loss, for one of their number was killed and two others so seriously wounded as to render it necessary to hold them upon their horses while recrossing the river. One of our men is supposed to be mortally wounded.[293]

Early in March the anxieties of the Potomac Valley residents were realized when a heavy freshet resulted from the simultaneous breaking up of the large ice flows in the river and considerable downpours of rain. The canal banks and the towpath were washed in many places, but with the

---

[291] Hagerstown *Mail*, February 25, 1865.
[292] Lowdermilk, *History of Cumberland*, 420–422, and New York *Times*, February 26, 1865.
[293] New York *Times*, February 26, 1865, and Ray Eldon Hiebert and Richard K. MacMaster, *A Grateful Remembrance: The Story of Montgomery County, Maryland* (Rockville, 1976), 175.

exception of some logs being removed from the cribs on the Virginia side of Dam No. 5, there were no serious breaches or injuries to the masonry work. After quick remedial repairs, the canal was ready for navigation about March 20. However, business was not actively resumed until April 1, because the coal shippers had not made satisfactory arrangements for transportation.[294]

Following a period of negotiations, the canal company agreed on March 9 to rent the property on the west side of the Rock Creek Basin to the federal government until the end of the war. Earlier on September 8, 1864, the New York-based Mayer interests that had rented the land in March notified canal officials that they were no longer interested in the property as a result of the delay in gaining possession of it. Accordingly, the company issued writs of ejectment against the defiant tenants, who then rented their properties to the Quartermaster Department. On November 14 the Circuit Court of the District of Columbia ruled in favor of the canal company by dispossessing the tenants of their claims to the land. However, the military already had established facilities on the property, and the canal company was forced to continue renting the land to the government at the same monthly rates that had been negotiated by the ex-tenants.[295]

Meanwhile, the Civil War was drawing to a close. After completing his "march to the sea," Union General William T. Sherman struck northward through the Carolinas on February 1 to unite with Grant in Virginia. Within six weeks, the capitals and major cities of both North and South Carolina were in Federal hands. On April 2 Grant broke the Confederate position at Five Forks, 16 miles southwest of Petersburg, and Lee's Army of Northern Virginia was forced to retreat westward. After the ragged 28,000 man army was surrounded near Appomattox Court House, Lee surrendered his command to Grant on April 9.[296]

After the commencement of navigation on April 1, commerce on the waterway proceeded at a slow pace and came to a standstill by April 26. The end of the war meant the reduction of choice government contracts for manufactured goods with an inevitable reflection on the coal trade. With the restoration of normal competition, the Cumberland coal interests began to look for ways to decrease costs and attract customers in the northern markets. The high rates previously paid for mining and transportation of coal could not be continued. As the miners and the boatmen were unwilling to see their wages and profits reduced, wage disputes between the miners and the coal companies led to a month-long suspension of mining in the coal fields. At the same time, the boatmen put pressure on the canal board to aid their cause on the declining coal trade by reducing the toll on coal shipments, but it rejected such recommendations. As a result of these developments, the amount of coal shipped on the canal up to June 1 was 61,677 tons compared to 101,390 tons during the same period in 1864. The total revenue collected from tolls for the current season was $65,097.44 compared with $74,988.58 over the same period the previous year.[297]

In his annual report to the company stockholders on June 5, President Spates provided information on the condition of the canal and the state of its financial affairs. Among his observations were the following:

> The canal is now in good navigable condition, but to put it in thorough and permanent order, make it reliable for uninterrupted navigation, and afford proper facilities to the largely increasing trade upon it, considerable expenditures will still be required. It is pro-

---

[294] *Thirty-Seventh Annual Report* (1865), 3, and Masters to Board of Directors, March 2, 1865, Ltrs. Recd., C & O Co.
[295] *Proceedings of the President and Board of Directors*, K, 399–400, 402–403, 486, and Ringgold to Moore, March 9, 1865, Ltrs. Sent, C & O Co.
[296] Allan Nevins, *The War for the Union* (4 books, New York, 1971), Book IV, 309–312.
[297] *Thirty-Seventh Annual Report* (1865), 6–7.

posed to do this during the present season as far as the revenues of the Company will admit consistent with other indispensable obligations....

Since the accession of the present Board in February 1862, the state of the country bordering the Canal, owing to the various military operations and restrictions, has been such as to render all matters connected with its business very precarious. The aggregate revenues of the Company for the years 1861 and 1862, were respectively in 1861, $75,741.90, in 1862, $72,624.95, whilst the maintenance of the Canal restricted by these inadequate means and the exhausted credit of the Company, was in 1861, $105,607.82, in 1862, $86,651.26, thus increasing the already overburdened debts of the Company for these two years, a further sum of $43,892.23 in addition to accumulating interest on obligations of the Company for repairs &c., which had hitherto been regularly paid, amounting to about $30,000.

During the years 1863 and 1864 however, notwithstanding the frequent interruptions and restrictions still continued by the course of the war, these disadvantages have been overcome in a great measure, and after the payment of all obligations incurred by the incumbent Board, [$171,367.10 of] claims previously existing have been liquidated and paid...

There still remain floating or current debts of the Company [$301,024.25] to be provided for from their surplus revenues, after the proper maintenance and improvements required to render the Canal effective and durable, which it is proposed to liquidate as early as practicable....[298]

---

[298] *Ibid,* 3–5. In response to an order of the Speaker of the Maryland House of Delegates, Spates had delivered a similar report to that body on March 13. Spates to Speaker, House of Delegates, March 13, 1865, Ltrs. Sent, C & O Co.

VII. THE CANAL IN THE AFTERMATH OF THE CIVIL WAR

The canal emerged from the Civil War on both a depressing note and a promising one. The waterway itself had suffered great physical damage from the military operations of the opposing armies. Furthermore, the military continued to occupy the Potomac Aqueduct and part of the Rock Creek mole, to the detriment of the canal's business. When the Quartermaster Department continued to insist on its right to occupy a portion of the wharves on the mole for a government coaling station, the canal company testily reacted by filing claims against the War Department for losses sustained as a result of military use of the waterway during hostilities. On May 2, 1866, the company informed Maryland Congressman Francis Thomas, a former canal president that

> during the whole war the canal was freely used by the Government for transportation without compensation being made in the payment of tolls, that considerable damages were done to the works by the operations of the military and great losses sustained by restrictions imposed by them upon general transportation, and for these the Company have filed claims in the War Department for the years 1861 and 1862 $75,391.96—1863 & 1864 $292,330, making an aggregate sum of $367,721.96.[299]

Later on September 5, 1866, the directors appealed directly to President Andrew Johnson

> to relieve from military occupation and turn over to the Alexandria Canal Company the Potomac Aqueduct, which belongs to that Company, and is at present the obstacle to the early opening of that Canal.[300]

On the other hand, the financial condition of the company had measurably improved as a result of the revival of trade after 1863. Bankruptcy, which had threatened the company in the late 1850s, no longer seemed to be so near. The improved commercial and financial status of the company made it possible to undertake the sorely needed improvements such as the raising of the Georgetown bridges, that had been postponed and those in progress, such as the new masonry Dam No. 5, that had come to a halt during the war years.[301]

The physical condition of the canal in 1865 was much worse than it had been before the war. Despite growing trade and revenues and some increase in repair expenditures toward the end of the conflict, the waterway had been generally neglected. The destruction of its works during the hostilities had been serious, and in addition, it had not received the attention required for normal maintenance. Only the most necessary repairs had been made, and then often in a hasty and slip-shod fashion. Evidence of the general state of the canal's deterioration was demonstrated by the occurrence of numerous breaches on the Georgetown, Monocacy, Antietam, and Cumberland Divisions between April and August in 1865.[302] It was reported that there were many trees bor-

---

[299] Ringgold to Thomas, May 2, 1866, Ltrs. Sent, C&O co. Also see, Ringgold to Rucker, May 29, 1866, Ltrs. Sent, C&O Co., and Moore to Ringgold, May 28, 1866, Ltrs. Recd., C&O Co. After further negotiations, the military finally agreed to relinquish its claims to the mole wharves on January 31, 1868. Godey to Ringgold, January 10, 1868, Ltrs. Recd., C&O Co. and Proceedings of the President and Board of Directors, L, 56.

[300] Proceedings of the President and Board of Directors, K, 511. After a number of similar appeals and considerable negotiations, the military relinquished control of the aqueduct. In July 1868 construction was begun on a wooden highway toll bridge built over the rewatered trunk.

[301] Sanderlin, *Great National Project*, 222-223.

[302] Ringgold to Greene, December 1, 1865, Ltrs. Sent, C&O Co., and Proceedings of the President and

dering the canal that had overgrown to the point that they were interfering with the passage of boats and the use of the towpath.[303] Many of the lock gates needed to be replaced, and the heavy horse traffic on the towpath had worn it down at many points.[304] The tidelocks in Georgetown were out of repair after being damaged by government occupation and mismanagement, and the Rock Creek Basin was largely filled in by the deposits of the creek. Moreover, the prism of the trunk was shrinking as a result of siltation deposits accumulating on the inner slopes and the floor of the canal. Hence it was no longer possible for two loaded boats to pass at many points along the canal.[305]

In November 1865 the canal company hired Charles P. Manning, a reputable civil engineer, to examine the waterway and to report on its condition and the repairs and improvements that were needed.[306] In a comprehensive report filed on May 31, 1866, he made the following observations:

> It is unnecessary for me to remind the Board that for several seasons previous to the last period of suspended navigation, no repairs beyond those of absolute necessity were either attempted or accomplished; nor that, consequently, the need of repairs during the past winter, and prospectively, for the current season of navigation has been and still is excessive.
>
> Though I feel confident that free navigation can and will be maintained, without much difficulty during the current season, I fear that the ordinary gradual deposit of sediment added to the large amount which has already accumulated to an extent sufficient, in many places, to reduce the channel of the Canal to an area much less than is required for the passage of two loaded boats, will, at no far distant period, cause an entire suspension of navigation, during the business season of, possibly, a whole year, in order that the original proper dimensions of the trough may be thoroughly restored.
>
> To mitigate, if not to effectively prevent the occurrence of this apprehended misfortune, the active and constant employment of a number of dredging boats, during the season navigation, is deemed essential, therefore, I advise the immediate construction of two more of these valuable machines, similar to the four now in use upon the line of the canal.
>
> In general the trough of the Canal is free from dangerous, or even injurious leaks; but that portion of it which traverses the cavernous lime-stone district between South and North mountains, has always been, and still is subject to very dangerous leaks and consequent breaches, for which there appears to be no effectual remedy, short of the elevation of the entire body of the Canal (bottom, towpath, &c.,) to a height of two feet or more above its present levels, wherever the most obstinate and dangerous of these leaks are known to exist, or continually threaten to break forth.
>
> In general the masonry of the aqueducts, culverts and Locks is both substantial and in good repair, the only exception requiring special remark being the aqueduct that spans the Conococheague River, which fine structure was wantonly and most seriously injured by rebel soldiers during the late rebellion. At present

---

Board of Directors, K, 442
[303] Proceedings of the President and Board of Directors, K, 438
[304] Cameron to President and Directors, November 9, 1865, Ltrs. Recd., C&O Co.
[305] Proceedings of the President and Board of Directors, K, 489–490
[306] Ibid, K, 465

the navigation is maintained over this dilapidated aqueduct by means of a substantial wooden trunk which is supported upon the original arches of the masonry and quite secure from the damaging effects of ordinary floods.

Generally speaking the lock gates are in excellent condition; but there are many that should be taken out and replaced by new ones as rapidly as circumstances may permit, and numbers thus removed might then be sufficiently repaired to answer all the purposes of reliable substitutes, or duplicates in cases of accident. These perishable appendages of the Canal are liable to great abuse at the hands of reckless boatmen, and therefore are a constant source of both anxiety and expense.

In relation to the dams, I have to say, that the "Little Falls" and "Seneca" (Nos. 1 & 2,) are in a somewhat dilapidated and inefficient state; and that the one at Harper's Ferry (No. 3,) commonly known as "The Government Dam," is in ordinarily good condition. The two first named of these structures are composed of brush and loose stones, and the last named of wooden crib-work, filled with loose stones and sheathed with timber and planks. Dam No. 4 is not only in sound condition, but being exclusively a structure of stone, is regarded as thoroughly permanent, if not quite imperishable.

Two thirds of Dam No. 5 are new, and made exclusively of stone, the remaining third being composed partly of temporary crib work filled with loose stone, but mainly of the original structure, which was built after the fashion of the one at Harper's Ferry.

Dam No. 6, is in general good condition, and regarded as a permanent structure, though formed of crib-work, filled with loose stones and sheathed with timber and planks, similar in most respects to Dam No. 3, but of better form and more substantial construction. The remaining Dam (at the terminus of the Canal in Cumberland) is exclusively of stone, and in perfect order.

Of these Dams Nos. 1 and 2 need unusual repairs, requiring altogether an expenditure of perhaps, no less than twenty-five thousand dollars, in order to restore them to thorough usefulness.

Dam No. 5 should be completed without delay, and preparations have been made and are now in progress to accomplish the major part, if not all of the unfinished stone-work during the coming summer and autumn. To complete this work an expenditure of about sixty thousand dollars will be required.

Of the remaining Dams, No. 3 needs only ordinary repairs. No. 4 a little back-filling of loose stones or gravel, and the one at Cumberland substantially nothing.

Owing to the great draught of water from Dam No. 1, chiefly requisite for milling, rather than the legitimate purposes of the Canal, the time is rapidly approaching, if it has not already arrived, when the construction of a new and larger feeder-canal, in lieu of, and entirely apart from the existing narrow and unsubstantial one at this Dam, should be commence and diligently prosecuted to an early completion.

At present the consumption of water for milling purposes in Georgetown exceeds four millions of gallons per hour, or enough to furnish lockage to tide water for *forty loaded boats* and a like number of *empty ones back again*.

The cost of constructing the proposed new feeder will probably be less than, but will not exceed twenty five thousand dollars.

Many of the lock keepers' houses need considerable repairing, and nearly all of these buildings, more or less restoration to a condition of necessary comfort. The expenditure of perhaps, five thousand dollars for this purpose, would accomplish all that is pressingly needed.[307]

The restoration and improvement of the canal began almost immediately after the conclusion of the war. On April 12, three days after Lee surrendered to Grant at Appomattox Court House, the board received word that the Corporation of Georgetown had agreed that the bridges over the canal east and west of the Market House were to be raised to a height of 11 feet above the water line. Accordingly, a contract was let to C. C. Carman for the raising and repair of the bridge west of the Market and the reconstruction of the bridge east of the Market.[308] In July the bridges at Lock No. 68 and at Patterson's Creek that had been destroyed by the Rebels were ordered to be rebuilt.[309] Construction of the masonry dam replacing the temporary structure at Dam No. 5 was soon resumed. By June 4, 1866, some 400 feet had been completed from the Virginia abutment with about 300 feet remaining to be done before it was finished to the Maryland shore. Plans were also considered for the improvement of Dams Nos. 1-3.[310] During the winter of 1865–66, many portions of the canal were dredged, and large amounts of sediment were removed from the prism. Other winter projects included repairs to the masonry works, the replacement of deteriorating lock gates, and work on the waste weirs.

In June 1866 the canal company finally came to an agreement with the corporate authorities of Georgetown concerning the manner of raising the bridges over the canal. After the Georgetown aldermen authorized the substitution of permanent iron bridges for the stone structures at Congress, Jefferson, Washington, and Greene Street, a contract was let to Duvall & Co. on August 9. The new structures, costing $22,000 were completed by early 1867.[311]

In anticipation of the resumption of trade through Georgetown, the company hired an engineer in the spring of 1867 to draw up plans and estimates for the restoration of the tidelock and tumbling dam at the mouth of Rock Creek. A contract was let to Deeter & Maynard for the work that was to cost an estimated $9,000.[312] At the same time, the company employed its dredging machines to restore the canal to its original dimensions from the mouth of Rock Creek to the Foundry above Georgetown.[313]

The repair of Civil War damages to the canal continued until 1869. In June of that year the stockholders were informed that during the preceding twelve months $169,258.40 had been spent on ordinary repairs and $10,453.42 on extraordinary repairs. Commenting on these large expenditures, President Spates stated:

> Whilst the above-mentioned expenditures may be considered heavy, yet the condition of the canal was such after the close of the war, from the fact of its being

---

[307] *Thirty-Eighth Annual Report* (1866), C&O Co., 6–9

[308] Proceedings of the President and Board of Directors, K, 422; Smith to Spates, April 10, 1865, Ltrs. Recd., C&O Co.; and *Ordinances and Resolutions of the Corporation of Georgetown, from January, 1865, to January, 1866* (Georgetown, 1866), 19. For more information on this topic, see Edwin C. Bearss, "The Bridges, Historic Structures Report—Part II" (NPS Mss., 1968), 40–42.

[309] Proceedings of the President and Board of Directors, K, 434

[310] *Thirty-Eighth Annual Report* (1866), C&O Co., 4–5

[311] Proceedings of the President and Board of Directors, K, 501–502, 508; Ringgold to Wallack, October 20, 1866, Ltrs. Sent, C&O Co.; and Ordinance of the Corporation of Georgetown, June 26, 1866, Ltrs. Recd., C&O Co. Also see, Bearss, "Bridges," 42–44

[312] *Thirty-Ninth Annual Report* (1867), C&O Co., 5

[313] *Fortieth Annual Report* (1868), C&O Co., 4

continually damaged by the contending armies, as to employ a large force to enable the Board to place its condition beyond any ordinary contingency. This, the Board, with judgment and discreetness, have done; and they now have the pleasure of reporting to the Stockholders the canal fully recovered from all damages growing out of the war. The whole line is now in thorough, complete, and safe condition.

During the past ten years little or nothing had been done towards repairing and improving lock-houses, bridges, culverts, aqueducts, locks, lock-gates, and waste-weirs of the Company; many of them had become entirely unfit for use and were becoming worthless, rendering it absolutely essential to the requirements of the Company to have them repaired. This the Board have done, and, although at heavy cost, they now present a comfortable and substantial condition, and the fact may now be confidently stated that the condition of the canal in all its departments is such as to justify a largely decreased expenditure during the current year, unless overtaken by unseen and unexpected disaster.[314]

Despite the progress in the restoration of the waterway, the canal company faced numerous difficulties during the postwar years. Heavy water freshets occurred in the Potomac Valley in 1865 and 1866, and a severe ice freshet in the spring of 1868 did considerable damage to the waterway.[315] The wage disputes between the Allegany County miners and the coal companies that had interfered with the coal trade in May and June 1865 again erupted in the spring of 1866.[316] As a result of the deflationary tendency of coal prices and the decreasing demand for that product, the board reduced tolls from ½ cent to 4/10 of a cent a tom per mile in September 1866 and to 1/4 of a cent in March 1868.[317]

The state of flux in Maryland politics during the Reconstruction era also had detrimental effects on the canal company. The Union coalition which had ruled the state since 1862 was undermined by the collapse of the Confederacy. Soon, political forces moved to establish a more natural realignment, a conservative reaction to the Radical Constitution of 1864 appeared, and Democrats commenced efforts to revitalize their decimated party. By 1867 Maryland's period of "Self-Reconstruction" had come to an end and a more stable party alignment had emerged. Augmented by Conservative Unionists, new voters, and returning veterans, the Democrats became the dominant party in Maryland and would remain so for many years to come under the leadership of Arthur P. Gorman.[318]

The political instability in Maryland during the period of party realignment in the aftermath of the war was demonstrated by the return of local political influence to the canal. The brief postwar period between 1865 and 1870 witnessed four changes in canal administration. Alfred Spates, who had served as president since January 1861, was replaced by Jacob Snively in June 1865 only to return in August 1867. In June 1869 Josiah Gordon became president, but he was replaced in June 1870 by James E. Clarke.[319]

Along with the frequent political upheavals, charges of fraudulence were placed against former canal officials. On December 9, 1869, the company's Committee of Accounts accused

---

[314] *Forty-First Annual Report* (1869), C&O Co., 4–5
[315] *Thirty-Ninth Annual Report* (1867), 5–6; *Fortieth Annual Report* (1868), 7; and Mans to President and Directors, July 11, 1868, Ltrs. Recd., C&O Co.
[316] *Thirty-Eighth Annual Report* (1866), 3–5, and *Thirty-Ninth Annual Report* (1867), 3
[317] Proceedings of the President and Board of Directors, K, 511, L, 82
[318] Richard Walsh and William Lloyd Fox, eds., *Maryland: A History, 1632–1974* (Baltimore, 1974), 377–392.
[319] Sanderlin, *Great National Project*, 224, 304.

Alfred Spates with nine separate charges of falsely obtaining for his own purposes appropriations amounting to between $5.000 and $80,000 for work already paid for during the period from February 1865 to October 1868. Division Superintendent George W. Spates was also charged with one count of misappropriation of funds.[320] Both men maintained their innocence, claiming that they were the victims of the fractious political infighting then taking place in the state.[321] Alfred Spates appeared to vindicate himself by being elected to the State Senate from Allegany County in 1869, but the controversy continued unabated.[322] On February 9, 1870, the board ordered the company counsel, George A. Pearre, to demand from the two men the money they owed the company or face court suit.[323]

When the two accused men rebuffed the counsel, formal suits were initiated in the Circuit Court of Allegany County against Alfred Spates and in the Circuit Court of Montgomery County against George W. Spates. Although the evidence presented indicated a strong probability of misconduct, a citizens' committee from Cumberland appealed to the directors on October 12 to drop the charges.[324] Although they refused to do so at that time by a 4-3 vote, all charges were finally dropped without further investigation on December 8. The action was taken on the grounds that the suit had been brought by ex-president Josiah Gordon and thus was "not authorized by the present or the former Board, and there being no prospect of successful prosecution."[325]

Despite unsettled trade conditions, political interference, and the expenditure of large sums of money for the restoration of the waterway, the financial condition of the company continued to improve. Canal trade increased each year with tonnage totals of 372,335 in 1865, 383,408 in 1866, 521,402 in 1867, 552,987 in 1868, and 723,938 in 1869.[326] Receipts from tolls averaged nearly $340,000 a year during the same period, thereby allowing the company to pay off its floating debt and enabling it to resume the payment of its long-term obligations.[327] Thus, the stage was set for the "golden years" of the canal's history in the early 1870s when the waterway would experience its most stable and prosperous period.

---

[320] Proceedings of the President and Board of Directors, L, 233–246. Earlier in July 1866, Alfred Spates had come under suspicion when it was found that in February 1865 he had withdrawn the $13,000 appropriation from the U. S. Treasury that had been authorized by Congress for the raising of the Georgetown bridges. After he was voted out as president of the company in June, he kept the Treasury check without making any account of his transaction in the company's financial records. Under the threat of a suit in the federal courts, Spates returned the check to Jacob Snively, his successor, in September 1866. Ringgold to Roman, July 28, 1866, and Ringgold to Snively, September 19, 1866, Ltrs. Sent, C&O Co., and Proceedings of the President and Board of Directors, K, 507–508

[321] A. Spates to Poe, November 15, 1869, and Garden to Stockholders, February 5, 1870, in Spates Papers.

[322] A. Spates to Poe, November 15, 1869, and Gordon to Stockholders, February 15, 1870, in Spates Papers

[323] Proceedings of the President and Board of Directors, L, 281, and Baltimore *American*, February 18, 1870, in Spates Papers

[324] *Ibid,* L, 370

[325] *Ibid,* L, 381

[326] Sanderlin, *Great National Project,* 307

[327] *Ibid,* 307,309; *Thirty-Ninth Annual Report* (1867), 6; and Proceedings of the President and Board of Directors, L, 226–231.

APPENDIX A

DISCOVERY AND DEVELOPMENT OF
GOLD VEINS NEAR GREAT FALLS

During the past 110 years more than 5,000 ounces of gold, valued at more than $150,000, have been produced in Maryland. Almost all of this total has been extracted from small mines in the southern part of Montgomery County. The extensive group of workings near Great Falls was the most productive of the vein systems. Here were located the Ford, Watson, and Maryland mines, the latter being the largest and furnishing the greatest yields.[1]

As early as 1827, Professor Ducatelle, a noted mineralogist of the period, stated that the region around Great Falls gave strong indications of the presence of gold.[2] Several years later, when Mrs. Trollope, the outspoken Englishwoman who was traveling in America preparatory for her publication on American manners, visited the residence of a German consul near Great Falls, she noted that traces of gold were found.[3] However, it was not until the Civil War period that actual free samples of gold were found in the area. Although there is some controversy surrounding the discovery of gold near Great Falls, most authoritative sources agree that the discovery was made in 1861 near the present site of the Maryland mine by a member of a regiment under the command of Colonel Edward A. Baker, a United States Senator from Oregon and a close friend of President Lincoln.[4]

Shortly after the firing on Fort Sumter, Baker was commissioned by Lincoln to raise three regiments or infantry in Philadelphia. One of these, the 71st Pennsylvania, was placed under his command and was referred to informally as the "First California Regiment." This designation was apparently in honor of Colonel Isaac J, Wistar of Philadelphia, who was in charge of the enrolling work and who had commanded Indian Rangers in California and Oregon in the late 1840s during the Mexican War. The regiment was moved to Fortress Monroe, where it remained until after the Battle of First Manassas on July 21, 1861. Following that northern defeat, the regiment was transferred to the Virginia side of the Potomac opposite Washington, where it was engaged, along with other commands, in building Fort Ethan Allen near Chain Bridge and strengthening the capital's defenses. The 71st Pennsylvania crossed the Potomac on September 30 and marched nine miles to Great Falls, where it camped for the night. On October 1, it reached Rockville, and after spending the next night at Seneca Mills, the regiment encamped near Poolesville from the 3rd to the 20th. During this period, it is likely that small detachments remained on picket duty along the river from Great Falls to Seneca Creek. After the bloody Union defeat on October 21 in the Battle of Ball's Bluff, in which the regiment lost its leader and 312 men, the reorganized 71st Pennsylvania was assigned to picket duty along the Potomac between Conrad's Ferry and Point of Rocks until the spring of 1862.[5]

Following the war, several members of the 71st Pennsylvania organized a group that bought the farm on which the original discovery was made. Considerable prospecting and devel-

---

[1] John C. Reed, Jr., and John C. Reed, *Gold Veins Near Great Falls, Maryland*, (Geological Survey Bulletin 1286, 1969), 1. The location and annual production of the Montgomery County gold mines may be seen on the map and graph on the following pages.
[2] John Thomas Scharff, *History of Western Maryland* (2 vols., Philadelphia, 1882), I, 676.
[3] James E. Mooney, ed., *Domestic Manners of the Americans by Mrs. Trollope* (Barre, 1969), 183-202, 227-234
[4] Reed and Reed, *Gold Veins Near Great Falls*, 4. and Edgar T. Ingalls, *The Discovery of Gold at Great Falls, Maryland* (N. P., 1960), 1-17. Map and chart from Reed and Reed, *Gold Veins Near Great Falls*, 2-4
[5] Charles H. Banes, *History of the Philadelphia Brigade* (Philadelphia, 1876), 2-32.

oping work was done, and in 1867 a shaft was sunk to a depth of about 100 feet at the future site of the Maryland mine. At least 7 ounces of gold were produced in 1868 and 4 ounces in 1869, but the work was soon abandoned.[6]

FORD MINE

During the 1880s, gold was discovered in the vicinity of the Ford Mine by George Kirk, a Georgia prospector. By February 1890, the veins were being worked by extensive open cuts on both sides of Cool Spring Branch, and a small mill was in operation near the mouth of the branch. Underground development at the Ford Mine commenced about 1890.

WATSON MINE

In the early 1900s considerable prospecting and development work were done on the veins along Carroll Branch, between the Maryland Mine and the Ford Mine, by the Great Falls Gold Mining Company. That area, which included the site of the Watson Mine, contained seven veins, the most important being the Potomac Vein that was explored by a 135-foot adit. The operations in that area, which continued until 1909, consisted of numerous pits and trenches and a few shallow shafts with short drafts and crosscuts.

MARYLAND MINE

About 1900 the property on which the Maryland Mine is located was taken over by the Maryland Gold Mining Company. A 135-foot shaft was sunk, and the mine was explored by drifts on the 50-foot and 100-foot levels. In 1903 a new shaft was started west of the vein and south of the old shaft. This shaft intersected the vein at a depth of 200 feet and was bottomed at 210 feet in 1906. The mine was shut down in 1908, but it was reopened briefly by the Empress Gold Mining Company of Philadelphia in 1912.

The most systematic exploration of the Great Falls veins began in 1915 when the Atlantic Development Company acquired the Ford Mine. Within three years the company had acquired tracts totaling 2,100 acres that included nearly all the known vein system. A. A. Hassan, a mining geologist and consulting engineer, directed an exploration program of extensive trenching, vein stripping, and diamond drilling. Reportedly, the operations found that a vein north of the Maryland Mine extended to a depth of 456 feet and that veins near the Ford Mine were at least 500 feet in depth.

American entry into World War I led to the closing of the mines in the fall of 1817. The Maryland Mine was reopened in the spring of 1918, and some development work and mining was conducted until 1922 when the mine was closed and the property sold.

After the price of gold was increased to $35 an ounce in 1934, the Maryland Mining Company was organized in October of the following year. The Maryland Mine was reopened, and a new mill was installed. Between 1936 and 1940 about 6,000 tons of ore was produced, yielding more than 2,500 ounces of gold valued at $90,000. The mine was closed in 1940, and no operations have been undertaken in the area since that time with the exception of some individual prospecting.[7]

---

[6] Reed and Reed, *Gold Veins Near Great Falls*, 5, and Ingalls, *Discovery of Gold*, 1–17
[7] Reed and Reed, *Gold Mines Near Great Falls*, 5–7 and Ingalls, *Discovery of Gold*, 1–17. Other sources that are of value in interpreting the "gold mine" story at Great Falls are: S. F. Simmons, "Notes on the Gold Deposits of Montgomery County, Maryland," *American Institute of Mining Engineers Transactions*, XVIII,

APPENDIX B

STATEMENT OF BOATS & NAMES OF OWNERS &C HELD BY THE U. S. GOVERNMENT FROM BOOKS OF THE QUARTERMASTER, U. S. A., WASHINGTON, D. C., APRIL 17, 1861[2]

BOAT NAME	OWNER	BOAT VALUE	FURNITURE VALUE	DATE SEIZED	WHERE LYING
P. B. Petrie[1]	John Rinehart	$900	—	—	Georgetown
John Humbert	John Rinehart	$1,000	$4	Feb. 17, 1862	Alexandria
F. & A. H. Dodge[1]	John Moffutt	$800	$2.50	Feb. 16, 1862	Liverpool Point
Kate McCormack	John McCormack	$900	$3	Feb. 17, 1862	Georgetown
S. B. Harrison[1]	Daniel Shives	$500	—	Feb. 17, 1862	Liverpool Point
Capt. Wm. T. Aud	Not Known	$1,300	—	Feb. 16, 1862	Fortress Monroe
Molly	Pat Broderick	$1,200	—	Feb. 16, 1862	Fortress Monroe
Dr. J. Robertson	Mertens & Snyder	$600	—	Feb 18. 1862	Liverpool Point
G. Brent	Benjamin Mitchell	$1,000	—	Feb. 16, 1862	Georgetown
Independence[1]	Jacob Zeigler	$700	$5	Feb. 18, 1862	Liverpool Point
R. R. Gregory[1]	Nancy Bowers	$700	$3	Feb. 16, 1862	Liverpool Point
Odd Fellow[1]	John Snyder	$500	$7	Feb. 13, 1862	Liverpool Point
Emperor[1]	John Young	$850	$2	Feb. 13, 1862	Liverpool Point
Geo. W. Hetsyer[1]	John H. Martin	$600	—	Feb. 18, 1862	Liverpool Point
J. Murray	Patrick Broderick	$1,000	—	Feb. 16, 1862	Georgetown
John Fitzpatrick[1]	A. J. Boose	$400	$6	Feb. 13, 1862	Liverpool Point
Union1	A. J. Boose	$400	—	Feb. 20, 1862	Liverpool Point
Hard Times[1]	A, J, Boose	$700	$6	Feb. 13, 1862	Liverpool Point
John F. Bear	Frederick Bear	$800	$8	Feb. 13, 1862	Georgetown
Jane Louisa	American Coal Co.	$700	$4	Feb. 22, 1862	Georgetown
Samuel Luman	J. H. Kindle	$700	$4	Feb. 22, 1862	Georgetown
J. Arnold[1]	W. W. Faulkwell	$700	$4	Feb. 18, 1862	Liverpool Point
Juniatta[2]	William Elder	$700	$3	Feb. 13, 1862	Liverpool Point
Maria Thompson[1]	American Coal Co.	$400	—	Feb. 18, 1862	Liverpool Point
Stephen Castleman[2]	George Hughes	$500	$5	Feb. 13, 1862	Liverpool Point
G. Hough	C. Hughes	$800	$10	Feb. 18, 1862	Georgetown
L. V. Savins[1]	John Savins	$850	$6	Feb. 18, 1862	Liverpool Point
J. M. Barnes	S. B. Barnes	$800	$1.50	Feb. 18, 1862	Fortress Monroe
Kate Barnes	S. B. Barnes	$1,100	—	Feb. 18, 1862	Georgetown
Mt. Savage	American Coal Co.	$700	$5	Feb. 18, 1862	Georgetown
W. E. Webster	John A. Reid	$1,00	—	Feb. 18, 1862	Georgetown
Three Brothers	John Spencer	$1,00	$4	Feb. 18, 1862	Fortress Monroe
Wm. Kissner[2]	Abner Meryman	$700	—	Feb. 18, 1862	Liverpool Point
M. E. Stonebreaker	American Coal Co.	$700	$5	Feb. 18, 1862	Georgetown
Thos. James	John A. Rinehart	$700	$5	Feb. 18, 1862	Georgetown
Geo. H. Mandy[1]	Peter Snyder	$900	$5	Feb. 18, 1862	Liverpool Point
D. Morrissey	Not Known	$750	$4	Feb. 26, 1862	Georgetown
Three Sisters	John Byroads	$1,000	$10	Feb. 21, 1862	Fortress Monroe
Y. Marmaduke[1]	Salem Cooper	$800	$8	Feb. 19, 1862	Liverpool Point

[1] Blst. Plaster
[2] Blst. Stone
Document in Spates Papers

391–411; C. W. Ostrander, "Gold in Montgomery County, Maryland," *Maryland Natural History Society Bulletin*, IX, 32–34; Titus Ulke, "Gold Mining Past and Present Near Washington, D. C.," *Rocks and Minerals*, XIV, 299–305; and W. H. Weed, *Notes on the Gold Veins Near Great Falls, Maryland* (U. S. Geological Survey Bulletin 260), 128–131.

BOAT NAME	OWNER	BOAT VALUE	FURNI-TURE VALUE	DATE SEIZED	WHERE LYING
J. M. Cross[1]	William Jordan	$800	—	Feb. 18, 1862	Liverpool Point
M. E. McCoy[1]	John L. Jordan	$1,000	—	Feb. 17, 1862	Liverpool Point
G. T. J. McKaig[1]	Martin Smith	$650	—	Feb. 22, 1862	Liverpool Point
Martin Hoffman[1]	Cons. Coal & Transp.	$350	—	Feb. 22, 1862	Liverpool Point
A. C. Blackman	Charles Wenner	$1,300	—	Feb. 27, 1862	Georgetown
Liberty[1]	Martin Smith	$800	—	Feb. 22, 1862	Liverpool Point
Prince Rupert[1]	Martin Smith	$800	$4	Feb. 22, 1862	Georgetown
Col. Dinlop	Charles Weinner	$1,150	$5	Feb. 17, 1862	Georgetown
Lauretta	D. Spates	$800	$4	Feb. 21, 1862	Liverpool Point
Wila Kate	Cons. Coal & Transp.	$650	—	Feb. 22, 1862	Liverpool Point
Jas. Buchanan	R. B. Carlisle	$1,000	$5	Feb. 18, 1862	Georgetown
Lloyd Lowe	Pat Brady	$800	$5	Feb. 18, 1862	Georgetown
Jno. A. Rinehart[1]	S. Weston	$900	$4	Feb. 22, 1862	Liverpool Point
Sir Jno. Franklin[1]	Owen Ardinger	$450	$5	Feb. 20, 1862	Liverpool Point
Georetta Ardinger	Henry Arts	$1,000	$6	Feb. 21, 1862	Georgetown
F. Benton[2]	Not Known	$1,000	—	Feb. 20, 1862	Liverpool Point
R. Gregory[1]	Not Known	$800	—	Feb. 20, 1862	Liverpool Point
Jno. R. Wilson	Hamilton Douns	$250	$5	Feb. 20, 1862	Liverpool Point
R, M. Borden	Charles McCarlde	$1,000	—	Feb. 20, 1862	Fortress Monroe
Elie Wade	Not Known	$400	—	Feb. 26, 1862	Discharged & Gone up the Canal

[1] Blst. Plaster
[2] Blst. Stone
Document in Spates Papers

HISTORIC RESOURCE STUDY
CHESAPEAKE & OHIO CANAL NHP

12.
LOCKKEEPERS AND BOATMEN ON THE C & O CANAL

BY HARLAN D. UNRAU
HISTORIAN, C&O CANAL RESTORATION TEAM, SENECA
DENVER SERVICE CENTER
1976

CONTENTS

I. THE LOCKKEEPERS 785

    A. INTRODUCTION 785
    B. DUTIES AND COMPENSATION 785
    C. FAMILY AND SEXUAL ROLES 794
    D. PEFORMANCE RECORD 796
    E. DRUNKENNESS 798
    F. NEGLECT OF DUTY 799
    G. ABANDONMENT OF LOCKS 800
    H. ABSENCE WITHOUT PROVIDING AN ADEQUATE SUBSTITUE 800
    I. SALE OF INTOXICATING BEVERAGES BY LOCKKEPERS 801
    J. REPUTABLE LOCK KEEPERS 803
    K. THE LOCK HOUSES: 1828–1850 804

II. THE BOATMEN 806

    A. INTRODUCTION 806
    B. CHARACTERISTICS OF BOATMEN: 1830–1850 806
    C. CHARACTERISTICS OF BOATMEN: 1851–1889 808
    D. CHARACTERISTICS OF BOATMEN: 1891–1924 814
    E. TYPICAL EXPERIENCES IN THE LIVES OF "CANALERS" 818
    F. THE EMERGENCE OF LABOR UNIONISM AMONG THE CANAL BOATMENT IN THE 1870'S 821
    G. FEED AND GROCERY STORES 831
    H. HAILING PLACE OF BOATMENT 836
    I. RACIAL DISCRIMINATION AGAINST BLACK BOAT MASTERS 838
    J. RELIGION ON THE TOWPATH 838
    K. CANAL SONGS 839
    L. STORIES AND REMINISCIENCES OF CANAL DAYS ... 841

APPENDIXES 843

    A. SPECIFICATION OF A LOCKKEEPER'S HOUSE, CA. OCTOBER 1828 843
    B. ESTIMATE OF THE EXPENSE OF A LOCKKEEPER'S HOUSE, CA. OCTOBER 1828 845
    C. SPECIFICATION FOR A LOCKKEEPERS HOUSE 30 X 18 FEET .. 846
    D. REGISTER OF FINES COLLECTED BETWEEN 1877–1880 ... 848

I. THE LOCK KEEPERS

A. INTRODUCTION

From the earliest period of navigation on the canal in the fall of 1830, the administration organization of the line was a mere formality, because the board of directors retained too much authority for itself. As a result, the character and conduct of the superintendents were not as important in the operation of the canal as they might have been. In the absence of an effective line of authority, the character of the lock keepers became important to the welfare of the canal. On the basis of what little is known of the lock tenders, they do not, as a group, seem to have been outstanding for their enthusiasm or reliability. Despite the important role which devolved upon them in the course of the directors' conduct of canal administration, apparently little was done to upgrade the quality of their services.[1]

B. DUTIES AND COMPENSATION

Several months before the canal was watered between Dams Nos. 1 and 2, the board authorized President Charles F. Mercer to nominate lock keepers for the line and determine the rate of compensation for those individuals. The annual wages of the tenders were not to exceed $150 for a single lock, $200 for two locks, and $250 for three locks.[2]

On August 7, 1830, Mercer recommended various individuals to serve as lock keepers and the rate of compensation each was to receive. As the company was beginning to experience its first financial difficulties, the pay of the tenders was considerably less than the maximum allowances earlier set by the board. The decrease in wages, however, was to be partially compensated for by allowing the tenders to use company land for gardening purposes. The keepers and their compensation, which were approved by the directors, were:

> Lock No. 5.—Whalen, keeper; compensation of $100 and use of Lockhouse No. 3. Together with the use of the company's ground below Guard Gate No. 1 and the embankment connecting it with the towpath of the new canal in its vicinity.

> Lock No. 6—William Conner, keeper; compensation of $100 and use of Lockhouse No. 4 together with the use of the company's ground between, at, next above, and below Dam No. 1 as far down as the guard gate and embankment.

> Lock No. 7—Robert Brooke, keeper; compensation to be the use of the lands between the canal and the river and such islands as had been purchased for the company from George French together with the use of Lockhouse No. 5.

> Lock No. 8—Solomon Drew, keeper; compensation of $100 and the use of the Lockhouse No. 6.

---

[1] . Walter S. Sanderlin, *The Great National Project: A History of the Chesapeake & Ohio Canal*, (Baltimore, 1946), 185

[2] *Proceedings of the President and Board of Directors*, B, 135. When compared with the wages being paid to the skilled and unskilled laborers then at work on the construction of the canal, the wages of the tenders appear to be rather low considering their responsibilities. The average wages for the unskilled workers on the line in the early 1830s were $13 per month (based on 26 working days), while those of skilled artisans were as much as $20 per month. Using a 9-month construction season as a basis, these figures would translate into annual wages of $117 for unskilled workers and $180 for skilled laborers.

Locks Nos. 9-10—Thomas Burgess, keeper; compensation of $150 and the use of Lockhouse No. 7.

Lock No. 11—(Mr.) Edmonston, keeper; compensation of $100 and the use of Lockhouse No. 8.

Locks Nos. 12-14—Charles L. Sears, keeper; compensation of $200 and the use of Lockhouse No. 9.

Locks Nos. 15-16—(No name given), keeper; compensation of $200 and the use of Lockhouse No. 10.

Locks Nos. 17-18—William Roberts, keeper; compensation of $200 and the use of Lockhouse No. 11.

Locks Nos. 19-20—William Roberts, keeper; compensation to be the use of Lockhouse No. 12 together with the use of the company's ground between the canal and the river that had been purchased from Moreen D. Loper and the Beall heirs.

Lock No. 21—(Mr.) Fuller, keeper; compensation of $50, the use of Lockhouse No. 13, and the use of the company's land bought from William Scott.

Lock No. 22—(Mr.) Wright, Keeper; compensation of $100, the use of Lockhouse No. 14, and the use of the company's land lying between the canal and the river below Muddy Branch.

Lock No. 23 and Guard Lock No. 2—Lewis Sewell, keeper; compensation to the use of Lockhouse No. 15 together with the use of Long-Acre and the company's ground between the canal and the river as far up the river as within 100 yards of Lock No. 24.[3]

In September the board approved a resolution requiring that at least one acre be attached to each lock for the use of the tender. On their plot the tenders were to raise gardens for their supply of fresh vegetables and to raise chickens, hogs and cows for their supply of eggs, milk, and meat.[4] The grounds set aside for these purposes were to be fenced with materials taken from company shanties that were to be dismantled near Dam. No. 1.[5]

Several weeks after the water had been admitted into the canal between Locks Nos. 5 and 23, the board made a change in one of the appointments and took the first steps toward a formal definition of the lock tenders' duties. On November 20 W. W. Fenlon, who already had applied for permission to commence a packet service between Georgetown and Great Falls, was confirmed as the keeper of Locks Nos. 15-20, since William Roberts had declined taking charge over his assigned locks. At the same time, the board directed Mercer to instruct the new tenders in the

---

[3] *Ibid*, B, 157–59.

[4] *Ibid*, B, 188.

[5] *Ibid*, B, 148. Later, as lock houses were built further up the valley, the board specified that the lots around the structures be fenced with "good post and rail fences." Whenever possible, locust posts were to be used. *Ibid*, E, 47, and Ingle to Elgin, Apr. 22, 1836, Ltrs. Sent, C & O Co.

proper manner of operating the locks. Moreover, each lock keeper was to be supplied with tools that were to be used for the preservation and repair of the portion of the canal under his care.[6]

Less than a week later, the board determined to make some special arrangements with Fenlon for having taken charge of Locks Nos. 15-20. In addition to a salary increase to $400 per year, Mercer was authorized to spend $200 for the addition of a kitchen to Lockhouse No. 12, $500 for an additional building, and $100 for other outhouses. These outlays would enable Fenlon to establish a hotel at Great Falls, which was soon named Crommelin House. Within eight months it was decided to make further improvements to Fenlon's hotel at company expense, the principle projects being the outside plastering of the lockhouse, the construction of a second story, and the erection of a porch in front of the stone center portion of the house.[7]

Similar improvements were also made to the lockhouse at Seneca Falls. The sum of $1,000 was authorized in July 1830 for additions to this structure, which was named Rushville. Peyton Page was named as the new lock tender as well as the new boat registrar at that location in March 1831 at a yearly wage of $250.[8]

The following June the board authorized President Mercer to appropriate eight per cent of the tender's annual salary for the construction of stables and a tavern near the lockhouse. The outbuildings were not to exceed the sum of $300, and they were to be rented by the tender.[9]

Mercer informed the board on July 1, 1831, that he had found it necessary to increase the wages of the lock keepers. Accordingly, he had raised their pay to the maximum limits set by the directors on July 7, 1830.[10]

On July 16 Mercer submitted to the board a draft of the regulations for the lock keepers and the boatmen, which he had been ordered to prepare several months earlier. The regulations for the lock tenders' districts and listed the duties that the tenders were expected to perform as follows:

> DISTRIBUTION OF THE CHESAPEAKE & OHIO CANAL, FOR THE PURPOSES OF NAVIGATION, INSPECTION, AND REPAIRS, INTO LOCK KEEPERS DISTRICTS.
>
> The first Lock-keeper's District shall extend from the eastern termination of the Canal in Washington, to the waste weir next above the old locks at the Little Falls of Potomac, and shall include the basin between Georgetown and Washington, as well as those locks.
>
> The second Lock-keeper's District shall extend from the first, as high up as to include the waste weir next above the United States powder magazine, and shall also include the dam and feeder at the Little Falls.
>
> The third Lock-keeper's District shall extend from the second, to the lower end of the external slope of protection wall next above the culvert over Cabin John Run.
>
> The fourth Lock-keeper's District shall extend from the third district, to the first culvert above his dwelling house.
>
> The fifth Lock-keeper's District shall extend from the fourth, to the waste weir through the berm of the canal next below the entrance of the Rocky Run Feeder.

---

[6] *Ibid*, B, 224–225. C, 401, and Fenlon to Board of Directors Nov. 6, 1830, Ltrs. Recd., C & O Co.

[7] *Proceedings of the President and Board of Directors*, B, 238, 245, 307, 383–84.

[8] *Ibid*, B 148, 290, 383.

[9] *Ibid*, B, 384.

[10] *Ibid*, B, 396–97

The sixth Lock-keeper's District shall extend from the fifth, to the lower end of the first high vertical protection wall above, and shall embrace Rock Run Dam and Feeder.

The seventh Lock-keeper's District shall extend from the sixth to the lower end of the first external slope or protection wall above the Great Falls of Potomac.

The eighth Lock-keeper's District shall extend from the seventh, to the first high bluff above the culvert over Watt's branch.

The ninth Lock-keeper's District shall extend from the eighth, to the lower end of the first external slope or protection wall above the culvert over Muddy Branch.

The tenth Lock-keeper's District shall extend from the ninth, to the upper end of the external slope or protection wall next above the Seneca Aqueduct.

If a District Lock-keeper shall, at any time, discover, that any of the works on the Canal, within his district, are out of repair, he shall immediately report the fact in person or by express, which, for that purpose, he is authorized to hire, to the Superintendent of repairs, and if from the nature of the repairs required, or of the damage apprehended, time be not allowed without farther injury to the Canal or its appurtenances, to wait the orders of the Superintendent, the Lock-keeper shall consider himself empowered, and he is required, at the cost of the Company, to take immediate steps, in the absence of the Superintendent, to repair the injury which has happened, or to prevent that which is apprehended. Of all expenses so incurred by him, for the benefit of the Company, he shall keep a fair account, a copy of which, he shall hand over to the Superintendent, as soon as his presence shall enable him to take charge of such repairs, the Superintendent shall repay to the Lock-keeper, the sums so expended. All such accounts shall be settled as soon as practicable, after they arise, and, at least, once in every month.

No Lock-keeper shall be entitled to receive his monthly pay, who shall have an unsettled account with the Company.

The District Lock-keepers shall be bound, if required, to provide by themselves, or their assistants, accommodation and subsistence, at a reasonable rate, not to exceed a given sum per week, for the Superintendent, and such hands or laborers as may be engaged in such repairs, or on any improvements upon, or alterations of the Canal.

Each Lock-keeper and Lock-keeper's assistant shall be furnished with 2 wheel-borrows, 3 shovels, a pick and a crow-bar, to be used in the improvement and repair of the Canal, whensoever required, and shall be held responsible for the good order and safe keeping of the same; and each District Lock-keeper, in his monthly return to the board, shall state the number and condition of the tools within his District.

In addition to his monthly pay, each District Lock-keeper shall be entitled to an enclosed lot, near his house.

Every Lock-keeper shall be at liberty, subject to the restraints and regulations of the existing laws, to accommodate the boatmen, and other travelers at his lock house, provided that under no circumstances whatever, shall any Lock-keeper, or his assistant, be allowed to sell or to supply on any terms, to any boatmen, traveler, or other person, any spirituous, or intoxicating liquor, or to allow the use or consumption of any such liquor within or upon his premises, unless particularly authorized so to do by the President and Directors of the Company; and for any violation of this rule, the offender shall be immediately discharged from the service of the Company.

In like manner any District or Assistant Lock-keeper, who shall at any time be found in a state of intoxication, shall be forthwith discharged.

Every District Lock-keeper, and his assistant, shall afford to the boatmen and all other persons navigating the canal, every aid and accommodation in his power, while he duly enforces the regulations for the protection of the Canal and its works–he shall instruct the boatmen how to navigate the Canal, to the best advantage, and especially to what part of their boat they should attach their tow or tracking line; how to track it with most comfort to themselves, and especially the manner of entering and passing out of the locks, and the use of their bow and stern strapping or snubbing ropes.

Every District Lock-keeper having reason to suspect a boat or float to have increased her cargo subsequent to the date of her waybill, is authorized to call upon the owner, master, or other person having charge of said boat or float for a sight of his waybill, to compare with the actual cargo of such boat, and if any augmentation of such cargo shall appear to have been made, subsequently to the date of the permit or waybill, to endorse a notice hereof, on such waybill, for the information of the Collector, and the other Lock-keepers.

All boats or floats left by their owners, or such persons as may have had charge thereof, either sunk in the canal or loosely floating thereupon, and all floating logs, planks or branches of trees, as well as other nuisances within the Canal, the Lock-keeper of the district within which the same may be, shall promptly cause to be removed or abated.

Every District Lock-keeper is required to pay particular attention to the orders regulating the height of water in the several levels between the locks of his district; and the Lock-keepers of the eighth and ninth districts, may be required to receive their orders through the Lock-keepers of the seventh or of the tenth district; and in like manner those of the second, third, and fourth, through the Lock-keepers of the first or fifth district.

In all cases, where practicable, the various levels shall be regulated by the use of the wastes and feeders of the Canal, reserving the side culverts and paddle gates of the locks for their appropriate use – that of filling and emptying the locks when required by the passage of boats.

Each District Lock-keeper shall see that obvious and suitable marks, by description stones or boards, be kept up, above and below each lock, to denote where a boat approaching the same, shall slacken its speed or await its turn for entering the Lock, if other boats have a right to precede it.

No Lock-keeper is authorized to practice himself, or to countenance others, in resisting, by violence, except in self-defense, any outrageous or disorderly conduct on the canal, but he shall take, at the cost of the Company, prompt measures to suppress and punish the same, by the judicial tribunals having cognizance thereof.[11]

When the canal was opened to navigation between Lock No. 5 and the Rock Creek Basin in September 1831, the board drew up a special set of rules for the keeper of Locks Nos. 1–4 as that position was crucial to the functioning of the waterway at its terminus. The duties of the Georgetown lock tender, in addition to the printed regulations for all lock keepers, were:

1. He was to have charge of Locks Nos. 1–4 and Tidelock A as well as supervisory responsibility for Lock District No. 1.
2. He was to hire two able-bodied assistants.
3. He was to "attend in Person" to his duty and was never to leave his district without permission from the president or board.

---

[11] *Ibid*, B, 314, 421–28.

James O'Reily was appointed to fill this position, and he and his assistants were to receive an annual wage of $500.[12]

From time to time additional duties were assigned to those lock tenders who were respected for their industriousness and consciousness, O'Reilly was authorized to undertake the duty of collecting tolls on boats which passed up the canal from Georgetown but did not use the Old Locks at Little Falls. The compensation for this job was $100 per year.[13]

In March 1832, the lock keeper at Lock No. 5 was authorized to examine the waybill of every boat ascending through his lock to insure that the captain had paid all his tolls on his last descent to Georgetown. He was to receive $50 per year for this additional work.[14]

As the canal extended westward, similar arrangements were made with the lock tenders at Harpers Ferry, Williamsport, and Hancock to act as toll collectors.[15]

From October 1834 to October 1837 the Georgetown lock keeper was assigned the additional duty of operating Tidelock B on the Washington Branch Canal for which job his salary was increased, to $1,200 per year.[16]

Some lock tenders were made responsible for the operation of pivot bridges at their locks, one such case being the keeper at Lock No. 30 who received an additional monthly stipend of $10 for his extra work.[17]

After the canal was completed to Cumberland in 1850, the directors approved new locks nearest to the guard or river locks were generally placed in charge of the operation of those structures along with an increased annual salary of $50.[18]

Regulations to govern the administration of the waterway. The new rules, which went into effect on April 1, 1851, defined the duties of the lock keepers as follows:

LOCK KEEPERS

128. It shall be the duty of all lock keepers to make a daily and particular examination of the locks under their charge, and of any other works which they may be directed, by order of the General Superintendent or of the Superintendents of repairs on whose division they are, to attend to; and to prevent by all lawful means within their power, any injury to said locks or other works, from the carelessness of boatmen or from malicious or disorderly persons.

129. They shall use their utmost exertions to keep the said locks or other works in the best possible order, and in case of any accident or injury to them, or to the canal in the vicinity of their stations, requiring immediate attention, they shall take the necessary measures to remedy the same and to prevent further injury; and in the meantime to send the earliest intelligence thereof to the Superintendent of repairs on that part of the canal.

---

[12] *Ibid*, C, 5–6.

[13] *Ibid*, C, 112–13.

[14] *Ibid*, C, 113. As long as the canal had its terminus at Dam No. 2, the tender at Lock No. 23 also was designated as a toll collector.

[15] *Ibid*, G, 149–50.

[16] *Ibid*, D, 181. In Oct. 1837, the lock house at the tide lock was completed and John Hilton was appointed as its tender at a yearly wage of $50. *Ibid*, E, 329.

[17] *Ibid*, M, 102.

[18] *Report to the Stockholders on the Completion of the Chesapeake & Ohio Canal to Cumberland* (Frederick, 1851), 139–40.

130. It shall be their duty, at all hours, by night as well as by day, unless otherwise ordered by the General Superintendent or Superintendent of repairs on that part of the canal, to pass all boats and floats presenting themselves at their locks, and entitled to pass the same under the regulations of the Company.

131. They shall not permit the boatmen to pass their boats or floats through any lock, except in the presence and under the direction of the keeper thereof or his assistant.

132. The lock keepers shall not absent themselves from their locks, on any occasion, without leave from the Superintendent of repairs on that part of the canal. They shall reside in the houses provided for them, at their respective stations; and shall be charged with the care and preservation of their respective houses and of the enclosures attached thereto; and also of any property of the Company that may be put in their keeping by the General Superintendent or the Superintendent of repairs on that part of the canal; and for any injury to the said house or enclosures or the said property, if occasioned by their neglect or carelessness, they shall be, respectively, liable.

133. Lock keepers, when repairs are making in the neighborhood of their locks, at points where, and at times when, there is difficulty in obtaining board and lodging for those persons employed upon such repairs, shall afford such accommodation, in the way of boarding and lodging, the whole or a part of the said persons, at fair and usual rates, as in the opinion of the Superintendent of repairs of that part of the canal, he can reasonably and with propriety be asked and required to afford.

134. Although, under these regulations, the lock keepers are, in many cases, authorized to impose fines; yet, except in cases of emergency, it is desired that they should forthwith report each violation of a regulation to the Superintendent of repairs on that part of the canal, with all the facts in the case, in order that the fine may be imposed by the said Superintendent; and that such other measures in relation to the said violation may be taken as in the judgment of the said Superintendent may be thought necessary.

135. All fines imposed by lock keepers shall be forthwith reported to the Superintendent of repairs on that part of the canal; and all moneys received by them for fines imposed by them shall be immediately paid over to the said Superintendent.

136. Any lock keeper who shall knowingly permit a boat or float to pass his lock or locks in violation of any provision of these regulations; or who shall himself neglect or refuse to comply promptly, with any one of such of these regulations as prescribes his duties, either towards the Company or those engaged in boating on the canal, shall be forthwith suspended from duty by the Superintendent of repairs on that part of the canal, on his becoming cognizant of the facts; and a report of the case shall be immediately made to the General Superintendent, by the said Superintendent, for his action thereon; and in the meantime the said Superintendent may appoint some person to fill, temporarily, the vacancy thus created.

137. Every lock keeper shall perform such other duties connected with the canal, as the General Superintendent may from time to time require of him.[19]

These regulations continued in effect with periodic slight modifications until the canal went into a receivership after the titanic flood of 1889.

The basic annual wages of the lock keepers remained generally unchanged from 1831 to 1853.[20]

---

[19] *By-Laws, Rules, and Regulations: In force on the Chesapeake & Ohio Canal, 1ˢᵗ April 1851* (Baltimore, 1894), 39–40.

On May 7 of the latter year, the board ordered that the tenders be paid annual salaries according to the following salary schedule beginning on June 1:

Locks Nos. 1-4	$600
Lock No. 23	$250
Lock No. 5	$300
Lock No. 24	$200
Lock No. 6	$200
Lock No. 25	$250
Lock No. 7	$200
Lock No. 26	$200
Lock No. 8	$200
Lock No. 27	$200
Locks Nos. 9-10	$300
Lock No. 28	$200
Lock No. 11	$200
Lock No. 29	$225
Lock No. 12-14	$325
Lock No. 30	$200
Lock No. 15	$200
Lock No. 31	$200
Lock No. 16	$200
Lock No. 32	$225
Locks Nos. 17-18	$300
Lock No. 33	$200
Locks Nos. 19-20	$300
Lock No. 34	$200
Lock No. 21	$200
Lock No. 35	$325
Lock No. 22	$200
Lock No. 37	$200
Lock No. 38	$250
Lock No. 57	$200
Lock No. 39	$200
Lock No. 58	$200
Lock No. 40	$200
Lock No. 59	$200
Guard Lock No. 4	$200
Lock No. 60	$200
Locks Nos. 41-42	$300
Lock No. 61	$200
Lock No. 43	$200
Lock No. 62	$200
Lock No. 44	$200

---

[20] During this period, the average annual wages for a skilled factory worker in the North (based on a 7-day week of 12-14 hour days) ranged between $200 to $500. Unskilled workers, women, and children received annual wages ranging from $50 to $300. When compared with these figures, the majority of the lock tenders received annual wages that put them in the middle of the unskilled working class. T. Harry Williams, Richard N. Current, and Frank Freidel, *A History of the United States to 1877* (3rd ed., New York, 1969), 464–65.

Lock No. 63 1/3-66	$400
Guard Lock No. 5	$200
Lock No. 67	$200
Locks Nos. 45-46	$300
Lock No. 68	$200
Locks Nos. 47-50	$400
Locks Nos. 69-71	$400
Locks Nos. 51-52	$300
Lock No. 72	$200
Lock No. 53	$200
Locks Nos. 73-74	$275
Locks Nos. 54-55 and Guard Lock No. 6	$300
GuardLock No. 8	$250
Lock No. 56	$200[21]

From May 1853 to September 1859 when another general pay increase went into effect there were a few modifications in the salaries of some lock tenders that were the result of special circumstances. In reply to a complaint from Samuel Morany, the tender of Locks Nos. 47-50, that his pay was too low to employ an assistant, the board agreed in January 1855 to increase his yearly stipend to $500.[22]

In May 1855 the directors granted John Shelly, the tender at Lock No. 70, a yearly wage increase to $225 because the company owned no ground at the lock house on which he could plant a garden.[23]

As the canal trade had increased to the point that the keeper at Lock Nos. 63 1/3, 64 2/3, and 66 needed to hire additional assistance, the directors in September 1855 allowed him a monthly increase of up to $20 at the discretion of the Superintendent of the Cumberland Division.[24]

For undetermined reasons, the annual salaries of the keepers at Lock No. 12 and at locks nos. 13-14 were raised drastically in October 1860 to $300 and $400 respectively.[25]

During the next decade the pay of the lock keepers rose rapidly. On May 1, 1864, another salary increase went into effect as follows:

Locks 6-62, 67-72, 75	$5 per month
Locks 63 1/3, 64 2/3, 66	$600 per year
Locks 73 and 74	$500 per year
Guard Lock 8	$400 per year[26]

The following month the tender of Lock No. 5 and Guard Lock No. 1 was given a $60 per year raise.[27]

---

[21] Iron to Lambie, May 7, 1853, Ltrs. Sent, C & O Co.
[22] *Proceedings of the President and Board of Directors*, I, 140.
[23] *Ibid*, I, 169.
[24] *Ibid*, I, 446.
[25] *Ibid*, K, 131.
[26] *Ibid*, K, 383.
[27] *Ibid*, K, 390

As of June 1, 1865, the pay of the keepers at Locks Nos. 9-10, 13-14, 17-18, and 19-20 was increased to $50 per month.[28]

In August 1865 this rate increase was extended to all tenders of two locks along the canal.[29]

The final general pay increase of which there is any record took effect on May 1, 1870, when the pay of all tenders of single locks was raised to $50 per month and that of all keepers of two locks was increased to $75 per month. Along with this last pay increase the board passed a resolution requiring each single lock keeper to hire one assistant and each double lock tender to employ two assistants.[30]

C. FAMILY AND SEXUAL ROLES

The canal company never set down written criteria for the qualifications of lock keepers. However a cursory review of the company records indicates that the directors preferred married men with large families. It was presumed that married men would provide more responsible service along the numerous isolated stretches of the canal than would those who were single. Large families were favored both because of their stabilizing tendencies and because they provided more hands to do the work. A large number of children was also an advantage to those lock keepers who were responsible for more than one lock, because their older offspring could be put to work operating the locks, thus relieving the tender of the need to hire an assistant.[31]

At times women held the position of lock keeper but these generally were the widows of the original tender. In March 1835 the board decided that all women lock keepers would be discharged after May 1, in the interest of more efficient operation.[32]

The employment of women violated the general social mores of that era, but even more important, the physical strength and endurance necessary to operate a lock was thought to be better suited to men.

There were a number of exceptions made to the ruling, which banned female lock tenders, as a number of women served in this capacity during the operation of the canal. In response to an entreaty from Mary Ross to be continued as the tender of Locks Nos. 12-14, the board voted in March 1835 to suspend its order in her case.[33] The following month the directors agreed to keep Elizabeth Burgess as the tender of Lock No. 11, provided that she hires a capable assistant.[34]

On the death of her husband in September, Mrs. Eliza Page was appointed temporarily as the registrar and lock keeper at Rushville. When she refused to act any longer as the registrar or lock-keeper in October the board voted to abolish the office of registrar at that place and to employ a lock tender on a temporary basis.[35]

The unpleasant experience with Mrs. Page caused the board that same month to reissue its order banning the employment of women as lock keepers after March 1, 1836.[36]

---

[28] *Ibid*, K, 426–27.

[29] *Ibid*, K, 438, and Ringgold to Masters, Aug. 15, 1870, Ltrs. Sent, C & O Co.

[30] *Ibid*, L, 314–15. This salary increase did not apply to the tenders of the Georgetown locks or the Cumberland Lock.

[31] Sanderlin, *The Great National Project*, p, 185.

[32] *Proceedings of the President and Board of Directors*, D, 264.

[33] *Ibid*, D, 267.

[34] *Ibid*, D, 273.

[35] *Ibid*, D, 401, 416.

[36] *Ibid*, D, 421.

Despite the new directive the board continued to make exceptions based on the circumstances of each case. On March 30, 1836, it was determined to continue the employment of Mrs. Susan Cross as the tender of Lock No. 21 "until the 1st day of May, and no longer."[37]

One of the most interesting cases in which a woman was appointed as a lock tender occurred in December 1842 after the drowning of James O'Reilly, the highly-respected keeper of the Georgetown locks since 1831. On the morning of December 14 O'Reilly's body was found in the opening of the culvert gate of Lock No. 3, presumably having fallen into the canal while turning the crank about 7 O'clock A.M. John Y. Young, the division superintendent, immediately hired Philip Gormly, who lived near Lock No. 4, as a temporary replacement. O'Reilly's assistants and his oldest son were continued as aides to Gormly.[38]

That same day Clement Cox, an influential Georgetown resident, informed the board that O'Reilly had left a large family of females and small children. His oldest son, James, Jr., however was 25 to 30 years old, well educated, and "entirely exemplary in his habits." Although the young man had been known formerly as a wild brawler, he had served as secretary of the Temperance Society of his church for nearly three years. As he would now be the sole bread-winner for the family, Cox urged that he be given the lock keeper's job.[39]

The board also received a petition signed by 21 boat owners and captains and Georgetown citizens recommending O'Reilly's widow as the lock tender. In the opinion of the signers of the memorial, such an act would be a fitting tribute to "a most worthy citizen and honest man." With the aid of her eldest son, the petitioners were convinced that Mrs. O'Reilly would render credible service to the company.[40]

Accordingly, the board appointed Mrs. O'Reilly as her husband's successor on December 20.[41]

There were other exceptions to the ruling against the employment of female lock tenders in the following years. In April 1844 Mrs. James Davis was appointed to succeed her deceased husband as the keeper at Lock No. 28.[42]

Four years later in April 1846 the board was notified that Asa Farman, the keeper of Locks Nos. 12-14, had died, leaving a widow and six children. Although Rebecca Farman continued to operate the locks with the aid of a brother and two of her sons, the board felt that she could not handle three locks. Accordingly, she was transferred to Lock No. 15, and Hezekiah Metts, the operator of that lock replaced her as he had "sufficient assistants."[43]

In 1848 Mary A. Brewer took over as tender of Lock No. 16 for her deceased husband Thomas. That same year Sarah Conner replaced her late husband Hugh as keeper of Lock No. 53, a post which he had held since April 1839 when the canal between Dams Nos. 5-6 was opened to navigation.[44]

In 1850 there were two female lock tenders listed on the canal company payroll. Lucy A. Metts, the widow of Frederick Metts, operated Lock No. 5 and Guard Gate No. 1 until March 10,

---

[37] *Ibid*, E, 36.

[38] Young to President and Directors, Dec. 14, 1842, and Cox to Ingle, Dec. 15, 1842, Ltrs. Recd, C & O Co.

[39] Cox to President and Directors, Dec. 14, 1842, Ltrs. Recd., C & O Co.

[40] Petition to President and Directors of the Chesapeake & Ohio Canal Company, Dec. 18, 1842, Ltrs. Recd., C & O Co.

[41] *Proceedings of the President and Board of Directors*, F, 512.

[42] *Ibid*, G, 146

[43] Elgin to Coale, Mar. 5, 1846, Ltrs. Recd., C & O Co., and *Proceedings of the President and Board of Directors*, G, 397-98.

[44] *Twentieth Annual Report* (1848), C & O Co., Appendix E, 26-27.

at which time she was transferred to Lock No. 16 for the remainder of the year. Sarah Connor was still at her post at Lock No. 53.[45]

Company records indicate that at least five women served as lock tenders during the 1860s and the 1870s. After a change in the canal's administration in June 1860, the new board replaced all of the waterway's lock keepers. Two of the new appointees were Mrs. Adeleade Hill at Lock No. 12 and Mrs. Egan at Lock No. 60.[46]

In November 1864 it was reported that John Rench, the keeper of Lock No. 30, had died and that George Hardy, the tender of Locks Nos. 35 and 36, had been drafted into the Union Army. In both cases, the women and children remained to attend the locks.[47]

On the death of G. W. Case, the lock keeper at Great Falls, the board appointed his widow to succeed him in August 1872.[48]

D. PERFORMANCE RECORD

Despite the precautions taken by the board in selecting the lock tenders, a cursory review of the company records reveals that many of the lock men were undisciplined and irresponsible. Although most were conscientious in their work, many were dismissed for drunkenness, neglect of duty, and absence without notice or without providing a substitute. Frequent complaints were made about the sale of liquor by lock keepers to boatmen and workers, and the disorderly results of this practice.

The formulation of detailed regulations and the organization of canal employees with assigned duties did not insure the orderly operation of the work. On the contrary, every conceivable abuse was reported at one time or another. Canal property was misused, tools were lost or stolen, repair materials were damaged or stolen, and the towpath and aqueducts used as a wagon roads and bridle paths. Repeated directions to the lock keepers to enforce the rules strictly indicate a laxness or indifference on the part of the tenders and boatmen alike.[49]

There were general complaints about the performance of the lock tenders almost from the first day of navigation. In May 1831 an article appeared in the *National Intelligencer* describing an excursion to Great Falls on a packet boat. The reports noted that the "hands at some of the locks are not as dexterous in the management of them perhaps as longer practice will make them." Thus, the passenger who was "not on his guard may chance [to] get a jolt or two."[50]

By the spring of 1832, the directors had become alarmed by the numerous reports of the irresponsibility and negligence of the lock tenders. On March 24 they ordered the Superintendent to interview each lock tender "to ascertain them that are acquainted with the extent of their respective districts and the various duties required of them." He was to report to President Mercer "the name of every lock keeper, whom he shall find, upon examination, to be ignorant of his duty or in any way negligent or remiss in its performance." Furthermore, the directors ordered him to "especially instruct" the lock tenders to make daily or weekly inspections of the embankments on both sides of the canal, within their respective districts in order to ascertain whether any leak exists or is threatened in any part thereof; whether any musk rats have made lodgments therein, and if any, the entrance of habitations...to pass thro' the several viaducts or culverts of the canal

---

[45] *Report to the Stockholders on the Completion of the Chesapeake & Ohio Canal to Cumberland*, 139–40.

[46] *Proceedings of the President and Board of Directors*, K, 192–93.

[47] *Ibid*, K, 405.

[48] *Ibid*, M, 49.

[49] Sanderlin, *The Great National Project*, 185-186.

[50] Washington *National Intelligencer*, quoted in Niles' Register, XL (May 21, 1831), 206.

within their district...or...by looking thro' the same, whether any leak exists thereon, and that, where any such leaks are discovered, they be promptly stopped or effectual measures be taken to prevent their enlargement.[51]

After several locks had been damaged in the spring of 1833 as a direct result of the negligence of the lock tenders, the board took further action to impress those individuals with the importance of enforcing the company's regulations. In June the directors determined that each of the lock keepers be "distinctly informed" that they would henceforth.

> be held responsible for any damage done his lock, by violently entering the same, or using iron pointed poles, while in the same, unless in each case of injury he report the number and description of the boat, by which such injury is occasioned; and when practicable, the name or names of the person or persons, having the same in charge, to the Collector in Georgetown, before the boat shall have returned thro' his lock. In like manner, he shall be held responsible for any injury done, by any boat to the gates, or pointing or projecting stone of his lock: and the cost of repairing such injury, shall in each case, be deducted from his next month's wages.

The directors put "teeth" into this directive by requiring that the superintendent would henceforth certify that the locks were in "good order" each month before the lock tenders were paid.[52]

Throughout the years of the canal's operation, the board frequently had to direct the lock tenders to enforce the rules of the company, often with the threat of dismissal if they refused to cooperate. In June 1833 the lock tenders were ordered to prevent any sharp-pointed scow from entering the canal after July 1 – this despite the fact that such a regulation had been in effect for nearly two years.[53]

The following month the directors were notified that there was "a regular travel of all kinds of carriages on the towing path" and also "crossing on the coping of the Monocacy Aqueduct," both of which were violation of company regulations resulting in past from the laxness of the lock keepers and in past from the antagonistic attitudes of the local residents.[54]

An accident at Lock No. 44, in which $60 worth of flour was lost through the negligence of the lock tenders led to an edict in June 1836 which stipulated that the tenders would be held responsible for all damages to boat cargoes which resulted from their "neglect of duty".[55]

In December 1837 the president of the Frederick and Harper's Ferry Road Company complained to the canal board that persons traveling on the turnpike were avoiding tolls by crossing the pivot bridge at Lock No. 31 and using the towpath for the distance between the lock and Harpers Ferry. Anxious to cooperate with the road company as well as to protect its works, the lock keeper was ordered to enforce the company rules and to prohibit persons from crossing the

---

[51] *Proceedings of the President and Board of Directors*, C, 111. As an inducement for the lock tenders to rid the canal of the muskrat problem, the board ordered the superintendent to pay a bounty of 25 cents for every such animal, which was killed on the canal, in its embankments, or in the riverside of the waterway.

[52] *Ibid*, C, 368–69.

[53] *Ibid*, C, 392.

[54] Elgin to Directors, July 10, 1833, Ltrs. Recd., C & O Co. Within two weeks, the board ordered that posts be placed on the towpath to prevent carriages from using the aqueduct. *Proceedings of the President and Board of Directors*, C, 401. A similar problem occurred in September 1841 when Thomas Dawson of Montgomery County continued to use the towpath as a road for his carts and wagons. Elgin to Directors, Sept. 15, 1841, Ltrs. Recd., C & O Co.

[55] *Proceedings of the President and Board of* Directors, E, 69.

bridge unless they were on canal business or were passing to or from Caspar Wever's Mill for whose immediate use the bridge had been constructed.[56]

When the board received word that many lock keepers and toll collectors were permitting boats to pass through their locks without certifying the manifests of their cargoes, it notified those individuals at Georgetown, Williamsport, and Hancock in April 1844 that such future violations would be grounds for dismissal.[57]

Frequent complaints that some of the lock tenders were refusing to pass boats through the locks at night aroused an angry board in February 1848 to order all the lock tenders to be responsible for such operations 24 hours a day.[58]

Aside from specific orders and threats of dismissal for the irresponsible performance of the lock tenders, the board attempted several other solutions to upgrade the services rendered by those individuals. In January 1843 a form of agreement delineating the duties of the lock keeper and the prerogatives of the company to dismiss him for non-performance was drawn up by President James M. Coale and adopted by the board for use in all future employment matters.[59]

On at least two occasions – August 15, 1849, and October 12, 1866 the board acted to increase the responsibility of the division superintendents by authorizing them to dismiss and replace any lock-keeper on their divisions for reasons of misconduct or negligence, providing that the directors were informed at their next meeting.[60]

This approach was used since the board was far removed from the waterway and incidents reported to it at its monthly meetings were often investigated long after their occurrence, thus allowing the tenders to carry out a "cover-up" of their alleged misdeeds and thereby encouraging a lack of respect for the enforcement powers of the superintendents.[61]

At other times, the superintendents were directed to report any lock keeper who was not performing his duties.[62]

E. DRUNKENNESS

Drunkenness among the lock tenders proved to be continuing problem for the board. One of the most notorious cases in which a lock tender was dismissed for drunkenness occurred in 1844. In April Ebenezer Steel, the owner of a warehouse near Locks Nos. 45–46, informed the board that John Herbert, the keeper of those locks, was drinking heavily. Herbert, who was an old man with a large family, countered these charges by arguing that Steel merely wanted his assistant, who had little to do other than receive periodic shipments of grain and flour, to be lock keeper so that he would not have to pay him wages. Moreover, Steel often did not provide a full statement of his shipments, and he could get away with even more dishonesty if Herbert was out of the way.[63]

---

[56] *Ibid*, E, 345; Thomas to Thomas, Dec. 15, 1837, Ltrs. Recd., C & O Co.; and Ingle to Elgin, Dec. 20, 1837, Ltrs. Sent, C & O Co.
[57] *Proceedings of the President and Board of Directors*, G, 150.
[58] *Ibid*, H, 144–45.
[59] *Ibid*, G, 2.
[60] *Ibid*, H, 288, K, 520.
[61] *Proceedings of Stockholders*, C, 592–94.
[62] *Circular to Superintendents*, William R. Hutton, 1870, Ltrs. Recd., C & O Co.
[63] Herbert to President and Directors, April 10, 1844, Ltrs. Recd., C & O Co.

Later, a petition signed by 19 residents in the vicinity of the two locks was submitted to the board. Among other things, the petitioners noted that Herbert was an "attentive" and "faithful" lock tender who deserved to be keep on the job.[64]

Following a short investigation of the case, Chief Engineer Charles B. Fisk recommended that Herbert be continued as lock tender and the board accepted the proposal.[65]

Fresh charges of heavy drinking were again leveled against Herbert in August 1844. It was reported that he had left the locks under the charge of his son-in-law during a drunken spree in the middle of the month. After a similar report in November, the directors removed him from the payroll as of December 1 and selected Henry Harsh as his replacement.[66]

There were other dismissals for drunkenness. In November 1844 it was reported that William H. Henderson, the keeper at Locks Nos. 17 and 18, was "intemperate in his habits, and guilty of neglect of duty." Among other complaints against him were charges that he was living alone, employing no assistants, and remaining absent from duty for days on end. Hence he was removed from his job as of December 1 and replaced by Horace Benton.[67]

In March 1846 the board was informed that Robert C. Fields, the tender at Lock No. 21, had kept his level "very irregular at times, putting boats aground, while he (was) absent on his drunken frolics without permission of the Superintendent."[68]

Accordingly, he was fired as of May 1 and replaced by Samuel M. Fisher.[69]

F. NEGLECT OF DUTY

There are numerous instances where lock tenders were either warned or dismissed. One of the most serious incidents to occur as the result of a lock-tender's drunken behavior occurred on September 11, 1875, at Lock No. 22. Arriving late one night, the *Excelsior*, owned by Richard A. Moore, commenced locking operation with the aid of the tender. As the keeper was so drunk that he could "not act straight," he failed to heed the warnings of the boat's steersman and opened the lower gate paddles before the boat was in place. Hence the boat struck the mitre sill, broke apart, and sank with its 113-ton coal cargo. As a result, Moore collected more than $1,300 in damages and the unnamed lock man was dismissed.[70]

For neglecting their duties. In August 1837 Phinas Janney, one of the canal's directors, reported that recently he had crossed over the Potomac River from Shepherdstown to descend the canal. Although he had notified the keeper of the river lock of his approach, the tender did not arrive at the lock until the boatmen had locked the vessel through it and were ready to descend the canal. From other sources there appear to have been numerous instances where the tender had arrived at the lock too late to be of any service.[71]

---

[64] Petition to President and Directors, April 15, 1844, Ltrs. Recd., C & O Co.

[65] *Proceedings of the President and Board of Directors*, G, 146.

[66] *Ibid*, G, 209-210, and Stone to Coale, Aug. 29, 1844, Ltrs. Recd., C & O Co.

[67] *Proceedings of the President and Board of Directors* G, 210. Henderson refused to leave the lock house, claiming that the structure had not been built on company-owned land. Instead, he asserted that the company had taken improperly some vacant land in 1834 and constructed the residence. Thus, a special order from the board was necessary to force him to vacate the premises. Young to President and Directors, Dec. 10, 1842, Ltrs. Recd., C & O Co.

[68] Elgin to Coale, Mar. 5, 1846, Ltrs. Recd., C&O Co.

[69] *Proceedings of the President and Board of Directors*, G, 397.

[70] Petition and Affidavit of Richard A. Moore to the President and Directors of the Chesapeake & Ohio Canal Company, Jan. 12, 1876, Ltrs. Recd., C & O Co.

[71] Ingle to Rodgers, Aug. 30, 1837, Ltrs. Sent, C & O Co.

The board received word in October 1842 that the keeper of the Georgetown locks was providing adequate service at Locks Nos. 1–4 but was giving scant attention to the Tidelock. It was recommended that a lock house be built near the Rock Creek Basin Dam and that the Georgetown lock tender be relieved of that responsibility along with a cut in his $600 annual salary. The proposal was rejected, and the directors ordered the tender to give "more efficient and prompt attention to the Tidelock."[72]

On several occasions, there were reports that the lock tender's [performance] of their duties resulted in breaches and high-water problems. In April 1834 the directors were notified that several lock keepers had failed to inspect their districts for some time; thus, a breach had developed in the canal banks near Harpers Ferry.[73]

From the fall of 1860 to the spring of 1862 there were seven periods of high water on the Potomac, each of which caused flooding below Dam No. 4. In each case, it was reported the keeper who was responsible for putting the planks in the stop lock at that location either had failed to do so or had done so in an improper manner thus allowing the water to knock them out.[74]

In March 1877 the directors received word that there was a breach between Locks Nos. 10 and 11 which had been caused by the lock tender's poor method of repairing an earlier leak. There was also a break at the tumbling waste on the Four Mile Level, which the tender had failed to report since the previous autumn.[75]

G. ABANDONMENT OF LOCKS

Some lock tenders simply left their locks unattended without notice to the company when they took other employment or when they had serious disagreements with canal officials. In June 1848 Superintendent William S. Elgin appointed John H. Boozell to be the keeper of Lock No. 25 and the Edward's Ferry River Lock, subject to the confirmation of the board. He had taken this action, according to his report to the directors, because Asa Aud, the former tender, "had gone off." The board quickly approved the action.[76]

Later in April 1863 Samuel Smart was appointed to replace the tender at Locks Nos. 1–4 who had left his job, and in June 1874 John W. Mimmis was given the job of C. Shanks who had "quit" as the keeper of Lock No. 12.[77]

When some of the tenders of double locks were unsuccessful in their bid to secure a larger salary advance then that granted to the single lock keepers, S. C. Rogers abandoned Locks Nos. 45-46 in protest in May 1864 and was replaced by Obadiah Barger.[78]

H. ABSENCE FROM LOCK WITHOUT PROVIDING AN ADEQUATE SUBSTITUTE

For a long period of time, many of the lock tenders took advantage of their isolated locations by leaving their locks in charge of unqualified substitutes while they attended to personal business.

---

[72] *Proceedings of the President and Board of Directors*, H, 555–56.

[73] *Ibid*, D, 80–81.

[74] Embrey and Son to Dellinger, Apr. 26, 1862, Ltrs. Recd., C & O Co.

[75] Latchford to Gorman, Mar. 24, 1877, Ltrs., Recd., C & O Co.

[76] *Ibid*, H, 178–79, and Elgin to Board of Directors, Ltrs. Recd., C & O Co.

[77] *Proceedings of the President and Board of Directors* K, 322–24, and Maus to Gorman, June 2, 1874, Ltrs. Recd., C & O Co.

[78] *Proceedings of the President and Board of Directors*, K, 384.

Five such cases were reported in August 1844 alone. In that month the directors were informed that John Herbert, the tender of Locks Nos. 45-46 who was later fired for drunkenness, had left his locks for two days in the charge of Joseph Duke, his son-in-law who lived in the lock house with him. Joseph Hollman, the keeper at Lock No. 44, had never attended his lock in person, leaving the job to his employees at his sawmill in Williamsport. On one day of that month even these men had been absent with the lock left in the hands of one of the men's wives. Isaac Dodd had left Lock No. 43 in charge of his young son for one day. That same day Henry Boyd had left his locks to be operated by his wife's sister. Levi R. Shaw also had left an inadequate substitute at guard Lock No. 4 for one day.[79]

Following the recitation of the information and similar reports from other superintendents on the line, the board determined to put a stop to the growing problems arising from the lock keepers' chronic absences from their duties. On December 20, 1844, the directors issued a new order prohibiting any employee from leaving the portion of the canal under his charge for any reason without the prior consent of the division superintendent. The superintendents were to report any infractions immediately and stern disciplinary action was promised for offenders.[80]

Apparently, this order was effective in solving the problem, because no reports of similar abuses were found in the company records for nearly twenty years.

In fact, only two other cases of chronic absence without approved substitutes were found in a cursory survey of the company papers. In November 1864 Obadiah Barger, a long-time canal employee, complained that he had been removed two months earlier as tender of Locks Nos. 45-46 without just cause, and that Susan Newcomer, who had been appointed to replace him, never had appeared at the locks. Instead she had hired a young person to operate the locks without notifying the division superintendent. When the directors heard that Mrs. Newcomer had delegated her authority in violation of the company regulations, she was dismissed from the payroll and Barger was reinstated to his job.[81]

An interesting case occurred in September 1876 when John T. Hill, who had worked for the company for ten years, was dismissed from his duty as the tender at Lock No. 16. Although he had a good employment record, Hill left the lock in the charge of his assistant every afternoon when he went to get his cow for milking. When he was discharged, Hill had nine friends sign a petition to the directors vouching for his orderly character, his membership in the Sons of Temperance, and his responsible care of the lock. The latter point was buttressed by the fact that the same lock gates had been in place for eleven years.[82]

There was no indication in the company records as to whether the board took any action on the petition.

I. SALE OF INTOXICATING BEVERAGES BY LOCK KEEPERS.

Soon after navigation on the canal commences in the fall of 1830 the board considered a ban prohibiting the lock keepers from selling intoxicating beverages. Such a ban was first issued June 10, 1831, and the following month on July 16 it was incorporated into the formal company regulations.[83]

---

[79] Stone to Coale, Aug. 29, 1844, Ltrs. Recd., C & O Co.

[80] *Proceedings of the President and Board of Directors*, G, 219.

[81] *Ibid*, K, 405–06, and Barger to Brengle, Spetes, and Watson (three letters), Nov. 4, 1864, Ltrs. Recd., C & O Co.

[82] Prettyman to Gorman, Sept. 11, 1876, Ltrs. Recd., C & O Co.

[83] *Proceedings of the Stockholders*, A, 182, and *Proceedings of the President and Board of Directors*, B, 410–19.

Two exceptions were made in this ruling when the lock keepers at Crommelin and Rushville were permitted to establish taverns, but, otherwise, an attempt was made to enforce the prohibition along the line. There were numerous complaints of violations by the lock tenders, one of the most notorious being A. S. Adams at Lock No. 33.[84]

The board experienced little success in its efforts to prohibit the illicit liquor trade. After numerous reports of disorderly conduct near Great Falls and Rushville that were the result of drinking at the lock houses at those two locations the board in November 1844 revoked the privileges that it had granted the lock tenders effective May 1, 1845.[85]

Soon, however appeals by the boatmen and local people pressured the directors into reversing their stand and allow the sale of liquor at those locations.

The existence of grog shops in many of the lock houses continued to be a nuisance to the efficient operation of the canal. In May 1848 J. F. Lewis complained to the board that one of his boats had been damaged and its cargo of flour partially destroyed at Lock No. 26 because of the carelessness of James Fitch, the lock tender, and his assistant. When the matter was investigated, it was found that the captain of the boat had been drinking when he arrived at the lock, and upon being informed that Fitch was repairing a break on the level below the lock, he had gone into the lock house to purchase more liquor. At midnight the boat, which had been left untied near the canal banks, was found sinking to the bottom of the waterway and the flour floating on the surface of the water. The boat captain, who was drunk by this time, solicited the aid of the assistant lock keeper to recover some of the flour. With the aid of several other boatmen the assistant recovered what flour he could. For his services, the assistant agreed to accept three barrels of flour, and the lock tender took one barrel of fine flour in payment for the captain's beverage bill.[86]

The board received the full report on this incident on June 5. At the same time, it was represented to the directors that many of the boatmen and company hands were getting drunk while on the job because of the numerous grog shops in the lock houses. Accordingly, the board determined to prohibit "the sale, barter or disposal of intoxicating liquors at any of the lock houses" with the exception of "the tavern stands at Rushville & Crommelin." The order was to be enforced by the division superintendents.[87]

The following year the board took steps to eliminate the sale of liquor at the Crommelin and Rushville taverns. In September the directors voted to discontinue the rental of these two structures as taverns and to use them only as lock houses for tenders at Locks Nos. 19–20 and Lock No. 23 and Guard Lock No. 2 respectively. Since the living accommodations at both places were superior to other lock houses, it was determined to pay each tender $100 per year. Henceforth the sale of liquor was to be prohibited at both locations after July 1, 1850.[88]

Both of the lock keepers at Crommelin and Rushville appealed the decision to cut their wages to $100, claiming that the closing of their taverns had hurt them financially.[89]

In response, the board raised their annual salaries to the level of $200 that was the standard for all tenders of two locks.[90]

The board continued adamant in its stand against the sale of liquor along the line of the canal. In 1858 Henry Busey, the tender at Locks Nos. 19–20, was permitted to reestablish a hotel

---

[84] *Proceedings of the President and Board of Directors*, E, 69.
[85] *Ibid*, G, 210–11.
[86] Elgin to Coale, May 6, 1848, Ltrs. Recd., C&O Co.
[87] *Proceedings of the President and Board of Directors*, H, 319.
[88] *Ibid*, H, 296–97.
[89] *Ibid*, H, 322–443.
[90] Coale to Collins, May 31, 1850, and Ringgold to Lambre, July 1, 1851, Ltrs. Sent, C & O Co.

or "ordinary" at Crommelin House for the accommodation of visitors to the "Great Falls" provided that no alcoholic beverages were served. George W. Case, the keeper of the locks at Great Falls from 1858 to 1872, was allowed the privilege of continuing to operate the hotel under the same conditions.[91]

J. REPUTABLE LOCK KEEPERS

While many of the lock tenders were undisciplined and indifferent to their jobs, there were some whose abilities and devotion to their duties was recognized and rewarded. The case of James O'Reilly, the keeper of Locks Ns. 1–4 and Tidelock A from 1831 to 1842 has been mentioned already. His reputation for honesty and integrity was so well documented that he was appointed by the board to serve as collector in Georgetown in 1834. In return, the directors rented two of the company buildings in that town to him, one of which was to serve as his office.[92]

Another man with similar credentials was William S. Elgin who served as the tender of Lock No. 33 and the Shenandoah River Lock and as Collector at Harpers Ferry throughout the 1840s and early 1850s.[93]

Some lock tenders were promoted to positions as division superintendents in recognition of their responsible contribution to the operation of the canal. Along these individuals were the aforementioned Elgin and John Y. Young, who served the company throughout the 1830s and 1840s as a lock tender and superintendent of the Georgetown Division. One of the most respected superintendents of that division in the 1840s was John Lambie, who began his employment with the company as the tender at Locks Nos. 9–10 on May 1, 1847. Three superintendents whose service to the company extended into the 1870s received their initial canal experience as lock keepers: A. K. Stake at Locks Nos. 41–42 from April 1, 1847, to July 1, 1848; Lewis G. Stanhope at the same locks from July 1, 1848, into the early 1850s; and Overton G. Lowe, the first individual to be assigned to Lock No. 56 when the waterway was opened to Cumberland in October 1850.[94]

There were other events throughout the canal operating history that indicated a large degree of reliability on the part of most of the lock tenders. During the spring and summer of 1841 when the company finances were desperately low, the keepers and other officers either were not paid for months or received their pay in depreciated scrip, which had a reduced value of nearly 50 percent.[95]

Despite the fact that they were not paid for months, there is no indication that many of the tenders left the line during this period. A similar set of events occurred in the fall of 1859 when the tenders and canal laborers went unpaid for some months. In December of that year, those individuals were reported to be "in a very destitute state for want of the pay due to them, and were unable to procure necessary supplies for their families." Again there were no reports that any of the lock tenders left their locks. To forestall such an occurrence, the board, determined to pay the tenders and laborers with "certificates of indebtedness." [96]

The lock tenders demonstrated their loyalty to the canal company under similar circumstances during the waning years of the independent existence of the waterway. Following the

---

[91] Hening et al to President and Directors, Mar. 1, 1858, Ltrs. Recd., C & O Co., and *Proceedings of the President and Board of Directors*, K, 28–29, 352.

[92] O'Reilly to Ingle, Apr. 23, 1834, Ltrs. Recd., C & O Co., and *Proceedings of the President and Board of Directors*, D, 228, F, 412.

[93] *Report to the Stockholders on the Completion of the Canal to Cumberland*, 139–140.

[94] *Ibid.*,

[95] *Proceedings of the Stockholders*, B, 486.

[96] *Proceedings of the President and Board of Directors*, K, 147–48.

heavy flood in November 1877, all the company officers, toll collectors, and lock keepers, who were not involved in the repair work, were removed from the company payroll so "that expenditures were restricted to the actual cost of repairs and office expenses." A significant number of locks men joined the repair crews as common laborers, thus expediting the restoration of the waterway.[97]

As the canal trade continued to decline during the 1880s, the canal company took various steps to cut its operating expenses. During the winter of 1883-84 the pay of the lock tenders was reduced by 50 percent.[98]

In June 1885 it was reported that most of the tenders were waiting patiently for their overdue wages. Only a few keepers in Washington County had presented problems to the directors because their wages had not been paid for some months.[99]

In 1889 just prior to the major flood in late May the company reported again that the tenders as a whole were faithfully carrying out their duties although they had not been paid for sometime.[100]

K.   THE LOCK HOUSES: 1828-1850

Two general specifications were drawn up by company engineers for the construction of the lock houses. According to the 1828 specifications for the lock houses, the structures were to be of stone, having dimensions of 30 feet by 18 feet. There was to be an earthen-floored cellar beneath the kitchen six feet in the clear with 22-inch thick walls. The principal story of the house was to be two feet above ground surface with 20-inch thick walls. That part not over the cellar was to have a stone footing all around of six more inches. The space between the ground and the bottom floor was to have three 9-inch by 4-inch slits to be covered over with perforated iron or copper plates. The ceiling was to be eight feet above the floor. The attic story was to have 18-inch thick walls, which were to rise three feet between the top of the floor and the square. The peak of the roof was to be six feet above the side walls. The stone work was to be laid in clay mortar with the exception of three inches on the outside of the walls above the ground surface and the inside of the cellar which was to be laid in lime mortar.

The chimney was to be built in the center of the house and to have a stone foundation while the stalk could be built of stone or bricks. There was to be a fireplace in each of the lower rooms. The outside doors were to have stone sills and steps, while the window sills could be either of stone or of painted and sanded locust timber. All the door and window lintels were to be of stone.

The floors of the lock houses were to be of 1 1/4 inch heart pine that did not exceed six inches in width. The front door was to have a stock lock, the kitchen door an inside bolt, the parlor door a seven-inch nob lock, and the rest thumb latches. The windows in the principal story were to be 10-inch by 12-inch glass panes, while those in the upper story were to be 8-inch by 10-inch glass. A 10-inch by 12-inch glass sash was to be put over the front door to light the entry. The roof was to consist of 18-inch cypress shingles, not less than four inches wide and 5/8 inch thick.

The principal story was to be divided into two rooms divided by a stud partition. The two rooms in the attic story were to be separated by a 1 ½ inch plank partition. The ceilings and stud

---

[97] *Fiftieth Annual Report* (1878), C & O Co., 9-10.
[98] *Fifty-Sixth Annual Report* (1884), C & O Co., 19.
[99] *Fifty-Seventh Annual Report* (1879), C & O Co., 9.
[100] *Sixty-First Annual Report* (1889), C & O Co., 10-11.

partitions were to be lathed and, together with the walls, finished with three coats of lime mortar made with glue and clear sand.[101]

In February 1836 a revised specification for the lock houses was adopted which incorporated a few changes. The houses were still to be 30 feet by 18 feet, but they could be of stone or brick at the option of the contractor. If the walls were of brick they were to be 13 ½ inches thick; if they were of stone they were to be 20 inches thick. The houses were to have full basements that were provided with drains protected by iron gratings. The lintels and sills of the doors and windows were to be of locust. All the outside and inside woodwork was to be given two or three coats of English white lead oil paint. The outside doors were to have Pennsylvania or German locks with iron handles. All of the masonry, except for the top 1 ½ feet, was to be laid in lime mortar. The top portion was to be laid in water cement. Virtually all of the other details were similar to the 1828 specifications.[102]

When the canal was finally completed between Dam No. 6 and Cumberland in 1847–50, the company attempted to save money and to speed construction by delaying the erection of lock houses on that portion of the line. When the final segment of the canal was opened to navigation, the lock houses above the Cacapon River were built. Apparently no single specification was used as some of the structures were of frame or log construction and had various designs and dimensions.

---

[101] *Specification of a Lock Keepers House, ca. October 1828, Drawings and other Records Concerning Construction.* The estimated cost for such a structure was $828.46. A copy of this specification may be seen in Appendix A.

[102] *Specification for a Lock Keeper's House, February 10, 1836, Drawings and Other Records Concerning Construction,* C & O Co. The estimated cost for such a structure was $950. A copy of this specification may be seen in Appendix B.

II. THE BOATMEN

A. INTRODUCTION

The life of the boatmen on the canal was one of hard work, long hours, and little pay. The daring adventure of their employment coupled with their isolation from much of the world outside of the canal made the independent-minded boatmen a rough and ready lot. They usually formed a class apart from their neighbors in the Potomac Valley, intermarrying within their own group. Their children were frequently born and raised in the trade and generally had little exposure to the educational or social refinements of the emerging American culture of the 19th century. The boatmen were constantly brawling among themselves for precedence at locks or because of some real or fancied slur. Their life was at best irregular and unpredictable, and the "canallers" exhibited those characteristics in their lifestyles. Some dawdled along the line or amused themselves in drunken revelry, taking their time in making the run. Others were more ambitious, driving their teams and boats at full speed night and day, caring little for themselves, their mules or boats, or canal property. The boatmen were constantly at odds with the company over toll rates and freight charges and with the lock keepers over operating procedures or personal slights. Usually, the "canallers" shunned the larger towns along the canal, for it cost too much to feed their teams, and they felt out of place. Even while wintering along the line they had their own settlements on the fringes of the towns or often quite far from them.[103]

B. CHARACTERISTICS OF THE BOATMEN: 1830–1850

Although many of the "canallers" were hard working and conscientious, the canal company records are filled with references to the brawling, unpredictable, and quarrelsome behavior of the boatmen. In their relationships with each other and with company officials, they exhibited a fierce independence and contentiousness that often ignored or opposed any show of authority by the company officials.

The rigors of life in the largely agrarian and forested Potomac Valley had its effect on the brash behavior of the early boatmen. It appears that they were constantly brawling among themselves for precedence at locks, because of some real or fancied slur, or for exercise. On April 2, 1831, Daniel Van Slyke, the superintendent of the canal, reported that since the water had been admitted into the canal two weeks earlier:

> it is with great difficulty we have been able to preserve order among the boatmen, who in striving to push forward for a preference in passing the several locks are sometimes disposed to injure each other's boats as a means of carrying their point. An unfortunate instance of this kind happened on Wednesday last at the locks on the 9th section. A strongly constructed boat ran her bow against a gondola loaded with flour, and so much injured her as to render it necessary to transship the load. But no damage was done to the cargo.

---

[103] Sanderlin, *The Great National Project*, 186–88, and *Baltimore Evening Sun*, Aug. 9–13, 1937. In his book, Sanderlin sketches some of the characteristics of the boatmen from information that he obtained in interviews with George Nicholson, General Manager of the canal from 1890 to 1838, "Charley" Egan and Harvey Mayhew, former boatmen, Frank Lee Carl, a newspaper correspondent and local historian in Cumberland, and Edward Oswald, Clerk of the Washington County Circuit Court at Hagerstown. In the series of five *Baltimore Evening Sun* articles, Lee McCardell discussed the life of the boatmen basing most of his material on two extensive interviews with Captains Charlie (Scot) Eaton of Cumberland and Denton (Dent) Shupp of Williamsport.

Van Slyke went on to suggest that some regulations be adopted by the board to help the lock tenders preserve order.

> so that the boats may pass the locks by turn as they arrive, as it frequently occurs that fifteen or twenty boats arrive at a lock within half an hour. Hence the contention for right of preference, which I believe would be allayed if it was known that they must be permitted to pass only by turn as they arrive.[104]

During the following month, Van Slyke informed the directors that the boatmen particularly resented the priority given to the packet *Charles F. Mercer* in passing the locks. As this policy already had triggered angry protests, he advised the board to print the order on handbills to be left with the lock tenders and distributed among the boatmen. Unless this were done, it would be virtually impossible to enforce the policy.[105]

The boatmen were constantly at odds with the company over toll rates and in the early days took unusual ways of expressing their dissatisfaction. W. W. Fenelon, the owner of the first packet service between Georgetown and Great Falls, staged a drunken demonstration in Georgetown in September 1831, which was reported to company officials by a local resident:

> Being at the break, at Baker's, at about 6 o'clock, we heard a thundering noise of wild music and saw a large cavalcade (of) colors flying & having got near, it proved to be Mr. Fenelon, with his teams and crew with the colors of the Packet floating in high glee; he proceeded and paraded down Bridge Street, made a stop upon the new bridge, and re freshing himself and his crew after much music gave the word of command for High Street reeling in saddle all the way; a gang of Negroes and boys thronging the street until nearly dark. Now, sir, their ostensible object of all that fuss, is a loud complaint about the tolls, which gives him a pretext to pour abuses on the institution and bias the mind of the people at large.[106]

The directors were irritated particularly by the quality of the boats operating on the canal. No one was willing to undertake to fulfill their dreams of steamers and double-decked packets. In fact, the boatmen generally refused to meet even the minimum requirements of the company regulations. Complaints were frequently made of iron-shod boats, leaky scows, drifting rafts, and sunken gondolas obstructing navigation.[107]

Not only were the boats affecting the flow of traffic on the waterway, but they also were causing damage to the locks. This growing problem was reported to the board in December 1838 as follows:

> many of the canal boats navigating the canal are armed on their sides with iron, and do great damage to the locks as they pass through. Many of the stone scows (their ends being at right angles) have their corners plated with iron, and entering the locks they frequently strike the coping and other parts of the lock and do great damage. By examining the locks in Georgetown you will readily perceive what damage has already been done.[108]

---

[104] Van Slyke to Mercer, Apr. 2, 1831, Ltrs. Recd., C & O Co.
[105] Van Slyke to Directors, May 26, 1831, Ltrs. Recd., C & O Co.
[106] Rodier to Ingle, Sept. 8, 1831, Ltrs. Recd, C & O Co.
[107] *Proceedings of the President and Board of Directors*, C, 30, and Stone to Ringgold, June 6, 1847, Ltrs. Recd, C & O Co.
[108] Easby to Directors, Dec. 19, 1838, Ltrs. Recd., C & O Co.

By the enforcement of regulations, the provision of dry docks, the assessment of fines, and the levy of a 100 percent rate discrimination against rafts, the company sought to drive undesirable craft off the waterway and to encourage the construction of new and larger boats. In this effort they were partly successful, assisted by the need for larger and sturdier boats to handle the growing demands of the trade. Nevertheless the lumber trade and the incidental trade of the numerous valley farmers, who after building their own craft designed to last for only one trip (usually to be sold at Georgetown for firewood), made the struggle for better boats a never ending one.[109]

The formulation of detailed regulations for the operation of the canal adopted in July 1831 and February 1835 did not insure the orderly conduct of business on the waterway. On the contrary, every conceivable abuse was reported at one time or another. The board immediately saw the necessity of securing some definite delegation of police power from the parties to the charter in order to gain the authority to enforce its regulations.[110]

Repeated directions for the enforcement of the rules indicate a laxness or indifference on the part of the officials and boatmen alike. Regulations which were regularly singled out for stricter enforcement were those that prohibited the use of iron-shod poles for propulsion, the navigation of the canal by boats that did not conform to the company specifications, the negligent practices that caused damage to locks, and the schemes of boatmen to defraud the company of toll payments.[111]

C. CHARACTERISTICS OF THE BOATMEN: 1851–1889

Many of the characteristics of the early boatmen also were exhibited by those who plied the waterway after its completion to Cumberland in 1850. The same problems of violent behavior, disregard of company regulations and property, and reckless navigation practices by the boatmen continued to plague the waterway.

On April 1, 1851, a new system of by-laws, rules, and regulations for the government, management, and operation of the waterway went into effect. Printed as a 47-page booklet, the regulations covered every facet of the canal's operation in detail and clearly defined the monetary penalty for every offense of the boatmen. This set of regulations, which remained in effect until 1889, was the most comprehensive effort of its kind to be undertaken by the board. The booklets were printed in great quantities and distributed to every boatmen and canal official.[112]

In the months immediately following their adoption, the new regulations appeared to have the desired effect upon the "canallers." That this was the case was evidenced by the following report made to the company stockholders by President William Grason on June 2, 1851:

> We have every reason to believe, as far as we can judge, from the short period which has elapsed since the by-laws of the company went into operation on the first of April last, that very beneficial results have, and will attend them; in the company...and producing a

---

[109] Sanderlin, *The Great National Project*, 188.

[110] *Proceedings of the Stockholders*, A, 173, and *Proceedings of the President and Board of Directors*, B, 206. This subject is covered more fully in Chapter 12 of this study.

[111] Bryan to Ingle, Aug. 15, 1831, Ltrs. Recd., C & O Co. and *Proceedings of the President and Board of Directors* B, 290, C, 30. To aid the tenders in the enforcement of the regulation against the use of iron-shod poles, the directors authorized in August 1831 the construction of a shed at Lock No. 23 where wooden poles could be stored. The boatmen would be given such poles free of charge if they turned in their iron poles. Bryan Ingle, Aug. 15, 1831, Ltrs. Recd., C&O Co.

[112] *By-Laws, Rules, and Regulations: In force on the Chesapeake & Ohio Canal*, 1–47

degree of order and regularity on the past of those navigating the canal, which has heretofore not existed. Although, as was to be supposed, in any new system of regulations, some opposition would, in the outset, be manifested by those to whom any restraint would be irksome, we have reason to believe, that all well-disposed persons engaged in navigating the canal, regard these regulations as wholesome and necessary, acting both as a protection to the works, of the company, insuring more regularity, and less frequent interruptions to the navigation of the canal, and, at the same time, preventing collisions with some of the boatmen, who have hitherto been disorderly. Under all circumstances, there has been less objection than could have been expected, and the boatmen have very generally quietly acquiesced in, and readily complied with the provision of the regulations.

Few infractions of the new regulations had been reported by the officers on the line of the canal. The amount of fines that had been imposed was $140, of which $80 had been written by the directors for sufficient reasons.[113]

Needless to say, the peaceful acquiescence to the company regulations by the boatmen did not last for long. The abrasive behavior of many of the boatmen soon became a great concern to the directors as they sought to maintain the orderly operation of the waterway. Among the most conspicuous examples of the revival of their destructive spirit were the (1) disregard of company rules and officials, (2) clamoring for access to the coal wharves on the congested Georgetown level, (3) reckless navigation practices which led to boating accidents and to the destruction of works on the canal, (4) incidents of physical violence vis-à-vis the lock tenders, (5) reluctance to meet the minimum requirements of the company regulations relative to the quality of the barges, and (6) attempts to defraud the company of its rightful tolls.

1. Disregard of Company Rules and Officials

By the fall of 1851 there were widespread reports of boatmen who were ignoring both the company regulations and the attempts of canal officials to enforce the rules. One common case was the insistence of boat captains to use grab hooks while passing through the locks. This persistent practice, which tended to cause injury to the masonry of the locks, was considered to be of such a serious nature that the board at one time considered revoking the license of any captain who refused to comply with the regulations.[114]

Another practice, which indicated the boatmen's lack of respect for the company regulations and the canal officials who attempted to enforce the rules, was that of refusing to pay fines. At first this was a minor problem as evidenced by the fact that all but $10 of the total amount of $140 levied in fines during the first three months of operation under the new rules in 1851 was paid. However, by the late 1870s nearly 70 percent of the fines were never paid. One of the worst years in this respect was 1877 in which only $45.47 was collected by canal authorities out of the total of $126.52 assessed.[115]

One of the most notorious incidents in this regard occurred in May 1874 when George Reed, captain of the *Mayfield and Heiston*, was fined $20 for illegally mooring his boat in the Cumberland basin. Refusing to pay the fine, he prepared to leave Cumberland with a barge cargo of coal destined for Georgetown. Because he refused to pay the fine, the collector at Cumberland would not give him a waybill. When the lock tenders at Lock No. 74 attempted to prevent him

---

[113] *Proceedings of the Stockholders*, D, 409.
[114] *Proceedings of the President and Board of Directors*, H, 476.
[115] *Fines Paid and Unpaid for 1877*, Ltrs. Recd., C & O Co.

from continuing his journey until the fine was paid and a waybill was served, Reed forced his way through the lock. This event brought an additional fine of $50 and a warning from President Gorman that a repetition of such an act would result in another $50 penalty. Nevertheless, the boat was allowed to proceed to Georgetown without further hindrance. After Reed deposited his cargo in Georgetown, he was confronted by canal officials and served notice that he owed the company $120 in fines and $4.08 for a waybill. Again, he defiantly ignored the remonstrance of the agents, commenced his return to Cumberland without a waybill, and forced his way through the locks despite the protests of the collectors at Georgetown, Lock No. 5, and Harpers Ferry. When Reed arrived in Cumberland, his boat was seized with the aid of the police and confiscated until he paid the sum of $124.08.[116]

2. Clamoring for Access to the Coal Wharves on the Congested Georgetown Level

As trade on the waterway increased, the method of expediting canal traffic on the Georgetown level soon became a major obstacle to the continued growth of business. Unloading and transfer facilities were unable to handle the increasing tonnage, which was brought to them. As a result, boats lined up in the canal awaiting their turn to unload. Not only were the delays annoying and costly to the boatmen, shippers and company alike, but the congestion on the Georgetown level was a problem in itself. The waterway was not wide enough to accommodate both the ordinary traffic to and from the basin or the aqueduct and the clamoring boatmen awaiting access to the coal wharves.

Complaints about the congestion and confusion on the Georgetown level forced the directors to take steps to alleviate the problem. In October 1864 the superintendent of the Georgetown Division was authorized to employ a harbormaster to regulate the boats at that place.[117]

Further reports by Georgetown citizens of brawling among the annoyed boatmen as they struggled to achieve quick access to the coal wharves led to the board's decision in April 1866 to invest the harbor master "with police authority to enable him more effectually to discharge the duties of his office."[118]

By 1871 the problem had become serious. Frequently there was a line of 60 to 80 boats along the canal bank and occasionally the string of loaded boats stretched from one half to one mile in length. As the boatmen jostled for position, some barges ran aground causing delays to the other boats.[119]

In their frustration, many "canallers" disregarded the company regulations and began lining up two, three, and four abreast in an effort to get closer to the wharves.[120]

Some of the more contentious boatmen attempted to get to the wharves out of turn, and when they were refused service they would moor their barges next to the unloading vessels, thereby causing jams and confusion. Two of the most flagrant examples of such practices were cases where a Maryland Coal Company boat obstructed traffic on the canal for six hours while "lying double" and another barge owned by the same company that blocked the navigation for twelve hours after trying to get ahead of eighteen boats in line at the Welch Wharf.[121]

---

[116] Pope to Gorman, May 6, 1874, Weber to Gorman, May 20, 1874, and Wenner to Gorman, June 8, 1874, Ltrs, Recd., C & O Co.
[117] *Proceedings of the President and Board of Directors*, K, 402.
[118] *Ibid,* K, 482.
[119] *Forty-Second Annual Report* (1870), C & O Co., 25.
[120] Hayden to Clark, June 14, 1871, Ltrs. Recd., C & O Co.
[121] *Report on Fines Imposed on Boats* by R. G. Connell, Harbormaster, Mar. 22, 1871," Ltrs. Recd., C&O Co.

The board soon initiated a series of steps to relieve the congestion and to restore order, regularity, and authority in the control and movements of boats on the Georgetown level. As the harbormaster was ill equipped to control the growing problem by himself, the directors authorized the employment of an assistant.[122]

New regulations were enacted which were strictly enforced, and a contract was let to build the Georgetown Incline Plane.[123]

3. Reckless Navigation Practices

There were numerous instances where the reckless navigation practices of the boatmen led to accidents that caused damage both to the barges and canal structures. At times boat races were held up and down the canal–the fastest–known time for a light boat from Georgetown to Cumberland was 62 hours set by Raleigh Bender of Sharpsburg while the best-known time for a loaded boat from Cumberland to Williamsport was 35 hours set by Dent Shupp of the latter town with 128 tons of coal. To set such records the boatmen walked along the towpath feeding the mules handfuls of hay while boating and giving them feed and water while passing through a lock.[124]

In their haste to gain time in navigation, the captain, often ignored the company regulations for passing. Hence a number of boat collisions occurred, one of the most notable involving a freight boat and a packet in July 1855. As a result of the accident, the passenger vessel was sunk and the freight boat's captain received a stiff fine.[125]

The reckless maneuvering of the boatmen and their lack of concern for canal property was manifested in other ways. Over the years Aqueduct No. 3 was the site of numerous accidents as a result of careless boatmen who refused to slacken their speed to negotiate the sharp bend immediately upstream. After a number of accidents in which boats struck and damaged the sidewalls of the aqueduct, the board in March 1870 issued an order that all barges were to slack their speed at least fifty yards from the approaches of the structure. The order was printed on handbills for distribution, and a watchman was stationed at the aqueduct to see that the boatmen complied with the directive.[126]

One of the most frequent results of the careless practices of the boatmen was the damage done to the lock gates. When the "canallers" were in a hurry, they often failed to slacken their speed sufficiently as they approached a lock. At other times, the impatient boatmen attempted to "lock through" without waiting for the service of the lock tenders. Such practices led to the numerous incidents in which the boats would strike and break the gates, thereby interrupting navigation for as much as a day until a new gate was put in.[127]

During one 4-year period from 1877 to 1880 there were nine occasions where boatmen were fined for running into or breaking lock gates.[128]

The negligent navigation practices of the boatmen sometimes caused greater damage to their vessels than to the canal structures. In one case, the *Loretto* struck the upper abutment of the

---

[122] Hutton to Clarke, Mar. 31, 1871, Ltrs. Recd., C & O Co.

[123] Both of these subjects are covered more fully in Chapter 12 of this study.

[124] *Baltimore Evening Sun*, Aug. 9–13, 1837.

[125] *Proceedings of the President and Board of Directors*, I, 193.

[126] Hutton to Thomas, March 19, 1870, Ltrs. Recd., C & O Co.

[127] Grimm to Chesapeake & Ohio Canal Company, Apr. 22, 1871, McMachaw to President and Directors, Mar. 11, 1874, Fletchall to President and Directors, June 17, 1875, and Fletchall to Gorman, July 18, 1876, Ltrs. Recd., C & O Co.

[128] Register of Offenses, 1877–1881, C & O Co.

Lock No. 15 and broke a hole in its side about one foot square. The boat sank, causing a 24-hour suspension of the navigation.[129]

Many of the boating accidents were attributable to the intoxication of the "canallers." One bizarre incident occurred in June 1873 when the American Coal Company boat *Henry C. Flagg* struck the gates of Lock No. 74 with such force that all four were knocked out and the vessel sank in the lock chamber, thus disrupting navigation for 48 hours. An investigation of the incident revealed that the boat had left Cumberland on the charge of two black hands, as its captain, Mr. Mulligan, was on a drunken spree in Shantytown. When the boat arrived at Lock No. 75, the lock keeper demanded a waybill, which the crew did not possess. When the hands agreed to wait until the captain arrived with the document, the tender noticed that the boat was filling with water because of several leaks. Since the hands did not have a pump, the keeper fearing the boat would sink ordered them to pull on to the short level below the lock. Soon the intoxicated captain arrived with the waybill and, disregarded the tender's entreaty to pump out the boat, ordered his hands to get the barge moving. They dutifully pulled the boat alongside the *F. C. Young*, which was about to enter Lock No. 74, thereby creating a jam in the mouth of the lock. While Captain Mulligan went to a nearby store, his crew borrowed a pump and commenced to extract the water from the boat. After the crew of the *F. C. Young* maneuvered their boat back to loosen the jam, the crew of the *Henry C. Flagg* pulled their boat into the lock. No effort was made to snub the boat; thus it struck the lower lock gates and knocked them out, the upper gates slammed shut and broke, letting water from the upper level run over the boat and causing it to sink.[130]

Many mules were also lost as a result of the negligent practices of the boatmen. One such example occurred near the brickyard on the Logwall Level in May 1873. As two boatmen were passing each other, the driver of one of the mule teams urged his animals on with a series of violent gestures. The driver theatrics frightened the team of the other boat, causing the two mules to jump over a high embankment. One of the mules was killed and the other was injured.[131]

4. Incidents of Physical Violence

As the lock tenders and the boatmen came into frequent contact, there were numerous instances of fighting between the two groups. Because both the lock men and the "canallers" were independent, rough and ready individuals, the initiative for the incidents of physical violence generally appears to have been taken by the latter. At the same time, it is clear that the lock tenders were often quick tempered and eager to respond to any provocative challenge flung at them.

One of the most celebrated incidents occurred at Lock No. 75 in July 1874. The quarrel commenced when the *Okonoka* was "locking through" early one morning. The towline of the boat caught on the lock railing and tore it loose. Furthermore Captain John Byroad insisted on scrubbing the sides of his boat with a broom while still in the lock. As another boat was waiting, John M. Bloss, the tender, ordered him to pull the barge out of the lock. Byroad refused whereupon one of Bloss' sons opened the berm gate. The gate's beam pinned one of Byroad's sons against the side of the boat where he was scrubbing. An argument and fisticuffs resulted in which one of Bloss' sons was knocked off the boat by the captain's wife. After a flurry of rock throwing between the boys of the boatmen and the lock tender, one of the latter's sons injured a son of the former with a club. When the tender's boys were chased to the lock house, they returned with a revolver and double-barreled shotgun both of which misfired when they tried to use them. As the

---

[129] Maus to Gorman, Nov. 30, 1872, Ltrs. Recd., C & O Co.

[130] Malvany to Gorman, June 25, 1873, Ltrs. Recd., C & O Co.

[131] Garrett to President and Board of Directors, July 2, 1873, Ltrs. Recd., C & O Co.

boat continued on its journey, the tender followed it all the way to Cumberland on horseback, brandishing a club and threatening that he would 'settle up the damage Old Bitch.'"[132]

At times the mere threat of violence by the boatmen so intimidated the lock tenders that they were unable to fulfill their duties. An example of this situation took place when the lock keepers were ordered to enforce the prohibition against Sunday navigation in the late 1860s and early 1870s. When the tenders attempted to prevent some boats from passing through the locks on the Sabbath, the boatmen threatened to fight any individuals who got in their way and proceeded up the canal busting the padlocks on the lock gates as they went. When some of the lock tenders attempted to stop the boatmen, violence erupted and reports of rioting and "depredations" spread along the line. The boatmen quickly gained the upper hand in the struggle, and the company soon gave up its attempts to enforce a "Sunday Law."[133]

5. Quality of the Boats

Many of the boatmen continued to be reluctant to meet even the minimum requirements of the regulations regarding the quality of the boats operating on the canal. There were numerous complaints of leaky scows, iron-shod boats, and sunken wrecks obstructing navigation. From 1855 to 1858 some 34 barges were broken or sunk as a result of either poor construction or inattention to periodic maintenance work.[134]

While the quality of the canal boats tended to improve with the growth of trade in the post-Civil War era, there were still reports of boats sinking because of their "bad condition."[135]

One of the more bizarre stories in this regard was that of a boat which started sinking at Cumberland when it was loaded. The crew pumped the water out and began the trip to Georgetown, all the while pumping to keep the vessel afloat. The barge finally sank just above Lock No. 5, impeding the flow of traffic for eleven hours.[136]

Some of the captains insisted on putting "sand streaks" along the sides of their boats in violation of the company rules, thereby causing them to get stuck in the lock chambers for more than an hour.[137]

The problems caused by boats unfit for navigation became a critical issue by 1872 since the board was anxious to maintain an efficiently operating waterway to accommodate the expanding trade. Accordingly, a committee was appointed in that year to re-register all the vessels on the canal. At the time of registration, the vessels were to be examined to see that their dimensions and state of repair conformed to company regulations. Those boats that were deemed unseaworthy were to have their applications for registration certificates rejected.[138]

Despite these efforts the canal faced increasing problems with leaky and sunken boats during the remaining years of its independent existence. Among the many incidents of this kind was the sinking of the *Lezer Ragen* at Lock No. 15 in July 1876. Leaking badly before it left Cumberland, the vessel was kept afloat by its crew until it ran into the abutments of several locks

---

[132] Byroad to Gorman, July 18, 1874, Bloss to Gorman. July 18, 1874, and Mulvany to Gorman, July 24, 1879, Ltrs. Recd., C & O Co.

[133] *Proceedings of the President and Board of Directors*, K, 518, L, 317, 169, 422, 435–36, and "Report on Sunday Law," May 19, 1870, Ltrs. Recd., C & O Co.

[134] *Proceedings of the President and Board of Directors*, K, 67.

[135] Hutton to Clarke, June 24, 1870, Ltrs. Recd., C & O Co.

[136] Maus to Gorman, Oct. 23, 1872, Ltrs. Recd., C & O Co.

[137] Gaimm to Chesapeake & Ohio Canal Company and Clarke to Mulvany, Apr. 20, 1871, Ltrs. Recd., C & O Co.

[138] Mulvany to Gorman, June 28, 1872, and Resloy to Gorman, Mar. 7, 1873, Ltrs. Recd., C & O Co., and *Williamsport Pilot*, Feb. 8, 1873, in Arthur P. Gorman Collection,. University of North Carolina Library, Chapel Hill.

below Great Falls. As it proceeded out of the chamber of Lock No. 15, the boat sank and its bow settled down on some rocks, at the mouth of the lock, cutting a large hole in its bottom.[139]

Similar stories abound of unseaworthy vessels throughout the period including that of the *Bertha M. Young*. As the boat was leaking badly, its crew convinced the steamer *Scrivenes* that was passing by, to tow it while they pumped the water out. When it became apparent that the pumping efforts were futile, the boat was allowed to sink one night on level no. 36 and abandoned, resulting in a delay of 36 hours to canal navigation.[140]

During the four-year period from 1877 to 1880 the company issued twenty citations for sunken boats or vessels that required the aid of canal hands to pump water in an effort to prevent their sinking.[141]

6. Attempts to Defraud the Canal Company of Tolls

At times the rebellious boatmen attempted to earn higher profits by attempting to defraud the company of its tolls. This was done most often when the boats were carrying a small cargo which could be hidden under the hatches and which did not weigh the boat down to a great extent. In May 1873 the *B. L. Slack* left Georgetown with 225 sacks of salt hidden under its hatches, although its waybill listed it as an empty boat. It was not until the barge reached Harpers Ferry that a company agent discovered the scheme on a tip from the mule driver that the captain was attempting to avoid the payment of $22.50 in tolls.[142]

There were numerous other instances in which captains made an effort to conceal a portion of their cargoes from the eyes of the company collectors.[143]

D. CHARACTERISTICS OF THE BOATMEN: 1891–1924

In 1902 the receivers took steps toward the establishment of complete control over freight charges on the waterway. The Canal Towage Company, sponsored by the canal receivers and the Consolidation Coal Company both of which were dominated by the Baltimore & Ohio Railroad, was organized along the lines first suggested by Arthur P. Gorman in the mid-1870s. The primary function of this enterprise was to provide economy and regularity in the runs of the waterway. To do this, the company supplied the boats, teams and equipment, and established a regular schedule for the boatmen to follow. Under this new arrangement, all that the captain was expected to furnish was the deck gear, the long and short fallboards, the feed, and troughs. The Canal Towage Company also cut freight rates from 65 cents per ton to 45 cents per ton and controlled the distribution of cargoes. As a result, the service and the efficiency of canal navigation were improved, but in so doing the last shred of independence for the "canallers" was destroyed. The canal lost much of its romance as the boats began to be numbered instead of named and to be uniform and utilitarian rather than colorfully individualistic.[144]

---

[139] Fleteball to Gorman, July 18, 1876, Ltrs. Recd., C & O Co.

[140] Moore to Gorman, Aug. 31, 1878, Ltrs. Recd., C & O Co.

[141] *Register of Offenses, 1877–1881*, C & O Co.

[142] Pope to Gorman, June 15, 1873, Ltrs. Recd., C & O Co.

[143] Herbert to President and Directors, Apr. 10, 1844, Ltrs. Recd., C & O Co.

[144] Although most of the boats had been named for their owners or members of their captains' families, many had been given colorful names over the years. A list of the coal boats navigating the canal in 1870 contained the following names: *Eagle, Vigilant, Invincible, Defiance, Emerald, Unexpected, Hawk, Owl, Peacock, Wren, Dalia, Energy, Hero, General Grant, Washington Irving, Kattskill, Rip Van Winkle, Brownbones, Napoleon Bonaparte, Six Days,* and *Wave*. Weber to Clarke, June 28, 1870, Ltrs. Recd., C & O Co.

Spirited, unruly, flamboyant, and lackadaisical boatmen were alike undesirable to the company, and the rougher ones were not permitted to use its boats. There was no longer room for romantic characters such as Captain John Malott of Williamsport whose mules were known for the white sheepskins with tasseled red rosettes that they wore on their tossing bell bows and whose boats were decorated with flags and political banners during campaigns. Traffic became regularized on a timetable basis.[145]

The transition in the position of the boatmen in the changing canal scene had been in progress for some three decades. The growth of marked distinctions in canal society after the Civil War–officials, shippers, and "canallers"–mirrored in microcosm the development of the capitalist, middle, and laboring classes in the nation as a whole. The emergence of the waterway as a moneymaking, big business enterprise in the early 1870s tended to increase the difference by exerting pressure on the groups to maintain the *status quo* in order not to disturb the canal's prosperity. The impact of the economic depression, which reached the canal in 1876, heightened the pressure on the boatmen. The directors insisted that the long-term benefits of maintaining the waterway as a going concern outweighed the immediate hardships to the boatmen, which might result. For this reason, strikes were crushed, wages and freight charges slashed, and canal trade regularized. The "canallers" were caught in a squeeze between the efforts of the coat companies and the canal company to reduce expenses. The coal companies, together with the boat builders, sought to increase their profits by maintaining boat rents and sale prices at high levels, reducing freight rates and calling for lower toll charges. To meet their continuing expenses, boatmen needed high freight charges. But the canal company, seeking to cut transportation costs to stay in competition with the Baltimore & Ohio and at the same time attempting to maintain tolls at a profitable level, demanded lower boat rents, sale prices, and freight charges. The Canal Towage Company represented the culmination of the late 19th century trends towards lower charges and complete control over coal transportation. Independent boatmen could not compete with the Canal Towage Company and its sponsors. A comparison of receipts and expenses of independent boatmen before the organization of the Canal Towage Company and the boats operated by that company indicates that the profits of the latter were some 42 percent greater than those of the former:

INDEPENDENT BOATMEN

Receipts	
90 tons @ 65 cents per ton	$58.50
Expenses	
Boat rent	$15.00
Mule hire	16.00
Waybills	4.80
Feed	5.00
	$40.80
Profit Per Trip	$17.70

CANAL TOWAGE COMPANY BOATS

Receipts	
90 tons @ 45 cents per ton	$40.50
Expenses	
Waybills	$4.80
Feed	4.00
	$ 9.80

---

[145] Sanderlin, *The Great National Project*, 268–269, and *Baltimore Evening Sun*, August 12, 1937.

Profit Per Trip $30.70[146]

There is little documentary information on the boatmen following the organization of the Canal Towage Company. The only significant problem to arise with the boatmen occurred in 1918 when the canal carried coal for the government proving grounds at Indianhead, Maryland, some 30 miles down the Potomac River from Washington. The movement of coal down the canal was held up during the early part of the navigation season by labor troubles, which were resolved in part by granting higher wages to the boatmen operating the 80-boat fleet of the Canal Towage Company,.[147]

The only comprehensive study of the canal boatmen and their families during the operation of the waterway was undertaken in 1921 by the U. S. Department of Labor. The survey is interesting, because it offers data on the social, economic, and educational characteristics of the "canallers" in the waning years of the canal's existence.

The great majority of the captains on the canal had their wives and children with them on the boats. Of the 66 captains on the payroll of the Canal Towage Company, 59 were married men.[148] Of these, 41 had their children with them during the boating season. The number of children found accompanying their families was 135 (70 boys and 65 girls), of which 48 were under 7 years of age. In addition to these children, there were 7 boys employed on the canal boats as deck hands by captains to whom they were not related. The ages of the 7 boys were as follows: one, 11 years; four, 14 years; one, 15 years; and one, 16 years.

All the captains and their wives included in the study were Native American whites. Seven of the captains and five of the wives were illiterate. One captain, who had begun boating with his father when he was five years of age, reported that altogether he had gone to school for 29 months. By the time he reached the fourth grade the children of his own age had long since completed the grammar school grades, and he was ashamed to enter classes with younger boys and girls. Regretting his own lack of education he said that when his daughter reached school age he should stop boating.

The principal activities in operating a boat on the canal consisted of driving the mules and steering the boat. It was generally the child's job to drive the mules during the day either walking besides the mules on the towpath or riding the leader. Steering the boat by means of a "stick" which controlled the rudder could be accomplished by the pilot standing or sitting against it. Hence the mother of the family often handled the steering while attending to household tasks. Young children could steer light boats, while the older boys and men usually handled the steering chores for heavily loaded boats.

The ages of the children working on the boats ranged from 5 to 17, but those aged 14 years composed the greatest number in any single age grouping. However, the 11-year-olds composed the second highest number in any age category.

One of the boating households consisted of four persons–the captain, the assistant deck hand, the captain's wife, and their 11-year-old daughter. The girl had been driving, steering, and doing housework on the boat for several years, but she did not like boating and was very lonesome. Her father said that she could do anything that a hired hand could do, but he felt that it was necessary to employ a man because "you have to rest once in a while." Among other things, the captain observed that the "women and children are as good as the men" and "if it weren't for the children the canal wouldn't run a day."

---

[146] Sanderlin, *The Great National Project*, 269–270, and *Washington Evening Star*, July 11, 1905.

[147] *Washington Evening Star*, September 26, 1918.

[148] By 1921 the canal boats were operating in fleets, thereby necessitating fewer captains.

In 1920 most of the captains received less than $1,250 from their boat work. About two-thirds of them supplemented their earnings either by winter employment or by incidental work during the season. For example, one man owned towing mules, which he hired out. Other captains secured small loads of incidental freight consisting of general merchandise, farm products, or supplies for the pleasure parks and summer campgrounds in the neighborhood of the canal. The captains were paid a uniform freight rate per ton amounting to $75 or $80 per trip.

The average size of the cabins on the canal boats was approximately 10 feet by 12 feet. All cabins had two bunks, one of which was set into the inner wall of the main cabin and the other located in the so-called "stateroom" which was partitioned off from the main cabin by a diagonal wall. The bunks were 36 inches wide–sufficient space for one person but ordinarily occupied by two. In addition to the cabin bunks, the feed box extending across the deck at the center of the boat was ordinarily used for sleeping purposes. This box, 4 feet high and 4 feet wide, provided a fairly comfortable bed by spreading blankets over the hay and other feed. It was used in some cases by the deck hands and occasionally by the children. Often in hot weather the floor of the deck was used as a bed, but some mothers stated that they were afraid to let the children sleep outside of the cabin.

In spite of the narrow berths, most families regarded them as adequate sleeping space for four persons. The feed box provided two additional sleeping places. Of the 41 families in the study, however, ten had seven members and nineteen had more than four persons. The most distressing instance of congestion existed where a family of nine lived on a boat. The mother said that she made a bed for the children on the floor, but "when you get seven down there, there ain't room left to walk around without stepping on them." The floors of the cabins were frequently bare, but fourteen families reported having linoleum coverings. One family stated that it was impossible to use any sort of covering as the floors leaked and were always damp.

The hours of travel on the canal were almost continuous. Fifteen hours a day was the minimum reported by any of the boat families. Eighteen hours the most frequently reported, but several families stated that they worked longer. One family had operated its boat without taking any intervals for rest. "It never rains, snows, or blows for a boatman, and a boatman never has no Sunday," said another. "Tell we see some folks along the way, dressed up and a-goin' to Sunday School." One captain and his wife who reported working 15 hours a day employed no crew but depended on the assistance of two children, a girl 14 years of age and a boy of 5. The girl did almost all the driving, usually riding mule back, and the parents steered. The little boy helped with the driving but not for more than a mile or two at a time. The boat was kept moving until the girl could drive no longer; then the boat was tied up for the night. "We'd boat longer if the driver felt like it," said the father.

Water for drinking and cooking purposes was secured from springs along the canal and stored in barrels or kegs. Water for washing clothes was obtained from the canal itself. Most of the families complained of mosquitoes.

Of the families visited for the study, five lived the year round on their boats, one having done so for eighteen years. All of the other families occasionally visited and spent the off-season in maintained houses along the canal. The dwellings were chiefly small detached wooden or log houses located in or near towns in the vicinity of the waterway within one mile of schools.

Numerous accidents had occurred among the boatmen's children. Forty-five children had fallen into the canal more or less frequently, eleven had been kicked by mules, one had been burned, one cut with an axe, and one dragged by a mule over a lock gate. One mother reported that her four children had many accidents. The oldest had his nose broken by a kick from a mule, and, with the exception of the baby, all had fallen into the canal many times. Once when a lock tender had closed the gates too soon, the boat's awning had been dragged off the deck taking the children with it, thus pinning them between the gate and the boat.[149]

E. TYPICAL EXPERIENCES IN THE LIVES OF THE 'CANALLERS'

The following narrative offers some typical features of the lives of the "canallers." The material is based primarily on three sources: Walter S. Sanderlin, *The Great National Project: A History of the Chesapeake & Ohio Canal* (Baltimore, 1946), pp. 186–188; *Baltimore Evening Sun*, August 9–13, 1937; and Ella E. Clark and Thomas F. Hahn, eds., *Life On the Chesapeake & Ohio Canal, 1859* (York, 1975), pp. 1–48. As these sources describe the canal experiences of the boatmen from the late 1850s to the early 1900s, the following data should be considered as representative only of that period.

1. Preparations for the Journey from Cumberland to Georgetown

In preparing for a journey down the 185-mile length of the canal, the boatman needed to obtain feed and provisions for his family and mules. Hay and feed for the mules was purchased at various establishments across from the coat loading wharves at the basin in Cumberland, the most popular store being Coulehan's on Wineow Street. Groceries were procured up Wineow Street at Dennis Murphy's or John McGrinnis' or at Coulehan's. The usual staples taken along on a trip consisted of flour, sugar, coffee, smoked meat, and dry salt belly. As the sale of liquor was outlawed along the canal, alcoholic beverages also were purchased at the stores along the canal basin or at the numerous saloons, which operated in Shantytown around and behind the boatyards. Among the most popular drinking establishments that the boatmen frequented while waiting for a load of coal (or upon reaching Cumberland after a long journey up the canal) were Old Aunt Susan Jones' Rising Sun Saloon, Mis' Palmer's Red Tin Shanty, and the bars owned by George Burns, Ed Cooney, Gus Hensel, Dora Ogle, and Cherry Clark. If the captain's family was not large enough to provide the needed help on the boat, he made arrangements to hire a deck hand or two.

2. The Journey Down the Canal Begins

When all preparations were made, the captain backed his boat up to the coal chutes at the loading basin. The coal was dumped out of the railroad cars on a trestle over the chutes and passed down the chutes into the holds of the barge. After having received a waybill from the canal company collector, the boat commenced its run down the canal. A normal trip to Georgetown took about five 18-hour days. Although some boats ran all night, most tied up in groups of six or seven between 10 p.m. and 4 a.m.

The usual schedule of work both for the mules and the people was six hours of work and six hours of rest. Members of the captain's family generally slept in the cabin if there was room. Hired hands or older members of large families slept in the hay house, which had bunks on one side and feed on the other. Some boatmen took Sunday off to attend church services in the small towns along the canal, but most of the "canallers," who generally appeared to be an irreverent and irreligious lot, boated seven days a week if loads were available.

3. The Procurement of Food and Provisions on the Journey

---

[149] Ethel M. Springer, *Canal Boat Children*, Children's Bureau, Department of Agriculture, 1921, reprinted in *Monthly Labor Review*, 1923, 3–11.

Most everything that was needed in the way of groceries or feed could be purchased along the canal. There were numerous stores at many of the locks and in the villages in the vicinity of the canal that catered to the needs of the boatmen. In addition, most of the lock tenders raised milk cows, chickens, and gardens, the surplus of which was sold to the "canallers." Some of the boatmen, however, carried some chickens and one or two pigs on their boats to cut their expenses. The boatmen's diet was supplemented with fish taken from the canal.

4. The Role of Women on the Boats

The duties of women on the canal boats included cooking, child rearing, steering, washing, and sewing. It was often the woman's duty to help steer the boat and feed the mules. The cooking was done on the cabin stove, which was usually heated with burned corncobs from the stable. Some of the boats had more modern stoves, known as Star Light coal burners, made with coke tin by the Cumberland firm of William Moorehead and Lew Metz. Two of the most popular dishes among the boatmen were turtle soup made from turtles caught in the canal and blackberry pie made from berries that grew wild along the towpath. The women had their babies on the boats; if possible, the boat would stop at a town where services of a midwife could be obtained. Then the journey was resumed the following day with the man handling most of the cooking chores unless he had older children. The washing of clothes and bathing of children often was done at the side of the canal in the moonlight after the boat had tied up for the night. The sewing or mending of clothes and awnings for the barge frequently was done while the woman leaned against the "stick" that guided the boat's rudder. If the husband died, the widow often ran the boat herself, several such examples being Mis' Ziegler, Nancy McCoy, and Clara Dick.

5. The Children on the Boats

To prevent the little children from falling into the canal, there was usually a ringbolt in the cabin roof. The smallest children were buckled into a leather or rope harness and tied fast with a line to the ringbolt. By the age of six, most children were put to work driving the mules. Most captains got their start on the canal in that manner. The mules were driven with a four-strand plaited whip by the child walking along beside them on the towpath. The children were permitted frequently to ride the lead mule to protect their feet and to prevent them from tiring. The "canallers" children generally had little opportunity for schooling. Many times a teen-age boy was hired as a deck hand, a job for which he seldom received more than $10 per month.

6. Approaching a Lock

When a boat approached a lock, the steersman got out his boat horn, generally a tin bugle, and blew the three notes of "Red Rover." Supposedly the boat horn was saying "Lock Ready! Lock Ready!" If there was no horn available, the steersman or driver, whoever had the loudest voice, would yell: "yea-a-a-a-a-a lock!" or "Hey-y-y-y-y-y lock!" Some boatmen used conch shells to announce their approach. During the day, the lock tender often saw the boat before he heard the call, but at night he had to be awakened.

7. The Mules

The mules, many of which came from Kentucky, were broken in by hitching them to logs. New mules, or "Greenies," often sat down and refused to move. This problem was solved by hitching several trained mules to the "sitdowners" and dragging it along until standing up was more comfortable than sitting down. The mules were hard on their shoes, and, thus, they were reshod on an average of once a month.

Mules were generally purchased when they were 2 ½ years old. As a rule, they lasted some 15 years before they became too old and infirm to be of value. Each boatman usually kept two teams of two or three mules each with his barge. Good experienced mules often did not require a driver. They slacked off automatically by instinct when a boatman was snubbing a boat into a lock and once through a lock they took off on the cue of the steersman's whistle. If a boatman wished to change his teams, the mules reacted to verbal commands. Generally, the mules were changed while the boat was passing through a lock–a feat that required fast work. A short fallboard, much like a cleated gangplank, was thrown over the side of the boat when the water in the lock chamber was at its highest level, and a fresh team from the stable in the bow was herded out quickly. Reckless boatmen would change teams while the boat was moving by jumping a fresh team into the canal and swimming them to shore, while the gangplank was hurriedly thrown down on the towpath and the old team rushed on to the boat. This latter practice led to the drowning of many mules.

8. Dogs on the Canal

A good dog was a great help with the mules and was sometimes used to drive them. Sam Poffenberger had a bulldog named "Rough" who could swim across the canal basin at Cumberland with a towline around his neck. This was a great help when the mules and boats were separated on opposite sides of the basin.

9. Wintering Along the Canal

When the canal got icy, a canal company scow, loaded with pig iron, started up the waterway from Georgetown to serve as an icebreaker. Homeward-bound boats, all light and heading for winter quarters, formed a procession behind the ice breaker. As many as 40 mules from the boats in the procession would be hooked to the icebreaker's towline. The animals would haul the boat up on the ice and her weight would break a channel through which the boats would pass. The entire convoy would help pump water out of a barge if the ice broke a hole in it. The members of the procession also would hack at the ice with their axes if necessary. If a boat was frozen solid, the captain and crew closed it up and rode the mules home.

The boatmen tied up their boats as close to their homes as possible. The most popular communities where the boatmen spent the winter months were Monocacy Basin, Point of Rocks, Brunswick, Sharpsburg Landing, Williamsport, Hancock, and Cumberland. Of these communities, Sharpsburg was considered the greatest producer of boatmen over the years. A few boatmen lived on their boats year-round, and a few maintained homes where their families lived throughout the year.

In the early spring, the "canallers" would return to their boats. Before resuming navigation in the new season, they would house clean the barges, make necessary repairs, and give the vessels a fresh coat of paint. Once that work was done, the awning was spread over a portion of the deck and operations were commenced.

F. THE EMERGENCE OF LABOR UNIONISM AMONG THE CANAL BOATMEN IN THE 1870s

During the early 1870s the Boatmen's Union of Cumberland emerged as a strong force on behalf of the interests of the "canallers." As the first manifestation of labor unionism on the canal, this organization reflected the growing interest in such labor activities across the United States in the decade after the Civil War. During this period, two national labor organizations-- the National Labor Union in 1866 and the Knights of Labor in 1869–were formed for the purpose of exercising their economic and political power to better the lot of the common working man in America.[150]

Organizing efforts were also occurring among the western Maryland coal miners at this time, and wage disputes between the miners and the coal company operations led to the first strike in May and June of 1865.[151]

The first recorded strike by the canal boatmen occurred at Cumberland in July 1871. The two-day work stoppage was joined by the dock laborers in that town. According to the word received by President James C. Clarke on August 28, the difficulty

> was occasioned by a few irresponsible men urged on by a few of the boatmen who were stated to have been imposed on by the Maryland (Coal) Co. by being obliged to pay a bonus. We (The Maryland Coal Company) reduced the freight, to (the) same basis on outside boats (those vessels not employed by the coal company) or five cents per ton, but to those running our own boats we have the spring rates of $1.45 per ton.

The informer went on to express his fears that another strike was brewing among the boatmen:

> Now the Maryland (Coal) Co. pays only $1.40 to all classes of boats, and still exacts the bonus . . . and the result of another strike is threatened. If it were to be confined merely to those who aggrieved, no one would object, but you may rest assured if a dozen of the men see fit to make the trouble, all will become involved and this will incur the daily loss of $25,000. If once begun, the loss all round will amount to hundreds of thousands. Why should these vast interests be paralyzed...by a few discontented men, hiring roughs to intimidate the well disposed.[152]

Sometime during the remainder of the 1871 boating season an eleven-day strike of the boatmen and Cumberland dock workers took place.[153]

It is apparent that the canal company attempted to prevent the labor unrest by ordering that the participating boatmen be fined for their activities. Later the board had second thoughts about the wisdom of this policy, and on January 12, 1872, it authorized Coale to remit the money collected in those cases that merited such consideration. The balance of the money collected was to be appropriated to the treasury of the Boatmen's Benevolent Society, an organization that had been formed, recently to foster the welfare of the "canallers."[154]

---

[150] Foster Rhea Dulles, *The United States Since 1865* (Ann Arbor, 1969), 68–81, and Michael Martin and Leonard Gelber, *The New Dictionary of American History* (Revised, New York, 1965), 335, 340–41, 425.

[151] *Thirty-Seventh Annual Report* (1865), C & O Co., 6.

[152] Slack to Clarke, Aug. 28, 1871, Ltrs. Recd., C & O Co., and *Proceedings of the President and Board of Directors*, M, 426–427.

[153] *Proceedings of the Stockholders*, E, 182.

[154] *Proceeding of the President and Board of Directors*, M, 506.

There were no further labor difficulties along the canal until January 1873. In that month, the president of the Boatmen's Benevolent Society sent a stern letter to the canal board protesting against the directors' proposal to raise the toll on coal from 46 cents to 51 cents per ton. The letter, which indicated the increasing militancy of the society, read as follows:

> The Boatmen's Benevolent Society do petition your honorable body against any increase of tolls on coal, as we consider such an advance an injury to the business and interest of the canal; also ruinous to the interest of the boatmen, to keep the cost of transportation on the canal at the basis of last season would require an equivalent decrease of freight, to which we the boatmen will not submit. Gentlemen, this association desires that the toll on coal should remain at the same rates as that of last Season. We refer you to the decrease of freight on coal by way of (the) canal, for the last two seasons of ten cents per ton. Submitting to a deduction of five cents each season, and any advance on tolls at this time in all probability would cause a further decrease, and for this reason just stated we earnestly enter our protest.[155]

The underlying reasons for the boatmen's concern over the canal directors' proposal to increase the toll on coal were given in a report in the *Williamsport Pilot* of January 11. According to the newspaper's editor, the boatmen at that town all felt

> that such an increase will only amount to a tax upon them. They are certain that in the end they will have to pay it. The past season was altogether an unprofitable one. In fact many boatmen actually lost money, and we much doubt if half the coal could be shipped over the canal during the coming season if the tolls are increased. It should be remembered that hay and feed commanded an unusual price, and of the first name article the prairies of Illinois had to be depended for a supply, which is sufficient to indicate its price.
> The coal companies have every advantage of the boatmen; they can regulate freights with a rule as imperious as the Czar of Russia. They of course will put freights down just in proportion as the canal company raises tolls.[156]

Despite the protests of the boatmen the canal board approved the five-cent increase in the toll on coal on February 13. The boatmen were angered still further on March 11 when a petition from the Boatmen's Benevolent Society requesting the suppression of the illicit liquor traffic along the line of the canal received no comment from the directors. Consequently, a strike was called, but apparently it was of short duration because company officials reported that it merely caused a delay in commencing the coal shipments in March.[157]

---

[155] Rosewann to Gorman and Directors, Jan. 1, 1873, Ltrs. Recd., C & O Co., and *Proceedings of the President and Board of Directors*, M, 94.

[156] *Williamsport Pilot*, Jan. 11, 1873, in Gorman Collection. The increasing militancy of the boatmen was also in part an effort to make up for financial losses sustained in November 1872 when an epidemic had killed many horses and mules along the canal. The epidemic was of such severity that the company estimated that it reduced the total tonnage for the canal by over 20,000 tons that month. *Forty-Fifth Annual Report* (1873), C & O Co., 3. Mulvany to Gorman, Nov. 9 and 16, 1872, Ltrs. Recd., C & O Co., and *Williamsport Pilot*, Dec. 21, 1872, in Gorman Collection.

[157] *Proceedings of the President and Board of Directors*, M, 102, & *Forty-Fifth Annual Report* (1873), C & O Co., 3.

There was relative labor calm on the canal until August 24, 1874, when the boatmen again called a strike at Cumberland, demanding that the current freight rates be raised from $1.25 to $1.35 for transporting a ton of coal from Cumberland to Tidewater.[158]

The following day a mob of some 200 persons marched to the coal loading wharves and, using threats of violence, prevented the loading of any boats manned by captains who were transporting coat at $1.25 per ton. The strikers camped on the wharves with rations of "bread and beer" and vowed to poison the mules and injure the crew of any boat that loaded at the lower rate.[159]

On August 26 the striking boatmen held a public meeting at Cumberland to consider their grievances, and the principal address was given by Mr. McCardell, the editor of the *Cumberland Times*. The "canallers" took the position that the coal companies could not afford to pay more than the present reduced freight rates–$1.20 and $1.25 per ton to Georgetown and Alexandria respectively–and that the boatmen could not afford to carry coal at those rates. Furthermore, the canal company should reduce the toll on coal to 36 cents per ton and give the extra 15 cents to the boatmen instead of to the company bondholders. The boatmen resolved to adhere to their demand that the freight rates should be at the level that was agreed upon in the spring–$1.35 per ton to Georgetown and $1.40 to Alexandria. Committees were appointed to provide liaison between the coal mine operators and the boatmen and to address the canal company with a petition to carry out the "McCardell Plan."[160]

Although the strike was called to address the specific grievances of the boatmen, the canal board received word that other factors were involved in the labor unrest. There were indications that some of the coal companies were promoting the strike. There was an over-supply of boats for the coal trade, and the coal companies were embroiled in "considerable competition...with no little cutting and gouging." The only company that was not involved in the work stoppage was the Borden Coal Company, which agreed to pay the higher freight rate demanded by the boatmen. Thus 9 to 12 of its boats were leaving Cumberland every day unmolested for the trip to Georgetown.[161]

By September 1 the striking boatmen had increased their numbers by enrolling some 200 captains in a "secret association." Many of the boatmen of the Maryland Coal Company, who had originally opposed the strike, now were in full support. The boatmen had increased the rates to Williamsport, Shepherdstown, and Antietam, as well as to Georgetown and Alexandria. The canal basins at Cumberland were blocked entirely by boats. However, there was little excitement reported, as the boatmen were "moving about quietly," but manifesting "a determined spirit to stand firm, and refuse to load, except upon the terms demanded."[162]

Two days later on September 3 President Gorman received word that the strike was about to be broken. The Consolidation Coal Company had decided the previous day to load its boats at the higher freight rates, and the agent of the New Central Coal Company had been instructed by his firm's headquarters in New York City to yield to the demands of the "canallers." However,

---

[158] Weber to Gorman, Aug. 24, 1874, Ltrs. Recd., C & O Co.

[159] Greene to Gorman, September 14, 1874, Ltrs. Recd., C & O Co. The coal companies appealed to the local authorities to disperse the unruly crowd, but upon consultation with the State's Attorney, it was decided not to intervene unless there was an overt act of violence. As the few boatmen who were willing to work for the lower freight rate were intimidated quickly into abandoning their boats, there were no such incidents.

[160] Weber to Gorman, August 26, 1874, Ltrs. Recd., C& O Co.

[161] *Ibid.*

[162] Weber to Gorman, September 1, 1874, Ltrs. Recd., C&O Co. The "secret association" referred to in this letter is the first reference to the organization of a boatmen's labor union.

the Maryland, American, Hampshire, Georges' Creek, Blaen Avon, and Atlantic Coal Companies had not indicated a change of position.[163]

When the strike still had not been settled by September 8, President Gorman requested from the various coal companies information relative to their understanding of the stalemate and to the causes, which led up to it. One such reply was given by J. W. Pearce, the Agent of the Maryland Coal Company:

> To show how the general public are deceived by the operations of Monopolies, and the "outside appearance of affairs when local Journals familiar with the Causes, either from fear of losing popularity for some pet Candidate for office or other interests; conceal the real evil under the cloak of ignorance of the cause, and only briefly notice the passing event – will you give some space in your valuable paper to this statement, so as to let the people of the State of Maryland understand how one of their great public works is paralyzed by the operations of a ring of Conspirators who are enriching themselves by despoiling the Stock Holders of the Companies they are employed by; and the people, whose public work they abuse. As will appear by reference to the Cumberland papers, "a strike has been in progress for some time among the Boatmen on the Ches & Ohio Canal!"
>
> From this brief notice the Stockholders of Coal Cos. and the public would naturally suppose it originated in a demand of the Boatmen for higher freights. If, however, you will go to the bottom of the trouble you will find it has been 'hatched up & egged on' by the agents or Managers of some of the Coal Cos., in conjunction with a part of the Boat Building interest at Cumberland.
>
> Their object is to keep up a high rate of freight on the Canal, so that they may be enabled to dispose of Boats at enormous prices. In furtherance of this object by maintaining the Freight, they Crowd their lines with more boats than are required to carry their coal; thus depriving their Companies of the advantages of lower rates, and The Boatmen to whom those high-priced Boats are sold of the necessary amount of freighting to enable them at any promised rate, to make money by good running.
>
> When the great 'law of supply and demand' begins to operate in favor of another Company who have been shipping Coal on a *lone business basis*, and who endeavor to have their Coal freighted as *Cheaply* as possible, by telling its Boatmen to buy Boats and supplies at the *lowest* market rates, instead of *forcing* them into paying exorbitant prices, and by giving *steady* employment to large numbers of otherwise unemployed Boatmen, thus largely more than paying their expenses (for while lying idle waiting for their Companies to load them, the expenses are as great as when running) them; in order to bring things back to that happy state where the Coal Cos. shall pay the Boatmen enough to enable them *to lie idle* and thus prosper the Boat business at the expense of the Coal Trade; a few irresponsible & reckless boatmen are employed to get up 'a Strike' and *by force* prevent these men (who are glad to get loads even at lower rates than the 'Ring' proposes) from doing as they see fit with their own labor & property; and so it comes to pass, that in order that a few 'Conspirators' may grow rich, a stoppage of work for weeks is caused; to the injury of the Miners; the Cumberland & Pennsylvania Rail Road—that brings Coal to the Canal—the Boatmen, the Ches & Ohio Canal, the various Coal wharves & schooners engaged in the Trade, and often causing loss & embarrassment to the Coal Companies. Were it not for this forcible interference the principle on which the Maryland Coal Co has been working this season—'Dispatch in loading and unloading for

---

[163] Weber to Gorman, September 3, 1874, Ltrs. Recd., C&O Co.

> a Concession in freights,' would become general, to the improvement of profits by the Canal Co, the Boatmen and the Coal Cos. For 3 loads per month @ $1 per Ton for 112 Tons is $366.00, which would require $1.50 per Ton to equal it,, with only 2 loads per month, and Two loads per month this season, is over the average, in such Companies as have let the Agents put in more Boats than the business required.
>
> There has been much talk and abuse of the Canal Co for not paying dividends on account of being 'a political machine,' the foregoing facts have much to do with its small receipts; for high Freights & Tolls inevitably drive the Coal Trade from the Canal to the Rail Roads.-[164]

As the strike wore on, the canal board considered various means to break the stalemate. They considered the passage of an order to prohibit the future navigation of all boats whose owners had been "instrumental in promoting strikes or disaffection among the boatmen." The directors also considered the expansion of the proposed ban to include the boats "owned in whole or in part" by the Cumberland boat builders who had encouraged the unrest. The board apparently gave up these ideas since their enactment would have alienated some of the coal companies on whose trade the canal depended and some of the boat builders on whom the "canallers" relied for the construction, maintenance, and repair of their barges.[165]

The devastating impact of the strike on the canal's trade and revenue was assessed by President Gorman at a board meeting on September 10. Had it not been for the work stoppage the tonnage and revenue for August would have exceeded any previous month in the history of the waterway. During the period from August 26–31, the average shipments on the canal per day were 1,394 compared with a pre-strike daily average of 4,925. Thus, the work stoppage had been responsible for the loss of 21,186 tons of trade during the last six days of that month. Gorman concluded by expressing his fears that the frequent recurrence of strikes by the boatmen would not only reduce the revenues of the company but that they would force the coal companies to take their trade to the railroads. Accordingly, he recommended that a committee be appointed to investigate the causes of the strike and to confer with the coal companies concerning an effective solution to the recurring problem.[166]

> The investigation of the strike by the committee uncovered serious abuses in the system of boating then in operation on the canal, which tended to support the boatmen's position. While the strikes, which drove the canal trade to the railroad, were suicidal to the boatmen, it was found that the "canallers" could not pay their expenses at the $1.25 freight rate. Accordingly, the boatmen had been taught to believe that (1) higher freight rates were the sole remedy, (2) the coal companies would not accede to the higher freights unless the canal company reduced its tolls, and (3) the canal company, as a semi-political corporation, should eliminate the toll on loaded boats.

The committee concluded that the boatmen's reasons for their financial difficulties were inaccurate. In its report, the members informed the board that the real reason for the plight of the boatmen was the exorbitant cost and the unfair purchase terms of the canal boats. A large proportion of boats on the waterway had been built by local capitalists in Cumberland at an average cost of about $1,400 each. The usual custom was for the builder to make arrangements with the agent of one of the Allegany County coal companies to take the boat into the company's line (i.e., to

---

[164] Pearce to Gorman, Sept. 8, 1874, Ltrs. Recd., C & O Co.
[165] Ray to Gorman, Sept. 9, 1874, Ltrs. Recd., C & O Co.
[166] *Proceedings of the President and Board of Directors*, M, 176–77.

transport that company's coal exclusively). The builder would then sell the boat to a "canaller" who was usually poor and unable to pay for the purchase with cash. The builder would advance the sum of $800 to $1,200 to the boatman, and this amount was to be repaid in regular installments to be deducted at the end of each trip on the amount paid for freight.

The boatmen were helpless to resist such practices, because they were forced to agree to the terms if they wanted to work. Hence they commenced their work by paying not only a fair value for their boats but also an "extortionate" bonus. Added to these expenses were the cost of their teams and outfits at greatly inflated prices.[167] Thus, the boatmen needed higher freight rates from the coal companies to pay the average trippage costs of $35 to $40 and to live. In most cases, it would take the boatmen three or four years of hard labor to pay off their debts if the freight rate was $1.35 per ton.

Once a boat was paid off, the boatmen were subject to other unfair monopolistic practices. As soon as a boat was paid for, the Cumberland boat builders often had a new one ready to take its place. The agent of the coal company would then remove the old boat from the line so as to make room for the new one for the profits to be derived from it. This practice had continued for so long that there were a large number of boats owned by regular boatmen who were not in the line of any coal company. Those individuals were compelled to obtain loads wherever and from whomever they could or to pay trippage to gain admission back into a line. Thus, there were about 100 boats more than were needed for the coal trade on the waterway.

In the spring of 1874 the Borden Mining Company determined to take advantage of the large pool of "outside" boats by employing a sufficient number of them to carry its coal. The company set down three conditions for this arrangement: (1) to employ a sufficient number of boats to accommodate the trade; (2) to keep the boats in port no longer than 24 hours; and (3) to enable boats to make 3 ½ trips per month without paying trippage.

> Some of the boatmen accepted this proposition at a reduced freight rate of $1.25 per ton, and within a short period all of the coal companies had reduced their rates. This state of affairs continued until August 25 when the boatmen paying trippage found that they could not make a living while the boats not paying trippage were realizing fair profits. It was found that the "outside" boats making 3 ½ trips per month at a freight rate of $1.25 were producing gross receipts of $490 per month. On the other hand, the "line" boats, which averaged about 2 ½ trips per month at the same freight rate, were realizing monthly gross receipts of $350 from which approximately $75 had to be subtracted for trippage.

The committee concluded its report by urging the canal board to induce the coal companies to break up the system of "middlemen" in the sale of the canal boats. If the boats were furnished at a fair price and the boatmen were given constant employment, the cost of transportation would be reduced and the "canallers" would realize greater profits. At the same time, the committee fully endorsed the company policy of providing police protection to the coal companies during the strike. Furthermore the members supported the strict enforcement of the company rules, which imposed heavy penalties on any person interfering with the loading of a boat or preventing any boat from proceeding on the canal by intimidation or threats of personal violence.[168]

---

[167] The average cost of mules during the 1870s and 1880s varied greatly. Common mules varied from $25 to $200 a head or $250 a pair. A team of four good, experienced mules together with their harnesses sold for prices of up to $1,400. Such sales were made on terms similar to those on boats. *Baltimore Evening Sun*, Aug. 12, 1937.

[168] *Proceedings of the President and Board of Directors* M, 180-85.

Normal operations on the canal were not resumed until late September when all of the coal companies agreed to pay the $1.35 freight rate demanded by the Boatmen's Union. Apparently, the last company to agree to the higher rate was the Maryland Coal Company, which had transferred its daily 1,000-ton trade to the railroad shortly after the strike commenced. When the company resumed its shipments on the canal, it reemployed a number of its old boatmen at the increased rate. Then the strikers attempted unsuccessfully to dictate to the company what boats it should employ.[169]

The Boatmen's Union continued to harass the movement of those 'outside' boats whose owners continued to ship at lower rates, but there were no more reports of violence during the remainder of the boating season.[170]

Prior to the opening of navigation on the canal in 1875, the Boatmen's Union met in Cumberland to adopt the freight rates for the year. The rates, which were not to be subject to any fees, bonuses for loading, or drawbacks, were as follows:

To Hancock	$ .50
To Williamsport	.70
To Shepherdstown	.90
To Antietam	.90
To Harpers Ferry	.95
To Knoxville	$1.00
To Point of Rocks	$1.05
To Georgetown	$1.35
To All Points in Washington	$1.40
To 1st and 2nd Boat Yard, Alexandria, Canal	$1.37
To Four Mile Run	$1.38
To Alexandria	$1.40

At the same time, the Boatmen's Union organized itself into a mutual life insurance association and contemplated certain other cooperative ventures for the benefit of the "canallers." The official membership of the union was reported to be 324 with control over 374 boats.[171]

The Boatmen's Union continued its efforts to intimidate the nonunion boatmen. On the night of January 8 three boats tied up near Lock No. 38 and one boat on the Four-Mile level were burned. Had it not been for the quick arrival of the fire engine from Shepherdstown, the whole fleet of boats lying at Shepherdstown would have caught fire.[172]

During the winter of 1874–1875, the canal company leased the Lynn-owned Potomac Wharf at Cumberland for a period of two years, thus putting it in a position to reduce the exorbitant wharf fees charged by the private wharf owners in that town. Such an action, coupled with earlier efforts to lower wharf charges in Georgetown, would make it possible for the company to reduce soon the cost of transporting coal over the waterway by some 12 cents per ton.[173]

---

[169] *Ibid,* M, 180.

[170] Brandt to Gorman, Oct. 27, 1874, Ltrs. Recd., C & O Co.

[171] *Cumberland Times,* Jan. 23, 1875, in Gorman collection. As there were some 539 boats registered on the canal at this time, the union, according to this report, controlled about 70 percent of the vessels plying the waterway.

[172] McGraw to Gorman, Jan. 9, 1875, Ltrs. Recd, C & O Co.

[173] *Cumberland Daily News,* Mar. 2, 1875, and *Cumberland Daily Times,* Mar. 20, 1875, in Gorman Collection, and *Forty-Seventh Annual Report* (1875), 19–21.

AVERAGE BOATMEN'S EXPENSES PER DAY
as reported in the *Williamsport Pilot*, Feb 20, 1875

CAPTAIN	$1.00
STEERSMAN	.83
DRIVER (2 @ 50¢ each)	1.00
BOARD FOR HANDS	2.00
ANIMAL FEED	2.00
ANIMAL SHOEING	.25
LINES	.50
TRIPPAGE	3.50
TOLLS	.40
	$11.48

COST OF TRANSPORTING ONE TON OF COAL ON
THE CHESAPEAKE & OHIO CANAL 1873–75,
as reported in the *Cumberland Daily Times*, Mar. 20, 1875

TOLLS	$ .510
WHARFAGE AT CUMBERLAND	.080
COMMISSION TO AGENTS	.025
FREIGHT RATE (185 MILES)	1.350
WHARFAGE AND HANDLING AT GEORGETOWN	.250
	$2.215

When navigation resumed in March, members of the Boatmen's Union commenced a series of threats against the nonunion boatmen at the Potomac Wharf. Efforts were made to frighten them from loading their boats by telling them that their mules would be poisoned and that all boats would be prevented from descending below Sharpsburg. Accordingly, the canal company requested that the Mayor of Cumberland authorize the canal's watchman at the wharf to arrest those who were disrupting the operation of the canal.[174]

On April 6, 1875, the canal board ordered a general reduction of charges, including toll, wharfage, and freights. This was done in order to maintain its competitive position in the coal trade with the Baltimore & Ohio Railroad and to placate the Boatmen's Union. The toll on coal was reduced by 8 cents to 43 cents per ton, and the freight and wharfage rates were decreased by 10 cents and 2 cents respectively.[175]

Boatmen's Union still was not satisfied completely with the financial arrangements for the 1875 boating season. A delegation from the union met with the board on April 13 and proposed a compromise solution to the stalemate. The union members would boat at a freight rate of $1.25 for the season and rescind their claim of demurrage if the boat owners would reduce trippage fees to a flat rate of $30 and the canal company would reduce its $4.08 toll on loaded boats by 50 percent. Next a group of boat owners, headed by Frederick Mertens of Cumberland, met with the board, and after a heated debate, they agreed to the boatmen's demands provided the company would do the same. Accordingly, the directors passed the following resolution:

---

[174] Tilghman to Gorman, April 1, 1875, Ltrs. Recd., C & O Co.

[175] *Proceedings of the President and Board of Directors*, M, 210–11.

Whereas the Boatmen cannot secure a reduction in their trippage of more than five (5) dollars, and therefore cannot afford to reduce the charges for freight 10 cents per ton, without some relief on the part of the Company.

Therefore, resolved, that so long as the rates for freighting coal to Georgetown shall not exceed $1.25 per ton, the toll on through boats shall be charged at the rate of $2.04, each way, and the rate for way coal boats shall be 1 ¼ cents per mile, each way, during the present season of navigation.[176]

Although their demands had been met, some of the union members remained embittered. As a result, a series of incidents were perpetrated against the nonunion "canallers" and the property of the canal company. On the night of April 14 the towpath was cut at a point about 3/4 mile below Grove's warehouse on the Antietam Division. It was reported that "depredations of some kind" were being committed every night in the vicinity of Sharpsburg.[177]

Several days after the towpath was cut, a boat was stoned near Harpers Ferry, because the captain was transporting coal at "ruinous rates." In commenting on this incident, the *Williamsport Pilot*, which was supporting the Boatmen's Union, informed its readers that those boatmen who contracted to transport coal at lower rates deserved no sympathy if their boats were burned. Such independent action was an invitation to the union members "to take more effectual measures" for getting rid of such boats.[178]

Some union men attacked the *Kate Prather* captained by Lewis F. Fernsner on the night of April 20 at a point some three miles below Cumberland, breaking the boat's windows and shutters with stones.[179]

On the same evening the *J. Baker* was stoned on the Antietam Division.[801]

To find out and prosecute the parties that were perpetrating these incidents, the canal company had its officials scour the countryside for leads and information. Furthermore, the company pressured Washington and Allegany County officials into conducting grand jury investigations into the problem. As a result, four leaders of the Boatmen's Union–James Hitechew, Taylor Reid, Peter Wolf, and Thomas O'Donnell–were indicted by the grand jury at Cumberland. After a lengthy trial in the Allegany County Circuit Court the four men were convicted on January 24, 1876, of forming a "conspiracy to control the rate of freight on coal transported over the C & O Canal." When the men were brought up for sentencing two days later, the judge "called attention to the gravity of the offense, and admonished boatmen, coal companies, and all others, that any combination to control prices by which the business of the community" was interrupted was "illegal and contrary to the common law." However, as this was the first case of its kind to be tried in the county, the magistrate made the penalty as light as possible, imposing a fine of $25 plus the prosecution costs amounting to $18.40 on each man.[181]

There was relative calm among the boatmen on the canal until June 21, 1877, when a group of "canallers" struck again to protest a decrease in the freight rates. A number of boatmen tied up their vessels on the first level west of Seneca where they awaited some redress from their grievances, far from the reach of the coal companies and the canal directors. At the upper end of the line, some 24 boats tied up at Lock No. 74 where they effectively closed the canal to traffic

---

[176] *Ibid*, M, 212; Ketchese to Gorman, Apr. 9, 1875, Ltrs. Recd., C & O Co.; and *Cumberland News*, Apr. 17, 1875, in Gorman Collection.

[177] McGraw to Stake, Apr. 15, 1875, Ltrs. Recd., C & O Co.

[178] *Williamsport Pilot*, Apr. 17, 1875, and *Baltimore American*, Apr. 29, 1875, in Gorman Collection.

[179] Tilghman to Gorman, Apr. 21, 1875, Ltrs. Recd., C&O Co.

[180] McGraw to Gorman, May 4, 1875, Ltrs. Recd., C&O Co.

[181] *Cumberland Times*, Jan. 26, 1876, in Gorman Collection.

pending a successful resolution of their demands. The strike lasted for two months, during which trade on the canal sank to negligible proportions. The men finally resumed their runs on August 20, but by that time many canal skippers had made arrangements with the railroad for the transportation of their business for the rest of the year.[182]

The canal company records indicate that there was relative calm on the canal in 1878 and 1879. In April of the latter year a petition signed by numerous boatmen was presented to the directors, asking that the charge for trimming boats at the company wharves in Cumberland be reduced from $1.35 to 75 cents per boat. A cursory review of the board's proceedings indicates that no action was taken on the requests and that no overt incidents resulted.[183]

The financial distress of the boatmen led to another two-month strike beginning in late June of 1880. The plight of the "canallers" was the result of the general nationwide business depression and the consequent deflationary tendency of coal prices. The price of a ton of coal on board vessels at Georgetown, which had been $4.65 in 1872, had fallen to $2.60 by 1879. Because of this decline the amount paid for transporting a ton of coal from Cumberland to Georgetown and placing it on board a vessel at the latter port had fallen also from $2.24 in 1872 to $1.35 in 1879. The breakdown of these latter figures shows the desperate situation in which the boatmen were trapped:

	1872	1879
Received by boatmen	$1.35	$ .75
Wharfage at Cumberland and Georgetown	.43	.04
Transfer fees at Georgetown	.00	.20
Canal company tolls	.46	.36
	$2.24	$1.35

The 1879 rates provided neither the boatmen, the wharf owners, nor the canal company with adequate revenue, but little could be done to increase them so long as the value of coal on board vessels at Georgetown remained less than $3 per ton.[184]

The eight-week strike, which extended from late June to late August, had a serious impact on the revenues of the canal company. The average weekly coal tonnage carried on the canal during the three months prior to the strike was 21,374 tons, while the average weekly tonnage during the strike was 13,870 tons. It was estimated that the strike resulted in a loss of some 75,000 tons of coal and some $45,000 in revenues to the company.[185]

The strike not only hurt the company's financial condition, but it also led to serious rioting at Sharpsburg landing, Williamsport and Millstone Point in July and August. Boats were stoned at these three localities, and other acts of violence were perpetrated in an effort to disrupt the entire navigation on the waterway. The company requested that the Washington County Commissioners send all available "sheriffs, detectives, and agents" to the three locations to investigate and to suppress the violence. In September the County Commissioners reported that the total cost of its anti riot operations had cost more than $3,000. At the request of the State's Attorney for Washington County the canal company reimbursed the County Commissioners for $1,000 of this sum.[186]

---

[182] *Fiftieth Annual Report* (1878). C & O Co., 3, 6; *Proceedings of the President and Board of Directors*, N, 4; and Stanhope to Gorman July 1, 1877, Ltrs. Recd., C & O Co.

[183] *Proceedings of the President and Board of Directors*, N, 81.

[184] *Fifty-First Annual Report* (1879), C & O Co. p.12, and *Fifty-Second Annual Report* (1880), C & O Co., .7.

[185] *Proceedings of the President and Board of Directors* N, .117–19.

[186] *Ibid,* N, 120–121.

No boatmen's strikes occurred on the canal during the remainder of the 1880s-a decade marked by trade stagnation, financial depression and physical deterioration of the canal company and the waterway itself. In fact, there appears to have been little union activity among the boatmen during this period. The one exception took place in February 1883 when a petition signed by ten boatmen at Williamsport was sent to the board requesting a redress of six grievances.[187]

The six demands were as follows: (1) the reduction of trimming rates for loaded boats at Cumberland from $1.30 to 75 cents, (2) the cleaning out of regular trying-up places and the planting of posts along the canal so that boats could tie up at night on the berm bank; (3) the enforcement of a Sunday law that would compel all boats to tie up at 12 o'clock midnight on Saturday; (4) the clearing-out of the basin at Cumberland that led from the Basin Wharf to the main stem of the canal so that boats could navigate that course; (5) the reduction of tolls and wharfage from 55 cents to 45 cents; and (6) the removal of the Baltimore & Ohio Railroad treating from the towpath between Locks Nos. 73 -75. The canal directors responded to the petition by promising to reduce tolls and wharfage fees at Cumberland to 40 cents per ton on coal and to decrease the cost of terminal facilities at Georgetown by 10 cents, but took no other action.[188]

G. FEED AND GROCERY STORES

The boatmen on the canal required large quantities of staples, groceries, and vegetables for themselves, their families, and their hired hands. Among the items that the boatmen needed were flour, sugar, coffee, smoked meats, dry salt belly, and bread. The "canallers" also were in need of large amounts of hay, feed, and provender for their mules employed on the waterway. The mules consumed an annual minimum of 25,000 barrels of corn, 3,840 bushels of oats, and several thousand tons of hay at a cost of some $60,000.[189]

Up until 1850s the boatmen generally purchased their food and feed in Georgetown or Cumberland before beginning their journey. Along the way, they would procure additional supplies in the small towns adjacent to the canal. Often they would buy vegetables from the lockkeepers, some of whom raised large gardens, and local farmers would sell the boatmen hay and feed.

By the late 1850s, however, the canal board had received numerous applications for permission to erect feed and grocery stores along the canal to accommodate the growing trade. Recognizing the need for such stores, the board on September 3, 1858, authorized the Engineer and General Superintendent to permit the construction of such stores where they were needed along the line of the canal. The following conditions were to be made a part of any agreement to construct such stores: (1) the ground rent was to be at least $12 per year; (2) no intoxicating beverages could be sold; (3) the businesses were not to interfere with the navigation of the canal; and (4) the company could revoke the privileges granted upon 30 days' notice.[190]

During the next three decades at least 27 grocery and feed stores were built along the line of the canal. Most of them were built in the decade after the Civil War. The location, type, proprietor, and date of these stores were as follows:

> Lock No. 6—On December 4, 1873, permission was granted to Levin B. Stine to erect a feed store.

---

[187] The boatmen who signed the document were E. P. Steffey, George W. McCardell, E. Donnelly, J. Morrison, W. C. McCardell, William Kimble, M. Stitzel, Henry Singer, H. C. Ardinger, and Victor Cushwa.
[188] Proceedings of the President and Board of Directors, N, 208–09.
[189] *Williamsport Pilot*, Feb. 8, 1873, in Gorman Collection.
[190] Proceedings of the President and Board of Directors, K, 61–62.

Lock No. 10—On February 13, 1873, permission was granted to Mikeal Q. McQuade to lease 60 feet of ground to build a provision and feed store.

Lock No. 13—Prior to August 1871, permission had been given to David Lorence to build a feed store. In that month his request to lease for ten years a plot of ground, 12 x 30 ft. for the purpose of enlarging his store was rejected.

Seven Locks—On December 4, 1873, permission was granted to Mrs. M. A. Douglas to rent land at the rate of $36 per year to build a feed store and to raise a large garden.

Lock No. 20—On June 24, 1851, the board authorized the General Superintendent to rent the Ball Room at Crommelin House for the use of the company in return for allowing Daniel Collins, the tender at Locks Nos. 19 and 20, to operate a grocery store in the building.

Lock No. 20—On October 12, 1869, Howard A. Garrett was granted permission to erect a feed store on the towpath side of the canal and to lease a plot of ground (50 x 28 feet and 16 feet from the lock wall) for ten years at an annual rent of $20. The lease was renewed at least once, because the Montgomery County Circuit Court records indicate that Garrett was still operating feed and provision store as late as 1887.

Lock No. 22—On March 9, 1870, permission was granted to George S. Garrett to build a feed store at the annual rent of $36. Some time later, the building was destroyed. Accordingly, he applied for and received permission on May 9, 1871, to build a new hay and feed store (20 x 24 feet) between the flume and the lock on the berm side of the canal.

Guard Lock No 2.—On December 8, 1870, permission was granted to John R. Connell to erect a feed store on the towpath near the guard lock. Connell operated the store for approximately one year and then vacated the premises. By May 1873 the store was vacant, and he was refusing to pay rent. On May 6 of that year, another contract was signed whereby Connell was permitted to build a new feed and supply store between Guard Lock No. 2 and Lock No. 23. The lease was for six years at an annual rental of $40.

Lock No. 23—On August 9, 1883, H. C. Ashly requested permission to build a store on the berm side of the canal at the lock, but there is no record of any action made relative to the request.

Lock No. 24—On January 7, 1873, E. M. Lowe was granted permission for the lease of land at the Seneca Lock for a feed store. Apparently, he moved a building from the Virginia side of the river and reconstructed it on the towpath side of the canal.

Edward's Ferry—On May 12, 1864, McVeirs and William Jones, Jr., were given permission to build a storehouse on the berm side of the canal near Edwards Ferry for the purpose of "vending food etc. to boatmen." The rent was to be $24 per year.

Edward's Ferry—Apparently, another store was being operated at Edward's Ferry prior to May 15, 1865, because on that date, Flitchall and Williams were permitted to build a porch on their store for an annual rent of $6.

Lock No. 25—On January 1, 1872, permission was granted to George W. Spates to lease a parcel of land on the berm side of Lock No. 25 (Frontage 25 feet and running back 36 feet) for the purpose of erecting a grocery and feed store. The lease was for ten years at $36 per year. On April 30, 1874, Spates assigned his lease to George C. Fisher, and in the Spring of 1876 the canal board approved another transfer of the lease to E. E. Jarboe.

Conrad's Ferry—On December 17, 1863, Daniel L. White was given permission to build a storehouse on the berm side of the canal at Conrad's Ferry at an annual rent of $12.

Lock No. 27—On June 15, 1866, M. Kindle was granted permission to build a grocery and feed store near the lock for an annual rent of $36.

Lock No. 28—On July 7, 1864, Greenbury Foot was given permission to erect a small building near the lock at an annual rent of $12.

Lock No. 29—On March 24, 1864, M. E. Alexander was given permission to build a storehouse on the berm side of the canal near the lock at a yearly rental of $12. The purpose of the store was to sell feed and provisions to the boatmen. On May 15, 1865, Alexander requested and received permission to sell groceries at his store. The board authorized John H. Rench on December 10, 1869, to build a second feed store on the company ground at the lock for an annual rental fee of $36.

Lock No. 30—On September 24, 1863, Mortimer Osborn was granted permission to put up a counter and shelves in a room at the lock house at Berlin for the purpose of selling dry goods and groceries. The privilege was to be for one year at an annual rental of $150 of which $100 was to be applied to his pay as lockkeeper.

Lock No. 33—On March 4, 1859, William Walsh requested permission to erect a feed store on a vacant piece of ground near the lock. Apparently, this store was later built above the flume of the lock.

Lock No. 37—Prior to December 1876, Joseph Lewis had operated a store on the berm side of the lock. In that month he requested that the lease be extended for five additional years. As his grocery business had been interfered with by the peddling and sale of produce on the towpath, he requested that his lease cover control of the towpath for marketing purposes.

Lock No. 39—On February 7, 1866, John J. Norman was granted permission to build a bakery and feed store at the lock for an annual rental fee of $36.

Lock No. 41—Prior to May 1, 1877, Charles Dellinger operated a stone storehouse and adjoining frame hay shed fronting on the lock. On this date, the lease was transferred to Daniel, his son, as he had died recently.

Williamsport—On January 11, 1866, Shoop and Leferre were granted permission to build a storehouse at Williamsport for an annual rental of $36. The following month on February 7 Franc Sharpless was given permission to build a store at Lock No. 44.

Lock No. 46—On August 10, 1865, F. W. Kindle was authorized to build a feed and grocery store. The lease was for ten years at an annual rent of $36.

Lock No. 50—On August 10, 1865, William J. Hassett was granted permission to build a feed store. The lease was for ten years at an annual rent of $36.

Lock No. 51—On March 8, 1866, Theophiles Barnett was permitted to construct a feed and grocery store at an annual rental fee of $36.

Lock No. 52—On April 12, 1865, A. B. Tancy was granted permission to erect a store for "vending groceries and feed" at an annual rental fee of $36.

Dam No. 6—On December 14, 1865, Adam Faith was permitted to build a feed store at an annual rental of $36.

Oldtown—Apparently, John Wilson was granted permission to erect a feed store "on the eastern side of the bridge and the berm bank of the canal at Oldtown" after March 3, 1859.[191]

In addition to the feed stores that were built along the canal to cater to the boatmen, there were a number of grocery and feed store establishments in Georgetown and Cumberland whose business consisted primarily in meeting the needs of the "canallers." By 1860, there were 17 flour and feed stores located near the canal in Georgetown, 13 of which were on Water Street and one each on Greene, Cherry, High, and Jefferson Streets. In that same year, there were 7 grocers, whose establishments were situated near the canal. Six of these were on Water Street and one on Market Street.[192]

As the trade of the canal grew so did the number of businesses in Georgetown that catered to the needs of the boatmen. By 1872 the number of flour and feed stores in the vicinity of the waterway had been consolidated into 7 principal establishments for the trade of the boatmen:

E. M. Cropley & Co.,	184 Bridge Street
James H. Foster,	22 Bridge Street
William H. Gaskins,	5 High Street
J. Jackson and Bro.,	110 High Street
J. T. Lee & Co.,	Bridge near Greene
S. B. Lyddane,	140 High Street
D. F. Robinson,	78 Water Street

At the same time, the number of grocery stores near the line of the canal had increased to some 13:

---

[191] Ibid, K, 90, 93, 327, 351, 361, 370, 373–374, 380, 385, 393, 406, 416, 421, 425–426, 441–442, 458–459, 464, 469, 475–476, 480, 498, L, 207, 248, 289, 382–383, 430, 445, M, 84, 88, 134, N, 141, 224; Garrett to President and Directors, March 9, 1870, Garrett to Clarke, May 9, 1872, McQuade to Board of Directors, Jan. 6, 1873, Maus to Gorman, May 16, 1873, Bickler to Gorman, July 30, 1874, Jarboe to President and Directors, April 23, 1876, Lewis to Gorman, Dec.12, 1876, Dellinger to Gorman May 1, 1877, and Douglas to Gorman, May 1, 1877, Ltrs. Recd., C & O Co., and Montgomery County Circuit Court, 61, Land Record, Liber., E.B.P., 9, 367–368, 63, Land Record, Liber., E.B.P., 11, 44, and 94 Land Record, Liber, JA-6, 141.

[192] Boyd's Washington and Georgetown Directory (Washington 1860), 189–92.

Chesapeake & Ohio Canal Historic Resource Study
Unrau: 12. Lockkeepers and Boatmen

Henry Artz,	4 Market Street
A. H. Bradt,	Canal Street near Potomac Aqueduct
Buckley and Lyons,	30 Water Street
George M. Godey,	High and Beall
James Hartigan,	42 Water Street
John S. Hill,	83 Greene Street
Lewis and Leetch,	13 Water Street
E. T. Lyddane,	64 Market Street
M. McNally,	48 Water Street
Daniel O'Leary,	128 Water Street
B. F. Riley,	115 High Street
John H. Sis,	79 High Street
Somers & Smith	97 Water Street[193]

In the latter years of the operation of the canal as an independent entity, the number of the businesses in Georgetown catering to the boatmen declined along with the commerce on the waterway. Among the most important grocers to the "canallers" during this period were:

S. Cropley's Sons	Bridge Street and Market Space
A. H. Bradt,	On the Canal near the Coal Elevators
William A. Offutt and Brother,	Bridge and High
E. T. Lyddane,	115 High Street
John Lyddane	High and First

During this latter period the principal businesses near the canal that supplied the boatmen with feed were:

George W. Darby,	221 Bridge Street
Darby & Johnson,	Bridge and Montgomery
John Dugan & Bros.,	Bridge and Market
David B. Jackson,	110 High Street
William H. Lee,	48 Bridge Street
Edward Lyddane	81 Water Street
Thomas Woodward,	35 Jefferson Street[194]

During the 1870s and 1880s, there were a number of business establishments near the Cumberland basin where the boatmen purchased most of their groceries, provisions, and feed. Groceries and staples were generally purchased at:

Thomas Connell,	122 Wineow Street
William T. Coulehan,	40 Wineow Street
Arthur Dawson,	64 Wineow Street
T. Morris,	116 Wineow Street
William Murphy,	176 Wineow Street
John McGinnis,	123 Wineow Street

---

[193] *Boyd's Business Directory of the Cities of Alexandria, Georgetown, and Washington* (Washington, 1872), 50–52.

[194] T. H. S. Boyd, *The History of Montgomery County, Maryland* (Clarksburg, 1879), 145–57 and *Boyd's Directory of the District of Columbia* (Washington, D.C., 1880), 57–58.

Feed and hay were usually procured at:

John J. Humbird,	41 North Center Street
Smouse & Wilson,	77 North Center Street
John W. Willison,	7 Glenn Street
William T. Coulehan,	40 Wineow Street[195]

H. HAILING PLACE OF BOATMEN

The hailing place of the boatmen refers to the locality in which they maintained a residence. The "canallers" wintered at their homes, but sometimes wives and children lived there year-around. According to the canal company register of 1851, in which the homes of all the boatmen were listed for the first time, the majority of the "canallers" lived in Cumberland, Georgetown, Williamsport, Alexandria, and New York. The statistical breakdown for the 223 boatmen that registered their vessels that year is as follows:

Alexandria	14
Antietam	6
Baltimore	1
Barry	1
Bay State	1
Berlin	3
Big Pool	1
Boston	4
Brooklyn	1
Catoctin	1
Cedar Grove	1
Cedar Point	1
Chaney's Neck	2
Conrad's Ferry	1
Cumberland	41
Dam No. 3	2
Dam No. 4	3
Edwards Ferry	4
Falling Waters	1
Georgetown	30
Glenily	1
Goose Creek	3
Hancock	8
Harpers Ferry	5
High Rocks	1
Hock Hill	1
Honey Wood	1
Horse Pen	1
Jefferson County	2

---

[195] *Cumberland City Directory, Local Guide, and Business Mirror* (Cumberland, 1873), 32, 57; *Directory of Cumberland and Allegany County* (Cumberland, 1890) 176–177; and *Baltimore Evening Sun*, August 10, 1937.

Knoxville	3
Leesburg	2
Maryland	1
Mercerville	5
Miller's Basin	2
Millstone Point	1
Monocacy	2
Mount View	1
New York	14
Noland's Ferry	2
North Bend	2
Point of Rocks	1
Potomac Mills	1
Quarter Branch	1
Rochester	1
Seneca	2
Sharpsburg	1
Sharpsburg Landing	1
Shepherdstown	7
Spring Mill	3
Springland	1
Washington	8
Weverton	2
Williamsport	17[196]

The years 1873–74 are the last for which there are available company records listing the hailing places of the boatmen. By this time there were 539 "canallers" operating vessels on the waterway.

Trade on the canal had nearly reached its zenith by this time for the nationwide depression hit the waterway in 1876, and the commerce never again reached the totals of the early 1870s. In 1873–74 the majority of the boatmen lived in Cumberland, Williamsport, Sharpsburg, Maryland, New York, Bakersville and Hancock. A statistical breakdown of the hailing places of the boatmen in those years was as follows:

Cumberland	162	Knoxville	3
Williamsport	49	Antietam	3
Sharpsburg	49	White's Ferry	3
New York	36	Sandy Hook	2
Maryland	27	Berlin	2
Bakersville	26	Point of Rocks	2
Hancock	26	Frederick County	2
Washington County	19	Monocacy	2
Shepherdstown	13	Edward's Ferry	1
Clear Spring	10	Dam No. 4	1
Seneca	10	Hall Town, Va.	
Georgetown	9	Dam No. 5	1
Four Locks	9	Fair View, Md	1
Alexandria	8	Gainesville, Va.	'

---

[196] Record of Boat Registrations, 1851–1874, C&O Co.

Harpers Ferry	8	Boonsboro	1
Millstone Point	7	Allegany County	1
McCoy's Ferry	6	Oldtown	1
Cherry Run	5	Jefferson County	1
Weverton	5	Pennsylvania	1
Washington	5	Unknown or living on boats	20[197]

I. RACIAL DISCRIMINATION AGAINST BLACK BOAT MASTERS

Although blacks had served as deck hands on canal boats since the canal had been opened to navigation, the issue of blacks as boat captains did not arise until 1856. Apparently, several blacks either attempted to purchase boats or were hired by the owners of large fleets of vessels to be captains of several barges in that year. Upon the complaint of some white boatmen and local residents along the waterway, the directors requested the legal opinion of the company counsel, W. S. Cox as to the "competency of the Board to limit or prohibit the employment of free Negroes or slaves upon the canal as masters of boats." In his report on November 7, Cox responded that according to his understanding of Maryland statute law there were no applicable acts relative to the question of blacks as masters of boats. Accordingly, the board approved a measure on December 10 requiring that all boats navigating the canal after January 1, 1857, have "at least one white person above the age of 18 years, who shall act as master."[198]

Although a formal declaration by the board abrogating the racial ban against black barge masters could not be found, there was some relaxation of the policy in the post-Civil War Era. Undoubtedly, the change was a direct result of the outcome of the national conflict and the subsequent adoption of the thirteenth and fourteenth amendments to the Constitution. However, it is interesting to note that no blacks were enrolled as barge captains on the company boat registers until January 1878, 1st. In that year, four blacks were listed in that category as follows:

CAPTAIN	BOAT NAME	BOAT OWNER	EMPLOYER
Louis Roberson	Viola H. Weir	John T. Dixon	New Central Coal
Wilson Middleton	Dr. F. N. Davis	T. H. Davis	New Central Coal
Kirk Fields	John W. Carder	Frank Darkey	Hampshire Coal
J. M. Johnson	John Sammon	Michael Ouigley	Maryland Coal[199]

J. RELIGION ON THE TOWPATH

Although there probably were a number of mission efforts directed toward the canal boatmen by various religious societies and institutions along the canal, three such endeavors are deserving of note. They are the establishment of Grace Episcopal Church in Georgetown in 1855, the holding of Sunday School services in Cumberland in the 1880s, and the opening of the Mission on the Towpath just above the Potomac Aqueduct in 1894.

1. Grace Episcopal Church

---

[197] *Ibid.*

[198] *Proceedings of the President and Board of Directors* I, 303, 319. It is interesting to note that this issue arose on the canal about the same time that the controversial and much heralded Dred Scott Case was before the United States Supreme Court.

[199] Register of Boats Employed on the Canal, January I, 1878, C & O Co.

In 1855 three members of the vestry of St. John's Episcopal in Georgetown, Messrs. Thomas, Rittenhouse, and Ridgely, became interested in starting a mission for the numerous sailors and canal boatmen who frequented the Georgetown waterfront. Through their efforts and at their personal expense, a small frame church was built on what is now Wisconsin Avenue below M Street. Rev Henderson Suter, later the rector of Christ Church at Alexandria, established a Sunday School in connection with the mission, and regular services were held there with the assistance of several students from the Virginia Theological Seminary at Alexandria. One of the students, who was the son of the former rector at St. John's, was largely responsible for the growth of the congregation. Henry D. Cooke, a one-time vestryman at St. John's and a wealthy member of the banking firm of Jay Cooke & Company, soon became interested in the work of the mission. In 1865 he bought two lots on Brickyard Hill (presently 1041 Wisconsin Avenue) and made possible the construction and furnishing of the present church edifice with a personal donation of $25,000. For some years all of the operating expenses of the mission were borne by St. John's. Later the work was taken over by Christ Church, Georgetown, and eventually Grace Episcopal Church became an independent parish.[200]

2. American Sunday School Union

In the late 1880s, the canal company granted a permit to the American Sunday School Union to hold Sabbath classes on an abandoned boat near Cumberland. The classes were taught by a local woman, and both adults and children were welcome. Attendance averaged about 35 per week. It is likely that similar classes were held in many of the towns along the canal for the benefit of the "canallers."[201]

3. Mission on the Towpath

The Mission On The Towpath was established in 1874 by Mrs. S. E. Safford for canal men and their families about ¼ mile above the Potomac Aqueduct. The mission was located in a low, one-story brick building "almost under the eaves of the Independent Ice Company" that had served originally as the office of the Foxhall Foundry. Here the boatmen's children were taught to read and write, and the adults were instructed in industrial arts and assisted in locating temporary housing in winter when the canal was closed to navigation. Sometime after 1905 the mission was moved to another building on the old Foxhall Foundry site. In December 1913, the mission was closed, due in part to the reduced number of boats operating on the waterway.[202]

K.   CANAL SONGS

Although most of the boatmen's songs were never written down or collected, the words of several tunes appeared in an article in the *Baltimore Evening Sun* of August 13, 1937. In the article Lee McCardell, the writer, interviewed a number of former boatmen, canal employees, and valley inhabitants during the sesquicentennial celebration at Cumberland.

---

[200] *One Hundred and Fifty years in the Life of St. John's Church, Georgetown* (Washington, D.C., 1946), 143; Mary Mitchell, *Divided Town* (Barre, 1968), 139; *Washington Evening Star*, October 14, 1870; and Rose Trexler Mitchell, comp., *Parish Register of Grace Protestant Episcopal Church, Georgetown, D.C., 1863–1900* 1963, iv–v.
[201] Misc. Mss., C & O Co.
[202] *Washington Evening Star*, July 11, 1905, and Thomas F. Hahn, *Towpath Guide to the Chesapeake & Ohio Canal*, Section One (Rev. ed., York 1974), 18.

One of the songs noted in the article was a three-verse ditty that Sam Graham, the captain of the *Rufus Stride*, had composed on his numerous journeys along the waterway. The last two lines of each verse were dedicated to his mule team, which usually had been driven by one of his three sons–Jake, Ben, or Charlie the words of the song were as follows:

> Comin' down the Big Pool,
> Water mighty wide,
> Pitch out your Quarter
> To see the cat fly;
> Captain, Captain,
> A quarter mighty small,
> Pitch out your pocketbook
> Manifest an'all!
> An' a ram-jam now,
> Git alon, Old Bones!
>
> I come down to Williamsport,
> Seven o'clock at night,
> And the first word I heerd
> Was a 'what boat's that?'
> A left foot an' lousy
> Just gettin' fat . . . .
> (Editor's Note-Censored!
> We can't print that)
> An' a ram-jam now,
> Git along, Old Bones!
>
> I come down the Log Wall
> An' give a mighty yell.
> The hames ketched a fire
> an' the driver ketched hell.
> The captain played the fiddle
> An' the steersman played the flute.
> An' the cook poured coffee
> In the Old Man's boot!
> An' a ram-jam now
> Git alon, Old Bones!

One of the most popular songs among the boatmen was the jingle "Johnny Howard," a ballad about a young canal hand who was hung on St. Patrick's Day for the brutal murder of his boat captain at the Oldtown Cut. The words of this doleful tune, of which only a few were still in the memory of the boatmen that McCardell interviewed, were as follows:

> Johnny Howard
>
> His name was Johnny Howard
> And a nice young man was he,
> he boated on the water
> For many a night and day . . .

> (One night at the Oldtown Cut the captain
> came on deck with a hatchet in his hand and announced)
> Johnny, before I take water,
> One of us must die . . .
>
> (Whereupon Johnny picked up a spreader stick and
> laid the captain low. He was scared but a black hand
> driving the mules reassured him:)
>
> The Negro said, Johnny, You
> need not run away,
> For I will swear it self-defense
> Upon that fatal day.

One other song is mentioned in the article by McCardell. The ballad had four verses but the words to only one stanza were given:

> I've waded through many a valley
> I've traveled the tall mountain hill,
> But there's nothing my spirit can rally
> Like the breadth of old Sideling Hill.[203]

L. STORIES AND REMINISCENCES OF CANAL DAYS

There are a number of sources of colorful stories about life along the canal during its operating period as well as reminiscences about canal days by former canal employees and boatmen. Among the most interesting and entertaining sources are:

> 1. There are a series of taped conversations with 14 former boatmen and canal employees on file at the Harpers Ferry Training Center and at the Chesapeake & Ohio Canal National Historical Park Headquarters.
>
> 2. The only recorded manuscript of a journey on the waterway during the canal's operating period was written by an anonymous unemployed New England man who served on the crew of a barge on a round-trip voyage from Cumberland to Alexandria and return in 1859. About thirty years later, he wrote his memories of the voyage. The anonymous manuscript reached the City Library Association of Springfield, Massachusetts, at an unknown date, and in 1923, it was given to the Library of Congress. The manuscript was first edited by Ella E. Clark and published in the *Maryland Historic Magazine*, in June 1960, and in 1975 it was reprinted as a booklet under the title *Life on the Chesapeake & Ohio Canal 1859* edited by Ella E. Clark and Thomas F. Hahn.
>
> 3. A number of colorful stories about the persons associated with the canal as well as its operation are found in George Hooper Wolfe, who worked as a hand on a boat crew in his youth during the waning years of the canal's operation, relates some of the most interesting occurrences, tales, and legends that are associated with life along the canal.

---

[203] *Baltimore Evening Sun*, August 13, 1937.

4. Sprinkled throughout the *Towpath Guide to the Chesapeake & Ohio Canal* by Thomas F. Hahn are numerous stories of fiction and fact concerning life along the canal during its operating period.

5. In the *Baltimore Evening Sun* of August 10–12, 1937, there are two extensive interviews with Captain Charlie (Scott) Eaton of Cumberland and Captain Denton (Dent) Shupp of Williamsport. Both of these interviews by Lee McCardell consist of rambling reminiscences concerning the boatmen's and lock keeper's lives along the waterway.

APPENDIX A

CA. OCT. 1828

SPECIFICATION OF A LOCK KEEPERS HOUSE

MASONRY—The building to be of stone and to be 30 x 18 feet over the walls, with a cellar under the kitchen part 6 feet in the clear, with a floor of earth, the walls to be 22 inches thick, and have a projection on the outside of 6 inches all round, and at least one course of stone high the cellar door to have stone steps, and a locust frame with grooves to receive the doors, which are to have substantial strap hinges and be fastened in the usual way with a padlock; there will be a window on each side consisting of a single sash each of 10 x 12 glass & 3 lights in width, each to shut in an oaken frame, the sash, to have hinges, to open upwards.

PRINCIPAL STORY—The floor to be 2 feet above the surface of ground; the walls to be 20 inches thick, and that part not over the cellar to have a footing of stone all around of 6 inches more, one course of stone high, the space between the ground and the bottom of floor to have 3 slits in each side, 9 x 4 inches, to be covered with perforated iron or copper plates, to exclude vermin, and admit air, under the end where there is no cellar: the height in the clear of the story to be 8 feet between floor & ceiling.

ATTIC STORY—The walls to be 18 inches thick and three feet high from the top of floor to the square: The peak of the roof to be 6 feet above side walls: The stone to be laid in clay mortar excepting 3 inches on the outside of the walls above ground and the inside of the cellar which 3 inches is to be good lime mortar and well pointed.

CHIMNEY STALK—To be begun as near the surface of the ground as a good foundation can be obtained, one side to be supported by the cross wall of cellar, the foundation to be of stone 8 x 4 feet to top of arch of oven where it will be 6 x 4 feet the stalk may be of brick or stone; if built of stone, the openings of the fireplaces, the insides of the flues, & the oven should be of brick; and the top above the roof should be hammered; or built of hard bricks, and good mortar: the kitchen flue to be 18 x 12 and that of the parlor 12 x 12 inches after they are plastered. The outside doors to have stone sills, and stone steps; the window sills should be of stone, or locust painted and sanded. All the lintels of the doors & windows are to be of stone.

CARPENTER WORK—Joists of first floor to be 3 x 9 inches: of 2d floor 3 x 8 inches. Floors, to be of 1 ¼ heart pine planed and tongued and grooved. Doors to be of 1 ¼ heart pine not to exceed 6 inches in width to be battened and fastened with wrought nails the outside doors, to have jamb casings of 2 inch heart pine, let into the sills and framed at the top the outside doors to have substantial strap hinges put on with screws, the front door to have a good stock lock, and the kitchen door an inside bolt, the parlor door to be furnished with a good 7 inch nob lock, all the rest of the doors to have thumb latches.

Windows Those in the principal story to have 10 x 12 glass, those in the upper story to have 8 x 10 glass: The casings to be 1 1/4 inch yellow pine plank.

A sash of 10 x 12 glass is to be put over the front door to light the entry.

ROOF—To have 10 pairs of rafters, 4 inches deep at top and 6 inches at lower end and three inches thick to be framed together at top and be secured by a brace at a point on the rafter that will afford a clear head way of 6 feet 4 inches in the attic story; the horizontal slope of foot of rafters to project 6 inches over the face of the wall & to have a plansier or casing, spiked to them, to extend to face of wall, the shingles to project 4 inches over that, making in all 10 inches of projection; the lower ends of rafters to be notched into a wall plate, and spiked to it; said wall plate to be 4 inches thick, and spiked to pieces of 3 x 4 scantling; built angling into top of wall, a rafter of 1 ½ inch plank to be built in the center of gables to project like the others: Sheeting, to be 3/4 boards, laid close, the shingles to be cypress, of good quality 18 inches long, & to show 5 ½ inches to the weather & not less than 4 inches wide [here a word is missing due to torn ms., but it is probably] and 5/8 thick.

CARPENTER WORK OF INSIDE—The inside doors to have plain jamb casings; the washboards and surface to be plain, only single beaded; the mantle pieces to have plain pilasters, and moldings to support the shelf: The spaces to the right & left of front entry to have stud partitions, the space between chimney stalk & back wall to have a two inch plank partition, the space between the fireplace and door of stairway to be stud partition the stair to be plain with a nosing. The partition separating the rooms in attic story, to be 1 ½ inch plank: The small closet to be finished in a plain manner.

PLASTERING—The ceilings, and stud partitions, to be lathed and those, as well as the walls to be finished with three coats of good lime mortar, made with glue and proper proportions of good clean sand.

APPENDIX B

CA. OCT. 1828

ESTIMATE OF THE EXPENSE OF A LOCKKEEPERS HOUSE

Stone and Brick

60	Cubic yards digging in foundation	@ $ .20 per yd.	12.00
124	Perches stone laid in clay, 3 inches in lime mortar	@ $ 2.50 per p.	310.00
4000	Bricks of good quality laid in lime mortar	@ $10.00 per m.	40.00
60	Running feet blue stone in steps, lintels & sills	@ $ .25 per ft.	15.00

Lumber

3250	Feet common white pine plank	@ $ .50 per 100 ft.	48.75
1822	Feet 4/5 hart pine	@ $ 2.75 per m.	50.18
4000	Shingles	@ $10.00 per m.	40.00
150	Pounds of nails	@ $ .08	12.00
	Hardware		17.62

Workmanship

8	Squares flooring including laying joists roof	A 4.00 per s.	32.00
	Roof		32.56
6	Doors at 3.75 = $22.50 + 2 mantle pieces at $8		30.50
330	Feet washboard & surface a 4¢ = $13.20 + stair at $11		24.20
150	Feet partitions at 5¢ = $7.50 + Closet at $6.00		13.50
7	Windows = $42 + cellar door and frames at $7.50		49.50
	Plastering on walls	A 22¢ per yd.	32.50
	Plastering on laths	A 30¢ per yd.	34.80
	Painting		30.00
	Crane for fireplace		3.50
			$828.46

Drawings and other Records Concerning Construction, C & O Co.

APPENDIX C

FEBRUARY 10, 1836

SPECIFICATION FOR A LOCK-KEEPERS HOUSE (30 BY 18 FEET) TO BE ERECTED ON THE LINE OF THE CHESAPEAKE & OHIO CANAL.

MASONRY—The building to be of brick or stone, at the option of the contractor.

CELLAR—There will be a cellar under the whole house, six feet in the clear, with a floor of earth. The cellar walls will be of stone, 22 inches thick, and shall project 2 inches outside of and around the building. The foundation course of these cellar walls shall project 6 inches outside of the 22 inches. The level of the foundation walls shall be at least one foot below the cellar floor. The cellar door shall have some steps, and a locust frame, with substantial strap hinges, and fastened in the usual way with a padlock. There will be two windows in the cellar, one on each side of the house, consisting each of a single six light sash of 8 by 10 glass, shutting in a locust frame, the sash having hinges to open upwards. From the cellar there shall be a good and sufficient drain, protected by an iron grate.

CHIMNEY—The chimney shall be in the middle of the building; its foundation shall be on level with the cellar walls, and may be either brick or stone; no wood shall be used to support the chimney, unless at such distance below the hearths, as shall, in the opinion of the Engineer, be safe from fire. Above the floor of the principal story the chimney shall be of brick.

PRINCIPAL STORY—The principal story will be eight feet in the clear between the floor and ceiling, and its walls will be 14 ¼ inches if of brick and 20 inches if of stone. The walls of the attic story, lengthwise of the building, will be the same thickness as the principal story. The end walls of the attic will only be 9 inches if of brick and 12 inches if of stone. From the top of the chamber floor to the square will be 3 ½ feet. The peak of the roof will be six feet above the side walls. In the clear, between the floor and ceiling of the attic, will be six feet three inches.

ROOMS—There will be two rooms in each story. The washboards and surface will be plain. To each of the two lower rooms, there shall be an outer door; there shall also be a door leading from one to the other of these rooms. There shall be a door for the stairs leading from one story to the other; and also between the two upper rooms.

DOORS—The doors (five in number, exclusive of the cellar door) shall all be plain paneled, each having a Pennsylvania or German lock, with iron handles. The outside doors will have locust sills and locust lintels; they will have jamb casings of two inch heart pine let into the sills, and framed at top; they shall also have substantial strap hinges, put on with screws.

WINDOWS—In the lower story there will be five windows of twelve lights, 10 by 12. In the upper story there will be four windows of nine lights each, 10 by 12, glass. The casings will be of 1 ¼ inch yellow pine plank. The sills and lintels will be of locust.

PLASTERING—The whole interior of the building above the cellar shall be plastered, except the partition separating the two rooms in the attic story, which will be of 1 ½ inch plank. The plaster shall be finished in the most durable manner, with two coats.

STAIRS AND CLOSETS—The stairs will be plain, and of such rise, and tread, and width, as the Engineer may direct. The closets, two in number, one in each of the lower two rooms, will be finished in a plain manner, with battened doors.

FIREPLACES—There will be two fireplaces, one in each of the lower rooms; each having a mantelpiece, with two pilasters; an iron crane shall be put in the kitchen fireplace.

JOISTS—The joists of the first floor shall be three by twelve inches; of the second, three by ten inches; sixteen inches apart, from center to center, of good yellow pine.

FLOORS—The floors are to be 1 ¼ inch heart pine, planed, and tongued and grooved.

ROOF—The roof will have sixteen pairs of rafters, five inches deep at the top, and eight inches deep at the lower end, and three inches thick, framed together at top, and secured by a collar seam at the point that shall give the required height of six feet three inches in the clear in the upper story. The method of securing the foot of the rafters shall be in the most substantial manner, by means of wad plates properly connected with the top of the brick work, of not less than four inches in thickness and nine inches in width. The projection over the wall, and the finish at the foot of the rafters, shall be such as to present a workmanship appearance. The sheathings will be of three-fourth inch board, laid close; the shingles of the best quality of cypress, eighteen inches long, showing 5 ½ inches to weather, and not less than four inches wide and five-eighths thick.

PAINTING—All of the woodwork outside shall have three coats, and the inside two coats of the best English white lead oil paint, well put on.

MATERIALS &C.—The quality of the brick and of the stone work of the whole building shall be such as the Engineer shall approve of; and the bond, also, of the brick and stone work shall be such as he shall direct.
    The whole of the masonry, from the foundation up, shall be laid in good and approved lime mortar, except 1 ½ feet in height at the top of the stone masonry, which shall be laid in mortar made of the best water cement.

PLAN—A plan shall be furnished by the Engineer to the contractor, showing the exact position of doors, windows, closets, etc.

APPENDIX D

COPY OF A REGISTER OF FINES COLLECTED
ON THE CANAL BETWEEN 1877–1880

DATE	BOAT	CAPTAIN	OFFENCE	FINE
May 30, 1877	Ed Bayer & H. C. Clamohan	Thomas Fisher	Passing through lock without waybill	$10.00
Oct. 22, 1877	R. Cropley's scow		Knock out gate in Lock No. 5	$25.00
Nov. 12, 1877	Five Bros.	Joseph Little	Run into crib at Lock No. 9	$10.00
Jun 3, 1878	Ludlow Patton		Shutting off fire while filling level and locking through without permission	$10.00
Jul 4, 1878	John Sherman		Unloading and raising	$62.70
Aug 30, 1878	Steamer Scrivenes		Allowing the Bertha M. Young in tow to sink on Level 36 and abandoning her at night without giving notice, causing navigation to be suspended 36 hrs.	$50.00
May 5, 1879	W. J. Booth	Jacob Hooker	Running into and breaking gate at Lock No. 40	$40.00
Jan 14, 1880	Harry & Ralph		Running into gate at Darbey's Lock	$5.00
Jan 17, 1880	P. Heim	Mertens	Running into gate at Lock No. 61	$10.00
Jun 1880	Walter Thompson		Running into and breaking gate at Lock No. 75	$25.00
Apr 24, 1880	Five Bros.	Joseph Little	¾ day pumping by Jacob Sheets and by Adam Keefer	$1.50
Apr 25, 1880	Five Bros.	Joseph Little	Pumping boat 2 days – 2 men @ $2 per day	$4.00
Apr 29, 1880	Adam Sherman	Capt. Bowers	Pumping boat 1 hand, 1½ day @ $1 per day	$1.50
May 14, 1880	Laura P. Agnew	Capt. Hedely	Services 1 hand, 2 days @ $1 per day	$2.00
May 27, 1880	G. W. Kscdr	Poffenberger	Pumping	$5.50
May 28, 1880	G. W. Kscdr	Poffenberger	Pumping	$5.50
May 29, 1880	G. W. Kscdr	Poffenberger	Pumping	$4.40
June 12, 1880	G. L. Booth		Pumping	$4.40
June 18, 1880	Mollie		Pumping 2½ days @ $1.10 per day	$2.75
June 19, 1880	City of Hamburg		Pumping 2 men ½ day each	$1.10

Date	Boat/Party		Reason	Amount
June 19, 1880	City of Hamburg		Pumping 4 men ½ day each	$2.20
June 26, 1880	A. J. McAllister		Pumping 2½ days @ $1.10	$2.75
June 27, 1880	Annie & Lizzie		Pumping 1½ days @ $1.10	$1.65
June 28, 1880	Annie & Lizzie		Pumping 2 hands	$2.20
July 14, 1880	G. T. Gertell		Pumping and bailing	$6.40
Aug 16, 1880	F. Gorman		Pumping	$1.10
Aug 19, 1880	Hatton & Bessin	Capt. Sharman	Pumping	$3.30
Aug 22, 1880	Ernst & Holland		Tying up on towpath	$5.00
Aug 28, 1880	Harris McDonald		Pumping	$2.20
Aug 30, 1880	U. S. Bracher		Pumping	$4.40
Sept 2, 1880	G. M. Ryan		Hoisting water and slamming gate	$5.00
Sept 2, 1880	Stonebreaker		Hoisting water and slamming gate	$5.00
Oct 24, 1880	Joseph Clark		Laying on towpath	$5.00
Oct 24, 1880	O. of Sheridan Line		Running into gate at Darbey's Lock	$5.00
Nov 2, 1880	W. H. Lowe		Laying on towpath	$5.00
Nov 2, 1880	Denton Prather		Laying on towpath	$5.00

Lightning Source UK Ltd.
Milton Keynes UK
UKHW041028311218
334695UK00023B/372/P